QUANTITATIVE METHODS:
APPLICATIONS TO MANAGERIAL DECISION MAKING

TO THE STUDENT

A Study Guide for the textbook is available through your college bookstore under the title Study Guide to accompany **QUANTITATIVE METHODS: APPLICATIONS TO MANAGERIAL DECISION MAKING** by **Robert E. Markland and James R. Sweigart**. The Study Guide, prepared by Shawnee Vickery of Michigan State University, can help you with course material by acting as a tutorial, review, and study aid. If the Study Guide is not in stock, ask the bookstore manager to order a copy for you.

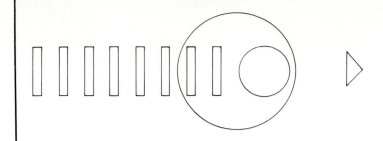

QUANTITATIVE METHODS:
APPLICATIONS TO MANAGERIAL DECISION MAKING

ROBERT E. MARKLAND
JAMES R. SWEIGART
University of South Carolina

JOHN WILEY & SONS
New York   Chichester   Brisbane   Toronto   Singapore

Library of Congress Cataloging-in-Publication Data:

Markland, Robert E.
  Quantitative methods.

  Includes indexes.
  1. Management science.   2. Operations research.
I. Sweigart, James R.   II. Title.

T56.M2745   1987   658.4'03   87-2025
ISBN 0-471-87885-5

Printed in the United States of America

10 9 8 7 6 5 4 3 2 1

NOTES FOR THE STUDENT

This text is designed for the survey course in quantitative methods which is typically required for under-graduate students majoring in business administration. It is intended to provide such students with a thorough understanding of quantitative methods, including material to test both their strengths and weaknesses. It is oriented toward the business student who will most likely pursue a career in an organization requiring managerial ability and decision-making skill, both of which can be enhanced by an understanding of quantitative methods.

In writing this textbook we attempted to achieve the following objectives.

1. To familiarize the student with a wide array of quantitative methods (i.e., operations research/management science techniques) that are currently being used by decision makers.

2. To present the material at a reasonable mathematical level, generally no higher than finite mathematics and college algebra.

3. To integrate the use of microcomputers in solving operations research/management science problems.

4. To write the material in a manner that is very student oriented.

This textbook has a very strong emphasis on applications. Numerous short examples and illustrations are provided throughout the book and these examples illustrate exactly how the various techniques are applied. At the end of each chapter we have included an "application review." Each of these application reviews describes a real-world scenario involving an actual company that has benefited from the use of quantitative methods.

The mathematical level of this textbook is generally that of finite mathematics and college-level algebra. It also employs various concepts from probability and statistics. However, for those of you who have forgotten what you learned in your probability and statistics course, (or simply sold your book), review chapters for this area (Chapters 2 and 3) are included for your benefit. Also, Appendices A and B contain brief reviews of calculus and matrix algebra. Matrix algebra is used extensively in the book but calculus is employed only to a very minor extent. The mathematical foundation for each quantitative technique is introduced and illustrated by means of examples, in a simple, straightforward manner.

The result of the microcomputer revolution is that it is now much easier to solve various kinds of operations research/management science problems. In the text we illustrate the application of several well-known and readily available microcomputer problem-solving software packages. Use of this microcomputer software can greatly alleviate the tediousness associated with problem solving in this area. It is also very beneficial to have knowledge of, and experience with, such software packages because you are likely to use various software packages in your job.

We have attempted to write this material in a manner that is very student oriented. Numerous examples, illustrations, drawings, and tables are included within the book. We have tried to make these examples as realistic as possible, without making them overly difficult. Key terms are highlighted throughout the book, and each chapter contains a glossary of important terms and definitions.

Since problem solving is an important part of any quantitative methods course, we have included numerous problems at the end of the various chapters. To enhance your learning process, we provide answers to the even-numbered problems at the end of the book.

One key point that you should keep in mind as you use this book is that it is more than just a collection of techniques. What we are trying to develop in you as a student is a philosophy of problem solving and decision making which emphasizes a rational, logical, "scientific" approach. If you can develop such an approach, it will serve you well in the future, regardless of the type of job or position in which you are working.

NOTES FOR THE INSTRUCTOR

From the instructor's perspective we have attempted to make this textbook both comprehensive and teachable. The book contains twenty-three chapters, which cover virtually all of the topics associated with the field of operations research/management science. The general topical organization of the textbook is shown in the following diagram. Within this general topical organization, the set of topics that will be emphasized is left to the discretion of the individual instructor. The material we generally try to cover in a one-semester course is marked with asterisks in the diagram. Obviously, it may be difficult to cover all of these topics in a single-semester course.

Within each chapter we have tried to present the material in a concise, straightforward manner. Each chapter basically considers one major topical area which is thoroughly explained, using numerous examples. We have also tried to avoid complex mathematical notation and involved formulas wherever possible.

The book also contains many learning aids for the student. Each chapter begins with a chapter outline which provides an overview of what will be covered in the chapter. Key concepts and definitions are highlighted throughout the chapter. Numerous tables, figures, and illustrations are provided. Also, at the end of each chapter, a glossary of the key terms for that chapter is provided. Each chapter also includes a set of reference materials. Finally, the solutions to all of the even-numbered problems at the end of the various chapters are included in the back of the book.

At the end of each chapter is a series of discussion questions and a problem set. These discussion questions and problems can be assigned to students as homework. The discussion questions and problems are organized in a manner that follows the order of presentation of the material in the chapter. They provide a range from the very easy to the very challenging. The Instructor's Manual which accompanies the text contains the detailed solutions to all of the problems, brief answers to the discussion questions, and transparency masters of key figures and tables.

Accompanying the book is a Study Guide (written by Shawnee Vickery of Michigan State University). This comprehensive and thorough study guide follows the topical coverage of the text and contains solved problems and numerous examples, as well as other explanatory material.

In preparing this book we have thoroughly classroom tested all of the material. We have used preliminary versions of the book for four semesters in various courses. Hopefully, many of the "rough spots" and errors have been eliminated.

TOPICAL ORGANIZATION OF THE TEXTBOOK

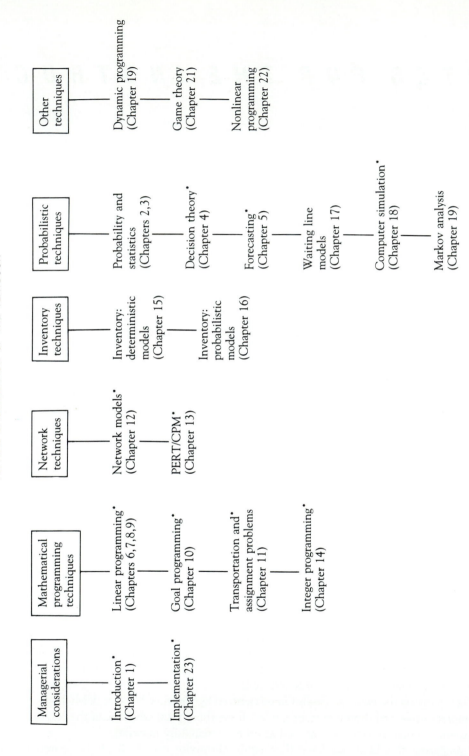

ACKNOWLEDGMENTS

We wish to acknowledge the assistance of a large number of people in the writing of this textbook. First, we would like to thank the large group of students who assisted us in classroom testing the material. Second, we greatly appreciate the advice and suggestions of our colleagues here in the management science department. We are particularly indebted to Marc Schniedersjans (University of Nebraska–Lincoln) who provided many useful comments on the goal programming chapter and to Steve Nahmias (University of Santa Clara) who made detailed suggestions for the PERT/CPM chapter. Several graduate students at the University of South Carolina, including Hope Baker, Eliott Minor, Ken McLeod, and Eric Brown, also were very helpful in solving problems and examples. Administrative support for the project was provided by Dean James F. Kane, and typing was done by Julia Moton and Leigh Hopkins. We are also most appreciative of the editorial assistance of Cheryl Mehalik, our editor at Wiley, and for the many suggestions made by the reviewers: Shawnee Vickery (Michigan State University), Suresh Chand (Purdue University), Tom Gulledge (Louisiana State University), Don R. Robinson (Illinois State University), Sheldon R. Epstein (Seton Hall University), Ralph Badinelli (Virginia Tech University), Ed Baker (University of Miami), and Steve Nahmias (University of Santa Clara).

Finally, we would like to express our deep appreciation for the continuing support of our wives and children.

Robert E. Markland
James R. Sweigart

To

Mylla, Kevin, and Keith

Robert E. Markland

Cindy, Susannah, Lindsey, and Shawn

James R. Sweigart

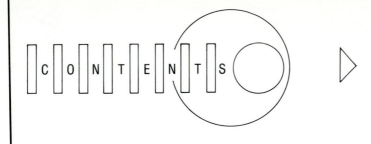

C O N T E N T S

CHAPTER 1

INTRODUCTION

1.1 INTRODUCTION

One fact of modern life is that the organizations with which we all interact, and in which many of us earn our livelihoods, are very complex. These complex organizations generate difficult problems that require decisions. For example, consider the large array of factors that must be analyzed as a company ponders the introduction of a new product. This decision will require an appraisal of the company's competitive position, its financial position, its production capacity, its ability to design, produce, package, and distribute a new product, as well as related activities such as advertising and promotion, hiring and training of new workers, and organizational restructuring. Clearly, the problems associated with the introduction of a new product will affect every facet of an organization.

In this complex decision-making environment, it has become increasingly more difficult for managers to consider all of the many factors, with their associated interactions, that affect the outcome of a decision. As a result, a need has arisen for a more rigorous and scientific approach to analyzing complex decision problems. In recent years, many new and important quantitative methods have been developed for improving the decision-making process. This textbook provides a survey of these quantitative decision-making techniques. Its emphasis is on showing exactly how these techniques can be used to contribute to improved decision making. Throughout this textbook we will attempt to provide numerous examples and applications that will illustrate how quantitative methods have been successfully applied.

The ability to use quantitative analysis in the decision-making process can be enhanced by the study of mathematical methods such as those introduced in this book. Such an ability will improve the overall effectiveness of the manager, and should also be complementary to the qualitative decision-making skills of the manager. Furthermore, even if the manager is not directly involved in making quantitative analyses, he or she should develop an understanding of what quantitative methods are available and how they can facilitate decision making, so that they can direct and evaluate the work of others.

The field of knowledge that encompasses quantitative approaches to decision making is very broad and includes several areas from applied mathematics. Two of the most widely used names for this area of study are *management science* (MS) and *operations research* (OR). We shall refer to these terms frequently and interchangeably throughout the remainder of this book. In both instances, the terms refer to the application of quantitative methods to decision making in business, industrial, governmental, and military organizations, with an objective of improving the quality of managerial decisions.

The operations research/management science (OR/MS) approach to problem solving generally incorporates most, or all, of the following characteristics:

1. Applies the scientific method to develop the problem-solving methodology.
2. Adopts a systems approach to the modeling process.
3. Utilizes a team concept in the modeling process.
4. Makes extensive use of computers in obtaining solutions to problems.

We now discuss each of these characteristics of the OR/MS approach to problem solving in further detail.

1.1.1 THE SCIENTIFIC METHOD IN QUANTITATIVE MODELING

The major distinguishing feature of operations research or management science is its emphasis on the use of the scientific method in decision making. Faced with a complex problem, a manager may rely on intuition or casual observation to make a decision. Or the manager may rely on the experience that he or she, or others have had. These approaches to making decisions, however, are not very systematic and are highly subjective. They do not provide for improving the managerial decision process, and it may be difficult to even determine how decisions were made based on their application. Conversely, the management science approach, which incorporates the basic elements of the scientific method, does facilitate a rational, systematic way of solving managerial decision problems.

The basic steps of the scientific method can be summarized as follows:

1. Observation of the problem situation.
2. Problem definition.
3. Formulation of a hypothesis related to the problem.
4. Experimentation and testing of the hypothesis.
5. Verification and validation of the results of the experiment.

In using the scientific method to make decisions, the manager will often follow these steps in an informal manner. That is, the manager will not perform a carefully controlled scientific experiment in order to make a decision. Nevertheless, the process involved in these steps can be very helpful in developing a rational, consistent approach to decision making.

1.1.2 THE SYSTEMS APPROACH IN QUANTITATIVE MODELING

In solving managerial decision problems the scientific method is usually employed in a broader context that is often referred to as the *systems approach*. In this context the organization is viewed as a system, composed of many component parts. Overall, the manager's goal is to achieve the objectives of the organization in total. By trying to achieve the best possible solution to some problem involving a part of the organization, however, the overall goals of the organization may not be achieved. This is referred to as *suboptimization* in the systems approach. To avoid suboptimization from a systems perspective, the manager may have to be satisfied with a less than perfect solution to a problem involving some particular part of the organization. That is to say, suboptimization with respect to the components of the system may be necessary for the overall good of the total organization.

1.1.3 THE TEAM CONCEPT IN QUANTITATIVE MODELING

Many complex managerial problems are simply too difficult to be solved by a single manager, working alone. Consequently, it is common for a team of specialists and experts to be formed to apply quantitative approaches to managerial problems. In a typical managerial decision-making problem this team might consist of specialists in operations research, computer programming, finance, and accounting. This interdisciplinary team approach also reinforces the total system concept as it facilitates the blending of several viewpoints in decision making.

Quantitative modeling emphasizes this team concept of problem solving. It recognizes that a much broader perspective and a much more thorough analysis of a problem situation typically results when a group interacts to solve a problem.

1.1.4 THE ROLE OF THE COMPUTER IN QUANTITATIVE MODELING

Many, if not most, meaningful quantitative modeling efforts are of a scope and complexity that require computerization for testing hypotheses and obtaining solutions. Indeed, the development and proliferation of operations research/management science has been enhanced by the development and distribution of high-speed digital computers. These techniques typically require long, complex calculations. High-speed digital computers that are capable of performing these complex calculations, at incredible speeds, are a critical factor in the acceptance and use of an operations research/management science methodology. There are still large-scale problems that cannot be solved using current quantitative techniques and existing computers. Such problems are important areas for basic research, but their ultimate solution will also be dependent on continuing development in the computer area.

In recent years much attention has been focused on the interface of operations research/management science with *management information systems* (MIS). Management information systems are computer-based systems for collecting, analyzing, and reporting information to managers. Many management information systems employ a *data base*, which is simply a large set of raw data structured according to some predefined set of rules. In addition to providing information for the manager, a data base often can be used to provide input data to support a quantitative modeling effort. The evolution in which the management science model is embedded in the overall management information system has resulted in a special type of information system called a *decision support system* (DSS). A decision support system attempts to provide timely and relevant information to the decision maker. It also allows the decision maker to interact with, and make changes to, the model, thereby enhancing the decision-making process. Decision support systems are the subject of a great deal of current attention, in both academic and industrial circles. Rapid developments in this area of interface between OR/MS and MIS offers an exciting future.

With the tremendous growth in the availability of minicomputers and microcomputers in organizations of all sizes, easy access to a wide range of quantitative techniques is now possible. Virtually all of the quantitative analysis techniques that you will study in this book have been computerized, and can be accessed on a microcomputer using various software programs. These software programs allow managers to solve large problems relatively easily, as the computer is supplied the necessary data and makes the required computations. Consequently, we stress the role of the computer in decision making throughout this book.

1.2 A HISTORICAL OVERVIEW

The use of quantitative approaches in managerial decision making is a relatively recent development. Very early in this century, industrial engineers began applying scientific techniques to industrial problems. In the early 1900s Frederick W. Taylor studied worker capacities and developed time standards for various jobs. Henry L. Gantt devised a scheduling system for loading jobs on machines that minimized job completion delays. Frank and Lilian Gilbreth founded the field of time and motion study, and were the first to use motion pictures to analyze manufacturing processes.

Other notable scientific achievements soon followed these early successes. By 1912, George Babcock had formulated some basic principles for establishing the most economical size of a production quantity, or lot, of parts. In 1915, his work was expanded into a prototype inventory model by F. W. Harris of the Westinghouse Company. During World War I, Thomas Edison studied antisubmarine warfare, and compiled statistics for determining the best methods for both evading and detecting submarines. The Danish engineer, A. K. Erlang, invented queuing theory to analyze the fluctuations of demand for automatic dialing telephone facilities. T. C. Fry applied probability theory to engineering problems. Walter Shewart formulated statistical quality-control methods. L. H. C. Tippett proposed a method for measuring delays in textile operations using probability theory. Horace C. Levinson utilized mathematical models to analyze and explain consumer behavior.

During World War II the scientist entered the environment of military decision making. The first notable use of scientific research in military operations occurred in Great Britain, under the direction of the distinguished physicist P. M. S. Blackett. This type of scientific activity was called "operational research" in England, since it was primarily concerned with problems associated with the operational use of radar. By 1942 the same type of scientific activity had been introduced within the U.S. military environment. In the U.S. Air Force, it became known as "operational analysis" and in the U.S. Army and Navy it was called "operations research and operations evaluation." During World War II, numerous interdisciplinary study teams of mathematicians and scientists were formed to assist in the analysis of military operations. Notable achievements were made in determining how to protect a convoy, how to organize radar defenses, and how to most effectively drop bombs to destroy submarines.

Following World War II, industrial operations research groups were formed in both England and the United States, as an attempt was made to transfer the newly developed, and successfully applied, techniques of military operations research to business decision making. During this same time, a general industrial expansion was occurring, and decision making in many organizations was increasing in complexity. In England, in particular, new types of management problems, caused by the nationalization of industry and wartime destruction of industrial facilities, were approached using operations research techniques.

At least three other major factors can be identified as providing strong impetus to the growth of the field of operations research during the post–World War II time period. First, the growth, product diversity, technological developments, and competitive and social pressures of the postwar industrial environment all served to enhance the need for precision in decision making and implementation. A second important factor was the growth and widespread interest in basic research in the field. This led to rapid and important advances in the state of the art following World War II. A prime example of this type of advancement was the development of the simplex method for the solution of linear programming problems, as accomplished by George Dantzig in 1947. A third factor that provided a great thrust to the field was the development of the high-speed digital computer in this same time period. This development enabled very complex operations research problems to be solved.

Operations research as a field of study also found its way into university curricula. In 1948, the Massachusetts Institute of Technology established a course in the nonmilitary applications of operations research. In the spring of 1952, Columbia University presented its first course in operations research, and similar courses were also developed by the Case Institute of Technology and Johns Hopkins University. Several professional societies, composed of individuals actively working in the field, soon were formed. Rapid proliferation of knowledge concerning the field also occurred through numerous books and journals.

1.3 THE PROCESS OF QUANTITATIVE MODELING

The process of quantitative modeling is shown pictorially in Figure 1.1. Every OR/MS project does not follow the exact steps shown in the figure, but many such projects follow these general guidelines. The activities generally involved in quantitative modeling can be summarized from Figure 1.1 by the following six steps.

1.3.1 ANALYSIS AND PROBLEM DEFINITION

The quantitative modeling process begins with the observation and description of a "real-world" problem. Quite often the real-world problem will initially be described in very broad terms. Examples of broadly defined problems might include: excessive inventories, poor coordination of production with sales, excessive cost of distribution, or poor utilization of field salespersons. From such broad problem descriptions, well-defined problems that can be approached quantitatively must be developed.

This problem-definition process is largely an art and will require the skill and experience of the manager, as well as considerable effort, imagination,

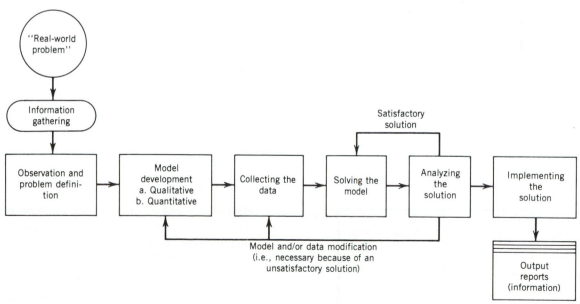

FIGURE 1.1   THE PROCESS OF QUANTITATIVE MODELING.

and assistance from others. It necessarily requires the gathering of information concerning the problem. As a part of the problem-definition process, it is often useful to perform some sort of a cost/benefit analysis. Such a cost/benefit analysis would include an estimate of the cost of completing the quantitative modeling study and an estimate of the potential economic benefits to be obtained from the study. Obviously, the results of such a cost/benefit analysis can be used to decide whether or not to continue the study at all, or whether or not to scale down the scope of the study.

1.3.2 MODEL DEVELOPMENT

Assuming that the project has been approved, the next step involves the development or selection of an appropriate quantitative model. This quantitative model should represent, in a mathematical framework, the physical situation being studied. As a preliminary step to the determination of the appropriate quantitative model it is often useful to describe the problem situation by an informal or qualitative model. Such a model is very descriptive in nature, but it does provide a useful framework for determining the more formal quantitative model.

Model development is the key to the quantitative modeling process. A model is nothing more than a representation of a real-life situation. Three basic types of models are shown in Figure 1.2. All of us have had experiences with *iconic* models, which are physical representations of real objects, using a different scale. For example, a model automobile is an iconic model. Another type of model is an *analog* model, in which one physical property is used to represent another physical property. For example, the temperature gauge on an automobile is an analog model that represents the heat level of the automobile's cooling system. A third type of model is a *symbolic* or *mathematical* model in which we employ a set of mathematical symbols and relationships to represent some real physical situation. An example of a simple mathematical model is the following equation describing the profit obtained from selling x number of units at price p, with a cost c:

$$\text{Profit} = \text{revenue} - \text{cost} = xp - xc \qquad (1.1)$$

In the mathematical modeling process two major types of models are employed. The first type is the *descriptive* model, in which the model simply represents or describes some particular physical situation but does not indicate any preferred course of action. Descriptive models help us to understand the behavior of a system, but they don't allow us to determine the "best" course of action with respect to it. A simple mathematical model relating a salesperson's commission income to the number of units sold is an example of a descriptive model. The second type is the *normative* model, which is prescriptive in nature. The normative model, which is also sometimes referred to as an optimization model, prescribes the course of action that the manager should use in order to achieve some specific objective.

As we construct normative models of decision problems we generally seek to satisfy a specific objective, such as maximizing profit or minimizing labor cost, subject to some restriction upon the availability of resources. The success of the quantitative modeling approach will depend on the mathematical accuracy with which the model's objective and restrictions can be described, and the extent to which they represent the real-world situation being examined.

Construction of a typical mathematical model is depicted pictorially in Figure 1.3. As shown in the figure, it requires the specification of four major elements

1. A SET OF CONTROLLABLE INPUTS The controllable inputs are the *decision activities* or *decision variables* that are under the control of the decision maker. The values of the decision variables are determined by solving the model, and a specific decision is provided when the decision variables take on specific values.

2. A SET OF UNCONTROLLABLE INPUTS The uncontrollable inputs are the *uncontrollable activities* or *uncontrollable variables* that are not under the control of the decision maker. The

Iconic Model	Model Automobile
Analog Model	Temperature Gauge
Mathematical Model	Profit $= xp - xc$

FIGURE 1.2 THREE BASIC TYPES OF MODELS.

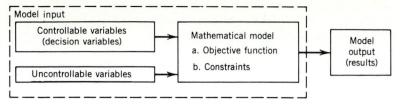

FIGURE 1.3 CONSTRUCTION OF A TYPICAL MATHEMATICAL MODEL.

uncontrollable inputs result from the environment that encompasses the problem situation.

a. *Known value:* This type of uncontrollable variable is referred to as a *parameter* or *coefficient* of the model, and is known with certainty. A model in which all of the uncontrollable variables are known and cannot vary is referred to as a *deterministic model.*

b. *Unknown value:* This type of uncontrollable variable is not known with certainty. If any of the uncontrollable variables are not known with certainty and are subject to variation, the model is referred to as a *stochastic* model.

It should also be noted that controllable variables and uncontrollable variables may be divided into two types: discrete and continuous. *Discrete variables* are those that can only take on one of a finite, or countably infinite number of values (in general, they must be integers or whole numbers). *Continuous variables* are those that can take on a continuum of values (i.e., they can be integers or nonintegers).

3. THE OBJECTIVE FUNCTION The objective function is a mathematical expression that relates the problem's objective to changes in the values of the decision variables. The objective function measures the desirability of the consequences of a decision.

4. A SET OF CONSTRAINTS The constraints restrict the range of the decision variables as a result of technological, economic, or physical restrictions related to the problem.

EXAMPLE (DETERMINISTIC MODEL)

To illustrate the construction of a simple deterministic model, consider the following production-scheduling situation. The owner of a factory that produces circuit boards for minicomputers has 400 production hours of available

labor each week, and a circuit board requires 2 hours to complete. Each circuit board results in a $5 profit. Therefore, the uncontrollable variables in this situation are known with certainty. The decision problem for this situation is the following: How many circuit boards should be scheduled for production each week in order to maximize profit? The mathematical model for this simple production-scheduling problem where x = (unknown) number of circuit boards to be produced per week, is:

$$\text{Maximize (profit)} = \$5x \quad \text{Objective function} \quad (1.2)$$

$$\text{Subject to:} \quad \left.\begin{array}{l} 2x \leq 400 \\ \text{with } x \geq 0 \end{array}\right\} \text{Constraints} \quad (1.3)$$

The optimal solution to this problem can easily be determined as $x = 200$, with an associated profit of $1000. Note that in this example the decision solution variable, x = number of circuit boards, is a continuous variable, even though it takes on a discrete value (i.e., $x = 200$). Note also that the two constraints are satisfied. The detailed construction of the specific mathematical model for this production-scheduling problem is shown in Figure 1.4.

EXAMPLE (STOCHASTIC MODEL)

As an example of a stochastic model, consider the situation faced by a fast-food restaurant as it tries to determine how many employees to have working at a particular time of the day. This decision would probably be based on past sales records that would then be used to derive a frequency distribution of sales by time of day. The uncontrollable variable in this stochastic situation is the level of demand by time of day, and is not known with certainty. As a result, the manager would try to have enough employees working at a particular time of day in order to achieve a certain probability of meeting demand.

1.3.3 COLLECTING THE DATA

The third step in the quantitative modeling process involves the collection and preparation of the data for the model. In essence the data that are required

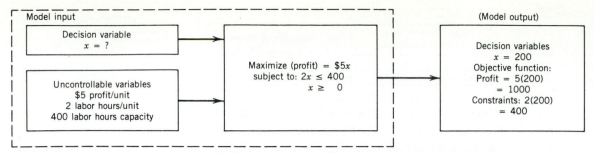

FIGURE 1.4 CONSTRUCTION OF A MATHEMATICAL MODEL FOR PRODUCTION SCHEDULING PROBLEM.

are those which describe the uncontrollable variables of the model. This information might be collected from company records, or it might result from an experiment or test, or it might be obtained from a survey. In the example shown above the $5 profit per item would probably be obtained from accounting data, while the 400 hours of production labor available each week and the 2 hours of production labor required for each circuit board would probably be obtained from the production manager. Data collection is a very important part of the quantitative modeling process, and it must be approached with care and diligence. It should also be mentioned that data collection may be done concurrently with model development, or in the case of certain types of statistical models it may even be done prior to model development.

1.3.4 SOLVING THE MODEL

Once the model has been constructed, and the input data have been collected, a solution for the model can be obtained. In solving the model, experimentation is used. Quite often we try to determine an "optimal" solution for the model. Referring to our previous example, solution of the model involved the determination of the value of the decision variable x (e.g., number of circuit boards to be produced) that maximized profit while not causing a violation of the production labor hours constraint.

The solution to the quantitative model typically will employ an *algorithm*. An algorithm is a set of procedures or rules that is followed in a step-by-step or iterative manner, which converges to the best solution for a given model. A particular algorithm has a specific set of rules that apply to a specific problem. One example is the "simplex" algorithm that is used to solve linear programming problems.

There are a large number of algorithms in existence, and many more are currently being developed.

The digital computer often plays an important role in obtaining a solution to the model, since the algorithms that are used can be programmed on the computer. In this fashion, the digital computer is used to perform the calculations within the iterative process.

1.3.5 ANALYZING THE SOLUTION TO THE MODEL

After the solution to the model has been obtained, it must be carefully analyzed to determine just how good the solution really is. Assuming that the modeler has proceeded carefully and accurately at each step of the modeling process, it is reasonable to expect that the solution to the model will be a good solution. However, this solution must be validated and examined carefully. Quite often it may be useful to test the model on a small "test" problem for which the results can be obtained by hand calculations, or for which the results are known. If the solution to the test problem is satisfactory, then the model can be utilized to solve full-scale problems. If the model testing and validation identifies problems or errors, then the model itself may have to be restructured or more accurate input data may have to be collected. Therefore, analysis of the solution to the model may result in a feedback looping process with the model formulation and/or data collection steps.

1.3.6 IMPLEMENTING THE SOLUTION TO THE MODEL

The final step in the process of quantitative modeling is perhaps the most difficult aspect of the entire process. This step involves implementing the solution to the model, which basically entails the "selling" of the results to management. Perhaps the best way to ensure that implementation will eventually be successful is to elicit management involvement and support from the initiation of the project onward. Also, the quantitative modeler must be very careful to present the results of the project in terms that can be understood by management, and must stress the benefit and contribution of the model. This may necessitate putting an emphasis on some of the more qualitative aspects of the modeling process.

Another important aspect of the implementation step is the provision of meaningful information concerning the model's solution to management. This is typically done by means of a set of computer-produced management reports. As we noted earlier many decision support systems are built around quantitative models.

1.4 QUANTITATIVE METHODS TO BE STUDIED

At this point it is useful to briefly preview the quantitative methods we consider in this book, and then indicate the types of problems to which they can be applied.

Probability concepts (Chapter 2) and *probability distributions* (Chapter 3) are useful for problems involving uncertainty.

Decision theory (Chapter 4) is applicable to situations in which the decision maker has several alternative courses of action but is also confronted with an uncertain future set of possible events. *Utility theory* (Chapter 4) is applied to problems in which expected monetary value is inappropriate.

Forecasting (Chapter 5) is fundamental to the practice of management, and involves using past behavior as an indicator of future conditions. Among the topics addressed in this chapter are qualitative forecasting methods, averaging methods, exponential smoothing, and causal forecasting using linear regression.

Linear programming (Chapters 6, 7, 8, 9) is discussed in considerable detail, as it is an extremely valuable and widely used method for choosing among alternatives subject to resource constraints, where the relationships can be described linearly. Graphical procedures, the simplex method, and postop-

timality aspects of linear programming are covered in these chapters.

Goal programming (Chapter 10) is a technique that extends linear programming to allow the consideration of multiple objectives or goals, rather than the single objective of linear programming.

Transportation, Transshipment, and *Assignment problems* (Chapter 11) concern logistical problems involving space and time. The transportation problem involves the optimum transportation or physical distribution of goods and services from several supply origins to several demand destinations. The transshipment problem is a special type of transportation problem in which the product or commodity is allowed to pass through intermediate transfer points before it reaches its final destination. The assignment problem involves the assignment of a fixed number of resources to a fixed number of activities, on a one-to-one basis.

Network models (Chapter 12) are applicable to subway, highway, and transportation systems, to information retrieval and processing, and in the planning and control of research and development projects. Network models can be used to find the shortest route through a network, or to maximize the flow through a network, or to find the minimum path connecting a number of points in a network.

PERT (program evaluation review technique) and *CPM* (critical path method) (Chapter 13) enable managers to more effectively manage the resources associated with large, complex projects.

Integer programming models (Chapter 14) are used for the same types of problems as linear programming, except that integer programming allows for solutions in integer (whole number) quantities.

Inventory analysis (Chapters 15 and 16) is used to control total inventory cost, which is composed of the cost of purchasing or producing inventory, carrying inventory, and being out of stock of inventory.

Waiting line models (Chapter 17) are used to improve the efficiency of service facilities in which the demand and timing of the demand of the customer, the time duration of the servicing operations, and the behavior of the customers as they arrive for service and/or wait in the queue are characterized by uncertainty.

Computer simulation (Chapter 18) is a procedure in which a model of the problem is constructed and tested in a trial-and-error manner to generate a series of solutions. The decision maker then makes a choice from among the solutions that have been generated. Simulation is one of the most widely used quantitative techniques.

Dynamic programming (Chapter 19) is a quantitative technique that is particularly applicable to sequential decision-making situations in which the same type of decision must be made at each stage of the problem.

Markov analysis (Chapter 20) is a stochastic procedure in which the decision maker tries to analyze and describe the current behavior of some variable in order to predict the future behavior of that same variable.

Game theory (Chapter 21) is used to develop competitive strategies in decision-making situations involving two or more knowledgeable opponents who are striving to attain some objective.

Calculus-based solution procedures and nonlinear programming (Chapter 22) is an introduction to the use of calculus in quantitative decision making as well as to problems that have nonlinear components.

1.5 QUANTITATIVE ANALYSIS IN PRACTICE

The use of quantitative analysis in practical decision-making situations has been the subject of frequent surveys. In 1965 Schumacher and Smith[1] reported findings from a survey of operations research activities as determined from a mail questionnaire sent to 168 companies in *Fortune* magazine's top 500. This study indicated heavy usage of operations research in production scheduling, inventory control, and forecasting.

Prasad,[2] in 1966, reported the results of a content analysis of 354 articles that were published in the journal, *Management Science*, during the period January 1955 to September 1964. The greatest frequency of application for these articles was seen to be in the production functional area.

A large-scale field study was conducted by Radnor, Rubenstein, and Bean[3] during the mid-1960s within 66 major U.S. corporations. Their findings indicated that management science activities began in the early 1950s in research and development, engineering, manufacturing, and financial areas of most corporations. Their findings suggested that there was a contraction of management science activities in all functional areas, except finance and corporate planning during the 1960s. As Radnor, Rubenstein and Bean indicate, this is probably not surprising since the finance function usually has control of the important data sources that are required by the management science function. Also, in many corporations the location of the computer operation in the controller's area has given impetus to the development of management science.

An interesting survey of the uses of management science was made by Turban,[4] and involved 107 of the largest corporations in the United States. Turban traced the activities of management science groups over time and concluded that more sophisticated and difficult problems had been considered as management science became a more mature activity.

The original Radnor, Rubenstein, and Bean study was updated by Radnor, Rubenstein, and Tansik in 1970[5] and by Radnor and Neal in 1973.[6] These latter articles indicated that operations research/management science activities were still in a transitional state within most organizations, with their position undergoing fairly steady improvement in terms of significance and acceptance. Radnor and Neal also found that there was an increasing dif-

[1]C. C. Schumacher and B. E. Smith, "A sample survey of industrial operations research activities II," *Operations Research*, **13**(6) (November/December 1965), 1023–1027.

[2]S. Benjamin Prasad, "Problem-solving trends in management science," *Management Science,* **13**(1) (October 1966), C10–C16.

[3]Michael Radnor, Albert H. Rubenstein, and Albert S. Bean, "Integration and utilization of management science activities in organizations," *Operations Research Quarterly,* **19**(2) (June 1968), 117–141.

[4]Efraim Turban, "How they're planning OR at the top," *Industrial Engineering,* **1**(12) (December 1969), 16–20; also "A sample survey of operations research activities at the corporate level," *Operations Research,* **20**(3) (May/June 1972), 708–721.

[5]Michael Radnor, Albert H. Rubenstein, and David A. Tansik, "Implementation in operations research and R and D in government and business," *Operations Research,* **18**(7) (1970), 967–991.

[6]Michael Radnor and Rodney D. Neal, "The progress of management science activities in large U.S. industrial corporations," *Operations Research,* **21**(2) (March/April 1973), 427–450.

fusion of operations research/management science techniques into various functional areas within business organizations, particularly in capital-intensive industries. They concluded that the most important finding from their latest study was that operations research/management science was in a "success phase" in its development history.

Gaither,[7] in 1975, made a study of the use of operations research in manufacturing firms. He found a high frequency of utilization of statistical analysis, simulation, and linear programming. Of special interest was the fact that PERT/CPM was identified as the method most frequently used by the manufacturing firms surveyed.

In 1976, Fabozzi and Valente[8] reported on a survey of the *Fortune* 500 firms in the United States concerning the use of mathematical programming. Their survey findings indicated that the most important area of application of mathematical programming was in production management (determination of product mix, production scheduling, plant, equipment, and manpower scheduling). The second most important area of application was financial and investment planning (capital budgeting, cash-flow analysis, portfolio analysis, cash management). Linear programming was found to produce good results for 76 percent of the firms responding, while nonlinear programming produced 57 percent, and dynamic programming 53 percent.

In 1977, Ledbetter and Cox reported on a survey of the *Fortune* 500 firms listed in 1975. One hundred seventy-six of these firms responded and indicated that regression analysis, linear programming, and simulation were the most frequently used operations research techniques in their firms. Their findings were quite similar, in this regard, to those reported earlier by Turban, and are summarized in Table 1.1.

A survey of practitioners in government, industry, and universities was made by Shannon, Long, and Buckles in 1980. Their study focused on both the respondents' familiarity with various quantitative methods and on whether or not they had actually applied the specific method. A summary of their findings is shown in Table 1.2.

Finally, a recent survey by Forgionne involved a random sample of 500 large corporations and disclosed some interesting findings concerning the use of OR/MS in these large companies. A summary of Forgionne's findings for the 125 large companies that responded to his survey is presented in Table 1.3.

Review Tables 1.1, 1.2, and 1.3, noting that you have had, or will take, a separate course in statistical analysis. Also, review chapters on statistical analysis (Chapter 2, Probability Concepts, and Chapter 3, Probability Distributions) are included in this book. Additionally, we have included a chapter on statistical decision theory (Chapter 4, Decision Theory and Utility Theory) and a chapter on statistical forecasting (Chapter 5, Forecasting). Each of the other methods listed in these tables is the subject of one or more chapters in this book. So by studying the quantitative methods discussed later, you should obtain a good background in those methods that are actually being used in practice.

1.5.1 PROFESSIONAL SOCIETIES

As a result of the rapid growth and proliferation of quantitative approaches to decision making, several professional societies devoted to this area and its related activities have been founded in the United States. In 1952 the Operations Research Society of America (ORSA) was founded, and began publication of the journal *Operations Research.* In 1953 The Institute of Management Science (TIMS) was initiated, and began publication of the journal *Management Science.* Today, these two professional organizations hold two national meetings jointly each year, and publish *Interfaces,* a quarterly journal that highlights practical applications of management science and operations research, and *OR/MS Today,* a bimonthly newsletter concerning the activities of the two organizations. In 1969, the Decision Sciences Institute (DSI) was begun and started publishing a journal *Decision Sciences.*

In addition to these U.S.-based professional societies, there are similar groups in more than 50 foreign countries. One such group is the Operational Research Society of the United Kingdom, founded in 1950, which publishes the *Journal of the Operational Research Society.*

---

[7]N. Gaither, "The adoption of operations research techniques by manufacturing organizations," *Decision Sciences,* **6**(4) (October 1975), 797–813.

[8]F. J. Fabozzi and J. Valente, "Mathematical programming in American companies: A sample survey," *Interfaces,* **7**(1) (November 1976), 93–98.

TABLE 1.1 USE OF OPERATIONS RESEARCH TECHNIQUES

	NUMBER OF RESPONDENTS	DEGREE OF USE (%)				
		NEVER				VERY FREQUENTLY
TECHNIQUES		1	2	3	4	5
Regression analysis	74	9.5	2.7	17.6	21.6	48.6
Linear programming	78	15.4	14.1	21.8	16.7	32.0
Simulation (in production)	70	11.4	15.7	25.7	24.3	22.9
Network models	69	39.1	29.0	15.9	10.1	5.8
Queuing theory	71	36.6	39.4	16.9	5.6	1.4
Dynamic programming	69	53.6	36.2	7.2	0.0	2.9
Game theory	67	69.7	25.4	8.9	6.0	0.0

Source: W. N. Ledbetter and J. F. Cox, "Are OR techniques being used?," *Industrial Engineering* (February 1977), p. 19.

TABLE 1.2 FAMILIARITY WITH, AND USE OF, OPERATIONS RESEARCH TECHNIQUES

METHOD	FAMILIARITY RANK	USAGE (PERCENT)
Linear programming	1	83.8
Simulation	2	80.3
Network analysis	3	58.1
Queuing theory	4	54.7
Decision trees	5	54.7
Integer programming	6	38.5
Nonlinear programming	7	32.5
Markov processes	8	31.6
Replacement analysis	9	38.5
Game theory	10	13.7
Goal programming	11	20.5

Source: R. E. Shannon, S. S. Long, and B. P. Buckles, "Operations research methodologies in industrial engineering: A survey," *AIIE Transactions*, **12**(4) (1980), p. 363.

1.5.2 QUANTITATIVE METHODS PERIODICALS

Another indication of the rapid growth and widespread use of quantitative decision-making methods is the large number of journals that regularly publish articles in this area. A listing of some of the major periodicals that contain articles of interest to the user of quantitative decision-making methods is shown.

1. Computers and Operations Research
2. Decision Sciences
3. European Journal of Operational Research
4. Interfaces
5. International Journal of Production Research
6. Journal of Financial and Quantitative Analysis
7. Journal of the Operational Research Society
8. Journal of Operations Management
9. Management Science
10. Naval Research Logistics Quarterly
11. Omega-International Journal of Management Science
12. Operations Research
13. Production and Inventory Management
14. Simulation

TABLE 1.3 USE OF OR/MS TECHNIQUES IN 125 LARGE COMPANIES

METHODOLOGY	FREQUENCY OF USE		
	NEVER	MODERATE	FREQUENT
Statistical analysis	1.6	38.7	59.7
Computer simulation	12.9	53.2	33.9
PERT/CPM	25.8	53.2	21.0
Linear programming	25.8	59.7	14.5
Queuing theory	40.3	50.0	9.7
Nonlinear programming	53.2	38.7	8.1
Dynamic programming	61.3	33.9	4.8
Game theory	69.4	27.4	3.2

Source: G. A. Forgionne, "Corporate management science activities: An update," *Interfaces*, **13**(3) (June 1983), p. 20.

1.6 WHY SHOULD I BE INTERESTED IN QUANTITATIVE APPROACHES TO DECISION MAKING?

Many undergraduate business students approach the study of quantitative methods with at least fear, if not downright loathing! Perhaps they have had a bad experience with an earlier statistics course, or they may not feel comfortable with courses that are mathematically oriented. They often feel that such courses are too "technical" and don't really offer much of value to someone interested in becoming a manager. Or they don't see how such a course relates to other functional areas of business, such as marketing or finance. The manifestation of these feelings can be summed up by the question: "Why should I be interested in quantitative approaches to decision making?"

A quick, and perhaps flippant, answer might be the same one that your mother told you about eating spinach: "Because it's good for you." Hopefully, we can suggest here, and illustrate throughout the remainder of this book, several reasons why you should be interested in quantitative approaches to decision making.

First, as we have stressed throughout this chapter, there has been a tremendous explosion in the use of quantitative methods for decision making throughout business, the public sector, and governmental and military organizations in recent years. This trend is becoming even more pronounced with the widespread availability of microcomputers. As a result, wherever your career path leads, you will undoubtedly be exposed to quantitative decision making, probably using a microcomputer. For example, as a manager faced with making decisions concerning the allocation of sales personnel to sales territories you might have to base your decision on an analysis done using linear programming. Or, you could become involved with decisions involving inventory control, or the routing of delivery vehicles. All of these decision-making situations utilize quantitative methods. In short, quantitative methods are an important and growing facet of the decision-making process for the progressive manager.

Second, because of the great growth in the use of quantitative methods, career opportunities in this field, or related fields, are truly outstanding. The demand for well-trained, highly motivated quantitative methods personnel far exceeds the supply. One can expect very good starting positions, with rapid advancement possibilities. Among the many types of jobs available with a quantitative methods focus are the following.

1. QUANTITATIVE ANALYSTS   A broad term used to describe individuals who apply quantitative methods to solve organizational decision problems. Specific types of quantitative analysts include

   a. Management scientists or operations researchers, who deal with large-scale organizational problems, usually as a corporate staff. They work throughout the company, in a team fashion, on a wide variety of problems.

   b. Production planners or schedulers, who focus on production planning and scheduling problems in a manufacturing environment.

   c. Inventory control analysts, who work with inventory-control problems.

   d. Financial analysts, who use quantitative methods to make investment decisions, do portfolio analysis, and make buy-or-lease decisions.

   e. Marketing researcher, who use quantitative methods to make new product decisions, survey consumer tastes, make market demand estimates, and develop marketing strategies.

   f. Forecasting analysts, who develop short- or long-term demand or sales forecasts and use these forecasts to assist in production planning and inventory control.

2. MANAGEMENT CONSULTANTS   Many large consulting firms exist that have a specific emphasis on the use of quantitative decision-making techniques. Most of the large accounting firms now have divisions that actively do consulting work of this nature.

3. INFORMATION SYSTEMS ANALYSTS   These individuals specialize in developing and implementing computer systems. Many of these computer systems are built around quantitative techniques, so the people involved with such systems also have strong quantitative backgrounds and interests.

1.7 SUMMARY

In this chapter we presented an introduction to quantitative modeling of decision problems. We saw that the quantitative approach to decision making applies the scientific method, adopts a systems modeling approach, utilizes a team concept, and makes extensive use of computers. Next, we explored the steps that are involved in quantitative modeling, placing particular emphasis on the model development step. The quantitative methods studied in this textbook were then discussed and summarized. The practice of quantitative analysis, as reported in several surveys, was then reviewed. Finally, we discussed why quantitative approaches to decision making should be important to you as a student.

GLOSSARY

Algorithm   A set of procedures, which is followed in an iterative manner and which converges to the optimum solution for a specific problem.

Analog Model   A model in which one physical property is used to represent another physical property.

Constraint   A mathematical function that limits or restricts resource utilization or allocation with respect to the decision variables of the model.

Continuous Variables   Variables that can take on a continuum of values.

Controllable Variables   Those variables that are under the control of the decision maker.

Data Base   A set of data which is structured according to some predefined set of rules.

Decision Support System   A type of management information system in which the manager is provided information that facilitates assessing future conditions and making decisions.

Decision Variables   The unknowns that are to be determined by solving the model.

Descriptive Model   A model that describes some problem situation but does not indicate any preferred course of action.

Deterministic Model   A model in which the functional relationships and parameters are known with certainty.

Discrete Variables   Variables that can take on one of a finite, or countably infinite, number of values.

Iconic Model   A scaled physical representation of a real system.

Management Information Systems   Computerized systems for collecting, analyzing, and reporting information to managers.

Management Science/Operations Research   Application of quantitative methods to decision making in business, industrial, governmental, and military organizations with an objective of improving the quality of managerial decisions.

Mathematical Model   A model in which a set of mathematical symbols and functional relationships are used to represent some physical situation.

Normative Model A model that describes the functional relationships between the variables of a system and prescribes a course of action for the decision maker to follow in meeting some defined objective.

Objective Function A mathematical function defining the relationship among the decision variables in terms of optimizing some measure of effectiveness.

Optimal Solution The solution that is optimal with respect to the underlying objective of the problem.

Parameters The known values or constants of the model.

Predictive Model A model used to make a forecast of the future.

Qualitative Model A descriptive model of the real system.

Stochastic Model A model that incorporates uncertainty in its functional relations and uncontrollable variables.

Suboptimization Failing to achieve the overall goals of the organization by concentrating on solving a problem involving only a part of the organization.

Systems Approach An approach to decision making in which the organization is viewed as a system composed of many parts.

Uncontrollable Variables Those variables that are not under the control of the decision maker.

Selected References

Anderson, David R., Dennis J. Sweeney, and Thomas A. Williams. 1976. *Quantitative Methods for Business*. St. Paul, Minn.: West.

Bell, Colin E. 1977. *Quantitative Methods for Administration*. Homewood, Ill.: Irwin.

Bierman, Harold, Charles P. Bonini, and Warren H. Hausman. 1977. *Quantitative Analysis for Business Decisions*. Homewood, Ill.: Irwin.

Churchman, C. W., R. L. Ackoff, and E. L. Arnoff. 1967. *Introduction to Operations Research*. New York: Wiley.

Davis, K. Roscoe, and Patrick G. McKeown. 1981. *Quantitative Models for Management*. Boston: Kent.

Dinkel, John J., Gary A. Kochenberger, and Donald R. Plane. 1978. *Management Science: Text and Applications*. Homewood, Ill.: Irwin.

Eppen, Gary D., and F. J. Gould. 1979. *Quantitative Concepts For Management*. Englewood Cliffs, N.J.: Prentice–Hall.

Hesse, Rick, and Gene Woolsey. 1980. *Applied Management Science*. Chicago: Science Res. Associates.

Hillier, Frederick S., and Gerald J. Lieberman. 1980. *Introduction to Operations Research*. San Francisco: Holden–Day.

Krajewski, Lee J., and Howard E. Thompson. 1981. *Management Science: Quantitative Methods In Context*. New York: Wiley.

Lee, Sang M., Laurence J. Moore, and Bernard W. Taylor. 1981. *Management Science*. Dubuque, Iowa: W. C. Brown.

Levin, Richard I., David S. Rubin, and Joel P. Stinson. 1986. *Quantitative Approaches to Management*. New York: McGraw–Hill.

Markland, Robert E. 1983. *Topics In Management Science.* New York: Wiley.

Shore, Barry. 1978. *Quantitative Methods For Business Decisions: Text and Cases.* New York: McGraw–Hill.

Trueman, Richard E. 1981. *An Introduction to Quantitative Methods for Decision Making.* New York: Holt, Rinehart & Winston.

Wagner, Harvey M. 1975. *Principles of Operations Research.* Englewood Cliffs, N.J.: Prentice–Hall.

Discussion Questions

1. Describe and contrast the qualitative and quantitative approaches to decision making.

2. Why is it important for the manager to be able to blend the qualitative and quantitative approaches to decision making?

3. List and discuss the six major steps in the quantitative modeling process.

4. What is the significance and importance of model building in the quantitative modeling process?

5. What is the difference between a descriptive and a normative model?

6. Describe the major elements in a typical mathematical model.

7. What is the difference between a discrete and a continuous variable?

8. Why is implementation a difficult aspect of the quantitative modeling process?

9. Why is the study of quantitative methods of importance to the prospective manager?

10. What are some of the job possibilities involving quantitative methods? Consult the "help wanted" ads in the *Wall Street Journal* and your local newspaper.

Introduction to Chapter Ending Application Reviews

At the end of most of the 23 chapters of this book we have included application reviews. These application reviews have been extracted from the literature of the field. They are intended to provide the reader with a better understanding of how quantitative methods are used, and how various companies have benefitted from their use.

Each application review describes the company involved and focuses on an application that is related to that chapter. The application reviews are written in a manner that avoids technical details and stresses the managerial implications of the application of the particular quantitative method.

Chapter 1 is intended to provide an introduction to quantitative methods, and does not stress any particular solution technique. Consequently, we have included an application review of the Burger King Corporation at the end of this chapter. The Burger King Corporation has a long history of successfully applying quantitative methods in a number of areas related to improving productivity and is a company in which quantitative methods have had a major impact. Also, it is one of the authors' favorite fast-food restaurants!

Application Review

Burger King Corporation—A Success Story In Productivity Improvement

The Burger King Corporation operates one of the most successful fast-food restaurant systems, involving more than 3000 restaurants worldwide. In 1981 it had total worldwide sales of more than $2 billion. An average franchised restaurant in its system grosses more than $700,000 annually.

The Burger King Corporation has increasingly made use of quantitative methods to more effectively manage its restaurant operations, as the introduction of drive-through service and new menu items have transformed a simple operation into a sophisticated production process. As the Burger King Corporation develops new products, systems, and procedures, it must then convince its individual restaurant franchises to adopt them as a means of improving profitability.

The Burger King Corporation has a large Operations Research Department at its Miami headquarters. This group has established itself through a series of high-impact projects that have greatly improved restaurant operations, productivity, and profitability. Areas in which various quantitative methods have been used include the following.

Waiting line analysis was utilized to develop a "hospitality system," or multichannel service facility type of restaurant. This was accomplished by expanding the restaurant building backwards, and placing the sandwich preparation board perpendicular to the counter, thus allowing more sandwich preparation employees to work simultaneously. These changes reduced the average customer service time and greatly increased overall sales.

Linear programming was employed to determine the least-cost formulation for individual meat packers; and to determine the least-cost distribution pattern for meat packers to restaurants. This resulted in an annual cost savings of $2 million for Burger King Corporation.

Simulation modeling was used to analyze the entire operation of a particular restaurant. The general-purpose restaurant simulation model that was developed has the capability of representing any restaurant type currently in the system as well as new restaurant designs. It has been used extensively to measure the effect on restaurant productivity and profitability that would result from changes in restaurant service configuration, the introduction of new products, changes in restaurant size, and location of new restaurants. Benefits both to franchises and the parent corporation have been substantial.

In summary, Burger King Corporation is a success story in productivity improvement. This productivity improvement has been largely achieved through its use of quantitative methods.

Source: Swart, William, and Luca Donno, "Simulation modeling improves operations, planning, and productivity of fast food restaurant," *Interfaces,* **11**(6) (December 1981), pp. 35–47.

2

PROBABILITY CONCEPTS

2.1 INTRODUCTION

Probability theory has been with us for a very long time. The formalization of the mathematics of probability as it applies to games of chance occurred around the eighteenth century. The eighteenth-century mathematicians Karl Gauss and Pierre Laplace are credited with the first application of probability concepts to other fields. Today, however, application to problems in the social and physical sciences is commonplace.

Probability is one of the fundamental components of the decision-making process. Since probability is used as a measure of uncertainty, we rely on it either explicitly or implicitly on a daily basis. We rely on probability to make choices such as what we wear on a particular day or whether we should cancel a planned outdoor activity because of the likelihood of inclement weather. We make a conscious decision about the amount of time we spend studying for certain topics that could be on an examination by the perceived likelihood of inclusion of the topic on the exam by the professor. In business, probability plays an important role in investment and marketing strategies, inventory policy, production planning, facility expansion/facility phase out, waiting line analysis, and the like. Clearly there are very few decisions in our personal or professional lives that are not based on the concept of probability.

In this chapter and the next a brief review of the basic concepts in probability theory and some standard probability distributions are presented. These chapters are not meant to replace a basic course in probability and statistics, but rather to provide a concise review of familiar concepts. Table 2.1 lists

TABLE 2.2 EXAMPLES OF EXPERIMENTS/OUTCOMES

EXPERIMENT	OUTCOME
Toss a coin	Head, tail
Take an examination	A, B, C, D, F
Roll a die	1, 2, 3, 4, 5, 6
Play a game of chess	Win, lose, draw

the topics covered in this textbook that directly incorporate some aspect of probability theory.

2.2 FUNDAMENTAL CONCEPTS

2.2.1 THE EXPERIMENT AND THE SAMPLE SPACE

The foundation of probability concepts is the *random experiment*. An *experiment* is the process through which an observation or outcome is recorded. If an experiment is repeated, each repetition yields exactly one outcome in the set of possible outcomes. An outcome may be, but will not necessarily be, a numerical value. Several examples of experiments and associated outcomes are given in Table 2.2. The *set* of all possible outcomes for an experiment is called the *sample space* for the experiment. A single element in the sample space is called a *sample point* or a *simple event*.

Before we can identify the sample space for a given situation we must clearly identify the purpose of the experiment. For example, an insurance salesperson conducts a sales call and we are interested in recording the result of the call. What is the result

TABLE 2.1 CHAPTERS USING PROBABILITY CONCEPTS

CHAPTER	TITLE
4	Decision Theory and Utility Theory
5	Forecasting
13	PERT/CPM
16	Inventory Analysis: Probabilistic Models
17	Waiting Line Models
18	Computer Simulation
20	Markov Analysis
21	Game Theory

of interest? Is it simply success or failure? Or is the outcome of interest the amount of the sale that could then be used for computing the average amount of the sale per call? Clearly the physical process of conducting a sales call can define several experiments. We will let S denote the sample space. The situation described above can define two distinct experiments.

EXPERIMENT 1:
Conduct a sales call and record success or failure.

$$S = \{sale, no\ sale\}$$

EXPERIMENT 2:
Conduct a sales call and record the amount of sale. Assume that only policies with face values of $10,000, $25,000, $50,000, $100,000, and $250,000 are available.

$$S = \{0;\ 10,000;\ 25,000;\ 50,000;$$
$$100,000;\ 250,000\}$$

Consider the experiment that involves the tossing of two coins; a nickel and a dime, and the observation of the sequences of heads and tails after the toss. How many sample points are there for this experiment and what are they?

A schematic approach that is useful in enumerating the sample points is called the *tree diagram*. Figure 2.1 gives the tree diagram for the nickel/dime tossing experiment. Here Step 1 corresponds to tossing the nickel and Step 2 corresponds to tossing the dime. The sample space for this experiment is:

$$S = \{(H, H),\ (H, T),\ (T, H),\ (T, T)\}$$

where *H* denotes "Heads" and *T* denotes "Tails." Position in the ordered pair (x, y) also has significance in this representation of the sample points. The first position records the result of the toss of the nickel, while the second position records the result of the toss of the dime.

As another illustration of the concepts introduced thus far we consider the case of BGS Construction Company. BGS is involved in the design, construction, and installation of custom kitchens. The management of BGS is interested in charac-

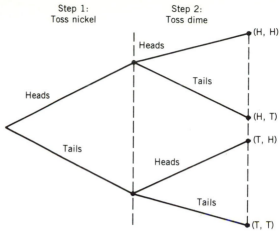

FIGURE 2.1 TREE DIAGRAM FOR COIN TOSSING EXPERIMENT.

terizing the number of weeks required for the completion of a job (contract), the design phase through installation phase. In the past the design phase has required 1 or 2 weeks, the construction phase has required either 2 or 3 weeks, and the installation phase has required 1, 2, or 3 weeks. Management would prefer to complete all jobs within 6 weeks.

The selection of a job along with the amount of time required to complete the three phases may be viewed as an experiment. The sample space for this experiment is constructed using the tree diagram in Figure 2.2. Here a sample point is designated by (x, y, z), where x represents the number of weeks required for the design phase, y represents the number of weeks required for the construction phase, and z represents the number of weeks required for the installation phase.

An *event* is defined as a subset of the sample space. Each element of the sample space forms a subset and this "trivial" subset is often called a simple event. Suppose that the event of particular interest to management is the subset of sample points that represents contract completion time of 6 weeks or less. Label this event A. Then,

$$A = \{(1, 2, 1);\ (1, 2, 2);\ (1, 2, 3);\ (1, 3, 1);$$
$$(1, 3, 2);\ (2, 2, 1);\ (2, 2, 2);\ (2, 3, 1)\}$$

Thus 8 out of 12 sample points comprise event A and *event A is said to occur* if any one of these 8 events occur. The primary question of interest is then: How likely is it for the event A to occur? Or:

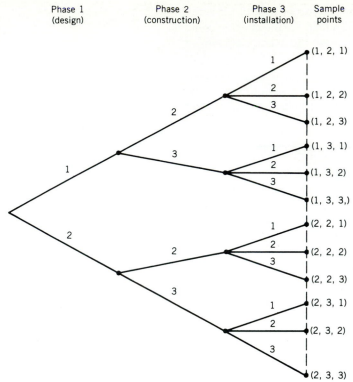

| Phase 1
(design) | Phase 2
(construction) | Phase 3
(installation) | Sample
points |

FIGURE 2.2   SAMPLE SPACE FOR THE BGS CONSTRUCTION ILLUSTRATION.

What is the probability that event A occurs? To answer either question we must determine how to assign probabilities to sample points as well as events.

2.2.2 DEFINING PROBABILITY

In order to define the probability of occurrence of an event we must define the probabilities of individual outcomes (sample points) from an experiment. Keep in mind the idea that a probability is a numerical value that measures the likelihood of occurrence for an individual outcome of an experiment. There are several ways that individual outcomes to an experiment are assigned probabilities. In any case, the probability of occurrence of a sample point is the proportion of time that the sample point under consideration is expected to occur. With this in mind it is logical that any explicit definition of probability must satisfy the following basic rules.

1. The probability value assigned to a sample point must be between 0 and 1, inclusive.

2. The sum of the probabilities of *all* sample points must be *exactly* one.

Historically three methods have been used to define probability

1. the classical approach;
2. the relative frequency approach;
3. the subjective approach.

The first two approaches define what is often called an *objective probability*.

The *classical approach* is based on the assumption that every sample point in the sample space has an equally likely chance to be the outcome of the experiment. Thus if there are n sample points in the sample space, the probability of each sample point is $1/n$. If we let $E_1, \ldots , E_n$ represent the sample points and $P(E_i)$ indicate the probability of E_i, then $P(E_i) = 1/n$, $i = 1, \ldots , n$. Also

$$\sum_{i=1}^{n} P(E_i) = \sum_{i=1}^{n} \frac{1}{n} = 1 \qquad (2.1)$$

TABLE 2.3 SAMPLE POINTS FROM FIGURE 2.1

LABEL	SAMPLE POINT
E_1	(H, H)
E_2	(H, T)
E_3	(T, H)
E_4	(H, H)

We note the consistency of this definition with the two previously stated rules.

The classical approach is appropriate in many gambling problems where the assumption of equally likely outcomes is reasonable. The sample space for the experiment represented in Figure 2.1 is listed in Table 2.3. We could argue, for this experiment, that each of the outcomes is equally likely. Thus

$$P(E_1) = P(E_2) = P(E_3) = P(E_4) = \tfrac{1}{4} \quad (2.2)$$

There are certainly many situations where this approach is not appropriate. In fact the relative frequency approach is more general and is probably a more widely accepted approach to probability definition than the classical approach. The relative frequency approach can be applied in most situations where the classical approach is used, and the resultant probabilities from the two approaches should be approximately the same.

The *relative frequency approach* is generally based on the observation of past occurrences. Suppose that we repeat the experiment of tossing a nickel and a dime 10,000 times. The results are reported in Table 2.4. In the relative frequency approach, the probability of E_i is the number of times that the sample point E_i is observed divided by the number of times the experiment is repeated. For this case, the probabilities $P(E_i)$ are listed in Table 2.5. If the experiment is repeated an infinitely large number of times,

TABLE 2.4 RESULT OF 10,000 REPETITIONS OF COIN TOSSING EXPERIMENT

SAMPLE POINT	FREQUENCY
E_1	2512
E_2	2500
E_3	2502
E_4	2486
	10,000

TABLE 2.5 RELATIVE FREQUENCY PROBABILITIES FOR COIN TOSSING EXPERIMENT

SAMPLE POINT	$P(E_i)$
E_1	$2512/10,000 = .2512$
E_2	$2500/10,000 = .2500$
E_3	$2502/10,000 = .2502$
E_4	$2486/10,000 = .2486$

these probabilities should be the same as the probabilities in the classical approach. It should be noted that in this case the relative frequency probabilities may be viewed as estimates for the classical probabilities. It is not difficult to imagine why the classical probability is sometimes called a *theoretical probability*, while the relative frequency probability is often termed an *empirical probability*.

In the BGS Construction example there is clearly no reason to assume that all 12 sample points are equally likely, and thus the relative frequency approach can be used if historical information is available. Suppose such information is available in the form of records for 250 completed contracts in the period January 1, 1979 to January 1, 1984. The information is given in the form of a *relative frequency/probability* table, Table 2.6. Consider the sample point E_7. This sample point represents the situation where 2 weeks is required for the design phase, 2 weeks for the construction phase, and 1 week for the installation phase. This outcome was observed in 35 out of 250 records. Thus the probability that an arbitrarily selected record will result in this outcome is 35/250.

There are many situations in which outcomes are not equally likely and for which relative frequency data are not available. In such a case, we must rely on experience and general information surrounding a possible outcome as well as intuition. A probability estimate without specific relative frequency information is called a *subjective probability*.

For example, perhaps you have done extensive reading on an upcoming presidential election and you believe that the probability of a particular candidate running is about .75. This is a subjective probability. A prominent expert in presidential races, however, claims that the probability of that particular candidate running is only .40. Both of these probabilities are subjective probabilities and both represent educated guesses based on available in-

TABLE 2.6 RELATIVE FREQUENCY/PROBABILITY TABLE FOR BGS ILLUSTRATION

SAMPLE POINT	FREQUENCY	$P(E_i)$
E_1: (1, 2, 1)	10	10/250 = .04
E_2: (1, 2, 2)	10	10/250 = .04
E_3: (1, 2, 3)	20	20/250 = .08
E_4: (1, 3, 1)	15	15/250 = .06
E_5: (1, 3, 2)	30	30/250 = .12
E_6: (1, 3, 3)	15	15/250 = .06
E_7: (2, 2, 1)	35	35/250 = .14
E_8: (2, 2, 2)	55	55/250 = .22
E_9: (2, 2, 3)	35	35/250 = .14
E_{10}: (2, 3, 1)	10	10/250 = .04
E_{11}: (2, 3, 2)	10	10/250 = .04
E_{12}: (2, 3, 3)	5	5/250 = .02
	250	1.00

formation. Certainly in this case it is likely that the information base is different for these two individuals, but even if the information base is the same, it is likely that the two individuals will give different subjective probabilities. Subjective probabilities express the *opinion* of an individual.

Subjective probabilities are frequently used in making business decisions. Estimating the impact of a new advertising campaign or estimating demand for a new, innovative service is likely to involve a subjective probability. Finally, it should be noted that in situations where the relative frequencies approach may be possible, a more acceptable estimate may be obtained by combining historical information with management's subjective probability estimates.

2.2.3 COMPUTING THE PROBABILITY OF AN EVENT

As defined earlier, an *event* is a collection of sample points. Recall the meaning of event A for the BGS Construction Company example. A is the set of all sample points that satisfies the condition that the contract is completed in 6 weeks or less.

$$A = \{(1, 2, 1); (1, 2, 2); (1, 2, 3); (1, 3, 1);$$
$$(1, 3, 2); (2, 2, 1); (2, 2, 2); (2, 3, 1)\}$$

The event A above is said to occur if the sample point (1, 2, 1) is observed, if the sample point (1, 2, 2) is observed, and so on. In general, the *event A is said to occur* if any one of the sample points that is used to define A occurs. As another example, define B as the event: 7 weeks are required to complete the project.

$$B = \{(1, 3, 3); (2, 2, 3); (2, 3, 2)\}$$

Again event B is said to occur if any one of these three sample points occurs.

The probability of occurrence of an event is defined in terms of the probabilities of the sample points that comprise an event. The *probability that event A occurs*, denoted $P(A)$, is said to be *equal* to the *sum* of the probabilities of the sample points that comprise A. In our previous examples

$$P(A) = P(1, 2, 1) + P(1, 2, 2) + P(1, 2, 3)$$
$$+ P(1, 3, 1) + P(1, 3, 2)$$
$$+ P(2, 2, 1) + P(2, 2, 2) + P(2, 3, 1)$$
$$= .04 + .04 + .08 + .06 + .12$$
$$+ .14 + .22 + .04$$
$$= .74 \qquad (2.3)$$
$$P(B) = P(1, 3, 3) + P(2, 2, 3) + P(2, 3, 2)$$
$$= .06 + .14 + .04$$
$$= .24 \qquad (2.4)$$

We know then that the probability of completing the contract in 6 weeks or less is .74, and that probability of completing the contract in exactly 7 weeks is .24.

In some situations the identification of all sample points in an experiment and the assignment of probabilities to each of the sample points is virtually impossible. On the other hand we may know the probabilities associated with certain events that are not necessarily single sample points. In such cases it is necessary to compute probabilities of events that are constructed from events with known probabilities. The remainder of the chapter deals primarily with the computation of such probabilities.

2.3 EVENT RELATIONS

In this section we introduce the event relations: union, intersection, complement, mutually exclusive, and collectively exhaustive. We accomplish this via an example involving the experiment of sequentially tossing a coin and then rolling a die. The sample space for this experiment, the T-R experiment, is listed in Table 2.7. Define the following events.

C: result of coin toss is a head;

D: result of coin toss is a tail;

E: roll of die results in a face number greater than 3;

F: roll of die results in a face number less than or equal to 3.

First we consider how events may be combined when some outcomes may be explained by the occurrence of more than one event. For example, the event that consists of sample points E_1, E_2, E_3 can

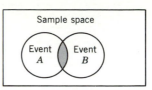

FIGURE 2.3 REPRESENTATION OF THE INTERSECTION OF *A* AND *B*.

be expressed as obtaining a head when tossing the coin *and* obtaining a face with number less than or equal to 3 when rolling the die.

The event that occurs when both events *A* and *B* occur is called the *intersection* of events *A* and *B* and is denoted as

$$(A \cap B) \quad \text{or} \quad (A \text{ and } B \text{ both occur})$$

$A \cap B$ is illustrated as the shaded region in Figure 2.3. We note that the event $\{E_1, E_2, E_3\}$ can be represented as $C \cap F$ where C and F are defined in the previous list of events.

The event that occurs when any one of two events *A* and *B* occurs is called the *union* of those events and is denoted as

$$(A \cup B) \quad \text{or} \quad \text{(either } A \text{ or } B \text{ occurs,} \\ \text{or both } A \text{ and } B \text{ occur)}$$

$A \cup B$ occurs if at least one of the following is true: *A* occurs, *B* occurs, both *A* and *B* occur. $A \cup B$ is depicted as the shaded region in Figure 2.4. For the T-R experiment

$$C \cup F = \{E_1, E_2, E_3, E_4, E_5, E_6, E_7, E_8, E_9\}$$

TABLE 2.7 SAMPLE SPACE FOR T-R EXPERIMENT

SAMPLE POINT	COIN	DIE	SAMPLE POINT	COIN	DIE
E_1	H	1	E_7	T	1
E_2	H	2	E_8	T	2
E_3	H	3	E_9	T	3
E_4	H	4	E_{10}	T	4
E_5	H	5	E_{11}	T	5
E_6	H	6	E_{12}	T	6

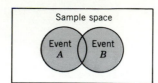

FIGURE 2.4 REPRESENTATION OF THE UNION OF *A* AND *B*.

1. *C* and *D* are mutually exclusive;
2. *E* and *F* are mutually exclusive;
3. *C* and *D* are collectively exhaustive;
4. *E* and *F* are collectively exhaustive;
5. *C, E, F* are collectively exhaustive but not mutually exclusive.

and $C \cup F$ is the set of outcomes where either a head or a face number less than or equal to 3 occurs.

The *complement* of event *A* is the event consisting of all sample points in *S* that are not in *A*. The complement of *A* will be denoted as $\overline{A}$. In set notation,

$$\overline{A} = S - A$$

where *S* denotes the sample space. $\overline{A}$ is depicted as the shaded region in Figure 2.5. In the T-R experiment we note that

$$\overline{C} = D \quad \text{and} \quad \overline{D} = C$$
$$\overline{E} = F \quad \text{and} \quad \overline{F} = E$$

It should also be noted that the complement of an event $\overline{A}$ is *A*.

Two events *A* and *B* are *mutually exclusive* if the occurrence of one event precludes the occurrence of the other event. If two events *A* and *B* are mutually exclusive, then it is true that $A \cap B = \emptyset$ ($\emptyset$: the empty set or the null set). A collection of events is said to be *collectively exhaustive* if the collection of sample points in this set of events is the entire sample space. We note that the collection of all simple events for an experiment is both collectively exhaustive and mutually exclusive. In the T-R example the following statements are valid.

2.4 THE ADDITION LAW

The addition law permits the computation of the probability that at least one of two events occurs. Using the language of the previous section, we want to compute the probability of an event that is expressed as the union of two events.

Recall that $P(A)$ is defined to be equal to the sum of the probabilities of the sample points that comprise *A*. This definition also applies to an event such as $A \cup B$, $A \cap B$, $\overline{A}$, and so on. It is clear that the event $A \cap B$ occurs when both *A* and *B* occur. Thus *A* and *B* both contain the sample points that comprise $A \cap B$. The significance of this observation is that $P(A)$ and $P(B)$ both include the sum of the probabilities of the sample points in $A \cap B$. In effect the expression $P(A) + P(B)$ actually reflects a double counting of the sample points in $A \cap B$ (see Figure 2.6). Thus, if our objective is to calculate $P(A \cup B)$, we must account for this double counting by subtracting $P(A \cap B)$ from $P(A) + P(B)$. The result is called the *addition law*

$$P(A \cup B) = P(A) + P(B) - P(A \cap B) \quad (2.5)$$

As an example of the application of the addition law consider the following situation. It is known that the probability that a certain movie will get an award for good directing is .44, the probability that it will get an award for special effects is .64, and the probability that it will get both awards is .09. We are interested in the probability that the

FIGURE 2.5 ILLUSTRATION OF THE COMPLEMENT OF AN EVENT.

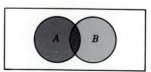

FIGURE 2.6 THE ADDITION LAW.

movie will get either or both awards. To answer this question define the following events.

A: the movie receives an award for good directing;

B: the movie receives an award for special effects.

From the previous information we know that $P(A) = .44$, $P(B) = .64$, $P(A \cap B) = .09$. Therefore, using the addition law,

$$P(A \cup B) = P(A) + P(B) - P(A \cap B)$$
$$= .64 + .44 - .09$$
$$= .99 \qquad (2.6)$$

The probability that the movie will receive either or both of the awards is .99.

As another example, suppose that in a production batch of 500 television sets, 20 have a scratched case and 10 have a serious mechanical defect, while there are 5 that have both a scratched case and a serious mechanical defect. If you purchase a television set from this batch, what is the probability of obtaining a defective set? Let A and B define the events as follows.

A: the purchased television has a scratched case;

B: the purchased television has a serious mechanical defect.

From the frequency information just given, we have

$$P(A) = 20/500 = .04$$
$$P(B) = 10/500 = .02 \qquad (2.7)$$
$$P(A \cap B) = 5/500 = .01$$

The probability that you purchase a TV that is not perfect is denoted as $P(A \cup B)$ and

$$P(A \cup B) = P(A) + P(B) - P(A \cap B)$$
$$= .04 + .02 - .01$$
$$= .05 \qquad (2.8)$$

2.4.1 THE ADDITION LAW AND MUTUALLY EXCLUSIVE EVENTS

We should note the special case of the addition law when the two events A and B are mutually exclusive.

If A and B are mutually exclusive, then A and B have no sample points in common. The intersection of the two sets A and B is said to be empty and is denoted by $\emptyset$. If $A \cap B = \emptyset$, then $P(A \cap B) = 0$ and the addition law becomes

$$P(A \cup B) = P(A) + P(B) \qquad (2.9)$$

This special case applies to the computation of $P(A \cup \overline{A})$, where $\overline{A}$ denotes the complement of A. Since the complement of A is the set of sample points not in A, $A \cup \overline{A} = S$ and $A \cap \overline{A} = \emptyset$. Thus $P(A \cap \overline{A}) = 0$ and

$$P(A \cup \overline{A}) = P(A) + P(\overline{A}) \qquad (2.10)$$

Also A and $\overline{A}$ are collectively exhaustive, so that $P(A \cup \overline{A}) = 1$, and we have established the relationship between $P(A)$ and $P(\overline{A})$. That is,

$$P(A) + P(\overline{A}) = 1 \qquad \text{or}$$
$$P(\overline{A}) = 1 - P(A) \qquad (2.11)$$

2.5 CONDITIONAL, JOINT, MARGINAL PROBABILITIES

Often two events are related in such a way that the probability of occurrence of one event depends on whether the second event has or has not occurred. Such a probability is called a *conditional probability* and we will develop this concept through the following example.

In a relatively conservative community each of the 60 families owns either a Chevrolet, a Ford, or a Plymouth. Also the only colors that these families will drive are red, white, and blue. There are 25 Chevrolets, 15 Fords, and 20 Plymouths. For each of these models the distribution of colors is given in Table 2.8. For example, there are 5 automobiles out of 60 that are Chevrolets and red. In other words, the two events, Chevrolet and red, occur jointly. Thus Table 2.8 is often referred to as a *joint frequency table*.

Using the relative frequency approach to define probability, the joint frequency table can be converted to a *joint probability table*. This is accomplished by dividing each frequency by the total number of observations (sample points). The probability that a family in this community owns a Chevrolet ($P(C)$)

TABLE 2.8 DISTRIBUTION OF AUTOMOBILE MODELS AND COLORS

	RED	WHITE	BLUE	TOTAL
Chevrolet	5	15	5	25
Ford	10	5	0	15
Plymouth	5	10	5	20
Total	20	30	10	60

is 25/60; also $P(F) = 15/60$ and $P(P) = 20/60$. The probability that a family owns a red car ($P(R)$) is 20/60; also $P(W) = 30/60$, $P(B) = 10/60$. The six probabilities just listed are often called *marginal probabilities*. In fact, whenever the probability of an event is expressed as the sum of the probabilities of a set of mutually exclusive events, this probability may be called a marginal probability. The probability that a family in the community will own a red Chevrolet is 5/60. In other words, this is the probability that a randomly selected family has a car that is red *and* is a Chevrolet. Actually this probability may be expressed as $P(R \cap C)$. This probability along with the other entries in the body of the table are referred to as *joint probabilities*.

Now suppose that we know that a particular family owns a Chevrolet. What is the probability that this family owns a red Chevrolet? To answer this question let's first go back to the joint frequency table, where we note that there are a total of 25 Chevrolets and only 5 of them are red. Therefore, the probability that this family will have a red car is 5/25. (The sample space for this experiment has 25 sample points.) As another example, suppose that we know that the family has a red car: what is the probability that this family owns a Chevrolet? In this case, we note that there are a total of 20 cars, 5 of which are Chevrolets. The requested probability is thus 5/20.

What we have described in the previous paragraph is the concept of a *conditional probability*. A conditional probability involves the computation of the probability of event A occurring under the condition that event B has occurred. This is denoted as

$$P(A|B) \qquad \text{``the probability of A given B''} \qquad (2.12)$$

We note that the examples previously given are

consistent with the formal definition of conditional probability given next.

$$P(A|B) = \frac{P(A \cap B)}{P(B)} \qquad (2.13)$$

Also,

$$P(B|A) = \frac{P(A \cap B)}{P(A)} \qquad (2.14)$$

Once again, the probability that a family owns a red car given that the family owns a Chevrolet is

$$P(R|C) = \frac{P(R \cap C)}{P(C)} = \frac{5/60}{25/60} = 5/25 \qquad (2.15)$$

As another example, we determine the probability that a family owns a Plymouth, given that we know the car is not red. From the joint frequency table we observe that there a total of 40 cars that are not red and that 15 of the cars that are not red are Plymouths. Therefore, the concept of a relative frequency probability allows us to say that the probability that a family owns a Plymouth given that the family does not own a red car is 15/40. Stated symbolically we must compute $P(P|\overline{R})$. Using the formula for this conditional probability, we need to evaluate

$$P(P|\overline{R}) = \frac{P(P \cap \overline{R})}{P(\overline{R})} \qquad (2.16)$$

Looking at the joint probability table (Table 2.9), we see that $P(P \cap \overline{R}) = P(P \cap W) + P(P \cap B)$. Also we observe that $P(\overline{R}) = P(W) + P(B)$. Thus

$$P(P|\overline{R}) = \frac{P(P \cap W) + P(P \cap B)}{P(W) + P(B)}$$

$$= \frac{10/60 + 5/60}{30/60 + 10/60} = 15/40 \qquad (2.17)$$

TABLE 2.9 JOINT PROBABILITY TABLE FOR AUTOMOBILE DISTRIBUTION

	RED(R)	WHITE(W)	BLUE(B)	TOTAL
Chevrolet (C)	5/60	15/60	5/60	25/60
Ford (F)	10/60	5/60	0	15/60
Plymouth (P)	5/60	10/60	5/60	20/60
Total	20/60	30/60	10/60	60/60

Conditional probabilities are often a very important part of decision models and often can only be assessed subjectively by the "experts" involved in the particular application. Assessing conditional probabilities can be very tedious and care must be taken to assure that the basic properties of probability, as discussed in Section 2.22, are not violated. In many situations it is much easier to obtain an estimate for a conditional probability as compared to a joint probability. To determine whether the conditional probability estimates are consistent with one another it is often useful to construct a joint probability table from these conditional probabilities. This process will then help to identify any inconsistencies and force a reevaluation of the subjective conditional probability estimates.[1]

Before discussing the multiplication rule we note the relationship between mutually exclusive events and conditional probability. If events A and B are mutually exclusive and if B occurs, then it must be the case that A does not occur. In other words, the event "B given A" can never occur and thus its probability is zero. Also from the definition of conditional probability

$$P(A|B) = \frac{P(A \cap B)}{P(B)} = \frac{0}{B} = 0 \qquad (2.18)$$

2.6 THE MULTIPLICATION LAW

Just as the addition rule is used to compute the probability of an event that is the union of two events, the multiplication law is used to calculate the probability of the intersection of two events. The multiplication law is obtained by algebraically

rewriting the definition of a conditional probability, given in (2.13) and (2.14).

From (2.13)

$$P(A \cap B) = P(B|A)P(A) \qquad (2.19)$$

and from (2.14)

$$P(A \cap B) = P(A|B)P(B) \qquad (2.20)$$

The multiplication law is useful when we are interested in computing a joint probability and have available conditional probability information involving the event of the interest. For example, suppose the probability that it will rain tomorrow is .60 and the probability that the temperature will be above 85°F if it does not rain is .60. What is the probability that it does not rain and the temperature is above 85°F? To answer this question define the following events.

A: it rains tomorrow;

$\overline{A}$: it does not rain tomorrow;

B: the temperature is above 85°F.

We know that $P(A) = .60$, $P(\overline{A}) = .40$, $P(B|\overline{A}) = .60$. What we want to determine is $P(B \cap \overline{A})$. Using the multiplication law

$$P(B \cap \overline{A}) = P(B|\overline{A})P(\overline{A})$$
$$= (.60)(.40) = .24 \qquad (2.21)$$

Therefore, the probability that it will not rain *and* the temperature will be above 85°F is .24.

2.6.1 THE MULTIPLICATION LAW AND INDEPENDENCE

The multiplication law is impacted by a concept not previously discussed, the independence/dependence

---

[1] For an in-depth look at this problem see: Herbert Moskowitz and Rakesh K. Sarin, "Improving the consistency of conditional probability assessments for forecasting and decision making," *Management Science*, **29**(6) (June 1983), 735–749.

of two events. Two events A and B are *independent* if

$$P(B|A) = P(B) \quad \text{or if}$$
$$P(A|B) = P(A) \quad (2.22)$$

If two events are not independent they are said to be *dependent*. If A and B are independent, then $P(B|A) = P(B)$ and

$$\frac{P(A \cap B)}{P(A)} = P(B|A)$$
$$= P(B) \quad (2.23)$$

Then (2.23) can easily be rewritten as

$$P(A \cap B) = P(A) P(B) \quad (2.24)$$

Equation 2.24 is the multiplication law when events A and B are independent. This *special case* says that the probability of a joint event is the product of the individual event probabilities if the events are independent. On the other hand, if $P(A|B) \neq P(A)$, then the occurrence of event A is dependent upon the occurrence or nonoccurrence of event B.

To illustrate this special case we consider a situation involving the donation of blood at a local blood bank. The probability that a donor arriving at a blood bank in a large metropolitan area will have an RH$^+$ factor is .70. Let

A: the first donor has an RH$^+$ factor;

B: the next donor has an RH$^+$ factor.

It is reasonable to assume that the RH factor of the first donor does not make it more or less likely that the second donor has a particular RH factor. The probability that both the first donor and the next donor will have an RH$^+$ factor is given by

$$P(A \cap B) = P(A)P(B) = (.70)(.70) = .49 \quad (2.25)$$

The probability that the first donor will have an RH$^+$ factor and the next donor an RH$^-$ factor is given by

$$P(A \cap \bar{B}) = P(A)P(\bar{B}) = (.70)(.30) = .21 \quad (2.26)$$

The probability that the first will have RH$^-$ and the next RH$^+$ is given by

$$P(\bar{A} \cap B) = P(\bar{A})P(B) = (.30)(.70) = .21 \quad (2.27)$$

And finally the probability that they both will have an RH$^-$ factor is given by

$$P(\bar{A} \cap \bar{B}) = P(\bar{A})P(\bar{B}) = (.30)(30) = .09 \quad (2.28)$$

The above probabilities in (2.25), (2.26), (2.27), and (2.28) can be summarized in the form of a joint probability table (see Table 2.10).

From this table we also note the independence of events A and B.

$$P(A|B) = \frac{P(A \cap B)}{P(B)} = \frac{.49}{.7} = .7 = P(A) \quad (2.29)$$

and

$$P(B|A) = \frac{P(A \cap B)}{P(A)} = \frac{.49}{.7} = .7 = P(B) \quad (2.30)$$

Finally we note that if A and B are mutually exclusive events, A and B are dependent events

$$P(A|B) = \frac{P(A \cap B)}{P(B)} = \frac{0}{P(B)} = 0 \quad (2.31)$$

Clearly $P(A|B) \neq P(A)$ in this case.

2.7 BAYES'S THEOREM

The $P(A)$ and $P(A|B)$ both denote the probability of occurrence of event A. However, $P(A|B)$ denotes

TABLE 2.10 JOINT PROBABILITY TABLE BLOOD DONOR ILLUSTRATION

	SECOND: RH$^+$(B)	SECOND: RH$^-$($\bar{B}$)	TOTAL
First: RH$^+$ (A)	.49	.21	.70
First: RH$^-$ ($\bar{A}$)	.21	.09	.30
Total	.70	.30	1.00

the probability of A given additional information, that is, the occurrence or nonoccurrence of event B. In a given situation $P(A)$ is referred to as a *prior probability* and $P(A|B)$ is referred to as a *posterior probability*. A posterior probability is a *revision* of a prior probability using new or additional information.

A posterior probability is then a conditional probability. In this context the concept of conditional probability will be used as the foundation for an important tool in decision making known as Bayes's rule. Bayes's rule is used to update the probability assignment by incorporating new information. We now show how this important probability relationship is constructed using the definition of conditional probability.

We note that Eq. 2.14 can be written as

$$P(A \cap B) = P(B|A)P(A) \qquad (2.32)$$

Substituting for $P(A \cap B)$ in (2.13), we obtain

$$P(A|B) = \frac{P(B|A)P(A)}{P(B)} \qquad (2.33)$$

Bayes's theorem for two mutually exclusive and collectively exhaustive events, A and $\overline{A}$, is obtained by observing that $P(B)$ can be calculated as follows

$$P(B) = P(B \cap A) + P(B \cap \overline{A}) \qquad (2.34)$$

Using the multiplication rule, we also observe that

$$P(B) = P(B|A)P(A) + P(B|\overline{A})P(\overline{A}) \qquad (2.35)$$

Combining (2.34) and (2.35) we obtain what is called Bayes's theorem:

$$P(A|B) = \frac{P(B|A)P(A)}{P(B|A)P(A) + P(B|\overline{A})P(\overline{A})} \qquad (2.36)$$

To illustrate the use of Bayes's theorem we consider a characterization of 250 mortgages that have been defaulted during the last year in a particular geographic region. These mortgages are either conventional (C) or FHA ($\overline{C}$), and they are for an amount less than \$40,000 (L) or for an amount of \$40,000 or more ($\overline{L}$). We know that for an arbitrarily selected mortgage (from these 250) the prob-

ability of it being conventional is 44. We also know that the probability of the loan being under \$40,000 if the financing was conventional is .455, and that the probability that the loan is under \$40,000 if the loan was FHA is .571. If we are handed the file for a defaulted loan and we know it was for an amount under \$40,000, what is the probability that this mortgage was conventional?

$$P(C) = .44, \ P(\overline{C}) = .56$$
$$P(L|C) = .455$$
$$P(L|\overline{C}) = .571 \qquad (2.37)$$

The probability of interest is $P(C|L)$. Using Bayes's theorem, we can write

$$
\begin{aligned}
P(C|L) &= \frac{P(L|C)P(C)}{P(L|C)P(C) + P(L|\overline{C})P(\overline{C})} \\
&= \frac{(.455)(.44)}{(.455)(.44) + (.571)(.56)} \\
&= .385 \qquad (2.38)
\end{aligned}
$$

Suppose that we are also interested in computing the probability of the loan being FHA if we know that it is for less than \$40,000. Then

$$
\begin{aligned}
P(\overline{C}|L) &= \frac{P(L|\overline{C})P(\overline{C})}{P(L|\overline{C})P(\overline{C}) + P(L|C)P(C)} \\
&= \frac{(.571)(.56)}{(.571)(.56) + (.455)(.44)} \\
&= .615 \qquad (2.39)
\end{aligned}
$$

It is also noted that $P(\overline{C}|L) + P(C|L) = 1$ or $P(\overline{C}|L) = 1 - P(C|L)$, so that $P(\overline{C}|L) = 1 - .385 = .615$, as before. In the terminology used at the beginning of this section, .44 and .56 are termed the prior probabilities, while .385 and .615 are the posterior probabilities of C and $\overline{C}$, respectively. Given that we know the loan is for an amount under \$40,000, it is less likely that the loan is conventional and more likely that the loan is FHA.

The joint probability table for this situation is presented in Table 2.11. It is easy to see that given a joint probability table, the computation of a posterior probability does not require the use of Bayes's theorem.

$$P(C|L) = \frac{.20}{.52} = .385 \qquad (2.40)$$

TABLE 2.11 JOINT PROBABILITY TABLE FOR DEFAULTED MORTGAGES

TYPE OF MORTGAGE	AMOUNT OF LOAN		
	UNDER $40,000	$40,000 OR MORE	TOTAL
Conventional	.20	.24	.44
FHA	.32	.24	.56
Total	.52	.48	1.00

It is obvious then that Bayes's theorem involves the quotient of a joint probability and a marginal probability. The form of the expression for the marginal probability in Bayes's theorem provides an effective procedure for combining historical information to update probability assessment.

Bayes's theorem can be extended to the case where there are n mutually exclusive and collectively exhaustive events $A_1, A_2, \ldots, A_n$. In this case,

$$P(A_i|B) = \frac{P(B|A_i)P(A_i)}{\sum_{i=1}^{n} P(B|A_i)P(A_i)} \qquad (2.41)$$

$P(A_1), P(A_2), \ldots, P(A_n)$ are the prior probabilities, and Eq. 2.41 can be used to calculate the posterior probabilities for events $A_1, \ldots, A_n$. As a final example consider a situation where a computer contractor purchases a special computer chip from three vendors. The Ashley Company provides 30 percent of the chips, the Bati Company provides 25 percent, and the Cattail Company provides 45 percent. Past records indicate that 2 percent of the chips from Ashley have been defective. The corresponding defective rates for Bati and Cattail are 3 percent and 1.5 percent, respectively. The computer chips are used in the installation of printer systems and the vendor is not recorded at installa-

tion. A particular printer failure is blamed on a defective chip. We would like to know the probability that this chip was purchased from the Ashley Company. The information provided in this description is labeled and presented in Table 2.12. Given the notation in Table 2.12, we need to calculate $P(A|D)$. Bayes's theorem of (2.41) with $n = 3$ can be utilized to evaluate this probability.

$$
\begin{aligned}
P(A|D) &= \frac{P(D|A)P(A)}{P(D|A)P(A) + P(D|B)P(B) + P(D|C)P(C)} \\
&= \frac{(.02)(.40)}{(.02)(.40) + (.03)(.25) + (.015)(.35)} \\
&= .385 \qquad (2.42)
\end{aligned}
$$

Thus the probability that the defective chip was purchased from Ashley is approximately .385.

2.8   SUMMARY

In this chapter the basic concepts in probability theory were reviewed. Fundamental to the laws of probability are the facts that probability values must lie between zero and one, and that the sum of the probabilities of all possible outcomes to an experiment must be one. Alternative ways to assess probability were presented and it was observed that the

TABLE 2.12 COMPUTER CONTRACTOR HISTORICAL INFORMATION

EVENT	LABEL	PROBABILITY
Ashley provides chip	A	$P(A) = .40$
Bati provides chip	B	$P(B) = .25$
Catti provides chip	C	$P(C) = .35$
Defective, provided by Ashley	$D|A$	$P(D|A) = .02$
Defective, provided by Bati	$D|B$	$P(D|B) = .03$
Defective, provided by Catti	$D|C$	$P(D|C) = .015$

probability of an event could be obtained by summing the probabilities of the sample points that comprise the event. Additionally a number of event relations and several laws of probability were presented. The chapter concludes with an important rule, Bayes's theorem, that can be used to revise probability values if new or additional information is obtained.

GLOSSARY

Addition Law   A rule for computing the probability of a union of events.

Bayes's theorem   A process of revising a probability given new or additional information.

Classical Probability   A probability calculated assuming all sample points are equally likely.

Collectively Exhaustive Events   A collection of events with the property that at least one must occur.

Complement   The event consisting of all sample points in the sample space not in a given event.

Conditional Probability   A probability based on the occurrence or nonoccurrence of another event.

Dependent Events   Events that are not independent.

Event   A subset of the sample space.

Event Occurs   An event occurs if any one of the sample points comprising that event occurs.

Experiment   The process through which an observation or outcome is recorded.

Independent Events   Two events are independent if the probability of the occurrence of one event is not affected by the occurrence or nonoccurrence of the other event.

Intersection   The event that occurs when both of two events A and B occur.

Joint Probability   The probability of the intersection of events.

Marginal Probability   The sum of probabilities for a set of mutually exclusive events.

Multiplication Law   A rule for computing the probability of an intersection of events.

Mutually Exclusive   Two events are mutually exclusive if the occurrence of one precludes the occurrence of the other.

Posterior Probability   A revision of a prior probability based on additional information.

Prior Probability   A probability that does not consider the effect of the occurrence or nonoccurrence of another (or other) event(s).

Probability A numerical statement about the uncertainty associated with the occurrence or nonoccurrence of an event.

Probability of an Event The sum of the probabilities of the sample points that comprise that event.

Relative Frequency Probability Probability based on observation of past occurrences.

Sample Point or Simple Event A single element in the sample space.

Sample Space The set of all possible outcomes for an experiment.

Subjective Probability A probability estimate that is based primarily on nonquantified evidence.

Tree Diagram A schematic procedure for the complete enumeration of sample points.

Union The event that occurs when any one of two events A and B occurs.

Selected References

Chou, Y. 1975. *Statistical Analysis.* New York: Holt, Rinehart & Winston.

Clelland, R. C., J. S. deCani, and F. E. Brown. 1973. *Basic Statistics with Business Applications,* 2nd ed. New York: Wiley.

Feller, W. 1968. *An Introduction to Probability Theory and Its Applications,* vol. 1, 3rd ed. New York: Wiley.

Freund, J. E., and R. E. Walpole. 1980. *Mathematical Statistics,* 3rd ed. Englewood Cliffs, N.J.: Prentice–Hall.

Hogg, R. V., and A. T. Craig. 1970. *Introduction to Mathematical Statistics,* 3rd ed. New York: Macmillan.

Lapin, L. L. 1973. *Statistics for Modern Business Decisions.* New York: Harcourt Brace Jovanovich.

Mendenhall, W., and J. E. Reinmuth. 1982. *Statistics for Management and Economics,* 4th ed. Boston: Duxbury.

Neter, J., W. Wasserman, and G. Whitmore. 1973. *Fundamental Statistics for Business and Economics,* 4th ed. Boston: Allyn & Bacon.

Parzen, E. 1960. *Modern Probability Theory.* New York: Wiley.

Discussion Questions

1. Give an intuitive definition of a probability value and an example of an application of the concept of a probability.

2. Discuss the relationship between an experiment, sample points, and sample space.

3. Discuss the two properties that all probability values must satisfy.

4. Discuss the different approaches used to determine probability values.

5. What is meant by the terms mutually exclusive and collectively exhaustive?

6. Describe the components of a joint probability table.

7. How does the concept of a mutually exclusive event impact the addition

law and how is this related to the subtraction of a joint probability in the addition law?

8. What is the difference between a pair of events that are independent and a pair of events that are dependent? Give an example.

9. How does the concept of independence of events impact the multiplication law?

10. What is the relationship between independence and mutually exclusive events?

11. What is the primary objective of Bayes's theorem?

12. Is a posterior probability simply a conditional probability? If it is, why is Bayes's theorem important?

PROBLEMS

1. Clyde's Small Times Construction Company has placed bids for two contracts. The result of the bidding process of interest to Clyde is whether they are awarded a contract. View the bidding process as an experiment. List the sample points for this experiment.

2. The four Jacks, from a standard deck of 52 playing cards, are separated from the remaining cards. We sequentially select two cards from this subset of four cards. Treat the process of selection as an experiment.

   a. How many sample points are there for this experiment?
   b. List the sample points by constructing a tree diagram for this experiment.

3. Consider an experiment that consists of tossing a nickel, tossing a dime, and then rolling a die. List the sample points by constructing a tree diagram for this experiment.

4. Assume that the classical definition of probability is appropriate in the experiment defined in Problem 3. What is the probability of a simple event in this case? Let A represent the event: the roll of the die results in a 6. What is $P(A)$?

5. The number of accidents per week on a 5-mile stretch of an urban expressway has been recorded for the last 100 weeks. The data are given below.

NUMBER OF ACCIDENTS	NUMBER OF WEEKS
1	10
2	25
3	30
4	18
5	12
6	5
	100

The experiment involves the observation of the number of accidents per week.

   a. How many sample points are there in this experiment?
   b. Assign probabilities to the sample points. What definition did you use?
   c. Verify that the two basic rules for probability are satisfied for your assignment.
   d. Let A define the event: The number of accidents in a given week is less than 4. Calculate $P(A)$.

6. The sample space, S, for an experiment consists of six sample points:

$$S = \{E_1, E_2, E_3, E_4, E_5, E_6\}$$

Also

$$P(E_1) = .20$$
$$P(E_2) = .05$$
$$P(E_3) = .08$$
$$P(E_4) = .22$$
$$P(E_5) = .20$$
$$P(E_6) = .25,$$

and

$$A = \{E_1, E_5, E_6\}$$
$$B = \{E_1, E_3, E_4\}$$
$$C = \{E_2, E_3, E_5\}.$$

   a. Find $P(A)$, $P(B)$, $P(C)$.
   b. Find $P(A \cap B)$.
   c. Are A and B mutually exclusive? Explain.
   d. Find $P(A \cup B)$.
   e. Are A and B collectively exhaustive? Explain.
   f. Find $P(A \cap B \cap C)$.
   g. Find $P(\overline{A})$.
   h. Find $P(\overline{A \cup C})$.

7. Given mutually exclusive events A and B for which $P(A) = .30$ $P(B) = .60$, find

   a. $P(\overline{A})$
   b. $P(A \cup B)$
   c. $P(A \cap B)$
   d. $P(\overline{A} \cap \overline{B})$
   e. $P(\overline{A} \cup \overline{B})$

8. At the beginning of a week a college student with a limited budget decides whether to allocate \$25 or \$40 to food for the week. Since she is hungry by the end of the week if she spends \$25 or \$40, we

will assume that weekly decisions are independent of one another. However, the probability that she chooses to allocate $25 is .30 and the probability that she chooses to allocate $40 to .70. What is the probability that in two consecutive weeks she will spend no more than $65?

9. A company's management is proposing a policy change in expense reimbursement for its sales staff of 500. A member of the sales force operates in one of three sales regions and is either opposed or not opposed to the policy change. The frequency distribution for each of the categories follows.

OPINION	NORTH(N)	SOUTH(S)	WEST(W)	TOTAL
Opposed (O)	100	100	30	230
Not Opposed (F)	50	100	120	270
Total	150	200	150	500

Suppose a salesperson is randomly selected, let N represent the event that he is from the North, F represent the event that he is not opposed to the policy, and so on. Find each of the following probabilities.

a. $P(O)$
b. $P(\overline{O})$
c. $P(N)$
d. $P(N \cup S)$
e. $P(N \cup O)$
f. $P(N \cup \overline{O})$
g. $P(N \cap W)$
h. $P(O|N)$
i. $P(O|\overline{N})$
j. $P(O \cup F)$
k. $P(O|F)$

10. A small retailer frequently places special orders with a number of wholesalers. They are interested in determining the likelihood of receiving an order within a certain number of days. They have collected data that are shown in the following table on 500 orders over a 3-year period.

| AMOUNT OF ORDER | DAYS FROM ORDER TO RECEIPT | | | |
	UNDER 10	11–14	OVER 14	TOTAL
Under $1000	20	30	120	170
$1000–$5000	40	75	60	175
Over $5000	100	25	30	155
	160	130	210	500

a. Construct the joint probability table for this situation.
b. Compute and interpret the marginal probabilities for the joint probability table.
c. Suppose that event A represents the delivery of an order in 14 days or less. What is the probability that A occurs?
d. Suppose that event B represents an order of $5000 or less. What is the probability that B occurs?
e. What is $P(A \cap B)$?
f. Suppose that an order has been placed that is $5000 or less. What is the probability that it will be received in 14 days or less?
g. Are A and B independent events?

11. Suppose that you are seeking a loan and that you have applied to three banks. Assume that the three applications are evaluated independently.

LENDING AGENCY	PROBABILITY OF OBTAINING A LOAN
Bank A	.2
Bank B	.10
Bank C	.15

What is the probability of obtaining a loan from more than one source?

12. In an industrial area air pollution levels are divided into three ranges and labeled Stage 0, Stage 1, and Stage 2. Wind direction is related to pollution levels in the following table.

PROBABILITY OF POLLUTION LEVEL GIVEN WIND DIRECTION			
WIND DIRECTION	STAGE 0	STAGE 1	STAGE 2
South	.1	.3	.5
East	.2	.4	.5
West	.4	.2	0
North	.3	.1	0

Meteorological records indicate that wind prevails from the south 30 percent of the time, from the east 40 percent, from the west 20 percent, and from the north 10 percent.

a. Suppose that wind is from the east. What is the probability that there is a Stage 2 air pollution level?
b. Suppose that there is a Stage 2 air pollution level. What is the probability that the wind is from the east?
c. On a given day, what is the probability that wind is from the west and that there is a Stage 1 air pollution level?

13. Ten percent of a lot of 100 golf clubs is imperfect. Three clubs are selected at random. Construct a tree diagram for this situation. Compute the following.

    a. Exactly one imperfect club is selected.
    b. At least one imperfect club is selected.
    c. No imperfect club is selected.

14. An employment agency gives an aptitude test to clients being placed into positions that require a college education. The agency is not currently using this test in the placement decisions. In fact, the test results are not tabulated until a report from the employer is filed that specifies whether the client is performing at a satisfactory level or performing at an unsatisfactory level. For 200 clients the following information has been tabulated.

	NUMBER OF PEOPLE	
PERFORMANCE	SCORED BELOW 75	SCORED 75 OR ABOVE
Satisfactory	20	80
Unsatisfactory	60	40

Suppose that this information is judged to be an acceptable basis. What is the probability that a candidate

    a. will score below 75 and be unsatisfactory?
    b. will be unsatisfactory if he/she scores below 75?
    c. has scored below 75 if we know that the person has performed at an unsatisfactory level?

15. A manufacturer's quality control department classifies 35 percent of its units as defective. Of the items classified as nondefective ultimately 10 percent are found to be defective by the consumer. Also further testing showed that 30 percent of those classified as defective were, in reality, nondefective. What is the probability that a nondefective unit will actually be classified as nondefective?

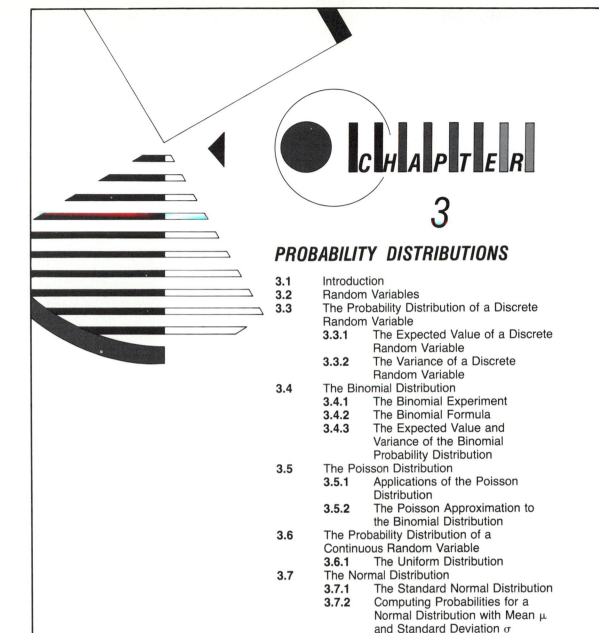

CHAPTER

3

PROBABILITY DISTRIBUTIONS

3.1 INTRODUCTION

In this chapter we extend the basic probability concepts introduced in Chapter 2 by introducing the concept of a probability distribution. We look at both discrete and continuous probability distributions. In particular, we examine in detail several of the most frequently encountered distributions.

1. The binomial distribution.
2. The Poisson distribution.
3. The uniform distribution.
4. The normal distribution.
5. The exponential distribution.

We compute the expected value for these distributions as well as their standard deviation and variance. We begin by building on the concept of an experiment, discussing the nature and attributes of random variables.

3.2 RANDOM VARIABLES

In many situations individual outcomes from an experiment may be represented by unique numerical values. A *random variable* is a function whose numerical value is determined by the outcome of a random experiment. Consider the example of an experiment that simply involves the tossing of a fair die. If we define the number of spots showing as a random variable, the values of the random variable will be 1, . . . ,6. On the other hand, the random variable could be defined as the square root of the number of spots showing, in which case the random variable assumes the values of 1, $\sqrt{2}$, . . . ,$\sqrt{6}$. Two very general observations should be made.

1. For each possible outcome there is exactly one associated numerical value.
2. For any given experiment the number of random variables that can be defined is unlimited.

Discrete random variables assume only a *finite* or a *countably infinite* number of values. These values, however, do not have to be integers. For example, the number of patrons at a local restaurant and the *fraction* of defective television sets produced on a given day at a particular plant are both examples of discrete random variables. The first assumes integer values, the second does not. If there is an upper bound on the number of sets produced per day, both random variables are also finite. On the other hand, the number of telephone calls placed in the United States during a certain time period would be an example of a countably infinite discrete random variable. By this we mean that the number of possible values of the random variable has no inherent limitation.

Continuous random variables take on any real value within some interval or collection of intervals. The number of pounds of particulate emissions from industry in an urban area and the number of gallons of water consumed weekly are two examples of continuous random variables. Typically, continuous random variables will involve *measurements*, while discrete random variables will involve *a counting process*.

Finally, we should note that it is a common practice to treat certain discrete variables as if they were continuous variables. Suppose that the sales of an inexpensive product are expected to be between 1,500,000 and 2,500,000 units. In many applications management scientists would assume that sales could take on any value in the specified range. Analysis is often simplified by using standard continuous models.

3.3 THE PROBABILITY DISTRIBUTION OF A DISCRETE RANDOM VARIABLE

A typical probability distribution for a discrete random variable may be developed from frequency information. Frequency information is obtained by repeating an experiment and recording the frequency of all outcomes. After the relative frequency information has been collected for a particular experiment and an appropriate discrete random variable has been defined, the identification of a *probability function* is straightforward. The *probability function* simply provides the probability that the random variable assumes a particular value. Let's identify the probability function as $f(x)$. The *probability distribution* for a discrete random variable can be represented by a formula, $y = f(x)$, a table, or a graph that gives the probability associated with every value of the random variable.

As an example consider Loveless Sports, Inc. Loveless can sell 0 through 6 professional-quality

TABLE 3.1 PROFESSIONAL RACQUETS SOLD PER DAY BY LOVELESS SPORTS, INC.	
SALES VOLUME	NUMBER OF DAYS
0	5
1	15
2	50
3	50
4	50
5	20
6	10
	200

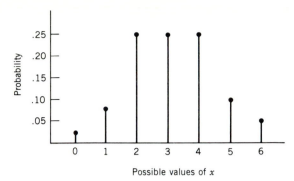

FIGURE 3.1 GRAPHICAL REPRESENTATION OF THE PROBABILITY DISTRIBUTION FOR NUMBER OF RACQUETS SOLD PER DAY.

racquets per day. Frequency information for 200 consecutive days is given in Table 3.1. Defining the random variable to be the number of racquets sold per day, the probability distribution for the number of racquets sold per day for Loveless is developed using the relative frequency definition of probability. The graphical representation of the probability distribution given in Table 3.2 is presented in Figure 3.1.

The properties stated in Section 2.2.2 for probability values must also hold for probability distributions. In our current notation these properties become

$$f(x) \geq 0$$
$$\sum_x f(x) = 1 \qquad (3.1)$$

These conditions state that the probability function is nonnegative and that the sum of all probabilities

TABLE 3.2 PROBABILITY DISTRIBUTION FOR NUMBER OF RACQUETS SOLD PER DAY	
x	$f(x)$
0	.025
1	.075
2	.250
3	.250
4	.250
5	.100
6	.050
	1.0

for a random variable must be one. In the Loveless example we see that

$$\sum_x f(x) = f(0) + f(1) + f(2) + f(3)$$
$$+ f(4) + f(5) + f(6)$$
$$= 0.25 + .075 + .25 + .25 + .25$$
$$+ .10 + .05 = 1.00 \qquad (3.2)$$

It is obvious that $f(x) \geq 0$, and thus the probability distribution in Table 3.2 is a valid one.

The probability distribution can also be used to provide additional probability information. For example, the probability that Loveless will sell fewer than two racquets is .10, that it will sell four or five racquets is .35, and so forth. Before we examine a measure for a probability distribution closely related to the concept of an average, we define what we mean by a cumulative probability.

The *cumulative probability* for a particular value of a random variable, X, is the sum of the probabilities of all occurrences of the random variable with numerical values less than or equal to X. We denote the cumulative probability distribution by $F(X)$, where

$$F(X) = P(x \leq X)$$
$$= \sum_{x \leq X} f(x) \qquad (3.3)$$

The cumulative probability distribution for the number of racquets sold per day is given in Table 3.3. The graphical representation of the cumulative

x	f(x)	F(x)
0	.025	.025
1	.075	.100
2	.250	.350
3	.250	.600
4	.250	.850
5	.100	.950
6	.050	1.00

TABLE 3.3 CUMULATIVE PROBABILITY DISTRIBUTION FOR NUMBER OF RACQUETS SOLD PER DAY

TABLE 3.4 THE EXPECTED VALUE OF A RANDOM VARIABLE

x	f(x)	x f(x)
0	.025	0(.025) = .000
1	.075	1(.075) = .075
2	.250	2(.250) = .500
3	.250	3(.250) = .750
4	.250	4(.250) = 1.000
5	.100	5(.100) = .500
6	.050	6(.050) = .300

$$\mu = E(x) = \sum_x x f(x) = 3.125$$

probability distribution is presented in Figure 3.2. Compare Figure 3.1 and Figure 3.2.

3.3.1 THE EXPECTED VALUE OF A DISCRETE RANDOM VARIABLE

The *expected value* or mean of a discrete random variable is a weighted sum of all possible values of the random variable where the weights are the probabilities associated with the individual values of the random variable. Mathematically, the expected value of the random variable x, denoted by μ, is given by

$$E(x) = \mu = \sum_x x f(x) \qquad (3.4)$$

Both μ and $E(x)$ are commonly used to denote the expected value of a random variable x.

The expected value of the random variable in the Loveless Sports, Inc., example is computed in

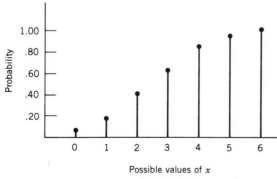

FIGURE 3.2 GRAPHICAL REPRESENTATION OF THE CUMULATIVE DISTRIBUTION FOR NUMBER OF RACQUETS SOLD PER DAY.

Table 3.4. The expected value of the random variable, the number of racquets sold per day, is 3.125. It is clear that on any given day we do not expect to sell 3.125 racquets. Even if the expected value had turned out to be an integer, we could not say that we expect the sales the next day (or the next time the experiment is repeated) to be this integer value. The expected value must be thought of as an average, a "long-run" average for the random variable. This means that if we record sales over an extended time period and compute average sales for that time period, the average should be close to 3.125. In other words, the expected value should provide a good estimate for the actual mean if the particular probability distribution given is a good model.

If it is the case that the probability distribution for racquet sales is valid in some future time interval, say the next six months, the expected value can be used to provide an estimate for sales expected over that time frame. Under such an assumption the expected sales for the next six month period would be (180)(3.125) = 562.5 racquets. Such a use of the expected value of a random variable can provide valuable information for the decision maker.

3.3.2 THE VARIANCE OF A DISCRETE RANDOM VARIABLE

The expected value that is a weighted sum of the random variable is a measure of central tendency for the random variable or probability distribution. Often it is important to know how values of the random variable are dispersed or scattered about the expected value or mean. The classical measure of dispersion is the *variance*. The computation of the variance is based on the deviation of the random variable x from its mean value, μ. The deviation, $x - \mu$, simply measures the distance of the random variable from its mean. The variance is computed by weighting the squared deviations by the respective probabilities of the random variable and summing over all values of the random variable. The variance is denoted as Var(x) or σ^2, and the mathematical expression for this measure is

$$\text{Var}(x) = \sigma^2 = \sum_x (x - \mu)^2 f(x) \qquad (3.5)$$

The *variance* is then defined to be the weighted sum of squared deviations.

The calculation of the variance for the number of racquets sold daily for Loveless Sports is given in Table 3.5. A related measure of variability is the *standard deviation*, σ, which is the positive square root of the variance. For Loveless Sports, the standard deviation of the number of racquets sold per day is

$$\sigma = \sqrt{1.861} = 1.364$$

The standard deviation is often preferred as a measure of variability over the variance, since it is measured in the same units as the random variable, and as such is easier to interpret.

A small standard deviation (or variance) relative to the expected value indicates that if the experiment that generates the random variable was repeated a large number of times, there would be a tendency for the observations of the random variable to be clustered close to the mean. A large value for the standard deviation relative to the mean would indicate, however, that observed values of the random variable would be widely dispersed from the mean. The concept of variance is very important in decision-making situations where sample information is used. In our discussion of the normal distribution we see how the variance/standard deviation is used in probability calculations.

3.4 THE BINOMIAL DISTRIBUTION

Many applications involve situations where there are exactly two mutually exclusive nonnumerical outcomes. For example, suppose that a sample of 100 individuals is subjected to a particular medical treatment. Each individual will either respond favorably or will not respond favorably to the treatment. In this situation and many others the numerical result of interest is how many times or in what proportion the dichotomous outcomes occur. In this example, the random variable of interest is the number of individuals in the sample of size 100 that respond favorably to the medical treatment. The probability distribution for this random variable, the binomial distribution, is the topic of this section.

The binomial distribution is easily illustrated by the process of coin tossing. Suppose that a fair coin is tossed four times. We may view this process as the four-stage experiment illustrated in Figure 3.3. In this experiment there are 16 equally likely sample points. We can easily calculate the probability of obtaining exactly three heads out of four

TABLE 3.5   VARIANCE CALCULATION

x	$x - \mu$	$(x - \mu)^2$	$f(x)$	$(x - \mu)^2 f(x)$
0	$0 - 3.125 = -3.125$	9.766	.025	$9.766(.025) =$ .244
1	$1 - 3.125 = -2.125$	4.516	.075	$4.516(.075) =$ .339
2	$2 - 3.125 = -1.125$	1.266	.250	$1.266(.250) =$ .317
3	$3 - 3.125 = 0.125$	0.016	.250	$0.016(.250) =$ .004
4	$4 - 3.125 = 0.875$	0.766	.250	$0.766(.250) =$ .192
5	$5 - 3.125 = 1.875$	3.516	.100	$3.516(.100) =$ .352
6	$6 - 3.125 = 2.875$	8.266	.050	$8.266(.050) =$ .413
			$\sigma^2 = \sum_x$	$(x - \mu)^2 f(x) = 1.861$

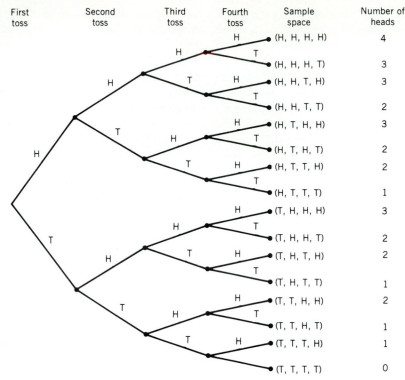

FIGURE 3.3   TREE DIAGRAM FOR FOUR COIN TOSSES.

by counting the number of equally likely sample points that involve three heads. Here

$$P(\text{exactly three heads}) = \frac{4}{16} = \frac{1}{4}$$

If we label x as the random variable that denotes the number of heads out of four, the probability distribution for x is given in Table 3.6. It should be clear that development of a distribution for the number of heads out of 12 tosses, for example, cannot be accomplished practically using a tree diagram. In such a case there would be a total of $4096(2^{12})$ sample points. We will discuss the procedure for calculating such probabilities, but first we delineate the general properties of a binomial random variable.

3.4.1 THE BINOMIAL EXPERIMENT

A sequence of coin tosses satisfies the properties of what is called a *Bernoulli process*. A list of the general properties of a Bernoulli process follows.

1. There are only two mutually exclusive outcomes possible on each repetition (trial) of the experiment. These outcomes are generally referred to as successes or failures.
2. The probability of success does not change from one trial to the next.
3. The trials are independent, which means that the outcome of one trial does not affect the outcome of another trial.

The discrete random variable that is defined to be the number of successes in n trials of an experiment that satisfies the properties of a Bernoulli process is said to have a *binomial distribution*. In situations where the binomial distribution is applicable, a for-

TABLE 3.6 PROBABILITY DISTRIBUTION FOR THE NUMBER OF HEADS OUT IN FOUR TOSSES

x	$f(x)$
0	1/16
1	4/16
2	6/16
3	4/16
4	1/16

mula has been developed to compute the probability for any possible value of the random variable.

3.4.2 THE BINOMIAL FORMULA

It can be shown that the number of experimental outcomes providing exactly x successes in n trials is given by

$$\frac{n!}{x!(n - x)!} \qquad (3.6)$$

where

$$n! = n(n - 1)(n - 2) \cdots (2)(1) \qquad (3.7)$$

and where 0! is defined to be 1. The probability of occurrence for an experimental outcome involving a particular arrangement of x successes and thus $(n - x)$ failures is given by

$$p^x(1 - p)^{n-x} \qquad (3.8)$$

In (3.8) p represents the probability of success, while $(1 - p)$ represents the probability of failure. The justification for the expression in (3.8) lies in Properties 2 and 3 for a Bernoulli process, as described in Section 3.4.1. Since the trials are independent, the order in which x successes and $n - x$ failures occur does not effect the probability of obtaining x successes. Also all of the sequences of trials that lead to x successes are mutually exclusive. Thus the probability of each of these simple events can be summed over the number of ways to obtain x successes in n trials.

$$\frac{n!}{x!(n - x)!} \qquad (3.9)$$

The result is a mathematical formula that specifies the binomial probability distribution where $f(x)$ is the probability of occurrence for an experimental outcome involving x successes and $n - x$ failures.

$$f(x) = \frac{n!}{x!(n - x)!} p^x(1 - p)^{n-x},$$
$$x = 0, 1, 2, \ldots, n \qquad (3.10)$$

Equation 3.10 indicates that if a random variable has a binomial distribution, then by specifying the number of trials (n) and the probability of success

on each trial (p), we can compute the probability for any particular number of successes (x) that is appropriate.

In the four coin toss example, $n = 4$ and $p = .5$. Therefore,

$$P(x = 2) = f(2) = \frac{4!}{2!(4 - 2)!}(.5)^2(1 - .5)^2$$
$$= (6)(1/2)^4$$
$$= 6/16 \qquad (3.11)$$

Table 3.6 is now developed using the *binomial formula*, Eq. 3.10, instead of Figure 3.3. The results are given in Table 3.7.

As another example of the application of the binomial distribution we consider the outcome of a random telephone survey to three individuals over 18 years of age. It is known that in the population of adults, 60 percent favor a particular referendum and 40 percent do not. We are interested in the probability that exactly two of three respondents favor the referendum.

We first check to determine whether the requirements for the binomial experiment are met.

1. The experiment is a sequence of three identical trials, one for each respondent contacted.
2. There are dichotomous outcomes: the respondent is in favor or not in favor.
3. The probability of each type of response is assumed to be the same for all respondents.
4. The opinion of one respondent is independent of the opinion of the other respondents.

TABLE 3.7 BINOMIAL DISTRIBUTION FOR THE NUMBER OF HEADS IN FOUR COIN TOSSES

x	$f(x)$
0	$\frac{4!}{0!4!}(1/2)^0(1/2)^4 = 1/16$
1	$\frac{4!}{1!3!}(1/2)^1(1/2)^3 = 4/16$
2	$\frac{4!}{2!2!}(1/2)^2(1/2)^2 = 6/16$
3	$\frac{4!}{3!1!}(1/2)^3(1/2)^1 = 4/16$
4	$\frac{4!}{4!0!}(1/2)^4(1/2)^0 = 1/16$
	1.00

Since the conditions for the binomial distribution are satisfied, we let x be the number of respondents out of three that favor the proposed referendum. Thus,

$$P(x = 2) = f(2) = \frac{3!}{2!(3-2)!}(.6)^2(.4)^1$$
$$= .432 \qquad (3.12)$$

Check this result with the tree diagram constructed in Figure 3.4.

If for example there were to be 20 individuals contacted instead of three, there may still be interest in the probability that exactly 2 of 20 respondents favor the referendum. In this case, x would be the number of respondents *out of 20* that favor the referendum. Then,

$$P(x = 2) = f(2) = \frac{20!}{2!(20-2)!}(.6)^2(.4)^{18}$$
$$= \frac{(20)(19)(18!)}{2!18!}(.6)^2(.4)^{18}$$
$$= 190(.6)^2(.4)^{18}$$
$$= .0000047 \qquad (3.13)$$

Tables have been developed that provide the probability of x successes in n trials for a binomial distribution. Such tables are generally easier to use than Eq. 3.7. Any collection of tables, however, cannot contain all binomial probability distributions. To use Table C.1 given in Appendix C, it is necessary to specify the values of n, p, and x for the appropriate distribution. Check your ability to read these tables by reproducing the results in Table 3.7 via the binomial tables.

3.4.3 THE EXPECTED VALUE AND VARIANCE OF THE BINOMIAL PROBABILITY DISTRIBUTION

Computing the expected value for the binomial distribution in Table 3.7, we have

$$\mu = \sum_x x f(x) = 0\left(\frac{1}{16}\right) + 1\left(\frac{4}{16}\right) + 2\left(\frac{6}{16}\right)$$
$$+ 3\left(\frac{4}{16}\right) + 4\left(\frac{1}{16}\right)$$
$$= 2 \qquad (3.14)$$

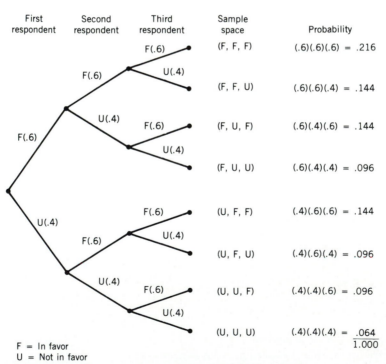

	First respondent	Second respondent	Third respondent	Sample space	Probability
			F(.6)	(F, F, F)	(.6)(.6)(.6) = .216
		F(.6)	U(.4)	(F, F, U)	(.6)(.6)(.4) = .144
		U(.4)	F(.6)	(F, U, F)	(.6)(.4)(.6) = .144
	F(.6)		U(.4)	(F, U, U)	(.6)(.4)(.4) = .096
		F(.6)	F(.6)	(U, F, F)	(.4)(.6)(.6) = .144
			U(.4)	(U, F, U)	(.4)(.6)(.4) = .096
	U(.4)	U(.4)	F(.6)	(U, U, F)	(.4)(.4)(.6) = .096
			U(.4)	(U, U, U)	(.4)(.4)(.4) = .064
					1.000

F = In favor
U = Not in favor

FIGURE 3.4 TREE DIAGRAM FOR THREE RESPONDENT SURVEY.

We note that this value could have been obtained by the simple formula

$$np = (4)\left(\frac{1}{2}\right) = 2 \qquad (3.15)$$

It can be shown that for the binomial probability distribution the expected value of the random variable is given by

$$\mu = np \qquad (3.16)$$

It can also be shown that the variance of the random variable that has a binomial distribution can be computed by the formula

$$\sigma^2 = np(1 - p) \qquad (3.17)$$

For the random variable in Table 3.7, the variance is

$$\sigma^2 = np(1 - p) = 4\left(\frac{1}{2}\right)\left(1 - \frac{1}{2}\right) = 1$$
$$\sigma = \sqrt{1} = 1 \qquad (3.18)$$

The mean of the random variable with a binomial distribution where $n = 4$ and $p = .5$ is 2. Also its variance and standard deviation are both equal to one.

3.5 THE POISSON DISTRIBUTION

Another discrete probability distribution of interest is the Poisson distribution, named after the early nineteenth-century French mathematician Siméon D. Poisson. The Poisson distribution is important in studying the waiting line models in Chapter 17.

The Poisson distribution is used in situations where events occur at random points in time or space. The arrival of customers at a service facility and the typographical errors in a manuscript serve as examples of random occurrence in time and space, respectively. Each of these situations represent a *Poisson process*. In a Poisson process the following conditions are met.

1. Over some specified time or space interval, the probability of occurrence of the event is constant, no matter when the specified interval begins.
2. The occurrence of the event is not dependent upon another occurrence of that event.

3. In a "small" interval of time or space the probability that two or more of the events of interest occur is negligible.

The Poisson distribution involves the random variable x that represents the number of rare events for an interval of time or space over which an average of λ such events can be expected to occur. The specification of this distribution is given in Eq. 3.19.

$$f(x) = \frac{\lambda^x e^{-\lambda}}{x!} \qquad \text{for} \quad x = 0, 1, 2, 3, \ldots \qquad (3.19)$$

where

$$e \doteq 2.71828$$

We note that x is a discrete but a countably infinite integer random variable. In this distribution a single parameter, λ, specifies (or determines) the exact probability distribution. (In the binomial distribution two parameters, n and p, were required.) Given λ we can use (3.19) or Table C.2 in Appendix C to calculate Poisson probabilities. It can be shown that both the mean and variance for this probability distribution are λ.

3.5.1 APPLICATIONS OF THE POISSON DISTRIBUTION

Suppose that we are interested in computing the probability that a telephone switchboard at a medical office building receives more than five calls in a given minute. Past experience for the switchboard at this medical office building suggests that an average of 120 incoming calls per hour are received by the switchboard. We will assume that the probability of receiving a call is the same for any short time segment within the hour and that the receipt of one call is not dependent upon the receipt of another call. Additionally, we expect an average of two calls per minute. Then we can calculate, for example, the probability of receiving exactly five calls in a given one minute interval. That is, $\lambda = (120/60) = 2$ and $x = 5$.

$$f(5) = \frac{2^5 e^{-2}}{5!}$$
$$= .0361 \qquad (3.20)$$

If it is the case that the switchboard can handle at most five incoming calls a minute, the probability that the switchboard is not overloaded during any given minute is written as

$$P(x \leq 5) = f(0) + f(1) + f(2) + f(3)$$
$$+ f(4) + f(5)$$
$$= \frac{2^0 e^{-2}}{0!} + \frac{2^1 e^{-2}}{1!} + \frac{2^2 e^{-2}}{2!} + \frac{2^3 e^{-2}}{3!}$$
$$+ \frac{2^4 e^{-2}}{4!} + \frac{2^5 e^{-2}}{5!}$$
$$= .1356 + .2707 + .2707 + .1804$$
$$+ .0902 + .0361$$
$$= .9837 \qquad (3.21)$$

Therefore, the probability that the switchboard will be overloaded during a given minute is .0163 = (1 − .9837). Again we note that Table C.2 in Appendix C could have been used instead of the direct calculations above.

To illustrate the use of the Poisson distribution in a situation not involving time we look at an example involving the construction of a concrete floor for a 100,000 square foot warehouse. In particular we are interested in the number of readily noticeable imperfections in the finished concrete. Again we will assume that the probability of imperfection is the same for any area of the same size and that occurrence or nonoccurrence of an imperfection in one area does not influence the occurrence or nonoccurrence of an imperfection in another area.

Suppose that we know that there is an average of 2 imperfections per 20 square feet. We want to calculate the probability of 10 imperfections for an arbitrarily located 100 square foot area on this 100,000 square foot floor. In this case $\lambda = (2)(5) = 10$, and 10 is the expected number of imperfections per 100 square feet. Thus we calculate $P(x = 10)$, where x is equal to the number of imperfections per 100 square feet, and where $\lambda = 10$.

$$P(x = 10) = f(10) = \frac{10^{10} e^{-10}}{10!}$$
$$= .1251 \qquad (3.22)$$

3.5.2 THE POISSON APPROXIMATION TO THE BINOMIAL DISTRIBUTION

If we look at Eq. 3.10 in Section 3.4, it is not difficult to observe that computational problems oc-

cur if n becomes large and if p or $1 - p$ become small. Binomial tables are seldom available for n greater than 100, and applications with n greater than 100 occur frequently. Fortunately, the Poisson distribution provides a good approximation to a binomial probability when n is large and $\lambda = \mu = np$ is small. There are a variety of rules that describe "small" in this context, but the one we accept here is that $n \geq 20$, while $p \leq .05$. Even if this definition is not satisfied, the approximation can still be used. In such a case, however, the approximation will not be as accurate.

As an example of the Poisson approximation to the binomial, consider the following situation. A manufacturer of riding lawn mowers purchases 10-horsepower engines in lots of 1000 from a supplier. He then installs one of these engines on each of the mowers. Historically, one engine per batch is defective. The manufacturer wants to assess the probability of three or fewer defectives in a batch of 1000 mowers. In reality we have a Bernoulli process where $n = 1000$ and the probability of success (i.e., a defective unit) is .001. Clearly, this is a case where the Poisson approximation to the binomial should be good. Here $\lambda = np = (1000)(.01) = 1$, and we are interested in calculating $P(x \leq 3)$, where x is the number of defectives out of 1000.

$$P(x \leq 3) = P(x = 0) + P(x = 1)$$
$$+ P(x = 2) + P(x = 3)$$
$$\doteq \frac{e^{-1}}{0!} + \frac{e^{-1}}{1!} + \frac{e^{-1}}{2!} + \frac{e^{-1}}{3!}$$
$$= .363 + .368 + .184 + .061$$
$$= .981 \qquad (3.23)$$

The probability that there will be three or fewer defectives in a batch of 1000 engines is *approximately* equal to .981.

As n gets larger and p becomes smaller, the Poisson approximation becomes better. Table 3.8 illustrates the quality of this approximation when $n = 25$ and $p = .01$.

3.6 THE PROBABILITY DISTRIBUTION OF A CONTINUOUS RANDOM VARIABLE

To this point we have only discussed discrete probability distributions, that is, situations where the random variable can take on only a finite number

TABLE 3.8 COMPARISON OF BINOMIAL PROBABILITY TO THE POISSON APPROXIMATION FOR $n = 25$ AND $p = .01$

x	BINOMIAL PROBABILITY	POISSON APPROXIMATION
0	.778	.779
1	.196	.195
2	.024	.024
3	.002	.002

of values (e.g., the binomial distribution) or a countably infinite number of values (e.g., the Poisson distribution). For a discrete probability distribution, there is a probability value associated with every possible value of the random variable. For a continuous random variable, such as the lifetime of a particular brand of picture tube for a new television set, associating a probability value for each possible value of the random variable is meaningless. Alternatively, we can only deal with the probability that the random variable falls within a given interval. What is the probability that the picture tube lasts between 5.2 and 6.5 years? We use a simple yet very useful continuous probability distribution, the *uniform distribution*, to illustrate the underlying concepts involved in probability distributions for continuous random variables.

3.6.1   THE UNIFORM DISTRIBUTION

We use the uniform probability distribution to illustrate some fundamental properties of continuous random variables. For example, the length of time between landings at a large metropolitan airport can be described by a random variable x, which takes on values between 1 and 5 minutes. It is reasonable to treat a variable in time as a continuous random variable. Recall that a continuous variable can take on *any* value within a given interval. We also assume that it is as likely for time between landings to be in the interval from 65 to 75 seconds as it is for time between landings to be in the interval from 280 to 290 seconds. In the uniform distribution it is equally likely for an observation of time between landings to be in any interval of a given fixed length such, as 10 seconds, 5 seconds, or 30 seconds. In other words, the length of the interval rather than the magnitude of the random variable within that interval determines the probability value.

The continuous random variable that satisfies the property just described is said to have the *uniform* probability distribution. A function that is used to compute probability values for a continuous random variable is called a *probability density function*. It must be noted that we do not talk about the probability of occurrence of a single value for a continuous random variable as we did for a discrete random variable. Since continuous random variables assume an uncountable number of values, assignment of probability values to the random variable would result in a violation of (3.1). Therefore, the probability of occurrence of a single value of a continuous random variable is zero and we deal only with the calculation of the probability that a continuous random variable is in a given interval.

If the random variable that represents time between landings has a uniform distribution, then for example

$$\begin{aligned} P(1 \le x \le 2) &= P(2 \le x \le 3) \\ &= P(3 \le x \le 4) \\ &= P(4 \le x \le 5) \end{aligned} \quad (3.24)$$

where x is measured in minutes. We also note that $P(1 \le x \le 2) = P(1 < x < 2)$, since $P(x = 1) = 0$ and $P(x = 2) = 0$ if x is continuous. Intuitively we would expect that

$$\begin{aligned} P(1 \le x < 2) &+ P(2 \le x < 3) + P(3 \le x < 4) \\ &+ P(4 \le x \le 5) = 1 \end{aligned} \quad (3.25)$$

since the four intervals involved are nonoverlapping and include all possible values of the variable x. Thus, since x has the uniform probability distribution

$$\begin{aligned} P(1 \le x < 2) &= P(2 \le x < 3) \\ &= P(3 \le x < 4) \\ &= P(4 \le x \le 5) \\ &= \frac{1}{4} \end{aligned} \quad (3.26)$$

The probability density function that describes the uniform probability distribution for time between arrivals is

$$f(x) = \begin{cases} \dfrac{1}{4} & \text{for } 1 \le x \le 5 \\ 0 & \text{elsewhere} \end{cases} \quad (3.27)$$

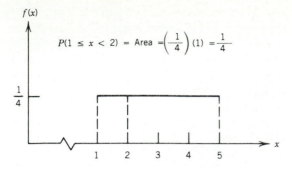

$$P(1 \leq x < 2) = \text{Area} = \left(\frac{1}{4}\right)(1) = \frac{1}{4}$$

FIGURE 3.5 THE UNIFORM PROBABILITY DENSITY FUNCTION FOR TIME BETWEEN ARRIVALS.

A graph of this probability density function is given in Figure 3.5. The area under the probability density function from 1 to 2 is 1/4. This is the probability that we previously assigned to $P(1 \leq x < 2)$. Indeed this is no coincidence.

The probability that $a \leq x \leq b$, where x is a continuous random variable, will be determined by the area under the probability density function between a and b. Any probability density function satisfies the following properties when the random variable can take on any value from a to b.

1. $f(x) \geq 0,$ for $a \leq x \leq b$ (3.28)
2. The area under the density function from a to b is 1.
3. $P(c \leq x \leq d)$, where $a \leq c$, $d \leq b$, is the area under the density function from c to d.

These properties can be rewritten if we recall the relationship between area and integral calculus.

1. $f(x) \geq 0,$ for $a \leq x \leq b$
2. $\int_a^b f(x)\, dx = 1$
3. $P(c \leq x \leq d) = \int_c^d f(x)\, dx$ (3.29)

If we accept the concept of probability as area we can easily answer a variety of probability questions about the time between landings in our initial example. For example, we may want to know the probability that the time between arrivals of two consecutive planes is between 90 seconds and 270

seconds. Alternatively, we compute

$$P(1.5 \leq x \leq 4.5) = (3)\left(\frac{1}{4}\right)$$
$$= .75 \qquad (3.30)$$

where .75 is the area under the density function from 1.5 to 4.5 minutes. If we want to know the probability that time between arrivals is greater than 90 seconds, we compute

$$P(x > 1.5) = P(1.5 < x \leq 5.0)$$
$$= (3.5)\left(\frac{1}{4}\right)$$
$$= .875 \qquad (3.31)$$

The general specification for the uniform probability density function is given by

$$f(x) = \begin{cases} \dfrac{1}{b-a} & \text{for } a \leq x \leq b \\ 0 & \text{elsewhere} \end{cases} \qquad (3.32)$$

In the example above $a = 1$ and $b = 5$.

Before examining several specific continuous probability distributions, we summarize several important principles involving continuous variables.

1. We only deal with the probability of the random variable taking on a value within a given interval. We do not talk about the probability of the random variable taking on a particular value.
2. The probability of the random variable taking on a value within a given interval is defined to be the area under the graph of the density function over that interval.

3.7 THE NORMAL DISTRIBUTION

The normal probability distribution is probably one of the most widely encountered probability models. Its probability density function takes on the form of a "bell-shaped" curve, as illustrated in Figure 3.6. The mathematical specification of the density function for this distribution is given in (3.33).

$$f(x) = \frac{1}{\sigma\sqrt{2\pi}} e^{-(x-\mu)^2/2\sigma^2} \qquad -\infty < x < \infty \quad (3.33)$$

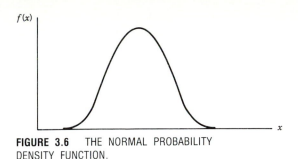

FIGURE 3.6 THE NORMAL PROBABILITY DENSITY FUNCTION.

where

μ = mean or expected value of x;

σ^2 = variance of x;

σ = standard deviation of x;

$\pi \doteq 3.14159$;

$e \doteq 2.71828.$ (3.34)

If values of μ and σ are given, the normal probability density function is specified. Recall that the magnitude of σ indicates the degree of dispersion for the random variable. Larger values of σ indicate a higher degree of dispersion (or spread) in the observations for the random variable. Since the area under the density function must be one, we would expect larger values of σ to be reflected in "flatter" bell-shaped curves. This is illustrated in Figure 3.7 for two normal distributions with a common mean of μ.

3.7.1 THE STANDARD NORMAL DISTRIBUTION

Since it is not practical to use the density function in (3.33) directly, we must examine the *standard*

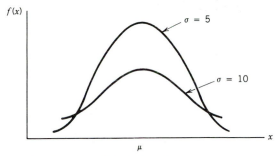

FIGURE 3.7 COMPARISON OF TWO NORMAL DISTRIBUTIONS.

normal distribution. Tables that allow us to compute areas under the normal probability density function are based on the standard normal distribution. The standard normal distribution has a mean of 0 and a standard deviation of 1. The graph of the standard normal distribution is given in Figure 3.8. The units on the x-axis actually measure the number of standard deviations from the mean of 0. The letter z is used to represent the standard normal random variable.

A standard normal probability table is given in Table C.3 of Appendix C. In this table numerical values are associated with standard deviation values. These values are actually cumulative probabilities. For example, if the standard deviation value z is 1.00, the associated numerical value .84134 is $P(z \le 1.00)$. Figure 3.9 illustrates the probabilities that are provided in the particular normal probability table given in Appendix C. These probabilities are actually areas under the probability density function from the lower bound on the random variable z ($-\infty$) to the specified value of z. We noted that this probability table provides cumulative probabilities so that $P(z \le 1)$ can be read directly from the normal probability table. We may also be interested in calculating $P(z > 1)$. To evaluate this probability value we recall that the entire area under the probability density function is equal to one. Therefore,

$$P(z \le 1) + P(z > 1) = 1 \qquad (3.35)$$

or

$$\begin{aligned} P(z > 1) &= 1 - P(z \le 1) \\ &= 1 - .84134 = .15866 \end{aligned}$$

This area is illustrated in Figure 3.10.

Calculating the probability that z is between two values may also be of interest. Suppose, for example, we want to know the probability that the standard normal random variable is within one standard deviation of the mean. In other words, calculate

$$P(-1 \le z \le 1) \qquad (3.36)$$

We observe that

$$P(z \le 1) = P(z \le -1) + P(-1 \le z \le 1) \quad (3.37)$$

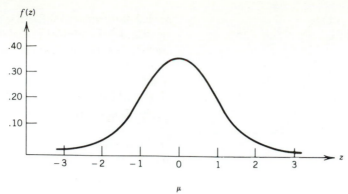

FIGURE 3.8   THE STANDARD NORMAL DISTRIBUTION.

Thus,

$$P(-1 \le z \le 1) = P(z \le 1) - P(z \le -1) \quad (3.38)$$

This actual probability, $.84134 - .15866 = .68268$, is represented as an area in Figure 3.11.

3.7.2   COMPUTING PROBABILITIES FOR A NORMAL DISTRIBUTION WITH MEAN μ AND STANDARD DEVIATION σ

Probabilities for any normal distribution can be calculated by first converting the normal distribution to the standard normal distribution (standardizing). The formula used to convert the normal random variable x with mean μ and standard deviation σ to the standard normal random variable z is

$$z = \frac{x - \mu}{\sigma} \quad (3.39)$$

In (3.39) σ is the magnitude of the standard deviation and $x - \mu$ is the deviation from the mean. Therefore, z represents the *number* of standard deviations that x lies away from its mean. For example,

if $\mu = 10$ and $\sigma = 5$, the observation of $x = 15$ is exactly one standard deviation away from the mean. The sign of z of course represents direction. Either the observation is above or it is below the mean.

To illustrate the use of (3.39) consider the following situation. Top Nut Peanut Oil, Inc., supplies customers with barrels containing about 100 gallons each. The actual volume of oil in a barrel can be described by a random variable that has a normal distribution. The standard deviation of volume is one-half gallon with a mean of 100 gallons. We want to know the probability that a barrel of peanut oil will contain at least 99 gallons. We need to calculate

$$P(x \ge 99) \quad (3.40)$$

Using $\mu = 100$ and $\sigma = .5$, Eq. 3.39 is used in the following calculations.

$$x \ge 99$$

$$x - 100 \ge 99 - 100$$

$$\frac{x - 100}{.5} \ge \frac{99 - 100}{.5}$$

$$\frac{x - 100}{.5} \ge -2 \quad (3.41)$$

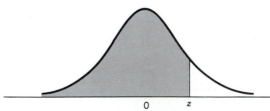

FIGURE 3.9   AREAS REPORTED IN THE STANDARD NORMAL PROBABILITY TABLE.

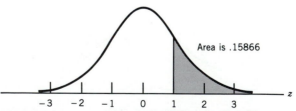

FIGURE 3.10   THE PROBABILITY THAT z IS GREATER THAN 1.0.

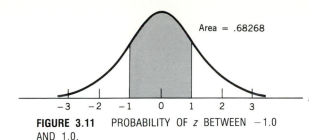

FIGURE 3.11 PROBABILITY OF z BETWEEN -1.0 AND 1.0.

Since $z = (x - 100)/.5$, we are calculating $P(z \geq -2)$. This equivalence is illustrated in Figure 3.12. Completing the calculation we have

$$P(z \geq -2) = 1 - P(z \leq -2)$$
$$= 1 - .02275$$
$$= .97725 \qquad (3.42)$$

Thus the probability that a barrel of peanut oil will contain at least 99 gallons is .97725. Suppose on the other hand we are interested in the probability that volume is between 99.8 gallons and 100.4 gallons. Then

$$P(99.8 \leq x \leq 100.4)$$
$$= P\left(\frac{99.8 - 100}{.5} \leq z \leq \frac{100.4 - 100}{.5}\right)$$
$$= P(-.4 \leq z \leq .8)$$
$$= P(z \leq .8) - P(z \leq -.4)$$
$$= .78814 - .34458$$
$$= .44356 \qquad (3.43)$$

The procedure illustrated via this example applies to any normal distribution. Values of the ran-dom variable x are converted to values of z using (3.39). Then the standard normal probability table can be used to calculate the probability of interest.

3.8 THE EXPONENTIAL DISTRIBUTION

In Section 3.5 we saw that the Poisson distribution is a discrete probability distribution for the number of events occurring in some interval of time or space. The Poisson distribution is expressed as

$$f(x) = \frac{\lambda^x e^{-\lambda}}{x!}, \qquad x = 0, 1, 2, \ldots \qquad (3.44)$$

where

x = number of events that occur for an interval of time over which an average of λ such events can be expected to occur

Additionally x can be redefined to be the number of events that occur over a time period t by replacing λ in (3.44) by λt. The probability distribution in (3.44) is then written as

$$f(x) = \frac{(\lambda t)^x e^{-\lambda t}}{x!}, \qquad x = 0, 1, 2, \ldots \qquad (3.45)$$

In this section we are interested in the probability distribution of the time between occurrence of events (interarrival time) instead of the probability distribution for the number of occurrences per

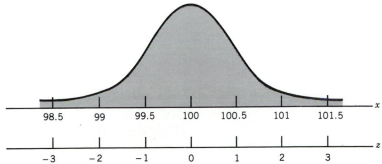

FIGURE 3.12 THE NORMAL DISTRIBUTION WITH $\mu = 100$, $\sigma = .5$ AND THE STANDARD NORMAL DISTRIBUTION.

time interval. We first note that the probability of no occurrence of the event of interest in time t is given as

$$P(x = 0) = f(0) = \frac{(\lambda t)^0 e^{-\lambda t}}{0!} = e^{-\lambda t} \quad (3.46)$$

If we let the random variable T denote the time between occurrence of events, T must be treated as a continuous random variable, since the event can occur at any time. The probability of no occurrences in time t is equal to the probability that the time between occurrences, T, is greater than t. Mathematically

$$P(T > t) = e^{-\lambda t} \quad (3.47)$$

and the probability distribution for T is called the *exponential distribution*. From (3.47) we can compute $P(T \leq t)$

$$
\begin{aligned}
P(T \leq t) &= 1 - P(T > t) \\
&= 1 - e^{-\lambda t} \quad (3.48)
\end{aligned}
$$

It can be shown that the general form for the probability density function for a random variable x with an exponential distribution is given in (3.49).

$$f(t) = \begin{cases} \lambda e^{-\lambda t} & \text{for } t \geq 0 \\ 0 & \text{otherwise} \end{cases} \quad (3.49)$$

The function $F(t) = 1 - e^{-\lambda t}$, where $t \geq 0$ is called the *cumulative density function* for the exponential distribution. Also, using integral calculus, it can be shown that mean and variance for the exponential distribution are as given in (3.50).

$$
\begin{aligned}
\mu &= 1/\lambda \quad (3.50) \\
\sigma^2 &= 1/\lambda^2
\end{aligned}
$$

To illustrate the use of the exponential distribution consider the following scenario. The arrivals at a service station follow a Poisson process and average two arrivals for a 5-minute interval. In other words, arrivals average 2/5 for a 1-minute interval. In this case, $\lambda = 2/5$ and $1/\lambda = 5/2$. The term $1/\lambda$ is interpreted as the average time between arrivals, which in this case is 2.5 minutes. Suppose that we are interested in computing the probability

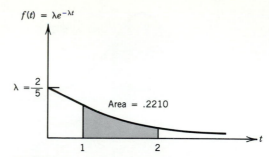

FIGURE 3.13   EXPONENTIAL DISTRIBUTION FOR INTERARRIVAL TIME AT A SERVICE STATION.

that the time between arrivals is somewhere between 1 and 2 minutes. To accomplish this we may use the area under the probability density function given in (3.49). In other words, we use this density function to compute $P(1 \leq t \leq 2)$ when $\lambda = 2/5$. Figure 3.13 illustrates this probability function while Figure 3.14 illustrates the same probability using the cumulative density function.

The calculation of the probability of an interarrival time in a specified interval is generally accomplished by using the cumulative density function.

$$
\begin{aligned}
P(1 \leq t \leq 2) &= P(t \leq 2) - P(t \leq 1) \\
&= 1 - e^{-(.4)(2)} - (1 - e^{-(.4)(1)}) \\
&= e^{-.4} - e^{-.8} \\
&= .6703 - .4493 = .2210 \quad (3.51)
\end{aligned}
$$

The calculation of probabilities for this distribution can be accomplished by evaluating values of e^{-x} that are given in Table C.5, Appendix C.

Both the exponential distribution and the Poisson distribution express the same process in different ways. The exponential distribution provides probabilities for the times between arrivals. The Poisson distribution involves a discrete random variable that provides probabilities for the number of arrivals in a specific interval of time. The exponential and Poisson distributions are very important in our study of queuing models in Chapter 17.

3.9   THE APPLICABILITY OF THE NORMAL DISTRIBUTION

An *empirical distribution* defines a probability distribution that was constructed from actual frequency

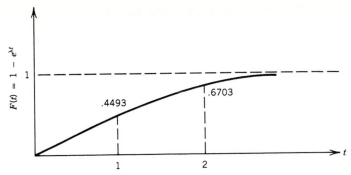

FIGURE 3.14 CUMULATIVE EXPONENTIAL DISTRIBUTION FOR INTER-ARRIVAL TIME AT A SERVICE STATION.

information. *Theoretical probability distributions* are not constructed from a particular set of frequency information, but rather appear to be representative of many empirical distributions. The binomial, Poisson, exponential, and normal distributions are examples of theoretical probability distributions.

The normal distribution has proved to be quite useful in modeling many different random variables that arise in applications. The normal distribution has also been used to approximate other theoretical distributions. For example, the Poisson and binomial distributions can be satisfactorily approximated using the normal distribution if certain conditions are satisfied. Aside from its role in empirical approximations, the assumption of a normal distribution gives acceptable results in many cases where the given probability distribution is not known to be normal.

The normal distribution also plays an integral role in statistical inference. The *central limit theorem*, which is fundamental to much of statistical inference, is based on the normal distribution. One form of this result can be stated as follows.

> If *n* random observations of a random variable with mean μ and variance σ^2 are obtained, the distribution of the average of *n* random observations (the sample mean) is approximately normally distributed (has a normal distribution) with mean μ and variance σ^2/n, when *n* is large.

The approximation becomes more accurate as *n* becomes large. This theorem, however, is true regardless of the form of the probability distribution from which the observations are drawn. The central limit theorem can be restated to apply to the sum of sample measurements

$$y = \sum_{i=1}^{n} y_i \qquad (3.52)$$

As *n* become large, y would also tend to possess a normal distribution, in repeated sampling, with mean $n\mu$ and standard deviation $\sigma\sqrt{n}$.

It is beyond the scope of our discussion here to go into more detail for any of the topics mentioned in this section. These issues are dealt with in more detail in most elementary statistics texts. They are mentioned here only because they do play an important role in the theoretical and conceptual development of a number of management science models.

3.10 SUMMARY

In this chapter we introduced the fundamental concepts involving random variables and probability distributions. We dealt with the difference between continuous and discrete random variables and the resultant differences in the computation of probabilities. A measure of central tendency, the mean, and a measure of variability, the variance/standard deviation, were also discussed.

Five theoretical probability distributions were examined: the binomial, the Poisson, the uniform, the normal, and the exponential. These distributions have a wide range of applicability and are supported by tables that permit the calculation of probabilities for particular values or intervals of values for the random variable of interest.

It should be noted that the field of probability and statistics is quite complex and contains much more than has been presented here. In this chapter and the last one we have presented only the topics that we feel the student must review in preparation for the topics that follow.

GLOSSARY

Binomial Probability Distribution   A discrete probability distribution for a random variable that is defined to be the number of successes in n trials of an experiment that satisfies the properties of a Bernoulli process.

Central Limit Theorem   An important result establishing the properties of the probability distribution for the sample mean.

Continuous Random Variable   A random variable that can take on any value in an interval.

Cumulative Probability   The probability associated with the occurrence of *all* values of the random variable less than or equal to a specified value.

Deviation   The distance of the random variable from its mean.

Discrete Probability Distribution   A relationship between a discrete random variable and the probability values associated with individual values of the random variable.

Discrete Random Variable   A random variable that can take on a finite or countably infinite number of values.

Expected Value   A weighted sum of all possible values of the random variable where the weights are the probabilities associated with the individual values of the random variable.

Exponential Distribution   A continuous probability distribution often used to model interarrival times of arrivals that follow a Poisson process.

Interarrival Time   The time between the occurrence of events.

Normal Probability Distribution   The continuous probability distribution with the density function of the bell-shaped curve. The distribution is specified by a mean value and by a standard deviation.

Poisson Probability Distribution   A probability distribution for a discrete random variable that represents the number of random events for an interval of time or space and that satisfies the properties of a Poisson process.

Probability Density Function   A function that is used to calculate probability for a continuous random variable.

Random Variable   Numerical values associated with the individual outcomes of an experiment.

Standard Deviation   The positive square root of the variance.

Standard Normal Distribution   A normal distribution with mean 0 and standard deviation 1.

Uniform Probability Distribution   A continuous probability distribution where the probability of a random variable being in an interval is a function of only the length of that interval.

Variance   The weighted sum of squared deviations where the weights are the probabilities associated with the individual values of the random variable. It is a measure of dispersion.

Selected References

Chou, Y. 1975. *Statistical Analysis*. New York: Holt, Rinehart & Winston.

Clelland, R.C., J.S. deCani, and F.E. Brown. 1973. *Basic Statistics with Business Applications*, 2nd ed. New York: Wiley.

Feller, W. 1968. *An Introduction to Probability Theory and Its Applications*, vol. 1, 3rd ed. New York: Wiley.

Freund, J.E., and R.E. Walpole. 1980. *Mathematical Statistics*, 3rd ed. Englewood Cliffs, N.J.: Prentice-Hall.

Hogg, R.V., and A.T. Craig. 1970. *Introduction to Mathematical Statistics*, 3rd ed. New York: Macmillan.

Lapin, L.L. 1973. *Statistics for Modern Business Decisions*. New York: Harcourt Brace Jovanovich.

Mendenhall, W., and J.E. Reinmuth. 1982. *Statistics for Management and Economics*, 4th ed. Boston: Duxbury.

Neter, J., W. Wasserman, and G. Whitmore. 1973. *Fundamental Statistics for Business and Economics*, 4th ed. Boston: Allyn & Bacon.

Parzen, E. 1960. *Modern Probability Theory*. New York: Wiley.

Discussion Questions

1. What is the difference between a discrete variable and a continuous variable? Give an example of each.

2. Discuss the relationship between a random variable and a probability distribution.

3. What is expected value? What does it measure? How is it computed for a discrete random variable?

4. What is variance? What does it measure? How is it computed for a discrete random variable?

5. Discuss the Bernoulli process. Give an example of a situation where the binomial distribution is applicable.

6. Discuss the Poisson process. Give an example of a situation where the Poisson distribution is applicable.

7. What is a probability density function? How is it used to calculate probabilities?

8. What is meant by a cumulative probability? Is cumulative probability interpreted differently for discrete probability distributions and continuous distributions?

9. Explain how cumulative probability is used in calculating probability for a random variable from a normal probability distribution.

10. Explain why the Poisson distribution and exponential distribution actually model the same process.

PROBLEMS

1. A fair die is rolled twice. Construct the probability distribution for the sum of the number of dots showing for the two successive rolls.

2. A jar contains four numbered balls. The selection of each is associated with a cash prize. The values of these prizes are $100, $200, $400, and $1000. If we successively select two balls (first one and then another out of the remaining three), construct the probability distribution for total winnings under the assumption that the selection is random.

3. Snow Packers, Inc., places an order for snowmobiles each September. The following probability distribution for demand is historically supported.

DEMAND	PROBABILITY
0	.10
1	.10
2	.30
3	.20
4	.20
5	.10

a. If the store orders four snowmobiles, what is the probability of selling all four?
b. What is the expected demand for snowmobiles?
c. What is the variance for demand? What is the standard deviation?
d. What is the probability that demand will lie within one standard deviation of the mean?

4. Freeze-Moore, Inc., sells refrigerators and maintenance agreements for these refrigerators. For refrigerators 1 to 3 years old Freeze-Moore has established a probability distribution of costs incurred per year.

COST	PROBABILITY
$0	.90
$25	.07
$75	.02
$150	.01

Currently, Freeze-Moore is selling the service agreement for $25 per year. Is that amount a reasonable selling price from Freeze-Moore's point of view?

5. A fair coin is tossed six times. Use the binomial formula to compute the probability of obtaining

   a. exactly three heads;
   b. exactly three tails;
   c. no tails;
   d. at least 4 heads;
   e. at most 3 heads.

6. Compute the probabilities in Problem 5 assuming that the coin is *not* fair. In fact, the probability of obtaining a head is .6 and the probability of obtaining a tail is .4.

7. Suppose that $n = 100$ parts are randomly chosen from a production process that yields 10 percent defectives. How many defectives are expected?

8. A fair coin is tossed 25 times in succession. Using the binomial tables in Appendix C, determine the probability that the number of heads obtained is

   a. less than or equal to 12;
   b. equal to 12;
   c. greater than 12;
   d. between 6 and 20, inclusively;
   e. less than 4 *or* greater than 20.

9. Compute the probabilities in Problem 8 assuming the coin described in Problem 6.

10. Construct the binomial probability distributions for $n = 5$, $p = .6$ and $n = 5$, $p = .4$. Compare the two distributions. Can you make any generalizations?

11. Five 6-year-old children work independently and simultaneously on a task. Each has a probability of .80 of successfully completing this task. View this situation as an experiment with five independent Bernoulli trials. Design the sample space and compute the probability of each simple event.

12. In Problem 11 define x to be the number of unsuccessful students. What is the distribution for x? What is the expected value and variance for x?

13. The number of tornadoes hitting an area in South Carolina each year is a random variable whose probability distribution is closely approximated with a Poisson distribution with $\lambda = 6$ (time—1 year). Find the probability that in a given year

a. exactly 4 tornadoes will hit South Carolina;
b. 4 or fewer tornadoes will hit South Carolina;
c. 6 to 7 tornadoes will hit South Carolina.

14. A local automobile tire retailer buys tires in lots of 750. Past experience confirms that 1 percent of all new tires purchased must be replaced within 30 days since they are defective. Find the probability that in a shipment of 750 tires there will be,

a. no defective tires;
b. zero or one defective tire;
c. more than three defective tires.

15. Answer the same questions posed in Problem 12 assuming a shipment of 1500 tires.

16. A gasoline distributor has found that his daily sales of gasoline follows a uniform distribution when daily sales range between 20,000 and 70,000 gallons. What is the probability that the distributor sells

a. between 20,000 and 40,000 gallons in a given day?
b. at most 60,000 gallons in a given day?
c. between 30,000 and 60,000 gallons in a given day?

17. Two baseball teams, A and B, score an average of three and four runs per game. Assume that runs are scored according to a Poisson process. What is the probability that team A will win if team B scores five runs in the game?

18. Customers arrive at a service center according to a Poisson process at an average of two per hour. What is the probability that more than five customers will arrive in a 2-hour period?

19. At the grand opening of the Diet-Rite Chocolate Shop, free snacks will be given to the first 500 customers. The free snack is either a chocolate-covered apple or a carob-covered apple. A market survey indicates that 60 percent of the customers will prefer the chocolate-covered apple. Diet-Rite has 300 chocolate-covered apples and 200 carob-covered apples available for the first 500 customers. What is the expected number of the first 500 customers that will have to settle for their second choice?

20. Okra Limited processes and packages frozen okra in 12-ounce packages. The packaging equipment has placed anywhere from $11\frac{1}{4}$ ounces to 13 ounces in a package. Okra Limited believes that the process follows a uniform distribution. Sketch the graph of this probability distribution. Determine the probability that an arbitrarily selected package will contain between 12 and $12\frac{1}{4}$ ounces.

21. In many cases measurement errors have been found to follow a normal distribution. It has been found that odometers equipped on a certain model car are not perfect. In fact, it has been found that

measurement error for these odometers has a normal distribution with mean 0 and standard deviation 1 mile for every 100 miles driven. The errors will be recorded as negative numbers if the measurement is under 100 for an actual distance of 100 miles. Determine the probability that an arbitrarily selected odometer will have a error that is

a. between 0 and 1.75;
b. 1.75 or more;
c. 1.75 or less;
d. between 0 and −1.75;
e. between −1.75 and 1.75;
f. between 1.5 and 1.75;
g. between −1.25 and −1.00;
h. greater than −2.05.

22. The lifetime of a high-intensity light bulb is normally distributed with a mean of 3000 hours and a standard deviation of 200 hours. Find the probability that one of these light bulbs will last

a. between 3000 and 3500 hours;
b. between 2500 and 3500 hours;
c. between 2000 and 3500 hours;
d. more than 2750 hours;
e. more than 3400 hours;
f. less than 2700 hours;
g. between 3400 and 3500 hours.

23. Easy Shaft manufactures electric motors. The average shaft for the $\frac{1}{3}$-horsepower motor it produces is .5 inches in diameter with a standard deviation of .01 inches. Shaft diameter is normally distributed. The motor will be classified as defective if the shaft diameter does not fall in the interval from .49 inches to .525 inches. What percent defectives should be expected for this production process?

24. The lifetime of a particular resistor used in the electrical system of a compact truck is normally distributed and has a standard deviation of 6 months. If 5 percent of these resistors wear out in less than four years, what is the expected life of the resistor?

25. Most tires on the market have a standard deviation of 2500 miles in treadwear and tread life tends to assume a normal distribution. What average treadwear rating should you purchase if you want to be 90 percent sure that a tire will last 35,000 miles?

26. The lifetime of an experimental energy-saving device has an exponential distribution with mean of 2 years. What is the probability that the device will last at least,

a. 2 years?
b. 3 years?
c. 1 year?

27. Customers arrive at a banking facility on Wednesday afternoons at the rate of one per minute. Assume that arrivals follow a Poisson process. What is the probability that the time between the next two successive arrivals will be

   a. shorter than 1.5 minutes?
   b. longer than 4 minutes?
   c. between 2 and 5 minutes?

28. What is the expected time between arrivals in Problem 27? What is the probability of occurrence of this expected interarrival time?

29. Three students begin working on an exam at 12:00 P.M. The time it takes a student to complete the exam follows the exponential distribution with a mean of 4 hours. Completion times for different students are independent. What is the probability that two of the three students will still be working on the exam at 5:00 P.M.?

30. The length of a service call has a normal distribution with mean 45 minutes and a standard deviation of 15 minutes. If 100 independent observations are taken from 100 randomly selected service calls, the average time can also be viewed as a random variable. What is the distribution of this random variable?

DECISION THEORY AND UTILITY THEORY

4.1 INTRODUCTION

Decision theory, or *decision analysis*, can be used in situations in which the decision maker has several alternative courses of action but it also faced with an uncertain future set of possible events. For example, a manufacturer of suntan lotion would try to manufacture large quantities of a product for the tanning season, assuming that good tanning weather (i.e., a long sunny summer) was predicted. If bad weather was predicted, however, the manufacturer would want to reduce the production quantity, so as not to have to maintain a large inventory. Unfortunately, the manufacturer would have to make this decision prior to the tanning season, without knowledge concerning the likelihood of a sunny summer. A decision-making problem such as this can be analyzed using a decision theory approach.

Decision theory has been applied to a wide range of problems. These problems have generally involved the interactions of alternatives and events whose uncertainties affect the desirabilities of various actions the decision maker can select. Among the problem situations that have been analyzed by decision theory are the following.

1. RESEARCH AND DEVELOPMENT   Should research be conducted in a certain area? Should we conduct experiments? What is the expected payoff from the research and development?

2. MARKETING APPLICATIONS   Should a new product be introduced? How should we advertise the new product? What is the best way to distribute the new product?

3. FINANCIAL DECISIONS   How should we determine our portfolio of investments? What new investments should be made? What is the expected return on our portfolio?

4. LAND DEVELOPMENT   How should we develop a piece of property we own? Would apartment or condominium development be more profitable? How large should the development be?

5. PERSONAL DECISIONS   Should you obtain a job or go to graduate school? What field of study should you select at college? What kind of automobile should you buy? Where should you live and work?

Initially, we provide an overview of the decision theory approach. We will see that it requires the decision maker to specify the payoffs that will result from choosing various alternatives given various possible states of nature. We then provide a summary of the types of decision-making situations that you can expect to encounter. We then provide detailed discussions of decision making under risk and uncertainty. Finally, we show how utility theory can be used for situations in which a monetary criterion is not appropriate.

4.2 AN OVERVIEW OF THE DECISION THEORY APPROACH

The decision theory approach to a problem situation involves three major steps. We introduce and illustrate these steps by means of an example involving a company, the Crabapple Microcomputer Company, that manufactures microcomputers and is contemplating the expansion of its manufacturing facilities.

STEP 1.   LIST ALL ALTERNATIVES:

The first step in the decision theory approach requires the decision maker to list all the alternative courses of action, or *decision alternatives*. For our problem situation, the Crabapple Microcomputer Company feels that it has three possible decision alternatives.

Decision Alternative 1.—Expand present manufacturing facility.
Decision Alternative 2.—Build a new manufacturing facility.
Decision Alternative 3.—License another manufacturer to build the microcomputer.

In decision theory, an alternative is defined to be a course of action or a strategy that can be selected by the decision maker. It is very important for the decision maker to list all possible alternatives, because a seemingly unimportant alternative may turn out to be the best choice in a particular situation.

STEP 2.   LIST ALL POSSIBLE FUTURE EVENTS:

The second step in applying decision theory requires the decision maker to develop an exhaustive list of possible future events. These future events are referred to as *states of nature*. It is assumed that the states of nature are defined to include everything that can happen (i.e., they are collectively exhaustive) and that only one of them can occur (i.e., they are mutually exclusive). The states of nature are not under the control of the decision maker.

For this problem situation the states of nature relate to future demand for the microcomputer. The Crabapple Microcomputer Company feels that the future events relating to demand for its microcomputer are

State of Nature 1.—High product demand.
State of Nature 2.—Moderate product demand.
State of Nature 3.—Low product demand.

Again, it is important for the decision maker to consider all possible states of nature. If you are optimistic about future events, don't forget about some of the bad outcomes. If the Crabapple Microcomputer Company ignores the possibility of "low product demand," it could have a lot of unsold computers in its inventory!

STEP 3.   CONSTRUCT A PAYOFF TABLE:

The third step in the decision analysis approach involves the specification of the outcomes resulting from selecting a certain decision alternative and then having a particular state of nature occur. This interaction between the decision alternative and the state of nature is referred to as the *payoff*. The payoffs may be specified in terms of profits, losses, revenues, costs, utilities, or other appropriate measurements. The payoff estimates are usually presented in terms of the interactions of the decision alternatives and the states of nature in the form of a *payoff table*.

Table 4.1 illustrates the nine possible payoffs for the Crabapple Microcomputer Company, as they have been estimated by the company's management.

The remainder of this chapter discusses how we apply this general decision theory approach to develop decision-making criteria for specific problem situations. As we shall see, there are several types of decision-making situations that can be encountered. The criterion we choose will be dependent on the type of decision-making situation that we are addressing. As you probably have already concluded, much of the value of decision theory is that it forces the decision maker to rationally and systematically structure information in making a decision.

4.3   TYPES OF DECISION-MAKING SITUATIONS

Four types of decision-making situations are typically encountered by the manager.

1.   DECISION MAKING UNDER CERTAINTY   In this situation the decision maker knows with certainty the state of nature for each decision alternative, (i.e., *perfect information* is available). The payoff for each alternative can be easily determined and the decision maker can make an optimal decision by selecting the largest payoff available. For example, assume that you can put $100 into a bank at a guaranteed interest rate of 6 percent per year or into a savings and loan association at a guaranteed interest rate of 8 percent per year. The choice obviously would be to put the money into the savings and loan association.

Finding situations in which perfect information is available is not always easy. Yet,

TABLE 4.1   PAYOFF TABLE—CRABAPPLE MICROCOMPUTER COMPANY

DECISION ALTERNATIVES	STATES OF NATURE		
	HIGH DEMAND	MODERATE DEMAND	LOW DEMAND
Expand present facility	$1,000,000	$500,000	− $100,000
Build new facility	2,500,000	1,200,000	− 500,000
License another manufacturer	1,500,000	800,000	− 50,000

Note: Payoffs are expressed in yearly profit dollars.

assuming certainty for a problem where information is not really known for certain often provides a reasonable approximation. For example, in later chapters in this book we study linear programming. In the analysis of linear programming problems, the available resources, the unit cost of producing a product, and the amount of resources required to produce a product are assumed to be known with certainty.

2. DECISION MAKING UNDER RISK   In this situation the decision maker does not have perfect information available, but can estimate the probability of occurrence for each state of nature. For example, assume that you are playing a game with a pair of dice. Then the probability of rolling a two on the pair of dice is 1/36, while the probability of rolling a seven on the pair of dice is 6/36. While this game is risky, you can make objective probability estimates concerning its outcomes.

   Or, assume that you are contemplating purchasing a fast-food restaurant franchise and locating it in a specific place. While you could not determine sales levels with certainty, you could make subjective probability estimates for various sales levels.

3. DECISION MAKING UNDER UNCERTAINTY   In this situation the decision maker cannot even estimate the probabilities associated with the various states of nature. For example, assume that you are asked to give the probability of IBM stock being at a certain price 10 years from now, or were asked to state the probability associated with the successful introduction of a new product.

4. DECISION MAKING UNDER CONFLICT   In this situation two or more decision makers have goals or objectives for which they are competing. As a result, the decision makers have to consider not only their own courses of action but also the courses of action that can be taken by their competitors. This type of decision-making situation is analyzed using *game theory*. Game theory is considered separately in Chapter 21.

As we discussed above, in decision-making situations involving certainty the state of nature is known for each decision alternative. This enables the decision maker to easily determine the payoff for each alternative, and make an optimal decision by simply selecting the largest payoff that is available. Consequently, we won't discuss decision making under certainty any further, and will concentrate our attention on decision making under risk and uncertainty. Certainty and uncertainty represent the two extremes of availability of information. Risk occurs at any point between these two extremes.

4.4 DECISION MAKING UNDER RISK

Decision making under risk involves situations in which probabilities are available for the various states of nature. For such situations we first identify the possible decision alternatives. Next, the states of nature are identified and their associated probabilities of occurrence are estimated. Then, the conditional payoff of a decision alternative under a given course of action is determined. In the context of decision making under risk we look at the expected monetary value and expected opportunity loss criteria and the concept of the expected value of perfect information.

4.4.1 EXPECTED MONETARY VALUE (EMV)

The most logical and straightforward approach to decision making under risk is to try to maximize the expected amount of money resulting from choosing a particular decision alternative. The *expected monetary value (EMV)* criterion requires the decision maker to construct a decision table that lists the outcomes for each decision alternative–state of nature and the probabilities for each state of nature. The expected monetary value for a particular alternative is then the sum of possible payoffs of that alternative, with each payoff being weighted by the probability of that payoff occurring. Thus, for any decision alternative i:

EMV (Decision alternative i) = (payoff from 1st state of nature − decision alternative i combination) · (probability of 1st state of nature) + (payoff from 2nd state of nature − decision alternative i combination) · (probability of 2nd state of nature) + · · · + (payoff from last state of nature − decision alternative *i* combination) · (probability of last state of nature) (4.1)

In general terms, we can state that the expected monetary value of a decision alternative a_i is given by

$$EMV(a_i) = \sum_{j=1}^{N} P(\theta_j)V(a_i, \theta_j) \qquad (4.2)$$

where

θ_j = state of nature *j*

$P(\theta_j)$ = the probability of occurrence of state of nature θ_j

$V(a_i, \theta_j)$ = the payoff associated with decision alternative a_i and state of nature θ_j

N = the number of possible states of nature; $j = 1, 2, \ldots, N$

with $P(\theta_j) \geq 0$ for all states of nature *j*

$$\sum_{j=1}^{N} P(\theta_j) = 1 \qquad (4.3)$$

To show how we actually compute the expected monetary value let us consider the Crabapple Microcomputer Company situation, and let us assume that the company's management has made an assessment of the probabilities associated with the three levels of projected demand for its microcomputer. In Table 4.2, the original payoff table for the Crabapple Microcomputer Company has been reproduced, with the probability assessments for the three states of nature (i.e., the projected demand

levels) added as the bottom row, and with the expected monetary value for each alternative shown in the last column. The expected monetary values for the three decision alternatives were calculated as follows.

$$
\begin{aligned}
EMV(a_1) &= \sum_{j=1}^{3} P(\theta_j)V(a_1, \theta_j) \\
&= (.4)(\$1,000,000) + (.4)(\$500,000) \\
&\quad + (.2)(-\$100,000) \\
&= \$400,000 + \$200,000 - \$20,000 \\
&= \$580,000 \qquad (4.4)
\end{aligned}
$$

$$
\begin{aligned}
EMV(a_2) &= \sum_{j=1}^{3} P(\theta_j)V(a_2, \theta_j) \\
&= (.4)(\$2,500,000) + (.4)(\$1,200,000) \\
&\quad + (.2)(-\$500,000) \\
&= \$1,000,000 + \$480,000 - \$100,000 \\
&= \$1,380,000 \qquad (4.5)
\end{aligned}
$$

$$
\begin{aligned}
EMV(a_3) &= \sum_{j=1}^{3} P(\theta_j)V(a_3, \theta_j) \\
&= (.4)(\$1,500,000) + (.4)(\$800,000) \\
&\quad + (.2)(-\$50,000) \\
&= \$600,000 + \$320,000 - \$10,000 \\
&= \$910,000 \qquad (4.6)
\end{aligned}
$$

The largest expected monetary value results from selecting the second decision alternative, "build new facility."

4.4.2 EXPECTED OPPORTUNITY LOSS

An alternative approach to decision making under risk is based on the idea that the decision maker

TABLE 4.2 EXPECTED MONETARY VALUE—CRABAPPLE MICROCOMPUTER COMPANY

DECISION ALTERNATIVES	STATES OF NATURE			EXPECTED MONETARY VALUE
	HIGH DEMAND (θ_1)	MODERATE DEMAND (θ_2)	LOW DEMAND (θ_3)	
Expand present facility (a_1)	$1,000,000	$500,000	−$100,000	$580,000
Build new facility (a_2)	2,500,000	1,200,000	−500,000	1,380,000
License another manufacturer (a_3)	1,500,000	800,000	−50,000	910,000
Probability	.4	.4	.2	

should try to minimize the loss associated with not selecting the best decision alternative. Using this approach, a second criterion for decision making under risk is the *expected opportunity loss* (EOL) criterion. The *opportunity loss*, or *regret*, is the difference between the optimal payoff for a particular state of nature and the actual payoff received for a particular state of nature–decision alternative combination, that is, the amount that is lost by not picking the best decision alternative. The general expression for the opportunity loss or regret function is

$$R(a_i, \theta_j) = V^*(\theta_j) - V(a_i, \theta_j) \qquad (4.7)$$

where

$R(a_i, \theta_j)$ = opportunity loss or regret associated with decision alternative a_i and state of nature θ_j

$V^*(\theta_j)$ = best payoff under state of nature θ_j

$V(a_i, \theta_j)$ = payoff associated with decision alternative a_i and state of nature θ_j

For the Crabapple Microcomputer Company, the opportunity loss associated with the first alternative, "expand present facility" and state of nature, "high demand," for example, is computed as

$$\begin{aligned} R(a_1, \theta_1) &= V^*(\theta_1) - V(a_1, \theta_1) \\ &= \$2{,}500{,}000 - \$1{,}000{,}000 \\ &= \$1{,}500{,}000 \end{aligned} \qquad (4.8)$$

Using Eq. 4.7 an opportunity loss table can be constructed, as is shown in Table 4.3.

Having constructed the opportunity loss table, the expected opportunity loss criterion uses the probabilities of the states of nature as weights for the opportunity loss values. The expected oppor-

tunity loss of a decision alternative, a_i, is then computed as

$$EOL(a_i) = \sum_{j=1}^{N} P(\theta_j)R(a_i, \theta_j) \qquad (4.9)$$

Let us see how this entire procedure would be done for the Crabapple Microcomputer Company.

STEP 1. CONSTRUCT THE OPPORTUNITY LOSS TABLE:

The opportunity losses for the Crabapple Microcomputer Company are obtained by applying Eq. 4.7 to the data presented in Table 4.1. The opportunity loss table for the Crabapple Microcomputer Company is shown in Table 4.3. In this opportunity loss table the opportunity loss for each decision alternative–state of nature combination was computed by subtracting the associated payoff for that combination from the best payoff in the same state of nature column, using the payoff figures presented earlier in Table 4.1.

STEP 2. COMPUTE THE EXPECTED OPPORTUNITY LOSS FOR EACH ALTERNATIVE:

Using this opportunity loss table and Eq. 4.9, the expected opportunity losses associated with the various decision alternatives are computed as

$$\begin{aligned} EOL(a_1) &= \sum_{j=1}^{3} P(\theta_j)R(a_1, \theta_j) \\ &= (.4)(\$1{,}500{,}000) + (.4)(\$700{,}000) \\ &\quad + (.2)(\$50{,}000) \\ &= \$600{,}000 + \$280{,}000 + \$10{,}000 \\ &= \$890{,}000 \qquad (4.10) \end{aligned}$$

TABLE 4.3 OPPORTUNITY LOSS TABLE—CRABAPPLE MICROCOMPUTER COMPANY

DECISION ALTERNATIVES	STATES OF NATURE			EXPECTED OPPORTUNITY LOSS
	HIGH DEMAND	MODERATE DEMAND	LOW DEMAND	
Expand present facility	$1,500,000	$700,000	$50,000	$890,000
Build new facility	0	0	450,000	$90,000
License another manufacturer	1,000,000	400,000	0	$560,000
Probability	.4	.4	.2	

$$EOL(a_2) = \sum_{j=1}^{3} P(\theta_j)R(a_2, \theta_j)$$

$$= (.4)(\$0) + (.4)(\$0)$$
$$+ (.2)(\$450,000)$$
$$= 0 + 0 + \$90,000$$
$$= \$90,000 \qquad (4.11)$$

$$EOL(a_3) = \sum_{j=1}^{3} P(\theta_j)R(a_3, \theta_j)$$

$$= (.4)(\$1,000,000) + (.4)(\$400,000)$$
$$+ (.2)(\$0)$$
$$= \$400,000 + \$160,000 + \$0$$
$$= \$560,000 \qquad (4.12)$$

The expected opportunity loss for each alternative is shown in the final column of Table 4.3. The smallest expected opportunity loss results from selecting the second decision alternative, "build new facility."

4.4.3 EXPECTED VALUE OF PERFECT INFORMATION

An important concept that is related to the criteria of expected monetary value and expected opportunity loss is the *expected value of perfect information* (*EVPI*). The expected value of perfect information, as its name suggests, is the value of the information that would allow the decision maker to be sure that the correct alternative was being chosen. This type of information can prevent the decision maker from making a very costly mistake.

In the two previous sections we have assumed that the executives of the Crabapple Microcomputer Company can estimate the probabilities associated with various demand levels. However, they do not know exactly what the demand level will be.

Let us now assume that information can be obtained that will change the decision situation from one of risk to one of certainty. Such information is called *perfect information*. Referring back to the opportunity loss table determined previously (see Table 4.3), we see that if one knew that there would be "high" demand, then the alternative selected would be "build new facility." Similarly, if one knew that there would be "moderate demand," then the alternative selected would be "build new facility." If one knew that there would be "low" demand, however, then the alternative selected

would be "license another manufacturer." Essentially, if we have perfect information, we will know exactly which of the various states of nature will occur.

We now see that if the state of nature "high demand" occurs, we will have selected the best decision alternative and the opportunity loss will be zero. Similarly, if the state of nature "moderate demand" occurs, we will have again selected the best decision alternative and the opportunity loss will again be zero. However, if the state of nature "low demand" occurs Crabapple Microcomputer Company will have an opportunity loss of $450,000 due to the fact that decision alternative "license another manufacturer" was not selected.

How can we compute the expected value of this perfect information? Using $P(\theta_1) = .4$, $P(\theta_2) = .4$, and $P(\theta_3) = .2$, and the opportunity loss values, we see that 80 percent of the time Crabapple Microcomputer Company would save $0, and 20 percent of the time it would save $450,000. Thus we can compute the expected value of perfect information (EVPI) as

$$EVPI = \sum_{j=1}^{N} P(\theta_j)R(a_i^*, \theta_j) \qquad (4.13)$$

where

θ_j = state of nature j

$P(\theta_j)$ = the probability of occurrence of state of nature θ_j

$R(a_i^*, \theta_j)$ = opportunity loss, or regret, associated with the best decision alternative a_i^* and state of nature θ_j

N = the number of possible states of nature j; $j = 1, \ldots, N$

For our decision situation, in which the best decision is alternative a_2

$$EVPI = \sum_{j=1}^{3} P(\theta_j)R(a_2^*, \theta_j)$$

$$= (.4)(\$0) + (.4)(\$0)$$
$$+ (.2)(\$450,000)$$
$$= 0 + 0 + \$90,000$$
$$= \$90,000 \qquad (4.14)$$

This value indicates that if we can obtain perfect

information, we could then expect to reduce the expected opportunity loss by $90,000. Viewed in another manner, the Crabapple Microcomputer Company should never pay more than $90,000 for information, no matter how good or reliable such information might be.

Observe further that the expected value of perfect information is equivalent to the minimum of the expected opportunity losses. Earlier (see Eqs. 4.10, 4.11, and 4.12) we computed the expected opportunity losses for the three alternatives to be

$$\text{EOL}(a_1) = \$890,000 \tag{4.15}$$

$$\text{EOL}(a_2) = \$90,000 \text{ (minimum)} \tag{4.16}$$

$$\text{EOL}(a_3) = \$560,000 \tag{4.17}$$

The minimum of these expected opportunity losses, $90,000, is seen to be equivalent to the expected value of perfect information that we computed using Eq. 4.13.

Alternatively, the expected value of perfect information can be computed using expected monetary values. Using this approach, the EVPI is the expected outcome with perfect information (i.e., the expected monetary value with perfect information) minus the expected outcome without perfect information (i.e., the maximum expected monetary value). Thus, we can express EVPI as follows

EVPI = expected monetary value with perfect information − maximum expected monetary value

This computation proceeds in two steps.

1. The expected monetary value with perfect information is determined as follows.

Expected monetary value with perfect information = (best outcome for 1st state of nature) · (probability of 1st state of nature) + (best outcome for 2nd state of nature) · (probability of 2nd state of nature) + · · · + (best outcome for last state of nature) · (probability of last state of nature) (4.18)

For the Crabapple Microcomputer Company

Expected monetary value with perfect information = ($2,500,000)(.4) + ($1,200,000)(.4) + (−$50,000)(.2) = $1,000,000 + $480,000 − $10,000 = $1,470,000 (4.19)

The maximum expected monetary value is $1,380,000 (see Table 4.2), which is the expected outcome without perfect information.

2. Now, the expected value of perfect information (EVPI) can be computed as:

EVPI = expected monetary value with perfect information − maximum expected monetary value
= $1,470,000 − $1,380,000
= $90,000 (4.20)

4.5 DECISION MAKING UNDER UNCERTAINTY

Decision making under uncertainty involves problem situations in which the probabilities associated with the potential outcomes are not known or cannot be estimated. For such situations, there are five criteria that can be used to make decisions. We discuss each of these five criteria, in the context of the microcomputer company problem presented earlier.

4.5.1 THE MAXIMAX CRITERION

The *maximax criterion* is an aggressive, or optimistic, criterion. Using this criterion, the decision maker arrays the maximum payoffs possible for the various decision alternatives, and then selects the decision alternative that is the maximum of these maximum payoffs.

To illustrate the application of the maximax criterion refer back to the payoff table for the Crabapple Microcomputer Company that was presented as Table 4.1. This table is reproduced as Table 4.4, and includes an extra column that indicates the maximum payoff associated with each decision alternative. In the final column of Table 4.4 the maximum value among the maximum payoffs, $2,500,000, is circled, and the decision alternative selected would be "build new facility."

TABLE 4.4   MAXIMAX CRITERION—CRABAPPLE MICROCOMPUTER COMPANY

DECISION ALTERNATIVES	STATES OF NATURE HIGH DEMAND	MODERATE DEMAND	LOW DEMAND	MAXIMUM PAYOFF
Expand present facility	$1,000,000	$500,000	−$100,000	$1,000,000
Build new facility	2,500,000	1,200,000	−500,000	2,500,000
License another manufacturer	1,500,000	800,000	−50,000	1,500,000

4.5.2   THE MAXIMIN CRITERION

The *maximin criterion* is a conservative, or pessimistic, criterion. It is sometimes referred to as the Wald criterion, after its originator, Abraham Wald. Using this criterion, the decision maker arrays the minimum payoffs possible for the various decision alternatives, and then selects the decision alternative that is the maximum of these minimum payoffs.

To demonstrate the application of the maximin criterion refer to Table 4.5, which is the original payoff table for the Crabapple Microcomputer Company with an extra column that indicates the minimum payoff associated with each decision alternative. In the final column of Table 4.5 the maximum value among the minimum payoffs, −$50,000, is circled, and the decision alternative selected would be "license another manufacturer."

4.5.3   THE CRITERION OF REALISM

The *criterion of realism* is a compromise between an optimistic and a pessimistic decision criterion, or between the maximin and maximax decision criteria. It is often called the Hurwicz criterion, after its originator, Leonid Hurwicz. Using this criterion the decision maker first selects a *coefficient of optimism*, α, which measures the decision maker's degree of optimism. The coefficient of optimism is between 0 and 1, with 0 indicating complete pessimism and 1 indicating complete optimism. Then, for each alternative the maximum payoff is multiplied by α, the minimum payoff is multiplied by $1 - \alpha$, and these two values are added to produce a weighted average payoff. This produces a set of weighted values, the highest of which represents the best alternative.

To illustrate the application of the criterion of realism, refer to Table 4.6, which is the original payoff table for the Crabapple Microcomputer Company with an extra column that summarizes the computation of the criterion of realism, or the weighted average, using a value of $\alpha = 0.6$. In the final column of Table 4.6 the largest weighted average payoff, $1,300,000, is circled, and the decision alternative selected would be "build new facility."

4.5.4   EQUALLY LIKELY CRITERION

The *equally likely criterion* is based on the assumption that since the probabilities of the future states of nature are unknown, it should be assumed that each state of nature is equally likely to occur. Consequently, each state of nature is assigned the same probability and the equally likely decision criterion selects the alternative with the highest average outcome.

TABLE 4.5   MAXIMIN CRITERION—CRABAPPLE MICROCOMPUTER COMPANY

DECISION ALTERNATIVES	STATES OF NATURE HIGH DEMAND	MODERATE DEMAND	LOW DEMAND	MINIMUM PAYOFF
Expand present facility	$1,000,000	$500,000	−$100,000	−$100,000
Build new facility	2,500,000	1,200,000	−500,000	−500,000
License another manufacturer	1,500,000	800,000	−50,000	−50,000

TABLE 4.6   CRITERION OF REALISM—CRABAPPLE MICROCOMPUTER COMPANY

| DECISION ALTERNATIVES | STATES OF NATURE | | | CRITERION OF REALISM (WEIGHTED AVERAGE) $\alpha = 0.6$ |
	HIGH DEMAND	MODERATE DEMAND	LOW DEMAND	
Expand present facility	$1,000,000	$500,000	−$100,000	$560,000
Build new facility	2,500,000	1,200,000	−500,000	1,300,000
License another manufacturer	1,500,000	800,000	−50,000	880,000

To demonstrate the application of the equally likely criterion refer to Table 4.7, which is the original payoff table for the Crabapple Microcomputer Company with an extra column that indicates the row average (i.e., assuming equal probabilities of 1/3 for each of the three states of nature) for each of the decision alternatives. In the final column of Table 4.7 the maximum of the average outcomes of each of the alternatives, $1,066,667, is circled, and the decision alternative selected would be "build new facility."

4.5.5   MINIMAX CRITERION

The *minimax criterion* is based on the concept of opportunity loss that was discussed earlier in the section on decision making under risk. It is sometimes referred to as the Savage criterion, or the minimax regret criterion, after its originator, L. J. Savage. The minimax criterion selects the decision alternative that minimizes the maximum opportunity losses over all alternatives. Initially, the maximum opportunity loss is computed for each decision alternative. Then the alternative with the minimum of these opportunity losses is selected.

To illustrate the application of the minimax criterion refer to Table 4.8, which is the opportunity loss table for the Crabapple Microcomputer Company with an extra column that indicates the max-

imum opportunity loss associated with each decision alternative. In the final column of Table 4.8 the minimum of the maximum opportunity losses, $450,000, is circled, and the decision alternative selected would be "build new facility."

4.6   DECISION TREES

A problem that can be analyzed using expected monetary values or expected opportunity losses can also be analyzed using a graphical approach called a *decision tree*. This graphical approach is often preferred by managers because it allows them to see exactly what is happening at each stage of the decision-making process by showing its natural or logical progression. It also affords the advantage of making the expected value computations (i.e., either expected monetary value or expected opportunity loss) easier because they can be made directly on the decision tree.

To illustrate the decision tree approach let us reconsider the Crabapple Microcomputer Company problem. Recall that the management of this company was trying to decide how to expand its operations, and was considering the expansion of its present manufacturing facility, the building of a new manufacturing facility, or the licensing of another manufacturer to build its microcomputer.

TABLE 4.7   EQUALLY LIKELY CRITERION—CRABAPPLE MICROCOMPUTER COMPANY

| DECISION ALTERNATIVES | STATES OF NATURE | | | ROW AVERAGE |
	HIGH DEMAND	MODERATE DEMAND	LOW DEMAND	
Expand present facility	$1,000,000	$500,000	−$100,000	$466,667
Build new facility	2,500,000	1,200,000	−500,000	1,066,667
License another manufacturer	1,500,000	800,000	−50,000	750,000

TABLE 4.8 MINIMAX CRITERION (USING OPPORTUNITY LOSS)—CRABAPPLE MICROCOMPUTER COMPANY

DECISION ALTERNATIVES	STATES OF NATURE			MAXIMUM OPPORTUNITY LOSS
	HIGH DEMAND	MODERATE DEMAND	LOW DEMAND	
Expand present facility	$1,500,000	$700,000	$50,000	$1,500,000
Build new facility	0	0	450,000	450,000
License another manufacturer	1,000,000	400,000	0	1,000,000

EXAMPLE (SIMPLE DECISION TREE)

A simple decision tree representing this decision situation is shown in Figure 4.1. Note that this decision tree presents the decisions and their outcomes in the natural, or chronological, order that is followed in the decision-making process. In this problem the decision maker must first decide whether to expand the present manufacturing facility, build a new manufacturing facility, or license another manufacturer to build its microcomputer. Once that decision is made, one of the possible states of nature (high product demand, moderate product demand, or low product demand) will occur.

Decision trees are constructed using a set of decision nodes and state of nature nodes. The following symbols are employed.

□ Denotes a decision node at which one of several alternatives may be chosen.

○ Denotes a state of nature, or chance, node at which one state of nature will occur.

In Figure 4.1, the initial node, node A, is marked □ as a square indicating that it is a decision node. Nodes 1, 2, and 3 are chance nodes, and are marked ○ as circles. Continuation down the branches out of these nodes is a chance event. Depending on the outcome of this chance event, a terminating point is reached. For this problem situation the terminating points are the payoffs associated with various decision alternative–state of nature combinations. These payoffs are, of course, the same payoffs that were presented earlier in Table 4.2.

The decision tree analysis is then completed (i.e., the problem is solved) by computing the expected monetary value associated with the initial decision node, node A. Using the probabilities previously assigned to the various states of nature (refer to Table 4.2), we work backward in the decision tree from the terminal events (payoffs). These probabilities are placed in parentheses next to each state of nature. Using these probabilities, the expected monetary values for each of the three chance nodes are computed as follows.

$$\begin{aligned} \text{EMV (chance node 1)} &= (.4)(\$1,000,000) + (.4) \\ &\quad (\$500,000) + (.2) \\ &\quad (-\$100,000) \\ &= \$400,000 + \$200,000 \\ &\quad - \$20,000 \\ &= \$580,000 \end{aligned} \quad (4.21)$$

$$\begin{aligned} \text{EMV (chance node 2)} &= (.4)(\$2,500,000) + (.4) \\ &\quad (\$1,200,000) + (.2) \\ &\quad (-\$500,000) \\ &= \$1,000,000 + \$480,000 \\ &\quad - \$100,000 \\ &= \$1,380,000 \end{aligned} \quad (4.22)$$

$$\begin{aligned} \text{EMV (chance node 3)} &= (.4)(\$1,500,000) + (.4) \\ &\quad (\$800,000) + (.2) \\ &\quad (-\$50,000) \\ &= \$600,000 + \$320,000 \\ &\quad - \$10,000 \\ &= \$910,000 \end{aligned} \quad (4.23)$$

The expected monetary values are then placed on their associated chance nodes (see Figure 4.1).

We are now able to compute the expected monetary value associated with the initial decision node, node A. This expected monetary value is simply the maximum of the expected monetary values of the three branches leading back into it, namely

$$\begin{aligned} \text{EMV (decision node A)} &= \text{maximum } \{[\$580,000], \\ &\quad [\$1,380,000], [\$910,000]\} \\ &= \$1,380,000 \end{aligned} \quad (4.24)$$

This largest expected monetary value results from selecting the second decision alternative, "build new facility."

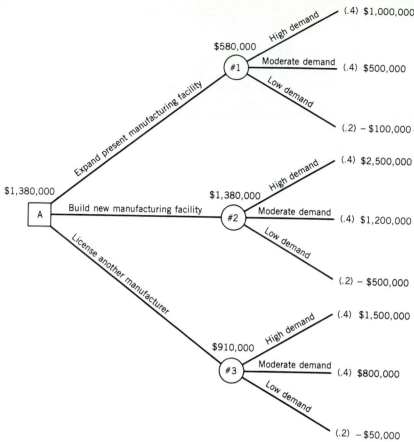

FIGURE 4.1   SIMPLE DECISION TREE—CRABAPPLE MICROCOMPUTER COMPANY.

We have, of course, obtained exactly the same results as we did previously from our expected monetary value analysis in Section 4.4.1.

It should also be mentioned that we could have constructed our decision tree using expected opportunity losses as payoffs instead of expected monetary values. If this were done, the expected opportunity loss associated with decision node A would be $90,000. This result is again exactly the same result that we obtained earlier from our expected opportunity loss analysis in Section 4.4.2.

EXAMPLE
(SEQUENTIAL DECISION TREE)

A decision tree approach is even more useful when a series of sequential decisions must be made. To illustrate, let us assume that the management of the Crabapple Microcomputer Company now has two decisions to make, with the second decision being dependent upon the outcome of the first decision. We assume that before making the decision concerning the expansion of its operations, the company can have a marketing research study made, at a cost of $5000. After the results of this survey are known, the management of the company can use the results to make a choice among its expansion opportunities.

Initially, recall that without any market research survey information the management of the Crabapple Microcomputer Company has made the following estimates of high, moderate, and low product demand.

$$P(\text{high demand}) = P(H) = .4$$
$$P(\text{moderate demand}) = P(M) = .4$$
$$P(\text{low demand}) = P(L) = .2 \quad (4.25)$$

These are the *prior probabilities*. They are demand estimates made before obtaining any additional information.

Now, let us assume that the company made several

TABLE 4.9 MARKET RESEARCH SURVEY RELIABILITY

RESULTS OF MARKET RESEARCH SURVEY	ACTUAL STATES OF NATURE		
	HIGH DEMAND (H)	MODERATE DEMAND (M)	LOW DEMAND (L)
Favorable (F)	$P(F|H) = .7$	$P(F|M) = .6$	$P(F|L) = .2$
Unfavorable (U)	$P(U|H) = .3$	$P(U|M) = .4$	$P(U|L) = .8$

marketing research studies previously and has kept data on the results of these previous studies. We assume that these results have been summarized, as follows, in Table 4.9. Observe that these probabilities are conditional probabilities. For example, the probability that the market research survey was favorable, given that high demand did occur, is .7, while the probability that the market research survey was unfavorable, given that high demand did occur, is .3.

The set of prior probabilities given by (4.25) and the

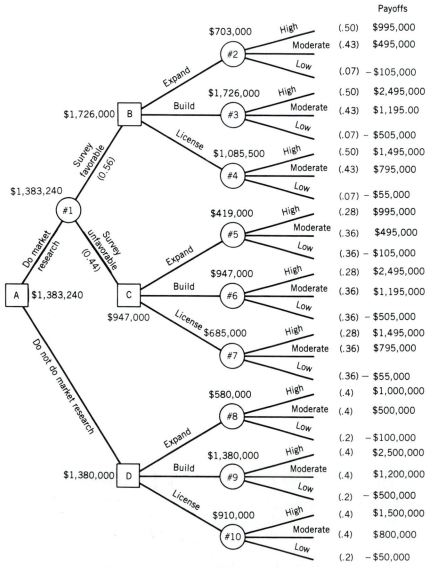

FIGURE 4.2 SEQUENTIAL DECISION TREE—CRABAPPLE MICROCOMPUTER COMPANY.

set of conditional probabilities shown in Table 4.9 are utilized later in determining a set of *posterior* probabilities, using Bayes's theorem. These posterior probabilities are then used in the sequential decision tree analysis.

The sequential decision tree for the Crabapple Microcomputer Company is presented in Figure 4.2. Initially, at decision node A, the management of the company must make a decision whether or not to conduct the market research study. If management decides not to conduct it (lower part of the decision tree), they will then move to decision node D. At decision node D they can either expand their present manufacturing facility, build a new manufacturing facility, or license another manufacturer. This decision will then lead to chance nodes 8, 9, or 10. Continuation down the branches out of these nodes is a chance event. Depending on the outcome of this chance event, a terminating point is reached, with an associated payoff. We assume that the probabilities associated with these chance events, and their associated payoffs, are the same as in the previous example. Therefore, this lower portion of the decision tree is identical to the simple decision tree presented in Figure 4.1. The reason is that the decision made without conducting the market research study is identical to the original decision.

The top part of the decision tree reflects the consequences associated with doing the market research study. The decision to conduct the market research survey immediately leads to chance node 1. At chance node 1, there are two branches, or two states of nature possible. For the top branch the survey is favorable, with an associated probability of .56. For the lower branch, the survey is unfavorable, with an associated probability of .44.

At chance node 1 we are computing the overall probabilities associated with the survey being either unfavorable or favorable. These probabilities are computed using the prior probabilities given by (4.25) and the conditional probabilities shown in Table 4.9, as follows.

P(survey favorable)

$\quad = P$(survey favorable|high demand)

$\qquad \cdot P$(high demand)

$\qquad + P$(survey favorable|moderate demand)

$\qquad \cdot P$(moderate demand)

$\qquad + P$(survey favorable|low demand)

$\qquad \cdot P$(low demand)

$\quad = P(F|H) \cdot P(H) + P(F|M) \cdot P(M)$

$\qquad + P(F|L) \cdot P(L)$

$\quad = (.7)(.4) + (.6)(.4) + (.2)(.2)$

$\quad = .56$ \hfill (4.26)

P(survey unfavorable)

$\quad = P$(survey unfavorable|high demand)

$\qquad \cdot P$(high demand)

$\qquad + P$(survey unfavorable|moderate demand)

$\qquad \cdot P$(moderate demand)

$\qquad + P$(survey unfavorable|low demand)

$\qquad \cdot P$(low demand)

$\quad = P(U|H) \cdot P(H) + P(U|M) \quad P(M)$

$\qquad + P(U|L) \cdot P(L)$

$\quad = (.3)(.4) + (.4)(.4) + (.8)(.2)$

$\quad = .44$ \hfill (4.27)

Depending on whether the survey is favorable or unfavorable, decision node B or decision node C will be reached. At either of these decision nodes, a decision to expand the present facility, build a new facility, or license another manufacturer will be made. These decisions will then lead to chance nodes 2 through 7. The payoffs associated with these chance nodes are the payoffs from the previous example minus the $5000 being spent for the market research survey. For example, at chance node 2, for the "high demand" branch, the payoff is $1,000,000 − $5000 = $995,000.

Let us now focus our attention on the probabilities associated with these chance nodes. These probabilities are *conditional* probabilities. For example, the probability .50 is the probability of high product demand *given* that the market research survey is favorable, and the probability .28 is the probability of high demand *given* that the market research survey is unfavorable.

These conditional probabilities were computed using Bayes's theorem. Bayes's theorem was discussed in Chapter 2, and you may want to review it before continuing. The use of Bayes's theorem allows the manager to revise his or her initial or *prior* probability assessments as a result of having new information.

The general form for Bayes's Theorem is as follows.

$$P(A_i|B) = \frac{P(A_i)P(B|A_i)}{\sum_{i=1}^{n} P(A_i)P(B|A_i)} \quad \text{(posterior probability)}$$

\hfill (4.28)

where

$\quad A_i$ = set of *n* mutually exclusive and exhaustive events

$\quad B$ = a known end effect or the outcome for an experiment

$\quad P(A_i)$ = the prior probability for event *i*

$\quad P(B|A_i)$ = the conditional probability of end effect, *B*, given the occurrence of A_i

The computed probability $P(A_i|B)$ is a conditional probability, and is called the *posterior* probability. It denotes the probability of the event A_i given additional information, that is, the occurrence or nonoccurrence of outcome B. This posterior probability is a revision of the prior probability using new or additional information.

Using Bayes's theorem we now can compute the (posterior) probabilities associated with chance nodes 2–7. At each chance node, the posterior probability, $P(A_i|B)$ is the probability of the event high demand, medium demand, or low demand given the outcome of either a favorable or unfavorable market survey report (i.e., given new information).

At chance nodes 2, 3, and 4 we are computing the probability of high, moderate, or low demand given that the market research study was *favorable*. In computing these posterior probabilities we will utilize the market research survey reliability data shown in Table 4.9, to update the prior probabilities given by (4.25). The posterior probabilities for nodes 2, 3, and 4 are computed as follows.

$P(H|F)$

$$= \frac{P(F|H) \cdot P(H)}{P(F|H) \cdot P(H) + P(F|M) \cdot P(M) + P(F|L) \cdot P(L)}$$

$$= \frac{(.7)(.4)}{(.7)(.4) + (.6)(.4) + (.2)(.2)}$$

$$= \frac{.28}{.56} = .50 \tag{4.29}$$

$P(M|F)$

$$= \frac{P(F|M) \cdot P(M)}{P(F|H) \cdot P(H) + P(F|M) \cdot P(M) + P(F|L) \cdot P(L)}$$

$$= \frac{(.6)(.4)}{(.7)(.4) + (.6)(.4) + (.2)(.2)}$$

$$= \frac{.24}{.56} = .43 \tag{4.30}$$

$P(L|F)$

$$= \frac{P(F|L) \cdot P(L)}{P(F|H) \cdot P(H) + P(F|M) \cdot P(M) + P(F|L) \cdot P(L)}$$

$$= \frac{(.2)(.2)}{(.7)(.4) + (.6)(.4) + (.2)(.2)}$$

$$= \frac{.04}{.56} = .07 \tag{4.31}$$

At chance nodes 5, 6, and 7 we are computing the probability of high, moderate, or low demand given that the market research study was *unfavorable*. Again, we use the market research reliability data shown in Table 4.9

to update the prior probabilities given by (4.25). The posterior probabilities for nodes 5, 6, and 7 are computed as follows.

$P(H|U)$

$$= \frac{P(U|H) \cdot P(H)}{P(U|H) \cdot P(H) + P(U|M) \cdot P(M) + P(U|L) \cdot P(L)}$$

$$= \frac{(.3)(.4)}{(.3)(.4) + (.4)(.4) + (.8)(.2)}$$

$$= \frac{.12}{.44} = .28 \tag{4.32}$$

$P(M|U)$

$$= \frac{P(U|M) \cdot P(M)}{P(U|H) \cdot P(H) + P(U|M) \cdot P(M) + P(U|L) \cdot P(L)}$$

$$= \frac{(.4)(.4)}{(.3)(.4) + (.4)(.4) + (.8)(.2)}$$

$$= \frac{.16}{.44} = .36 \tag{4.33}$$

$P(L|U)$

$$= \frac{P(U|L) \cdot P(L)}{P(U|H) \cdot P(H) + P(U|M) \cdot P(M) + P(U|L) \cdot P(L)}$$

$$= \frac{(.8)(.2)}{(.3)(.4) + (.4)(.4) + (.8)(.2)}$$

$$= \frac{.16}{.44} = .36 \tag{4.34}$$

Using these conditional probabilities we can compute the expected monetary value at chance nodes 2–7. For example, the expected monetary value at chance node 2 is computed as

EMV (chance node 2)
$$= (.50)(\$995,000) + (.43)(\$495,000)$$
$$+ (.07)(-\$105,000)$$
$$= \$497,500 + \$212,850 - \$7350$$
$$= \$703,000 \tag{4.35}$$

From the expected monetary values shown at chance nodes 2, 3, and 4, the largest expected monetary value, \$1,726,000 at chance node 3, is chosen for decision node 3. Similarly, from the expected monetary values shown at chance nodes 5, 6, and 7, the largest expected monetary value, \$947,000 at chance node 6, is chosen for decision node C.

Using the expected monetary values at decision nodes B and C, we can now compute the expected monetary value at chance node 1. Thus the expected monetary value at chance node 1 is

EMV (chance node 1)

$= (.56)(\$1,726,000) + (.44)(\$947,000)$

$= \$966,560 + \$416,680$

$= \$1,383,240$ (4.36)

The expected monetary value at chance node 1 is the expected monetary value associated with doing the market research survey. As we can see, the expected monetary value associated with conducting the survey is $1,383,240, which is larger than the expected monetary value of $1,380,000 for not conducting the survey. Consequently, the best decision is to conduct the market research survey.

4.7 EXPECTED VALUE OF SAMPLE INFORMATION

In our previous example Crabapple Microcomputer Company has selected a decision alternative involving building a new plant. This decision was reached by using a Bayes's procedure, employing sample information gained at a cost of $5000. Assume that as a part of its overall analysis, the company is interested in the value of this information compared to its cost. One way of measuring the value of this market research survey information is to compute the *expected value of sample information* (*EVSI*):

EVSI

$$= \begin{bmatrix} \text{expected value of} \\ \text{optimal decision with} \\ \text{sample information} \\ \text{(ignoring cost of sample)} \end{bmatrix}$$

$$- \begin{bmatrix} \text{expected value of} \\ \text{optimal decision} \\ \text{without sample} \\ \text{information} \end{bmatrix}$$ (4.37)

For the Crabapple Microcomputer Company the market research information can be considered to be the "sample" information. Recall that the decision tree calculations indicated that the expected value of the optimal decision *with* the market research information was $1,383,240, while the expected value of the optimal decision *without* the market research information was $1,380,000. The expected value of the optimal decision with the

market research information, however, included the cost of obtaining the information (i.e., $5000). Thus this amount must be added back to obtain the true expected value of the optimal decision with sample information. In other words, the expected value of the optimal decision with sample information is $1,383,240 + $5000 = $1,388,240. Using Eq. 4.37, the expected value of the market research (sample) information is

EVSI

$= [\$1,388,240] - [\$1,380,000] = \$8240$ (4.38)

Consequently, management of the Crabapple Microcomputer Company should be willing to pay up to $8240 for the marketing research information.

4.8 EFFICIENCY OF INFORMATION

The efficiency of information obtained by sampling may be compared to perfect information, under the assumption that perfect information has an efficiency of 100 percent. Under this assumption, the *efficiency of information*, E_I, is computed as

$$E_I = \frac{\text{EVSI}}{\text{EVPI}} \times 100$$ (4.39)

For the Crabapple Microcomputer Company example

$$E_I = \frac{\text{EVSI}}{\text{EVPI}} \times 100 = \frac{\$8240}{\$90,000} = 9.2\%$$

(*Note:* EVPI obtained from Eq. 4.14) (4.40)

Thus, by obtaining the sample information the Crabapple Microcomputer Company has only achieved 9.2 percent of the efficiency that it could have if it were able to secure perfect information. Again, this efficiency of information could be compared to the cost of obtaining it. Alternatively, a low efficiency of information rating could cause the decision maker to seek other types of information.

4.9 UTILITY THEORY

So far in this chapter we have made decisions using various criteria expressed in monetary terms. In practice, however, decision makers do not always make decisions on the basis of monetary criteria. Some decision makers are unwilling to accept potential losses in the present in order to realize greater potential gains in the future. This type of decision maker is a *risk avoider*. Other decision makers are willing to accept potential losses in the present in order to realize greater potential gains in the future. This type of decision maker is a *risk taker*.

To illustrate the phenomenon of risk aversion consider the following set of paired alternatives:

> A_1—You receive a $50,000 gift, tax free, with certainty;
>
> A_2—You receive a $102,000 gift, tax free, if on the flip of a fair coin it comes up heads. If it comes up tails, however, you receive nothing.
>
> B_1—You lose $125 with certainty;
>
> B_2—You lose $10,000, with a probability of $\frac{1}{100}$. You have a $\frac{99}{100}$ probability of losing nothing.

For each set of alternatives you must choose one alternative, that is, either A_1 or A_2, or either B_1 or B_2.

Based on a risk-aversion preference, most people would probably choose alternative A_1. However, note that the expected monetary value of alternative A_2 is

EMV (alternative A_2)

$$= \frac{1}{2} (\$102,000) + \frac{1}{2} (\$0)$$

$$= \$51,000 \qquad (4.41)$$

Thus, the expected monetary value of alternative A_2, $51,000, exceeds the certain payoff, $50,000, of alternative A_1.

Considering the second set of alternatives, the risk averter would probably choose alternative B_1 even though the expected monetary loss of alternative B_2 is

EML (alternative B_2)

$$= \frac{1}{100} (-\$10,000) + \frac{99}{100} (\$0)$$

$$= -\$100 \qquad (4.42)$$

Thus, the expected monetary loss of alternative B_2,

−$100, is less than the certain monetary loss, −$125, of alternative B_1.

These two examples reflect the difficulty with basing decision criteria solely on monetary payoffs. It is therefore reasonable to suggest that many decision makers may not always make decisions with respect to monetary values. An alternative approach to decision making involves expressing the value of an alternative in terms of its *utility*, and then using *expected utility* as a preferred decision criterion.

Utility is defined as the individual decision maker's measure of the value of a particular alternative taking into account the decision maker's preference for monetary return as opposed to avoiding risk. Von Neumann and Morgenstern developed an approach to decision making in which the decision maker attempts to choose the alternative that will maximize his or her expected utility.[1]

4.9.1 UTILITY FUNCTION CONSTRUCTION

The Von Neumann–Morgenstern *utility function* is measured on an *interval*, or *cardinal scale*. An interval scale is characterized by the lack of a specified origin and by the specification of an arbitrary unit for making measurements using the scale. A thermometer is an example of a device that uses interval measurement. For example, using the interval scale of a Fahrenheit thermometer, the freezing and boiling points of water are specified at 32° and 212°, respectively.

Let us now see how we would actually construct a utility function. Suppose that we have a decision-making situation involving the payoffs from a series of research and development projects. In Table 4.10 we present the monetary payoff table for a series of four research and development projects, given three possible states of nature. Using the monetary payoffs shown in this table, construction of the utility function proceeds in the following manner.

1. We determine the highest monetary payoff, $P_{max} = 20$, and the lowest monetary payoff, $P_{min} = 2$, in the payoff table. For these two

---

[1]John Von Neumann and Oskar Morgenstern, *Theory of Games and Economic Behavior*. Princeton, N.J.: Princeton Univ. Press, 1944.

TABLE 4.10 PAYOFF TABLE—RESEARCH AND DEVELOPMENT PROJECTS ($MILLIONS)

RESEARCH AND DEVELOPMENT PROJECTS	STATES OF NATURE		
	θ_1: LOW SUCCESS	θ_2: MODERATE SUCCESS	θ_3: HIGH SUCCESS
1	9	13	20
2	2	4	6
3	5	9	13
4	10	14	18

payoff values we arbitrarily assign the utility indexes of 1 and 0. That is

$$U(\$20,000,000) = 1.0$$
$$U(\$2,000,000) = 0 \quad (4.43)$$

Note that the selection of the utility values of 1 and 0 is arbitrary. We can actually use any two indexes for which the index of the larger monetary payoff exceeds the index of the smaller monetary payoff. At this point we have arbitrarily determined two points on the utility function.

2. Next, we determine a *certainty equivalent* that represents the monetary payoff for which the decision maker is indifferent to receiving the uncertain payoffs P_1 and P_2, each with probability .5, and the option of receiving the certainty equivalent with certainty. For our present problem situation, assume that we have presented the monetary payoff table to the company's vice president for research and development and that she has indicated that she has a certainty equivalent of $14,000,000 compared to receiving a payoff of $P_1 = \$20,000,000$ with probability of .5 and a pay-

off of $P_2 = \$2,000,000$ with probability .5. Since the vice president for research and development is indifferent to the riskless payoff of $P_1 = \$20,000,000$ and $P_2 = \$2,000,000$, it then follows that the utility associated with the certainty equivalent of $14,000,000 must be equal to the expected utility associated with $P_1 = \$20,000,000$ and $P_2 = \$2,000,000$. Therefore, we can state

$$U(\$14,000,000)$$
$$= .5\, U(\$20,000,000) + .5\, U(\$2,000,000)$$
$$= .5(1) + .5(0)$$
$$= .5 \quad (4.44)$$

In this manner we have determined a third point on our utility function.

3. We now repeat Step 2 a number of times until enough points have been determined to establish a smooth utility function curve. Note that we can arbitrarily select monetary payoff values to determine the utility of the certainty equivalent, as long as the monetary payoff values have known utility indexes. For example,

TABLE 4.11 MONETARY PAYOFFS AND ASSOCIATED UTILITY INDICES

DATA POINT	MONETARY PAYOFF (CERTAINTY EQUIVALENT)	UTILITY INDEX
1	$20,000,000	1.00
2	2,000,000	.00
3	14,000,000	.50
4	10,000,000	.25
5	16,000,000	.75

we used P_{max} and P_{min} to establish the third point on the utility function. Once the third point is established, it can then be used with either P_{max} or P_{min} to establish a fourth point, and so forth. For example, assume that the company's vice president for research and development now indicates that she has a certainty equivalent of $10,000,000 compared to receiving a payoff of $P_1 = \$14,000,000$ with probability of .5 and a payoff of $P_2 = \$2,000,000$ with probability .5. Therefore, we can state

$U(\$10,000,000)$
$= .5\ U(\$14,000,000)\ +\ .5\ U(\$2,000,000)$
$= .5(.50)\ +\ .5(0)$
$= .25$ (4.45)

In Table 4.11 we present a set of five points for which monetary payoffs and associated utility indexes have been determined.

4. From the data shown in Table 4.10, the utility function is drawn. This utility function for this problem situation is shown in Figure 4.3.

The utility function shown in Figure 4.3 is typical for a *risk seeker*. This type of decision maker gets more utility from a greater risk and higher potential payoff, and seeks situations where high payoffs might occur. Thus, as monetary value increases on this utility function, the utility increases at an increasing rate.

The opposite of a risk seeker is a *risk avoider*. This type of decision maker gets less utility from a greater risk and higher potential payoff, and tends to avoid situations where high losses might occur. Thus, as monetary value increases on this utility function, the utility increases at a decreasing rate.

Finally, we may encounter a decision maker who is *indifferent* to risk. Such a decision maker will have a utility function that is a straight line. Figure 4.4 shows the three types of utility function and the risk preferences associated with each of them.

Using the utility function presented in Figure 4.3, we can now replace the monetary payoffs shown in Table 4.10 by utility indices. The utility table

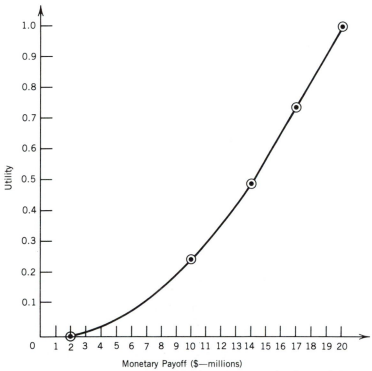

FIGURE 4.3   UTILITY FUNCTION—RESEARCH AND DEVELOPMENT EXAMPLE.

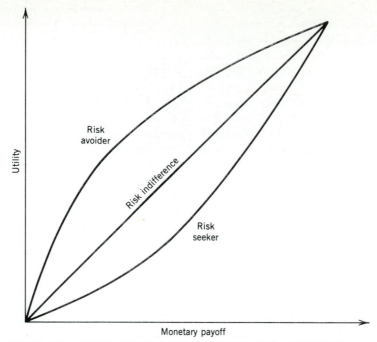

FIGURE 4.4 UTILITY FUNCTION AND ASSOCIATED RISK PREFERENCES.

constructed using the utility function shown in Figure 4.3 is presented in Table 4.12.

4.9.2 USING THE UTILITY FUNCTION

The utility function and utility table can be used in decision making in the same manner that monetary values were used previously in this chapter. To illustrate let us assume that the vice president for research and development has decided that there is a .3 probability associated with "low" success rate, a .4 probability associated with a "moderate" success rate, and a .3 probability associated with a "high" success rate for a given research and development project.

Using these subjective probabilities and the monetary payoffs presented earlier in Table 4.10, the expected monetary values for the four research and development projects can be calculated as follows:

EMV(R&D Project 1)
  = (.3)($9,000,000) + (.4)($13,000,000)
    + (.3)($20,000,000)
  = $2,700,000 + $5,200,000 + $6,000,000
  = $13,900,000   (4.46)

EMV(R&D Project 2)
  = (.3)($2,000,000) + (.4)($4,000,000)
    + (.3)($6,000,000)
  = $600,000 + $1,600,000 + $1,800,000
  = $4,000,000   (4.47)

EMV(R&D Project 3)
  = (.3)($5,000,000) + (.4)($9,000,000)
    + (.3)($13,000,000)
  = $1,500,000 + $3,600,000 + $3,900,000
  = $9,000,000   (4.48)

EMV(R&D Project 4)
  = (.3)($10,000,000) + (.4)($14,000,000)
    + (.3)($18,000,000)
  = $3,000,000 + $5,600,000 + $5,400,000
  = $14,000,000   (optimal)   (4.49)

Next, using the same subjective probabilities and the utilities shown in Table 4.11, the expected utilities for the four research and development projects can be calculated as follows:

EU(R&D Project 1)
  = (.3)(.20) + (.4)(.44) + (.3)(1.00)
  = .06 + .176 + .30
  = .536   (optimal)   (4.50)

TABLE 4.12 UTILITY TABLE—RESEARCH AND DEVELOPMENT PROJECTS

RESEARCH AND DEVELOPMENT PROJECTS	STATES OF NATURE		
	θ_1: LOW SUCCESS	θ_2: MODERATE SUCCESS	θ_3: HIGH SUCCESS
1	.20	.44	1.00
2	.00	.03	.08
3	.05	.20	.44
4	.25	.50	.80

EU(R&D Project 2)

$= (.3)(.00) + (.4)(.03) + (.3)(.08)$

$= .00 + .012 + .024$

$= .036$ (4.51)

EU(R&D Project 3)

$= (.3)(.05) + (.4)(.20) + (.3)(.44)$

$= (.015) + (.08) + (.132)$

$= .227$ (4.52)

EU(R&D Project 4)

$= (.3)(.25) + (.4)(.50) + (.3)(.80)$

$= (.075) + (.20) + (.240)$

$= .515$ (4.53)

From these two sets of computations we see that, based on expected monetary value, the decision maker would select research and development Project 4. Based on expected utility, however, the decision maker would select research and development Project 1. Therefore, the optimal decision made when risk preference is taken into consideration is different than that which would be made if only monetary payoffs are considered.

4.10 SOLVING DECISION THEORY PROBLEMS USING A COMPUTER

Computer software packages for solving decision theory problems are fairly common, particularly those for solving decision-tree-type problems. These types of packages help the analyst, or manager, by performing many of the tedious computations that are required to evelute all the branches of a decision tree.

One example of a microcomputer software package that can be used for solving decision tree problems is that developed by Chang and Sullivan.[2] To illustrate this software program we first used it to solve the simple decision tree shown in Figure

4.1. Input for the decision tree microcomputer program consists of a description of each branch, including its name, its starting node, its ending node, and an indication of whether the starting node is a chance node or a decision node. If the branch's starting node is a chance node, a probability associated with the branch must be specified, as well as the payoff associated with its ending node. Output from the microcomputer program applied to the simple decision tree (Figure 4.1) is presented in Table 4.13. In Table 4.13 the input for the problem is shown and then the solution is presented in terms of the four nodes of the decision tree, which have been relabeled in numerical order. The type of node is indicated, along with the (computed) expected value. If the node is a decision node, the preferred decision at that node is indicated. For node 1, which corresponds to decision node A in Figure 4.1, the decision is to "build the new manufacturing facility," which produces an expected monetary value of $1,380,000. This is, of course, the same solution that we obtained manually (see Eq. 4.24).

Next, we used this same software program to solve the sequential decision tree shown in Figure 4.2. Input for this problem was done in the same manner as previously described. Output from the microcomputer program applied to the sequential decision tree (Figure 4.2) is presented in Table 4.14. Again, the input data are shown first and then the solution is presented. For node 1, which corresponds to decision node A in Figure 4.1, the decision is to "do market research," which produces an expected monetary value of $1,383,240. This is, again, the same solution that we obtained manually (see Eq. 4.35).

---

[2]Yih-Long Chang and Robert S. Sullivan, *Quantitative Systems For Business*. Englewood Cliffs, N.J.: Prentice–Hall, 1985.

TABLE 4.13 MICROCOMPUTER PROGRAM OUTPUT: SIMPLE DECISION TREE (FIGURE 4.1)

Input Data Describing your Problem DT1—Decision Tree Page 1

Branch Number	Branch Name	Start Node	End Node	Start Node Type	Probability	Payoff/Cost
1	expand	1	2	1.000	0	0
2	build	1	3	1.000	0	0
3	license	1	4	1.000	0	0
4	hd2	2	5	2.000	0.400000	1,000,000
5	md2	2	6	2.000	0.400000	500,000
6	ld2	2	7	2.000	0.200000	−100,000
7	hd3	3	8	2.000	0.400000	2,500,000
8	md3	3	9	2.000	0.400000	1,200,000
9	ld3	3	10	2.000	0.200000	−500,000
10	hd4	4	11	2.000	0.400000	1,500,000
11	md4	4	12	2.000	0.400000	800,000
12	ld4	4	13	2.000	0.200000	−50,000

Decision Tree Analysis

Node	Type of Node	Expected Value	Decision
1	Decision	1,380,000	Build
2	Chance	580,000	
3	Chance	1,380,000	
4	Chance	910,000	

TABLE 4.14 MICROCOMPUTER PROGRAM OUTPUT: SEQUENTIAL DECISION TREE (FIGURE 4.2)

Input Data Describing your Problem DT2—Decision Tree Page 1

Branch Number	Branch Name	Start Node	End Node	Start Node Type	Probability	Payoff/Cost
1	DO	1	2	1.000	0	0
2	DONOT	1	5	1.000	0	0
3	FAV	2	3	2.000	0.560000	0
4	UNFAV	2	4	2.000	0.440000	0
5	EXPAND3	3	6	1.000	0	0
6	BUILD3	3	7	1.000	0	0
7	LICENSE3	3	8	1.000	0	0
8	EXPAND4	4	9	1.000	0	0
9	BUILD4	4	10	1.000	0	0
10	LICENSE4	4	11	1.000	0	0
11	EXPAND5	5	12	1.000	0	0
12	BUILD5	5	13	1.000	0	0
13	LICENSE5	5	14	1.000	0	0
14	H6	6	15	2.000	0.500000	995,000
15	M6	6	16	2.000	0.430000	495,000
16	L6	6	17	2.000	0.070000	−105,000
17	H7	7	18	2.000	0.500000	2,495,000
18	M7	7	19	2.000	0.430000	1,195,000
19	L7	7	20	2.000	0.070000	−505,000
20	H8	8	21	2.000	0.500000	1,495,000
21	M8	8	22	2.000	0.430000	795,000

TABLE 4.14 (CONTINUED)

22	L8	8	23	2,000	0.070000	−55,000
23	H9	9	24	2,000	0.280000	995,000
24	M9	9	25	2,000	0.360000	495,000
25	L9	9	26	2,000	0.360000	−105,000
26	H10	10	27	2,000	0.280000	2,495,000
27	M10	10	28	2,000	0.360000	1,195,000
28	L10	10	29	2,000	0.360000	−505,000
29	H11	11	30	2,000	0.280000	1,495,000
30	M11	11	31	2,000	0.360000	795,000
31	L11	11	32	2,000	0.360000	−55,000
32	H12	12	33	2,000	0.400000	1,000,000
33	M12	12	34	2,000	0.400000	500,000
34	L12	12	35	2,000	0.200000	−100,000
35	H13	13	36	2,000	0.400000	2,500,000
36	M13	13	37	2,000	0.400000	1,200,000
37	L13	13	38	2,000	0.200000	−500,000
38	H14	14	39	2,000	0.400000	1,500,000
39	M14	14	40	2,000	0.400000	800,000
40	L14	14	41	2,000	0.200000	−50,000

Decision Tree Analysis

Node	Type of Node	Expected Value	Decision
1	Decision	1,383,240	DO
2	Chance	1,383,240	
3	Decision	1,726,000	BUILD3
4	Decision	947,000	BUILD4
5	Decision	1,380,000	BUILD5
6	Chance	703,000	
7	Chance	1,726,000	
8	Chance	1,085,500	
9	Chance	419,000	
10	Chance	947,000	
11	Chance	685,000	
12	Chance	580,000	
13	Chance	1,380,000	
14	Chance	910,000	

4.11 SUMMARY

Decision theory, or decision analysis, is an important technique for quantitative decision making. The use of decision theory requires the delineation of alternative courses of action and possible states of nature. Then the resulting payoffs must be specified. In some situations, the decision maker attempts to define probabilities for the various states of nature occurring. The objective of decision theory then becomes that of identifying the best decision alternative given an uncertain or risky pattern of future events.

After discussing decision making under certainty and risk, we considered decision making under uncertainty. Herein, we reviewed the maximax criterion, the maximin criterion, the criterion of realism, the equally likely criterion, and the minimax criterion. Next, the graphical approach to decision theory through the use of decision trees was discussed and illustrated. We next examined how experimental or sample data can be employed to refine or improve decision making. Finally, we saw that it was often useful to make decisions based on utility rather than monetary values, which led to a discussion of the construction and utilization of utility functions for decision making.

GLOSSARY

Certainty Equivalent   Represents a monetary payoff for which the decision maker is indifferent to receiving the uncertain payoffs P_1 and P_2, each with probability .50, and the option of receiving the certainty equivalent with probability 1.00.

Criterion of Realism   A decision criterion that is a compromise between an optimistic and a pessimistic decision criterion, or between the maximin and maximax decision criteria.

Decision Alternatives   The possible courses of action the decision maker can take.

Decision Analysis or Decision Theory   A probability-oriented management science methodology that is useful in situations in which a decision maker is faced with several alternative courses of action but is also confronted with an uncertain future set of possible events.

Decision Making Under Certainty   A decision-making environment where the future states of nature are known.

Decision Making Under Conflict   A decision-making environment in which there are two or more decision makers who have goals for which they are competing.

Decision Making Under Risk   A decision-making environment where several states of nature may occur as a result of a decision or alternative, and the probabilities of these states of nature can be estimated.

Decision Making Under Uncertainty   A decision-making environment where several states of nature may occur, but the probabilities of these states of nature are not known.

Decision Tree   A graphical method for performing a decision analysis.

Efficiency of Information   The efficiency of the information obtained by sampling or experimentation as compared to perfect information, assuming that perfect information has an efficiency of 100 percent.

Expected Opportunity Loss (EOL) of a Decision Alternative   The sum of the probabilities associated with the states of nature times the associated opportunity loss values of the decision alternatives and states of nature.

Expected Monetary Value (EMV) of a Decision Alternative   The sum of the probabilities associated with the states of nature times the associated values of the decision alternatives and states of nature.

Expected Value of Perfect Information   A measure of the value of "perfect" information concerning the states of nature in decision theory, assuming such information could be obtained.

Expected Value of Sample Information   The expected value of the optimal decision with sample information minus the expected value of the optimal decision without sample information.

Equally Likely Decision Criterion   A decision criterion that places equally likely weight on all of the states of nature.

Interval Scale or Cardinal Scale A scale characterized by the lack of specified origin and by the specification of an arbitrary unit for making measurements using the scale.

Maximax Decision Criterion A decision criterion in which the decision maker arrays the "maximum" payoffs possible under the various decision alternatives and then selects the decision alternative that "maximizes" the maximum payoffs.

Minimax Decision Criterion A decision criterion in which the decision maker determines the "maximum" loss that would occur under each decision alternative and then selects the decision alternative that is associated with the "minimum" loss among the maximum losses.

Minimax Regret Decision Criterion A decision criterion in which the decision maker identifies the "maximum" opportunity loss or "maximum" regret for each decision alternative and then selects the decision alternative associated with the "minimum" maximum regret value.

Opportunity Loss or Regret The difference between the optimal payoff for a particular state of nature and the actual payoff received for a particular state of nature–decision alternative combination.

Payoff The outcome for a decision alternative–state of nature combination that results from selecting a certain decision alternative and then having a particular state of nature occur.

Payoff Table A tabular representation of the payoff estimates in terms of the interaction of the decision alternatives and the states of nature.

Prior Probabilities The probabilities of the states of nature prior to obtaining experimental information.

Posterior (Revised) Probabilities The probabilities of the state of nature after using Bayes's theorem to adjust the prior probabilities based upon given indicator information.

States of Nature All possible future events that might occur; it is assumed that these events are mutually exclusive and collectively exhaustive.

Utility Function A function that depicts the dependent relationship of utility upon monetary payoff.

Utility Scale A scale that measures the decision maker's preference, including a willingness to take or avoid risk.

Utility Theory A body of knowledge that suggests a utility-based criterion for decision making where the decision maker attempts to optimize expected utility rather than expected monetary value.

Selected References

Chernoff, H., and L.E. Moses. 1959. *Elementary Decision Theory*. New York: Wiley.

Hadley, G. 1967. *Introduction to Probability and Statistical Decision Theory*. San Francisco: Holden–Day.

Harrison, E. 1975. *The Managerial Decision Making Process*. Boston: Houghton Mifflin.

Luce, R.D., and H. Raiffa. 1957. *Games and Decisions*. New York: Wiley.

Martin, J.J. 1967. *Bayesian Decision Problems and Markov Chains*. New York: Wiley.

Newman, J.W. 1971. *Management Applications of Decision Theory*. New York: Harper & Row.

Pratt, J.W., H. Raiffa, and R.O. Schlaifer. 1965. *Introduction to Statistical Decision Theory*. New York: McGraw–Hill.

Raiffa, H. 1968. *Decision Analysis*. Reading, Mass.: Addison–Wesley.

Schlaifer, R.O. 1969. *Analysis of Decisions Under Uncertainty*. New York: McGraw–Hill.

Winkler, R.L. 1972. *Introduction to Bayesian Inference and Decision*. New York: Holt, Rinehart & Winston.

Discussion Questions

1. Describe what is involved in the decision theory approach.

2. What is an alternative? What is a state of nature?

3. Can the "state of nature" be a continuous variable? Why or why not?

4. Discuss the differences between decision making under certainty, decision making under risk, and decision making under uncertainty.

5. What is the "expected value of perfect information" dependent upon? How can it help the manager?

6. What criteria are employed for solving decision-making problems under uncertainty? Which result in an optimistic decision? Which result in a pessimistic decision?

7. What is the difference between an "expected value" approach and a "decision tree" approach to decision making?

8. When might a decision tree approach to decision making be appropriate?

9. What is the difference between the prior and posterior probabilities?

10. How is Bayes's theorem employed in the decision-making process?

11. What is the "expected value of sample information" dependent upon? How is it used?

12. What is the purpose of utility theory?

13. What characterizes a risk seeker? What characterizes a risk avoider? How do the utility curves for the two types of decision makers differ?

14. Describe the process for determining the utility function.

15. Can decision making based on expected utility yield a different result compared to decision making based on expected monetary value? Why or why not?

PROBLEMS

1. Suppose that you are a decision maker having four decision alternatives and four states of nature. On the basis of your analysis of the problem environment you have developed the following payoff table.

DECISION	STATES OF NATURE			
ALTERNATIVES	θ_1	θ_2	θ_3	θ_4
a_1	14	9	8	5
a_2	11	10	10	7
a_3	8	12	12	8
a_4	6	12	12	12

Additionally, you have a considerable amount of historical data that have enabled you to make the following probability estimates for the occurrences of the states of nature.

$$P(\theta_1) = .4$$

$$P(\theta_2) = .2$$

$$P(\theta_3) = .1$$

$$P(\theta_4) = .3$$

a. Using an expected monetary value decision criterion, which decision alternative should be selected?
b. Using an expected opportunity loss decision criterion, show that the same decision alternative as that in part a should be selected.
c. What is the expected value of perfect information for this problem situation?
d. If the probabilities associated with the states of nature change to

$$P(\theta_1) = .1$$

$$P(\theta_2) = .3$$

$$P(\theta_3) = .4$$

$$P(\theta_4) = .2$$

does the selection of the optimum decision alternative also change?

2. Given the following payoff table

DECISION	STATES OF NATURE		
ALTERNATIVES	θ_1	θ_2	θ_3
a_1	$1000	$3000	$1500
a_2	900	1100	800
a_3	700	600	600
Probability	.3	.5	.2

a. compute the expected monetary value of each of the alternatives and select the best alternative;
b. develop the opportunity loss table and compute the expected opportunity loss for each alternative;
c. determine the expected value of perfect information for this problem situation.

3. You are an investor trying to choose between two alternative investments, stocks or mutual funds. The return for each investment under two possible economic conditions are as follows.

INVESTMENT ALTERNATIVES	STATES OF NATURE	
	FAVORABLE ECONOMIC CONDITIONS	UNFAVORABLE ECONOMIC CONDITIONS
Stocks	$8000	−$3000
Mutual funds	6000	1000
Probability	.7	.3

a. Using the probabilities shown, compute the expected monetary value of each investment alternative and select the best alternative.
b. What probabilities for the two economic conditions would have to exist before the investor would be indifferent to investing in stocks or in mutual funds?

4. Janet Higgins has recently purchased a ski resort in Boone, North Carolina. Her financial success in this new venture will mostly depend upon the weather conditions (i.e., snowfall) during the winter months. Probabilities associated with three levels of snowfall have been obtained from the local weather bureau. Janet has developed the following payoff table, with associated probabilities for her new venture.

	STATES OF NATURE		
	HEAVY SNOWFALL	MODERATE SNOWFALL	LIGHT SNOWFALL
Season return	$150,000	$50,000	−$25,000
Probability	.3	.4	.3

Janet is contemplating an offer from a syndicate of local investors who wish to lease the ski resort from her for $50,000 annually. Should she accept their offer or should she operate the ski resort herself?

5. A local golf professional buys used golf balls from a used golf ball company. The golf balls are purchased at a cost of $4 per dozen and sold at a price of $8 per dozen. Any golf balls left at the end of the month are sold to a local driving range for $2 per dozen. The monthly demand for golf balls, and the probabilities of occurrence of demand, are as follows.

MONTHLY DEMAND (DOZENS OF GOLF BALLS)	PROBABILITY OF MONTHLY DEMAND
10	.10
11	.20
12	.20

MONTHLY DEMAND (DOZENS OF GOLF BALLS)	PROBABILITY OF MONTHLY DEMAND
13	.30
14	.20

For this type problem, the alternative actions are the amounts to be stocked (i.e., between 10 and 14 dozen golf balls) and the states of nature are the demands.

a. Construct the payoff matrix for this problem and determine the amount that should be stocked.
b. Construct the opportunity loss table and determine the amount to stock based on the economic opportunity loss of each alternative.
c. Compute the EVPI for the problem situation.

6. The owner of Greenstreets, a campus restaurant, must decide how many cases of lettuce to stock each week in order to meet demand. The probability distribution of demand is

WEEKLY DEMAND (CASES)	PROBABILITY OF WEEKLY DEMAND
5	.10
6	.20
7	.15
8	.15
9	.30
10	.10

Each case costs the owner $7, and she sells it in salads for $12. Unsold cases are sold to a pet store for $2. If a shortage exists the profit of $5 per case is considered to be a cost.

a. Construct the payoff matrix for this problem and determine the amount that should be stocked.
b. Construct the opportunity loss table and determine the amount to stock based on the economic opportunity loss of each alternative.
c. Compute the EVPI for this problem situation.

7. A real estate investor is considering three alternative investment locations. The probability associated with these three investments will be affected by the mortgage interest rate associated with purchasing these properties. The payoff matrix under uncertainty for this problem situation has been determined to be

INVESTMENT ALTERNATIVES	MORTGAGE INTEREST RATES		
	LOW	MODERATE	HIGH
Location A	$150,000	$100,000	$20,000
Location B	100,000	25,000	−10,000
Location C	90,000	40,000	5,000

Determine the best investment under conditions of uncertainty using each of the following decision criteria.

a. Maximax criterion.
b. Maximin criterion.
c. Criterion of realism.
d. Equally likely criterion.
e. Minimax criterion.

8. The Great Southwestern Land Company owns 10,000 acres of land in western New Mexico that may have oil producing potential. The company is faced with a decision whether to explore extensively for oil, to lease the land, or to sell it. For each of these three alternatives, three states of nature may exist: θ_1, a large oil deposit; θ_2, a small oil deposit; θ_3, no oil deposit. The payoff table associated with the various states of nature is as follows.

DECISION ALTERNATIVES	STATES OF NATURE		
	θ_1: Large	θ_2: Small	θ_3: None
Explore extensively	$10,000,000	$4,000,000	-$500,000
Lease land	5,000,000	2,000,000	750,000
Sell land	1,000,000	1,000,000	1,000,000

Determine the best investment under conditions of uncertainty using each of the following criteria.

a. Maximax criterion.
b. Maximin criterion.
c. Criterion of realism.
d. Equally likely criterion.
e. Minimax criterion.

9. Ocean Breeze Condominiums, Inc., has recently purchased land near Myrtle Beach, South Carolina, and is attempting to determine the size of the condominium development it should build. Three sizes of developments are being considered: small, medium, and large. At present the market for condominiums in the Myrtle Beach area is uncertain because of a weak economy and overbuilding. Management of the company has prepared the following payoff table.

DECISION ALTERNATIVES	STATES OF NATURE		
	LOW DEMAND	MEDIUM DEMAND	HIGH DEMAND
Small development	$500,000	$500,000	$ 500,000
Medium development	300,000	800,000	800,000
Large development	-100,000	600,000	1,000,000

a. Assuming that nothing is known about the demand probabilities, determine the recommended decision under the maximax, maximin, and minimax criteria.
b. If P(low demand) = .30, P(medium demand) = .40, and P(high de-

mand) = .30, what is the recommended decision under the expected monetary value criterion?

c. What is the expected value of perfect information for this situation?

10. Southern Ski, Inc., located in Charlotte, North Carolina, is contemplating its seasonal order of ski equipment. The manager of this store must decide whether to order a large, medium, or small amount of ski equipment prior to the beginning of the ski season, since the delivery time for the equipment is approximately 2 months. Sales of the ski equipment are a function of the skiing conditions in the northwestern areas of North Carolina throughout the skiing season. Subjective estimates that the seasonal skiing conditions will be excellent, good, or poor, are .7, .2, and .1, respectively. The expected profit for each action and state of nature is given in the following table.

DECISION ALTERNATIVES	STATES OF NATURE		
	θ_1: EXCELLENT SEASON	θ_2: GOOD SEASON	θ_3: POOR SEASON
a_1: Large order	$5000	$2000	−$200
a_2: Medium order	3000	1000	500
a_3: Small order	1000	800	400

a. Using an expected value decision criterion, which decision alternative should be selected?

b. The Charlotte Weather Bureau has compiled extensive data related to seasonal weather predictions. These data have been compiled in probabilistic form as indicated in the following table.

FORECASTED SKIING WEATHER IS	ACTUAL SKIING WEATHER IS		
	EXCELLENT	GOOD	POOR
Excellent	.7	.2	.1
Good	.2	.6	.2
Poor	.1	.2	.7

For example, P(Forecast of excellent skiing weather|actual excellent skiing weather) = .7.

Construct a decision tree and determine the expected value of the optimal decision taking the sample information under consideration.

c. What is the expected value of the sample information for this situation?
d. What is the expected value of perfect information for this situation?
e. What is the efficiency of information for this situation?

11. Boffo Productions, Inc., is contemplating the production of a new horror movie. It can either produce and sell the film, or it can produce and lease the film. Under either of these two options, the film can go into limited distribution, U.S. distribution, or worldwide

distribution. The profits expected to accrue to Boffo Productions, Inc., for this situation are summarized in the following table.

DECISION ALTERNATIVES	STATES OF NATURE		
	θ_1: LIMITED DISTRIBUTION	θ_2: U.S. DISTRIBUTION	θ_3: WORLDWIDE DISTRIBUTION
a_1: Produce and sell	−$200,000	$1,500,000	$2,000,000
a_2: Produce and lease	200,000	1,000,000	2,000,000

Boffo Productions, Inc., has made subjective estimates concerning the probabilities associated with the extent of the film's distribution. These estimates are as follows:

$$P(\theta_1: \text{Limited distribution}) = .2$$
$$P(\theta_2: \text{U.S. distribution}) = .6$$
$$P(\theta_3: \text{Worldwide distribution}) = .2$$

a. Using an expected value decision criterion, which decision alternative should be selected?
b. Boffo Productions, Inc., can purchase a market research study that will indicate more clearly the probability associated with the three levels of distribution. Previous studies of a similar nature have indicated the following.

FORECASTED LEVELS OF DISTRIBUTION	ACTUAL LEVELS OF DISTRIBUTION		
	θ_1: LIMITED	θ_2: UNITED STATES	θ_3: WORLDWIDE
Limited	.5	.3	.1
United States	.3	.5	.3
Worldwide	.2	.2	.6

For example, $P(\text{forecast of limited distribution}|\text{actual limited distribution}) = .5$.

Construct a decision tree and determine the expected value of the optimal decision taking the sample information under consideration.

c. What is the expected value of the sample information for this situation?
d. What is the expected value of perfect information for this situation?
e. What is the efficiency of information for this situation?

12. Work Problem 1 using a decision tree approach.

13. Work Problem 2 using a decision tree approach.

14. A diving and salvage company must decide whether to continue searching a certain area in the Caribbean. If they continue to search and find the ship, they estimate the find to be worth $10,000,000. If they continue to search and do not find the ship, they lose

$1,000,000. If they stop searching, they take the risk another searcher will find the ship. They have computed a loss of $5,000,000 if they stop searching, and the ship is found by another searcher. Finally, if they abandon the search, and in fact the ship is never found, this would be worth $750,000 (the remaining funds allocated for the project). This is an extremely risky endeavor, and the owner estimates they only have a one in ten chance of finding the ship.

a. Construct the payoff matrix. What are the alternatives? What are the possible states of nature?
b. Using an expected value decision criterion, which decision alternative should be selected?
c. Consider the following information. The company has the option of hiring a famous historian to investigate the location of the ship further. The fee is not cheap, though in similar circumstances when the historian has said a ship wreck is in a certain location, the ships have been found 2 out of 5 times. This historian has also graciously offered the following information for consideration by the company's owner.

| THE HISTORIAN'S | THE SHIP IS | |
OPINION IS TO	FOUND	NOT FOUND
Look	.8	.1333
Not look	.2	.8667

That is, P(historian will say look|ship is eventually found) = .8.

Construct a decision tree to incorporate this new information.

d. The historian charges a flat fee of $100,000. Based on the decision tree, would the owner be wise to hire the historian? Why or why not?

15. A manufacturing firm is considering the purchase of a stamping machine. The firm is in a volatile industry, however, and sensitive to changes in the economy. Based on past experience, the manager estimates a 70 percent chance of a rise in the economy over the next year, and a 30 percent chance of a decline. The expected contribution to the company for each action and state of nature is included in the following table. The manager also has the option of hiring a local consulting firm who for $75 will provide predictions for the economy over the next year. The consulting firm has advised the manager that the predictions are accurate 80 percent of the time when a rise actually occurs and 70 percent of the time when a decline actually occurs.

DECISIONS	θ_1: RISE	θ_2: DECLINE
a_1: Purchase	300	−500
a_2: No purchase	100	25
$P(\theta_i) =$	.7	.3

a. Using an expected monetary value decision approach, which decision alternative should be selected if the manager chooses not to consider the consultant's predictions?

b. Using a decision tree approach, and ignoring the cost of the forecast, is the expected value more or less if the forecast is considered.

c. Given the cost of the forecast, should the manager purchase it? Why or why not?

16. Consider the following table, which presents monetary payoffs for a series of three investments, given three states of nature related to stock market conditions.

	STATES OF NATURE		
INVESTMENT OPPORTUNITIES	θ_1: DECLINING STOCK MARKET	θ_2: STABLE STOCK MARKET	θ_3: INCREASING STOCK MARKET
a_1: Computer stock	$100,000	$200,000	$400,000
a_2: Growth mutual fund	500,000	600,000	700,000
a_3: Oil company stock	300,000	350,000	400,000

Discussions with a wealthy entrepreneur who is considering investing in these three opportunities suggest that she is initially indifferent to receiving a certain payoff of $500,000 compared to receiving a payoff of $P_1 = \$700,000$ with probability .5 and a payoff of $P_2 = \$100,000$ with probability .5. Continue this process, using your own set of certainty equivalents and determine a set of corresponding utility indices. (Determine at least five points.)

17. Use the utility indices you determined in Problem 16 to draw a utility function. Then construct a utility table to replace the payoff table for Problem 16. Assume that the wealthy entrepreneur has estimated that there is a .2 probability associated with a "declining stock market," a .5 probability associated with a "stable stock market," and a .3 probability associated with an "increasing stock market." Determine the expected monetary values and the expected utilities for the three real estate projects. What is the best decision based on an expected monetary value decision criterion? What is the best decision based on an expected utility decision criterion?

18. Consider the following table, which presents the monetary payoffs associated with the three subdivision plans, given three states of nature relating to real estate sales.

SUBDIVISION DEVELOPMENT PLANS	STATES OF NATURE		
	θ_1: POOR SALES	θ_2: AVERAGE SALES	θ_3: GOOD SALES
Small development	$-\$100,000$	$150,000	$250,000

SUBDIVISION DEVELOPMENT PLANS	STATES OF NATURE		
	θ_1: POOR SALES	θ_2: AVERAGE SALES	θ_3: GOOD SALES
Medium development	−500,000	250,000	500,000
Large development	−1,000,000	400,000	900,000

Conversations with the developer have led to the following assessment of his monetary payoffs and associated utility indices.

POINT	MONETARY PAYOFF	UTILITY INDEX
1	−$1,000,000	.00
2	900,000	1.00
3	500,000	.75
4	250,000	.50
5	150,000	.25

Use these utility indices to construct a utility function. Determine a utility table to replace the payoff table shown above.

19. Assume that the developer has talked to other real estate developers and has estimated that there is a .25 probability associated with poor sales, a .50 probability associated with average sales, and a .25 probability associated with good sales. Determine the estimated monetary values and the estimated utilities for the three development plans. What is the best decision based on an expected monetary value decision criterion? What is the best decision based on an expected utility decision criterion?

Application Review

Evaluation of Air Quality Control Equipment at Ohio Edison Company Using Decision Analysis

During 1979, the Ohio Edison Company (electric utility) negotiated with the U.S. Environmental Protection Agency (EPA) on a program to achieve compliance with the Clean Air Act. The Clean Air Act set limits on the amount of sulfur dioxide and particulates (small particles of ash) that could be released from a power plant. At its W.H. Sammis power generating plant, located on the Ohio River in eastern Ohio, the company determined that it could comply with sulfur dioxide limits by burning coal with sufficiently low sulfur content, or by installing costly equipment called "scrubbers" that removed sulfur dioxide from the power plant's flue gas. To comply with particulate limits, it could install either fabric filters or electrostatic precipitators. The fabric filters used thousands of fiberglass bags to collect the particulate matter from the flue gas. The electrostatic precip-

Source: Madden, Thomas J., Michael S. Hyrnick, James A. Hodde (February 1983), *Interfaces,* Vol. 13, No. 1, pp. 66–75.

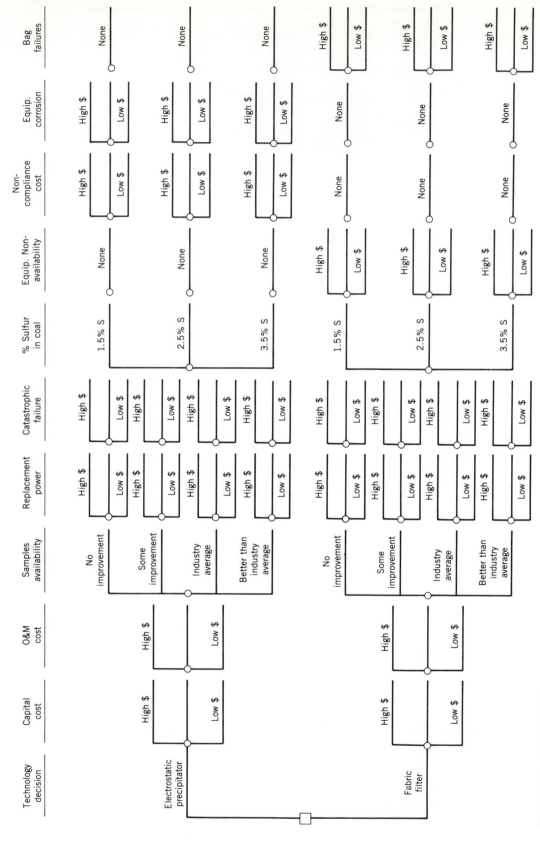

FIGURE 4.5 DECISION TREE—PARTICULATE CONTROL TECHNOLOGY.

itators used electric fields to impart positive electrical charges to flue gas particles, and then removed them from the flue gas.

This firm decided to use decision theory to make a choice between electrostatic precipitators and fabric filters for particulate control at two of its large coal-fired power generating units at the Sammis facility. Decision theory was selected as being appropriate because of the risk associated with the particulate control equipment and because of the need for a reliable and cost-effective method.

After considerable analysis the firm was able to define a decision tree for this problem. This decision tree is shown in Figure 4.5. The first (square) node shown in the decision tree represents the basic decision to be made, namely the choice between the electrostatic precipitator and the fabric filter. The remaining (circles) nodes in the decision tree are uncertainties represented by probability distributions. The uncertainties are variables that affect the revenue requirements, which are the annual funds that would have to be collected from the utility customers to cover the cost of installing and operating the equipment. Since these requirements varied from year to year, a "levelized revenue requirement" was calculated. This levelized revenue requirement had the same value for all years, and when it was substituted for the actual stream of annual revenue requirements, it yielded the same present value.

The levelized revenue requirements were computed, using the decision tree shown in Figure 4.5, by a computerized model that was designed for that purpose. The probability distributions at each of the uncertainty nodes were used to determine the expected levelized revenue requirements for each of the two alternatives. It was determined that the electrostatic precipitators had an expected levelized revenue requirement of $31.2 million per year, $1 million per year lower than the expected levelized revenue requirement of the fabric filter. Based on this use of decision theory the company decided to install electrostatic precipitators on the three largest units at the W.H. Sammis Plant.

FORECASTING

5.1 INTRODUCTION

Forecasting is a critical element in virtually every decision made by the manager, and is crucial to the management process in any organization. Accurate forecasting enables the manager to select the right combination of human and material resources to produce the physical goods or services required from the firm. This chapter introduces several methods that can be used to help forecast how the operations of an organization will proceed in the future.

Forecasting generally involves using information from the past to make decisions concerning the future. Managers have always faced a dilemma in this regard, namely that of whether and how to use the past to tell beforehand what will happen in the future. In this respect some managers attempt to make a distinction between a prediction and forecast. Herein a *prediction* is defined to be the use of subjective judgment or experience in making an estimate of the future, while a *forecast* is defined to be the extrapolation of past data into the future using some scientific, or statistical, method. We do not attempt to make a fine distinction between forecasts and predictions in this book, but in this chapter, as its title suggests, our major emphasis will be on forecasting rather than prediction. In practice, prediction is often related to a specific situation, and few explicit predictive models are available. It should be emphasized, however, that it may be possible to make very accurate subjective estimates of future occurrences.

A great many forecasting techniques are statistical in nature. As such, they are based on the statistical concepts you reviewed in Chapters 2 and 3. The ability to make a good forecast is also of importance to other quantitative techniques. For example, in Chapters 15 and 16 you will study inventory control. Inventory control techniques are based on the ability to forecast the future demand for an item.

Also, it is often very useful to initially calculate a forecast by some scientific method, and then use subjective judgment to further refine the forecast. For example, if a manager is aware of a planned advertising campaign with respect to a particular product, he or she would certainly want to use this information in increasing demand forecasts made from extrapolation of past data.

The forecasting process has seven major steps.

1. Determination of the objective for the forecast.
2. Determination of the time period for which forecasts are to be made.
3. Selection of the forecasting methodology or technique to be employed.
4. Data gathering and refinement.
5. Making the forecast.
6. Measuring the forecasting error.
7. Tracking the forecasting error and evaluating the forecasting error.

We describe and discuss these steps in the forecasting process throughout the remainder of this chapter.

5.2 SELECTING A FORECASTING METHOD

The basic problem facing the individual attempting to make a forecast is the selection of a forecasting method that will allow the achievement of a "good" estimate of future conditions. Since there are a myriad of forecasting techniques in existence, and each has a special use, special care must be taken to select the correct technique for a particular forecasting problem. While the selection of an appropriate forecasting technique for a particular situation may be difficult and based to an extent on intuition and experience, it is useful to review some of the major factors that should be considered in the selection of a forecasting technique prior to studying the actual forecasting techniques. It should also be emphasized that the manager, as well as the forecaster, who is often a staff person, has an important role in the selection of an appropriate forecasting technique. The better a manager understands the types of forecasting techniques and their advantages and disadvantages, the more likely it is that an accurate forecast will be obtained.

5.2.1 TIME SPAN CONSIDERATIONS

As an illustration let us consider production planning that involves the use of the firm's manufacturing facilities, a process that necessarily interrelates and overlaps with other management processes.

Production planning takes place at several different levels in the corporation. Most commonly, production planning will focus on day-to-day, week-to-week, or month-to-month problems concerning the use of people, machines, and raw materials. In some instances, however, it may be necessary to consider capacity planning problems that extend considerably further into the future. Thus, the time span involved in the forecasting problem may be an important consideration in the choice of the appropriate forecasting technique. Forecasting problems can be classified according to three time spans.

1. SHORT RANGE Current operations and the immediate future.

2. INTERMEDIATE RANGE Operations in the next one to three years.

3. LONG RANGE Operations beyond three years.

Table 5.1 summarizes some of the uses and characteristics of forecasts made for various time spans and various functions in an organization.

5.2.2 FORECASTING OBJECTIVES

Definition of forecasting objectives prior to actually making a forecast is a critical necessity. Definition of such forecasting objectives includes an appraisal of the purpose of the forecast, that is, how is the forecast to be used? For example, the manager may be interested in a forecast of anticipated yearly demand for a new product that must be produced using a special piece of equipment. In this instance, a fairly gross forecast may be sufficient to allow the manager to make a decision concerning the acquisition of the new equipment. In another instance, the manager may need to actually schedule the work force for a particular time period. The forecast of demand for this time period, translated into production requirements, would need to be made with a fairly high degree of accuracy.

Tradeoffs between cost and accuracy are a vital consideration in the choice of a forecasting technique. Forecasting accuracy tends to improve as more rigorous, mathematically sophisticated forecasting methods are employed. The more sophisticated forecasting approaches also tend to be more costly, however. The costs associated with the choice of a particular forecasting method are of three types.

1. The development costs associated with the particular forecasting method. This typically includes the cost of writing and/or modifying a computer program to apply a given forecasting method.
2. The data storage costs for the forecasting method, usually computer data storage costs.
3. The costs associated with repeated use of the forecasting method, usually computer running-time costs.

Figure 5.1 plots the relative cost of making forecasts versus the relative accuracy of forecasts, using a representative set of forecasting techniques that vary in sophistication. In the hypothetical situation represented by Figure 5.1, there is an optimal cost region that produces a reasonable balance between

TABLE 5.1 FORECASTING—TIME SPAN CONSIDERATIONS

TYPE OF FORECAST	TIME SPAN OF FORECAST	USE OF FORECAST	FORECASTING METHODS
Short range	Less than 1 year	Production scheduling Purchasing sales forecasting	Trend projection Moving average Exponential smoothing
Intermediate range	1 to 3 years	Budgeting Production planning Sales planning	Regression Time series analysis
Long range	3 years or more	Capital budgeting Plant location or expansion	Delphi method Market research

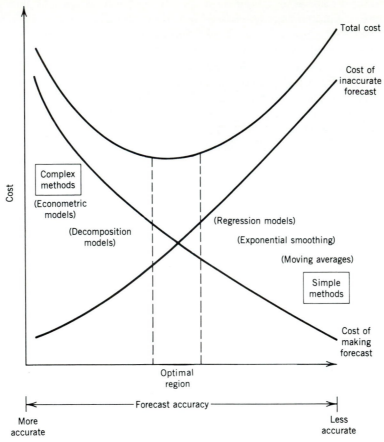

FIGURE 5.1   COST VS. ACCURACY—FORECASTING METHODS.

cost and accuracy. The forecaster should attempt to choose a forecasting technique that lies within this optimal region.

5.2.3 PRODUCT LIFE CYCLE CONSIDERATIONS

In attempting to make a choice of an appropriate forecasting technique for a particular situation, consideration should also be given to the life cycle of the product for which a forecast is being sought. In general, a successful product will pass through five demand stages in its product life cycle. These five demand stages are shown in Figure 5.2. At each stage in the product life cycle, the production planning decisions that must be made are quite different, and these decisions require quite different kinds of forecasting information. For example, in the product

development stage good forecasting results might be obtained by using a consensus of opinions obtained from top executives of the firm. Then, as the product moved into the testing and introduction and rapid growth of demand stages, it might be more appropriate to apply some sort of statistical forecasting technique.

5.2.4 DEMAND PATTERNS OVER TIME

An accurate forecasting method is one that produces results that are consistent with the actual *demand pattern* over time. The demand pattern refers to the central tendency, or the general form of the time series. Herein two somewhat conflicting phenomena must be considered. First, the forecaster would like for the forecast to be *stable* in terms of maintaining consistency when there are random fluctuations or

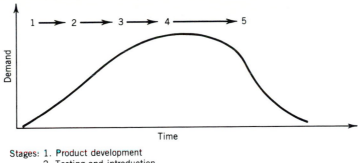

Stages: 1. Product development
2. Testing and introduction
3. Rapid growth and demand
4. Steady state demand
5. Phase out

FIGURE 5.2 DEMAND STAGES IN PRODUCT LIFE CYCLE.

noise in the demand pattern. These random fluctuations are not representative of true changes in the demand pattern, and a good forecasting method should not overforecast or shift too quickly in a response to them. Second, the forecaster would like for the forecast to be *responsive* to true changes in the base level of demand. If there is a major change in the demand pattern, a good forecasting method should recognize the shift, and take action to modify the forecast accordingly. Tradeoffs between these two desirable, but conflicting, characteristics are a major consideration in the choice of a forecasting method for a particular forecasting problem.

5.3 APPROACHES TO FORECASTING

As noted previously, there are two broad approaches to forecasting: subjective predictions based on intuition, and formalized statistical models. The intuitive approach is based on the manager's experience as related to making a judgment concerning future demand. Qualitative data and information about special events are used in making the subjective predictions. The statistical modeling approach relies on objective historical data and systematically uses this historical data to determine a summary value, which is then used as a forecast of the future. There are two basic types of models that are used within the statistical approach to forecasting.

1. Time series analysis and projection models.
2. Causal models.

Time series analysis and projection models are typically used when there are several years of demand data for the product being considered, and the underlying relationships and trends of these data appear to be measurable and relatively stable. Causal models are typically used when the forecaster has several years of demand data for the product being considered, and has also determined the relationships between the product demand and other economic or socioeconomic factors.

Within the broad approaches to forecasting previously discussed there are numerous individual forecasting techniques. An excellent review of forecasting techniques according to qualitative methods, time series analysis and projection methods, and causal models appeared in a *Harvard Business Review* article by Chambers, et al.[1] This review has been summarized in Tables 5.2, 5.3, and 5.4, in terms of the forecasting techniques and their associated cost and accuracy. Although this article was published several years ago, the forecasting techniques shown in these tables are still widely used in practice today. The computer cost figures shown in these tables refer to the costs associated with making forecasts using a large mainframe computer. It should be noted that virtually all of these forecasting techniques are now available in microcomputer packages, often at less cost than shown in the tables. Typical of the microcomputer-based forecasting

---

[1]John S. Chambers, Satinder K. Mullick, and Donald S. Smith, "How to choose the right forecasting technique," *Harvard Business Review,* **49**(4) (July–August 1971), 55–64.

TABLE 5.2 QUALITATIVE FORECASTING METHODS

FORECASTING TECHNIQUE	COST OF MAKING FORECAST	ACCURACY OF FORECAST
Delphi method	$100–$2500 (with a computer)	Short term: Fair to very good Intermediate term: Fair to very good Long term: Fair to very good
Market research	$5000–$10,000 (with a computer)	Short term: Excellent Intermediate term: Good Long term: Fair to good
Panel consensus	$1000–$5000 (with a computer)	Short term: Poor to fair Intermediate term: Poor to fair Long term: Poor
Historical analogy	$1000–$3000 (with a computer)	Short term: Poor Intermediate term: Good to fair Long term: Good to fair

Source: Chambers, John S., Satinder K. Mullick, and Donald S. Smith, "How to choose the right forecasting technique" (July/August 1971), *Harvard Business Review,* Vol. 49, No. 4, p. 55.

packages that are currently in existence are the following.

1. XTRAPOLATOR: Stratix Company, Woodenville, WA 98072—Twelve competing forecasting methods ($195).
2. SMART FORECASTS: Smart Software, Belmont, MA 02178—Ten forecasting methods with graphics capability ($495).
3. STATE SPACE FORECASTING: Scientific Systems, Inc., Cambridge, MA 02140—Five forecasting methods with graphics capability ($395).

In this chapter, we do not attempt to consider all of the forecasting methods summarized in these three tables. Instead, we focus on selected techniques that have proved to be useful in forecasting applications. The forecasting techniques that we consider in the chapter can be summarized as follows.

5.4 MEASURING FORECASTING ERROR

As part of the forecasting process, and in order to evaluate alternative forecasting methods, forecast-

TABLE 5.3 TIME SERIES ANALYSIS AND PROJECTION METHODS

FORECASTING TECHNIQUE	COST OF MAKING FORECAST	ACCURACY OF FORECAST
Moving average	$100–$1000 (with a computer)	Short term: Poor to good Intermediate term: Poor Long term: Very poor
Exponential smoothing	$100–$1000 (with a computer)	Short term: Fair to good Intermediate term: Poor to good Long term: Very poor
Box–Jenkins	$1000–$5000 (with a computer)	Short term: Very good to excellent Intermediate term: Poor to good Long term: Very poor
X-11 (decomposition)	$1000–$5000 (with a computer)	Short term: Very good to excellent Intermediate term: Good Long term: Very poor

Source: Chambers, John S., Satinder K. Mullick, and Donald S. Smith, "How to choose the right forecasting technique" (July/August 1971), *Harvard Business Review,* Vol. 49, No. 4, p. 55.

TABLE 5.4 CAUSAL METHODS

FORECASTING TECHNIQUE	COST OF MAKING FORECAST	ACCURACY OF FORECAST
Regression model	$100–$1000 (with a computer)	Short term: Good to very good Intermediate term: Good to very good Long term: Good
Econometric model	$10,000–$25,000 (with a computer)	Short term: Good to very good Intermediate term: Very good to excellent Long term: Good to excellent
Input–output model	$50,000–$100,000 (with a computer)	Short term: Not used in short term Intermediate term: Good to very good Long term: Good to excellent

Source: Chambers, John S., Satinder K. Mullick, and Donald S. Smith, "How to Choose the Right Forecasting Technique" (July/August 1971), *Harvard Business Review*, Vol. 49, No. 4, p. 55.

ing effectiveness must be measured. Usually, some measure of forecast error is employed to evaluate the effectiveness of the forecast.

Forecast error is defined to be the numerical difference between the forecasted demand and the actual demand, in a specific time period i.

Forecast error$_i$

$$= \text{forecasted demand}_i - \text{actual demand}_i \quad (5.1)$$

Obviously, the forecaster would like the forecasting errors to be as small as possible, and would choose a forecasting method to accomplish this objective.

There are numerous ways of measuring forecasting errors. We will now discuss several of the more commonly used measures of forecasting errors, dividing them into two categories: (1) absolute measures, and (2) relative measures.

5.4.1 ABSOLUTE MEASURES OF FORECASTING ERROR

Absolute measures of forecasting error are so named because the error measurements employed are made in an absolute manner without any consideration given to the underlying level of demand. Three commonly used absolute measures of forecasting error are

1. Standard deviation of forecasting errors

$$= \sqrt{\frac{\sum_{i=1}^{N} (\text{forecasted demand}_i - \text{actual demand}_i)^2}{N - 1}}$$

$$(5.2)$$

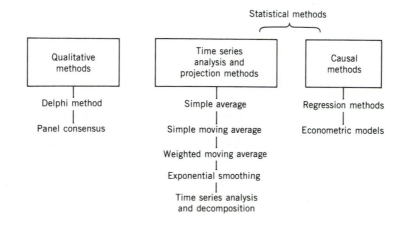

Statistical methods

Qualitative methods — Delphi method — Panel consensus

Time series analysis and projection methods — Simple average — Simple moving average — Weighted moving average — Exponential smoothing — Time series analysis and decomposition

Causal methods — Regression methods — Econometric models

2. Mean absolute deviation (MAD) of forecasting errors

$$= \frac{\text{sum of absolute deviations for all periods}}{\text{total number of periods evaluated}}$$

$$= \frac{\sum_{i=1}^{N} |\text{forecasted demand}_i - \text{actual demand}_i|}{N} \qquad (5.3)$$

3. Bias of forecasting errors

$$= \frac{\text{sum of algebraic deviations for all periods}}{\text{total number of periods evaluated}}$$

$$= \frac{\sum_{i=1}^{N} (\text{forecasted demand}_i - \text{actual demand}_i)}{N} \qquad (5.4)$$

In practice, the standard deviation of the forecasting errors or the mean absolute deviation of the forecasting errors are most commonly used. A slight preference for MAD may exist among practitioners, as it is easier to compute. Note that MAD is the average of several absolute deviations that are measured without regard to their sign. It measures the extent but not the direction of the forecasting error. Under the assumption that the forecasting errors are normally distributed, the following relationship between the standard deviation and the mean absolute deviation can be stated.

$$\text{Standard deviation} = 1.25 \, (\text{MAD}) \qquad (5.5)$$

The bias of the forecasting errors measures the absolute directional tendency of the forecast errors. It tells the forecaster if overforecasting or underforecasting is occurring.

To illustrate the computations involved in using these three absolute measures of forecasting error, consider the following example.

EXAMPLE (ABSOLUTE MEASURES OF FORECASTING ERROR)

An electronics company that manufactured a computer for the "home-hobbyist" market estimated its monthly demand for the first quarter of the year to be 1000 units per month. Later, the actual demands were observed to be 900, 1200, 800, and 1300, respectively. The three absolute measures of forecasting accuracy for this situation would be computed as follows:

1. Standard deviation of forecasting errors

$$= \sqrt{\frac{\begin{array}{c}(1000 - 900)^2 + (1000 - 1200)^2 \\ + (1000 - 800)^2 + (1000 - 1300)^2\end{array}}{4 - 1}}$$

$$= \sqrt{\frac{(100)^2 + (-200)^2 + (200)^2 + (-300)^2}{3}}$$

$$= \sqrt{\frac{(10,000) + (40,000) + (40,000) + (90,000)}{3}}$$

$$= \sqrt{\frac{180,000}{3}} = \sqrt{60,000} = 244.9 \text{ units} \qquad (5.6)$$

2. Mean absolute deviation of forecasting errors

$$= \frac{\begin{array}{c}|1000 - 900| + |1000 - 1200| \\ + |1000 - 800| + |1000 - 1300|\end{array}}{4}$$

$$= \frac{100 + 200 + 200 + 300}{4} = \frac{800}{4} = 200 \text{ units} \qquad (5.7)$$

3. Bias of forecasting errors

$$= \frac{\begin{array}{c}(1000 - 900) + (1000 - 1200) \\ + (1000 - 800) + (1000 - 1300)\end{array}}{4}$$

$$= \frac{(100) + (-200) + (200) + (-300)}{4}$$

$$= \frac{-200}{4} = -50 \text{ units} \qquad (5.8)$$

5.4.2 RELATIVE MEASURES OF FORECASTING ERROR

Relative measures of forecasting error take into account the relative magnitude of the forecasting errors with respect to the underlying demand level.

Two commonly used relative measures of forecasting error are

1. Coefficient of variation of forecasting error

$$= \frac{\text{standard deviation of forecasting error}}{\text{mean of the actual demand}}$$

$$= \frac{\sqrt{\sum_{i=1}^{N} (\text{forecasted demand}_i - \text{actual demand}_i)^2 / N - 1}}{\left(\sum_{i=1}^{N} \text{actual demand}_i\right) \Big/ N} \tag{5.9}$$

2. Relative forecasting error

$$= \frac{\sum_{i=1}^{N} (\text{forecasted demand}_i - \text{actual demand}_i)}{\sum_{i=1}^{N} \text{actual demand}_i} \tag{5.10}$$

Note that both of these relative measures of forecasting error are defined with respect to the actual level of demand that is occurring. The coefficient of variation scales the standard deviation of the forecasting error by the average demand level. The relative forecasting error is simply a relative measure of the bias present in the forecast.

To illustrate the computations involved in using these two relative measures of forecasting error, let us apply them to the same data for which we previously computed the three measures of absolute forecasting error.

EXAMPLE (RELATIVE MEASURES OF FORECASTING ERROR)

An electronics company with forecasted demand of 1000 for 4 months experiences actual demands of 900, 1200, 800, and 1300, respectively for the 4-month period.

1. Coefficient of variation of forecasting errors

$$= \frac{\text{standard deviation of forecasting error}}{\text{mean of actual demand}}$$
$$= \frac{244.9}{4200/4} = \frac{244.9}{1050} = 0.23 (23\%) \tag{5.11}$$

2. Relative forecasting error

$$= \frac{\sum_{i=1}^{N} (\text{forecasted demand}_i - \text{actual demand}_i)}{\sum_{i=1}^{N} \text{actual demand}_i}$$

$$= \frac{-200}{4200} = -0.05 (-5\%) \tag{5.12}$$

Note that both of these relative measures are expressed in dimensionless terms. Alternatively, they are often expressed as percentages.

5.5 QUALITATIVE FORECASTING METHODS

5.5.1 DELPHI METHOD

The Delphi method is probably the most commonly applied qualitative approach to forecasting. Originally developed at the RAND Corporation, it is a group process that seeks to obtain a refined consensus forecast. Application of the Delphi method begins with the selection of a group of experts who are willing to answer questions concerning a particular forecasting problem. These experts may often be a mixture of persons from inside and outside the company. The objective of the Delphi approach is to obtain a reliable consensus of opinion from this group of experts as to the forecast, while eliminating undesirable group interaction. To accomplish this objective, the coordinator of the Delphi group begins by asking each of the members of the group to make a written estimate with respect to the forecasting problem. The coordinator then collates, edits, and summarizes these estimates. This summary is then given back to members of the Delphi group and they are asked to make a second, more refined, estimate. The entire process is then repeated, until the coordinator feels that a reasonable consensus of opinion has been achieved. During this process the individualized answers help to ensure the anonymity that is necessary to reduce the effect of a particularly aggressive or socially dominant individual. The danger of conformity to a majority opinion, very common in committee decision making, can be avoided by presentation of the summarization in terms of quartile responses. It should be noted that the Delphi process does not necessarily produce a single answer, but instead, the final answer may be expressed in terms of a narrow statistical range.

One important aspect of the Delphi group is that each expert need not be proficient in exactly the same aspect of the problem being studied. Indeed, diversity in the makeup of the Delphi group is often desirable, so that information concerning the entire problem area can be obtained.

A major advantage of the Delphi method is that it eliminates much of the personal conflict or dominance by one individual that is so often a part of group decision making. The disadvantages of the Delphi method are its low level of reliability, the oversensitivity of its results to any ambiguities included in the questionnaires used in the process, and the difficulty associated with determining the degree of expertise that has been incorporated in the forecast.

5.5.2 PANEL CONSENSUS

One of the most widely used and influential qualitative approaches to forecasting involves the simple utilization of the opinions and intuition of a panel of experts. This qualitative approach to forecasting is similar to the Delphi method, and is based on the assumption that a panel of experts can arrive at a better, more accurate forecast than can one person. As with the Delphi method, the panel of experts is queried as to their opinions with respect to a particular forecasting problem. Unlike the Delphi method, however, secrecy between members of the panel is not maintained, and communication is encouraged. This means that panel consensus forecasts are often influenced by the dominant personality of the panel, or by other social factors, and thus may not reflect a true consensus.

Two general approaches to panel consensus forecasting are commonly used. In the first approach, the "top-down" approach, the panel consists of the chief executives of the firm. Each member of this panel is asked to make an independent fore-

cast. These individual estimates are then reviewed and discussed, and are converted by group judgment into a companywide forecast. In the second approach, the "bottom-up" approach, the panel is composed of the company's salespeople, who are asked to make estimates of their customers' demands. These estimates are then reviewed and consolidated at successively higher levels until a companywide consensus forecast is obtained.

The major advantages of the panel consensus approach to forecasting is that it is simple to use, involves knowledgable people in the forecasting process, and encourages interaction. Its major disadvantages are its low level of reliability and its oversensitivity to the dominance of a strong individual, or individuals, within the panel of experts.

5.6 STATISTICAL FORECASTING METHODS

Statistical forecasting methods are applicable when three general conditions are met.

1. There is a reliable set of information about the past, usually referred to as *time series data;*
2. This set of information can be expressed in quantitative terms;
3. It can reasonably be assumed that the pattern of demand exhibited by the set of past information will continue into the future.

Analysis and forecasting of statistical data are generally divided into time series analysis and projection methods (see Table 5.2), and causal methods (see Table 5.3). We now consider selected methods in each of these two categories.

5.6.1 TIME SERIES ANALYSIS AND PROJECTION METHODS

5.6.1.1 AVERAGING MODELS

One way of forecasting future demand is based on the assumption that market demand forces will remain constant over time. Then, a good estimate of future demand can be obtained by determining some sort of average of past demand. There are several ways of determining this average of past demand.

Simple Average. The simple average is an average of past demand in which the demands of all past periods are equally weighted. The simple average is computed as

Simple average (SA)

$$= \frac{\text{sum of demands for all past periods}}{\text{number of demand periods}}$$

$$= \frac{D_t + D_{t-1} + \cdots + D_{t-(N-1)}}{N} \quad (5.13)$$

where

$$D_t = \text{demand in the current period;}$$

$$D_{t-1} = \text{demand in the past period;}$$

$$D_{t-(N-1)} = \text{demand in the last period for which data were available;}$$

$$N = \text{total number of time periods.}$$

Note that in the calculation of the simple average the demands from all previous periods are equally influential (equally weighted) in determining the average that is then used as the forecast of the future.

To illustrate the computation of a simple average, consider the following example.

EXAMPLE

Donna Formsby owns and operates a store that sells sporting equipment used by runners. She has experienced demand for one of her best selling running shoes for the current month and the past 5 months, according to the following pattern.

$$D \text{ current month, } t = 150 \text{ pairs of shoes}$$

$$D \text{ past month, } t - 1 = 100 \text{ pairs of shoes}$$

$$D \text{ 2 months ago, } t - 2 = 130 \text{ pairs of shoes}$$

$$D \text{ 3 months ago, } t - 3 = 110 \text{ pairs of shoes}$$

$$D \text{ 4 months ago, } t - 4 = 170 \text{ pairs of shoes}$$

$$D \text{ 5 months ago, } t - 5 = 180 \text{ pairs of shoes}$$

$$
\begin{aligned}
\text{Simple average} &= \frac{\begin{array}{c} D_t + D_{t-1} + D_{t-2} + D_{t-3} \\ + D_{t-4} + D_{t-5} \end{array}}{N} \\[2mm]
&= \frac{\begin{array}{c} 150 + 100 + 130 + 110 \\ + 170 + 180 \end{array}}{6} \\[2mm]
&= \frac{840}{6} \\[2mm]
&= 140 \quad\quad (5.14)
\end{aligned}
$$

A forecast for the next month would thus be 140 pairs of shoes. Referring to the example given above, note what the simple averaging process accomplishes. While the demand in any one period may be above or below the average, the average demand tends to be representative of the true underlying demand pattern. As the number of periods used to calculate the average increases, the averaging process tends to reflect the central tendency of the demand process, and the effect of extreme random deviations is reduced.

One major advantage of the simple average method is that the demand in all past periods enters equally into the calculation. If the true demand pattern actually changes over time, however, the simple average may not be truly reflective of the most recent past, and hence the future, since all past demand periods are equally weighted. This disadvantage is somewhat overcome by using a simple moving average.

Simple Moving Average. A simple moving average is an average computed for a specified number of recent time periods. In this averaging process, each period a new demand data point becomes available and is included in the average, while the oldest demand observation is excluded. Again, a specific number of observations are used in the averaging process. Once the number of past periods to be used in the calculation has been selected, it is held constant, and the demands within this time frame are equally weighted. The average "moves" in the sense that after each demand period elapses, the demand for the newest period is added, and the demand for the oldest period is deleted, before the next calculation is made.

The simple N-period moving average is computed as

Moving average (MA)

$$= \frac{\text{sum of demands for last } N \text{ periods}}{\begin{array}{c}\text{number of periods used in}\\\text{the moving average } (N)\end{array}}$$

$$= \frac{D_t + D_{t-1} + \cdots + D_{t-(N-1)}}{N} \qquad (5.15)$$

where

D_t = demand in the current period;

D_{t-1} = demand in the past period;

$D_{t-(N-1)}$ = demand in the last period for which the moving average is computed;

N = number of periods used in the moving average.

To illustrate the computation of a moving average, consider the following example.

EXAMPLE

Ms. Formsby has collected a year's worth of data concerning the demand experienced for her running shoes.

She would like to determine 3-month moving averages for her year's worth of data. The following table summarizes her computations.

In Table 5.5 the 3-month moving averages in column 4 are based on the observed demand for the current month and the two previous months. At the end of month three, the 3-month moving average is the average for months 1, 2, 3, namely, $(150 + 100 + 130)/3 = 126.67$. This moving average would then be the forecast for month four. The last figure in column 4, 190.00, is the moving average associated with months 9, 10, and 11, and it would be used as the forecast for month twelve. Similarly, the 5-month moving averages in column 5 are based on the observed demand for the current month and the four previous months. At the end of month five, the 5-month moving average is the average for months 1, 2, 3, 4, 5, namely, $(150 + 100 + 130 + 110 + 170)/5 = 132.00$. This moving average would then be the forecast for month six. The last figure in column 5, 194.00, is the moving average associated with months 7, 8, 9, 10, and 11, and it would be used as the forecast for month twelve.

TABLE 5.5 MOVING AVERAGES—RUNNING SHOE DATA

(1) MONTH	(2) TIME PERIOD	(3) OBSERVED DEMAND	(4) 3-MONTH MOVING AVERAGE	(5) 5-MONTH MOVING AVERAGE
Jan.	1	150	—	—
Feb.	2	100	—	—
Mar.	3	130	—	—
Apr.	4	110	126.67	—
May	5	170	113.33	—
June	6	180	136.67	132.00
July	7	190	153.33	138.00
Aug.	8	210	180.00	156.00
Sept.	9	180	193.33	172.00
Oct.	10	200	193.33	186.00
Nov.	11	190	196.67	192.00
Dec.	12	220	190.00	194.00

The advantage of the moving average method is that it effectively smooths out abrupt fluctuations in the demand pattern and can provide a stable estimate of demand. The stability of response to a change in the demand pattern is somewhat controlled by the choice of the number of time periods included in the moving average. The basic disadvantage of the moving average forecasting method, however, is that of inaccuracy, because of an inability to rapidly respond to a change in the demand pattern.

Weighted Moving Average. A weighted moving average is a moving average in which the forecaster assigns more weights to certain time periods. The varying of the weights is usually done to allow recent demand data to influence the forecast more than older demand data. In this manner a more rapid response to recent changes in the demand pattern is provided.

The N-period weighted moving average is computed as

Weighted moving average (WMA)
$$= W_t D_t + W_{t-1} D_{t-1}$$
$$+ \cdots + W_{t-(N-1)} D_{t-(N-1)} \quad (5.16)$$

where

$$0 \leq W_t \leq 1.0 = \text{weight for period } t;$$
$$0 \leq W_{t-1} \leq 1.0 = \text{weight for period } t - 1;$$
$$\vdots \qquad\qquad \vdots$$
$$0 \leq W_{t-(N-1)} \leq 1.0 = \text{weight for period } t$$
$$- (N - 1)$$
$$W_t + W_{t-1} + \cdots + W_{t-(N-1)} = 1.0$$

The weighted moving average process can be illustrated by the following example.

EXAMPLE

Andy's Deli wishes to forecast demand for its "Super Sub" sandwich for the forthcoming week. It has experienced sandwich demand in the last three weeks of $D_t = 750$, $D_{t-1} = 725$, $D_{t-2} = 690$, respectively. It wishes to weight these demands as $W_t = .60$, $W_{t-1} = .30$, and $W_{t-2} =$ .10, respectively. The three-period weighted moving average is computed as:

Three period weighted moving average (WMA)
$$= W_t D_t + W_{t-1} D_{t-1} + W_{t-2} D_{t-2}$$
$$= (.60)(750) + (.30)(725) + (.10)(690)$$
$$= 450 + 217.5 + 69 = 736.5 \quad (5.17)$$

The advantage of the weighted moving average forecasting process is that it allows the forecaster to use judgment in weighting more heavily the demand experience of recent months. The forecaster can also allow for a trend in demand, or for a seasonality effect, by carefully choosing the weighting coefficients. The disadvantage of this forecasting process is that the choice of the weights is still a subjective process in which errors can occur.

Exponential Smoothing. Exponential smoothing is a special type of a weighted moving average. As noted in our previous discussion, there are two major limitations to the general use of moving averages. First, the data required to compute moving averages can be extensive if the number of periods used in the moving average is large, and if the number of items requiring a forecast is also large. Second, in the moving average forecasting process equal weight is given to each of the past N demands, and no weight is given to demand in periods prior to ($t - N + 1$). In general, we observed that the true demand pattern is more likely to be reflected in the demand evidenced in more recent time periods. Thus recent demand values should be given relatively more weight in the forecasting process than should older demand observations. Exponential smoothing considers both of the problems that are inherent in the use of a moving average.

Exponential smoothing is so named because of the special way it weights each of the past demands. The pattern of weights is *exponential* in that demand for the most recent time period is weighted most heavily, and then the weights placed on successively older time periods decay exponentially. To illustrate, let us now examine the computational aspects of *single*, or *first-order exponential smoothing*. The equation used in first-order exponential smoothing to produce a forecast uses only three pieces of data: (1) the actual demand for the most recent time period, (2) the forecast made for the most recent time period, and (3) the exponential smoothing constant. The general form of the first-order exponential smoothing equation is

$$F_{t+1} = \alpha D_t + (1 - \alpha)F_t \qquad (5.18)$$

where

F_{t+1} = forecast of next period's demand;

D_t = actual demand in most recent period;

F_t = forecasted demand in most recent period;

α = exponential smoothing constant, $0.0 \leq \alpha \leq 1.0$.

The implications of exponential smoothing can be better explained if we expand the general form of the first-order exponential smoothing equation just presented. To do this, we first expand Eq. 5.18 by replacing F_t with its components as follows.

$$\begin{aligned} F_{t+1} &= \alpha D_t + (1 - \alpha)[\alpha D_{t-1} + (1 - \alpha)F_{t-1}] \\ &= \alpha D_t + \alpha(1 - \alpha)D_{t-1} + (1 - \alpha)^2 F_{t-1} \quad (5.19) \end{aligned}$$

We continue expanding by replacing F_{t-1} with its components, F_{t-2} with its components, etc., with the resulting equation being

$$\begin{aligned} F_{t+1} = \alpha D_t &+ \alpha(1 - \alpha)D_{t-1} \\ &+ \alpha(1 - \alpha)^2 D_{t-2} + \alpha(1 - \alpha)^3 D_{t-3} \\ &+ \cdots + \alpha(1 - \alpha)^{N-1} D_{t-(N-1)} \quad (5.20) \end{aligned}$$

Note that in Eq. 5.20 the weights applied to each of the past demand values decrease exponentially, hence the name exponential smoothing. Note also that the exponential smoothing process is nonlinear. The smoothing constant, α, is a number between 0 and 1, and is chosen in a manner to make the forecasted values fit the past data in an accurate manner. The choice of $\alpha = .0$ would result in a forecast that would not be adjusted in any way, regardless of the demand that occurred. This would be a constant forecast, and it would also be totally unresponsive to changes in the actual demand pattern. Conversely, the choice of $\alpha = 1.0$ would result in a forecast that would always equal the last actual demand value. This would be a very responsive forecast, but it would also be very unstable with respect to any fluctuations in the actual demand pattern.

Let us now consider the effect of the choice of $\alpha = .3$, a smoothing constant value that is often used in practice. In Table 5.6 we indicate how the numerical value of the weighting coefficient exponentially decays over time (e.g., for $\alpha = .3$). A plot of the data in the last column of Table 5.6 is shown in Figure 5.3. This plot highlights the ex-

TABLE 5.6 WEIGHTS ASSIGNED TO DATA IN PAST TIME PERIODS, EXPONENTIAL SMOOTHING, $\alpha = .3$

TIME PERIOD	WEIGHTING COEFFICIENT	NUMERICAL VALUE OF WEIGHTING COEFFICIENT IF $\alpha = .3$
t	$\alpha(1 - \alpha)^0$	.3
$t - 1$	$\alpha(1 - \alpha)^1$	.21
$t - 2$	$\alpha(1 - \alpha)^2$	.147
$t - 3$	$\alpha(1 - \alpha)^3$	.1029
$t - 4$	$\alpha(1 - \alpha)^4$	.072
$t - 5$	$\alpha(1 - \alpha)^5$	.051
.	.	.
.	.	.
.	.	.
$t - (N - 1)$	$\alpha(1 - \alpha)^{N-1}$	$(.3)(.7)^{N-1}$

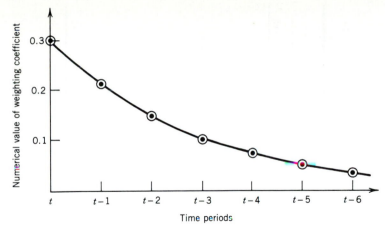

FIGURE 5.3 WEIGHT ASSIGNED TO DATA IN PAST TIME PERIODS, EXPONENTIAL SMOOTHING, $\alpha = 0.3$.

ponential decay that occurs over time with respect to the weights used with the data. As can be seen in Figure 5.3, the exponential smoothing model with an $\alpha = .3$ weights the most current demand with a value of .3, but weights demand from five periods ago with a weight of .05.

The application of single exponential smoothing can be illustrated by the following situation. The Le Gourmet Company manufactures food processors and is interested in using exponential smoothing to make a series of monthly forecasts over a 1-year time horizon. Table 5.7 shows the forecasting results from using exponential smoothing, with values of $\alpha = .1, .5, .9$ over the 1-year period.

One problem that exists with actually applying exponential smoothing is that in the first period for which a forecast is to be made (F_{t+1}) we have no forecast for the previous period (F_t). This problem can be resolved by averaging the demands for several early periods to get an initial forecast, or more simply, the forecaster can use the first observed value as the first forecast. This was done in the example shown in Table 5.7. Thus the observed value of demand in period 1 $(F_{t=1})$ was used as the forecast of demand in period 2 $(F_{t+1=2})$. Then forecasts were made for period 3, using the first-order exponential smoothing equation as follows. For

$$\alpha = .1: F_{t=3} = \alpha D_{t=2} + (1 - \alpha)F_{t=2}$$
$$= (.1)(120) + (1 - .1)(110)$$
$$= 12 + 99 = 111 \tag{5.21}$$

$$\alpha = .5: F_{t=3} = \alpha D_{t=2} + (1 - \alpha)F_{t=2}$$
$$= (.5)(120) + (1 - .5)(110)$$
$$= 60 + 55 = 115 \tag{5.22}$$

$$\alpha = .9: F_{t=3} = \alpha D_{t=2} + (1 - \alpha)F_{t=2}$$
$$= (.9)(120) + (1 - .9)(110)$$
$$= 108 + 11 = 119 \tag{5.23}$$

The effect that the choice of the value of α has on the exponential smoothing process can be seen in Figure 5.4. Note that a value of $\alpha = .9$ produces very little smoothing in the forecast, but instead reacts very quickly to changes in the demand pattern. Conversely, a value of $\alpha = .1$ gives considerable smoothing, but is relatively unresponsive to changes in the demand pattern.

Since exponential smoothing is nothing more than a special type of a weighted moving average, a relationship between the value of α used in exponential smoothing and the number of months, N, used in the moving average, can be determined. This relationship has been shown to be

$$\alpha = \frac{2}{N + 1} \tag{5.24}$$

Using this relationship, the following equivalence table can be derived.

As Table 5.8 illustrates, the larger the value of α, the smaller the corresponding value of N, and vice versa. This explains why very little smoothing

TABLE 5.7 FORECASTED FOOD PROCESSOR DEMAND USING EXPONENTIAL SMOOTHING

MONTH	TIME PERIOD	OBSERVED DEMAND (000 UNITS)	FORECAST	α = .1 DEVIATION	|DEVIATION|	FORECAST	α = .5 DEVIATION	|DEVIATION|	FORECAST	α = .9 DEVIATION	|DEVIATION|
						EXPONENTIALLY SMOOTHED FORECASTS					
Jan.	1	110	—	—	—	—	—	—	—	—	—
Feb.	2	120	110	10.0	10.0	110	10.0	10.0	110	10.0	10.0
Mar.	3	150	111	39.0	39.0	115	35.0	35.0	119	31.0	31.0
Apr.	4	180	114.9	65.1	65.1	132.5	47.5	47.5	146.9	33.1	33.1
May	5	120	121.4	−1.4	1.4	156.3	−36.3	36.3	176.7	−56.7	56.7
June	6	100	121.3	−21.3	21.3	138.2	−38.2	38.2	125.7	−25.7	25.7
July	7	90	119.2	−29.2	29.2	119.1	−29.1	29.1	102.6	−12.6	12.6
Aug.	8	140	116.3	23.7	23.7	104.6	−35.4	35.4	91.3	48.7	48.7
Sept.	9	170	118.7	51.3	51.3	112.3	57.7	57.7	135.1	34.9	34.9
Oct.	10	190	123.8	66.2	66.2	141.2	48.8	48.8	166.5	23.5	23.5
Nov.	11	200	130.4	69.6	69.6	165.6	34.4	34.4	187.7	12.3	12.3
Dec.	12	220	137.4	82.6	82.6	182.8	37.2	37.2	198.8	21.2	21.2
				MAD = 459.4/11 = 41.8			MAD = 409.6/11 = 37.2			MAD = 309.7/11 = 28.2	

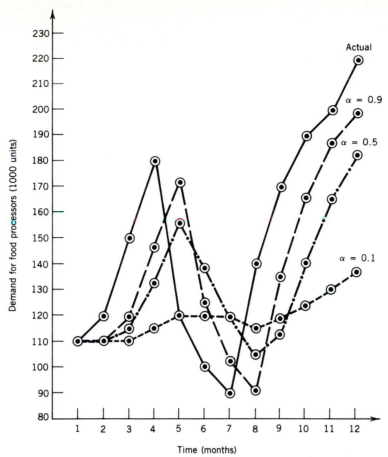

FIGURE 5.4 FOOD PROCESSOR DEMAND—ACTUAL AND EXPONENTIALLY SMOOTHED FORECASTS.

TABLE 5.8 EQUIVALENCE BETWEEN N (MOVING AVERAGES) AND α (EXPONENTIAL SMOOTHING)

NUMBER OF PERIODS, N, USED IN MOVING AVERAGE	VALUE OF α USED IN EXPONENTIAL SMOOTHING
1	1.00
2	.67
3	.50
4	.40
5	.33
6	.29
8	.22
10	.18
12	.15
24	.08
36	.05

is achieved with a large value of α, while a great deal of smoothing is achieved with the small value of α.

Exponential smoothing has as its advantages its operating simplicity and the fact that its requirements for data are very minimal. Its main disadvantage, however, is that the forecaster must choose a value of α. This choice is usually made through a trial-and-error process in which the forecaster chooses a value for α that minimizes some measure of the forecast error. Referring back to the data shown in Table 5.7, the "best" value of α on the basis of providing the smallest MAD (28.2) is .9. The reason that this value of α produces the best fitting forecast can be evidenced by referring to Figure 5.4, in which it can be observed that the actual demand pattern over time has a great deal of variability. Thus a higher value of α must be used in order to make the exponentially smoothed forecast responsive to the fluctuating demands.

5.6.1.2 TIME SERIES ANALYSIS AND DECOMPOSITION

A time series is a sequence of data points measured at constant intervals of time. Monthly sales or demand figures are examples of time series data. One of the oldest and most commonly used approaches to forecasting involves the analysis and decomposition of time series. In using this approach we assume that the time series we are trying to forecast consists of an underlying pattern plus or minus some random error.

Time series value = underlying pattern
$$\pm \text{ random error} \quad (5.25)$$

Figure 5.5 illustrates the actual observations of a time series representing the sales of the "Duke" graphite tennis racket. The solid line in Figure 5.5 is the underlying pattern for this particular time series, and the distances between the pattern and the actual observations are the random errors. Observe that these random errors can be positive or negative.

In applying time series analysis and decomposition methods to a set of data such as that portrayed in Figure 5.5 we first attempt to break the past data

into components. These components are then projected into the future. The four components most commonly employed are

1. The trend component (T_t);
2. The cyclical component (C_t);
3. The seasonal component (S_t);
4. The irregular, or random, component (I_t).

Each of these components will now be considered in more detail.

Trend Component. The trend component describes the long-run, or average, movement of the data over time, and can be increasing, decreasing, or unchanged. Determination of the trend component may require a great deal of data. For example, we might have to review 10 to 15 years of sales data in order to determine that there was a gradual increase in sales volume over time.

The trend component may be either linear or nonlinear. Typical trend patterns for various time series are shown in Figure 5.6. Obviously, many combinations of these patterns can occur.

In time series analysis there are at least three methods of estimating the trend component.

1. Inspect the plot of the time series data and draw a trend curve that fits the data points.
2. Fit a trend line to the data using the method of least squares. (This method is discussed in

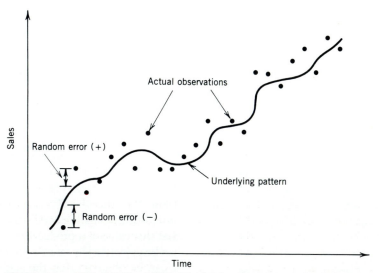

FIGURE 5.5 TIME SERIES—SALES OF "DUKE" GRAPHITE TENNIS RACKET.

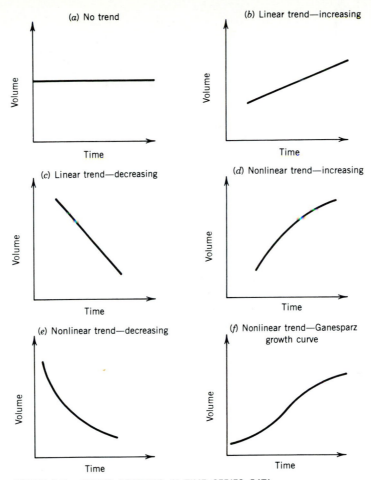

FIGURE 5.6   TREND PATTERNS IN TIME SERIES DATA.

further detail in the later section of this chapter dealing with regression.)

3. Compute a moving average for the time series, whose average length, N, is equal to the length of seasonality. The purpose of this moving average is to eliminate seasonality and irregularity, and thus isolate the trend component. (We discuss this procedure in more detail in the numerical example to be presented at the end of this section.)

Cyclical Component.   The cyclical component refers to the recurrent upward and downward wavelike conditions that occurs over time due to general economic conditions. The frequency of this cyclical component is longer than a year, and is generally attributable to business cycles (i.e., ex-

pansion, recession). It may vary between countries, industries within a country, or companies within an industry.

The cyclical pattern in a time series is often manifested by alternating sequences of data points above and below the trend time. Figure 5.7 shows the graph of a time series that has an obvious cyclical component.

Determining the cyclical component in a time series is often very difficult. It requires knowledge of the level of economic, industry, or company activity for the period of time encompassed by the time series. Such knowledge can frequently be based only on judgment or experience. In summary, determination of the cyclical component of time series is a subject that is beyond the scope of this book.

Seasonal Component.   The seasonal component of a time series consists of periodic fluctuations

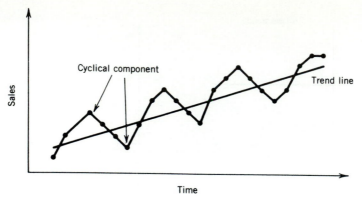

FIGURE 5.7 TIME SERIES EXAMPLE—CYCLICAL COMPONENT.

of constant length that are caused by seasonal influences such as weather, month of the year, or timing of holidays. For example, ice cream and soft drink sales can be expected to be greater in the warm summer months than in the winter. The seasonal component in a time series is often isolated by means of a moving average. This is shown in greater detail in the next example.

Irregular or Random Component. The irregular component of a time series consists of the random fluctuations that cannot be explained by the trend, cycle, or seasonal components. These random variations are of a short, erratic nature, follow no discernible pattern, and cannot be forecast. The irregular component represents the error between the combined effect of the trend, cycle, and seasonal components and the actual data. It is unpredictable, and because of this random error forecasts are never 100 percent accurate.

It is assumed that these four components act in an independent manner, and that the factors that caused them to occur in the past will continue into the future. Figure 5.8 below shows a typical time series and its decomposed components. Note that while it would be difficult to extrapolate the actual time series, it would not be as hard to project the components of the time series, with the obvious exception of the irregular component. There is a major danger in this approach when a change occurs in the factors that have influenced demand in the past. When this occurs a *turning point* is encountered, and there can be a major error in extrapolating past patterns into the future.

There are several alternative approaches to decomposing a time series. The general mathematical representation of the decomposition approach is

$$X_t = f(T_t, C_t, S_t, I_t) \qquad (5.26)$$

where

X_t = time series value (actual data) in period t;

T_t = trend component in period t;

C_t = cyclical component in period t;

S_t = seasonal component in period t;

I_t = irregular component in period t.

The exact functional form of Eq. 5.26 depends on the actual decomposition method that is employed. Two common functional forms are

$$X_t = T_t + C_t + S_t + I_t$$
$$\text{(Additive Model)} \qquad (5.27)$$

$$X_t = T_t \times C_t \times S_t \times I_t$$
$$\text{(Multiplicative Model)} \qquad (5.28)$$

Time series analysis and decomposition methods are some of the oldest approaches to forecasting, having been used in the early 1900s by economists. The decomposition method most widely used today is known as Census II, and was developed by the Bureau of the Census of the U.S. Department of Commerce, under the direction of Julius Shiskin.

To illustrate the decomposition approach, let us consider the quarterly data for sales of videocassette recorders for a particular retailer shown in Table 5.9 and plotted in Figure 5.9. We begin our

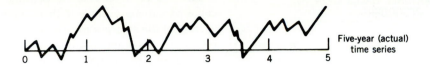

Five-year (actual)
time series

Trend component

Seasonal component

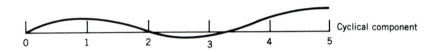

Cyclical component

Irregular component

FIGURE 5.8   A TIME SERIES AND ITS DECOMPOSED COMPONENTS.

analysis with the isolation of the seasonal component of this time series.

The computational procedure for identifying each quarter's seasonal influence uses a moving average to measure the combined trend—cyclical ($T_t \cdot C_t$) component of the time series. Herein we seek to eliminate the seasonal and random components S_t and I_t. Since we are working with quarterly data, we use four data values in each moving average. For example, the first moving average is

$$\text{First moving average}$$
$$= \frac{570 + 500 + 700 + 740}{4}$$
$$= \frac{2510}{4} = 627.5 \qquad (5.29)$$

Continuing the moving average process, we next add the value of 670 for the first quarter of 1982 and drop the value of 570 for the first quarter of 1981. Thus the second moving average is

$$\text{Second moving average}$$
$$= \frac{500 + 700 + 740 + 670}{4}$$
$$= \frac{2610}{4} = 652.5 \qquad (5.30)$$

The moving average calculation for this entire set of time series data is summarized in Table 5.10. Notice that the four quarter moving averages are centered between the four quarters used in their computation. For example, the first moving average

TABLE 5.9 QUARTERLY SALES DATA FOR VIDEOCASSETTE RECORDERS

YEAR	QUARTER	SALES (UNITS)
1981	1	570
	2	500
	3	700
	4	740
1982	1	670
	2	610
	3	770
	4	830
1983	1	700
	2	650
	3	740
	4	770
1984	1	720
	2	680
	3	900
	4	930

is centered between quarters two and three. The centered moving average is then computed as the average of the adjacent moving averages and is centered on the corresponding quarter. For example, the centered moving average for quarter three in 1981 is computed as

Centered moving average

$$= \frac{627.5 + 652.5}{2} = \frac{1280}{2} = 640 \quad (5.31)$$

A plot of the centered moving average superimposed on the actual time series is shown in Figure 5.10. Observe that the moving average values have smoothed out the fluctuations in the data. The moving averages were computed for four quarters of data and therefore do not include the fluctuations due to seasonal influences. Additionally, since the random movements tend to average out to zero over a

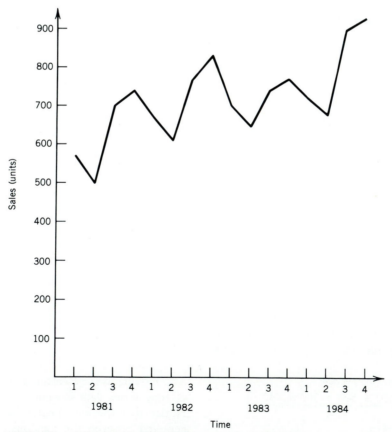

FIGURE 5.9 QUARTERLY SALES—VIDEOCASSETTE RECORDERS.

TABLE 5.10 MOVING AVERAGE CALCULATIONS FOR VIDEOCASSETTE RECORDER TIME SERIES DATA

YEAR	QUARTER	SALES (UNITS)	FOUR QUARTER MOVING AVERAGE	CENTERED MOVING AVERAGE
1981	1	570		
	2	500	627.5	
	3	700	652.5	640.00
	4	740	680.0	666.25
1982	1	670	697.5	688.75
	2	610	720.0	708.75
	3	770	727.5	723.75
	4	830	737.5	732.50
1983	1	700	730.0	733.75
	2	650	715.0	722.50
	3	740	720.0	717.50
	4	770	727.5	723.75
1984	1	720	767.5	747.50
	2	680	807.5	787.50
	3	900		
	4	930		

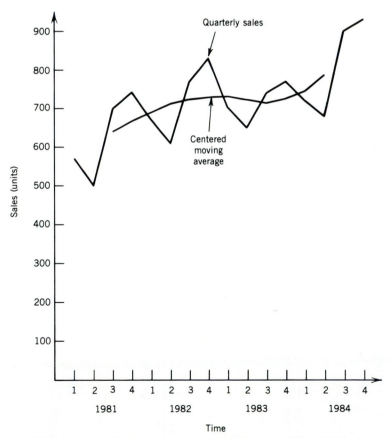

FIGURE 5.10 QUARTERLY SALES AND CENTERED MOVING AVERAGE—VIDEO-CASSETTE RECORDERS.

number of quarters, this moving average process has also eliminated these random influences.

In the plot shown in Figure 5.10 the centered moving average values represent the trend—cyclical component of the time series. Assuming that we are using a multiplicative model of the form

$$X_t = T_t \times C_t \times S_t \times I_t \qquad (5.32)$$

we know the actual time series values (the X_t) and the combined trend—cyclical component (T_tC_t). Thus we can compute the combined seasonal—random component as

$$S_tI_t = \frac{X_t}{T_tC_t} \qquad (5.33)$$

These computations are summarized in Table 5.11, in which we can see that the results for the third quarter for years 1981, 1982, and 1983, are 1.094, 1.064, and 1.031, respectively. We can therefore conclude that in all three years the seasonal—random component appears to have an above-average influence in the third quarter. Since year-to-year changes in the seasonal—random component can be attributed primarily to the random component,

we can now proceed to average the S_tI_t values to eliminate this random influence and obtain a "true" estimate of the third quarter seasonal component. Proceeding, we obtain

$$
\begin{aligned}
\text{Seasonal component, } & S_t \\
\text{(third quarter)} & \\
= & \frac{1.094 + 1.064 + 1.031}{3} \\
= & \frac{3.189}{3} = 1.063 \qquad (5.34)
\end{aligned}
$$

In Table 5.12 the computations for the seasonal components for all four quarters for the videocassette recorder sales data are summarized. As can be seen in this table, the fourth quarter is the best quarter for sales and the second quarter is the worst. These sales data also show a very pronounced seasonal pattern.

Now that we have identified the seasonal component in this time series we can deseasonalize the data and identify the trend in the time series. Using the notation of our multiplicative model, we have

$$X_t = T_t \times C_t \times S_t \times I_t \qquad (5.35)$$

TABLE 5.11 COMPUTATION OF SEASONAL—RANDOM COMPONENT OF VIDEOCASSETTE RECORDER TIME SERIES DATA

YEAR	QUARTER	SALES (X_t)	FOUR QUARTER CENTERED MOVING AVERAGE (T_tC_t)	SEASONAL–RANDOM COMPONENT $S_tI_t = X_t/T_tC_t$
1981	1	570		
	2	500		
	3	700	640.00	1.094
	4	740	666.25	1.111
1982	1	670	688.75	0.973
	2	610	708.75	0.861
	3	770	723.75	1.064
	4	830	732.50	1.133
1983	1	700	733.75	0.954
	2	650	722.50	0.900
	3	740	717.50	1.031
	4	770	723.75	1.064
1984	1	720	747.50	0.963
	2	680	787.50	0.863
	3	900		
	4	930		

TABLE 5.12 SEASONAL COMPONENT CALCULATIONS—VIDEOCASSETTE RECORDER SALES DATA

QUARTER	SEASONAL—RANDOM COMPONENT VALUES $(S_t I_t)$	SEASONAL FACTOR (S_t)
1	0.973, 0.954, 0.963	0.963
2	0.861, 0.900, 0.863	0.874
3	1.094, 1.064, 1.031	1.063
4	1.111, 1.133, 1.064	1.103

Using the seasonal factors that we have just determined, we can compute the value of the combined trend, cyclical, and random components as

$$\frac{X_t}{S_t} = T_t \cdot C_t \cdot I_t \qquad (5.36)$$

Therefore, we can divide each time series observation by its appropriate seasonal factor to remove the effect of seasonality from the time series data. The deseasonalized sales data computations are shown in Table 5.13. A graph of the deseasonalized sales data is shown in Figure 5.11.

Looking at this graph, we see that these data have an upward trend that can be approximated linearly. For a linear trend, the estimated trend values can be expressed as a linear function of time

$$T_t = b_0 + b_1 t \qquad (5.37)$$

where

T_t = trend value for videocassette recorder sales in period t;

b_0 = intercept of the trend line;

b_1 = slope of the trend line;

t = time period.

The procedure that is most often used to determine the linear function that best approximates a linear trend is based upon the least squares method,

TABLE 5.13 DESEASONALIZED TIME SERIES DATA— VIDEOCASSETTE RECORDERS

YEAR	QUARTER	SALES (X_t)	SEASONAL FACTOR (S_t)	DESEASONALIZED SALES DATA $X_t/S_t = T_t \cdot C_t \cdot I_t$
1981	1	570	0.963	592
	2	500	0.874	572
	3	700	1.063	659
	4	740	1.103	671
1982	1	670	0.963	696
	2	610	0.874	698
	3	770	1.063	724
	4	830	1.103	752
1983	1	700	0.963	721
	2	650	0.874	744
	3	740	1.063	696
	4	770	1.103	698
1984	1	720	0.963	748
	2	680	0.874	778
	3	900	1.063	847
	4	930	1.103	843

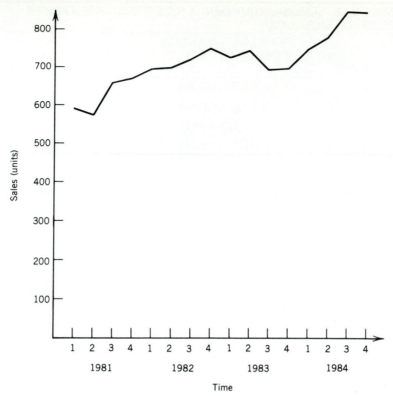

FIGURE 5.11 DESEASONALIZED SALES—VIDEOCASSETTE RECORDERS.

which identifies the values of b_0 and b_1 that minimize the sum of the squared forecast errors. That is

$$\text{Minimize} \sum_{t=1}^{n} (X_t - T_t)^2 \qquad (5.38)$$

where

$T_t = b_0 + b_1 t = $ forecast trend line;

$X_t = $ actual value of the time series in period t;

$n = $ number of periods.

Besides being described in detail in many books on elementary statistics, the least squares method is also used in the discussion of regression in Section 5.6.2. The appropriate formulas for computing the values of b_0 and b_1 using this approach are as follows.

$$b_i = \frac{n \sum_{t=1}^{n} tX_t - \sum_{t=1}^{n} t \sum_{t=1}^{n} X_t}{n \sum_{t=1}^{n} t^2 - \left(\sum_{t=1}^{n} t\right)^2} \qquad (5.39)$$

$$b_0 = \overline{X} - b_1 \bar{t} \qquad (5.40)$$

where

$$\overline{X} = \frac{\sum_{t=1}^{n} X_t}{n} = \text{average value of the time series;}$$

$$\bar{t} = \frac{\sum_{t=1}^{n} t}{n} = \text{average value of } t.$$

In the example currently being considered, the X_t values are the deseasonalized data. Using the deseasonalized data, the trend line computation is made as follows.

$$\bar{t} = \frac{\sum_{t=1}^{n} t}{n} = \frac{136}{16} = 8.5 \qquad (5.41)$$

$$\overline{X} = \frac{\sum_{t=1}^{n} X_t}{n} = \frac{11,445}{16} = 715.313 \qquad (5.42)$$

t	DESEASONALIZED SALES DATA (X_t)	tX_t	t^2
1	592	592	1
2	572	1144	4
3	659	1977	9
4	671	2684	16
5	696	3480	25
6	698	4188	36
7	724	5068	49
8	752	6016	64
9	727	6543	81
10	744	7440	100
11	696	7656	121
12	698	8376	144
13	748	9724	169
14	778	10,892	196
15	847	12,705	225
16	843	13,488	256
Total $\Sigma t = 136$	$\Sigma X_t = 11,445$	$\Sigma tX_t = 101,973$	$\Sigma t^2 = 1496$

$$b_1 = \frac{n \sum_{t=1}^{n} tX_t - \sum_{t=1}^{n} t \sum_{t=1}^{n} X_t}{\sum_{t=1}^{n} t^2 - \left(\sum_{t=1}^{n} t\right)^2}$$

$$= \frac{(16)(101,973) - (136)(11,445)}{(16)(1496) - (136)^2}$$

$$= \frac{75,048}{5440} = 13.796 \qquad (5.43)$$

$$b_0 = \overline{X} - b_1 t = 715.313 - 13.796(8.5)$$

$$= 715.313 - 117.266 = 598.047 \qquad (5.44)$$

Therefore, the trend line for the deseasonalized data is

$$T_t = b_0 + b_1 t$$

$$= 598.047 + 13.796t \qquad (5.45)$$

If we now assume that this trend will continue into the future, we can make trend projections for the next four quarters (i.e., for the year 1985). For example, substituting $t = 17$ into Eq. 5.45 yields the trend projection for the first quarter of 1985.

$$T_{17} = b_0 + b_1(t = 17)$$

$$= 598.047 + (13.796)(17) = 598.047 + 234.532$$

$$= 832.579 \; (\sim 833 \text{ units}) \qquad (5.46)$$

In similar fashion, we could make trend projections for the last three quarters of 1985, using $t = 18$, 19, and 20, respectively. This has been done, and is summarized in Table 5.14, where we have also used the seasonal factors obtained earlier (refer back to Table 5.12) to adjust the trend projection in order to arrive at the quarterly forecast shown in the final column. We could attempt to further adjust our forecast for the possible cyclical effect, but we have no knowledge of what the cyclical effect might be in this situation, and its determination is beyond the scope of this book.

5.6.2 CAUSAL METHODS

Causal forecasting methods assume that the factor, or dependent variable, to be forecasted has a cause–effect relationship with one or more independent variables. For example, the forecaster may want to

TABLE 5.14 QUARTERLY FORECASTS FOR VIDEOCASSETTE RECORDER SALES

YEAR	QUARTER	TREND PROJECTION	SEASONAL FACTOR	ADJUSTED QUARTERLY FORECAST
1985	1	833	0.963	802
	2	846	0.874	739
	3	860	1.063	914
	4	874	1.103	964

predict demand for a product (dependent variable) as a function of these independent variables.

1. Advertising expenditure for the product;
2. Price of the product;
3. Consumer discretionary income.

Thus, when a causal forecasting model is employed, the forecaster attempts to determine the underlying relationship between the dependent variable and the independent variable(s) and then uses this relationship to forecast future values of the dependent variable. In a sense, the use of a causal model allows the interjection of subjectivity into the forecasting process in the choice of the independent variables to be considered.

5.6.2.1 REGRESSION METHODS

As was previously noted, the forecaster often wants to study the relationship that may exist between several variables, hoping that a relationship can be found that is useful in forecasting a particular variable. The forecast will be expressed as a function of a certain number of factors that determine its outcome. Such forecasts will not necessarily use time as the variable to explain demand, and therefore can be employed for forecasting horizons of longer duration than those for which time series analysis and projection methods are used. Causal forecasting approaches such as these are known as *regression methods*. It is important to note at the outset of our discussion that while regression methods reveal and measure relationships among variables, they do not prove that an underlying causal relationship actually exists.

In performing a regression analysis for forecasting purposes, the following steps are necessary.

1. Select the variable you are interested in forecasting (Y, the dependent variable), and those variables that you know from theory or experience are functionally related to $Y(X_1, X_2, \ldots, X_m$, the independent variables). For example, the demand for a product (quantity sold) might be expressed solely as a function of the price of the product

Demand for product, Y
$$= f(\text{price of product, } X_1) \quad (5.47)$$

or it might be expressed as a function of several factors, such as the price of product, GNP level, advertising expenditures, and research and development expenditures

Demand for product, Y
$$= f(\text{price of product, } X_1; \text{ GNP level, } X_2; \text{ advertising expenditures, } X_3; \text{ research and development expenditures, } X_4) \quad (5.48)$$

When there is only one independent variable present (as in Eq. 5.47), the method of *simple regression* is appropriate. When two or more independent variables are used (as in Eq. 5.48), the method of *multiple regression* is appropriate. Note that both simple and multiple regression involve functional forms of relationships that extend beyond simply using time factors.

2. Collect data that indicate the corresponding values of the dependent and independent variable(s) being considered. This sample of data should be taken in a careful and accurate manner, and the larger the sample, the more accurate the regression results will be.

3. Plot the relationship between the dependent

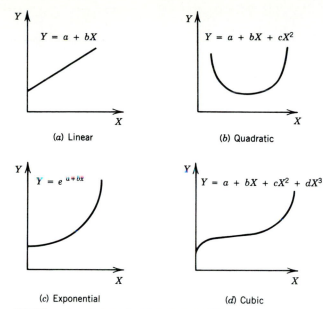

FIGURE 5.12   PLOTS OF DIFFERENT FORMS OF FUNCTIONAL RELATIONS.

variable, Y, and each of the independent variables, X_i, $i = 1, 2, \ldots, m$. This plot, called a *scatter diagram*, is used to determine the form of the relationship between the dependent and independent variables. Some typical relationships are shown in Figure 5.12. Standard regression methods can deal only with linear relationships, that is, the parameters of the regression equation can only be estimated using linear relationships. This is not a major limitation, however, because many nonlinear functions can be transformed into linear functions. For example, consider the nonlinear (exponential) relationship shown in Figure 5.12c.

$$Y = e^{a+bX} \qquad (5.49)$$

Taking the natural logarithm of both sides of Eq. 5.49 gives

$$\log_e Y = (a + bX)(\log_e e)$$
$$= a + bX, \quad \text{since } \log_e e = 1 \quad (5.50)$$

Thus, by using the $\log_e Y$ instead of Y, we have determined a linear functional form. Equation 5.50 is a linear relationship and its parameters,

a and b, can be estimated using simple regression.

4. Propose a regression model that relates the dependent variable to the independent variable (s), using the scatter diagram (s). This is probably the most difficult aspect of regression modeling, and typically requires the judgement and experience of the forecaster. In most instances the most appropriate form that can be employed is the multivariate linear model

$$Y = a + b_1 X_1 + b_2 X_2 + b_3 X_3$$
$$+ \cdots + b_m X_m \quad (5.51)$$

Recall that we indicated that multiple regression involves the determination of the mathematical relationship between a dependent variable and two or more independent variables. The mathematical complexities of multiple regression are beyond the scope of an introductory text such as this, however, so we focus our attention on simple linear regression as a means of providing an introduction to the general concept of regression analysis.

5. Compute the coefficients of the regression model. Remember that we are now focusing

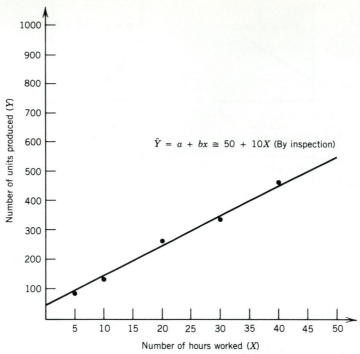

FIGURE 5.13 FORECASTING NUMBER OF UNITS PRODUCED AS A FUNCTION OF NUMBER OF HOURS WORKED.

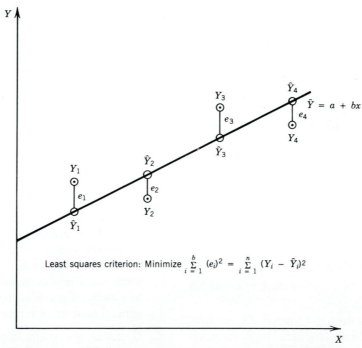

FIGURE 5.14 SIMPLE LINEAR REGRESSION—LEAST SQUARES METHOD.

on the simple linear regression relationship $Y = a + bX_1$ and wish to determine the value of a, called the *regression constant* or *intercept*, and the value of b, called the *slope*. There are several methods that can be used to estimate the values of a and b, with the most straightforward being that of simply plotting the historical observations for the Y and X values and then drawing a straight line that seems to "fit" the points. The values of a and b can then be read directly off such a graph. Figure 5.13 presents such a graph, in which Y (dependent variable) is the number of units produced, and X (independent variable) is the number of hours worked. Note that this graph was produced using a very limited number of data points (five, in this instance). Note also that the values of a and b can be estimated directly from the straight line that has been passed through the five data points.

A straight line fitted in such an inspective manner is a useful approximation, but a more accurate procedure needs to be developed. The procedure that is employed is called the method of *least squares*. The rationale of the method of least squares is that the square of the distance between the actual observation and the fitted regression line should be minimized by the appropriate choice of a and b. To illustrate, consider Figure 5.14. In this figure the observed (actual) values are labeled Y_1 Y_2, Y_3, and Y_4; the points estimated by the fitted regression line are labeled $\hat{Y}_1$, $\hat{Y}_2$, $\hat{Y}_3$, and $\hat{Y}_4$; and the deviation from the fitted regression line are labeled e_1, e_2, e_3, and e_4. Each of the deviations can be computed as $e_i = Y_i - \hat{Y}_i$, and any value on the fitted regression line can be computed as $\hat{Y}_i = a + bX_i$. The least squares criterion is employed to determine the values of a and b in such a way that the sum of the squared deviations between the actual and forecasted values, $\Sigma_{i=1}^{n} (e_i)^2 = \Sigma_{i=1}^{n} (Y_i - \hat{Y}_i)^2$ is as small as possible. This implies that we should

$$\text{Minimize } \sum_{i=1}^{n} (Y_i - \hat{Y}_i)^2$$

$$= \sum_{i=1}^{n} [Y_i - (a + bX_i)]^2 \quad (5.52)$$

By differentiating[2] this expression with respect to a and b, and setting the corresponding derivatives equal to zero, we obtain

$$b = \frac{n \sum_{i=1}^{n} X_i Y_i - \sum_{i=1}^{n} X_i \sum_{i=1}^{n} Y_i}{n \sum_{i=1}^{n} X_i^2 - \left(\sum_{i=1}^{n} X_i\right)^2}$$

$$= \frac{\sum_{i=1}^{n} (X_i - \bar{X})(Y_i - \bar{Y})}{\sum_{i=1}^{n} (X_i - \bar{X})^2} \quad (5.53)$$

$$a = \frac{\sum_{i=1}^{n} Y_i}{n} - b \frac{\sum_{i=1}^{n} X_i}{n} = \bar{Y} - b\bar{X} \quad (5.54)$$

WHERE

n = number of observations (data points) used to fit the regression line.

To illustrate the procedure involved in computing a and b, Table 5.15 uses the example shown earlier in Figure 5.13. The relevant computations and the resulting equations for the regression line were obtained using Eqs. 5.52 and 5.53.

$$\bar{Y} = \frac{1290}{5} = 258 \qquad \bar{X} = \frac{105}{5} = 21 \quad (5.55)$$

$$b = \frac{n \sum_{i=1}^{n} X_i Y_i - \sum_{i=1}^{n} X_i \sum_{i=1}^{n} Y_i}{n \sum_{i=1}^{n} X_i^2 - \left(\sum_{i=1}^{n} X_i\right)^2}$$

$$= \frac{5(35,650) - (105)(1290)}{5(3025) - (105)^2}$$

$$= \frac{178,250 - 135,450}{15,125 - 11,025}$$

$$= \frac{42,800}{4100} = 10.4 \quad (5.56)$$

[2]For purposes of simplicity we omit the detailed steps involved in this differentiation process and focus only on its results. A brief introduction to differentiation is provided in Appendix B.

TABLE 5.15 SIMPLE LINEAR REGRESSION COMPUTATIONS

DATA POINT i	UNITS PRODUCED Y_i	HOURS WORKED X_i	Y_i^2	X_i^2	X_iY_i
1	90	5	8100	25	450
2	140	10	19,600	100	1400
3	260	20	67,600	400	5200
4	340	30	115,600	900	10,200
5	460	40	211,600	1600	18,400
Totals	$\sum_{t=1}^{5} Y_i = 1290$	$\sum_{i=1}^{5} X_i = 105$	$\sum_{i=1}^{5} Y_i^2 = 422{,}500$	$\sum_{i=1}^{5} X_i^2 = 3025$	$\sum_{i=1}^{5} X_iY_i = 35{,}650$

$$a = \overline{Y} - b\overline{X} = 258 - 10.4(21)$$
$$= 258 - 218.4 = 39.6 \qquad (5.57)$$

Thus,

$$\hat{Y} = a + bX = 39.6 + 10.4X. \qquad (5.58)$$

Note the agreement between what we have just computed and what we obtained earlier by simple inspection of Figure 5.13.

6. Compute a measure of the efficiency or accuracy of the fitted regression model and measure the degree of correlation among the variables. One commonly used measure of the efficiency of the fitted regression model is the standard error of the estimate,[3] defined as

Standard error of the estimate (SEE)

$$= \sqrt{\frac{\sum_{i=1}^{n} (Y_i - \hat{Y}_i)^2}{n - 2}} \qquad (5.59)$$

The standard error of the estimate is similar to the standard deviation except that it is based on the mean square vertical deviations of the actual observations from the fitted regression line rather than on the deviations from the mean. Computations of the standard error of the estimate allow the forecaster to compare regression models and to make statements about confidence intervals for the predicted values of Y_i. If we assume that demand is normally distributed about the fitted regression line, as shown in Figure 5.15, a 68 percent confidence interval is obtained by moving ± 1 standard errors of the estimate from the predicted value. Similarly, a 95 percent confidence interval is obtained by moving ± 2 standard errors of the estimate from the predicted values.

For example, if the fitted regression model is

$$\hat{Y}_i = 100 + 10X_i \qquad (5.60)$$

then the predicted value of $\hat{Y}_i$ for $X_i = 2$ is

$$\hat{Y}_i = 100 + 10(2) = 120 \qquad (5.61)$$

If the corresponding value of SEE $= 5$, then the forecaster can state the following. 68 percent confidence interval

$$\text{Prob}(\hat{Y}_i - 1 \text{ SEE} \leq \text{true value of } Y_i$$
$$\leq \hat{Y}_i + 1 \text{ SEE}) = .68$$

$$\text{Prob}(120 - 5 \leq \text{true value of } Y_i$$
$$\leq 120 + 5) = .68$$

$$\text{Prob}(115 \leq \text{true value of } Y_i$$
$$\leq 125) = .68 \qquad (5.62)$$

---

[3]For simple linear regression, in general, the denominator in this expression is $n - k$, where k is the number of regression constants.

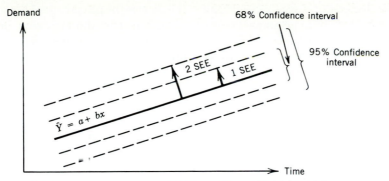

FIGURE 5.15   CONFIDENCE INTERVALS—FITTED REGRESSION LINE.

95 percent confidence interval

$$\text{Prob}(\hat{Y}_i - 2\ \text{SEE} \leq \text{true value of } Y_i$$
$$\leq \hat{Y}_i + 2\ \text{SEE}) = .95$$

$$\text{Prob}(120 - 2(5) \leq \text{true value of } Y_i$$
$$\leq 120 + 2(5)) = .95$$

$$\text{Prob}(110 \leq \text{true value of } Y_i$$
$$\leq 130) = .95 \tag{5.63}$$

Naturally, the smaller the value of the standard error of the estimate, the more accurate the model is.

A second commonly used measure of model efficiency is the *correlation coefficient*, r. The correlation coefficient is a relative measure of the association between the independent and dependent variables. It can vary from 0 (indicating no correlation) to ±1 (indicating perfect correlation). When the correlation coefficient is greater than zero, the two variables are said to be positively correlated, and when it is less than zero they are said to be negatively correlated. A *positive* correlation coefficient indicates that the independent and dependent variables increase or decrease in the same manner. A *negative* correlation coefficient indicates that the independent variable increases while the

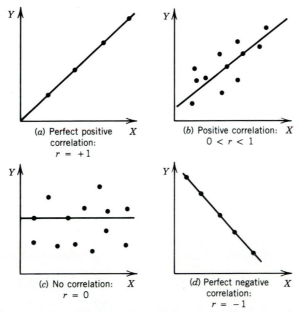

(a) Perfect positive correlation:
$r = +1$

(b) Positive correlation:
$0 < r < 1$

(c) No correlation:
$r = 0$

(d) Perfect negative correlation:
$r = -1$

FIGURE 5.16   EXAMPLES OF VARIOUS VALUES OF THE CORRELATION COEFFICIENT.

dependent variable decreases, or vice versa. Figure 5.16 shows four plots that illustrate various values of the correlation coefficient. The sign of the correlation coefficient is always the same as the sign of the regression coefficient, b, in a simple regression model. The correlation coefficient is computed as

Correlation coefficient (r)

$$= \frac{n \sum_{i=1}^{n} X_i Y_i - \sum_{i=1}^{n} X_i \sum_{i=1}^{n} Y_i}{\sqrt{\left[n \sum_{i=1}^{n} X_i^2 - \left(\sum_{i=1}^{n} X_i \right)^2 \right] \left[n \sum_{i=1}^{n} Y_i^2 - \left(\sum_{i=1}^{n} Y_i \right)^2 \right]}}$$

(5.64)

The square of the correlation coefficient, referred to as the *coefficient of determination*, is also a useful measure of regression model accuracy. It can be shown that the coefficient of determination is the ratio of the variation in the data explained by the fitted regression line to the total variation in the data. The coefficient of determination is computed as

$$r^2 = \frac{\text{Sum of explained variation in the data}}{\text{Sum of total variation in the data}}$$

$$= \frac{\sum_{i=1}^{n} (\hat{Y}_i - \bar{Y})^2}{\sum_{i=1}^{n} (Y_i - \bar{Y})^2}$$

$$= \frac{\left(n \sum_{i=1}^{n} X_i Y_i - \sum_{i=1}^{n} X_i \sum_{i=1}^{n} Y_i \right) es2}{\left[n \sum_{i=1}^{n} X_i^2 - \left(\sum_{i=1}^{n} X_i \right)^2 \right] \left[n \sum_{i=1}^{n} Y_i^2 - \left(\sum_{i=1}^{n} Y_i \right)^2 \right]}$$

(5.65)

It indicates the percentage of the total variation that is explained by the regression line, and measures how well the observations fit around the regression line.

The calculation of the standard error of the estimate, the correlation coefficient, and the coefficient of determination can be illustrated using the data from our previous example. These computations are summarized in Table 5.16 and what follows.

Standard error of the estimate (SEE)

$$= \sqrt{\frac{\sum_{i=1}^{n} (Y_i - \hat{Y}_i)^2}{n - 2}} = \sqrt{\frac{323.2}{5 - 2}} = \sqrt{\frac{323.2}{3}}$$

$$= \sqrt{107.73} = 10.4$$

(5.66)

Correlation coefficient (r)

$$= \frac{n \sum_{i=1}^{n} X_i Y_i - \sum_{i=1}^{n} X_i \sum_{i=1}^{n} Y_i}{\sqrt{\left[n \sum_{i=1}^{n} X_i^2 - \left(\sum_{i=1}^{n} X_i \right)^2 \right] \left[n \sum_{i=1}^{n} Y_i - \left(\sum_{i=1}^{n} Y_i \right)^2 \right]}}$$

$$= \frac{5(35,650) - (105)(1290)}{\sqrt{[(5)(3025) - 11,025][5(422,500) - 1,664,100]}}$$

$$= \frac{178,250 - 135,450}{\sqrt{[4100][448,400]}}$$

$$= \frac{42,800}{42,877} = 0.998$$

(5.67)

TABLE 5.16 COMPUTATION OF STANDARD ERROR OF THE ESTIMATE, CORRELATION COEFFICIENT, AND COEFFICIENT OF MULTIPLE DETERMINATION

Y_i	X_i	Y_i	$(Y_i - \hat{Y}_i)$	$(Y_i - \hat{Y}_i)^2$	$(Y_i - \bar{Y})$	$(Y_i - \bar{Y})^2$	$(\hat{Y}_i - \bar{Y})$	$(\hat{Y}_i - \bar{Y})^2$
90	5	9.16	−1.6	2.56	−168	28,224	−166.4	27,689
140	10	143.6	−3.6	12.96	−118	13,924	−114.4	13,087
260	20	247.6	12.4	153.76	2	4	−10.4	108
340	30	351.6	−11.6	134.56	82	6724	93.6	8761
460	40	455.6	4.4	19.36	202	40,804	197.6	39,046
				$\sum_{i=1}^{5} = 323.2$		$\sum_{i=1}^{5} = 89,680$		$\sum_{i=1}^{5} = 88,691$

Coefficient of determination (r^2)

$$= \frac{\sum_{i=1}^{n} (\hat{Y}_i - \overline{Y})^2}{\sum_{i=1}^{n} (Y_i - \overline{Y})^2}$$

$$= \frac{88,691}{89,680} = 0.989 \qquad (5.68)$$

The computations summarized in Table 5.16 and Eqs. 5.66–5.68 are not too complicated, mainly because a small number of data points (i.e., five) were considered. Even the computations of the parameters of the simple regression equation become difficult as the number of data points increases, however. Also, while we really aren't going to consider multiple regression, the determination of the parameters of the multiple regression equation is always a difficult task to do manually.

In practice today, most simple and multiple regression analyses are done using computer packages that only require the user to input data. Among the computer packages that perform regression analyses are the following.

1. BMD (Biomedical Computer Programs);
2. SPSS (Statistical Packages for the Social Sciences);
3. SAS (Statistical Analysis System).

The latter two packages have been available on mainframe computers for several years, and recently have been implemented on microcomputers.

When we attempt to use regression methods in making forecasts, what we are doing is making a statistical inference from a particular sample to the parent population. In order to use regression analysis to make valid inferences about the parent population from the sample data, certain assumptions must be satisfied.

Assumption 1. Linearity: The fitting of a straight line to sample data assumes that the true, or population, relationship must also be linear. This underlying (linear) relationship may be expressed in the form

$$\hat{Y}_i = a + bX_i + \epsilon_i \qquad (5.69)$$

where a and b are the true (but unknown) parameters of the regression line, and ϵ_i is the deviation of an actual value, Y_i, from the value $\hat{Y}_i$, predicted by the regression line

$$\epsilon_i = Y_i - \hat{Y}_i \qquad (5.70)$$

Assumption 2. Homoscedasticity: This refers to the property in which the standard deviations of the ϵ_i values are the same for all the values of the X_i. In other words, homoscedasticity means that there is a uniform scatter or dispersion of data points about the regression line. In Figure 5.17, examples illustrating when this assumption is valid and when it is invalid are presented. In the uniform scatter plot the data points are uniformly dispersed around the regression line. In the nonuniform scatter plot the data points are narrowly dispersed around the regression line for small values of X, but they become widely dispersed as the value of X increases.

Assumption 3. Independence of the ϵ_i: This assumption means that the deviation of one data point with respect to the regression line is not related to the deviation of any other data point with respect to the regression line. This assumption of independence of the ϵ_i about the regression line is often not met for time series data, as time series data often have a definite cycle in which data points are related (i.e., are not independent). In Figure 5.18, examples illustrating independence and dependence of the ϵ_i values are shown. In the plot showing independence there is no particular pattern to the data points. In the plot showing dependence however, there is a definite cyclical pattern to the data points.

Assumption 4. Normal Distribution of the ϵ_i: This assumption means that the distribution of data points above and below the regression line follows a normal curve. This will result in the ϵ_i values being

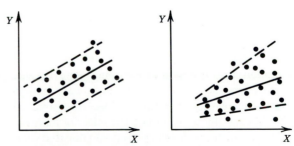

FIGURE 5.17 EXAMPLES OF UNIFORM AND NONUNIFORM SCATTER OF POINTS ABOUT THE REGRESSION LINE.

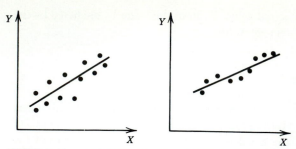

FIGURE 5.18 INDEPENDENCE AND DEPENDENCE OF THE ϵ_i VALUES.

normally distributed, with a mean value of zero. The regression line will pass through the expected values of the Y_i, given the values of the X_i.

When these four assumptions are met for the sample data used to compute the regression equation, the linear regression coefficients and the standard error of the estimate computed from the sample are good estimates of the true population values.

Two other problems sometimes arise in the use of regression methods. The first problem is known as *multicollinearity*, and exists in multiple regression models when two or more variables are themselves highly correlated. When multicollinearity occurs, the significance and accuracy of the multiple regression results can be affected. Usually, the forecaster tries to minimize the effects of multicollinearity by eliminating one of the pair of independent variables that have a high ($\geq .70$) simple correlation. Even though we are not going to consider multiple regression to any great extent, you should be aware of multicollinearity.

A second problem is that of *spurious correlation*, which occurs when two or more variables have the appearance of being highly correlated when, in reality, they are not. For example, there has long been a high correlation between church attendance figures and alcoholic consumption in the United States. This high correlation has probably been due mainly to the general increase in population over time. The problem of spurious correlation is fairly common to business and economic data because many of the factors underlying the data are increasing or decreasing over time. Thus, the forecaster should carefully try to isolate the effect of increases or decreases due to time before concluding that some strong relationship exists between a set of variables.

5.6.2.2 ECONOMETRIC MODELS

Another type of causal approach to forecasting involves econometric models. An econometric model is a set of simultaneous linear equations involving several interdependent variables. Econometric models typically employ systems of multiple regression equations to predict sales for a single firm, sales for an entire industry, demand for a particular product or commodity, or economic factors for a geographic region. Each of the regression equations in an econometric model involves the effect of particular external, or exogenous, variable(s) on the dependent variable that is being forecast.

An example of a very simplistic econometric model has been suggested by Makridakis and Wheelwright.[4] It consists of the following system of simultaneous equations.

$$
\begin{aligned}
\text{Sales} &= f(\text{GNP, price, advertising}) \\
\text{Production cost} &= f(\text{number of units produced, inventories, labor costs, material cost}) \\
\text{Selling expenses} &= f(\text{advertising, other selling expenses}) \\
\text{Advertising} &= f(\text{sales}) \\
\text{Price} &= f(\text{production cost, selling expenses, administrative overhead, profit})
\end{aligned}
$$
(5.71)

This set of five simultaneous equations expresses sales and its independent variables (i.e., GNP, price and advertising) as a function of each other and other external factors. For example, price is related to production cost, which in turn is a function of several other variables.

The objective in econometric modeling is to simultaneously solve all of the regression equations and obtain the parameters of the model. Unfortunately, a large number of equations may be necessary in order to capture the complex interactions among the large number of interdependent variables that affect the variable being forecasted. Thus, econometric models tend to become very complex, and econometric analysis usually requires strong technical expertise and a large-scale computer. As noted

[4]Spyros Makridakis and Steven C. Wheelwright, *Forecasting: Methods and Applications*. New York: Wiley, 1977, p. 231.

earlier in Table 5.4, econometric analysis tends to produce accurate forecasting results, but it is also expensive to accomplish. For this reason, its use tends to be restricted to large organizations that have the technical and computer capability necessary for its successful implementation.

There are several commercially available econometric models currently available. Among them are

1. Chase Manhattan Bank Econometrics Model;
2. Data Resources, Inc., Econometrics Model;
3. General Electric Forecasting Service Model.

The Wharton Econometrics model, for example, has over 200 equations and 80 external variables. It was very costly to develop, and is costly to maintain. The cost of using such services, however, is only a small fraction of the cost of developing and maintaining one's own econometric model.

5.7 SUMMARY

In this chapter we have provided an introduction to some of the basic methods used in forecasting. First, we indicated the factors that need to be considered in selecting a forecasting method. Next, we considered two broad categories of forecasting, namely qualitative forecasting and statistical forecasting approaches. Both of these broad approaches were then addressed in detail, and several specific forecasting techniques in each category examined. Measures for evaluating forecasting accuracy were also considered. In conclusion, it is important to emphasize that forecasting is a major field of inquiry. In this chapter we have only presented a brief introduction to this vast and important area of study.

GLOSSARY

Alpha   A constant whose value is between 0 and 1 that is used in computing an exponentially smoothed forecast for a time series.

Bias   A measure of forecasting error that is computed as the algebraic sum of the actual forecasting errors for all periods divided by the total number of periods evaluated. The bias measures the average of the forecast errors and indicates any tendency of overforecast or underforecast.

Causal Forecasting Model   A type of forecasting model that assumes that the factor to be forecast exhibits a cause–effect relationship with one or more other factors. Regression models and econometric models are examples of this type of forecasting approach.

Census II   A time series decomposition method of forecasting that has been developed and utilized by the U.S. Bureau of the Census.

Decomposition Method   An approach to forecasting in which the time series is analyzed and decomposed into trend, cyclical, seasonal, and random components. These components are then extrapolated into the future, and recombined to produce forecasts.

Delphi Method   A qualitative forecasting approach that systematically uses the judgment of a group of experts in arriving at a forecast.

Demand Pattern   General tendency of the time series, which is typically composed of trend, cycle, seasonal, and irregular components.

Dependent Variable   In regression analysis the variable being predicted or forecast as a function of one or more related variables is called the dependent variable.

Econometric Forecasting   An approach to forecasting that involves solving for the parameters of a simultaneous set of regression equations.

Forecasting Horizon   The length of time into the future for which forecasts are made. The forecasting horizon may be short-term (1 to 6 months), intermediate term (6 months to 2 years), or long-term (2 years to 5 years), depending on the purpose for which the forecast is to be used.

Homoscedasticity   The condition in which the error terms in a forecast have a constant variance over the range of the forecast.

Independent Variable   In regression analysis the variable used to predict the value of the dependent variable is called the independent variable.

Multicollinearity   The condition that exists when two or more variables are highly correlated.

Noise   The presence of randomness in a set of data.

Qualitative Forecasting   Qualitative forecasting relies on the judgment, experience, or intuition of the forecaster, and is most appropriate when information about the past cannot be obtained, or when it cannot be assumed that the past pattern will continue into the future.

Quantitative Forecasting   Quantitative forecasting rests on the assumption that quantitative information about the past is available, and that the pattern inherent in the past data can be expected to continue into the future.

Residual   The error term in a forecast that is computed by subtracting the forecast value from the actual value.

Single Exponential Smoothing   The most basic type of exponential smoothing in which the parameter α ($0.0 \leq \alpha \leq 1.0$) is used to smooth past data values and produce a forecast.

Spurious Correlation   The condition that exists when two or more variables have the appearance of being highly correlated, when they are not.

Selected References

Box, G.E.P., and G.M. Jenkins. 1976. *Time Series Analysis: Forecasting and Control.* San Francisco: Holden–Day.

Brown, R.G. 1963. *Smoothing, Forecasting and Prediction of Discrete Time Series.* Englewood Cliffs, N.J.: Prentice–Hall.

Chisholm, Roger K., and Gilbert R. Whitaker, Jr. 1971. *Forecasting Methods.* Homewood, Ill.: Irwin.

Centrom, M. 1971. *Industrial Applications of Technological Forecasting.* New York: Wiley.

Gross, C., and R. Peterson. 1976. *Business Forecasting.* Boston: Houghton–Mifflin.

Johnston, J. 1966. *Econometric Methods.* Englewood Cliffs, N.J.: Prentice–Hall.

Judge, George G., William E. Griffiths, R. Carter Hill, and Tsoug-Chao Lee. 1980. *The Theory and Practice of Econometrics.* New York: Wiley.

Makridakis, S., and S. Wheelwright. 1978. *Forecasting Methods and Applications.* New York: Wiley/Hamilton.

Wheelwright, S., and S. Makridakis. 1977. *Forecasting Methods for Management.* New York: Wiley.

Valentine, Lloyd M., and Carl A. Dauten. 1983. *Business Cycles and Forecasting.* Cincinnati: South-Western.

Discussion Questions

1. What is meant by the term "forecast"?

2. What is the difference between forecasting and prediction? Present an example of each.

3. What is a qualitative forecasting method?

4. What is a quantitative forecasting method?

5. What is a time series analysis forecasting method?

6. What is a causal forecasting method?

7. Explain why the forecasting time horizon is important in the choice of a forecasting method.

8. What are some of the factors that need to be considered in choosing a forecasting model?

9. Explain what is meant by the cost–accuracy tradeoff in forecasting model selection.

10. What is involved in time series analysis?

11. What are the advantages and disadvantages of making forecasts using moving averages?

12. What are the advantages and disadvantages of making forecasts using exponential smoothing?

13. What are the advantages and disadvantages of making forecasts using regression methods?

14. What are ways of measuring the forecasting error in an absolute manner?

15. What are ways of measuring the forecasting error in a relative manner?

16. What is an econometric forecasting model?

17. Name and describe the four components into which time series data are decomposed.

PROBLEMS

1. The Imprudent Insurance Company has had claims experience of the following nature for the past year.

MONTH	NUMBER OF CLAIMS
Jan.	1150
Feb.	1180
Mar.	1200

MONTH	NUMBER OF CLAIMS
Apr.	1000
May	1050
June	1100
July	1250
Aug.	1200
Sept.	1280
Oct.	1300
Nov.	1350
Dec.	1300

Using these data it would like to make forecasts for months 6–12 using the following models

a. Moving Average—3 periods
b. Moving Average—5 periods
c. Exponential Smoothing—$\alpha = .1$
d. Exponential Smoothing—$\alpha = .5$
e. Exponential Smoothing—$\alpha = .9$

In making these forecasts, use the actual data for months 3, 4, and 5 to initialize model a; the actual data for months 1, 2, 3, 4, and 5 to initialize model b; the average of the data for months 1, 2, 3, 4, and 5 to initialize models c, d, and e.

2. For Problem 1, for each of the forecasting models, compute the following measures of forecasting accuracy.

a. Standard deviation;
b. Mean absolute deviation;
c. Bias;
d. Coefficient of variation;
e. Relative forecasting error.

What conclusions can be drawn by comparing these measures of forecasting accuracy for the various forecasting models?

3. The Runner's Delight Company has had sales experience for its "Tike Nightfall" running shoe of the following nature for the past two years.

MONTH	YEAR 1	YEAR 2
Jan.	500	1300
Feb.	550	1700
Mar.	480	1500
Apr.	510	1800
May	490	2100

MONTH	YEAR 1	YEAR 2
June	530	2500
July	600	2700
Aug.	650	2600
Sept.	720	2900
Oct.	750	3200
Nov.	890	3500
Dec.	1050	4000

Using these data it would like to make forecast for months 8–24 using the following models

a. Moving average—7 months
b. Exponential smoothing—$\alpha = .2$
c. Exponential smoothing—$\alpha = .5$
d. Exponential smoothing—$\alpha = .9$

In making these forecasts, use the actual data for months 1–7 to initialize model a; the average of the data for months 1–7 to initialize models b, c, and d.

4. For Problem 3, for each of the forecasting models, compute the following measures of forecasting accuracy.

a. Standard deviation;
b. Mean absolute deviation;
c. Bias;
d. Coefficient of variation;
e. Relative forecasting error.

What conclusions can be drawn by comparing these measures of forecasting accuracy for the various forecasting models?

5. A company that manufactures camp stoves has experienced the following monthly demand.

MONTH	DEMAND FOR CAMP STOVE
Jan.	650
Feb.	700
Mar.	810
Apr.	800
May	900
June	980

a. Using a 3-month simple average, what would the forecast have been for April, May, and June?

b. Using a 3-month simple moving average, what would the forecast have been for April, May, and June?

c. Using a 3-month weighted moving average (weights of .2, .3, and .5), what would the forecast have been for April, May, and June?

d. Which of these three forecasting methods would you recommend for this company? Why?

6. A diesel engine manufacturer has experienced quarterly demand for its largest diesel engine as follows.

QUARTER NUMBER	DIESEL ENGINE DEMAND
1	50
2	52
3	48
4	50
5	49
6	46
7	48
8	44

a. Calculate a weighted moving average forecast for quarter 9, using a 3-quarter moving average model with the most recent period being weighted three times as heavily as each of the previous two periods.

b. Does the forecasting result you obtained in part a and a visual examination of the data indicate a better weighting scheme? Why?

7. A bank wishes to make a forecast of its future check processing requirements. It has collected the following set of data.

MONTH	ACTUAL NUMBER OF CHECKS PROCESSED	
	(YEAR 1)	(YEAR 2)
Jan.	52,000	72,000
Feb.	55,000	78,000
Mar.	58,000	84,000
Apr.	62,000	80,000
May	60,000	88,000
June	57,000	96,000
July	63,000	110,000
Aug.	65,000	105,000
Sept.	62,000	115,000
Oct.	70,000	130,000
Nov.	75,000	135,000
Dec.	77,000	140,000

a. Using these data make exponentially smoothed forecasts with α values of .1, .3, .5, .7, and .9.

b. Using these data make moving average forecasts with N values of 3, 5, and 7 months.

c. Assuming that the past pattern will extend into the future, what values of α and N should management select in order to minimize the forecasting errors? (*Note:* Select your own measure of forecasting error.)

8. Sales of the "Premier" leather briefcase have grown steadily during the past 10 years. Robert Maccum, President of the company, predicted in 1974 that sales of the "Premier" leather briefcase would be 500,000 units in 1975. Using the following information, and exponential smoothing with $\alpha = .30$, develop forecasts for 1976 through 1985.

YEAR	SALES
1975	545,000
1976	540,000
1977	550,000
1978	575,000
1979	600,000
1980	590,000
1981	620,000
1982	660,000
1983	710,000
1984	725,000
1985	?

9. For Problem 8, compute the following measures of forecasting accuracy

a. Standard deviation;
b. Mean absolute deviation.

10. Analyze the forecasting errors for the time series in Problem 8 by using a smoothing constant of $\alpha = .6$. Which smoothing constant produces the most accurate forecast?

11. The number of subassemblies used in a particular production process each week in the last 12 weeks is as follows.

WEEK	SUBASSEMBLIES USED IN PRODUCTION
1	400
2	410
3	430
4	440
5	460

WEEK	SUBASSEMBLIES USED IN PRODUCTION
6	450
7	480
8	520
9	580
10	600
11	610
12	630

The production manager, Ms. Jane Bryson, had originally forecast that 375 subassemblies would be used in week one. Using the information just presented and exponential smoothing with $\alpha = .25$, develop forecasts for weeks 2 through 12.

12. For Problem 11, compute the following measures of forecasting accuracy

   a. Coefficient of variation;
   b. Relative forecasting error.

13. Analyze the forecasting errors for the time series in Problem 11 by using a smoothing constant of $\alpha = .5$. Which smoothing constant produces the most accurate forecast?

14. The number of participants in a youth soccer program has had the following pattern over an 8-year time span.

YEAR	NUMBER OF PARTICIPANTS
1977	150
1978	230
1979	300
1980	450
1981	540
1982	600
1983	750
1984	800

   a. Plot this time series. What sort of a trend pattern is indicated by your plot?
   b. Estimate the trend equation from your plot.
   c. Determine the trend equation for this time series. (*Note:* Do not try to deseasonalize the time series.)

15. The percentage of games won for Hi Studley, football coach at Bearskin Tech, for the past 10 years is as follows.

YEAR	PERCENTAGE OF GAMES WON
1975	.800
1976	.750
1977	.600
1978	.750
1979	.500
1980	.500
1981	.400
1982	.500
1983	.400
1984	.333

a. Plot this time series. What sort of a trend pattern is indicated by your plot?

b. Estimate the trend equation from your plot.

c. Determine the trend equation for this time series. (*Note:* Do not try to deseasonalize the time series.)

16. Textbook sales at Ron Piley, and Daughters, have had the following pattern over the last 10 years.

YEAR	TOTAL TEXTBOOK SALES
1975	1,200,000
1976	1,400,000
1977	1,800,000
1978	2,200,000
1979	2,000,000
1980	2,100,000
1981	2,400,000
1982	3,000,000
1983	2,800,000
1984	3,100,000

a. Plot this time series. What sort of a trend pattern is indicated by your plot?

b. Estimate the trend equation from your plot.

c. Determine the trend equation for this time series. (*Note:* Do not try to deseasonalize the time series.)

17. A firm that manufactures disc brake systems for automobiles has kept records concerning its per unit costs over the past several years. In the table the firm's cost per unit over the 8-year time period is presented.

YEAR	COST/UNIT
1977	37.00
1978	35.00
1979	32.00
1980	33.00
1981	29.00
1982	25.00
1983	27.00
1984	26.00

   a. Plot this time series. What sort of a trend pattern is indicated by your plot?

   b. Estimate the trend equation from your plot.

   c. Determine the trend equation for this time series. (*Note:* Do not try to deseasonalize the time series.)

18. The quarterly sales data for a particular type of women's ski jacket for the past 4 years are as follows.

QUARTER \ YEAR	SALES, THOUSANDS			
	1981	1982	1983	1984
Quarter 1	$470	$570	$600	$620
Quarter 2	400	510	550	580
Quarter 3	600	570	640	800
Quarter 4	640	730	670	830

   a. Determine the four-quarter moving average values for this time series.

   b. Plot the quarterly sales data and the four-quarter moving average values.

   c. Determine the seasonal factors for the four quarters.

   d. Using these seasonal factors, deseasonalize the sales data.

   e. Graph the deseasonalized sales data.

   f. Determine the trend equation for these deseasonalized sales data.

19. The quarterly advertising cost data for a Mexican food chain for the past 4 years are shown in the table.

QUARTER \ YEAR	ADVERTISING COST, THOUSANDS			
	1981	1982	1983	1984
Quarter 1	$8	$12	$16	$21
Quarter 2	10	14	18	22
Quarter 3	7	15	18	24
Quarter 4	11	17	20	26

   a. Determine the four-quarter moving average values for this time series.

   b. Plot the quarterly advertising cost data and the four-quarter moving average values.

   c. Determine the seasonal factors for the four quarters.

   d. Using the seasonal factors, deseasonalize the advertising cost data.

e. Graph the deseasonalized cost data.

f. Determine the trend equation for these deseasonalized cost data.

20. The quarterly attendance figures for the St. Andrews Multi-Cinema in Columbia, South Carolina, for a 4-year period is shown in the table.

QUARTER / YEAR	ATTENDANCE, THOUSANDS			
	1980	1981	1982	1983
Quarter 1	60	76	88	98
Quarter 2	68	78	94	104
Quarter 3	72	82	98	110
Quarter 4	80	90	100	116

a. Determine the four-quarter moving average values for this time series.

b. Plot the quarterly attendance data and the four-quarter moving average values.

c. Determine the seasonal factors for the four quarters.

d. Using these seasonal factors, deseasonalize the attendance data.

e. Graph the deseasonalized attendance data.

f. Determine the trend equation for these deseasonalized attendance data.

21. Determine the linear regression equation for the following data.

Month	1	2	3	4	5	6	7	8	9	10	11	12
Demand	31	36	36	37	38	43	45	50	55	60	63	69

Using the computed linear regression equation, what would be the next month forecast?

22. Consider the following set of cost and production data for the Able Company.

TOTAL COST (in $1000)	UNITS PRODUCED (in 1000s)
35	5
13	2
40	6
52	7
65	10
60	9

a. Determine the linear regression equation for this set of data.

b. Compute the standard error of the estimate (SEE)

c. Compute the correlation coefficient, r

d. Compute the coefficient of determination, r^2

23. Data on test scores of various salespeople and their subsequent productivity are shown in the following table.

SALESPERSON	TEST SCORE	SALES PRODUCTIVITY ($000)
A	50	450
B	70	610
C	60	500
D	40	400
E	30	280
F	100	1000
G	90	800
H	65	570
I	80	740
J	55	500
K	70	610
L	75	680
M	60	550
N	40	350
O	45	380

a. Plot these data on a graph with the test scores as the X-axis and the sales productivity as the Y-axis.

b. Determine the linear regression equation for this set of data.

c. What sales productivity would you expect for a salesperson having a test score of 85?

d. Compute SEE.

e. Compute r.

f. Compute r^2.

g. Compute a 95 percent confidence interval for the forecast you made for the salesperson having a test score of 85.

24. The manufacturer of a new type of women's lipstick, "Fire and Ice," is trying to determine how television advertising expenditures affect lipstick sales. Sales revenue and advertising expenditure data indicate the following.

TIME PERIOD	LIPSTICK SALES ($000)	ADVERTISING EXPENDITURES ($000)
1	100	20
2	110	30
3	130	35
4	180	40
5	220	50
6	290	55
7	350	60
8	410	70

TIME PERIOD	LIPSTICK SALES ($000)	ADVERTISING EXPENDITURES ($000)
9	460	90
10	500	100
11	520	100
12	540	110
13	600	150
14	650	150
15	700	170

a. Plot these data on a graph with the lipstick sales as the y-axis and the advertising expenditures as the x-axis.
b. Determine the linear regression equation for this set of data.
c. What level of lipstick sales would you expect for an advertising expenditure of $200,000?
d. Compute SEE.
e. Compute r^2.
f. Compute r.
g. Compute a 95 percent confidence interval for the forecast you made for an advertising expenditure of $200,000.

Application Review 1

Use of the Delphi Technique In a Dutch Elm Disease Sanitation Program

At the beginning of 1977 the city of Minneapolis, Minnesota, had approximately 200,000 elm trees distributed among private land, boulevard strips, parks, and wild areas. The city was committed to maintaining an "urban forest" atmosphere and was greatly concerned about the problem associated with Dutch elm disease.

The Dutch elm disease fungus was first discovered in the United States in 1930 on the East Coast. Since then it spread westward and has destroyed elm trees all over the United States. The Dutch elm disease fungus is spread by English Bark Beetles that breed in the diseased trees, and there is no effective chemical treatment for the disease. Basically, diseased elm trees must be removed before they become a breeding ground for the fungus-carrying beetle.

In 1977, Minneapolis lost 31,745 trees to Dutch elm disease. This loss was approximately 16 percent of the city's existing tree population, and 450 percent of the loss that had originally been forecast.

As a result of the 1977 experience, the city's Park Board, which had responsibility for the management and control of the Dutch elm disease problem, became greatly concerned. They utilized a management science consulting team from the University of Minnesota in formulating the problem and developing a model for its solution.

The management science team quickly realized that to a large extent the problems encountered in 1977 were due to the large disparity between the 7000 trees that were forecasted to be lost and the 31,754 trees that were actually lost.

Source: Chervany, Norman L., John C. Anderson, P. George Benson, and Arthur V. Hill, "A management science approach to a Dutch elm disease sanitation program" (April 1980), *Interfaces,* Vol. 10, No. 2, pp. 108–114.

Although the original forecast had been done in a conscientious manner by the Park Board, it was based on limited historical data. Further, there were no relevant Dutch elm disease forecasting models available in the tree pathology literature.

Because of the scarcity of historical data and the lack of specific forecasting models, it was decided to develop the forecast of future losses based on the opinions of four Dutch elm disease experts. These four experts were the Director of Forestry for the Park Board, two professors from the Department of Plant Pathology at the University of Minnesota, and a research entomologist from the U.S. Forestry Service. The first three experts were selected because of their intimate knowledge of the geographical and climatological conditions in Minneapolis, while the last expert was chosen because of his extensive research experience in Dutch elm disease pathology and control.

To initiate the forecasting process a five-stage interview process was employed to solicit a probability distribution for each of the four experts concerning the total number of infected trees to be expected in Minneapolis in 1978. Additionally, the experts were asked to develop scenarios for explaining the occurrence of either an extremely low or an extremely high number of diseased elms in 1978. Next, the Delphi process was used to allow each of the four experts to evaluate the forecasts of the other three experts, and to make changes in their forecasts if so desired.

All four of the experts stood firm with their original forecasts. These forecasts were then averaged, using equal weights, to obtain a single probability distribution reflecting the combined beliefs of all four experts.

Once it had been developed, the aggregate distribution was used as a forecast for a simulation study of the management process involved in identifying and removing diseased elms. The modal forecast value for diseased elms for 1978, using this aggregate distribution, was in the range of 20,000 to 22,500 trees. The actual number of tree losses from Dutch elm disease in 1978 totaled 20,817. Consequently, this Delphi-based forecasting approach, using the panel of four experts, proved to be very accurate and was a major positive input to the overall management and control of the Dutch elm disease problem.

Application Review 2
Cereal Consumption Forecasting Using Regression

In the mid-1970s the Ralston Purina Company of St. Louis, Missouri, found that it had a need for developing an "industry forecasting system" for a number of its major products. The term "industry forecast" was defined to mean total industry sales in pounds or, in effect, U.S. domestic consumption demand. It was desired that the industry forecasting system provide the following types of forecasts.

1. A 1-year forecast on a monthly basis;
2. A 2-year forecast on a quarterly basis;
3. A 5-year forecast on a yearly basis.

The company was concerned about three major industries: (1) ready-to-eat cereals; (2) cat foods; and (3) dog foods. Initial forecasting efforts focused on the ready-to-eat cereals industry.

The data sources available for this forecasting project were twofold in nature. First, historical industry sales volume and sales dollar data were available from the

Source: Unpublished Ralston Purina Company Technical Report. The author would like to acknowledge the assistance of P. Michael Hattery in this forecasting project, as well as the administrative support of Dr. P. K. Misra.

company's marketing research department. Approximately 52 time periods of data were available. Second, external government documents were a source of various types of time series data.

The choice of the forecasting methodology to be employed in this particular situation was dependent on the following factors.

1. The context of the forecast;
2. The relevance and availability of historical data;
3. The degree of forecasting accuracy desired;
4. The time horizon to be forecast;
5. The cost–benefit (or value) of the forecast to the company;
6. The time available for making the forecasting analysis.

Observe that these factors are basically the same as those discussed in Section 5.2. In making the choice of a forecasting methodology, three broad types of forecasting techniques were considered. These techniques were

1. Qualitative techniques;
2. Times series analysis and projection techniques;
3. Causal models.

Since the major objective for this project was the development of a *long-range* forecasting methodology, a causal forecasting technique was selected as being most appropriate, because causal models are good for predicting turning points and preparing long-range forecasts. A number of causal models were considered, including the following.

1. Regression models;
2. Econometric models;
3. Input–output models;

Among these causal models, it was decided that a regression model offered the most potential, from a cost–benefit and accuracy standpoint. From a time cost standpoint it simply was not possible to develop either an econometric or an input–output model, for U.S. cereal consumption. Similarly, it was not possible to easily identify leading indicator time series, and even if such time series could have been identified, they are not very accurate with respect to long-term forecasting.

Having made the decision to employ a regression approach to forecasting, the next consideration was that of the general form of the forecasting model. The general form of the regression forecasting model that was developed was as follows.

$$\text{Total U.S. cereal consumption (per time period)}$$
$$= f(\text{trend variable, external variables, seasonality}) \qquad (5.71)$$

Using this general model, the trend variable was isolated from the U.S. cereal consumption data. The initial test results indicate that a trend was present in the data, with a curvilinear trend model providing the best fit.

Next, a series of external variables was analyzed. It was determined that the price level for cereals and the income level of the United States were two exogenous variables that had a causal relationship to U.S. cereal consumption. The Consumer Price Index was employed to express both of these external variables in "real" or constant dollar terms.

Finally, a series of seasonal factors was computed using the original U.S. cereal consumption data.

A number of regression equations having the general form indicated by (5.71) and utilizing the trend variable and external variables were derived and tested. The best fitting regression equation that was obtained was found to have the following form.[5]

Total U.S. cereal consumption
$$= f(\text{curvilinear trend, real price level, real income level}) \qquad (5.72)$$

This regression equation had a coefficient of determination, $r^2 = .840$. Thus, a very good fitting regression equation was obtained.

---

[5]Specific regression coefficients are not presented because of proprietary reasons.

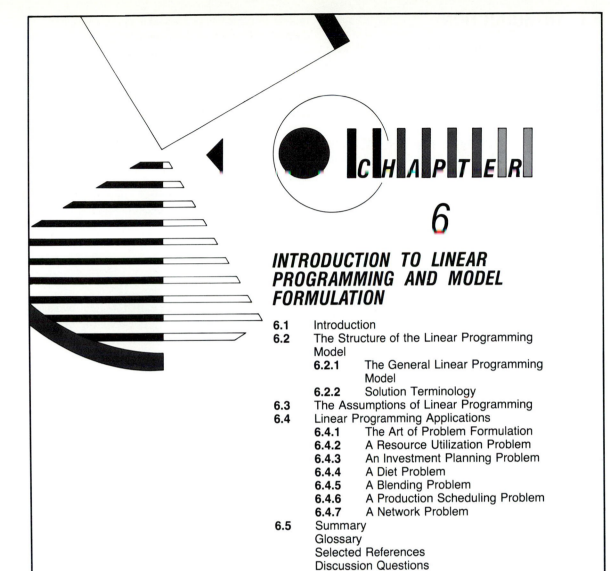

CHAPTER

6

INTRODUCTION TO LINEAR PROGRAMMING AND MODEL FORMULATION

6.1 INTRODUCTION

Linear programming should not be confused with computer programming. A computer program is a set of instructions to be executed by the computer. A linear program is a model that can be used to determine how to achieve an objective while satisfying all the basic requirements for a problem situation. It is a mathematical procedure that is applicable when the objective and requirements can be expressed as functions that are linear.

Linear programming typically deals with the problem of allocating limited resources in a fashion that maximizes return or minimizes cost. As a model, linear programming has been widely used in a variety of applications, including production planning, capital budgeting, advertising/promotion planning, product distribution, investment planning, and the analysis of governmental regulations. Undoubtedly, linear programming has had the widest impact of all modern quantitative methods. It has literally helped to save business and government billions of dollars.

In this chapter the primary concern is the formulation of the linear programming model for a variety of situations. The following chapter provides graphical representations of two-variable linear programming models and is used to introduce some of the fundamental concepts used in the solution procedure for linear programming. Chapters 8 and 9 deal with the mathematical solution, analysis, and interpretation of the model results.

6.2 THE STRUCTURE OF THE LINEAR PROGRAMMING MODEL

The structure of a linear programming model will be introduced by looking at a very simple product-mix application. In this product-mix problem several products are competing for the same production capacity. The problem is to decide which products should be produced and the production level of each. The actual selection is a function of both the limited resources and a specified objective. We assume that the objective is profit maximization.

A company is planning to produce two new products that we simply label A and B. These products have per unit profits of $5 and $8, respectively. Each unit of product

must be processed on two assembly lines for required production times as shown in Table 6.1.

In this situation management needs to determine how many units of product A and how many units of product B to produce in order to maximize profit given the limited resources of 60 and 40 hours on the two assembly lines. To formulate this problem as a mathematical programming model we symbolically represent the decisions required. That is, we let x_1 and x_2 represent the number of units of product A and product B to be produced. Also Z will represent profit. The profit function can then be constructed as

$$Z = 5x_1 + 8x_2 \qquad (6.1)$$

The variables x_1 and x_2 are called *decision variables* or *activity variables* and (6.1) is called the *objective function* for the model being constructed.

The limited resources must then also be related to the stated decision variables. The total number of hours on assembly line 1 used by the production of x_1 units of product A and x_2 units of product B is $(12x_1 + 4x_2)$. Similarly, the total number of hours used by the production of x_1 units of product A and x_2 units of product B is $(6x_1 + 5x_2)$. The restrictions on resource utilization are then

$$12x_1 + 4x_2 \le 60$$
$$6x_1 + 5x_2 \le 40 \qquad (6.2)$$

Since production quantities cannot be negative, we also require

$$x_1, x_2 \ge 0 \qquad (6.3)$$

The mathematical model that represents the decision problem stated above has as its objective (6.1), while (6.2) forms the set of *constraints* for this model. Equation 6.3 is called the *nonnegativity* con-

TABLE 6.1 REQUIRED PRODUCTION TIME

HOURS/UNIT	PRODUCT A	PRODUCT B	HOURS AVAILABLE
Line 1	12	4	60
Line 2	6	5	40

ditions for the model. Optimizing an objective subject to a set of restrictions is called *mathematical programming*. The mathematical problem that we have constructed here is a *linear programming model*, since all the functional relationships used to structure the model are linear.

To summarize, in the mathematical language of linear programming, the problem is to determine the values of x_1 and x_2 so as to

$$\text{Maximize } Z = 5x_1 + 8x_2 \qquad (6.4)$$

subject to (the restrictions)

$$12x_1 + 4x_2 \leq 60$$
$$6x_1 + 5x_2 \leq 40 \qquad (6.5)$$

with

$$x_1, x_2 \geq 0 \qquad (6.6)$$

6.2.1 THE GENERAL LINEAR PROGRAMMING MODEL

In the previous introductory example there were two limited resources (time on two assembly lines) to be allocated between two competing activities (two products). Now suppose that there are m limited resources to be allocated between n competing activities. The resources are indexed by i, where $i = 1, \ldots, m$ and the activities are indexed by j, where $j = 1, \ldots, n$. We let x_j be the level of activity j, and Z be the numerical value of the measure of benefit. We also define c_j to be the increase in Z that would result from a one unit increase in x_j. The parameter b_i denotes the amount of resource i available and a_{ij} represents the amount of resource i needed

for one unit of activity j. The set of data for this situation is given in Table 6.2.

Using the data from Table 6.1 we can formulate the general linear programming model for allocating m resources to n activities.

$$\text{Maximize } Z = c_1x_1 + c_2x_2 + \cdots + c_nx_n \qquad (6.7)$$

subject to

$$a_{11}x_1 + a_{12}x_2 + \cdots + a_{1n}x_n \leq b_1$$
$$a_{21}x_1 + a_{22}x_2 + \cdots + a_{2n}x_n \leq b_2$$
$$\vdots \qquad \vdots \qquad \qquad \vdots \qquad \vdots \qquad (6.8)$$
$$a_{m1}x_1 + a_{m2}x_2 + \cdots + a_{mn}x_n \leq b_m$$

with

$$x_1, x_2, \ldots, x_n \geq 0 \qquad (6.9)$$

We will refer to (6.7), (6.8), and (6.9) as the *standard form* for the linear programming problem. The standard form of the linear programming model is rewritten in (6.10), (6.11), and (6.12), using summation notation.

$$\text{Maximize } Z = \sum_{j=1}^{n} c_jx_j \qquad (6.10)$$

subject to

$$\sum_{j=1}^{n} a_{ij}x_j \leq b_i, \qquad i = 1, \ldots, m \qquad (6.11)$$

with

$$x_j \geq 0, \qquad j = 1, \ldots, n \qquad (6.12)$$

TABLE 6.2 DATA FOR THE GENERAL LINEAR PROGRAMMING MODEL

RESOURCE \ ACTIVITY	RESOURCE REQUIRED/UNIT				RESOURCE AVAILABLE
	1	2	$\cdots$	n	
1	a_{11}	a_{12}	$\cdots$	a_{1n}	b_1
2	a_{21}	a_{22}	$\cdots$	a_{2n}	b_2
$\vdots$	$\vdots$	$\vdots$	$\vdots$	$\vdots$	$\vdots$
m	a_{m1}	a_{m2}	$\cdots$	a_{mn}	b_m
Change in Z/Unit	c_1	c_2	$\cdots$	c_n	

Equation 6.10 is called the *objective function*, Eq. 6.11 is referred to as the set of *constraints*, and Eq. 6.12 is called the set of *nonnegativity conditions*. The x_j are called *decision variables*. The a_{ij}, b_i, and c_j are referred to as the *parameters* of the model.

We should note that the standard form of the linear programming model is not the only legitimate linear programming model. The objective may be to minimize rather than to maximize. Also some constraints may be of the form

$$a_{i1}x_1 + a_{i2}x_2 + \cdots + a_{in}x_n \geq b_i \qquad (6.13)$$

or

$$a_{i1}x_1 + a_{i2}x_2 + \cdots + a_{in}x_n = b_i \qquad (6.14)$$

Additionally the nonnegativity conditions may be deleted for a variable, allowing x_j to be unrestricted in sign. Any of the variations mentioned may be incorporated into the model of (6.10), (6.11), and (6.12) with the result being a linear programming model.

6.2.2 SOLUTION TERMINOLOGY

Any specification of the variables $(x_1, x_2, \ldots, x_n)$ that satisfy (6.11) in the linear programming model (6.10), (6.11), and (6.12) is called a *solution*. A *feasible solution* is a solution that also satisfies the nonnegativity conditions, (6.12). For example, in model (6.4), (6.5), and (6.6), $(x_1, x_2) = (2, 2)$ is a feasible solution; $(x_1, x_2) = (5, 2)$ is not a solution, while $(x_1, x_2) = (-1, 5)$ is a solution but not a feasible solution. Solution (5, 2) violates the first constraint in (6.5), and $(-1, 5)$ violates one of the nonnegativity solutions. It is also possible that a linear programming problem has no feasible solutions. For example, if the constraint $x_1 \geq 6$ was added to (6.5), there would be no solution that satisfies both $x_1 \geq 6$ and $12x_1 + 4x_2 \leq 60$.

Given a set of feasible solutions, the purpose of linear programming is to find the "best" feasible solution. An *optimal solution* is a feasible solution that has the largest value for the objective function if the objective is to maximize, or the smallest value if the objective is to minimize. An optimal solution either maximizes or minimizes an objective over the entire feasible region. Frequently, a linear programming problem will have a single optimal solution—

a *unique optimal solution*. In other cases, there will be an infinite number of solutions that give the optimal value of the objective function—*multiple optimal solutions*. On the other hand, the linear programming problem may not have an optimal solution even if the problem has at least one feasible solution. This situation occurs when the constraints do not prevent increasing the value of the objective indefinitely if the objective is to maximize, or decreasing the value of the objective indefinitely if the objective is to minimize. In such cases the solution to the linear programming model is said to be *unbounded*. Finally, we note that the objective value associated with an optimal solution is called the *optimal value* of the linear program.

6.3 THE ASSUMPTIONS OF LINEAR PROGRAMMING

The mathematical structure of the linear programming model presented in the previous section is only part of the formulation process. We need to be aware of the implicit assumptions surrounding the structure of this model and the solution techniques used to solve the mathematical problem. The three basic assumptions of all linear programming models are: *linearity*, *divisibility*, and *determinism*. The linearity assumption is mathematically straightforward, but has several very significant implications.

Technically, we say that decision variables must only appear in linear relationships in the linear programming problem. A linear relationship involving n decision variables $x_1, x_2, \ldots, x_n$ is an expression of the form $c_1x_1 + c_2x_2 + \cdots + c_nx_n$, where $c_1, \ldots, c_n$ are specified real numbers. One implication of this mathematical form is that economies of scale are not assumed. For example, in model (6.4), (6.5), and (6.6) it is assumed that profit increases at the constant rate of \$5 per unit if product A is produced. This means that there are no economies of scale that would cut production costs and increase the per unit profit. Another way of saying the same thing is to note that profit per unit will not increase as the production level increases. We also note that to calculate total profit we simply add profit from product A $(5x_1)$ to profit from product B $(8x_2)$. This points to another implicit assumption specified by the linear model—there are no interactions between the variables. In the context of the model in (6.4),

(6.5), and (6.6), this means that the production level of product A does not affect the profitability of product B, and the production level of product B does not affect the profitability of product A.

The two important implications of a linear relationship discussed in the previous paragraph are often referred to as the *proportionality* and *additivity* assumptions, respectively. Of course, these assumptions also apply to resource utilization as modeled by the linear relationships in the constraint set. There are situations where the linearity assumptions are not accurate approximations of the real-world situation being modeled. In such cases nonlinear relations must be employed to construct the model and nonlinear programming methods must be used to solve the problem. The nonlinear programming model is discussed in Chapter 22.

The divisibility assumption simply means that we are treating the variables as continuous rather than discrete variables. Again, this is generally an approximation and if this approximation is not reasonable, another solution methodology called integer programming is employed. Integer programming is the topic of Chapter 14. Finally, we assume that all the parameters (the b_i, c_j, and a_{ij}) in the linear programming model are deterministic. That is, they are known with certainty. In reality these parameters are often estimates and since we treat these estimates as being the actual value of the parameters in the solution process, it is important to at least examine the implications of inaccuracies after we have determined the optimal solution to the deterministic model. Chapter 9, on *postoptimality analysis* (or *sensitivity analysis*), deals with determining how much the individual parameters can vary before the optimal solution changes.

6.4 LINEAR PROGRAMMING APPLICATIONS

As mentioned earlier, linear programming has been successfully applied to a wide spectrum of problems across many different fields. The typical decision problem confronted by management in various settings, however, is the optimal allocation of scarce resources. Linear programming is often applicable in such problem settings. After the applicability of linear programming has been determined, the real-world problem is structured by the development or formulation of a representative mathematical model.

The art of problem formulation is discussed in Section 6.4.1. The remainder of this chapter is then devoted to the presentation of a variety of examples that demonstrate the process of linear programming model formulation.

6.4.1 THE ART OF PROBLEM FORMULATION

Many individuals that employ linear programming models and other management science models have more difficulty with the problem formulation process than the actual computational procedures used to solve the model. The ability to represent a real-world situation with a mathematical model is an art. The art of problem formulation comes with practice, a good deal of patience, and a thorough understanding of the problem being modeled.

Although each problem situation is different, with practice and thus experience, even the more complicated formulations do not appear quite so elusive. There are, however, some general procedures that can facilitate the development of this art. First, it is important to identify the overall objective for the situation and give a clear, concise, verbal statement of that objective. At the same time, the identification of the factors over which the decision maker has control is of vital importance. A concise statement of each condition that constrains the achievement of the objective is also very desirable.

After the problem has been properly identified verbally, the verbal descriptions must be transformed into mathematical statements. The following process is generally effective in accomplishing this task.

STEP 1: Identify the decision variables, the x_j.

STEP 2: Identify the objective function coefficients, the c_j.

STEP 3: Construct the objective function.

STEP 4: Identify the resource availabilities, the b_i.

STEP 5: Relate resource availability to resource utilization. In other words, identify the a_{ij}.

STEP 6: Construct the constraints for the model.

In these six steps the identification of appropriate decision variables is most critical. In the process of identifying the decision variables, the units of measurement should be clearly stated. The clear identification of units of measurement in Step 1 and a repeated check for consistency in the remaining steps will facilitate the development of a valid model. It should be noted that the decision variables for the model representation of a particular situation are not necessarily unique. There may be many ways to define an appropriate set of decision variables for a given problem situation. If it appears impossible to represent the constraints of the problem with the set of decision variables defined initially, a different specification of the decision variables may be required. Remember that the set of decision variables that is used to construct the objective function must also be used to construct the constraint relationships. We now proceed to illustrate the formulation process using some typical application categories. At the same time we show the solutions to these illustrative examples. These solutions can be used to check the formulation process, by determining whether the computed solution is a reasonable solution. The solutions here were obtained using a microcomputer. The role of the computer in the linear programming solution process is discussed in Chapter 8.

6.4.2 A RESOURCE UTILIZATION PROBLEM

The Colonial Chair Company has an excess of 30.25 hours of hand labor and 25 hours of machine time available per week. The production of three novelty items to use this excess capacity is being considered. A wooden toy requires 40 minutes of labor and 20 minutes of machine time per unit. A small toy chest requires 20 minutes of labor and 25 minutes of machine time. A decorative picture frame requires 45 minutes of labor and 15 minutes of machine time.

The per unit profit figures for these items are $4, $3, and $5, respectively. It is known, however, that demand for toy chests will not exceed 12 units per week and demand for picture frames will be at least 6 units per week. Thus the manufacturer has decided that if toy chests are produced, 12 or fewer units will be produced, and 6 or more picture frames must be produced.

We want to formulate a mathematical model that will determine maximum profit if the excess production capacity is utilized to produce one or all of these three novelty items. We formulate this problem as a linear programming model by defining the decision variables, constructing the objective function, constructing the constraints, and then listing the entire model. Before doing this, it is often useful to combine the problem parameters in tabular form. In this situation the resulting table, called a resource requirements table, is given below.

Decision Variables   Management wants to maximize profit, and to do so must decide on how many units of each item to produce. There are three decision variables, each of which represents the number of units of an item to be produced. The quantities can be represented symbolically as

$$x_1 = \text{the number of wooden toys to produce}$$

$$x_2 = \text{the number of toy chests to produce}$$

$$x_3 = \text{the number of picture frames to produce}$$

The Objective Function   The objective of the Colonial Chair Company is to maximize total profit. Total profit consists of the sum of the individual profits from each of the three items. Mathematically our objective is

$$\text{Maximize } Z = 4x_1 + 3x_2 + 5x_3 \qquad (6.15)$$

| | RESOURCE REQUIREMENTS | | | | |
PRODUCT	LABOR (MIN/UNIT)	MACHINE TIME (MIN/UNIT)	MAXIMUM PRODUCTION	MINIMUM PRODUCTION	PROFIT ($/UNIT)
Wooden toy	40	20	—	—	4
Toy chest	20	25	12	—	3
Picture frame	45	15	—	6	5
Available time (min)	1815	1500			

WHERE

Z = total profit per week;
$4x_1$ = profit from x_1 wooden toys;
$3x_2$ = profit from x_2 toy chests;
$5x_3$ = profit from x_3 picture frames.

The Constraint Set This problem has two limited production resources and two conditions that bound the number of units that are produced. We note that if x_1 wooden toys are produced, $40x_1$ minutes of labor are consumed, if x_2 toy chests are produced, $20x_2$ minutes of labor are consumed, and if x_3 picture frames are produced, $45x_3$ minutes of labor are consumed. Therefore, if x_1, x_2, x_3 units of the respective items are produced simultaneously, a total of $(40x_1 + 20x_2 + 45x_3)$ minutes of labor are consumed. Since there are a total of 1815 minutes available for the week, we must satisfy the condition

$$40x_1 + 20x_2 + 45x_3 \leq 1815 \qquad (6.16)$$

Similarly

$$20x_1 + 25x_2 + 15x_3 \leq 1500 \qquad (6.17)$$

where 1500 is the number of minutes of machine time available. Additionally, we note that not more than 12 toy chests will be produced:

$$x_2 \leq 12 \qquad (6.18)$$

Also at least six picture frames will be produced:

$$x_3 \geq 6 \qquad (6.19)$$

The only other condition that must be imposed is that the decision variables may not assume any negative value, the nonnegativity conditions

$$x_1, x_2, x_3 \geq 0 \qquad (6.20)$$

The complete linear programming model for this situation is obtained by combining (6.15) through (6.20):

$$\text{Maximize } Z = 4x_1 + 3x_2 + 5x_3 \qquad (6.21)$$

subject to

$$40x_1 + 20x_2 + 45x_3 \leq 1815$$
$$20x_1 + 25x_2 + 15x_3 \leq 1500$$
$$x_2 \leq 12$$
$$x_3 \geq 6 \qquad (6.22)$$

with

$$x_1, x_2, x_3 \geq 0 \qquad (6.23)$$

The solution to this model will maximize total profit Z and simultaneously satisfy all the constraints (6.22) and (6.23). We note that even the most simple models may involve a combination of the constraint types ($\leq, \geq, =$), as discussed in Section 6.2.1. It should be noted that the constraints in linear programming models can be measured in different units. The units in the first two constraints of (6.22) are minutes. The third and fourth constraints are measured in units of the individual products. The units of measurement within a particular constraint must be consistent, however. In the first constraint of (6.22) the terms $40x_1$, $20x_2$, $45x_3$, and the right-hand side (1815) all represent minutes of labor.

The optimal solution to the model (6.21), (6.22), and (6.23) is $x_1 = 0$, $x_2 = 12$, $x_3 = 35$, and the optimal value of the linear programming problem is \$211. The optimal solution involves the production of 12 toy chests and 35 picture frames. No wooden toys are produced. At the same time, we note that if this solution is implemented, all the available labor (1815 minutes) is utilized

$$40(0) + 20(12) + 45(35) = 1815. \qquad (6.24)$$

On the other hand, 675 minutes of machine time are not utilized

$$20(0) + 25(12) + 15(35) = 825 \quad \text{and}$$
$$1500 - 825 = 675 \qquad (6.25)$$

It should be noted that there is no reason to expect that the decision variables will have integer optimal values. In fact, changing a single parameter value in the resource requirements table will likely result in a noninteger optimal solution.

6.4.3 AN INVESTMENT PLANNING PROBLEM

Amvest, Inc., has $500,000 available for investment and seeks to determine how much of this amount is to be invested in each of four available investment alternatives: stock X, stock Y, bond X, and bond Y. A maximum of $105,000 may be invested in bonds of type X and a maximum of $100,000 may be invested in bonds of type Y. Annual net return is listed in Table 6.3.

Amvest is aware of the fact that there is a considerable amount of risk associated with investment in stock X. Therefore, Amvest has determined that it will not invest an amount in stock X that exceeds one-fourth of its total investment. Also the total amount invested in stock Y must be at least three times the amount invested in stock X. Additionally, Amvest requires that its investment in bonds must be at least as great as one-half its investment in stocks.

Decision Variables In this situation management wants to maximize return and thus the total amount of money available after an investment period of one year. Amvest must therefore decide how much money to invest in each of the four alternatives. There are four decision variables

$$x_1 = \text{amount of money invested in stock } X$$
$$x_2 = \text{amount of money invested in stock } Y$$
$$x_3 = \text{amount of money invested in bond } X \quad (6.27)$$
$$x_4 = \text{amount of money invested in bond } Y$$

The Objective Function The objective of Amvest is to maximize the total amount available for reinvestment after one year. Mathematically, the objective is

Maximize Z
$$= 1.20x_1 + 1.10x_2 + 1.09x_3 + 1.11x_4 \quad (6.27)$$

TABLE 6.3 ANNUAL NET RETURN ON INVESTMENT

Stock X	20%
Stock Y	10%
Bond X	9%
Bond Y	11%

WHERE

Z = total amount available after one year;

$(1 + c_j)x_j$ = amount available after one year from an investment of x_j in alternative j, having an annual return of c_j.

The Constraint Set The most obvious restriction in this problem is that the money available for investment is limited to $500,000. We note that the total investment limit is reflected by the constraint

$$x_1 + x_2 + x_3 + x_4 \leq 500,000 \quad (6.28)$$

The second condition stated requires that the total investment in stock X cannot exceed one fourth of the total investment. That is,

$$x_1 \leq 0.25(x_1 + x_2 + x_3 + x_4) \quad \text{or}$$
$$0.75x_1 - 0.25x_2 - 0.25x_3 - 0.25x_4 \leq 0 \quad (6.29)$$

Also, the total amount invested in stock Y must be at least three times the amount invested in stock X.

$$x_2 \geq 3x_1 \quad \text{or} \quad x_2 - 3x_1 \geq 0 \quad \text{or}$$
$$3x_1 - x_2 \leq 0 \quad (6.30)$$

Amvest requires that its investment in bonds must be at least 50 percent of its investment in stocks. Since $x_1 + x_2$ represents its total investment in stocks and $x_3 + x_4$ represents total investment in bonds, we require

$$x_3 + x_4 \geq 0.50(x_1 + x_2) \quad \text{or}$$
$$0.5x_1 + 0.5x_2 - x_3 - x_4 \leq 0 \quad (6.31)$$

Finally, limited bond availability requires

$$x_3 \leq 105,000$$
$$x_4 \leq 100,000 \quad (6.32)$$

Upon adding the nonnegativity conditions to conditions (6.27) through (6.32), we obtain the complete model

Maximize Z
$$= 1.20x_1 + 1.10x_2 + 1.09x_3 + 1.11x_4 \quad (6.33)$$

TABLE 6.4 OPTIMAL INVESTMENT STRATEGY FOR AMVEST

AMOUNT INVESTED	AMOUNT INVESTED + RETURN
$x_1 = \$83,333.33$	$100,000.00
$x_2 = 250,000.00$	275,000.00
$x_3 = 66,666.67$	72,666.67
$x_4 = 100,000.00$	111,000.00
	$558,666.67

subject to

$$x_1 + x_2 + x_3 + x_4 \leq 500,000 \quad (6.34)$$

$$0.75x_1 - 0.25x_2 - 0.25x_3 - 0.25x_4 \leq 0$$

$$3x_1 - x_2 \leq 0$$

$$0.5x_1 + 0.5x_2 - x_3 - x_4 \leq 0$$

$$x_3 \leq 105,000$$

$$x_4 \leq 100,000$$

with

$$x_1, x_2, x_3, x_4 \geq 0 \quad (6.35)$$

The solution to this reinvestment problem is given in Table 6.4.

6.4.4 A DIET PROBLEM

The Fatkat Company is considering the production of a new cat food, Super Chow. The new cat food must meet certain standards with respect to its calorie, protein, and vitamin content. The cat food can be blended from four ingredients. The standards for the cat food and the calorie, protein, and vitamin content of the four basic ingredients are shown in Table 6.5. The cost per pound for each of the four ingredients is also shown. The Fatkat Company needs to determine the quantities of the various ingredients that should be blended to meet the established standards for the cat food while minimizing cost.

Decision Variables Since there are no production goals or limits and no restriction on the amount of each of the four ingredients available, it is possible to base the formulation on the production of one pound of cat food. The linear programming model will be constructed so that the optimal mix will be

the same whether we produce 100 pounds or 10,000 pounds. The four decision variables individually represent the proportion of a pound of an ingredient used in the production of one pound of cat food. Specifically, we let x_j ($j = 1, 2, 3, 4$) represent the proportion of a pound of ingredient j to be blended in one pound of cat food.

The Objective Function The objective in this situation is to minimize the cost of producing one pound of cat food. The objective is written as,

Minimize Z
$$= 0.25x_1 + 0.20x_2 + 0.22x_3 + 0.30x_4 \quad (6.36)$$

WHERE

Z = total cost per pound of cat food;

$c_j x_j$ = cost per pound of Super Chow attributed to ingredient j.

The Constraint Set In this situation there are three conditions that must be satisfied. They relate to a maximum number of units of calories and minimum levels of protein and vitamins per pound of cat food. The left-hand side of each of these constraints represents the number of units of each nutritional element of interest in a pound of cat food. Mathematically, these three constraints are,

$$2000x_1 + 2500x_2 + 2250x_3 + 1750x_4 \leq 2500$$

$$110x_1 + 160x_2 + 130x_3 + 130x_4 \geq 120$$

$$150x_1 + 90x_2 + 100x_3 + 120x_4 \geq 100 \quad (6.37)$$

Additionally, we limit the analysis to production of one pound

$$x_1 + x_2 + x_3 + x_4 = 1 \quad (6.38)$$

Combining (6.36), (6.37), (6.38), and the non-negativity conditions, the linear programming model for this diet problem is

Minimize Z
$$= 0.25x_1 + 0.20x_2 + 0.22x_3 + 0.30x_4 \quad (6.39)$$

TABLE 6.5 STANDARDS OF FOUR BASIC INGREDIENTS

NUTRITIONAL COMPONENT	UNITS OF NUTRITIONAL COMPONENT PER POUND OF INGREDIENT				TOTAL NUTRITIONAL REQUIREMENT PER POUND
	INGREDIENT 1	INGREDIENT 2	INGREDIENT 3	INGREDIENT 4	
Calories	2000	2500	2250	1750	≤ 1500
Protein	110	160	130	130	≥ 120
Multivitamin	150	90	100	120	≥ 100
Cost per Pound	$0.25	$0.20	$0.22	$0.30	

subject to

$$2000x_1 + 2500x_2 + 2250x_3 + 1750x_4 \leq 2500$$

$$110x_1 + 160x_2 + 130x_3 + 130x_4 \geq 120$$

$$150x_1 + 90x_2 + 100x_3 + 120x_4 \geq 100$$

$$x_1 + x_2 + x_3 + x_4 = 1 \qquad (6.40)$$

with

$$x_1, x_2, x_3, x_4 \geq 0 \qquad (6.41)$$

The optimal solution to the model formulated is given in Table 6.6. In order to meet the nutritional requirements and minimize cost we would use one-sixth of a pound of Ingredient 1 and five-sixths of a pound of Ingredient 2 to produce one pound of cat food. The cost per pound would be $0.20833.

6.4.5 A BLENDING PROBLEM

The blending problem is closely related to the diet problem. In this category of problems a product can be made from a variety of raw materials, each having a particular composition and price. The exact composition of the product is subject to the availability of the raw materials and the minimum and maximum constraints on certain product ingredients. This example is also used to illustrate the use of double subscripts.

The Noled Company wholesales two grades of unleaded gasoline, Superior and Regular. Both grades are composed of one or more blending elements. The data concerning the three blending elements are given in Table 6.7. The supply figures represent the maximum available supply for the three blending elements. Both of these grades of gasoline must meet a minimum standard for octane rating. The demand figures shown in Table 6.8 represent the minimum demand per day required for each grade of gasoline. The minimum demand will be incorporated so that at least the specified daily amounts can be produced. It is assumed that there is a market for all blended gasoline subject to the supply limitations.

Decision Variables The decision in this situation involves the amount of each blending element used in the production of the two grades of gasoline. We let x_{ij} represent the number of barrels of blending element i used in the production of gasoline of brand j. Here, $i = 1, 2, 3$ and $j = 1, 2$, where $j = 1$ represents Superior and $j = 2$ represents Regular. If instead we were considering the production of 5 grades of gasoline and 10 different blending elements, the merit of double subscripting would be quite obvious. Double subscripts (or in many cases more than two subscripts) facilitate the systematic

TABLE 6.6 OPTIMAL SOLUTION TO THE DIET MODEL

OBJECTIVE VALUE	DECISION VARIABLES	NUTRITIONAL REQUIREMENTS PROVIDED	
$Z = 0.20833$	$x_1 = 0.1667$ pounds	Calories	2316.67
	$x_2 = 0.8333$ pounds	Protein	151.67
	$x_3 = 0$	Multivitamin	100
	$x_4 = 0$		

TABLE 6.7 THE THREE BLENDING ELEMENTS

BLENDING ELEMENT	OCTANE RATING	COST ($/BARREL)	SUPPLY PER DAY (BARRELS)
1	100	28	5000
2	95	25	7500
3	85	20	7500

representation of a large number of variables. Subscripting also allows us to incorporate summation notation and provides a concise representation of a particular model or class of models.

The Objective Function The objective in this situation is to maximize total profit. For every barrel of blending element i used in the production of gasoline of grade j there is a specified profit per barrel input. For example, the profit from one barrel of blending element 1 used in the production of the Superior grade is $(35 - 28) = 7$. The corresponding per unit profit is 2, however, if it is used in the production of Regular grade. The entire objective function may then be specified as follows.

Maximize Z

$$= (35 - 28)x_{11} + (35 - 25)x_{21}$$
$$+ (35 - 20)x_{31} + (30 - 28)x_{12}$$
$$+ (30 - 25)x_{22} + (30 - 20)x_{32} \qquad (6.42)$$

WHERE

Z = total profit;

$c_{ij}x_{ij}$ = total profit from the blending component of type i used to produce gasoline of type j.

The Constraint Set In this blending problem there are three different sets of constraints involved. First,

there are the supply availability constraints. Second, there are the demand requirement constraints. Third, the minimum octane standards must be met. The supply availability constraints must individually specify that the total amount of blending element of type i may not exceed the supply limit. These constraints are

$$x_{11} + x_{12} \leq 5000$$
$$x_{21} + x_{22} \leq 7500$$
$$x_{31} + x_{32} \leq 7500 \qquad (6.43)$$

As noted earlier demand conditions will be imposed so that we must produce at a specified level or above this level.

$$x_{11} + x_{21} + x_{31} \geq 10,000$$
$$x_{12} + x_{22} + x_{32} \geq 5000 \qquad (6.44)$$

We assume that one barrel of blending element of type 1 and one barrel of blending element of type 2 will yield two barrels of gasoline with a combined octane rating of $(100 + 95)/2 = 97.5$. Thus

$$\frac{100x_{11} + 95x_{21} + 85x_{31}}{x_{11} + x_{21} + x_{31}} \qquad (6.45)$$

TABLE 6.8 DEMAND FIGURES SHOWING MINIMUM DAILY REQUIREMENTS

GRADE OF GASOLINE	MINIMUM OCTANE STANDARD	SELLING PRICE ($/BARREL)	DEMAND PER DAY (BARRELS)
Superior	95	35	10,000
Regular	90	30	5,000

represents the combined octane rating of (x_{11} + x_{21} + x_{31}) barrels of Superior gasoline. The assumption here is that mixing one gallon of each blending element will result in 3 gallons of gasoline with an octane rating of $(100 + 95 + 85)/3 = 93.33$. The left-hand sides of the constraints in (6.46) are then a weighted average of the octane ratings, with the weights being the barrels of blending element i used in product j. The relevant constraints are then

$$\frac{100x_{11} + 95x_{21} + 85x_{31}}{x_{11} + x_{21} + x_{31}} \geq 95$$

$$\frac{100x_{12} + 95x_{22} + 85x_{32}}{x_{12} + x_{22} + x_{32}} \geq 90 \qquad (6.46)$$

Equation 6.46 can be written as

$$100x_{11} + 95x_{21} + 85x_{31} \geq 95(x_{11} + x_{21} + x_{31})$$

$$100x_{12} + 95x_{22} + 85x_{32} \geq 90(x_{12} + x_{22} + x_{32}) \qquad (6.47)$$

and then as

$$5x_{11} - 10x_{31} \geq 0$$

$$10x_{12} + 5x_{22} - 5x_{32} \geq 0 \qquad (6.48)$$

The expressions (6.42), (6.43), (6.44), and (6.46) are then combined with the nonnegativity conditions to form the model for the blending problem.

$$\text{Maximize } Z = 7x_{11} + 10x_{21} + 15x_{31} + 2x_{12} + 5x_{22} + 10x_{32} \qquad (6.49)$$

subject to

$$x_{11} + x_{12} \leq 15,000 \qquad (6.50)$$

$$x_{21} + x_{22} \leq 7500$$

$$x_{31} + x_{32} \leq 7500$$

$$x_{11} + x_{21} + x_{33} \geq 10,000$$

$$x_{12} + x_{22} + x_{32} \geq 5000$$

$$5x_{11} - 10x_{31} \geq 0$$

$$10x_{12} + 5x_{22} - 5x_{32} \geq 0$$

with

$$x_{ij} \geq 0 \qquad i = 1, 2, 3, \qquad j = 1, 2. \qquad (6.51)$$

The optimal solution to the blending problem is summarized in Table 6.9. We note that the octane ratings of the two grades of gasoline produced to maximize profit are exactly 95 and 90, respectively. This can be verified by substituting the optimal x_{ij} values into the constraints in (6.46).

Note that the constraints of (6.37) for the diet problem also involve blending. They are very similar but yet different. The constraints in (6.37) were constructed assuming that one unit is mixed. If additionally there were resource constraints, the first constraint in (6.37) would be written as

$$\frac{2000x_1 + 2500x_2 + 2250x_3 + 1750x_4}{x_1 + x_2 + x_3 + x_4} \leq 2500$$

$$(6.52)$$

TABLE 6.9 OPTIMAL SOLUTION TO THE BLENDING PROBLEM

BLENDING ELEMENT i USED IN GASOLINE TYPE j	BARRELS USED	CONTRIBUTION TO PROFIT
x_{11}	5000	\$35,000
x_{21}	2500	25,000
x_{31}	2500	37,500
x_{12}	0	0
x_{22}	5000	25,000
x_{32}	5000	50,000
		\$172,500

The left-hand side would again be a weighted average that represents calories per pound.

6.4.6 A PRODUCTION SCHEDULING PROBLEM

Scheduling production over several time periods is another important application of linear programming. In many multiperiod scheduling situations the manufacturer seeks to balance the cost of overtime production against the cost associated with carrying inventory from one period to the next. The following example illustrates the linear programming formulation of a multiperiod planning situation.

Slippery Stick, Inc., produces hockey sticks during July, August, September, and October. These hockey sticks are also sold in these 4 months and the forecasted demand for this time period is given in Table 6.10. Slippery Stick wants to plan production so that at least 1800 units will be available in July, at least 2200 units available in August, and so forth. Because of production limits and demand variations, management has found that in some months excess production will be required, which in turn will result in holding (storage) costs. The per unit cost of production using regular time is $20. The company can produce 2400 hockey sticks per month in regular shifts. By using overtime, an additional 800 hockey sticks per month can be produced. Because of higher labor costs for overtime, a $7 per unit cost increase results for a hockey stick not produced during the regular shift. Management has also estimated that a storage cost of $3 per month will be incurred for any hockey stick that is produced in a month and not sold in that month. Management would like to determine a production schedule that minimizes the total cost of production and storage. We assume that there are no hockey sticks in stock on July 1 and that there will be no inventory on November 1.

Decision Variables The delineation of the optimal production schedule involves three sets of decision variables. The first two sets of primary decision variables designate the number of hockey sticks produced in a given month on a regular shift or using overtime. The third set of decision variables could actually be defined in terms of the primary variables, but it is often more convenient to incorporate these "secondary" or "accounting" variables directly into the mathematical model. We denote the variables in the decision process as follows.

$x_j (j = 1, \ldots, 4)$ is the number of hockey sticks produced in month j using regular time;

$y_j (j = 1, \ldots, 4)$ is the number of hockey sticks produced in month j using overtime,

$I_j (j = 1, 2, 3)$ is the number of hockey sticks carried over from the end of month j to the beginning of month $j + 1$.   (6.53)

The Objective Function The stated objective in this situation is to minimize the total cost of production and storage. The total cost of production is the regular time production costs plus the overtime production costs. The actual specification of the objective is then,

$$\text{Minimize } Z = 20 \sum_{j=1}^{4} x_j + 27 \sum_{j=1}^{4} y_j + 3 \sum_{j=1}^{3} I_j \quad (6.54)$$

TABLE 6.10 FORECASTED DEMAND

j	MONTH	FORECASTED DEMAND (HOCKEY STICKS)
1	July	1800
2	August	2200
3	September	3400
4	October	2800
Total		10,200

$20 \sum_{j=1}^{4} x_j$ = the total cost of regular time production;

$27 \sum_{j=1}^{4} y_j$ = the total cost of overtime production;

$3 \sum_{j=1}^{3} I_j$ = the total storage cost.

The Constraint Set The constraints in this problem involve the production limits and the demand requirements. The production limits simply specify that regular time and overtime production are bounded

$$x_j \le 2400 \qquad j = 1, \ldots, 4$$
$$y_j \le 800 \qquad j = 1, \ldots, 4 \qquad (6.55)$$

The constraints involving demand are generally constructed in the following way.

Beginning inventory + production
$$- \text{ demand} = \text{ending inventory} \qquad (6.56)$$

or

Beginning inventory + production
$$- \text{ ending inventory} = \text{demand} \qquad (6.57)$$

We note that total production in month j is $x_j + y_j$ and use form (6.57) to specify the demand constraints for this situation

$$x_1 + y_1 - I_1 = 1800$$
$$I_1 + x_2 + y_2 - I_2 = 2200$$
$$I_2 + x_3 + y_3 - I_3 = 3400$$
$$I_3 + x_4 + y_4 \qquad = 2800 \qquad (6.58)$$

To understand the formulation of this set of constraints it is important to note that the ending inventory in month k is the beginning inventory in month $k + 1$. The nonnegativity conditions on the I_j is of particular significance in this formulation,

since it directly prohibits any shortage. Combining (6.54), (6.55), and (6.58) gives the complete production scheduling model.

$$\text{Minimize } Z = 20 \sum_{j=1}^{4} x_j + 27 \sum_{j=1}^{4} y_j + 3 \sum_{j=1}^{3} I_j \qquad (6.59)$$

subject to

$$x_j \le 2400 \qquad j = 1, \ldots, 4$$
$$y_j \le 800 \qquad j = 1, \ldots, 4$$
$$x_1 + y_1 - I_1 = 1800$$
$$I_1 + x_2 + y_2 - I_2 = 2200$$
$$I_2 + x_3 + y_3 - I_3 = 3400$$
$$I_3 + x_4 + y_4 \qquad = 2800 \qquad (6.60)$$

with

$$x_j, y_j \ge 0 \qquad j = 1, \ldots, 4$$
$$I_j \ge 0 \qquad j = 1, \ldots, 3. \qquad (6.61)$$

Please note the significance of the distinction between the sets of variables described earlier. From (6.56) and (6.58) we see that

$$I_1 = x_1 + y_1 - 1800$$
$$I_2 = I_1 + x_2 + y_2 - 2200$$
$$\quad = x_1 + y_1 - 1800 + x_2 + y_2 - 2200$$
$$\quad = x_1 + x_2 + y_1 + y_2 - 4000$$
$$I_3 = x_1 + x_2 + y_1 + y_2 - 4000$$
$$\qquad + x_3 + y_3 - 3400$$
$$\quad = x_1 + x_2 + x_3 + y_1 + y_2 + y_3 - 7400 \qquad (6.62)$$

Also from the last constraint in (6.60) we see that

$$\sum_{j=1}^{4} x_j + y_j = 10,200 \qquad (6.63)$$

The expressions (6.63), (6.60), and the conditions $I_1, I_2, \ge 0$ form the constraint set for a linear programming model that does not explicitly involve

TABLE 6.11 PRODUCTION SCHEDULE AND INVENTORY RECORD

MONTH	REGULAR PRODUCTION	OVERTIME PRODUCTION	ENDING INVENTORY
1	2400	0	600
2	2400	0	800
3	2400	200	0
4	2400	400	0

the variables I_1, I_2, I_3 and is equivalent to the model in (6.59), (6.60), and (6.61). This model follows

Minimize Z

$$= 20 \sum_{j=1}^{4} x_j + 27 \sum_{j=1}^{4} y_j$$
$$+ 3((x_1 + y_1 - 1800)$$
$$+ (x_1 + x_2 + y_1 + y_2 - 4000)$$
$$+ (x_1 + x_2 + x_3 + y_1 + y_2 + y_3 - 7400)) \quad (6.64)$$

subject to

$$x_j \leq 2400 \qquad j = 1, \ldots, 4$$
$$y_j \leq 800 \qquad j = 1, \ldots, 4$$
$$x_1 + y_1 \geq 1800$$
$$\sum_{j=1}^{2} (x_j + y_j) \geq 4000$$
$$\sum_{j=1}^{3} (x_j + y_j) \geq 7400$$
$$\sum_{j=1}^{4} (x_j + y_j) = 10{,}200 \quad (6.65)$$

with

$$x_j, y_j \geq 0 \qquad j = 1, \ldots, 4 \quad (6.66)$$

The elimination of the inventory variables from the formulation does not eliminate any constraints from the model. It does not really represent a significant reduction in the mathematical complexity of the problem. It does help to explain why we described these inventory variables as secondary variables earlier. They are not required but do facilitate the formulation process.

The optimal solution for the 4-month planning horizon for this problem is given in Table 6.11. The total cost for overtime and inventory, given this production schedule, is $8400.

An Alternative Formulation An alternative formulation for the production scheduling problem involves a single set of decision variables having three subscripts. Explicitly,

x_{ijk} = is the number of hockey sticks produced in month i for demand in month j with labor of type k.

Here, $i = 1, \ldots, 4$; $j = i, \ldots, 4$; and $k = 1$ labels regular time production, while $k = 2$ labels overtime production. The relevant variables are listed in Table 6.12. We note that inventory levels must be accounted for indirectly in this case. In fact the difference between the first and second subscripts is used to compute holding cost. The entire formulation is given as follows.

TABLE 6.12 PRODUCTION VARIABLES

MONTH 1		MONTH 2		MONTH 3		MONTH 4	
x_{111}	x_{112}						
x_{121}	x_{122}	x_{221}	x_{222}				
x_{131}	x_{132}	x_{231}	x_{232}	x_{331}	x_{332}		
x_{141}	x_{142}	x_{241}	x_{242}	x_{341}	x_{342}	x_{441}	x_{442}

Minimize Z

$$= 20(x_{111} + x_{121} + x_{131} + x_{141} + x_{221} + x_{231}$$
$$+ x_{241} + x_{331} + x_{341} + x_{441}) + 27(x_{112} + x_{122}$$
$$+ x_{132} + x_{142} + x_{222} + x_{232} + x_{242} + x_{332}$$
$$+ x_{344} + x_{442}) + 3(x_{121} + x_{122} + x_{231}$$
$$+ x_{232} + x_{341} + x_{342}) + 6(x_{131} + x_{132}$$
$$+ x_{241} + x_{242}) + 9(x_{141} + x_{142}) \qquad (6.67)$$

subject to

$$x_{111} + x_{121} + x_{131} + x_{141} \leq 2400$$

$$x_{221} + x_{231} + x_{241} \leq 2400$$

$$x_{331} + x_{341} \leq 2400$$

$$x_{441} \leq 2400$$

$$x_{112} + x_{122} + x_{132} + x_{142} \leq 800$$

$$x_{222} + x_{232} + x_{242} \leq 800$$

$$x_{332} + x_{342} \leq 800$$

$$x_{442} \leq 800$$

$$x_{111} + x_{112} = 1800$$

$$x_{121} + x_{122} + x_{221} + x_{222} = 2200$$

$$x_{131} + x_{132} + x_{231} + x_{232} + x_{331} + x_{332} = 3400$$

$$x_{141} + x_{142} + x_{241} + x_{242} + x_{341} + x_{342}$$
$$+ x_{441} + x_{442} = 2800 \quad (6.68)$$

with

$$x_{ijk} \geq 0 \qquad i = 1, \ldots, 4;$$
$$j = i, \ldots, 4; k = 1, 2. \quad (6.69)$$

The solution to the model in (6.67), (6.68) and (6.69) is given in Table 6.13. Verify that it is equivalent to the solution given for model in (6.59), (6.60), and (6.61).

6.4.7 A NETWORK PROBLEM

The final example of this chapter involves an application that falls into a general category of linear programming models known as network models. This group of models is examined in detail in Chapter 12.

Dartmor Motors, Inc., imports and distributes cars through two ports of entry, Charleston and Jacksonville. There are four demand locations, Philadelphia, Atlanta, Dayton, and Chicago. For July the import quantities are shown in Figure 6.1.

Table 6.14 gives the per unit shipping costs and the permissible shipping routes between pairs of cities. Management needs to determine how many cars should be shipped from Charleston and Jacksonville to each of the other cities to either be delivered there or transferred to another city. Management is interested in determining the distribution plan that minimizes the total shipping cost for the 750 cars imported in July. Figure 6.2 represents the distribution network for Dartmor Motors. It is constructed from the information already presented in Figure 6.1 and Table 6.14.

Even though this illustration involves only six cities, there are a number of feasible solutions to this problem, of which Table 6.15 gives three. There are of course many other feasible solutions. This illustration points to the complexity of this type of distribution problem when there are 1000 or even 100 locations involved.

Decision Variables   The decisions involved in this distribution problem require the delineation of the number of cars shipped from one city to another. Here

x_{ij} = number of cars shipped from city i to city j where index numbers are identified from Figure 6.2

TABLE 6.13 OPTIMAL PRODUCTION SCHEDULE FOR SLIPPERY STICK, INC.

PRODUCTION PERIOD	REGULAR TIME	OVERTIME
July	$x_{111} = 1800$ $x_{121} = 600$	
August	$x_{221} = 1600$ $x_{231} = 800$	
September	$x_{331} = 2400$	$x_{332} = 200$
October	$x_{441} = 2400$	$x_{442} = 400$

FIGURE 6.1 DARTMOR DISTRIBUTION REQUIREMENTS.

TABLE 6.14 SHIPPING COSTS PER CAR

FROM \ TO	SHIPPING COSTS PER CAR			
	PHILADELPHIA	ATLANTA	DAYTON	CHICAGO
Charleston	$300	100	—	—
Jacksonville	—	150	400	—
Atlanta	200	—	175	225
Dayton	—	—	—	100

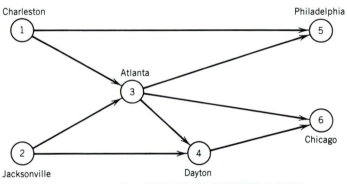

FIGURE 6.2 DISTRIBUTION NETWORK FOR DARTMOR MOTORS.

TABLE 6.15 FEASIBLE SOLUTIONS FOR DARTMOR MOTORS

ROUTE	SOLUTION 1 (CARS)	SOLUTION 2 (CARS)	SOLUTION 3 (CARS)
Charleston to Philadelphia	0	200	100
Charleston to Atlanta	250	50	150
Jacksonville to Dayton	0	450	200
Jacksonville to Atlanta	500	50	300
Atlanta to Philadelphia	200	0	100
Atlanta to Chicago	300	0	250
Atlanta to Dayton	150	0	0
Dayton to Chicago	0	300	50

TABLE 6.16 DECISION VARIABLES LISTED BY CITY OF ORIGIN

CHARLESTON	JACKSONVILLE	ATLANTA	DAYTON
x_{13}	x_{23}	x_{34}	x_{46}
x_{15}	x_{24}	x_{35}	
		x_{36}	

Table 6.16 lists all the decision variables for this situation.

The Objective Function   The objective in this situation is to determine the number of cars to ship from each possible origin to each permissible destination to minimize total distribution cost while meeting the demand requirements. The objective is

$$\text{Minimize } Z = \sum_i \sum_j c_{ij} x_{ij} \qquad (6.70)$$

where c_{ij} is the per unit cost of shipping from city i to city j and the summation extends over the entire set of decision variables. The sum in (6.70) gives the total cost of shipping all the cars imported. The actual objective function in this illustration is

Minimize Z
$$= 100x_{13} + 300x_{15} + 150x_{23} + 400x_{24}$$
$$+ 175x_{34} + 200x_{35} + 225x_{36} + 100x_{46} \qquad (6.71)$$

The Constraint Set   The constraint set in this problem is based entirely on the relationship

$$\text{Flow in } - \text{ flow out} = \text{demand} \qquad (6.72)$$

TABLE 6.17 OPTIMAL DISTRIBUTION PLAN FOR DARTMOR MOTORS

AMOUNT OF TRANSFER FROM CITY i TO CITY j	COST OF TRANSFER FROM CITY i TO CITY j
$x_{13} = 50$	$5000
$x_{15} = 200$	60,000
$x_{23} = 50$	7500
$x_{24} = 450$	180,000
$x_{46} = 300$	30,000
	$282,500

for each city in the network. Here "flow in" refers to the number of cars shipped to a city and "flow out" refers to the number of cars shipped out of a city. Thus there are six constraints in this model.

Charleston:
$$250 - x_{13} - x_{15} = 0 \qquad \text{or}$$
$$x_{13} + x_{15} = 250$$

Jacksonville:
$$500 - x_{23} - x_{24} = 0 \qquad \text{or}$$
$$x_{23} + x_{24} = 500$$

Atlanta:
$$x_{13} + x_{23} - x_{34} - x_{35} - x_{36} = 100$$

Dayton:
$$x_{24} + x_{34} - x_{46} = 150$$

Philadelphia:
$$x_{15} + x_{35} = 200$$

Chicago:
$$x_{36} + x_{46} = 300 \qquad (6.73)$$

The entire distribution network model is obtained by combining (6.71) and (6.73).

$$\text{Minimize } Z = 100x_{13} + 300x_{15} + 150x_{23}$$
$$+ 400x_{24} + 175x_{34} + 200x_{35}$$
$$+ 225x_{36} + 100x_{46} \qquad (6.74)$$

subject to

$$x_{13} + x_{15} = 250 \;.$$
$$x_{23} + x_{24} = 500$$
$$x_{13} + x_{23} - x_{34} - x_{35} - x_{36} = 100$$
$$x_{24} + x_{34} - x_{46} = 150$$
$$x_{15} + x_{35} = 200$$
$$x_{36} + x_{46} = 300 \qquad (6.75)$$

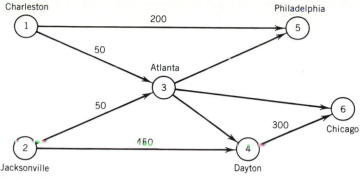

FIGURE 6.3 OPTIMAL SHIPPING ROUTES FOR DARTMOR MOTORS.

with

$$x_{ij} \geq 0 \qquad (6.76)$$

The optimal solution to the distribution problem and total shipping cost is indicated in Table 6.17. Figure 6.3 indicates the flow of cars associated with the optimal solution.

6.5 SUMMARY

In this chapter we have attempted to introduce the basic structure of the linear programming model and related terminology. We have discussed the implicit assumptions utilized whenever a linear programming model is applied, as well as the art of problem formulation. We have presented a variety of applications of linear programming in order to help the reader better comprehend the structure of linear programming as it relates to "real-world" problem solving. The next chapter focuses on the conceptual development of the solution process to be presented in Chapter 8. Graphical analysis is the tool used in this development.

GLOSSARY

Constraints   An equation or inequality that rules out certain combinations of values for the variables involved.

Decision Variables   Variables that represent decisions or components of decisions that must be made in a problem solving situation.

Deterministic Coefficients   A property of linear programming that specifies that all parameters in the model are known constants.

Divisibility   A property of linear programming that means that all variables are continuous.

Feasible Solution   A solution that satisfies all the constraints.

Infeasible   A property of linear programming problem meaning that there is no solution that satisfies the constraints.

Linear Programming   A mathematical procedure for allocating scarce resources while measuring some benefit or cost.

Linear Programming Model   A mathematical model with a linear objective function, linear constraints, and nonnegative variables.

Linearity   A property of linear programming meaning that the marginal measure of profitability and the marginal utilization of each resource are assumed to be constant over the entire range of the decision variables.

Multiple Optimal Solutions   Two or more solutions that give the optimal value to the linear program.

Nonnegativity Conditions   Conditions that specify all the variables in the model to be greater than or equal to zero.

Objective Function   A mathematical function expressed in terms of decision variables, which is to be optimized (maximized or minimized). In linear programming this mathematical function is linear.

Optimal Solution   A feasible solution that maximizes or minimizes the objective function.

Optimal Value   The value of the objective associated with optimal solution.

Unbounded   A property of linear programming meaning that the objective value can be made indefinitely large and positive for a maximization problem or indefinitely large in absolute value and negative for a minimization problem. In each case, none of the constraints are violated.

Solution   Any set of values for the variables.

Selected References

Bazaraa, Mokhtar S., and John J. Jarvis. 1977. *Linear Programming and Network Flows.* New York: Wiley.

Bradley, Stephen P., Arnoldo C. Hax, and Thomas L. Magnanti. 1977. *Applied Mathematical Programming.* Reading, Mass.: Addison–Wesley.

Budnick, Frank S., Richard Mojena, and Thomas E. Vollmann. 1977. *Operations Research for Management.* Homewood, Ill.: Irwin.

Charnes, A., and W. W. Cooper. 1961. *Management Models and Industrial Applications of Linear Programming,* vols. 1 and 2. New York: Wiley.

Cooper, Leon, and David Steinberg. 1974. *Methods and Applications of Linear Programming.* Philadelphia, Pa.: Sanders.

Dantzig, George B. 1963. *Linear Programming and Extensions.* Princeton, N.J.: Princeton Univ. Press.

Greenberg, Michael R. 1978. *Applied Linear Programming For the Socio-economic and Environmental Sciences.* New York: Academic Press.

Hadley, G. 1962. *Linear Programming.* Reading, Mass.: Addison–Wesley.

Hillier, Fredrick S., and Gerald J. Lieberman. 1980. *Introduction to Operations Research,* 3rd ed. San Francisco: Holden–Day.

Hughes, Ann J., and Dennis E. Grawoig. 1973. *Linear Programming: An Emphasis on Decision Making.* Reading, Mass.: Addison–Wesley.

Ignizo, James P. 1982. *Linear Programming In Single and Multiple Objective Systems.* Englewood Cliffs, N.J.: Prentice–Hall.

Llewellyn, Robert W. 1964. *Linear Programming.* New York: Holt, Rinehart & Winston.

Luenberger, David G. 1973. *Introduction to Linear and Nonlinear Programming.* Reading, Mass.: Addison–Wesley.

Markland, Robert E. 1983. *Topics in Management Science,* 2nd ed. New York: Wiley.

Taha, Hamdy A. 1982. *Operations Research: An Introduction,* 3rd. ed. New York: Macmillan.

Thompson, Gerald E. 1971. *Linear Programming: An Elementary Introduction.* New York: Macmillan.

Wagner, Harvey M. 1969. *Principles of Operations Research: With Applications to Managerial Decisions.* Englewood Cliffs, N.J.: Prentice–Hall.

Discussion Questions

1. Is an optimal solution a feasible solution? Is a feasible solution an optimal solution? Explain.

2. Is the linearity assumption typically realistic in applications?

3. What is the primary difference between a linear equality and a linear inequality in the context of a linear programming problem?

4. If the objective of a linear programming problem is to minimize a function, what do we mean by an unbounded solution in this context?

5. How do you transform constraints of the form

$$\frac{4x_1 + 5x_2 + 5x_3}{x_1 + x_2 + x_3} \geq 3$$

so that they can be used in linear programming?

6. Explain the structure of the second formulation to the production scheduling problem given in Section 6.4.6.

7. Discuss the basic difference between the diet problem and the blending problem as they are presented in Sections 6.4.4 and 6.4.5.

PROBLEMS

1. A company produces two products, A and B, that have profits of $10 and $9, respectively. Each unit of product must be processed on two machines for the required production time as follows.

PRODUCT	HOURS/UNIT	
	MACHINE 1	MACHINE 2
A	12	6
B	6	8
Total Available Hours	60	40

Formulate a linear programming model to determine the production quantities that will maximize profit.

2. The Chicken Dog Meat Packing Company produces a meat filler product in 500 pound batches. The mixture contains three basic

ingredients: chicken, turkey, and cereal. The ingredients cost $3, $4, and $2 per pound, respectively. Each batch is mixed according to the following specifications.

a. The mix cannot contain more than 150 pounds of cereal;
b. There must be at least 100 pounds of chicken in the mixture;
c. The mixture must contain at least twice as much turkey as chicken.

Formulate a linear programming model to determine the composition of the optimal mix.

3. A local convenience store makes two types of sandwiches as a service to its early morning customers. They make a profit of $1.00 each from the submarine sandwich and $1.50 from the feedmill sandwich. Given the composition of these two sandwich types and the ingredient availability, formulate the model that determines how many sandwiches of each type to make if the store can sell all the sandwiches it can make.

INGREDIENT	SUBMARINE	FEEDMILL	AMOUNT AVAILABLE
Ham	4 oz.	4 oz.	80 oz.
Turkey	2 oz.	4 oz.	64 oz.
Cheese	3 oz.	4 oz.	64 oz.

4. A furniture manufacturer makes wooden desk chairs, desks, and rocking chairs. From past experience it was learned that at least twice as many desks as desk chairs should be made. Also no more than 20 rocking chairs should be made. There are 10,000 board feet of wood available and a work force of the equivalent of 1000 work hours per day. A desk chair uses 10 board feet, a desk requires 60 board feet, and a rocking chair requires 15 board feet. Two hours of labor are required for the desk chair, 10 for a desk, and 3 for a rocking chair. The profit is $10 for chairs, $50 for desks, and $20 for rocking chairs. Formulate a model to maximize profit for this situation.

5. A manufacturing company is attempting to effectively allocate 100 employess to three primary functions in its plant. The three functions are cutting, assembling, and finishing. Because of limited floor space, no more than 25 employees should be assigned to the cutting function. Also it is known that cutting and finishing together should not exceed the number of employees involved in the assembling operation by more than 10 employees. A recent productivity study conducted by the company indicated that the daily profit contributions made by each employee in the three functions are $20, $15, and $18, respectively. Any employee not assigned to one of these primary functions may be utilized in an external function that results in a daily profit contribution of $10 per employee. Formulate

a linear programming model to determine the optimal allocation of employees.

6. The community of Westover sponsors an annual fund raising drive to support its recreation facilities. Calls for donations are made via a local television station, a local radio station, and a community based newspaper. Westover has decided to allocate $5000 to such advertising. Audience reached per advertisement, cost per advertisement, and the maximum number of advertisements per media type are shown in the following table.

	TELEVISION	RADIO	NEWSPAPER
Audience reached per advertisement	100,000	25,000	50,000
Cost per advertisement	$500	$75	$150
Usage limits	10	20	10

Also the total number of advertisements on television and radio cannot exceed 15. Formulate the linear programming model to maximize the total audience reached.

7. Rockey Quarries hauls crushed rock from its two quarries to three asphalt contractors. Rockey, the manager wants to determine how to supply these three contractors from his two quarries so as to minimize the total number of miles traveled by his fleet of trucks. The following table shows distances between quarries and contractors as well as daily quarry capacity and contractor demand, both in truckloads.

QUARRY	CONTRACTOR			QUARRY CAPACITY
	1	2	3	
1	10	9	14	100
2	6	12	8	200
Contractor demand	75	125	100	300

Formulate a linear programming model that can be used to determine the optimal daily trucking schedule.

8. Clearview, Mfg., manufactures 5-inch color television sets. Clearview has orders for 1600 and 2200 units to be delivered on April 1 and July 1, respectively. Each unit requires a control module that is produced "in house" or by a subcontractor. The cost to manufacture in house is $5.00. Subcontracting costs are currently $5.50 for units produced in the first quarter, and this cost is expected to increase to $6.50 for modules produced after March 31. The inven-

tory holding cost to keep a single module from the first quarter to the second quarter is estimated to be $2.00. This is somewhat high because of the risk of obsolescence. Clearview's production capacity is 1800 modules per quarter. The subcontractor can provide 250 modules in the first quarter and 325 in the second quarter. Formulate a linear programming model to assist in production planning for the first two quarters of this year. Assume no beginning or ending inventory level.

9. The Hi-Lo Brokerage firm needs to invest an undisclosed amount of money for one of its clients. The client has her own ideas about the distribution of the funds being invested. She requests that Hi-Lo select whatever stocks and/or bonds they feel advisable, but within the following guidelines

    a. Municipal bonds should make up at least 15 percent of the investment;
    b. At least 30 percent of the investment should be invested in electronics firms;
    c. For every dollar invested in nuclear waste disposal at least $3 should be invested in day care;
    d. At most 60 percent of the total investment may be invested in electronics firms and nuclear waste disposal.

The analysts noted these guidelines and prepared a list of recommended stocks and bonds and the corresponding rates of return.

INVESTMENT	PROJECTED RATE OF RETURN (%)
Columbia Municipal Bonds	7.0
Data Systems, Inc.	8.2
Compute Quik, Inc.	7.4
E-Z Day Care	9.4
United Nuke Dispose-Less	20.2

The client's goal is to maximize projected return on investment. Formulate this resulting portfolio selection problem as a linear programming model.

10. Lazy-Back makes three types of wooden chairs. Each is manufactured in a four-stage process. The company is able to obtain all the raw materials it needs. The available production capacity during the 80-hour production workweek is as follows.

| PROCESS | WEEKLY CAPACITY IN NUMBER OF CHAIRS | | |
	CHAIR 1	CHAIR 2	CHAIR 3
1	400	800	1000
2	2000	400	300
3	800	1000	800
4	600	500	600

It is assumed that there are 80 hours of labor available for each process and that we are interested only in finished chairs and not work in process. The contributions to profit for the three types of chairs are $15.50, $22.50, and $27.50, respectively. Formulate as a linear programming problem.

11. Hot-Pot Enterprises of Readi, Pennsylvania, produces and sells hand-made copper tea pots. Hot-Pot is attempting to plan its operations for the next year, which is divided into four periods for planning purposes. The production capacity, demand, and production costs vary from one period to the next. The exact parameters are given in the following table.

PERIOD	FALL	WINTER	SPRING	SUMMER
Production Capacity	55	70	55	30
Demand	35	30	30	60
Production/Cost Unit	$40	$30	$45	$50
Selling Price/Unit	$75	$60	$75	$75

Additionally, it costs $3 per unit to carry a unit over in inventory from the end of one season to the beginning of the next. Assume that they begin the fall season with a beginning inventory of 10 and that they want to complete the year with an inventory of 15. Hot-pot wants to know how many tea pots should be produced each season. Formulate as a linear programming model.

12. Icemore, Inc., services ice making machines in a summer tourist area. Given past records they are planning for a demand of 4000 hours of labor in May, 6000 in June, 5500 in July, and 3000 in August. Icemore has 40 service persons available May 1. Each worker averages 150 hours of productive work per month. Newly hired service persons must be trained for one month so that during their first month they do not provide any productive time. Furthermore, training is done on a one-to-one basis using experienced service people. This reduces a service person's productive time by 40 hours a month. There is a turnover of 10 percent among the experienced workers and all trainees give at least one month of productive service. There are no layoffs. An experienced service person is paid $2000 a month, while a trainee is paid $1000 a month.

Formulate a linear programming model to determine the number of trainees that must be hired in May, June, and July.

13. Market Analysis, Inc., is in the business of evaluating consumer response to new media services. In particular, a client is interested in evaluating the response to an innovative educational television network for all ages. The client's contract calls for a door-to-door, personal interview survey with the following requirements.

a. Survey at least 350 households with no children;
b. Survey at least 350 households with children;
c. Survey at least 100 households with children under 5 years of age;
d. Survey at least 100 households with children 5 years or older (one household may satisfy both c and d, but may only count in one category);
e. At least 50 percent of the families should be contacted at night;
f. At least 60 percent of the families with children should be contacted at night;
g. At least 1250 households should be contacted.

The following interview cost structure is assumed

| | INTERVIEW COST | |
HOUSEHOLD	DAY	EVENING
No children	$ 6	$ 8
Children <5	$10	$ 8
Children ≥5	$ 8	$10

Formulate a linear program to minimize interview costs and meet the seven stated requirements.

14. Ducky Feedmill produces duck food from four ingredients: corn, sorghum, wheat, and synthetic vitamins. The company produces the duck food in 1000 pound batches. The cost per pound of each ingredient is given in the following table.

INGREDIENT	COST/LB.
Corn	$0.10
Sorghum	$0.15
Wheat	$0.15
Vitamins	$0.25

Each batch must be mixed according to the following specifications.

a. The mix must contain at least 10 percent of the vitamin supplement;
b. The mix cannot contain more than 40 percent corn;
c. Corn and wheat must make up at least 50 percent of the mix;
d. The ratio of sorghum and wheat to corn cannot be more than 3 to 2.

Formulate a linear programming model that minimizes total batch cost.

15. Jetlag Transport, Inc., operates weekly air cargo flights from Hong Kong to San Francisco. Three types of merchandise are loaded into three compartments of the cargo plane. The capacity for both volume and weight follows.

AIR CARGO CAPACITIES		
COMPARTMENT	WEIGHT (TONS)	VOLUME (CU. FT.)
Front	50	2000
Center	100	5000
Rear	50	4000

The available cargo, revenue per ton transported, and the relationship between weight and volume for the cargo is listed below. Any amount of the merchandise available may be selected.

CARGO INFORMATION			
MERCHANDISE	WEIGHT (TONS)	VOLUME (CU. FT./TON)	REVENUE ($/TON)
Clothing	75	200	$ 600
Auto parts	150	45	$1000
Furniture	100	75	$ 400

Jetlag can select the merchandise available in any way it chooses as long as the plane is loaded evenly. By this we mean that the ratio of loaded cargo weight to weight capacity must be identical for the three compartments. Formulate a linear programming model to maximize revenue.

16. J. R. Department Stores, Ltd., is planning for the expansion of its network of stores. Currently they are planning for one additional store in Fort Rollins. The store is to have 75,000 square feet of useable floor space and the total investment cannot exceed $1.5 million. Currently they are attempting to allocate this space among four departments. Past experience and the best forecasts available indicate the following profitability.

DEPARTMENT	PROFIT PER SQUARE FOOT
Men's clothing	$3.00
Women's clothing	$5.00
Housewares	$2.50
Auto supplies	$2.75

Different departments require different rates of investment per square foot.

DEPARTMENT	INVESTMENT PER SQUARE FOOT
Men's clothing	$12
Women's clothing	$15
Housewares	$10
Auto supplies	$20

Additionally, the women's clothing department cannot be more than 15 percent larger than the men's clothing department. Also the space for auto supplies should be less than 25 percent of the total space allocated to the other three departments. Minimum sizes for each department are also specified.

DEPARTMENT	MINIMUM SIZE IN SQUARE FEET
Men's clothing	10,000
Women's clothing	15,000
Housewares	8000
Auto supplies	5000

    a. Formulate a linear programming model to determine the optimal space allocation.

    b. How would this formulation be modified if we wanted to simultaneously determine the optimal store size?

17. Built-Mor manufactures four different models of its Security Van. The per unit profit for each model is given in the following table.

MODEL	A	B	C	D
Net Profit ($000)	10	8	6	12

The company has $1.5 million capital to invest in production and a capability of 15,000 person days. The capital and labor requirements for each product are given below.

MODEL	REQUIRED CAPITAL PER UNIT ($000)	REQUIRED PERSON DAYS PER UNIT
A	25	240
B	14	100
C	10	180
D	30	275

The marketing department insists that model C must make up at least 35 percent of the total number of security vans produced. Formulate a linear program to determine the best production plan if

    a. The company's objective is profit maximization;

    b. The company's objective is to produce the maximum number of security vans.

18. An entering college student has $5000 to invest now that will be used to begin a small business upon graduation 4 years in the future. At the beginning of each year he can invest money in 1-, 2-, or 3-year time deposits. The bank he deals with exclusively pays 10 percent on a 1-year deposit, 22 percent (total) on a 2-year deposit, and 35 percent (total) on a 3-year deposit. Formulate a linear programming model to determine how to maximize total available cash at the end of the fourth year. There are severe penalties for early withdrawal of funds!

19. A custom kitchen builder has three shops. The shops require 800, 1000, and 600 board feet of lumber per week, respectively. The lumber comes from three different lumber companies. The lumber companies A, B, C sell the lumber for $0.50, $0.45, and $0.55 per board foot, respectively. Lumber companies A and B can provide a maximum of 1000 board feet per week, while the supply at lumber company C is virtually unlimited. The shipping costs must be paid by the buyer and these costs are listed below.

LUMBER	SHOP		
COMPANY	A	B	C
A	$0.025	0.04	0.05
B	0.03	—	0.03
C	0.02	0.05	—

The costs in the above table are the costs of shipping per board foot. Shipping from Lumber Company B to Shop B and Lumber Company C to Shop C are too expensive to consider. Additionally, Lumber Company A will not ship more than 500 board feet to any one customer. Formulate a linear programming model that will minimize the total cost of lumber acquisition.

20. Print-Rite assembles printers for personal computers. These printers are assembled at five different points along the production line. Each production line consists of five work teams with different levels of skill. Each team can be assigned to any of the five assembly points. The following table gives the time, in minutes, to perform the tasks at each assembly point for the individual teams.

	ASSEMBLY POINT				
TEAM	1	2	3	4	5
A	20	26	40	30	26
B	22	24	30	32	18
C	24	26	28	36	18
D	20	24	36	30	20
E	20	26	30	40	24

Formulate a linear programming model that will minimize the total assembly time for a printer.

Application Review

Central Carolina Bank and Trust Company (CCB)—A Successful Application of Linear Programming To Financial Planning

In early 1975, CCB had assets of about $360 million, including an investment securities portfolio of $100 million. The management of CCB was concerned with coordinating the activities of the bank to maximize the interest rate differentials between fund sources and uses of the funds. The bank established a Financial Planning Committee that was charged with integrating the following functions.

1. Interest rate forecasting;
2. Forecasting demand for bank services;
3. Liquidity management policy;
4. Funds allocation.

Concurrently, the development of a balance sheet optimization model using linear programming was authorized. Since the Financial Planning Committee was comprised of all senior bank officers, and their acceptance of the model was critical to implementation, they were also asked to assist in the development and implementation of the model.

The bank's financial goal was to maximize returns to shareholders. This goal was translated into achieving a target end of the period balance sheet position that produced the greatest profit. With this characterization of the bank's financial planning issues, the Financial Planning Committee began to develop the model. After considering the options available the committee decided to utilize a single-period model, and the model was formulated.

The decision variables in the developed model were tied directly to asset and liability/equity categories available to the bank. These categories are delineated below.

Asset Category	Liabilities/Equities
Cash	Demand deposit account
Treasury securities	Savings accounts
Agency securities	Savings certificates
Tax-exempt securities	Money market certificates
Other short-term instruments	State funds
Consumer loans	Certificates of deposit
Commercial loans	Repurchase agreements
Real estate loans	Federal funds sold

Source: Balbirer, Sheldon D., and David Shaw, "An Application of linear programming to bank financial planning" (October 1981), *Interfaces*, Vol. 11, No. 5, pp. 77–82.

Asset Category	Liabilities/Equities
Other assets	Other liabilities
Federal funds sold	Capital notes
	Equity accounts

The decision variables represented the amount of money (dollars) in each identified category. Associated with each category are the appropriate maturities or options. Thus, there are a number of decision variables for each category.

Since the objective was profit maximization, net yields or costs were determined for each asset and liability category. There were, of course, a number of restrictions on the bank's ability to select an end of the period balance sheet position. These restrictions were reflected by five categories of constraints.

1. Maximum activity level constraints;
2. Turnover constraints;
3. Policy constraints;
4. Legal/regulatory constraints;
5. Funds flow constraints.

Collectively these constraints represent a wide variety of operational, legal, and financial policy considerations.

The bank's financial records provided most of the required data. The major data input required to implement the model are listed here.

1. Expected yields on all securities and loan categories;
2. Expected interest rates on deposits and money market liabilities;
3. Administrative and/or processing costs on major loan and deposit categories;
4. Expected loan losses, by loan type, as a percentage of outstanding loans;
5. Maturity structure of all asset and liability categories;
6. Forecasts of demand for bank services.

The systems that were developed to satisfy the above data requirements proved to be beneficial in the sense that information that was not previously available was provided to management.

The goal of intimately involving senior managers in the modeling process was reflected in the assigned responsibility for generating all data input. Senior management assumed this responsibility and in the implementation process the coordination of changes in the model's parameters was the responsibility of the senior vice president for funds management.

The model was utilized on a continuing basis and resolved before each monthly meeting of the Financial Planning Committee. To obtain updated information the funds' manager solicited forecasts from other bank officers on any significant shift in the expected demand for bank services.

Forecasts of future interest rates were also developed at this point and a list of the changes to the model's input parameters were forwarded to the data processing department and a revised run was obtained. If there was significant uncertainty associated with these forecasts, multiple runs were obtained.

A run of the model produced a target balance sheet as well as a ranking of bank services. The target balance sheet gave targets for each balance sheet category and displayed additional information on lower or upper bounds. The model also used duality theory (introduced in Chapter 9) to rank the bank services according to their desirability. This output provided the marketing department with guidelines for their advertising and promotional activities.

Each time the Financial Planning Committee met, the current balance sheet position and the strategies implied by the model solution were analyzed. Since most of the committee was involved in the formulation process and was familiar with the model's strengths and weakness, the model solution was used to set general guidelines. Modifications based on nonquantifiable and/or subjective factors were then incorporated. The application of the management science model allowed for the input of experienced managers and provided a forum for communication. Top management at CCB believes that the education provided through the modeling process and the resulting communication are just as important as the actual solutions generated directly by the model.

7

GRAPHICAL ANALYSIS IN LINEAR PROGRAMMING

7.1 INTRODUCTION

In this chapter we examine the structure of the linear programming model through graphical methods. It should be noted that graphical analysis does not provide a practical way to solve realistic problems. It does, however, provide very important intuitive instruction on the structure of the algebraic methods used to solve and analyze a general linear programming problem.

Graphical analysis in linear programming is restricted to problems with two decision variables. Graphical representation of a linear problem is awkward in three decision variables, and impossible if more than three decision variables are involved. With two decision variables (2-dimensions) the graphical representation involves the graphing of systems of linear equalities and inequalities. We initially look at the analysis of a maximization problem with all less than or equal to constraints.

7.2 THE GRAPHICAL METHOD: THE MAXIMIZATION PROBLEM

The Dandy Serve Company produces mugs and snack plates for local souvenir shops. The mugs and snack plates are manufactured in a two-stage process. There are 300 minutes of time available for the completion of the first-stage process, and 400 minutes available for the completion of the second-stage process. Additionally, mugs require handpainting, which is restricted by a total of 150 minutes of available skilled labor. The remaining production/profit information is given in Table 7.1. Dandy needs to determine how many mugs and snack plates to produce with the available resources while maximizing profit. The linear programming model for this situation is given in (7.1), (7.2), and (7.3).

$$\text{Maximize } Z = 2x_1 + 4x_2 \qquad (7.1)$$

subject to

$$2.5x_1 + 3x_2 \le 300$$
$$5x_1 + 2x_2 \le 400$$
$$2x_2 \le 150 \qquad (7.2)$$

with

$$x_1, x_2 \ge 0 \qquad (7.3)$$

x_1 = number of snack plates produced

x_2 = number of mugs produced

We begin the graphical solution procedure by exhibiting a graph that can be used to display possible solutions to Dandy's product mix problem. The graph, shown in Figure 7.1, measures x_1 on the horizontal axis and x_2 on the vertical axis. Every point on the graph (x_1, x_2) corresponds to a possible solution. Figure 7.1 depicts a possible solution with $x_1 = 40$ and $x_2 = 60$.

We need to initially represent only those points that correspond to feasible solutions to the linear programming problem. Generally both x_1 and x_2 must be nonnegative. These conditions require a feasible solution to be in the first quadrant of the graph in Figure 7.1. This portion of that graph is shown in Figure 7.2. In all future graphical representations of linear programming we draw only the first quadrant.

The constraint that represents the stage 1 process was given as

$$2.5x_1 + 3x_2 \le 300. \qquad (7.4)$$

To graph this inequality we first graph the corresponding equality

$$2.5x_1 + 3x_2 = 300 \qquad (7.5)$$

TABLE 7.1 PRODUCTION REQUIREMENTS FOR THE DANDY SERVE COMPANY

PRODUCT	PRODUCTION TIME (MIN)			PROFIT ($/UNIT)
	STAGE 1	STAGE 2	PAINTING	
Snack plates	2.5	5	—	2
Mugs	3	2	2	4

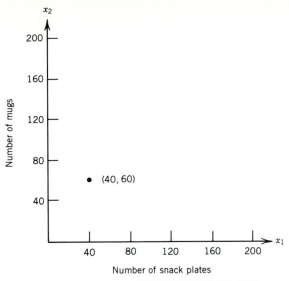

FIGURE 7.1   GRAPHICAL REPRESENTATION OF SOLU-
TION POINT FOR DANDY SERVE.

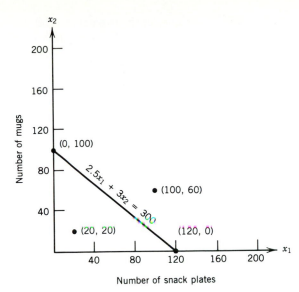

FIGURE 7.3   STAGE 1 PROCESS CONSTRAINT LINE.

as a line in our two-dimensional graph. The line
may be graphed by identifying two points that satisfy
this equality and drawing a line through these two
points. If the line does not pass through the point
(0, 0), the two points can be easily determined by
identifying the x_1 and x_2 intercepts. That is, when
$x_1 = 0$, $3x_2 = 300$, and $x_2 = 100$. Similarly, when
$x_2 = 0$, $2.5x_1 = 300$, and $x_1 = 120$. The line is
graphed in Figure 7.3.

We are not interested in the equality (7.4)

alone. The inequality (7.4) can be written as the
set of points that satisfy either of the following.

$$2.5x_1 + 3x_2 = 300 \qquad (7.6)$$

$$2.5x_1 + 3x_2 < 300 \qquad (7.7)$$

Obviously any point on the line (7.6) satisfies the
constraint (7.4). Now we must identify all points

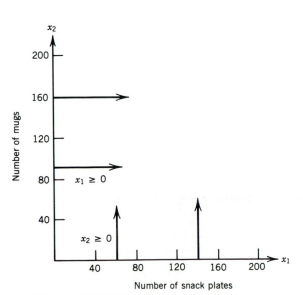

FIGURE 7.2   THE NONNEGATIVITY CONDITIONS.

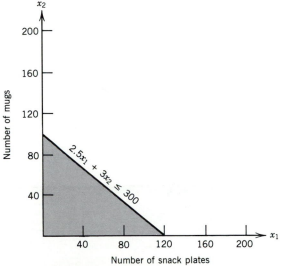

FIGURE 7.4   FEASIBLE SOLUTIONS FOR STAGE 1
PROCESS CONSTRAINT.

that satisfy (7.4). Consider the two points (100, 60) and (20, 20). Clearly the first does not satisfy (7.4) while the second does. It can be shown that if a point satisfies the constraint (and does not lie on the line), all points to the side of the line on which that point lies satisfy the given constraint. The shaded region in Figure 7.4 shows all the points that satisfy the constraint

$$2.5x_1 + 3x_2 \leq 300 \qquad (7.8)$$

In a similar fashion we graphically represent all feasible solutions to the remaining two constraints. Figure 7.5 gives the feasible solutions to the stage 2 process constraint, while Figure 7.6 gives the feasible solutions to the handpainting constraint.

Now that we have looked at the feasible solutions to the constraints individually we must look at the solutions that are feasible to all constraints simultaneously. To find these solutions that are indeed feasible to the linear programming problem stated in (7.1), (7.2), and (7.3) we draw all constraints on one graph and shade the region that satisfies all constraints simultaneously. The resulting shaded region in Figure 7.7 is called the *feasible region*. Any point on the boundary of the feasible region or within the feasible region is called a feasible solution.

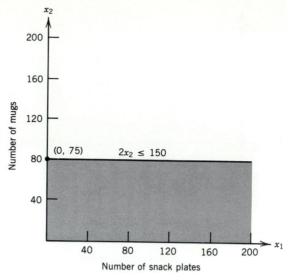

FIGURE 7.6 FEASIBLE SOLUTIONS FOR HANDPAINTING CONSTRAINT.

Once the feasible region is identified we can find the optimal solution to Dandy Serve's problem. Since an optimal solution is a feasible solution, we must identify the best feasible solution in the feasible region. Also, since there are an infinite number of feasible solutions, evaluating and comparing associated objective values is not possible. Therefore, we must develop a systematic procedure for determining the best feasible solution.

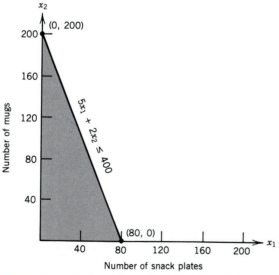

FIGURE 7.5 FEASIBLE SOLUTIONS FOR STAGE 2 PROCESS CONSTRAINT.

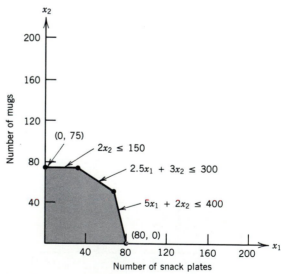

FIGURE 7.7 FEASIBLE REGION FOR DANDY SERVE.

We first select an arbitrary profit level and determine all feasible solutions that yield the selected profit or objective value. For example, suppose $Z = 120$, then from (7.1) x_1 and x_2 must satisfy the linear relationship

$$2x_1 + 4x_2 = 120 \qquad (7.9)$$

This is simply the equation of a line and is graphed in Figure 7.8, which also shows the feasible region. We see that any point on the line $2x_1 + 4x_2 = 120$ that is in the feasible region for the linear programming problem is a feasible solution with an objective value of 120. We must ask the following question: Are there any feasible solutions with objective values greater than 120?

It is instructive to rewrite the objective function

$$Z = 2x_1 + 4x_2 \qquad (7.10)$$

by solving for x_2 in terms of x_1 and Z. That is,

$$4x_2 = -2x_1 + Z$$

$$x_2 = -\frac{1}{2} x_1 + \frac{1}{4} Z \qquad (7.11)$$

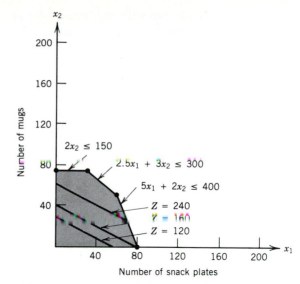

FIGURE 7.9 SELECTED PROFIT LINES FOR DANDY SERVE.

The coefficient of x_1 is the slope of the line, and $(1/4)Z$ is the x_2 intercept. We note that the slope of this line is independent of the value given for Z. Thus for any specified value of Z the profit line (7.10) has a slope of $-1/2$. Furthermore, different specifications for Z result in parallel profit lines. To verify this we substitute profit values of $Z = 120$, $Z = 160$, and $Z = 240$ into the second equation in (7.11).

$$\text{For } Z = 120 \qquad x_2 = -\frac{1}{2} x_1 + 30$$

$$\text{For } Z = 160 \qquad x_2 = -\frac{1}{2} x_1 + 40$$

$$\text{For } Z = 240 \qquad x_2 = -\frac{1}{2} x_1 + 60$$

These three profit lines are illustrated in Figure 7.9. Additionally, we observe that as Z increases, the profit lines are further from the origin. We can think of moving the profit line further from the origin in such a way that it remains parallel to the profit lines that are already graphed. If we do this, eventually the profit line *will no longer* touch the feasible region. When this happens the corresponding value for Z is not a feasible objective value for the linear programming problem. A point in the feasible region

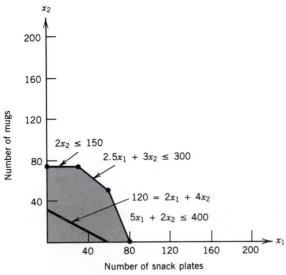

FIGURE 7.8 FEASIBLE SOLUTIONS WITH PROFIT OF $120.

that lies on the profit line with the largest value of Z is an optimal solution to the linear program under consideration.

We should now be able to identify the optimal solution to the Dandy Serve problem. The last point reached on the feasible region is indicated in Figure 7.10. The term $(x_1{}^*, x_2{}^*)$ is used to denote the coordinates of the optimal solution to the linear program in (7.1), (7.2), and (7.3). Determining the exact values of these coordinates from the graph is not advisable. We note that the optimal solution is at a point that is the intersection of the stage 1 process constraint and the handpainting constraint. Thus to find these coordinates we simply need to solve the following pair of equations simultaneously

$$2.5x_1 + 3x_2 = 300 \qquad (7.12)$$

$$2x_2 = 150 \qquad (7.13)$$

Solving (7.13) for x_2 yields $x_2 = 75$, and substituting this value in (7.12) we have

$$2.5x_1 + 3(75) = 300$$

$$2.5x_1 = 300 - 3(75)$$

$$x_1 = 30 \qquad (7.14)$$

Therefore, $(x_1{}^*, x_2{}^*) = (30, 75)$ and we can verify that the optimal objective value is 360 by substituting these values in (7.10)

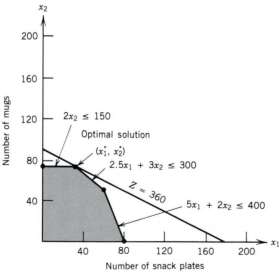

x_2

200

160

Number of mugs

120 — $2x_2 \leq 150$

Optimal solution

(x_1^*, x_2^*)

80 — $2.5x_1 + 3x_2 \leq 300$

$Z = 360$

40 — $5x_1 + 2x_2 \leq 400$

40   80   120   160   200 x_1

Number of snack plates

FIGURE 7.10   OPTIMAL SOLUTION FOR DANDY SERVE.

$$2(30) + 4(75) = 360 \qquad (7.15)$$

We observe that in order to maximize profit, Dandy Serve should produce 30 snack plates and 75 mugs. We also note that in developing the graphical solution to a two-decision variable problem, the exact values of the decision variables can be found by first using the graphical procedure to find the optimal point on the graph, and then solving a pair of simultaneous equations to find the exact coordinates.

At this point it is instructive to observe and interpret the result when $(x_1{}^*, x_2{}^*)$ is substituted into the left-hand sides of the three constraints in (7.2): Stage 1 process constraint

$$2.5(30) + 3(75) = 300 \qquad (7.16)$$

Stage 2 process constraint

$$5(30) + 2(75) = 300 \qquad (7.17)$$

Handpainting constraint

$$2(75) = 150 \qquad (7.18)$$

This means that we have fully utilized all the stage 1 production time and handpainting time, but we have only utilized 300 minutes of stage 2 production time, and thus 100 minutes of the available time remains. The stage 1 process constraint and the handpainting constraint are said to be *tight* (or met as equalities) at the point where $(x_1, x_2) = (30, 75)$. The stage 2 process constraint is not tight at this point, and we say that there is a *positive slack* for this constraint at the point $(x_1, x_2) = (30, 75)$. The significance of unused resource (slack) will be made clear in the following section. First, however, we summarize the graphical procedure developed here.

It should be noted again that the graphical procedure is used for instructive purposes and is reasonable only for linear programming problems with two decision variables. The steps for the graphical solution procedure for a maximization problem are outlined as follows.

1. Determine the feasible region for the linear programming problem.
2. Specify a value for Z and graph all points that yield this value of Z (a profit line).

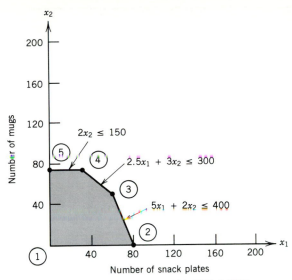

x_2

Number of mugs

200

160

120

80

$2x_2 \leq 150$

⑤

④

$2.5x_1 + 3x_2 \leq 300$

40

③

$5x_1 + 2x_2 \leq 400$

②

①

40   80   120   160   200

x_1

Number of snack plates

FIGURE 7.11   EXTREME POINTS FOR THE DANDY SERVE PROBLEM.

3. "Move" the profit line toward a larger value until further movement places the profit function outside the feasible region. (This means moving the profit line away from the origin if all the objective function coefficients are positive.)

4. A feasible point that lies on the profit line with the largest objective value is an optimal solution.

7.3   EXTREME POINTS AND THE SLACK VARIABLE

Look again at the feasible region for the Dandy Serve Company. Figure 7.11 labels five points on the boundary of the feasible region that make up the vertices or "cornerpoints" of the feasible region. In linear programming terminology these vertices are called *extreme points* of the feasible region. The coordinates of the feasible region are given in Table 7.2. We note again that each extreme point is the intersection of two constraints for the problem (one or both can be a nonnegativity constraint). For example, extreme point 3 is the intersection of the two process constraints and is the solution to the simultaneous equations that follow

$$2.5x_1 + 3x_2 = 300$$

$$5x_1 + 2x_2 = 400 \qquad (7.19)$$

TABLE 7.2   COORDINATES OF EXTREME POINTS FOR DANDY SERVE

EXTREME POINT	COORDINATES
1	(0, 0)
2	(80, 0)
3	(60, 50)
4	(30, 75)
5	(0, 75)

Each of the extreme points is a solution to the linear programming problem (7.1), (7.2), and (7.3). Therefore, we can compute the amount of resource used and thus the amount of resource unused for each solution. These computations are given in Table 7.3.

It should be evident that the decision variables (x_1, x_2) are not the only variables in this linear programming problem. Associated with each extreme point (or with a solution) there are uniquely specified values for the variables

S_1 = number of hours of unused stage 1 time

S_2 = number of hours of unused stage 2 time

S_3 = number of hours of unused handpainting time

$$\qquad (7.20)$$

Consider the stage 1 constraint

$$2.5x_1 + 3x_2 \leq 300 \qquad (7.21)$$

This constraint can be written as

$$300 - 2.5x_1 - 3x_2 \geq 0 \qquad (7.22)$$

where the left-hand side of this inequality is S_1, unused resource. Therefore, (7.21) can be replaced by the two conditions

$$S_1 \geq 0$$

$$300 - 2.5x_1 - 3x_2 = S_1 \qquad (7.23)$$

These two conditions can also be rewritten as

$$S_1 \geq 0$$

$$2.5x_1 + 3x_2 + S_1 = 300 \qquad (7.24)$$

TABLE 7.3 RESOURCE UTILIZATION AT EXTREME POINTS

EXTREME POINTS RESOURCE (HRS)	HOURS REQUIRED	HOURS AVAILABLE	HOURS UNUSED
1. (0, 0)			
Stage 1	$2.5(0) + 3(0) = 0$	300	300
Stage 2	$5(0) + 2(0) = 0$	400	400
Handpainting	$2(0) = 0$	150	150
2. (80, 0)			
Stage 1	$2.5(80) + 3(0) = 200$	300	100
Stage 2	$5(80) + 2(0) = 400$	400	0
Handpainting	$2(0) = 0$	150	150
3. (60, 50)			
Stage 1	$2.5(60) + 3(50) = 300$	300	0
Stage 2	$5(60) + 2(50) = 400$	400	0
Handpainting	$2(50) = 100$	150	50
4. (30, 75)			
Stage 1	$2.5(30) + 3(75) = 300$	300	0
Stage 2	$5(30) + 2(75) = 300$	400	100
Handpainting	$2(75) = 150$	150	0
5. (0, 75)			
Stage 1	$2.5(0) + 3(75) = 225$	300	75
Stage 2	$5(0) + 2(75) = 150$	400	250
Handpainting	$2(75) = 150$	150	0

Mathematically we have shown that the set of solutions to (7.21) is the same as the set of solutions to (7.24), and the constraint set of (7.1), (7.2), and (7.3) can be written in equality form as follows.

$$2.5x_1 + 3x_2 + S_1 \qquad\qquad = 300 \qquad (7.25)$$
$$5x_1 + 2x_2 \qquad + S_2 \qquad = 400$$
$$2x_2 \qquad\qquad + S_3 = 150$$
$$x_1, x_2, S_1, S_2, S_3 \geq 0 \qquad (7.26)$$

The objective function remains unchanged, but for completeness may be written as

$$\text{Maximize } Z = 2x_1 + 4x_2 + 0S_1 + 0S_2 + 0S_3 \qquad (7.27)$$

The variables S_1, S_2, S_3 are called the *slack variables* for the three inequality constraints. If a slack variable is zero at an extreme point, the associated constraint is said to be *binding* or *tight* at that extreme point. At the optimal extreme point, (30, 75), the stage 1 and handpainting constraints are binding or tight while the stage 2 constraint is not.

The ability to convert inequality constraints to equivalent equality constraints is more than a math-ematical exercise. While it is not practical to work with large systems of inequalities, it is practical to deal with large systems of linear equations. Chapter 8 exploits the structure of a linear programming problem as a system of linear equalities to develop an algorithm to find the optimal solution.

Before proceeding to briefly discuss our obvious preoccupation with extreme points, let us look at the correspondence between solutions to system (7.25) and (7.26) and the extreme points listed in Table 7.2. This relationship is summarized in Table 7.4. The S_1, S_2, and S_3 coordinates are simply obtained from system (7.25), by substituting the x_1 and x_2 coordinates from Table 7.2.

As a final comment we note that only three (the number of equations) of five variables are greater than zero for each extreme point. Again this is no coincidence. Do you see any pattern in the way the zero and nonzero variables are changing as we compare extreme point 1 to extreme point 2, extreme point 2 to extreme point 3, and so on?

7.4 EXTREME POINTS AND OPTIMALITY

Let us begin by examining the optimal solution to (7.1), (7.2), and (7.3) if the objective function

TABLE 7.4 EXTREME POINTS AND SLACK VARIABLES

EXTREME POINT	COORDINATES (x_1, x_2)	COORDINATES $(x_1, x_2, S_1, S_2, S_3)$
1	(0, 0)	(0, 0, 300, 400, 150)
2	(80, 0)	(80, 0, 100, 0, 150)
3	(60, 50)	(60, 50, 0, 0, 50)
4	(30, 75)	(30, 75, 0, 100, 0)
5	(0, 75)	(0, 75, 75, 250, 0)

coefficient of x_1 is changed from 2 to 3.5. In other words,

$$\text{Maximize } \bar{Z} = 2x_1 + 4x_2 \qquad (7.28)$$

is replaced by

$$\text{Maximize } Z = 3.5x_1 + 4x_2 \qquad (7.29)$$

As in the analysis of Section 7.2, we arbitrarily select a value for Z and graph the resulting line. $Z = 280$ is chosen and shown in Figure 7.12. By moving this profit line in a parallel fashion, we note that the optimal solution occurs at the corner point (60, 50). Here the optimal value of the linear programming problem is 410. It will be noted that the objective line $Z = 410$ and the constraint line $2.5x_1 + 3x_2 = 300$ are very difficult to distinguish in Figure 7.12.

In the case when the slope of the objective is close to the slope of a binding constraint, the graph may not be sufficient to determine the optimal solution. In such a case, we may compare the slopes of the two lines. Here the slope of the objective is $-3.5/4$ and the slope of the relevant constraint is $-2.5/3$. Since the slope of the objective is greater in absolute value than the slope of the constraint, the objective line that passes through (60, 50) will not intersect the feasible region at another point. Thus we can conclude that the optimal solution occurs at (60, 50). Also it can be verified that the objective value at the corner point (30, 75) is 405.

It was not a coincidence that the optimal solution to the linear programming problem with objective (7.29) also occurred at an extreme point. The intuitive argument for establishing optimality at an extreme point using the graphical analysis presented in Section 7.2 can be established mathematically. The result is the following theorem.

> **Theorem:** The optimal feasible solution, if it exists, will occur at one or more of the extreme points.

Thus, if we are seeking an optimal solution to a linear programming problem, we need only identify the extreme points for the feasible region and evaluate the objective values for these extreme points. The identification and evaluation of extreme points *without* the use of graphical analysis is the primary topic developed in Chapter 8.

7.4.1 ALTERNATIVE OPTIMAL SOLUTIONS

We began Section 7.4 with the consideration of the objective $Z = 3.5x_1 + 4x_2$. In this section we begin

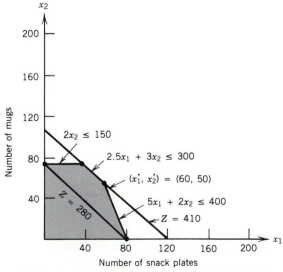

FIGURE 7.12 OPTIMAL SOLUTION FOR DANDY SERVE: OBJECTIVE $Z = 3.5x_1 + 4x_2$.

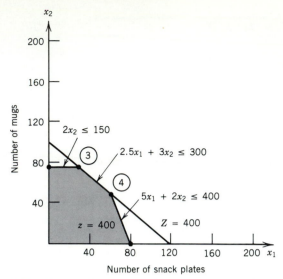

FIGURE 7.13 ALTERNATE OPTIMAL SOLUTIONS FOR DANDY SERVE: OBJECTIVE $Z = \frac{10}{3}x_1 + 4x_2$.

by considering problem (7.1), (7.2), and (7.3) with the modified objective:

$$\text{Maximize } Z = \left(\frac{10}{3}\right) x_1 + 4x_2 \qquad (7.30)$$

Figure 7.13 depicts the graphical analysis. Note the objective values for extreme points 3 and 4. Extreme point 3

$$\frac{10}{3} (60) + 4(50) = 400 \qquad (7.31a)$$

extreme point 4

$$\frac{10}{3} (30) + 4(75) = 400 \qquad (7.31b)$$

The graphical analysis indicates that both extreme points 3 and 4 are optimal solutions. The linear programming problem defined by objective (7.30) and the constraints of (7.1), (7.2), and (7.3) is said to have alternate optimal solutions.

We also observe that the coordinates to any point on the line segment from (60, 50) to (30, 75) can be computed by the expression

$$\lambda(60, 50) + (1 - \lambda) (30, 75),$$
$$\text{where } 0 \leq \lambda \leq 1 \qquad (7.32)$$

If $\lambda = 1/5$, then

$$\frac{1}{5} (60, 50) + \left(1 - \frac{1}{5}\right) (30, 75)$$
$$= (12, 10) + (24, 60) = (36, 70) \qquad (7.33)$$

The objective value for this point (which is not an extreme point) is

$$\left(\frac{10}{3}\right) (36) + 4(70) = 400 \qquad (7.34)$$

From this we observe that if a linear programming problem has an optimal solution, either it is unique or there are an infinite number of optimal solutions!

7.4.2 THE SLOPE OF THE OBJECTIVE FUNCTION

From a graphical point of view, the analysis of the three objective functions considered thus far

$$Z = 2x_1 + 4x_2$$
$$Z = 3.5x_1 + 4x_2$$
$$Z = \frac{10}{3} x_1 + 4x_2 \qquad (7.35)$$

differed only because of the slopes of the objective functions. Algebraically we solve for x_2 in terms of x_1, and the coefficient of x_1 is the slope of the respective objective function. The results are now listed.

$$x_2 = -\frac{1}{2} x_1 + \frac{Z}{4}$$
$$x_2 = -\frac{7}{8} x_1 + \frac{Z}{4}$$
$$x_2 = -\frac{5}{6} x_1 + \frac{Z}{4} \qquad (7.36)$$

The slopes of the three objectives are then $-1/2$, $-7/8$, and $-5/6$, respectively. Also the equality associated with the constraint,

$$2.5x_1 + 3x_2 \leq 300 \qquad (7.37)$$

has a slope of $-5/6$. Another observation of significance at this point is that if a linear programming problem has alternate optimal solutions, then the

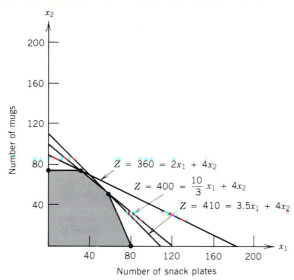

$$Z = 360 = 2x_1 + 4x_2$$

$$Z = 400 = \frac{10}{3}x_1 + 4x_2$$

$$Z = 410 = 3.5x_1 + 4x_2$$

FIGURE 7.14 A COMPARISON OF THREE OBJECTIVE FUNCTIONS FOR DANDY SERVE.

slope of the objective and the slope of a binding constraint are equal.

Figure 7.14 presents the three objective functions presented in (7.35) and illustrates the impact of increasing the objective function coefficient of variable x_1 if the objective function coefficient of variable x_2 is fixed (remains at 4). We see that as the coefficient of x_1, say c_1, increases, the objective function line becomes "steeper." As c_1 increases, the slope of the objective becomes closer to the slope of the constraint $25x_1 + 2x_2 \le 300$. As we observed earlier, when these slopes are equal, there are alternate optimal solutions and there is a choice for the optimal extreme point. Thus what we observe is that c_1 can increase from 2 to 10/3 without changing the optimal extreme point. When $c_1 = 10/3$, there are two optimal extreme points, and when c_1 is greater than 10/3 the optimal corner point or extreme point changes. The implications here are very important. As long as the objective function coefficient of x_1 is in the interval [2, 10/3] (while $c_2 = 4$), the optimal solution would mean the implementation of the solution: produce 30 snack plates and 75 mugs. In reality input parameters to the linear programming problem are approximations. Therefore, if the "true" per unit profit for snack plates is somewhere between 2 and 10/3, the production of 30 snack plates and 75 mugs will be optimal. On the other hand, if $c_1 = 3.4$, then the

production of 60 snack plates and 50 mugs is optimal.

Problems 23 and 24 at the end of this chapter extend the analysis presented in this section. What we are touching on here is a graphical approach to the primary topic developed in Chapter 9. Over what range can an input parameter vary without changing the optimal extreme point solution? This type of information is essential to the decision maker's interpretation and consequent implementation of the model results, and is called *sensitivity analysis*.

7.5 THE MINIMIZATION PROBLEM

Benson Assembly, Inc., fabricates custom metal doorframes. The fabrication process is very simple. In fact, fabrication only involves the completion of two 4-inch welds. There are two categories of employees that can be utilized for this task. The experienced employee can fabricate 30 frames per hour, and 98 percent of these frames are approved by the quality control inspectors. The inexperienced employee completes 20 frames per hour, with 95 percent approved by quality control.

The experienced employee is paid $12 per hour, while the inexperienced employee is paid $8 per hour. Each error costs the company $5, and Benson requires that a minimum of 2400 doorframes (not necessarily defect free) must be fabricated in an 8-hour shift. Finally, the labor pool limits Benson's staffing solution, since there are only 8 experienced workers available and 12 inexperienced workers available.

Benson faces the problem of determining a minimum cost solution to its staffing problem. It is obvious that the decision to be made is: How many experienced and how many inexperienced workers should be employed? Thus, the decision variables for this problem are

x_1 = the number of experienced workers hired

x_2 = the number of inexperienced workers hired

Incorporating the cost of unacceptable units, the per unit costs (per hour) are computed as follows

$$c_1: \$12 + \$5(0.02)(30) = \$15$$

$$c_2: \$\ 8 + \$5(0.05)(20) = \$13 \qquad (7.38)$$

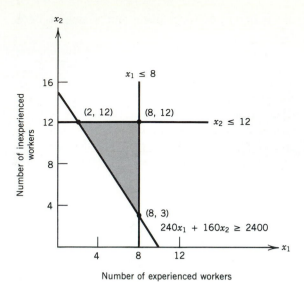

FIGURE 7.15 FEASIBLE REGION FOR
BENSON ASSEMBLY.

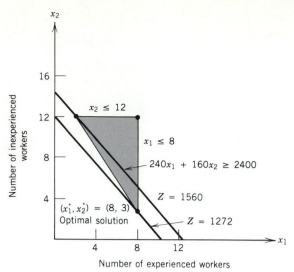

FIGURE 7.16 OPTIMAL SOLUTION FOR
BENSON ASSEMBLY.

Therefore, if the objective is stated as minimizing total cost for an 8-hour shift, the completed model is as follows.

$$\text{Minimize } Z = 120x_1 + 104x_2 \qquad (7.39)$$

subject to

$$
\begin{aligned}
x_1 &\leq 8 \\
x_2 &\leq 12 \\
(30)(8)x_1 + (20)(8)x_2 &\geq 2400 \qquad (7.40)
\end{aligned}
$$

with

$$x_1, x_2 \geq 0 \qquad (7.41)$$

Since only two decision variables are involved, a graphical procedure can be used to solve this linear programming problem. Figure 7.15 displays the feasible region to problem (7.39), (7.40), and (7.41) and three extreme points of this feasible region.

To determine the optimal value of $Z = 120x_1 + 104x_2$ we proceed in a fashion similar to the procedure developed in Section 7.2. We first specify a value for Z and graph all points that yield this value of Z. The line $Z = 1560$ is initially plotted in Figure 7.16. We observe that a total cost of 1560 is a feasible cost for this problem. This is not the optimal

value of the linear programming problem, since a small decrease in Z results in a line that passes through the feasible region also. As in Section 7.2 we think of moving the objective line in a direction until further movement places this line outside the feasible region. In a minimization problem with all positive objective function coefficients this means that Z decreases as the objective line is "moved toward" the origin.

The values of x_1 and x_2 that minimize total cost are 8 and 3, respectively. For a cost of $120(8) + 104(3) = 1272$, exactly 2400 doorframes will be fabricated, all available experienced workers are used, and there are nine inexperienced workers that are not utilized. Whether the linear programming problem involves a maximization objective or a minimization objective, the optimal feasible solution, if it exists, will occur at one or more of the extreme points. Thus, the analysis of a linear programming problem is much the same for both problems.

7.5.1 THE SURPLUS VARIABLE

In Section 7.3 we introduced the concept of a slack variable. Slack variables are associated with less-than-or-equal-to constraints. On the other hand, it will also be necessary to write a linear equality equivalent to the greater-than-or-equal-to constraint. In model (7.39), (7.40), and (7.41) the only "≥" constraint is

$$240x_1 + 160x_2 \geq 2400 \qquad (7.42)$$

Inequality (7.42) can be rewritten as

$$240x_1 + 160x_2 - 2400 \geq 0 \qquad (7.43)$$

where the left-hand side of this inequality, S_3, is defined to be *surplus* or the number of doorframes fabricated that exceed the requirement of 2400. Inequality (7.43) can also be written as

$$240x_1 + 160x_2 - 2400 = S_3$$
$$S_3 \geq 0 \qquad (7.44)$$

Mathematically, (7.42) and (7.44) are equivalent and (7.44) can be rewritten in the more conventional form

$$240x_1 + 160x_2 - S_3 = 2400$$
$$S_3 \geq 0 \qquad (7.45)$$

Problem (7.39), (7.40), and (7.41) can then be rewritten with equality constraints

Minimize $Z = 120x_1 + 104x_2$
$$+ 0S_1 + 0S_2 + 0S_3 \quad (7.46)$$

subject to

$$
\begin{array}{rcrcrcrcr}
x_1 & & & + S_1 & & & & = & 8 \\
& & x_2 & & + S_2 & & & = & 12 \\
240x_1 & + & 160\,x_2 & & & - S_3 & & = & 2400 \quad (7.47)
\end{array}
$$

with

$$x_1, x_2, S_1, S_2, S_3 \geq 0 \qquad (7.48)$$

S_1 and S_2 are slack variables as defined in Section 7.3, and S_3 is a *surplus variable*. Again, if a surplus variable is equal to zero at an extreme point, the constraint is said to be *binding* or *tight* at that extreme point. Table 7.5 lists the extreme points for problem (7.39), (7.40), and (7.41) and the corresponding solution to the equality constraint representation of (7.46), (7.47), and (7.48). Again S_1, S_2, and S_3 are computed by substituting the (x_1, x_2) values (as obtained from Figure 7.15) into (7.47).

7.6 SPECIAL PROBLEMS IN DETERMINING OPTIMAL SOLUTIONS

In this section we discuss three special situations that can occur in solving linear programming problems. These situations are refered to as *redundancy*, *infeasibility*, and *unboundedness*. We illustrate these special problems with examples involving two decision variables.

7.6.1 REDUNDANCY IN LINEAR PROGRAMMING

Redundancy refers to individual constraints in the set of constraints that define the feasible region. A particular constraint is said to be *redundant* if that constraint can be omitted without changing the set of feasible solutions to the linear programming problem under consideration.

Suppose that in the Dandy Serve example production of more than a combined total of 120 snack plates and mugs is prohibited. This condition is expressed as

$$x_1 + x_2 \leq 120 \qquad (7.49)$$

TABLE 7.5 EXTREME POINTS AND SLACK/SURPLUS VARIABLES FOR BENSON MANUFACTURING

EXTREME POINT	COORDINATES (x_1, x_2)	COORDINATES $(x_1, x_2, S_1, S_2, S_3)$
1	(8, 3)	(8, 3, 0, 4, 0)
2	(2, 12)	(2, 12, 6, 0, 0)
3	(8, 12)	(8, 12, 0, 0, 1440)

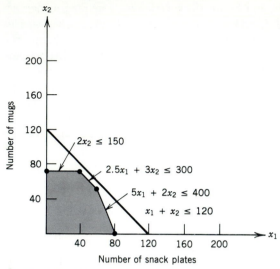

$2x_2 \leq 150$

$2.5x_1 + 3x_2 \leq 300$

$5x_1 + 2x_2 \leq 400$

$x_1 + x_2 \leq 120$

Number of mugs

Number of snack plates

FIGURE 7.17 REDUNDANCY AND THE FEASIBLE REGION.

and the modified linear programming model for Dandy Serve is as follows.

$$\text{Maximize } Z = 2x_1 + 4x_2 \qquad (7.50)$$

subject to

$$2.5x_1 + 3x_2 \leq 300 \qquad (7.51)$$
$$5x_1 + 2x_2 \leq 400$$
$$2x_2 \leq 150$$
$$x_1 + x_2 \leq 120$$

with

$$x_1, x_2 \leq 0 \qquad (7.52)$$

Figure 7.17 illustrates the fact that the constraint $x_1 + x_2 \leq 120$ does not limit the set of feasible solutions to (7.50), (7.51), and (7.52). In fact, the two constraints

$$2.5x_1 + 3x_2 \leq 300$$
$$5x_1 + 2x_2 \leq 400 \qquad (7.53)$$

together require that $x_1 + x_2 \leq 120$. Thus, the constraint $x_1 + x_2 \leq 120$ is a redundant constraint. The set of extreme points for (7.1), (7.2), and (7.3) and the set extreme points for (7.50), (7.51), and (7.52) are identical. We do want to note, however, that the extreme point representation that incorporates slack variables is slightly different than the summary in Table 7.4. To see this we write the constraint set for problem (7.25) in equality form.

$$2.5x_1 + 3x_2 + S_1 \qquad\qquad = 300 \quad (7.54)$$
$$5x_1 + 2x_2 \qquad + S_2 \qquad\qquad = 400$$
$$2x_2 \qquad\qquad + S_3 \qquad = 50$$
$$x_1 + x_2 \qquad\qquad\qquad + S_4 = 120$$

with

$$x_1, x_2, S_1, S_2, S_3, S_4 \geq 0 \qquad (7.55)$$

Table 7.6 lists the extreme points for problem (7.50), (7.51), and (7.52) and their coordinates in terms of the slack variables given in (7.54). We observe that S_4 is not zero for any extreme point. If the slack or surplus variable associated with an inequality is greater than zero at every extreme point of the feasible region, then the constraint is redundant.

TABLE 7.6 EXTREME POINT REPRESENTATION FOR PROBLEM (7.50), (7.51), AND (7.52)

EXTREME POINT	COORDINATES (x_1, x_2)	COORDINATES $(x_1, x_2, S_1, S_2, S_3, S_4)$
1	(0, 0)	(0, 0, 300, 400, 150, 120)
2	(80, 0)	(80, 0, 100, 0, 50, 40)
3	(60, 50)	(60, 50, 0, 0, 50, 10)
4	(30, 75)	(30, 75, 0, 100, 0, 15)
5	(0, 75)	(0, 75, 75, 250, 0, 45)

7.6.2 INFEASIBILITY IN LINEAR PROGRAMMING

Infeasibility occurs when there is no possible solution to the linear programming problem that satisfies all the constraints and nonnegativity conditions. Infeasibility simply means that the feasible region does not exist.

To illustrate the problem of infeasibility, suppose the management of Dandy Serve suggests that at least 60 mugs and at least 60 snack plates be produced. This means that we must add to the original problem formulation the constraints

$$x_1 \geq 60$$

$$x_2 \geq 60 \tag{7.56}$$

We see in Figure 7.18 that there is no point that satisfies (7.56) as well as the constraints from (7.1), (7.2), and (7.3). In this illustration there is no feasible solution, simply because there are not enough resources to meet the constraints for the production problem. Sixty snack plates and 60 mugs require 330 minutes of stage 1 labor and 420 minutes of stage 2 labor. There are only 300 minutes of stage 1 labor and 400 minutes of stage 2 labor available.

If infeasibility is encountered in practice, the first thing to determine is whether a mistake has been made in the formulation process. Often, infeasibility is the direct result of the misspecification

of a constraint. If there are no obvious formulation errors, then it is important to further analyze the structure of the model by carefully evaluating resource availability as well as implicit minimum (maximum) levels for the decision variables.

7.6.3 THE UNBOUNDED SOLUTION

The solution to a linear programming problem is *unbounded* if the value of the objective may be made infinitely large (for a maximization problem) without violating any of the constraints. If the objective function involves profit maximization and the solution is unbounded, then any level of profit can be achieved. Certainly, something has been omitted in such a situation! Generally, the cause is an error in formulation, such as a constraint being inadvertently omitted in the formulation process.

To illustrate the nature of an unbounded solution consider the following linear programming problem

$$\text{Maximize } Z = 2x_1 + 3x_2 \tag{7.57}$$

subject to

$$x_1 - x_2 \leq 2$$

$$-3x_1 + x_2 \leq 4 \tag{7.58}$$

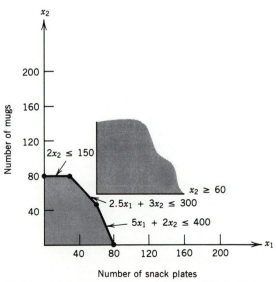

FIGURE 7.18 INFEASIBILITY IN LINEAR PROGRAMMING.

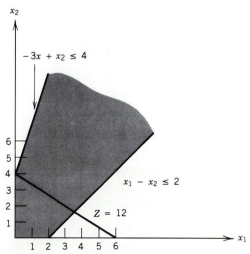

FIGURE 7.19 UNBOUNDEDNESS IN LINEAR PROGRAMMING.

with

$$x_1, \ x_2 \leq 0 \qquad (7.59)$$

Figure 7.19 shows the feasible region for (7.57), (7.58), and (7.59). The feasible region extends infinitely. Graphed also in Figure 7.19 is the equation $Z = 12$. It is easy to see that no matter how large the selected value of Z, the resulting line will graphically intersect this "open-ended" feasible region. In other words, no matter what objective value we pick, there will always be a feasible solution with a larger objective value. Thus, the solution to (7.57), (7.58), and (7.59) is unbounded, and we say that there is no optimal solution to this linear programming problem.

7.7 SUMMARY

The graphical approach to the solution of linear programming problems was not presented as an effective way to solve linear programming problems. Rather it was viewed as an instructional tool to present some of the basic concepts in the solution of general linear programming problems.

In the graphical approach, the feasible region and optimal extreme points were determined from the graph and simultaneous equations were solved to find the *exact* coordinates of these extreme points. The simultaneous equations solved involved two equations and two variables. The solution of simultaneous equations forms the basis of the simplex method for solving linear programming problems, which is presented in Chapter 8.

With this in mind, we also presented a procedure for converting linear inequalities to linear equalities. Slack variables were used to convert less-than-or-equal-to constraints to equality constraints, while surplus variables were used to convert greater-than-or-equal-to constraints to equality form. In this process we also required that the slack and surplus variables satisfy nonnegativity conditions.

Additionally, four special situations in linear programming were illustrated: redundancy, infeasibility, unboundedness, and alternative optimal solutions. Redundancy involved the inclusion of a constraint that could be omitted without changing the set of feasible solutions. In the case of infeasibility, there are no feasible solutions. In the case of unboundedness, the objective value can be made infinitely large for a maximization problem or infinitely small for a minimization problem. In the case of alternate optimal solutions (alternate optima), two extreme points are optimal as well as all the points in the line segment connecting them.

GLOSSARY

Feasible Region   The set of all feasible solutions to the linear programming problem.

Extreme Point   Feasible solution points occurring at the vertices or "corners" of the feasible solution. In two dimensions, extreme points are determined by the intersection of two constraint lines.

Redundancy   A particular constraint is said to be redundant if it can be omitted without changing the set of feasible solutions.

Slack Variable   A variable added to the left-hand side of a "$\leq$" constraint. A slack variable is used to convert the "$\leq$" constraint to an equality and is nonnegative.

Surplus Variable   A variable subtracted from the left-hand side of a "$\geq$" constraint. A surplus variable is used to convert the "$\geq$" constraint to an equality and is nonnegative.

Tight (Binding) Constraint   An inequality constraint is said to be tight at a particular point if the slack (or surplus) variable is equal to zero at that point.

(Please review the glossary for Chapter 6 for additional terminology.)

Selected References

Bazaraa, Mokhtar S., and John J. Jarvis. 1977. *Linear Programming and Network Flows.* New York: Wiley.

Bradley, Stephen P., Arnoldo C. Hax, and Thomas L. Magnanti. 1977. *Applied Mathematical Programming.* Reading, Mass.: Addison–Wesley.

Budnick, Frank S., Richard Mojena, and Thomas E. Vollmann. 1977. *Operations Research for Management.* Homewood, Ill.: Irwin.

Charnes, A., and W. W. Cooper. 1961. *Management Models and Industrial Applications of Linear Programming,* vols. 1 and 2. New York: Wiley.

Cooper, Leon, and David Steinberg. 1974. *Methods and Applications of Linear Programming.* Philadelphia, Pa.: Sanders.

Dantzig, George B. 1963. *Linear Programming and Extensions.* Princeton, N.J.: Princeton Univ. Press.

Greenberg, Michael R. 1978. *Applied Linear Programming For the Socio-economic and Environmental Sciences.* New York: Academic Press.

Hadley, G. 1962. *Linear Programming.* Reading, Mass.: Addison–Wesley.

Hillier, Fredrick S., and Gerald J. Lieberman. 1980. *Introduction to Operations Research,* 3rd ed. San Francisco: Holden–Day.

Hughes, Ann J., and Dennis E. Grawoig. 1973. *Linear Programming: An Emphasis on Decision Making.* Reading, Mass.: Addison–Wesley.

Ignizo, James P. 1982. *Linear Programming In Single and Multiple Objective Systems.* Englewood Cliffs, N.J.: Prentice–Hall.

Llewellyn, Robert W. 1964. *Linear Programming.* New York: Holt, Rinehart & Winston.

Luenberger, David G. 1973. *Introduction to Linear and Nonlinear Programming.* Reading, Mass.: Addison–Wesley.

Markland, Robert E. 1983. *Topics in Management Science,* 2nd ed. New York: Wiley.

Taha, Hamdy A. 1982. *Operations Research: An Introduction,* 3rd. ed. New York: Macmillan.

Thompson, Gerald E. 1971. *Linear Programming: An Elementary Introduction.* New York: Macmillan.

Wagner, Harvey M. 1969. *Principles of Operations Research: With Applications to Managerial Decisions.* Englewood Cliffs, N.J.: Prentice–Hall.

Discussion Questions

1. Discuss the basic differences/similarities to the graphical approach for solving maximization versus minimization problems.

2. Discuss the implications of the following statement: Either a linear programming problem has a unique optimal solution or an infinite number of optimal solutions.

3. State a condition necessary for a linear programming problem to have alternate optimal solutions.

4. How does redundancy impact the determination of the optimal solution in linear programming?

5. State a condition necessary for a linear programming problem to be unbounded.

6. If a linear programming problem is unbounded or infeasible, we say this problem has no optimal solution. There is, however, a significant difference. What is it?

7. Give an intuitive argument, based on the graphical approach, for the fact that optimal solutions in linear programming occur at extreme points.

8. Slack and surplus variables are restricted to be nonnegative. Why is this necessary?

9. Suppose we have a linear programming problem with an equality constraint. Describe the feasible region for this problem.

10. Give two feasible solutions to the Dandy Serve problem, (7.1), (7.2), and (7.3), not on the boundary to the feasible region. Describe these solutions via the coordinates $(x_1, x_2, S_1, S_2, S_3)$. Discuss any structural difference between these two solutions and the extreme point solutions.

PROBLEMS

1. Consider the following graph and the associated constraint set:

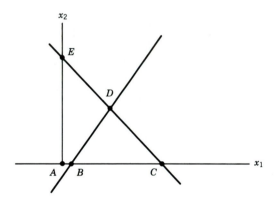

$$x_1 - x_2 \geq 1$$

$$x_1 + x_2 \leq 7$$

$$x_1, x_2 \geq 0 \qquad\qquad \text{(E.1)}$$

    a. Give the coordinates of the points A, B, C, D, E as indicated on the graph.

    b. What are the extreme points for feasible regions to (E.1)?

    c. If the problem has the objective function, Maximize $Z = 3x_1 + x_1$, what is the optimal extreme point?

    d. If the problem has the objective function, Minimize $Z = 3x_1 + x_2$, what is the optimal extreme point?

2. Replace (E.1) with the modified constraint set

$$x_1 - x_2 \leq 1$$

$$x_1 + x_2 \leq 7$$

$$x_1, x_2 \geq 0 \qquad\qquad \text{(E.2)}$$

    a. What are the extreme points for the feasible region to (E.2)?

b. Answer 1c for constraint set (E.2).
c. Answer 1d for constraint set (E.2).

3. Replace (E.1) with the modified constraint set

$$x_1 - x_2 \leq 1$$
$$x_1 + x_2 \geq 7$$
$$x_1, x_2 \geq 0 \tag{E.3}$$

a. What are the extreme points for the feasible region to (E.3)?
b. Answer 1c for constraint set (E.3).
c. Answer 1d for constraint set (E.3).

4. Replace (E.1) with the modified constraint set

$$x_1 - x_2 \geq 1$$
$$x_1 + x_2 \geq 7$$
$$x_1, x_2 \geq 0 \tag{E.4}$$

a. What are the extreme points for the feasible region to (E.4)?
b. Answer 1c for constraint set (E.4).
c. Answer 1d for constraint set (E.4).

5. Consider the linear programming problem

$$\text{Maximize } Z = x_1 + 2x_2$$

subject to

$$x_1 \leq 10$$
$$x_2 \leq 10$$
$$x_1 + x_2 \leq 15$$

with

$$x_1, x_2 \geq 0$$

a. Graphically show the feasible region for the problem.
b. What are the coordinates for the extreme points to the feasible region?
c. What is the optimal solution?
d. Solve if the objective is changed to $Z = 2x_1 + x_2$.

6. Consider the following modification of Problem 5.

$$\text{Minimize } Z = x_1 + 2x_2$$

subject to

$$x_1 \leq 10$$

$$x_2 \leq 10$$

$$x_2 + x_2 \geq 15$$

with

$$x_1, x_2 \geq 0$$

Answer questions a–d in Problem 5.

7.   Consider the following modification of Problem 5.

$$\text{Maximize } Z = x_1 + 2x_2$$

subject to

$$x_1 \leq 10$$

$$x_2 \leq 10$$

$$x_1 + x_2 = 15$$

with

$$x_1, x_2 \geq 0$$

Answer questions a–d in Problem 5. Are the nonnegativity constraints redundant in this situation?

8.   Solve the following problem graphically

$$\text{Maximize } Z = 3x_1 + 4x_2$$

subject to

$$2x_1 + 4x_2 \leq 80$$

$$x_1 + 5x_2 \leq 70$$

with

$$x_1, x_2 \geq 0$$

9.   Consider the following linear programming problem.

$$\text{Maximize } Z = 5x_1 + x_2$$

subject to

$$2x_1 + 3x_2 \leq 12$$
$$3x_1 + x_2 \leq 9$$
$$x_1 - x_2 \leq 1$$

with

$$x_1, x_2 \geq 0$$

a. Give the coordinates to all the extreme points to the feasible region.
b. Find the optimal solution to this problem.

10. Solve the following problem graphically

$$\text{Minimize } Z = 100x_1 + 120x_2$$

subject to

$$2x_1 + x_2 \geq 60$$
$$x_1 + 4x_2 \geq 100$$

with

$$x_1, x_2 \geq 0$$

11. Solve the following problem graphically

$$\text{Minimize } Z = x_1 + x_2$$

subject to

$$x_1 + x_2 \geq 4$$
$$2x_2 \leq 6$$
$$3x_1 + x_2 \leq 9$$

with

$$x_1, x_2 \geq 0$$

12. Solve the following problem graphically

$$\text{Minimize } Z = -3x_1 - 4x_2$$

subject to

$$2x_1 + 4x_2 \leq 80$$
$$x_1 + 5x_2 \leq 70$$

with

$$x_1, x_2 \geq 0$$

13. Solve the following problem graphically

$$\text{Minimize } Z = 25x_1 + 35x_2$$

subject to

$$2x_1 + 4x_2 \geq 22$$
$$x_1 \quad\quad \leq 4$$
$$x_2 \leq 3$$

with

$$x_1, x_2 \geq 0$$

14. Solve the following problem graphically

$$\text{Maximize } Z = 4x_1 + 3x_2$$

subject to

$$5x_1 - 4x_2 \leq 40$$
$$x_2 \leq 30$$
$$x_1 + x_2 \geq 20$$

with

$$x_1, x_2 \geq 0$$

15. Consider the following linear programming problem

$$\text{Maximize } Z = 20x_1 + 35x_2$$

subject to

$$3x_1 + 2x_2 \geq 12$$
$$-x_1 + 2x_2 \leq 12$$
$$x_1 - 2x_2 \geq 4$$
$$x_1 + x_2 \leq 12$$

with

$$x_1, x_2 \geq 0$$

a. Give the coordinates to all the extreme points to the feasible region.
b. Find the optimal solution to this problem.

16. Verify graphically that the following problem has alternate optimal solutions.

$$\text{Maximize } Z = 4x_1 + 2x_2$$

subject to

$$8x_1 + 4x_2 \leq 40$$
$$5x_1 + 8x_2 \leq 80$$
$$6x_1 + x_2 \leq 24$$

with

$$x_1, x_2 \geq 0$$

a. Give the coordinates of three optimal solutions to this problem.
b. Does this problem have a redundant constraint? If it does, identify it.

17. Write the constraints of Problem 16 in equality form and give the coordinates of the extreme points in the form $(x_1, x_2, S_1, S_2, S_3)$.

18. Write the constraints of Problem 15 in equality form and give the coordinates of the extreme points in the form $(x_1, x_2, S_1, S_2, S_3, S_4)$.

19. Solve Problem 1, Chapter 6, graphically.

20. A manufacturer makes two types of desks, the conventional model and the micro-support model. The conventional model requires $120 to produce and 40 cubic feet of storage space. The micro-support model costs $80 to produce and requires 40 cubic feet of storage space. The micro-support model yields a $100 per unit profit, while the conventional model yields a $75 per unit profit. Use graphical analysis to determine the optimal number of each type of desk to produce if the objective is to maximize profit. We must operate under the constraints that production cost cannot exceed $160,000 and that the total available storage space is 60,000 cubic feet.

21: Write the constraints of the model in Problem 20 in equality form. Interpret the values of *all* variables at each of the extreme points for this problem.

22. For the following problem

$$\text{Minimize } Z = x_1 + 2x_2$$

subject to

$$2x_1 - 3x_2 \le 7$$

$$x_1 + 2x_2 \le 10$$

with

$$x_1, x_2 \ge 0$$

find the coordinates of the extreme points where both slack variables are zero.

23. For model (7.1), (7.2), and (7.3) verify the following.

   a. If the objective function coefficient of x_1 is in the interval [2, 10/3], then the optimal solution occurs at extreme point 4.
   b. If the objective function coefficient of x_1 is the interval [10/3, 3.5], then the optimal solution occurs at extreme point 3.

24. For model (7.1), (7.2), and (7.3) verify the following.

   a. If the objective function coefficient of x_1 is in the interval [0, 10/3], then the optimal solution occurs at extreme point 4.
   b. If the objective function coefficient of x_1 is in the interval [10/3, 10], then the optimal solution occurs at extreme point 3.

25. For Problem 5, find the minimum increase in the objective function coefficient of x_1 that will result in a change of the optimal solution.

26. For problem 8, find the minimum increase in the objective function coefficient of x_2 that will result in a change of the optimal solution.

27. For Problem 10, find the minimum increase in the objective function coefficient of x_1 that will result in a change of the optimal solution.

28. For Problem 10, find the minimum increase in the objective function coefficient of x_2 that will result in a change of the optimal solution.

29. The owner of the Happy Hog Ranch must determine the appropriate mix of two types of pig food: Heavenly Hash and Butter Rump. Heavenly Hash costs $0.35 per pound and Butter Rump costs $0.70 per pound. Four essential ingredients are contained in each type of pig food. The following table indicates the minimum daily requirements and the percent of each ingredient per pound of food.

INGREDIENT	HEAVENLY HASH (%/LB)	BUTTER RUMP (%/LB)	MINIMUM DAILY REQUIREMENT (LB)
1	40	50	60
2	15	5	25

INGREDIENT	HEAVENLY HASH (%/LB)	BUTTER RUMP (%/LB)	MINIMUM DAILY REQUIREMENT (LB)
3	15	35	60
4	24	10	60

Using graphical analysis, find the least cost daily blend for the Happy Hog Ranch.

30. A company produces two different brooms: Sweep Easy and Light Sweep. The per unit profit for Sweep Easy is $2.00, while the per unit profit for Light Sweep is $3.50. The production of brooms requires three operations. Sweep Easy requires 20 minutes for operation 1, 12 minutes for operation 2, and 24 minutes for operation 3. Light Sweep requires 10 minutes for operation 1, 12 minutes for operation 2, and 4 minutes for operation 3. A production run lasts 24 hours. Additionally, the marketing department suggests that at most twice as many Sweep Easy brooms should be produced. Use graphical analysis to determine how many brooms of each type should be used to maximize profit.

31. Suppose that in Problem 26 our objective would be to minimize unused time for the three machines. How would the formulation change? Is graphical analysis still appropriate? Explain.

32. Assume that the objective in Problem 1, Chapter 6 is to minimize the underutilization of available machine time. Solve this modified problem using graphical analysis.

33. Solve Problem 3, Chapter 6 using graphical analysis.

Application Review

Crude Oil Sales at Elk Hills: Using LP to Evaluate Competitive Bids

The Naval Petroleum Reserves in California (NPRC) are a major source of crude oil in the United States. The Elk Hills field is jointly owned by the federal government and Chevron, USA. The Department of Energy administers the federal government's interest in the oil field.

Production began at Elk Hills in July 1976, with production in excess of 150,000 barrels of oil per day (BOPD). In order to bring these fields into production sales contracts with private companies needed to be secured, so that the oil could be moved to the marketplace. This case study examines how the bid award structures were developed. Particular attention is given to the role of linear programming in the development of the resulting procedures.

Source: Jackson, Bruce L., and John Michael Brown, "Using LP for crude oil sales at Elk Hills: A case study" (June 1980), *Interfaces,* Vol. 10, No. 3, pp. 65–69.

Until 1976, production at Naval Petroleum Reserve was minimal. With the enactment of PL 94-258 (the Naval Petroleum Act of 1976), the federal government was faced with a mandate to produce and sell crude oil to the highest qualified bidders. The only qualification was that no company could receive more than 20 percent of the oil produced. First we examine the initial bid and evaluation procedures for Elk Hills oil sales.

The initial sales at Elk Hills were based on an evaluation procedure called the "line item approach." A *line item* was defined as the average daily production expected to be available at each of six delivery points during the contract period. Bidders were allowed to bid on the entire line item or a portion of the line item. The bids were made by offering a bonus price based on the highest price offered for a similar grade oil produced from nongovernmental fields in the area. After the bids were opened, all bids on a line item were ranked from highest to lowest, beginning with line item 1. In some cases, a bidder reached the 20 percent limit on line item 1 and was not eligible for subsequent line items, even though its bid for other line items would have proved to be more attractive to the seller.

A simple example illustrates the deficiency in the line item approach as implemented by the federal government. It is assumed that a sales contract is offered for two line items.

Line item 1—Sell 10,000 BOPD from shipping point A
Line item 2—Sell 10,000 BOPD from shipping point B

Also no single bidder may receive more than 15,000 BOPD. Suppose that two bidders, company C and company D, respond as follows.

BIDDER	SHIPPING POINT	MAXIMUM QUALITY DESIRED	BONUS ($)
Company C	A	10,000	+0.10
Company D	A	10,000	+0.09
Company C	B	10,000	+0.20
Company D	B	10,000	+0.15

If the bid evaluator proceeded using the line item evaluation procedure, considering the quantity available at shipping point A first, all of line item 1 would be awarded to company C and the second line item would be split between companies C and D. Specifically:

LINE ITEM	AWARDEE	AMOUNT	BONUS
1	C	10,000	+0.10
2	C	5000	+0.20
2	D	5000	+0.15
Average bonus per barrel = $0.1375/BBL			

On the other hand, if the evaluator started with line item 2, the award would be made as follows.

LINE ITEM	AWARDEE	AMOUNT	BONUS
2	C	10,000	+0.20
1	C	5000	+0.10
1	D	5000	+0.09
Average bonus per barrel = $0.1475/BBL			

Obviously order of award was significant and the objective of revenue maximization was not being achieved.

Recognizing the problem, a simple linear programming model was developed to assist in the task of revenue optimization. Utilizing the two shipping point, two company example, the model was constructed as follows. The decision variables are

AC = quantity of oil to be awarded to company C from shipping point A

AD = quantity of oil to be awarded to company D from shipping point A

BC = quantity of oil to be awarded to company C from shipping point B

BD = quantity of oil to be awarded to company D from shipping point B

R = revenue

The actual illustrative model is

$$\text{Maximize } R = (0.10)AC + (0.09)AD + (0.20)BC + (0.15)BD \quad (7.60)$$

subject to

$$AC + AD \leq 10{,}000 \quad (7.61)$$
$$BC + BD \leq 10{,}000$$
$$AC + BC \leq 15{,}000$$
$$AD + BD \leq 15{,}000$$
$$AC \leq 10{,}000$$
$$AD \leq 10{,}000$$
$$BC \leq 10{,}000$$
$$BD \leq 10{,}000$$

with

$$AC, AD, BC, BD \geq 0 \quad (7.62)$$

A model of the type presented in (7.60), (7.61), and (7.62) served as the basis for evaluating bids with the objective of maximizing total revenue. The linear program model had a major shortcoming even though it was an integral part of the overall bid evaluation scenario. The model allows any quantity to be awarded that is less than or equal to the quantity the bidder offered to purchase, although it may be uneconomical to accept less than 200 BOPD for a given vendor. Thus bidders were asked to specify both a maximum quantity and a minimum quantity desired at the offered bonus price.

The incorporation of this reality into the model required the inclusion of binary variables into the linear programming model. The result was a mixed integer programming (MIP) model. The resulting MIP model was eventually adopted for use at Elk Hills. The linear programming approach not only assisted the government but also provided an additional benefit to the bidders. For example, if a company could only use 5000 BOPD during the contract year, they could make several bids that totaled more than 5000 BOPD. This allowed the bidders the flexibility needed without fear of receiving more oil than they could use.

In July 1978, the MIP model was approved for use by the Assistant Secretary of Energy for Resource Applications. The method was utilized in the crude oil sale conducted at Elk Hills on December 18, 1978. There were a total of 21 companies that bid, making a total of 62 bids for a sale that was 300 percent oversubscribed. The total cost of the computer run, including the keypunching, was estimated to be less than $2500. On the other hand, the sale resulted in an equivalent increase in revenue, based on the increased bonus price alone, of over $7,000,000 for the sale period. In this situation a relatively simple linear programming model assisted in overall revenue maximization, enhanced the revenue derived from the sale, and provided the bidders for government crude oil with greater flexibility in structuring their bids.

CHAPTER

8

THE SIMPLEX METHOD

8.1 INTRODUCTION

In Chapter 7 we noted that the graphical approach to linear programming is inappropriate when the number of decision variables is greater than two. We can, however, solve linear programming problems with many decision variables by using an iterative procedure called the *simplex method*. This method permits us to evaluate a sequence of extreme points in such a way that each additional extreme point examined gives an objective value that is at least as good as the previous extreme point examined. The procedure continues until an extreme point with a better objective value cannot be generated. At that point we are able to conclude whether we have found the optimal solution to the linear programming problem.

The simplex method is examined in detail in this chapter. We begin by developing the concept of a basic feasible solution and examining the relationship between such solutions and extreme points. An algebraic approach to linear programming is then presented. We also show how these calculations can be efficiently organized by using what is called the *simplex tableau*. These methods are first developed considering a maximization problem with all less-than-or-equal-to constraints. Dealing with greater-than-or-equal-to and equality constraints is slightly more complex and requires the use of additional variables called *artificial variables*. The solution to the minimization problem is then discussed. We also briefly discuss unconstrained variables, alternate optima, infeasibility, unboundedness, degeneracy, and redundancy in the context of the simplex method and simplex tableau. We conclude the chapter with a discussion of the role of the computer in linear programming applications.

8.2 BASIC SOLUTIONS AND EXTREME POINTS

Before developing the relationship between basic solutions and extreme points and presenting an algebraic approach to the solution of a linear programming problem, we present a specific model that is used extensively in both Chapters 8 and 9.

Rollins Unlimited produces two types of skateboards, the Deluxe and the Professional. The production process involves the mounting of the wheel assembly to the premanufactured boards and the precision adjustment of the wheel assembly units. Rollins has available 1200 wheel assembly units, 50 hours of labor available for wheel assembly mounting, and 60 hours of labor available for the precision adjustment. Mounting the wheel assembly unit requires 2 minutes for the Deluxe boards and 3 minutes for the Professional boards. Precision adjustment requires 1 minute for the Deluxe board and 4 minutes for each Professional board. The projected per unit profits for the Deluxe and Professional skate boards are $3 and $4, respectively.

If the objective of Rollins is profit maximization given the specified limited resources, the model for this situation can be written as follows. Let

x_1 = number of Deluxe skateboards to be produced

x_2 = number of Professional skateboards to be produced

$$\text{Maximize } Z = 3x_1 + 4x_2 \quad \text{(profit)} \quad (8.1)$$

subject to

$$x_1 + x_2 \leq 1200 \quad \text{(Limited wheel assembly units)}$$

$$2x_1 + 3x_2 \leq 3000 \quad \text{(Minutes of mounting labor)}$$

$$x_1 + 4x_2 \leq 3600 \quad \text{(Minutes of adjustment labor)} \quad (8.2)$$

with

$$x_1, x_2 \geq 0 \quad (8.3)$$

The feasible region and the optimal objective line are given in Figure 8.1. The two-dimensional coordinates for the extreme points of the feasible region are given in Table 8.1.

8.2.1 THE BASIC SOLUTION

In this section the concept of a basic solution is developed. Basic solutions are important, since every extreme point can be represented as a basic solution. To introduce the concept of a basic solution to a linear system of equations, we use a particular linear

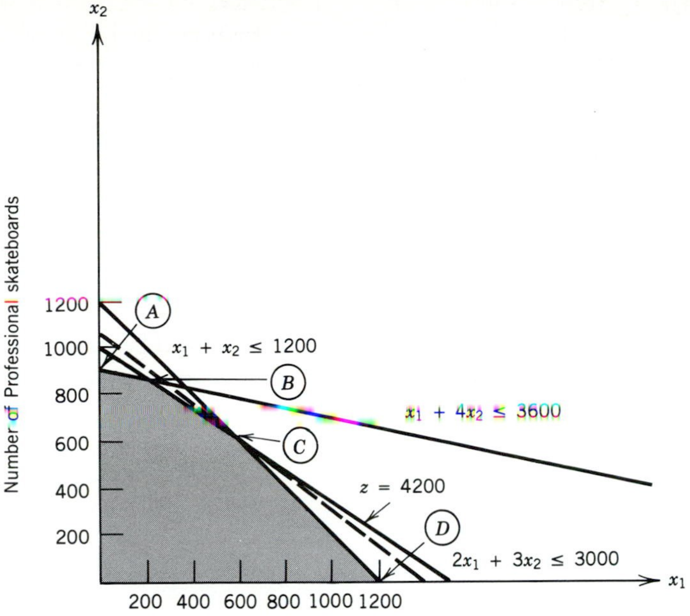

x_2
Number of Professional skateboards
1200
1000
800
600
400
200
A
B
C
D
$x_1 + x_2 \le 1200$
$x_1 + 4x_2 \le 3600$
$z = 4200$
$2x_1 + 3x_2 \le 3000$
x_1
200 400 600 800 1000 1200
Number of Deluxe skateboards

FIGURE 8.1 THE ROLLINS UNLIMITED ILLUSTRATION.

system of equations. System (8.4) is the equality representation of the set of constraints (8.2).

$$
\begin{aligned}
x_1 + x_2 + S_1 \qquad\qquad &= 1200 \\
2x_1 + 3x_2 \qquad + S_2 \qquad &= 3000 \\
x_1 + 4x_2 \qquad\qquad + S_3 &= 3600
\end{aligned} \tag{8.4}
$$

with

$$x_1,\ x_2,\ S_1,\ S_2,\ S_3 \ge 0 \tag{8.5}$$

In (8.4) S_1, S_2, S_3 are slack variables and represent unused wheel assembly units, unused labor (in minutes) for mounting, and unused labor (in minutes) for adjustment, respectively. The representation of the extreme points in terms of the five variables used in (8.2) is given in Table 8.2.

The five coordinate representations of the extreme points for problem (8.1), (8.2), and (8.3) define all *feasible basic solutions* for system (8.4) and (8.5). A *basic solution* to a linear system of three equations in five variables is obtained by setting two variables equal to zero and solving the resulting linear system in three equations and three variables. The number of possible basic solutions is then $5!/[3!(5 - 3)!] = 10$, the number of unique ways (combinations) of selecting three variables from a set of five variables. The set of all basic solutions

TABLE 8.1 EXTREME POINTS FOR ROLLINS UNLIMITED

EXTREME POINT	COORDINATES (x_1, x_2)
O	(0, 0)
A	(0, 900)
B	(240, 840)
C	(600, 600)
D	(1200, 0)

TABLE 8.2 EXTREME POINT REPRESENTATION FOR ROLLINS UNLIMITED

EXTREME POINTS	COORDINATES $(x_1, x_2, S_1, S_2, S_3)$
O	(0, 0, 1200, 3000, 3600)
A	(0, 900, 300, 300, 0)
B	(240, 840, 120, 0, 0)
C	(600, 600, 0, 0, 600)
D	(1200, 0, 0, 600, 2400)

to system (8.4) and (8.5) is given in Table 8.3. The variables set equal to zero are in parentheses. In the more general context, a basic solution to a linearly independent system of equations in n variables and m equations $(n > m)$ is obtained by setting $(n - m)$ variables to zero and solving the resultant linear system in m equations and m variables simultaneously. The *maximum* number of possible basic solutions in this case is $n!/[m! \, (n - m)!]$. This number, as you can easily verify, can be quite large. Certainly, the infeasible basic solutions are of little value to us. Still, the number of solutions that are basic and feasible (*basic feasible solutions*) can be very large. By feasible we mean that all variables are greater-than-or-equal-to zero. If one variable is less than zero, the basic solution is said to be *infeasible*.

Recognizing a priori that we are not interested in infeasible basic solutions and that the number of basic feasible solutions is probably too large to enumerate completely, the goal becomes one of systematically generating basic feasible solutions. Each basic solution generated is required to be better than the one previously generated. The simplex algorithm, which is the primary topic of this chapter, sequentially (or iteratively) examines a subset of basic feasible solutions terminating with the optimal solution. As mentioned earlier, every extreme point can be represented as a basic feasible solution. Since it is known that an optimal solution corresponds to at least one extreme point, this means that the *only* feasible solutions that need to be examined are basic solutions. Thus a procedure based on the sequential

generation of basic feasible solutions provides a viable approach to the identification of an optimal solution to the linear programming problem.

8.2.2 ADJACENT EXTREME POINTS AND BASIC FEASIBLE SOLUTIONS

We explained earlier that in a system of n variables and m equations we can generate basic solutions by equating $n - m$ variables to zero and solving the resulting system in m variables and m equations simultaneously. The variables that are set equal to zero are called the *nonbasic variables* and the remaining variables are called *basic variables*. The set of basic variables is called a *basis*.

Let's look again at the constraint set of problem (8.1), (8.2), and (8.3), written in equality form

$$
\begin{array}{rcrcrcrcrcl}
x_1 &+& x_2 &+& S_1 &&&&& =& 1200 \\
2x_1 &+& 3x_2 &&&+& S_2 &&& =& 3000 \\
x_1 &+& 4x_2 &&&&&+& S_3 &=& 3600 \quad (8.6)
\end{array}
$$

with

$$ x_1, \, x_2, \, S_1, \, S_2, \, S_3 \geq 0 \qquad (8.7) $$

If we set $x_1 = x_2 = 0$, the solution to the resulting three-variable, three-equation system has the obvious solution $S_1 = 1200$, $S_2 = 3000$, and $S_3 = 3600$. The terms x_1 and x_2 are nonbasic variables and S_1, S_2, and S_3 are the basic variables in the basic solution $(x_1, \, x_2, \, S_1, \, S_2, \, S_3) = (0, \, 0, \, 1200,$

TABLE 8.3 BASIC SOLUTIONS TO SYSTEM (8.4) AND (8.5)

BASIC SOLUTIONS					FEASIBLE/
x_1	x_2	S_1	S_2	S_3	INFEASIBLE
(0)	(0)	1200	3000	3600	Feasible
(0)	900	300	300	(0)	Feasible
240	840	120	(0)	(0)	Feasible
600	600	(0)	(0)	600	Feasible
1200	(0)	(0)	600	2400	Feasible
(0)	1200	(0)	− 600	− 1200	Infeasible
(0)	1000	200	(0)	− 400	Infeasible
3600	(0)	− 2400	− 4200	(0)	Infeasible
1500	(0)	− 300	(0)	2100	Infeasible
400	800	(0)	− 200	(0)	Infeasible

3000, 3600). A basic variable can also be related explicitly to the form in which the linear system is written. A variable is said to be *basic in an equation* only if it has a coefficient of one in that equation and if that variable has coefficients of zero in the remaining equations. In the basic solution above that represents the origin (0, 0), S_1 is basic in the first equation of (8.6), S_2 is basic in the second equation of (8.6), and S_3 is basic in the third equation of (8.6). We now look at a procedure for generating equivalent linear systems that provide easy identification of other basic solutions.

Every basic solution to a linear independent system of equations can be represented by an equivalent linear system in which the basic variables have coefficients of one in the equations where they are basic and zero coefficients elsewhere. Rewriting the linear system of equations is accomplished by the use of *elementary row operations*. The elementary row operations that will be used here are as follows.

1. An equation may be multiplied by a nonzero number.
2. An equation may be replaced by the result of adding or subtracting a multiple of another equation to it.

It must be understood that use of elementary row operations to identify basic solutions requires that the linear system of equations is independent. This means that it is not possible to eliminate any equation in the system by the use of elementary row operations. The application of these two elementary row operations to a system of simultaneous linear equations will not change the solutions of the system of equations. These row operations, however, will change the coefficients of the variables and the values of the right-hand sides. The objective of the application of these row operations is to rewrite the linear system in a form that allows us to simply read basic solutions from the set of equations as we did for solution (0, 0, 1200, 3000, 3600).

Recall that extreme points can be represented as basic solutions. Using a sequence of elementary row operations the linear system of equations can be written so that one of the previously basic variables becomes nonbasic and one of the previously nonbasic variables becomes basic. We call this process the *exchange of a single basic and a single nonbasic variable*, and the two associated basic solutions (or

extreme points) are said to be *adjacent extreme points*. In Figure 8.1 this means that extreme point A is adjacent to extreme point B, extreme point B is adjacent to extreme point C, and so on. To illustrate the process involved, consider the following two adjacent extreme points

$$(0, 0, 1200, 3000, 3600)$$

$$(0, 900, 300, 300, 0)$$

By the definition of a nonbasic variable we know that a variable that is greater than zero cannot be a nonbasic variable. Therefore, in the second basic solution x_2, S_1, and S_2 must be basic variables, while x_1 and S_3 are nonbasic variables. The variable that becomes nonbasic (was basic) is S_3, while the variable that becomes basic (was nonbasic) is x_2. Variable S_3 is sometimes called the *departing variable*, while x_2 is called the *entering variable*. Variable S_3 is leaving the set of basic variables (the basis), while x_2 is entering the set of basic variables.

Using elementary row operations to rewrite this system will require that x_2, S_1, S_2 be basic. Since S_1 and S_2 were previously basic in the first and second equations of (8.6) (and remain basic), x_2 will become basic in the third equation. Thus x_2 must have a coefficient of one in the third equation of (8.6) and zero coefficients elsewhere. To accomplish this we first multiply the third equation by (1/4). System (8.6) becomes

$$
\begin{array}{llll}
x_1 + & x_2 + S_1 & = 1200 & (8.8) \\
2x_1 + & 3x_2 & + S_2 & = 3000 & (8.9) \\
0.25x_1 + & x_2 & + 0.25S_3 = & 900 & (8.10)
\end{array}
$$

Now we see that the coefficient of x_2 in (8.9) will become 0 if we multiply (8.10) by (-3) and add it to (8.9).

$$
\begin{array}{llll}
2x_1 + 3x_2 & + S_2 & = & 3000 \\
-0.75x_1 - 3x_2 & - 0.75S_3 & = & -2700 \\
\hline
1.25x_1 & + S_2 - 0.75S_3 & = & 300
\end{array}
$$

System (8.8), (8.9), and (8.10) is now

$$
\begin{array}{llll}
x_1 + x_2 + S_1 & & = 1200 & (8.11) \\
1.25x_1 & + S_2 - 0.75S_3 = & 300 & (8.12) \\
0.25x_1 + x_2 & + 0.25S_3 = & 900 & (8.13)
\end{array}
$$

Finally, the coefficient of x_2 in Eq. 8.11 will become zero if we multiply (8.13) by (-1) and add the result to (8.11)

$$
\begin{array}{r}
x_1 + x_2 + S_1 = 1200 \\
-0.25x_1 - x_2 \qquad\qquad -0.25S_3 = -900 \\
\hline
0.75x_1 \qquad + S_1 \qquad -0.25S_3 = 300
\end{array}
$$

System (8.11), (8.12), and (8.13) is now

$$0.75x_1 \quad + S_1 \qquad\qquad -0.25S_3 = 300 \tag{8.14}$$
$$1.25x_1 \qquad\qquad + S_2 - 0.75S_3 = 300 \tag{8.15}$$
$$0.25x_1 + x_2 \qquad\qquad + 0.25S_3 = 900 \tag{8.16}$$

and (8.14), (8.15), and (8.16) has S_1 basic in (8.14), S_2 basic in (8.15), and x_2 basic in (8.16), with the values of 300, 300, and 900, respectively. Variables x_1 and S_3 are zero, since they are not basic. It must be noted that the set of solutions to system (8.8), (8.9), and (8.10) is the same as the set of solutions to system (8.14), (8.15), and (8.16). What we have done is establish another equivalent representation of that system, one from which we can read another basic solution by inspection.

The set of elementary row operations used in the transformation of system (8.8), (8.9), and (8.10) to system (8.14), (8.15), and (8.16) is called a *pivot operation*. The *pivot operation* is a sequence of elementary row operations that exchanges a basic and nonbasic variable. The maximum number of elementary row operations required in a pivot operation is the same as the number of equations in a linear system. The variable that is to become basic is referred to as the *pivot variable* (column) and the equation in which the variable is to become basic is called the *pivot equation* (row). The pivot equation will be selected so that the new basic solution remains feasible. The coefficient of the pivot variable in the pivot equation is called the *pivot element*.

Let's illustrate this procedure again by representing the basic solution (240, 840, 120, 0, 0) given system (8.14), (8.15), and (8.16) as the starting point. Here the pivot variable is x_1 and the pivot equation is (8.15). Multiplying the pivot equation by the reciprocal of the pivot element $1/(1.25)$, we obtain the following.

$$0.75x_1 \quad + S_1 \qquad\qquad -0.25S_3 = 300 \tag{8.17}$$
$$x_1 \qquad\qquad + 0.8S_2 - 0.60S_3 = 240 \tag{8.18}$$
$$0.25x_1 + x_2 \qquad\qquad + 0.25S_3 = 900 \tag{8.19}$$

To eliminate the coefficient of x_1 in Eq. 8.17 we multiply the pivot equation (8.18) by (-0.75) and add it to (8.17)

$$
\begin{array}{r}
0.75x_1 \qquad + S_1 \qquad -0.25S_3 = 300 \\
-0.75x_1 \qquad\qquad -0.6S_2 + 0.45S_3 = -180 \\
\hline
S_1 - 0.6S_2 + 0.20S_3 = 120
\end{array}
$$

System (8.17), (8.18), and (8.19) then becomes

$$S_1 - 0.6S_2 + 0.2S_3 = 120 \tag{8.20}$$
$$x_1 \qquad + 0.8S_2 - 0.6S_3 = 240 \tag{8.21}$$
$$0.25x_1 + x_2 \qquad\qquad + 0.25S_3 = 900 \tag{8.22}$$

The final elementary row operation in this pivot requires that the coefficient of x_1 in (8.22) be eliminated. To accomplish this we multiply the pivot equation by (-0.25) and add it to (8.22).

$$
\begin{array}{r}
-0.25x_1 \qquad\qquad -0.2S_2 + 0.15S_3 = -60 \\
0.25x_1 + x_2 \qquad\qquad + 0.25S_3 = 900 \\
\hline
x_2 \qquad -0.2S_2 + 0.40S_3 = 840
\end{array}
$$

System (8.20), (8.21), and (8.22) is then

$$S_1 - 0.6S_2 + 0.2S_3 = 120 \tag{8.23}$$
$$x_1 \qquad + 0.8S_2 - 0.6S_3 = 240 \tag{8.24}$$
$$x_2 \qquad -0.2S_2 + 0.4S_3 = 840 \tag{8.25}$$

Here S_1 is basic in Eq. 8.23, x_1 is basic in Eq. 8.24, x_2 is basic in Eq. 8.25, and S_1, x_1, and x_2 have values of 120, 240, 840, respectively. Finally, we give the representation of the basic solution $(x_1, x_2, S_1, S_2, S_3) = (600, 600, 0, 0, 600)$ using (8.23), (8.24), and (8.25) as the initial representation of the linear system under consideration. In this case, S_3 is the pivot variable, (8.23) is the pivot equation, and the pivot element is (0.2). The result of this pivot operation is

$$5S_1 - 3S_2 + S_3 = 600 \tag{8.26}$$
$$x_1 \quad + 3S_1 - S_2 \qquad = 600 \tag{8.27}$$
$$x_2 - 2S_1 + S_2 \qquad = 600 \tag{8.28}$$

To this point we have looked only at the constraints and have not incorporated the objective function into the analysis. The objective function is critical in the analysis, since its inclusion into the linear system permits us to eliminate the explicit consideration of some (in some cases, many) basic solutions. The objective function coefficients, when incorporated into system (8.6) and (8.7), allow us to consider only basic solutions that improve the value of the objective function. Coefficients are modified to be consistent with the basic solutions for the set of constraints.

We first note that the objective function $Z = 3x_1 + 4x_2$ could have been written as

$$-Z + 3x_1 + 4x_2 = 0 \qquad (8.29)$$

Then Eq. 8.29 may be incorporated into system (8.6) and (8.7)

$$
\begin{aligned}
x_1 + x_2 + S_1 &= 1200 \\
2x_1 + 3x_2 \quad + S_2 &= 3000 \\
x_1 + 4x_2 \quad\quad + S_3 &= 3600 \\
-Z + 3x_1 + 4x_2 &= 0 \qquad (8.30)
\end{aligned}
$$

The pivot operation could also incorporate the objective function equation. To see this we repeat (8.14), (8.15), and (8.16) and add the objective function

$$
\begin{aligned}
0.75x_1 \quad + S_1 \quad - 0.25S_3 &= 300 \\
1.25x_1 \quad\quad + S_2 - 0.75S_3 &= 300 \\
0.25x_1 + x_2 \quad\quad + 0.25S_3 &= 900 \\
-Z + 3x_1 + 4x_2 &= 0 \\
&\qquad (8.31)
\end{aligned}
$$

Then pivot equation [the third equation in (8.31)] is multiplied by -4 and added to the objective function [the last equation in (8.31)]:

$$
\begin{array}{c}
- x_1 - 4x_2 \quad - S_3 = -3600 \\
\underline{-Z + 3x_1 + 4x_2 \qquad\qquad = \quad 0} \\
-Z + 2x_1 \qquad\quad - S_3 = -3600 \qquad (8.32)
\end{array}
$$

Completing the pivot operation, the system (8.31) becomes

$$
\begin{aligned}
0.75x_1 \quad + S_1 \quad - 0.25S_3 &= 300 \\
1.25x_1 \quad\quad + S_2 - 0.75S_3 &= 300 \\
0.25x_1 + x_2 \quad\quad + 0.25S_3 &= 900 \\
-Z + 2x_1 \qquad\quad - S_3 &= -3600 \\
&\qquad (8.33)
\end{aligned}
$$

Here $-Z = -3600$ or $Z = 3600$. Thus when $x_2 = 900$, $S_1 = 300$, and $S_2 = 300$, the value of the objective is 3600. If we continue to incorporate the objective function into the pivot operations that resulted in systems (8.23), (8.24), and (8.25) and (8.26), (8.27), and (8.28), the specific results would be as follows

$$
\begin{aligned}
S_1 - 0.6S_2 + 0.2S_3 &= 120 \\
x_1 \quad + 0.8S_2 - 0.6S_3 &= 240 \qquad (8.34) \\
x_2 - 0.2S_2 + 0.4S_3 &= 840 \\
-Z \quad - 1.6S_2 + 0.2S_3 &= -4080
\end{aligned}
$$

$$
\begin{aligned}
5S_1 - 3S_2 + S_3 &= 600 \\
x_1 \quad + 3S_1 - S_2 &= 600 \qquad (8.35) \\
x_2 - 2S_1 + S_2 &= 600 \\
-Z \quad - S_1 - S_2 &= -4200
\end{aligned}
$$

Thus we observe from (8.34) and (8.35) that the objective values associated with extreme points (240, 840, 120, 0, 0) and (600, 600, 0, 0, 600) are 4080 and 4200, respectively.

The pivot operation is the basis of the simplex method, that is, an algorithm for computing the optimal solution to linear programming problems. The pivot operation is completely determined by the selection of the pivot element that is itself determined by the chosen pivot variable and pivot equation. Since the pivot variable must be basic in the pivot equation, the sequence of elementary operations that comprise the pivot is completely and uniquely determined. Our choices for the pivot element in this section have been determined by knowing a priori the coordinates of the adjacent extreme point. These coordinates were available simply because we were able to graph the feasible region. In the next section we will not rely on the geometry of the problem to select the pivot element.

8.3 THE SIMPLEX METHOD

The simplex method is the name given to the solution procedure for solving a linear programming problem. This method, which was developed by George Dantzig in 1947, is an iterative procedure that leads to the optimal solution in a finite number of steps.[1] The simplex method is algebraic in nature and is based on the representation of extreme points as basic feasible solutions to a linear system of equations. The sequential representation of extreme points is accomplished by the use of the algebraic procedure known as a pivot operation. As we observed in Section 8.2.2, this operation is accomplished via a carefully selected set of elementary row operations, which is completely determined with the selection of the pivot element. The algebraic selection of the pivot element and the representation of the linear programming problem in tabular form are the primary new ideas presented in this section.

The procedures presented here and in Section 8.2.2 are relatively straightforward, but require many elementary row operations. Although most linear programming problems are solved using the algorithm as programmed and executed on a digital computer, we must be able to provide a clear interpretation of the results. The objective here is then to develop a thorough understanding of the linear programming solution. We feel this is possible only through a firm understanding of the simplex method.

8.3.1 THE INITIAL SIMPLEX TABLEAU

For a linear programming problem with all less-than-or-equal-to constraints, the simplex method begins with a basic feasible solution and then moves from one basic feasible solution to the next until an optimal basic feasible solution is found. This requirement must be reflected in the way the constraint set is written, which must be as follows.

1. Each constraint must be converted to an equation.
2. In every equation there must be a variable that is basic in that equation.
3. The right-hand side (RHS) of every equation must be a nonnegative constant.

The model for Rollins Unlimited is written in the form that satisfies the above conditions

$$\text{Maximize } Z = 3x_1 + 4x_2 + 0S_1 + 0S_2 + 0S_3 \quad (8.36)$$

subject to

$$
\begin{aligned}
x_1 + x_2 + S_1 & = 1200 \\
2x_1 + 3x_2 + S_2 & = 3000 \\
x_1 + 4x_2 + S_3 &= 3600 \quad (8.37)
\end{aligned}
$$

with

$$x_1, x_2, S_1, S_2, S_3 \geq 0 \quad (8.38)$$

After the linear programming problem is written in a form that satisfies the previous list, we are in a position to construct the *initial simplex tableau*. The *simplex tableau* provides a convenient means for keeping track of and performing the calculations necessary during the simplex solution procedure.

We adopt the following notation.

c_j = objective function coefficient for variable j

b_i = right-hand-side value for constraint i

a_{ij} = coefficient of variable j in constraint i

The portion of the simplex tableau that reflects all the input parameters is given in Table 8.4. Thus the objective function coefficients are written first and the constraint coefficients and RHS values follow. The vertical line above may be viewed as an equality line.

Notation that will be helpful as we continue our development of the simplex method and supporting material is as follows:

c row: a row of objective function coefficients;

b column: a column of right-hand-side values of the constraint equations;

A matrix: a matrix with m rows and n columns of the coefficients of the variables in the constraint equations.

TABLE 8.4 INPUT PARAMETERS FOR GENERAL LINEAR PROGRAMMING MODEL

c_1	c_2	$\cdots$	c_n	
a_{11}	a_{12}	$\cdots$	a_{1n}	b_1
a_{21}	a_{22}	$\cdots$	a_{2n}	b_2
$\vdots$	$\vdots$	$\vdots \vdots \vdots$	$\vdots$	$\vdots$
a_{m1}	a_{m2}	$\cdots$	a_{mn}	b_m

---

[1] This may not be the case if the condition of degeneracy exists. In such a case, the simplex method may cycle, but this is extremely rare. See Section 8.6.4.

TABLE 8.5 INPUT PARAMETETS USING MATRIX NOTATION

c row	
A matrix	b column (solution values)

TABLE 8.6 INPUT PARAMETERS FOR ROLLINS UNLIMITED EXAMPLE

3	4	0	0	0	
1	1	1	0	0	1200
2	3	0	1	0	3000
1	4	0	0	1	3600

TABLE 8.7 COLUMN LABELS FOR ROLLINS UNLIMITED EXAMPLE

c_j	3	4	0	0	0	
	x_1	x_2	S_1	S_2	S_3	
	1	1	1	0	0	1200
	2	3	0	1	0	3000
	1	4	0	0	1	3600

The portion of the simplex tableau in Table 8.4 is represented using this notation in Table 8.5. The particular model input (8.36), (8.37), and (8.38) is written in this form in Table 8.6. Using the notation in the list on page 222, $c_2 = 4$, $b_3 = 3600$, $a_{21} = 2$, and so on. The first column of the tableau in Table 8.6 is called the x_1 column, the second, the x_2 column, and so forth. To help us remember this, we add some additional labeling to our partial tableau (Table 8.7). Since the simplex method starts with a basic solution and iteratively represents additional basic solutions, labeling the basic variables has become an important part of the information reflected by a simplex tableau. Variable S_1 is basic in the first equation or row 1, S_2 is basic in row 2, and S_3 is basic in row 3. These variables are labeled in the basis column. The objective function coefficients of the basic variables are listed in an additional column labeled by c_j. The objective function coefficients of the slack variables are all zero, as indicated in problem (8.36), (8.37), and (8.38). This information as well as the objective function coefficients of the basic variables is incorporated into the tableau in Table 8.8. It can be observed that a column with a "1" as the only nonzero entry is associated with each basic variable. These columns are known as unit columns or unit vectors. These unit vectors make reading the solution from the given tableau trivial. If S_1, S_2, and S_3 are basic, x_1 and x_2 must be nonbasic. Therefore, the constraints are simply

$$(1)\ (0) + (1)\ (0) + (1)S_1 + (0)S_2 + (0)S_3 = 1200$$
$$(2)\ (0) + (3)\ (0) + (0)S_1 + (1)S_2 + (0)S_3 = 3000$$
$$(1)\ (0) + (4)\ (0) + (0)S_1 + (0)S_2 + (1)S_3 = 3600$$

$$(8.39)$$

or

$$S_1 \qquad\qquad = 1200$$
$$\qquad S_2 \qquad = 3000$$
$$\qquad\qquad S_3 = 3600 \qquad (8.40)$$

It should be obvious that the b_i are the solution values of the basic variables. This is reflected in the labeling of the tableau in Table 8.9.

Before generating another basic solution, additional information regarding the objective function must be incorporated into the tableau. Two additional rows labeled Z_j and $c_j - Z_j$ are utilized.

8.3.2 CHOOSING THE PIVOT COLUMN

The objective value associated with the basic solution represented in Table 8.9 is zero. Our goal is to use this basic feasible solution to generate another basic feasible solution that has a larger objective value. To do this we have to change the set of basic variables. We select one of the current nonbasic variables to become basic. The question we must deal with is: Which one? Clearly, the objective function coefficients will ultimately determine which of the decision variables will be basic, and thus the optimal solution. Therefore, the objective function needs to be reflected in the tableau. In section 8.2.2 we observed how the objective function could be incorporated into the linear system of equations that represents the constraints. Instead of incorporating the objective function directly as an equation in a linear system, we use the format of the tableau presented thus far to generate the same information. Two additional rows are added to the tableau: a Z_j row and a $c_j - Z_j$ row.

We first devise a simple procedure for computing Z_j and $c_j - Z_j$. The initial basic feasible so-

TABLE 8.8 BASIC VARIABLE LABELS FOR ROLLINS UNLIMITED EXAMPLE

	c_j	3	4	0	0	0	
c_b	BASIS	x_1	x_2	S_1	S_2	S_3	
0	S_1	1	1	1	0	0	1200
0	S_2	2	3	0	1	0	3000
0	S_3	1	4	0	0	1	3600

TABLE 8.9 SOLUTION LABELS FOR THE ROLLINS UNLIMITED EXAMPLE

	c_j	3	4	0	0	0	
c_b	BASIS	x_1	x_2	S_1	S_2	S_3	SOLUTION
0	S_1	1	1	1	0	0	1200
0	S_2	2	3	0	1	0	3000
0	S_3	1	4	0	0	1	3600

lution for problem (8.36), (8.37), and (8.38) is $x_1 = 0$, $x_2 = 0$, $S_1 = 1200$, $S_2 = 3,000$, and $S_3 = 3600$. It is also noted that the following three equations must be satisfied

$$x_1 + x_2 + S_1 \qquad\qquad = 1200$$
$$2x_1 + 3x_2 \qquad + S_2 \qquad = 3000$$
$$x_1 + 4x_2 \qquad\qquad + S_3 = 3600 \qquad (8.41)$$

with

$$x_1, x_2, S_1, S_2, S_3 \geq 0 \qquad (8.42)$$

Suppose the initial basic feasible solution is modified so that x_1 is one and x_2 remains at zero. Then $S_1 = 1199$, $S_2 = 2998$, and $S_3 = 3599$. Thus S_1 decreases by one, S_2 decreases by two, and S_3 decreases by 1 when $x_1 = 1$ and $x_2 = 0$. The objective function value changes by the sum of the weighted changes of the basic variables S_1, S_2, and S_3, where the weights are the objective function coefficient of the individual variables. The change in the objective function value due to changes in the current basic variables is labeled as Z_j. The Z_1 value is computed as described above

$$Z_1 = (0)(1) + (0)(2) + (0)(1) = 0$$

In this case the value Z_1 represents the decrease in the value of the objective function due to a one-unit increase in the value of the nonbasic variable x_1. The net change per unit change of the two non-basic variables is equal to the per unit individual profits, 3 and 4, respectively. This means that increasing x_1 or x_2 increases the value of the objective function. It follows that the $c_j - Z_j$ values for basic variables are always equal to zero.

The complete initial simplex tableau is given in Table 8.10. The number in the solution column in the Z_j row is the value of the objective function. This value is obtained by multiplying the values of the basic variables, as listed in the solution column, by the corresponding objective function coefficients. Again, $c_j - Z_j$ indicates the net increase in the objective value per unit increase in variable j, provided, of course, that the solution generated is feasible. The rule for choosing the pivot variable or pivot column is based on these values.

Pivot Column Selection Rule: (Maximization Problem)

The nonbasic variable with the largest $c_j - Z_j$ value for all $c_j - Z_j \geq 0$ is the pivot variable.

The variable that is nonbasic and becomes basic is often called the *entering variable*. For the tableau in Table 8.10, x_2 is the entering variable. The pivot column selection rule is made operational in the following fashion. Any nonbasic variables with a positive $c_j - Z_j$ value will improve the value of the objective function. Choose the largest $c_j - Z_j$ value (if there is a tie, break it arbitrarily) and use it to select the variable that is to enter the basis. Before proceeding to choose the pivot row we should note the relationship between the tableau in Table 8.10

TABLE 8.10 INITIAL SIMPLEX TABLEAU FOR THE ROLLINS UNLIMITED EXAMPLE

c_b	c_j BASIS	3 x_1	4 x_2	0 S_1	0 S_2	0 S_3	SOLUTION
0	S_1	1	1	1	0	0	1200
0	S_2	2	3	0	1	0	3000
0	S_3	1	4	0	0	1	3600
	Z_j	0	0	0	0	0	0
	$c_j - Z_j$	3	4	0	0	0	

and the objective represented in (8.30). The objective function coefficients of x_1, x_2, S_1, S_2, and S_3 are the respective $c_j - Z_j$ values given in Table 8.10. This is no concidence. If we use this tableau representation of the linear programming problem and represent the extreme points in systems (8.33), (8.34), and (8.35), the $c_j - Z_j$ values will also be equal to the objective function coefficients in those systems. The point that needs to be emphasized here is that the tableau presented does not provide any additional information over the linear system of equations in Section 8.2.2. It simply provides a convenient form to perform the calculations necessary to find the optimal solution to a linear programming problem.

8.3.3 CHOOSING THE PIVOT ROW

After the entering variable has been selected we must determine which basic variable must become nonbasic. In other words we must select the *departing variable* or the *pivot row*. If we consider the initial tableau in Table 8.10, we note that the pivot column selection rule implies that the entering variable is x_2. If x_2 becomes basic, then either S_1, S_2, or S_3 must be nonbasic. Consider the implications of each of these variables becoming zero individually. The constraint information below is taken directly from Table 8.10 and takes into account the fact that x_1 remains nonbasic; that is, $x_1 = 0$ for this analysis.

$$x_2 + S_1 \qquad\qquad = 1200$$
$$3x_2 \qquad + S_2 \qquad = 3000$$
$$4x_2 \qquad\qquad + S_3 = 3600 \qquad (8.43)$$

If $S_1 = 0$, then $x_2 = 1200/1 = 1200$;

If $S_2 = 0$, then $x_2 = 3000/3 = 1000$;

If $S_3 = 0$, then $x_2 = 3600/4 = 900$.

It can easily be seen that if x_2 is larger than the smallest of the three ratios in (8.43), at least one of the basic variables becomes negative. For example, suppose that $x_2 = 1000$. This in turn implies that the departing variable is S_2 and requires that $S_3 = -400$. The resulting solution would be infeasible. The smallest ratio computed tells us which constraint is the most restrictive when x_2 is introduced into the solution. This ratio then determines the departing variable and identifies the pivot row.

The rule for selecting the pivot row follows.

Pivot Row Section Rule:

If the jth column is the pivot column, compute all ratios b_i/a_{ij}, where $a_{ij} > 0$. Select the variable basic in the row with the minimum ratio to leave the basis. The row with the minimum ratio is the pivot row.

In general the Z_j row can be calculated by multiplying the elements in the c_b column by the corresponding elements in the individual variable columns in the partial tableau of Table 8.9, and by adding these products. The particular calculations follow.

$$Z_1 = (0)(1) + (0)(2) + (0)(1) = 0$$
$$Z_2 = (0)(1) + (0)(3) + (0)(4) = 0$$
$$Z_3 = (0)(1) + (0)(0) + (0)(0) = 0$$
$$Z_4 = (0)(0) + (0)(1) + (0)(0) = 0$$
$$Z_5 = (0)(0) + (0)(0) + (0)(1) = 0$$

In general, for a nonbasic variable the Z_j value represents the decrease in the value of the objective function due to a one-unit increase in the value of a given nonbasic variable. For a basic variable the

Z_j value is simply the objective function coefficient of the jth variable.

For a nonbasic variable in a maximization problem, c_j indicates a per unit increase in the value of the objective function, while Z_j represents a per unit decrease. The term $c_j - Z_j$ then represents a net change to the objective value. The $c_j - Z_j$ terms for all the variables in problem (8.36), (8.37), and (8.38) are calculated below.

$$c_1 - Z_1 = 3 - 0 = 3$$

$$c_2 - Z_2 = 4 - 0 = 4$$

$$c_3 - Z_3 = 0 - 0 = 0$$

$$c_4 - Z_4 = 0 - 0 = 0$$

$$c_5 - Z_5 = 0 - 0 = 0$$

To illustrate the above criterion for selecting the pivot row, a new column listing the appropriate ratios may be added to the tableau in Table 8.10. The element circled in Table 8.11 is common to the pivot column and pivot row and is called the *pivot element*.

In order to improve the current solution of $x_1 = 0$, $x_2 = 0$, $S_1 = 1200$, $S_2 = 3000$, and $S_3 = 3600$, we should increase x_2 to 900 with a corresponding profit of $3600. In producing 900 Professional skateboards we have utilized all the labor available for precision adjustment, reducing S_3 from 3600 to zero. Again, x_2 becomes basic and S_3 becomes nonbasic. The pivot operation described in Section 8.2.2 is used to develop a tableau where S_1 is basic in the first equation, S_2 is basic in the second equation, and x_2 is basic in the third equation.

8.3.4 THE PIVOT OPERATION AND THE OPTIMAL SOLUTION

It is obvious from the previous section that introducing x_2 into the basis to replace S_3 improves the solution. This new basic feasible solution is $x_1 = 0$, $x_2 = 900$, $S_1 = 300$, $S_2 = 300$, and $S_3 = 0$. We must, however, determine if this new basic feasible solution can be improved. To answer this question we will have to rewrite the initial simplex tableau and use the pivot column selection rule to determine a new pivot column.

Consider the following portion of the simplex tableau.

A matrix	b column

This portion of the simplex tableau is modified using the pivot operation. After the pivot is complete, the Z_j and $c_j - Z_j$ rows are computed, and the pivot column and row selection rules are applied to select the new pivot element.

The pivot operation transforms the simplex tableau so that it represents an equivalent system of constraint equations. By equivalent we mean that the new system has the same set of solutions as the previous system. From a computational point of view, our goal is to transform the x_2 column from

$$\begin{pmatrix} 1 \\ 3 \\ 4 \end{pmatrix} \quad \text{to} \quad \begin{pmatrix} 0 \\ 0 \\ 1 \end{pmatrix}.$$

This transformation changes all columns in the A matrix and b column and the transformed b column reflects the new values of the basic variables.

Remembering that the numbers in the A matrix and b column are coefficients of variables in particular equations and right-hand-side values for these equations, we can restate the pivot operation assuming that A has m rows and n columns.

Pivot Operation:

Suppose the jth column is the pivot column and the kth row is the pivot row. Then the element

TABLE 8.11 INITIAL PIVOT ELEMENT SELECTION FOR ROLLINS UNLIMITED

c_b	BASIS	c_j 3	4	0	0	0	SOLUTION	RATIOS
		x_1	x_2	S_1	S_2	S_3		
0	S_1	1	1	1	0	0	1200	1200/1 = 1200
0	S_2	2	3	0	1	0	3000	3000/3 = 1000
0	S_3	1	④	0	0	1	3600	3600/4 = 900
	Z_j	0	0	0	0	0	0	
	$c_j - Z_j$	3	4	0	0	0		

a_{kj} *is the pivot element. The pivot operation consists of m elementary row operations organized as follows:*

1. *Divide the pivot row, $(a_{k.}, b_k)$ by the pivot element a_{kj}. Call the result $(\bar{a}_{k.}, \bar{b}_k)$.*
2. *For every other row $(a_{i.}, b_i)$, replace that row by $(a_{i.}, b_i) + (-a_{ij})(\bar{a}_{k.}, \bar{b}_k)$. In other words, multiply the revised pivot row by the negative of the a_{ij}th element and add it to the row under consideration.*

The pivot operation for a linear programming problem involving m constraints involves at most m elementary row operations.

To illustrate the pivot operation previously described, let us start from the simplex tableau of Table 8.11 with the circled pivot element. Again the first step in the pivot operation is to divide the pivot row by the pivot element (i.e., 4). The result follows

$$(1/4 \quad 4/4 \quad 0/4 \quad 0/4 \quad 1/4, \quad 3600/4)$$

Next we modify row 2 by multiplying the revised pivot row by -3 and adding it to row 2

$$
\begin{array}{r}
(-0.75 \quad -3 \quad 0 \quad 0 \quad -0.75, \quad -2700) \\
+ (\ \ 2 \qquad 3 \quad 0 \quad 1 \qquad 0\ , \qquad 3000) \\
\hline
(\ \ 1.25 \qquad 0 \quad 0 \quad 1 \quad -0.75, \qquad 300)
\end{array}
$$

Finally, we replace row 1 by itself plus (-1) times the result in the revised pivot row

$$
\begin{array}{r}
(-0.25 \quad -1 \quad 0 \quad 0 \quad -0.25, \quad -900) \\
+ (\ \ 1 \qquad 1 \quad 1 \quad 0 \qquad 0\ , \qquad 1200) \\
\hline
(\ \ 0.75 \qquad 0 \quad 1 \quad 0 \quad -0.25, \qquad 300)
\end{array}
$$

The results of these calculations replace the original A matrix and b column in Table 8.11 as shown in Table 8.12. Now we are ready to determine the possible impact of bringing another nonbasic variable into the basis. We do this by again computing Z_j and $c_j - Z_j$

$$
\begin{aligned}
Z_1 &= (0)(0.75) &+ (0)(1.25) &+ (4)(0.25) &= 1 \\
Z_2 &= (0)(0) &+ (0)(0) &+ (4)(1) &= 4 \\
Z_3 &= (0)(1) &+ (0)(0) &+ (4)(0) &= 0 \\
Z_4 &= (0)(0) &+ (0)(1) &+ (4)(0) &= 0 \\
Z_5 &= (0)(-0.25) &+ (0)(-0.75) &+ (4)(0.25) &= 1
\end{aligned}
$$
$$(8.44)$$

Also, the objective value is

$$(0)(300) + (0)(300) + 4(900) = 3600 \quad (8.45)$$

Finally, substracting Z_j from c_j we get the complete new simplex tableau shown in Table 8.13. The $c_j - Z_j$ row indicates that bringing x_1 into the basis increases the value of the objective function. For each Deluxe skateboard produced, the objective will increase by \$2. We also note the interpretation of the coefficients in the x_1 column. These coefficients indicate by how much the variables in the basis will change if one Deluxe skateboard is produced. To determine the maximum number of Deluxe skateboards that can be produced with a "marginal profit" of \$2, we compute the ratios involving these three coefficients and the current solution values. Since the minimum ratio is $300/1.25 = 240$, the second row is the pivot row and the variable that leaves the basis is S_2. The pivot element of 1.25 is indicated in Table 8.14. We can use it to compute the new values of the basic variables without going through the complete pivot operation.

$$x_2 = \frac{300}{1.25} = 240$$

$$S_1 = 300 - (0.75)(240) = 120$$

$$x_2 = 900 - (0.25)(240) = 840$$

TABLE 8.12 INITIAL PIVOT OPERATION IN THE ROLLINS UNLIMITED EXAMPLES

c_b	c_j BASIS	3 x_1	4 x_2	0 S_1	0 S_2	0 S_3	SOLUTION
0	S_1	0.75	0	1	0	-0.25	300
0	S_2	1.25	0	0	1	-0.75	300
4	x_2	0.25	1	0	0	0.25	900

TABLE 8.13 SECOND SIMPLEX TABLEAU FOR THE ROLLINS UNLIMITED EXAMPLE

c_b	c_j BASIS	3 x_1	4 x_2	0 S_1	0 S_2	0 S_3	SOLUTION
0	S_1	0.75	0	1	0	-0.25	300
0	S_2	1.25	0	0	1	-0.75	300
4	x_2	0.25	1	0	0	0.25	900
	Z_j	1	4	0	0	1	3600
	$c_j - Z_j$	2	0	0	0	-1	

Also the new objective should be

$$3600 + 2(240) = 4080$$

where 2 is the marginal profit associated with the production of Deluxe skateboards. A more precise economic interpretation of the $c_j - Z_j$ values is given in Chapter 9. We can check this interpretation by evaluating the objective function directly

$$Z = 3(240) + 4(840) = 4080$$

After the pivot operation is complete, the $c_j - Z_j$ values are recomputed for the new set of basic variables, the basis. We continue to pivot as long as we can find a nonbasic variable that will increase the value of the objective function. In other words, we continue as long as we can find a $c_j - Z_j > 0$. When all $c_j - Z_j$ values are less than or equal to zero, the optimality condition is said to be satisfied.

Optimality Condition for Linear Programming:

The optimal solution to a linear programming problem with a maximization objective has been found when $c_j - Z_j \leq 0$ for all variable columns in the simplex tableau.

The remaining simplex tableaus for the current problem are given in Tables 8.15 and 8.16. In Table 8.15 we note that the optimality condition for linear programming is satisfied ($c_j - Z_j \leq 0$ for all j), and thus the optimal solution suggests the production of 600 Deluxe skateboards and 600 Professional skateboards. The slack variables S_1, S_2, and S_3 assume values of 0, 0, and 600, respectively. This means that we used all 1200 wheel assembly units, all 3000 minutes of assembly labor, and that we did *not* use 600 minutes of labor allocated to precision adjustment. Under the optimal solution the first two constraints are said to be tight while the third is not.

8.4 SOLVING A LINEAR PROGRAMMING PROBLEM WITH MIXED CONSTRAINTS

Our ability to solve the problem in (8.1), (8.2), and (8.3) rested on two important conditions

1. The right-hand sides of all constraints were greater than or equal to zero.

TABLE 8.14 PIVOT ELEMENT SELECTION: SECOND ITERATION FOR THE ROLLINS UNLIMITED EXAMPLE

c_b	c_j BASIS	3 x_1	4 x_2	0 S_1	0 S_2	0 S_3	SOLUTION	RATIOS
0	S_1	0.75	0	1	0	-0.25	300	300/0.75
0	S_2	(1.25)	0	0	1	-0.75	300	300/1.25
4	x_2	0.25	1	0	0	0.25	900	900/0.25
	Z_j	1	4	0	0	1	3600	
	$c_j - Z_j$	2	0	0	0	-1		

TABLE 8.15 THIRD SIMPLEX TABLEAU FOR THE ROLLINS UNLIMITED EXAMPLE

c_b	c_j BASIS	3 x_1	4 x_2	0 S_1	0 S_2	0 S_3	SOLUTION	RATIOS
0	S_1	0	0	1	-0.6	(0.2)	120	120/0.2
3	x_1	1	0	0	0.8	-0.6	240	—
4	x_2	0	1	0	-0.2	0.4	840	840/0.4
	Z_j	3	4	0	1.6	-0.2	4080	
	$c_j - Z_j$	0	0	0	-1.6	0.2		

2. All the constraints were of the less than or equal to variety.

The second condition guaranteed that we had a basic variable in every equation that represented the constraint set. Of course, the basic variable in each of these constraints was initially the added slack variable. The first condition guaranteed that the initial basic solution was feasible.

Satisfying the first condition is not difficult. If a constraint does not have a nonnegative right-hand side, we simply multiply both sides of the constraint by -1. We assume that constraints are always written in the form where the right-hand side is a constant. In other words, a constraint would not be written as

$$x_1 + x_2 \leq 0.25 (5 - 2x_1 - 3x_2) \qquad (8.46)$$

Rather, the constraint would be algebraically written as

$$1.5x_1 + 1.75x_2 \leq 1.25 \qquad (8.47)$$

Consider the following three constraints

$$2x_1 + 3x_2 = -5$$
$$1.5x_1 + 1.75x_2 \leq -1.25$$
$$3x_1 - 2x_2 \geq -2 \qquad (8.48)$$

Each of these constraints could be rewritten in the form that satisfies the first condition. We simply need to multiply both sides of the constraints by (-1). We also need to recall that multiplying both sides of an inequality by (-1) reverses the direction of the inequality. Note that the constraints in (8.49) are equivalent to the constraints in (8.48).

$$-2x_1 - 3x_2 = 5$$
$$-1.5x_1 - 1.75x_2 \geq 1.25$$
$$-3x_1 + 2x_2 \leq 2 \qquad (8.49)$$

The constraints should always be written with positive right-hand sides before adding the slack and surplus variables.

To illustrate the procedure for dealing with linear programming problems that do not have all less-

TABLE 8.16 FOURTH SIMPLEX TABLEAU FOR THE ROLLINS UNLIMITED EXAMPLE

c_b	c_j BASIS	3 x_1	4 x_2	0 S_1	0 S_2	0 S_3	SOLUTION
0	S_3	0	0	5	-3	1	600
3	x_1	1	0	3	-1	0	600
4	x_2	0	1	-2	1	0	600
	Z_j	3	4	1	1	0	4200
	$c_j - Z_j$	0	0	-1	-1	0	

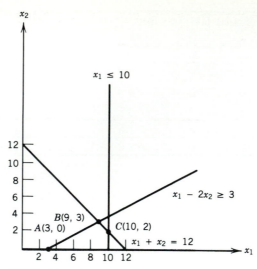

FIGURE 8.2 FEASIBLE REGION FOR PROBLEM (8.50), (8.51), AND (8.52).

than-or-equal-to constraints, we consider the following linear programming problem.

$$\text{Maximize } Z = 5x_1 + x_2 \qquad (8.50)$$

subject to

$$x_1 \qquad\qquad \leq 10$$

$$x_1 - 2x_2 \geq\ 3$$

$$x_1 + \ x_2 = 12 \qquad (8.51)$$

with

$$x_1,\ x_2 \geq 0 \qquad (8.52)$$

Writing all constraints in equality form, (8.50), (8.51), and (8.52) become

$$\text{Maximize } Z = 5x_1 + x_2 + 0S_1 + 0S_2 \qquad (8.53)$$

subject to

$$x_1 \qquad\quad + S_1 \qquad = 10$$

$$x_1 \ - 2x_2 \qquad - S_2 =\ 3$$

$$x_1 \ + \ x_2 \qquad\qquad = 12 \qquad (8.54)$$

with

$$x_1,\ x_2,\ S_1,\ S_2 \geq 0 \qquad (8.55)$$

The feasible region to (8.50), (8.51), and (8.52) is shown in Figure 8.2. It is the *line segment* connecting points B and C. The basic solution representation of the points indicated in Figure 8.2 are given in Table 8.17. Point A is, however, not a basic *feasible* solution. If we look at the constraint set (8.54), we note that S_1 is basic in the first equation, but there are no variables that are basic in the second and third equations. We also know that the simplex method can only operate on basic solutions, and this means that there must be a basic variable in every equation.

Equality constraints and greater-than-or-equal-to constraints will generally be without basic variables when we attempt to construct the initial simplex tableau. We know, however, that to apply the simplex method there must be a basic variable in each equation. In order to generate an initial basic feasible solution, a variable is added to each equation without a basic variable. This variable is called an *artificial variable*, and as long as this variable is

TABLE 8.17 BASIC SOLUTION REPRESENTATION OF POINTS LABELED IN FIGURE 8.2

POINT	(x_1, x_2)	(x_1, x_2, S_1, S_2)
A	(3, 0)	(3, 0, 7, 0)
B	(9, 3)	(9, 3, 1, 0)
C	(10, 2)	(10, 2, 0, 3)

TABLE 8.18 INCORPORATION OF ARTIFICIAL VARIABLES IN THE SIMPLEX TABLEAU

BASIS	x_1	x_2	S_1	S_2	A_1	A_2	SOLUTION
S_1	1	0	1	0	0	0	10
A_1	1	-2	0	-1	1	0	3
A_2	1	1	0	0	0	1	12

greater than zero the associated constraint is not satisfied. Consider the constraint

$$x_1 - 2x_2 - S_2 = 3 \qquad (8.56)$$

If we rewrite this constraint adding the artificial variable, say A_1, it becomes

$$x_1 - 2x_2 - S_2 + A_1 = 3 \qquad (8.57)$$

Now A_1 is basic in this equation since it has zero coefficients in the remaining constraint equations. Variable A_1 is assumed to be nonnegative, and as long as $A_1 > 0$,

$$x_1 - 2x_2 - S_2 < 3 \qquad (8.58)$$

and thus the original constraint is not satisfied. We also add an artificial variable to the third constraint

$$x_1 + x_2 + A_2 = 12 \qquad (8.59)$$

When entered into the simplex tableau, these variables are treated as any other variable in the computations. We will not, however, have a feasible solution as long as an artificial variable is greater than zero. We can see that the initial basic solution to the linear system represented in Table 8.18 is $x_1 = 0$, $x_2 = 0$, $S_1 = 10$, $S_2 = 0$, $A_1 = 3$, $A_2 =$ 12 (the origin in Figure 8.2). This solution is not feasible to problem (8.50), (8.51), and (8.52), and any subsequent solution involving an artificial variable that is greater than zero will not be feasible.

The problem that must be dealt with in this context is one of making sure that the artificial variables will be driven from the basis if the linear programming problem under consideration has a feasible solution. This can be done by assigning large negative coefficients to the artificial variables in the objective function. If the objective coefficients of the artificial variables are for example, $-1,000,000$, even small values for the artificial variable will have a significant negative impact on the value of the objective function. As a result, the artificial variables will be driven from the basis as soon as possible.

Instead of attempting to determine how large the negative coefficient should be in an individual problem, we assume an arbitrarily large negative coefficient and denote it as $-M$. This notation also makes it somewhat easier to identify the elements in the simplex tableau that are dependent upon the objective coefficients of the artificial variables. The complete problem that is used to construct the initial simplex tableau is given in (8.60), (8.61), and (8.62), and the corresponding initial simplex tableau is constructed in Table 8.19.

$$\text{Maximize } Z = 5x_1 + x_2 + 0S_1$$
$$+ 0S_2 - MA_1 - MA_2 \qquad (8.60)$$

TABLE 8.19 INITIAL SIMPLEX TABLEAU FOR ARTIFICIAL VARIABLE ILLUSTRATION

c_b	c_j BASIS	5 x_1	1 x_2	0 S_1	0 S_2	$-M$ A_1	$-M$ A_2	SOLUTION
0	S_1	1	0	1	0	0	0	10
$-M$	A_1	1	-2	0	-1	1	0	3
$-M$	A_2	1	1	0	0	0	1	12
	Z_j	$-2M$	M	0	M	$-M$	$-M$	$-15M$
	$c_j - Z_j$	$5 + 2M$	$1 - M$	0	$-M$	0	0	

subject to

$$x_1 \quad\quad + S_1 \quad\quad\quad\quad\quad = 10$$

$$x_1 - 2x_2 \quad\quad - S_2 + A_1 \quad\quad = 3$$

$$x_1 + \;x_2 \quad\quad\quad\quad\quad + A_2 = 12 \quad\quad (8.61)$$

with

$$x_1,\, x_2,\, S_1,\, S_2,\, A_1,\, A_2 \geq 0 \quad\quad (8.62)$$

The pivot column is the x_1 column since $5 + 2M$ is the largest positive $c_j - Z_j$ value and the second row is the pivot row. Therefore, A_1 is driven from the basis, and the result of the simplex iteration is given in Table 8.20. The solution delineated in Table 8.20 is $x_1 = 3$, $x_2 = 0$, $S_1 = 7$, $S_2 = 0$, $A_1 = 0$, and $A_2 = 9$. Inequality $A_2 > 0$ implies that we still have not found a feasible solution. We actually have represented point A in Figure 8.2. We see that $11 + 3M > 5 + M$, so that x_2 is the entering variable and A_2 is the departing variable. Thus after the next simplex iteration we should have a feasible solution! The solution represented in Table 8.21 is $x_1 = 9$, $x_2 = 3$, $S_1 = 1$, $S_2 = 0$, and $A_1 = A_2 = 0$. Since both A_1 and A_2 are zero, we have found a feasible solution to problem (8.50), (8.51), and (8.52). When a feasible solution is obtained, the artificial variables have zero values. Furthermore, when a feasible solution is obtained and the artificial variables are nonbasic variables, these variables may be dropped from the simplex tableau, since they have accomplished the desired result. Artificial variables permit the use of the simplex method to generate an initial basic feasible solution. When these artificial variable columns are eliminated, there is no problem in using the generated feasible solution to determine the optimal solution. When these columns are eliminated, however, we may lose information that is useful in sensitivity analysis.

The solution in Table 8.22 is feasible but not optimal. One additional pivot is required to move us from point B to point C in Figure 8.2. The result of the pivot and the optimal tableau is given in Table 8.23.

We should note that the basic simplex procedure has not changed with the addition of the artificial variables. The addition has, however, allowed us to use the simplex method to find an initial

basic feasible solution. After the initial feasible solution is found, these variables may be omitted. On the other hand, artificial variable columns are often kept in the simplex tableau, since they do provide information that is of value in certain types of sensitivity analysis.

In summary, we note several important points in constructing the initial simplex tableau for any linear programming problem with a maximization objective.

1. Write all constraints with variables on the left-hand side and a *nonnegative* constant on the right-hand side.
2. Convert all inequality constraints to equalities by adding or subtracting slack or surplus variables.
3. Add an artificial variable to each constraint that is a greater-than-or-equal-to constraint or an equality constraint (after the constraint has been modified to have a nonnegative right-hand side).
4. All artificial variables are indicated in the objective function with a coefficient of $-M$.

We now have the ability to solve any linear programming problem with a maximization objective. The next section deals with a minor modification that allows us to handle the minimization problem as well.

8.5 SOLVING THE MINIMIZATION PROBLEM

Consider now the problem of solving a linear programming problem with a minimization objective. Again we use the simplex method that requires the generation of basic solutions. Thus our goal is to select a pivot element so that the next generated basic solution will have an objective value lower than the objective value associated with the previous basic solution. The selection of the pivot row is based on the condition that all basic variables must be greater than or equal to zero. This condition must be satisfied independently of the form of the objective, and thus there is no difference in the selection of the pivot row for a minimization as compared to a maximization problem.

The difference in the selection of the pivot

TABLE 8.20 SECOND SIMPLEX TABLEAU FOR ARTIFICIAL VARIABLE ILLUSTRATION

	c_j	5	1	0	0	$-M$	$-M$	
c_b	BASIS	x_1	x_2	S_1	S_2	A_1	A_2	SOLUTION
0	S_1	0	2	1	1	-1	0	7
5	x_1	1	-2	0	-1	1	0	3
$-M$	A_2	0	3	0	1	-1	1	9
	Z_j	5	$-10-3M$	0	$-5-M$	$5+M$	$-M$	$15-9M$
	$c_j - Z_j$	0	$11+3M$	0	$5+M$	$-5-2M$	0	

TABLE 8.21 THIRD SIMPLEX TABLEAU FOR ARTIFICIAL VARIABLE ILLUSTRATION

	c_j	5	1	0	0	$-M$	$-M$	
c_b	BASIS	x_1	x_2	S_1	S_2	A_1	A_2	SOLUTION
0	S_1	0	0	1	1/3	$-1/3$	$-2/3$	1
5	x_1	1	0	0	$-1/3$	1/3	2/3	9
1	x_2	0	1	0	1/3	$-1/3$	1/3	3
	Z_j	5	1	0	$-4/3$	4/3	11/3	48
	$c_j - Z_j$	0	0	0	4/3	$-M-\dfrac{4}{3}$	$-M-\dfrac{11}{3}$	

TABLE 8.22 MODIFIED SIMPLEX TABLEAU FOR ARTIFICIAL VARIABLE ILLUSTRATION

	c_j	5	1	0	0	
c_j	BASIS	x_1	x_2	S_1	S_2	SOLUTION
0	S_1	0	0	1	1/3	1
5	x_1	1	0	0	$-1/3$	9
1	x_2	0	1	0	1/3	3
	Z_j	5	1	0	$-4/3$	48
	$c_j - Z_j$	0	0	0	4/3	

TABLE 8.23 OPTIMAL SIMPLEX TABLEAU FOR ARTIFICIAL VARIABLE ILLUSTRATION

	c_j	5	1	0	0	
c_j	BASIS	x_1	x_2	S_1	S_2	SOLUTION
0	S_2	0	0	3	1	3
5	x_1	1	0	1	0	10
1	x_2	0	1	-1	0	2
	Z_j	0	0	4	0	52
	$c_j - Z_j$	0	0	-4	0	

column is very simple and is justified by recalling the primary interpretation of the $c_j - Z_j$ values. The $c_j - Z_j$ value associated with a nonbasic variable indicates the per unit change of the objective if the nonbasic variable becomes a basic variable in the process of applying the pivot operation. Therefore, if $c_j - Z_j < 0$, the effect of entering the variable into the basis is to decrease the value of the objective. The rule for choosing the pivot variable or pivot column is then as follows

Pivot Column Selection Rule: (Minimization Problem)

The nonbasic variable with the largest $|c_j - Z_j|$ value, for all $c_j - Z_j < 0$, is the pivot variable.

The optimal solution is found when the $c_j - Z_j$ values for all variables in the problem are greater to or equal to zero. To illustrate the row rule for selecting the variable that will become basic, we consider the following problem

$$\text{Minimize } Z = 1200y_1 + 3000y_2 + 3600y_3 \quad (8.63)$$

subject to

$$y_1 + 2y_2 + y_3 \geq 3$$
$$y_1 + 3y_2 + 4y_3 \geq 4 \quad (8.64)$$

with

$$y_1, y_2, y_3 \geq 0 \quad (8.65)$$

(The fact that the variables are labeled as y_j has no sigificance here. This problem is referenced in Chapter 9 where this labeling is significant.) The inequality constraints are converted to equality constraints and problem (8.63), (8.64), and (8.65) is rewritten as follows

$$\text{Minimize } Z = 1200y_1 + 3000y_2 + 3600y_3 \quad (8.66)$$

subject to

$$y_1 + 2y_2 + y_3 - S_1 = 3$$
$$y_1 + 3y_2 + 4y_3 - S_2 = 4 \quad (8.67)$$

with

$$y_1, y_2, y_3, S_1, S_2 \geq 0 \quad (8.68)$$

Since there is no obvious initial basic feasible solution, the use of artificial variables is required. We have already learned how to incorporate artificial variables in the constraints, but we must reevaluate the role of the artificial variables in the objective function. In the maximization problem, large negative coefficients were assigned to the artificial variables in the objective function. Thus any positive value for the artificial variable has a significant negative impact on the objective value. On the other hand, if large positive coefficients are assigned to the artificial variables in the objective, any positive value for the artificial variable has a significant positive impact on the objective value. Certainly for a minimization objective this is not desirable and the net effect of incorporating artificial variables into a minimization objective would be to drive these variables from the basis as soon as possible. Problem (8.63), (8.64), and (8.65) with artificial variables included is then as follows

$$\text{Minimize } Z = 1200y_1 + 3000y_2 + 3600y_3 + MA_1 + MA_2 \quad (8.69)$$

subject to

$$y_1 + 2y_2 + y_3 - S_1 + A_1 = 3$$
$$y_1 + 3y_2 + 4y_3 - S_2 + A_2 = 4 \quad (8.70)$$

with

$$y_1, y_2, y_3, S_1, S_2, A_1, A_2 \geq 0 \quad (8.71)$$

TABLE 8.24 INITIAL SIMPLEX TABLEAU FOR MINIMIZATION ILLUSTRATION

c_b		c_j	1200	3000	3600	0	0	M	M	
	BASIS		y_1	y_2	y_3	S_1	S_2	A_1	A_2	SOLUTION
M	A_1		1	2	1	-1	0	1	0	3
M	A_2		1	③	4	0	-1	0	1	4
	Z_j		2M	5M	5M	$-M$	$-M$	M	M	7M
	$c_j - Z_j$		$1200 - 2M$	$3000 - 5M$	$3600 - 5M$	M	M	0	0	

TABLE 8.25 SECOND SIMPLEX TABLEAU FOR MINIMIZATION ILLUSTRATION

		1200	3000	3600	0	0	M	M	SOLUTION
c_b	BASIS	y_1	y_2	y_3	S_1	S_2	A_1	A_2	
M	A_1	$1/3$	0	$-5/3$	-1	$(2/3)$	1	$-2/3$	$1/3$
3000	y_2	$1/3$	1	$4/3$	0	$-1/3$	0	$1/3$	$4/3$
	Z_j	$\left(\dfrac{1}{3}M + 1000\right)$	3000	$\left(-\dfrac{5}{3}M + 4000\right)$	$-M$	$\left(\dfrac{2}{3}M - 1000\right)$	M	$\left(-\dfrac{2}{3}M + 1000\right)$	$\dfrac{1}{3}M + 4000$
	$c_j - Z_j$	$\left(-\dfrac{1}{3}M + 200\right)$	0	$\left(\dfrac{5}{3}M - 400\right)$	M	$\left(-\dfrac{2}{3}M + 1000\right)$	0	$\left(\dfrac{5}{3}M - 1000\right)$	

TABLE 8.26 THIRD SIMPLEX TABLEAU FOR MINIMIZATION ILLUSTRATION

c_b	c_j BASIS	1200 y_1	3000 y_2	3600 y_3	0 S_1	0 S_2	M A_1	M A_1	SOLUTION
0	S_2	1/2	0	−5/2	−3/2	1	3/2	−1	1/2
3000	y_2	1/2	1	1/2	−1/2	0	1/2	0	3/2
	Z_j	1500	3000	1500	−1500	0	1500	0	4500
	$c_j - Z_j$	−300	0	2100	1500	0	M − 1500	M	

The initial simplex tableau is given in Table 8.24. Initially the "largest negative" $c_j - Z_j$ value is $(3000 - 5M)$, and thus y_2 enters the basis and A_2 leaves the basis (Table 8.25). After the first iteration, the solution is still not feasible, and the largest negative $(c_j - Z_j)$ value is $(-2/3M + 1000)$. Thus S_2 becomes basic while A_2 becomes nonbasic (Table 8.26). The current solution is now feasible but not optimal. The artificial variables have served their purpose. We carry these columns along in Table 8.27, since the complete tableau will be utilized in Chapter 9. We note that all $c_j - Z_j \geq 0$, so that we have computed the optimal tableau. The optimal solution is $y_1 = 1$, $y_2 = 1$, and $y_3 = 0$, and the optimal objective value is 4200.

Solving a linear programming problem with a minimization objective is different from a maximization problem in the following two aspects.

1. Constructing the initial simplex tableau typically involves artificial variables, since greater-than-or-equal-to or equality constraints are involved. (A minimization problem with all less-than-or-equal-to constraints would have the obvious solution where all decision variables are zero.) For the minimization problem the artificial variables are included in the objective function with large positive coefficients; for a maximization problem that requires the use of artificial variables, the artificial variables are included in the objective function with large negative coefficients.

2. The criterion for selecting the pivot variable is shifted from selecting the largest positive $c_j - Z_j$ value to selecting the "largest negative" $c_j - Z_j$ value, and the solution is optimal when all $c_j - Z_j$ values are nonnegative.

There are other alternatives available in dealing with minimization problems. Perhaps the most popular alternative is to convert every minimization problem to a maximization problem. If Z is used to denote the objective function, it can be shown that minimizing Z is equivalent to maximizing −Z. For example, $3 = \min(3, 5) = -\max(-3, -5) = -(-3) = 3$. What we mean is that the values of the variables that solve these two problems are the same. The difference is that the objective values are opposite in sign. In other words,

$$\text{Minimum } Z = -(\text{Maximum } -Z) \quad (8.72)$$

Problem (8.63), (8.64), and (8.65) would be written as

$$\text{Maximize } Z = -1200y_1 - 3000y_1 - 3600y_3 \quad (8.73)$$

subject to

$$y_1 + 2y_2 + y_3 \geq 3$$
$$y_1 + 3y_2 + 4y_3 \geq 4 \quad (8.74)$$

TABLE 8.27 OPTIMAL SIMPLEX TABLEAU FOR MINIMIZATION ILLUSTRATION

c_b	c_j BASIS	1200 y_1	3000 y_2	3600 y_3	0 S_1	0 S_2	M A_1	M A_2	SOLUTION
1200	y_1	1	0	−5	−3	2	3	−2	1
3000	y_2	0	1	3	1	−1	−1	1	1
	Z_j	1200	3000	−3000	−600	−600	600	600	4200
	$c_j - Z_j$	0	0	600	600	600	(M − 600)	(M − 600)	

TABLE 8.28 INITIAL SIMPLEX TABLEAU FOR PROBLEM (8.73), (8.74), AND (8.75)

		c_j	-1200	-3000	-3600	0	0	$-M$	$-M$	
c_b	BASIS		y_1	y_2	y_3	S_1	S_2	A_1	A_2	SOLUTION
$-M$	A_1		1	2	1	-1	0	1	0	3
$-M$	A_2		1	③	4	0	-1	0	1	4
	Z_j		$-2M$	$-5M$	$-5M$	M	M	$-M$	$-M$	$-7M$
	$c_j - Z_j$		$2M - 1200$	$5M - 3000$	$5M - 3600$	$-M$	$-M$	0	0	

TABLE 8.29 OPTIMAL SIMPLEX TABLEAU FOR PROBLEM (8.73), (8.74), AND (8.75)

c_b	c_j BASIS	-1200 y_1	-3000 y_2	-3600 y_3	0 S_1	0 S_2	$-M$ A_1	$-M$ A_2	SOLUTION
-1200	y_1	1	0	-5	-3	2	3	-2	1
-3000	y_2	0	1	3	1	-1	-1	1	1
	z_j	-1200	-3000	3000	600	600	-600	-600	-4200
	$c_j - z_j$	0	0	-600	-600	-600	$(600 - M)$	$(600 - M)$	

with

$$y_1, y_2, y_3 \geq 0. \qquad (8.75)$$

The initial tableau would be as given in Table 8.28. The optimal tableau would be written as shown in Table 8.29. Note that the only difference relates to the optimality criterion. That is, the solution is optimal when all $c_j - Z_j$ values are less than or equal to zero. Both ways of dealing with minimization problems are widely accepted. We use the first method presented throughout the remainder of the text.

8.6 TYPES OF SOLUTIONS AND PROBLEMS IN APPLYING THE SIMPLEX METHOD

In this section we discuss the process of recognizing linear programming problems that are infeasible, unbounded, or have alternate optimal solutions. It is important to be able to identify these situations via the simplex tableau, since graphical analysis is a luxury we do not generally have in solving problems that arise from real applications. We also discuss the concept of degeneracy in linear programming and its potential impact on the solution process. Finally, unconstrained variables and redundancy are discussed.

8.6.1 THE INFEASIBLE LINEAR PROGRAMMING PROBLEM

A linear programming problem is infeasible if it has no solution that satisfies the constraints and nonnegativity conditions for the problem. This means that the feasible region is empty.

Consider this linear programming problem that was presented in Section 7.6.2.

$$\text{Maximize } Z = 2x_1 + 4x_2 \qquad (8.76)$$

subject to

$$2.5x_1 + 3x_2 \leq 300 \qquad (8.77)$$
$$5x_1 + 2x_2 \leq 400$$
$$2x_2 \leq 150$$
$$x_1 \qquad \geq 60$$
$$x_2 \geq 60$$

with

$$x_1, x_2 \geq 0 \qquad (8.78)$$

Figure 7.18 illustrates the fact that this linear programming problem is infeasible. We attempt to solve this problem using the simplex method and observe the results. In the simplex method either an obvious initial basic feasible solution is available or artificial variables must be used to find a feasible solution. A solution is feasible when the artificial variables in the problem are all zero. If the simplex method cannot do this, the linear programming problem will be infeasible. The simplex solution procedure to this problem is presented in Tables 8.30–8.33.

We note that in the final simplex tableau, all $c_j - Z_j$ values are less than or equal to zero, since M is a large positive number. Therefore, the optimality conditions are satisfied, and there is no basis for selecting another pivot column. However, $A_2 = 10$ and the constraint $x_2 \geq 60$ is not satisfied. Thus there is no feasible solution to this problem. Table 8.34 gives the coordinates of the solutions generated in the simplex tableau in Tables 8.30, 8.31, 8.32, and 8.33. Figure 8.3 illustrates these extreme points graphically. Points 2 and 3 satisfy $x_2 \geq 60$ and point 4 satisfies $x_1 \geq 60$. None of the points generated is feasible to both of these constraints, and finally the optimality condition ($c_j - Z_j \leq 0$) for the linear programming problem with a maximization objective is satisfied.

We can show that a linear programming problem is infeasible by generating a basic solution that satisfies the optimality conditions for the problem but still has an artificial variable that is greater than zero in solution. Any linear programming problem that involves "$\geq$" or "$=$" constraints has the potential for being infeasible. Also, it is important to note that infeasibility in real applications generally points to a model formulation error or unfounded expectations.

8.6.2 THE UNBOUNDED LINEAR PROGRAMMING PROBLEM

In a maximization problem, a linear program is unbounded if the objective function can be made infinitely large without violating any of the constraints. The simplex method automatically exhibits this condition. Consider again the problem used to

TABLE 8.30 INITIAL SIMPLEX TABLEAU FOR INFEASIBILITY ILLUSTRATION

		2	4	0	0	0	0	$-M$	0	$-M$	
c_b	BASIS	x_1	x_2	S_1	S_2	S_3	S_4	A_1	S_5	A_2	SOLUTION
0	S_1	2.5	3	1	0	0	0	0	0	0	300
0	S_2	5	2	0	1	0	0	0	0	0	400
0	S_3	0	2	0	0	1	0	0	0	0	150
$-M$	A_1	1	0	0	0	0	-1	1	0	0	60
$-M$	A_2	0	①	0	0	0	0	0	-1	1	60
	Z_j	$-M$	$-M$	0	0	0	M	$-M$	M	$-M$	$-120M$
	$c_j - Z_j$	$2+M$	$4+M$	0	0	0	$-M$	0	$-M$	0	

TABLE 8.31 SECOND SIMPLEX TABLEAU FOR INFEASIBILITY ILLUSTRATION

c_b		2	4	0	0	0	0	$-M$	0	$-M$	
	c_j										
	BASIS	x_1	x_2	S_1	S_2	S_3	S_4	A_1	S_5	A_2	SOLUTION
0	S_1	(2.5)	0	1	0	0	0	0	3	-3	120
0	S_2	5	0	0	1	0	0	0	2	-2	280
0	S_3	0	0	0	0	1	0	0	2	-2	30
$-M$	A_1	1	0	0	0	0	-1	1	0	0	60
4	x_2	0	1	0	0	0	0	0	-1	1	60
	Z_j	$-M$	4	0	0	0	M	$-M$	-4	4	$240 - 6M$
	$c_j - Z_j$	$2 + M$	0	0	0	0	$-M$	0	4	$-M - 4$	

TABLE 8.32 THIRD SIMPLEX TABLEAU FOR INFEASIBILITY ILLUSTRATION

	c_j	2	4	0	0	0	0	-M	0	-M	
c_b	BASIS	x_1	x_2	S_1	S_2	S_3	S_4	A_1	S_5	A_2	SOLUTION
2	x_1	1	0	0.4	0	0	0	0	1.2	-1.2	48
0	S_2	0	0	-2	1	0	0	0	-4	④	40
0	S_3	0	0	0	0	1	0	0	2	-2	30
-M	A_1	0	0	-0.4	0	0	-1	1	-1.2	1.2	12
4	x_2	0	1	0	0	0	0	0	-1	1	60
	Z_j	2	4	(0.8 + 0.4M)	0	0	M	-M	(-1.6 + 1.2M)	(1.6 - 1.2M)	336 - 12M
	$c_j - Z_j$	0	0	(-0.8 - 0.4M)	0	0	-M	0	(1.6 - 1.2M)	(-1.6 + .02M)	

TABLE 8.33 FINAL SIMPLEX TABLEAU FOR INFEASIBILITY ILLUSTRATION

c_b	$c_j \to$ BASIS	2 x_1	4 x_2	0 S_1	0 S_2	0 S_3	0 S_4	-M A_1	0 S_5	-M A_2	SOLUTION
2	x_1	1	0	-0.2	0.3	0	0	0	0	0	60
-M	A_2	0	0	-0.5	0.25	0	0	0	-1	1	10
0	S_3	0	0	1	0.5	1	0	0	0	0	50
-M	A_1	0	0	0.2	-0.3	0	-1	1	0	0	0
4	x_2	0	1	0.5	-0.25	0	0	0	0	0	50
	Z_j	2	4	(1.6 + 0.3M)	(-0.4 + 0.05M)	0	M	-M	M	-M	320 - 10M
	$c_j - Z_j$	0	0	(-1.6 - 0.3M)	(0.4 - 0.05M)	0	-M	0	-M	0	

TABLE 8.34 EXTREME POINTS GENERATED FOR INFEASIBILITY ILLUSTRATION

TABLEAU	COORDINATES (x_1, x_2)
Initial	(0, 0)
Second	(0, 60)
Third	(48, 60)
Final	(60, 50)

illustrate this situation graphically, problem (7.57), (7.58), and (7.59), rewritten as follows.

$$\text{Maximize } Z = 2x_1 + 3x_2 \qquad (8.79)$$

subject to

$$x_1 - x_2 \leq 2$$
$$-3x_1 + x_2 \leq 4 \qquad (8.80)$$

with

$$x_1, x_2 \geq 0 \qquad (8.81)$$

The initial simplex tableau for this problem is given in Table 8.35. The simplex method generates a sequence of adjacent extreme points. These points are illustrated in Figure 8.4, which also shows an un-

bounded feasible region. We note that there is no new extreme point adjacent to the extreme point (0, 4). This dilemma is reflected in the second simplex tableau, Table 8.36. The pivot column is chosen to be the x_1 column, but there is no row that can serve as the pivot row. Additional insight is provided by looking at the equations the second tableau represents.

$$-2x_1 + S_1 + S_2 = 6$$
$$-3x_1 + x_2 + S_2 = 4 \qquad (8.82)$$

Since $S_2 = 0$, (8.82) may be rewritten as follows

$$-2x_1 + S_1 = 6$$
$$-3x_1 + x_2 = 4 \qquad (8.83)$$

If $x_1 = 10$, $S_1 = 26$ and $x_2 = 34$; if $x_1 = 100,000$, $S_1 = 200,006$ and $x_2 = 300,004$. This should indicate that x_1 can become infinitely large and still satisfy the constraints to the problem. Additionally, each unit of x_1 increases the objective value by 11 [the $(c_j - Z_j)$ value]. The conclusion must be that the objective increases without bound.

In summary, an unbounded solution is recognized in a maximization problem when it is possible to select a pivot column but not a pivot row. The same criterion is used in identifying an unbounded

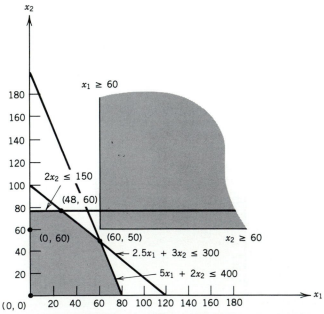

FIGURE 8.3 SEQUENCE OF POINTS REPRESENTED BY TABLEAUS FOR PROBLEM (8.76), (8.77), AND (8.78).

TABLE 8.35 INITIAL SIMPLEX TABLEAU FOR UNBOUNDED ILLUSTRATION

c_b	c_j BASIS	2 x_1	3 x_2	0 S_1	0 S_2	SOLUTION
0	S_1	1	-1	1	0	2
0	S_2	-3	①	0	1	4
	Z_j	0	0	0	0	0
	$c_j - Z_j$	2	3	0	0	

solution for a problem with a minimization objective. It is important to remember that unbounded solutions in real applications generally point to a model formulation error.

8.6.3 ALTERNATE OPTIMAL SOLUTIONS

If two or more solutions yield the optimal objective value, the linear programming problem is said to have alternate optimal solutions. When using the simplex method, we recognize the fact that there are alternate optima from the optimal simplex tableau. If the $c_j - Z_j$ value is zero for one or more of the *nonbasic* variables in the solution, there will be alternate optima. To illustrate this point again, we take our illustration from Chapter 7.

Consider the problem

$$\text{Maximize } Z = \frac{10}{3} x_1 + 4x_2 \qquad (8.84)$$

subject to

$$2.5x_1 + 3x_2 \le 300$$
$$5x_1 + 2x_2 \le 400$$
$$2x_2 \le 150 \qquad (8.85)$$

with

$$x_1, x_2 \ge 0 \qquad (8.86)$$

The solution follows in Tables 8.37, 8.38, and 8.39. The third tableau (Table 8.39) is an optimal tableau. We note, however, that the $c_j - Z_j$ value for S_3, a nonbasic variable, is zero. Let's pivot to make S_3 basic. The result is in Table 8.40. Alternate optimal solutions can be generated by continuing to pivot after an optimal tableau has been generated. The pivot column would be selected from the set of nonbasic variables that have zero $c_j - Z_j$ terms. Graphically this means that the objective function is par-

allel to one of the binding constraints. The occurrence of alternate optima is illustrated graphically for this problem in Figure 8.5.

8.6.4 THE CONCEPT OF DEGENERACY IN LINEAR PROGRAMMING

A feasible solution to a linear programming problem is said to be degenerate if one or more of the basic variables has a value of zero. Degeneracy occurs whenever two rows satisfy the criterion of selection as a pivot row. Consider the following problem.

$$\text{Maximize } Z = 4x_1 + 3x_3 \qquad (8.87)$$

subject to

$$x_1 - x_2 \quad\quad \le 2$$
$$2x_1 \quad\quad + x_3 \le 4$$
$$x_1 + x_2 + x_3 \le 3 \qquad (8.88)$$

with

$$x_1, x_2, x_3 \ge 0 \qquad (8.89)$$

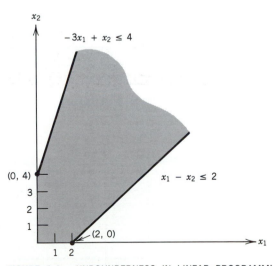

FIGURE 8.4 UNBOUNDEDNESS IN LINEAR PROGRAMMING.

TABLE 8.36 SECOND SIMPLEX TABLEAU FOR UNBOUNDED ILLUSTRATION

	c_j	2	3	0	0	
c_b	BASIS	x_1	x_2	S_1	S_2	SOLUTION
0	S_1	-2	0	1	1	6
3	x_2	-3	1	0	1	4
	Z_j	-9	3	0	3	12
	$c_j - Z_j$	11	0	0	-3	

TABLE 8.37 INITIAL SIMPLEX TABLEAU FOR ALTERNATIVE OPTIMAL ILLUSTRATION

	c_j	$\frac{10}{3}$	4	0	0	0	
c_b	BASIS	x_1	x_2	S_1	S_2	S_3	SOLUTION
0	S_1	2.5	3	1	0	0	300
0	S_2	5	2	0	1	0	400
0	S_3	0	②	0	0	1	150
	Z_j	0	0	0	0	0	0
	$c_j - Z_j$	$\frac{10}{3}$	4	0	0	0	

TABLE 8.38 SECOND SIMPLEX TABLEAU FOR ALTERNATE OPTIMAL ILLUSTRATION

	c_j	$\frac{10}{3}$	4	0	0	0	
c_b	BASIS	x_1	x_2	S_1	S_2	S_2	SOLUTION
0	S_1	⬭2.5	0	1	0	-1.5	75
0	S_2	5	0	0	1	-1	250
4	x_2	0	1	0	0	0.5	75
	Z_j	0	4	0	0	2	300
	$c_j - Z_j$	$\frac{10}{3}$	0	0	0	-2	

TABLE 8.39 THIRD SIMPLEX TABLEAU FOR ALTERNATE OPTIMAL ILLUSTRATION

	c_j	$\frac{10}{3}$	4	0	0	0	
c_b	BASIS	x_1	x_2	S_1	S_2	S_3	SOLUTION
$\frac{10}{3}$	x_1	1	0	0.4	0	-0.6	30
0	S_2	0	0	-2	1	2	100
4	x_2	0	1	0	0	0.5	75
	Z_j	$\frac{10}{3}$	4	$\frac{4}{3}$	0	0	400
	$c_j - Z_j$	0	0	$-\frac{4}{3}$	0	0	

TABLE 8.40 FOURTH SIMPLEX TABLEAU FOR ALTERNATE OPTIMAL ILLUSTRATION

c_b	c_j BASIS	$\frac{10}{3}$ x_1	4 x_2	0 S_1	0 S_2	0 S_3	SOLUTION
$\frac{10}{3}$	x_1	1	0	-0.2	0.3	0	60
0	S_3	0	0	-1	0.5	1	50
4	x_2	0	1	0.5	-0.25	0	50
	Z_j	$\frac{10}{3}$	4	$\frac{4}{3}$	0	0	400
	$c_j - Z_j$	0	0	$-\frac{4}{3}$	0	0	

The initial simplex tableau follows in Table 8.41. We see that x_1 is the entering variable, and there is a tie for the minimum ratio. It is not difficult to see that no matter which row is chosen as the pivot row (1 or 2), the result of the pivot will be a degenerate solution. Let's choose the first row as the pivot row (Tables 8.42–8.45).

The fifth tableau (Table 8.45) is the optimal tableau and the basic optimal solution is not degenerate. This example illustrates two important facts: first, degeneracy may occur but may be eliminated as the simplex method continues; second, the objective may not change for a number of iterations.

We see that the objective value is 8 for the second, third, and fourth tableax. For each of those basic solutions $x_1 = 2$, $x_2 = 0$, $x_3 = 0$. The same extreme point is being represented three times in three different ways.

Degeneracy occurs because there is not always a unique algebraic representation of an extreme point. A single extreme point may have many basic solution representations. That is exactly what was happening above. The simplex method provided three representations of that extreme point ($x_1 = 2$, $x_2 = 0$, $x_3 = 0$) before it moved on to an adjacent extreme point. One of the problems at the end of this

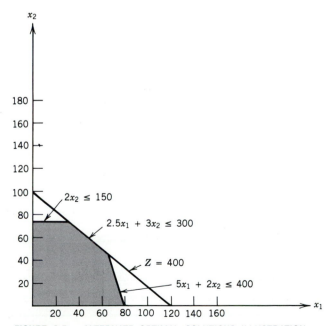

FIGURE 8.5 ALTERNATE OPTIMAL SOLUTIONS ILLUSTRATION.

TABLE 8.41 INITIAL SIMPLEX TABLEAU FOR DEGENERACY ILLUSTRATION

c_b	BASIS	c_j → 4	0	3	0	0	0	SOLUTION	RATIOS
		x_1	x_2	x_3	S_1	S_2	S_3		
0	S_1	①	−1	0	1	0	0	2	2/1 = 2
0	S_2	②	0	1	0	1	0	4	4/2 = 2
0	S_3	1	1	1	0	0	1	3	3/1 = 3
	Z_j	0	0	0	0	0	0	0	
	$c_j - Z_j$	4	0	3	0	0	0		

TABLE 8.42 SECOND SIMPLEX TABLEAU FOR DEGENERACY ILLUSTRATION

c_b	BASIS	c_j → 4	0	3	0	0	0	SOLUTION	RATIOS
		x_1	x_2	x_3	S_1	S_2	S_3		
4	x_1	1	−1	0	1	0	0	2	—
0	S_2	0	②	1	−2	1	0	0	0/2
0	S_3	0	2	1	−1	0	1	1	1/2
	Z_j	4	−4	0	4	0	0	8	
	$c_j - Z_j$	0	4	3	−4	0	0		

TABLE 8.43 THIRD SIMPLEX TABLEAU FOR DEGENERACY ILLUSTRATION

c_b	BASIS	c_j → 4	0	3	0	0	0	SOLUTION	RATIOS
		x_1	x_2	x_3	S_1	S_2	S_3		
4	x_1	1	0	0.5	0	0.5	0	2	2/0.5
0	x_2	0	1	⓪.5	−1	0.5	0	0	0/0.5
0	S_3	0	0	0	1	−1	1	1	—
	Z_j	4	0	2	0	2	0	8	
	$c_j - Z_j$	0	0	1	0	−2	0		

TABLE 8.44 FOURTH SIMPLEX TABLEAU FOR DEGENERACY ILLUSTRATION

c_b	BASIS	c_j → 4	0	3	0	0	0	SOLUTION	RATIOS
		x_1	x_2	x_3	S_1	S_2	S_3		
4	x_1	1	−1	0	1	0	0	2	2/1
3	x_3	0	2	1	−2	1	0	0	—
0	S_3	0	0	0	①	−1	1	1	1/1
	Z_j	4	2	3	−2	3	0	8	
	$c_j - Z_j$	0	−2	0	2	−3	0		

TABLE 8.45 FIFTH SIMPLEX TABLEAU FOR DEGENERACY ILLUSTRATION

c_b	BASIS	c_j →	4	0	3	0	0	0	SOLUTION
			x_1	x_2	x_3	S_1	S_2	S_3	
4	x_1		1	-1	0	0	1	-1	1
3	x_3		0	2	1	0	-1	2	2
0	S_1		0	0	0	1	-1	1	1
	Z_j		4	2	3	0	1	2	10
	$c_j - Z_j$		0	-2	0	0	-1	-2	

chapter asks you to solve the same problem, initially choosing the second row as the pivot row. More advanced texts discuss procedures for choosing the pivot row when there is a tie for the minimum ratio. Generally, the choice affects the number of iterations required to find the optimal solution. Degeneracy can cause some difficulties in the application of the simplex method. It is theoretically possible for the simplex algorithm to alternate among a set of basic feasible solutions without ever increasing the value of the objective function. This phenomenon is called *cycling* and if it occurs the simplex algorithm will never terminate. Fortunately, cycling has not proved to be a major problem, since an occurrence has not been reported in an actual application. Degeneracy, on the other hand, is very common.

8.6.5 UNCONSTRAINED VARIABLES

Occasionally we encounter applications that require one or more of the decision variables to be unconstrained in sign. In other words, these variables can assume either positive or negative values. For example, in models involving inventory, the negative value of an inventory variable indicates a shortage, and in situations where backordering is possible, a negative value for the inventory variable represents a backorder quantity. Consider the inventory constraints (6.58) for the production scheduling problem in Section 6.4.6.

$$x_1 + y_1 - I_1 = 1800$$
$$I_1 + x_2 + y_2 - I_2 = 2200$$
$$I_2 + x_3 + y_3 - I_3 = 3400$$
$$I_3 + x_4 + y_3 = 2800 \qquad (8.90)$$

The variables I_1, I_2, and I_3 could be unconstrained in sign. If I_j is positive, there is inventory in month j that can be carried to month $J + 1$. On the other hand, if I_j is negative then there has been a shortage in month j and this shortage may be satisfied by production in month $J + 1$.

Although variables that are unconstrained in sign occur in applications, the simplex method requires that all variables are nonnegative. Fortunately, linear programming problems with unconstrained variables can be converted to an algebraically equivalent problem with all nonnegative variables. This is accomplished by expressing each of the unconstrained variables as the difference between two nonnegative variables. If the variable x_1 is unconstrained in sign, then

$$x_1 = x_1' - x_1'' \qquad (8.91)$$

where $x_1' \geq 0$ and $x_1'' \geq 0$. For example, if $x_1 = 3$, then $x_1' = 3$ and $x_1'' = 0$, and if $x_1 = -3$, then $x_1' = 0$ and $x_1'' = 3$.

To illustrate this substitution we rewrite the inventory conditions in (8.90) allowing the I_j to be unconstrained.

$$x_1 + y_1 - I_1' + I_1'' = 1800$$
$$I_1' - I_1'' + x_2 + y_2 - I_2' + I_2'' = 2200$$
$$I_2' - I_2'' + x_3 + y_3 - I_3' + I_3'' = 3400$$
$$I_3' - I_3'' + x_4 + y_4 = 2800 \qquad (8.92)$$

If $I_1' > 0$, then there is a positive ending inventory in month 1, and if $I_1'' > 0$, then there is a shortage in month 1. The fact that I_1'' is included in the second equation of (8.92) indicates that we will attempt to meet demand in month 1 before meeting demand in subsequent months. In other words, backordering is applicable. On the other hand, if backordering is not possible, system (8.92) would be rewritten as follows

$$x_1 + y_1 - I_1' + I_1'' = 1800$$

$$I_1' + x_2 + y_2 - I_2' + I_2'' = 2200$$

$$I_2' + x_3 + y_3 - I_3' + I_3'' = 3400$$

$$I_3' + x_4 + y_4 = 2800 \qquad (8.93)$$

Certainly the substitution, $I_j = I_j' - I_j''$, where $I_j' \geq 0$ and $I_j'' \geq 0$ must reflect the fact that we cannot have a positive ending inventory and backorder simultaneously. In other words, I_j' and I_j'' cannot both be greater than zero or $(I_j')(I_j'') = 0$.

Returning to (8.91) where $x_1 = x_1' - x_1''$ we note that if $x_1 = 3$ while $x_1' = 8$ and $x_1'' = 5$, there would be a serious problem in justifying the validity of the basic substitution, (8.91), suggested here. Fortunately, this representation can be ruled out if we are interested only in the basic solutions to a linear programming problem. Examine, for example, the simplex tableaus for problem (8.76), (8.77), and (8.78) given in Tables 8.30–8.33. Note that in each tableau the coefficients in the A_1 column can be obtained by multiplying the coefficients in the S_4 column by -1. The same relationship holds between the S_5 and A_2 columns, and it can be shown that if two columns differ only in sign, the result of the pivot operation is that these two columns will still only differ in sign. The point of this argument is simply that x_1' and x_1'' cannot both be basic at the same time, and thus the product of x_1' and x_1'' must always be zero. This means that the representation of x_1 where

$$x_1 = x_1' - x_1''$$

is unique when used in the context of linear programming. To illustrate this principle we consider a specific linear programming problem.

$$\text{Maximize } Z = 10x_1 + 15x_2 \qquad (8.94)$$

subject to

$$x_1 + 3x_2 \leq 6$$

$$4x_1 + 5x_2 \leq 10 \qquad (8.95)$$

with

$$x_1 \geq 0, \ x_2 \quad \text{unconstrained in sign} \qquad (8.96)$$

To solve this problem using the simplex method, this problem is reformulated as follows

$$\text{Maximize } Z = 10x_1 + 15x_2' - 15x_2'' \qquad (8.97)$$

subject to

$$x_1 + 3x_2' - 3x_2'' \leq 6$$

$$4x_1 + 5x_2' - 5x_2'' \leq 10 \qquad (8.98)$$

with

$$x_1, x_2', x_2'' \geq 0 \qquad (8.99)$$

The initial simplex tableau can then be constructed as usual in Table 8.46. We see that the new basic variable is x_2', which means that x_2'' is nonbasic and thus zero. One simplex iteration illustrates again that the columns x_2' and x_2'' differ only in sign (see Table 8.47). As we can see, the simplex computations do not change. Dealing with variables that are unconstrained in sign is basically a formulation

TABLE 8.46 INITIAL SIMPLEX TABLEAU FOR UNCONSTRAINED VARIABLE ILLUSTRATION

c_b		c_j	10	15	-15	0	0	
	BASIS		x_1	x_2'	x_2''	S_1	S_2	SOLUTION
0	S_1		1	③	-3	1	0	6
0	S_2		4	5	-5	0	1	10
	Z_j		0	0	0	0	0	0
	$c_j - Z_j$		10	15	-15	0	0	

TABLE 8.47 SECOND SIMPLEX TABLEAU FOR UNCONSTRAINED VARIABLE ILLUSTRATION

c_b	c_j BASIS	10 x_1	15 x_2'	-15 x_2''	0 S_1	0 S_2	SOLUTION
15	x_2'	$\dfrac{1}{3}$	1	-1	$\dfrac{1}{3}$	0	2
0	S_2	$\dfrac{7}{3}$	0	0	$\dfrac{-5}{3}$	1	0
	Z_j	5	15	-15	5	0	30
	$c_j - Z_j$	5	0	0	-5	0	

technique that provides a linear programming equivalent with all variables constrained to be greater than or equal to zero.

8.6.6 REDUNDANT CONSTRAINTS

A constraint is redundant if it can be removed from the formulation without affecting the set of *feasible solutions* to the linear programming problem. Redundant constraints are not easily identified and cause no problem if the constraints are all of the "≤" or "≥" type. If this is the case and there is a redundant constraint, the result is that the slack or surplus variable associated with that constraint will be basic in every basic feasible solution to the problem. On the other hand, redundancy involving equality constraints may lead to computational difficulties. This problem is handled in more advanced texts and is typically discussed in the context of the linear dependence of systems of equations.

8.7 USING THE COMPUTER TO SOLVE LINEAR PROGRAMMING PROBLEMS

We have emphasized the computational aspects of linear programming in this chapter. We believe that learning the simplex process significantly increases the understanding of linear programming and the ability to interpret and intelligently implement the solution. It does become obvious rather quickly that solving linear programming problems via hand calculations is not practical or desirable. Fortunately, the evolution of linear programming has been paralleled by the development of the high-speed digital computer. At the same time a number of computer programming (software) packages for solving linear programming problems have been developed. Three basic types of computer packages for linear program-

ming are available: the batch program, the time-shared or interactive package, and programs that are implemented on microcomputers. The batch program requires the user to prepare the input in advance in the form of a file that is read by the program, or the input may be punched on cards. All the input data and the control statements that specify the parameters for the program are simultaneously submitted to the computer, and the program is placed in queue for execution. At a later time the output is printed and retrieved by the user. In the case of the interactive package, the user provides input and receives output via a remote terminal, often a cathode-ray tube (CRT) or a microcomputer. Data for the interactive packages are submitted in parts as queried by the computer package. With the increased availability of the sophisticated microcomputer has come the development of a number of interactive computer packages dedicated for use on the microcomputer. Ramesh Sharda provided an informative survey of many available microcomputer codes in *Interfaces*.[2]

We now briefly describe five computer packages. First, a popular interactive linear programming package, LINDO, is examined.[3] Two interactive economical microcomputer packages are also discussed. Finally, two batch programs are considered. The first is one of many codes designed to solve textbook-size problems. The second is a commercial code designed to solve very large linear programming problems quickly.

The LINDO computer package was developed by Linus E. Schrage of the University of Chicago.

---

[2]Ramesh Sharda, "Linear programming on microcomputers: A survey," *Interfaces,* **14** (November/December 1984), 27–28.

[3]Linus Schrage, *Linear Programming with LINDO.* Palo Alto, Calif.: The Scientific Press, 1981.

```
LINDO
[LINDO (UC 1 APRIL 84)]
[:]
MAX 3×1 + 4×2
[?]
ST
[?]
×1 + ×2 < 1200
[?]
2×1 + 3×2 < 3000
[?]
×1 + 4×2 < 3600
[?]
END
[:]
LOOK ALL
MAX 3×1 + 4×2
SUBJECT TO
        2)  ×1 + ×2 = 1200
        3) 2×1 + 3×2 = 3000
        4)  ×1 + 4×2 = 3600
END
```

FIGURE 8.6 DATA INPUT SESSION WITH LINDO (COMPUTER RESPONSES ARE BRACKETED).

This package allows the user to interact with the computer in a conversational mode. After the computer software has been accessed, the user responds to simple requests for information. After the data have been entered (correctly), the command "GO" is issued, a solution is available at the computer terminal.

The model for Rollins Unlimited, (8.1), (8.2), and (8.3), is solved using the five computer packages. We begin with a description of a portion of the LINDO computer session for this problem. Figure 8.6 describes the input portion of the session. This package is very natural to use since the objective function and constraints are typed as they would appear from the written formulation. In this package the symbol ":" indicates that the computer is waiting for further instructions and "?" indicates it is waiting for further input about the problem being solved. Even though "<" is input, it can be seen from the computer response to the LOOK ALL instruction that "<" was read as "≤". The LOOK ALL command simply permits a check of the users input. After the input is verified to be correct, the user issues the command GO and the problem is solved. Figure 8.7 shows the solution information provided by LINDO. In Chapter 9 we will see that the re-

duced cost and dual price information reflect the $Z_j - c_j$ values associated with the activity variables and slack variables. One of the options for this package (and most other linear programming packages) is sensitivity analysis. The format seen in Figure 8.7 is typical. This information should be referred to in Chapter 9 when the sensitivity analysis for Rollins Unlimited is presented. We will not present the sensitivity analysis output for the remaining computer packages discussed here. The typical tableau format for LINDO is given in Figure 8.8. This particular tableau is the optimal tableau.

As mentioned earlier there are many linear programming packages for microcomputers. The programming package by Warren J. Erickson and Owen P. Hall, Jr., includes linear programming and additionally 12 other computer models for management science.[4] The package provides all the information needed to run the programs as well as a floppy disk that contains the operating system and all the programs necessary to implement the computer models.

---

[4]Warren J. Erickson and Owen P. Hall, Jr., *Computer Models for Management Science.* Reading, Mass.: Addison-Wesley, 1986.

```
[:]
GO
     LP OPTIMUM FOUND AT STEP 2
                OBJECTIVE FUNCTION VALUE
  1)          4199.99609
VARIABLE               VALUE            REDUCED COST
        X1          600.000000              0.0
        X2          600.000000              0.0
     ROW        SLACK OR SURPLUS         DUAL PRICES
        2)            0.0                 1.000000
        3)            0.0                 1.000000
        4)         599.999512             0.0
NO. ITERATIONS=            2
DO RANGE(SENSITIVITY) ANALYSIS?
[?]
  Y
         RANGES IN WHICH THE BASIS IS UNCHANGED
                  OBJ COEFFICIENT RANGES
     VARIABLE     CURRENT        ALLOWABLE         ALLOWABLE
                  COEF           INCREASE          DECREASE
        X1       3.000000       1.000000          0.333333
        X2       4.000000       0.500000          1.000000
                  RIGHTHAND SIDE RANGES
     ROW         CURRENT        ALLOWABLE         ALLOWABLE
                 RHS            INCREASE          DECREASE
        2     1200.00000        300.000000        119.999939
        3     3000.00000        199.999893        600.000000
        4     3600.00000        INFINITY          599.999512
```

FIGURE 8.7 SOLUTION INFORMATION FROM LINDO.

The information about the size of the program and the actual input parameters are queried one piece of information at a time. Figure 8.9 describes the questions that are asked sequentially by this package. There are a variety of output options. Figure 8.10 illustrates the option where the initial and optimal tableaus are printed. It should be noted that the columns printed in the tableau are only the columns associated with the nonbasic variables.

Another microcomputer package that is considerably more flexible in terms of problem size, input form, problem modification, and so forth, was developed by Paul A Jensen.[5] This package also contains a number of the computer models, including integer programming for 0–1 variables and dynamic programming. Figure 8.11 shows the summary input, while Figure 8.12 gives one output option

that traces the pivot operations. The linear programming model in this package additionally has an option that gives detailed information on the progress of the simplex technique.

We now briefly discuss two batch programs. The first is one of many codes designed to solve textbook-size problems.[6] The input file is very easy to construct, and the code will handle problems having up to 30 constraints and up to 79 variables (including slack, surplus, and artificial variables). The second code discussed can be used to solve very large linear programming problems quickly. *IBM Mathematical Programming System Extended/370*[7] is available on large IBM installations. It does, however, require a fairly complicated input data format and is generally not used for classroom instruction.

The batch computer code designed for classroom instruction has input requirements similar to

[5]Paul A. Jensen, *MICROSOLVE/Operations Research, Introduction to Operations Research.* Oakland, Calif.: Holden Day, 1983.

[6]Robert E. Markland, *Topics In Management Science.* New York: Wiley, 1983, pp. 179–182.

[7]*IBM Mathematical Programming System Extended/370.* White Plains, New York: IBM Corporation, 1985.

```
THE TABLEAU
   ROW   (BASIS)                     X1      X2    SLK    2   SLK    3
     1  ART                         0.0     0.0       1.000       1.000
     2           X1                 1.000   0.0       3.000      -1.000
     3           X2                 0.0     1.000    -2.000       1.000
     4  SLK       4                 0.0     0.0       5.000      -3.000


   ROW       SLK      4
     1        0.0          4200.000
     2        0.0           600.000
     3        0.0           600.000
     4        1.000         600.000
```

FIGURE 8.8   TABLEAU FORMAT FOR LINDO.

those for the LINDO code. The objective and constraint parameters are input sequentially into specified data fields, and the input file is submitted to the batch program. The computer output for Rollins Unlimited is shown in Figures 8.13 and 8.14. You will note some minor labeling differences between this output and the tableau used in the text. The major difference is that the Z_j row is not printed. The "DELTA" row does, however, list the $c_j - Z_j$ values and the P(I) column lists the variables that are basic in each equation.

The MPS-360 code will also be discussed briefly. The following is a description of the MPS-360 application to the Rollins Unlimited problem.

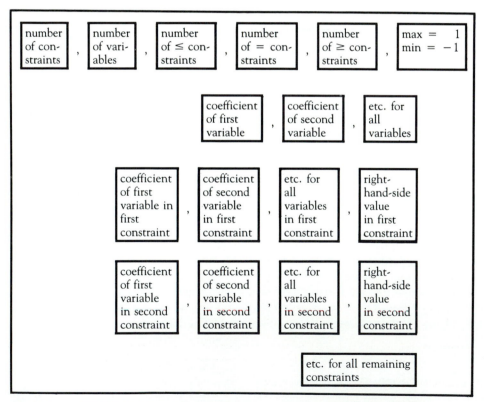

FIGURE 8.9   FORMAT OF INPUT FOR ERICKSON/HALL LINEAR PROGRAMMING PACKAGE.

```
***************************
*                         *
*   LINEAR PROGRAMMING    *
*        ANALYSIS         *
*                         *
***************************

**  INFORMATION ENTERED  **

NUMBER OF CONSTRAINTS       3
NUMBER OF VARIABLES         2
NUMBER OF <= CONSTRAINTS    3
NUMBER OF  = CONSTRAINTS    0
NUMBER OF >= CONSTRAINTS    0

MAXIMIZATION PROBLEM

3 X 1 + 4 X 2

SUBJECT TO

1 X 1 + 1 X 2 <= 1200

2 X 1 + 3 X 2 <= 3000

1 X 1 + 4 X 2 <= 3600

** TABLEAU OUTPUT **

ITERATION 0

BASIS

X 3 = 1200
X 4 = 3000
X 5 = 3600

BASIS        1     2

 X 3         1     1

 X 4         2     3

 X 5         1     4

C(J)-Z(J)    3     4
** TABLEAU OUTPUT **

ITERATION 3

BASIS

X 1 = 600
X 2 = 600
X 5 = 600

BASIS       4      3

X 5        -3      4.99

X 1        -1      2.99

X 2        .99    -2

C(J)-Z(J)  -1     -1

** RESULTS **

          VARIABLE ORIGINAL COEFF.
VARIABLE  VALUE    COEFF.   SENS.

X 1       600      3        0
X 2       600      4        0

CONSTRAINT ORIGINAL SLACK OR SHADOW
NUMBER     RHS      SURPLUS  PRICE

1          1200     0        1
2          3000     0        1
3          3600     599.99   0

OBJECTIVE FUNCTION VALUE : 4200
```

FIGURE 8.10 SAMPLE OUTPUT FROM ERICKSON/HALL LINEAR PROGRAMMING PACKAGE.

```
                    CONSTRAINT MATRIX BY COLUMNS FOR PROBLEM ROLLINS

    CONST.          WHEEL           MOUNT           ADJ
    VAR.

    X 1              1               2               1

    X 2              1               3               4

    SLK- 1           1               0               0

    SLK- 2           0               1               0

    SLK- 3           0               0               1


                   <=              <=              <=

    RHS             1200            3000            3600

    VAR.            X 1             X 2             SLK- 1          SLK- 2          SLK- 3

    OBJMAX          3               4               0               0               0

    BNDS            999999          999999          999999          999999          999999
```

FIGURE 8.11 SUMMARY INPUT FOR MICROSOLVE.

Input Data. The input data supplied are printed as shown in Figure 8.15. The Rollins Unlimited problem has three constraints that are WAUNITS (Wheel Assembly UNITS), WAHOURS (Wheel Assembly HOURS), and PAHOURS (Precision Adjustment HOURS). The symbol L indicates that the constraints are less-than-or-equal-to constraints. The symbol N associated with the OBJFUNC indicates that OBJFUNC is the objective function. The data are listed by decision variable. For example, $\times 1$ appears in the objective function with a coefficient of 3.0 and in each of the three constraints with respective coefficients of 1.0, 2.0, and 1.0. The right-hand-side values for the three constraints are given in the RHS section.

Optimal Objective Function Value. After three simplex iterations, the optimal solution is obtained. The value of the objective function at optimality is $4200, as shown in Figure 8.16.

Optimal Solution Values: Resource Activity. In the optimal solution, the WAUNITS and WAHOURS constraints are at their respective upper limits (UL) of 1200 wheel assembly units and 3000 wheel assembly hours. Therefore, there is no slack activity for these two constraints. The values under the Dual Activity Column in Figure 8.17 are the shadow prices associated with each constraint. This concept will be introduced in Chapter 9. The

constraint PAHOURS is not at its limit with slack activity of 600 hours. The symbol BS indicates that the slack variable associated with the constraint PAHOURS is in the basis in the optimal solution and all the available hours of precision adjustment time are not utilized.

Optimal Solution Values: Decision Variables. The decision variables $\times 1$ and $\times 2$ are in the basis (BS) in the optimal solution at respective values of 600 Deluxe skateboards and 600 Professional skateboards. The objective function coefficient for each basic variable is given in the Input Cost column of Figure 8.18.

8.8 SUMMARY

In this chapter a detailed presentation of the simplex method has been provided. The simplex method was introduced in 1947 and continues to be of substantial value because it is fast, it has many applications, and it can answer important questions about the sensitivity of solutions to variations in the input data. The simplex method has provided an extremely efficient method for solving complex linear programming problems with thousands of constraints.

Mathematicians in the USSR have recently

```
                    PRIMAL SIMPLEX ALGORITHM

PHASE 2

                  BASIC SOLUTION-PHASE 2 -ITER. 1

          VAR.          NAME          VALUE         STATUS
           1            x1            0             ZERO
           2            x2            0             ZERO
           3            SLK- 1        1200          BASIC- 1
           4            SLK- 2        3000          BASIC- 2
           5            SLK- 3        3600          BASIC- 3

                    OBJECTIVE =  0

x2 ENTERING BASIS GOING UP
SLK- 3 LEAVING BASIS BY GOING TO ZERO

                  BASIC SOLUTION-PHASE 2 -ITER. 2

          VAR.          NAME          VALUE         STATUS
           1            x1            0             ZERO
           2            x2            900           BASIC- 3
           3            SLK- 1        300           BASIC- 1
           4            SLK- 2        300           BASIC- 2
           5            SLK- 3        0             ZERO

                    OBJECTIVE = 3600

x1 ENTERING BASIS GOING UP
SLK- 2 LEAVING BASIS BY GOING TO ZERO

                  BASIC SOLUTION-PHASE 2 -ITER. 3

          VAR.          NAME          VALUE         STATUS
           1            x1            240           BASIC- 2
           2            x2            840           BASIC- 3
           3            SLK- 1        120           BASIC- 1
           4            SLK- 2        0             ZERO
           5            SLK- 3        0             ZERO

                    OBJECTIVE = 4080

SLK- 3 ENTERING BASIS GOING UP
SLK- 1 LEAVING BASIS BY GOING TO ZERO

                  BASIC SOLUTION-PHASE 2 -ITER. 4

          VAR.          NAME          VALUE         STATUS
           1            x1            600           BASIC- 2
           2            x2            600           BASIC- 3
           3            SLK- 1        0             ZERO
           4            SLK- 2        0             ZERO
           5            SLK- 3        600           BASIC- 1

                    OBJECTIVE = 4200
```

FIGURE 8.12   SOLUTION TO ROLLINS ILLUSTRATION WITH MICROSOLVE.

TABLEAU NUMBER 0   ROLLINS UNLIMITED PROBLEM   VALUE = 0.0

	2 DECISION VARIABLES		3 CONSTRAINTS		THE OBJECT IS TO MAXIMIZE VALUE OF OBJECTIVE FUNCTION	
	1	2	3	4	5	
P(I)						
3	1.000E+00	1.000E+00	1.000E+00	0.0	0.0	1.200E+03
4	2.000E+00	3.000E+00	0.0	1.000E+00	0.0	3.000E+00
5	1.000E+00	4.000E+00	0.0	0.0	1.000E+00	3.600E+03
REAL VAR. C(J)	3.00000	4.00000	0.0	0.0	0.0	
SOLUTION	0.0	0.0	1.2000E+03	3.0000E+03	3.6000E+03	
DELTA	3.000E+00	4.000E+00	0.0	0.0	0.0	

VARIABLE 2 MUST REPLACE VARIABLE 5 IN ROW 3 OF BASIS

FIGURE 8.13   INITIAL SOLUTION FOR ROLLINS UNLIMITED—BATCH CODE FOR TEXTBOOK PROBLEMS.

TABLEAU NUMBER 3   ROLLINS UNLIMITED PROBLEM   VALUE = 4.199961E+03

THE OBJECT IS TO MAXIMIZE VALUE OF OBJECTIVE FUNCTION

P(I)	2 DECISION VARIABLES		3 CONSTRAINTS			
	1	2	3	4	5	
5	0.0	0.0	5.000E+00	-3.000E+00	1.000E+00	6.000E+02
1	1.000E+00	0.0	3.000E+00	-1.000E+00	0.0	6.000E+02
2	0.0	1.000E+00	-2.000E+00	1.000E+00	0.0	6.000E+02
REAL VAR. C(J)	3.00000	4.00000				
SOLUTION	6.0000E+02	6.0000E+02	0.0	0.0	6.0000E+02	
DELTA	0.0	0.0	-1.000E+00	-1.000E+00	0.0	-1.000E+00

FINAL TABLEAU   **OPTIMUM** SOLUTION

FIGURE 8.14 OPTIMAL SOLUTION FOR ROLLINS UNLIMITED—BATCH CODE FOR TEXTBOOK PROBLEMS.

```
                    EXECUTOR.          MPS/360 V2-M6
NAME               ROLLINS
ROWS
  N  OBJFUNC
  L  WAUNITS
  L  WAHOURS                                                                    *
  L  PAHOURS
COLUMNS
       X1          OBJFUNC          3.00000     WAUNITS          1.00000
       X1          WAHOURS          2.00000     PAHOURS          1.00000
       X2          OBJFUNC          4.00000     WAUNITS          1.00000
       X2          WAHOURS          3.00000     PAHOURS          4.00000
RHS
     RHSVAL        WAUNITS       1200.00000     WAHOURS       3000.00000
     RHSVAL        PAHOURS       3600.00000
ENDATA
```

FIGURE 8.15   MPS-370 INPUT.

```
                      EXECUTOR.   MPS/360   V2-M6
      SOLUTION            (OPTIMAL)

      TIME  =             0.02 MINS. ITERATION NUMBER =        3

                          ...NAME...        ...ACTIVITY...     DEFINED AS

                          FUNCTIONAL         4200.00000        OBJFUNC
                          RESTRAINTS                           RHSVAL
```

FIGURE 8.16   MPS-370 OUTPUT: OBJECTIVE FUNCTION INFORMATION.

```
              EXECUTOR.   MPS/360   V2-M6
SECTION 1 - ROWS
NUMBER   ...ROW..  AT   ...ACTIVITY...  SLACK ACTIVITY  ..LOWER LIMIT.  ..UPPER LIMIT.  DUAL ACTIVITY

     1   OBJFUNC   BS     4200.00000     4200.00000-         NONE            NONE          1.00000
     2   WAUNITS   UL     1200.00000           .            NONE         1200.00000        1.00000-
     3   WAHOURS   UL     3000.00000           .            NONE         3000.00000        1.00000-
     4   PAHOURS   BS     3000.00000      600.0000          NONE         3600.00000            .
```

FIGURE 8.17   MPS-370 OUTPUT: RESOURCE ACTIVITY.

```
              EXECUTOR.   MPS/360   V2-M6
SECTION 2 - COLUMNS

NUMBER   .COLUMN.  AT   ...ACTIVITY...  ..INPUT COST..  ..LOWER LIMIT.  ..UPPER LIMIT.  REDUCED COST.
     5    X1       BS      600.00000       3.00000            .             NONE             .
     6    X2       BS      600.00000       4.00000            .             NONE             .
```

FIGURE 8.18   MPS-370 OUTPUT: DECISION VARIABLES.

developed a new algorithm for linear programming that is called the ellipsoid method. The development was reported in front-page articles in newspapers throughout the world. This suggests the economic significance of linear programming today. Unfortunately this new algorithm has so far not provided significant evidence of outperforming the simplex method in practice. In 1984, Dr. Narendra Karmarkar, a mathematician at AT&T Bell Laboratories, reported another radically different procedure for handling linear programming problems. In the simplex method, the computer searches from vertex to vertex of a multidimensional polytope to find the best one. In this most recent development, the computer goes into the interior of the polytope and creates a sequence of spheres inside the polytope that converge on the desired vertex (a basic solution).

It is unclear where these new approaches will lead and the impact on current computational practice for solving moderately sized linear programming problems. It is clear, however, that linear programming is a practical tool of great theoretical interest. Perhaps the most important consequence of these theoretical breakthroughs is the rekindled interest in both practical and theoretical aspects of linear programming. Hopefully these new approaches will lead to computational tools that will allow us to solve large-scale problems in linear/integer programming that are currently too large to solve.

GLOSSARY

Artificial Variable   A variable with no physical interpretation that is used to find an initial basic feasible solution to a linear programming problem.

Basic Feasible Solution   A basic solution where all variables are greater than or equal to zero.

Basic in an Equation   A variable that is basic in an equation has a coefficient of one in that equation and zero coefficients in all other equations.

Basic Solution   A solution to a system of m equations and n variables obtained by setting $n - m$ variables to zero and solving for the remaining variables.

Basic Variable   A variable in a basic solution that is not nonbasic.

Basis   The set of basic variables in a basic solution.

Degenerate Solution   Any basic solution in which one or more of the basic variables has a zero value.

Elementary Row Operations   Algebraic operations that can be used to rewrite a system of equations without changing the solution(s) to the system.

Nonbasic Variable   A variable in a basic solution that is equated to zero in identifying a basic solution.

Pivot Element   The coefficient of the pivot variable in the pivot row.

Pivot Equation (Row) (Departing Variable)   The row in the simplex tableau that is identified by the variable that is basic and becomes nonbasic.

Pivot Operation   A sequence of elementary row operations that exchanges a basic and nonbasic variable in a basic solution.

Pivot Variable (Column) (Entering Variable)   The variable that is nonbasic and becomes basic as the result of the pivot operation.

Simplex Method (Simplex Algorithm) A method for solving a linear programming problem that utilizes the pivot operation to examine a sequence of basic solutions that improve the objective value until the optimal solution is found.

Simplex Tableau A tabular representation of the linear programming problems that facilitates the simplex calculations.

Unconstrained Variable A variable that can assume both positive and negative values.

Selected References

Bazaraa, Mokthar S., and John J. Jarvis. 1977. *Linear Programming and Network Flows.* New York: Wiley.

Bradley, Stephen P., Arnoldo C. Hax, and Thomas L. Magnanti. 1977. *Applied Mathematical Programming.* Reading, Mass.: Addison–Wesley.

Budnick, Frank S., Richard Mojena, and Thomas E. Vollmann. 1977. *Operations Research for Management.* Homewood, Ill.: Irwin.

Charnes, A., and W. W. Cooper. 1961. *Management Models and Industrial Applications of Linear Programming,* vols. 1 and 2. New York: Wiley.

Cooper, Leon, and David Steinberg. 1974. *Methods and Applications of Linear Programming.* Philadelphia, Pa.: Sanders.

Dantzig, George B. 1963. *Linear Programming and Extensions.* Princeton, N.J.: Princeton Univ. Press.

Greenberg, Michael R. 1978. *Applied Linear Programming For the Socio-economic and Environmental Sciences.* New York: Academic Press.

Hadley, G. 1962. *Linear Programming.* Reading, Mass.: Addison–Wesley.

Hillier, Fredrick S., and Gerald J. Lieberman. 1980. *Introduction to Operations Research,* 3rd ed. San Francisco: Holden–Day.

Hughes, Ann J., and Dennis E. Grawoig. 1973. *Linear Programming: An Emphasis on Decision Making.* Reading, Mass.: Addison–Wesley.

Ignizo, James P. 1982. *Linear Programming In Single and Multiple Objective Systems.* Englewood Cliffs, N.J.: Prentice–Hall.

Llewellyn, Robert W. 1964. *Linear Programming.* New York: Holt, Rinehart & Winston.

Luenberger, David G. 1973. *Introduction to Linear and Nonlinear Programming.* Reading, Mass.: Addison–Wesley.

Markland, Robert E. 1983. *Topics in Management Science,* 2nd ed. New York: Wiley.

Taha, Hamdy A. 1982. *Operations Research: An Introduction,* 3rd. ed. New York: Macmillan.

Thompson, Gerald E. 1971. *Linear Programming: An Elementary Introduction.* New York: Macmillan.

Wagner, Harvey M. 1969. *Principles of Operations Research: With Applications to Managerial Decisions.* Englewood Cliffs, N.J.: Prentice–Hall.

Discussion Questions

1. How are the basic variables determined for the initial simplex tableau?

2. Discuss the relationship between basic solutions and extreme points. How does the concept of degeneracy fit into this relationship?

3. Explain the rule for selecting the pivot variable.

4. Explain the rule for selecting the pivot equation.

5. How do you know when to stop pivoting in linear programming? Distinguish between a maximization problem and a minimization problem.

6. If a negative right-hand side exists in a constraint for a linear programming problem, is it possible to solve this problem using linear programming? Explain.

7. Why are artificial variables used in the simplex method? Will there ever be artificial variables in the optimal basis? Explain.

8. How is the simplex method used to establish that a linear programming problem has no feasible solutions?

9. How does degeneracy occur in linear programming? How does it affect the calculations from that point to the optimal tableau?

10. How do you determine if a linear programming problem is unbounded?

11. How do you determine if a linear programming problem has alternate optimal solutions?

12. Discuss the uniqueness of the representation of unconstrained variables presented in Section 8.6.5.

PROBLEMS

1. Continue from the system (8.26), (8.27), and (8.28) to represent the remaining extreme point in the Rollins Unlimited illustration, $(x_1 = 1200, x_2 = 0)$.

2. Solve the following linear programming problem using the simplex method.

$$\text{Maximize } Z = 3x_1 + 2x_2$$

subject to

$$4x_1 + x_2 \leq 200$$
$$x_1 + x_2 \leq 80$$
$$x_1 + 3x_2 \leq 180$$

with

$$x_1, x_2 \geq 0$$

3. Solve the following linear programming problem using the simplex method.

$$\text{Maximize } Z = 3x_1 + 4x_2$$

subject to

$$x_1 + x_2 \leq 1000$$
$$x_1 + 2x_2 \leq 1600$$
$$3x_1 + x_2 \leq 2400$$

with

$$x_1, x_2 \geq 0$$

4. Solve the following linear programming problem using the simplex method.

$$\text{Maximize } Z = 5x_1 + 7x_2$$

subject to

$$x_1 \leq 10$$
$$x_1 + x_2 = 12$$
$$x_1 - 2x_2 \geq 3$$

with

$$x_1, x_2 \geq 0$$

5. Add the constraint $3x_1 + 2x_2 \geq 12$ to Problem 4 and solve the resulting linear programming problem.

6. Replace the objective in Problem 4 with maximize $Z = 5x_1 + x_2$, and solve the resulting linear programming problem.

7. Solve the following problem using the simplex method.

$$\text{Minimize } Z = 5x_1 + 7x_2$$

subject to

$$x_1 \leq 10$$
$$x_1 + x_2 \leq 12$$
$$x_1 - 2x_2 \geq 3$$

with

$$x_1, x_2 \geq 0$$

8. Solve the following problem using the simplex method.

$$\text{Maximize } Z = 100x_1 + 60x_2 + 80x_3$$

subject to

$$8x_1 + 4x_2 + 6x_3 \leq 1200$$
$$5x_1 + 4x_2 + 5x_3 \leq 700$$
$$8x_1 + 3x_2 + 6x_3 \leq 1000$$

with

$$x_1, x_2, x_3 \geq 0$$

9. Solve the following problem using the simplex method.

$$\text{Maximize } Z = 19x_1 + 17x_2 + 11x_3$$

subject to

$$2x_1 + 3x_2 + 2x_3 \leq 360$$
$$2x_1 + 2x_2 + 2x_3 \leq 360$$
$$4x_1 + x_2 + 3x_3 \leq 360$$

with

$$x_1, x_2, x_3 \geq 0$$

10. Solve the following problem using the simplex method.

$$\text{Maximize } Z = 20x_1 + 40x_2$$

subject to

$$2x_1 + x_2 \leq 8000$$
$$2x_1 + 4x_2 \leq 16,000$$

with

$$x_1, x_2 \geq 0$$

11. Solve the following problem using the simplex method.

$$\text{Maximize } Z = 2x_1 + 5x_2 + 8x_3$$

subject to

$$6x_1 + 8x_2 + 4x_3 \leq 96$$
$$2x_1 + x_2 + 4x_3 \leq 40$$
$$5x_1 + 3x_2 + 2x_3 \leq 60$$

with

$$x_1, x_2, x_3 \geq 0$$

12. Solve the following problem using the simplex method.

$$\text{Maximize } Z = 3x_1 + 6x_2 + 2x_3$$

subject to

$$3x_1 + 4x_2 + x_3 \leq 2$$
$$x_1 + 2x_2 + 2x_3 \leq 1$$

with

$$x_1, x_2, x_3 \geq 0$$

13. Solve the following problem using the simplex method.

$$\text{Maximize } Z = 2x_1 + 7x_2$$

subject to

$$-x_1 + x_2 \leq 3$$
$$-x_1 - x_2 \leq -5$$

with

$$x_1, x_2 \geq 0$$

14. Solve the example problem in Section 8.6.4 by choosing the second row as the initial pivot row.

15. Solve the following problem using the simplex method.

$$\text{Minimize } Z = 0.5x_1 + 0.5x_2 + 2x_3$$

subject to

$$x_1 + 2x_2 + 3x_3 \geq 115$$
$$2x_1 + x_2 + 8x_3 \geq 200$$
$$2x_1 + 2x_3 \geq 50$$

with

$$x_1, x_2, x_3 \geq 0$$

16. Solve the following problem using the simplex method.

$$\text{Minimize } Z = x_1 + x_2 - 2x_3$$

subject to

$$x_1 - x_2 + x_3 \leq 8$$
$$x_1 - x_2 - 2x_3 = 4$$
$$2x_1 + x_2 - 3x_3 \geq 12$$

with

$$x_1, x_2, x_3 \geq 0$$

17. Solve the following problem using the simplex method.

$$\text{Minimize } Z = 3x_1 + 2x_2 + x_3$$

subject to

$$2x_1 \qquad + x_3 \leq 10$$
$$x_1 + 2x_2 \qquad = 6$$
$$x_1 + 2x_2 - 3x_3 \geq 20$$
$$x_1 + 4x + 2x_1 \geq 5$$

with

$$x_1, x_2, x_3 \geq 0$$

18. Solve the following problem using the simplex method.

$$\text{Maximize } Z = 4x_1 + 2x_2$$

subject to

$$8x_1 + 4x_2 \leq 40$$
$$5x_1 + 8x_2 \leq 80$$
$$6x_1 + x_2 \leq 24$$

with

$$x_1, x_2 \geq 0$$

19. Solve the following problem using the simplex method.

$$\text{Maximize } Z = 20x_1 + 35x_2$$

subject to

$$-x_1 + 2x_2 \leq 12$$

$$x_1 + x_2 \leq 12$$

$$3x_1 + 2x_2 \geq 12$$

$$x_1 - 2x_2 \geq 4$$

with

$$x_1, \ x_2 \geq 0$$

20. Solve the following problem using the simplex method.

$$\text{Maximize } Z = x_1 + x_2$$

subject to

$$3x_1 + 5x_2 \leq 200$$

$$2x_1 + 3x_2 \leq 1200$$

$$-3x_1 + 2x_2 \geq 400$$

with

$$x_1 \text{ unrestricted, } x_2 \geq 0$$

21–40. Solve the linear programming models that you formulated for problems 1–20 in Chapter 6.

Application Review

Land Development and Linear Programming: The Lakedale Experience

Lakedale is a large real estate developer and resort company that combines large-scale resort and land-development businesses and holds several thousand acres of undeveloped land. Lakedale decided to develop a strategic plan to assist them in their long-range planning and to help develop a consensus about future development goals among the board of directors, community groups, and major lenders. This was important to obtain financing for development, necessary zoning approvals, and community support for financing.

Lakedale decided to attempt to use management science techniques to handle the complex tradeoffs systematically. These techniques were expected to improve the owner's expected discounted cash flow, management, and provide a comprehensive and defensible position for approval by both internal and external constituencies. Linear programming was viewed as being relatively inexpensive to use

Source: Winokur, Herbert S., Jr., John B. Frick, and James C. Bean. "The affair between the land developer and the management scientist," *Interfaces* (October 1981), Vol. 11, No. 5, pp. 50–56.

and understand, and valuable in developing plans to allocate investments to different types of development over time. The comprehensive planning methodology sought by management was to be used by management to respond to possible criticisms of the strategic plan. Lakedale lacked a master land-use plan and many recent decisions had been based on ad hoc analysis. These decisions had become increasingly vulnerable to criticisms of individuals who hoped to maintain the status quo as Lakedale matured.

The linear programming model developed sought to maximize the expected present value of future cash flows subject to constraints related to public policy considerations, previous development decisions, and existing commitments to property owners. The constraints included such factors as the development rate, the mix of real estate products offered, the adequacy of the utilities and recreational facilities, and the desired balance between resort and real estate development. The general form of the model used follows.

$$\text{Maximize} \sum_{t=1}^{T} d^t \sum_{i \in I_t} \sum_{s=0}^{t-1} p_{i(t-s)s} x_{i(t-s)} \tag{8.100}$$

subject to

$$\sum_{i \in I_t} \sum_{s=0}^{t-1} \delta_{ri(t-s)s} x_{i(t-s)} \leq R_0^r, \qquad r \in \mathbf{R}, \quad t = 1, \ldots, T \tag{8.101}$$

$$x_{it} \leq W_{it} + \sum_{i \in I_t} \sum_{s=0}^{t-1} w_{i'i(t-s)s} x_{i'(t-s)}, \qquad i \in I_t, \quad t = 1, \ldots, T \tag{8.102}$$

with

$$l_{it} \leq x_{it} \leq u_{it} \tag{8.103}$$

WHERE

x_{it} = dollar level of investment of type i in period t;

d = discount rate;

p_{its} = return in dollars, s periods after a \$1 investment of type i in period t;

$\mathbf{R}$ = set of scarce resources;

R_0^r = initial availability of resource r;

d_{rits} = incremental consumption of resource r, s periods after a \$1 investment of type i in period t;

$w_{i'its}$ = incremental demand for investment i, s periods after a \$1 investment of type i' in period t;

W_{it} = a demand constant for the product of investment of type i in period t.

The constraints in (8.101) reflect the limitations arising from scarce resources, such as revenue, land, and golf course capacity. The constraints in (8.102) are demand limitations. The constraints in (8.103) set upper and lower bounds on the levels of investment. These limitations arise from regulatory and political constraints.

This model used a large amount of subjective data as well as normal planning

TABLE 8.48 SUMMARY OF SELECTED RESULTS FROM THE LAKEDALE PLANNING CASE: 20-YEAR LAND SELLOUT

CASE	LAND SOLD AS DEVELOPED LOTS (ACRES)	UNDEVELOPED LAND SALES (ACRES)	SHELTER SALES (UNITS)	HOTEL OCCUPANCY (%)	AVERAGE RECREATIONAL FACILITIES REVENUES ($ MILLIONS)	YEARS FOR BUILDOUT	RELATIVE PRESENT VALUE	LIMITING FACTORS
Master plan case, orderly development of a large shelter program	5500	500	3500	80	7	25	1.0	The resort is essentially self-financing in the early years with the initial land-sales proceeds funding the development of a balanced shelter program
Master plan case with total sellout within 20 years	4500	1500	3000	80	7	20	0.9	Land is wholesaled near the end due to a lack of available capacity in the recreational facilities and the desire to meet to target sellout date
Emphasize the development of the resort	2000	4000	400	85	7	30	0.6	The early emphasis on the resort delays the development of a viable real estate program due to the unavailability of funds for investment in infrastructure
Continue current policies of short-term maximization of profits by each department	4500	1500	600	70	5	15	0.3	The continuation of current practices leads to inadequate recreational facilities, which forces wholesale sales of land
Expand recreational facilities, sellout as fast as possible	4000	2000	400	50	4	10	0.2	The added recreational facilities reduce the present value due to the limited revenues generated by residents relative to hotel guests

data that enabled management to integrate expert judgments. Many of the subjective data were obtained from market research studies that centered on product selection and pricing. Each product was assumed to generate revenue, operating costs, capital costs over time, and place demand on support facilities such as golf courses and utilities. For example, housing demand required an earlier utility investment and involved greater initial golf course usage than land sales. Land sales, however, produce higher initial cash flows.

The land-use plan provided the basic structure for the linear programming model where land-use planning typically seeks to minimize development costs and maximize housing density. The model in (8.100), (8.101), (8.102), and (8.103) generated a development plan yielding housing densities well below what was politically acceptable and far below what had been achieved in the past. The model was constructed with $T = 20$ measured in years. The problem had 122 rows and 343 variables (including slacks). Several versions of model input were used with the number of iterations ranging from 250 to 450 and solution times from 6 to 8 seconds. A summary of the relative present-value net operating cash flows from the alternative development plans considered is provided in Table 8.48.

The model required under six man-weeks to develop. Data collection turned out to be the constraining activity. The model was also inexpensive, with the incremental cost totaling under $25,000. An important part of the development process was that the model was acceptable as a viable framework for evaluating tradeoffs and was used to integrate the judgments of the consultants in the detailed planning. The results of the model were presented to the board of directors, lenders, community groups, and regulatory agencies to gain support for the long-range development plans of Lakedale. The model's ability to evaluate second-order effects of various tradeoffs helped defend the proposed plans. The model helped to justify the solution that it may be necessary to forgo increasing short-run profits to preserve what appears to be surplus capacity in the future.

Lakedale profited from the skills of the management scientists. In this case, the development and application of the planning model increased the ability of management to develop a comprehensive and *dependable* development plan at a reasonable cost in a reasonable amount of time.

CHAPTER

9

POSTOPTIMALITY ANALYSIS

9.1 INTRODUCTION

Determining the optimal solution to a linear programming problem is not the end of the problem analysis. Often, the optimal simplex tableau provides additional economic information that in turn provides more insight than the optimal basic feasible solution itself. The analysis of the optimal simplex tableau is known as postoptimality analysis.

Postoptimality analysis relates to two major topics: *duality* and *sensitivity analysis*. The dual of a linear programming model is an alternative form of the model that contains information on the value of the resources utilized. Sensitivity analysis examines the impact of changes in the input parameters on the optimal solution. This is extremely important since it allows us to assess the impact of error in the specification of input parameters for the linear programming model. In practice the results of sensitivity analysis are very important in the implementation of the model results.

In this chapter we first discuss duality in linear programming and the economic interpretation of the dual linear programming problem. The remainder of the chapter is devoted to a variety of issues in sensitivity analysis.

9.2 DUALITY

For every linear programming problem that we can construct there is another related linear programming problem that incorporates the same input parameters. As a pair of linear programming problems one problem is called the *primal problem* and the other is called the *dual problem*. A fundamental relationship between the primal and dual problems is as follows: if the primal problem has a finite optimal (bounded) solution, then the dual problem is also bounded and the optimal objective values of these two linear programming problems are the same. Much work has been done in the study of a linear programming problem, and its dual and the results of

this effort comprise a body of knowledge called *duality theory*. We do not get into this extensive body of knowledge in any depth; rather we examine the construction of the dual problem, first from a mechanical point of view and then from an economic point of view.

9.2.1 CONSTRUCTION OF THE DUAL

To illustrate the construction of the dual and examine the economic interpretation of the dual, consider the Rollins Unlimited illustration of Chapter 8. Rollins produces two types of skateboards: the Deluxe and the Professional. The resource information is summarized in Table 9.1 and the model is stated in (9.1), (9.2), and (9.3).

$$\text{Maximize } Z = 3x_1 + 4x_2 \qquad (9.1)$$

subject to

$$
\begin{aligned}
x_1 + x_2 &\leq 1200 \\
2x_1 + 3x_2 &\leq 3000 \\
x_1 + 4x_2 &\leq 3600 \qquad (9.2)
\end{aligned}
$$

with

$$x_1, x_2 \geq 0 \qquad (9.3)$$

WHERE

x_1 = number of Deluxe skateboards produced;
x_2 = number of Professional skateboards produced.

The dual form for the model (9.1), (9.2), and (9.3) has a minimization objective and is given in (9.4), (9.5), and (9.6).

$$\text{Minimize } Z = 1200y_1 + 3000y_2 + 3600y_3 \qquad (9.4)$$

TABLE 9.1 RESOURCE REQUIREMENTS FOR ROLLINS UNLIMITED

RESOURCE	DELUXE	PROFESSIONAL	TOTAL AVAILABLE RESOURCES
Wheel assembly unit	1 unit	1 unit	1200 units
Mounting time	2 minutes	3 minutes	3000 minutes
Precision adjustment time	1 minute	4 minutes	3600 minutes

subject to

$$y_1 + 2y_2 + y_3 \geq 3$$

$$y_1 + 3y_2 + 4y_3 \geq 4 \qquad (9.5)$$

with

$$y_1, y_2, y_3 \geq 0 \qquad (9.6)$$

The specific relationships between this primal and dual pair of linear programming problems, (9.1), (9.2), and (9.3), and (9.4), (9.5), and (9.6), are given later. These relationships can be used to write the dual for a general linear problem. We refer to (9.1), (9.2), and (9.3) as the primal problem and (9.4), (9.5), and (9.6) as the dual problem.

1. The variables in the dual problem, the dual variables, y_1, y_2, and y_3, are associated with the individual constraints in the primal problem. For each constraint in the primal there is one dual variable and thus the number of constraints in the primal is the same as the number of variables in the dual. Also one constraint in the dual corresponds to each variable in the primal.
2. The right-hand-side values of the inequality constraints in the primal become the objective function coefficients in the dual.
3. The objective function coefficients in the primal problem become the right-hand-side values for the constraints in the dual problem.
4. The constraint coefficients for a single variable in the primal problem become the constraint coefficients for the corresponding constraint in the dual problem.
5. It is assumed that all constraints in the primal problem are "$\leq$", all the variables in the primal are nonnegative, and that the objective is to maximize.
6. It is also assumed that the dual has all "$\geq$" constraints, the dual variables are nonnegative, and that the objective is to minimize.

In general if the primal has n variables and m constraints, the primal/dual pair of linear programming problems can be written as follows. Primal problem

$$\text{Maximize } Z^P = \sum_{j=1}^{n} c_j x_j \qquad (9.7)$$

subject to

$$\sum_{j=1}^{n} a_{ij} x_j \leq b_i, \qquad i = 1, \ldots, m \qquad (9.8)$$

with

$$x_j \geq 0, \qquad j = 1, \ldots, n \qquad (9.9)$$

dual problem

$$\text{Minimize } Z^D = \sum_{i=1}^{m} b_i y_i \qquad (9.10)$$

subject to

$$\sum_{i=1}^{m} a_{ij} y_i \geq c_j, \qquad j = 1, \ldots, n \qquad (9.11)$$

with

$$y_i \geq 0, \qquad i = 1, \ldots, m \qquad (9.12)$$

We again note that the number of constraints in the primal is the number of variables in the dual and the number of variables in the primal is the number of constraints in the dual. One of the pair may have considerably fewer constraints. If this is the case, it may be computationally more efficient to solve the problem with the fewest constraints. Computational efficiency is, however, only one of the reasons for considering duality. The economic information provided by the dual is also of considerable importance.

9.2.2 THE PRIMAL AND DUAL SOLUTIONS

In this section a comparison of the solutions to the primal and dual problems is made. The primal/dual pairs used in this discussion are problems (9.1), (9.2), and (9.3), and (9.4), (9.5), and (9.6). The optimal simplex tableaux for these two problems are taken from Chapter 8. The dual problem was actually solved in Section 8.5 in the presentation of the simplex method for the minimization problem. The optimal tableaux are given in Tables 9.2 and 9.3.

Table 9.4 compares the primal and dual solu-

TABLE 9.2 OPTIMAL SIMPLEX TABLEAU FOR THE PRIMAL PROBLEM: (9.1), (9.2), AND (9.3)

c_b	c_j BASIS	3 x_1	4 x_2	0 S_1	0 S_2	0 S_3	SOLUTION
0	S_3	0	0	5	-3	1	600
3	x_1	1	0	3	-1	0	600
4	x_2	0	1	-2	1	0	600
	Z_j	3	4	1	1	0	4200
	$c_j - Z_j$	0	0	-1	-1	0	

tions for problems (9.1), (9.2), and (9.3), and (9.4), (9.5), and (9.6). Values S_1^P, S_2^P, S_3^P are used to denote the slack variables in the primal problem, and S_1^D and S_2^D are used to denote the surplus variables in the dual problem. It was stated in Section 9.2.1 that dual variables are associated with individual constraints in the primal problem. This association is taken one step further. Dual variables are associated with the slack variables for the constraints in the primal problem. In other words, there is a relationship between y_1 and S_1^P, y_2 and S_2^P, and y_3 and S_3^P. Also, with each dual constraint there is an associated primal variable and there is a relationship between primal variables and the surplus variables in the dual problem. Specifically, this relationship is between x_1 and S_1^D and between x_2 and S_2^D.

One of the most important mathematical results in duality concludes that the following products must be zero.

$$(y_1)(S_1^P) = 0$$
$$(y_2)(S_2^P) = 0$$
$$(y_3)(S_3^P) = 0 \qquad (9.13)$$

and

$$(x_1)(S_1^D) = 0$$
$$(x_2)(S_2^D) = 0 \qquad (9.14)$$

In other words, a dual variable and its associated slack variable cannot both be *greater* than zero simultaneously. Alternatively, if a dual variable is greater than zero, then its associated constraint must be tight (met as an equality or in other words, the slack variable must be zero). Conditions (9.13) and (9.14) are individually known as the *complementary slackness conditions* and provide very important information about the solutions to the primal and dual linear programming problems. We examine the economic implications of the complementary slackness conditions in the next section.

Returning to Tables 9.2 and 9.3, we observe that both of the tableaux are not necessary. The optimal dual solution can be read from the optimal primal tableau. Also, the optimal primal solution can be read from the optimal dual tableau. First consider Table 9.2. If we examine the absolute values of the $c_j - Z_j$ values we see that x_1 is associated with 0, x_2 with 0, S_1^P with 1, S_2^P with 1, and S_3^P

TABLE 9.3 OPTIMAL SIMPLEX TABLEAU FOR THE DUAL PROBLEM: (9.4), (9.5), AND (9.6)

c_b	c_j BASIS	1200 y_1	3000 y_2	3600 y_3	0 S_1	0 S_2	M A_1	M A_2	SOLUTION
1200	y_1	1	0	-5	-3	2	3	-2	1
300	y_2	0	1	3	1	-1	-1	1	1
	Z_j	1200	3000	3000	-600	-600	600	600	4200
	$c_j - Z_j$	0	0	600	600	600	$(M - 600)$	$(M - 600)$	

TABLE 9.4 COMPARISON OF THE OPTIMAL PRIMAL AND DUAL SOLUTIONS

$x_1 = 600$	$S_1^D = 0$
$x_2 = 600$	$S_2^D = 0$
$S_1^P = 0$	$y_1 = 1$
$S_2^P = 0$	$y_2 = 1$
$S_3^P = 600$	$y_3 = 0$
$Z^P = 4200$	$Z^D = 4200$

with 0. Also, as mentioned previously, x_1 is associated with S_1^D, S_1^P with y_1, and so on. As you might expect, the values of all variables in the dual problem can be read from the primal tableau using this association

$$|c_j - Z_j| = 0 \quad \text{for} \quad x_1 \Rightarrow S_1^D = 0 \quad (9.15)$$

$$|c_j - Z_j| = 0 \quad \text{for} \quad x_2 \Rightarrow S_2^D = 0$$

$$|c_j - Z_j| = 1 \quad \text{for} \quad S_1^P \Rightarrow y_1 = 1$$

$$|c_j - Z_j| = 1 \quad \text{for} \quad S_2^P \Rightarrow y_2 = 1$$

$$|c_j - Z_j| = 0 \quad \text{for} \quad S_3^P \Rightarrow y_3 = 0$$

Similarly, the primal solution can be read from Table 9.3.

$$c_j - Z_j = 0 \quad \text{for} \quad y_1 \Rightarrow S_1^P = 0 \quad (9.16)$$

$$c_j - Z_j = 0 \quad \text{for} \quad y_2 \Rightarrow S_2^P = 0$$

$$c_j - Z_j = 600 \quad \text{for} \quad y_3 \Rightarrow S_3^P = 600$$

$$c_j - Z_j = 600 \quad \text{for} \quad S_1^D \Rightarrow x_1 = 600$$

$$c_j - Z_j = 600 \quad \text{for} \quad S_2^D \Rightarrow x_2 = 600$$

Of course, the objective values for the pair of primal/dual solutions are identical.

9.2.3 THE INTERPRETATION OF THE DUAL MODEL

Interpretation of the dual linear programming model depends to a large extent on the interpretation of the solution to the primal problem. The key to the interpretation is suggested by the relationship between the optimal primal and dual tableaux discussed in the previous section. The values of the dual variables are the absolute values of the $c_j - Z_j$ terms associated with the slack variables in the primal problem. To interpret these values, consider Table 9.2. Suppose one wheel assembly unit was withheld from the production process. In other words, $S_1 = 1$ in the final solution. If $S_1 = 1$, the following equations from Table 9.2 give the new values for x_1, x_2, and S_3.

$$5S_1 + S_3 = 600$$

$$x_1 + 3S_1 = 600$$

$$x_2 - 2S_1 = 600 \quad (9.17)$$

The new values of S_3, x_1, and x_2 are $S_3 = 595$, $x_1 = 597$, and $x_2 = 602$. The new value of the objective is:

$$Z = 3(597) + 4(602) = 4199 \quad (9.18)$$

The net change is a decrease of one for the objective. Decreasing the availability of one wheel assembly unit will decrease profit by one. The value of that unit of resource to Rollins is $1 in lost profit plus the per unit cost of the resource that was used to compute the value of the objective function coefficients. This value represents an opportunity cost. If we remove one unit of this resource from production, we forgo profit of $1. We also show in Section 9.4 that if one additional wheel assembly unit was available (1201 instead of 1200), then the optimal solution would be $S_3 = 605$, $x_1 = 603$, and $x_2 = 598$. The new objective value is then

$$Z = 3(603) + 4(598) = 4201 \quad (9.19)$$

In other words, increasing the availability of one wheel assembly unit will increase profit by one. This value can also be viewed as a shadow price, meaning that if we could purchase an additional wheel assembly unit, the maximum surcharge we should be willing to pay for that resource would be $1. That is, if we can purchase a wheel assembly unit at a price that is up to $1 more than the price used to compute the objective function coefficients, the objective function value increases. Either an increase of one unit in the availability of the resource or a decrease in the availability of one unit will change the value of the objective function by $1. Thus, the values of dual variables are often referred to as marginal values of resources. In the Rollins Unlimited case the marginal value of a wheel assembly unit is 1, the marginal value of one minute of assembly time is 1, and the marginal value of one minute of precision adjustment time is 0.

Before proceeding to a discussion of the structure of the dual problem, it is important to observe that the interpretation of the dual variable as a marginal value of a resource must be qualified. This qualification is best discussed by an example. Suppose we decided to withdraw 150 wheel assembly units from the production process. Then, using Eq. 9.17, $S_1 = 150$, and thus $S_3 = -150$, $x_1 = 150$, and $x_2 = 900$. Variable $S_3 = -150$ simply means that $x_1 = 150$ and $x_2 = 900$ is not a feasible solution to problem (9.1). Requiring $S_1 = 150$ is equivalent to replacing the first constraint in problem (9.1), (9.2), and (9.3) by

$$x_1 + x_2 \leq 1050 \qquad (9.20)$$

Solving this modified problem using the simplex method gives the following optimal solution

$$x_1 = 200$$
$$x_2 = 850$$
$$S_2 = 50$$
$$Z = 4000 \qquad (9.21)$$

Using the marginal value of a wheel assembly unit to compute profit if 150 units are withdrawn from production proves to be incorrect. The actual new profit is 4000, not 4050. The point of this discussion is that this interpretation is subject to particular numerical intervals that include the available resources used to compute the optimal linear programming solution. These particular intervals can be computed using techniques developed later in this chapter in the context of sensitivity analysis. To illustrate what is happening in this situation consider Figures 9.1 and 9.2. Figure 9.1 indicates the original Rollins Unlimited problem, while Figure 9.2 represents a reduction in the right-hand side of the first constraint [see (9.20)]. The optimal basic

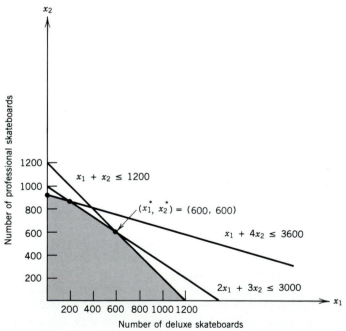

FIGURE 9.1   THE ROLLINS UNLIMITED ILLUSTRATION—FIRST CONSTRAINT: $x_1 + x_2 \leq 1200$.

solution to the original problem is

$$(x_1, x_2, S_1, S_2, S_3) = (600, 600, 0, 0, 600) \quad (9.22)$$

while the optimal basic solution to the modified problem is

$$(x_1, x_2, S_1, S_2, S_3) = (200, 850, 0, 50, 0) \quad (9.23)$$

A change in this right-hand side forced a change in the set of basic variables (a basis change). This change of the basis results in a change in the values assigned as marginal values of resources. Sensitivity analysis then determines both a maximum increase and a maximum decrease in the value of the specified parameter for which there will not be a change in the basis. Thus sensitivity analysis is important in the interpretation of the values of the dual variables. Note also in Figure 9.2 that the feasible region was significantly changed and that the constraint

$$2x_1 + 3x_2 \leq 3000 \quad (9.24)$$

is, in fact, now redundant.

We have examined the meaning of the numerical values of dual variables and observed that dual variables may be viewed as marginal values of resources, shadow prices of resources, or opportunity costs associated with resources. We now examine the interpretation of the dual linear programming problem. Again we examine the interpretation in the context of the Rollins Unlimited problem.

If Rollins Unlimited wants to impute or assign values to available resources, it would not assign a value to the resources greater than the profit provided collectively from these resources. On the other hand, Rollins would not want to assign a value to the available resources that is less than the profit that can be earned by these resources. At this point, it is interesting to observe the relationship between the two functions $Z = 3x_1 + 4x_2$ and $Z = 1200y_1 + 3000y_2 + 3600y_3$. The following mathematical derivation follows from the systematic use of the constraints first in the dual problem and then in the primal problem.

$$3x_1 + 4x_2 \leq (y_1 + 2y_2 + y_3)x_1 + (y_1 + 3y_2 + 4y_3)x_2$$

(Since $y_1 + 2y_2 + y_3 \geq 3$ and $y_1 + 3y_2 + 4y_3 \geq 4$ in the dual problem)

$$3x_1 + 4x_2 \leq y_1(x_1 + x_2)$$
$$+ y_2(2x_1 + 3x_2) + y_3(x_1 + x_2) \quad (9.25)$$

(By a rearrangement of terms)

$$3x_1 + 4x_2 \leq 1200y_1 + 3000y_2 + 3600y_3$$

(Since $x_1 + x_2 \leq 1200$, $2x_1 + 3x_2 \leq 3000$ and $x_1 + 4x_2 \leq 3600$ in the primal problem.)

In other words, every dual feasible solution has an objective value that is greater than or equal to the objective value for any primal feasible solution. Thus we can see the justification for the minimization objective in the dual problem. If the value of resources is to be equal to the profit earned by the resources and mathematically

$$3x_1 + 4x_2 \leq 1200y_1 + 3000y_2 + 3600y_3 \quad (9.26)$$

equality can only be obtained by minimizing the dual objective. Thus

1200(wheel assembly units)
  × (value of one wheel assembly unit)
  + 3000(minutes mounting time)
  × (value of one-minute mounting time)
  + 3600(minutes adjustment time)
  × (value of one-minute adjustment time)
  = 600(Deluxe skateboards)
  × 3(per unit profit of the Deluxe skateboard)
  + 600(Professional skateboards)
  × 4(per unit profit of the Professional skateboard)
    = 4200

It is also logical to assume that the marginal values of the resources used to produce a product should be equal to the profit contribution of that product. Consider the product: Deluxe skateboards. The optimal solution calls for the production of 600 Deluxe skateboards. The total value of resources

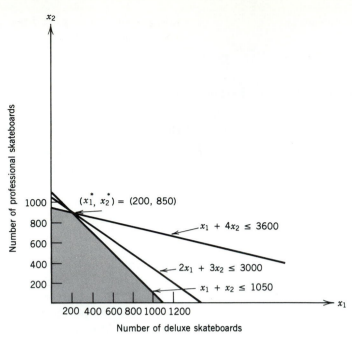

FIGURE 9.2 THE ROLLINS UNLIMITED ILLUSTRATION—FIRST CON-
STRAINT: $x_1 + x_2 \leq 1050$.

used to produce 600 Deluxe skateboards is given as follows.

600(Deluxe skateboards) × 1(wheel assembly unit)

   × (value of one wheel assembly unit)

   + 600(Deluxe skateboards)

   × 2(minutes mounting time)

   × (value of one minute mounting time)

   + 600(Deluxe skateboards)

   × 1(minute adjustment time)

   × (value of one-minute adjustment time)

   = 600(Deluxe skateboards)

   × 3(per unit profit of the Deluxe skateboard)

     = 1800

Also the optimal solution calls for the production of 600 Professional skateboards, so we would also need to satisfy the following.

600(Professional skateboards) × 1(wheel assembly unit)

   × (value of one wheel assembly unit)

   + 600(Professional skateboards)

   × 3(minutes mounting time)

   × (value of one-minute mounting time)

   + 600(Professional skateboards)

   × 4(minutes adjustment time)

   × (value of one-minute adjustment time)

   = 600(Professional skateboards)

   × 4(per unit profit of the professional skateboard)

     = 2400

The set of values that satisfies the three previous conditions follows.

Value of one wheel assembly unit = \$1

Value of one-minute mounting time = \$1

Value of one-minute precision adjustment time = \$0

The values are precisely the marginal values of the resources as suggested by the optimal tableau to (9.1), (9.2), and (9.3). We note that no value was assessed to adjustment time, since that particular resource was not fully utilized. We did not use all of this time ($S_3 = 600$), and thus additional time would be of *no* value in the production process.

Recall the dual form (9.4), (9.5), and (9.6)

Minimize $Z = 1200y_1 + 3000y_2 + 3600y_3$ (9.27)

subject to

$$y_1 + 2y_2 + y_3 \geq 3$$

$$y_1 + 3y_2 + 4y_3 \geq 4 \qquad (9.28)$$

with

$$y_1, y_2, y_3 \geq 0 \qquad (9.29)$$

The first constraint can be interpreted as requiring that the value of the three resources used in producing a single Deluxe skateboard must be at least as great as the profit for one Deluxe skateboard

y_1 = value of a wheel assembly unit used to produce a Deluxe skateboard

$2y_2$ = value of mounting time used to produce a Deluxe skateboard

y_3 = value of precision adjustment time used to produce a Deluxe skateboard

Substituting the values of the dual variables, we obtain

$$1(1) + 2(1) + 1(0) = 3$$

Similarly, the second constraint can be interpreted as requiring that the value of the three resources used in producing a single Professional skateboard must be at least as great as the profit for one Professional skateboard

y_1 = value of a wheel assembly unit used to produce a Professional skateboard

$3y_2$ = value of mounting time used to produce a Professional skateboard

$4y_3$ = value of precision adjustment time used to produce a Professional skateboard

Substituting the values of the dual variables, we obtain

$$1(1) + 3(1) + 4(0) = 4$$

In this case, the value of the resources used to produce each product is equal to that product's per unit profit. If the primal solution is considered, we note that both products were produced. Recall the com-

plementary slackness conditions. They require the following

$$\text{if } x_1 > 0, \qquad \text{then } S_1^D = 0$$

$$\text{if } x_2 > 0, \qquad \text{then } S_1^D = 0 \qquad (9.30)$$

or

$$\text{if } S_1^D > 0, \qquad \text{then } x_1 = 0$$

$$\text{if } S_2^D > 0, \qquad \text{then } x_2 = 0 \qquad (9.31)$$

Thus, the complementary slackness conditions are interpreted in the following fashion. If a product is produced, the marginal value of the resources used to produce one unit of that product is equal to the product's per unit profit (marginal profit). This is the case since the associated variable is basic and c_j (marginal profit) is equal to Z_j (marginal value of resources). It can be argued in a similar fashion that if the marginal value of the resources required to produce one unit of product is greater than the product's per unit profit, the product will not be produced. We observe that the dual constraints reflect accepted economic theory.

Finally, we observe that the objective function reflects the total marginal value of the resources available

$$Z^D = (1200)(1) + (3000)(1) + 3600(0)$$

$$= 4200 \qquad (9.32)$$

As we argued earlier, the total value imputed to the available resources should be the same as profit associated with the use of the available resources in production

$$Z^P = 3(600) + 4(600) = 4200 \qquad (9.33)$$

Again, it should be noted that it is never necessary to solve both the primal and the dual problem. To obtain the valuable information provided by the dual, we only need the optimal tableau from the primal problem.

9.2.4 ADDITIONAL PRIMAL/ DUAL RELATIONSHIPS

The procedure used to write the dual linear programming problem presented in Section 9.2.1 assumes that all the constraints in the maximization problem are less-than-or-equal-to constraints. We now consider the problem of writing the dual to a linear programming problem that has mixed constraints. Consider the following example.

$$\text{Maximize } Z = 20x_1 + 30x_2 \tag{9.34}$$

subject to

$$x_1 + 2x_2 \le 400 \tag{9.35}$$

$$2x_1 + 15x_2 \ge 1000 \tag{9.36}$$

$$3x_1 + x_2 = 500 \tag{9.37}$$

with

$$x_1, x_2 \ge 0 \tag{9.38}$$

Mathematically, the constraints (9.36) and (9.37) can be rewritten in an equivalent form. Initially, constraint (9.36) is modified by multiplying both sides of the constraint by -1

$$-2x_1 - 15x_2 \le -1000 \tag{9.39}$$

Next we observe that constraint (9.37) can be replaced by two inequalities

$$3x_1 + x_2 \le 500$$

$$3x_1 + x_2 \ge 500 \tag{9.40}$$

The second condition can be modified by multiplying by -1 as before. Inequality (9.37) is then replaced by the pair of inequalities

$$3x_1 + x_2 \le 500$$

$$-3x_1 - x_2 \le -500 \tag{9.41}$$

Combining (9.35), (9.39), and (9.41), the original problem is rewritten as

$$\text{Maximize } Z = 20x_1 + 30x_2 \tag{9.42}$$

subject to

$$x_1 + 2x_2 \le 400$$

$$-2x_1 - 15x_2 \le -1000$$

$$3x_1 + x_2 \le 500$$

$$-3x_1 - x_2 \le -500 \tag{9.43}$$

with

$$x_1, x_2 \ge 0 \tag{9.44}$$

The dual to (9.42), (9.43), and (9.44) can now be written using the techniques in Section 9.2.1.

$$\text{Minimize } Z = 400y_1 - 1000y_2 + 500y_3 - 500y_4 \tag{9.45}$$

subject to

$$y_1 - 2y_2 + 3y_3 - 3y_4 \ge 20$$

$$2y_1 - 15y_2 + y_3 - y_4 \ge 30 \tag{9.46}$$

with

$$y_1, y_2, y_3, y_4 \ge 0 \tag{9.47}$$

Problem (9.45), (9.46), and (9.47) may be slightly rewritten to gain additional insight to the process of writing this dual problem

$$\text{Minimize } Z = 400y_1 - 1000y_2 + 500(y_3 - y_4) \tag{9.48}$$

subject to

$$y_1 - 2y_2 + 3(y_3 - y_4) \ge 20$$

$$2y_1 - 15y_2 + (y_3 - y_4) \ge 30 \tag{9.49}$$

with

$$y_1, y_2, y_3, y_4 \ge 0 \tag{9.50}$$

The representation of a variable unconstrained in sign was discussed in Section 8.6.5. Examining (9.48), (9.49), and (9.50), we find that the difference $(y_3 - y_4)$ appears in both constraints as well as the objective function. This difference can be used to represent a single variable that is unconstrained in sign. Thus the dual problem actually has the form indicated in (9.51), (9.52), and (9.53)

$$\text{Minimize } Z = 400y_1 - 1000y_2 + 500y_3 \tag{9.51}$$

subject to

$$y_1 - 2y_2 + 3y_3 \ge 20$$

$$2y_1 - 15y_2 + y_3 \ge 30 \tag{9.52}$$

with

$$y_1, \; y_2 \geq 0, \quad y_3 \text{ unconstrained} \qquad (9.53)$$

The general relationship that is being developed in this section is the following.

> If the primal problem has an equality constraint, the corresponding variable in the dual is unconstrained in sign.

Furthermore, it can be argued that if there is an unconstrained variable in the primal problem, then that variable corresponds to a constraint in the dual problem that is an equality.

This can be seen by writing the dual constraints in model (9.48), (9.49), and (9.50) that correspond to variables y_3 and y_4

$$3x_1 + x_2 \leq 500$$
$$-3x_1 - x_2 \leq -500$$

or

$$3x_1 + x_2 \leq 500$$
$$3x_1 + x_2 \geq 500$$

or

$$3x_1 + x_2 = 500$$

The key to writing the dual to any linear programming problem is to write it in a form where the objective is to maximize and the constraints are all "$\leq$", or where the objective is to minimize and the constraints are all "$\geq$".

9.3 THE DUAL SIMPLEX METHOD

The dual simplex method is an alternate form of the simplex method that was presented in Chapter 8. The simplex method of Chapter 8, the primal simplex method, begins with a solution where all basic variables are nonnegative and the goal is to satisfy the optimality conditions for the problem ($c_j - Z_j \leq 0$ for a maximization problem, or $c_j - Z_j \geq 0$ for a minimization problem). On the other hand, the dual simplex method begins with a solution that satisfies the optimality conditions and the goal is to satisfy the feasibility conditions (all basic variables are greater than or equal to zero).

The dual simplex method is studied, not because it is more efficient than the primal simplex method, but because it is very useful in performing sensitivity analysis. The dual simplex method is similar to the primal simplex method with only a few minor alterations. One major difference between these two methods is in the construction of the initial solution. In the dual simplex method all "$\geq$" constraints are multiplied by -1. The purpose of this modification is to provide basic variables in these constraints. The surplus variables then serve as the initial basic variables in these constraints. Of course, these variables will have negative values. Once the initial solution is determined, the only real difference between the two methods is in the procedure for selecting the pivot element.

The dual simplex method may be used to solve both maximization problems and minimization problems. The procedure, however, will be discussed and then illustrated for a minimization problem. As such the initial solution must satisfy the condition that $c_j - Z_j \geq 0$ for all j. If all the $c_j - Z_j \geq 0$ and all the values of the basic variables are nonnegative ($b_i \geq 0$), the solution is both feasible and optimal. Otherwise, the pivot element is selected. In the dual simplex method the pivot row is selected first and then the pivot column is selected.

1. The pivot row is selected by the negative b_i or solution value with the largest absolute value.
2. The pivot column is determined by locating all the negative coefficients in the pivot row. These negative coefficients are divided into the $c_j - Z_j$ values in the respective columns. The negative ratio that is smallest in absolute value identifies the pivot column.

If there are no negative coefficients in the pivot row, Step 2 cannot be completed. This means that there is no feasible solution to the problem. Otherwise, the pivot row and pivot column identify the pivot element and the pivot operation is performed. This process continues until all the b_i values are nonnegative or until a pivot column cannot be found. To illustrate the dual simplex algorithm consider the following example.

$$\text{Minimize } Z = 1200y_1 + 3000y_2 + 3600y_3 \qquad (9.54)$$

TABLE 9.5   INITIAL DUAL SIMPLEX TABLEAU

c_b	BASIS	c_j					SOLUTION
		1200	3000	3600	0	0	
		y_1	y_2	y_3	S_1	S_2	
0	S_1	-1	-2	-1	1	0	-3
0	S_2	-1	-3	-4	0	1	-4
	Z_j	0	0	0	0	0	0
	$c_j - Z_j$	1200	3000	3600	0	0	

TABLE 9.6   SECOND DUAL SIMPLEX TABLEAU

c_b	BASIS	c_j					SOLUTION
		1200	3000	3600	0	0	
		y_1	y_2	y_3	S_1	S_2	
0	S_1	-0.75	-1.25	0	1	-0.25	-2
3600	y_3	0.25	0.75	1	0	-0.25	1
	Z_j	900	2700	3600	0	-900	3600
	$c_j - Z_j$	300	300	0	0	900	

TABLE 9.7   THIRD DUAL TABLEAU

c_b	BASIS	c_j					SOLUTION
		1200	3000	3600	0	0	
		y_1	y_2	y_3	S_1	S_2	
3000	y_2	0.6	1	0	-0.8	0.2	1.6
3600	y_3	-0.2	0	1	0.6	-0.4	-0.2
	Z_j	1080	3000	3600	-240	-840	4080
	$c_j - Z_j$	120	0	0	240	840	

TABLE 9.8   OPTIMAL DUAL SIMPLEX TABLEAU

c_b	BASIS	c_j					SOLUTION
		1200	3000	3600	0	0	
		y_1	y_2	y_3	S_1	S_2	
3000	y_2	0	1	3	1	-1	1
1200	y_1	1	0	-5	-3	2	1
	Z_j	1200	3000	3000	-600	-600	4200
	$c_j - Z_j$	0	0	600	600	600	

subject to

$$y_1 + 2y_2 + y_3 \geq 3$$

$$y_1 + 3y_2 + 4y_3 \geq 4 \qquad (9.55)$$

with

$$y_1, y_2, y_3 \geq 0 \qquad (9.56)$$

As in the primal simplex method the constraints are first converted to equality constraints

$$y_1 + 2y_2 + y_3 - S_1 \qquad = 3$$

$$y_1 + 3y_2 + 4y_3 \qquad - S_2 = 4 \qquad (9.57)$$

Then these constraints are multiplied by -1, so that S_1 and S_2 are basic in the two constraints, respectively

$$-y_1 - 2y_2 - y_3 + S_1 \qquad = -3$$

$$-y_1 - 3y_2 - 4y_3 \qquad + S_2 = -4 \qquad (9.58)$$

The initial tableau is then constructed, as shown in Table 9.5. Notice that the optimality conditions are satisfied. The pivot row is determined by the largest negative b_i value, -4, in this problem. Therefore, the second row is the pivot row. The negative coefficients in the pivot row are -1, -3, -4 and we compute,

$$\text{Minimum} \left\{ \left| \frac{1200}{-1} \right|, \left| \frac{3000}{-3} \right|, \left| \frac{3600}{-4} \right| \right\} = 900$$

The third column is the pivot column and y_3 enters the basis while S_2 departs. The result of the pivot is shown in Table 9.6. Now the first row must be the pivot row and the pivot column is selected by computing

$$\text{Minimum} \left\{ \left| \frac{300}{-0.75} \right|, \left| \frac{300}{-1.25} \right|, \left| \frac{900}{-0.25} \right| \right\} = 240$$

Column 2 is the pivot column and y_2 enters the basis and S_1 leaves the basis. The result of the pivot is shown in Table 9.7. In the final iteration y_1 enters and y_3 departs and the optimal dual simplex is shown in Table 9.8.

The dual simplex method would not be applied to a maximization problem that has any positive objective coefficients, since the optimality conditions will not be satisfied initially. Dual simplex iterations will be applied, however, to both maximization and minimization problems in the context of sensitivity analysis. The only difference in the application of dual simplex iteration to the maximization problem is in the selection of the pivot column. For the maximization problem all $c_j - Z_j$ are nonpositive and the ratios computed for the selection of the pivot column are all nonnegative. Therefore, the pivot column is chosen by the smallest positive ratio.

9.4 SENSITIVITY ANALYSIS

The input parameters that are used to construct the linear programming model are rarely known with certainty, although one of the primary assumptions of linear programming is that these parameters are deterministic. To help evaluate the implications of such an assumption we examine the effects of parameter changes on the optimal solution to the linear programming problem. The analysis of parameter changes and the impact on the optimal solution is called *sensitivity analysis* or *postoptimality analysis*. Specifically if there is a change or error in an input parameter, the change in the optimal solution is determined from the optimal simplex tableau for the original problem.

Obviously an optimal solution that is not sensitive to minor input parameter changes is desired. It is much easier to justify the implementation of a model solution that will not change significantly if there is a small change in an estimated input parameter. A significant change is defined as a change in the set of basic variables. Therefore, sensitivity analysis often involves the determination of a range of change for an input parameter that will not induce a basis change.

In this section we discuss changes in the objective function coefficients, the c_j, and changes in the right-hand-side constraints, the b_i. We also examine the addition of a new constraint and the addition of a new variable. We briefly discuss changes in the constraint coefficients, the a_{ij}. Sensitivity analysis is presented using a maximization problem with less-than-or-equal-to constraints. In particular, the Rollins Unlimited example of Chapter 8 is used. Modification of the techniques presented to encompass the minimization problem and greater-to-or-

TABLE 9.9 INITIAL SIMPLEX TABLEAU FOR ROLLINS UNLIMITED

c_b	c_j BASIS	3 x_1	4 x_2	0 S_1	0 S_2	0 S_3	SOLUTION
0	S_1	1	1	1	0	0	1200
0	S_2	2	3	0	1	0	3000
0	S_3	1	4	0	0	1	3600
	Z_j	0	0	0	0	0	0
	$c_j - Z_j$	3	4	0	0	0	

equal-to constraints is also discussed. Before proceeding with the discussion of sensitivity analysis, the concept of the basis matrix and the basis inverse matrix is introduced. This concept can serve as a useful tool in certain sensitivity calculations.

9.4.1 THE BASIS MATRIX

Consider the initial and optimal simplex tableaux (Tables 9.9 and 9.10) for Rollins Unlimited.

The basis associated with the optimal solution, the optimal basis, is the set of variables $\{S_3, x_1, x_2\}$. The basis matrix for this solution consists of the columns associated with this set of variables in the coefficient matrix (the A matrix) in the initial simplex tableau. The basis matrix is a square matrix with the number of rows being the number of constraints in the problem. In the Rollins Unlimited example the initial coefficient matrix is

$$A = \begin{matrix} & x_1 & x_2 & S_1 & S_2 & S_3 \\ & \begin{bmatrix} 1 & 1 & 1 & 0 & 0 \\ 2 & 3 & 0 & 1 & 0 \\ 1 & 4 & 0 & 0 & 1 \end{bmatrix} \end{matrix}$$

The basis matrix for the optimal solution is

$$B = \begin{matrix} & S_3 & x_1 & x_2 \\ & \begin{bmatrix} 0 & 1 & 1 \\ 0 & 2 & 3 \\ 1 & 1 & 4 \end{bmatrix} \end{matrix}$$

The inverse of matrix B is called the basis inverse matrix (B^{-1}). It can be identified from the optimal simplex tableau in the following way. First, identify the set of variables basic in the initial simplex tableau. The columns in the optimal simplex tableau

associated with the initial set of basic variables (i.e., S_1, S_2, S_3) can be used to construct B^{-1}. Here

$$B^{-1} = \begin{matrix} & S_1 & S_2 & S_3 \\ & \begin{bmatrix} 5 & -3 & 1 \\ 3 & -1 & 0 \\ -2 & 1 & 0 \end{bmatrix} \end{matrix}$$

It can be easily verified that indeed

$$B^{-1}B = I$$

Also it should be verified that

$$B^{-1}A = \begin{matrix} & x_1 & x_2 & S_1 & S_2 & S_3 \\ & \begin{bmatrix} 0 & 0 & 5 & -3 & 1 \\ 1 & 0 & 3 & -1 & 0 \\ 0 & 1 & -2 & 1 & 0 \end{bmatrix} \end{matrix}$$

$B^{-1}A$ represents the coefficient matrix for the optimal simplex tableau in Table 9.10. Also,

Original Right-Hand Side		Current Optimal Right Hand Side	

$$[B^{-1}]\begin{bmatrix} 1200 \\ 3000 \\ 3600 \end{bmatrix} = \begin{bmatrix} 600 \\ 600 \\ 600 \end{bmatrix} = \begin{bmatrix} S_3 \\ x_1 \\ x_2 \end{bmatrix}$$

Thus multiplying B^{-1} by the original right-hand side gives the optimal values of the basic variables. It should be noted that the simplex method can be presented and implemented using only matrix methods and the concept of a basis matrix. We leave this to more advanced texts.[1] What is needed here is the ability to identify the basis inverse matrix.

---

[1] See, for example; Bazaraa, Mokhtar S., and John J. Jarvis, *Linear Programming and Network Flows.* New York: Wiley, 1977.

TABLE 9.10 OPTIMAL SIMPLEX TABLEAU FOR ROLLINS UNLIMITED

c_b	BASIS	c_j					SOLUTION
		3	4	0	0	0	
		x_1	x_2	S_1	S_2	S_3	
0	S_3	0	0	5	-3	1	600
3	x_1	1	0	3	-1	0	600
4	x_2	0	1	-2	1	0	600
	Z_j	3	4	1	1	0	4200
	$c_j - Z_j$	0	0	-1	-1	0	

9.4.2 CHANGES IN THE RIGHT-HAND-SIDE VALUES

Often the right-hand-side values for a constraint represents the amount of resources available. It is not uncommon for the availability of resources to be slightly different than what was expected when the model was initially constructed. Thus a study of the sensitivity of the optimal solution to changes in these values is vital.

Suppose for example that there are $1200 + \Delta$ wheel assembly units available rather than 1200 units. Here Δ represents the change in the original parameter with value 1200. The initial simplex tableau would then be shown in Table 9.11. Notice that the coefficients for Δ in the solution column are the same as the coefficients of S_1. If we iterate using the simplex method, solution columns for the four simplex tableaux of the Rollins Unlimited example are as given in Table 9.12. This, of course, assumes that the right-hand side of the first constraint is $1200 + \Delta$. It should be noted by looking at Tables 8.11, 8.13, 8.15, and 8.16 that the S_1 column coefficients and the coefficients of Δ in the solution columns reported in Table 9.12 are identical. This is no coincidence. If two columns in the simplex tableau are identical, the result of a se-

quence of elementary row operations would leave these two columns identical. The optimal simplex tableau for this change is given in Table 9.13. Alternatively the basis inverse matrix can be used to establish the solution column in Table 9.13.

$$[B^{-1}] \begin{bmatrix} 1200 + 1\Delta \\ 3000 + 0\Delta \\ 3600 + 0\Delta \end{bmatrix} = \begin{bmatrix} 600 + 5\Delta \\ 600 + 3\Delta \\ 600 + -2\Delta \end{bmatrix} \quad (9.59)$$

If we change the right-hand side of the first constraint from 1200 to $(1200 + \Delta)$, the only impact on the optimal tableau is in the solution column. The basis will not change as long as the basic variables remain greater than or equal to zero.

$$S_3 = 600 + 5\Delta \geq 0$$
$$x_1 = 600 + 3\Delta \geq 0 \quad (9.60)$$
$$x_2 = 600 - 2\Delta \geq 0$$

The three conditions in (9.60) can be simplified to read

$$\Delta \geq -120$$
$$\Delta \geq -200 \quad (9.61)$$
$$\Delta \leq 300$$

TABLE 9.11 INITIAL SIMPLEX TABLEAU FOR ROLLINS UNLIMITED: $1200 + \Delta$ WHEEL ASSEMBLY UNITS

c_b	BASIS	c_j					SOLUTION
		3	4	0	0	0	
		x_1	x_2	S_1	S_2	S_3	
0	S_1	1	1	1	0	0	$1200 + 1\Delta$
0	S_2	2	3	0	1	0	$3000 + 0\Delta$
0	S_3	1	4	0	0	1	$3600 + 0\Delta$
	Z_j	0	0	0	0	0	0
	$c_j - Z_j$	3	4	0	0	0	

These three inequalities must be satisfied simultaneously, and the set of values for Δ that will do this are

$$-120 \leq \Delta \leq 300 \qquad (9.62)$$

For example, if in reality we only had 1100 wheel assembly units available, $\Delta = -100$ and

$$S_3 = 600 + 5\,(-100) = 100$$
$$x_1 = 600 + 3\,(-100) = 300$$
$$x_2 = 600 - 2\,(-100) = 800 \qquad (9.63)$$

The corresponding value of the objective function is 4100. This is what is expected from our interpretation of the dual variable that is associated with the first constraint. As long as the right-hand side of the first constraint, (b_1), does not increase by more than 300 or decrease by more than 120, the current basis will remain optimal. The range for b_1 is then

$$1200 - 120 \leq b_1 \leq 1200 + 300 \qquad (9.64)$$

or

$$1080 \leq b_1 \leq 1500$$

Now, suppose the actual number of wheel assembly units available is 1050. Then

$$S_3 = 600 + 5\,(-150) = -150$$
$$x_1 = 600 + 3\,(-150) = 150$$
$$x_2 = 600 - 2\,(-150) = 900 \qquad (9.65)$$

This solution is not feasible and the final tableau would be represented as shown in Table 9.14. The tableau in Table 9.14 satisfies the criterion for applying the dual simplex method: the solution satisfies the optimality conditions but is not feasible. The pivot element is circled in Table 9.14. The result of the pivot is given in Table 9.15. The solution in Table 9.15 is optimal if $b_1 = 1050$. It is very important to note that the availability of wheel assembly units decreased by 150 while the objective decreased by 200. In Table 9.10 the shadow price of resource 1 is given as 1. The interpretation of the

dual variable as a shadow price/opportunity cost/marginal value is limited and must be tied to the sensitivity analysis for the availability of the corresponding resource. The shadow price of resource 1 is 1 *only if* the availability of that resource is restricted to be between 1080 units and 1500 units.

Now consider the second resource and suppose 3000 is replaced by $3000 + \Delta$. Performing a sensitivity analysis on this parameter, we construct the set of conditions that must be satisfied.

$$S_3 = 600 - 3\Delta \geq 0; \quad -3\Delta \geq -600$$
$$x_1 = 600 - \Delta \geq 0; \quad -\Delta \geq -600$$
$$x_2 = 600 + \Delta \geq 0; \quad \Delta \geq -600 \qquad (9.66)$$

or

$$\Delta \leq 200$$
$$\Delta \leq 600$$
$$\Delta \geq -600 \qquad (9.67)$$

Thus $-600 \leq \Delta \leq 200$ and $2400 \leq b_2 \leq 3200$. As long as we have between 2400 and 3200 minutes of mounting time available, the current basis is optimal.

Finally consider the third resource and suppose 3600 is replaced by $3600 + \Delta$. Then the conditions that must be satisfied are

$$S_3 = 600 + \Delta \geq 0; \quad \Delta \geq -600$$
$$x_1 = 600 + 0\Delta \geq 0; \quad \Delta \text{ not restricted}$$
$$x_2 = 600 + 0\Delta \geq 0; \quad \Delta \text{ not restricted} \qquad (9.68)$$

or

$$\Delta \geq -600 \qquad (9.69)$$

In other words, the availability of this resource can be reduced by 600 units without changing the optimal basis. Any increase will have no effect. This should be an intuitive result. Variable $S_3 = 600$ implies that we already have 600 minutes of precision adjustment time unused. An increase in this resource will have no effect other than increasing the amount of unused resource. Compare the results of the computations in this section and Section 9.4.3 to Figure 8.8.

TABLE 9.12 SOLUTION COLUMNS FOR SIMPLEX TABLEAUX FOR 1200 + Δ AVAILABLE WHEEL ASSEMBLY UNITS

	INITIAL TABLEAU	SECOND TABLEAU	THIRD TABLEAU	OPTIMAL TABLEAU
Solution—Row 1	$1200 + \Delta$	$300 + \Delta$	$120 + \Delta$	$600 + 5\Delta$
Solution—Row 2	$3000 + 0\Delta$	$300 + 0\Delta$	$240 + 0\Delta$	$600 + 3\Delta$
Solution—Row 3	$3600 + 0\Delta$	$900 + 0\Delta$	$840 + 0\Delta$	$600 - 2\Delta$

TABLE 9.13 OPTIMAL SIMPLEX TABLEAU FOR ROLLINS UNLIMITED: 1200 + Δ WHEEL ASSEMBLY UNITS

c_b	c_j BASIS	3 x_1	4 x_2	0 S_1	0 S_2	0 S_3	SOLUTION
0	S_3	0	0	5	-3	1	$600 + 5\Delta$
3	x_1	1	0	3	-1	0	$600 + 3\Delta$
4	x_2	0	1	-2	1	0	$600 - 2\Delta$
	Z_j	3	4	1	1	0	$4200 + \Delta$
	$c_j - Z_j$	0	0	-1	-1	0	

TABLE 9.14 MODIFIED SIMPLEX TABLEAU FOR 1050 WHEEL ASSEMBLY UNITS

c_b	c_j BASIS	3 x_1	4 x_2	0 S_1	0 S_2	0 S_3	SOLUTION
0	S_3	0	0	5	$\boxed{-3}$	1	-150
3	x_1	1	0	3	-1	0	150
4	x_2	0	1	-2	1	0	900
	Z_j	3	4	1	1	0	4050
	$c_j - Z_j$	0	0	-1	-1	0	

TABLE 9.15 OPTIMAL SIMPLEX TABLEAU FOR 1050 WHEEL ASSEMBLY UNITS

c_b	c_j BASIS	3 x_1	4 x_2	0 S_1	0 S_2	0 S_3	SOLUTION
0	S_2	0	0	$-5/3$	1	$-1/3$	50
3	x_1	1	0	$4/3$	0	$-1/3$	200
4	x_2	0	1	$-1/3$	0	$1/3$	850
	Z_j	3	4	$8/3$	0	$1/3$	4000
	$c_j - Z_j$	0	0	$-8/3$	0	$-1/3$	

TABLE 9.16 OPTIMAL SIMPLEX TABLEAU FOR ROLLINS UNLIMITED: PER UNIT PROFIT FOR DELUXE SKATEBOARDS IS $3 + \Delta$

c_h	c_j BASIS	$3 + \Delta$ x_1	4 x_2	0 S_1	0 S_2	0 S_3	SOLUTION
0	S_3	0	0	5	-3	1	600
$3 + \Delta$	x_1	1	0	3	-1	0	600
4	x_2	0	1	-2	1	0	600
	Z_j	3	4	$1 + 3\Delta$	$1 - \Delta$	0	$4200 + 600\Delta$
	$c_j - Z_j$	0	0	$-1 - 3\Delta$	$-1 + \Delta$	0	

9.4.3 CHANGES IN COEFFICIENTS OF THE OBJECTIVE FUNCTION

Changes in objective function coefficients can also be analyzed by considering the impact on the optimal simplex tableau. Consider first the objective function coefficient c_1, of variable x_1. This coefficient changes from c_1 to $c_1 + \Delta$. The problem is one of determining a set of permissible values of Δ so that the set of basic variables does not change. The changes in the optimal simplex tableau are indicated in Table 9.16. The solution in the table remains optimal as long as

$$-1 - 3\Delta \leq 0$$
$$-1 + \Delta \leq 0 \qquad (9.70)$$

or

$$-\frac{1}{3} \leq \Delta \leq 1 \qquad (9.71)$$

The objective coefficient could be underestimated by as much as $1 and overestimated by as much as $1/3 without changing the optimal basis. In this case, only the value of the objective func-

tion changes. There is no effect on the values of basic variables if the basis does not change, and if $8/3 \leq c_1 \leq 4$, there is no basis change. On the other hand, if $c_1 = 2 (\Delta = -1)$, $c_1 - Z_1 = +2$ for variable S_1 and there will be a basis change. It can be verified by performing one additional pivot with the simplex method, that the new optimal solution would be $x_1 = 240$, $x_2 = 840$, while the objective value is 3840.

Similarly, if c_2 is replaced by $c_2 + \Delta$, the conditions that must be satisfied are read from the tableau in Table 9.17. The solution in Table 9.17 remains optimal as long as

$$-1 + 2\Delta \leq 0$$
$$-1 - \Delta \leq 0 \qquad (9.72)$$

or

$$-1 \leq \Delta \leq \frac{1}{2} \qquad (9.73)$$

Again if $-1 \leq \Delta \leq 1/2$ or if $3 \leq c_2 \leq 9/2$ there will be no basis change. If $c_2 = 7/2$, for example, the only change in the solution will be that $Z = 4200 + 600(-1/2) = 3900$.

TABLE 9.17 OPTIMAL SIMPLEX TABLEAU FOR ROLLINS UNLIMITED: PER UNIT PROFIT FOR PROFESSIONAL SKATEBOARDS IS $4 + \Delta$

c_h	c_j BASIS	3 x_1	$4 + \Delta$ x_2	0 S_1	0 S_2	0 S_3	SOLUTION
0	S_3	0	0	5	-3	1	600
3	x_1	1	0	3	-1	0	600
$4 + \Delta$	x_2	0	1	-2	1	0	600
	Z_j	3	$4 + \Delta$	$1 - 2\Delta$	$1 + \Delta$	0	$4200 + 600\Delta$
	$c_j - Z_j$	0	0	$-1 + 2\Delta$	$-1 - \Delta$	0	

TABLE 9.18 OPTIMAL SIMPLEX TABLEAU FOR ROLLINS UNLIMITED: CONTRIBUTION TO PROFIT FOR UNUSED WHEEL ASSEMBLY UNITS IS Δ

c_b	c_j BASIS	3 x_1	4 x_2	$0 + \Delta$ S_1	0 S_2	0 S_3	SOLUTION
0	S_3	0	0	5	-3	1	600
3	x_1	1	0	3	-1	0	600
4	x_2	0	1	-2	1	0	600
	Z_j	3	4	1	1	0	4200
	$c_j - Z_j$	0	0	$\Delta - 1$	-1	0	

The examples used to this point involved changes in objective function coefficients of basic variables. Changing objective function coefficients of nonbasic variables is more simple. In this case, only the $c_j - Z_j$ value associated with the nonbasic variable is changed. Even if the objective function coefficient of variable S_1 is zero, a sensitivity analysis of that coefficient can be performed. For example, suppose that the associated resource that is not utilized also contributes to profit. Then if this coefficient changes from 0 to $0 + \Delta$, there is only one change in the optimal tableau as is noted in Table 9.18.

The previous tableau remains optimal as long as $\Delta \leq 1$ or as long as the objective function coefficient of S_1 is less than or equal to 1. A summary of the sensitivity analysis for the objective function coefficients is given in Table 9.19.

9.4.4 THE ADDITION OF A CONSTRAINT

The addition of a constraint after the linear programming model has been solved can occur for a variety of reasons. A mistake could have been made, and some important information omitted from the original formulation of the problem. Also a new set of circumstances may have developed and require an additional constraint. In any case, when a constraint must be added after the model is solved, it is not necessary to re-solve the entire problem.

To illustrate the principle involved we again consider the Rollins Unlimited example. In the construction of the original model it did not appear that there would be any restriction on the amount of labor required for packaging the skateboards. Other demands in the company, however, have since placed a bound on the labor available for packaging this product line. In fact, there will only be 1400 minutes available. Also, one minute is required for packaging a Deluxe skateboard and 1.75 minutes for packaging a Professional skateboard. This requires the addition of the constraint

$$x_1 + 1.75x_2 \leq 1400 \qquad (9.74)$$

Writing the constraints from the optimal tableau in Table 9.10, we obtain the following

$$5S_1 - 3S_2 + S_3 = 600$$
$$x_1 - 3S_1 - S_2 = 600$$
$$x_2 - 2S_1 + S_2 = 600 \qquad (9.75)$$

Adding the new constraint (9.74) to (9.75), we obtain the following system

$$5S_1 - 3S_2 + S_3 = 600$$
$$x_1 + 3S_1 - S_2 = 600$$
$$x_2 - 2S_1 + S_2 = 600$$
$$x_1 + 1.75x_2 + S_4 = 1400 \qquad (9.76)$$

TABLE 9.19 SUMMARY OF SENSITIVITY ANALYSIS FOR ALL OBJECTIVE FUNCTION COEFFICIENTS

VARIABLE	CHANGE (Δ)	RANGE OF c_j
x_1 (basic)	[1/3, 1]	[8/3, 4]
x_2 (basic)	[−1, 1/2]	[3, 9/2]
S_1 (nonbasic)	(−∞, 1]	(−∞, 1]
S_2 (nonbasic)	(−∞, 1]	(−∞, 1]
S_3 (basic)	[−1/5, 1/3]	[−1/5, 1/3]

TABLE 9.20 MODIFIED SIMPLEX TABLEAU FOR ROLLINS UNLIMITED: AN ADDITIONAL PACKAGING CONSTRAINT

c_b	c_j BASIS	3 x_1	4 x_2	0 S_1	0 S_2	0 S_3	0 S_4	SOLUTION
0	S_3	0	0	5	-3	1	0	600
3	x_1	1	0	3	-1	0	0	600
4	x_2	0	1	-2	1	0	0	600
0	S_4	0	0	0.5	-0.75	0	1	-250
	Z_j	3	4	1	1	0	0	4200
	$c_j - Z_j$	0	0	-1	-1	0	0	

The new slack variable for constraint (9.74), S_4, is basic in the fourth equation, and S_3 is basic in the first equation. There are no variables that satisfy the criteria for being basic in the second and third equations.

When a constraint must be added after the optimal solution is computed, that constraint cannot generally be added to the optimal simplex tableau without some additional calculations. Several elementary row operations may be required to write the new constraint in a form so that we have a basic variable in each equation. Variable x_1 was initially basic in the second equation and x_2 was initially basic in the third equation. The system in (9.76) will be written to reestablish these variables as basic variables in the second and third equations. The calculations are given below.

$$
\begin{aligned}
-1(x_1 \qquad\quad + 3S_1 - S_2 \qquad\qquad &= 600) \\
\underline{x_1 + 1.75x_2 \qquad\qquad\quad + S_4 &= 1400} \\
1.75x_2 - 3S_1 + S_2 + S_4 &= 800
\end{aligned}
$$

$$(9.77)$$

and

$$
\begin{aligned}
-1.75(\quad x_2 - \quad 2S_1 + \quad S_2 \qquad\qquad &= 600) \\
\underline{1.75x_2 - \quad 3S_1 + \qquad S_2 + S_4 &= 800} \\
0.5S_1 - 0.75S_2 + S_4 &= -250
\end{aligned}
$$

$$(9.78)$$

The result of these calculations is that S_3 is basic in the first equation, x_1 is basic in the second equation, x_2 is basic in the third equation, and S_4 is basic in the fourth equation. This solution, however, is not feasible, $S_4 = -250$. The result in (9.78) can now be added to the optimal tableau, and the complete modified tableau is given in Table 9.20.

The solution in Table 9.20 satisfies the optimality conditions, but is not feasible. The dual simplex method is applicable and is applied in this situation. The pivot element is circled in Table 9.20. The result of the pivot is given in Table 9.21.

The additional constraint limits production

TABLE 9.21 OPTIMAL SIMPLEX TABLEAU FOR ROLLINS UNLIMITED: AN ADDITIONAL PACKAGING CONSTRAINT

c_b	c_j BASIS	3 x_1	4 x_2	0 S_1	0 S_2	0 S_3	0 S_4	SOLUTION
0	S_3	0	0	3	0	1	-4	1600
3	x_1	1	0	7/3	0	0	$-4/3$	933 1/3
4	x_2	0	1	$-4/3$	0	0	4/3	266 1/3
0	S_2	0	0	$-2/3$	1	0	$-4/3$	333 1/3
	Z_j	3	4	5/3	0	0	4/3	3866 1/3
	$c_j - Z_j$	0	0	$-5/3$	0	0	$-4/3$	

TABLE 9.22 MODIFIED SIMPLEX TABLEAU FOR ROLLINS UNLIMITED: AN ADDITIONAL DECISION VARIABLE

c_b	c_j BASIS	3 x_1	4 x_2	2.5 x_3	0 S_1	0 S_2	0 S_3	SOLUTION
0	S_3	0	0	3	5	-3	1	600
3	x_1	1	0	2	3	-1	0	600
4	x_2	0	1	-1	-2	1	0	600
	Z_j	3	4	2	1	1	0	4200
	$c_j - Z_j$	0	0	0.5	-1	-1	0	

and reduces the objective from 4200 to $4200 - 1(333\ 1/3) = 3866\ 2/3$. The new optimal solution calls for the production of 933 1/3 Deluxe skateboards and 266 1/3 Professional skateboards.

This work is unnecessary if the current solution is still feasible after the constraint has been added. Therefore, it is important to first check for feasibility by substituting the optimal value of the decision variables into the constraint or constraints that are being added. If $x_1 = 600$ and $x_2 = 600$,

$$600 + 1.75(600) = 1650 \nleq 1400 \qquad (9.79)$$

In summary, feasibility should first be checked. If the current solution is *not* feasible, the added constraint should be rewritten using elementary row operations before it is added to the current optimal tableau. Finally, dual simplex iterations are performed either to regain a feasible solution or to verify that there is no feasible solution to the modified problem.

9.4.5 ADDING A VARIABLE

Suppose that Rollins is now considering an addition to the two skateboards already being produced—the

Suburban. The Suburban requires one wheel assembly unit, one minute of mounting time, and one minute for precision adjustment. The per unit profit of the Suburban is $2.50. The modified model incorporating the new decision variable x_3 is listed.

$$\text{Maximize } Z = 3x_1 + 4x_2 + 2.5x_3 \qquad (9.80)$$

subject to

$$x_1 + x_2 + x_3 \leq 1200$$
$$2x_1 + 3x_2 + x_3 \leq 3000$$
$$x_1 + 4x_3 + x_3 \leq 3600 \qquad (9.81)$$

with

$$x_1,\ x_2,\ x_3 \geq 0 \qquad (9.82)$$

WHERE

x_3 = number of Suburban skateboards produced.

The question of importance here is whether the current solution should be modified to include

TABLE 9.23 OPTIMAL SIMPLEX TABLEAU FOR ROLLINS UNLIMITED: AN ADDITIONAL DECISION VARIABLE

c_b	c_j BASIS	3 x_1	4 x_2	2.5 x_3	0 S_1	0 S_2	0 S_3	SOLUTION
2.5	x_3	0	0	1	5/3	-1	1/3	200
3	x_1	1	0	0	$-1/3$	1	$-2/3$	200
4	x_2	0	1	0	1/3	0	1/3	800
	Z_j	3	4	2.5	27/6	1/2	1/6	4300
	$c_j - Z_j$	0	0	0	$-27/6$	$-1/2$	$-1/6$	

the production of the Suburban skateboard. The decision variable x_3 will be initially incorporated into the optimal tableau as a nonbasic variable. The value of the $c_j - Z_j$ term for x_3 is of vital importance, as it tells us whether the current solution continues to remain optimal when this variable is included.

Since the dual variables can be used to represent the marginal value of resources, we can compute the total marginal value of resources used to produce one Suburban skateboard

$$(1)(1) + (1)(1) + (1)(0) = 2$$

The preceding calculation reflects the fact that optimal marginal values of the resources are 1, 1, and 0, respectively, and that production of the Suburban skateboard requires one unit of each resource.

Since the per unit profit is 2.5 and greater than the marginal value of the resources needed to produce one unit of that product, production of the Suburban skateboard should be considered. In fact, what we have done using the interpretation of the dual variable is calculate $Z_j(= 2)$ for x_3, and thus $c_j - Z_j = 0.5$. Thus the current solution would not be optimal and variable x_3 would need to be incorporated in Table 9.2.

Even though we have calculated Z_j and $c_j - Z_j$ for x_3, we have not dealt with the inclusion of the constraint coefficients into the optimal tableau. This will require the use of the basis inverse matrix. Since $B^{-1}A$ gives the constraint coefficients for the optimal tableau, the constraint coefficient for x_3 can be calculated by

$$B^{-1}\begin{bmatrix} 1 \\ 1 \\ 1 \end{bmatrix} = \begin{bmatrix} \text{variable } x_3 \\ \text{coefficients} \end{bmatrix} \qquad (9.83)$$

or

$$\begin{bmatrix} 5 & -3 & 1 \\ 3 & -1 & 0 \\ -2 & 1 & 0 \end{bmatrix}\begin{bmatrix} 1 \\ 1 \\ 1 \end{bmatrix} = \begin{bmatrix} 3 \\ 2 \\ -1 \end{bmatrix} \qquad (9.84)$$

The modified simplex tableau is given in Table 9.22.

The pivot element is selected and an additional pivot is performed using the standard simplex method (Table 9.23).

The new optimal solution involves the production of 200 Deluxe skateboards, 800 Professional skateboards, and 200 Suburban skateboards. The objective increases by $(0.5)(200) = 100$, and all the resources are utilized in this solution.

9.4.6 CHANGES IN THE CONSTRAINT COEFFICIENTS

Sensitivity of the optimal solution to changes in the constraint coefficients, the a_{ij}, is also important. The difficulty of the analysis depends on whether the change involves a basic or a nonbasic variable. When the a_{ij} coefficient of a nonbasic variable is changed, the range of this coefficient over which the optimality of the basic solution will not be affected can be computed rather simply. In fact, the only change in the optimal tableau will be in the $c_j - Z_j$ value for the nonbasic variable involved in the change.

Unfortunately, changes in the a_{ij} coefficient of a basic variable can result in numerous changes in the optimal simplex tableau. It is easy to imagine the complexity of this problem, if we observe that the initial pivot element may be changed $(a_{ij} + \Delta)$. In this case, the quantity Δ could appear in any row of any column in the tableau. It is possible for the final tableau to become infeasible as well as nonoptimal. Given the complexity of the impact of this single change in a constraint coefficient, a systematic approach to sensitivity analysis for this case is difficult to develop. Even in special cases where such methods have been developed, the results cannot be obtained directly from the final tableau. Generally, subsequent simplex iterations (primal or dual) are required. Often the best way to perform a sensitivity analysis of a constraint coefficient of a basic variable is to incorporate the change into the initial problem and resolve.

9.5 SENSITIVITY ANALYSIS CONTINUED

In this section sensitivity analysis on a problem with a minimization objective and greater-than-or-equal-to constraints is discussed. We note that there are no significant changes in the analysis. To reillustrate the minor modifications and review the relationship

TABLE 9.24 OPTIMAL SIMPLEX TABLEAU FOR DUAL TO ROLLINS UNLIMITED

c_b	BASIS	c_j								SOLUTION
		1200	3000	3600	0	0	M	M	
		y_1	y_2	y_3	S_1	S_2	A_1	A_2	
1200	y_1	1	0	-5	-3	2	3	-2	1
3000	y_2	0	1	3	1	-1	-1	1	1
	Z_j	1200	3000	-3000	-600	-600	600	600	4200
	$c_j - Z_j$	0	0	600	600	600	$(M - 600)$	$(M - 600)$	

between the primal and dual problems we consider the dual to the Rollins Unlimited problem.

$$\text{Minimize } Z = 1200y_1 + 3000y_2 + 3600y_3 \quad (9.85)$$

subject to

$$y_1 + 2y_2 + y_3 \geq 3$$
$$y_1 + 3y_2 + 4y_3 \geq 4 \quad (9.86)$$

with

$$y_1, y_2, y_3 \geq 0 \quad (9.87)$$

The optimal simplex tableau for this problem is given in Table 9.24.

Sensitivity analysis for a problem involving a minimization objective involves a minor modification in studying variation in objective function coefficients. Simply, the $c_j - Z_j$ must remain greater than or equal to zero. For example, suppose the coefficient of y_1 changes from 1200 to $1200 + \Delta$. The resulting simplex tableau is given in Table 9.25.

The A_1 and A_2 columns (the artificial variables columns) can be ignored in this analysis. Thus the conditions that must be satisfied are

$$600 + 5\Delta \geq 0$$
$$600 + 3\Delta \geq 0$$
$$600 - 2\Delta \geq 0 \quad (9.88)$$

or

$$\Delta \geq -120$$
$$\Delta \geq -200$$
$$\Delta \leq 300 \quad (9.89)$$

Then $-120 \leq \Delta \leq 300$ and $1080 \leq c_1 \leq 1500$. We note that the range on c_1 is the same as the range for the right-hand-side constant for the first constraint in the primal problem. Is this a surprise? Table 9.26 summarizes the sensitivity calculations for the objective function coefficients.

Change in the sensitivity analysis for the right-hand-side constraints for greater-than-or-equal-to constraints is slightly more subtle. Yet the analysis is not difficult if we recall the reasoning behind the analysis in Section 9.4.2. To recall the precise analysis used consider a change in the right-hand-side constant of the first constraint. Change 3 to $3 + \Delta$ and the initial simplex tableau is given in Table 9.27.

We again notice that the coefficients for Δ in the solution column are the same as the coefficients of A_1. Again if two columns are the same in the simplex column, we would expect that the results of a sequence of elementary row operations would leave these two columns identical. This fact is reflected in Table 9.28.

In order to maintain a feasible solution the solution values must remain nonnegative. That is,

$$1 + 3\Delta \geq 0$$
$$1 - \Delta \geq 0 \quad (9.90)$$

or

$$-\frac{1}{3} \leq \Delta \leq 1 \quad (9.91)$$

and the right-hand side of the first constraint can vary between 2 2/3 and 4 without changing the optimal basis. Furthermore, any change of the parameter between a decrease of 1/3 and an increase of 1 will change the objective value by 600Δ. Again

TABLE 9.25 OPTIMAL SIMPLEX TABLEAU FOR DUAL TO ROLLINS UNLIMITED: OBJECTIVE FUNCTION COEFFICIENT CHANGE

c_b	c_j BASIS	$1200 + \Delta$ y_1	3000 y_2	3600 y_3	0 S_1	0 S_2	M A_1	M A_2	SOLUTION
$1200 + \Delta$	y_1	1	0	-5	-3	2	3	-2	1
3000	y_2	0	1	3	1	-1	-1	1	1
	z_j	$1200 + \Delta$	3000	$-3000 - 5\Delta$	$-600 - 3\Delta$	$-600 + 2\Delta$	$600 + 3\Delta$	$600 - 2\Delta$	$4200 + \Delta$
	$c_j - z_j$	0	0	$600 + 5\Delta$	$600 + 3\Delta$	$600 - 2\Delta$	$(M - 600 - 3\Delta)$	$(M - 600 + 2\Delta)$	

TABLE 9.26 SENSITIVITY OF OBJECTIVE FUNCTION COEFFICIENTS: PROBLEM (9.85), (9.86), AND (9.87)

COEFFICIENT	CHANGE	RANGE
1200	$[-120, 300]$	$[1080, 1500]$
3000	$[-600, 200]$	$[2400, 3200]$
3600	$[-600, +\infty]$	$[3000, +\infty]$

The primary difference between sensitivity analysis for greater-than-or-equal-to constraints and less-than-or-equal-to constraints involves the use of the artificial variable columns rather than the slack variable columns. Note that the surplus variable columns differ from their corresponding artificial variable columns in sign only. Therefore, if the artificial variable columns are not maintained in the simplex calculations after a feasible solution is found, we still could be able to perform this type of sensitivity analysis.

it should be verified that this analysis is consistent with the sensitivity for the objective function coefficient of x_1 in the primal problem.

The same analysis could be performed using the basis inverse matrix. Recall the basis inverse matrix was identified in the optimal simplex tableau by the columns that were initially associated with basic variables. In this case, the artificial variables were initially basic and

$$
\begin{array}{cc} & A_1 \quad A_2 \\ B^{-1} = & \begin{bmatrix} 3 & -2 \\ -1 & 1 \end{bmatrix} \end{array}
$$

Variable B^{-1} can be used in the following way

$$
\begin{bmatrix} 3 & -2 \\ -1 & 1 \end{bmatrix} \begin{bmatrix} 3 + \Delta \\ 4 \end{bmatrix} = \begin{bmatrix} 1 + 3\Delta \\ 1 - \Delta \end{bmatrix} \quad (9.92)
$$

9.6 SUMMARY

The interpretation of the optimal solution to a linear programming model is enhanced by the duality relationships in linear programming and sensitivity analysis. The primal/dual relationship in linear programming and related economic implications have been presented in this chapter. Procedures for examining changes in input parameters were also developed. These procedures, sensitivity analysis, involved single parameter changes. Simultaneous changes in several input parameters was not a topic discussed in this chapter, but is a topic that is developed in more advanced texts.

The economic information provided by duality

TABLE 9.27 INITIAL SIMPLEX TABLEAU FOR DUAL TO ROLLINS UNLIMITED: RIGHT-HAND-SIDE CHANGE

c_b	c_j BASIS	1200 y_1	3000 y_2	3600 y_3	0 S_1	0 S_2	M A_1	M A_2	SOLUTION
M	A_1	1	2	1	-1	0	1	0	$3 + 1\Delta$
M	A_2	1	3	4	0	-1	0	1	$4 + 0\Delta$
	Z_j	2M	5M	5M	$-M$	$-M$	M	M	$7M + M\Delta$
	$c_j - Z_j$	$1200 - 2M$	$3000 - 5M$	$3600 - 5M$	M	M	0	0	

TABLE 9.28 OPTIMAL SIMPLEX TABLEAU FOR DUAL TO ROLLINS: RIGHT-HAND-SIDE CHANGE

c_b	c_j BASIS	1200 y_1	3000 y_2	3600 y_3	0 S_1	0 S_2	M A_1	M A_2	SOLUTION
1200	y_1	1	0	-5	-3	2	3	-2	$1 + 3\Delta$
3000	y_2	0	1	3	1	-1	-1	1	$1 - \Delta$
	Z_j	1200	3000	3000	-600	-600	600	600	$4200 + 600\Delta$
	$c_j - Z_j$	0	0	600	600	600	$M - 600$	$M - 600$	

relationships and sensitivity analysis is invaluable and often more useful than the actual solution itself. The appropriate implementation of a model solution depends upon the evaluation of the additional information provided by sensitivity analysis and duality theory. The study of duality and sensitivity analysis is an extremely important part of the methodology of linear programming.

GLOSSARY

Basis Inverse Matrix   The inverse of the basis matrix.

Basis Matrix   A square matrix whose columns are the constraint coefficients in the original model for the variables that are basic in that solution.

Complementary Slackness Conditions   An important relationship between a basic solution in the primal problem and the corresponding basic solution in the dual problem.

Dual Problem   A linear programming problem that has a specific structural relationship to another linear programming problem called the *primal* linear programming problem.

Dual Simplex Method   A linear programming algorithm designed to deal with solutions that satisfy the optimality criteria for the problem but are infeasible.

Duality Theory   The study of a linear programming problem and its dual.

Marginal Value of Resource (Shadow Price, Opportunity Cost)   The value of an additional unit of resource.

Postoptimality Analysis   The study of the relationship between the primal and dual solutions and sensitivity analysis.

Sensitivity Analysis   An analysis of the impact of individual input parameter changes on the optimal solution.

Selected References

Bazaraa, Mokhtar S., and John J. Jarvis. 1977. *Linear Programming and Network Flows.* New York: Wiley.

Bradley, Stephen P., Arnoldo C. Hax, and Thomas L. Magnanti. 1977. *Applied Mathematical Programming.* Reading, Mass: Addison-Wesley.

Budnick, Frank S., Richard Mojena, and Thomas E. Vollmann. 1977. *Operations Research for Management.* Homewood, Ill.: Irwin.

Charnes, A., and W.W. Cooper. 1961. *Management Models and Industrial Applications of Linear Programming,* vols. 1 and 2. New York: Wiley.

Cooper, Leon, and David Steinberg. 1974. *Methods and Applications of Linear Programming.* Philadelphia, Pa.: Sanders.

Dantzig, George B. 1963. *Linear Programming and Extensions.* Princeton, N.J.: Princeton Univ. Press.

Greenberg, Michael R., 1978. *Applied Linear Programming For the Socioeconomic and Environmental Sciences.* New York: Academic Press.

Hadley, G. 1962. *Linear Programming.* Reading, Mass.: Addison-Wesley.

Hillier, Fredrick S., and Gerald J. Lieberman. 1980. *Introduction to Operations Research*, 3rd ed. San Francisco: Holden-Day.

Hughes, Ann J., and Dennis E. Grawoig. 1973. *Linear Programming: An Emphasis on Decision Making*. Reading, Mass: Addison-Wesley.

Ignizo, James P. 1982. *Linear Programming In Single and Multiple Objective Systems*. Englewood Cliffs, N.J.: Prentice-Hall.

Llewellyn, Robert W. 1964. *Linear Programming*. New York: Holt, Rinehart & Winston.

Luenberger, David G. 1973. *Introduction to Linear and Nonlinear Programming*. Reading, Mass.: Addison-Wesley.

Markland, Robert E. 1983. *Topics in Management Science*, 2nd ed. New York: Wiley.

Taha, Hamdy A. 1982. *Operations Research: An Introduction*, 3rd ed. New York: Macmillan.

Thompson, Gerald E. 1971. *Linear Programming: An Elementary Introduction*. New York: Macmillan.

Wagner, Harvey M. 1969. *Principles of Operations Research: With Applications to Managerial Decisions*. Englewood Cliffs, N.J.: Prentice-Hall.

Discussion Questions

1. Discuss the importance of sensitivity analysis on the interpretation of the linear programming solution.

2. Is it ever necessary to solve both the primal problem and the dual problem? Explain.

3. What is a shadow price? Precisely how is this value related to the price you would be willing to pay for additional resources?

4. Discuss the impact of equality constraints and variables unconstrained in sign on duality.

5. A linear programming problem has 50 variables and 240 constraints. Discuss the advantages of solving the dual problem.

6. Discuss the role of the dual simplex method in sensitivity analysis.

7. How do we identify the basis inverse matrix in (a) a problem with all less-than-or-equal-to constraints? (b) A problem with mixed constraints?

8. Interpret the complementary slackness conditions in the context of a product-mix problem with all less-than-or-equal-to constraints.

9. How does change in a right-hand side affect the optimal graphical solution of a linear programming problem?

10. Examining the impact of changing a constraint coefficient of a nonbasic variable can be approached by elementary sensitivity techniques. Is this statement justified? Explain.

PROBLEMS

1. Construct the dual to the following linear programming problem.

$$\text{Maximize } Z = 2x_1 + 3x_2 + 4x_3$$

subject to

$$x_1 + x_2 + x_3 \leq 20$$

$$x_1 \qquad + x_3 \leq 15$$

$$x_1 + x_2 \qquad \leq 10$$

$$x_2 + x_3 \leq 5$$

with

$$x_1,\ x_2,\ x_3 \geq 0$$

2. Construct the dual to the following linear programming problem.

$$\text{Maximize } Z = x_1 + 2x_2 + 3x_3 + 4x_4$$

subject to

$$x_1 + \left(\frac{1}{2}\right)x_2 + \left(\frac{1}{3}\right)x_3 + \left(\frac{1}{4}\right)x_4 \leq 40$$

$$2x_1 + x_2 + x_3 \qquad \leq 80$$

with

$$x_1,\ x_2,\ x_3,\ x_4 \geq 0$$

3. Construct the dual to the following linear programming problem.

$$\text{Minimize } Z = 3x_1 + 4x_2 + x_3$$

subject to

$$x_1 + 4x_2 + 6x_3 \geq 38$$

$$x_1 + 2x_2 \qquad \geq 28$$

with

$$x_1,\ x_2,\ x_3 \geq 0$$

4. Construct the dual to the following linear programming problem.

$$\text{Maximize } Z = 4x_1 + x_2$$

subject to

$$4x_1 + 5x_2 \leq 8$$

$$x_1 + 3x_2 = 5$$

with

$$x_1, \ x_2 \geq 0$$

5. Construct the dual to the following linear programming problem.

$$\text{Minimize } Z = -3x_1 + 5x_2$$

subject to

$$x_1 + \ x_2 \geq 200$$
$$5x_1 + 6x_2 \geq 900$$

with

$$x_2 \geq 0, \ x_1 \text{ unrestricted in sign}$$

6. Construct the dual to the following linear programming problem.

$$\text{Maximize } Z = \left(\frac{1}{2}\right)x_1 + \left(\frac{1}{3}\right)x_3 + 3x_3$$

subject to

$$x_1 + \ x_2 + x_3 \geq 50$$
$$x_2 + x_3 = 10$$
$$2x_1 + 3x_2 + x_3 \leq 75$$

with

$$x_1, \ x_2, \ x_3 \geq 0$$

7. Construct the dual to the following linear programming problem.

$$\text{Maximize } Z = x_1 + 8x_2$$

subject to

$$-3x_1 + 8x_2 \geq -10$$
$$x_1 + \ x_2 = -4$$
$$3x_1 + 7x_2 \leq \ \ 35$$

with

$$x_1, \ x_2 \geq 0$$

8. Construct the dual to the following linear programming problem.

$$\text{Maximize } Z = x_1 + 8x_2$$

subject to

$$-3x_1 + 8x_2 \geq -10$$
$$x_1 + x_2 = -4$$
$$3x_1 + 7x_2 \leq 35$$

with

$$x_1, x_2 \text{ unrestricted in sign}$$

9. Construct the dual to the following linear programming problem.

$$\text{Maximize } Z = 2x_1 + 3x_2$$

subject to

$$x_1 + x_2 \leq 2$$
$$-3x_1 + x_2 \leq 4$$

with

$$x_1, x_2 \geq 0$$

Find the solution to the given problem and its dual.

10. Write the dual to the following linear programming problem.

$$\text{Maximize } Z = 2x_1 + 4x_2$$

subject to

$$2.5x_1 + 3x_2 \leq 300$$
$$5x_1 + 2x_2 \leq 400$$
$$2x_2 \leq 150$$
$$x_1 \geq 60$$
$$x_2 \geq 60$$

with

$$x_1, x_2 \geq 0$$

We note that the above problem is infeasible (see Section 8.6.1). Solve the dual problem. Interpret the result.

11. Solve the following problem using the dual simplex method.

$$\text{Minimize } Z = 200x_1 + 80x_2 + 180x_3$$

subject to

$$4x_1 + x_2 + x_3 \geq 3$$
$$x_1 + x_2 + 3x_3 \geq 2$$

with

$$x_1, x_2, x_3 \geq 0$$

12. Solve the following problem using the dual simplex method.

$$\text{Minimize } Z = 1000x_1 + 1600x_2 + 2400x_3$$

subject to

$$x_1 + x_2 + 3x_3 \geq 3$$
$$x_1 + 2x_2 + x_3 \geq 4$$

with

$$x_1, x_2, x_3 \geq 0$$

13. Solve the following problem using the dual simplex method.

$$\text{Minimize } Z = 180(x_1 + x_2 + x_3)$$

subject to

$$x_1 + x_2 + 2x_3 \geq 19$$
$$1.5x_1 + x_2 + 0.5x_3 \geq 17$$
$$x_1 + x_2 + 1.5x_3 \geq 11$$

with

$$x_1, x_2, x_3 \geq 0$$

14. Solve the following problem using the dual simplex problem.

$$\text{Minimize } Z = x_1 + 2x_2$$

subject to

$$x_1 \leq 10$$
$$x_2 \leq 10$$
$$x_1 + x_2 \geq 15$$

with

$$x_1, x_2 \geq 0$$

15. Consider the following linear programming model.

$$\text{Maximize } Z = 7x_1 + 5x_2 + 9x_3$$

subject to

$$x_1 + x_2 \le 4$$
$$2x_1 + 3x_3 \le 2$$
$$x_1 + 3x_2 + x_3 \le 3$$

with

$$x_1, x_2, x_3 \ge 0$$

The optimal simplex tableau follows.

	c_j	7	5	9	0	0	0	
c_b	BASIS	x_1	x_2	x_3	S_1	S_2	S_3	SOLUTION
0	S_1	0	0	$-4/3$	1	$-1/3$	$-1/3$	7/3
7	x_1	1	0	3/2	0	1/2	0	1
5	x_2	0	1	$-1/6$	0	$-1/6$	1/3	2/3
	Z_j	7	5	29/3	0	8/3	5/3	31/3
	$c_j - Z_j$	0	0	$-2/3$	0	$-8/3$	$-5/3$	

a. Perform a sensitivity analysis for each of the objective function coefficients (including the coefficients of the slack variables).
b. Perform a sensitivity analysis for each of the right-hand-side values.

16. Consider the following linear programming model.

$$\text{Minimize } Z = 7x_1 + 5x_2 + x_3$$

subject to

$$x_1 - 3x_2 \le 3$$
$$5x_1 - 3x_3 \ge 7$$
$$2x_2 - 5x_3 \ge 4$$

with

$$x_1, x_2, x_3 \ge 0$$

The optimal simplex tableau follows.

	c_j	7	5	1	0	0	M	0	M	
c_b	BASIS	x_1	x_2	x_3	S_1	S_2	A_1	S_3	A_2	SOLUTION
0	S_1	0	0	-6.9	1	0.2	-0.2	-1.5	1.5	7.6
7	x_1	1	0	-0.6	0	-0.2	0.2	0	0	1.4
5	x_2	0	1	-2.5	0	0	0	-0.5	0.5	2.0
	Z_j	7	5	-16.7	0	-1.4	1.4	-2.5	2.5	19.8
	$c_j - Z_j$	0	0	17.7	0	1.4	$(M - 1.4)$	2.5	$(M - 2.5)$	

a. Perform a sensitivity analysis for each of the objective function coefficients (including the coefficients of the slack variables).
b. Perform a sensitivity analysis for each of the right-hand-side values.

17. A manufacturing company produces three types of desk lamps, Lamp 1, Lamp 2, and Lamp 3. Each lamp requires the use of three limited resources, Resource 1, Resource 2, and Resource 3. Lamp 1 requires one unit of Resource 1, three units of Resource 2, and two units of Resource 3. Lamp 2 requires two units of Resource 1 and eight units of Resource 3. Lamp 3 requires one unit of Resource 1 and two units of Resource 2. Lamp 1 yields a $6 per unit profit, Lamp 2 a $2 per unit profit, and Lamp 3 an $8 per unit profit. There are 500 units of Resource 1 available, 460 units of Resource 2, and 840 units of Resource 3. The linear programming formulation of this problem for maximizing profit is

$$\text{Maximize } Z = 6x_1 + 2x_2 + 8x_3$$

subject to

$$x_1 + 2x_2 + x_3 \leq 500$$
$$3x_1 \qquad + 2x_3 \leq 460$$
$$2x_1 + 8x_2 \qquad \leq 840$$

with

$$x_1, x_2, x_3 \geq 0$$

The optimal tableau for this problem is given in the following tableau.

	c_j	6	2	8	0	0	0	
c_b	BASIS	x_1	x_2	x_3	S_1	S_2	S_3	SOLUTION
0	S_1	-1	0	0	1	-0.5	-0.25	60
8	x_3	1.5	0	1	0	0.5	0	230
2	x_2	0.25	1	0	0	0	0.125	105
	Z_j	12.5	2	8	0	4	0.25	2050
	$c_j - Z_j$	-6.5	0	0	0	-4	-0.25	

a. Perform a sensitivity analysis for each of the objective function coefficients (including the coefficients of the slack variables).
b. Perform a sensitivity analysis for each of the right-hand-side values.
c. Perform a sensitivity analysis for the addition of the constraint

$$x_1 + x_2 + x_3 \leq 300$$

d. Perform a sensitivity analysis for the addition of another decision variable x_4. The constraint coefficients for each constraint are 1 and the objective function coefficient is 10.

18. Using the optimal solution for Problem 17, answer the following questions.

    a. What is the optimal production schedule for this manufacturing firm? Are there alternative optimal production schedules?

    b. What are the optimal values of the dual decision variables?

    c. What are the optimal values of the dual surplus variables?

    d. What are the shadow prices for the three resources? How are these values interpreted?

    e. How is the $c_j - Z_j$ value for decision variable 1 interpreted?

    f. What is the basis inverse matrix for the optimal solution in Problem 17? What is the basis matrix?

19. Consider a production problem with initial simplex, Tableau A, and final tableau, Tableau B. The objective for the firm is to maximize profits subject to three resource constraints. The firm's outputs are x_1, x_2, x_3. Variables S_1, S_2, S_3 are the slack variables corresponding to the three resources—raw materials, machine hours, and labor days.

TABLEAU A

c_b	c_j BASIS	4 x_1	5 x_2	6 x_3	0 S_1	0 S_2	0 S_3	SOLUTION
0	S_1	2	3	4	1	0	0	60
0	S_2	1	1	1	0	1	0	40
0	S_3	2	3	0	0	0	1	50
	Z_j	0	0	0	0	0	0	0
	$c_j - Z_j$	4	5	6	0	0	0	

TABLEAU B

c_b	c_j BASIS	4 x_1	5 x_2	6 x_3	0 S_1	0 S_2	0 S_3	SOLUTION
6	x_3	0	0	1	1/4	0	−1/4	5/2
0	S_2	0	−1/2	0	−1/4	1	−1/4	25/2
4	x_1	1	3/2	0	0	0	1/2	25
	Z_j	4	6	6	3/2	0	1/2	115
	$c_j - Z_j$	0	−1	0	−3/2	0	−1/2	

    a. Write both the primal and dual problems.

    b. Give both the primal and dual optimal solutions and illustrate the complementary slackness conditions.

    c. Give the economic interpretation of each dual variable.

    d. For variable x_1 give the range over which the objective function coefficient can vary without changing the optimal solution. Answer the same question for variables x_2 and x_3.

    e. Give the basis inverse matrix.

    f. Use the basis inverse matrix to assess the impact of a simultaneous reduction of 10 units for each of the three resources.

g. Give the interval for raw materials over which the current basis remains optimal. Answer the same question for machine hours and labor days.

h. If the firm receives an inquiry about the possibility of producing a fourth output that requires 6 pounds of raw material, 2 hours of machine time, and 2 worker days of labor per unit, and would contribute a profit of $9 per unit, should the firm add the fourth output to production line? Explain.

i. Answer Question h if the per unit profit was $12.

j. The production process is to be modified so that a second raw material is utilized. The resulting constraint is $2x_1 + 4x_2 + 2x_3 \leq 50$. Assume that the remaining parameters in the problem are not changed. What is the optimal solution with this additional constraint?

20. Consider Problem 3 of Chapter 6. The linear programming model for this situation follows.

$$\text{Maximize } Z = 1.00x_1 + 1.50x_2$$

subject to

$$4x_1 + 4x_2 \leq 80$$

$$2x_1 + 4x_2 \leq 64$$

$$3x_1 + 4x_2 \leq 64$$

with

$$x_1, x_2 \geq 0$$

where

$$x_1 = \text{number of submarine sandwiches made;}$$

$$x_2 = \text{number of feedmill sandwiches made.}$$

The optimal tableau for this problem is also given.

c_b	c_j BASIS	1.00 x_1	1.50 x_2	0 S_1	0 S_2	0 S_3	SOLUTION
0	S_1	0	0	1	1	-2	16
1.5	x_2	0	1	0	0.75	-0.5	16
1.0	x_1	1	0	0	-1	1	0
	Z_j	1	1.5	0	0.125	0.25	24
	$c_j - Z_j$	0	0	0	-0.125	-0.25	

a. What is the shadow price of one ounce of ham? How is it interpreted? Over what range is the interpretation valid?

b. What is the shadow price of one ounce of turkey? How is it interpreted? Over what range is the interpretation valid?

c. What is the shadow price of one ounce of cheese? How is it interpreted? Over what range is the interpretation valid?
d. Suppose 50 ounces of turkey is available instead of 64. What is the optimal solution to this revised problem?
e. Suppose 76 ounces of cheese is available instead of 64. What is the optimal solution to this revised problem?
f. Perform a sensitivity analysis on the objective function coefficients.
g. Suppose the feedmill sandwich provides a profit of $2.10 instead of $1.50. What is the optimal solution to this revised problem?

21. Consider Problem 4 of Chapter 6. The linear programming model for this situation follows.

$$\text{Maximize } Z = 10x_1 + 50x_2 + 20x_3$$

subject to

$$2x_1 - x_2 \leq 0$$
$$x_3 \leq 20$$
$$10x_1 + 60x_2 + 15x_3 \leq 10{,}000$$
$$2x_1 + 10x_2 + 3x_3 \leq 1000$$

with

$$x_1, x_2, x_3 \geq 0$$

where

x_1 = number of desk chairs produced;

x_2 = number of desks produced;

x_3 = number of rocking chairs produced.

The optimal tableau for this problem is also given.

	c_j	10	50	20	0	0	0	0	
c_b	BASIS	x_1	x_2	x_3	S_1	S_2	S_3	S_4	SOLUTION
0	S_1	2.2	0	0	1	−0.3	0	0.1	94
20	x_3	0	0	1	0	1	0	0	20
0	S_3	−2	0	0	0	3	1	−6	4060
50	x_2	0.2	1	0	0	−0.3	0	0.1	94
	Z_j	10	50	20	0	5	0	5	5100
	$c_j - Z_j$	0	0	0	0	−5	0	−5	

a. What is the shadow price of an hour of labor? How is it interpreted? Over what range is the interpretation valid?
b. Perform a sensitivity analysis on the availability of wood.

c. What is the maximum increase in the per unit profit of desks that will not change the optimal basis?

d. What is the maximum decrease in the per unit profit of rocking chairs that will not change the optimal basis?

e. Does this model have alternate optimal solutions? If so, what are they?

22. An auto specialty shop fabricates custom seats of two types, Plush (x_1) and Extraplush (x_2), using excess labor and material. The specialty shop has resource constraints for production time, cubic feet of compressed fiber, and square yards of leather. The LP model for profit maximization follows.

$$\text{Maximize } Z = 70x_1 + 80x_2 \quad \text{(Profit \$)}$$

subject to

$$2x_1 + x_2 \le 19 \quad \text{(Production, hours)}$$

$$x_1 + x_2 \le 14 \quad \text{(Leather, square yards)}$$

$$x_1 + 2x_2 \le 20 \quad \text{(Fiber, cubic feet)}$$

with

$$x_1, x_2 \ge 0$$

The optimal simplex tableau is as follows.

c_b	c_j BASIS	70 x_1	80 x_2	0 S_1	0 S_2	0 S_3	SOLUTION
70	x_1	1	0	2/3	0	-1/3	6
0	S_2	0	0	-1/3	1	-1/3	1
80	x_2	0	1	-1/3	0	2/3	7
	Z_j	70	80	20	0	30	980
	$c_j - Z_j$	0	0	-20	0	-30	

a. Write the dual and give the optimal values of the dual decision variables as well as the dual surplus variables.

b. Give the amount of each resource used under the optimal solution.

c. What is the shadow price for one hour of production time? How is it interpreted? Over what range is this interpretation valid?

d. By what amount, if any, can we decrease the availability of leather without changing the optimal solution?

e. Over what range can the objective function coefficient of x_1 vary without changing the optimal solution?

f. Suppose that after the second seat is produced, the time required to produce each additional seat decreases. Can sensitivity analysis be used to determine the impact of such a change? Is linear programming an appropriate model in this situation? Explain.

Application Review

Production Planning in a Sri Lanka Coconut Mill: The Introduction of Linear Programming as a Planning Tool

Sri Lanka is an agricultural country that depends primarily on the export of tea, rubber, and coconut for its export earnings. The study that is summarized here examines the production strategy of S.A. Silva and Sons, Ltd., the largest coconut miller in Sri Lanka. Production planning using mathematical programming techniques had not been attempted before in Sri Lanka and was supported by a company management that was open to evaluating techniques that could improve management. The study sought to answer a number of questions.

1. Is the current production plan one that would maximize profits? If not, what is the optimal production plan?
2. Are current capital expenditure plans optimal?
3. What are the most profitable marketing avenues?
4. What are the benefits of the existing sales contracts and how can they be improved?
5. Can a rule-of-thumb production plan be developed that would eliminate or minimize the need for using computerized planning techniques?

The operations of S.A. Silva and Sons, Ltd., at its three mills are listed.

1. Every month the management decides on the quantity of nuts, copra, and parings that must be purchased, the amounts of various grades of desiccated coconut to be produced, and the amount of charcoal that can be made.
2. Coconuts are sorted and are sent for desiccated coconut and copra production.
3. The good quality coconuts selected for desiccated coconut production are sent to the mill where two types of desiccated coconut are produced, fancy grade and two categories of granulates.
4. Remaining nuts are sent to the kiln for copra manufacture.
5. The desiccated coconut is graded and sold and the other by-products, such as shells, parings, and desiccated coconut waste, replenish the stocks of shells and copra.
6. Coconut oil and poonac are produced from copra, parings, and desiccated coconut waste, and are sold. The resulting shells are used to manufacture charcoal and shell flour and the remaining shells are stored for charcoal production.

Since this was the first time linear programming was utilized, the analysis had to be understandable by the layman. Model simplication was achieved by grouping variables and making certain assumptions. For example, each product was considered to be produced by a single process, although various stages produce intermediate products that are raw materials for other processes in the mill. The model was formulated as a profit maximization problem where the variables were grouped as follows.

1. Purchase of coconuts, copra, and parings.
2. Production of intermediate products, copra, and parings.

Source: Cobraal, R. Amil, "Production planning in a Sri Lanka coconut mill using parametric linear programming," *Interfaces* (June 1981), Vol. 11, No. 3, pp. 16–23.

3. Production of commodities for sale: oil from copra and parings, oil from waste desiccated coconut; shell flour, charcoal, granulate desiccated coconut.
4. Sales of desiccated coconut, oil, poonac, charcoal, shell flour, and shells.
5. Storing shells for later charcoal production.

The constraints used represented inventory size, plant capacity, and process or sales limits. A single-period model was designed to simulate the activities in a single month. There is a variability in product yields, called *out-turns* in the coconut milling industry. For the linear programming formulation, fixed out-turn rates for the products were assumed. The model was validated for July 1974, since product out-turns in this month were closest to the average rates used in the linear programming model. Table 9.29 gives a comparison of the model output and the actual July 1974 production. The model also worked well when the out-turns were furthest away from the average rates used in the model.

Sensitivity analysis was performed on important sales policy variables and on critical constraints. The sensitivity analysis performed here was an extension of the methods presented in this chapter, called *parametric analysis*. Parametric analysis allows a parameter to change beyond the limits defined by standard sensitivity techniques. Thus changes in the model solution are examined at critical parameter-change limits where the basis changes. For example, sensitivity analysis for the quantity of medium-grade desiccated coconut showed that although medium-grade desiccated coconut received a premium price due to the current constraint, producing it was not the optimal strategy. It was not optimal because resources were forced from more profitable oil production to satisfy the contractural requirements.

Using the shadow prices for the optimal linear programming solution and solutions generated by a type of sensitivity analysis, further analysis was performed.

1. HATCHETING AND PARING CAPACITY It was found that there was no need for a proposed capital investment to increase this capacity.

TABLE 9.29 COMPARISON OF ACTUAL JULY 1974 PRODUCTION WITH LP MODEL RESULTS AT 1.1 MILLION RUPEES PRODUCTION COST

	JULY PRODUCTION	LP MODEL RESULTS
Nuts purchased	2,789,650	2,247,169
Copra bought (candies)[a]	74	0
Parings bought (candies)	0	39
Copra made (candies)	160	176
Parings made (candies)	328	278
Total desiccated coconut (pounds)	500,000	600,000
Fancy grade desiccated coconut (pounds)	40,380	33,400
Oil made (tons)	76	80
Poonac (tons)	38	40
Charcoal (tons)	10	10
Shell flour (tons)	56	50
Waste desiccated coconut (pounds)	12,320	30,000

[a]A "candy" is a unit of 560 pounds.

2. SHELL FLOUR SALES   Analysis showed that shell flour has a very high marginal revenue. This high shadow price suggested an investment in developing the market for additional shell flour.

3. CHARCOAL PLANT CAPACITY   Since there is no difficulty selling charcoal, the marginal revenue specifies a maximum that should be spent in order to increase the charcoal plant capacity.

4. OIL PRODUCTION   There is a substantial need to increase oil plant capacity. Due to foreign exchange difficulties, however, it is doubtful that plant capacity can be increased.

The company's management agreed that such techniques could be useful, but still preferred to make production decisions based on experience. In addition to the expected skepticism of the unfamiliar quantitative analysis, management indicated several other reasons that prevented them from implementing the recommendations: long-term contractual obligations for the sale of desiccated coconut, the idling of desiccated coconut producing equipment, and the inability to lay off skilled labor.

There is an interesting epilogue to this case. Two years after the study there was a serious drought and a resulting substantial increase in coconut oil prices relative to that of desiccated coconut. As a result management was forced to restrict desiccated coconut production in favor of coconut oil at production. Thus the production strategy that evolved began to resemble the one suggested by the model.

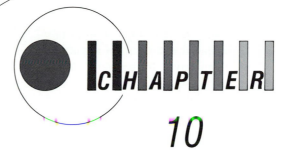

CHAPTER 10

GOAL PROGRAMMING

10.1 INTRODUCTION

In many instances maximization of profits, or minimization of costs, may not be the only objective that an organization seeks. Quite often, the maximization of profits may be one of several objectives, such as maintaining a stable work force, increasing market share, or minimizing pollution. In previous chapters we made an extensive study of linear programming, a technique that focuses on the attainment of a single objective. In contrast, in this chapter we consider an important new technique for the analysis and solution of problems involving multiple goals and objectives. Known as *goal programming*, it allows the decision maker to include multiple goals or objectives in the problem formulation.

Goal programming can be thought of as an extension of linear programming that allows the decision maker to include conflicting objectives while still obtaining a solution that is optimal with respect to the decision maker's specification of goal priorities. It is based on the idea that the modern manager does not really attempt to optimize, rather he or she tries to "satisfice."[1] Therefore, the goal-programming approach involves the decision maker in a process that attempts to achieve a "satisfactory" level of achievement for several objectives, rather than an "optimal" outcome for a single objective (as is done in linear programming). Essentially, the manager attempts to make a decision that results in a solution that comes as close as possible to reaching all goals. It utilizes the well-developed and tested technique of linear programming, while still allowing for the simultaneous consideration of a number of objectives. Perhaps its major advantage is that it more realistically reflects the way that managers actually make decisions by allowing them to incorporate a number of goals and objectives in the decision-making process.

Goal programming was first developed by Charnes and Cooper in the early 1960s.[2] It was further refined by Ijiri in the mid-1960s,[3] and major applications were developed by Lee,[4] Jaaskelainen,[5] and Ignizio[6] in the 1970s.

Goal programming has become a widely accepted and applied technique in business, governmental, and nonprofit organizations. It has been utilized in portfolio selection, media planning, academic resource allocation, determination of school busing plans, production scheduling, and health planning.

In the material that follows in this chapter we first focus on the formulation of various types of goal-programming models. We then see how these various models can be solved. Then we consider special problems and sensitivity analysis in goal programming.

10.2 A GOAL-PROGRAMMING EXAMPLE

To illustrate how goal-programming models are formulated let us consider a very simple production scheduling situation. We initially formulate it as a linear programming problem, and then we reformulate it as a goal-programming problem. The Pegasus Company manufactures three models of running shoes, the "Mercury" model, the "Flying Feet" model, and the "Swift Runner" model. The resource requirements and profits associated with these three models of running shoes are presented in Table 10.1. The Pegasus Company currently has a production capacity of 200 hours of labor available each day and a daily supply of 100 pounds of material.

The linear programming formulation of this situation would be as follows.

Maximize (total profit) Z
$$= \$10x_1 + \$7x_2 + \$5x_3 \quad (10.1)$$

subject to

$$3x_1 + 2x_2 + 1x_3 \leq 200 \quad \text{(Labor hour availability)}$$

$$2x_1 + 1x_2 + 1x_3 \leq 100 \quad \text{(Material availability)}$$

$$(10.2)$$

[1]The "satisficing" concept is discussed in detail in J.G. March and H.S. Simon, *Organizations*. New York: Wiley, 1981.

[2]A. Charnes and W.W. Cooper, *Management Models and Industrial Applications of Linear Programming*. New York: Wiley, 1961.

[3]Y. Ijiri, *Management Goals and Accounting for Control*. Chicago, Ill.: Rand McNally, 1965.

[4]S.M. Lee, *Goal Programming for Decision Analysis*. Philadelphia, Pa.: Auerbach, 1972.

[5]V. Jaaskelainen, *Accounting and Mathematical Programming*. Helsinki, Finland: Research Institute for Business and Economics, 1973.

[6]J.P. Ignizio, *Goal Programming and Extensions*. Lexington, Mass: Heath, 1976.

TABLE 10.1 RESOURCE REQUIREMENTS AND PROFITS

RUNNING SHOE MODEL	RESOURCE REQUIREMENTS		PROFITS ($/PAIR)
	LABOR (HR./PAIR)	MATERIALS (LB./PAIR)	
Mercury	3	2	10
Flying Feet	2	1	7
Swift Runner	1	1	5

with

$$x_1, \ x_2, \ x_3 \geq 0 \qquad (10.3)$$

WHERE

x_1 = number of pairs of "Mercury" model produced daily;

x_2 = number of pairs of "Flying Feet" model produced daily;

x_3 = number of pairs of "Swift Runner" model produced daily.

For this simple problem situation, however, let us assume that the management of Pegasus Company has developed the following set of goals, which are considered to be of equal importance to the company.

1. Achieve a satisfactory profit level of at least $750 per day.
2. Avoid any layoffs of workers, (i.e., fully utilize the labor hour availability).
3. Produce at least 50 pairs of the "Swift Runner" model daily.

Management of the Pegasus Company would like to achieve these goals as completely as possible. It has decided that a goal-programming approach would be desirable, since it would allow the consideration of these multiple goals.

10.2.1 DEVELOPING A SET OF CONSTRAINTS

The key to a goal-programming problem formulation is that each goal or objective is written in the form of a constraint. In this problem situation management's first goal is to achieve a satisfactory profit level, defined to be at least $750 per day. To incorporate the $750 per day profit goal into the problem, we first define the following deviational variables.

d_1^+ = overachievement of the daily profit goal of $750 (i.e., the amount by which the actual daily profit exceeds the daily profit goal)

d_1^- = underachievement of the daily profit goal of $750 (i.e., the amount by which the actual daily profit fails to meet the daily profit goal)

Since we cannot have both underachievement and overachievement of a goal simultaneously, either one or both of these deviational variables will be equal to zero. That is, $d_1^+ \times d_1^- = 0$. The daily profit goal constraint can now be written as

$$10x_1 + 7x_2 + 5x_3 - d_1^+ + d_1^- = 750 \quad (10.4)$$

The deviational variables, d_1^- and d_1^+, represent the number of dollars less than $750 ($d_1^-$, underachievement) and the number of dollars exceeding $750 ($d_1^+$, overachievement) for the level of production determined by the values of x_1, x_2, and x_3. For example, if the final solution to the problem is $x_1 = 50$, $x_2 = 20$, and $x_3 = 30$, the total daily profit would be $10(50) + $7(20) + $5(30) = $790. This would mean that $d_1^+ = $40 and $d_1^- = $0. At this level of production the daily profit goal of $750 would be overachieved by $790 − $750 = $40. Alternatively, if $x_1 = 40$, $x_2 = 20$, and $x_3 = 30$, the total daily profit would be $10(40) + $7(20) + $5(30) = $690. This would mean that $d_1^+ = $0, and $d_1^- = $60. At this level of production the daily profit goal of $750 would be underachieved by $750 − $690 = $60.

Management's second goal is to fully utilize the labor hour availability, thereby avoiding any layoff of workers. This goal constraint is defined as

$$3x_1 + 2x_2 + 1x_3 - d_2^+ + d_2^- = 200 \quad (10.5)$$

where d_2^+ is the overachievement (i.e., overtime) and d_2^- is the underachievement associated with the daily labor hour goal.

The third goal of the management of the Pegasus Company is to produce at least 50 pairs of the "Swift Runner" model daily. This goal constraint is defined as

$$x_3 - d_3^+ + d_3^- = 50 \quad (10.6)$$

where d_3^+ is the overachievement of this goal and d_3^- is the underachievement of this goal.

In the formulation of a goal-programming model, it is also possible to include constraints that do not contain deviational variables. The final constraint in this problem formulation is a constraint upon material availability, and is included just as it would be in any linear programming problem. This type of constraint is often called a *resource* or *structural* constraint in the goal-programming formulation. This structural constraint is defined as

$$2x_1 + 1x_2 + 1x_3 \leq 100 \quad (10.7)$$

Observe that we do not include a structural constraint for the labor hour availability. Such a structural constraint is not needed, since we already defined a goal constraint associated with fully utilizing the labor hour availability, namely (10.5).

10.2.2 DEVELOPING A GOAL-PROGRAMMING OBJECTIVE FUNCTION

In this problem situation management of the Pegasus Company has three basic goals that are of equal interest. For the first goal, management wishes to avoid not achieving at least $750 per day in profits. This is accomplished in the objective function as follows

$$\text{Minimize } Z = 1d_1^- + 0d_1^+ \quad (10.8)$$

For the second goal, management wishes to avoid any layoffs (i.e., it prefers overtime to the under-utilization of its labor force). This is accomplished by expanding the objective function shown in

(10.8) as follows

$$\text{Minimize } Z = 1d_1^- + 0d_1^+ + 1d_2^- + 0d_2^+ \quad (10.9)$$

Finally, for the final goal, management wishes to avoid not producing at least 50 pairs of the "Swift Runner" model daily. This is accomplished by expanding the objective function shown in (10.9) as follows

$$\text{Minimize } Z = 1d_1^- + 0d_1^+ + 1d_2^- + 0d_2^+ + 1d_3^- + 0d_3^+ \quad (10.10)$$

Note that the objective function shown in (10.10) reflects management's equal weighting of the three goals. Also note that the goal-programming objective function Z is not a one-dimensional value such as profit. Rather, Z is a multidimensional function composed of three deviations, with the first deviation measured in profit dollars, the second deviation measured in labor hours, and the third deviation measured in number of pairs of shoes. In Eq. 10.10 we have presented the multidimensional objective function for our goal-programming problem as the *summation* of the three deviations. We must be careful to realize that the "value" of the goal-programming objective function only refers to the summation of these three deviations. Some authors emphasize this point by writing the objective function with commas replacing the plus signs.

10.2.3 THE COMPLETE GOAL-PROGRAMMING MODEL

The complete goal-programming model for this problem situation can now be summarized as follows.

$$\text{Minimize } Z = d_1^- + d_2^- + d_3^- \quad (10.11)$$

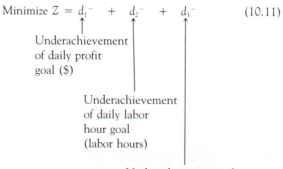

Underachievement of daily profit goal ($)

Underachievement of daily labor hour goal (labor hours)

Underachievement of daily production goal of "Swift Runner" model shoe (number of pairs of shoes)

subject to

$$10x_1 + 7x_2 + 5x_3 - d_1^+ + d_1^- = 750$$

(Daily profit goal)

$$3x_1 + 2x_2 + 1x_3 - d_2^+ + d_2^- = 200$$

(Daily labor hour utilization goal)

$$1x_3 - d_3^+ + d_3^- = 50$$

(Daily production—"Swift Runner" model)

$$2x_1 + 1x_2 + 1x_3 \leq 100$$

(Material availability constraint)

$$(10.12)$$

with

$$x_1, x_2, x_3, d_1^+, d_1^-, d_2^+, d_2^-, d_3^+, d_3^- \geq 0 \quad (10.13)$$

Note that this formulation has three goal constaints that reflect the three equally important goals that are being sought. It is a *multiple-goal model*. In this case, the underachievement of each of these goals is given a mathematical weight (i.e., any real number) of one in the objective function. If one goal were felt to be more important than another goal, it could be given a larger mathematical weight. Such a model is referred to as a *weighted linear goal programming model*. We could, of course, have a single-goal model. Such a *single-goal model* represents the simplest form of a goal-programming model. Also observe that the three goal constraints have different dimensions, or units of measure. The first goal constraint is measured in dollars, the second in labor hours, and the third in production units (i.e., pairs of shoes). Note finally that these three goals are in conflict, since the satisfaction of the daily profit goal will not necessarily satisfy the daily labor hour utilization goal nor the daily production goal for the "Swift Runner" model shoe. This is exactly the type of situation for which the goal-programming procedure was developed, as these goals are in conflict and cannot be satisfied simultaneously. The final constraint upon material availability is included just as it would be in any linear programming problem.

Just as with linear programming, the decision variables in a goal-programming model must be nonnegative, and all of the deviational variables must be greater than or equal to zero. These nonnegativity requirements are summarized by (10.13).

10.3 GOAL PROGRAMMING: PRIORITIZED GOALS

In many goal-programming situations, the decision maker will inherently favor the achievement of one goal over another. In such situations the use of goal programming is predicated on the ability of the manager to priority rank the goals associated with the model. The goals are given an ordinal ranking, and are called *preemptive priority factors*. These preemptive priority factors have the relationship

$$P_1 >>> P_2 >>> \cdots >>> P_j >>> P_{j+1} \quad (10.14)$$

where $>>>$ means "very much greater than." Note that this priority ranking is absolute. Therefore, the P_1 goal is so much more important than the P_2 goal that the P_2 goal will never be attempted until the P_1 goal is achieved to the greatest extent possible, and the P_2 goal is so much more important than the P_3 goal that P_3 goal will never be attempted until the P_2 goal is achieved to the greatest extent possible, and so on. In mathematical terms, the preemptive priority relationship implies that multiplication by a number $n > 0$, however large n may be, cannot make a lower priority goal as important as a higher priority goal (i.e., $P_j > nP_{j+1}$). In formulating a goal-programming model having prioritized goals, these preemptive priority factors are incorporated into the objective function as weights for the deviational variables.

To illustrate the formulation of such a goal-programming model reconsider the Pegasus Company situation. Let us now assume that the management of the Pegasus Company has taken a careful look at the three goals that it previously had ranked as being equally important, and has prioritized these goals as shown in Table 10.2.

The goal-programming model for this new problem situation can be summarized as follows.

$$\text{Minimize } Z = P_1 d_3^- + P_2 d_1^- + P_3 d_2^- \quad (10.15)$$

subject to

$$10x_1 + 7x_2 + 5x_3 - d_1^+ + d_1^- = 750$$
$$3x_1 + 2x_2 + 1x_3 - d_2^+ + d_2^- = 200$$
$$1x_3 - d_3^+ + d_3^- = 50$$
$$2x_1 + 1x_2 + 1x_3 \leq 100 \quad (10.16)$$

TABLE 10.2 PEGASUS COMPANY PRIORITIZED GOALS

GOAL	PRIORITY	DEVIATIONAL VARIABLE
1. Produce at least 50 pairs of the "Swift Runner" model daily.	P_1	d_3^-
2. Achieve the satisfactory profit level of at least $750 per day.	P_2	d_1^-
3. Avoid any layoffs of workers.	P_3	d_2^-

with

$$x_1, \ x_2, \ x_3, \ d_1^+, \ d_1^-, \ d_2^+, \ d_2^-, \ d_3^+, \ d_3^- \geq 0 \quad (10.17)$$

Solution of the new problem requires that the goals specified in the objective function be minimized, in the order of their priority. Consequently, the value of the deviational variable associated with the highest preemptive priority, d_3^-, must first be minimized to the fullest possible extent. Then, when no further improvement is possible for this goal, the value of the deviational variable associated with the next highest preemptive priority, d_1^-, is minimized, and so forth. Once again, the objective function Z is a multidimensional function that represents the sum of the deviations from the prioritized goals. Remember, however, that the deviations from the goals represented in this objective function are to be minimized *individually* in order of their priority.

10.4 GOAL PROGRAMMING: WEIGHTED GOALS

An additional capability of goal programming is the ability to weight goals within the same priority level. In order to do so, however, the goals within this same priority level must be *commensurable*, or measured in the same units. To illustrate this capability, consider the following problem situation. Pawley's Island Hammocks, Inc. produces an excellent quality outdoor hammock. Its production facility consists of two production lines. The first is staffed with skilled workers who can produce an average of four hammocks per hour, and the second is staffed with less experienced employees who can produce only two hammocks per hour. The normal working hours for each production line are 40 hours per week. Because the first production line is more efficient but more costly than the second production line, the operating costs of the two production lines are

basically the same. The production manager for this firm has prioritized the production objectives for the following week as follows.

P_1: Produce at least 250 hammocks weekly.
P_2: Avoid the overutilization of regular working hours for both production lines.
P_3: Avoid the underutilization of regular working hours for both production lines.

Additionally, with respect to the last two prioritized objectives, the production manager wishes to weight them differentially. For priority two, he feels that it is twice as important to avoid the overutilization of production line 2 as line 1, while for priority three, it is three times as important to avoid underutilization of production line 1 as line 2. Observe that for both priority two and three the goals within these priority levels are measured in the same units (i.e., regular working hours).

To formulate this problem situation as a goal-programming model, let us define the following set of variables.

x_1 = number of hours that production line 1 is in operation weekly

x_2 = number of hours that production line 2 is in operation weekly

d_1^+ = overachievement of hammock production goal

d_1^- = underachievement of hammock production goal

d_2^+ = overutilization of production line 1

d_2^- = underutilization of production line 1

d_3^+ = overutilization of production line 2

d_3^- = underutilization of production line 2

Using this set of variables, the complete goal-programming model can be formulated as follows

$$\begin{aligned} \text{Minimize } Z = \ & P_1 d_1^- + 1 P_2 d_2^+ \\ & + 2 P_2 d_3^+ + 3 P_3 d_2^- + 1 P_3 d_3^- \quad (10.18) \end{aligned}$$

subject to

$$4x_1 + 2x_2 - d_1^+ + d_1^- = 250 \text{ hammocks}$$
$$\text{(Production goal constraint)}$$

$$x_1 \quad - d_2^+ + d_2^- = 40 \text{ hours}$$
$$\text{(Operating time goal constraint, line 1)}$$

$$x_2 - d_3^+ + d_3^- = 40 \text{ hours}$$
$$\text{(Operating time goal constraint, line 2)}$$

$$(10.19)$$

with

$$x_1, x_2, d_1^+, d_1^-, d_2^+, d_2^-, d_3^+, d_3^- \geq 0 \quad (10.20)$$

Note that in the objective function underachievement of the weekly production goal of 225 hammocks is given the top priority. Within the second priority level, overutilization of production line 2 is given a differential weight of two compared to production line 1. Finally, at the third priority level, underutilization of production line 1 is given a differential weight of three compared to production line 2.

10.5 OVERVIEW: GOAL-PROGRAMMING MODELS

The examples presented in the previous section can be summarized by the following general goal-programming model

$$\text{Minimize } Z = \sum_{k=1}^{k} \sum_{i=1}^{l} P_k(w_{ik}^+ d_i^+ + w_{ik}^- d_i^-) \quad (10.21)$$

subject to

$$\sum_{j=1}^{n} a_{ij} x_j - d_i^+ + d_i^- = b_i, \quad \text{for}$$
$$i = 1, 2, \ldots, I \quad (10.22)$$

plus any original linear programming constraints involving the x_j, with

$$x_j, d_i^-, d_i^+ \quad + \geq 0 \quad (10.23)$$

WHERE

P_k = the preemptive priority ($P_k >>> P_{k+1}$) assigned to goal k;

w_{ik}^+, w_{ik}^- = the cardinal weights assigned to the deviational variables of goal i at priority level k;

d_i^-, d_i^+ = the negative and positive deviations associated with goal i;

a_{ij} = the technological coefficient associated with x_j in goal i;

b_i = the ith goal level.

In this general goal-programming model, note the following characteristics common to goal-programming models:

1. The objective function requires minimizing the weighted sum of the deviational variables, which may also be prioritized. Prioritization will be done in a preemptive manner, with the weights for the deviational variables reflecting the relative "penalty" for each unit deviation from the corresponding goal's target value.
2. Each of the goals of the model appears in a separate constraint with the right-hand-side value reflecting the target value for that goal.
3. Other constraints, reflecting limitations upon resources, are included just as they would be in any linear programming model.
4. Deviational variables are included for each of the goal constraints, and reflect the possible overachievement or underachievement of that goal.
5. All variables of the model—that is, both the decision variables, the x_j, and the deviational variables, the d_i^- and d_i^+—are restricted to be equal to, or greater than, zero.

A few other situations may arise in the formulation of goal-programming models. Instead of seeking to satisfy a goal exactly, we may have a case of a one-sided goal where g_k represents only a bound on the goal to be achieved. If g_k is a *lower bound goal*, it is written as the following inequality constraint

$$\sum_{j=1}^{n} a_{jk} x_i \geq g_k \qquad (10.24)$$

Then, any amount in excess of the goal g_k is acceptable, but any deviation below g_k should be avoided if possible. Thus we would change the linear programming formulation of the goal-programming model by deleting d_k^+ from the objective function, since we would only want to minimize the d_k^- deviation. Both d_k^+ and d_k^- would still appear in the constraint for the goal g_k, however, since it would be possible for both types of deviations to occur.

Similarly, if g_k is an *upper bound goal*, it is written as the following inequality constraint

$$\sum_{j=1}^{n} a_{jk} x_j \leq g_k \qquad (10.25)$$

Thus any amount in excess of the goal g_k is unacceptable, but any deviation below g_k is acceptable. Thus we would change the linear programming model by deleting d_k^- from the objective function, since we would only want to minimize the d_k^+ deviation. Both d_k^+ and d_k^- would still appear in the constraint for the goal g_k, however, since it would be possible for either type of deviation to occur.

10.6 SOLVING GOAL-PROGRAMMING PROBLEMS

The computational approaches used to solve goal-programming problems are based on the simplex procedure of linear programming. The choice of a com-

putational approach for a specific goal-programming problem is dependent on the structure of the goal-programming model that is being considered. Let us now consider various computational approaches to goal programming, using the goal-programming models that were formulated earlier in the chapter.

10.6.1 SOLVING GOAL-PROGRAMMING PROBLEMS USING STANDARD LINEAR PROGRAMMING TECHNIQUES

Recall that in considering the production scheduling situation of the Pegasus Company (i.e., refer back to Section 10.2) we initially developed a linear programming formulation, as given by (10.1), (10.2), and (10.3). The solution to this simple linear programming problem is $x_1 = 0$, $x_2 = 100$, $x_3 = 0$, with a total profit of $Z = \$700$.

We then reconsidered this problem situation with the addition of three equally ranked goals. Recall that the complete formulation for this equally ranked goals model was given by (10.11), (10.12), and (10.13). This goal-programming model can also be solved using standard linear programming techniques. The initial tableau for this problem is shown in Table 10.3. In constructing this initial tableau, the initial basic variables are d_1^- (deviational variable), d_2^- (deviational variable), d_3^- (deviational variable), and S_1 (slack variable). In this initial basic feasible solution $d_1^- = 750$, $d_2^- = 200$, $d_3^- = 50$, and $S = 100$. This solution is $\$750$ below (i.e., $d_1^- = 750$) the daily profit goal, 200 hours below (i.e., $d_2^- = 200$) the daily labor hours goal, and 50 units below (i.e., $d_3^- = 50$) the daily production goal for the "Swift Runner" model.

In Table 10.3 note that we have chosen not to show the current value of the objective function Z_j. Although we could compute such a value as the

TABLE 10.3 EQUALLY RANKED GOALS MODEL: INITIAL TABLEAU

c_b	BASIS	0 x_1	0 x_2	0 x_3	0 d_1^+	1 d_1^-	0 d_2^+	1 d_2^-	0 d_3^+	1 d_3^-	0 S_1	SOLUTION	TEST RATIOS
1	d_1^-	10	7	5	-1	1	0	0	0	0	0	750	$750/10 = 75$
1	d_2^-	3	2	1	0	0	-1	1	0	0	0	200	$200/3 = 66.7$
1	d_3^-	0	0	1	0	0	0	0	-1	1	0	50	—
0	S_1	②	1	1	0	0	0	0	0	0	1	100	$100/2 = 50$
	Z_j	13	9	7	-1	1	-1	1	-1	1	0		
	$c_j - Z_j$	-13	-9	-7	1	0	1	0	1	0	0		

TABLE 10.4 EQUALLY RANKED GOALS MODEL: FINAL TABLEAU

c_b	BASIS	0 x_1	0 x_2	0 x_3	0 d_1^+	1 d_1^-	0 d_2^+	1 d_2^-	0 d_3^+	1 d_3^-	0 S_1	SOLUTION
1	d_1^-	-4	0	-2	-1	1	0	0	0	0	-7	50
0	x_2	2	1	1	0	0	0	0	0	0	1	100
1	d_3^-	0	0	1	0	0	0	0	-1	1	0	50
0	d_2^+	1	0	1	0	0	1	-1	0	0	2	0
	Z_j	-4	0	-1	-1	1	0	0	-1	1	-7	
	$c_j - Z_j$	4	0	1	1	0	0	1	1	0	7	

sum of the current values of the three deviational variables (i.e., $Z_j = d_1^- + d_2^- + d_3^- = 750 + 200 + 50 = 1000$), this sum has no real meaning since it is composed of deviations that are measured in different units.

Since we are minimizing the objective function, we selected the smallest $c_j - Z_j$ value to enter the basis (i.e., x_1). Pivoting is accomplished using the usual simplex process, and the problem is solved in the usual manner. The final tableau (optimal solution) for this problem is shown in Table 10.4. This optimal solution indicates that 100 units of x_2 ("Flying Feet" model shoe) should be produced. This will minimize the equally ranked goals objective function to the greatest extent possible. The daily profit goal of $750 will be underachieved by $50, however, as indicated by the fact that the underachievement deviational variable $d_1^- = 50$. Similarly, the daily production goal of 50 pairs of "Swift Runner" shoes is underachieved by 50 pairs (i.e., none are produced). This is indicated by the fact that the underachievement deviational variable $d_3^- = 50$. Note finally that this solution *exactly* achieves the desired daily labor hour goal of 200 hours. This is indicated by the fact that d_2^- is not basic in the optimal solution, and that while d_2^+ is basic in the optimal solution, its value is $d_2^+ = 0$.

10.6.2 THE MODIFIED SIMPLEX METHOD OF GOAL PROGRAMMING

In Section 10.3 we formulated a goal-programming model having prioritized goals. The prioritized goal-programming model that was developed was given by (10.15), (10.16), and (10.17). Recall also that the priority rankings for this problem, P_1, P_2, and P_3, were preemptive. Therefore, to solve this prob-

lem we first want to minimize the deviation (d_3^-) associated with priority 1, then we want to minimize the deviation (d_1^-) associated with priority 2, and finally we want to minimize the deviation (d_2^-) associated with priority 3. To accomplish this, we must modify the simplex procedure to take into account these priority rankings.

In Table 10.5, the initial modified simplex tableau for the prioritized goal-programming model is presented. Using this modified simplex tableau, there are a number of characteristics of the *modified simplex method of goal programming* that we now explain.

1. The variables entry criterion (i.e., select the variable having the most negative $c_j - Z_j$ value as the variable to enter the basis for a minimization problem) is no longer expressed as a single row at the bottom of the simplex tableau. Instead, there is a separate Z_j row and $c_j - Z_j$ row for each of the P_1, P_2, P_3 preemptive priorities. This is necessary because we cannot add deviations from the production goal (P_1) to deviations from the profit goal (P_2) to deviations from the worker layoff goals (P_3), since their units are different. Thus we need three separate priority rows to properly account for each of the priorities. The usual practice is to place the priority rows from bottom to top in the simplex tableau. The Z_j values associated with the respective rows indicate the contributions to the objective function of the deviation associated with that priority level. For example, observe that $d_1^- = 750$, and recall that d_1^- was the deviation associated with priority 2. Observe further that the corresponding Z_j value associated with priority 2 is equal to 750.

TABLE 10.5 PRIORITY RANKED GOALS MODEL: INITIAL TABLEAU

c_b	BASIS		x_1 0	x_2 0	x_3 0	d_1^+ 0	d_1^- P_2	d_2^+ 0	d_2^- P_3	d_3^+ 0	d_3^- P_1	S_1 0	SOLUTION	TEST RATIOS
P_2	d_1^-		10	7	5	-1	1	0	0	0	0	0	750	$750/5 = 150$
P_3	d_2^-		3	2	1	0	0	-1	1	0	0	0	200	$200/1 = 200$
P_1	d_3^-		0	0	①	0	0	0	0	-1	1	0	50	$50/1 = 50$
0	S_1		2	1	1	0	0	0	0	0	0	1	100	$100/1 = 100$
	P_3	Z_j	3	2	1	0	0	-1	1	0	0	0	200	
		$c_j - Z_j$	-3	-2	-1	0	0	1	0	0	0	0		
	P_2	Z_j	10	7	5	-1	1	0	0	0	0	0	750	
		$c_j - Z_j$	-10	-7	-5	1	0	0	0	0	0	0		
	P_1	Z_j	0	0	1	0	0	0	0	-1	1	0	50	
		$c_j - Z_j$	0	0	-1	0	0	0	0	1	0	0		

2. The $c_j - Z_j$ value for any *column* is shown in the priority rows at the bottom of the tableau. For example, $c_1 - Z_1 = -3P_3 - 10P_2$; $c_2 - Z_2 = -2P_3 - 7P_2$; $c_3 - Z_3 = -1P_3 - 5P_2 - 1P_1$, and so forth.

3. In selecting the variable to enter the basis, we begin with the highest priority, P_1, and select as the variable to enter the basis that variable having the most negative value in that row. Thus, in Table 10.5, variable x_3 is chosen to enter the basis, since $c_3 - Z_3 = -1$ is the most negative value for priority P_1. If there was no negative $c_j - Z_j$ value in the P_1 row, we would have moved up in the tableau to the next most important priority, P_2, and would have examined the $c_j - Z_j$ values in that row. If there are no negative values in any of the priority rows, the optimal solution has been obtained.

4. In selecting the variable to remove from the basis, the usual linear programming variable removal criterion is employed. Accordingly, we compute the appropriate ratios for column three, and $50/1 = 50$ is the smallest positive value. Thus, row three (variable d_3^-) will be replaced in the next tableau. The pivot element "1" at the intersection of row three and column three has been circled in Table 10.5.

5. If we encounter a negative $c_j - Z_j$ value in one of the priority rows that has a positive $c_j - Z_j$ value in one of the priority rows beneath it, we do not consider it further. This

is done because the positive value means that deviations from the lower (and therefore more important) goal would be *increased* if we entered the associated variable into the basis. This must be avoided, since it will not improve the solution, and in fact will make it worse.

From the initial goal programming simplex tableau shown in Table 10.5 we proceed in the manner encompassed by the five steps just discussed. The resulting simplex tableaux are shown below in Tables 10.6 to 10.8.

The optimal solution to this goal-programming problem is presented in the final goal-programming simplex tableau shown as Table 10.8. From the optimal solution presented we see that daily production is

$$x_2 = 50 \text{ pairs of "Flying Feet" model shoes}$$

$$x_3 = 50 \text{ pairs of "Swift Runner" model shoes}$$

This solution meets the first prioritized goal, namely the daily production of 50 pairs of "Swift Runner" model shoes, and is indicated by the fact that $d_3^- = 0$ in the optimal solution. The second prioritized goal is underachieved by $150, and is indicated by the fact that $d_1^- = 150$ in the optimal solution. The third prioritized goal is underachieved by 50 hours, and is indicated by the fact that $d_2^- = 50$ in the optimal solution.

In summary, for the set of priority goals and resource constraints given by (10.15), (10.16), and (10.17), the Pegasus Company should produce

TABLE 10.6 PRIORITY RANKED GOALS MODEL: SECOND TABLEAU

c_b	BASIS		0 x_1	0 x_2	0 x_3	0 d_1^+	P_2 d_1^-	0 d_2^+	P_3 d_2^-	0 d_3^+	P_1 d_3^-	0 S_1	SOLUTION	TEST RATIOS
P_2	d_1^-		10	7	0	−1	1	0	0	5	−5	0	500	500/10 = 50
P_3	d_2^-		3	2	0	0	0	−1	1	1	−1	0	150	150/3 = 50
0	x_3		0	0	1	0	0	0	0	−1	1	0	50	—
0	S_1		②	1	0	0	0	0	0	1	−1	1	50	50/2 = 25
P_3	Z_j		3	2	0	0	0	−1	1	1	−1	0	150	
	$c_j - Z_j$		−3	−2	0	0	0	1	0	−1	1	0		
P_2	Z_j		10	7	0	−1	1	0	0	5	−5	0	500	
	$c_j - Z_j$		−10	−7	0	1	0	0	0	−5	5	0		
P_1	Z_j		0	0	0	0	0	0	0	0	0	0	0	
	$c_j - Z_j$		0	0	0	0	0	0	0	0	1	0		

TABLE 10.7 PRIORITY RANKED GOALS MODEL: THIRD TABLEAU

c_b	BASIS		0 x_1	0 x_2	0 x_3	0 d_1^+	P_2 d_1^-	0 d_2^+	P_3 d_2^-	0 d_3^+	P_1 d_3^-	0 S_1	SOLUTION	TEST RATIOS
P_2	d_1^-		0	2	0	−1	1	0	0	0	0	−5	250	250/2 = 125
P_3	d_2^-		0	$\frac{1}{2}$	0	0	0	−1	1	$\frac{1}{2}$	$-\frac{1}{2}$	$-\frac{3}{2}$	75	75/$\frac{1}{2}$ = 150
0	x_3		0	0	1	0	0	0	0	−1	1	0	50	—
0	x_1		1	⑴⁄₂	0	0	0	0	0	$\frac{1}{2}$	$-\frac{1}{2}$	$\frac{1}{2}$	25	25/$\frac{1}{2}$ = 50
P_3	Z_j		0	$\frac{1}{2}$	0	0	0	−1	1	$\frac{1}{2}$	$-\frac{1}{2}$	$-\frac{3}{2}$	75	
	$c_j - Z_j$		0	$-\frac{1}{2}$	0	0	0	1	0	$-\frac{1}{2}$	$\frac{1}{2}$	$\frac{3}{2}$		
P_2	Z_j		0	2	0	−1	1	0	0	0	0	−5	250	
	$c_j - Z_j$		0	−2	0	1	0	0	0	0	0	5		
P_1	Z_j		0	0	0	0	0	0	0	0	0	0	0	
	$c_j - Z_j$		0	0	0	0	0	0	0	0	1	0		

TABLE 10.8 PRIORITY RANKED GOALS MODEL: FINAL TABLEAU

c_b	BASIS		0 x_1	0 x_2	0 x_3	0 d_1^+	P_2 d_1^-	0 d_2^+	P_3 d_2^-	0 d_3^+	P_1 d_3^-	0 S_1	SOLUTION
P_2	d_1^-		−4	0	0	−1	1	0	0	−2	2	−7	150
P_3	d_2^-		−1	0	0	0	0	−1	1	−1	1	−2	50
0	x_3		0	0	1	0	0	0	0	−1	1	0	50
0	x_2		2	1	0	0	0	0	0	1	−1	1	50
P_3	Z_j		−1	0	0	0	0	−1	1	−1	1	−2	50
	$c_j - Z_j$		1	0	0	0	0	1	0	1	−1	2	
P_2	Z_j		−4	0	0	−1	1	0	0	−2	2	−7	150
	$c_j - Z_j$		4	0	0	1	0	0	0	2	−2	7	
P_1	Z_j		0	0	0	0	0	0	0	0	0	0	0
	$c_j - Z_j$		0	0	0	0	0	0	0	0	1	0	

TABLE 10.9   WEIGHTED PRIORITY RANKED GOALS MODEL: INITIAL TABLEAU

c_b	BASIS		0 x_1	0 x_2	0 d_1^+	P_1 d_1^-	$1P_2$ d_2^+	$3P_3$ d_2^-	$2P_2$ d_3^+	$1P_3$ d_3^-	SOLUTION	TEST RATIOS
P_1	d_1^-		4	2	-1	1	0	0	0	0	250	$250/4 = 62.5$
$3P_3$	d_2^-		1	0	0	0	-1	1	0	0	40	$40/1 = 40$
$1P_3$	d_3^-		0	1	0	0	0	0	-1	1	40	—
	P_3	Z_j	3	1	0	0	-3	3	-1	1	160	
		$c_j - Z_j$	-3	-1	0	0	3	0	1	0		
	P_2	Z_j	0	0	0	0	0	0	0	0	0	
		$c_j - Z_j$	0	0	0	0	1	0	2	0		
	P_1	Z_j	4	2	-1	1	0	0	0	0	250	
		$c_j - Z_j$	-4	-2	1	0	0	0	0	0		

(daily) 50 pairs of "Flying Feet" model shoes and 50 pairs of "Swift Runner" model shoes. If this is done

1. the daily production goal of 50 pairs of "Swift Runner" model shoes will be exactly satisfied ($d_3^- = 0$);
2. the daily profit goal of $750 will be underachieved ($d_1^- = 150$), since $10($x_1 = 0$) + $7($x_2 = 50$) + $5($x_3 = 50$) = $600 (<$750 by $150);
3. the daily labor hour goal of 200 hours will be underachieved ($d_2^- = 50$), since $3($x_1 = 0$) + 2($x_2 = 50$) + 1($x_3 = 50$) = 150$ hours (<200 hours by 50 hours).

Weighted priority goal-programming models are also solved using the modified simplex procedure previously illustrated. Let us reconsider the Pawley's Island Hammocks, Inc. problem situation presented in Section 10.4. The weighted goal-programming formulation of this problem was given by (10.18), (10.19), and (10.20). Recall that the priority rankings for this problem were preemptive and that the deviational variables associated with the second and third priority factors, P_2 and P_3, were weighted.

The initial goal-programming simplex tableau for this problem is presented in Table 10.9. The modified simplex procedure discussed earlier is again used to solve the problem. For the sake of brevity, the intermediate goal-programming simplex tableaux will not be illustrated. The final goal-programming simplex tableau (optimal solution) is presented in Table 10.10.

TABLE 10.10   WEIGHTED PRIORITY RANKED GOALS MODEL: FINAL TABLEAU

c_b	BASIS		0 x_1	0 x_2	0 d_1^+	P_1 d_1^-	$1P_2$ d_2^+	$3P_3$ d_2^-	$2P_2$ d_3^+	$1P_3$ d_3^-	SOLUTION
$1P_2$	d_2^+		0	0	$-\frac{1}{4}$	$\frac{1}{4}$	1	-1	$\frac{1}{2}$	$-\frac{1}{2}$	2.5
0	x_1		1	0	$-\frac{1}{4}$	$\frac{1}{4}$	0	0	$\frac{1}{2}$	$-\frac{1}{2}$	42.5
0	x_2		0	1	0	0	0	0	-1	1	40
	P_3	Z_j	0	0	0	0	0	0	0	0	0
		$c_j - Z_j$	0	0	0	0	0	3	0	1	
	P_2	Z_j	0	0	$-\frac{1}{4}$	$\frac{1}{4}$	1	-1	$\frac{1}{2}$	$-\frac{1}{2}$	2.5
		$c_j - Z_j$	0	0	$\frac{1}{4}$	$-\frac{1}{4}$	0	1	$\frac{3}{2}$	$\frac{1}{2}$	
	P_1	Z_j	0	0	0	0	0	0	0	0	0
		$c_j - Z_j$	0	0	0	1	0	0	0	0	

The final goal-programming simplex tableau shown in Table 10.10 indicates that $x_1 = 42.5$ hours of production line 1 and $x_2 = 40$ hours of production line 2 are required. This result exactly satisfies the first priority goal (the desired production of 250 hammocks), since

$$4(x_1 = 42.5) + 2(x_2 = 40)$$
$$= 250 \quad \text{(Exactly)} \quad (10.26)$$

Thus in the optimal solution the deviational variable, d_1^-, is equal to zero. With respect to the second priority goals, we cannot avoid overutilization of the first production line and still satisfy the first priority. Thus in the optimal solution $d_2^+ = 2.5$ (i.e., we utilize 42.5 hours on production line 1). Note that with respect to the second priority the most heavily weighted second priority goal (i.e., avoid overutilization of production line 2) is satisfied exactly. The third priority goals, which involve the underutilization of production lines 1 and 2, are satisfied. Thus we overutilize production line 1 (i.e., by 2.5 hours) and we exactly utilize the production hours available on production line 2. Therefore, we observe that $d_2^- = 0$ in the optimal solution.

10.7 SPECIAL PROBLEMS IN GOAL PROGRAMMING

The computational procedures that are used in goal programming are based upon the simplex algorithm of linear programming. Therefore, just as in linear programming, a number of special problems can occur in solving goal-programming problems. These special problems are now briefly reviewed.

10.7.1 ALTERNATIVE OPTIMAL SOLUTIONS

Alternative optimal solutions can occur in goal programming, just as in linear programming, and will be indicated by the presence of an entire column of zeros in the $c_j - Z_j$ rows for a nonbasic variable with the existence of at least one positive a_{ij} element in the corresponding column. The alternative optimal solution is determined by computing a new tableau, using the standard iterative procedure described above.

10.7.2 UNBOUNDED SOLUTIONS

In most real-world goal-programming problems unbounded solutions do not occur, since every goal is constrained and the goal tends to be set at a level that is not easily reached. It is possible, however, to omit important constraints in a goal-programming problem, as well as have an unrealistic priority structure. When this happens, an unbounded solution could occur. Such an unbounded solution would require the decision maker to reanalyze the goal structure of the problem.

10.7.3 INFEASIBLE SOLUTIONS

Infeasible solutions occur in linear programming where absolute constraints, which are always present, may be incompatible. In goal programming, infeasibility is generally not a problem, because deviational variables are employed in an attempt to satisfy various goals, which are written as constraints. Nevertheless, a type of infeasibility can occur in goal programming if we establish a set of absolute objectives at the highest priority level. An infeasibility for this situation represents an unimplementable solution and is indicated by a solution with a negative $c_j - Z_j$ value for some nonbasic variable associated with the highest priority level (i.e., with some absolute goal). This means that the satisfaction of this absolute objective was not completely achieved. In practice, this indicates that either the absolute objectives should be modified (i.e., they do not have to be as absolute as first stated) or that changes in the problem environment (e.g., increases in the limited resources) need to be considered.

10.7.4 TIE FOR ENTERING BASIC VARIABLE

A tie for the entering basic variable can occur between the $c_j - Z_j$ values in any row (i.e., for any priority level) of the goal-programming tableau. It is quite possible that two or more columns can have exactly the same negative $c_j - Z_j$ value at this highest unattained priority goal. As in linear programming, this tie can be broken arbitrarily.

10.7.5 TIE FOR LEAVING BASIC VARIABLE

In the goal-programming simplex process, the variable selected for removal from the basis is determined as the smallest ratio that is computed when the coefficients of the incoming column are divided into the Solution values. If two or more rows have the same ratio, the tie may be broken by selecting the row having the highest associated priority level (i.e., by referring to the priority levels as indicated in the $\bar{c}_b$ column). In some instances, however, the variables being considered for removal will not have associated priority levels. In such cases, the tie can be broken arbitrarily. Theoretically, this could cause degeneracy in goal-programming problems, but this has not occurred in practice.

10.8 SENSITIVITY ANALYSIS IN GOAL PROGRAMMING

Application of goal programming, particularly when preemptive priorities are utilized, may afford a number of difficulties for the decision maker. As discussed by Zeleny,[7] the preemptive weights version of goal programming has a number of problems associated with its use. For example, if this approach is incompatible with the utility preferences of the decision maker, it can lead the solutions that are dominated, and it can fail to identify an unbounded solution.

The preemptive weights used in goal programming are based upon the ordering of the vectors in a solution according to the importance of their components. It can be shown, however, that no utility function can be constructed that is compatible with the ordering required by the use of the preemptive weights. Consequently, decision makers who utilize utility functions are not likely to accept the results of preemptive goal programming.

A goal-programming solution can also turn out to be dominated, which means that it will not be the best solution among the alternative solutions that are available. In goal programming, goals are

set a priori, without being able to explore the feasible region for the solution. Therefore, the goal-programming approach, using preemptive or other types of weighting systems, can lead to suboptimal, or dominated solutions, because of its reliance on the principle of satisficing. Similarly, an unbounded solution can go undetected when goal programming is used, since the goals are determined a priori to the feasible region of the solution being examined.

As was the case for linear programming, sensitivity analysis can be very valuable in goal programming. Because of the problems just noted, and because of the general uncertainty concerning the model parameters in real-world problems, sensitivity analysis should be a part of the goal-programming process. A detailed discussion of sensitivity analysis in goal programming is beyond the level of this textbook, but the following are among the sensitivity analysis questions the decision maker should examine.

1. How does changing the priority rankings affect the optimal solution?
2. How does changing the target levels of the goals affect the optimal solution?
3. What are the relative tradeoffs among the goals of the problem?

Changes in the priority ranking in the objective function can have a major impact on the optimal solution. One type of sensitivity analysis in goal programming involves the determination of the impact on the optimal solution of reordering the priority rankings.

As noted previously, goal programming is a satisficing procedure that tries to attain prespecified target levels for various goals. Another type of sensitivity analysis tries to determine the impact of changes in the prespecified target level for various goals.

A final type of sensitivity analysis involves the examination of the relative tradeoffs among the goals of the problem. To do this the decision maker examines the optimal tableau to see if any of the deviational variables can be reduced. If any of them can, it will involve a tradeoff with a variable that is already basic, and will thereby reduce the level of a goal in the optimal solution. The extent of this

---

[7]M. Zeleny, *Multiple Criteria Decision Making.* New York: McGraw-Hill, 1982, p. 295.

tradeoff can be determined by analyzing the optimal tableau.

10.9 SOLVING GOAL-PROGRAMMING PROBLEMS USING A COMPUTER

There are several computer software packages available for solving goal-programming problems. These software packages are available for both mainframe computers and for microcomputers. The quantity and availability of goal-programming software packages is limited, however, compared to that available for linear programming or the transportation method.

Typical of the goal-programming software packages that are available are two computer programs described by Schniederjans.[8] The first program, written in FORTRAN, can be used on macro- (i.e., mainframe) or minicomputer systems. The parameter limits dimensioned in this code are 150 goal constraints, 150 decision variables, and 10 preemptive priority levels. The second program, written in BASIC, is designed to be used on a personal or microcomputer system. The parameter limits in this code are 35 goal constraints, 10 decision variables, and 9 preemptive priority levels.

To illustrate the use of the microcomputer program we solve the prioritized goal-programming model given earlier by (10.15), (10.16), and (10.17). You will recall that this goal-programming formulation had three goal constraints, each with a positive and a negative deviational variable. It also had one structural constraint. The microcomputer program requires that in the initial basic feasible solution the basic variables are the negative deviational variables (i.e., the d_i^-). This means that each constraint that does not have a negative deviational variable, d_i^-, must be given one in order to determine the initial basic feasible solution. Consequently, the structural constraint is written with both a positive and a negative deviational variable, and in the objective function the positive deviational variable is given the highest priority P_1. This

---

[8]Marc J. Schniederjans, *Linear Goal Programming.* Princeton, N.J.: Petrocelli, 1984, p. 113 and 201.

ensures that the structural constraint will be satisfied as a less-than-or-equal-to inequality. This restructured goal-programming problem being solved by the microcomputer code is as follows.

$$\text{Minimize } Z = P_1 d_4^+ + P_2 d_3^- + P_2 d_1^- + P_3 d_2^- \quad (10.27)$$

subject to

$$
\begin{aligned}
10x_1 + 7x_2 + 5x_3 - d_1^+ + d_1^- &= 750 \\
3x_1 + 2x_2 + 1x_3 - d_2^+ + d_2^- &= 200 \\
1x_3 - d_3^+ + d_3^- &= 50 \\
2x_1 + 1x_2 + 1x_3 - d_4^+ + d_4^- &= 100 \quad (10.28)
\end{aligned}
$$

with

$$x_1, x_2, x_3, d_1^+, d_1^-, d_2^+, d_2^-, d_3^+, d_3^-, d_4^+, d_4^- \geq 0 \quad (10.29)$$

The solution produced by the microcomputer program appears in Figure 10.1.

Note that the output produced by this program closely parallels the tableaux shown as Tables 10.5, 10.6, 10.7, and 10.8. The solution produced by this program indicates that $d_1^- = 150$, $d_2^- = 50$, $x_3 = 50$, and $x_2 = 0$, with the daily profit goal being underachieved by $150 and daily labor hour goal being underachieved by 50 hours. These results are, of course, identical to those we obtained by working the problem manually.

10.10 SUMMARY

Decision making in modern organizations often involves situations in which the manager would like to consider more than one goal or objective. Analyzing problems with goal programming provides the manager with the ability to consider multiple goals or objectives. It is an important procedure for the solution of multiobjective decision-making problems. In this chapter we have shown how several types of goal-programming problems can be formulated and solved, and have outlined special problems and sensitivity analysis issues in goal programming. An application review that shows how goal programming has been used in practice is included at the end of the chapter.

```
D 1  -  3                          WT  1
D 2  -  4                          WT  1
D 3  -  2                          WT  1
D 4  -  0                          WT  0
D 1  +  0                          WT  0
D 2  +  0                          WT  0
D 3  +  0                          WT  0
D 4  +  1                          WT  1

COEFFICIENTS IN TABLEAU:

D 1-      750.00     10.00   7.00   5.00   1.00   0.00    0.00    0.00   -1.00
     0.00      0.00    0.00
D 2-      200.00      3.00   2.00   1.00   0.00   1.00    0.00    0.00    0.00
    -1.00      0.00    0.00
D 3-       50.00      0.00   0.00   1.00   0.00   0.00    1.00    0.00    0.00
     0.00     -1.00    0.00
D 4-      100.00      2.00   1.00   1.00   0.00   0.00    0.00    1.00    0.00
     0.00      0.00   -1.00

VALUES IN ZJ-CJ:

P 4       200.00      3.00   2.00   1.00   0.00   0.00    0.00    0.00    0.00
    -1.00      0.00    0.00
P 3       750.00     10.00   7.00   5.00   0.00   0.00    0.00    0.00   -1.00
     0.00      0.00    0.00
P 2        50.00      0.00   0.00   1.00   0.00   0.00    0.00    0.00    0.00
     0.00     -1.00    0.00
P 1         0.00      0.00   0.00   0.00   0.00   0.00    0.00    0.00    0.00
     0.00      0.00   -1.00
PIVOT COLUMN = 3
PIVOT ROW = 3

COEFFICIENTS IN TABLEAU:

D 1-      500.00     10.00   7.00   0.00   1.00   0.00   -5.00    0.00   -1.00
     0.00      5.00    0.00
D 2-      150.00      3.00   2.00   0.00   0.00   1.00   -1.00    0.00    0.00
    -1.00      1.00    0.00
X 3        50.00      0.00   0.00   1.00   0.00   0.00    1.00    0.00    0.00
     0.00     -1.00    0.00
D 4-       50.00      2.00   1.00   0.00   0.00   0.00   -1.00    1.00    0.00
     0.00      1.00   -1.00

VALUES IN ZJ-CJ:

P 4       150.00      3.00   2.00   0.00   0.00   0.00   -1.00    0.00    0.00
    -1.00      1.00    0.00
P 3       500.00     10.00   7.00   0.00   0.00   0.00   -5.00    0.00   -1.00
     0.00      5.00    0.00
P 2         0.00      0.00   0.00   0.00   0.00   0.00   -1.00    0.00    0.00
     0.00      0.00    0.00
P 1         0.00      0.00   0.00   0.00   0.00   0.00    0.00    0.00    0.00
```

FIGURE 10.1 MICROCOMPUTER PROGRAM OUTPUT: PRIORITIZED GOAL-PROGRAMMING MODEL.

```
COEFFICIENTS IN TABLEAU:

D 1-       250.00      0.00   2.00   0.00   1.00   0.00    0.00   -5.00   -1.00
            0.00      0.00   5.00
D 2-        75.00      0.00   0.50   0.00   0.00   1.00    0.50   -1.50    0.00
           -1.00     -0.50   1.50
X 3         50.00      0.00   0.00   1.00   0.00   0.00    1.00    0.00    0.00
            0.00     -1.00   0.00
X 1         25.00      1.00   0.50   0.00   0.00   0.00   -0.50    0.50    0.00
            0.00      0.50  -0.50

VALUES IN ZJ-CJ:

P 4         75.00      0.00   0.50   0.00   0.00   0.00    0.50   -1.50    0.00
           -1.00     -0.50   1.50
P 3        250.00      0.00   2.00   0.00   0.00   0.00    0.00   -5.00   -1.00
            0.00      0.00   5.00
P 2          0.00      0.00   0.00   0.00   0.00   0.00   -1.00    0.00    0.00
            0.00      0.00   0.00
P 1          0.00      0.00   0.00   0.00   0.00   0.00    0.00    0.00    0.00
            0.00      0.00  -1.00
PIVOT COLUMN = 2
PIVOT ROW = 4

COEFFICIENTS IN TABLEAU:

D 1-       150.00     -4.00   0.00   0.00   1.00   0.00    2.00   -7.00   -1.00
            0.00     -2.00   7.00
D 2-        50.00     -1.00   0.00   0.00   0.00   1.00    1.00   -2.00    1.00
           -1.00     -1.00   2.00
X 3         50.00      0.00   0.00   1.00   0.00   0.00    1.00    0.00    0.00
            0.00     -1.00   0.00
X 2         50.00      2.00   1.00   0.00   0.00   0.00   -1.00    1.00    0.00
            0.00      1.00  -1.00

VALUES IN ZJ-CJ:

P 4         50.00     -1.00   0.00   0.00   0.00   0.00    1.00   -2.00    0.00
           -1.00     -1.00   2.00
P 3        150.00     -4.00   0.00   0.00   0.00   0.00    2.00   -7.00   -1.00
            0.00     -2.00   7.00
P 2          0.00      0.00   0.00   0.00   0.00   0.00   -1.00    0.00    0.00
            0.00      0.00   0.00
P 1          0.00      0.00   0.00   0.00   0.00   0.00    0.00    0.00    0.00
            0.00      0.00  -1.00

SOLUTION VARIABLES ARE:

D 1-                           150
D 2-                           50
X 3                            50
X 2                            50

UNACHIEVED GOALS ARE:

P 3                            150
P 4                            50
```

FIGURE 10.1 CONTINUED

GLOSSARY

Commensurable Goals Goals that are measured in the same units.

Conflicting Goal Two goals are conflicting if the level of achievement of one of the goals cannot be increased without simultaneously reducing the level of achievement of the other goal.

Deviational Variables Auxiliary variables in a goal constraint equation that measure the underachievement or overachievement of the specified aspiration level. A negative deviation variable ($d_i^- \geq 0$) reflects the amount by which aspiration level i is underachieved, while a positive deviational variable ($d_i^+ \geq 0$) indicates the amount by which aspiration level i is exceeded, where $d_i^- \cdot d_i^+ = 0$.

Deviations Failure to achieve a particular goal will result in a positive or negative deviation from the goal.

Differential Weights Cardinal weights used in weighted linear goal programming to weight deviational variables.

Goal A numerical expression of an objective in terms of the aspiration level associated with that objective.

Goal Constraints A set of constraints that corresponds to the goals expressed by the decision maker.

Goal Programming A technique that extends linear programming to allow the consideration of multiple objectives or goals, rather than the single objective of a linear programming formulation.

Lower Bound Goal A goal from which a positive deviation is acceptable but a negative deviation is to be avoided.

Modified Simplex Method of Goal Programming A modification of the simplex algorithm used in solving preemptive linear goal programming problems that allows for the achievement of the highest priority goal before considering the next highest priority goal, and so on.

Nonconflicting Goals Two goals are nonconflicting if the level of achievement of one of the goals can be increased without simultaneously reducing the level of achievement of the other goal.

Preemptive Priority Factors Priority factors $P_j(j = 1, \ldots, K$; where K is the number of objectives in the model) that have the following relationship

$$P_1 >>> P_2 >>> \cdots >>> P_j >>> P_{j+1}$$

where $>>>$ implies "infinitely greater than".

Preemptive Priority Goal Programming A frequently used goal-programming formulation in which the deviational variables in the objective function are assigned preemptive priority factors that represent an ordinal ranking of goals. Each of the goals is considered in order of priority; low-priority goals may be satisfied only after higher priority goals have been satisfied to the fullest possible extent. Deviational variables in the objective function that are associated with incommensurable goals are assigned different priority factors.

Resource or Structural Constraints   The set of constraints involving resource utilization that are included in the goal-programming formulation. These constraints are typically the same as those that would appear in the linear programming formulation of the problem.

Satisficing   A concept that states that the decision maker may often be satisfied with achieving a satisfactory level for multiple objectives rather than determining the optimal level for a single objective.

Upper Bound Goal   A goal from which a negative deviation is acceptable, but a positive deviation is to be avoided.

Weighted Linear Goal Programming   A goal-programming formulation in which the deviational variables in the objective function are assigned cardinal weights, thus allowing solution by the simplex algorithm.

Selected References

Charnes, A., and W. W. Cooper. 1961. *Management Models and Industrial Applications of Linear Programming.* New York: Wiley.

Cohen, J. L. 1978. *Multiobjective Programming and Planning.* New York: Academic Press.

Fatseas, V. A. 1973. *Multi-Goal Decision Model Solutions by Goal Programming.* Sydney, Australia: Univ. of New South Wales Press.

Halter, A. N., and G. W. Dean. 1971. *Decisions Under Uncertainty.* Cincinnati, Ohio: South-Western.

Ignizio, J. P. 1976. *Goal Programming and Extensions.* Lexington, Mass.: Heath.

Ignizio, J. P. 1982. *Linear Programming in Single & Multiple Objective Systems.* Englewood Cliffs, N.J.: Prentice-Hall.

Ijiri, Y. 1965. *Management Goals and Accounting for Control.* Chicago, Ill.: Rand McNally.

Jaaskelaninen, V. 1973. *Accounting and Mathematical Programming.* Helsinki, Finland: Research Institute for Business and Economics.

Lee, S. M. 1972. *Goal Programming for Decision Analysis.* Philadelphia, Pa.: Auerbach.

Lee, S. M., and L. J. Moore. 1975. *Introduction to Decision Science.* New York: Petrocelli/Charter.

Schniederjans, M. J. 1984. *Linear Goal Programming.* Princeton, N.J.: Petrocelli.

Zeleny, M. 1982. *Multiple Criteria Decision Making.* New York: McGraw-Hill.

Discussion Questions

1. Discuss the similarities and differences of goal programming and linear programming.

2. What advantage does goal programming afford the decision maker, as compared to linear programming?

3. Explain how deviational variables are used in goal programming.

4. What is the difference between a goal constraint and a structural constraint in goal programming?

5. What does the term "satisficing" mean in the context of goal programming?

6. What does it mean to prioritize goals in a goal-programming model? How does this prioritization affect the solution to the model?

7. How does the modified simplex tableau used in goal programming differ from the simplex tableau used in linear programming?

8. What are preemptive priority factors in goal programming?

9. Explain what is meant by a weighted goal-programming model. How can such a model be solved?

10. Explain how the weighting of prioritized goals affects the solution to a goal-programming model.

11. How is optimality determined when the modified goal-programming algorithm is employed?

PROBLEMS

1. The production manager of the Kent Company is faced with the problem of job allocation between his two production teams. The production rate of team A is 6 units per hour, while the production rate of team B is 4 units per hour. Both production teams work 40 hours per week. The production manager has prioritized the following goals for the coming week.

   P_1: Avoid underachievement of the desired production level of 600 units.
   P_2: Avoid overtime operations for team A beyond 5 hours.
   P_3: The sum of the overtime for both teams (i.e., 80 hours) should be minimized.
   P_4: Any underutilization of regular working hours should be avoided.

   Formulate and solve as a goal-programming model.

2. Reformulate the preceding problem with priority 3 and priority 4 assigned differential weights according to the relative productivity of the two teams.

3. The Super Stick Corporation produces two types of industrial adhesives: "Regular" and "Extra Strength." A batch (1000 gallons) of Regular requires 10 production hours and a batch (1000 gallons) of Extra Strength requires 12 production hours. The sales forecast for the coming week for the Regular adhesive is 20,000 gallons (i.e., 200 production hours), and for the Extra Strength adhesive is 25,000 gallons (i.e., 300 production hours). The Super Stick Corporation has a regular-time available production capacity of 450 hours. If more than 450 hours are required, overtime costs are incurred. If less than 450 hours are used, layoff costs result. If the sales forecasts are not met, however, the company suffers from loss of goodwill,

and if the sales forecasts are exceeded, inventory costs are incurred. Formulate and solve as a goal-programming model, in order to minimize overtime, layoffs, loss of goodwill, and inventory costs.

4. Joe Studley is a wrestler for Irmo High School and must lose weight in order to compete in the 175-pound weight class in the South Carolina state wrestling tournament. He has developed a weekly weight loss diet plan based on five food items. The calories and protein associated with one unit of these items and their unit costs are shown in the following table.

FOOD ITEM	CALORIES/ UNIT	PROTEIN/ UNIT	COST/ UNIT
Cottage cheese	200	1.2	1.20
Fruit	225	2.5	0.70
Yogurt	175	1.0	1.30
Whole wheat bread	250	1.2	0.90
Granola bar	300	1.8	1.50

Joe has a weekly food budget of $35.00, and must restrict his weekly intake of calories to at most 15,000 in order to lose weight. In order to be strong enough to wrestle effectively, Joe must have a weekly intake of at least 50 milligrams of protein. Joe's favorite food item is the granola bar, followed by yogurt, fruit, cottage cheese, and whole wheat bread, and he would prefer at least 10 units of each. Formulate and solve as a goal-programming model.

5. A foundry produces three types of large metal castings. To produce casting A requires four hours, to produce casting B requires two hours, and to produce casting C requires one hour. The foundry has a regular time capacity of 40 hours per week. The current weekly demand for its castings are as follows

Casting A—20 castings;
Casting B—20 castings;
Casting C—25 castings.

The manager of the foundry has established the following set of operating goals, which are considered to be of equal importance.

a. Avoid any weekly underutilization of production capacity.
b. Avoid weekly overtime operation of the plant beyond 10 hours.
c. Satisfy the weekly needs of a new prospective customer for 15 "A" castings and 20 "C" castings.
d. Satisfy the weekly demand for castings.

Formulate and solve as a goal-programming model.

6. The foundry manager, after considering the solution to the equally weighted goal programming problem, has decided to prioritize the

goals. The four goals shown previously are prioritized as follows:

P_1: Satisfy the weekly demand for castings.
P_2: Avoid weekly overtime operation of the plant beyond 10 hours.
P_3: Satisfy the weekly needs of a new prospective customer for 15 "A" castings and 20 "C" castings.
P_4: Avoid weekly underutilization of production capacity.

Formulate and solve as a goal-programming model.

7. The Chariot Corporation has just opened a new hotel in Columbia, South Carolina. It is currently attempting to hire a staff for this new hotel. The staff will be composed of 100 professional people and 200 nonprofessional people. If possible, the Chariot Corporation wishes to recruit minorities and women. The estimated costs associated with recruiting are shown in the following table.

	PROFESSIONAL PEOPLE	NONPROFESSIONAL PEOPLE
Women	1100	500
Minorities	1500	700
All Other	800	400

The Chariot Corporation has established a budget of $200,000 for its recruiting efforts. The management of the Chariot Corporation has established the following overall recruiting goals.

Goal 1: Have at least 50 percent of the new work force consist of women.
Goal 2: Have at least 35 percent of the new work force consist of minorities. (Note: A minority woman is counted both as a woman and a minority employee.)
Goal 3: Minimize the overall cost of recruiting.

Formulate and solve as a goal-programming model.

8. Solve the following goal-programming problem

$$\text{Minimize } Z = P_1 d_1^- + P_2 d_3^+ + 4P_3 d_2^- + 3P_3 d_3^-$$

subject to:

$$x_1 + 2x_2 - d_1^+ + d_1^- = 100$$
$$2x_1 \qquad - d_2^+ + d_2^- = 80$$
$$x_2 - d_3^+ + d_3^- = 70$$

with

$$x_1, x_2, d_1^-, d_1^+, d_2^-, d_2^+, d_3^-, d_3^+ \geq 0$$

9. Solve the following goal-programming problem

$$\text{Minimize } Z = 2P_1d_1^- + 3P_2d_2^- + 2P_2d_3^- + 2P_3d_4^+$$

subject to:

$$5x_1 + 3x_2 - d_1^+ + d_1^- = 1500$$
$$x_1 \quad\quad - d_2^+ + d_2^- = 700$$
$$x_2 - d_3^+ + d_3^- = 400$$
$$d_2^+ \quad - d_4^+ + d_4^- = 200$$

with

$$x_1,\ x_2,\ d_1^-,\ d_1^+,\ d_2^-,\ d_2^+,\ d_3^-,\ d_3^+,\ d_4^-,\ d_4^+ \geq 0$$

10. Solve the following goal-programming problem

$$\text{Minimize } Z = P_1d_1^- + P_2d_2^+ + 4P_3d_3^+ + 3P_3d_4^+ + 4P_4d_4^- + 3P_4d_3^-$$

subject to:

$$3x_1 + 5x_2 - d_1^+ + d_1^- = 100$$
$$x_1 \quad\quad - d_2^+ + d_2^- = 15$$
$$x_2 - d_3^+ + d_3^- = 10$$
$$x_1 \quad\quad - d_4^+ + d_4^- = 8$$

with

$$x_1,\ x_2,\ d_1^-,\ d_1^+,\ d_2^-,\ d_2^+,\ d_3^-,\ d_3^+,\ d_4^-,\ d_4^+ \geq 0$$

11. Solve the following goal-programming problem

$$\text{Minimize } Z = P_1d_1^+ + P_2d_4^- + 3P_3d_2^- + P_4d_2^+ + 3P_4d_3^+$$

subject to:

$$4x_1 + 2x_2 - d_1^+ + d_1^- = 2500$$
$$3x_1 + 5x_2 - d_2^+ + d_2^- = 1000$$
$$x_2 - d_3^+ + d_3^- = 400$$
$$x_1 \quad\quad - d_4^+ + d_4^- = 100$$

with

$$x_1,\ x_2,\ d_1^-,\ d_1^+,\ d_2^-,\ d_2^+,\ d_3^-,\ d_3^+,\ d_4^-,\ d_4^+ \geq 0$$

12. Dynamic Marketing Programs, Inc. has developed three 2 year marketing programs for a condominium builder. The condominium builder is willing to spend up to $80,000 on marketing in year 1 and up to $70,000 in year 2. Relevant data for each of the three marketing programs are given in the following table.

MARKETING PROGRAM	UNITS OF NET PROFIT	UNITS SOLD	COST (YR. 1)	COST (YR. 2)
1	$500,000	30	70,000	50,000
2	$400,000	30	10,000	30,000
3	$500,000	20	40,000	20,000

Dynamic Marketing Programs has a goal of maximizing units sold and net profit. Formulate as a goal-programming problem.

13. The High Flyer Investment Company has developed a list of seven investment alternatives, with corresponding financial factors, for a 10-year investment horizon. These investments, with their corresponding financial factors, are presented in the following table:

INVESTMENT ALTERNATIVE	LENGTH OF INVESTMENT (YEARS)	ANNUAL RATE OF RETURN(%)	RISK COEFFICIENT	GROWTH POTENTIAL(%)
1. Treasury bills	4	9	1	0
2. Common stock	7	13	5	18
3. Corporate bonds	8	12	4	10
4. Real estate	6	23	8	32
5. Growth mutual fund	10	18	6	20
6. Savings and loan	5	10	3	7
7. Cash	0	0	0	0

Management of the High Flyer Investment Company has established the following unranked goals for its investment portfolio.

Goal 1: Achieve a return on investment of at least 15 percent.
Goal 2: Limit the weighted risk factor of the investment portfolio to 5 percent or less.
Goal 3: Achieve an average growth potential for the investment portfolio of 10 percent or more.
Goal 4: Limit the average length of investment for the portfolio to 6 years or less.
Goal 5: Keep the portfolio fully invested (i.e., the proportions of funds invested in the various alternatives must sum to 1.00).

Formulate and solve this problem using goal programming.

14. Calhoun County is faced with the challenge of designing a busing program for the students in its four school districts in order to achieve racial desegregation in its three schools. The following table summarizes the busing cost and mileage data for every district-to-school

SCHOOL DISTRICT	RACE	SCHOOL 1 TRANSPORTATION COST ($)	MILES	SCHOOL 2 TRANSPORTATION COST ($)	MILES	SCHOOL 3 TRANSPORTATION COST ($)	MILES	TOTAL NUMBER
1	Black	35	4	70	8	105	12	460
	White	35	4	70	8	105	12	30
2	Black	45	5	65	7	120	14	260
	White	45	5	65	7	120	14	110
3	Black	85	10	30	3	45	5	30
	White	85	10	30	3	45	5	520
4	Black	65	7	45	5	30	3	50
	White	65	7	45	5	30	3	390
	School Capacity	700		550		550		1850 / 1850

combination, and also indicates the number of students of each race in each district and the capacities of the three schools.

The mileage figures represent the average miles traveled by a student within the county, based on shortest routes from strategic community bus stops to schools. The transportation costs are a function of these shortest route distances.

The Calhoun County School Board has the following prioritized goals for its busing program.

Goal 1: Achieve a racial balance in each school that corresponds to the overall racial proportions of Calhoun County. (For example, if 40 percent of the students in Calhoun County are black, then 40 percent of the students in each of the schools must be black.)

Goal 2: Minimize the total transportation cost of the busing program.

Goal 3: Limit the distance (average) traveled by students to 8 miles.

Goal 4: Avoid either overcrowding or underutilizing any of the schools.

Additionally, the structural constraints of the problem must ensure that every child is assigned to a school. Formulate and solve this problem using goal programming.

15. Sid's Uncle Harry died recently leaving Sid a substantial sum of money ($100,000). Sid, who was a liberal arts major in college, and who knows very little about investing money has asked you to come up with a plan to best invest the money he has inherited. After careful consideration, you decide to split the money in some fashion among real estate, blue chip stocks, mutual funds, and gold. Over the course of a year your best estimate of the rates of return on real estate and blue chip stocks is 15 percent and 13 percent, respectively. The estimated return on mutual funds is 14 percent. Gold is a risky investment, although the potential payoff is big. You estimate that there is a 40 percent chance that gold will have a *negative* rate of return of 10 percent, and a 60 percent chance of a positive rate of return of 30 percent. Together, you and Sid have established the following goals in priority order:

a. Diversify the investment to minimize risk. Invest no more than 30 percent of the total $100,000 in any one plan.

b. Sid is something of a gambler, and wishes to invest at least $30,000 in gold.

c. The amount invested in gold should not exceed the amount invested in blue chip stocks and mutual funds.

d. You have located a promising piece of real estate at a good price. Sid would like to buy it if possible (cost of property, $32,000).

e. Provide a return on investment for the first year of $20,000.

Formulate and solve as a goal-programming model.

16. Laura is at home on a leave of absence from her job, and is trying to balance her time out between work and play. Laura's favorite things to do on vacation are first, to simply lay outside and enjoy the sun, and second to work out at the gym. While there is no

charge for the sun, the local gym charges $10 per hour for the use of its facilities. Since Laura is on a non-paying vacation and must finance her time at the gym, she has decided to do a little net fishing since her parents live on the water, and the boat, nets, and gas are available to her free of charge. From past experience, Laura knows that she will earn on the average $12.50/hour while fishing. Laura would like to meet the following goals, in priority order:

a. Spend at least 6 hours each day either sunbathing or otherwise relaxing.
b. Spend at least 3 hours each day at the gym.
c. Spend no more time fishing than she does either sunbathing or at the gym.
d. Earn at least $30 in excess of what she spends at the gym.

(*Note:* Consider the day to be 12 hours long.) Formulate and solve as a goal-programming model.

17. The Dixie Manufacturing Company produces a particular product that may be manufactured on one of two different assembly lines, or may be purchased from an outside source if desired. Although this product may actually be procured at a cheaper cost from an outside source, the quality is not as good as for those items manufactured by Dixie. The company has assigned a quality control rating to each option, and this information, along with the pertinent cost and production data is included in the following table:

	ASSEMBLY LINE 1	ASSEMBLY LINE 2
Machine hours required per unit	0.5	1.0
Machine cost per hour	$8.00	$5.00
Machine hours available	50	100
Man hours required per unit	5	4
Cost per man hours	$6.00	$8.00
Regular-time man hours available	200	150
Quality control rating	8	9

Overtime is limited to 50 percent of available regular-time man hours. If the item is purchased from an outside source, the per unit cost is $25; however, the quality control rating is only 7. Given the following priorities, formulate and solve the model using goal-programming procedures, achieving the following.

a. Meet customer demand of 150 units per week.
b. Maintain an average quality control rating of 8 or better.
c. Minimize the total cost of production for the week.
d. Limit overtime on assembly line 2, as well as underutilization of man hours on line 2. Limiting overtime is considered three times as important as limiting underutilization of man hours.
e. Minimize overtime on line 1.

18. A small midwest oil company requires a key ingredient for one of its specialized fuels, which it may purchase in any combination from three possible sources. One of the desirable quantities is the percent of a certain additive, ethyl-A, in the ingredient. The pertinent data are included in the table.

	SOURCE		
	A	B	C
Cost per gallon	$0.50	$0.75	$0.25
Shipping cost per gallon	$0.10	$0.08	$0.05
Percent Ethyl-A	70%	90%	60%

Management has determined the following priorities.

a. Because of a previously negotiated arrangement, the company desires to purchase at least 60 percent of its total demand of 10,000 gallons per week from source A.
b. Limit shipping costs to $1000 per week.
c. Maintain an average percent of ethyl-A of 80 percent or better.
d. Minimize the total cost of the purchase, including the shipping cost.

Formulate and solve as a goal-programming model.

19. A hospital administrator is reevaluating how to best assign the nursing hours available among four different units, intensive care, pediatric care, prenatal/delivery, and emergency care. Since the hospital is on a tight budget and must operate with less than the desired level of staffing, the administrator must make some tradeoffs between cost and staffing. Consider the following table:

	INTENSIVE CARE	PEDIATRICS	PRENATAL/ DELIVERY	EMERGENCY CARE
Minimum required hours per week	840	336	168	504
Recommended hours per week	1176	672	336	1008
Critically quotient	0.8	0.4	0.6	1.0

The "minimum required hours per week" is a "bare bones" level and must be maintained if the hospital is to offer quality care. The "recommended hours per week" provide the best level of staffing, and is based upon past experience for hospitals of this size. The "critically quotient" measures the importance of proper staffing and is measured on a scale from zero to one with one being the most critical. The administrator has 2000 hours of regular-time nursing hours available per week. Formulate and solve a goal-programming problem to help the administrator make the assignments, given the following priorities.

a. Meet the minimum required hours in each ward.
b. Limit overtime to 25 percent of regular-time hours.
c. Meet the recommended number of hours for each unit according to the criticality quotients.

Application Review

Using Goal Programming to Locate a Trucking Terminal

The liquid food division of the Truck Transport Corporation of East St. Louis, Illinois, had a distribution network consisting of five trucking terminals. Management of the company had decided to relocate its East St. Louis trucking terminal. The East St. Louis terminal, however, operated as many as 30 independent truck drivers throughout the United States, Mexico, and Canada, and most of the independent truck drivers' homes were within a 100-mile radius of the East St. Louis terminal. This meant that the site relocation decision needed to be made using a mixture of objective cost factors and the personal preferences of the independent truck drivers. Furthermore, the decision had to be made based on consideration of the personal preferences of the firm's customers, primarily those of the perceived service improvements associated with a proposed site location.

Based on these considerations a goal-programming model was constructed. The structure of this goal-programming model involved five goals, or priority levels.

1. A P_1 priority level that was intended to require a solution that satisfied two combined transportation problems.

   a. A transportation problem that allowed the five trucking terminals to supply the necessary average number of trips required by the firm's 12 major customers.

   b. A transportation problem that allowed the five trucking terminals to supply the firm's most productive truck drivers (i.e., some 22 drivers) with their requested number of trips.

2. A P_2 priority level that was designed to allow truck drivers to avoid new truck terminal assignments that were considered to be undesirable because of the dissatisfaction with the new terminal managers.

3. A P_3 priority level that was designed to allow potential customers to avoid new truck terminal assignments that were considered to be undesirable because of the dissatisfaction with the new terminal managers.

4. A P_4 priority level that was structured to minimize the cost of transportation between the five trucking terminals and the truck drivers' homes.

5. A P_5 priority level that was structured to minimize the cost of transportation between the five trucking terminals and the 12 major customers.

The complete goal-programming model for this problem situation had 170 decision variables, 128 deviational variables, and 65 goal constraints. The model was solved using a modified FORTRAN computer program on an IBM 370/168 system, and required a little more than 8 minutes of execution time for each run. The results of applying the model to five new alternative terminal site locations is shown on page 342 in Table 10.11, in terms of the deviations from the goals.

In Table 10.11 it can be seen that the P_1 priority (required number of trips), the P_2 priority (driver preference), and the P_3 priority (customer preference) are totally satisfied at each of the five alternative site locations. It can also be seen that the choice of any site will raise the cost of doing business. Obviously, minimizing the increase in cost is the relevant criterion for site selection, and site 2

Source: Schniederjans, Marc J., N. K. Kwak, and Mark C. Helmer, "An application of goal programming to resolve a site location problem," *Interfaces* (June 1983), Vol. 12, No. 3, pp. 65–72.

TABLE 10.11 TEST RESULTS: TRUCKING TERMINAL SITE LOCATION (DEVIATIONS FROM GOALS)

PRIORITY	GOAL ACHIEVEMENT BY SITE				
	1	2	3	4	5
P_1 (required trips)	0	0	0	0	0
P_2 (driver preference)	0	0	0	0	0
P_3 (customer preference)	0	0	0	0	0
P_4 (transportation cost: drivers/$1000)	17.3	3.2	10.2	25.1	8.0
P_5 (transportation cost: customers/$1000)	13.7	1.4	1.6	23.0	2.5

causes the least increase in cost for the truck drivers and for the trucking firm's customers. Consequently, site 2 was recommended for the new terminal.

Six months after moving the terminal to the new site, the operations manager reported the following.

1. The company's records indicated that driver turnover was consistent with normally expected turnover for that time of year.
2. None of the major customers altered their business with the trucking firm during this period for any reason other than the usual seasonal needs.
3. No significant increase in transportation costs for the truck drivers occurred, nor did any of the 22 truck drivers complain about decreased profitability as a result of the new terminal location.

In summary, this application of goal programming facilitated an excellent decision with respect to the new site location for the trucking terminal.

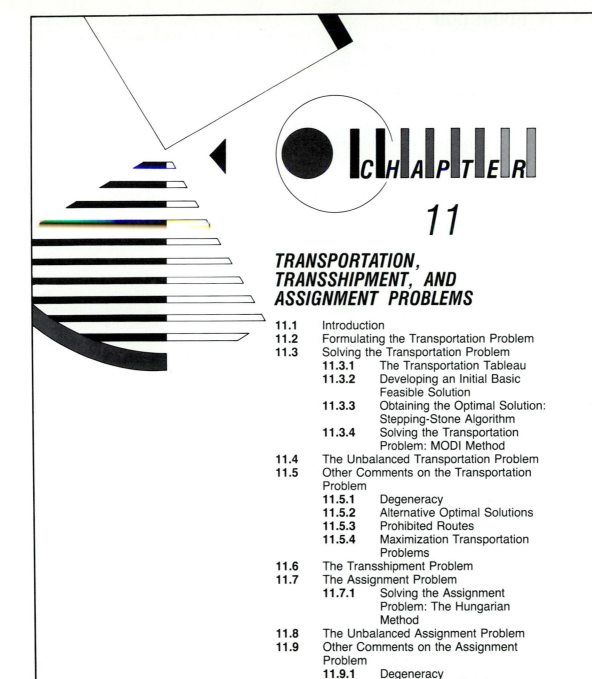

CHAPTER 11

TRANSPORTATION, TRANSSHIPMENT, AND ASSIGNMENT PROBLEMS

11.1 INTRODUCTION

The *transportation* and *assignment problems* are two special types of linear programming problems that arise frequently in practice. They are of considerable importance because the solution of these types of problems results in a least-cost distribution network, or the optimal assignment of a set of resources to a set of activities. *The transshipment problem* is an extension of the transportation problem in which each origin and destination can also be a transshipping point of shipment from other origins or destinations.

Since the transportation and assignment problems are really linear programming problems, they could be solved using the simplex procedure that was discussed in previous chapters. Their special structure, however, allows us to develop more efficient algorithms for their solution. In this chapter we focus on the development and use of these special algorithms.

11.2 FORMULATING THE TRANSPORTATION PROBLEM

The *transportation problem* deals with the transportation or physical movement of goods or services from a number of sources to a number of destinations, at a minimum total transportation cost. In general, there will be a fixed amount or limited supply of goods or services at each source, or *supply origin*, and a fixed amount or required quantity will be needed at each terminal, or *demand destination*.

To illustrate, consider Figure 11.1, which presents the United States physical distribution system for the Foxworth Corporation, a producer of home air conditioners. As can be seen in the figure, these air conditioners are produced at three factories (origins) and must be shipped to three warehouses (destinations).

Within this physical distribution system, each factory has a specified weekly productive capacity, and each warehouse has a specified weekly demand for the air conditioners. There is also a unique unit cost associated with transporting an air conditioner from each factory to each warehouse. The supply availabilities at the three origins, the demand requirements at the three destinations, and the transportation costs ($/air conditioner unit) are as shown in Table 11.1. The structure of this transportation problem involves a set of nine shipping routes, with their associated costs, for the nine possible origin-to-destination movements. The requirements (or

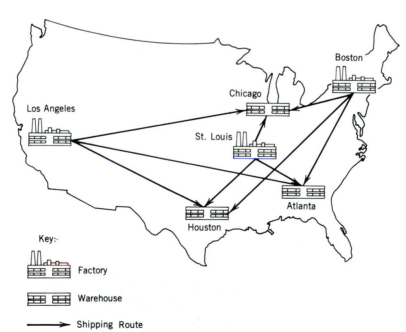

FIGURE 11.1 UNITED STATES PHYSICAL DISTRIBUTION SYSTEM— FOXWORTH CORPORATION.

TABLE 11.1 SUPPLY, DEMAND, AND TRANSPORTATION COSTS

SUPPLY ORIGINS (FACTORIES)	DEMAND DESTINATIONS (WAREHOUSES)			ORIGIN AVAILA-BILITIES (UNITS)
	D_1: CHICAGO	D_2: HOUSTON	D_3: ATLANTA	
O_1: LOS ANGELES	90	80	100	1000
O_2: ST. LOUIS	20	40	50	1900
O_3: BOSTON	40	90	60	1600
DESTINATION REQUIREMENTS (UNITS)	700	2000	1800	4500

constraints) of the problem are that demand at each warehouse (destination) must be met without exceeding the availability, or productive capacity, at each factory (origin). Solution of the transportation problem requires the determination of how many units should be shipped from each origin to each destination, in a manner that satisfies all of the destination demands, while minimizing the total associated cost of transportation.

The Foxworth Corporation transportation situation is presented as a network model in Figure 11.2. In simple terms, a network is just an arrangement of branches or routes that are connected at various points through which physical goods move from point to point. The factories and warehouses represent the connecting points of the transporta-

tion network, and the distribution routes are its branches. In this network model, each of the three factories ($i = 1, 2, 3$) can supply air conditioners to each of the three warehouses ($j = 1, 2, 3$). The total supply at the three factories is 4500 units, which exactly equals the total demand from the three warehouses. This type of problem is called a *balanced transportation problem*. In practice, most transportation problems are not "balanced"; however, we will use this balanced transportation problem to initiate our discussion of the solution of transportation problems in general. The nine possible distribution routes for the Foxworth Corporation are shown in Figure 11.2. Along each of these distribution routes, the unknown amount to be shipped is denoted as the decision variable x_{ij} (e.g.,

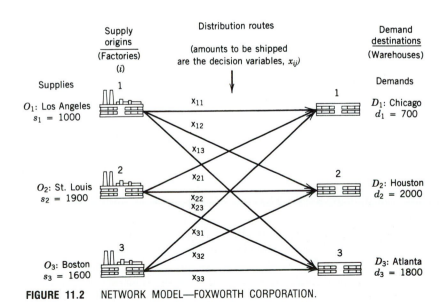

FIGURE 11.2 NETWORK MODEL—FOXWORTH CORPORATION.

the amount to be shipped from origin $i = 1$ to destination $j = 1$ is denoted by the decision variable, x_{11}).

The balanced transportation problem depicted by the network model shown in Figure 11.2 can be formulated as a linear programming problem as follows. Let

x_{ij} = number of air conditioners shipped from factory i to warehouse j (11.1)

$$\text{Minimize } Z = \$90x_{11} + \$80x_{12} + \$100x_{13}$$
$$+ \$20x_{21} + \$40x_{22} + \$50x_{23}$$
$$+ \$40x_{31} + \$90x_{32} + \$60x_{33}$$

subject to

$x_{11} + x_{12} + x_{13} = 1000$

(Supply, origin 1, Los Angeles)

$x_{21} + x_{22} + x_{23} = 1900$

(Supply, origin 2, St. Louis)

$x_{31} + x_{32} + x_{33} = 1600$

(Supply, origin 3, Boston) (11.2)

$x_{11} + x_{21} + x_{31} = 700$

(Demand, destination 1, Chicago)

$x_{12} + x_{22} + x_{32} = 2000$

(Demand, destination 2, Houston)

$x_{13} + x_{23} + x_{33} = 1800$

(Demand, destination 3, Atlanta)

with

$$\text{all } x_{ij} \geq 0 \qquad (11.3)$$

The objective function for this linear programming formulation represents the total transportation cost associated with all origin-to-destination movements. The constraints of this linear programming formulation depict the total amount that can be supplied by each factory using all possible shipping routes, and the total amount that is demanded at each warehouse using all shipping routes. The constraints are represented as equalities, because the problem is balanced (i.e., all of the supplies at the origins must be distributed and all of the demands at the destinations must be satisfied).

In general, the mathematical formulation of a transportation problem with m origins and n destinations can be described as follows. Let

s_i = the supply of the product available at origin i

d_j = the demand for the product at destination j

c_{ij} = the unit cost associated with shipping one unit of product from origin i to destination j

x_{ij} = the unknown quantity to be shipped from origin i to destination j

Minimize

$$Z = \sum_{i=1}^{m} \sum_{j=1}^{n} c_{ij} x_{ij} \qquad (11.4)$$

subject to

$$\sum_{j=1}^{n} x_{ij} = s_i$$

(Supply, $s_i > 0$, at origin i; $i = 1, 2, \cdots, m$) (11.5)

$$\sum_{i=1}^{m} x_{ij} = d_j$$

(Demand, $d_j > 0$, at destination j; $j = 1, 2, \cdots, n$) (11.6)

with

$$\text{all } x_{ij} \geq 0 \qquad (i = 1, 2, \cdots, m;$$
$$j = 1, 2, \cdots, n) \qquad (11.7)$$

Additionally, the balanced condition of the transportation problem is expressed as

$$\sum_{i=1}^{m} s_i = \sum_{j=1}^{n} d_j \qquad (11.8)$$

Consequently, the total amount available at the m origins will exactly satisfy the total amount demanded at the n destinations. As we show later in this chapter, the condition expressed by (11.8) is really no more restrictive than one in which the constraints given by (11.5) and (11.6) could have $\leq$ signs. For purposes of developing a solution procedure for the transportation problem, however, we initially concentrate our efforts on the balanced form of the transportation problem.

Since this balanced transportation problem can be formulated as a standard linear programming problem as shown in (11.4), (11.5), (11.6), and (11.7), we could apply the simplex algorithm to solve such a transportation problem. Even very small transportation problems quickly explode, however, into large linear programming problems. For example, our very small problem with three origins and three destinations results in a simplex tableau with six constraints, nine decision variables, and six artificial variables. Fortunately, the transportation problem has a very simple and special structure in which all of the coefficients in the constraint equations are ones. This special structure can be used in the development of two algorithms that are computationally more efficient than the simplex method.

11.3 SOLVING THE TRANSPORTATION PROBLEM

Having seen how to formulate transportation problems and having developed the general mathematical structure of transportation problems, we now proceed to develop two procedures for solving transportation problems. The special structure of the transportation problem is utilized in the construction of these two algorithms.

11.3.1 THE TRANSPORTATION TABLEAU

In developing the two solution procedures we will find it convenient to consider the special structure of the transportation problem depicted in a unique tabular form called the *transportation tableau*. The transportation tableau has the general form shown in Table 11.2.

This matrix tableau has m rows and n columns. Each row in this tableau corresponds to a supply origin and each column corresponds to a demand destination. The entries in the final column are the supply availabilities at the origins, and the entries in the bottom row are the demand requirements at the destinations. An x_{ij} entry in cell (i, j) denotes the number of units distributed from origin i to destination j. The corresponding transportation cost per unit allocated is c_{ij}, and is recorded in the small box in the upper-right-hand corner of each cell. The sum of the x_{ij} in the cells across row i must equal the supply, s_i, for that row. The sum of the x_{ij} in the cells down column j must equal the demand, d_j,

TABLE 11.2 TRANSPORTATION TABLEAU (BALANCED TRANSPORTATION PROBLEM)

FROM ORIGINS \ TO DESTINATIONS		1	2	$\cdots$	j	$\cdots$	n	ORIGIN SUPPLY
		c_{11}	c_{12}		c_{1j}		c_{1n}	
	1	x_{11}	x_{12}	$\cdots$	x_{1j}	$\cdots$	x_{1n}	s_1
		c_{21}	c_{22}		c_{2j}		c_{2n}	
	2	x_{21}	x_{22}	$\cdots$	x_{2j}	$\cdots$	x_{2n}	s_2
ORIGINS	$\vdots$	$\vdots$	$\vdots$		$\vdots$		$\vdots$	$\vdots$
		c_{i1}	c_{i2}		c_{ij}		c_{in}	
	i	x_{i1}	x_{i2}	$\cdots$	x_{ij}	$\cdots$	x_{in}	s_i
	$\vdots$	$\vdots$	$\vdots$		$\vdots$		$\vdots$	$\vdots$
		c_{m1}	c_{m2}		c_{mj}		c_{mn}	
	m	x_{m1}	x_{m2}	$\cdots$	x_{mj}	$\cdots$	x_{mn}	s_m
DESTINATION DEMAND		d_1	d_2	$\cdots$	d_j	$\cdots$	d_n	$\Sigma s_i = \Sigma d_j$

TABLE 11.3 TRANSPORTATION TABLEAU: FOXWORTH CORPORATION

TO DESTINATIONS FROM ORIGINS	D_1: CHICAGO	D_2: HOUSTON	D_3: ATLANTA	ORIGIN AVAILABILITY
O_1: LOS ANGELES	90 ⑦⑩⓪ ⟶	80 ③⓪⓪	100	1000
O_2: ST. LOUIS	20	40 ⑰⓪⓪ ⟶	50 ②⓪⓪	1900
O_3: BOSTON	40	90	60 ⑯⓪⓪	1600
DESTINATION DEMAND	700	2000	1800	4500

for that column. The lower-right-hand box reflects the fact that the total amount available at the m supply origins exactly satisfies the total amount required at the n demand destinations.

The transportation tableau for the Foxworth Corporation problem is shown in Table 11.3. In this tableau we have not specified any values for the decision variables, the x_{ij}. To do this we must determine an initial basic feasible solution for the problem.

11.3.2 DEVELOPING AN INITIAL BASIC FEASIBLE SOLUTION

From our previous discussion concerning the formulation of the transportation problem (see Section 11.2) it can be seen that in the balanced transportation problem there are m supply constraints related to the origins and n demand constraints related to the destinations. This results in a total of $(m + n)$ constraints. Recall that in a typical linear programming problem, the number of basic variables in a basic feasible solution is equal to the number of constraints for the problem. The set of $m + n$ constraints for the balanced transportation problem, however, always has one *redundant* constraint (i.e., any one of the constraints is automatically satisfied whenever the other $m + n - 1$ constraints are satisfied). This occurs because we are assuming that the "balance" between supply and demand, as given by (11.8), is required. This means that any set of x_{ij} that satisfies all but one of the constraints must

automatically satisfy the remaining constraint in order for (11.8) to be satisfied. To illustrate this property for the Foxworth Corporation problem let us assume that we have arbitrarily specified the following set of $m + n - 1 = 3 + 3 - 1 = 5$ x_{ij} values.

$$
\begin{array}{lll}
x_{11} = 0 & x_{12} = 0 & x_{13} = 1000 \\
x_{21} = 0 & x_{22} = 1100 & x_{23} = 800 \\
x_{31} = 700 & x_{32} = 900 & x_{33} = 0
\end{array}
$$

Observe that these x_{ij} values satisfy the first five constraints given by (11.2), namely

$$
\begin{array}{l}
x_{11} + x_{12} + x_{13} = 1000 \\
\quad 0 + 0 + 1000 = 1000 \; \checkmark \\
x_{21} + x_{22} + x_{23} = 1900 \\
\quad 0 + 1100 + 800 = 1900 \; \checkmark \\
x_{31} + x_{32} + x_{33} = 1600 \\
\quad 700 + 900 + 0 = 1600 \; \checkmark \\
x_{11} + x_{21} + x_{31} = 700 \\
\quad 0 + 0 + 700 = 700 \; \checkmark \\
x_{12} + x_{22} + x_{32} = 2000 \\
\quad 0 + 1100 + 900 = 2000 \; \checkmark
\end{array}
$$

The remaining constraint must also be satisfied in order for the balance equation (11.8) to hold. We can also verify that this remaining constraint is satisfied by these x_{ij} values, namely

$$x_{13} + x_{23} + x_{33} = 1800$$
$$1000 + 800 + 0 = 1800 \checkmark$$

Therefore, a basic feasible solution to a balanced transportation problem must contain exactly $m + n - 1$ basic variables.[1] It is represented in the transportation problem tableau (see Table 11.2) as having exactly $(m + n - 1)$ positive x_{ij} (allocations), with the sum of the allocations for each row being equal to the supply availability, s_i, for that row, and with the sum of the allocations for each column being equal to the demand requirement, d_j, for that column.

There are numerous methods available for developing an initial basic feasible solution for a transportation problem. We now proceed to discuss three of the more widely used methods.

Northwest Corner Rule. The simplest method for determining the initial basic feasible solution to a transportation problem is the *northwest corner rule*. To apply the northwest corner rule, the following steps are taken.

1. Start at the northwest corner cell in the tableau [i.e., cell (1, 1) in the upper-left-hand corner] and allocate as much as possible to x_{11} without violating either the supply or demand constraints [i.e., set $x_{11} = \min(s_1, d_1)$].

2. This allocation will exhaust the supply at origin 1 and/or satisfy the demand at destination 1. Consequently, no more units can be allocated to the exhausted row or column and it is eliminated from further consideration. Then, we next allocate as much as possible to the adjacent cell in the row or column that has not been eliminated. For example, if $s_1 > d_1$, we would then move to cell (1, 2) and set $x_{12} = \min(s_1 - d_1, d_2)$. Conversely, if $s_1 < d_1$, we would move to cell (2, 1) and set $x_{21} = \min(d_1 - s_1, s_2)$. If both a row and

column are exhausted simultaneously, move diagonally to the next cell. This will produce degeneracy, a condition that is discussed further later.

3. Proceed in the same manner until all supply availabilities have been exhausted and all demand requirements have been met.

The initial basic feasible solution for the Foxworth Corporation problem, obtained by using the northwest corner rule, is presented in Table 11.4.

Observe first that we are using the same tableau format that was introduced earlier in Table 11.3. Applying the northwest corner rule, the first allocation is $x_{11} = 700$, which is the $\min(s_1 = 1000, d_1 = 700) = 700$. This exactly satisfies the demand requirement at destination 1, Chicago. Since $s_1 > d_1$, we then move to cell (1, 2) and set $x_{12} = 300$, which is the $\min(s_1 - d_1, d_2) = \min(1000 - 700 = 300, 2000) = 300$. This completely utilizes the origin availability for the first origin, Los Angeles. We then proceed downward and to the right, in stair-step fashion, until all row (origin) availabilities have been utilized and all column (destination) requirements have been met. The arrows in Table 11.4 indicate the order in which the basic variables (i.e., allocations to the cells) are selected. Observe that the initial basic feasible solution obtained by use of the northwest corner rule has $m + n - 1 = 3 + 3 - 1 = 5$ strictly positive allocations (i.e., five of the x_{ij} cell values are greater than zero). The total transportation cost associated with this initial basic feasible solution is as shown in Table 11.5. Observe that the northwest corner rule is a very simple method for obtaining an initial basic feasible solution. It will not generally produce a good (i.e., low total transportation cost) initial basic feasible solution, however, since it will tend to make allocations to those cells lying along the diagonal of the tableau, and these cells may not necessarily be the least costly.

Matrix Minima Rule. A second procedure for determining an initial basic feasible solution involves the repeated determination of the minimum cost cells for the entire matrix, or tableau. This procedure tries to minimize the total transportation cost by systematically making allocations to the various cells in order of the magnitude of the unit costs

---

[1] In general, these $m + n - 1$ basic variables will be strictly positive (i.e., >0). If one or more of these $m + n - 1$ basic variables is equal to zero, however, we have a "degenerate" solution. Degeneracy in transportation problems is discussed further in a later section of this chapter.

TABLE 11.4 INITIAL BASIC FEASIBLE SOLUTION-FOXWORTH CORPORATION-NORTHWEST CORNER RULE

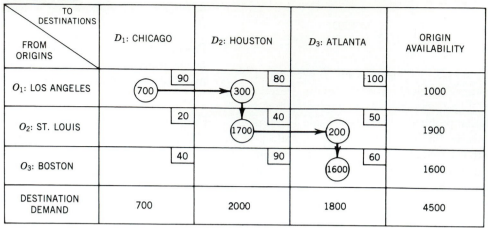

TO DESTINATIONS / FROM ORIGINS	D_1: CHICAGO	D_2: HOUSTON	D_3: ATLANTA	ORIGIN AVAILABILITY
O_1: LOS ANGELES	90 (700)	80 (300)	100	1000
O_2: ST. LOUIS	20	40 (1700)	50 (200)	1900
O_3: BOSTON	40	90	60 (1600)	1600
DESTINATION DEMAND	700	2000	1800	4500

associated with the cells. To apply the *matrix minima rule,* the following steps are taken.

1. Examine the entire transportation tableau and determine the cell having the smallest unit transportation cost, c_{ij}. If a tie between two or more cells occurs, the tie may be broken arbitrarily. For the minimum cost cell, we set $x_{ij} = \min(s_i, d_j)$, and eliminate from further consideration either row i, if supply availability s_i is exhausted, or column j, if demand requirement d_j is satisfied. Consequently, if $x_{ij} = s_i$, we decrease d_j by s_i, and if $x_{ij} = d_j$, we decrease s_i by d_j.

2. For the remaining cells that are feasible (i.e., those cells to which no allocation has been made, or whose row or column has not been eliminated), select the minimum cost cell and allocate as much as possible.

3. Proceed in the same manner until all supply availabilities have been exhausted and all demand requirements have been satisfied.

The initial basic feasible solution for the Foxworth Corporation problem, obtained by using the matrix minima rule, is presented in Table 11.6.

Applying the matrix minima rule, the first allocation is made to cell (2, 1) since $c_{21} = 20$ is the minimum cost cell for the entire transportation tableau. The number of units allocated is $x_{21} = \min(s_2 = 1900, d_1 = 700) = 700$. This exactly satisfies the demand requirement at destination 1, Chicago, so column 1 is eliminated from further consideration and x_{11} and x_{31} are no longer feasible. We also reduce the supply availability at origin 2 by 700 units. The next allocation is made by determining the minimum cost cell among the six remaining cells. This minimum cost cell is $c_{22} = 40$.

TABLE 11.5 TOTAL TRANSPORTATION COST: NORTHWEST CORNER RULE

SHIPPING ROUTE	TRANSPORTATION COST
Los Angeles → Chicago	700 units × $90/unit = $ 63,000
Los Angeles → Houston	300 units × $80/unit = 24,000
St. Louis → Houston	1700 units × $40/unit = 68,000
St. Louis → Atlanta	200 units × $50/unit = 10,000
Boston → Atlanta	1600 units × $60/unit = 96,000
	Total $261,000

TABLE 11.6 INITIAL BASIC FEASIBLE SOLUTION-FOXWORTH CORPORATION-MATRIX MINIMA RULE

TO DESTINATIONS / FROM ORIGINS	D_1: CHICAGO	D_2: HOUSTON	D_3: ATLANTA	ORIGIN AVAILABILITY
O_1: LOS ANGELES	90	80 (800)	100 (200)	1000
O_2: ST. LOUIS	20 (700)	40 (1200)	50	1900
O_3: BOSTON	40	90	60 (1600)	1600
DESTINATION DEMAND	700	2000	1800	4500

The number of units allocated is $\min(s_2 - 700 = 1200, d_2 = 2000) = 1200$. This exactly satisfies the supply availability at origin 2, St. Louis, so row 2 is eliminated from further consideration and x_{23} is no longer feasible. This process is then repeated throughout the entire tableau, as indicated by the arrows that show the order in which the basic variables are selected. Observe that the initial basic feasible solution obtained by use of the matrix minima rule has $m + n - 1 = 3 + 3 - 1 = 5$ positive allocations. The total transportation cost associated with this initial basic feasible solution is as shown in Table 11.7.

Vogel's Approximation Method. A third and final method for determining an initial basic feasible solution is known as *Vogel's approximation method*

(VAM).[2] It involves making allocations in a manner that will minimize the "penalty cost" for allocating to the wrong cell. To apply Vogel's approximation method, the following steps are taken.

1. Calculate the penalty cost for each row and each column. This is done as follows. For each row, we determine the difference between the lowest cost, c_{ij}, and the next lowest cost, c_{it}. This difference represents the "penalty" that will be incurred if instead of shipping over the best route (i.e., the route having cost c_{ij}) we are forced to ship over the second best route (i.e., the route having cost c_{it}). This computation is made for each of the m rows and n columns, and results in $m + n$ values.

TABLE 11.7 TOTAL TRANSPORTATION COST: MATRIX MINIMA RULE

SHIPPING ROUTE	TRANSPORTATION COST		
Los Angeles → Houston	800 units × $80/unit	=	$ 64,000
Los Angeles → Atlanta	200 units × $100/unit	=	20,000
St. Louis → Chicago	700 units × $20/unit	=	14,000
St. Louis → Houston	1200 units × $40/unit	=	48,000
Boston → Atlanta	1600 units × $60/unit	=	96,000
	Total		$242,000

[2]More details concerning this method can be found in: N. V. Reinfeld and W. R. Vogel, *Mathematical Programming*. Englewood Cliffs, N.J.: Prentice-Hall, 1958).

TABLE 11.8 INITIAL BASIC FEASIBLE SOLUTION-FOXWORTH CORPORATION-VOGEL'S APPROXIMATION METHOD

TO DESTINATIONS / FROM ORIGINS	D_1: CHICAGO	D_2: HOUSTON	D_3: ATLANTA	ORIGIN AVAILABILITY
O_1: LOS ANGELES	90	80 (100)	100 (900)	1000
O_2: ST. LOUIS	20	40 (1900)	50	1900
O_3: BOSTON	40 (700)	90	60 (900)	1600
DESTINATION DEMAND	700	2000	1800	4500

2. Select the row or column that has the largest penalty cost (breaking any tie arbitrarily). Allocate as much as is possible to the cell having the smallest c_{ij} value in the row or column selected. Thus, for the smallest c_{ij} value in the selected row or column, $x_{ij} = \min(s_i, d_j)$. By making this allocation, the penalties associated with more costly allocations are avoided.

3. Adjust the supply availabilities and demand requirements to reflect the allocation made. Eliminate from further consideration any row for which the supply has been exhausted, or any column for which demand has been satisfied.

4. Proceed in the same manner until all supply availabilities have been exhausted and all demand requirements have been met. Note that each time we return to Step 1 a new set of penalty costs must be computed.

The initial basic feasible solution for the Foxworth Corporation problem, obtained by using Vogel's approximation method, is presented in Table

TABLE 11.9 SUMMARY TABLE: VOGEL'S APPROXIMATION METHOD

	DIFFERENCES							
	ROW			COLUMN			LARGEST	
STEP	1	2	3	1	2	3	DIFFERENCE	ALLOCATION
1	10	20	20	20	40	10	40, column 2	$x_{22} = 1900$ { Eliminate row 2
2	10		20	50	10	40	50, column 1	$x_{31} = 700$ { Eliminate column 1
3	20		30		10	40	40, column 3	$x_{33} = 900$ { Eliminate row 3
4	20						20, row 1	$x_{21} = 100$ { Eliminate column 2
5								$x_{14} = 900$ { Eliminate row 1 and column 3

TABLE 11.10 TOTAL TRANSPORTATION COST: VOGEL'S APPROXIMATION METHOD

SHIPPING ROUTE	TRANSPORTATION COST
Los Angeles → Houston	100 units × $80/unit = $ 8,000
Los Angeles → Atlanta	900 units × $100/unit = 90,000
St. Louis → Houston	1900 units × $40/unit = 76,000
Boston → Chicago	700 units × $40/unit = 28,000
Boston → Atlanta	900 units × $60/unit = 54,000
	Total $256,000

11.8. The steps taken in applying Vogel's approximation method are summarized in Table 11.9.

In Step 1 we first compute the $m + n = 3 + 3 = 6$ row and column differences for the entire tableau. Observing that the 40 is the largest difference in column 2, we select column 2 for the first allocation. The cell having the smallest cost in column 2 is cell $(2, 2)$, since $c_{22} = 40$. We then set $x_{22} = \min(s_2 = 1900, d_2 = 2000) = 1900$. This eliminates row 2 from further consideration, and the demand requirement for column 2 is reduced to $2000 - 1900 = 100$ units. In Step 2 we recompute the differences for the remaining rows (i.e., row 2 being eliminated) and the remaining columns. We see that 50 in column 1 is the largest difference, so we select column 1 for the second allocation. The cell having the smallest cost in column 1 is cell $(3, 1)$, since $c_{31} = 40$. We then set $x_{31} = \min(s_3 = 1600, d_1 = 700) = 700$. This eliminates column 1 from further consideration, and the supply availability for origin 3 is reduced to $1600 - 700 = 900$. This process is then repeated throughout the entire tableau, as indicated by the arrows, which show the order in which the basic variables are selected. The initial basic feasible solution obtained by use of Vogel's approximation method has $m + n - 1 = 3 + 3 - 1 = 5$ positive allocations. The total transportation cost associated with this initial basic feasible solution is as shown in Table 11.10. Observe that Vogel's approximation method has resulted in an initial basic feasible solution that has a lower total transportation cost than that obtained by use of the northwest corner rule, but a higher total transportation cost than that obtained by using the matrix minima rule. In general, use of Vogel's approximation method produces an initial basic feasible solution that is very near the optimal solution. Its use, however, also requires more work than either the northwest corner rule or the matrix minima rule.

11.3.3 OBTAINING THE OPTIMAL SOLUTION: STEPPING-STONE ALGORITHM

Once we have determined the initial basic feasible solution, the next step is to determine if the total transportation cost associated with this initial basic feasible solution can be reduced. One method for doing this requires the evaluation of each of the unoccupied cells (i.e., each of the unused shipping routes) to determine the effect upon the total transportation cost of transferring one unit from an occupied cell to the unoccupied cell. This process is called the *stepping-stone algorithm,* and takes its name from the fact that a closed loop of occupied cells (basic variables), with the occupied cells thought of as stones in a pond representing the entire tableau, are used to evaluate each unoccupied cell (i.e., each nonbasic variable).

We now employ the initial basic feasible solution obtained from use of the northwest corner rule to illustrate how to obtain the optimal solution by means of the stepping-stone algorithm. This table is reproduced as Table 11.11. Recall that the initial basic feasible solution obtained by using the northwest corner rule is not the optimal solution to the problem. The stepping-stone algorithm involves two steps.

1. Each unoccupied cell is evaluated for the "net-cost" effect of transferring one unit from an

TABLE 11.11 INITIAL BASIC FEASIBLE SOLUTION-STEPPING-STONE ALGORITHM

TO DESTINATIONS / FROM ORIGINS	D_1: CHICAGO	D_2: HOUSTON	D_3: ATLANTA	ORIGIN SUPPLY
O_1: LOS ANGELES	(700) ⌐90	(300) ⌐80	⌐100	1000
O_2: ST. LOUIS	⌐20	(1700) ⌐40	(200) ⌐50	1900
O_3: BOSTON	⌐40	⌐90	(1600) ⌐60	1600
DESTINATION DEMAND	700	2000	1800	4500

occupied cell to the unoccupied cell. This transfer must be made in a manner that maintains the row and column balance of the transportation problem (i.e., each row supply is exactly allocated and each column requirement is exactly satisfied).

2. After all of the unoccupied cells have been evaluated, a reallocation is made to the unoccupied cell for which it is indicated that the greatest per-unit net-cost savings would occur.

These two steps are repeated until there are no unoccupied cells for which an improvement in the total

transportation cost (i.e., the objective function of the problem) would occur.

To begin our analysis let us consider cell (1, 3), which is currently unoccupied and represents the Los Angeles → Atlanta shipping route (Table 11.12). This unoccupied cell, and indeed every unoccupied cell in the tableau, represents a nonbasic variable. For any nonbasic cell to enter the solution (i.e., become basic) it must contribute to a reduction in the value of the objective function. Assume that we now decide to allocate one unit to cell (1, 3), $x_{13} = 1$. We now have 1801 units in column three, which violates the demand requirement at

TABLE 11.12 EVALUATION OF TRANSFERRING ONE UNIT TO CELL (1,3)

TO DESTINATIONS / FROM ORIGINS	D_1: CHICAGO	D_2: HOUSTON	D_3: ATLANTA	ORIGIN SUPPLY
O_1: LOS ANGELES	(700) ⌐90	(300) −1 ⌐80	+1 ⌐100	1000
O_2: ST. LOUIS	⌐20	(1700) +1 ⌐40	(200) −1 ⌐50	1900
O_3: BOSTON	⌐40	⌐90	(1600) ⌐60	1600
DESTINATION DEMAND	700	2000	1800	4500

destination three, Atlanta. To compensate, we must subtract one unit from either cell (2, 3), $x_{23} = 200$ or cell (3, 3), $x_{33} = 1600$ in column three. Subtracting one unit from cell (2, 3), $x_{23} = 200 - 1 = 199$, will balance column three at 1800 units once more. Now, however, row two has only 1899 units (i.e., $x_{22} = 1700$, $x_{23} = 199$, $x_{22} + x_{23} = 1700 + 199 = 1899$). Consequently, we must add one unit to cell (2, 2), $x_{22} = 1700 + 1 = 1701$, which will balance row two at 1900 units once more.

Now, however, column two has 2001 units (i.e., $x_{22} = 1701$, $x_{12} = 300$, $x_{22} + x_{12} = 1701 + 300 = 2001$). Thus, one unit must be subtracted from x_{12}, $x_{12} = 300 - 1 = 299$, which will balance column two at 2000 units once more. Note that row one is now completely balanced even though we just subtracted one unit from x_{12}. This is because we originally added one unit to x_{13}, the unoccupied cell. The closed loop for cell (1, 3) that we have just analyzed can be summarized as follows.

UNOCCUPIED CELL   CLOSED LOOP

x_{13} x_{13} $\rightarrow$ x_{23} $\rightarrow$ x_{22} $\rightarrow$ x_{12} $\rightarrow$ x_{13}

                            $(+1)$ (-1) $(+1)$ (-1)

The evaluation of transferring one unit to cell (1, 3) is shown in Table 11.12. The general procedure for tracing out the closed loop for evaluating an unoccupied cell is as follows.

1. Begin with the unoccupied cell to be evaluated and place a $+1$ in this unoccupied cell. This indicates that we are evaluating the effect of moving one unit into this unoccupied cell [i.e., moving one unit into this unoccupied cell (i, j) will incur a cost of $+c_{ij}$].

2. Draw an arrow from the unoccupied cell being evaluated to an occupied cell in the same row, or to an occupied cell in the same column. Place a -1 in the cell to which the arrow was drawn. This signifies that we are compensating for the $+1$ unit moved into the unoccupied cell by subtracing (shifting) one unit from either an occupied cell in its same row or an occupied cell in its same column [i.e., moving one unit from this occupied cell (k, j) will save a cost equal to c_{kj}]. This shifting is necessary in order to maintain the row or column balance. The direction initially taken from the unoccupied cell will have no effect on the determination of the closed loop. The same closed loop will result regardless of the direction initially taken from the unoccupied cell.

3. Move from the occupied cell just selected, horizontally or vertically (but never diagonally) to another occupied cell. Draw an arrow to

this occupied cell and place a $+1$ in the cell to which the arrow was drawn, again to maintain the row or column balance.

4. Repeat the process of moving from occupied cell to occupied cell until you loop back to the original unoccupied cell. At each step of the looping process the $+1$ and -1 allocations are alternated in order to maintain the row or column balance. Remember, what we are doing is evaluating the effect of moving one unit into an unoccupied cell (i.e., making that cell basic) and compensating by removing one unit from an occupied cell (i.e., making that cell nonbasic).

5. Throughout the looping process we maintain the important restriction that there is exactly one positive allocation $(+1)$ and exactly one negative allocation (-1) in any row or column through which the loop happens to pass. Again, this restriction is necessary to maintain the row or column balance. Physically, this means that as we trace out the closed loop, orthogonal (90° or right-angle) turns will be made only at the occupied cells. It is also important to note that the number of cells involved in the closed-loop process will always be an even integer equal to or greater than 4 (i.e., 4, 6, 8, . . .). Finally, the looping process described earlier will result in one unique closed path for each unoccupied cell.

It is important to recognize that both occupied

and unoccupied cells can be skipped over in the construction of a closed loop. To illustrate, consider the following arbitrarily constructed example in which cell (1, 1) is being evaluated.

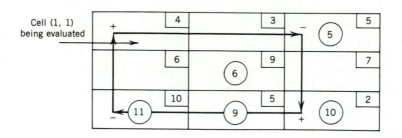

Also, the closed loop can cross over itself. To illustrate, consider the following arbitrarily constructed example in which cell (2, 1) is being evaluated.

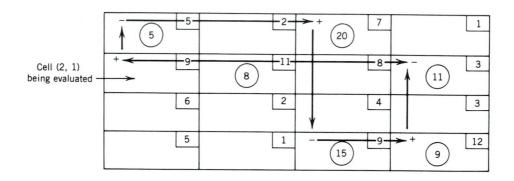

After the closed loop has been constructed, the "net cost" associated with reallocating one unit to the unoccupied cell is determined. For cell (1, 3), referring back to Table 11.12 we see that if $x_{13} = 1$, a cost of \$100 (i.e., the transportation cost for one unit being moved from origin one to destination three) will be incurred. This must be offset by the decrease of x_{23} by one unit, however, which will reduce cost by \$50. This in turn will be offset by the addition of one unit to x_{22}, which will increase cost by \$40. Finally, this will be offset by the decrease of x_{12} by one unit, which will reduce cost by

---

TABLE 11.13 SUMMARY COMPUTATIONS FOR UNOCCUPIED CELLS: INITIAL BASIC FEASIBLE SOLUTION

UNOCCUPIED CELL	CLOSED LOOP	CLOSED-LOOP INCREASE AND DECREASE	= NET COST CHANGE
(1, 3)	$x_{13} \to x_{23} \to x_{22} \to x_{12} \to x_{13}$	$+c_{13} - c_{23} + c_{22} - c_{12}$ $+\$100 - 50 + 40 - 80$	$= +\$10$
(2, 1)	$x_{21} \to x_{22} \to x_{12} \to x_{11} \to x_{21}$	$+c_{21} - c_{22} + c_{12} - c_{11}$ $+\$20 - 40 + 80 - 90$	$= -\$30$
(3, 1)	$x_{31} \to x_{11} \to x_{12} \to x_{22} \to x_{23} \to x_{33} \to x_{31}$	$+c_{31} - c_{11} + c_{12} - c_{22} + c_{23} - c_{33}$ $+\$40 - 90 + 80 - 40 + 50 - 60$	$= -\$20$
(3, 2)	$x_{32} \to x_{22} \to x_{23} \to x_{33} \to x_{32}$	$+c_{32} - c_{22} + c_{23} - c_{31}$ $+\$90 - 40 + 50 - 60$	$= +\$40$

$80. In summary, the "net cost" associated with allocating one unit to cell (1, 3) can be summarized as follows

$$\text{Net cost, cell } (1, 3) = + c_{13} - c_{23} + c_{22} - c_{12}$$
$$= + \$100 - \$50 + \$40 - \$80$$
$$= + \$10$$

Consequently, if one unit is reallocated to cell (1, 3), a net cost increase of $10 in the total transportation cost would result. Therefore, x_{13} would not be chosen as an entering basic variable, since to do so would increase rather than decrease the total transportation cost.

The effect of allocating one unit to each of the other occupied cells is evaluated in exactly the same manner. The computations for all of the unoccupied cells are summarized in Table 11.13.

In this table we see that we can decrease the objective function by making an allocation to either the currently unoccupied cell (2, 1) or the currently unoccupied cell (3, 1). Since allocating to cell (2, 1) results in a per-unit transportation cost decrease of $30 that is greater than the per-unit transporta-

tion cost decrease of $20 associated with cell (3, 1), cell (2, 1) is initially chosen as the cell to which an allocation is made. The question now becomes: How large an allocation can we make to cell (2, 1)?

The amount that can be allocated to cell (2, 1) is first of all restricted by the supply availability at origin 2 (i.e., 1900 units) and the demand requirement at destination 1 (i.e., 700 units). Moreover, the amount that can be allocated to cell (2, 1) is restricted by the amount that can be transferred along the closed loop that was used to evaluate cell (2, 1). Referring back to Table 11.13, we see that for every unit allocated to cell (2, 1), a unit is subtracted from cells (2, 2) and (1, 1) along the closed loop. Recall that these are the cells marked with a -1 during the closed-loop evaluation process. Therefore, the amount of the allocation to a chosen unoccupied cell is always the *minimum* amount in the cells on the closed loop that are marked with a -1 during the unoccupied cell evaluation process. The limit on the number of units that can be allocated to cell (2, 1) is equal to the minimum of the number of units currently allocated to either cell (1, 1) or cell (2, 2). This is because one of these two cells will provide the units that will move into cell (2, 1). Diagramatically

In these two diagrams each of the cells along the closed loop has been marked with a $+1$ or -1. The number of units to be allocated to cell (2, 1) would be computed as

$$\text{Allocation to cell } (2, 1) = \text{minimum}$$
$$\begin{pmatrix} \text{amount in} & \text{amount in} \\ \text{cell } (1, 1) \text{ or} & \text{cell } (2, 2) \\ = 700 & = 1700 \end{pmatrix}$$
$$= 700 \qquad (11.10)$$

To maintain a basic feasible solution, and keep the row (supply) and column (demand) balanced, the

minimum value in these two cells (700) must be moved into cell (2, 1). To summarize, we move 700 units from cell (1, 1) to cell (2, 1), which means that $x_{21} = 700$ (i.e., x_{21} is now a basic variable). Since cell (1, 1) has been reduced to zero, $x_{11} = 700 - 700 = 0$ (i.e., x_{11} is now a nonbasic variable). To compensate for this move, in terms of maintaining the row/column balance, cell (1, 2) is increased by 700 units, which means that $x_{12} = 300 + 700 = 1000$ units. Finally, we reduce the amount in cell (2, 2) by 700 units, which means that $x_{22} = 1700 - 700 = 1000$ units. We have, of course, simply moved 700 units around the closed

TABLE 11.14 SECOND BASIC FEASIBLE SOLUTION-STEPPING-STONE ALGORITHM (OPTIMAL SOLUTION) (REALLOCATION TO CELL (2,1): x_{21} BECOMES BASIC, x_{11} BECOMES NONBASIC)

TO DESTINATIONS / FROM ORIGINS	D_1: CHICAGO	D_2: HOUSTON	D_3: ATLANTA	ORIGIN SUPPLY
O_1: LOS ANGELES	+30 · · · · · 90	(1000) · · · 80	+10 · · · · 100	1000
O_2: ST. LOUIS	(700) · · · · 20	(1000) · · · 40	(200) · · · · 50	1900
O_3: BOSTON	+10 · · · · · 40	+40 · · · · · 90	(1600) · · · 60	1600
DESTINATION DEMAND	700	2000	1800	4500

path that we used to originally evaluate unoccupied cell (2, 1). The new transportation tableau, in which the reallocation of 700 units to cell (2, 1) has been made, is shown in Table 11.14.

We now must evaluate the unoccupied cells in this second tableau, using the stepping-stone process, to see if there are any further allocations possible that will reduce the total transportation cost. Table 11.15 presents a summary of the computations for the unoccupied cells in this second solution tableau (i.e., for the second basic feasible solution). Since the net cost changes for all of the unoccupied cells are positive, we know that no further reallocations can be made to reduce the total transportation cost. Consequently, the minimum cost shipping plan is as shown in Table 11.16. Observe finally that the optimal solution has a minimum cost of $240,000,

which is only $2000 lower than the minimum cost obtained by using the matrix minima method to determine an initial basic feasible solution.

11.3.4 SOLVING THE TRANSPORTATION PROBLEM: MODI METHOD

The *modified distribution method*, or *MODI method*, offers an alternative approach to the stepping-stone algorithm for evaluating the unoccupied cells in a transportation tableau. The MODI method is based on the dual formulation of the transportation problem.

Consider the general formulation of the original Foxworth Corporation problem, which had

TABLE 11.15 SUMMARY OF COMPUTATIONS FOR UNOCCUPIED CELLS: SECOND BASIC FEASIBLE SOLUTION

UNOCCUPIED CELL	CLOSED LOOP	CLOSED-LOOP INCREASE AND DECREASE	= NET COST CHANGE
(1, 1)	$x_{11} \rightarrow x_{12} \rightarrow x_{22} \rightarrow x_{21} \rightarrow x_{11}$	$+c_{11} - c_{12} + c_{22} - c_{21}$ $+\$90 - 80 + 40 - 20$	= +$30
(1, 3)	$x_{13} \rightarrow x_{12} \rightarrow x_{22} \rightarrow x_{23} \rightarrow x_{13}$	$+c_{13} - c_{12} + c_{22} - c_{23}$ $+\$100 - 80 + 40 - 50$	= −$10
(3, 1)	$x_{31} \rightarrow x_{21} \rightarrow x_{23} \rightarrow x_{33} \rightarrow x_{31}$	$+c_{31} - c_{21} + c_{23} - c_{33}$ $+\$40 - 20 + 50 - 60$	= +$10
(3, 2)	$x_{32} \rightarrow x_{33} \rightarrow x_{23} \rightarrow x_{22} \rightarrow x_{32}$	$+c_{32} - c_{33} + c_{23} - c_{22}$ $+\$90 - 60 + 50 - 40$	= +$40

TABLE 11.16 MINIMUM TOTAL TRANSPORTATION COST

SHIPPING ROUTE	SHIPPING COST		
Los Angeles → Houston	1000 units × $80/unit =	$	80,000
St. Louis → Chicago	700 units × $20/unit =		14,000
St. Louis → Houston	1000 units × $40/unit =		40,000
St. Louis → Atlanta	200 units × $50/unit =		10,000
Boston → Atlanta	1600 units × $60/unit =		96,000
	Total		$240,000

$m = 3$ rows (origins) and $n = 3$ columns (destinations). Written as a primal form linear programming problem, this formulation would be as follows.

$$\text{Minimize } Z = c_{11}x_{11} + c_{12}x_{12} + c_{13}x_{13} + c_{21}x_{21}$$
$$+ c_{22}x_{22} + c_{23}x_{23} + c_{31}x_{31} + c_{32}x_{32} + c_{33}x_{33}$$
$$(11.11)$$

subject to

$$x_{11} + x_{12} + x_{13} = s_1$$
$$x_{21} + x_{22} + x_{23} = s_2$$
$$x_{31} + x_{32} + x_{33} = s_3 \qquad (11.12)$$
$$x_{11} + x_{21} + x_{31} = d_1$$
$$x_{12} + x_{22} + x_{32} = d_2$$
$$x_{13} + x_{23} + x_{33} = d_3$$

with

$$\text{all } x_{ij} \geq 0 \qquad (11.13)$$

In this primal formulation, a c_{ij} value represents the unit cost associated with shipping one unit of product from origin i to destination j, an x_{ij} value represents the unknown quantity to be shipped from origin i to destination j, s_i is the fixed supply availability at origin i, d_j is the fixed demand requirement at destination j, and we seek to minimize the total cost associated with shipping all units from origins to destinations.

If we now define u_1, u_2, and u_3 as the three dual variables associated with the three origin (supply) constraints of the primal linear programming problem, and v_1, v_2, v_3 as the three dual variables associated with the three destination (demand) constraints of the primal linear programming problem,

we can construct the following dual formulation of the problem.

$$\text{Maximize } Z = (s_1 u_1 + s_2 u_2 + s_3 u_3)$$
$$+ (v_1 d_1 + v_2 d_2 + v_3 d_3) \quad (11.14)$$

subject to

$$u_1 + v_1 \leq c_{11}$$
$$u_1 + v_2 \leq c_{12}$$
$$u_1 + v_3 \leq c_{13}$$
$$u_2 + v_1 \leq c_{21}$$
$$u_2 + v_2 \leq c_{22} \qquad (11.15)$$
$$u_2 + v_3 \leq c_{23}$$
$$u_3 + v_1 \leq c_{31}$$
$$u_3 + v_2 \leq c_{32}$$
$$u_3 + v_3 \leq c_{33}$$

with u_i, v_j unrestricted in sign (since all constraints in the primal were equalities).

In this dual formulation the u_i and v_j dual variables are the implicit values associated with the various origins and destinations. Thus, u_i is the value of one unit of the product at origin i, or the implicit worth of origin i (per unit). Similarly, v_j is the value of one unit of the product delivered at destination j, or the implicit worth of destination (per unit). In the objective function of this dual problem, the s_i are the units available at the i origins, and the d_j are the amounts required at the destinations. The objective function we are seeking to maximize is the total value associated with the i origins and j destinations.

In the dual problem formulation, each constraint includes one u variable and one v variable only. Additionally, for each dual constraint, the subscript of u_i and v_j match the double subscript of c_{ij}, the right-hand-side value. Thus, if u_i and v_j are dual variables corresponding to the i origin constraints ($i = 1, 2, \ldots, m$) and the j destination constraints ($j = 1, 2, \ldots, n$), the corresponding dual to the transportation problem is given by

$$\text{Maximize } Z = \sum_{i=1}^{m} s_i u_i + \sum_{j=1}^{n} d_j v_j \quad (11.16)$$

subject to

$$u_i + v_j \leq c_{ij} \qquad \text{for all } i, j \quad (11.17)$$

with u_i, v_j unrestricted in sign.

As noted in our discussion of duality theory in Chapter 9, for each primal basic variable in any basic feasible solution, the corresponding dual constraint must be satisfied strictly as an equality (i.e., according to the property of complementary slackness). This means that

$$u_i + v_j = c_{ij} \quad \text{for all basic } x_{ij} \ (x_{ij} > 0)$$

$$\text{(i.e., for each occupied cell)} \quad (11.18)$$

and the remaining dual constraints will all be inequalities of the form

$$u_i + v_j \leq c_{ij} \quad \text{for all nonbasic } x_{ij} \ (x_{ij} = 0)$$

$$\text{(i.e., for each unoccupied cell)} \quad (11.19)$$

For the occupied cells, which represent the basic variables of the problem, we have $m + n - 1$ equations in $m + n$ unknowns, as given by (11.18). This set of equations can be solved by assigning an arbitrary value to any one of the u_i or v_j, and then determining the values of the remaining u_i and v_j. We assign an arbitrary value to any one of the u_i or v_j because we have fewer equations (i.e., $m + n - 1$) than unknowns (i.e., $m + n$), and we must do this in order to be able to solve the set of equations.

For the unoccupied cells, which represent the nonbasic variables of the problem, the value of $c_{ij} - u_i - v_j$ represents the amount by which each unit of x_{ij} would change the value of the objective function. Once all the u_i and v_j have been determined, the entering basic variable (if there is one) can be determined by calculating $c_{ij} - u_i - v_j$ for each unoccupied cell. If $c_{ij} - u_i - v_j \geq 0$ for each unoccupied cell, then we are optimal. Otherwise, we make the maximum permissible allocation to the unoccupied cell having the smallest (largest negative) value of $c_{ij} - u_i - v_j < 0$.

TABLE 11.17 INITIAL BASIC FEASIBLE SOLUTION-FOXWORTH CORPORATION-NORTHWEST CORNER RULE

TO DESTINATIONS / FROM ORIGINS	D_1: CHICAGO	D_2: HOUSTON	D_3: ATLANTA	ORIGIN SUPPLY	u_i
O_1: LOS ANGELES	90 ⑦⁰⁰	80 ③⁰⁰	100	1000	0
O_2: ST. LOUIS	20	40 ①⁷⁰⁰	50 ②⁰⁰	1900	−40
O_3: BOSTON	40	90	60 ①⁶⁰⁰	1600	−30
DESTINATION DEMAND	700	2000	1800	4500	
v_j	90	80	90		

TABLE 11.18 COST CHANGE COMPUTATIONS

UNOCCUPIED CELL	NET COST CHANGE COMPUTATION
$(1, 3)$	$c_{13} - u_1 - v_3 = 100 - 0 - 90 = +10$
$(2, 1)$	$c_{21} - u_2 - v_1 = 20 - (-40) - 90 = -30$
$(3, 1)$	$c_{31} - u_3 - v_1 = 40 - (-30) - 90 = -20$
$(3, 2)$	$c_{32} - u_3 - v_2 = 90 - (-30) - 80 = +40$

The savings in computational effort afforded by the MODI method become more apparent when we consider an actual problem situation. To demonstrate the MODI method, we refer back to the initial basic feasible solution to the Foxworth Corporation problem that we originally obtained by using the northwest corner rule. The initial transportation tableau for this problem is duplicated as Table 11.17. Observe that this table has an additional column, which indicates the values of the u_i, and an additional row, which indicates the values of the v_j. The values of the u_i and v_j were computed in the following manner.

First, the transportation costs corresponding to the variables in the initial basic feasible solution are

$$c_{11} = 90$$
$$c_{12} = 80$$
$$c_{22} = 40 \qquad (11.20)$$
$$c_{23} = 50$$
$$c_{33} = 60$$

Accordingly, the set of $m + n - 1 = 3 + 3 - 1 = 5$ simultaneous linear equations to be solved is

$$u_1 + v_1 = c_{11} = 90$$
$$u_1 + v_2 = c_{12} = 80$$
$$u_2 + v_2 = c_{22} = 40 \qquad (11.21)$$
$$u_2 + v_3 = c_{23} = 50$$
$$u_3 + v_3 = c_{33} = 60$$

Arbitrarily setting $u_1 = 0$, we obtain

$$0 + v_1 = 90 \rightarrow v_1 = 90$$
$$0 + v_2 = 80 \rightarrow v_2 = 80$$
$$u_2 + 80 = 40 \rightarrow u_2 = -40 \qquad (11.22)$$
$$-40 + v_3 = 50 \rightarrow v_3 = 90$$
$$u_3 + 90 = 60 \rightarrow u_3 = -30$$

TABLE 11.19 SECOND BASIC FEASIBLE SOLUTION—MODI METHOD (OPTIMAL SOLUTION)

TO DESTINATIONS / FROM ORIGINS	D_1: CHICAGO	D_2: HOUSTON	D_3: ATLANTA	ORIGIN SUPPLY	u_i
O_1: LOS ANGELES	90 / +30	80 / (1000)	100 / +10	1000	0
O_2: ST. LOUIS	20 / (700)	40 / (1000)	50 / (200)	1900	-40
O_3: BOSTON	40 / +10	90 / +40	60 / (1600)	1600	-30
DESTINATION DEMAND	700	2000	1800	4500	
v_j	60	80	90		

Now, for any unoccupied cell, the net cost change associated with allocating one unit to the unoccupied cell can be computed as $c_{ij} - u_i - v_j$. These computations are made as shown in Table 11.18. These values are, of course, exactly the same as those obtained by use of the stepping-stone algorithm (refer back to Table 11.13). Note, however, that our use of the MODI method has required much less work, as the tedious process of tracing out the closed loops has been eliminated, and the chances of making numerical errors have been reduced.

As was the case for the stepping-stone algorithm, the value of -30 associated with cell (2, 1) indicates that the present solution is not optimal. The amount allocated to cell (2, 1) is determined in exactly the same manner as was done for the stepping-stone procedure. Accordingly, 700 units are reallocated to cell (2, 1) resulting in the second basic feasible solution shown in Table 11.19.

In Table 11.19, the u_i, v_j, and the values of the $c_{ij} - u_i - v_j$; for the unoccupied cells must be recomputed. This has been done for the transportation tableau shown in this tableau, with the net cost changes for the unoccupied cells shown in the unoccupied cells. Since the net cost changes for all of the unoccupied cells in this tableau are positive, we have obtained the optimal solution. This optimal solution is, of course, identical to the optimal solution to this same problem obtained earlier by using the stepping-stone algorithm (refer back to Table 11.14).

11.4 THE UNBALANCED TRANSPORTATION PROBLEM

In our discussion thus far we have considered only the balanced transportation problem in which supply equals demand. In many real-world situations, however, supply exceeds demand, or vice versa. When an *unbalanced transportation problem* is encountered, we need to convert the unbalanced transportation problem into a balanced transportation problem in order to be able to apply either the stepping-stone or the MODI method.

The first case we consider is one that occurs when supply exceeds demand. The mathematical formulation of this type of unbalanced transportation problem is as follows.

CASE 1: UNBALANCED TRANSPORTATION PROBLEM—SUPPLY EXCEEDS DEMAND

$$\text{Minimize } Z = \sum_{i=1}^{m} \sum_{j=1}^{n} c_{ij}\, x_{ij} \qquad (11.23)$$

subject to

$$\sum_{j=1}^{n-1} x_{ij} \leq s_i \qquad i = 1, 2, \ldots, m$$
$$\sum_{i=1}^{m} x_{ij} = d_i \qquad j = 1, 2, \ldots, n-1 \qquad (11.24)$$

with

$$x_{ij} \geq 0 \qquad \text{all } i \text{ and } j \qquad (11.25)$$

Note that in the first set of m constraints we sum from $j = 1$ to $n - 1$ rather than the usual $j = 1$ to n. The reasons for doing this are explained later. Also, the first set of m constraints now contains a $\leq$ sign rather than an equality sign, indicating that we physically have more units available at the origins than are required at the destinations.

Now, the first m inequalities can be converted to m equalities by the addition of m slack variables. These slack variables are denoted as x_{in}; $i = 1, 2, \ldots, m$. The constraint set originally given by (11.24), rewritten as equalities becomes

$$\sum_{j=1}^{n-1} x_{ij} + x_{in} = s_i \quad i = 1, 2, \ldots, m \qquad (11.26)$$

$$\sum_{i=1}^{m} x_{ij} = d_j \qquad j = 1, 2, \ldots, n-1 \qquad (11.27)$$

If we now sum (11.26) over i and sum (11.27) over j, and subtract the second summation from the first summation, we obtain

$$\sum_{i=1}^{m} s_i - \sum_{j=1}^{n-1} d_j = \sum_{i=1}^{m} x_{in} \qquad (11.28)$$

Therefore, the sum of the slack variables is a constant, and is equal to the difference between the sum of the supplies at the origins and the sum of the demands at the

TABLE 11.20 REFORMULATED FOXWORTH CORPORATION PROBLEM—UNBALANCED PROBLEM (SUPPLY AT BOSTON INCREASED TO 1900 UNITS)

TO DESTINATIONS / FROM ORIGINS	D_1: CHICAGO	D_2: HOUSTON	D_3: ATLANTA	DUMMY D_4: DESTINATION	ORIGIN SUPPLY	u_i
O_1: LOS ANGELES	90 / +30	80 / (800)	100 / (200)	0 / −40	1000	0
O_2: ST. LOUIS	20 / (700)	40 / (1200)	50 / −10	0 / 0	1900	−40
O_3: BOSTON	40 / +20	90 / +50	60 / (1600)	0 / (300)	1900	−40
DESTINATION DEMAND	700	2000	1800	300	4800	
v_j	60	80	100	40		

destinations. This means that in order to convert an unbalanced transportation problem into a balanced transportation problem, we simply add one additional column to the transportation tableau. This additional column represents an additional destination that has a demand requirement that is equal to the amount by which the original supply exceeds the original demand. This additional column is referred to as a *slack* or *dummy destination*. The costs associated with this dummy column, the c_{in} associated with the slack variables, the x_{in}, are all zero. Thus we are considering the slack units to be shipped at zero cost. Having made these modifications, the unbalanced transportation problem has been converted into a balanced transportation problem, and it can be solved in the usual manner.

To illustrate an unbalanced transportation problem in which supply exceeds demand, let us reconsider the Foxworth Corporation problem, with the supply at origin 3, Boston, increased to 1900 units. The modified transportation tableau is shown in Table 11.20. In Table 11.20 observe first that we have added one dummy destination (column) with demand requirement given by

Demand requirement at dummy destination

$$= \sum_{i=1}^{m} s_i - \sum_{j=1}^{n-1} d_j$$
$$= 4800 - 4500 \qquad (11.29)$$
$$= 300$$

The transportation costs associated with this dummy destination column are all zero. Observe next that we have determined an initial basic feasible solution for this problem, with $m + n - 1 = 3 + 4 - 1 = 6$ cells occupied, using the matrix minima method. In determining this initial basic feasible solution, we utilize one cell in the dummy destination column, and the total transportation cost is $242,000. Using the MODI method to evaluate the costs associated with moving into the unoccupied cells for this initial basic feasible solution, we see that a per-unit savings of $40 can be achieved by making an allocation to cell (1, 4). We next determine that it is possible to move 200 units into cell (1, 4). Making this reallocation, we obtain the second basic feasible solution shown in Table 11.21.

In this second basic feasible solution, the total transportation cost is $234,000. Employing the MODI method once again, we see that a per-unit savings of $20 can be achieved by making an allocation to cell (3, 1). We next determine that it is possible to move 100 units into cell (3, 1). Making this reallocation, we obtain the third basic feasible solution shown in Table 11.22. In this solution all of the unoccupied cells have positive evaluations, indicating that we have determined the optimal solution. The minimum cost shipping plan is as shown in Table 11.23.

The second case we consider is that which occurs when demand exceeds supply. The mathematical formulation of this type of unbalanced transportation problem is as follows.

TABLE 11.21 SECOND BASIC FEASIBLE SOLUTION—UNBALANCED PROBLEM

TO DESTINATIONS / FROM ORIGINS	D_1: CHICAGO	D_2: HOUSTON	D_3: ATLANTA	DUMMY D_4: DESTINATION	ORIGIN SUPPLY	u_i
O_1: LOS ANGELES	90 / +30	80 / (800)	100 / +160	0 / (200)	1000	0
O_2: ST. LOUIS	20 / (700)	40 / (1200)	50 / +150	0 / +40	1900	−40
O_3: BOSTON	40 / −20	90 / +10	60 / (1800)	0 / (100)	1900	0
DESTINATION DEMAND	700	2000	1800	300	4800	
v_j	60	80	−60	0		

TABLE 11.22 THIRD BASIC FEASIBLE SOLUTION—UNBALANCED PROBLEM

TO DESTINATIONS / FROM ORIGINS	D_1: CHICAGO	D_2: HOUSTON	D_3: ATLANTA	DUMMY D_4: DESTINATION	ORIGIN SUPPLY	u_i
O_1: LOS ANGELES	90 / +30	80 / (700)	100 / +20	0 / (300)	1000	0
O_2: ST. LOUIS	20 / (600)	40 / (1300)	50 / +10	0 / +40	1900	−40
O_3: BOSTON	40 / (100)	90 / +30	60 / (1800)	0 / +20	1900	−20
DESTINATION DEMAND	700	2000	1800	300	4800	
v_j	60	80	80	0		

TABLE 11.23 MINIMUM COST SHIPPING PLAN

SHIPPING ROUTE	TRANSPORTATION COST
Los Angeles → Houston	700 units × $80/unit = $ 56,000
Los Angeles → Dummy Destination	300 units × $ 0/unit = 0
St. Louis → Chicago	600 units × $20/unit = 12,000
St. Louis → Houston	1300 units × $40/unit = 52,000
Boston → Chicago	100 units × $40/unit = 4,000
Boston → Atlanta	1800 units × $60/unit = 108,000
	Total $232,000

CASE 2. UNBALANCED TRANSPORTATION PROBLEM—DEMAND EXCEEDS SUPPLY

$$\text{Minimize } Z = \sum_{i=1}^{m} \sum_{j=1}^{n} c_{ij} x_{ij} \qquad (11.30)$$

subject to

$$\sum_{j=1}^{n} x_{ij} = a_i \qquad i = 1, \ldots, m-1$$

$$\sum_{j=1}^{m-1} x_{ij} \leq b_j \qquad j = 1, \ldots, n \qquad (11.31)$$

with

$$x_{ij} \geq 0 \qquad \text{for all } i, j \qquad (11.32)$$

Now we have a situation in which the resource requirements exceed the supply availabilities. Consequently, rather than introducing a slack or dummy destination to receive an unused supply, we must now introduce a slack or dummy origin from which we can obtain the unfilled demand capacity. We add one more row to the tableau, that is, we add an additional source having an availability equal to the difference between the destination requirements and the supply availability. In general, the costs associated with this dummy row, the c_{mj} associated with the slack variables, the x_{mj}, are set equal to zero. In this case, however, we are really indicating that a certain amount of the requirement at the real destination will be

satisfied from fictitious, or nonexistent, origins. Thus, it may be preferable to make the costs associated with this dummy origin equal to some reasonable set of "penalty" costs, which typically would be higher than the costs associated with the other (real) origins. Alternatively, they can be set equal to zero, as was done for the case in which supply exceeded demand. Having made these modifications, we have converted this unbalanced transportation problem into a balanced transportation problem, and it can be solved in the usual manner.

11.5 OTHER COMMENTS ON THE TRANSPORTATION PROBLEM

Certain complications can arise in actually solving transportation problems. In this section we discuss some of these complications and consider ways in which they may be resolved.

11.5.1 DEGENERACY

A basic feasible solution to a transportation problem is *degenerate* if less than $m + n - 1$ of the x_{ij} values are strictly positive (i.e., > 0). In this case, less than $m + n - 1$ strictly positive allocations will be necessary to utilize all of the supply availabilities and satisfy all of the demand requirements. Degeneracy can occur during the determination of the initial basic feasible solution, or it can occur during sub-

TABLE 11.24 INITIAL BASIC FEASIBLE SOLUTION—NORTHWEST CORNER RULE (DEGENERATE SOLUTION—ONLY FIVE OCCUPIED CELLS)

TO DESTINATIONS / FROM ORIGINS	D_1	D_2	D_3	D_4	ORIGIN SUPPLY
O_1	(35) 3	6	7	6	35
O_2	(15) 4	(175) 5	8	7	190
O_3	5	3	(65) 5	(35) 5	100
DESTINATION DEMAND	50	175	65	35	325

TABLE 11.25 INITIAL BASIC FEASIBLE SOLUTION—ADDITION OF DUMMY CELL (2,3)

TO DESTINATIONS / FROM ORIGINS	D_1	D_2	D_3	D_4	ORIGIN SUPPLY	u_i
O_1	㉟ 3	+2 6	+0 7	−1 6	35	0
O_2	⑮ 4	⑰⑤ 5	⓪ 8	−1 7	190	1
O_3	+4 5	+1 3	㊚ 5	㉟ 5	100	−2
DESTINATION DEMAND	50	175	65	35	325	
v_j	3	4	7	7		

sequent iterations made using either the stepping-stone algorithm or the MODI method when there is a tie for the basic variable leaving the solution. Unfortunately, when degeneracy occurs it is impossible to apply either the stepping-stone algorithm or MODI method. Without the $m + n - 1$ occupied cells (i.e., without $m + n - 1$ x_{ij} values strictly positive) it is impossible to evaluate all the closed paths or solve the $m + n - 1$ MODI equations.

CASE 1: DEGENERACY OCCURRING IN THE INITIAL BASIC FEASIBLE SOLUTION

To illustrate a situation in which degeneracy occurs in the initial basic feasible solution, consider the tableau shown in Table 11.24, in which the northwest corner rule was used to select the initial basic feasible solution. The occupied cells are circled.

TABLE 11.26 SECOND BASIC FEASIBLE SOLUTION—OPTIMAL SOLUTION (DEGENERATE OPTIMAL SOLUTION)

TO DESTINATIONS / FROM ORIGINS	D_1	D_2	D_3	D_4	ORIGIN SUPPLY	u_i
O_1	㉟ 3	+2 6	+1 7	⓪ 6	35	0
O_2	⑮ 4	⑰⑤ 5	+1 8	0 7	190	1
O_3	+3 5	0 3	㊚ 5	㉟ 5	100	−1
DESTINATION DEMAND	50	175	65	35	325	
v_j	3	4	6	6		

TABLE 11.27 INITIAL BASIC FEASIBLE SOLUTION—NORTHWEST CORNER RULE

TO DESTINATIONS / FROM ORIGINS	D_1	D_2	D_3	D_4	ORIGIN SUPPLY	u_i
O_1	5 / ⑤⓪	2 / ③⓪	1 / −4	2 / −5	80	0
O_2	4 / −3	4 / ④⓪	7 / ①⓪	3 / −6	50	2
O_3	6 / +2	2 / +1	4 / ②⓪	6 / ①⓪	30	−1
DESTINATION REQUIREMENT	50	70	30	10	160	
v_j	5	2	5	7		

Observe that as we apply the northwest corner rule, we make allocation of 175 units to cell (2, 2), which simultaneously exhausts the supply at origin 2 and satisfies the demand at destination 2. As a result, our initial basic feasible solution has only five occupied cells when there should be six (i.e., $m + n - 1 = 3 + 4 - 1 = 6$). Thus, a degenerate solution exists. Observe further that were we to try to use the stepping-stone algorithm on this tableau, we could not proceed to determine closed loops for most of the unoccupied cells in the tableau. For example, no closed loop exists for cell (2, 4).

To alleviate this situation and to allow us to proceed, a fictitious, or dummy, allocation of 0 units must be made to one of the unoccupied cells in order to reestablish the $m + n - 1$ occupied cells condition. Usually there will be more than one unoccupied cell to which the dummy allocation can be made. The cell chosen will be one that will then allow all other unoccupied cells to be evaluated using either the stepping-stone algorithm or the MODI method. In this case, two possible candidates for the dummy allocation are cells (2, 3) and cells (3, 2), since they are the cells to which an allocation would have been made using the northwest corner method. Selecting cell (2, 3) as the cell to receive the dummy allocation of 0 units results in Table 11.25. Having specified a basic feasible solution having $m + n - 1$ occupied cells, we can proceed to obtain a solution. Using the MODI method we see that a reallocation can be made to either cell (1, 4) or cell (2, 4). Choosing cell (1, 4), we next see that the maximum allocation to cell (1, 4) is 0 units (i.e., the dummy allocation originally made to cell 2, 3). Making this reallocation we obtain Table 11.26. In this transportation tableau, all of the unoccupied cells have positive values, so we have obtained the optimal solution. Note,

however, that this optimal solution is still degenerate, since it has only five cells with x_{ij} values greater than zero.

CASE 2: DEGENERACY OCCURRING BECAUSE OF A TIE FOR THE LEAVING BASIC VARIABLE

Let us now consider the situation in which the solution becomes degenerate because of a tie for the leaving basic variable. To illustrate, consider Table 11.27, which presents an initial feasible solution to a transportation problem obtained by using the northwest corner rule. The occupied cells are circled. In this tableau each of the unoccupied cells has been evaluated using the MODI method, and net cost changes for the respective unoccupied cells are indicated. In the tableau it is seen that an allocation should be made to cell (2, 4), since it has the most negative value. Note that there is a tie for the leaving basic variable, since either $x_{23} = 10$ or $x_{34} = 10$ can be replaced by $x_{24} = 10$. Allocating the maximum feasible amount of 10 units results in the second basic feasible solution shown in Table 11.28. Note that when the allocation of 10 units is made to cell (2, 4), the solution becomes degenerate, since both cell (2, 3) and cell (3, 4) are reduced to zero (i.e., $x_{23} = 0$ and $x_{34} = 0$, as $x_{24} \rightarrow 10$). In essence, two basic variables have left the solution, while only one variable has entered. We now have only five occupied cells instead of the required $m + n - 1 = 3 + 4 - 1 = 6$. Once again, we would be unable to evaluate most of the unoccupied cells in the tableau, as we cannot determine the entire set of u_i and v_j values.

To alleviate this situation and to allow us to proceed, we once again must make a dummy allocation of 0 units

TABLE 11.28 SECOND BASIC FEASIBLE SOLUTION (DEGENERATE—ONLY FIVE OCCUPIED CELLS)

TO DESTINATIONS / FROM ORIGINS	D_1	D_2	D_3	D_4	ORIGIN SUPPLY	u_i
O_1	(50) · 5	(30) · 2	1	2	80	0
O_2	4	(40) · 4	7	(10) · 3	50	2
O_3	6	2	(30) · 4	6	30	(Cannot determine)
DESTINATION REQUIREMENT	50	70	30	10	160	
v_j	5	2	(Cannot determine)	1		

to one of the unoccupied cells in order to reestablish the $m + n - 1$ occupied cells condition. In general, the 0 allocation can be made to either of the two cells that have been reduced to zero. Let us assume that we make the allocation to cell (2, 3). The tableau in which this has been done is shown as Table 11.29. Applying the MODI method, we see that a reallocation should be made to cell (1, 3). A maximum reallocation of 0 can be made, since the closed loop for this cell contains the 0 in cell (2, 3) as the minimum amount to be subtracted. Making this reallocation, we obtain the third basic feasible solution shown in Table 11.30. Applying the MODI method, we see that a reallocation should be made to

either cell (2, 1) or cell (3, 2). Choosing cell (2, 1), the maximum reallocation possible is 40 units. Making this reallocation, we obtain the fourth basic feasible solution shown in Table 11.31. Applying the MODI method, we see that a reallocation should be made to cell (3, 2). The maximum reallocation possible is 30 units. Making this reallocation, we obtain the fifth basic feasible solution shown in Table 11.32. Applying the MODI method, we see that a reallocation should be made to cell (1, 4). The maximum reallocation possible is 10 units. Making this reallocation, we obtain the sixth basic feasible solution shown in Table 11.33. Since all the unoccupied cells now have net cost change evaluations that are positive, we

TABLE 11.29 SECOND BASIC FEASIBLE SOLUTION-ADDITION OF DUMMY CELL (2,3)

TO DESTINATIONS / FROM ORIGINS	D_1	D_2	D_3	D_4	ORIGIN SUPPLY	u_i
O_1	(50) · 5	(30) · 2	-4 · 1	$+1$ · 2	80	0
O_2	-3 · 4	(40) · 4	(0) · 7	(10) · 3	50	2
O_3	$+2$ · 6	$+1$ · 2	(30) · 4	$+6$ · 6	30	-1
DESTINATION REQUIREMENT	50	70	30	10	160	
v_j	5	2	5	1		

TABLE 11.30 THIRD BASIC FEASIBLE SOLUTION

TO DESTINATIONS / FROM ORIGINS	D_1	D_2	D_3	D_4	ORIGIN SUPPLY	u_i
O_1	(50) 5	(30) 2	(0) 1	+1 2	80	0
O_2	−3 4	(40) 4	+4 7	(10) 3	50	2
O_3	−2 6	−3 2	(30) 4	+2 6	30	3
DESTINATION REQUIREMENT	50	70	30	10	160	
v_j	5	2	1	1		

have obtained the optimal solution. This optimal solution is still degenerate, however, since only five of the occupied cells are strictly positive.

11.5.2 ALTERNATIVE OPTIMAL SOLUTIONS

A transportation problem can have more than one optimal solution (i.e., alternative optimal solutions). This will be indicated by the presence of an unoccupied cell with a net cost change equal to zero.

This means that an alternative allocation pattern is possible, and that this alternative allocation pattern will produce the same total transportation cost.

11.5.3 PROHIBITED ROUTES

In many practical transportation problems it will be desirable to discourage or prevent shipment of a product from a certain origin to a certain destination. This can be accomplished by assigning an arbitrarily large cost, for example, $c_{ij} = +M$, as the cost coefficient for the cell corresponding to this

TABLE 11.31 FOURTH BASIC FEASIBLE SOLUTION

TO DESTINATIONS / FROM ORIGINS	D_1	D_2	D_3	D_4	ORIGIN SUPPLY	u_i
O_1	(10) 5	(70) 2	(0) 1	−2 2	80	0
O_2	(40) 4	+3 4	+7 7	(10) 3	50	−1
O_3	−2 6	−3 2	(30) 4	−1 6	30	3
DESTINATION REQUIREMENT	50	70	30	10	160	
v_j	5	2	1	4		

TABLE 11.32 FIFTH BASIC FEASIBLE SOLUTION

FROM ORIGINS \ TO DESTINATIONS	D_1	D_2	D_3	D_4	ORIGIN SUPPLY	u_i
O_1	(10) — 5	(40) — 2	(30) — 1	−2 — 2	80	0
O_2	(40) — 4	+3 — 4	+7 — 7	(10) — 3	50	−1
O_3	+1 — 6	(30) — 2	+3 — 4	+2 — 6	30	0
DESTINATION REQUIREMENT	50	70	30	10	160	
v_j	5	2	1	4		

origin → destination movement. The use of +M as the cost coefficient for the cell will effectively prohibit entry of the associated cell into the basic solution, and such an allocation will not be a part of the final solution. The solution process then proceeds in the normal fashion.

11.5.4 MAXIMIZATION TRANSPORTATION PROBLEMS

It is not unusual to encounter a transportation problem in which the objective is the maximization of profits rather than the minimization of costs. Such maximization transportation problems can still be solved using the stepping-stone algorithm or MODI method. One of the two following modifications must be made, however.

1. The profit maximization transportation problem is solved in exactly the same manner as the cost minimization transportation problem, except that costs c_{ij} are replaced by profits p_{ij} and the test of optimality is reversed. Thus, in the profit maximization transportation

TABLE 11.33 SIXTH BASIC FEASIBLE SOLUTION (OPTIMAL SOLUTION)

FROM ORIGINS \ TO DESTINATIONS	D_1	D_2	D_3	D_4	ORIGIN SUPPLY	u_i
O_1	+2 — 5	(40) — 2	(30) — 1	(10) — 2	80	0
O_2	(50) — 4	+1 — 4	+5 — 7	(0) — 3	50	1
O_3	+3 — 6	(30) — 2	+3 — 4	+4 — 6	30	0
DESTINATION DEMAND	50	70	30	10	160	
v_j	3	2	1	2		

TABLE 11.34 PRODUCTION UNIT TO WHOLESALE DISTRIBUTOR SHIPMENT— COST MATRIX

TO FROM	LOS ANGELES	HOUSTON	ATLANTA	PITTSBURGH
PROVO	60	115	175	155
DENVER	50	45	120	200
KANSAS CITY	130	60	125	125

problem, when all the unoccupied cell evaluations are zero or negative, the solution is optimal.

2. The profit maximization transportation problem is transformed by subtracting all of the p_{ij} from the largest p_{ij}. This transformation scales the original problem into a new problem involving relative costs. To illustrate consider the following two cells in a transportation tableau in which the profits associated with the cells are shown in the right-hand corners.

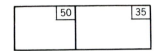

In the profit maximization problem we would try to allocate as much as possible to the cell having the largest profit, namely $p_{ij} = 50$. If we now perform the transformation of subtracting the p_{ij} from the largest p_{ij}, we obtain

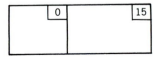

Now, in a relative cost sense we would try to allocate as much as possible to the cell having the smallest relative cost, namely $p_{ij} = 0$, so we see that the two problems are equivalent. The new relative cost problem can then be solved in the usual cost minimization manner. The total maximum profit is calculated by multiplying the optimal values of the basic variables, the x_{ij}, by the original profits, the p_{ij}.

11.6 THE TRANSSHIPMENT PROBLEM

An interesting and important extension of the transportation problem involves situations in which each origin and destination can also be an intermediate (or transshipping) point of shipment from, or to, the other origins or destinations. This situation is referred to as the *transshipment problem,* and is basically a generalization of the transportation problem in which there may be not only pure origins and pure destinations, but also transshipment points that can be both origins and destinations. Fortunately, the transshipment problem can be solved as a transportation problem after it has been reformulated into the tableau format of the standard transportation problem.

To illustrate the procedure for transforming a transshipment problem situation into a transportation problem, let us consider an example. The Hempstead Company manufactures ceiling fans at three production facilities and supplies these ceiling fans to four large wholesale distributors. The pro-

TABLE 11.35 PRODUCTION UNIT TO PRODUCTION UNIT SHIPMENTS— COST MATRIX

TO FROM	PROVO	DENVER	KANSAS CITY
PROVO	0	80	95
DENVER	80	0	30
KANSAS CITY	95	30	0

TABLE 11.36 WHOLESALE DISTRIBUTOR TO WHOLESALE DISTRIBUTOR SHIPMENTS—COST MATRIX

FROM \ TO	LOS ANGELES	HOUSTON	ATLANTA	PITTSBURGH
LOS ANGELES	0	90	65	150
HOUSTON	90	0	60	120
ATLANTA	65	60	0	85
PITTSBURGH	150	120	85	0

duction units are located in Provo, Utah; Denver, Colorado; and Kansas City, Missouri. The wholesale distributors are located in Los Angeles, Houston, Atlanta, and Pittsburgh.

First, the Hempstead Company can make shipments from its production units to wholesale distributors. The costs associated with these types of shipments are shown in the cost matrix in Table 11.34. This set of transportation costs is the same as it would be for a normal transportation problem involving only the production units and the wholesale distributors.

Second, the Hempstead Company can also make shipments between its production units. The costs associated with these types of shipments are shown in the cost matrix in Table 11.35. This set of transportation costs is based on the idea that production unit to production unit shipments are allowed. This might be desirable, for example, if excess storage space was available at the production units.

Third, the Hempstead Company can also make shipments between its wholesale distributors. The costs associated with these types of shipments are

shown in the cost matrix in Table 11.36. Again, this set of costs is based on wholesaler to wholesaler shipments being possible, or desirable, perhaps because of excess storage space.

Fourth, the Hempstead Company can also make shipments from its wholesale distributors to its production units. This is allowed, again, because of potential excess storage space at the production units. Obviously, the wholesale distributor to production unit transportation costs are identical to those presented earlier as the production unit to wholesale distributor transportation costs.

The Hempstead Company has determined that the weekly supply availabilities at Provo, Denver, and Kansas City are 25 truckloads, 75 truckloads, and 50 truckloads, respectively. The weekly demand requirements at Los Angeles, Houston, Atlanta, and Pittsburgh are 25 truckloads, 30 truckloads, 50 truckloads, and 45 truckloads, respectively. The Hempstead Company would like to determine the shipping schedule that will minimize the total transportation cost for this transshipping situation.

Using the cost data shown in the previous cost matrixes, we initially construct a combined cost ma-

TABLE 11.37 STRUCTURE OF COMBINED TRANSPORTATION COST MATRIX

FROM \ TO	PRODUCTION UNITS	WHOLESALE DISTRIBUTORS
PRODUCTION UNITS	From Production Unit to Production Unit	From Production Unit to Wholesale Distributor
WHOLESALE DISTRIBUTORS	From Wholesale Distributor to Production Unit	From Wholesale Distributor to Wholesale Distributor

TABLE 11.38 COMBINED COST MATRIX—TRANSSHIPMENT PROBLEM

FROM \ TO	PRODUCTION UNIT			WHOLESALE DISTRIBUTOR				SUPPLY AVAILABILITY
	PROVO	DENVER	KANSAS CITY	LOS ANGELES	HOUSTON	ATLANTA	PITTSBURGH	
PRODUCTION UNIT								
PROVO	0	80	95	60	115	175	155	25
DENVER	80	0	30	50	45	120	200	75
KANSAS CITY	95	30	0	130	60	125	125	50
WHOLESALE DISTRIBUTOR								
LOS ANGELES	60	50	130	0	90	65	150	0
HOUSTON	115	45	60	90	0	60	120	0
ATLANTA	175	120	125	65	60	0	85	0
PITTSBURGH	155	200	125	150	120	85	0	0
DEMAND REQUIREMENTS	0	0	0	25	30	50	45	

TABLE 11.39 TRANSSHIPMENT PROBLEM IN TRANSPORTATION TABLEAU FORMAT

FROM \ TO	PRODUCTION UNIT			WHOLESALE DISTRIBUTOR				SUPPLY AVAILABILITY
	PROVO	DENVER	KANSAS CITY	LOS ANGELES	HOUSTON	ATLANTA	PITTSBURGH	
PRODUCTION UNIT — PROVO	0	80	95	60	115	175	155	175
DENVER	80	0	30	50	45	120	200	225
KANSAS CITY	95	30	0	130	60	125	125	200
WHOLESALE DISTRIBUTOR — LOS ANGELES	60	50	130	0	90	65	150	150
HOUSTON	115	45	60	90	0	60	120	150
ATLANTA	175	120	125	65	60	0	85	150
PITTSBURGH	155	200	125	150	120	85	0	150
DEMAND REQUIREMENTS	150	150	150	175	180	200	195	

trix that summarizes information for all four of the shipping options allowable for the transshipment problem. Remember that the transshipment problem has a structure such that the production units can ship to other production units as well as to the wholesale distributor. Similarly, the wholesale distributors can ship to other wholesale distributors as well as to the production units. The structure of this combined transportation cost matrix is as shown in Table 11.37. The combined cost matrix for the transshipment problem situation being analyzed, using the corresponding transportation cost information, is presented in Table 11.38. Observe that in this table, the actual supply availabilities are for the production units and the actual demand requirements are for the wholesale distributors.

The second step in the transformation process involves the determination of the appropriate modified supply availabilities at the expanded set of origins and the determination of the appropriate modified demand requirements at the expanded set of destinations. In the transshipment problem each origin and each destination represents either a potential point of supply or potential point of demand. This means that the supply availabilities for the new rows and the demand requirements for the new columns must reflect the fact that any location (origin or destination) can now serve as a supply or demand point for all other locations. In the example currently being considered, the total supply availability and the total demand requirement is 150 truckloads per week. This is the total amount that can be transshipped through any location. Thus, each of the new origins (rows) is assigned an availability equal to the total transshipment quantity and each of the new destinations (columns) is assigned a requirement equal to the total transshipment quantity. Additionally, the total transshipment amount of 150 truckloads per week is added to each of the original supply availabilities and to each of the original destination requirements. For example, at the Los Angeles wholesale distributor the demand requirement is now 25 truckloads/week + 150 truckloads/week = 175 truckloads/week. Of this amount 25 truckloads per week are actually required at Los Angeles, while the remaining 175 truckloads/week − 25 truckloads/week = 150 truckloads/week could be routed to Los Angeles for transshipment to other demand destinations. The complete transshipment problem that has been reformulated in transportation tableau format is presented in Table 11.39.

The transportation problem equivalent of the transshipment problem, as presented in Table 11.39

TABLE 11.40 OPTIMAL SOLUTION—TRANSSHIPMENT PROBLEM

FROM \ TO		PRODUCTION UNIT			WHOLESALE DISTRIBUTOR				SUPPLY AVAILABILITY
		PROVO	DENVER	KANSAS CITY	LOS ANGELES	HOUSTON	ATLANTA	PITTSBURGH	
PRODUCTION UNIT	PROVO	0 (150)	80	95	60 (25)	115	175	155	175
	DENVER	80	0 (150)	30	50	45 (75)	120	200	225
	KANSAS CITY	95	30	0 (150)	130	60 (5)	125	125 (45)	200
WHOLESALE DISTRIBUTOR	LOS ANGELES	60	50	130	0 (150)	90	65 (0)	150	150
	HOUSTON	115	45	60	90 (100)	0 (50)	60	120	150
	ATLANTA	175	120	125	65	60 (150)	0	85	150
	PITTSBURGH	155	200	125	150	120	85	0 (150)	150
DEMAND REQUIREMENTS		150	150	150	175	180	200	195	

TABLE 11.41 MINIMUM TRANSPORTATION COST SHIPPING PLAN

SHIPPING ROUTE	TRANSPORTATION COST
Provo → Los Angeles	25 units × $60/unit = $ 1500
Denver → Houston	75 units × $45/unit = 3375
Kansas City → Houston	5 units × $60/unit = 300
Kansas City → Pittsburgh	45 units × $125/unit = 5625
Houston → Atlanta	50 units × $60/unit = 3000
	Total $13,800

Transshipment brackets: Denver → Houston, Kansas City → Houston, and Houston → Atlanta.

may now be solved using either the stepping-stone algorithm or the MODI method. The optimal solution for this problem is presented in Table 11.40. The minimum transportation cost shipping plan is as shown in Table 11.41.

11.7 THE ASSIGNMENT PROBLEM

The assignment problem is a special type of linear programming problem. Its structure is such that each of n resources must be assigned to each of n activities, on a one-to-one basis. There are an equal number of origins and destinations, and each origin supply and each destination requirement equals one. Thus, each resource must be assigned to one, and only one, activity. A cost c_{ij} is associated with using resource i for activity j, and the objective of the assignment problem is to minimize the total cost of assigning all resources to all activities.

EXAMPLE

To illustrate the structure of a typical assignment problem consider the following problem situation. The manager of the computer center at Bohonkus Technical College has four programming jobs that she wishes to assign to four programmers. From the nature and length of the programming jobs, the manager of the computer center can estimate the cost associated with assigning a particular programmer to a particular programming job. These costs are shown in Table 11.42. The assignment problem for this situation requires the assignment of the four programming jobs to the four programmers on a one-to-one basis.

The assignment problem can be written mathematically as the following linear programming problem.

$$\text{Minimize } Z = \sum_{i=1}^{n} \sum_{j=1}^{n} c_{ij} x_{ij} \qquad (11.33)$$

subject to

$$\sum_{i=1}^{n} x_{ij} = 1 \qquad \text{for } j = 1, 2, \ldots, n$$
$$\qquad (11.34)$$
$$\sum_{j=1}^{n} x_{ij} = 1 \qquad \text{for } i = 1, 2, \ldots, n$$

with

$$x_{ij} = 0 \quad \text{or} \quad 1 \qquad \text{for all } i \text{ and } j \qquad (11.35)$$

TABLE 11.42 PROGRAMMING COST BY PROGRAMMER AND PROGRAMMING JOB

PROGRAMMER \ PROGRAMMING JOB	1	2	3	4
BOB	11	7	9	13
SUE	9	14	8	11
JIM	6	10	8	9
ANN	10	13	12	11

TABLE 11.43 TRANSPORTATION TABLEAU FOR THE ASSIGNMENT PROBLEM

RESOURCE	ACTIVITY A_1	A_2	$\cdots$	A_n	AVAILABILITY
R_1	C_{11}	C_{12}	$\cdots$	C_{1n}	1
R_2	C_{21}	C_{22}	$\cdots$	C_{2n}	1
$\vdots$	$\vdots$	$\vdots$	$\ddots$	$\vdots$	$\vdots$
R_n	C_{n1}	C_{n2}	$\cdots$	C_{nn}	1
REQUIREMENT	1	1	$\cdots$	1	n

WHERE

x_{ij} = assignment of resource i to activity j; c_{ij} = cost associated with assignment of resource i to activity j.

The assignment problem specified by (11.33), (11.34), and (11.35) is a *balanced assignment problem*, since the number of activities is exactly equal to the number of resources (i.e., $i = j = n$).

For the assignment problem example shown in Table 11.42, its linear programming formulation can be written as follows. Let

x_{ij} = assignment of programmer i to programming job j

Minimize $Z = 11x_{11} + 7x_{12} + 9x_{13}$
$$+ 13x_{14} + 9x_{21} + 14x_{22} + 8x_{23} + 11x_{24}$$
$$+ 6x_{31} + 10x_{33} + 8x_{33} + 9x_{34}$$
$$+ 10x_{41} + 13x_{42} + 12x_{43} + 11x_{44} \quad (11.36)$$

subject to

$$x_{11} + x_{12} + x_{13} + x_{14} = 1$$
$$x_{21} + x_{22} + x_{23} + x_{24} = 1$$
$$x_{31} + x_{32} + x_{33} + x_{34} = 1$$
$$x_{41} + x_{42} + x_{43} + x_{44} = 1$$
$$\quad (11.37)$$
$$x_{11} + x_{21} + x_{31} + x_{41} = 1$$
$$x_{12} + x_{22} + x_{32} + x_{42} = 1$$
$$x_{13} + x_{23} + x_{33} + x_{43} = 1$$
$$x_{14} + x_{24} + x_{34} + x_{44} = 1$$

with

$$x_{ij} = 0 \quad \text{or} \quad 1 \qquad \text{for all } i \text{ and } j \quad (11.38)$$

You might want to compare this linear programming formulation of the assignment problem to the linear programming formulation of the transportation problem that was presented in Section 11.2. Observe that the assignment problem is a special type of transportation problem in which $m = n$, supply availability $s_i = 1$ for $i = 1, 2, \ldots, n$; demand requirement $d_j = 1j = 1, 2, \ldots, n$; and

$$\sum_{i=1}^{n} s_i = \sum_{j=1}^{n} d_j = n \quad (11.39)$$

The transportation tableau corresponding to the assignment problem is shown in Table 11.43.

11.7.1 SOLVING THE ASSIGNMENT PROBLEM: THE HUNGARIAN METHOD

Because of the special structure of the assignment problem it can be solved most efficiently by a solution procedure known as the *Hungarian method.*[3] The Hungarian method is based on two features of the structure of the assignment problem.

---

[3]Named after D. Konig, a Hungarian mathematician who first proved (1916) a theorem required for the development of the method. See C.W. Churchman, R.L. Ackoff, and E.L. Arnoff, *Introduction to Operations Research.* New York: Wiley, 1967, pp. 347–368, for a discussion of the history and development of the Hungarian method.

First, each resource must be assigned to one and only one of the activities and vice versa. An optimal assignment will involve a one-to-one matching of the n resources to the n activities. In an optimal solution we will have exactly one $x_{ij} = 1$ in each row (and column). We seek to make this assignment in a manner that minimizes the overall cost of the assignment, using the cost matrix defined by the transportation tableau.

Second, in the transportation tableau for the assignment problem a constant can be added to or subtracted from all cost values in a row, or all cost values in a column, without having any effect on the set of optimal assignments. For example, if four units are subtracted from the values in the ith row and two units are added to the values in the jth column, then the objective function for the assignment problem would become

$$\text{Minimize } Z = \sum_{i=1}^{n} \sum_{j=1}^{n} c_{ij} \, x_{ij} - 4 \sum_{j=1}^{n} x_{ij}$$

$$+ 2 \sum_{i=1}^{n} x_{ij}$$

$$= \sum_{i=1}^{n} \sum_{j=1}^{n} c_{ij} \, x_{ij} - 4 + 2 \quad (11.40)$$

since

$$\sum_{j=1}^{n} x_{ij} = 1 \quad \text{and} \quad \sum_{i=1}^{n} x_{ij} = 1 \quad (11.41)$$

as specified by the constraints for the assignment problem (see 11.34). Subtracting a constant from, or adding a constant to the objective function does not change the set of optimal assignments, since every basic feasible solution would have the same amount subtracted from, or added to, the objective function.

The concepts just illustrated can be generalized to the case in which a_i is subtracted from each value in the ith row for $i = 1, 2, \ldots, n$, and b_j is subtracted from each value in the jth column of the transportation tableau for the assignment problem for $j = 1, 2, \ldots, n$. The new objective function for the assignment problem would become

$$\text{Minimize } Z = \sum_{i=1}^{n} \sum_{j=1}^{n} c_{ij} \, x_{ij} - \sum_{i=1}^{n} a_i \sum_{j=1}^{n} x_{ij}$$

$$- \sum_{j=1}^{n} b_j \sum_{i=1}^{n} x_{ij}$$

$$= \sum_{i=1}^{n} \sum_{j=1}^{n} c_{ij} \, x_{ij} - \sum_{i=1}^{n} a_i - \sum_{j=1}^{n} b_j \quad (11.42)$$

Again, subtracting the constants $\sum_{i=1}^{n} a_i$ and $\sum_{j=1}^{n} b_j$ from the original objective function will not change the set of basic feasible solutions, or the optimal set of assignments.

The Hungarian method for efficiently solving the assignment problem initially involves converting the original cost matrix into an equivalent cost matrix having only positive or zero elements. This process is called *matrix reduction* and results in the original cost matrix being transformed into an *opportunity cost matrix*. Matrix reduction is done by subtracting the smallest cost value in each row from all cost values in that row and then, if necessary, subtracting the smallest cost value in each column from all cost values in that column. The new cost matrix is the opportunity cost matrix, and the zero entries in this opportunity cost matrix represent the relative cost assignment of resources to activities and vice versa. The determination of a zero in a particular row or column cell signifies the best possible assignment relative to other cells in that row or column. The assignments are then made to the cell having zero entries, and if it is possible to make one assignment in each row and each column, we will have determined the optimal solution to the assignment problem.

EXAMPLE

Let us illustrate the matrix reduction procedure by solving the assignment problem presented earlier in Table 11.42.

Using the matrix reduction procedure we begin by row reducing the original cost matrix. This re-

TABLE 11.44 ROW REDUCED COST MATRIX

PROGRAMMER \ PROGRAMMING JOB	1	2	3	4	ROW REDUCTION
BOB	4	0	2	6	7
SUE	1	6	0	3	8
JIM	0	4	2	3	6
ANN	0	3	2	1	10

TABLE 11.45 OPPORTUNITY COST MATRIX (ROW REDUCED AND COLUMN REDUCED)

PROGRAMMER \ PROGRAMMING JOB	1	2	3	4	ROW REDUCTION
BOB	4	[0]	2	5	7
SUE	1	6	[0]	2	8
JIM	[0]	4	2	2	6
ANN	0	3	2	[0]	10
COLUMN REDUCTION	0	0	0	1	

TABLE 11.46 ASSIGNMENTS

PROGRAMMER	JOB	REQUIRED PROGRAMMING COST ($)
BOB	2	7
SUE	3	8
JIM	1	6
ANN	4	11
Minimum total programming cost		32

quires that we subtract the minimum cost element in each row from all other cost elements in that row. Table 11.44 presents the row reduced cost matrix.

The same procedure is then repeated for each column. Table 11.45 presents the complete opportunity cost matrix that has been both row and column reduced.

The opportunity cost matrix presented in Table 11.45 has the zero elements necessary for determining the optimal assignment. To minimize the total programming cost, assignments can be made by inspection. The assignments are indicated in this table by boxes around the appropriate zero elements, as shown in Table 11.46. Observe that this optimal assignment has one programmer assigned to each job and vice versa.

EXAMPLE

Unfortunately, the optimal assignment is not always obtained in as easy a manner as it was for the previous example. Let us now consider a second assignment problem that requires the expansion and modification of our basic solution procedure. In this second assignment problem, the owner of Andrews Auto Service is contemplating the assignment of five automobile repair jobs to his five mechanics. He has made an estimate of the time each mechanic will require to repair each automobile. The cost of repairing an automobile is directly related to the time spent in repairing the automobile, since all the mechanics are paid at the same hourly rate. Therefore, in this problem we substitute times for costs. The times for the various repair jobs being done by the various mechanics are shown in Table 11.47.

TABLE 11.47 AUTO REPAIR TIMES IN HOURS BY MECHANIC AND AUTOMOBILE REPAIR JOB—ANDREWS AUTO SERVICE

MECHANIC	FORD—BRAKES	PLYMOUTH—ENGINE	CHEVROLET—TRANSMISSION	BUICK—ELECTRICAL	DATSUN—STEERING
AL	9	7	11	10	13
TIM	6	9	4	8	7
JERRY	8	5	4	6	9
TOM	9	5	8	11	7
BILL	4	6	7	5	11

TABLE 11.48 ROW REDUCED COST MATRIX—ANDREWS AUTO SERVICE PROBLEM

AUTOMOBILE REPAIR JOB / MECHANIC	FORD— BRAKES	PLYMOUTH— ENGINE	CHEVROLET— TRANSMISSION	BUICK— ELECTRICAL	DATSUN— STEERING	ROW REDUCTION
AL	2	0	4	3	6	7
TIM	2	5	0	4	3	4
JERRY	4	1	0	2	5	4
TOM	4	0	3	6	2	5
BILL	0	2	3	1	7	4

TABLE 11.49 INITIAL OPPORTUNITY COST MATRIX—ANDREWS AUTO SERVICE PROBLEM

MECHANIC \ AUTOMOBILE REPAIR JOB	FORD—BRAKES	PLYMOUTH—ENGINE	CHEVROLET—TRANSMISSION	BUICK—ELECTRICAL	DATSUN STEERING	ROW REDUCTION
AL	2	0	4	2	4	7
TIM	2	5	0	3	1	4
JERRY	4	1	0	1	3	4
TOM	4	0	3	5	0	5
BILL	0	2	3	0	5	4
COLUMN REDUCTION	0	0	0	1	2	

TABLE 11.50 TEST FOR OPTIMALITY—ANDREWS AUTO SERVICE PROBLEM

MECHANIC \ AUTOMOBILE REPAIR JOB	FORD— BRAKES	PLYMOUTH— ENGINE	CHEVROLET— TRANSMISSION	BUICK— ELECTRICAL	DATSUN— STEERING
AL	2	0	4	2	4
TIM	2	5	0	3	1
JERRY	4	1	0	1	3
TOM	4	0	3	5	0
BILL	0	2	3	0	5

Proceeding with the matrix reduction procedure, we begin by row reducing the original cost matrix. The resultant row reduced cost matrix is shown in Table 11.48. In this table it is not possible to make a set of five assignments. Therefore, we next column reduce the table, subtracting the minimum element in each column from every entry in that column. Table 11.49 presents the initial opportunity cost matrix that has been both row reduced and column reduced.

For an optimal assignment to exist, we need to be able to make five unique one-to-one assignments in Table 11.49. Upon inspecting the table we see that this cannot be done. Both Tim and Jerry have the "Chevrolet—Transmission" repair job as their only minimum assignment. Also, Bill is the only mechanic that can be assigned to either the "Ford—Brakes" repair job or the "Buick—Electrical" repair job. A simple way of determining if the required number (i.e., in this case, five) of unique assignments can be made is to draw the minimum number of straight lines, horizontally and vertically, required to cross out all zeros. If the minimum number of lines drawn equals the number of rows or columns in the opportunity cost matrix, then an optimal assignment can be made. Drawing the minimum number of lines for the opportunity cost matrix (Table 11.49) results in Table 11.50, which we then test to see if an optimal assignment can be made. As can be seen in this table, only four lines are required to cross out all zeros. (Note that these four lines could have been drawn in different positions.) Therefore, the required five unique one-to-one assignments do not exist.

In order to obtain an optimal solution, we need to uncover other potential cells with small relative costs in the opportunity cost matrix. To do this we examine the costs in all those cells not covered by a straight line. The straight lines we have drawn serve to "protect" the zero elements already obtained, while the uncovered elements become the candidates for further reduction. We determine the minimum cost element that is not covered by a straight line, and subtract this value from all of the uncovered elements. This will create zeros at one or more of the uncovered elements. The same value

TABLE 11.51 REVISED OPPORTUNITY COST MATRIX—ANDREWS AUTO SERVICE PROBLEM

MECHANIC \ AUTOMOBILE REPAIR JOB	FORD— BRAKES	PLYMOUTH— ENGINE	CHEVROLET— TRANSMISSION	BUICK— ELECTRICAL	DATSUN— STEERING
AL	2	[0]	5	2	4
TIM	1	4	[0]	2	0
JERRY	3	0	0	[0]	2
TOM	4	0	4	5	[0]
BILL	[0]	2	4	0	5

TABLE 11.52 ASSIGNMENTS

MECHANIC	AUTO REPAIR JOB	REQUIRED REPAIR TIME (HRS)
Al	Plymouth—Engine	7
Tim	Chevrolet—Transmission	4
Jerry	Buick—Electrical	6
Tom	Datsun—Steering	7
Bill	Ford—Brakes	4
	Minimum total time	28 Hours

is then added to every element at the intersection of two straight lines. By adding this value to every element at the intersection of two lines, we maintain the same relative differences between the elements. Note that the minimum value is 1 in positions "Tim—Datsun—Steering", "Jerry—Plymouth—Engine", and "Jerry—Buick—Electrical." Therefore, we subtract 1 from the values in the first, second, fourth, and fifth columns for both rows two and three. A 1 is then added to the values at the intersection of row one and column three, at the intersection of row four and column three, and at the intersection of row five and column three. These changes result in the revised opportunity cost matrix presented in Table 11.51. The test for optimality is now repeated, and we see that it requires a minimum of five straight lines to cover all of the zeros in the revised opportunity cost matrix. (Note again that these five lines could have been drawn in different positions.) From Table 11.51 we see that we now have the zero elements necessary for determining the optimal solution. The optimal assignments of mechanics to auto repair jobs can now be made by inspection. The assignments are indicated in Table 11.51 by boxes around the appropriate zero elements, and are summarized in Table 11.52. Observe that this optimal assignment has one mechanic assigned to each repair job and vice versa.

11.8   THE UNBALANCED ASSIGNMENT PROBLEM

If the number of resources is not equal to the number of activities in an assignment problem, it is referred to as an unbalanced assignment problem. Since each of the resources must be assigned to each of the activities on a one-to-one basis, the unbalanced condition is removed by adding a row or rows of dummy resources, or a column or columns of dummy activities, until the number of resources exactly equals the number of activities. The costs of all the elements of the dummy row(s) or column(s) are set equal to zero, since any assignment made to a dummy row or column will not actually occur.

To illustrate this type of problem, consider the unbalanced assignment problem shown in Table 11.53. In this problem, there are four engineers to be assigned to three projects, with assignment costs as indicated.

To apply the Hungarian method to this problem, a dummy column is added with zero costs, so that the original problem is expressed as a square matrix of size $n = 4$. This new cost matrix is shown in Table 11.54.

In the matrix shown in this table, the smallest element in each row is zero, and this matrix thus represents a row reduced cost matrix. Performing a column reduction on Table 11.54 leads to the opportunity cost matrix shown in Table 11.55. This total opportunity cost matrix has all of the zero elements necessary to obtain an optimal solution. The optimal solution for this unbalanced assignment problem, shown by boxes around the zero elements in Table 11.55 is summarized in Table 11.56.

TABLE 11.53 PROJECT COST BY ENGINEER AND PROJECT

ENGINEER	PROJECT		
	1	2	3
Jim	1000	1700	1400
Ellen	1100	1900	1800
Roger	1600	1400	1600
Pat	1400	2300	1200

TABLE 11.54 BALANCED ASSIGNMENT PROBLEM

ENGINEER \ PROJECT	1	2	3	DUMMY
Jim	1000	1700	1400	0
Ellen	1100	1900	1800	0
Roger	1600	1400	1600	0
Pat	1400	2300	1200	0

11.9 OTHER COMMENTS ON THE ASSIGNMENT PROBLEM

The same types of complications that arise in solving transportation problems occur in solving assignment problems. In this section we review some of these complications and consider ways in which they may be resolved.

11.9.1 DEGENERACY

An assignment problem is a type of transportation problem whose tableau is a square matrix consisting of n rows and n columns. Therefore, since the assignment problem is really a special type of transportation problem, a basic feasible solution to an assignment problem should have $n + n - 1$ occupied cells (i.e., $n + n - 1$ of the x_{ij} variables in an assignment problem would have a value equal to one). An optimal solution to an assignment problem, however, will always involve a one-to-one matching of the n resources to the n activities. Consequently, the number of basic variables in the solution to an $n \times n$ assignment problem (i.e., the number of variables $x_{ij} = 1$) is exactly n. This means

that an optimal solution to an assignment problem is degenerate.

11.9.2 ALTERNATIVE OPTIMAL SOLUTIONS

An assignment problem can have more than one optimal solution (i.e., alternative optimal solutions). This will be indicated by there being more than one set of the n required assignments in the opportunity cost matrix. For example, in a particular row of the opportunity cost matrix there would be two or more zero elements that could be used in combination with other zero elements in the matrix to make more than one of the required one-to-one assignments.

11.9.3 PROHIBITED ASSIGNMENTS

In many practical assignment problems it may be desirable or necessary to prohibit the assignment of a certain resource to a certain activity. This can be accomplished by assigning an arbitrarily large cost, for example, $c_{ij} = +M$, as the cost coefficient for the cell corresponding to this resource → activity assignment. The solution process then proceeds in the normal fashion.

TABLE 11.55 OPPORTUNITY COST MATRIX

ENGINEER \ PROJECT	1	2	3	DUMMY	ROW REDUCTION
Jim	[0]	300	200	0	0
Ellen	100	500	600	[0]	0
Roger	600	[0]	400	0	0
Pat	400	900	[0]	0	0
COLUMN REDUCTION	1000	1400	1200	0	

TABLE 11.56 OPTIMAL SOLUTION FOR UNBALANCED ASSIGNMENT PROBLEM

TABLE 11.56 OPTIMAL SOLUTION FOR UNBALANCED ASSIGNMENT PROBLEM

ASSIGNMENT	COST
Jim → Project 1	$1000
Roger → Project 2	1400
Pat → Project 3	1200
Ellen → Dummy (Idle)	0
Minimum total cost	$3600

11.9.4 MAXIMIZATION ASSIGNMENT PROBLEMS

Assignment problems that require the maximization of an objective function utilize the following solution procedure.

1. Select the largest cell value in the profit matrix.

2. Construct a new cost matrix by subtracting each of the cell values of the original profit matrix from the largest cell value in the profit matrix.

3. Proceed to find the assignment producing the optimum (minimum) cost for the converted problem, using the Hungarian method discussed previously. This minimum-cost assignment for the converted problem will be the maximum-profit assignment for the original problem.

This procedure is the same as the procedure we discussed and illustrated for solving the maximization transportation problem (refer to Section 11.5.4).

11.10 SOLVING TRANSPORTATION, TRANSSHIPMENT, AND ASSIGNMENT PROBLEMS USING A COMPUTER

Numerous computer programs are in existence for solving transportation, transshipment, and assignment problems. These programs are available in both mainframe and microcomputer versions.

Transshipment problems, because of their size, are usually good candidates for solution using the computer. In Section 11.6 we considered a transshipment problem that had seven origins and seven destinations. For illustrative purposes we have solved this transshipment problem using a mainframe computer program called TRANSP. This transportation problem code was developed by Professor L. Douglas Smith of the University of Missouri-St. Louis, who kindly made it available to the authors of this book. This code will accommodate transportation (or transshipment problems) having not more than 20 origins and 20 destinations. The code generates the initial basic feasible solution using the row minima rule and then solves the problem using the MODI method. Output from use of this program for the transshipment problem is shown in Figure 11.3. As you can see from this output, the minimum transportation cost shipping plan is as shown in Table 11.57.

TABLE 11.57 MINIMUM TRANSPORTATION COST SHIPPING PLAN

ORIGIN	DESTINATION	QUANTITY	UNIT COST	COST ($)
1(Provo)	4(Los Angeles)	25	60	1500
2(Denver)	5(Houston)	75	45	3375
3(Kansas City)	5(Houston)	5	60	300
3(Kansas City)	7(Pittsburgh)	45	125	5625
5(Houston)	6(Atlanta)	50	60	300
				13,800

```
                    TRANSPORTATION COST MATRIX
                    WITH SUPPLIES AND DEMANDS
                            INDICATED


            1      2      3      4      5      5      7
    1       0     80     95     60    115    175    155    175
    2      30      0     30     50     45    120    200    225
    3      95     30      0    130     50    125    125    200
    4      60     50    130      0     90     55    150    150
    5     115     45     60     90      0     50    120    150
    6     175    120    125     65     60      0     55    150
    7     155    200    125    150    120     55      0    150
          150    150    150    175    190    200    195


    ORIGIN       SHADOW PRICE
       1               0
       2             -20
       3              -5
       4             -60
       5             -65
       6            -125
       7            -130
    DESTIN       SHADOW PRICE
       1               0
       2              20
       3               5
       4              60
       5              65
       6             125
       7             130
    FINAL ALLOCATION SORTED BY SUPPLY POINTS


    ORIGIN    DESTIN    QUANTITY    UNIT COST       COST
       1         1        150           0             0
       1         4         25          60          1500
    ─────────────────────────────────────────────────────
    TOTAL                 175                       1500


       2         2        150           0             0
       2         5         75          45          3375
    ─────────────────────────────────────────────────────
    TOTAL                 225                       3375


       3         3        150           0             0
       3         5          5          60           300
       3         7         45         125          5525
    ─────────────────────────────────────────────────────
    TOTAL                 200                       5925
```

FIGURE 11.3   MAINFRAME COMPUTER PROGRAM OUTPUT, TRANSSHIPMENT PROBLEM.

```
                        ARC PARAMETERS AND FLOWS

ARCS THAT START AT AL

        GO TO          ARC NO       LOWER       UPPER       COST        FLOW

        FORD           1            0           1           9           0
        PLYM           2            0           1           7           1
        CHEV           3            0           1           11          0
        BUICK          4            0           1           10          0
        DATS           5            0           1           13          0
        SLACK          6            0           1           999999      0

ARCS THAT START AT TIM

        GO TO          ARC NO       LOWER       UPPER       COST        FLOW

        FORD           7            0           1           6           0
        PLYM           8            0           1           9           0
        CHEV           9            0           1           4           1
        BUICK          10           0           1           8           0
        DATS           11           0           1           7           0
        SLACK          12           0           1           999999      0

ARCS THAT START AT JERRY

        GO TO          ARC NO       LOWER       UPPER       COST        FLOW

        FORD           13           0           1           8           0
        PLYM           14           0           1           5           0
        CHEV           15           0           1           4           0
        BUICK          16           0           1           6           1
        DATS           17           0           1           9           0
        SLACK          18           0           1           999999      0

ARCS THAT START AT TOM

        GO TO          ARC NO       LOWER       UPPER       COST        FLOW

        FORD           19           0           1           9           0
        PLYM           20           0           1           5           0
        CHEV           21           0           1           8           0
        BUICK          22           0           1           11          0
        DATS           23           0           1           7           1
        SLACK          24           0           1           999999      0
```

FIGURE 11.4   MICROCOMPUTER PROGRAM OUTPUT, ASSIGNMENT PROBLEM.

```
ARCS THAT START AT BILL

        GO TO        ARC NO        LOWER        UPPER        COST        FLOW

        FORD          25             0            1             4           1
        PLYM          26             0            1             6           0
        CHEV          27             0            1             7           0
        BUICK         28             0            1             5           0
        DATS          29             0            1            11           0
        SLACK         30             0            1         999999          0


  NO ARCS ORIGINATE AT NODE FORD

  NO ARCS ORIGINATE AT NODE CHEV

  NO ARCS ORIGINATE AT NODE BUICK

  NO ARCS ORIGINATE AT NODE DATS

ARCS THAT START AT SLACK

        GO TO        ARC NO        LOWER        UPPER        COST        FLOW

        FORD          31             0            1         999999          0
        PLYM          32             0            1         999999          0
        CHEV          33             0            1         999999          0
        BUICK         34             0            1         999999          0
        DATS          35             0            1         999999          0

                        NODE  PARAMETERS

            NODE        NAME        POTENTIAL        EXT.FLOW

             1          AL          999990             1
             2          TIM         999993             1
             3          JERRY       999993             1
             4          TOM         999992             1
             5          BILL        999995             1
             6          FORD        999999            -1
             7          PLYM        999997            -1
             8          CHEV        999997            -1
             9          BUICK       999999            -1
            10          DATS        999999            -1
            11          SLACK            0             0
```

FIGURE 11.4 (CONTINUED)

TABLE 11.58 OPTIMAL SOLUTION

ARCS THAT START AT	GO TO	ARC NUMBER	LOWER	UPPER	COST ($)	FLOW
Al	Plymouth	2	0	1	7	1
Tim	Chevrolet	9	0	1	4	1
Jerry	Buick	16	0	1	6	1
Tom	Datsun	23	0	1	7	1
Bill	Ford	25	0	1	4	1
					28	

In Section 11.7 we addressed an assignment problem involving five mechanics and five auto repair jobs. For illustrative purposes we have solved this 5 × 5 assignment problem using a microcomputer package: *Microsolve/Operations Research* by Paul A. Jensen.[4] This package includes several programs that can be used to solve transportation, transshipment, or assignment problems having as many as 50 nodes and 300 routes. Output from use of this microcomputer package for the assignment problem is shown in Figure 11.4. As you can see from this output, the solution summarized in Table 11.58 is optimal.

11.11 SUMMARY

In this chapter we have discussed the transportation problem and the assignment problem. These types of problems are encountered frequently in practice, and a large number of applications involving transportation or assignment problems have been reported. We observed that both of these types of problems have special structures, which can be exploited in determining an optimal solution. The special structures of both of these problems allowed them to be solved by very efficient algorithms. We have presented and discussed these algorithms, and have demonstrated how they can be applied.

GLOSSARY

Assignment Problem   A linear programming problem having a special structure in which each of n resources must be assigned to each of n activities, on a one-to-one basis.

Balanced Assignment Problem   An assignment problem in which the number of activities is exactly equal to the number of resources.

Balanced Transportation Problem   A transportation problem in which the total amount available at the origins exactly satisfies the total amount required at the destinations.

Degenerate Solution   A feasible solution to a transportation problem is degenerate if less than $m + n - 1$ of the x_{ij} values are strictly positive.

Demand Destination   A customer demand location characterized by a required quantity of goods or services.

Hungarian Method   An efficient solution procedure for the assignment problem based on a theorem developed by a Hungarian mathematician.

---

[4]Paul A. Jensen, *Microsolve/Operations Research.* Oakland, Calif.: Holden–Day, 1983.

Matrix Minima Rule   A procedure used to determine an initial basic feasible solution to the transportation problem.

Matrix Reduction   Conversion of the original cost matrix of the assignment problem into an equivalent cost matrix having only positive or zero elements.

Modified Distribution Algorithm or MODI Method   An algorithm for the solution of the transportation problem.

Northwest Corner Rule   A procedure used to determine an initial basic feasible solution to the transportation problem.

Opportunity Cost Matrix   The cost matrix that results from matrix reduction of the original cost matrix of the assignment problem.

Orthogonal Turns   Ninety-degree or right-angle turns made within a transportation tableau.

Slack or Dummy Destination   The additional column added to a tableau in a transportation problem where supply exceeds demand, having a demand requirement equal to the excess supply.

Slack or Dummy Origin   An additional row added to a tableau in a transportation problem where demand exceeds supply, having a supply availability equal to the excess demand.

Stepping-Stone Algorithm   An algorithm for the solution of the transportation problem.

Supply Origin   A supply location having a fixed amount or limited quantity of goods or services.

Transportation Problem   A special type of linear programming problem that involves the transportation or physical distribution of goods and services from several supply origins to several demand destinations.

Transshipment Problem   A special type of transportation problem in which the product or commodity is allowed to pass through intermediate transfer points before it reaches its final destination.

Unbalanced Assignment Problem   An assignment problem where the number of resources is not equal to the number of activities.

Unbalanced Transportation Problem   A transportation problem in which we physically have more units available at the origins than are required at the destinations; or a transportation problem in which resource requirements exceed supply availabilities.

Vogel's Approximation Method   A procedure used to determine an initial basic feasible solution to the transportation problem.

Selected References

Anderson, D. R., D. J. Sweeney, and T. A. Williams. 1974. *Linear Programming for Decision Making.* St. Paul, Minn.: West.

Bazarra, M. S., and J. J. Jarvis. 1977. *Linear Programming and Network Flows.* New York: Wiley.

Hughes, A. J., and D. E. Graowig. 1973. *Linear Programming: An Emphasis on Decision Making.* Reading, Mass.: Addison–Wesley.

Llewellyn, R. W. 1964. *Linear Programming.* New York: Holt, Rinehart & Winston.

Kwak, N. K. 1973. *Mathematical Programming With Business Applications.* New York: McGraw–Hill.

Strum, J. E. 1972. *Introduction to Linear Programming.* San Francisco: Holden–Day.

Discussion Questions

1. Why does a basic feasible solution to a balanced transportation problem having m origins and n destinations have only $m + n - 1$ basic variables, assuming it is not degenerate?

2. Illustrate how the transportation tableau describes the linear programming formulation of the transportation problem.

3. Why does use of the northwest corner rule generally not result in an initial basic feasible solution that is close to the optimal solution?

4. Why is Vogel's approximation method a good method for determining an initial basic feasible solution to a transportation problem?

5. What does a value of zero for the net cost change for an unoccupied cell indicate?

6. Why does degeneracy cause a problem in applying either the stepping-stone algorithm or the MODI method?

7. Describe the relationship between the transportation and the transshipment problem.

8. Why will adding a constant d to each cost in row i or each cost in column j of the transportation tableau not cause a change in the optimal allocation to the cells of the transportation tableau? Will the value of the objective function change?

9. Describe the relationship between the transportation and the assignment problems.

10. Why won't the optimal solution to an assignment problem always be obtained by simply row and column reducing the original cost matrix?

11. Describe how unbalanced assignment problems are solved.

12. Why is the solution to an assignment problem always degenerate?

PROBLEMS

1. A snack-food manufacturer has three plant and four distribution warehouses. The shipping costs from the three plants to the four distribution warehouses and the plant availabilities and warehouse requirements are shown as follows. The manufacturer wishes to develop a shipping plan that will minimize its total shipping cost.

PLANT \ WAREHOUSE	A	B	C	D	PLANT AVAILABILITY
1	6.50	4.00	3.00	5.00	250
2	6.00	8.50	7.00	4.00	300
3	5.00	6.00	9.00	10.00	125
WAREHOUSE REQUIREMENT	130	155	200	190	675

    a. Determine an initial basic feasible solution using the northwest corner rule.

    b. Determine the optimum solution using the stepping-stone algorithm.

2. A particular transportation problem has the following costs, origin availabilities, and destination requirements.

ORIGIN \ DESTINATION	COSTS				ORIGIN AVAILABILITY
	A	B	C	D	
1	7	6	2	11	60
2	4	10	8	7	30
3	10	4	10	6	100
DESTINATION REQUIREMENT	30	50	40	70	190

    a. Determine an initial basic feasible solution using the northwest corner rule.

    b. Determine the optimum solution using the stepping-stone algorithm.

3. Omnipotent Oil Corporation has three refineries that produce gasoline, which is then shipped to four large storage facilities. The total quantities (1000 barrels) produced by each refinery and the total requirements (1000 barrels) for each storage facility, as well as the associated shipping costs are shown as follows. Omnipotent Oil Corporation wishes to determine a shipping schedule that will minimize its total shipping costs.

REFINERY \ STORAGE FACILITY	S_1	S_2	S_3	S_4	REFINERY AVAILABILITY
R_1	90	80	60	70	25
R_2	55	85	35	75	20
R_3	45	45	90	85	15
STORAGE REQUIREMENT	10	15	20	15	60

a. Determine an initial basic feasible solution using the northwest corner rule.
b. Determine the optimal solution using the stepping-stone algorithm.

4. Solve the transportation problem having the following costs, origin availabilities, and destination requirements. Use the northwest corner rule to obtain an initial basic feasible solution, and use the stepping-stone algorithm to obtain the optimal solution.

ORIGIN \ DESTINATION	D_1	D_2	D_3	D_4	D_5	D_6	ORIGIN AVAILABILITY
O_1	3	4	3	6	7	5	50
O_2	3	3	2	1	4	1	70
O_3	6	5	7	11	8	4	95
O_4	6	4	10	6	7	9	25
DESTINATION REQUIREMENT	25	50	40	25	60	40	240

5. A particular transportation problem has the following costs, supply availabilities, and demand requirements.

ORIGIN \ DESTINATION	D_1	D_2	D_3	ORIGIN AVAILABILITY
O_1	7	8	5	110
O_2	3	1	4	60
O_3	5	2	4	100
DESTINATION REQUIREMENT	80	120	70	

a. Find the initial basic feasible solution using the matrix minima method. Is it optimal? Explain.
b. Find the initial basic feasible solution using Vogel's approximation method. Is it optimal? Explain.
c. What is the optimal solution to this problem?

6. Given the following transportation problem

DESTINATION ORIGIN	D_1	D_2	D_3	D_4	ORIGIN AVAILABILITY
O_1	6	9	7	+M	50
O_2	3	5	8	10	80
O_3	+M	6	4	7	40
O_4	3	9	6	4	90
DESTINATION REQUIREMENT	50	40	70	80	

a. find the initial basic feasible solution using Vogel's approximation method;

b. solve the problem using the stepping-stone algorithm;

c. formulate this problem as a general linear programming model.

7. Oranges are grown, harvested, and stored in warehouses in Orlando, Tampa, and Fort Lauderdale. These warehouses then supply oranges to wholesale grocery firms in Atlanta, Charlotte, Birmingham, and Knoxville. The following shipping costs per ton and supply-and-demand requirements exist.

WAREHOUSES / WHOLESALERS	ATLANTA	CHARLOTTE	BIRMINGHAM	KNOXVILLE	WAREHOUSE SUPPLY
ORLANDO	8	7	5	9	100
TAMPA	3	9	6	4	200
FORT LAUDERDALE	4	7	6	3	300
WHOLESALER DEMAND	150	100	140	200	

a. Determine an initial basic feasible solution for this problem using the matrix minima method.

b. Solve the problem using the MODI method.

8. Dusty Melon grows canteloupes at three locations in South Carolina; Walterboro, Kingstree, and Edgefield. The canteloupes are then sent to farmers' markets located in Columbia, Charleston, and Spartan-burg, South Carolina. The transportation cost per truckload of can-

teloupes for every farm to market combination are given in the
following cost matrix.

FARMERS' MARKET FARM	COLUMBIA	CHARLESTON	SPARTANBURG
WALTERBORO	50	75	60
KINGSTREE	30	35	30
EDGEFIELD	40	65	70

The supply availabilities of canteloupes (in truckloads) for the farm
operations are as follows.

Walterboro 40
Kingstree   60
Edgefield   50

The demand requirements of canteloupes (in truckloads) at the farmers' markets are as follows.

Columbia   50
Charleston 30
Spartanburg 90

Develop a shipping schedule that minimizes total transportation cost.

9. Solve the following transportation problem. Use the northwest corner rule to obtain an initial basic feasible solution.

DESTINATION ORIGIN	D_1	D_2	D_3	D_4	D_5	D_6	ORIGIN AVAILABILITY
O_1	1	3	5	7	8	1	60
O_2	3	4	2	7	9	1	80
O_3	5	8	4	5	6	10	20
O_4	7	2	3	8	9	11	160
DESTINATION REQUIREMENT	100	40	20	60	40	60	

10. Solve the following plant-to-warehouse transportation problem
whose initial basic feasible solution is shown in the following tableau.

PLANT \ WAREHOUSE	W_1	W_2	W_3	W_4	PLANT AVAILABILITY
P_1	(50) 7	(30) 4	3	4	80
P_2	6	(40) 6	(10) 9	5	50
P_3	8	4	(20) 6	(10) 8	30
WAREHOUSE REQUIREMENT	50	80	30	10	

11. Solve the following transportation problem using the MODI method. Obtain the initial basic feasible solution using the matrix minima method.

ORIGIN \ DESTINATION	D_1	D_2	D_3	D_4	D_5	D_6	ORIGIN AVAILABILITY
O_1	14	12	10	8	6	8	75
O_2	11	16	14	12	9	11	90
O_3	10	12	15	17	12	10	30
O_4	8	7	12	14	18	17	135
DESTINATION REQUIREMENT	105	60	30	45	30	60	

12. Solve the following transportation problem that involves a shoe manufacturer that has three distribution centers that must supply four shoe wholesalers. The initial feasible solution for the problem is as follows.

DISTRIBUTION CENTER \ WAREHOUSE	W_1	W_2	W_3	W_4	DISTRIBUTION CENTER AVAILABILITY
DC_1	(30) 4	8	5	6	30
DC_2	(10) 5	(20) 3	(30) 0	(0) 4	60
DC_3	5	8	7	(40) 4	40
WAREHOUSE REQUIREMENT	40	20	30	40	

13. The Tertz Auto Rental Company has a problem in connection with the distribution of its rental cars. It has a shortage of rental cars in certain cities and an oversupply of rental cars in other cities. The imbalances are as follows.

CITY	SHORTAGE	OVERAGE
New York		100
Boston		150
Philadelphia		60
Washington, D.C.	40	
Atlanta		80
Miami	60	
New Orleans	80	
St. Louis	50	
Chicago	70	

The costs associated with distributing the rental cars are presented in the following table.

FROM \ TO	WASHINGTON	MIAMI	NEW ORLEANS	ST. LOUIS	CHICAGO
NEW YORK	60	45	75	90	135
BOSTON	M	75	105	135	150
PHILADELPHIA	45	15	30	60	90
ATLANTA	45	75	90	105	M

Formulate and solve as a transportation problem.

14. A farm cooperative in central Missouri wishes to distribute its products to four large storage depots. It has produced the following:

Corn	150,000 bushels
Wheat	750,000 bushels
Oats	1,500,000 bushels
Soybeans	400,000 bushels

The demand requirements for these four crops are as follows.

Storage Depot 1	400,000 bushels
Storage Depot 2	850,000 bushels
Storage Depot 3	400,000 bushels
Storage Depot 4	1,200,000 bushels

The distribution costs for this supply–demand situation are as follows.

PRODUCT	STORAGE DEPOT 1	STORAGE DEPOT 2	STORAGE DEPOT 3	STORAGE DEPOT 4
CORN	30	25	40	25
WHEAT	45	25	45	35
OATS	35	20	30	20
SOYBEANS	50	40	50	50

Determine the minimum cost shipping plan.

15. An electric motor manufacturer has three major production facilities that supply three large distribution warehouses. The following network diagram indicates the cost per railroad car shipment of motors for the factory-to-factory, warehouse-to-warehouse, and factory-to-warehouse shipments that are possible in this network.

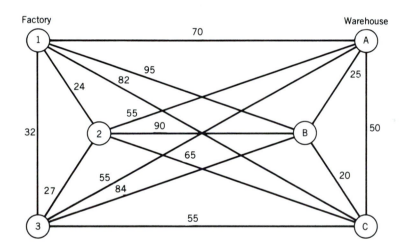

The supply of motors (in railroad car shipments) for each factory and the demand for motors at each warehouse (in railroad car shipments) are as follows.

FACTORY-SUPPLY		WAREHOUSE-DEMAND	
Factory 1	90	Warehouse A	75
Factory 2	135	Warehouse B	90
Factory 3	150	Warehouse C	210

Formulate and solve as a transshipment problem.

16. A company produces men's suits in three cities for outlet stores in three other cities. The shipping costs per unit and the supply and demand data are as follows.

PLANT \ OUTLET	ST. LOUIS	CHICAGO	NEW YORK	SUPPLY
Phoenix	34	27	30	1000
Dallas	23	26	38	1500
Atlanta	26	35	24	2000
DEMAND	1800	1200	1500	

The company can also ship between sources and between destinations if such routes provide cheaper transportation. The unit shipping costs for these routes are as follows.

PLANT-TO-PLANT

FROM \ TO	PHOENIX	DALLAS	ATLANTA
Phoenix	0	4	7
Dallas	4	0	6
Atlanta	7	6	0

WAREHOUSE-TO-WAREHOUSE

FROM \ TO	ST. LOUIS	CHICAGO	NEW YORK
St. Louis	0	5	7
Chicago	5	0	6
New York	7	6	0

Formulate and solve as a transshipment problem.

17. A furniture manufacturer has four lathe operators to be assigned to four lathes. The hourly costs to operate each lathe by each lathe operator are as follows.

LATHE OPERATOR \ LATHE	1	2	3	4
Joe	13	13	9	17
Jim	11	11	11	11
Sam	15	10	8	14
Hank	7	10	11	12

Formulate and solve as an assignment problem.

18. Janice Philipps is the manager of the computer service bureau at a large corporation. She currently has a backlog of six disk copying jobs which she wishes to assign to six technicians. The time requirements, by disk copying job, by technician, are as follows.

TECHNICIAN \ DISK COPYING JOB	1	2	3	4	5	6
Jan	6	4	3	5	9	7
Bill	2	6	11	8	3	10
Sue	4	7	13	9	4	9
Tom	5	3	2	8	7	4
Mary	3	6	9	5	2	6
Joe	5	7	3	8	4	6

Formulate and solve as an assignment problem.

19. Mr. Wally Fin, the head men's swimming coach at the local university needs to assign four swimmers to four important races. His four best swimmers and the fastest times (in seconds) they have achieved in each of the four races are as follows.

SWIMMER \ RACE	50 METERS	100 METERS	200 METERS	400 METERS
Bill	25.2	150.4	275.2	500.1
Joe	27.0	152.6	280.3	502.3
Bob	25.1	148.7	278.2	506.4
Tom	26.4	160.2	270.6	508.3

Formulate and solve as an assignment problem.

20. Consider the following matrix which gives the profits associated with a particular customer buying a particular product.

CUSTOMER \ PRODUCT	A	B	C	D	E
1	5	7	3	9	4
2	6	2	8	5	7
3	5	3	9	4	2
4	11	7	6	5	3
5	8	6	4	9	7

Formulate and solve as an assignment problem.

Application Review

Scheduling Umpire Crews For the American Baseball League

Play Ball! This cry rings out many times each summer as the 28 major league baseball teams compete for their respective league pennants and the World Series championship. Most of us take for granted that our favorite teams will be playing games almost every day from April until October. But, have you ever thought about the scheduling of these games, and in particular the scheduling of their umpire crews?

Consider, for example, the American League, which is composed of 14 teams that are organized into two divisions. The Western Division has teams in Seattle, Oakland, California, Texas, Kansas City, Minnesota, and Chicago. The Eastern Division has teams in Milwaukee, Detroit, Cleveland, Toronto, Baltimore, New York, and Boston. The scheduling of games for each season is itself a formidable problem. The game schedule for each of these 14 teams is made giving consideration to factors such as the number of games played against other teams both within and outside a division, the split between home games and road trips, travel time, and possible conflicts in cities that also have a team in the National League (e.g., Chicago or New York).

Similar, but perhaps more difficult decisions arise in the scheduling of umpires. This scheduling requires some seven crews, since there are 14 teams in each league. Each crew is assigned to one of the seven concurrent series. These series may be two-, three-, or four-game series and therefore each team may not play each day. This umpire crew scheduling problem is complicated by further restrictions, the most important of which are summarized as follows.

1. An umpire crew cannot travel from city A to city B if the last game in city A is a night game and there is an afternoon game in city B the next day.

Source: James R. Evans, John E. Hebert, and Richard F. Deckro, "Play Ball! The Scheduling of Sports Officials," *Perspectives In Computing* (Spring 1984), Vol. 4., No. 1, pp. 18–29.

2. An umpire crew cannot travel from the West Coast to Chicago or any Eastern Division city without a day off between cities.
3. An umpire crew traveling in or out of Toronto must have a day off unless the crew is coming from or going to New York, Boston, or Cleveland.
4. An umpire crew traveling from a night game in Seattle, Oakland, or Los Angeles cannot be assigned to Kansas City or Texas for a game the next day, even if it is a night game.
5. No umpire crew should be assigned to the same team for more than two series in a row.

Obviously, the American League would also like to minimize the cost associated with the scheduling of its crews, and this cost is a direct function of the airline travel (i.e., total airline miles) involved.

The umpire crew scheduling problem for the American League has been investigated and solved as a seven-crew assignment problem subject to the travel restrictions and balance objectives just noted. In the first series in the season, the umpire crews are assigned arbitrarily. Thereafter, reassignment of crews is done using the assignment algorithm, with potential assignments that might violate the restrictions being blocked by setting the appropriate c_{ij} to a large value. Each problem solution is designed to minimize the total travel distance involved for all

TABLE 11.59 UMPIRE CREW ASSIGNMENT: FROM SERIES SIX TO SERIES SEVEN

CREW	FROM	TO
7	Cleveland	Seattle
4	Oakland	Oakland
6	Kansas City	California
1	Texas	Texas
5	California	Milwaukee
3	Detroit	Cleveland
2	New York	New York

Mileage = 5237

CREW	CUMULATIVE MILEAGE
1	3336
2	2936
3	2514
4	4371
5	4593
6	3245
7	3662

seven crews. In practice, the algorithm employed ranks the 10 best solutions so that the scheduler has more flexibility in the choice of assignments. Complete crew schedules are provided in four-week segments that are summarized in a series of reports that are used by the supervisor of umpires to finalize the official assignments. An example of one typical umpire crew assignment is shown in Table 11.59.

CHAPTER 12

NETWORK MODELS

12.1 INTRODUCTION

Network models are a very important part of quantitative decision making. Many practical real-world problems can be formulated in a network fashion. For example, the planning of distribution networks, communications systems, and large-scale projects is a common application of network models. Solutions to such problems, using network models, can be very effectively conveyed to managers, since network models can be presented as diagrams of real-world problem situations. Other problems that physically don't seem to have a network structure nevertheless can be modeled as networks. For example, a certain type of cash management problem involving accounts receivable can be modeled using a "lock box" location network. Also, network models are very efficient in terms of problem size and solution speeds. They often can be solved using reasonable amounts of computer time, when other modeling approaches are computationally unrealistic.

In Chapter 11 we saw that a transportation problem could be represented graphically as a network. In this chapter we study three special types of network models. First, we consider the shortest route problem, which involves the determination of the minimum total distance from some starting point to some ending point in a network. The trip routing provided by the AAA Automobile Club is an example of a shortest route network. Second, we examine the minimum spanning-tree problem, which involves the determination of a set of branches of a network that connects all the nodes of the network

in a fashion that minimizes the total length of the branches used to reach these points. A subway system is an example of a minimum spanning-tree network. Finally, we address the maximum-flow problem in which we seek to allocate the flows in the branches of a network in a manner that maximizes the overall flow in the network. A natural-gas pipeline system is one example of a maximum-flow network.

12.2 TERMINOLOGY AND NOTATION FOR NETWORK PROBLEMS

Before we begin our study of network models it is instructive to define certain basic terms.[1] Initially, let us define a *network* as a set of junction points called *nodes* or *events* that are connected by flow routes called *branches* or *activities* (or "arcs," "links," "connectors," or "edges"). Figure 12.1 is an example of a simple network, in which the circles are the nodes and the lines connecting the circles are the branches.

The nodes in a network typically represent physical locations, such as cities, airports, terminals, or pumping stations. The branches typically represent connecting roads, air routes, pipelines, or cables.

The origin in a network is called the *source node,* and the destination is called the *sink node.* A source node has an orientation such that all flow moves away from it, and a sink node has an ori-

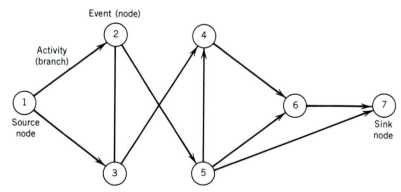

FIGURE 12.1 A SIMPLE NETWORK.

[1]For a more detailed discussion, see Mokhtar S. Bazaraa and John J. Jarvis, *Linear Programming and Network Flows.* New York: Wiley, 1977, pp. 404–407.

entation such that all flow moves into it. In Figure 12.1, Node 1 is the source node and Node 7 is the sink node.

We can attribute a sense of direction to a branch by indicating which node is to be considered the point of origin. Such a branch is called *directed,* or *oriented,* and when drawing a network we indicate the orientation of a branch by an arrowhead. For example, in Figure 12.1 "branch 1 to 2" is a directed branch, and in this branch the direction is from Node 1 to Node 2. A branch that does not have a sense of direction attached to it is called *undirected*

and is not marked with an arrowhead. In Figure 12.1, "branch 2 to 3" is an undirected branch. In most instances, we can replace an undirected branch with a pair of directed branches whose directions are opposite.

A *path* in a network is a specific sequence of branches from the source node to the sink node in which the initial node of each branch is the same as the ending node of the preceding branch in the sequence. In Figure 12.1, one path between Node 1 and Node 7 is composed of the branches 1 to 2, 2 to 5, 5 to 7, as follows:

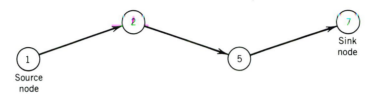

A *chain* in a network has a similar structure to a path, except that not all branches are necessarily directed toward the sink node. In Figure 12.1, one chain is composed of the branches 3 to 4, 5 to 4, 5 to 6, as follows:

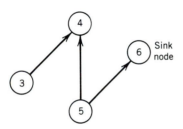

Note that every path in a network is a chain, but not vice versa.

A *circuit* in a network is a path in which the source node and the sink node are the same. A circuit is simply a closed path. An example of a circuit is the following:

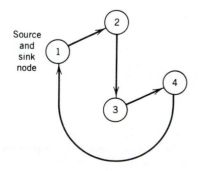

A *cycle* in a network is a closed chain. An example of a cycle is the following:

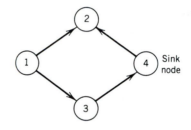

Note that every circuit in a network is a cycle, but not vice versa.

A network is called *connected* if there is a path connecting every pair of nodes in the network. The network shown in Figure 12.1 is connected. If we removed branches 2 to 5 and 3 to 4 however, we would no longer have a connected network.

An undirected, connected network that contains no cycles is called a *tree.* Therefore, between any two nodes of the tree there is a unique chain joining the two nodes. An example of a tree is the following network.

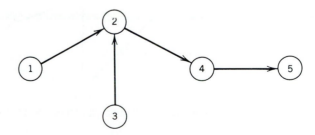

TABLE 12.1	EXAMPLES OF FLOW NETWORKS	
NODES	BRANCHES	FLOW
Intersections	Highways	Automobiles
Valves	Pipeline segments	Natural gas
Ports	Shipping lanes	Ships
Cities	Rivers	Barges
Work stations	Conveyors	Products

A *spanning tree* is a tree that includes every node in the network, so the tree shown here is also a spanning tree.

In many practical situations some sort of physical flow takes place in the branches of the network. Examples of common networks involving physical flows are shown below in Table 12.1.

The basic definitions just presented are used throughout the material that follows. Additional definitions are introduced with respect to specific network models.

12.3 THE SHORTEST ROUTE PROBLEM

The shortest route problem is concerned with finding the shortest route from an origin to a destination through a connected network, given the distances associated with the respective branches of the network. One very common type of shortest route problem involves the determination of the shortest dis-

tance, in miles, from an origin city to a destination city, where the network branches are the individual highways, with associated distances, that connect one city to another. Shortest time problems are often of equal interest to shortest route problems, and such problems arise frequently in connection with transportation networks, delivery systems, and communications networks.

Although the shortest route problem can be formulated and solved using linear programming, a simpler and more efficient solution procedure has been developed. This procedure is now presented and illustrated by means of an example.

The Boffa Trucking Company operates a fleet of trucks from its home base in Denver. It has just contracted to deliver a number of loads of chemicals from Denver to Pittsburgh. In Figure 12.2 a highway network is presented for this situation. It indicates which routes Boffa's trucks can take, as well as the distances between the various nodes of the network. The objective in this problem situation is to determine the shortest shipping route from Denver to Pittsburgh.

Note that the branches in this highway network are undirected so that travel may occur from Node i to Node j or from Node j to Node i, and the travel distance is the same in either case. In this network, however, there is a restriction that travel must originate at Node 1 (Denver) and terminate at Node 7 (Pittsburgh). Therefore, travel cannot return from Nodes 2, 3, or 4 to Node 1 (origin), and travel cannot return from Node 7 (destination) to Nodes 5 or 6.

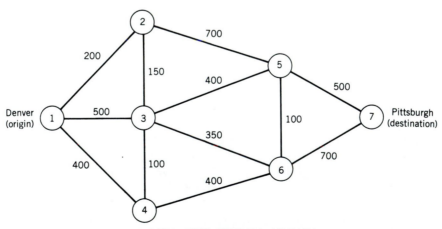

FIGURE 12.2 HIGHWAY NETWORK—BOFFA TRUCKING COMPANY.

12.3.1 SOLUTION PROCEDURE FOR THE SHORTEST ROUTE PROBLEM

The solution procedure for the shortest route problem that we employ was originally developed by Dijkstra.[2] The essence of the procedure involves fanning out from the origin node, successively identifying the next node that has the shortest route from the origin node. The procedure not only determines the shortest route from the origin node to the destination node, it also identifies the shortest route from the origin node to every other node in the network.

Use of the procedure assumes that the direct distance, d_{ij}, between any two nodes in the network of n nodes is given, and that all such distances are nonnegative. The procedure begins by assigning to all nodes a label that is either temporary or permanent. The temporary label represents the upper bound on the shortest distance from the source node to the node being evaluated; the permanent label is the actual shortest distance.

To begin, the source node is assigned a permanent label of zero. All of the other nodes are assigned temporary labels equal to the direct distance from the source node to the node being examined. If any node cannot be reached directly from the source node, it is assigned a temporary label of $+\infty$. The algorithm then proceeds to examine the temporarily labeled nodes, and makes them, one at a time, permanent labels. As soon as the sink node receives a permanent label, the shortest route from the source node to the sink node has been determined.

The iterative steps of Dijkstra's algorithm can be summarized as follows.

STEP 0 INITIALIZATION STEP

A permanent label of zero is assigned to the source node. All other nodes are assigned temporary labels that are set equal to the direct distances from the source node to the nodes being examined. If any node cannot be reached directly from the source node it is assigned a temporary label of $+\infty$.

---

[2]E. W. Dijkstra, "A note on two problems in connections with graphs," *Numerische Mathematik*, **1** (1959), 269–271.

STEP 1

All of the nodes having temporary labels are examined and the node having the minimum of the temporary labels is selected and declared permanent. If there are ties between temporary labels, break the tie arbitrarily.

STEP 2

Suppose that Node T has been assigned a permanent label most recently. The remaining nodes with temporary labels are examined, by comparing, one at a time, the temporary label of each node to the sum of the permanent label of Node T and the direct distance from Node T to the node being examined. The minimum of these two distances is assigned as the new temporary label for the node. Note that if the old temporary label for the node being examined is still minimal, then it will remain unchanged during this step.

STEP 3

Now select the minimum of the temporary labels and declare it permanent. If there are ties, select one, but only one, and declare it permanent. If the node just declared permanent is the sink node, the algorithm terminates and the shortest route has been determined. Otherwise return to Step 2.

After the algorithm terminates, the shortest path is identified by retracing the path backward from the sink node to the source node, selecting the nodes that were permanently labeled at each step. Alternatively, the shortest path may be identified by determining which of the nodes have permanent labels that differ exactly by the length of the connecting arc.

Before illustrating Dijkstra's algorithm, we should emphasize that it can be applied to either a directed or nondirected network. In actuality the shortest route problem involves finding which path connecting two specified nodes minimizes the sum of the branch distances along the path. Thus it is not really necessary to travel in any specific direction along this path. It should also be mentioned that frequently d_{ij} does not equal d_{ji}. Also, some nodes may not be connected directly, a situation that can be indicated by letting the corresponding $d_{ij} = +\infty$.

Let us now apply Dijkstra's algorithm to the network presented earlier in Figure 12.2. Initially, the origin node, Node 1, is permanently labeled as zero, and all other nodes are assigned temporary labels equal to their direct distance from Node 1.

Thus, the node labels at the initialization step, denoted by $L(0)$, are

NODES	1	2	3	4	5	6	7
	*						
$L(0)$	0	200	500	400	$+\infty$	$+\infty$	$+\infty$
Preceding Node	—	1	1	1	—	—	—

Observe that an asterisk (*) has been placed over Node 1, indicating that Node 1 has been permanently labeled. Additionally, we have included a row marked "Preceding Node," which indicates the preceding node on the route from the source node to the other nodes. At Step 0 we have considered Nodes 1, 2, 3, 4, and Node 1 has been assigned a permanent label. The permanently labeled node at the initialization step is shown in Figure 12.3, and is indicated by the dashed line. At the initialization step it consists only of Node 1.

At iteration 1 the smallest of the temporary labels is made permanent. Thus, Node 2 is assigned a permanent label, since it is the smallest of the temporary labels. The node labels at iteration 1, denoted by $L(1)$, are

NODES	1	2	3	4	5	6	7
	*	*					
$L(1)$	0	200	500	400	$+\infty$	$+\infty$	$+\infty$
Preceding Node	—	1	1	1	—	—	—

The permanently labeled nodes at iteration 1 are shown by the dashed lines in Figure 12.4, and consist of Nodes 1 and 2. Note also that branch (1, 2), shown in boldface, is identified as the shortest route connecting the permanently labeled nodes (i.e., Nodes 1 and 2). At iteration 2, we examine each of the temporarily labeled nodes that can directly be connected to Node 2 (i.e., the node that was just labeled as a permanent node). For each of the temporarily labeled nodes we determine the sum of the permanent label of Node 2 and the direct distance from Node 2 to the temporarily labeled node. We then compare this sum to the current temporary label of the node, and the smaller of the two num-

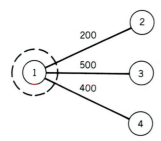

FIGURE 12.3 INITIALIZATION STEP—PERMANENTLY LABELED NODE.

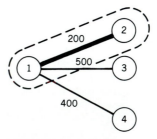

FIGURE 12.4 ITERATION 1— PERMANENTLY LABELED NODES.

bers becomes the new temporary label for that node. To illustrate, since Nodes 3 and 5 are the temporarily labeled nodes connected to Node 2

New temporary label for Node 3
= minimum of (200 + 150
= 350, 500) = 350

New temporary label for Node 5
= minimum of (200 + 700
= 900, +∞) = 900

Then, the smallest of the temporary labels is made permanent. The node labels at iteration 2, denoted by $L(2)$, are

NODES	1	2	3	4	5	6	7
$L(2)$	0	200	350	400	900	+∞	+∞
Preceding Node	—	1	2	1	2	—	—

At iteration 2, Node 3 is assigned a permanent label and the permanently labeled nodes, shown in Figure 12.5, consist of Nodes 1, 2, and 3. Note that branch (1, 3) has been deleted (as shown by the dotted line), since branch (2, 3) has been identified as part of the shortest route from Node 1 to Node 3.

At iteration three, we examine each of the temporarily labeled nodes that can be connected to Node 3. For each of the temporarily labeled nodes, we determine the sum of the permanent label of Node 3 and the direct distance to the temporarily labeled node. We then compare this sum to the current temporary label of the node, and the smaller of the two numbers becomes the new temporary label for that node. To illustrate, since Nodes 4, 5, and 6 are the temporarily labeled nodes connected

to Node 3

New temporary label for Node 4
= minimum of (350 + 100
= 450, 400) = 400

New temporary label for Node 5
= minimum of (350 + 400
= 750, 900) = 750

New temporary label for Node 6
= minimum of (350 + 350
= 700, +∞) = 700

Then, the smallest of the temporary labels is made permanent. The node labels at iteration 3, denoted by $L(3)$, are

NODES	1	2	3	4	5	6	7
$L(3)$	0	200	350	400	750	700	+∞
Preceding Node	—	1	2	1	3	3	—

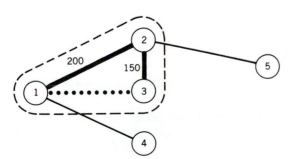

FIGURE 12.5   ITERATION 2—PERMANENTLY LABELED NODES.

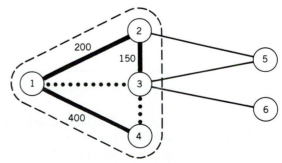

FIGURE 12.6   ITERATION 3—PERMANENTLY LABELED NODES.

At iteration 3, Node 4 is assigned a permanent label and the shortest route, shown in Figure 12.6, consists of Nodes 1, 2, 3, and 4. Note that branch (3, 4) has been deleted (as shown by the dotted line), since branch (1, 4) has been identified as the shortest route from Node 1 to Node 4.

At iteration 4, we examine each of the temporarily labeled nodes that can be connected to Node 4. For each of the temporarily labeled nodes we determine the sum of the permanent label of Node 4 and the direct distance to the temporarily labeled node. We then compare this sum to the current temporary label of the node, and the smaller of the two numbers becomes the new temporary label for that node. To illustrate, since Node 6 is the temporarily labeled node connected to Node 4

New temporary label for Node 6
= minimum (400 + 400
= 800, 700) = 700

Then, the smallest of the temporary labels is made permanent. The node labels at iteration 4, denoted by $L(4)$, are

NODES	1	2	3	4	5	6	7
$L(4)$	0	200	350	400	750	700	$+\infty$
Preceding Node	—	1	2	1	3	3	—

At iteration 4, Node 6 is assigned a permanent label and the shortest route, shown below in Figure 12.7, consists of Nodes 1, 2, 3, 4, and 6. Note that branch (4, 6) has been deleted (as shown by the dotted line), since branch (3, 6) has been identified as part of the shortest route from Node 1 to Node 6.

At iteration five, we examine each of the temporarily labeled nodes that can be connected to Node 6. For each of the temporarily labeled nodes we determine the sum of the permanent label of Node 6 and the direct distance to the temporarily labeled node. We then compare this sum to the current temporary label of the node, and the smaller of the two numbers becomes the new temporary label for that node. To illustrate, since Nodes 5 and 7 are the temporarily labeled nodes connected to Node 6

New temporary label for Node 5
= minimum (700 + 100
= 800, 750) = 750

New temporary label for Node 7
= minimum (700 + 700
= 1400, $+\infty$) = 1400

Then, the smallest of the temporary labels is made permanent. The node labels at iteration 5, denoted by $L(5)$, are

NODES	1	2	3	4	5	6	7
$L(5)$	0	200	350	400	750	700	1400
Preceding Node	—	1	2	1	3	3	6

At iteration 5, Node 5 is assigned a permanent label, and the shortest route, shown in Figure 12.8, consists of Nodes, 1, 2, 3, 4, 5, and 6. Note that branches (2, 5) and (5, 6) have been deleted (as shown by the dotted lines), since branches (3, 5) and (3, 6) have been identified as part of the shortest routes from Node 1 to Nodes 5 and 6.

At iteration 6, we examine each of the temporarily labeled nodes that can be connected to Node 5. For each of the temporarily labeled nodes, we determine the sum of the permanent label of Node 5 and the direct distance to the temporarily labeled node. We then compare this sum to the current temporary label of the node, and the smaller of the two numbers becomes the new temporary label for that node. To illustrate, since Node 7 is the only temporarily labeled node connected to node 5

New temporary label for Node 7
= minimum (750 + 500
= 1250, 1400) = 1250

Then, the smallest of the temporary labels is made permanent. The node labels at iteration 6, denoted by $L(6)$, are

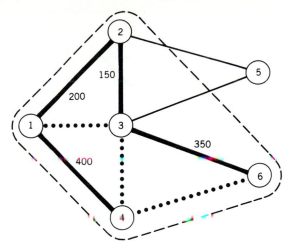

FIGURE 12.7 ITERATION 4—PERMANENTLY LABELED NODES.

NODES	1	2	3	4	5	6	7
$L(6)$	0	200	350	400	750	700	1250
Preceding Node	—	1	2	1	3	3	5

We have now permanently labeled the sink node (Node 7), so the algorithm terminates and the shortest route from Node 1 to Node 7 is 1250 miles. Observe that we have actually determined the shortest distance from Node 1 to every other node in the network, since every node has been permanently labeled in iteration 6.

To determine the sequence of nodes in the shortest route from Node 1 to Node 7, we work backward from Node 7, using the "Preceding Node" row. Thus, Node 5 is the immediate predecessor of Node 7. Similarly, Node 3 precedes Node 5, Node 2 precedes Node 3, and Node 1 precedes Node 2. Therefore, the shortest route from Node 1 to Node 7 is 1→ 2 → 3 → 5 → 7 with a total distance of 1250 miles. The optimal solution, after six iterations, is shown in Figure 12.9. Note also that the shortest route from Node 1 to Node 6 is 1 → 2 → 3 → 6.

12.4 THE MINIMUM SPANNING-TREE PROBLEM

An important variation of the shortest route problem is known as the minimum spanning-tree prob-

lem. Once again we are given a network consisting of a set of nodes and branches, with the length of the various branches being known. The minimum spanning-tree problem, however, involves choosing the branches for the network that have the shortest total length while providing a route between each pair of nodes. In solving this problem, we choose

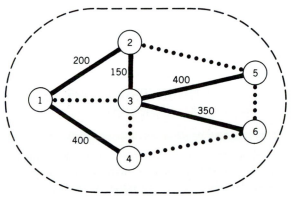

FIGURE 12.8 ITERATION 5—PERMANENTLY LABELED NODES.

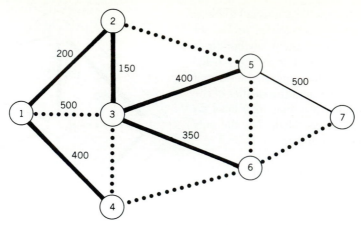

FIGURE 12.9 OPTIMAL SOLUTION: BOFFA TRUCKING COMPANY—SHORTEST ROUTE PROBLEM.

the branches in a manner such that the resulting network forms a tree that "spans" (i.e., is connected to) all the nodes of the given network. This spanning tree cannot have any "cycles," or sequences of branches connecting two nodes. In summary, the problem is simply to find the tree that reaches all the nodes of the network with a minimum total branch length.

The minimum spanning-tree problem is important in a number of practical situations. Its most important application is in the planning of transportation networks, such as bus or subway systems. In such applications, the nodes of the network are the various terminals or stops, and the branches are the distances between the nodes via highways, subway tracks, and so forth. The problem, then, is to specify the transportation lanes that would serve all the terminals in a minimum total distance. Other applications of the minimum spanning tree arise in the planning of distribution networks and communication systems.

12.4.1 SOLUTION PROCEDURE FOR THE MINIMUM SPANNING-TREE PROBLEM

The minimum spanning-tree problem can be solved in a simple, orderly manner. The steps involved in the solution procedure are as follows.

1. Select any node of the network arbitrarily and connect it to its nearest node; that is, choose the shortest possible branch to another node, without worrying about the effect this would have on a later decision.
2. Identify the unconnected node that is closest to a connected node, and then connect these two nodes.
3. Repeat Step 2 until all nodes have been connected.

The resulting network will be a minimal spanning tree. It is interesting to note that this solution procedure is one in which making the best short-run decision at each step (i.e., simply choose the shortest possible branch to another node) will eventually result in the best long-run decision (i.e., we will determine the minimum spanning tree). This is unusual, as making short-run optimal decisions usually doesn't result in the long-run optimal decision.

Ties for the nearest node (Step 1) or for the closest unconnected node (Step 2) can be broken arbitrarily and the solution process will still yield an optimal solution. Such ties indicate that there may be multiple optimal solutions to the problem, which can be identified by tracing out the spanning trees for all possible ways of breaking ties.

Let us now consider an example that illustrates the application of the minimum spanning-tree solution procedure. We again utilize the highway network for the Boffa Trucking Company, which is reproduced in Figure 12.10. Assume that, for the network shown in the figure, we are interested in specifying a set of communication lines paralleling

414   *NETWORK MODELS*

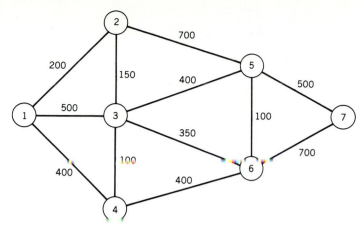

FIGURE 12.10   MINIMUM SPANNING TREE—COMMUNICATIONS NET-
WORK EXAMPLE.

the branches of this highway network that will connect, or span, all of the nodes. We further assume
that any unspecified distances in the figure are greater
than the branch distances already shown. For example, no branch distance is shown for branch (1,
5), but it is assumed that the length of branch (1,
5) is greater than the lengths of branches (1, 2),
(1, 3), and (1, 4), respectively. Using the information summarized on Figure 12.10, the step-by-
step solution of the problem is summarized below.

To begin the solution procedure we arbitrarily
select a node at which to start. A logical node to
begin with is Node 1, although any starting node
can be chosen and the resultant minimum spanning
distance will be the same. Now, the unconnected
node closest to Node 1 is Node 2. Therefore, we

connect Node 1 to Node 2, and the connected nodes
(shown in boldface) after the first iteration are as
shown in Figure 12.11.

We next consider both Nodes 1 and 2, and
observe that the unconnected node closest to either
Node 1 or Node 2 is Node 3 (which is closest to
Node 2). Therefore, we connect Node 3 to Node
2, and the connected nodes after the second iteration are as shown in Figure 12.12.

We next consider Nodes 1, 2, and 3, and observe that the unconnected node closest to either
Nodes 1, 2, or 3 is Node 4 (which is closest to Node
3). Observe further that we do not consider connecting Node 3 to Node 1, because Node 1 is already
connected to Node 2, and if we connected Node 1
to Node 3 we would produce a cycle (cycles are

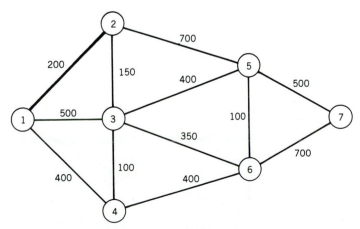

FIGURE 12.11   ITERATION 1—CONNECTED NODES.

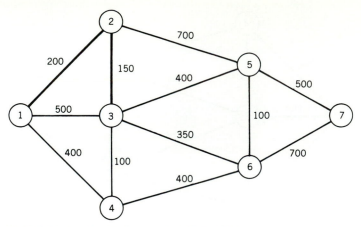

FIGURE 12.12 ITERATION 2—CONNECTED NODES.

prohibited in our spanning tree). Therefore, we connect Node 4 to Node 3, and the connected nodes after the third iteration are as shown in Figure 12.13.

We next consider Nodes 1, 2, 3, and 4, and observe that the unconnected node closest to either Nodes 1, 2, 3, or 4 is Node 6 (which is closest to Node 3). Therefore, we connect Node 6 to Node 3, and the connected nodes after the fourth iteration are as shown in Figure 12.14.

We next consider Nodes 1, 2, 3, 4, and 6, and observe that the unconnected node closest to either Nodes 1, 2, 3, 4, or 6 is Node 5 (which is closest to Node 6). Therefore, we connect Node 5 to Node 6, and the connected nodes after the fifth iteration are as shown in Figure 12.15.

We next consider Nodes 1, 2, 3, 4, 5, and 6, and observe that the unconnected node closest to

either Nodes 1, 2, 3, 4, 5, or 6, is Node 7 (which is closest to Node 5). Therefore, we connect Node 7 to Node 5. All nodes are now connected, so we have determined the desired solution to this problem. The minimum spanning-tree solution, shown in Figure 12.16, has a total length of 1400 miles.

12.5 THE MAXIMUM-FLOW PROBLEM

In the maximum- or maximal-flow problem we consider a connected network consisting of a single origin (source), a single destination (sink), and branches connecting intermediate nodes. Within the maximum-flow network some, or all, of the branches may be directed. In this instance, the ori-

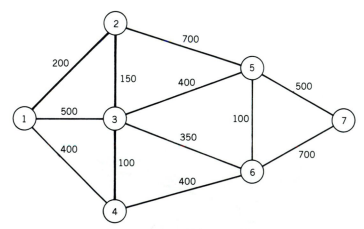

FIGURE 12.13 ITERATION 3—CONNECTED NODES.

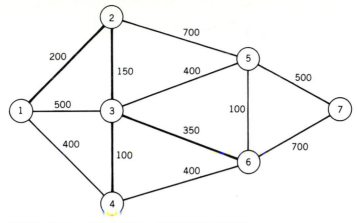

FIGURE 12.14   ITERATION 4—CONNECTED NODES.

entation of the branch is assumed to be the feasible direction of flow along the particular branch. We assume that there is conservation of flow (i.e., flow into the node equals flow out of the node) at each node other than the source and the sink. The source node has an orientation such that all flow moves away from it, and the sink node has an orientation such that all flow moves toward it. Additionally, it is important to recognize that a branch in a maximal-flow network need not be directed because it may be feasible to have flow in either direction along a branch. A two-way street is an example of a non-oriented branch, while a one-way street is an example of an oriented branch.

In the maximum-flow problem, the flow capacity of a branch in a specified direction is defined to be the upper limit of the feasible magnitude of the rate (or total quantity) of flow in the branch in that direction. The flow capacity of a branch may be any nonnegative quantity, including infinity. An oriented branch will have a flow capacity equal to a nonnegative quantity in one direction and a flow capacity equal to zero in the other direction. The maximum-flow problem is to determine the feasible steady-state pattern of flows through the network that maximizes the total flow from the source to the sink.

As an example of a typical maximum-flow problem consider the electrical transmission network for Southern Utilities Company presented below in Figure 12.17. The source node (Node 1) in this network is the power generating station, and the sink node (Node 7) represents the destination city to which the electrical power is directed. The

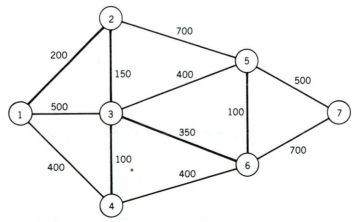

FIGURE 12.15   ITERATION 5—CONNECTED NODES.

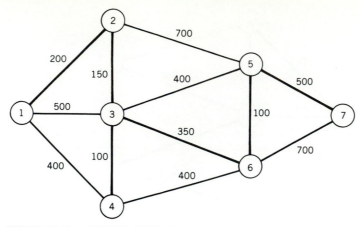

FIGURE 12.16 OPTIMAL SOLUTION: COMMUNICATIONS NETWORK—
MINIMUM SPANNING-TREE PROBLEM.

TOTAL LENGTH OF MINIMUM SPANNING TREE = (200 + 150 +
100 + 350 +
100 + 500)
= 1400 MILES

other nodes of the network represent switching stations, at which the electrical flow of the branches of the network can be regulated. The capacities of the various branches of the network are shown on the respective branches. For example, $c_{12} = 9$ and $c_{21} = 0$.

A second typical maximum-flow problem might involve the maximization of information flow through a computer network. The central processing unit would be the source, and some type of output device would become the sink. The branches of the network would then become the various channels be-

tween the central processing unit and the output device. The objective in this situation would be to plan the selection and utilization of the various channels in a manner that would maximize the total information flow through the network.

12.5.1 SOLUTION PROCEDURE FOR THE MAXIMUM-FLOW PROBLEM

The solution procedure used to solve maximum-flow problems consists of the following steps.

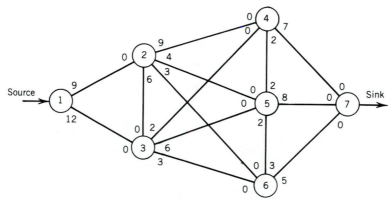

FIGURE 12.17 ELECTRICAL TRANSMISSION NETWORK—SOUTHERN UTILITIES COMPANY.

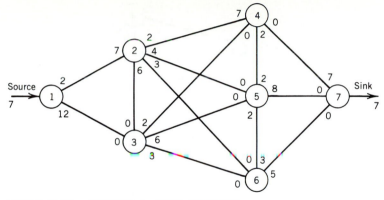

FIGURE 12.18 ITERATION 1—FLOW CAPACITIES.

1. Find a path through the network, from the source node to the sink node, which has some available flow capacity on each branch of the selected path. If no such path exists, the net flows already assigned constitute the maximum-flow pattern.

2. Search this path for the branch with the smallest flow capacity. Denote this capacity as c_{ij}^*, and increase the flow in each branch on this path by c_{ij}^*.

3. Decrease the flow capacity of each branch on the selected path by c_{ij}^*.

4. Increase the flow capacity, in the opposite direction, of each branch in the selected path by c_{ij}^*. (*Note:* this step is done in order to identify the potential flow redirection possible for each branch on the selected path.)

5. Return to Step 1 and repeat the process outlined in Steps 2, 3, and 4 until no paths with positive flow capacity remain.

6. Compute the net flows in all branches of the network.

Let us now apply the steps of the solution procedure to the electrical transmission network shown in Figure 12.17. At iteration 1, path $1 \rightarrow 2 \rightarrow 4 \rightarrow 7$ is arbitrarily selected and the maximum possible flow of seven units is assigned. Observe that the maximum flow for this path is restricted by the capacity of branch (4, 7), namely, $c_{47} = 7$. Figure 12.18 shows the revision of the flow capacities along the selected path, $1 \rightarrow 2 \rightarrow 4 \rightarrow 7$, after iteration 1. Note that the flow capacities in the direction from

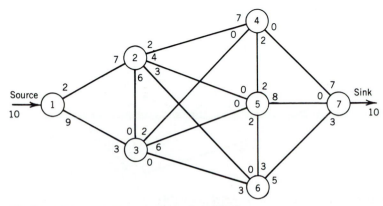

FIGURE 12.19 ITERATION 2—FLOW CAPACITIES

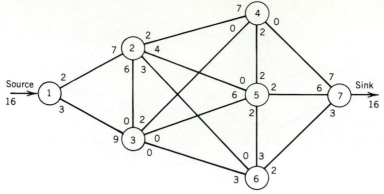

FIGURE 12.20   ITERATION 3—FLOW CAPACITIES.

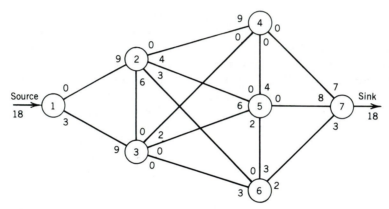

FIGURE 12.21   ITERATION 4—FLOW CAPACITIES.

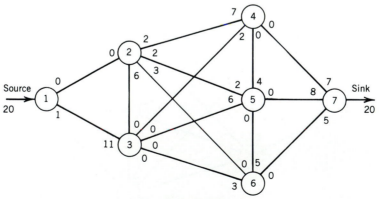

FIGURE 12.22   ITERATION 5—FLOW CAPACITIES.

TABLE 12.2 DETERMINATION OF NET FLOW FOR BRANCH (2, 4)

ITERATION	BRANCH	FLOW ALLOCATION	
1	$(2 \rightarrow 4)$	7	} 9
4	$(2 \rightarrow 4)$	2	
5	$(4 \rightarrow 2)$	2	

Note: Net flow in branch $(2 \rightarrow 4) = 9 - 2 = 7$.

the source node to the sink node have been decreased, while the flow capacities in the direction from the sink node to the source node have been increased by equal amounts. For example, $c_{12} = 9 - 7 = 2$ and $c_{12} = 0 + 7 = 7$.

At iteration 2, path $1 \rightarrow 3 \rightarrow 6 \rightarrow 7$ is arbitrarily selected, and the maximum possible flow of three units is assigned. Figure 12.19 shows the revisions of the flow capacities along the selected path, $1 \rightarrow 3 \rightarrow 6 \rightarrow 7$, after iteration 2.

At iteration 3, path $1 \rightarrow 3 \rightarrow 5 \rightarrow 7$ is arbitrarily selected, and the maximum possible flow of six units is assigned. Figure 12.20 shows the revisions of the flow capacities along the selected path, $1 \rightarrow 3 \rightarrow 5 \rightarrow 7$, after iteration 3.

At iteration 4, path $1 \rightarrow 2 \rightarrow 4 \rightarrow 5 \rightarrow 7$ is arbitrarily selected, and the maximum possible flow of two units is assigned. Figure 12.21 shows the revisions of the flow capacities along the selected path, $1 \rightarrow 2 \rightarrow 4 \rightarrow 5 \rightarrow 7$, after iteration 4.

At iteration 5, *two* paths, $1 \rightarrow 3 \rightarrow 4 \rightarrow 2 \rightarrow 6 \rightarrow 7$ and $1 \rightarrow 3 \rightarrow 4 \rightarrow 2 \rightarrow 5 \rightarrow 6 \rightarrow 7$, remain with positive flow capacity. A maximum possible flow of two units can be assigned to either of these two paths. Let us assume that we decide to use path $1 \rightarrow 3 \rightarrow 4 \rightarrow 2 \rightarrow 5 \rightarrow 6 \rightarrow 7$, and assign the maximum flow of two units to it. Figure 12.22 shows the revisions of the flow capacities along the selected path, $1 \rightarrow 3 \rightarrow 4 \rightarrow 2 \rightarrow 5 \rightarrow 6 \rightarrow 7$, after iteration 5.

Observe that at iteration 5 an allocation of two units has been assigned to branch (2, 4), that is, in the "wrong" direction since the original flow network for this problem (see Figure 12.17) indicated a zero flow capacity for branch (4, 2). The actual net flow for branch (2, 4), that is, in the "right" direction, however, may be determined as shown in Table 12.2. Therefore, the net flow for branch $(2 \rightarrow 4)$ will be seven units. The effect will be to reroute two units of the nine units of flow that had been assigned to branch $(2 \rightarrow 4)$ to branch $(2 \rightarrow 5)$. The two units of flow will then be sent to Nodes 6 and 7.

Examining the source node (Node 1) for the network shown in Figure 12.22, we see that there is remaining flow capacity for branch $1 \rightarrow 3$ (i.e., one unit). There is, however, no flow capacity for any of the branches leading out of Node 3. There-

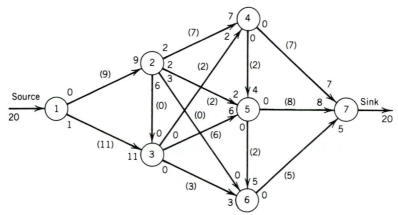

FIGURE 12.23 OPTIMAL SOLUTION: SOUTHERN UTILITIES COMPANY—MAXIMUM FLOW PROBLEM.

TABLE 12.3 SUMMARY OF FLOW ALLOCATIONS TO THE BRANCHES OF THE NETWORK

ITERATION	ALLOCATION	1→2	1→3	2→3	2→4	2→5	2→6	3→4	3→5	3→6	4→2	4→5	4→7	5→6	5→7	6→7
1	7 units to 1 → 2 → 4 → 7	7			7								7			
2	2 units to 1 → 3 → 6 → 7		3							3						3
3	6 units to 1 → 3 → 5 → 7		6						6						6	
4	2 units to 1 → 2 → 4 → 5 → 7	2			2							2			2	
5	2 units to 1 → 3 → 4 → 2 → 5 → 6 → 7		2			2		2			2			2		2
	Total allocation	9	11	0	9	2	0	2	6	3	2	2	7	2	8	5
	Original capacity	9	12	6	9	4	3	2	6	3	0	2	7	2	8	5
	Final capacity	0	1	6	2	2	3	0	0	0	7	0	0	0	0	0
	Unused capacity	0	1	6	2	2	3	0	0	0	7	0	0	0	0	0

Note: Maximum flow = 20. Also, net flow in branch (2 → 4) = 9 − 2 = 7 units.

fore, no further flow allocation can be made, and we have obtained the optimal solution. The final network (optimal solution) after five iterations is reproduced in Figure 12.23. The final flow allocation for each branch is shown in parentheses, and the direction of flow for each branch is indicated by arrows. The final flow capacities for the various branches are also shown.

The flow allocations to the various branches of the network are summarized in Table 12.3, and the individual allocations to each branch at each iteration are presented. Also shown are the original branch capacities, the final branch capacities, and the unused branch capacities after the final allocation. Observe that the actual net flow in branch $(2 \rightarrow 4) = 9 - 2 = 7$ units.

12.6 SOLVING NETWORK PROBLEMS USING A COMPUTER

Computer programs for solving network problems are readily available in both mainframe and microcomputer versions. Typical of the latter are the programs included in the microcomputer package: *Computer Models for Management Science* by Erickson and Hall.[3] It includes programs that can be used to solve small shortest route, minimum spanning-tree, and maximal-flow problems. We now illustrate these programs in terms of the examples presented earlier in this chapter.

In Section 12.3 we considered a highway network shortest route problem. Referring back to Figure 12.2, you can see that this highway network has 7 nodes and 12 branches (or arcs). The length of each branch is shown directly above that branch. Input for the shortest route program includes the number of nodes, the number of branches, and the lengths of the branches. The output from this program is shown in Figure 12.24. As you can see from this output, the shortest route is defined by the nodes $1 \rightarrow 2 \rightarrow 3 \rightarrow 5 \rightarrow 7$, with a total distance of 1250

miles. The program can also be used to find the shortest route to any node in the network, but requires a separate run for each starting and ending node combination.

In Section 12.4 we addressed a minimum spanning-tree problem involving a communications network. Referring back to Figure 12.10 you can see that this communication network has 7 nodes and 12 branches (or arcs). The length of each branch is shown directly above that branch. Input for the minimum spanning-tree program includes the number of nodes, the number of branches, and the lengths of the branches. The output from this program is shown in Figure 12.25. As you can see from this ouput, the minimum spanning-tree has a length of 1400 miles. The branches that are connected to form it are also shown in the output.

In Section 12.5 we presented an electrical transmission network maximum-flow problem. Referring back to Figure 12.17, you can see that this electrical transmission network has 7 nodes and 16 branches. Note that there are 16 branches because there is two-way flow in two of the branches (i.e., $4 \leftrightarrows 5$ and $5 \leftrightarrows 6$). The maximum flow permitted in each branch is shown directly above that branch. Input for the maximum-flow program includes the number of nodes, the number of branches, and the maximum flows allowed in the branches. The output from the program is shown in Figure 12.26. As you can see from this output, the maximum total network flow is 20 units. The flow in each of the branches of the network is also shown in the output.

12.7 SUMMARY

In this chapter we have considered a set of problems that can conveniently be solved by constructing and analyzing a network. Network problems are encountered in a wide variety of managerial decision-making situations, including the planning of transportation and distribution systems, the specification of terminals in a mass-transit system, and the structuring of material-flow systems, such as pipelines. For these network problems, and the maximum-flow problem, we developed and utilized algorithms that were based on the unique structures of these particular problems.

[3]Warren J. Erickson and Owen P. Hall, Jr., *Computer Models for Management Science.* Reading, Mass. Addison–Wesley, 1986.

```
     *************************
     *                       *
     *     SHORTEST ROUTE    *
     *        ANALYSIS       *
     *                       *
     *************************

     **  INFORMATION ENTERED  **

     NUMBER OF NODES  7
     NUMBER OF LINKS  12
     TYPE:  SYMMETRIC

LINK      START      END       DISTANCE      REVERSE
          NODE       NODE                    DISTANCE

  1         1          2          200          200
  2         1          3          500          500
  3         1          4          400          400
  4         2          3          150          150
  5         3          4          100          100
  6         2          5          700          700
  7         3          5          400          400
  8         3          6          350          350
  9         4          6          400          400
 10         5          7          500          500
 11         5          6          100          100
 12         6          7          700          700

          **  RESULTS  **

START               END                  DISTANCE
NODE                NODE

  1                  2                     200
  2                  3                     150
  3                  5                     400
  5                  7                     500

     TOTAL DISTANCE  1250

     **  END OF ANALYSIS  **
```

FIGURE 12.24   MICROCOMPUTER PROGRAM OUTPUT—SHORTEST ROUTE PROBLEM.

```
*************************
*                       *
*      SPANNING TREE     *
*        ANALYSIS        *
*                       *
*************************

** INFORMATION ENTERED **

    NUMBER OF NODES:  7
    NUMBER OF LINKS:  12
```

LINK NUMBER	START NODE	END NODE	LINK LENGTH
1	1	2	200
2	1	3	500
3	1	4	400
4	2	3	150
5	2	5	700
6	3	4	100
7	3	5	400
8	3	6	350
9	4	6	400
10	5	6	100
11	5	7	500
12	6	7	700

```
            ** RESULTS **

MINIMUM SPANNING TREE
```

START NODE	END NODE	LINK LENGTH
1	2	200
2	3	150
3	4	100
3	6	350
6	5	100
5	7	500

```
TOTAL LENGTH = 1400
```

FIGURE 12.25   MICROCOMPUTER PROGRAM OUTPUT—MINIMUM SPANNING TREE PROBLEM.

```
        ************************
        *                      *
        *    MAXIMUM FLOW       *
        *    ANALYSIS           *
        *                      *
        ************************

        **  INFORMATION ENTERED  **

           NUMBER OF NODES:  7
           NUMBER OF LINKS:  16

LINK          START          END          FLOW
              NODE           NODE

1             1              2            9
2             1              3            12
3             2              3            6
4             2              4            9
5             2              5            4
6             2              6            3
7             3              4            2
8             3              5            6
9             3              6            3
10            4              5            2
11            4              7            7
12            5              4            2
13            5              6            2
14            5              7            8
15            6              5            3
16            6              7            5


                **  RESULTS  **

OPTIMAL FLOW OVER ALL PATHS FROM
NODE 1 TO NODE 7 :

FLOW     NODES     THAT     DEFINE     EACH     PATH

7        1        2        4        7
2        1        2        5        7
6        1        3        5        7
3        1        3        6        7
2        1        3        4        5        6        7
```

FIGURE 12.26   MICROCOMPUTER PROGRAM OUTPUT—MAXIMUM-FLOW PROBLEM.

```
OPTIMAL FLOW OVER EACH LINK:

START        END          FLOW
NODE         NODE

  1            2            9
  1            3           11
  2            4            7
  2            5            2
  3            4            2
  3            5            6
  3            6            3
  4            5            2
  4            7            7
  5            6            2
  5            7            8
  6            7            5

MAXIMUM TOTAL NETWORK FLOW:  20

        ** END OF ANALYSIS **
```

GLOSSARY

Activity (Branch)   Connector between the nodes of the network.

Chain   A sequence of branches in a network with the property that not all of the branches are necessarily directed toward the ending node.

Circuit   A path in a network in which the initial and ending nodes are the same node.

Connected Graph   A graph in which there is a path connecting every pair of nodes in the graph.

Cycle   A chain that begins and ends at the same node.

Directed or Oriented Branch   A branch characterized by a sense of direction indicating which node is to be considered the point of origin.

Event (Node)   A junction point in a network.

Flow   Physical movement along a branch of a network.

Flow Capacity   The upper limit to the feasible magnitude of the rate (or total quantity) of flow in the branch in that direction.

Maximum-(Maximal-) Flow Problem   Concerns the maximum amount of flow that can enter into and exit from some connected network during a given period of time.

Minimum Spanning-Tree Problem   Involves choosing the branches for the network that have the shortest total length while providing a route between each pair of nodes.

Network   A set of junction points, called nodes, that are connected by flow routes called branches.

Path A specific sequence of branches in a network in which the initial node of each branch is the same as the ending node of the preceding branch.

Shortest Route Problem Involves the determination of the minimum total distance from the origin to the destination in a network.

Trees An undirected, connected network that contains no cycles.

Selected References

Battersby, Albert. 1970. *Network Analysis for Planning and Scheduling*. New York: Wiley.

Bazaraa, Mokhtar S., and John J. Jarvis. 1977. *Linear Programming and Network Flows*. New York: Wiley.

Conway, R.W., W.L. Maxwell, and L.W. Miller. 1967. *Theory of Scheduling*. Reading, Mass.: Addison–Wesley.

Elmaghraby, Salah E. 1970. *Some Network Models in Management Science*. Berlin/ New York: Springer-Verlag.

Frank, Howard, and Ivan T. Frisch. 1971. *Communication, Transmission and Transportation Networks*. Reading, Mass.: Addison–Wesley.

Hu, Te Chiang. 1969. *Integer Programming and Network Flows*. Reading, Mass.: Addison–Wesley.

Potts, R.B., and R.M. Oliver. 1972. *Flows in Transportation Networks*. New York: Academic Press.

Whitehouse, George E. 1973. *Systems Analysis and Design Using Network Techniques*. Englewood Cliffs, N.J.: Prentice–Hall.

Discussion Questions

1. Why is it often advantageous to consider managerial problems in a network framework?

2. Why is Dijkstra's shortest route algorithm preferable to linear programming for solving shortest route problems?

3. Explain how Dijkstra's shortest route algorithm converges to a solution.

4. What is the difference between the solution procedure of the shortest route problem and the minimum spanning-tree problem?

5. Why isn't the solution procedure for the minimum spanning-tree problem dependent on the choice of a starting node?

6. Is the solution procedure for the shortest route problem dependent on the choice of a starting node? Why or why not?

7. In the maximum-flow solution procedure, the remaining capacity of a branch is updated each time flow is assigned to a branch. If the allocated flow to branch (i, j) is in the direction $i \rightarrow j$, capacity c_{ij} is decreased while capacity c_{ji} is increased. Explain why these adjustments are made, and indicate how these adjustments ensure that the maximum-flow patterns will be identified.

8. Explain how the minimum spanning-tree solution procedure converges to a solution.

9. Explain how the maximum-flow solution procedure converges to a solution.

PROBLEMS

1. Find the shortest route for the following highway network, where the distances shown are in hundreds of miles.

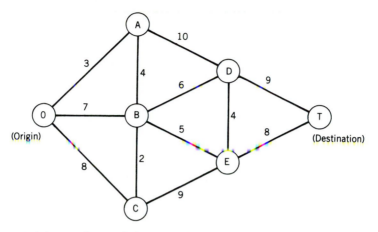

2. A hiker wishes to hike through a wilderness area in as few days as possible. Possible branches between various shelters in this wilderness are shown in the following network (branch numbers represent the number of days required to hike between nodes of that branch). What route should be taken to minimize travel time?

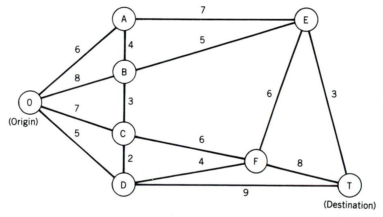

3. Find the shortest route for the following railroad network, where the branch distances are in hundreds of miles.

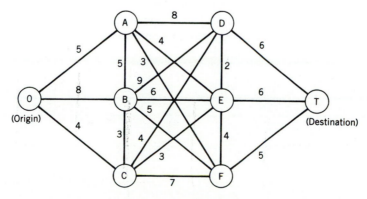

4. Find the shortest route for the following electrical transmission network, where the branch distances are in hundreds of miles.

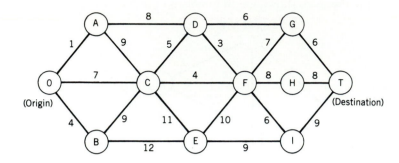

5. Sunbird Airlines operates a fleet of small airplanes to provide commuter flights between a number of small southeastern cities. The flight distances between these cities are shown in the following network.

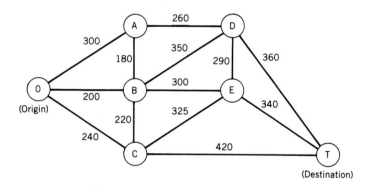

Find the shortest route from the origin to the destination.

6. The city of New Vista has a comprehensive monorail system that connects eight of its major shopping centers as well as its two main cultural centers. Each monocab is assigned a round-trip route between two of the centers; every 10 minutes a monocab departs from one center to another. A one-way monorail trip between two centers averages 30 minutes. Determine the minimum route from the east side of New Vista (Center 1) to the west side of New Vista (Center 10) given the following list of monorail routes and their associated distances.

MONORAIL ROUTES	DISTANCE (MI)
Center 1 to Center 2	4.0
Center 1 to Center 4	5.0
Center 1 to Center 5	8.5

MONORAIL ROUTES	DISTANCE (MI)
Center 2 to Center 4	4.2
Center 2 to Center 3	4.5
Center 3 to Center 4	4.8
Center 3 to Center 6	5.2
Center 4 to Center 5	6.5
Center 4 to Center 6	5.5
Center 5 to Center 6	5.0
Center 5 to Center 7	4.2
Center 5 to Center 8	7.0
Center 6 to Center 8	6.5
Center 7 to Center 8	4.5
Center 7 to Center 9	5.0
Center 8 to Center 9	6.3
Center 8 to Center 10	5.5
Center 9 to Center 10	4.5

Find the shortest route from Center 1 to Center 10.

7. Find the minimum spanning-tree for the network shown in Problem 1.

8. Find the minimum spanning-tree for the network shown in Problem 2.

9. Find the minimum spanning-tree for the network shown in Problem 3.

10. Find the minimum spanning-tree for the network shown in Problem 4.

11. Find the minimum spanning-tree for the network shown in Problem 5.

12. The city of New Vista (see Problem 6) wishes to establish a communications network between each of its eight shopping centers and two cultural centers, in a manner that connects every center. Determine the minimum spanning-tree for the communications network.

13. For the following pipeline network, find the maximum oil flow from the source to the sink, given that the flow capacity from Node i to Node j is the number along branch (i, j) nearest Node i.

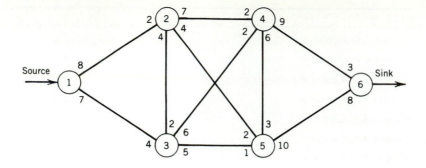

14. For the following highway network, find the maximum vehicle flow from the source to the sink, given that the flow capacity from Node *i* to Node *j* is the number along branch (*i*, *j*) nearest Node *i*.

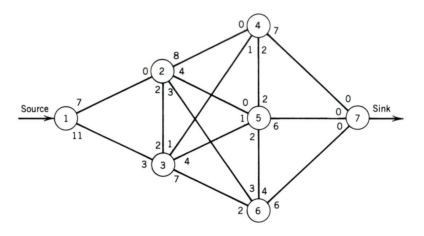

15. For the following pipeline network, find the maximum natural-gas flow from the source to the sink, given that the flow capacity from Node *i* to Node *j* is the number along branch (*i*, *j*) nearest Node *i*.

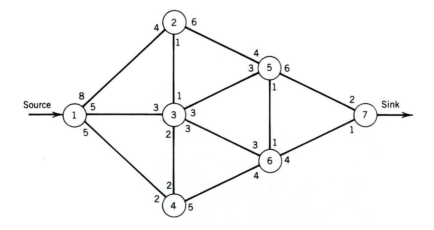

16. For the following electrical transmission network, find the maximum energy flow from the source to the sink, given that the flow capacity from Node i to Node j is the number along branch (i, j) nearest Node i.

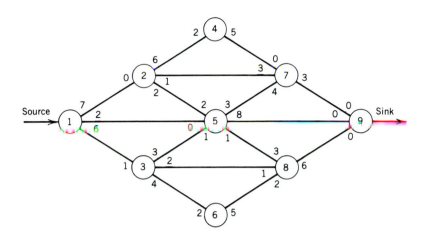

17. Ski Snowflake is attempting to plan a system of chair lifts for its proposed ski facility to be built in Boone, North Carolina. Its ski facility begins at the bottom of the mountain and ends at the top. There are six intermediate points, however, at which skiers can leave their chair lifts, or they can continue on to the top of the mountain. Potential flow capacities for the chair lifts are determined and structured in terms of the following network.

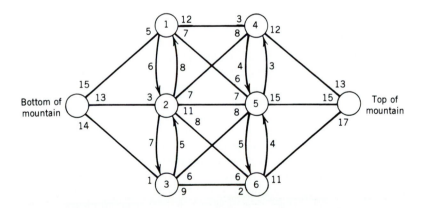

(*Note:* Flow capacities are in thousands of persons per hour.) Determine the size (capacities) of chair lifts to be built to maximize the flow of people from the bottom of the mountain to the top. Specify the maximum flow.

18. Determine the maximum flow for the following network.

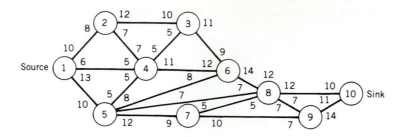

Application Review 1

The Passenger-Mix Problem at Frontier Airlines

Since airline deregulation has gone into effect, there have been major changes in the competitive structure of the airline industry. Prior to deregulation, competition among airline carriers was limited by the Civil Aeronautics Board (CAB) in two of the three major areas of airline marketing, route authority and pricing. The airlines were able to compete only in terms of the amount of capacity (number of flights) to be made available by any one carrier over any one route.

Deregulation of the airline industry by the CAB has created many challenges and opportunities. Foremost among the challenges is the opportunity to set prices more adaptively and to change them more rapidly.

The basic problem faced by the airline industry is often called the "pricing and passenger-mix" problem. Solution of the problem is complicated by the following factors.

1. The existence of a multitude of prices (fares), with varying degrees of restrictions limiting the availability of all but the highest priced seats.
2. Numerous flights operated by a number of airlines over various routings, any one of which (or combinations of two or more) can be used by passengers to each of their destinations.
3. Varying degrees of demand for the seats on any one airline's flight segment over time.

By exploring different pricing and routing options, and seeking the best mix of passengers, an airline can structure a more effective reservation system as well as improve its overall profitability.

Frontier Airlines, a Denver-based carrier, has addressed this problem using a network modeling approach, utilizing a minimum-cost (maximum-revenue) network-flow model with special side constraints. In it, one set of branches corresponded to the various flight segments, while another set corresponded to the various passenger itineraries as they were differentiated by fare classes. Flow on the forward (former) branches represented the number of passengers on a flight segment, and flow on the backward (latter) branches represented the number of passengers on each passenger itinerary at each of the various fare classes. The flow on each of the forward arcs was limited by the capacity of the aircraft, and flow on each of the backward branches was limited by the demand for the passenger

Source: Fred Glover, Randy Glover, Joe Lorenzo, and Claude McMillan, "The passenger-mix problem in the scheduled airlines," *Interfaces* (June 1982), Vol. 12, No. 3, pp. 73–80.

itinerary and the fare class represented by that branch. An increment of revenue was associated with each unit of flow on each backward branch, and this increment of revenue was set equal to the price of the ticket at the associated fare class for that branch. A set of additional constraints was imposed on the problem formulation. These constraints prohibited the sum of flows on passenger-itinerary/fare-class branches from exceeding the intended flight-segment branch capacities.

The maximum-revenue network-flow model designed for Frontier Airlines accommodated a network composed of 600 flights and 30,000 passenger itineraries with up to five fare classes per passenger itinerary. The number of special side constraints ranged from about 1800 to 2400. Solution of the network model determined the flow on each branch that maximized revenue on Frontier Airlines' network, without violating the aircraft capacity constraints and the demand for the various personal itineraries at their associated fare classes. It was of major value to Frontier Airlines in pricing, as well as in overall planning and scheduling.

Application Review 2

Improving the Distribution of Industrial Gases at Air Products and Chemicals, Inc.

The major products of the industrial gas industry are oxygen, nitrogen, hydrogen, argon, and carbon monoxide. In the industry's early years, the gases were sold in highly compressed form in heavy metal cylinders. Air Products and Chemicals, Inc., a leading supplier of industrial gases, was founded by the late Leonard P. Pool, in 1940, on the basic idea of the "on-site" production of industrial gases, primarily oxygen. Air Products and Chemicals, Inc., built oxygen-generating facilities adjacent to large-volume users, so that oxygen could be piped directly from the generating facility to the point of use. This procedure reduced distribution costs and was a technical and economic success. It enabled Air Products and Chemicals, Inc., to grow very rapidly, and was the foundation for subsequent high-technology innovations in distribution.

Today, Air Products and Chemicals, Inc., is one of the world's largest industrial gas producers. It has grown from a company with sales of $8300 in 1940 to an international corporation with sales exceeding $1.5 billion in 1982. Throughout its history a spirit of innovative progress has flourished in its distribution function. By the middle 1970s, the plants, trucks, and other equipment used by Air Products and Chemicals, Inc., for the manufacture and distribution of liquid gases were highly engineered and automated. This was in sharp contrast to the completely manual system for scheduling the delivery of these liquid gases. The company determined that its competitive edge in the industrial gas industry would depend on automation of delivery scheduling.

This goal resulted in the development of an on-line computerized routing and scheduling system. This advanced decision support system included on-line data entry functions, customer usage forecasting, a time/distance network, a mathematical optimization model (which produced daily delivery schedules), and an interactive schedule change interface.

Within this large computer system the travel time and distance between combinations of customers and between each customer and depot was an important input to the scheduling module. The common approach of computing straight-

Source: Walter L. Bell, et al., "Improving the distribution of industrial gases with an on-line computerized routing and scheduling optimizer," *Interfaces* (December 1983), Vol. 13, No. 6, pp. 4–23.

line distances from coordinates of latitude and longitude and then adjusting by some factor of road miles was judged to be too inaccurate for this application, especially in metropolitan areas. Furthermore, it provided no information about travel times.

To achieve the necessary level of detail for distances and travel speeds, a vendor was contracted to develop a computerized data base of the network of highways in the United States. The data base contained about 65,000 road segments (links) and about 40,000 intersections of road segments (nodes). For each road segment, the length of the segment and the toll cost were specified. Additionally, five characteristics were specified for each road segment and were then used to compute the travel speed.

The shortest path algorithm was then used to determine each possible intercustomer distance and travel time. The criterion used to determine the shortest path was not solely distance, but was a travel-cost value found from a combination of travel time, distance, and tolls. The output from the shortest path model sector of the computer system then became an input to the vehicle routing optimizer sector of the system. Overall, the computer system provided a number of benefits to Air Products and Chemicals, Inc., including savings from avoiding capital expenditures of approximately $445,000.

13

PERT/CPM

13.1 INTRODUCTION

The *Program Evaluation and Review Technique* (PERT) and *Critical Path Method* (CPM) are two of the best known and most widely used techniques of management science. They are typically used in situations where managers have responsibilities for planning, scheduling, and controlling large projects that are composed of many activities performed by a variety of people in various work areas. PERT and CPM have been effective procedures for complex project management problems. Although PERT and CPM utilize the same terminology and have the same objectives, they were developed independently.

The Program Evaluation and Review Technique was developed in 1958 for the planning and control of the efforts involved in the development of the Fleet Ballistic Missile (Polaris) submarine. PERT is typically used for projects that involve research and development work in which the planning effort and the manufacturing of component parts is new and is usually being attempted for the first time. In using PERT, the time estimates that are made cannot be predicted with certainty, and probabilistic concepts are employed.

The Critical Path Method originated in 1957, when consultants from the Remington Rand UNIVAC Division of Sperry Rand Corporation were asked by the DuPont Corporation of Wilmington, Delaware, to help devise a scheduling technique to be used in the construction, maintenance, and shutdown of chemical process plants. CPM is typically used for construction projects in which a single, or deterministic, time estimate is made for each job or activity.

13.2 THE FRAMEWORK OF PERT/CPM NETWORK ANALYSIS

In the previous chapter we considered a series of network models in which the branches of the network represented connections between points in the network, with these points being represented by nodes. We defined a path in these network models to consist of a sequence of branches between nodes with the direction of travel, or flow, specified.

In this chapter a project is viewed as a group of jobs or operations that are performed in a certain sequence to reach an objective. Each one of the jobs or operations that is part of a project is time and resource consuming, incurs a cost, and is referred to as an *activity*. Each activity has a beginning point and an ending point that are points in time. The points in time are known as *events*, and can be considered as milestones of the project. A *path* for this project is a sequence of related activities which is resource- and time-consuming.

A mathematical model satisfying the previous definitions can then be visualized as a network in which nodes, corresponding to events, are joined by branches, corresponding to activities. This network becomes a convenient method of depicting the sequential nature of the project. As an illustration, consider the following simple network for building a wooden deck on a house, which could be represented as follows.

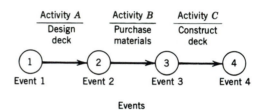

The first step in the PERT/CPM project scheduling process is to specify *all* of the jobs or activities that constitute the project. The development of a complete and accurate set of activities is the key step in the project scheduling process, since the entire scheduling process is based on the list of activities.

To illustrate the specification of the activities that constitute a project consider Table 13.1, which lists all of the activities required for planning and conducting a soccer tournament at Azalea State University. In constructing Table 13.1 a careful analysis of the entire project would be made. Observe that the table lists all of the activities, along with descriptions of the activities, and indicates additional information in the column labeled "Immediate Predecessors." The immediate predecessors for a particular activity are those activities that must be completed immediately prior to the beginning of the given activity. For example, referring to the table, we see that work on activity A can begin anytime, since beginning activity A does not depend

TABLE 13.1 ACTIVITY LIST: AZALEA STATE UNIVERSITY SOCCER TOURNAMENT

ACTIVITY	DESCRIPTION OF ACTIVITY	IMMEDIATE PREDECESSORS
A	Determine tournament site	–
B	Select and invite teams	A
C	Make concession arrangements	B
D	Make team housing arrangements	C
E	Print programs and tickets	B
F	Sell programs and tickets	E
G	Complete final planning	C
H	Schedule games, game fields	D
I	Schedule practices, practice fields	G,H
J	Conduct tournament	F,I

on the completion of any prior activities. Activity I, however, cannot be started until both activities G and H have been completed. This information concerning the immediate predecessors is very important because it will allow us to specify the interdependencies among the activities of the project. This in turn will allow us to specify the network for the project.

After specifying the relationships among all the activities in the project, the next step in the PERT/CPM scheduling process involves constructing the network that connects all of the activities. As just illustrated, the network consists of a set of numbered circles (nodes) that are interconnected by arrows (branches).

There are several important rules connected with the handling of events and activities in a network that should be followed in order to maintain the correct structure for the network. The following rules are most important.

1. Each defined activity is shown by a unique branch.
2. Branches show only the relationship between different activities; the lengths of the branches have no significance.
3. Branch direction indicates the general progression in time. The branch head represents the point in time at which an "activity completion event" takes place. In a similar man-

ner, the branch tail represents the point in time at which an "activity start event" occurs.
4. When a number of activities terminate at one event, this indicates that no activity starting from that event may start before all activities terminating at this event have been completed.
5. Events are identified by numbers. An effort should be made to have each event identified by a number higher than the immediately preceding event.
6. Activities are identified by the numbers of their starting events and ending events, and are specified by capital letters.
7. Two or more activities are not allowed to share the same beginning and ending events. In a situation like this in which two or more activities can be done concurrently, a *dummy activity* is used to ensure that the proper activity relationships are depicted by the network. Dummy activities have no duration or cost.

EXAMPLE 1

To illustrate these rules, consider the following examples. When an activity is dependent on the completion of many other activities, the network should be structured as follows.

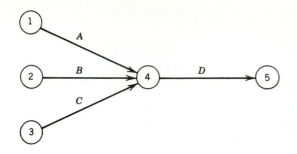

In this situation, activity D is shown to start only after A, B, and C are completed.

EXAMPLE 2

If the completion of an activity is the milestone for the start of a number of activities, the network model will be shown as follows.

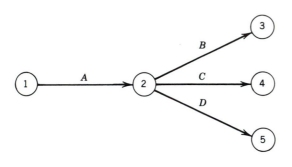

In this situation, B, C, and D can start only after the completion of A.

EXAMPLE 3

If two activities in a project must be done concurrently, one way to present these activities would be to join two events by two or more branches corresponding to each activity. Because all activities are uniquely identified by their beginning and ending event number, however, a dummy activity should be introduced and the ambiguity that would have arisen is eliminated, as follows.

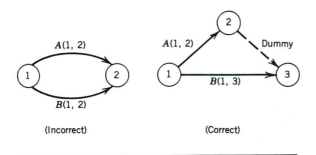

Using the preceding rules we can now construct a network describing the events and activities associated with the Azalea State University soccer tournament. This network is presented in Figure 13.1. Note that each activity (branch) is denoted by a capital letter, and each event (node) is represented by a circled number. Check the network shown in the figure to see that it does indeed maintain the immediate predecessor relationships among the various activities shown in Table 13.1.

13.2.1 ACTIVITY TIME ESTIMATES IN CPM AND PERT

Once the network for the project has been constructed we must next obtain information on the time required to complete each activity. This information is then used to compute the total time required to complete the project and the time required to complete the various activities that comprise the project.

As noted previously, the Critical Path Method is typically used for construction projects. In such situations managers will often have the knowledge and historical information necessary to make accurate time estimates. Thus, a single, or deterministic, time estimate is made for each job or activity.

Unlike the Critical Path Method, the Program Evaluation and Review Technique is commonly employed for projects having a significant amount of time uncertainty. To use PERT, three time estimates are made for each activity, as follows.

1. OPTIMISTIC. An estimate of the minimum time an activity will take; a result that will occur only if everything goes according to plan.
2. MOST LIKELY. An estimate of the normal time an activity will take; a result that would occur most frequently if the same activity could be repeated a number of times.
3. PESSIMISTIC. An estimate of the maximum time an activity will take; a result that will occur only if everything goes badly. This estimate should reflect the possibility of initial failure and fresh start. The possibility of a catastrophic event should not be considered,

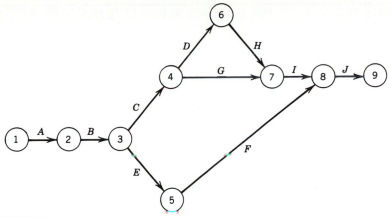

FIGURE 13.1 NETWORK—AZALEA STATE UNIVERSITY SOCCER TOURNAMENT.

however, unless it is an inherent risk of the activity.

In developing three time estimates for an activity, the judgment of competent personnel should be utilized. The three time estimates are considered to be related in the form of a unimodal probability distribution, with m, the most likely time, being the modal value. Because a, the optimistic time, and b, the pessimistic time, may vary in their relationship to m, this probability distribution may be skewed to the right or to the left. These relationships are shown in Figure 13.2.

After considerable research into the relationship between these three time estimates, the original research team decided that the beta distribution seemed to fit their general properties. This distribution was chosen because it is the only unimodal distribution restricted to a closed interval with a modal value that can be any value in that interval.

Two basic assumptions are made in order to convert m, a, and b into estimates of the expected value and variance of the elapsed time required by the activity.

The first basic assumption is that the activity times are beta distributed, as shown in Figure 13.2. Under this assumption, the expected activity time can be approximated as:

Expected activity time:

$$t_e = \frac{1}{6}[a + 4m + b] \qquad (13.1)$$

Equation 13.1 is used to compute the estimated expected value of the elapsed time required for an activity.

The second of these assumptions is that the standard deviation of the time required by the activity is equal to one-sixth of the range of reasonably

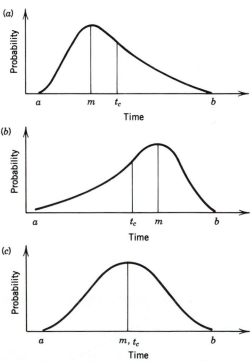

FIGURE 13.2 BETA PROBABILITY DISTRIBUTIONS—PERT ACTIVITY TIME ESTIMATES.

TABLE 13.2 ACTIVITY TIME ESTIMATES: AZALEA STATE UNIVERSITY SOCCER TOURNAMENT

ACTIVITY	TIME ESTIMATES		
	OPTIMISTIC	MOST LIKELY	PESSIMISTIC
A	2	3	5
B	3	5	8
C	10	13	20
D	5	8	11
E	4	7	8
F	17	20	21
G	5	7	12
H	2	3	5
I	1	2	3
J	1	1	1

possible time requirements. Using this assumption, the variance of the activity time can be computed as:

Variance of the activity time:

$$\sigma_{t_e}^2 = \left[\frac{(b - a)}{6} \right]^2 \qquad (13.2)$$

The underlying rationale for this assumption is that the tails of many probability distributions are known to lie at about three standard deviations from the mean, so that there would be a range of about six standard deviations between the tails. Equation 13.2 is used to compute the variance of the time required by an activity.

As an illustration of the PERT procedure with uncertain activity times, consider the time estimates

(in days) for the activities associated with the Azalea State University soccer tournament. The optimistic, most likely, and pessimistic time estimates for the soccer tournament are presented in Table 13.2. We assume that these time estimates were made by the group of persons responsible for staging the Azalea State University soccer tournament.

13.2.2 BASIC CONCEPTS USED IN DETERMINING THE CRITICAL PATH

After we have specified the activities and events for the project, drawn the project network, and made estimates of the activity times, we are ready to determine the minimum time required for completion

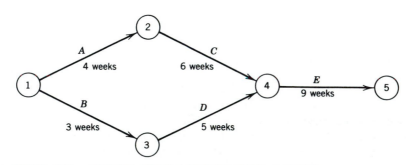

FIGURE 13.3 NETWORK EXAMPLE (ACTIVITY TIMES IN WEEKS).

of the entire project, which is equal to the longest time path through the network. This longest time path is referred to as the *critical path*.

Before we proceed to determine the critical path for the activities associated with the Azalea State University soccer tournament, let us illustrate some of the basic concepts that are used in the analysis. As an example, consider the simple network shown in Figure 13.3, where the numbers along the branches indicate the expected values of the elapsed time for the various activities.

For any particular event in a network, the *earliest time*, T_E, is defined as the time at which the event will occur if the preceding activities are started as early as possible. The earliest times for events 1, 2, 3, 4, and 5 are 0 weeks, 4 weeks, 3 weeks, 10 weeks, and 19 weeks, respectively. For any particular event in a network, the *latest time*, T_L, is defined as the latest time at which the event can occur without delaying the completion of the project beyond its earliest time. The latest times for events 1, 2, 3, 4, and 5 are 0 weeks, 4 weeks, 5 weeks, 10 weeks, and 19 weeks, respectively. The slack concept defines the *slack, S*, for an event as the difference between the latest time and earliest time for that event (i.e., $S = T_L - T_E$). The slacks for events 1, 2, 3, 4, and 5 are 0, 0, 2, 0, and 0, respectively. The slack value indicates how much delay in reaching an event can be tolerated without delaying the total project completion time.

When project activities are plotted according to the branch-diagramming technique described in the previous section, there can be numerous paths existing between the "start" and "end" of a project network. By adding the durations of all the various activities forming the paths, various "durations for project completion" are obtained. The longest of these durations is the critical time for project completion, and the path associated with it is the critical path. Thus, the critical path controls the project completion time.

The critical path for the project can also be defined as the path through the network such that the activities on this path have zero slack. In the previous example, the critical path is $A \rightarrow C \rightarrow E$. It is important to note that in determining the critical path for the network, we are simply identifying the set of branches (activities) of the network that are most critical in terms of the total time required for the project's completion.

13.2.3 DETERMINING THE CRITICAL PATH: AN EXAMPLE

The concepts just illustrated are utilized in the analysis of the Azalea State University soccer tournament. Given the project network and the associated activity times, we can calculate the expected completion time for the project and prepare a detailed schedule of the various activities of the project. Initially, we must compute the expected times and variances for the various activities of the network. The computations are summarized in Table 13.3.

Determination of the expected times and variances in Table 13.3 was done using Eqs. 13.1 and 13.2. For example, for activity C

$$\text{Expected time} \quad (t_C) = \frac{a + 4m + b}{6}$$

$$= \frac{10 + 4(13) + 20}{6}$$

$$= \frac{82}{6} = 13.67 \quad (13.3)$$

$$\text{Variance} \quad (\sigma_{t_C}^2) = \left(\frac{b - a}{6}\right)^2$$

$$= \left(\frac{20 - 10}{6}\right)^2$$

$$= \frac{100}{36} = 2.778 \quad (13.4)$$

In our subsequent discussions we utilize the concepts of earliest time and latest time. To facilitate our discussions we refer to the various activities of the network by their starting and ending nodes, using the (i, j) notation shown in this table.

Using the expected activity time information shown in Table 13.3, the Azalea State University soccer tournament network can now be redrawn as shown in Figure 13.4. Observe that above each branch of the network we have written the letter corresponding to that activity, and that below each branch of the network we have written the expected time of the activity.

In Table 13.3 we determined that the total expected time for all of the activities in the Azalea State University soccer tournment was 70.02 days. By referring to Figure 13.4, however, it is obvious that several of the activities can take place at the same time (for example, activities C and E can be done concurrently). In order to determine just how

TABLE 13.3 EXPECTED TIME AND VARIANCE COMPUTATIONS: AZALEA STATE UNIVERSITY SOCCER TOURNAMENT

ACTIVITY	STARTING AND ENDING NODES (i, j)	ACTIVITY TIME ESTIMATES			EXPECTED ACTIVITY TIME	VARIANCE
		OPTIMISTIC (a)	MOST LIKELY (m)	PESSIMISTIC (b)		
A	(1, 2)	2	3	5	3.17	0.250
B	(2, 3)	3	5	8	5.17	0.694
C	(3, 4)	10	13	20	13.67	2.778
D	(4, 6)	5	8	11	8.00	1.000
E	(3, 5)	4	7	8	6.67	0.444
F	(5, 8)	17	20	21	19.67	0.444
G	(4, 7)	5	7	12	7.50	1.361
H	(6, 7)	2	3	5	3.17	0.250
I	(7, 8)	1	2	3	2.00	0.111
J	(8, 9)	1	1	1	1.00	0.000
				Total	70.02	

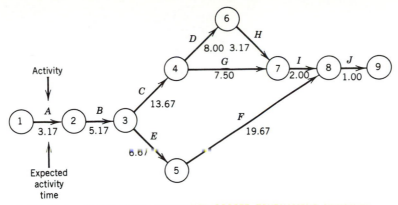

FIGURE 13.4 AZALEA STATE UNIVERSITY SOCCER TOURNAMENT NETWORK—
WITH EXPECTED ACTIVITY TIMES.

long the project will take, we determine the critical path for the entire network.

As noted earlier, the critical path is the longest time path route through the network. To determine the critical path for the network we need to determine the following quantities for each activity in the network.

1. EARLIEST START TIME (ES). The earliest time an activity can begin without violating the immediate predecessor relationships.
2. EARLIEST FINISH TIME (EF). The earliest time at which an activity can end.
3. LATEST START TIME (LS). The latest time an activity can begin without delaying the entire project.
4. LATEST FINISH TIME (LF). The latest time an activity can end without delaying the entire project.

We begin the computational process at the origin node for the network (i.e., Node 1). The earliest start time for the origin node is always set equal to zero. Since activity A has an expected activity time of 3.17 weeks, its earliest finish time is 3.17. In general, the earliest finish time can be computed as

$$\text{Earliest finish time} = \text{earliest start time} \\ + \text{expected activity time}$$

$$EF = ES + t_e \qquad (13.5)$$

Within the network, we represent the earliest start time and the earliest finish time for each activity in the manner shown below for activity A.

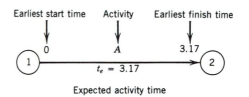

To compute these times for all of the activities in the network, we make a *forward* pass through the network, progressing from the origin node to the destination node. Since the activities that leave a node cannot be started until all of the predecessor activities have been completed, the following rule is used to determine the earliest start times for the activities.

Earliest Start Time Rule. The earliest start time for an activity leaving a node is equal to the *largest* of the earliest finish times for all activities entering the node.

To illustrate this rule, let us apply it to the portion of the Azalea State University soccer tournament network that involves Nodes 4, 6, 7, and 8, as shown here. From this diagram it can be seen that there is a single activity, activity C, leading into Node 4. The earliest finish time for activity C (previously computed as the sum of the expected activity times for activities A, B, and C) is 22.01

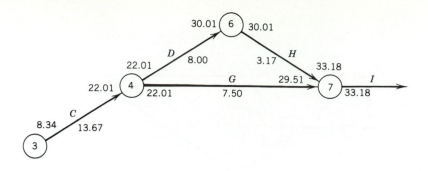

days. The earliest finish time for activity C (i.e., the activity leading into Node 4) then becomes the earliest start time for both activity D and activity G (i.e., the activities that lead out of Node 4). For activity I (i.e., the activity leaving Node 7) we observe that there are two activities (i.e., activities G and H) that lead into Node 7. Since activity G has an earliest finish time of 29.51 days and activity H has an earliest finish time of 33.18 days, the earliest start time for activity I is the larger of the two, 33.18 days. This same forward pass process is then done for the entire network. The Azalea State University soccer tournament network with earliest start times and earliest finish times shown over the respective activities is presented in Figure 13.5. From this figure the earliest finish time for activity J is 36.18 days. Since activity J is the last activity for the entire project, the earliest completion time for the entire project is 36.18 days.

The next step in finding the critical path for the network is to compute the latest start and finish times for each activity in the network. This is done by making a *backward* pass through the network. We start at the last activity, activity J, and assign a latest finish time of 36.18 days to it.

Remember that the latest finish time is the latest an activity can end without delaying the entire project. In general, the latest start time can be computed as

$$\text{Latest start time} = \text{latest finish time} - \text{expected activity time}$$
$$\text{LS} = \text{LF} - t_e \qquad (13.6)$$

For example, for activity J, the latest finish time is 36.18 days and the expected activity time is 1.00

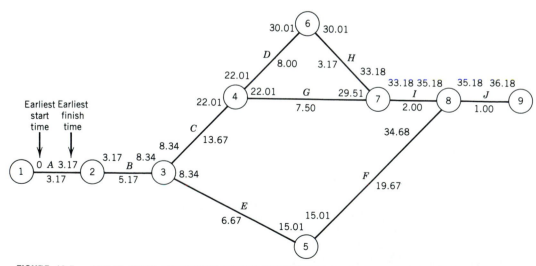

FIGURE 13.5 AZALEA STATE UNIVERSITY SOCCER TOURNAMENT NETWORK—WITH EARLIEST START TIME AND FINISH TIMES.

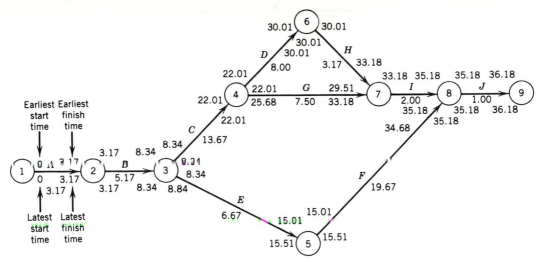

FIGURE 13.6 AZALEA STATE UNIVERSITY SOCCER TOURNAMENT NETWORK—WITH LATEST START TIMES AND FINISH TIMES.

days. The latest start time for activity J is then

$$
\begin{aligned}
LS(\text{activity } J) &= LF(\text{activity } J) \\
&\quad - t_e(\text{activity } J) \\
&= 36.18 - 1.00 \\
&= 35.18 \qquad (13.7)
\end{aligned}
$$

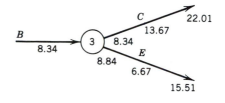

In performing the backward pass the following rule is used to determine the latest finish times for the activities.

Latest Finish Time Rule. The latest finish time for an activity that enters a node is equal to the *smallest* of the latest starting times for all activities leaving that node.

The latest finish time rule indicates that the latest time an activity can be finished is equal to the smallest value of the latest start times of the following activities.

The Azalea State University soccer tournament network with latest start times and latest finish times shown under the respective activities is presented in Figure 13.6.

In this figure note the application of the latest finish time rule at Node 3. The portion of the network involving activities moving in and out of Node 3 is as follows. The latest finish time for activity $B(LF = 8.34)$ is the smallest value of the latest start times for the activities (i.e., activities C and E) that leave Node 3.

After we have obtained the earliest start times, the earliest finish times, and the latest finish times for all of the activities in the network, we can determine the amount of free time, or slack, associated with each of the activities. As noted previously, slack is the amount of time an activity can be delayed without delaying the completion date for the project. The slack associated with a particular activity is computed as

$$
\begin{aligned}
\text{Slack} &= \text{latest start time} \\
&\quad - \text{earliest start time} \\
&= LS - ES \qquad (13.8)
\end{aligned}
$$

or

$$
\begin{aligned}
\text{Slack} &= \text{latest finish time} \\
&\quad - \text{earliest finish time} \\
&= LF - EF \qquad (13.9)
\end{aligned}
$$

In Table 13.4 a summary of ES, LS, EF, LF, and

ACTIVITY	EARLIEST START TIME (ES)	LATEST START TIME (LS)	EARLIEST FINISH TIME (EF)	LATEST FINISH TIME (LF)	SLACK (LS − ES) OR (LF − EF)	ON CRITICAL PATH?
A	0	0	3.17	3.17	0	Yes
B	3.17	3.17	8.34	8.34	0	Yes
C	8.34	8.34	22.01	22.01	0	Yes
D	22.01	22.01	30.01	30.01	0	Yes
E	8.34	8.84	15.01	15.51	0.50	No
F	15.01	15.51	34.68	35.18	0.50	No
G	22.01	25.68	29.51	33.18	3.67	No
H	30.01	30.01	33.18	33.18	0	Yes
I	33.18	33.18	35.18	35.18	0	Yes
J	35.18	35.18	36.18	36.18	0	Yes

slack times for the activities of the Azalea State University soccer tournament is presented. Referring to this table, we see that activity G has 3.67 days of slack time, since LS − ES = 3.67 (or alternatively, LF − EF = 3.67). This means that activity G can be delayed up to 3.67 days without causing the project to run longer than the total project completion time, 36.18 days. Observe, however, that activities A, B, C, D, H, I, and J have slack times equal to zero. This means that none of these activities can be delayed without delaying the completion of the entire project. These activities are called *critical activities* and the corresponding path is the critical path. The length of the critical path, as seen in Table 13.4, is the last (and hence largest) number in the EF or LF columns (36.18 days). The critical path is shown in Figure 13.7.

13.2.4 ANALYZING PROJECT COMPLETION-TIME VARIABILITY

We have just determined, by use of a critical path analysis, that the Azalea State University soccer tournament can be expected to be completed in 36.18 days. The tournament director, however, knows that Azalea State University will dismiss for spring break in 40 days and he is worried about the possibility that the tournament might not be completed within 40 days (i.e., before spring break).

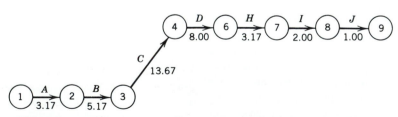

FIGURE 13.7 CRITICAL PATH—AZALEA STATE UNIVERSITY SOCCER TOURNAMENT.

Recall from our earlier analysis that there is variation in the times of the various activities. This means that since the critical path activities govern the expected project completion time, variation in the times of the activities on the critical path can cause a variation in the project completion time of 36.18 days.

The PERT procedure uses the variances in the times of the critical path activities to determine the variance in the project completion time. This variability in times can cause a longer than expected total project time, which will extend the project completion date. On the other hand, the variability in times for critical path activities can cause a shorter than expected total project time, which will shorten the project completion date. Observe also that the variability in times for activities that are not on the critical path will generally have no effect on the total project completion time, since there will be slack time associated with each of the noncritical path activities. If, however, the variability in time for an activity that was not on the critical path was large enough to cause it to be delayed in a manner that expended all of its slack time, then that activity would become part of a new critical path. This would result in an extension of the expected project completion time.

The PERT procedure assumes that the activity times are statistically independent and distributed according to the beta distribution. Because of the statistical independence of the activity times, the expected times (means) and variances along a particular path in a network can be summed to determine the total expected time and variance for the path. The PERT method also assumes that there are enough activities involved that the summed totals will be approximately *normally* distributed. This means that the total project completion time can be closely approximated by the normal distribution. This assumption is based on the *central limit theorem* of probability theory, which states that the sum of several independent variables tends toward normality. The normal probability distribution of the total project completion time can then be used to determine the probability of finishing the project in a specific time frame.

In the Azalea State University soccer tournament network the expected, or mean, project completion time, T_e, is given by the sum of the expected (mean) activity times for the activities along the critical path $A \to B \to C \to D \to H \to I \to J$. It is computed as follows.

Expected (or mean) project completion time:

$$
\begin{aligned}
T_e &= t_A + t_B + t_C + t_D + t_H \\
&\quad + t_I + t_J \\
&= 3.17 + 5.17 + 13.67 \\
&\quad + 8.00 + 3.17 + 2.00 + 1.00 \\
&= 36.18 \text{ days} \qquad (13.10)
\end{aligned}
$$

Similarly, the variance of the project completion time, σ^2, is given by the sum of the variances of the critical path activities. It is computed as follows:

Variance of project completion time:

$$
\begin{aligned}
\sigma^2 &= \sigma_A^2 + \sigma_B^2 + \sigma_C^2 + \sigma_D^2 \\
&\quad + \sigma_H^2 + \sigma_I^2 + \sigma_J^2 \\
&= 0.250 + 0.694 + 2.778 + 1.000 \\
&\quad + 0.250 + 0.111 + 0.000 \\
&= 5.08 \qquad (13.11)
\end{aligned}
$$

From basic statistics we know that the standard deviation is the square root of the variance. Consequently, we can compute the standard deviation of the project completion time as follows:

Standard deviation of project completion time:

$$
\begin{aligned}
\sigma &= \sqrt{\sigma^2} \\
&= \sqrt{5.08} \\
&= 2.25 \text{ days} \qquad (13.12)
\end{aligned}
$$

Having computed the expected project completion time, the variance of the project completion time, and the standard deviation of the project completion time, we can now proceed to determine the probability of staging the soccer tournament in 40 days or less. Recall that we indicated earlier that the total project completion time can be approximated by a normal distribution. Thus, we can depict the probability distribution (i.e., the normal distribution) for the total project completion time as shown in Figure 13.8. From the normal distribution shown in the figure, observe that there is a 50 percent probability that it will be completed in less than the expected 36.18 days and a 50 percent probability that it will exceed 36.18 days.

We are interested in determining the probability of staging the soccer tournament in $T = 40$ days, or less. Using the normal distribution, we must determine the probability that the expected project completion time is less than or equal to $T = 40$ days. This is shown graphically as the shaded area (i.e., the area under the curve from $-\infty$ to 40 days) in Figure 13.9. The standard normal equation can be applied to this situation, as follows.

Probability (meeting target project completion time of $T = 40$ days) $= P(T \le 40)$

$= \text{probability} \left(Z \le \dfrac{\text{target project completion time} - \text{expected project completion time}}{\text{standard deviation of project completion time}} \right)$

$= \text{probability} \left(Z \le \dfrac{T - T_e}{\sigma} \right) = \text{probability} \left(Z \le \dfrac{40.0 - 36.18}{2.25} \right)$

$= \text{probability} \left(Z \le \dfrac{3.82}{2.25} \right)$

$= \text{probability} \ (Z \le 1.70)$

$= 0.955$

$$(13.13)$$

where Z has a standard normal distribution. Note that we determine the probability associated with the Z value of 1.70 by referring to a normal distribution table (see Appendix C, Table C.3). This is also illustrated in Figure 13.9 with the area under the normal distribution curve to the left of 40 days shown as 0.955. Consequently, there is a 95.5 percent chance that the Azalea State University soccer tournament will be completed within the 40 day deadline.

In a similar manner, probability statements can be made about meeting target completion times at each node of the network. This is done by summing the expected activity times and the variances of the activity times on the longest path to each node being examined. Then, the normal distribution is utilized in the manner shown here, assuming that there are enough activities to justify the use of the central limit theorem.

13.3 MAKING TIME-COST TRADEOFFS

In our previous discussion we assumed that the time associated with completing an activity in a network was fixed. That is, in a CPM network we have a fixed time associated with each activity, and in a PERT network we determine a single expected time for each activity. In many projects, however, this situation may not be true, as the manager may have the ability to assign more resources to an activity, thereby shortening it. For example, more workers or overtime may be used to shorten the time for a particular activity in a project. Decreasing the proj-

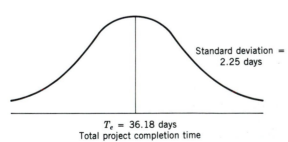

$T_e = 36.18$ days
Total project completion time

FIGURE 13.8 NORMAL PROBABILITY DISTRIBUTION FOR TOTAL PROJECT COMPLETION TIME.

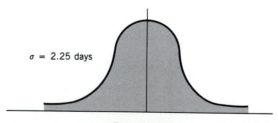

$T_e = 36.18$ days $T = 40.0$ days

FIGURE 13.9 PROBABILITY OF COMPLETION OF AZALEA STATE UNIVERSITY SOCCER TOURNAMENT PRIOR TO 40-DAY DEADLINE.

ect activity time will usually be accompanied by an increase in the activity cost. Consequently, it is useful to consider how to make appropriate time-cost tradeoffs. Extension of the typical critical path analysis for a project involves activity *time-cost analysis* and activity *crashing*.

In performing a time-cost analysis for the network two types of costs associated with each activity are estimated. These costs are the *normal-time cost* and the *crash-time cost,* and are associated with two time estimates for each activity, the *normal time* and the *crash time*. The normal time for a CPM network activity is simply the time estimate that is made for the activity. The normal time for a PERT network activity can be either the estimated most likely time, m, or the computed expected time, t_e. Now, the term "crashing" refers to the shortening of project duration by "crashing" or "rushing" one or more of the critical project activities to completion in less than normal time. For CPM networks, this requires that an additional crash time estimate be provided for each activity. For PERT networks, the crash-time estimate is usually the most optimistic time estimate, a.

In order to make the *time-cost analysis* reasonably simple, the relationship between normal-time cost and crash-time cost for an activity is assumed to be linear. A typical relationship for one activity is shown in Figure 13.10. As seen in the figure, the crash cost per unit of time can be estimated as the relative change in cost per unit change in time. For the example shown in the figure, the crash cost is $200 per day, computed as follows

$$\text{Crash cost per day} = \frac{\text{crash cost} - \text{normal cost}}{\text{normal time} - \text{crash time}}$$
$$= \frac{\$1000 - 400}{5 \text{ days} - 2 \text{ days}}$$
$$= \$200/\text{day} \qquad (13.14)$$

As noted earlier, the process of shortening the time required to complete a project is called crashing and is generally achieved by adding extra resources to an activity. Obviously, crashing a project will incur extra costs, so the manager is usually interested in crashing the project at the least additional cost.

The general procedure for crashing project ac-

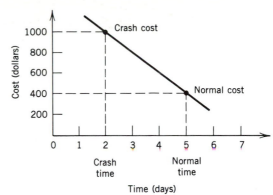

FIGURE 13.10 RELATIONSHIPS OF ACTIVITY TIMES AND ASSOCIATED COSTS.

tivities while minimizing additional cost involves four steps.

1. Determine the normal time critical path and identify the critical activities.
2. Compute the crash cost per time period for all activities in the network, using the formula given by (13.14).
3. Select the activity on the critical path that has the minimum crash cost per unit of time. Crash this activity to the maximum extent possible, or to the point at which the desired deadline has been achieved.
4. Revise the network by adjusting for the time and cost assigned to the crashed activity. Then check to see whether or not the critical path that has just been crashed is still the critical path for the network. (Often a reduction in an activity time along the original critical path will cause a previously noncritical path, or paths, to become critical.) If the original critical path is still the longest path through the network, return to Step 3. Otherwise, determine the new critical path, or paths, and then return to Step 3.

13.3.1 CRASHING A PROJECT: BASIC ANALYSIS

The following example illustrates the application of these steps to a specific project. The project to be analyzed is shown in network form in Figure 13.11.

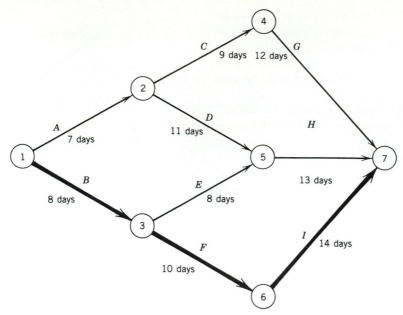

FIGURE 13.11 ORIGINAL PROJECT NETWORK—CRASHING EXAMPLE.

Note: Critical path 1→3→6→7 shown in boldface.
Critical path length = 32 days.

In the figure the normal activity times are shown directly below the letters representing the various activities. The critical path for this network, using these normal activity times, is $1 \rightarrow 3 \rightarrow 6 \rightarrow 7$, with a total expected completion time of 32 days. Let us assume that we would like to have a total project completion time of 29 days.

In Table 13.5 the normal and crash times and the normal and crash costs for the network shown in Figure 13.11 are presented. Note, for example, that for Activity A, the normal time is 7 days while the crash time is 6 days. This means that activity A can be shortened by one day if extra resources can be made available. Note also that the normal

TABLE 13.5 NORMAL AND CRASH DATA

	TIME (DAYS)		COST ($)		CRASH COST
ACTIVITY	NORMAL	CRASH	NORMAL	CRASH	PER DAY
A	7	6	600	750	150
B	8	6	750	900	75
C	9	7	900	1100	100
D	11	8	1100	1400	100
E	8	5	850	1200	116.66
F	10	7	1000	1300	100
G	12	10	1300	1500	100
H	13	11	1400	1500	50
I	14	10	1500	2000	125
Total			$9400		

cost for activity A is $600 per day, while the crash cost is $750 per day. Consequently, for activity A the crash cost per day is:

Crash cost/day (activity A)

$$= \frac{\text{crash cost} - \text{normal cost}}{\text{normal time} - \text{crash time}}$$

$$= \frac{\$750 - \$600}{7 \text{ days} - 6 \text{ days}} \qquad (13.15)$$

$$= \$150/\text{day}$$

We have established that the original critical path for the network shown in Figure 13.11 is path $1 \to 3 \to 6 \to 7$, or activities $B \to F \to I$. Examining the activities on this critical path, using Table 13.5, we observe the following.

Therefore, the activity that can be shortened in the cheapest manner is activity H, at an incremental cost of $50 per day. Thus, activity H should be crashed to the maximum extent possible (i.e., 2 days) and this would reduce the completion time for activities $A \to D \to H$ to $31 - 2 = 29$ days, at a total project cost of $9550 + 100 = $9650.

The project network with activity B crashed two days and activity H crashed two days is shown in Figure 13.13. The new critical path for the network is now path $1 \to 3 \to 6 \to 7$, or activities $B \to F \to I$. Note that this is the original critical path that was previously crashed to 30 days. Examining the remaining activities on this new critical path (i.e., activities F and I, since activity B has already been crashed to the maximum extent possible), we observe that activity F can be shortened in the cheapest manner at an incremental cost of

ACTIVITY	DAYS SHORTENED BY CRASHING	COST OF CRASHING ($)	CRASH COST PER DAY ($)
B	8 − 6 = 2	900 − 750 = 150	75
F	10 − 7 = 3	1300 − 1000 = 300	100
I	14 − 10 = 4	2000 − 1500 = 500	125

Consequently, the activity that can be shortened in the cheapest manner is activity B, at an incremental cost of $75 per day. Crashing activity B to the maximum extent possible (i.e., 2 days) would reduce the completion time for activities $B \to F \to I$ to $32 - 2 = 30$ days, at a total project cost of $9400 + $150 = $9550.

The project network with activity B crashed two days is shown in Figure 13.12. The new critical path for the network is now path $1 \to 2 \to 5 \to 7$, or activity $A \to D \to H$, with a total expected completion time of 31 days. Examining the activities on this new critical path, using Table 13.5, we observe the following.

$100/day. Note also that we only need to crash this activity by one day to reach the desired total project completion time for activities $B \to F \to I$ to $30 - 1 = 29$ days, at a total project cost of $9650 + $100 = $9750. The project network with activity B crashed two days, activity H crashed two days, and activity F crashed one day is shown in Figure 13.14.

We have now crashed activities $B \to F \to I$ twice and have reduced the completion time for path $1 \to 3 \to 6 \to 7$ to the desired 29 days. We have also crashed activities $A \to D \to H$ once, and have reduced the completion time for path $1 \to 2 \to 5 \to 7$ to the desired 29 days. We did not have to crash

ACTIVITY	DAYS SHORTENED BY CRASHING	COST OF CRASHING ($)	CRASH COST PER DAY ($)
A	7 − 6 = 1	750 − 600 = 150	150
D	11 − 8 = 3	1400 − 1100 = 300	100
H	13 − 11 = 2	1500 − 1400 = 100	50

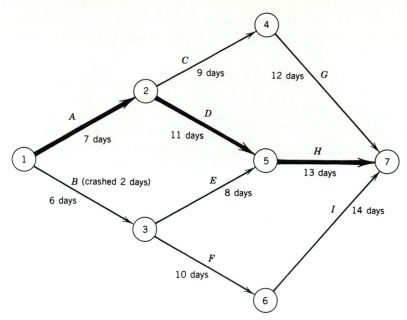

FIGURE 13.12   PROJECT NETWORK—ACTIVITY *B* CRASHED TWO DAYS.

Note: Critical Path 1→2→5→7 shown in boldface.
Critical path length = 31 days.

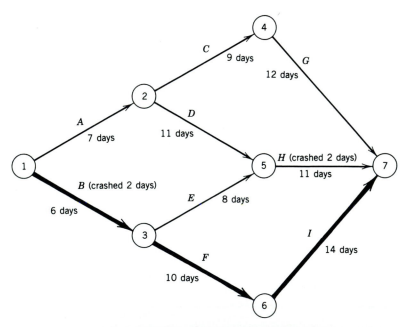

FIGURE 13.13   PROJECT NETWORK—ACTIVITY *B* CRASHED TWO DAYS; ACTIVITY *H* CRASHED TWO DAYS.

Note: Critical path 1→3→6→7 shown in boldface.
Critical path length = 30 days.

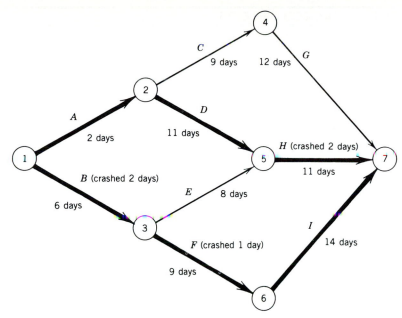

FIGURE 13.14 PROJECT NETWORK—ACTIVITY *B* CRASHED TWO DAYS; ACTIVITY *H* CRASHED TWO DAYS; ACTIVITY *F* CRASHED ONE DAY.

Note: Critical paths $\left\{\begin{array}{l} 1 \to 2 \to 5 \to 7 \\ 1 \to 3 \to 6 \to 7 \end{array}\right\}$ shown in boldface.
Critical path length = 29 days (desired completion time).

activities $A \to C \to G$ because the completion time for path $1 \to 2 \to 4 \to 7$ was originally 28 days. Similarly, we did not have to crash activities $B \to E \to H$ because the completion time for path $1 \to 3 \to 5 \to 7$ was originally 29 days.

The tradeoffs between total project completion time and increasing costs are summarized in Table 13.6. The relationship between the time-cost tradeoffs is illustrated in Figure 13.15. In practice, the procedure described earlier for making time-cost tradeoffs may be cumbersome to apply, particularly if large networks are involved. Its use requires continual monitoring of the network and the continual recalculation of the new critical path for the network, as well as the days shortened and the costs associated with crashing various activities. As we show in the following section, linear programming affords an effective way of making crashing decisions for a PERT/CPM network.

13.3.2 MAKING CRASHING DECISIONS USING LINEAR PROGRAMMING

Linear programming can be used as an alternative way of making crashing decisions. To illustrate its use, we apply it to the same project network that we analyzed previously (refer back to Figure 13.11 and Table 13.5).

We begin by defining the decision variables, letting:

x_i = time of occurrence of event i;

$$i = 1, 2, \ldots, 7$$

y_j = amount of time crashed for activity j;

$$j = A, B, \ldots, I$$

From Table 13.5 we observe that the normal time project cost is fixed at $9400. Thus, in order

TABLE 13.6 SUMMARY OF TIME-COST TRADEOFFS

STEP	ACTION	CRITICAL PATH	TOTAL PROJECT COMPLETION TIME	TOTAL PROJECT COMPLETION COSTS ($)
0	No crashing in network	$1 \rightarrow 3 \rightarrow 6 \rightarrow 7$	32	9400
1	Activity B crashed by 2 days	$1 \rightarrow 2 \rightarrow 5 \rightarrow 7$	31	9550
2	Activity H crashed by 2 days	$1 \rightarrow 3 \rightarrow 6 \rightarrow 7$	30	9650
3	Activity F crashed by 1 day	$1 \rightarrow 2 \rightarrow 5 \rightarrow 7$ $1 \rightarrow 3 \rightarrow 6 \rightarrow 7$	29	9750

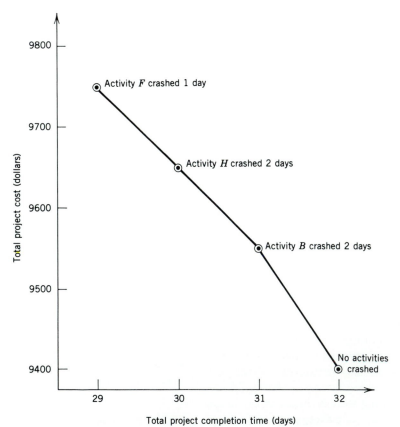

FIGURE 13.15 RELATIONSHIPS BETWEEN TIME AND COST.

to minimize that total project cost (normal-time project cost plus crash-time project cost) we need only to minimize the crash cost. The objective function for our linear programming model formulation can be written as

$$\text{Minimize (crash cost) } Z$$
$$= \$150y_A + \$75y_B + \$100y_C$$
$$+ \$100y_D + \$116.66y_E + \$100y_F$$
$$+ \$100y_G + \$50y_H + \$125y_I \quad (13.16)$$

Observe that these per-unit (crash cost per day) cost coefficients for the objective function were obtained from the far right-hand column of Table 13.5. Note also that the x_i variables, which indicate the times of the occurrences of the events, do not result in costs, and thus have coefficients of zero in the objective function.

The constraints for our linear programming model require that we meet the project completion date, limit the activity crash times, and describe the network. We address each of these types of constraints separately.

Project Completion-Date Constraint. The project completion constraint specifies that the last event must take place before the project deadline. In this illustration we wish to have a total project completion time of 29 days. Thus, the project completion-date constraint can be written as

$$x_7 \leq 29 \quad (13.17)$$

Activity Crash-Time Constraints. These constraints ensure that each activity is not crashed more than its maximum allowable crash time. The maximum allowable crash time for each activity is the difference between the normal time and the crash time (refer to the second and third columns of Table 13.5). These activity crash-time constraints can be

written as

$$y_A \leq 1$$
$$y_B \leq 2$$
$$y_C \leq 2$$
$$y_D \leq 3$$
$$y_E \leq 3 \quad (13.18)$$
$$y_F \leq 3$$
$$y_G \leq 2$$
$$y_H \leq 2$$
$$y_I \leq 4$$

Constraints Describing the Network. The final set of constraints for the linear programming model is required to describe the project network. These constraints are based on the following network requirements.

1. The occurrence time for an event must be equal to, or greater than, the activity completion time for all activities leading into the node that represents that event.
2. The start time for an activity is equal to the occurrence time of its preceding event.
3. The time required to complete an activity is equal to its normal time minus the length of time it is crashed.

We begin the development of this set of constraints by setting the event occurrence time for event 1 to zero. Thus, for event 1, we simply have $x_1 = 0$. For event 2

Occurrence time $\geq$ time required to + start time for
for event 2   complete activity A   activity A
$\underbrace{}$ $(x_1 = 0)$

Normal time $-$ Crash time
for activity   for activity
A   A

$$x_2 \geq 7 - y_A + 0 \quad (13.19)$$

or $x_2 + y_A \geq 7$. For event 3

$$x_3 \geq 8 - y_B + 0 \quad (13.20)$$

or $x_3 + y_B \geq 8$. For event 4

$$x_4 \geq 9 - y_C + x_2$$

(Note that activity C begins with event 2, x_2)

(13.21)

or $x_4 - x_2 + y_C \geq 9$. For event 5 (since two activities enter Node 5, we need the following two constraints)

$$x_5 \geq 11 - y_D + x_2 \quad \text{(For the path from activity } D\text{)}$$

(13.22)

or $x_5 - x_2 + y_D \geq 11$;

$$x_5 \geq 8 - y_E + x_3 \quad \text{(For the path from activity } E\text{)}$$

(13.23)

or $x_5 - x_3 + y_E \geq 8$. For event 6

$$x_6 \geq 10 - y_F + x_3 \quad (13.24)$$

or $x_6 - x_3 + y_F \geq 10$. For event 7 (since three activities enter Node 7, we need the following three constraints)

$$x_7 \geq 12 - y_G + x_4 \quad \text{(For the path from activity } G\text{)}$$

(13.25)

or $x_7 - x_4 + y_G \geq 12$;

$$x_7 \geq 13 - y_H + x_5 \quad \text{(For the path from activity } H\text{)}$$

(13.26)

or $x_7 - x_5 + y_H \geq 13$;

$$x_7 \geq 14 - y_I + x_6 \quad \text{(For the path from activity } I\text{)}$$

(13.27)

or $x_7 - x_6 + y_I \geq 14$.

To complete our linear programming model formulation we add the following nonnegativity restrictions

$$x_i \geq 0 \quad \text{for } i = 1, 2, \ldots, 7$$
$$y_j \geq 0 \quad \text{for } j = A, B, \ldots, I \quad (13.28)$$

Solving this linear programming model, which has 16 decision variables and 20 constraints, we obtain the following solution

$x_1 = 10$	$y_A = 0$
$x_2 = 7$	$y_B = 2$
$x_3 = 6$	$y_C = 0$
$x_4 = 17$ (Since the slack for	$y_D = 0$ (13.29)
activity C = 1 day)	
$x_5 = 18$	$y_E = 0$
$x_6 = 15$	$y_F = 1$
$x_7 = 29$	$y_G = 0$
	$y_H = 2$
	$y_I = 0$

The solution values of $y_B = 2$, $y_F = 1$, and $y_H = 2$ indicate that activity B must be crashed two days, activity F must be crashed one day, and activity H must be crashed two days. The crash cost will be minimized, as follows

Minimize (crash cost) $Z = \$150y_A + \$175y_B$
$$+ \$100y_C + \$100y_D$$
$$+ \$166.66y_E + 100y_F$$
$$+ \$100y_G + \$50y_H$$
$$+ \$125y_I$$
$$= \$150(0) + \$75(2)$$
$$+ \$100(0) + \$100(0)$$
$$+ \$166.66(0) + \$100(1)$$
$$+ \$100(0) + \$50(2)$$
$$+ \$125(0)$$
$$= \$350 \quad (13.30)$$

The total project completion cost is \$9400 (normal project completion-time cost) + \$350 (crash cost) = \$9750. Observe that these results are identical to those obtained in our previous analysis (refer back to Section 13.3.1). The project network as it appears before and after crashing by means of linear programming is shown in Figure 13.16.

13.4 PERT/COST

In our previous discussions of CPM and PERT we have concentrated on obtaining information relative to the time aspect of a project. In particular,

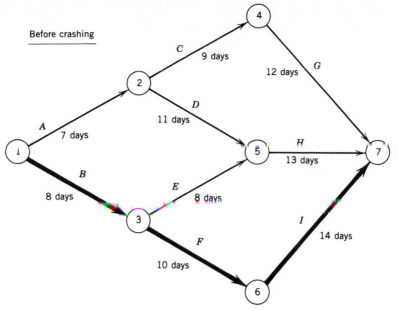

Before crashing

Note: Critical path: 1→3→6→7, Critical path length = 32 days.

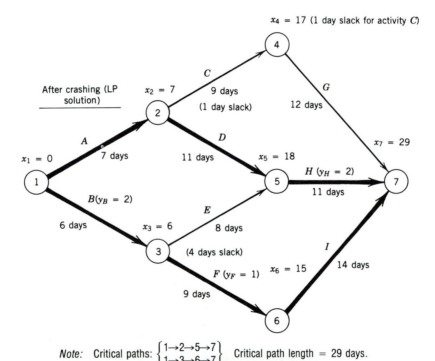

$x_4 = 17$ (1 day slack for activity C)

After crashing (LP solution)

$x_2 = 7$

$x_1 = 0$

$x_5 = 18$

$x_7 = 29$

$B(y_B = 2)$

$x_3 = 6$

$x_6 = 15$

Note: Critical paths: $\begin{cases} 1{\rightarrow}2{\rightarrow}5{\rightarrow}7 \\ 1{\rightarrow}3{\rightarrow}6{\rightarrow}7 \end{cases}$ Critical path length = 29 days.

FIGURE 13.16 PROJECT NETWORK—LINEAR PROGRAMMING ANALYSIS OF CRASHING.

our analysis has focused on the time information that can be used to schedule and control individual project activities, so that the project is completed within a certain time period.

In this section we present a technique called PERT/COST, which is a modification of PERT that enables the manager to plan, schedule, and control cost, as well as time. Initially, we consider how project costs can be planned and scheduled. Then we address the monitoring and controlling of cost as well as time. Our ultimate goal in using the PERT/COST approach is to maintain overall project completion costs within a specific budget.

To illustrate the PERT/COST technique, let us consider the project network shown in Figure 13.17. In this figure, the (computed) expected activity times in months are shown below the letters denoting the various activities.

13.4.1 PLANNING AND SCHEDULING PROJECT COSTS

The first step in the PERT/COST procedure is to subdivide the project into components that can be used to plan and schedule the costs associated with the project. This is basically a budgeting process in which we seek to determine how much will be spent in every time period.

The budgeting process involves four major steps, which are as follows.

1. For each activity in the project, determine the aggregate cost associated with that activity. This will be the budget for that activity.
2. Given the expected activity time for each activity, convert the budgeted cost for each activity into a cost per time period. In determining the cost per time period we assume that spending on any activity is done at a uniform rate over time.
3. Using the expected activity times, perform the critical path calculations to determine the critical path for the project.
4. Using the earliest and latest start times from the critical path calculations, determine the amount of money that should be spent during each time period in order to complete the project by a desired date.

We now apply this budgeting process to the network shown in Figure 13.17. We assume that a detailed cost analysis for this project network has been made and that the activity cost estimates, along with the expected activity times, are shown in Table 13.7. It should be mentioned that the large number of activities present in some PERT networks may be too detailed to allow control of project costs. If this

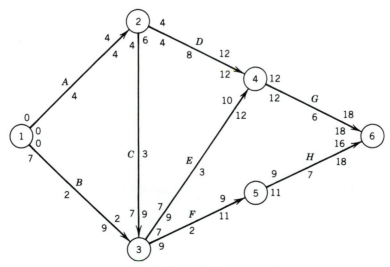

FIGURE 13.17   PROJECT NETWORK—PERT/COST EXAMPLE.

TABLE 13.7 EXPECTED ACTIVITY TIMES AND COST ESTIMATES

ACTIVITY	EXPECTED ACTIVITY TIME (MONTHS)	ESTIMATED COST (BUDGET) ($)	BUDGETED COST PER MONTH
A	4	20,000	$ 5,000
B	2	20,000	10,000
C	3	12,000	4,000
D	8	24,000	3,000
E	3	21,000	7,000
F	2	18,000	9,000
G	6	36,000	6,000
H	7	14,000	2,000
Total budgeted cost = 165,000			

occurs, related activities are often grouped to form a more manageable entity called a *work package.* Since the networks we consider in this chapter have a relatively small number of activities, however, we define work packages as having only a single activity. Observe that in Table 13.7 we have converted the estimated costs for the various activities into budgeted costs per month for the various activities. The total estimated cost (budget) for this project is $165,000.

Using the expected activity times shown in the table, we can compute the critical path for the project. Table 13.8 presents a summary of the critical path calculations. The critical path is composed of activities A, D, and G and has a duration of 18 months.

We can now proceed to develop a detailed budget for this project for the entire 18-month time horizon, utilizing the cost information from Table 13.7 and the activity schedule information from Table 13.8.

First, we proceed on the assumption that all activities begin at their earliest possible starting time. Using the budgeted cost per month information from Table 13.7 and the earliest start times shown in Table 13.8, we can prepare a month-by-month

TABLE 13.8 ACTIVITY SCHEDULE AND SLACK TIME

ACTIVITY	EARLIEST START TIME (ES)	LATEST START TIME (LS)	EARLIEST FINISH TIME (EF)	LATEST FINISH TIME (LF)	SLACK (S)	ON CRITICAL PATH?
A	0	0	4	4	0	Yes
B	0	7	2	9	7	No
C	4	6	7	9	2	No
D	4	4	12	12	0	Yes
E	7	9	10	12	2	No
F	7	9	9	11	2	No
G	12	12	18	18	0	Yes
H	9	11	16	18	2	No

TABLE 13.9 BUDGETED COSTS ($000), USING EARLIEST START TIMES

ACTIVITY	1	2	3	4	5	6	7	8	9	10	11	12	13	14	15	16	17	18	TOTALS
										MONTH									
A	5	5	5	5															20
B	10	10																	20
C					4	4	4												12
D					3	3	3	3	3	3	3	3							24
E								7	7	7									21
F								9	9										18
G													6	6	6	6	6	6	36
H										2	2	2	2	2	2	2			14
Total Cost/Month	15	15	5	5	7	7	7	19	19	12	5	5	8	8	8	8	6	6	165
Total Cost to Date	15	30	35	40	47	54	61	80	99	111	116	121	129	137	145	153	159	165	

TABLE 13.10 BUDGETED COSTS ($000), USING LATEST START TIMES

ACTIVITY	MONTH 1	2	3	4	5	6	7	8	9	10	11	12	13	14	15	16	17	18	TOTALS
A	5	5	5	5															20
B								10	10										20
C							4	4	4										12
D					3	3	3	3	3	3	3	3							24
E										7	7	7							21
F										9	9								18
G													6	6	6	6	6	6	36
H												2	2	2	2	2	2	2	14
Total Cost/Month	5	5	5	5	3	3	7	17	17	19	19	12	8	8	8	8	8	8	165
Total Cost to Date	5	10	15	20	23	26	33	50	67	86	105	117	125	133	141	149	157	165	165

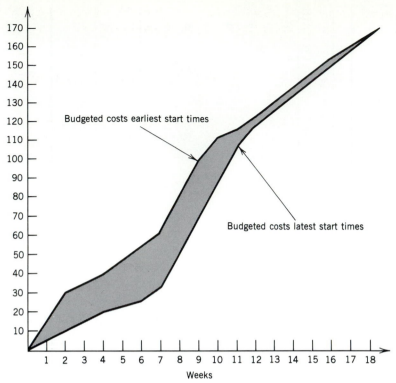

FIGURE 13.18 BUDGETED COST RANGES.

budgeted cost summary as shown in Table 13.9. To show how Table 13.9 is constructed let us focus our attention on activities A and B. The earliest start times for both of these activities is month 0. Activity A has a duration of four months, with a monthly budgeted cost of $5000. Activity B has a duration of two months, with a monthly budgeted cost of $10,000. Consequently, in months one and two, a total of $5000 + $10,000 = $15,000 will be spent monthly. Activity B is completed after two months, so in months three and four, the monthly spending will be at the rate of $5000/month. The remainder of Table 13.9 is constructed in a similar manner. Note also in this table that the total cost/week and the total cost to date are displayed in the bottom two rows of the table.

The activities that are on the critical path for the project must spend their budgets according to their earliest start times. The activities that are not on the critical path, however, can be started at a later time. This means that another budget can be constructed, using the latest starting times for each

activity. The procedure for computing budgeted costs when latest starting times are used is the same as when the earliest starting times are used. Table 13.10 presents the budgeted cost schedules when all activities are started at the latest starting times.

Assuming that the project proceeds according to its PERT time estimates, each activity will be started somewhere between its earliest and latest start times. This means that the cumulative activity costs should fall between those costs indicated for the earliest start cost schedule (Table 13.9) and the latest (Table 13.10). For example, using the data in these two tables, we see that by month five, the total project cost to date should be somewhere between $23,000 (latest starting date schedule) and $47,000 (earliest starting date schedule). Thus, the manager can choose a budget that falls within the budget ranges specified in these two tables. This budget range concept is illustrated in Figure 13.18. The budget ranges in the figure were established by plotting the total-to-date budgets for the earliest and latest starting times. As noted earlier, Figure 13.18

shows that the manager can use any budget in these feasible ranges and still complete the project on time.

13.4.2 MONITORING AND CONTROLLING PROJECT COSTS

Thus far we have gathered information that is useful for planning and scheduling project costs. However, our real objective is to monitor and control these project costs, in order to keep the project on schedule while minimizing cost overruns. In order to do this we must monitor actual costs for all completed and partially completed activities, and then compare these costs to budgeted costs. This will facilitate the identification of cost overruns, for which the manager can take corrective action.

Let us assume that we would like to determine how our project is going, and that it is now the ninth week of the 18-week project. Let us assume that we have collected the actual cost information and the percent completion data for each activity, as shown in Table 13.11. This current status information at the end of the ninth week indicates that activities A, B, and C have been completed; activities D and E have begun; and activities F, G, and H have not been started. We also see that for the activities that have begun, but have not been completed, activity D is 50 percent complete and activity E is 25 percent complete.

For each of the activities shown in Table 13.11, the value of the work completed is computed as

Value of work completed
$$= \text{(percent of completion)} \times \text{(total budgeted cost)} \tag{13.31}$$

As noted earlier, we monitor the actual costs for the various activities as the project proceeds, and these costs are shown as the column marked "Total Actual Cost" in Table 13.11. For each activity we can then determine the activity cost difference, which is computed as

Activity cost difference
$$= \text{total actual cost} - \text{value of work completed} \tag{13.32}$$

These activity cost differences are shown as the final column in the table. We observe that after nine weeks, we have cost underruns on activities A and E, and cost overruns on activities B, C, and D. Overall, the entire project has a cost overrun of $3750, or on a percentage basis there is a cost overrun of $3750/$69,250 = 5.42 percent. At this point, there is nothing that the manager can do with respect to the cost overruns on activities B and C, since they are 100 percent completed. Activity D, however, is in process and is only 50 percent complete. It should be reviewed immediately in terms

TABLE 13.11 ACTIVITY COST AND COMPLETION DATA: END OF MONTH 9

ACTIVITY	TOTAL BUDGETED COST ($)	PERCENT OF COMPLETION	VALUE OF WORK COMPLETED ($)	TOTAL ACTUAL COST ($)	ACTIVITY COST DIFFERENCE ($)
A	20,000	100	20,000	18,000	− 2000
B	20,000	100	20,000	22,000	2000
C	12,000	100	12,000	15,000	3000
D	24,000	50	12,000	13,000	1000
E	21,000	25	5250	5000	− 250
F	18,000	0	0	0	0
G	36,000	0	0	0	0
H	14,000	0	0	0	0
Total	165,000		69,250	73,000	3750

TABLE 13.12 PRICES, DISTRIBUTORS, AND SOFTWARE INTERFACES: SELECTED PROJECT MANAGEMENT MICROCOMPUTER SOFTWARE PACKAGES

SOFTWARE PACKAGE	PRICE ($)	DISTRIBUTOR	SOFTWARE INTERFACE
Harvard Total Project Manager	495	Harvard Software Inc. 521 Great Road Littleton, MA 01460 (617) 486-8431	Lotus *1-2-3* *VisiCalc* *dBASE II*
IIE Project Management	175 140 IIE members	Industrial Engineering and Management Press 25 Technology Park/Atlanta Norcross, GA 30092 (404) 449-0460	
IntePert	249	Schuchardt Software Systems 515 Northgate Drive San Rafael, CA 94903 (415) 492-9330	InteSoft products (*InteCalc*, *IntePlan*, etc.)
MacProject	150	Apple Computer, Inc. 20525 Mariani Avenue Cupertino, CA 95014 (408) 996-1010	*MacWrite* *MacPaint* *MacDraw*
MicroPERT 0	350	Sheppard Software Co. 4750 Clough Creek Road Redding, CA 96002 (916) 222-1553	
Microsoft Project	250	Microsoft Corporation 10700 Northup Way Box 97200 Bellevue, WA 98009 (206) 828-8088	*Multiplan* Microsoft *Chart* Lotus *1-2-3* *VisiCalc* *dBASE II*
PAC MICRO	990	AGS Management Systems Inc. 880 First Avenue King of Prussia, PA 19406 (215) 265-1550	
Project Manager Workbench	1150 advanced version	Applied Business Technology 365 Broadway, 6th Floor New York, NY 10013 (212) 219-8945	Lotus *1-2-3* *dBASE II*
QWIKNET	895	Project Software & Development, Inc. 20 University Road Cambridge, MA 02138 (617) 661-1444	PROJECT/2
SuperProject	395	SORCIM/IUS Micro Software 2195 Fortune Drive San Jose, CA 95131 (408) 942-1727	*SuperCalc*
Task Monitor	495	Monitor Software 960 North San Antonio Rd. Suite 210 Los Altos, CA 94022 (415) 949-1688	

TABLE 13.12 (CONTINUED)

SOFTWARE PACKAGE	PRICE ($)	DISTRIBUTOR	SOFTWARE INTERFACE
Time Line	395	Breakthrough Software Corp. 505 San Marin Drive Novato, CA 94947 (415) 898-1919	Lotus *1-2-3* *Symphony* *SuperCalc3* *Multiplan* *dBASE II*
VisiSchedule	195	Paladin Software Corp. 2895 Zanker Road San Jose, CA 95134 (408) 946-9000	*VisiCalc*

Source: A. A. Assad and E. A. Wasil, "Project management using a microcomputer," Working Paper MS/S #85-027, College of Business and Management, Univ. of Maryland, College Park, August 1985, p. 56.

of corrective actions that can be taken to make the total actual cost equal to the total budgeted cost.

PERT/COST offers a very effective cost-control extension of the basic PERT procedure. It does, however, have some drawbacks with respect to implementation. The most notable of these is that the cost monitoring and control systems may require a lot of data gathering and clerical effort. Thus, some of the benefits that accrue to the use of the PERT/COST system may be offset by increased personnel and data gathering efforts.

13.5 PROBLEMS IN THE APPLICATION OF CPM AND PERT

Although the use of CPM and PERT is widespread, these techniques do present difficulties in their application. Among these difficulties are the following.

1. It may be difficult to divide a project into a set of independent activities. Before a project begins it may be very difficult to subdivide the project into distinct activities. This is particularly true for research and development projects. Also, it may be difficult to decide where one activity ends and another starts. This makes the identification of a set of separate, independent activities for the planning of a project a major problem.

2. It may be difficult to firmly establish the precedence relationships among the various activities in the network. Often, not all precedence

relationships can be anticipated before a project begins. This is especially true for research and development types of projects. Second, use of CPM and PERT for network analysis implies a fixed and known ordering of activities. In many situations, the activities and their precedence relationships are contingent upon the outcome of previous activities. For example, the drilling of an oil well will often be contingent upon satisfactory results of seismic testing.

3. The PERT procedure is highly dependent on being able to accurately make activity time estimates. Obtaining accurate estimates may be a problem, as these estimates are subjective in nature and are made by humans operating in an uncertain environment.

4. The theoretical foundation of the PERT statistical procedure is subject to question. These theoretical assumptions have been examined by various researchers who have concluded that the assumptions used in PERT could lead to errors in the values of the expected activity times and the variance of the activity times. These theoretical problems, however, are not nearly as important as the practical problems associated with making accurate time estimates.

In actual practice, the problems noted here have not detracted from the use and popularity of CPM and PERT in decision making. Most managers seem to have concluded that their usefulness far

TABLE 13.13 HARDWARE REQUIREMENTS AND PROGRAM PACKAGES: SELECTED PROJECT MANAGEMENT MICROCOMPUTER SOFTWARE PACKAGES

		HARDWARE REQUIREMENTS			MAXIMUM PACKAGE CAPACITIES				
SOFTWARE PACKAGE	VERSION	MINIMUM MEMORY	DISK DRIVES	SUPPORTS COLOR DISPLAY	ACTIVITIES	PREDECESSORS	RESOURCE TYPES	RESOURCES PER ACTIVITY	ACTIVITY LABEL
Harvard Total Project Manager	1.0	384K	2 DS or HD	●	100 (384K)	2 unless milestones are created	20 (384K)	250 across all activities (384K)	8
IIE Project Management		48K	1 DS		500 for CPM 300 for PERT		1	1	NA
IntelPert	1.2	128K	2 DS or HD	●	1200–1700	NS	26	26	15
MacProject	1.0	128K	1 SS		200 (128K) 2000 (512K)	NS	50	6	NS
MicroPERT 0	3.2	192K	2 DS or HD	●	220	NS	NA	NA	30
Microsoft Project	1.01	128K	1 DS or HD	●	128	8	64	8	15
PAC MICRO	1.24	128K	2 DS or HD	●	400	3	100	1 category	30 on Gantt chart 8 on network
Project Manager Workbench	2.00	320K	1 DS or HD	●	LM	LM	100	3	27 on Gantt chart 11 on network
QWIKNET	2.0	384K	2 DS or HD	●	250	255 including successors	100	12	10
SuperProject	1.00	256K	2 DS or HD	●	LM	LM	LM	LM	16
Task Monitor	2.2	256K	2 DS or HD	●	LM	21	NA	NA	9
Time Line	1.0	256K	2 DS or HD	●	100–150	NS	16	16	30
VisiSchedule	1.10	64K	2 DS		50 (54K) 150 (96K)	9	9	NS	12

Source: A. A. Assad and E. A. Wasil, "Project management using a microcomputer," Working Paper MS/S #85-027, College of Business and Management, Univ. of Maryland, College Park, August 1985, p. 43.

Note: All packages ●except for MacProject operate on an IBM PC and are DOS 2.0 compatible. ●support a monochrome display, ●except for IIE Project Management support a dot-matrix printer; DS = double sided; SS = single sided; HD = hard disk; LM = limited by disk space and/or RAM; NA = not applicable; NS = not specified.

outweighs the difficulties associated with their application.

13.6 SOLVING PERT/CPM PROBLEMS USING A COMPUTER

Because the use of project management techniques (i.e., CPM and PERT) is so widespread, there is a large number of computer software packages available. A representative review of mainframe software as of 1981 may be found in Moder et al.[1] Gido[2] has provided a more current list that encompasses some 127 project management systems. Mainframe computer programs are in existence that can accommodate projects having 10,000 activities or more.

In the last few years, a wide variety of project management systems for microcomputers have emerged in the marketplace. These microcomputer systems have considerably smaller project size limits compared to the mainframe systems. Their advantages are that they are interactive and are more user-oriented.

A recent working paper by Assad and Wasil[3] presented a profile of the current capabilities of project management software together with a list of desired features. They also provided a detailed review and evaluation of 13 microcomputer software packages.

The prices, distributors, and software interfaces for these 13 microcomputer software packages are shown below in Table 13.12. As can be seen in this table, project management microcomputer software packages are readily available at fairly modest cost.

A summary of hardware requirements and program capabilities for the 13 software packages is presented in Table 13.13.

13.7 SUMMARY

In this chapter we have considered CPM, PERT, and PERT/COST as techniques for planning and controlling large projects. We developed procedures that allow for the identification of activities that must be completed on schedule if the entire project is to be completed on time. We further studied how progress on the project, from a time versus cost perspective, could be monitored and controlled. Finally, we studied how various activities within the project could be completed in less time, and developed a procedure for evaluating the various time-cost tradeoffs possible in such networks.

GLOSSARY

Activity In PERT/CPM terminology an activity is one of the jobs or operations that makes up a project and consumes time and resources.

Backward Pass A calculation procedure that moves backward through the network and determines the latest start and finish times for each activity.

Beta Distribution A continuous probability distribution used to describe the distribution of PERT time estimates.

Branch A line connecting junction points in a graph.

---

[1] Joseph J. Moder, Cecil R. Phillips, and E. Davis, *Project Management with CPM, PERT, and Precedence Diagramming.* New York: Van Nostrand, 1983.

[2] J. Gido, *Project Management Software Directory.* New York: Industrial Press, 1985.

[3] Arjang A. Assad and Edward A. Wasil, "Project management using a microcomputer," Working Paper MS/S #85-027, College of Business and Management, Univ. of Maryland, College Park, August 1985.

CPM (Critical Path Method)   A network procedure typically used for construction projects in which a single, or deterministic, time estimate is made for each job or activity.

Crash Activities   Reassigning some of the manpower from activities not on the critical path to activities on the critical path (assuming transference of labor skills).

Critical Activities   The activities on the critical path.

Critical Path   The "longest" path in a CPM or PERT network.

Dummy Activities   An activity that has no duration or cost, which is used to join two events if one event takes precedence over another event, and is not connected by a specific activity.

Earliest Finish Time   The earliest time at which an activity may be completed.

Earliest Start Time   The earliest time at which an activity may begin.

Earliest Time   The time at which the event will occur if the preceding activities are started as early as possible.

Event   In PERT/CPM terminology an event is the beginning or ending point in time for an activity.

Expected Activity Time   In PERT, the mean of the optimistic time, most likely time, and pessimistic time where the relationship between these activity time estimates is specified by a beta distribution.

Forward Pass   A calculation procedure that moves forward through the network and determines the latest start and finish times for each activity.

Immediate Predecessors   The activities that must immediately precede another given activity.

Latest Finish Time   The latest time at which an activity may be completed without holding up the entire project.

Latest Start Time   The latest time at which an activity may begin without holding up the entire project.

Latest Time   The latest time at which the event can occur without delaying the completion of the project beyond its earliest time.

Most Likely Time   In PERT, an estimate of the normal time an activity will take.

Network   A graphical description of a project of numbered circles (nodes) interconnected by a series of lines (branches or arcs).

Node   A junction point in a graph, or an event in PERT/CPM terminology.

Optimistic Time   In PERT, an estimate of the minimum time an activity will take.

Path   In PERT/CPM terminology a path in a network is a sequence of activities that is resource- and time-consuming.

PERT (Program Evaluation Review Technique)   A project-scheduling network technique typically employed in research and development work in which a probabilistic time estimate is made for each job or activity.

PERT/COST   A technique designed to assist in the planning, scheduling, and controlling of project costs.

Pessimistic Time   In PERT, an estimate of the maximum time an activity will take.

Slack   The slack for an event is the difference between its latest and earliest times. It indicates how much delay in reaching an event can be tolerated without delaying project completion.

Time-Cost Tradeoff Curve   Indicates the costs of a project associated with various project completion times.

Work Package   A natural grouping of interrelated project activities for purposes of cost control. A work package is a unit of cost control in a PERT/COST system.

Selected References

Antill, James M., and Ronald Woodhead. 1970. *Critical Path Methods in Construction Practice,* New York: Wiley–Interscience.

Archibald, Russell D., and Richard L. Villoria. 1967. *Network-Based Management Systems (PERT/CPM).* New York: Wiley.

Battersby, Albert. 1970. *Network Analysis for Planning and Scheduling.* New York: McGraw–Hill.

Conway, R. W., W. L. Maxwell, and L. W. Miller. 1967. *Theory of Scheduling.* Reading, Mass.: Addison–Wesley.

Elmaghraby, Salah E. 1970. *Some Network Models in Management Science.* New York: Springer-Verlag.

Evart, H. F. 1964. *Introduction to PERT.* Boston: Allyn & Bacon.

Martino, R. L. 1970. *Critical Path Networks.* New York: McGraw–Hill.

Miller, Robert Wallace. 1963. *Schedule, Cost and Profit Control with PERT: A Comprehensive Guide for Program Management.* New York: McGraw–Hill.

Moder, Joseph J., Cecil R. Phillips, and E. Davis. 1983. *Project Management with CPM, PERT and Precedence Diagramming.* New York: Van Nostrand.

Riggs, James L., and Charles O. Heath. 1966. *Guide to Cost Reduction Through Critical Path Scheduling.* Englewood Cliffs, N.J.: Prentice–Hall.

Wiest, J., and F. Levy, 1969. *A Management Guide to PERT-CPM.* Englewood Cliffs, N.J.: Prentice–Hall.

Discussion Questions

1. What is the basic difference between CPM and PERT?

2. What are "dummy" activities and when are they used?

3. What assumptions are made in computing the expected activity times and variances in a PERT network?

4. Is the slack concept relevant in analyzing a CPM network? Why or why not?

5. Describe briefly how you determine the critical path in a network.

6. Why is the identification of the critical path important to the scheduling and controlling of a project?

7. What is the meaning of slack in a network and how can it be computed?

8. Briefly discuss PERT/COST and how it is used.

9. What are some of the problems involved in using PERT/COST?

10. What do we mean by "crashing" activities?

11. Why would we want to "crash" an activity?

12. How do we compute the probability that a project will be completed by a certain point in time? What assumptions are made in this computation?

PROBLEMS

1. Construct a PERT/CPM network for a project having the following activities.

ACTIVITY	IMMEDIATE PREDECESSORS
A	—
B	—
C	A
D	B
E	C,D
F	C
G	E,F
H	G

2. The following set of activities and precedence relationships have been developed with respect to a construction project. Construct a PERT/CPM network appropriate for these activities.

ACTIVITY	IMMEDIATE PREDECESSORS
A	—
B	—
C	—
D	A
E	B
F	A
G	C,D
H	E
I	G,H
J	I,F

3. For the activities shown in Problem 1, assume that the following expected activity times have been determined.

ACTIVITY	EXPECTED ACTIVITY TIME (WEEKS)
A	3
B	6
C	5
D	8
E	9
F	7
G	11
H	6

Determine the total project completion time and the critical path.

4. For the construction project where activities and precedence relationships were shown in Problem 2 the following expected activity times have been computed.

ACTIVITY	EXPECTED ACTIVITY TIME (DAYS)
A	3
B	4
C	6
D	2
E	8
F	5
G	9
H	4
I	7
J	8

Determine the following

a. The ES and LS values for each activity.
b. The EF and LF values for each activity.
c. The slack for each activity.
d. The critical path for the project.

5. Given the following project network where the expected activity times (in days) are shown on each branch, determine the following

a. The ES and LS values for each activity.
b. The EF and LF values for each activity.
c. The slack for each activity.
d. The critical path for the project.

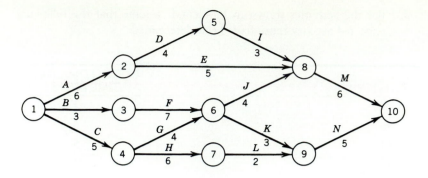

6. Consider the following PERT network.

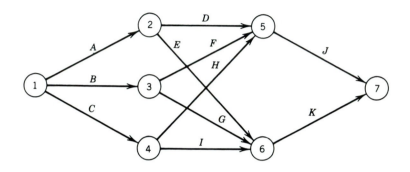

The PERT time estimates (in days) for each of these activities are given in the following table.

ACTIVITY	ESTIMATE	MOST LIKELY ESTIMATE	PESSIMISTIC ESTIMATE
A	3	6	8
B	4	6	8
C	7	9	12
D	6	9	11
E	5	8	11
F	3	6	8
G	4	7	12
H	6	8	10
I	7	10	12
J	5	7	9
K	4	7	11

Determine the following

a. The expected activity time and the variance of the expected activity time, for each activity.
b. The ES and LS values for each activity.
c. The EF and LF values for each activity.

d. The slack for each activity.
e. The critical path for the project.
f. The entire project must be completed in 25 days. Will there be difficulty in meeting this deadline?

7. Consider the following critical path network in which the time required (in weeks) is known for each activity and is given by the number below the corresponding branch.

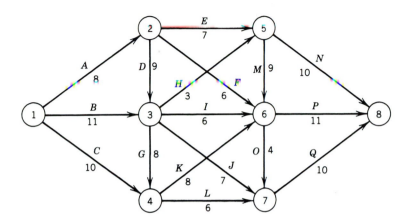

Determine the critical path for this network.

8. Consider the following PERT network that describes the activities associated with the introduction of a new microcomputer.

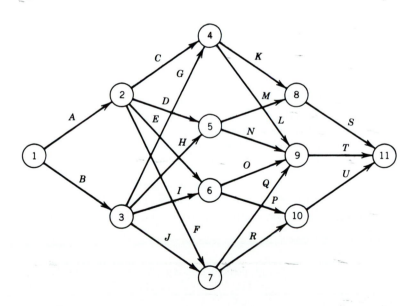

The PERT time estimate (in months) for each of the activities of this network are presented in the following table.

ACTIVITY	OPTIMISTIC ESTIMATE	MOST LIKELY ESTIMATE	PESSIMISTIC ESTIMATE
A	4	6	10
B	5	6	9
C	6	9	12
D	7	8	11
E	10	10	14
F	9	11	15
G	8	10	14
H	12	13	17
I	9	10	14
J	10	12	15
K	6	7	11
L	4	5	8
M	3	4	7
N	8	9	12
O	9	9	12
P	11	12	17
Q	7	7	13
R	6	9	13
S	8	8	14
T	9	10	15
U	4	5	10

Determine the following

   a. The expected activity time and the variance of the expected activity time for each activity.
   b. The ES and LS values for each activity.
   c. The EF and LF values for each activity.
   d. The slack for each activity.
   e. The critical path for the project.
   f. Assume that we would like to introduce the new microcomputer within 40 weeks. Will there be difficulty in meeting this deadline?

9. Consider the PERT network that describes the probable activities associated with staging a school carnival. The PERT time estimates (in weeks) for each of these activities are given in the following table.

	OPTIMISTIC ESTIMATE	MOST LIKELY ESTIMATE	PESSIMISTIC ESTIMATE
Solicit booths	4	5	6
Secure carnival site	1	2	4
Arrange refreshments	3	5	7

	OPTIMISTIC ESTIMATE	MOST LIKELY ESTIMATE	PESSIMISTIC ESTIMATE
Obtain prizes	6	8	12
Sell tickets	5	6	8
Sell programs	2	4	5
Sell refreshments	1	1	1
Run carnival booth	1	1	1

Determine the following

a. The expected activity time and the variance of the expected activity time for each activity.
b. The ES and LS values for each activity.
c. The EF and LF values for each activity.
d. The slack for each activity.
e. The critical path for the project.
f. The carnival committee wants to be sure that everything is completed within 18 weeks. How likely is this to happen?

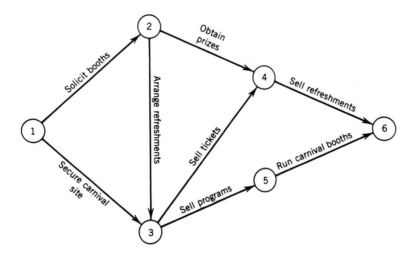

10. The following data relate to the project network shown on the following page.

ACTIVITY	OPTIMISTIC ESTIMATE (DAYS)	MOST LIKELY ESTIMATE (DAYS)	PESSIMISTIC ESTIMATE (DAYS)
A	4	6	8
B	5	9	11
C	6	9	12
D	4	9	9
E	5	7	12
F	7	7	9
G	4	7	10

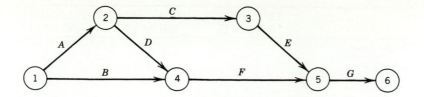

Determine the following

a. The expected activity time and the variance of the expected activity time for each activity.
b. The ES and LS values for each activity.
c. The EF and LF values for each activity.
d. The slack for each activity.
e. The critical path for the project.
f. Determine the probability that the project will be completed in 35 days or less.
g. Determine the probability that the project will require 30 or more days for completion.

11. The following data relate to the research and development project network shown below.

ACTIVITY	ACTIVITY TIME (DAYS)		ACTIVITY COST ($)	
	NORMAL	CRASH	NORMAL	CRASH
A	8	7	1000	1100
B	9	7	1300	1500
C	10	8	1600	1800
D	12	9	2000	2400
E	9	6	1500	2000
F	11	8	1800	2200
G	13	11	2400	2600
H	14	12	2600	2800
I	15	11	2800	3400

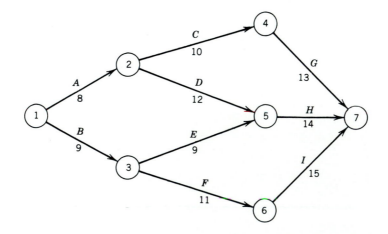

a. Determine the critical path for this network.
b. Assume that the research and development project manager wants to reduce the total completion time for the project to 30 days. Determine the time-cost tradeoff curve, and the associated activities to be crashed to achieve this objective.

12. In a project involving the development of a new production process, the various costs associated with various time reductions are as shown in the following table. (Assume activity B connects nodes 1 and 2, and a dummy activity connects 2 and 3.)

ACTIVITY	EVENT $i \rightarrow j$	NORMAL TIME (DAYS)	CRASH TIME (DAYS)	DAILY CRASH COST ($)
A	$1 \rightarrow 3$	5	3	100
B	$1 \rightarrow 2$	6	3	150
C	$2 \rightarrow 4$	5	4	200
D	$2 \rightarrow 5$	8	5	125
E	$3 \rightarrow 4$	9	6	175
F	$3 \rightarrow 5$	7	5	225
G	$3 \rightarrow 6$	10	6	200
H	$4 \rightarrow 7$	11	6	180
I	$4 \rightarrow 8$	12	8	200
J	$5 \rightarrow 6$	11	8	190
K	$5 \rightarrow 7$	10	7	150
L	$5 \rightarrow 8$	13	10	175
M	$6 \rightarrow 9$	9	6	225
N	$7 \rightarrow 9$	10	6	210
O	$8 \rightarrow 9$	11	7	200

a. Draw the network diagram for this project and determine the critical path, assuming that no activities are crashed.
b. Using the linear programming approach discussed in this chapter, determine the least cost sequence for completing the project in 35 days.
c. Construct a time-cost tradeoff curve for this problem showing the behavior of the incremental cost of crashing the project to 35 days.

13. For the example presented in Section 13.4.1, suppose that the revised estimated costs (budgeted costs) for the various activities are as follows.

ACTIVITY	ESTIMATED COST (BUDGET) ($)
A	25,000
B	30,000
C	16,000
D	14,000

ACTIVITY	ESTIMATED COST (BUDGET) ($)
E	28,000
F	24,000
G	45,000
H	16,000

Develop a revised total cost budget based on both an earliest start and a latest start schedule. Draw the graph detailing feasible budget cost ranges.

14. Joseph C. Lunch has been asked to stage a large tennis tournament. He has developed a set of activities that must be accomplished and he knows the earliest start time, the latest start time, the expected activity time, and the total budgeted cost for each activity. This information is presented in the following table.

ACTIVITY	EXPECTED ACTIVITY TIMES	EARLIEST START TIMES	LATEST START TIMES	TOTAL BUDGETED COST ($)
A	5	0	0	20,000
B	3	2	5	40,000
C	5	4	5	10,000
D	4	5	7	60,000
E	3	5	9	50,000

a. Using the earliest start times, determine Joe's total budget.
b. Using the latest start times, determine Joe's total budget.
c. Draw the graph detailing feasible budget cost ranges.

15. Assume that you have a project in which only one activity can be crashed. It can be crashed from 13 days to 11 days at an additional cost of $2000. The current daily overhead costs for this project are $1200. Should this activity be crashed? If it should, how much should it be crashed? Explain your answer.

Application Review
Use of PERT/CPM by the Forest Service

The Forest Service is the agency of the U.S. Department of Agriculture that administers the national forests located throughout the United States. In the late

Source: C. W. Dane, C. F. Gary, and B. M. Woodworth, "Factors affecting the successful application of PERT/CPM systems in a government organization," *Interfaces* (November 1979), Vol. 9, No. 5, pp. 94–98.

TABLE 13.14 ACTIVITIES ASSOCIATED WITH A NATIONAL FOREST TIMBER SALE

ACTIVITY	DURATION (DAYS)	RESOURCE REQUIRED
Engineer right of way	13–21	Survey crew
Send right of way data to regional office	1–3	None
Lay out sales boundary	3–11	Forester
Process right of way data and return location line	8–12	Central computer facility
Lay out location on ground	110–130	Survey crew
Cruise timber	17–23	Forester
Send cruise data to local computer; process and return	1–5	Local computer facility
Compare cruise results	1–3	Forester
Appraise sale	4–6	Appraisal forester

1970s, in the states of Oregon and Washington, 19 national forests covered 23 million acres of land and provided over 25 percent of the raw timber sold from national forest land in the continental United States.

Each of the national forests was administered by a forest supervisor, with a staff composed of technical specialists in personnel, engineering, and resources. Underneath the forest supervisor and his staff were three to five districts, each headed by a district ranger who supervised 20 to 100 people.

The most complex tasks facing the forest supervisors and district rangers in the western United States were those of scheduling and coordinating the people and activities required to prepare a portion of a forest for a timber sale. The activities and required resource skills for a typical timber sale are shown in Table 13.14. At any point in time, a particular district ranger could be supervising 50 timber sales concurrently, with each timber sale requiring as many as 30 different types of work skills. Obviously, this environment created a need for a high level of scheduling and coordination.

Because of the complex nature of the scheduling task that was faced by the Forest Service, many of the individual forest rangers attempted to apply PERT/CPM techniques to their scheduling activities. By 1970, the multiproject nature of the scheduling problem was recognized and a computer package, called "Critical Path Man Scheduling," was made available to all the administrators of the 19 national forests in the states of Oregon and Washington. This PERT/CPM program could accommodate 99 timber sales, containing up to 4500 activities involving 99 different resource craft skills.

Eventually, 18 of the 19 administrations in the region used some form of PERT/CPM in scheduling timber sales activites. Of the 18 administrations that introduced computerized PERT/CPM in scheduling timber sales, however, only four continued to use the technique for three or more years following its introduction. Those administrations that successfully used PERT/CPM for an extended period of time appeared to be positively influenced by the following two factors.

1. Level of person making the introduction of PERT/CPM: The higher the person was in the organizational structure, the more likely it was that the introduction of PERT/CPM would be successful.
2. Stated purpose for the introduction of PERT/CPM: The more broad and general the announced purpose for the introduction of PERT/CPM, the better was its chance for successful introduction.

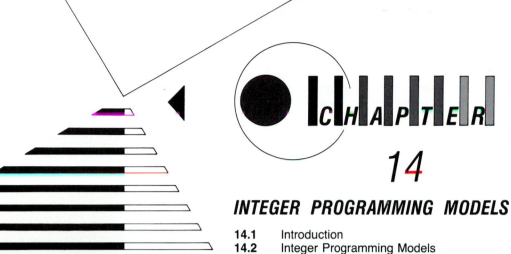

CHAPTER 14

INTEGER PROGRAMMING MODELS

14.1 INTRODUCTION

In the previous discussion of linear programming the assumption of divisibility was noted. This assumption permits the decision variables to take on noninteger values. In many applications the divisibility assumption does not cause any major problems. Producing 1.84 tons of steel or using 101.5 hours of time in a work center is quite easy to interpret. In some decision problems, however, the divisibility assumption is unacceptable. A solution to a distribution problem that requires the strategic location of 5.6 warehouses in a three-state region makes little sense.

The mathematical models examined in this chapter are referred to as integer linear programming (ILP) models. These models differ from the standard linear programming model only in the fact that at least one variable is restricted to assuming only integer values. It may be the case that an integer optimal solution is found when the ILP model is solved using the simplex method. In this case, we have found the optimal solution to the ILP problem. If the simplex method does not find an integer optimal solution, it is possible to round the noninteger optimal solution to an integer solution. This, however, can create two problems. First, it is possible that the "rounded" solution will not be feasible. Second, it is possible that the integer optimal solution will be quite different from the rounded continuous optimal solution. As an illustration of the issues involved in rounding continuous solutions consider the following simple example.

No-Risk Investors has $1,840,000 to invest in two types of high-risk construction projects. Type 1 projects require an investment of $320,000 while Type 2 projects require an investment of $230,000. The net profit for these two project types is $80,000 for Type 1 and $50,000 for Type 2. No-Risk needs to determine its investment strategy. The actual model that results follows.

$$\text{Maximize } Z = 80{,}000x_1 + 50{,}000x_2 \quad (14.1)$$

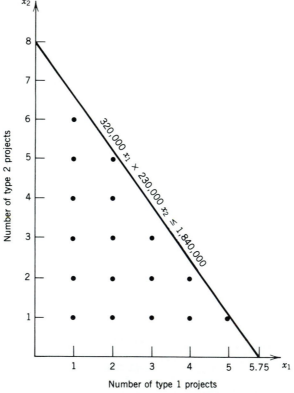

FIGURE 14.1 FEASIBLE INTEGER SOLUTIONS TO MODEL (14.1), (14.2), AND (14.3).

subject to

$$320{,}000x_1 + 230{,}000x_2 \leq 1{,}840{,}000 \qquad (14.2)$$

with

$$x_1, \, x_2 \geq 0 \qquad (14.3)$$

and

$$x_1, \, x_2 \text{ integer.}$$

WHERE

x_1 = number of projects of Type 1 undertaken; x_2 = number of projects of Type 2 undertaken.

If the integrality conditions are dropped and the resultant linear programming problem is solved, the optimal solution is

$$x_1 = 5.75$$
$$x_2 = 0$$
$$Z = 460{,}000$$

Certainly this solution cannot be implemented, and if we attempt to round the noninteger variable to its closest integer value ($x_1 = 6$, $x_2 = 0$), we quickly find that the solution is not feasible. Thus we must round 5.75 to 5, and we see that the corresponding value of $Z = 400{,}000$. On the other hand, it can be shown that the integer optimal solution to this problem is $x_1 = 5$ and $x_2 = 1$, where $Z = 450{,}000$. Simple rounding to meet the feasibility conditions would have cost No-Risk Investors $50{,}000$.

If the model is modified slightly, the impact of rounding becomes even more extreme. Suppose projects of Type 2 require an investment of $210{,}000$ and provide a $52{,}000$ profit. Also total investment

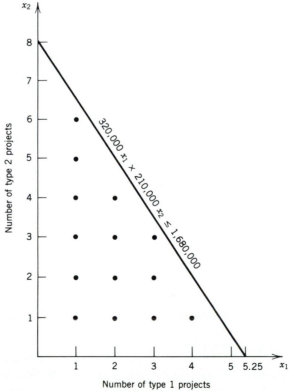

FIGURE 14.2 FEASIBLE INTEGER SOLUTIONS TO MODEL (14.4), (14.5), AND (14.6).

is limited to \$1,680,000. The modified model is

$$\text{Maximize } Z = 80{,}000x_1 + 52{,}000x_2 \quad (14.4)$$

subject to

$$320{,}000x_1 + 210{,}000x_2 \le 1{,}680{,}000 \quad (14.5)$$

with

$$x_1, x_2, \ge 0 \quad (14.6)$$

and x_1, x_2, integer. The continuous solution to this problem is $x_1 = 5.25$ and $x_2 = 0$ and the rounded solution is $x_1 = 5$, $x_2 = 0$, $Z = 400{,}000$. The integer optimal is, however, $x_1 = 0$ and $x_2 = 8$, where $Z = 416{,}000$. This optimal solution is not even close graphically to the rounded solution. Rounding does not guarantee a solution that is even close to the integer optimal solution. Figures 14.1 and 14.2 illustrate the feasible integer solutions to models (14.1), (14.2), and (14.3) and (14.4), (14.5), and (14.6).

Obviously, methods that deal directly with integer constraints are necessary in many situations. This chapter presents some of the fundamental concepts for this methodology. Additionally, the use of variables that are restricted to values of zero or one (binary variables) is examined.

14.2 INTEGER PROGRAMMING MODELS

There are three different categories of integer programming problems: the pure integer problem, the mixed integer problem, and the zero-one (0-1) or binary problem. In the pure integer problem all of the variables must assume integer values. In the mixed integer problem some of the variables, but not all, must assume integer values. In the 0-1 integer problem all of the variables must assume a value of zero or a value of one. These three problem types are illustrated by three separate examples.

14.2.1 A PURE INTEGER MODEL

The owner of a large jewelry store specializing in diamond sales has a supply of 1000 $\frac{1}{2}$-carat diamonds and 750 $\frac{1}{4}$-carat diamonds. She must decide how to utilize these diamonds, and has decided to limit the use to the artistic configuration of diamond rings, diamond earrings, and diamond necklaces. The three items require the following.

ITEM	1/2-CARAT DIAMONDS	1/4-CARAT DIAMONDS
Ring	3	5
Earrings (pair)	2	4
Necklace	12	6

Furthermore, the owner does not want to configure the diamonds into more than 125 items. The per-unit profit for diamond rings will be \$650, for earrings \$450, and for necklaces \$1250. The model for this situation follows.

$$\text{Maximize } Z = 650x_1 + 450x_2 + 1250x_3 \quad (14.7)$$

subject to

$$\begin{aligned}
3x_1 + 2x_2 + 12x_3 &\le 1000 \\
5x_1 + 4x_2 + 6x_3 &\le 750 \\
x_1 + x_2 + x_3 &\le 125 \quad (14.8)
\end{aligned}$$

with

$$x_1, x_2, x_3 \ge 0 \quad (14.9)$$

and x_1, x_2, x_3 integer,

$$x_1 = \text{number of rings}$$
$$x_2 = \text{number of earrings}$$
$$x_3 = \text{number of necklaces}$$

All the decision variables in this problem are restricted to be "whole" items. Since all the variables must be integer, the model is an example of a pure integer problem.

14.2.2 A MIXED INTEGER MODEL

A young investor has recently inherited \$125,000. He must wait one year for complete control of the funds but can decide within certain guidelines how to invest this money for a year. He can invest in a low-risk stock that can be purchased for $50.50 a share. The expected return for one share is $6. Also a higher risk stock can be purchased for $100.75 a share with an expected return per share of $15. Additionally any amount of money can be placed in an insured investment account that yields a 10 percent annual return. The amount invested in low-risk stock must be at least twice the amount invested in higher risk stock, and the amount placed in the insured investment account must be at least three times the amount invested in higher risk stock. The model for this situation is as follows.

$$\text{Maximize } Z = 0.10x_1 + 6x_2 + 15x_3 \quad (14.10)$$

subject to

$$x_1 + 50.5x_2 + 100.75x_3 = 125{,}000$$
$$50.5x_2 - 201.5x_3 \geq 0$$
$$x_1 \qquad\qquad - 302.25x_3 \geq 0 \quad (14.11)$$

with

$$x_1, x_2, x_3 \geq 0 \quad (14.12)$$

and x_2, x_3 integer

x_1 = amount placed in investment account

x_2 = number of shares of low-risk stock

x_3 = number of shares of high-risk stock

Either the investor buys a share of stock or he doesn't. It is not possible to purchase a fraction of a share. Thus two of the decision variables must be integer valued. On the other hand, any amount of money can be placed in the investment account. Variable x_1 is appropriately treated as a continuous variable. Any problem that involves both integer and continuous variables is a mixed integer problem.

14.2.3 A 0–1 INTEGER MODEL

A construction company has options to engage in six construction projects during the next two-year period. There is, however, only approximately $500,000 available for construction costs. The expected costs and expected net profits for the individual projects are listed in the table below.

Corporate policy places several additional restrictions on the project-selection decision.

1. Exactly one of projects A, B, and C must be selected.
2. Exactly one of projects B, C, D, E, and F must be selected.
3. At most, one of the two projects E and F can be selected.
4. At most, two of projects A, B, C, D, and E can be selected.

The model for the project selection follows, where $j = 1$ corresponds to project A, $j = 2$ corresponds to project B, and so forth.

$$\text{Maximize } Z = 180x_1 + 120x_2 + 100x_3$$
$$+ 140x_4 + 105x_5 + 200x_6 \quad (14.13)$$

CONSTRUCTION PROJECT	EXPECTED NET PROFIT ($000)	EXPECTED COST ($000)
A	180	125
B	120	90
C	100	60
D	140	120
E	105	75
F	200	150

subject to

$$125x_1 + 90x_2 + 60x_3 + 120x_4$$
$$+ 75x_5 + 150x_6 \leq 500{,}000 \quad (14.14)$$
$$x_1 + x_2 + x_3 \qquad\qquad = 1$$
$$x_2 + x_3 + x_4 + x_5 + x_6 = 1$$
$$x_5 + x_6 \leq 1$$
$$x_1 + x_2 + x_3 + x_4 + x_5 \leq 2$$

with

$$x_j = 0 \quad \text{or} \quad 1, \quad j = 1, \ldots, 6 \quad (14.15)$$

and

$$x_j = \begin{cases} 1, & \text{if project } j \text{ is taken} \\ 0, & \text{otherwise} \end{cases}$$

Here all the decision variables assume only values of zero or one. The first constraint is a budget constraint, while the remaining constraints represent the corporate policy that limits the selection process. These constraints are discussed in more detail in Section 14.6.1.

14.3 THE NATURE OF INTEGER PROGRAMMING SOLUTION PROCEDURES

Two primary methods exist for finding solutions to integer programming models: cutting plane methods and a search procedure known as the branch and bound procedure. Cutting plane methods systematically add special constraints called cutting planes that gradually modify the original continuous feasible region (the region specified by all the con-

straints except the integrality constraints) until a continuous optimal extreme point satisfies the integrality conditions. Cutting planes exclude certain portions of the continuous feasible region that do not contain feasible integer points. Search methods refer to the idea of enumerating a subset of feasible integer points. The method is based on the development of effective comparison methods that consider only a small portion of the feasible integer solutions explicitly. The remaining feasible integer solutions are eliminated implicitly by these comparison methods. The most prominent search method is called the branch and bound method. This method begins with the continuous optimal solution (using linear programming techniques) and iteratively separates the continuous feasible region into subproblems. In the process, portions of the continuous feasible region that contain no integer feasible solutions are deleted.

In this section we use a two-variable example to illustrate how cutting planes are utilized and also examine how a systematic search procedure such as the branch and bound method is applied to the same problem. The purpose of this presentation is to provide an intuitive understanding of the differences between the two primary solution methodologies for integer programming. A more detailed discussion of the branch and bound method is presented in Section 14.4. A more detailed discussion of the cutting plane methodology, including the actual construction of cutting planes, is beyond the scope of this textbook.

14.3.1 THE FUNCTION OF A CUTTING PLANE

There are a wide variety of procedures for constructing cutting planes. In this presentation we do not consider the construction of cutting planes. We assume that a cutting plane has been constructed

TABLE 14.1   OPTIMAL SIMPLEX TABLEAU

c_b	c_j BASIS	4 x_1	2 x_2	0 S_1	0 S_2	SOLUTION
4	x_1	1	0	0.375	-0.125	1.75
2	x_2	0	1	-0.125	0.375	2.75
	Z_j	4	2	1.25	0.25	12.5
	$c_j - Z_j$	0	0	-1.25	-0.25	

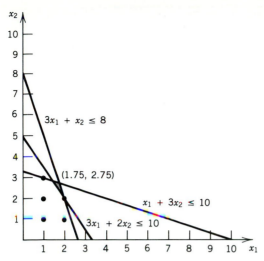

FIGURE 14.3 ADDITION OF CUTTING PLANE FOR (14.16), (14.17), AND (14.18).

and examine how the cutting plane is used. The algebraic and graphical impact is illustrated.

Consider the following integer programming problem and its optimal continuous solution presented in Table 14.1.

$$\text{Maximize } Z = 4x_1 + 2x_2 \qquad (14.16)$$

subject to

$$3x_1 + x_2 \le 8$$
$$x_1 + 3x_2 \le 10 \qquad (14.17)$$

with

$$x_1, x_2, \ge 0 \qquad (14.18)$$

and x_1, x_2 integer.

It can be shown that the constraint $3x_1 + 2x_2 \le 10$ satisfies the criterion of a cutting plane. In other words, it excludes a portion of the continuous feasible region that does not contain feasible integer solutions. Figure 14.3 illustrates the impact of this cutting plane graphically. The shaded region in the figure shows the portion of the continuous feasible region that is eliminated using this cutting plane. Cutting planes are incorporated into the optimal simplex tableau to determine if the addition of the cutting plane will allow us to compute the integer optimal solution using linear programming techniques. With the addition of this particular cutting plane the following problem is solved.

$$\text{Maximize } Z = 4x_1 + 2x_2 \qquad (14.19)$$

subject to

$$3x_1 + x_2 \le 8$$
$$x_1 + 3x_2 \le 10$$
$$3x_1 + 2x_2 \le 10 \qquad (14.20)$$

with

$$x_1, x_2 \ge 0 \qquad (14.21)$$

and x_1, x_2 integer. In solving problem (14.19), (14.20), and (14.21) as a linear programming problem the techniques of Section 9.4.4 are utilized. A new constraint must be incorporated into the tableau of Table 14.1. The result of this addition is given in Table 14.2. The pivot element is circled in Table 14.2, and the result of one dual simplex iteration is given in Table 14.3.

To summarize the steps taken to this point we note that optimal solution to problems (14.16),

TABLE 14.2 OPTIMAL SIMPLEX TABLEAU (CUTTING PLANE INCORPORATED)

c_b	c_j BASIS	4 x_1	2 x_2	0 S_1	0 S_2	0 S_3	SOLUTION
4	x_1	1	0	0.375	−0.125	0	1.75
2	x_2	0	1	−0.125	0.375	0	2.75
0	S_3	0	0	−0.875	(−0.375)	1	−0.75
	Z_j	4	2	1.25	0.25	0	12.5
	$c_j - Z_j$	0	0	−1.25	−0.25	0	

TABLE 14.3 OPTIMAL AND FEASIBLE SIMPLEX TABLEAU (CUTTING PLANE INCORPORATED)

c_b	c_j BASIS	4 x_1	2 x_2	0 S_1	0 S_2	0 S_3	SOLUTION
4	x_1	1	0	2/3	0	$-1/3$	2
2	x_2	0	1	-1	0	1	2
0	S_2	0	0	7/3	1	$-8/3$	2
	Z_j	4	2	2/3	0	2/3	12
	$c_j - Z_j$	0	0	$-2/3$	0	$-2/3$	

(14.17), and (14.18), and (14.19), (14.20), and (14.21) are identical. The cutting plane did not eliminate any feasible integer solutions. The linear programming solutions to problems (14.16), (14.17), and (14.18), and (14.19), (14.20), and (14.21) are different, however. The impact of the addition of a cutting plane to problem (14.16), (14.17), and (14.18) is that the linear programming solution to problem (14.19), (14.20), and (14.21) is integer, and thus the optimal solution to the original problem is

$$x_1 = 2$$
$$x_2 = 2 \qquad (14.22)$$
$$Z = 12$$

Certainly solutions to integer programming problems do not come this easy in general. Typically many cutting planes will be required to find the integer optimal solution using the simplex method. These cutting planes are added one at a time until the optimal extreme point is integer. For more information on the construction and utilization of cutting planes, see the references at the end of this chapter.

14.3.2 THE FUNCTION OF A SUBPROBLEM

The branch and bound method also eliminates portions of the continuous feasible region that cannot contain feasible integer solutions. This is accomplished by constructing two problems, called *subproblems*, with mutually exclusive feasible regions. In other words, a problem is "branched" into two subproblems. The branching is defined for any integer constrained variable that does not have an integer value when the linear programming solution is found. The branch and bound approach also begins with the linear programming solution to the original problem. Consider again problem (14.16), (14.17), and (14.18).

Both x_1 and x_2 assume noninteger values in the optimal linear programming solution. We arbitrarily select $x_1 = 1.75$ as the "branching" variable. To branch on a variable means that we exclude a set of points that contains no integer feasible solutions. Clearly, the set of points for which $x_1 > 1$ and $x_2 < 2$ satisfies this condition. These conditions on the variable x_1 are used to construct two subproblems. A subproblem is generated by adding an additional constraint to the original problem. The conditions $x_1 \leq 1$ and $x_1 \geq 2$ are then used to define two subproblems.

SUBPROBLEM 1

$$\text{Maximize } Z = 4x_1 + 2x_2 \qquad (14.23)$$

subject to

$$3x_1 + x_2 \leq 8$$
$$x_1 + 3x_2 \leq 10$$
$$x_1 \geq 2 \qquad (14.24)$$

with

$$x_1, x_2 \geq 0 \qquad (14.25)$$

and x_1, x_2 integer.

SUBPROBLEM 2

$$\text{Maximize } Z = 4x_1 + 2x_2 \qquad (14.26)$$

subject to

$$3x_1 + x_2 \leq 8$$
$$x_1 + 3x_2 \leq 10$$
$$x_1 \qquad \leq 1 \qquad (14.27)$$

with

$$x_1, x_2 \geq 0 \qquad (14.28)$$

and x_1, x_2 integer. The feasible regions for those two subproblems are shaded in Figure 14.4. The optimal continuous solution to (14.23), (14.24), and (14.25) is $x_1 = 2$, $x_2 = 2$, and $Z = 12$, while the optimal continuous solution to (14.26), (14.27), and (14.28) is $x_1 = 1$, $x_2 = 3$, and $Z = 10$. Since the solution to each of the subproblems using standard linear programming techniques is integer, we compare the two, choose the best, and conclude that $x_1 = 2$ and $x_2 = 2$ gives the optimal solution to problem (14.16), (14.17), and (14.18).

Since x_2 is also noninteger we could have instead branched on variable x_2. Again, any point that satisfies $2 < x_2 < 3$ cannot be integer, and the two defined subproblems are as follows.

SUBPROBLEM 1

$$\text{Maximize } Z = 4x_1 + 2x_2 \qquad (14.29)$$

subject to

$$3x_1 + x_2 \leq 8$$
$$x_1 + 3x_2 \leq 10$$
$$x_2 \geq 3 \qquad (14.30)$$

with

$$x_1, x_2 \geq 0 \qquad (14.31)$$

and x_1, x_2 integer.

SUBPROBLEM 2

$$\text{Maximize } Z = 4x_1 + 2x_2 \qquad (14.32)$$

subject to

$$3x_1 + x_2 \leq 8$$
$$x_1 + 3x_2 \leq 10$$
$$x_2 \leq 2 \qquad (14.33)$$

with

$$x_1, x_2 \geq 0 \qquad (14.34)$$

and x_1, x_2 integer. The feasible regions for these two subproblems are shaded in Figure 14.5. The optimal continuous solution to (14.29), (14.30), and (14.31)

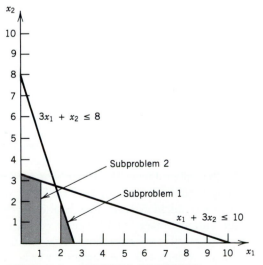

FIGURE 14.4 BRANCHING ON VARIABLE x_1.

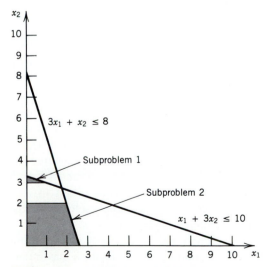

FIGURE 14.5 BRANCHING ON VARIABLE x_2.

is $x_1 = 1$, $x_2 = 3$, and $Z = 10$, while the optimal continuous solution to (14.32), (14.33), and (14.34) is $x_1 = 2$, $x_2 = 2$, and $Z = 12$. Again it can be concluded that $x_1 = 2$ and $x_2 = 2$ is the optimal solution to problem (14.16), (14.17), and (14.18).

This example again provides an oversimplification of an enumeration procedure for integer programming. The important question that should be asked is: What if one of the subproblem solutions is not integer? This problem is answered in the next section where the branch and bound procedure is described in detail. The purpose here was to provide an intuitive presentation of the cutting plane approach and the branching procedure in the branch and bound method. Cutting plane methods solve one linear programming problem and sequentially add additional constraints to that problem. The branch and bound approach involves the solution of subproblems and subproblems of subproblems. Here many linear programming problems are solved, and the subproblems differ from the original model only in that bounds are imposed on individual variables.

14.4   THE BRANCH AND BOUND METHOD

Both the cutting plane and branch and bound methods have played an important role in the development of the current integer programming solution technology. Currently, the branch and bound approach is the most efficient method for solving integer linear programming problems and mixed integer linear programming problems. Since many integer programming problems have upper and/or lower bounds on the decision variables, we often seek solutions to problems that have a finite number of feasible integer solutions. In such a case, an enumeration procedure provides a logical approach for determining an optimal solution. The general idea is to divide or partition the set of all feasible solutions in a given problem into smaller and mutually exclusive subsets. Bounds on the value of the best solution in each subset are then computed, thus allowing the elimination of certain subsets from further consideration. This method allows us to implicitly consider all of the feasible solutions without explicitly enumerating them.

The branch and bound procedure for a linear integer programming problem with a maximization objective is now summarized.

1.   FIND INITIAL BOUNDS   Ignore the integrality conditions and solve the problem as a linear programming problem. If the LP solution is integer, then the optimal solution to the integer programming problem has been found. Otherwise, the optimal objective value represents the *initial upper bound* to the integer programming problem. No integer solution can have a larger objective value than the upper bound. When a feasible integer solution is found, it serves as a *lower bound*, and certainly the optimal objective value will be no less than the largest lower bound (the current lower bound) identified. Thus we know that the optimal objective value is no greater than the upper bound and no less than the lower bound. This information allows us to implicitly eliminate many feasible solutions without the explicit enumeration of these solutions.

BRANCHING   An integer constrained variable that has a noninteger value in the optimal solution is selected for branching. This variable is used to *branch* the problem being considered into two subproblems. If the variable selected, x, has the value $(p.q)$, then one subproblem is formed by adding the constraint $x \geq p + 1$ and the other subproblem is formed by adding the constraint $x \leq p$. The addition of these mutually exclusive constraints creates two subproblems with nonoverlapping feasible regions and eliminates a set of continuous solutions.

BOUNDING   Each subproblem is solved using the simplex method (or sensitivity analysis techniques) and an upper bound is then computed for each subproblem. If any of the subproblems solved has an integer optimal solution, the objective value becomes the lower bound if it is greater than the current lower bound. At any point in the solution procedure there is *one* lower bound. The objective value of each subproblem serves as an upper bound for that subproblem. The lower bound for the integer programming solution indicates that any subproblem with an upper bound less than the current lower bound cannot contain an integer feasible solution that is better than the one associated with the current lower bound. Subproblems with upper bounds greater than or equal to the current lower *bound* will be further analyzed.

FATHOMING   Each subproblem is analyzed to determine if further branching is necessary. The possible states of a subproblem are listed here.

a. A subproblem has no feasible linear programming solution. In this case, the subproblem is *fathomed* (i.e., eliminated from further consideration).

b. A subproblem has a linear programming solution that is not integer and is worse than the current lower bound. This subproblem has an upper bound less than the current lower bound. Thus, this subproblem cannot provide the integer optimal solution, and it is fathomed.

c. A subproblem has a linear programming solution that is all integer, but its objective value is less than the current lower bound. In this case, the subproblem is also fathomed.

d. A subproblem does not have integer values for the integer variables and has a higher objective value than the current lower bound. This subproblem must be branched.

5. The branching continues until all subproblems are fathomed or have integer feasible solutions. In other words, the procedure continues until all upper bounds are less than or equal to the current lower bound.

Principles 1 to 5 are taken collectively to form the branch and bound approach. There are many issues that are important to the efficient implementation of this method that cannot be considered here. For example, the selection of the branching variable and the subproblem to be partitioned often make a difference in terms of the amount of effort required to compute the optimal solution.

The branch and bound procedure is now illustrated using a pure integer problem in which the subproblems can be solved graphically.

14.5   APPLICATION OF THE BRANCH AND BOUND METHOD

In this section we use the branch and bound method to solve the integer programming problems: a pure integer model, a mixed integer model, and a 0–1 integer model. The first two applications follow the

explicit procedure presented in Section 14.4 very closely, while the third, an assignment model, involves a minimization objective, with a slight modification of the procedure as presented in the previous section.

14.5.1   AN APPLICATION OF THE BRANCH AND BOUND PROCEDURE TO A PURE INTEGER MODEL

Consider the following problem

$$P_0: \text{Maximize } Z = 2x_1 + 3x_2 \qquad (14.35)$$

subject to

$$3x_1 + 2x_2 \leq 8$$
$$x_1 + 4x_2 \leq 10$$
$$2x_1 + 4x_2 \leq 11 \qquad (14.36)$$

with

$$x_1, x_2, \geq 0 \qquad (14.37)$$

and x_1, x_2 integer. When the integrality assumptions are ignored, the continuous optimal solution to the problem is $x_1 = 1.25$, $x_2 = 2.125$, and $Z = 8.88$. The graphical solution is shown in Figure 14.6. Since both of the variables are constrained to be integer, either can be selected for branching. No general

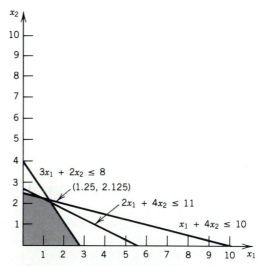

FIGURE 14.6   CONTINUOUS FEASIBLE REGION AND OPTIMAL SOLUTION TO P_0.

rule has been established for selecting the "branching variable" among the noninteger variables, although many rules have been proposed in the literature. In this illustration we select the variable that has the greatest fractional part. The resulting variable is x_1, and the feasible region is partitioned or subdivided. Branching on this variable generates two subproblems P_1 and P_2 with disjoint feasible regions.

$$P_1: \text{Maximize } Z = 2x_1 + 3x_2 \qquad (14.38)$$

subject to

$$3x_1 + 2x_2 \leq 8$$
$$x_1 + 4x_2 \leq 10$$
$$2x_1 + 4x_2 \leq 11$$
$$x_1 \qquad \geq 2 \qquad (14.39)$$

with

$$x_1, x_2 \geq 0 \qquad (14.40)$$

and x_1, x_2 integer.

$$P_2: \text{Maximize } Z = 2x_1 + 3x_2 \qquad (14.41)$$

subject to

$$3x_1 + 2x_2 \leq 8$$
$$x_1 + 4x_2 \leq 10$$
$$2x_1 + 4x_2 \leq 11$$
$$x_1 \qquad \leq 1 \qquad (14.42)$$

with

$$x_1, x_2 \geq 0 \qquad (14.43)$$

and x_1, x_2 integer. The feasible regions to subproblems P_1 and P_2 are labeled P_1 and P_2 in Figure 14.7. The optimal solution to subproblem P_1 is $x_1 = 2$, $x_2 = 1$, and $Z = 7$, while the optimal solution to subproblem P_2 is $x_1 = 1$, $x_2 = 2.25$, and $Z = 8.75$.

Since subproblem P_1 has an integer solution, this problem is not investigated further. The objective value of 7 is used, however, as a lower bound. In other words, we know that the optimal objective value is at least 7. The upper bounds for P_1 and P_2 are 7 and 8.75, respectively. The solution to sub-

problem 2 is not integer, and the objective value of 8.75 is greater than the lower bound of 7. Therefore, this subproblem cannot be fathomed, and branching from this subproblem is required. Since x_2 is the only noninteger variable in the optimal solution to subproblem 2, we branch on variable x_2. The resulting subproblems are as follows.

$$P_3: \text{Maximize } Z = 2x_1 + 3x_2 \qquad (14.44)$$

subject to

$$3x_1 + 2x_1 \leq 8$$
$$x_1 + 4x_2 \leq 10$$
$$2x_1 + 4x_2 \leq 11$$
$$x_1 \qquad \leq 1$$
$$x_2 \geq 3 \qquad (14.45)$$

with

$$x_1, x_2 \geq 0 \qquad (14.46)$$

and x_1, x_2 integer.

$$P_4: \text{Maximize } Z = 2x_1 + 3x_2 \qquad (14.47)$$

subject to

$$3x_1 + 2x_2 \leq 8$$
$$x_1 + 4x_2 \leq 10$$
$$2x_1 + 4x_2 \leq 11$$
$$x_1 \qquad \leq 1$$
$$x_2 \leq 2 \qquad (14.48)$$

with

$$x_1, x_2 \geq 0 \qquad (14.49)$$

and x_1, x_2 integer. It is easy to see from Figure 14.7 that subproblem P_3 has no feasible solution, and Figure 14.8 shows the feasible region to subproblem P_4. The optimal solution to subproblem P_4 is $x_1 = 1$, $x_2 = 2$, and $Z = 8$. Since $Z = 8$ is the new lower bound and since there is no upper bound with a value greater than 8, we have found the optimal solution to the original integer programming problem. It is noted that all other subproblems have either been branched or fathomed.

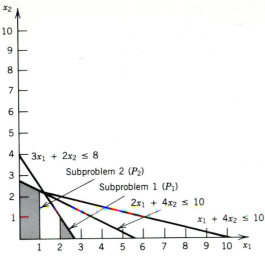

FIGURE 14.7 FEASIBLE REGIONS TO SUBPROBLEMS P_1 AND P_2.

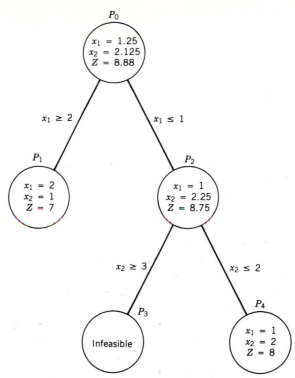

FIGURE 14.9 ENUMERATION TREE FOR BRANCH AND BOUND SOLUTION TO MODEL (14.35), (14.36), AND (14.37).

It is often convenient to present the various solutions as they are obtained by using an enumeration tree. The enumeration tree that is presented in Figure 14.9 shows the solutions for the subproblems solved as well as the added constraints. The enumeration tree is also often used to trace the sequence of subproblems solved in larger branch and bound problems.

Again we note that graphical analysis can be used only in the situation where there are two decision variables. For larger problems the simplex method must be used to solve the subproblems. Each new subproblem is obtained by adding a constraint to a previous subproblem. Thus the dual simplex method can be used, as in Section 9.4.4, to regain a feasible optimal solution where possible.

14.5.2 AN APPLICATION OF THE BRANCH AND BOUND PROCEDURE TO A MIXED INTEGER MODEL

Solving a mixed integer programming model using the branch and bound procedure is not much different from the application to the pure integer model. In a mixed integer model the subproblems are generated only by the variables that are constrained to be integers. There are really no other differences from the application presented in Section 14.5.2.

Consider the following mixed integer programming model.

$$P_0: \text{Maximize } Z = 125x_1 + 150x_2 \quad (14.50)$$

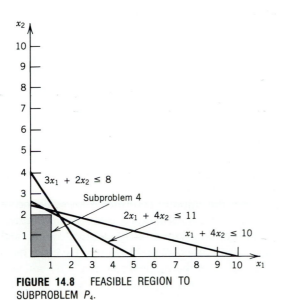

FIGURE 14.8 FEASIBLE REGION TO SUBPROBLEM P_4.

subject to

$$x_1 + 2x_2 \leq 24$$
$$4x_1 + x_2 \leq 32 \qquad (14.51)$$

with

$$x_1, x_2 \geq 0 \qquad (14.52)$$

and x_1 integer. Solving (P_0) as a linear programming problem, the continuous optimal solution is $x_1 = 40/7$, $x_2 = 64/7$, and $Z = 2085.71$. The feasible region for (P_0), without the integrality constraint on x_1, is illustrated in Figure 14.10. The initial upper bound for this problem is $Z = 2085.71$. A lower bound could also be obtained initially by simply rounding x_1 down to a value of 5. Thus if $x_1 = 5$, $x_2 = 64/7$, $Z = 1996.43$, and 1996.43 would serve as a lower bound. Caution should be taken in establishing initial lower bounds in this manner. The procedure is valid here *only* because all of the constraints are of the less-than-or-equal-to variety and the constraint coefficients are positive. Again it is noted that only the lower bound serves to fathom subproblems. If the objective value of the solved subproblem is less than 1996.43, that problem is fathomed or, in other words, is not subject to further branching. The upper bound gives a limit on the optimal value of the objective function and is often used to determine which subproblem should be examined next.

In problem P_0 only x_1 is constrained to be integer, so the two subproblems are constructed by constraining x_1 to be greater than or equal to 6 and x_1 to be less than or equal to 5, respectively. These two subproblems follow.

$$P_1: \text{Maximize } Z = 125x_1 + 150x_2 \qquad (14.53)$$

subject to

$$x_1 + 2x_2 \leq 24$$
$$4x_1 + x_2 \leq 32$$
$$x_1 \geq 6 \qquad (14.54)$$

with

$$x_1, x_2 \geq 0 \qquad (14.55)$$

and x_1 integer.

$$P_2: \text{Maximize } Z = 125x_1 + 150x_2 \qquad (14.56)$$

subject to

$$x_1 + 2x_2 \leq 24$$
$$4x_1 + x_2 \leq 32$$
$$x_1 \leq 5 \qquad (14.57)$$

with

$$x_1, x_2 \geq 0 \qquad (14.58)$$

and x_1 integer. The optimal solution to P_1 is $x_1 = 6$, $x_2 = 8$, and $Z = 1950$, while the optimal solution to P_2 is $x_1 = 5$, $x_2 = 9.5$, and $Z = 2050$. The feasible regions for these two subproblems are shown in Figure 14.11.

The solutions to both subproblems satisfy the integrality constraints for x_1. Subproblem P_1 is immediately fathomed because its objective value is less than the initially constructed lower bound of 1996.43. Since the solution to subproblem 2 satisfies the integer constraints of the original model, and there are no other subproblems that have not been fathomed, it is the optimal solution. The enumeration tree for this application is shown in Figure 14.12.

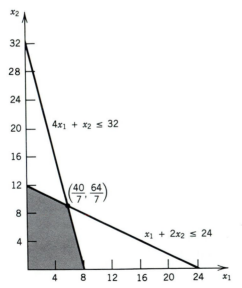

FIGURE 14.10 CONTINUOUS FEASIBLE REGION AND OPTIMAL SOLUTION TO P_0.

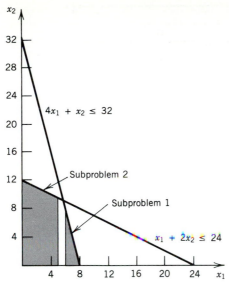

FIGURE 14.11   FEASIBLE REGIONS TO SUBPROBLEMS P_1 AND P_2.

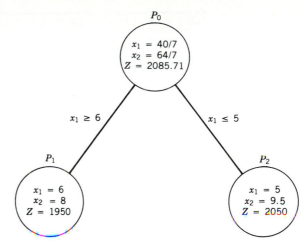

FIGURE 14.12   ENUMERATION TREE FOR BRANCH AND BOUND SOLUTION TO MODEL (14.50), (14.51), AND (14.52).

Before proceeding to the next application we illustrate how the dual simplex method is used to update the initial simplex tableau for the new subproblems. The optimal tableau to P_0 is given in Table 14.4. To solve problem P_1 we must add the constraint $x_1 \geq 6$ to the above tableau. This requires the addition of the surplus variable S_3 where

$$x_1 - S_3 = 6 \qquad (14.59)$$

After the required algebraic operations, the new constraint (14.59) is added to Table 14.4, and the result is given in Table 14.5. The pivot element is indicated, and the result of one dual simplex iteration follows in Table 14.6.

The solution in Table 14.6 is optimal, and we have utilized sensitivity techniques to solve problem P_1. If the branch and bound method is utilized to solve integer programming problems as in these two

applications, efficient methods *must* be employed to solve the individual subproblems.

14.5.3   AN APPLICATION OF THE BRANCH AND BOUND PROCEDURE TO A 0–1 INTEGER MODEL

We continue to illustrate the branch and bound procedure by applying this method to an assignment problem. The assignment problem is a 0–1 programming problem that was presented in Chapter 11, Section 7. An example used in Section 11.7.1, which involves the assignment of four programmers to four programming jobs, is used to illustrate the branch and bound method. A slightly modified cost table for the assignment of programmers to jobs is given in Table 14.7. A feasible solution to an assignment problem requires the assignment of exactly one resource (programmer) to each activity (programming job). In this problem there are a total of $4! = 24$ feasible assignments. We use the branch

TABLE 14.4   OPTIMAL SIMPLEX TABLEAU FOR P_0

c_b	BASIS	c_j				SOLUTION
		125	150	0	0	
		x_1	x_2	S_1	S_2	
150	x_2	0	1	$-1/7$	$4/7$	$64/7$
125	x_1	1	0	$2/7$	$-1/7$	$40/7$
	Z_j	125	150	$100/7$	$475/7$	$14600/7$
	$c_j - Z_j$	0	0	$-100/7$	$-475/7$	

TABLE 14.5 OPTIMAL SIMPLEX TABLEAU FOR P_1

c_b	BASIS	c_j 125 x_1	150 x_2	0 S_1	0 S_2	0 S_3	SOLUTION
150	x_2	0	1	$-1/7$	$4/7$	0	$64/7$
125	x_1	1	0	$2/7$	$-1/7$	0	$40/7$
0	S_3	0	0	$2/7$	$-1/7$	1	$-2/7$
	Z_j	125	150	$100/7$	$475/7$	0	$14600/7$
	$c_j - Z_j$	0	0	$-100/7$	$-475/7$	0	

and bound procedure to partially enumerate the feasible solutions to this assignment problem and in the process determine the optimal assignment. This application differs from the previous two in that no linear programming problems are solved. Also the objective is to minimize the cost of assignment. It should be observed that the minimization objective modifies the role of upper and lower bounds in this application.

In applying the branch and bound procedure to this problem we compute lower and upper bounds and use the upper bounds to fathom sets of solutions. In this enumeration process both feasible and infeasible assignments are listed. A lower bound is computed for each subset of assignments, while the upper bound is the best (of minimum value) objective value associated with a feasible solution to the assignment problem.

To illustrate the computation of a lower bound compute the sum of the minimum costs of the four columns: $6 + 7 + 8 + 9 = 30$. This cost reflects the following infeasible assignment.

Assign job 1 to Jim
Assign job 2 to Bob
Assign job 3 to Sue
Assign job 4 to Jim

This lower bound simply indicates that the cost of a feasible assignment cannot be less than 30.

In beginning the enumeration procedure for the assignment model presented in Table 14.7 we have a single lower bound of $Z_L = 30$. Since no upper bound has been determined, we let $Z_U = +\infty$. Initially, the set of feasible solutions is branched or partitioned into four subsets. Each of these four sets corresponds to the least cost assignment when a particular programmer is assigned to programming job 1. Viewing the cost information in Table 14.7 as a matrix, we determine the assignment in the following way. If programmer i is assigned to task j, row i and column j are deleted from the cost matrix and we compute the minimum costs in the remaining columns. The assignment then corresponds to these minimum costs. It should be noted that the achievement of feasibility is ignored when these minimum costs are computed and ties are broken arbitrarily or via some predetermined rule. We illustrate the computation of the lower bound in tabular form when programming job 1 is assigned to Bob in Table 14.8. The minimum cost assignment if job 1 is assigned to Bob involves the assignment of job 2 to Jim, job 3 to Sue, and job 4 to Jim. The lower bound associated with the set of feasible solutions where job 1 is assigned to Bob, $Z_L[1 - B]$,

TABLE 14.6 OPTIMAL AND FEASIBLE SIMPLEX TABLEAU FOR P_1

c_b	BASIS	c_j 125 x_1	150 x_2	0 S_1	0 S_2	0 S_3	SOLUTION
150	x_2	0	1	1	0	4	8
125	x_1	1	0	0	0	1	6
0	S_2	0	0	-2	1	-7	2
	Z_j	125	150	150	0	475	1950
	$c_j - Z_j$	0	0	-150	0	-475	

TABLE 14.7 PROGRAMMING COST BY PROGRAMMING JOB

PROGRAMMER	PROGRAMMING JOB 1	2	3	4
Bob (B)	11	7	9	13
Sue (S)	9	14	8	12
Jim (J)	6	10	8	9
Ann (A)	10	13	12	14

is 38. In other words, any feasible solution that involves the assignment of job 1 to Bob must cost at least 38. We also note that this is not a feasible solution. We now compute the remaining lower bounds for the assignment of job 1.

$$Z_L[1 - B] = 11 + 10(J) + 8(S) + 9(J) = 38$$
$$\text{(infeasible)}$$
$$Z_L[1 - S] = 9 + 7(B) + 8(J) + 9(J) = 33$$
$$\text{(infeasible)}$$
$$Z_L[1 - J] = 6 + 7(B) + 8(S) + 12(S) = 33$$
$$\text{(infeasible)}$$
$$Z_L[1 - A] = 10 + 7(B) + 8(S) + 9(J) = 34$$
$$\text{(feasible)} \quad (14.60)$$

The current lower bounds are 38, 33, and 33, while the current upper bound is 34. All solutions with a lower bound greater than the current upper bound can be fathomed. Thus the upper bound of 34 can be used to fathom all feasible solutions where job 1 is assigned to Bob. We must still investigate solutions where job 1 is assigned to Sue or Jim. The enumeration tree for the analysis thus far is shown in Figure 14.13. Branching subsets of feasible solutions with lower bounds less than the current upper bound are required. Generally, the subset with the smallest lower bound is chosen. In this case, the subset where job 1 is assigned to Sue is chosen for branching. This subset is then partitioned into three disjoint subsets, the first involving the assignment of job 2 to Bob, the second the assignment of job 2 to Jim, and the third the assignment of job 2 to Ann. Thus in the assignment of jobs 3 and 4 two rows and two columns are ignored in the cost matrix. The analysis when job 1 is assigned to Sue and job 2 to Bob is presented in Table 14.9. In this case, two rows and two columns are ignored in the cost matrix. From this table we can see that the lower bound associated with the assignment of job 1 to Sue and job 2 to Bob, $Z_L[1 - S, 2 - B]$, is 33, and this is not a feasible assignment. The set of bounds associated with the assignment of job 1 to

TABLE 14.8 LOWER BOUND COMPUTATION: PROGRAMMING JOB 1 ASSIGNED TO BOB

Programmer	Job 1	2	3	4
B	(11)			
S		14	(8)	12
J		(10)	8	(9)
A		13	12	14

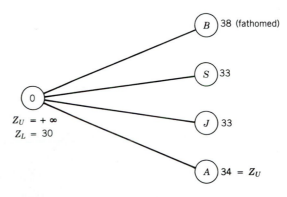

FIGURE 14.13 BRANCH AND BOUND EXAMPLE—JOB 1 ASSIGNED.

$Z_U = +\infty$
$Z_L = 30$

Programmer \ Job	1	2	3	4
B		⑦		
S	⑨			
J			⑧	⑨
A			12	14

Sue is listed:

$$Z_L[1 - S, 2 - B] = 9 + 7 + 8(J)$$
$$+ 9(J) = 33 \quad \text{(infeasible)}$$

$$Z_L[1 - S, 2 - J] = 9 + 10 + 9(B) \quad (14.61)$$
$$+ 13(B) = 41 \quad \text{(infeasible)}$$

$$Z_L[1 - S, 2 - A] = 9 + 13 + 8(J)$$
$$+ 9(J) = 39 \quad \text{(infeasible)}$$

The resulting enumeration tree is shown in Figure 14.14. The current lower bounds that are less than the upper bound are both 33. The subset of solutions

where job 1 is assigned to Jim will be chosen for branching. The computation of the lower bounds follows.

$$Z_L[1 - J, 2 - B] = 6 + 7 + 8(S)$$
$$+ 12(S) = 33 \quad \text{(infeasible)}$$

$$Z_L[1 - J, 2 - S] = 6 + 14 + 9(B) \quad (14.62)$$
$$+ 13(B) = 42 \quad \text{(infeasible)}$$

$$Z_L[1 - J, 2 - A] = 6 + 13 + 8(S)$$
$$+ 12(S) = 39 \quad \text{(infeasible)}$$

The resulting enumeration tree is shown in Figure 14.15.

The current lower bounds that are less than the upper bound of 34 are both 33. We choose to branch on the subset of solutions where job 1 is assigned to Sue and job 2 to Bob. The resulting lower bounds are computed as follows.

$$Z_L[1 - S, 2 - B, 3 - J] = 9 + 7 + 8$$
$$+ 14(A) = 38 \quad \text{(feasible)} \quad (14.63)$$

$$Z_L[1 - S, 2 - B, 3 - A] = 9 + 7 + 12$$
$$+ 9(J) = 37 \quad \text{(feasible)}$$

Since a current lower bound of 33 remains, we must also branch the subset of solutions where job 1 is assigned to Jim and job 2 to Bob. These lower bounds

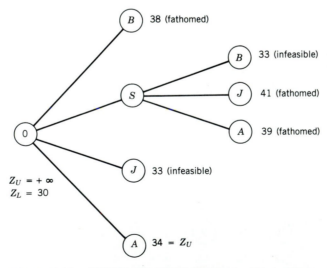

$$Z_U = +\infty$$
$$Z_L = 30$$

FIGURE 14.14 BRANCH AND BOUND EXAMPLE—JOB 1 ASSIGNED TO SUE.

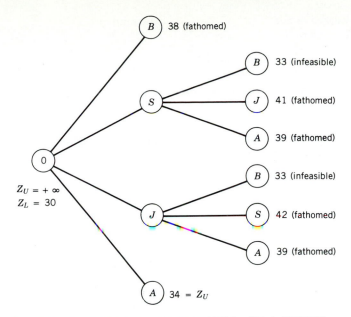

FIGURE 14.15 BRANCH AND BOUND EXAMPLE—JOB 1 ASSIGNED TO JIM.

are now computed

$$Z_L[1 - J, 2 - B, 3 - S] = 6 + 7 + 8 + 14(A) = 35 \quad \text{(feasible)} \quad (14.64)$$

$$Z_L[1 - J, 2 - B, 3 - A] = 6 + 7 + 12 + 12(S) = 37 \quad \text{(feasible)}$$

Figure 14.16 presents the complete enumeration tree. We observe from this figure that all lower bounds are greater than or equal to the current upper bound of 34. Thus the optimal solution has been determined

Programming job 1 is assigned to Ann
Programming job 2 is assigned to Bob

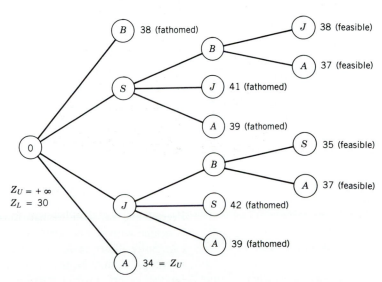

FIGURE 14.16 COMPLETE SOLUTION FOR THE BRANCH ASSIGNMENT PROBLEM.

Programming job 3 is assigned to Sue
Programming job 4 is assigned to Jim

Additionally, it should be noted that determining which subset to "branch on" is another problem of interest, and it does make a difference with respect to the number of assignments that need to be enumerated. In this case, a total of 14 assignments was enumerated. Total enumeration would have involved $4! = 24$ assignments. In large problems the reduction in problem size can be much more dramatic. The efficiency of the method is then linked directly to the generation of good upper and lower bounds quickly.

14.6 FORMULATING INTEGER PROGRAMMING MODELS INVOLVING 0–1 VARIABLES

An important use of integer variables in mathematical programming models is to incorporate "yes or no decisions" or "dichotomous alternatives" into the model. These integer variables are typically referred to as logical, binary, or 0–1 variables. These 0–1 variables have already been used in the construction of the illustration in Section 14.2.1. The dichotomous decisions involved in that situation are whether a project is selected or not selected. The assignment model of Section 14.5.3 also involves dichotomous decisions: either programmer i is assigned to programming task j or she is not assigned. In this section we examine some additional applications of 0–1 variables.

14.6.1 LOGICAL RESTRICTIONS

Mutually Exclusive and Multiple Choice Restrictions. Consider again the example of Section 14.2.3, where the selection of construction projects subject to stated policy is modeled as a 0–1 integer programming problem. Here the jth "yes-or-no" (select or don't select) decision is represented by the decision variable x_j where

$$x_j = \begin{cases} 1, & \text{if decision is yes} \\ 0, & \text{if decision is no} \end{cases} \qquad (14.65)$$

In general if there are a set of n mutually exclusive decisions where one "yes" decision precludes all others, the condition is represented by the following constraint

$$\sum_{j=1}^{n} x_j \leq 1 \qquad \begin{array}{l}\text{(at most one decision in} \\ \text{the set of decisions can} \\ \text{be yes)}\end{array} \qquad (14.66)$$

In particular, if at most one of the two projects, 5 and 6, can be selected, then the constraint

$$x_5 + x_6 \leq 1 \qquad (14.67)$$

is specified.

On the other hand, if exactly one decision out of the n decisions must be yes, then the following constraint would be used

$$\sum_{j=1}^{n} x_j = 1 \qquad \begin{array}{l}\text{(exactly one decision in} \\ \text{the set of decisions } must \\ \text{be yes)}\end{array} \qquad (14.68)$$

If exactly one out of the five projects 2, 3, 4, 5, and 6 must be selected, then the following constraint is appropriate

$$x_2 + x_3 + x_4 + x_5 + x_6 = 1 \qquad (14.69)$$

A slight extension of this type of constraint involves the situation where k out of n decisions is required to be yes. Two widely used multiple-choice constraints for such situations are listed below

$$\sum_{j=1}^{n} x_j = k \qquad \begin{array}{l}\text{(exactly } k \text{ of } n \text{ decisions} \\ \text{must be yes)}\end{array} \qquad (14.70)$$

$$\sum_{j=1}^{n} x_j \leq k \qquad \begin{array}{l}\text{(at most } k \text{ of } n \text{ decisions} \\ \text{can be yes)}\end{array} \qquad (14.71)$$

If at most two of the projects 1, 2, 3, 4, and 5 can be selected, then

$$x_1 + x_2 + x_3 + x_4 + x_5 \leq 2 \qquad (14.72)$$

Precedence or Conditional Relationships. If we continue with the construction project scenario we can easily illustrate several additional logical relationships. It may be the case that because of a by-product of one project a second project cannot be selected unless the first is selected. The logical condition (project k cannot be selected unless project m is selected) is written in the following form

$$x_k \leq x_m$$

or   (14.73)

$$x_k - x_m \leq 0 \qquad \text{(decision } m \text{ must be yes for decision } k \text{ to be yes)}$$

Another conditional relationship might involve the simultaneous selection or nonselection of two projects. The condition that projects k and m must both be selected or neither be selected would be written as follows.

$$x_k = x_m$$

or   (14.74)

$$x_k - x_m = 0 \qquad \text{(decisions } m \text{ and } k \text{ must be the same)}$$

k Out of N Constraints Must be Satisfied. In many situations it may be desirable to satisfy many criteria as part of an overall operating policy, although all of these criteria do not have to be met for the successful operation of the firm. In fact, it may not be possible for all the criteria to be met simultaneously. In such situations we require that a given number of conditions be satisfied. If we want to satisfy k out of N conditions, the mathematical structure of this condition would be

$$\begin{aligned} a_{11}x_1 + a_{12}x_2 + \cdots + a_{1n}x_n &\leq b_1 + My_1 \\ a_{21}x_1 + a_{22}x_2 + \cdots + a_{2n}x_n &\leq b_2 + My_2 \\ &\vdots \\ a_{N1}x_1 + a_{N2}x_2 + \cdots + a_{Nn}x_n &\leq b_N + My_N \end{aligned}$$
(14.75)

with

$$y_i = 0 \quad \text{or} \quad 1, \qquad i = 1, \ldots, N \quad (14.76)$$

and

$$\sum_{i=1}^{N} y_i = N - k \qquad (14.77)$$

In the above set of conditions M is an arbitrarily large positive number. The original set of constraints from which a subset is being selected is

$$a_{i1}x_1 + a_{i2}x_2 + \cdots + a_{in}x_n \leq b_i, \qquad i = 1, \ldots, N \quad (14.78)$$

Consider the first constraint that incorporates the 0–1 variable y_1

$$a_{11}x_1 + a_{12}x_2 + \cdots + a_{1n}x_n \leq b_1 + My_1 \quad (14.79)$$

If $y_1 = 0$, then (14.79) becomes

$$a_{11}x_1 + a_{12}x_2 + \cdots + a_{1n}x_n \leq b_1 + 0 \quad (14.80)$$

On the other hand, if $y_1 = 1$, then (14.79) becomes

$$a_{11}x_1 + a_{12}x_2 + \cdots + a_{1n}x_n \leq \text{arbitrarily large number} \quad (14.81)$$

Therefore, $y_i = 0$ requires that constraint i be satisfied, though $y_i = 1$ does not require that the constraint i be satisfied. The condition

$$\sum_{i=1}^{N} y_i = N - k \qquad (14.82)$$

implies that exactly k of the variables y_i be zero. This in turn means that exactly k of the N conditions must be satisfied.

Either/or Conditions. In other situations a choice must be made between two constraints, so that one, but not both, constraints must hold. Consider the following pair of conditions that represent the use of two different manufacturing procedures. One but not both will be relevant.

$$\begin{aligned} 4x_1 + 5x_2 &\leq 30 \\ 5x_1 + 3x_2 &\leq 45 \end{aligned}$$
(14.83)

Either of the constraints in (14.83) must hold. Here the 0–1 variables will be incorporated in a manner similar to the previous example.

$$\begin{aligned} 4x_1 + 5x_2 &\leq 30 + My \\ 5x_1 + 3x_2 &\leq 45 + M(1 - y) \end{aligned}$$
(14.84)

with

$$y = 0 \quad \text{or} \quad 1 \qquad (14.85)$$

and M is an arbitrarily large positive number. If $y = 0$, then the first condition in (14.84) becomes

$$4x_1 + 5x_2 \leq 30 \qquad (14.86)$$

and the second constraint in (14.84) becomes

$$5x_1 + 3x_2 \leq \text{arbitrarily large number} \qquad (14.87)$$

In this case, the first constraint of (14.83) must be satisfied, but the second constraint of (14.83) does not have to be satisfied. If on the other hand $y = 1$, the first constraint in (14.84) becomes

$$4x_1 + 5x_2 \leq \text{arbitrarily large number} \qquad (14.88)$$

and the second condition in (14.84) becomes

$$5x_1 + 3x_2 \leq 45 \qquad (14.89)$$

Here, we are requiring that at least one of the two conditions must hold.

A common application of the formulation concept presented here involves the fact that we often decide to engage in an activity only if the activity level is above some minimum level. For example, consider the following situation. The continuous variable x_j represents the amount of money in dollars invested in fund j. At least \$5000 must be invested, however, if any money is invested in fund j. Thus we must satisfy

$$x_j = 0$$

or

$$x_j \geq 5000 \qquad (14.90)$$

Assuming that the nonnegativity conditions hold, that is, $x_j \geq 0$, we can write (14.90) as

$$x_j \leq 0$$

or

$$5000 - x_j \leq 0 \qquad (14.91)$$

In turn, (14.91) can be written as

$$x_j \leq My$$

or

$$5000 - x_j \leq M(1 - y)$$
$$y = 0 \quad \text{or} \quad 1 \qquad (14.92)$$

or

$$x_j \leq My$$
$$x_j \geq 5000 - M(1 - y)$$
$$y = 0 \quad \text{or} \quad 1 \qquad (14.93)$$

We note that if $y = 0$, x_j must be equal to zero, and if $y = 1$, x_j must be greater than or equal to 5000.

The Fixed-Charge Condition. Many applications involve situations where a *fixed-charge* or *setup cost* is experienced if a particular activity is undertaken. The total cost of the activity must reflect both the fixed-charge for this activity and the variable cost of the activity. If x_j represents the activity level, c_j the per-unit activity cost, and k_j the fixed-charge, the total cost of engaging in activity j is

$$(k_j + c_j x_j) \qquad \text{if } x_j > 0$$

or

$$0 \qquad \text{if } x_j = 0 \qquad (14.94)$$

If the fixed-charge is part of the objective function in a mathematical programming model, we must be sure that the fixed-charge, k_j, is assessed only if x_j, the activity level, is *greater* than zero. Here it is necessary to use a 0–1 variable to impose the following conditional relationships:

if $x_j = 0$, then total cost $= 0$

if $x_j > 0$, then total cost $= k_j + c_j x_j$

This can be done by requiring that

$$x_j - My_j \leq 0 \qquad (14.95)$$

and writing total cost as $k_j y_j + c_j x_j$, where y_j is a 0–1 variable. Whenever $x_j > 0$, these constraints ensure that y_j assumes a value of one, so that

$$x_j \leq \text{arbitrarily large number}$$

and   (14.96)

$$\text{Total cost} = k_j(1) + c_j x_j$$

Alternately, if $x_j = 0$, the constraints allow y_j to assume a value of zero or one. Since the objective is to minimize, however, y_j will be zero and the total cost associated with that activity will also be zero.

Given this procedure for handling a fixed-charge situation, the general fixed-charge model for n activities is given below.

$$\text{Minimize } Z = \sum_{j=1}^{n} (c_j x_j + k_j y_j) \qquad (14.97)$$

subject to (original linear constraints)

$$x_j - M y_j \leq 0 \qquad (14.98)$$

with

$$x_j \geq 0 \qquad j = 1, \ldots, n$$

and

$$y_j = 0 \quad \text{or} \quad 1, \qquad j = 1, \ldots, n \qquad (14.99)$$

14.6.2   THE WAREHOUSE LOCATION PROBLEM

Often decisions must be made concerning tradeoffs between transportation costs and costs for operating distribution centers (warehouses). In general, management must determine which of m locations should be used for meeting the demand of n customers or markets. The decisions that must be made are the following.

1. Which warehouses should be opened?
2. What amount should be sent from warehouse i to customer j?

The decision variables for this problem are

$$y_i = \begin{cases} 1, & \text{if warehouse } i \text{ is opened} \\ 0, & \text{if warehouse } i \text{ is not opened} \end{cases}$$

$x_{ij} = $ amount shipped from warehouse i to location j

The relevant input parameters are

$f_i = $ fixed operating cost for warehouse i

$c_{ij} = $ per-unit operating cost at warehouse i plus the transportation cost for supplying customer j from warehouse i

$d_j = $ demand for customer j

$k_i = $ capacity at warehouse i

The model that minimizes total fixed and variable costs for the distribution problem just described follows.

$$\text{Minimize } Z = \sum_{i=1}^{m} \sum_{j=1}^{n} c_{ij} x_{ij} + \sum_{i=1}^{m} f_i y_i \qquad (14.100)$$

subject to

$$\sum_{i=1}^{m} x_{ij} = d_j, \qquad j = 1, \ldots, n$$

$$\sum_{j=1}^{n} x_{ij} - y_i k_i = 0, \qquad i = 1, \ldots, m \qquad (14.101)$$

with

$$x_{ij} \geq 0, \qquad i = 1, \ldots, m$$
$$j = 1, \ldots, n$$

and

$$y_i = 0 \quad \text{or} \quad 1, \qquad i = 1, \ldots, m \qquad (14.102)$$

It is easy to see that this classical model is a type of fixed charge model. It is a slight extension of what was presented in the previous section in that M is replaced by the value k_i, which is a bound on the variables associated with warehouse i.

The model presented here forms the basis for many complex distribution/location models. It is one of many standard (classical) integer programming models. We examine one more of these models before concluding the chapter.

14.6.3 THE CAPITAL BUDGETING/KNAPSACK PROBLEM

The capital budgeting model often involves a selection among n investment alternatives where the objective is to maximize return subject to constraints on the resources used in the investment. Some or all of the resources may be capital. In many cases, it makes no sense to consider partial investment in a project or activity. Thus the activity variables, x_j, are 0 or 1. Variable $x_j = 0$ means that the activity is not selected, while $x_j = 1$ means that the activity is selected.

If c_j is the contribution resulting from the jth investment, a_{ij} is the amount of resource i used in investment j, and if b_i is the amount of resource i available, the capital budgeting problem may be written as

$$\text{Maximize } Z = \sum_{j=1}^{n} c_j x_j \qquad (14.103)$$

subject to

$$\sum_{j=1}^{n} a_{ij} x_j \leq b_i, \qquad i = 1, \ldots, m \qquad (14.104)$$

with

$$x_j = 0 \quad \text{or} \quad 1, \qquad j = 1, \ldots, n \qquad (14.105)$$

The capital budgeting model may be enhanced by incorporating the appropriate logical relationships discussed earlier in this section.

The knapsack problem is a special case of the capital budgeting problem. A simple scenario for describing this model involves a hiker who wishes to fill his pack. The pack has limited size and each item has a different volume and value to the hiker. The objective is to maximize value while adhering to the volume constraint. The model has a single resource constraint and can be stated as follows:

$$\text{Maximize } Z = \sum_{j=1}^{n} c_j x_j \qquad (14.106)$$

subject to

$$\sum_{j=1}^{n} a_{ij} x_j \leq b \qquad (14.107)$$

with

$$x_j = 0 \quad \text{or} \quad 1, \qquad j = 1, \ldots, n \qquad (14.108)$$

Knapsack models are important since the study of this model has played a role in the development of efficient solution procedures for more complex integer programming problems. It should be noted that the example of Section 14.2.3 is a knapsack problem.

14.7 SUMMARY

In this chapter we have provided some of the basic ideas used in structuring and formulating integer programming models. At this same time, we have attempted to briefly present some basic approaches used to find solutions to integer programming problems. It does not take long to realize that integer programming problems are much more difficult to solve than linear programming problems. The concept of a cutting plane was presented and contrasted to branching, while the branch and bound procedure was presented in more detail. Both cutting plane methods and the branch and bound procedure have been an important part of the development of the integer programming solution technology. Currently, branch and bound methods are believed to be the most effective, and computer codes for the solution of integer programming problems are generally based on the branch and bound procedure. There are a variety of integer programming computer codes available. Both the LINDO and MICROSOLVE computer packages mentioned in Chapter 8 have the ability to solve 0–1 integer programming problems. IBM's MPSX-370 computer package is a commercial integer code that is available at many IBM computer installations. This is a very versatile code and has the ability to handle integer problems of significant size.

This chapter is by no means a comprehensive coverage of integer programming. There are many more interesting "classical" (or standard) integer programming models in the literature. There are other solution approaches, such as the Balas Additive Algorithm for the 0–1 integer model. There are also many heuristics developed for the efficient application of the branch and bound method. Nonetheless, our purpose here is to provide some basic knowledge in an area where research continues to provide more efficient solution methods for a set of very complex mathematical problems.

GLOSSARY

Binary Variables   Variables that are restricted to be 0 or 1.

Bounding   The process of finding a value for the objective function that cannot be exceeded for any feasible solution (for a maximization problem) in a given subproblem or for a set of feasible solutions.

Branch and Bound Method   An enumeration procedure used to solve integer programming problems where only a small portion of the feasible solutions are explicitly enumerated.

Branching   The partitioning of the feasible solutions of an integer programming problem into mutually exclusive subsets.

Capital Budgeting Problem   A 0–1 integer programming problem having multiple resource constraints.

Conditional Relationships   Situations that must reflect that one decision is dependent on another decision.

Continuous Feasible Region   The region associated with an integer programming problem that satisfies all the constraints except for the integrality conditions.

Cutting Plane   A constraint that does not eliminate any integer feasible solutions, but eliminates a portion of the continuous feasible region.

Cutting Plane Method   A procedure for solving integer programming problems that adds constraints, called cutting planes, until the optimal extreme point is integer.

Enumeration Tree   A graphical presentation of the subsets of solutions that are examined in the branch and bound procedure.

Fathoming   The process of using a feasible solution to eliminate sets of feasible solutions without explicit enumeration.

Fixed-Charge Condition   A situation that requires that a fixed-charge be accounted for if the level of a decision variable (or set of decision variables) is greater than zero.

Integer Linear Programming Model   A model that satisfies all of the four properties of a linear programming problem except the divisibility property.

Integrality Conditions   Constraints on the variables of a problem that require these variables to be integer.

Knapsack Problem   A 0–1 integer programming problem having a single resource constraint.

Mixed Integer Model   An integer programming model that has both integer and continuous variables.

Multiple-Choice Restriction   A condition where exactly one decision in a set of decisions is "yes."

Mutually Exclusive Constraints   A pair of constraints used to generate a pair of subproblems in the branch and bound procedure.

Mutually Exclusive Restriction   A condition that at most one decision in a set of decisions is "yes."

Pure Integer Model   An integer programming model where all variables assume integer variables.

Subproblem   A linear programming problem, generated from an integer programming problem, with a feasible region that is a subset of the original continuous feasible region.

Warehouse Location Problem   A fixed-charge problem that models the tradeoffs between transportation cost and the cost of operating distribution centers.

Zero-One (0–1) Integer Model   An integer programming model where all the variables are 0 or 1.

Selected References

Bradley, Stephen P., Arnoldo C. Hax, and Thomas L. Magnanti. 1977. *Applied Mathematical Programming.* Reading, Mass.: Addison–Wesley.

Budnick, Frank S., Richard Mojena, and Thomas E. Vollmann. 1977. *Operations Research for Management.* Homewood, Ill.: Irwin.

Garfinkel, Robert, and George L. Nemhauser. 1972. *Integer Programming.* New York: Wiley.

Greenberg, Harold. 1971. *Integer Programming.* New York: Wiley.

Hillier, Fredrick S., and Gerald J. Lieberman. 1980. *Introduction to Operations Research,* 3rd ed. San Francisco, Calif.: Holden–Day.

Hu, T.C. 1969. *Integer Programming and Network Flows.* Reading, Mass.: Addison–Wesley.

McMillan, Claude. 1975. *Mathematical Programming.* New York: Wiley.

Plane, Donald R., and Claude McMillan. 1971. *Discrete Optimization: Integer Programming and Network Analysis for Management Decisions.* Englewood Cliffs, N.J.: Prentice–Hall.

Salkin, Harvey M. 1975. *Integer Programming.* Reading, Mass.: Addison–Wesley.

Taha, Hamody A. 1975. *Integer Programming: Theory, Applications, and Computations.* New York: Academic Press.

Wagner, Harvey M. 1969. *Principles of Operations Research: With Applications to Managerial Decisions.* Englewood Cliffs, N.J.: Prentice–Hall.

Zionts, S. 1974. *Linear and Integer Programming.* Englewood Cliffs, N.J.: Prentice–Hall.

Discussion Questions

1. Discuss the primary difference(s) between linear and integer programming.

2. Discuss the problems with rounding a "continuous solution" to obtain an integer solution.

3. Discuss the basic conceptual differences between the cutting plane approach and the branch and bound approach to integer programming.

4. If the linear programming optimal solution to an integer programming problem is integer, is this solution optimal to the integer problem? Explain.

5. In using the branch and bound approach, how do you know when you have found the optimal solution to the integer programming problem?

6. What changes in the branch and bound solution procedure are required if a minimization problem is solved instead of a maximization problem?

7. Discuss the primary differences between the application of the branch and bound procedure to a general integer programming problem and the assignment problem.

8. Are there any major differences between the application of the branch and bound procedure to a pure integer problem as compared to a mixed integer problem?

9. In the fixed charge problem explain the impact of the constraints of the form $x_j - My_i \leq 0$.

10. In the warehouse location problem of Section 14.6.2, explain how the formulation might be changed if there were no capacity limitations on any of the warehouses.

PROBLEMS

1. Consider the following integer programming problem.

$$\text{Maximize } Z = 2x_1 + x_2$$

subject to

$$15x_1 + 7x_2 \leq 105$$
$$11x_1 + 15x_2 \leq 165$$

with

$$x_1, x_2 \geq 0$$

and x_1, x_2 integer.

   a. Find the continuous optimal linear programming solution to this problem.
   b. Find a feasible integer solution by rounding the solution found in part (a).
   c. Graph the feasible region to the integer programming problem, and find the integer optimal solution by complete enumeration.

2. Solve the following integer programming problem using the branch and bound method.

$$\text{Maximize } Z = 2x_1 + x_2$$

subject to

$$5x_1 + 2x_2 \leq 16$$
$$5x_1 + 6x_2 \leq 30$$

with

$$x_1, x_2 \geq 0$$

and x_1, x_2 integer.

3. Solve the following integer programming problem using the branch and bound method.

$$\text{Maximize } Z = x_1 + x_2$$

subject to

$$2x_1 + x_2 \leq 45$$
$$5x_1 + x_2 \leq 110$$
$$x_1 + 2x_2 \leq 55$$

with

$$x_1, x_2 \geq 0$$

and x_1, x_2 integer.

4. Solve the following integer programming problem using the branch and bound method.

$$\text{Maximize } Z = 5x_1 + x_2$$

subject to

$$2x_1 + 3x_2 \leq 12$$
$$3x_1 + x_2 \leq 9$$
$$x_1 - x_2 \leq 1$$

with

$$x_1, x_2 \geq 0$$

and x_1, x_2 integer.

5. Solve the following mixed integer programming problem using the branch and bound method.

$$\text{Maximize } Z = 3x_1 + 6x_2 + 8x_3$$

subject to

$$3x_1 + 4x_2 + 8x_3 \leq 24$$

$$2x_1 + 4x_2 - x_3 \leq 7$$

with

$$x_1, x_2, x_3 \geq 0$$

and x_2, x_3 integer.

6. Solve the following problem using the branch and bound procedure.

$$\text{Maximize } Z = x_1 + x_2 + x_3 + x_4$$

subject to

$$4x_1 + 8x_2 + 16x_3 + 15x_4 \leq 613$$

$$2x_1 + x_2 + 10x_3 + 10x_4 \leq 338$$

$$2x_1 + 3x_2 \leq 105$$

$$x_1 + 3x_3 \leq 205$$

$$x_1 + 3x_4 \leq 140$$

with

$$x_1, x_2, x_3, x_4 \geq 0$$

and x_1, x_2, x_3, x_4 integer.

7. Four limousines must be dispatched to pick up four prominent politicians and deliver them to a scheduled news conference. The round-trip costs for all possible alternatives are given in the following table. The politicians refuse to ride with each other, so each of the limousines will have to be used.

| | POLITICIAN | | | |
LIMOUSINE	A	B	C	D
1	125	115	120	145
2	130	115	125	155
3	115	95	100	135
4	140	125	145	130

a. If the objective is to minimize the total transportation cost, formulate as an integer programming problem.
b. Solve this problem using the branch and bound method.

8. A local newspaper must assign five paper carriers to five paper routes. The newspaper would, to the extent possible, like to satisfy the

preferences of the carriers. The carriers were asked to indicate their preferences with a 1 indicating a first choice and a 5 indicating a last choice. The results are tabulated in the following table.

CARRIER	ROUTE				
	A	B	C	D	E
1	2	4	3	1	5
2	1	2	3	4	5
3	5	4	3	2	1
4	3	2	4	5	1
5	3	4	5	1	2

    a. Formulate an integer programming model that minimizes the sum of the preference values for the five carriers.

    b. Solve this problem using the branch and bound method.

9. Consider a capital budgeting problem where five projects are being considered for implementation and are of three years' duration. The expected returns for each project and the yearly expenditures (in hundreds of thousands of dollars) are shown below. The objective is to select the projects that will maximize the total returns.

PROJECT	EXPENDITURES			RETURNS
	YEAR 1	YEAR 2	YEAR 3	
1	5	1	10	25
2	6	6	8	45
3	2	4	4	15
4	4	9	1	15
5	8	6	7	35
Maximum funds available	22	22	22	

Formulate as an integer programming problem.

10. Write the constraints for the capital budgeting problem in Problem 9 needed to reflect the following additional restrictions.

    a. Two of the projects 1, 2, 4, and 5 must be undertaken.

    b. Projects 3 and 5 must be undertaken simultaneously if at all.

    c. Project 1 or 2 must be undertaken, but not both.

    d. Project 5 cannot be undertaken unless projects 3 and 4 are also undertaken.

11. In a production planning situation there is a demand of 2500 units of a product that can be manufactured on three machines. The setup costs, the per-unit production costs, and the production capacity for the three machines are listed in the following table.

MACHINE	SETUP COST	PRODUCTION COST/UNIT	CAPACITY (UNITS)
1	500	3	900
2	150	12	900
3	350	5	1800

The objective is to minimize the total production cost of the lot of 2500 units. Formulate the problem as an integer programming problem.

12. A broker has been given $1,000,000 to invest. He will choose the investment from a list of 25 stocks. The net return from 10 dollars in stock i is r_i. Given the risks and expected returns for the 25 stocks involved, the following operating policy will be adhered to.

a. No more than $125,000 will be invested in a single stock.
b. If any amount is invested in a stock, at least $25,000 will be invested in it.

Formulate a mixed integer linear programming problem that maximizes return.

13. A manufacturer has the ability to produce flatbed railroad cars at three locations. These railroad cars are then shipped directly to one of four regional distribution centers. The fixed cost of production at each of these locations follows.

PLANT	SETUP COST
1	20,000
2	15,500
3	12,000

The per-unit distribution costs, plant capacities, and demands at the regional distribution centers are also given.

PLANT	DISTRIBUTION CENTERS				PRODUCTION CAPACITY
	I	II	III	IV	
1	750	1000	800	900	55
2	650	900	1250	500	50
3	800	525	675	775	30
Demand	20	15	30	35	

Formulate this problem of determining how to handle production as an integer programming problem. Assume that per-unit production costs, excluding the setup charges, are the same at all plants.

14. Reformulate the problem in Problem 13 if additionally when production is undertaken at a given plant, at least 15 units must be produced there.

15. A student in a management science class has the opportunity to take one page of notes (a sheet of paper 8 1/2 × 11 or 93.5 square inches) to the final exam. The comprehensive exam covers 10 chapters. The student already has condensed notes on the 10 chapters and knows how much space is required for each chapter. Further condensation would render the notes meaningless. Also the relative weights for each chapter are known a priori. This information follows.

CHAPTER	SPACE REQUIRED (IN².)	PERCENT OF COVERAGE ON EXAM
1	10	5
2	18	10
3	22	15
4	16	10
5	14	10
6	20	5
7	32	20
8	12	5
9	12	15
10	10	5

The student feels very uncomfortable with the material in Chapters 2, 3, 7, 8, and 9, and thus feels that he should have notes from at least three of these five chapters. Also the notes from Chapter 5 are of no value unless the notes from Chapter 4 are also included. Formulate an integer programming problem that will determine which notes should be included.

16. Joe is attempting to determine a minimum-cost food mixture that will meet the dietary standards given in the following table. Joe has four food sources that he can utilize. There are, however, ordering costs for these foods. The cost of ordering is a fixed charge that is also given in the table that follows.

	UNITS OF NUTRIENTS PER OUNCE OF FOOD SOURCE j			
	1	2	3	4
Nutrient A	200	50	100	50
Nutrient B	100	100	80	100
Nutrient C	130	80	90	150
Cost per ounce for food source	$0.45	$0.35	$0.38	$0.42
Ordering costs for food source	$5.00	$6.50	$7.50	$4.00

The required units of nutrients are 2000 for A, 1500 for B, and 1200 for C. Formulate a model that will determine the number of ounces of each food source that should be ordered to meet the required units of nutrients and minimize total cost.

17. Reformulate the model in Problem 16, so that only two of the three nutritional constraints must be satisfied.

18. Top-E manufactures walnut executive desks at two factories that must be supplied to three regional warehouses. The supply at each factory, the demand at each warehouse, as well as the relevant distances are given in the following table.

| | WAREHOUSE | | | |
FACTORY	YORK	WESTHAVEN	TROY	SUPPLY
Denmark	100 mi	200 mi	300 mi	35
Mount Joy	350 mi	60 mi	100 mi	30
Demand	20	15	30	

Trucks will be rented to transport these desks for $1.00 per mile, and this rental charge is independent of the number of desks transported. Formulate an integer programming model to determine the transportation plan for Top-E.

Application Review

Improving Transit Check-Clearing Operations at Maryland National Bank

One of the most important aspects of improving productivity in today's banking environment involves the clearing (i.e., collection of funds) of "transit" (out-of-town) checks. This problem became even more important due to the passage of the Depository Institution's Deregulation and Monetary Control Act of 1980. This law meant that beginning September 1, 1981 the Federal Reserve System began charging for its check-clearing and collection services.

Clearing of transit checks is a complex combinatorial problem for several reasons. First, a transit check can be cleared in at least three ways: one, the transit check can be cleared using the Federal Reserve System, and will cost the bank according to the origin and destination banks associated with that check; two, the check may be cleared by using a "correspondent" bank that will transport the check to the destination bank, and will charge the originating bank for this service; three, the check may be cleared by using direct courier service from the originating bank to the destination bank. Such a service is probably the fastest of the three, but it is also the most expensive in that a fixed charge for transportation is incurred while only a nominal check processing charge is assessed for the former two cases.

The decision concerning which transit check-clearing method to use is further compounded by several factors. First, the Federal Reserve System and each bank

Source: Robert E. Markland and Robert M. Nauss, "Improving transit check clearing operations at Maryland National Bank," *Interfaces* (February 1983), Vol. 13, No. 1, pp. 1–9.

in the United States has an *availability schedule* that details the number of days required to clear particular checks drawn on various banks in each region of the country. These availability schedules are quoted in terms of business days required for clearing, given presentation of a check by a particular time of day and day of week. Second, a separate check-clearing decision must be made for each destination bank. Third, while transit checks may be cleared most rapidly by sending checks directly to the bank on which they are drawn (i.e., a process commonly called a "direct" send), a number of alternative transportation options, with differing logistic and cost structures, are available at different times of the day. In summary, in order to select the least costly method of clearing transit checks it is necessary to consider reduction of the time required to clear the checks (commonly referred to as "float" reduction), within the time constraints imposed by availability schedules of the Federal Reserve System and individual banks, taking into account the per-check processing charges and the fixed charges associated with various transportation modes.

Given the general nature of the transit check-clearing problem as outlined above, it can be modeled as a large-scale 0–1 integer linear programming problem. Its structure is similar to the classical uncapacitated facility location problem, and can be summarized as follows.

$$x_{ijk} = \begin{cases} 1, & \text{if check type } i \text{ is cleared by method } j \text{ in time period } k \\ 0, & \text{if not} \end{cases}$$

$$y_{jk} = \begin{cases} 1, & \text{if clearing method } j \text{ is used in time period } k \\ 0, & \text{if not} \end{cases}$$

c_{ijk} = opportunity cost of float for checks of type i cleared by method j in time period k

v_j = variable (per-check) charge for clearing method j

f_{jk} = fixed cost of clearing method j in time period k

$J(i)$ = $\{j|$ check type i cleared by method $j\}$

d_{ik} = number of checks of check type i ready for clearing in time period k

where $i = 1, \ldots, n; j \in J(i); k = 1, \ldots, m, L = \{j|j \in J(i), i = 1, \ldots, n\}$. Then the transit check clearing problem may be formulated as

$$\text{Minimize} \sum_{i=1}^{n} \sum_{j \in J(i)} \sum_{k=1}^{m} c_{ijk} x_{ijk}$$

$$+ v_j d_{ik} x_{ijk} + \sum_{j \in L} \sum_{k=1}^{m} f_{ik} y_{jk} \qquad (14.109)$$

subject to

$$\sum_{j \in J(i)} x_{ijk} = 1, \qquad \text{all } i = 1, \ldots, n; k = 1, \ldots, m$$

$$x_{ijk} \leq y_{jk}, \qquad \text{all } i = 1, \ldots, n; j \in J(i): k = 1, \ldots, m \qquad (14.110)$$

with

$$x_{ijk} = 0, 1, \qquad \text{all } i = 1, \ldots, n; j \in J(i); k = 1, \ldots, m$$

$$y_{jk} = 0, 1, \qquad \text{all } j \in J(i); k = 1, \ldots, m \qquad (14.111)$$

TABLE 14.10. OPTIMAL SOLUTION PRESENTED BY DAY PROCESSED, TIME SLOT, AND ENDPOINT

TIME SLOT	FRD	DIRECT SEND	DAY SENT	BANK	ITEMS	DOLLARS	OPPORTUNITY COST OF $ FLOAT + PER-ITEM COST	AVAILABILITY
2130	111	New York 1	Wednesday	601	969	433,953	386.65	2.00
2130	113	Buffalo 1	Wednesday	406	268	69,022	72.09	2.00
2200	711	Chicago 2	Wednesday	242	781	140,989	138.84	2.00
2200	710	Chicago 2	Wednesday	242	901	1,040,016	448.67	1.00
2300	110	New York 1	Wednesday	607	886	791,896	345.81	1.00

Note: Day processed is Tuesday.

The objective function simply adds the opportunity cost of float, the variable (per-check) charges, and the fixed transportation charges. The first set of constraints in (14.110) requires that each check type i during each time period k be cleared by exactly one clearing method $j \in J(i)$. The second set of constraints in (14.110) assures that a check type i during time period k can only be cleared if the corresponding clearing method j in time period k is being used. An additional constraint

$$\sum_{j \in L} \sum_{k=1}^{m} y_{jk} \le K \qquad (14.112)$$

may also be added to the formulation if a limit is to be placed on the number (K) of direct sends that may be made.

Working within the actual check-processing environment of Maryland National Bank, Baltimore, Maryland, a computerized integer programming model has been developed, tested, implemented, and successfully utilized. Problem sizes (with facility location analogues) are on the order of 200 to 300 potential direct sends (facilities), 2000 cash letters (customers), and 15,000 to 20,000 cash letter arcs (facility-customer connections). Optimal solutions (with 0 suboptimality tolerance) are generated in about 60 seconds on an AMDAHL 470/V7.

Maryland National Bank typically clears about $600 million of checks daily. Use of the computerized model to improve the efficiency of transit check clearing has resulted in yearly savings in excess of $100,000 for Maryland National Bank.

The transit check-clearing model produces five types of computer-generated reports that are used by management for making decisions. One of these reports presents the optimal solution by ordering the pertinent information by the day processed, then by the time slots during that day, and finally by the appropriate destination (endpoint). A sample of this type of management report is presented in Table 14.10.

INVENTORY ANALYSIS: DETERMINISTIC MODELS

15.1 INTRODUCTION

Inventories typically represent a sizable portion of an organization's total assets. Inventory can be viewed as any economic resource that is held by an organization at a given point in time. Raw materials awaiting use in a production process, partially finished units of production (work in process), and finished production units are probably the most commonly recognized inventory items for a manufacturing organization. Finished goods waiting for sale are the common inventory items for retail organizations, cash is an important inventory item for banks, and for many service organizations human resources are the primary inventory items.

Inventory may assume diverse forms, but maintaining and managing inventory is a problem common to most manufacturing firms, retail outlets, service organizations, and governmental agencies. Inventory policies for most organizations are governed by a variety of objectives, three of which are minimizing the capital investment in inventory, providing an adequate level of customer service, and maximizing output efficiency. Finding an acceptable balance across these three objectives is at the heart of much of the analysis encountered in inventory planning.

In this chapter, the classical economic order quantity model and several variations of this model are presented. The models discussed represent the most fundamental of the mathematical inventory models. These models are deterministic models, that is, demand for a product or service is known with certainty and is constant. These deterministic models provide the framework for the stochastic models presented in Chapter 16.

15.2 THE INVENTORY DECISION

Inventories provide flexibility for operations in most organizations. The most obvious reason for maintaining an inventory is so that an order placed by a customer can be filled quickly; otherwise, the customer may order from a competitor! The threat of possible loss of revenue is, however, only one of many reasons for maintaining and carefully managing inventories.

In many situations inventory is not an option but rather a simple requirement. For example, agricultural products often involve periodic or seasonal production. The entire annual corn crop cannot all be consumed immediately and thus must be an inventory item for someone. The determination of which organization will hold the inventory item is a function of the ultimate use of the product and the product pricing strategy used by the producer.

The possibility of maintaining an inventory can contribute directly to production efficiency. Achieving economies of scale by large batch production is possible if items are placed in inventory. Maintaining a smooth production flow within an organization is often dependent upon adequate inventory. When one manufacturing activity cannot begin before another is complete, inventory provides a way to decouple the manufacturing process.

Inventory policy interacts with many other management decisions. Determining whether to maintain employees over periods of changing demand is indirectly a decision based on acceptable inventory levels. Inventory may also serve as management's goal to hedge inflation or protect itself from an intolerable interruption resulting from a labor dispute or another potentially disastrous event over which the organization itself has little control.

It is easy to see that inventory decisions have many facets. There are, however, only two basic decisions that must be made in inventory control: (1) how much to order and (2) when to order. The questions are quite simple, but finding good answers involves the consideration of a large number of factors.

1. The ordering cost.
2. The holding or storage cost.
3. The cost of a stockout or shortage cost.
4. The nature of future demand.
5. The impact of quantity discounts.
6. The impact of nonzero lead time.
7. The impact of ordering policy.

Before examining several simple inventory models we briefly discuss the factors listed above.

Each time an order is placed to meet unsatisfied demand or replenish inventory a fixed cost is incurred. The cost that is independent of the size of the order placed is called the *ordering cost*. The ordering costs involve the clerical work and supplies associated with the order, fixed transportation charges, and the cost of inspecting and paying for the order. In a production environment ordering costs are often called *setup costs*. Setup costs may also include clerical work and supplies. The primary costs in this situation are generally the labor and material costs associated with setting up a piece of machinery for the production of the order.

The *holding cost* or *storage cost* is the cost associated with maintaining units in inventory until they are used or sold. Opportunity cost or the cost of capital is the largest component of the holding cost, and is often determined by management to be the best return the company could achieve from alternative investments. The cost of maintaining storage facilities, insurance, taxes, and the cost associated with obsolescence are the common costs assigned to inventory maintenance, and are generally tied to the level of inventory. Determining the inventory level is by no means exact. Often the estimated average inventory or the excess of supply over demand for a fixed time period is used to assess inventory holding costs.

A *stockout* or *shortage cost* may occur when the demand for an item exceeds its supply. The cost associated with a shortage is dependent upon how management responds to a shortage. A back order occurs when the customer places an order for an item, finds that the supplier cannot fill that order, and waits for the next shipment to arrive. The assumption often made in models that permit backordering is that no sale is lost due to a stockout. If backordering is permitted, the relevant shortage costs may include the clerical costs and supplies associated with the backorder, costs associated with a "rush" or "priority" shipment, and perhaps a "goodwill" cost that reflects a future loss in sales.

The purpose of the backorder is to maintain customer "goodwill." If backordering is not permitted, the shortage will result in a loss of sales for the items not immediately available, and a "goodwill" cost if the unhappy customer takes its future business elsewhere. The computation of the shortage cost is dependent upon the organization and the individual situation. Often a fixed cost per shortage is assumed that is independent of the magnitude or duration of the shortage. Another approach is to assume a per-unit shortage cost per unit of time. No matter how shortages are handled, a significant portion of the cost relates directly to customer goodwill. This perceived cost is often estimated in terms of expected lost sales. In the models considered here we treat shortage cost as a fixed cost per unit per unit time.

Another important factor in inventory models is the nature of future demand. If demand is known with certainty, the model developed is called a deterministic inventory model. On the other hand, if demand is described by an appropriate probability distribution, the model developed is called a stochastic inventory model. This chapter deals with deterministic inventory models, while the next examines several stochastic inventory models.

In some situations the purchase cost is a function of the quantity of items ordered. In many situations the assumption that the per-unit cost is constant is reasonable. If *quantity discounts* are allowed for specific order sizes, however, those differential prices must be considered in the inventory decision. Quantity discounts generally reflect economies of scale in the production or distribution process.

Lead time is the time between the placement of the order and the receipt of the order. Lead time can be deterministic or stochastic just as demand can be deterministic or stochastic. We treat only the models that involve a deterministic lead time. Thus if orders are received in lots and we know when an order is needed, the order is placed an appropriate amount of time before the date needed. This amount of time is the deterministic lead time.

There are two basic types of order systems: the *order point system* and the *periodic review system*. An order point system assumes a continuous review, and an order is placed when the stock level falls below a prespecified level called a *reorder point*. In a periodic review system inventory levels are checked at discrete intervals, and orders are placed as needed. We only consider order-point systems here.

15.3 THE ECONOMIC ORDER QUANTITY MODEL

The simplest of the independent demand inventory models is known as the economic order quantity model or the EOQ model. The model presented addresses the problem of controlling the inventory of a *single item* at a *single location*. Additionally the following assumptions characterize this model.

1. Demand is known with certainty and is constant over time.
2. Lead time is zero, the order is received the instant it is placed.
3. The entire order is received as a single batch.

4. Inventory is replenished when the inventory is zero, and thus no shortages are allowed.
5. The order quantity, Q, is constant.
6. An infinite (continuous) time horizon is assumed.

The inventory level for the EOQ model is represented graphically in Figure 15.1. The constant order quantity is denoted by Q, and D represents the constant demand per unit time. The assumption of constant demand means for example that if demand for 4 weeks is 24 units, then demand in each of the 4 weeks will be 6. In general, this means that the demand over a specified time interval is dependent only on the length of the time interval. This assumption is reflected in the figure, where inventory falls from Q to 0 in the interval 0 to Q/D, from Q to 0 in the interval Q/D to $2Q/D$, and so forth. Here, Q/D represents the time between placement of orders. We note that the slopes of the lines that represent inventory level are constant and thus reflect the assumption that inventory is being depleted at a constant rate. We also note that since replenishment is instantaneous, inventory jumps from 0 to Q at the time the inventory is depleted.

Consider the situation where a department store carpet division sells 30,000 yards of carpet of a particular type and color per year. Every time the division places an order to the manufacturer, there is a fixed charge of $1000 independent of the size of the order. At the same time the estimated costs of holding one yard of carpet in inventory for a year is $2. The question that needs to be answered is: How many yards of carpet should be ordered each time an order is placed? Intuitively, we want to examine the tradeoff between the two costs and ultimately minimize the total cost that is the sum of the ordering costs and the holding costs. The quantity that minimizes total cost is called the *order quantity* or *economic lot size*.

The ordering cost, K, is a fixed charge for a single order. This charge reflects the clerical cost of preparing a purchase order, or a shop order if the items are to be manufactured rather than purchased. Costs of order expediting and processing an invoice are included if a purchase order is involved. For a shop order the main cost may be associated with machine setup. The holding cost, h, includes the cost to finance inventory and hold it in storage. If an item is ordered infrequently in large quantities, the holding costs will be larger than the holding costs when the item is ordered frequently and in smaller quantities. The cost to finance the inventory is an opportunity cost of the capital that is tied up in inventory. As mentioned earlier, holding costs also include the maintenance of the storage facility, insurace, inventory taxes, handling costs, and loss due to theft or obsolescence. The parameter, h, represents the holding cost, in dollars, per item per unit of time.

We now look at the development of the EOQ model in the context of the department store carpet division scenario described, where

$K = \$1000$, the cost of placing one order;

$h = \$2$, the cost of holding a yard of carpet in inventory for one year;

$D = 30{,}000$, yards of carpet demanded in one year.

The costs associated with the model are obtained as follows.

1. If the order quantity is Q, and the demand per unit time is D, the number of orders per unit time is D/Q. Thus,

$$\text{Total order cost (per unit of time)} = K(D/Q)$$
$$(15.1)$$

For the carpet division illustration

Total order cost (per year)

$$= \$1000 \left(\frac{30{,}000}{Q} \right) \quad (15.2)$$

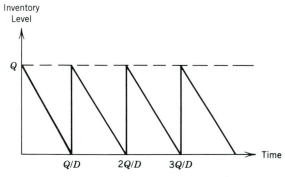

FIGURE 15.1   INVENTORY LEVELS FOR THE EOQ MODEL.

2. From Figure 15.1 we note that if Q is the order quantity and D is demand, the amount of time between the placement of orders is Q/D. The times 0 to Q/D, Q/D to $2Q/D$, and $2Q/D$ to $3Q/D$, are called *inventory cycles*. The EOQ model assumes that all inventory cycles are of equal length. Since inventory is uniformly depleted in a given inventory cycle, the average inventory in a cycle is given by

$$\frac{\text{Beginning inventory} - \text{ending inventory}}{2}$$

$$= \frac{Q - 0}{2} \quad (15.3)$$

Since all inventory cycles are of equal length, the average inventory level over time is $Q/2$ and

$$\text{Total holding cost (per unit of time)} = h(Q/2) \quad (15.4)$$

and if $h = 2$,

Total holding cost (per unit of time)
$$= 2(Q/2) = Q \quad (15.5)$$

3. The total cost of inventory per unit time is denoted by TC and is given by

Total inventory cost (per unit of time)
$$= K(D/Q) + h(Q/2) \quad (15.6)$$

In the carpet division illustration the total inventory cost per year is

$$TC = (1000)\left(\frac{30,000}{Q}\right) + 2\left(\frac{Q}{2}\right) \quad (15.7)$$

Our objective is to determine the optimal order quantity or economic order quantity, which by definition minimizes total cost. Figure 15.2 illustrates the general behavior of the ordering cost function and of the holding cost function as the order quantity Q varies. As the order quantity increases, fewer orders are required and total ordering cost decreases. On the other hand, as the order quantity increases, the average inventory level increases and so does the total holding cost.

In this figure the optimal order quantity, Q^*,

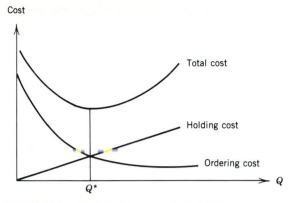

FIGURE 15.2 INVENTORY COSTS FOR THE EOQ MODEL.

occurs at the intersection of the holding cost function and the ordering cost function. Algebraically, Q^* can be solved by equating these two cost functions and solving for Q:

$$h\left(\frac{Q}{2}\right) = K\left(\frac{D}{Q}\right) \quad (15.8)$$

$$\frac{hQ^2}{2} = KD \quad (15.9)$$

$$Q^2 = \frac{2KD}{h} \quad (15.10)$$

Thus the optimal order quantity, Q^*, is given by

$$Q^* = \sqrt{\frac{2KD}{h}} \quad (15.11)$$

The optimal value of Q could also be determined via differential calculus.[1]

---

[1] To determine the EOQ using differential calculus, we differentiate $TC = K(D/Q) + h(Q/2)$ with respect to Q and set the derivative equal to zero

$$\frac{dTC}{dQ} = \frac{-KD}{Q^2} + \frac{h}{2} = 0 \quad \text{or} \quad Q^* = \sqrt{\frac{2KD}{h}}$$

To verify that we have found a relative minimum point we calculate the second derivative

$$\frac{d^2TC}{dQ^2} = \frac{2KD}{Q^3}$$

If $Q > 0$, then $(2KD)/Q^3 > 0$ and since the relevant second derivative is positive the computed value of Q, Q^*, will minimize total cost.

In any case, the optimal order quantity is given in (15.11). In the carpet division illustration,

$$Q^* = \sqrt{\frac{2(1000)(30000)}{2}} = \cong 5477 \text{ yards} \quad (15.12)$$

Every time an order is placed, 5477 yards of carpet are ordered. The number of orders per year (or per unit of time) are

$$\frac{D}{Q^*} = \frac{30,000}{5477} \cong 5.5 \quad (15.13)$$

and the number of days in an inventory cycle (the time needed to deplete an inventory of Q^*) is

$$\frac{Q^*}{D}(365) \cong 67 \text{ days} \quad (15.14)$$

In this situation, given the cost of ordering and the cost of holding inventory, an order should be placed about once every 67 days. Finally, the total yearly inventory cost is computed.

Total yearly inventory cost

$$= K\frac{D}{Q^*} + h\frac{Q^*}{2}$$

$$= (1000)\frac{(30,000)}{5477} + 2\left(\frac{5477}{2}\right)$$

$$= \$10,954 \quad (15.15)$$

15.4 THE EOQ MODEL WITH NONZERO LEAD TIME

Our second assumption in Section 15.3 was that lead time is zero or that when an order is placed it is received instantaneously. It is much more realistic to assume that an order is placed, and in a reasonable amount of time the order is received. The time between the placement of the order and the receipt of the order is called the *lead time* or *reorder lead time*. As long as the lead time is known with certainty, the economic order quantity will remain as computed in Section 15.3.

We now illustrate two relevant situations. First, lead time is less than the length of an inventory cycle; and second, lead time is greater than the length of the inventory cycle as determined by Q^*. Let C represent the length of the inventory cycle

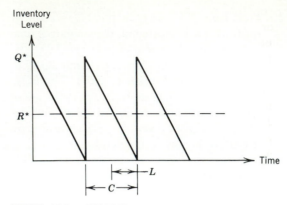

FIGURE 15.3   REORDER POINT: LEAD TIME LESS THAN INVENTORY CYCLE TIME.

and let L be the deterministic lead time. Recall that

$$C = Q^*/D \quad (15.16)$$

where C and L are measured in the unit of time as specified by demand. Also let R^* be the inventory level when the order must be placed to assure that there will be no shortage. Variable R^* is often called the *reorder point*. Figure 15.3 illustrates the case when $C > L$. Each time the inventory level reaches R^* an order must be placed so that it arrives when inventory is depleted. Figure 15.4 illustrates the situation when $C < L$.

In this situation the reorder point is again the inventory level used to specify when the order is placed. The order must now, however, be placed in a previous inventory cycle in order to satisfy demand. Thus at least one order will arrive during the lead time. This is illustrated in Figure 15.4, where

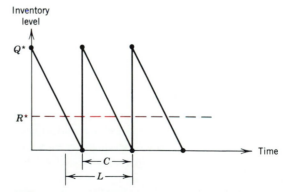

FIGURE 15.4   REORDER POINT: LEAD TIME GREATER THAN INVENTORY CYCLE TIME.

the order to replenish inventory at the end of the second inventory cycle must be placed before the order to replenish inventory at the end of the first inventory cycle arrives.

To determine the reorder point we observe that the total demand during lead time is equal to the reorder point plus the inventory that arrives during lead time. Suppose that L, C, and D are measured in years and consider the case where $C > L$. Then demand during lead time is $(L/C)Q^*$. Also,

$$
\begin{aligned}
R^* &= (L/C)Q^* \\
&= (L)(D/Q^*)Q^* \\
&= LD
\end{aligned}
\qquad (15.17)
$$

On the other hand if $C < L$, L/C represents the lead time in terms of a number of inventory cycles. We represent the fractional part of the quotient L/C as $F(L/C)$. In other words if C is 0.2 years and L is 90 days, we have

$$
F[(90/365)/0.2] = F(1.23) = 0.23 \qquad (15.18)
$$

Using this notation, if $C < L$

$$
R^* = F(L/C)Q^* \qquad (15.19)
$$

In the carpet division illustration of Section 15.3 we found that $Q^* = 5477$ yards, and the length of the inventory cycle was approximately 0.183 years or 67 days. Thus if lead time was 30 days, the reorder point would be approximately

$$
R^* = \frac{30}{365}(30,000) = 2466 \text{ yards} \qquad (15.20)
$$

If a perpetual inventory count was mandated, when the inventory level reaches 2466 yards of carpet, an order for 5477 yards of carpet is placed. If, on the other hand, the lead time was 75 days instead of 30 days

$$
F(75/67) = F(1.12) = 0.12 \qquad (15.21)
$$

Thus,

$$
R^* = (0.12)(5477) = 657 \text{ yards} \qquad (15.22)
$$

Again, each time the inventory level falls to 657 yards of carpet, an order is placed. It should also be noted that this order will not be used to meet demand in the following inventory cycle.

15.5 THE EOQ MODEL WITH A UNIFORM REPLENISHMENT RATE

In many situations it is reasonable to assume that the order is received as a batch. This is valid for most retail operations. In other situations, inventory is received gradually over a period of time. In a production setting this consideration is very important, since a production run may take a significant amount of time. The model developed in this section is of particular importance in the case of an organization that produces and inventories the same end item. This type of model is often called the *production lot size model* and designates that inventory is replenished directly from production.

The behavior of inventory in this situation is illustrated in Figure 15.5. Inventory is not replenished instantaneously, but is received as it is produced. Thus the inventory level gradually increases until the entire order Q is received, and then inventory is depleted to a zero level. At that point the production process is started again, and another inventory cycle begins. It should be noted that this process works only if items are being produced at a rate greater than the demand rate.

We now develop a variation of the EOQ model that allows for this gradual replenishment. For this model one of the six assumptions in Section 15.3 is relaxed: The entire order is received as a single batch. Again demand is constant and uniform, and no shortages are allowed. As before, this model is

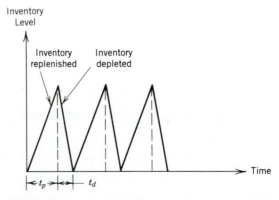

FIGURE 15.5 AN INVENTORY MODEL WITH A UNIFORM REPLENISHMENT RATE.

determined by the construction of the ordering cost function and the holding cost function. Again we find the optimal order quantity by equating these two costs. The ordering cost is not affected by the relaxation of this assumption, but the holding cost does change.

The development of this model requires the definition of one additional parameter, p. The uniform replenishment rate or production rate (p) is measured in the same unit of time as the demand rate. Replenishment or production is assumed to be uniform and at a constant rate over the length of the production run. This production time is designated by t_p in Figure 15.5. In contrast, t_d represents the time that inventory is being depleted and not replenished, while $t_p + t_d$ represents the length of an inventory cycle.

The costs for this model are developed as follows.

1. Again given that the order quantity is Q and that the demand per unit time is D, the number of orders per unit time is D/Q. Thus

$$\text{Total order cost per unit time} = K(D/Q)$$
$$(15.23)$$

2. To determine total holding cost we must recalculate the average inventory, first determining the maximum inventory level. It is not Q in this situation. The time required to receive an order is the length of the production run.

$$\text{Length of production run} = Q/p \quad (15.24)$$

Next we need to compute total demand during the period of production.

$$\text{Demand during production} = (Q/p)D \quad (15.25)$$

Thus inventory will be maximized precisely when production stops and when total production reaches the order quantity Q. Total production in an inventory cycle is Q, and demand during lead time is $(Q/p)D$. Therefore, when production stops, the inventory level must begin to decrease and

$$\text{Maximum inventory level}$$
$$= Q - (Q/p)D \quad (15.26)$$

Again average inventory is one-half of the maximum inventory level as in the case of the EOQ model for Section 15.3

Average inventory level

$$= \frac{1}{2}(Q - (Q/p)D)$$
$$= (Q/2)(1 - D/p) \quad (15.27)$$

$$\text{Total holding cost per unit time} = h(Q/2)(1 - D/p) \quad (15.28)$$

$$\text{Total inventory cost per unit time} = K(D/Q)$$
$$+ h(Q/2)(1 - D/p) \quad (15.29)$$

The relationships between ordering cost, holding cost, and total cost can again be illustrated by Figure 15.2. Minimum inventory cost once more occurs where the total cost function is minimized and where holding cost is equal to ordering cost. To find Q^* we equate these two expressions.[2]

$$K(D/Q) = h(Q/2)(1 - D/p)$$
$$KD = Q^2(h/2)(1 - D/p)$$
$$Q^2 = \frac{2KD}{h(1 - D/p)}$$
$$Q^* = \sqrt{\frac{2KD}{h(1 - D/p)}} \quad (15.30)$$

To illustrate the use of this model consider the following situation. Chinatown Manufacturing produces cases of egg rolls on a production line. The annual production capacity is 25,000 cases per year, while the estimated demand is 15,000 cases per year. When the egg rolls are produced the fixed costs associated with a production run are $500. The annual holding cost is estimated to be $50 a case per year. In this situation the economic order quantity Q^* is computed as follows

$$Q^* = \sqrt{\frac{2(500)(15,000)}{50(1 - (15,00/25000))}}$$
$$= 866 \text{ cases per order} \quad (15.31)$$

The total annual inventory cost using Q^* is also

_____

[2]Q^* can also be obtained by differentiating (15–29) with respect to Q, setting the derivative equal to zero, and solving for Q^*.

computed

$$\text{Total inventory cost} = 500 \left(\frac{15{,}000}{866}\right)$$
$$+ 50 \left(\frac{866}{2}\right)\left(1 - \frac{15{,}000}{25{,}000}\right)$$
$$= \$17{,}321 \text{ per year} \qquad (15.32)$$

The total number of production runs (or orders) per year is

$$\frac{D}{Q} = \frac{15{,}000}{866} = 17.3 \text{ production runs} \qquad (15.33)$$

The length of the production run, t_p, and the time during which the inventory is being depleted, t_d, are also computed. We first note that the length of the inventory cycle Q^*/D is 866/15,000 or 0.059 years or approximately 21 days, while

$$t_p = \frac{Q^*}{p} = \frac{866}{25{,}000}$$
$$= 0.035 \text{ years (12.6 days)} \qquad (15.34)$$

and

$$t_d = \frac{Q^*}{D} - \frac{Q^*}{p}$$
$$= \frac{866}{15{,}000} - \frac{866}{25{,}000}$$
$$= 0.023 \text{ years (8.4 days)} \qquad (15.35)$$

Also the maximum inventory level is computed

$$\text{Maximum inventory level}$$
$$= Q^* - \frac{Q^*}{p} D$$
$$= 866 - \frac{866}{25{,}000}(15{,}000) \qquad (15.36)$$
$$= 346.4 \text{ cases} \qquad (15.36)$$

15.6 THE EOQ MODEL: SHORTAGES ALLOWED

There are many situations where it is more economical to allow shortages and to backorder the unfilled demand. This would allow the organization to in-crease the length of the inventory cycle and reduce the high inventory levels that may be necessary to avoid any shortage. Allowing for shortages is especially important when the per-unit cost of holding inventory is high. In the EOQ model that allows shortages, the tradeoffs between ordering costs, holding costs, and shortage costs must be considered. The only assumption relaxed in this model is assumption 4 in Section 15.3. No shortages are allowed.

The inventory model that allows shortages is shown in Figure 15.6. The inventory cycle has been divided into two periods: t_1 is the amount of time in which there is inventory available; t_2 is the amount of time during which there is a shortage. During the period t_2 units are backordered, and the back orders are filled when the next shipment arrives. Thus if Q is the order quantity and S is the shortage level, $Q - S$ is the maximum inventory level in this model. There is a cost associated with shortage, and we label the per-unit cost of shortage U. We note that this cost is also specified for a unit of time consistent with the specification of demand.

In the development of this model we must add a shortage cost component and modify the holding cost function. The model is developed as follows.

1. There is no change in the ordering cost component from the simple EOQ model of Section 15.3. It remains

$$\text{Ordering cost per unit of time} = K\left(\frac{D}{Q}\right)$$
$$(15.37)$$

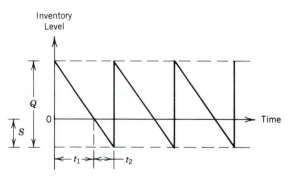

FIGURE 15.6 EOQ INVENTORY MODEL WITH SHORTAGES.

2. The holding cost is computed in the following way. From the figure it can be seen that inventory ranges from $Q - S$ to 0. Thus the average inventory level is $(Q - S)/2$ over the period of time when there are no shortages. Since the proportion of time when there is no shortage is given by $(Q - S)/Q$ and the average inventory level is $(Q - S)/2$, holding cost is computed as follows.

Holding cost per unit of time
$$= h((Q - S)/2)((Q - S)/Q)$$
$$= h(Q - S)^2/2Q \qquad (15.38)$$

3. The shortage cost is computed similarly. Again from the figure we can see that the shortage level ranges from 0 to S. Thus the average shortage level is $S/2$ over the period of time when there are shortages. Since the proportion of time when there is shortage is given by S/Q, shortage cost is computed as follows.

Shortage cost per unit of time
$$= U(S/2)(S/Q)$$
$$= US^2/2Q. \qquad (15.39)$$

4. Combining these individual costs we obtain the total cost function

Total inventory cost per unit of time
$$= K(D/Q) + h(Q - S)^2/2Q$$
$$+ US^2/2Q \qquad (15.40)$$

Figure 15.7 illustrates the relative behavior in the individual component cost and the total cost. In this model there are three individual component costs to consider, and there generally will not be a common point of intersection for these three cost functions. Thus an algebraic solution for Q^* cannot be derived, and differential calculus must be used to solve for both Q^* and S^*, the optimal maximum shortage level. Differential calculus can then be used to show that

$$Q^* = \sqrt{\frac{2KD}{h}\left(\frac{U + h}{U}\right)} \qquad (15.41)$$

and[3]

$$S^* = Q^*\left(\frac{h}{U + h}\right) \qquad (15.42)$$

To illustrate the use of this model consider the following example. Lift-All, Inc., produces 20-ton-capacity forklifts that are distributed directly to retailers. Lift-All purchases diesel engines for these forklifts and uses them to meet a demand that amounts to 2500 units per year. Since the engine mounting and installation is relatively simple, Lift-All will tolerate shortages of the engines. The per-unit shortage cost, however, is estimated to be $500 per year, while the per-unit holding cost is $200 per year. Also the cost of placing an order and receiving it is $3000 per order. The optimal order quantity for Lift-All is computed as follows.

$$Q^* = \sqrt{\frac{2KD}{h}\left(\frac{U + h}{U}\right)}$$
$$= \sqrt{\frac{2(3000)(2500)}{200}\left(\frac{500 + 200}{500}\right)}$$
$$= 324 \text{ engines per order} \qquad (15.43)$$

The maximum shortage level is

$$S^* = Q^*\left(\frac{h}{U + h}\right)$$
$$= 324\left(\frac{200}{500 + 200}\right)$$
$$= 92.6 \text{ engines} \qquad (15.44)$$

Using the optimal order quantity and the maximum shortage S^*, we can compute total inventory cost.

---

[3]In this case, the two partial derivatives $(\partial TC)/(\partial Q)$ and $(\partial TC)/(\partial S)$ are computed and set equal to zero

$$\frac{\partial TC}{\partial Q} = \frac{-KD}{Q^2} - \frac{h(Q - S)^2}{2Q^2} + \frac{h(Q - S)}{Q} - \frac{US^2}{2Q^2} = 0$$

$$\frac{\partial TC}{\partial S} = \frac{-h(Q - S)}{Q} + \frac{US}{Q} = 0$$

If these two equations are solved simultaneously, Eqs. (15.41) and (15.42) can be verified.

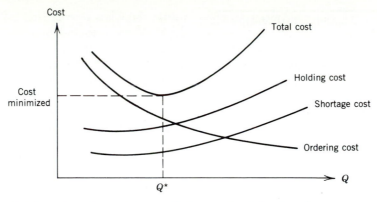

FIGURE 15.7 EOQ INVENTORY MODEL WITH SHORTAGES: COMPONENT COSTS.

Annual inventory cost

$$= K\left(\frac{D}{Q}\right) + h\frac{(Q-S)^2}{2Q} + U\frac{S^2}{2Q}$$

$$= 3000\left(\frac{2500}{324}\right) + 200\frac{(324-92.6)^2}{2(324)}$$

$$+ 500\frac{(92.6)^2}{2(324)}$$

$$= \$46{,}291 \qquad\qquad (15.45)$$

The maximum inventory is $Q - S = 231.4$ engines, while the total number of orders per year is $D/Q = 7.7$.

The time during which inventory exists in an inventory cycle, t_1, and the time during which there are shortages, t_2, are computed as follows.

$$t_1 = \frac{Q-S}{Q}\left(\frac{Q}{D}\right) = \frac{Q-S}{D}$$

$$= \frac{324-92.6}{2500}$$

$$= 0.09256 \text{ years}$$

$$\cong 33.8 \text{ days} \qquad\qquad (15.46)$$

$$t_2 = \left(\frac{S}{Q}\right)\left(\frac{Q}{D}\right) = \frac{S}{D}$$

$$= \frac{92.6}{2500}$$

$$= 0.03704 \text{ years}$$

$$\cong 13.5 \text{ days} \qquad\qquad (15.47)$$

Thus an inventory cycle lasts $33.8 + 13.5 = 47.3$ days.

15.7 QUANTITY DISCOUNTS

In this section we examine the use of the EOQ model in the situation where quantity discounts are offered. This section does not involve the relaxation of any of the assumptions of the economic order quantity model of Section 15.3. Quantity discounts occur when suppliers choose to provide incentives for the purchase of large quantities of a good. Quantity discounts are often reflected by lower unit costs on items purchased in larger lots.

In our discussion of the impact of quantity discounts, the total inventory cost function will be redefined to include the purchase price of all the units of the particular good or service. If we let the price per unit be denoted by C, CD represents the total purchase price of the item purchased in a given time period. Total inventory cost is then

$$\text{Total inventory cost per unit time}$$
$$= K(D/Q) + h(Q/2) + CD \qquad (15.48)$$

Since CD is independent of Q, the relationship between holding cost, ordering cost, and total cost is as illustrated in Figure 15.2. Thus the economic order quantity is given in (15.11):

$$Q^{\bullet} = \sqrt{\frac{2KD}{h}} \qquad\qquad (15.49)$$

To illustrate how quantity discounts can be analyzed, consider the carpet division illustration of Section 15.3. Here the carpet division can purchase

TABLE 15.1 QUANTITY DISCOUNT INFORMATION FOR THE CARPET DIVISION

DISCOUNT CLASS	ORDER SIZE	UNIT COST
1	0 to 7499	10.00
2	7500 to 9999	8.00
3	10,000 and over	7.50

carpet at the regular price of $10 a yard; at $8 a yard if 7500 yards or more are ordered at a time; or at $7.50 if 10000 or more yards are ordered at a time. This information is summarized in Table 15.1. Recall from Section 15.3 that the order cost, K, is $1000 and that the yearly demand, D, is 30,000 yards. Here we also account for the fact that a holding cost is a function of the price paid for an item in inventory. Suppose that the holding cost per unit per year is 10 percent of the unit price. Thus the per-unit holding costs for the classes in Table 15.1 are $1.00, $0.80, and $0.75 respectively.

Our first step in analyzing the impact of quantity discounts is to compute the economic order quantity, Q_1^*, for each class i. Using (15.48) we obtain the following

$$Q_1^* = \sqrt{\frac{2(1000)(30,000)}{1}} = 7746 \quad (15.50)$$

$$Q_2^* = \sqrt{\frac{2(1000)(30,000)}{0.8}} = 8660 \quad (15.51)$$

$$Q_3^* = \sqrt{\frac{2(1000)(30,000)}{0.75}} = 8944 \quad (15.52)$$

We observe that the purchase price of $10 is not applicable in this situation, since $Q_1^* = 7746 > 7500$. That is, if the economic order quantity is large enough to qualify for a discount, that discount will be accepted. Therefore, the Class 1 price can be automatically eliminated. Since $Q_2^* = 8660$ falls

within the Class 2 order size, taking advantage of the $8.00 price requires an order size of 8660 yards. Finally, we note that $Q_3^* = 8944 < 10,000$, and this order size does not qualify for the discount price of $7.50. The nearest order quantity that will allow for this price is 10,000 yards.

To complete the analysis we must compute the total cost of inventory for a year. We do this by evaluating the expression in (15.48). The information is summarized in Table 15.2. It is easy to see that the optimal decision is to place orders of 10,000 yards of carpet three times a year. It should again be noted that quantity discounts affect not only the purchase price of the inventory, but the per-unit holding costs are also impacted. By calculating the optimal order quantity necessary to take advantage of each discount level and using these order quantities to calculate total inventory cost (including the purchase price of inventory), it is possible to find the best order quantity when there are many quantity discount classes.

15.8 SENSITIVITY ANALYSIS AND THE EOQ MODEL

Like the linear programming model, the EOQ model is a deterministic model and the assumption was made that the holding cost, the ordering cost, and the demand are all known with certainty. Even though a great deal of effort is expended in determining the values of these parameters, however, they are at best good estimates. We now examine the impact on the optimal order quantity and total cost if the actual parameters differ from the estimated values of these parameters. The sensitivity analysis briefly discussed here differs from that employed in linear programming in that the simultaneous effect of changing several parameters is evaluated.

Recall from Section 15.3 that the economic

TABLE 15.2 TOTAL ANNUAL COST COMPARISONS FOR THE CARPET DIVISION

DISCOUNT CLASS	UNIT COST ($)	ORDER QUANTITY	ORDER COST ($)	HOLDING COST ($)	PURCHASE COST ($)	TOTAL ANNUAL COST
1	10	7746	—	Not relevant	—	
2	8	8660	3464	3464	240,000	246,928
3	7.5	10,000	3000	3750	225,000	231,750

order quantity Q^* is expressed as follows

$$Q^* = \sqrt{\frac{2KD}{h}} \qquad (15.53)$$

We assume that K, D, h are the estimated parameters and that K^a, D^a, h^a represent the *actual* values of these parameters. The true optimal economic order quantity is given in (15.54), while the estimated economic order quantity is given in (15.53).

$$Q^a = \sqrt{\frac{2K^aD^a}{h^a}} \qquad (15.54)$$

Define r as the ratio of the actual to estimated EOQ, and then

$$r = \frac{Q^a}{Q^*} = \frac{\sqrt{2K^aD^a/h^a}}{\sqrt{2KD/h}}$$

$$= \sqrt{\left(\frac{D^a}{D}\right)\left(\frac{K^a}{K}\right)\left(\frac{h}{h^a}\right)} \qquad (15.55)$$

To illustrate the use of (15.55), suppose that the estimated parameters for the simple EOQ model are $K = 1000$, $D = 30,000$, and $h = 2$. The demand, however, is actually 35,000. Then

$$r = \frac{Q^a}{Q^*} = \sqrt{\left(\frac{35,000}{30,000}\right)(1)(1)}$$

$$= 1.08 \qquad (15.56)$$

The result is interpreted in the following way. If demand is underestimated by 14.3 percent $(35,000 - 30,000)/30,000$, then the economic order quantity is underestimated by approximately 7.4 percent since

$$\left(\frac{Q^*}{Q^a} = \frac{1}{1.08}\right)$$

To verify this we note that $Q^* = 5477$ and thus,

$$Q^a = 1.08(Q^*)$$
$$= 1.08(5477)$$
$$= 5915, \quad \text{and} \quad \frac{5915 - 5477}{5915} = 0.074. \qquad (15.57)$$

On the other hand, suppose that $D^a = 35,000$,

$K^a = 800$, and $h^a = 2.5$. Then

$$r = \frac{Q^a}{Q^*} = \sqrt{\left(\frac{35,000}{30,000}\right)\left(\frac{800}{1000}\right)\left(\frac{2}{2.5}\right)}$$
$$= \sqrt{0.74667}$$
$$= 0.864 \qquad (15.58)$$

In this case, a simultaneous 14.3 percent underestimate of demand, a 25 percent overestimate of ordering cost, and a 20 percent underestimate of holding cost results in approximately a 15.7 percent overestimate in the economic order quantity.

Up to this point we have evaluated the impact of error on the economic order quantity. The critical impact is generally considered to be the effect on the total cost. For the simple EOQ model the minimal cost is

$$TC = K(D/Q^*) + h(Q^*/2) \qquad (15.59)$$

We assume that the estimated order quantity, Q^*, is implemented rather than the actual optimal order quantity Q^a, which is based on the real input parameters K^a, D^a, and h^a. The incurred total cost, TC^i, would then be

$$TC^i = K^a(D^a/Q^*) + h^a(Q^*/2) \qquad (15.60)$$

Since $r = Q^a/Q^*$ and $Q^* = Q^a/r$, the incurred total cost can be written as follows.

$$TC^i = \frac{K^a(D^a)(r)}{Q^a} + \frac{h^aQ^a}{2r} \qquad (15.61)$$

Substituting for Q^a in (15.61), we obtain the following expression.

$$TC^i = \frac{K^a(D^a)(r)}{\sqrt{\frac{2K^aD^a}{h^a}}} + \frac{h^a\sqrt{\frac{2K^aD^a}{h^a}}}{2r} \qquad (15.62)$$

Rewriting this expression, we obtain the following

$$TC^i = r\sqrt{\frac{K^aD^ah^a}{2}} + \frac{\sqrt{2K^aD^ah^a}}{2r}$$
$$= (r/2 + 1/2r)\sqrt{2K^aD^ah^a}$$
$$= \frac{1}{2}(r + 1/r)\sqrt{2K^aD^ah^a} \qquad (15.63)$$

At the same time we observe that the optimal total cost, TC^*, can be written as follows.

$$
\begin{aligned}
TC^* &= K^a(D^a/Q^a) + h^a(Q^a/2) \\
&= K^a\left(\frac{D^a}{\sqrt{2K^aD^a/h^a}}\right) + h^a\frac{\sqrt{2K^aD^a/h^a}}{2} \\
&= \frac{2K^aD^a + h^a(\sqrt{2K^aD^a/h^a})^2}{2\sqrt{2K^aD^a/h^a}} \\
&= \frac{2K^aD^a}{\sqrt{2K^aD^a/h^a}} = \frac{\sqrt{(2K^aD^a)^2}}{\sqrt{2K^aD^a/h^a}} \\
&= \sqrt{2K^aD^ah^a}
\end{aligned}
\tag{15.64}
$$

Therefore from (15.63) we observe that actual total cost is defined as

$$
TC^i = \left(\frac{r + 1/r}{2}\right)TC^* \tag{15.65}
$$

and

$$
\frac{TC^i}{TC^*} = \frac{r + 1/r}{2} \tag{15.66}
$$

To illustrate the relationship described in (15.66) suppose that the optimal order quantity is 5477 yards of carpet per order and we actually order 4732 yards. Then $r = Q^a/Q^* = 4732/5477 = 0.864$ and

$$
\frac{TC^i}{TC^*} = \frac{0.864 + 1/0.864}{2} = 1.01 \tag{15.67}
$$

Thus if the implemented order quantity is 13.6 percent less than the optimal order quantity, the impact on total cost is a mere 1 percent increase. In Table 15.3 we present the impact of total cost for a variety

TABLE 15.3 SENSITIVITY TO TOTAL COST

r	$\dfrac{r + 1/r}{2}$
0.50	1.25
0.75	1.04
0.84	1.01
0.90	1.006
1.11	1.006
1.19	1.01
1.33	1.04
2.00	1.25

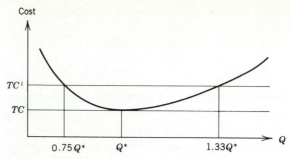

FIGURE 15.8 TOTAL COST CURVE: CHANGE IN ORDER QUANTITY.

of values for r. This table illustrates the relative insensitivity of total cost to the implementation of nonoptimal order quantities. We observe also that an order quantity 25 percent less than the optimal order quantity and an order quantity approximately 33 percent greater than the optimal order quantity both result in 4 percent increases in costs. This property is also illustrated in Figure 15.8. Fortunately, the results presented in Table 15.3 and supported by this figure are typical. The EOQ model is insensitive to small variations of error in the cost and demand estimates. This property provides for flexibility in the implementation of the results of the model.

15.9 MATERIAL REQUIREMENTS PLANNING

In the models discussed in the previous sections of this chapter we focus on what are often called *independent-demand* inventories. Many kinds of organizations maintain independent-demand inventories: wholesale distributors, retail businesses, auto repair businesses, hospitals, restaurants, and the like. On the other hand, manufacturing companies must manage what are often called *dependent-demand* inventories. Demand for a given item is said to be dependent if the inventory item is to become a part of another item. These dependent inventory items or *components* become part of what is called a *parent* item. Dependent-demand items are usually consumed within a production system itself, while independent-demand items are controlled by a demand external to the organization. An independent-demand item has no identifiable parent item within the organization that is maintaining the inventory.

The role of a dependent-demand inventory item

is more complex than that of an independent-demand inventory item. The purpose of an independent-demand inventory is simply to meet customer demand. The primary function of a dependent-demand inventory is to assure that the demand for the finished good can be met. To do this the demand for the finished good must be translated into detailed inventory requirements for the components that are used in the production process.

One of the most important techniques developed to deal with the unique problems of dependent-demand inventories or manufacturing inventories is called *material requirements planning* (MRP). The *master production schedule* is the key component in the use of an MRP system. The master production schedule is simply a schedule of when and how many units of a finished good are to be produced. After a master production schedule has been determined, it is then possible to determine the production requirements of individual components. These production requirements constitute the *bill of materials*. The bill of materials is a parts list that conforms to the actual manufacturing process and shows how each good is actually manufactured. We next consider a production situation for which the MRP approach to inventory control is appropriate. This simple example is used to illustrate the basic approach used in an MRP system.

Exerite Manufacturing produces exercise bikes. To assemble the final product Exerite needs wheel assembly units, frames, and accessory packages. The production of the wheel assembly units first uses the gear mechanism, and then the gear mechanism is used to construct the wheel, which in turn is used to construct the wheel assembly unit. Figure 15.9 displays the partial list of requirements described earlier and indicates the dependencies involved.

Suppose that the master production schedule calls for the final assembly of 4000 exercise bikes by the end of a 75 workday production period. This means that the frames, the wheel assembly units, and the accessory packages must be available so that assembly can be completed in this time frame. We assume the final assembly requires 10 workdays and concentrate initially on the production and inventory for the wheel assembly units. Table 15.4 gives the number of units in current inventory.

The initial question that must be answered deals with how many units of each component will be required to fill the demand of 4000 units. An answer

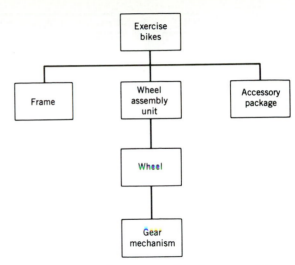

FIGURE 15.9   PARITAL BILL OF MATERIALS FOR THE EXERCISE BIKE.

to this question that ignores the dependency of inventory items is given in Table 15.5. The calculations ignore the important facts that 1400 wheels are already installed in the wheel assembly units and that 600 gear mechanism units are already part of the wheel. Accounting for these facts, which were ignored in the calculations of Table 15.5, the MRP analysis would proceed as follows.

Exercise bikes to be assembled—4000;
Total requirement for wheel assembly units—4000;
Wheel assembly units in inventory—1400;
Additional wheel assembly units required—2600.

Since each wheel assembly unit requires a wheel

Total requirement for wheels—2600;
Wheels in inventory— 600;
Additional wheels required—2000.

Also since each additional wheel requires a gear

TABLE 15.4   INVENTORY ON HAND FOR EXERITE

COMPONENT	UNITS IN INVENTORY
Wheel assembly unit	1400
Wheel	600
Gear mechanism	800

TABLE 15.5 ADDITIONAL COMPONENT REQUIREMENTS: DEPENDENCY IGNORED

COMPONENT	NUMBER OF UNITS NEEDED	NUMBER IN INVENTORY	ADDITIONAL REQUIRMENT
Wheel assembly unit	4000	1400	2600
Wheel	4000	600	3400
Gear mechanism	4000	800	3200

TABLE 15.6 ACCOUNTING FOR DEPENDENCY IN EXERITE MANUFACTURING

COMPONENT	ADDITIONAL REQUIREMENTS: DEPENDENCY IGNORED	ADDITIONAL REQUIREMENTS: DEPENDENCY INCORPORATED
Wheel assembly unit	2600	2600
Wheel	3400	2000
Gear mechanism	3200	1200

TABLE 15.7 LEAD TIMES FOR PRODUCTION OF WHEEL ASSEMBLY UNITS

COMPONENT	ADDITIONAL REQUIREMENTS	LEAD TIME (DAYS)
Wheel assembly unit	2600	10
Wheel	2000	5
Gear mechanism	1200	25

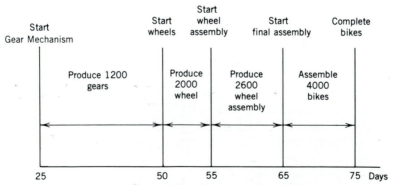

FIGURE 15.10 TIME PHASING FOR EXERITE MANUFACTURING.

TABLE 15.8 PLANNED ORDER RELEASES FOR EXERITE MANUFACTURING

EXERCISE BIKES

DAY	20	25	30	35	40	45	50	55	60	65	70	75	80
Total requirements												4000	
Inventory												4000	0
Net requirements												4000	
Planned order release										4000			

WHEEL ASSEMBLY UNIT

DAY	20	25	30	35	40	45	50	55	60	65	70	75	80
Total requirements										4000			
Inventory	1400	1400	1400	1400	1400	1400	1400	1400	1400	1400	0	0	0
Net requirements										2600			
Planned order release								2600					

WHEEL

DAY	20	25	30	35	40	45	50	55	60	65	70	75	80
Total requirements								2600					
Inventory	600	600	600	600	600	600	600	600	0	0	0	0	0
Net requirements								2000					
Planned order release							2000						

GEAR MECHANISM

DAY	20	25	30	35	40	45	50	55	60	65	70	75	80
Total requirements							2000						
Inventory	800	800	800	800	800	800	800	0	0	0	0	0	0
Net requirements							1200						
Planned order release		1200											

mechanism

Total requirement for gear mechanisms—2000;
Gear mechanisms in inventory— 800;
Additional gear mechanisms required—1200.

The MRP approach uses the dependent demand information to provide a list of additional component requirements that lead to lower inventory levels and thus lower inventory charges. Table 15.6 shows the improvement when the MRP approach is utilized.

The determination of net requirements for components is only part of the MRP approach. Additionally, MRP determines when these requirements are needed. MRP deals with this problem by using a procedure called *time phasing*. Time phasing allows an organization to determine specific points in time when component manufacturing must begin. Table 15.7 gives the amount of time it will take to produce the given components.

The information in Table 15.7, the fact that the final assembly of 4000 exercise bikes requires 10 working days, and the information on current inventory, allow us to detail the production requirements and the production schedule in Table 15.8. This table lists the total number of units required at points in time, the inventory level, net requirements, and the number of units ordered at a point in time (planned order release). The order releases are traced in the table and represented in Figure 15.10. This process is often called *time-phasing*. We see that if there were no other considerations, production would not have to begin until 25 days of the production period have passed. It should be understood that if MRP was actually used to produce exercise bikes, many more components would likely be identified. This would, of course, complicate the net requirements calculations as well as the time phasing aspect of MRP.

Through this simple example we hope to show the conceptual simplicity of the MRP approach. Nonetheless, it is not difficult to imagine the volume of calculations that must be performed to apply MRP in actual manufacturing situations where individual components can be used in many final products. Current computer technology does allow us to handle these massive calculations and permits MRP to provide a viable approach to inventory control involving dependent-demand items. Fortunately, there are a number of software companies that offer commercial MRP packages that have lead to the successful application of the MRP approach to inventory control. Again it should be emphasized that we have only provided the basic concepts of MRP in our discussion. A more complete discussion may be found in *Material Requirements Planning* by Joseph Orlicky (McGraw–Hill, 1975).

15.10 SUMMARY

In this chapter the basic deterministic model in inventory analysis, the EOQ model, was presented. In all the models presented we assumed that demand was known with certainty and was constant over time. Initially the simple EOQ model was presented and its assumptions discussed. As those individual assumptions were relaxed we were able to develop models that are more realistic in certain situations. The modifications lead to the discussion of nonzero lead time, continuous rather than batch replacement, shortages, and quantity discounts. We also recognized that the input parameters to the basic EOQ model were, at best, good estimates and discussed the sensitivity of the model output to deviations of the input parameter values. Finally, we distinguished between independent-demand inventory and dependent-demand inventories. The basic concepts involved in material requirements planning were also presented. MRP provides one popular approach in controlling dependent-demand inventories.

In the next chapter we relax the most basic of the EOQ model assumptions and attempt to deal explicitly with the reality of uncertain demand. Even with the strong assumptions we should note before proceeding that these models have been and continue to be very useful in the development of rational inventory policy.

GLOSSARY

Backordering The practice of accepting an order for items not in inventory and filling that order when the items become available.

Bill of Material   A sequential list of all the components that go into a finished product.

Cycle   The period of time between the placement of two consecutive orders.

Dependent-Demand Item   Items that are usually consumed within the production system itself.

Deterministic Inventory Model   Inventory models that assume demand is known with certainty and is constant over time.

Economic Order Quantity (EOQ)   The amount of an item that is produced or ordered in a single item model so that total inventory cost is minimized. (Also called economic lot size.)

Holding (Storage Cost)   The cost associated with maintaining an inventory until it is used or sold.

Independent-Demand Item   Items controlled by demand external to the organization, or items with no identifiable parent item.

Inventory   An economic resource that is held by an organization at a given point of time.

Inventory Models   Models associated with the maintenance and control of inventory in an organization.

Lead Time   The elapsed time between the placement of an order and the receipt of an order.

Master Production Schedule   A detailed schedule that shows how many units of each product are to be produced and when they should be produced.

Material Requirements Planning   A inventory control system that deals with production control and inventory control simultaneously.

Ordering Cost (Setup Cost)   The cost associated with placing an order.

Order Point System   An inventory system in which a perpetual inventory record is maintained. Replenishment orders are placed when the inventory drops below a prespecified reorder point.

Periodic Review Inventory System   An inventory system in which inventory levels are checked at specified points in time. Replenishment orders are placed at these times, if necessary.

Production Lot Size Model   A modification of the EOQ model that allows for the uniform (continuous) replenishment of inventory.

Production (Purchase) Costs   The cost associated with manufacturing or purchasing replenishment inventory.

Quantity Discounts   A discount on the total purchase price used to induce the purchase or order of large quantities of an item.

Reorder Point   The inventory level at which a replenishment order is placed in an order point inventory system.

Stochastic Inventory Model A model in which demand is not known with certainty and is described with an appropriate probability distribution.

Stockout (Shortage) Cost The cost that occurs when the demand for an item exceeds its supply.

Time Phasing A procedure used to determine specific points in time when component manufacturing must begin.

Selected References

Buffa, E.S., and W.H. Taubert. 1972 *Production—Inventory Systems: Planning and Control.* Homewood, Ill.: Irwin.

Dilworth, J.B. 1983 *Production and Operations Management.* New York: Random House.

Greene, J.H. 1974. *Production and Inventory Control.* Homewood, Ill.: Irwin.

Hadley, G., and T.M. Whitin. 1963. *Analysis of Inventory Systems.* Englewood Cliffs, N.J.: Prentice-Hall.

Hillier, F., and G.J. Lieberman. 1980. *Introduction to Operations Research.* 3rd ed. San Francisco: Holden-Day.

Holt, C.C., I. Modigliani, J.F. Muth, and H.A. Simon. 1960. *Production Planning, Inventories, and Work Force.* Englewood Cliffs, N.J.: Prentice-Hall.

Johnson, L.A., and D.C. Montgomery. 1974. *Operations Research in Production Planning, Scheduling, and Inventory Control.* New York: Wiley.

Orlicky, J.A. 1975. *Material Requirement Planning.* New York: McGraw-Hill.

Starr, M.K. and D.W. Miller. 1962. *Inventory Control: Theory and Practice.* Englewood Cliffs, N.J.: Prentice-Hall.

Trueman, R.E. 1974. *An Introduction to Quantitative Methods for Decision Making.* Chicago, Ill.: Holt, Rinehart & Winston.

Wagner, H.M. 1962. *Statistical Management of Inventory Systems.* New York: Wiley.

Whitin, T.M. 1957. *The Theory of Inventory Management.* Princeton, N.J.: Princeton Univ. Press.

Discussion Questions

1. Identify the major functions of inventory.

2. What is the "opportunity cost" of inventory.

3. What is the difference between an order point inventory system and a periodic review inventory system in terms of the order quantity, if we assume that demand is constant and uniform over time?

4. List and discuss each of the assumptions of the basic EOQ model.

5. Define the length of an inventory cycle in terms of the economic order quantity.

6. What are the common cost factors in inventory analysis? Discuss the cost tradeoff between these factors.

7. Discuss the differences between the basic EOQ model and the production lot size model. How do the assumptions between these models differ? How do the maximum inventory levels differ?

8. What is the impact of a replenishment rate that is less than the demand rate in the production lot size model?

9. Discuss the differences between the basic EOQ model and the EOQ model with shortages. How do the assumptions between these models differ? How do the maximum inventory levels differ?

10. How are deterministic lead times handled for inventory models with deterministic demand?

11. Describe the difference in the cost function when quantity discounts are evaluated.

12. What are the benefits of sensitivity analysis involving deterministic inventory models?

13. To what type of production planning and scheduling situation is material requirements planning (MRP) applicable?

14. Distinguish between independent-demand and dependent-demand environments.

PROBLEMS

1. Given the following annual demand, annual carrying cost, and cost per order, compute the economic order quantity, the total annual minimum cost, and the length of an inventory cycle.

$$D = 32,000 \text{ units per year}$$
$$K = \$500 \text{ per order}$$
$$h = \$0.35 \text{ per unit per year}$$

2. Given the following annual demand, monthly carrying cost, and cost per order, compute the economic order quantity, the total annual minimum cost, and the length of the inventory cycle.

$$D = 115,000 \text{ units per year}$$
$$K = \$2,100 \text{ per order}$$
$$h = 0.25 \text{ per unit per month}$$

3. L. Jones Department Store experiences an annual demand of 9000 supersoft pillows. The fixed cost associated with placing an order is $200, and it costs $3 a year to hold a pillow in inventory. Compute the economic order quantity, the minimum total annual inventory cost, the optimal number of orders per year, and the optimal time between orders.

4. Provide a schematic representation of the inventory system in Problem 3.

5. Sharky Tools utilizes 20,000 1/4-horsepower electric motors per year. Every time an order is placed, Sharky pays $750 plus $35 a motor. Also it costs $3.25 to hold a motor in inventory for a year. Compute the economic order quantity, the optimal number of orders per year, and the optimal time between orders.

6. Suppose it takes 30 days for an order of electric motors to arrive. What is the reorder point for Sharky Tools? Illustrate the order times in a schematic representation of the inventory system for Problem 5.

7. Suppose it takes 60 days for an order of electric motors to arrive. What is the reorder point for Sharky Tools? Illustrate the order times in a schematic representation of the inventory system for Problem 5.

8. For the production lot size model the production (replenishment) rate per year, the demand per year, the order cost, and the holding cost per year are given. Compute the economic order quantity and the minimum total cost for this situation.

$$D = 50,000 \text{ units per year}$$
$$p = 80,000 \text{ units per year}$$
$$K = \$900 \text{ per order}$$
$$h = \$0.75 \text{ per unit per year}$$

9. In Problem 8 what is the length of the inventory cycle (in days)? In a given inventory cycle compute the number of days during which the inventory is being replenished. What is the maximum inventory? What is the minimum inventory level? Provide a schematic representation of this inventory system.

10. Happy Day Pharmaceuticals produces a popular diet pill. The demand for this product is 5000 cases per month. The setup cost associated with the production of this type of pill is $15,000, and it costs $2 a month to hold a case of diet pills in inventory. Production is limited to 10,000 cases of pills per month. Compute

   a. the optimal production lot size;
   b. the number of days per month when production occurs;
   c. the maximum inventory level.

11. The Ultra Dark Brewery produces Black Swamp Beer, stores it in a warehouse, and supplies it to regional distributors as it is needed. Since all the equipment must be sanitized after producing a batch of Black Swamp, there is a fixed cost of $12,500 assessed to each production run. The cost of holding a case of beer in inventory for a year is $2.50, the demand for Black Swamp is 2000 cases per day, and the production capacity is 5000 cases per day. Compute

   a. the optimal number of cases to produce in a production run;
   b. the number of days per inventory cycle when production occurs;
   c. the maximum inventory level.

12. Compute the optimal order quantity and the minimum annual inventory cost for an inventory system that permits shortages. Given

is the yearly demand, the order cost, the holding cost per year, and the shortage cost per year.

$$D = 15,000 \text{ units per year}$$

$$K = \$800 \text{ per order}$$

$$h = \$5 \text{ per unit per year}$$

$$U = \$8 \text{ per unit per year}$$

13. Provide a schematic representation of the inventory system described in Problem 12. Indicate the maximum inventory level and the maximum shortage.

14. The True Test Hardware chain experiences an annual demand of 2500 for a particular type of freezer, the Quick Freeze. True Test feels that it must allow for the possibility of a stockout for this item, but realizes that the cost of backordering is about $100 a unit per year. The cost of holding the Quick Freeze in inventory for a year is $30, and the cost of placing an order for this item is only $25 per order. How many freezers will be backordered per inventory cycle if total inventory cost is minimized. What is the maximum amount of time a customer will have to wait for a freezer?

15. Assume that the following quantity discount schedule is appropriate.

ORDER SIZE (UNITS)	DISCOUNT (%)	UNIT COST ($)
0–50	0	100
51–150	5	95
151–∞	10	90

Suppose that the annual demand for the product being considered is 500 units, the ordering cost is $100 per order, and the inventory holding cost per year is 25 percent of the unit cost of the product. Compute the economic order quantity.

16. A local paint retailer is attempting to determine how paint should be ordered. The retailer experiences an annual demand of 10,000 gallons. If the retailer orders the paint by the case, it costs $8.00 per gallon, but if he orders by the truck (1000 gallons or more), the cost is $5.50 per gallon. The annual holding cost is 30 percent of the purchase price and it costs $50 to place an order. Should the dealer buy a truck load?

17. Cycle-Rite distributes competition bicycles. If they order 25 of fewer bicycles from the manufacturer, the cost is $575. If between 26 and 100 are ordered, there is a 15 percent discount, and if 100 or more are ordered, a 25 percent discount is given. The annual demand

experienced by Cycle-Rite is 450. It costs $45 to place an order, and the holding cost per unit is 25 percent of the purchase price. Compute the economic order quantity.

18. In Problem 1 the values for D, K, and h are estimated parameter values. Demand was incorrectly estimated, however, and has an actual value of 35,000. Compute the percentage error in the implemented economic order quantity.

19. In problem 2 the values for D, K, and h are estimated parameter values. All these parameters have been incorrectly estimated, however. The actual values are: $D = 120,000$, $K = \$1500$, and $h = 0.40$. Compute the percentage error in the implemented economic order quantity.

20. In problem 3, L. Jones incorrectly estimated demand. The actual demand is 10,000 supersoft pillows. Compute the percentage error in estimated *total cost* caused by the use of this incorrect value of demand.

21. For the Exerite Manufacturing example of Section 15.9, suppose that the beginning inventory levels for wheel assembly units, wheels, and gear mechanism units are 1600, 800, and 1000, respectively. Assuming demand for Exercise Bikes is 5000, determine the net requirements for the wheel assembly unit.

22. In Problem 21 assume a 75-day production period when 5000 Exercise Bikes can be assembled in 15 work days. Also assume that 100 gear mechanism units, 200 wheels, and 170 wheel assembly units can be produced per day. Present the relevant production schedule for Exerite Manufacturing.

Application Review

MRP Implementation: The Ajax Company Solution

MRP (material requirements planning) and other computerized production and inventory management systems are widely used in manufacturing operations. Implementation of computerized systems is not easy, since a variety of complex technical and behavioral problems must be managed. The Ajax Company is a producer of electric and gasoline chain saws, power tools, and other heavy-duty construction finishing equipment. The management of Ajax realized the need of an MRP system because of growing problems in scheduling and cost and quality control. Management also correctly perceived that the implementation of a MRP system required broad preparation. To facilitate implementation a task force consisting of three experienced people was formed. The task force had the responsibility

Source: Satish Mehra and M. Jerry Reid, "MRP implementation using an action plan," *Interfaces* (February 1982), Vol. 12, No. 1, pp. 69–73.

of developing a procedure that would result in the successful implementation of the proposed MRP system over a time period of two to three years.

As a first step, the task force identified the areas in the company that would be impacted most by the MRP system. The following areas were identified as being significantly related to the implementation of the proposed system

1. organization;
2. specific inventory function;
3. purchasing;
4. forecasting;
5. scheduling;
6. engineering changes.

The inventory process was reviewed carefully. Definitions of excess, obsolete, usable, and scrap items were evaluated. The areas of record maintenance and accuracy as well as the procedure for material disbursement from the warehouse were also examined. At the same time, the needs of an inventory control education and training program were established. The task force also determined that

1. there was no systematic procedure to revise/update lead times, and thus unnecessary and excessive exception reporting took place;
2. there was no continuous monitoring program for vendor performance or vendor-buyer relations;
3. there was no document outlining, well-defined objectives, and requirements of the forecasting system, and this was creating problems in the scheduling area;
4. problems of coordination were discovered to be acute and there was a need for an engineering change coordinator.

Having identified the areas to be impacted by the implementation of the MRP system, the task force developed an action plan.

During the development of the action plan, the task force also attempted to address the views of those to be directly involved in the operation of the proposed system. Thus a direct attempt was made to avoid any behavioral or personnel problems.

The action plan consisted of 19 activities and is summarized in Figure 15.11. For each activity estimated time duration, sequential information, and the overlapping of activities was incorporated. Completion of the 19 action assignments resulted in a smooth implementation of the MRP system for the Ajax Company. It took Ajax approximately two years for the entire 14-period implementation process. It should be noted that the action plan was broken into many more activities with specific individuals, departments, and committees identified with specific responsibilities.

ACTION ASSIGNMENTS	PERIOD													
	1	2	3	4	5	6	7	8	9	10	11	12	13	14
1(a) Evaluate existing manufacturing staff in terms of being able to understand, implement, and enforce modern MRP and inventory management systems	····													
1(b) Make staffing changes as required		··												
2(a) Evaluate the organizational structure to guarantee proper alignment for execution of MRP responsibilities	····													
2(b) Make organizational changes as required		··												
3(a) Consider changing reporting procedures of movement (material handlers) in the shop. Analyze their reporting vis-a-vis material control	····													
3(b) If appropriate, act on that decision		··												
4(a) Define objectives, duties, responsibilities and staffing requirements of inventory control section		····												
4(b) Select inventory control section			····											
5(a) Review excess, obsolete, and usable inventory definitions	····	····												
5(b) Determine schedule to scrap or identify nonusable inventory		····	····		····									
6. Guarantee inventory accuracy	····	····	····	····										
7(a) Identify all manual recordkeeping functions		····	····											
7(b) Eliminate manual records and enforce use of computer inventory records				····	····									
8(a) Select inventory control education and training coordinator		··												
8(b) Establish inventory control education and training program and schedule		····	····											
8(c) Audit results of education and training (test, performance)			·	····	····	····	····	····	····	····	····	····	····	····
9. Establish material location policy and procedure		····												

10. Enforce discipline with employees that disregard procedures relative to inventory control

11(a) Establish schedule to review and update lead times

11(b) Update lead times

12(a) Establish vendor performance

12(b) Implement and maintain program

13. Review blanket order practice and establish alternate procedure

14. Identify part usage information to be maintained

15(a) Select sales forecast project team

15(b) Define sales forecast objective and requirements

15(c) Develop sales forecast system

15(d) Implement and audit sales forecast system

16(a) Review possibility of maintaining a "stabilization stock" of finished goods inventory

16(b) Determine total investment and operating philosophy concerning finished goods inventory

16(c) Build "stabilization stock"

17(a) Establish schedule and program to review and update shop routings, machine center capacities, and labor standards

17(b) Implement schedule and audit results

18(a) Form a production scheduling project team

18(b) Define production scheduling objectives and requirements

18(c) Develop manual production scheduling system

18(d) Implement and audit manual production scheduling system

19(a) Define duties and responsibilities of the engineering change notice coordinator

19(b) Select change coordinator

FIGURE 15.11 THE ACTION PLAN.

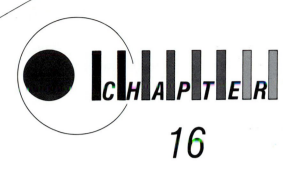

CHAPTER 16

INVENTORY ANALYSIS: PROBABILISTIC MODELS

16.1 INTRODUCTION

It is likely that there is uncertainty in the demand for a given product or service, in the amount of time required for an order to be processed and delivered, and in the production time or time needed to provide a service. In fact, there is uncertainty associated with practically every aspect of a production and distribution system. Although uncertainty was not incorporated into the models of Chapter 15, it was considered indirectly via sensitivity analysis. Recall that sensitivity analysis assesses the impact on changes in the model assumptions on the model solution or the implied decision.

This chapter deals with uncertainty more explicitly. Models are considered that directly incorporate a probability distribution for demand during lead time. Even when a probability distribution for demand is assumed, the two basic decisions presented in the previous chapter are still the important ones: When should an order be placed, and how much should be ordered? If demand is uncertain, however, stockouts may occur when a reorder point is specified. To avoid stockouts under demand uncertainty, a buffer inventory called a safety stock is often used. The EOQ model combined with the concept of a safety stock is discussed in the following section.

16.2 EOQ WITH SAFETY STOCK: A DISCRETE DISTRIBUTION FOR DEMAND DURING LEAD TIME

Certainly if inventory replenishment was instantaneous, and demand was stochastic, stockouts could always be avoided by ordering when inventory levels fall to zero. When the lead time is not zero, we must deal with the behavior of demand during lead time. Recall that lead time is the amount of time between the placement of the order and the receipt of the order, and the reorder point was defined to be the level of inventory remaining in stock that is equal to the deterministic demand during lead time. When demand is known with uncertainty, inventory is depleted to zero when the order arrives. When demand is not known with certainty, a stockout may very well occur before the order arrives.

In an attempt to avoid stockouts, an "extra" inventory often referred to as a *safety stock* is maintained. Figure 16.1 illustrates the inventory behavior when demand is uncertain. In the first cycle demand is less than the reorder point during lead time, and thus inventory at the beginning of the second inventory cycle exceeds Q. During the second inventory cycle a stockout occurs, since demand exceeds the reorder point during lead time. With the maintenance of a safety stock, it will generally be possible to meet demand even though demand exceeds the reorder point during lead time. Figure 16.2 illustrates this situation. The basic difference here is that even though demand exceeds the reorder point during lead time, a shortage does not occur.

In many ways the safety stock really does not affect the calculation of the reorder point, it simply increments the reorder point provided by the simple EOQ model by the amount of the safety stock. Our goal is still to avoid the utilization of the safety stock, but we realize that it is likely that some of the safety stock will be used at least once in the planning horizon; otherwise, there would be little value in maintaining a safety stock. Let SS be used to denote the safety stock level.

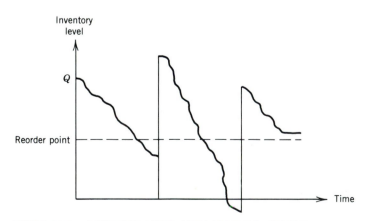

FIGURE 16.1 INVENTORY MODEL WITH UNCERTAIN DEMAND.

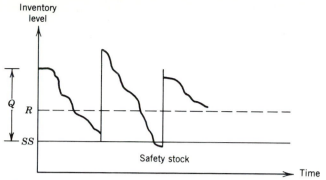

FIGURE 16.2   INVENTORY MODEL WITH SAFETY STOCK (*SS*).

What we analyze next is the relationship between the cost of a safety stock and the cost of the shortage that can be avoided with a given level of a safety stock. As noted in Figure 16.2, in some inventory cycles there will be more available inventory (other than safety stock) than is required. In other inventory cycles, units from the safety stock will be required to meet demand. In this analysis we set a reorder point that is equal to expected demand during lead time. Thus if actual demand is less than expected demand during lead time, the initial inventory level when an order arrives may be greater than $SS + Q$ (see Figure 16.2). On the other hand, if actual demand during lead time is greater than expected demand during lead time, the initial inventory level when an order arrives may be less than $SS + Q$. Since the reorder point is set to be the expected demand during lead time, it follows that unused inventory in some inventory cycles and safety stock required in other inventory cycles average out over an extended time horizon. This fact leads to the assumption that the average safety stock is equal to the initial number of units held as safety stock. Thus if SS is used to denote this level of safety stock, the total carrying cost of safety stock per unit time is $h(SS)$. In the example that follows, we examine the tradeoff between the carrying cost for safety stock and the stockout or shortage cost.

ABC Chemical uses a particular toxic waste product to produce an industrial strength cleaner. The demand for this cleaner is not known with certainty but can be described by a discrete probability distribution. The following is a probability distribution for the demand during lead time. Since the toxic waste is both expensive to handle and store, the ordering cost is estimated to be $2000 and the holding cost is estimated to be $8 per gallon per

DEMAND DURING LEAD TIME (GAL)	PROBABILITY
1000	.10
1500	.30
2000	.20
2500	.30
3000	.10

year. Shutting down the production process because of the unavailability of this toxic waste is very expensive and the associated shortage cost, S, is estimated to be $12 per gallon short. Note that the shortage cost is per unit, not per unit time. No back orders are permitted, and average annual demand is estimated to be 18,000 gallons. Lead time is approximately six weeks.

If we ignore the stochastic nature of demand and calculate the economic order quantity (no shortages, zero lead time), the results are as follows

$$Q^* = \sqrt{\frac{2KD}{h}}$$

$$= \sqrt{\frac{2(2000)(18000)}{8}}$$

$$= 3000 \text{ gallons per order} \qquad (16.1)$$

The number of orders placed per year would be $D/Q = 18,000/3000 = 6$ and the inventory cycle would be of length 2 months. If demand during lead time is known with certainty and is 2000 gallons, the reorder point would be 2000 gallons, and at that time an order would be placed for 3000 gallons. If demand was indeed known with certainty, there would be no shortage in this situation.

Unfortunately, this is not the case, but we do have demand during lead time described by a discrete probability distribution. Using this probability distribution, we can compute the expected demand during lead time

$$E(\text{demand}) = .10 \ (1000) + .30 \ (1500)$$
$$+ .20 \ (2000) + .30 \ (2500)$$
$$+ .10 \ (3000)$$
$$= 2000 \text{ gallons} \qquad (16.2)$$

We use a reorder point that is no less than expected demand during lead time.

If 2000 gallons is the reorder point, then 60 percent of the time $(P(D = 1000) + P(D = 1500) + P(D = 2000))$ there will be no stockout, 30 percent of the time there will be a stockout of 500 gallons, and 10 percent of the time there will be a stockout of 1000 gallons. This means that the expected shortage for a reorder point of 2000 is $.30(500) + .10(1000) = 250$ gallons. If on the other hand the reorder point is 2500 gallons, 90 percent of the time there will be no stockout and 10 percent of the time there will be a stockout of 500 gallons. This information is summarized in Table 16.1. Having computed the economic order quantity using the simple EOQ model, we know that

there will be 6 orders per year. Also given the cost per gallon short as $12 per gallon, we can compute the annual shortage costs for the three levels of safety stock, 0, 500, and 1000 gallons as follows. We note that (D/Q) is the number of inventory cycles per year.

Total annual shortage cost
$$= S(D/Q) \ (\text{expected shortage})$$

Total annual shortage cost for a safety stock of 0 gallons
$$= (\$12)(6)(250)$$
$$= \$18,000$$

Total annual shortage cost for a safety stock of 500 gallons
$$= (\$12)(6)(50)$$
$$= \$3600$$

Total annual shortage cost for a safety stock of 1000 gallons
$$= (\$12)(6)(0)$$
$$= 0$$

Assuming that average safety stock is equal to the initial number of units held as safety stock, we compute the annual holding cost of the safety stock, $h(SS)$.

TABLE 16.1 EXPECTED SHORTAGES FOR REORDER POINTS NO LESS THAN EXPECTED DEMAND

REORDER POINT	SAFETY STOCK	DEMAND DURING LEAD TIME	SHORTAGE	PROBABILITY OF SHORTAGE	EXPECTED SHORTAGE FOR REORDER POINT
2000	0	1000	0	.10	0
		1500	0	.30	0
		2000	0	.20	0
		2500	500	.30	150
		3000	1000	.10	100
					250
2500	500	1000	0	.10	0
		1500	0	.30	0
		2000	0	.20	0
		2500	0	.30	0
		3000	500	.10	50
					50
3000	1000	1000	0	.10	0
		1500	0	.30	0
		2000	0	.20	0
		2500	0	.30	0
		3000	0	.10	0
					0

TABLE 16.2 A COMPARISON OF SHORTAGE COST AND SAFETY STOCK HOLDING COST

SAFETY STOCK	ANNUAL SHORTAGE COST ($)	ANNUAL HOLDING COST ($)	TOTAL COST SAFETY STOCK ($)
0	18,000	0	18,000
500	3600	4000	7600
1000	0	8000	8000

Total annual holding cost for a safety stock of 0 gallons

$$= (\$8)(0)$$
$$= 0$$

Total annual holding cost for a safety stock of 500 gallons

$$= (\$8)(500)$$
$$= \$4000$$

Total annual holding cost for a safety stock of 1000 gallons

$$= (\$8)(1000)$$
$$= \$8000$$

These calculations are summarized in Table 16.2.

Thus the minimum total cost associated with the safety stock occurs when we have a safety stock of 500 and this minimum cost is $7600. We note that the cost difference between a safety stock level of 500 and a safety stock level of 1000 is minimal. Management would likely adopt the larger safety stock if there is any chance that the shortage costs were underestimated.

The "optimization" procedure just described involved a small number of comparisons. These simple comparisons were possible because of the nature of the probability distribution for demand during lead time. This probability distribution for demand was *discrete*. If there is no reason why demand during lead time could not assume a value of 2020 or 2021, or in fact any other value between 1000 and 3000, there may be justification for describing demand during lead time with a *continuous* probability distribution. This perhaps more realistic description of demand does, however, complicate the "optimization" procedure described in the example of this section. In the next section we examine the normal distribution for demand during lead time. Because of the difficulty of the computations, we do not attempt to compare the holding cost of safety stock and shortage costs as we did in this section. The analysis, which requires the use of integral calculus, is left to more advanced texts. We alternatively analyze the safety stock level *required to maintain a prespecified level of service.*

16.3 EOQ WITH SAFETY STOCK: A CONTINUOUS DISTRIBUTION FOR DEMAND DURING LEAD TIME

In the previous section we determined a safety stock level based on the fraction of demand that resulted in a stockout. In this process we directly incorporated the relevant inventory costs. The approach taken in this section to determine the amount of safety stock is useful when a shortage cost cannot be determined. At the same time, a different service level criterion is utilized. Instead of defining service level as the fraction of demand that results in a stockout, as in the previous section, we base our definition of service level on the average fraction of stockouts we are willing to allow. Alternatively, level of service could be based on the number of stockouts that we are willing to permit in a given time period. We use the first definition (as a fraction of stockouts) in the following illustration. For example, suppose that we are willing to tolerate one stockout out of 20 planned orders. In other words, 5 percent of the orders result in a stockout, and the service level we want to achieve is said to be a 95 percent service level. Thus, we require that for any one order placed there is only a 5 percent chance of a stockout. Also, we specify a reorder point for which there is a 5 percent chance that lead time demand will exceed the specified reorder point. The process of finding a reorder point that corresponds to a desired service level is illustrated in the following example involving ABC Chemical. Here it is assumed that demand during lead time follows a particular continuous probability distribution: the normal probability distribution.

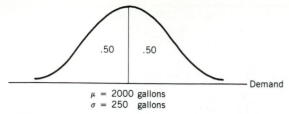

FIGURE 16.3 NORMAL DISTRIBUTION DURING LEAD TIME PROBABILITY.

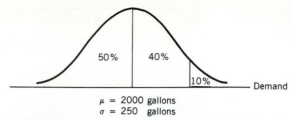

FIGURE 16.4 THE REORDER POINT FOR A NORMAL DISTRIBUTION OF DEMAND.

Suppose that demand during lead time for ABC Chemical is described by a normal probability distribution with a mean (μ) of 2000 gallons and standard deviation (σ) of 250 gallons. Figure 16.3 describes this situation. Average demand during the lead time is 2000 gallons, and using this amount as the reorder point, 50 percent of the time demand will exceed 2000 gallons and 50 percent of the time demand will be less than 2000 gallons. In other words, 50 percent of the time we would expect a stockout using this reorder point. This means that on average, one out of two orders would result in a stockout, and the corresponding service level is often referred to as a 50 percent service level. It should be noted at this point that a stockout occurrence is independent of the number of units short.

Suppose that ABC Chemical wants at most one out of ten orders to result in a stockout. In other words, ABC is aspiring to a 90 percent service level. The reorder point that corresponds to this service level would be a level of demand associated with a cumulative probability of .90. This means that $P(\text{demand} \leq R) = .90$, if R is defined to be that level of demand. Figure 16.4 illustrates the situation. As in the case of the discrete probability distribution during lead time, the safety stock is the difference between the reorder point and expected (or average) demand. Thus, if we are seeking a level of demand R so that

$$P(\text{demand} \leq R) = .90 \qquad (16.3)$$

we are seeking an observation from the normal distribution that is approximately 1.28 standard deviations above the mean of 2000 gallons. Figure 16.4 corresponds to a cumulative probability of .90 (see Table 3.C in Appendix C). Since 250 is the value of the standard deviation, σ, in the normal probability distribution of interest, the corresponding value of R is $(1.28)(250) = 320$ gallons above the mean. Thus the corresponding reorder point is $2000 + 320 = 2320$ gallons. Again, if this reorder point is used, only 10 percent of the inventory cycles should result in a stockout.

In more general terms, let Z denote the standard normal probability distribution where Z_α is a value of Z so that,

$$P(Z \leq Z_\alpha) = \alpha \qquad (16.4)$$

Then the safety stock required to provide a service level of α is computed as

$$\text{Safety stock} = Z_\alpha\sigma \qquad (16.5)$$

TABLE 16.3 REQUIRED SAFETY STOCK AT SELECTED SERVICE LEVELS

SERVICE LEVEL (%)	PROBABILITY OF A STOCKOUT	REQUIRED SAFETY STOCK: $Z_\alpha\sigma$
75	.25	.674 σ
80	.20	.842 σ
85	.15	1.036 σ
90	.10	1.282 σ
95	.05	1.645 σ
99.9	.001	3.090 σ

The reorder point, R, is then given by

$$R = \mu + Z_\alpha \sigma \qquad (16.6)$$

Table 16.3 gives the required safety stock for a variety of service levels.

As mentioned earlier, we only deal with the maintenance of a prespecified service level when the demand during lead time is continuous. We leave the cost analysis of the safety stock in this case to the more advanced texts.

16.4 DETERMINING THE ORDER QUANTITY USING PAYOFF ANALYSIS: A SINGLE-PERIOD INVENTORY MODEL

Up to this point we have modeled inventory systems that operate continuously and have many cycles. The *single-period* inventory model refers to a situation where a single order is placed for a good or service and at the end of that period there is either a shortage or there is a surplus of items that will be disposed of for salvage value. Single-period models are appropriate in situations involving seasonal or perishable items that cannot be carried in inventory to a future period. Seasonal clothing, certain agricultural products, and products with limited shelf life are often handled in the context of a single-period inventory model. Newspapers, magazines, and certain categories of popular books can also be viewed as seasonal items.

Dealing with inventory planning for items of this type may be viewed as a sequence of single-period models. Each inventory period is considered separately from the preceding inventory period and the only decision to be made involves how much of the product needs to be ordered for availability at the beginning of that period. The problem and its solution would indeed be quite simple if demand for this single period was known with certainty. We consider here the situation where demand can be described by a discrete probability distribution. The use of a payoff table to answer the question, How much should be ordered (or produced)? is presented in an illustration of a situation where the single-period approach to inventory management is appropriate.

A textbook distributor must determine how many management science texts to order from a publisher to meet the demand of regional campus bookstores. Orders are always received from the bookstores in multiples of 50 copies. The probability distribution for demand is estimated from historical information and is given in Table 16.4.

Each textbook purchased from the publisher costs $20 and is sold to the campus bookstores for $25. If the distributor does not sell the books, they must be returned to the publisher, and the publisher will refund only one-half of the original purchase price ($10). On the other hand, if there are not enough texts ordered to meet demand, the distributor must place a "rush order" for the text, and these texts will cost $25 each. A profit of zero as compared to $5 is then made on these texts. In general, let

$$P = \text{selling price (\$25)}$$
$$C = \text{purchase or production cost (\$20)}$$
$$C' = \text{purchase cost on units backordered (\$25)}$$
$$S = \text{salvage cost (\$10)}$$
$$Q = \text{order quantity}$$
$$D = \text{demand quantity}$$

Given this notation, the profit function assumes one of three forms, depending on the relationship between Q and D.

1. If $Q = D$

$$\begin{aligned} \text{Profit} &= \text{sales} - \text{purchase cost} \\ &= 25D - 20Q \end{aligned}$$

2. If $Q < D$

$$\begin{aligned} \text{Profit} &= \text{sales} - \text{purchase cost} \\ &= 25D - 20Q - 25(D - Q) \\ &= 5Q \end{aligned}$$

3. If $Q > D$

$$\begin{aligned} \text{Profit} &= \text{sales} - \text{purchase cost} + \text{salvage value} \\ &= 25D - 20Q + 10(Q - D) \\ &= 15D - 10Q \end{aligned}$$

TABLE 16.4 PROBABILITY DISTRIBUTION FOR TEXTBOOK DEMAND

DEMAND	PROBABILITY OF DEMAND
1000	.10
1050	.20
1100	.30
1150	.20
1200	.10
1250	.10

If we assume that the distributor will only order 1000, 1050, 1100, 1150, 1200, or 1250 textbooks, the profit equations can be used to compute profit under all combinations of order quantity and demand. These computations are summarized in Table 16.5, the conditional profit or payoff table.

We can now compute the expected profit associated with each order quantity by multiplying each of the conditional profits by the associated probabilities given in Table 16.4.

$$\text{Expected profit } (Q = 1000) = 1.0(5000)$$
$$= \$5000$$

TABLE 16.5 CONDITIONAL PAYOFF TABLE: TEXTBOOK DISTRIBUTION

ORDER QUANTITY	DEMAND	SALES	PURCHASE COST	SALVAGE VALUE	PROFIT
1000	1000	25,000	20,000	0	5000
	1050	26,250	21,250	0	5000
	1100	27,500	22,500	0	5000
	1150	28,750	23,750	0	5000
	1200	30,000	25,000	0	5000
	1250	31,250	26,250	0	5000
1050	1000	25,000	21,000	500	4500
	1050	26,250	21,000	0	5250
	1100	27,500	22,250	0	5250
	1150	28,750	23,500	0	5250
	1200	30,000	24,750	0	5250
	1250	31,250	26,000	0	5250
1100	1000	25,000	22,000	1000	4000
	1050	26,250	22,000	500	4750
	1100	27,500	22,000	0	5500
	1150	28,750	23,250	0	5500
	1200	30,000	24,500	0	5500
	1250	31,250	25,750	0	5500
1150	1000	25,000	23,000	1500	3500
	1050	26,250	23,000	1000	4250
	1100	27,500	23,000	500	5000
	1150	28,750	23,000	0	5750
	1200	30,000	24,250	0	5750
	1250	31,250	25,500	0	5750
1200	1000	25,000	24,000	2000	3000
	1050	26,250	24,000	1500	3750
	1100	27,500	24,000	1000	4500
	1150	28,750	24,000	500	5250
	1200	30,000	24,000	0	6000
	1250	31,250	25,250	0	6000
1250	1000	25,000	25,000	2500	2500
	1050	26,250	25,000	2000	3250
	1100	27,500	25,000	15000	4000
	1150	28,750	25,000	1000	4750
	1200	30,000	25,000	500	5500
	1250	31,250	25,000	0	6250

Expected profit $(Q = 1050)$ = .10(4500) + .90(5250)
                              = \$5175
Expected profit $(Q = 1100)$ = .10(4000) + .20(4750)
                                + .70(5500)
                              = \$5200
Expected profit $(Q = 1150)$ = .10(3500) + .20(4250)
                                + .30(5000) + .40(5750)
                              = \$5000
Expected profit $(Q = 1200)$ = .10(3000) + .20(3750)
                                + .30(4500) + .20(5250)
                                + .20(6000)
                              = \$4650
Expected profit $(Q = 1250)$ = .10(2500) + .20(3250)
                                + .30(4000) + .20(4750)
                                + .10(5500) + .10(6250)
                              = \$4225

Thus the payoff table analysis indicates that if our objective is to maximize profit, we should order 1100 books, and if demand exceeds 1100, we should rush order the balance and forego the profit on these books. This inventory strategy is based on the concept of maximum expected profit. It is a straightforward application of the concept of expected monetary value (EMV) presented in Chapter 4, Section 4.4. It should again be noted that this type of analysis is possible only if the order quantity and demand quantity combinations are finite.

16.5 MARGINAL ANALYSIS: A SINGLE-PERIOD INVENTORY MODEL

In the analysis of the previous section the payoff table approach to the single-period inventory model was possible only because all of the alternative demand levels for a given order quantity could be listed. If the probability distribution for demand is not discrete, then this type of analysis is not possible. In many situations the number of values demand can actually assume is so large that it is necessary to approximate demand with a continuous probability distribution. If this is the case, marginal analysis or incremental analysis provides a way for determining how much to order in a single-period inventory situation. Here we assume that the probability for demand follows the normal probability distribution.

The marginal analysis approach handles the order size problem by comparing the expected profit

of ordering an additional unit and not selling it. Consider the illustration of the previous section with one major change. The discrete probability distribution for demand given in Table 16.4 is replaced by the normal distribution for demand where the mean $\mu = 1115$ texts and the standard deviation $\sigma = 70$ texts. If a text is stocked and not sold, there is a marginal profit P_- that is the difference between the salvage value for the unit and the cost of that unit.

$$P_- = S - C$$
$$= \$10 - \$20 = -\$10 \qquad (16.7)$$

On the other hand, if an additional text is ordered and sold, the marginal profit P_+ is simply the difference between the selling price and cost.

$$P_+ = P - C$$
$$= \$25 - \$20 = \$5 \qquad (16.8)$$

For example, suppose that the inventory decision was to stock the mean or expected number of texts demanded. If 1116 texts were stocked instead of 1115, and 1116 texts were sold, the associated incremental or marginal profit is $P_+ = 5$. Alternatively, if only 1115 texts were sold, the incremental profit is $-\$10$. Table 16.6 summarizes these observations.

If these two marginal profits are weighted by the probability of occurrence of these marginal profits, we obtain the expected profit for stocking an additional unit. Specifically

Expected incremental profit
$$= P_+ P(D > 1115) + P_- P(D \leq 1115)$$
$$= (5)(.5) + (-10)(.5)$$
$$= -\$2.50 \qquad (16.9)$$

Since the expected profit for $Q = 1116$ is \$2.50 less than the profit for $Q = 1115$, we would want to avoid this expected loss and would stock 1115 texts instead of 1116. The next logical question is whether we should stock 1115 texts rather than 1114. If the expected marginal profit is greater than zero, we would stock the incremental unit. Obviously, from a practical point of view this type of pairwise comparison cannot continue until we happen to find an order quantity with an expected incremental profit of zero.

TABLE 16.6   INCREMENTAL LOSS FOR A SPECIFIED ORDER QUANTITY

ORDER QUANTITY	MARGINAL PROFIT	MARGINAL PROFIT APPLIES WHEN
Incremental unit stocked and sold ($Q = 1115$)	$P_+ =$ \$5	Demand > 1115
Incremental unit stocked and not sold ($Q = 1115$)	$P_- = -$\$10	Demand ≤ 1115

We can, however, define Q^*, the optimal order quantity, to be the quantity associated with an expected incremental profit of zero. The expected incremental profit for Q^* is defined in (16.10).

Expected incremental profit (Q^*)

$$= P_+ \, P(D > Q^*) + P_- \, P(D \leq Q^*) \quad (16.10)$$

We can compute Q^* by solving the following equation.

$$P_+ \, P(D > Q^*) + P_- \, P(D \leq Q^*) = 0 \quad (16.11)$$

Since $P(D > Q^*) = 1 - P(D \leq Q^*)$, we can write

$$P_+(1 - P(D \leq Q^*)) + P_- \, P(D \leq Q^*) = 0$$
$$(16.12)$$

Solving for $P(D \leq Q^*)$, we obtain

$$P(D \leq Q^*) = \frac{P_+}{P_+ - P_-} \quad (16.13)$$

If the distribution for demand is normally distributed, we are seeking a value for Q^* so that the shaded area in Figure 16.5 is $P_+/(P_+ - P_-)$. In the particular illustration presented here where $\mu = 1115$, $\sigma = 70$, $P_+ = 5$, and $P_- = -10$, we seek

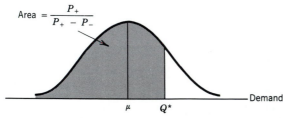

Area $= \dfrac{P_+}{P_+ - P_-}$

Demand

$\mu \quad Q^*$

FIGURE 16.5   COMPUTING Q^* WITH A NORMAL DISTRIBUTION FOR DEMAND.

Q^*, so that

$$P(D \leq Q^*) = \frac{5}{5 + 10} = \frac{1}{3} \quad (16.14)$$

Using a standardized normal probability table we seek a value of Z^*, so that

$$P(Z \leq Z^*) = \frac{1}{3} \quad (16.15)$$

and it is found that Z^* is approximately $-.43$. Therefore, Q^* is computed as

$$Q^* = \mu + Z^* \cdot \sigma$$
$$= 1115 - .43 \, (70)$$
$$\doteq 1115 - 30 = 1085 \quad (16.16)$$

If the probability distribution for demand is approximately normally distributed with mean 1115 and standard deviation 70, the textbook distributor should stock 1085 texts in this single-period inventory model.

Finally, it is important to note that the analysis presented is valid for any continuous probability distribution for demand. We simply must be able to find Q^* given that

$$P(D \leq Q^*) = K, \qquad \text{where } 0 \leq K \leq 1 \quad (16.17)$$

In other words, some functional description of the cumulative probability density function must be available.

16.6   SUMMARY

In this chapter we examined several structured procedures for dealing with stochastic rather than deterministic demand. The analysis depended upon the specification of the probability distribution of demand during lead time. We initially used the EOQ model as the basis for the order size decision in the inventory problem. The economic order quantity calculated was based on average demand over an extended period of time. Using expected demand during lead time, we were able to find the optimal safety stock if the demand distribution was discrete. If demand during lead time was continuous rather than discrete, we examined the safety stock issue in terms of a desired service level. Additionally, we looked at the single-period inventory problem. If the appropriate demand distribution was discrete, it was possible to find the optimal order quantity by a complete enumeration of alternatives summarized in a conditional payoff table. If the probability distribution was continuous for the single-period model, marginal or incremental analysis was used to find the optimal order quanity. Although the only continuous probability distribution considered was the normal distribution, the analysis presented for the multiperiod and single-period inventory situations works equally well for any continuous probability distribution for which we can characterize the cumulative probability distribution.

In this chapter and Chapter 15 we have examined inventory situations where relatively simple mathematical techniques can be used to provide insight into the inventory problem. For the most part, the models presented here are specific to the inventory problem with few generalizations to other applications. On the other hand, many of the other techniques presented in the text can be useful in inventory analysis. A good example is the production scheduling problem of Chapter 6, Section 6.4.6, where inventory levels are an integral part of the multiperiod planning problem. In very complicated inventory models involving stochastic components, simulation modeling (Chapter 18) may be the only feasible approach to the problem.

GLOSSARY

Cost of Safety Stock   The expected holding cost due to the maintenance of safety stock.

Marginal Analysis   A procedure for comparing impact, in terms of marginal expected profit, for stocking an additional unit of an item.

Safety Stock   The amount of stock used to prevent stockouts during lead time in stochastic inventory models.

Salvage Value   The value of an inventory item at the end of the period in a single-period inventory model.

Service Level   The percentage of stockouts that is deemed acceptable during a given period of time.

Single-Period Inventory Model   An inventory model that allows only one order to be placed and only considers demand for that one time period.

Stochastic Inventory Model   A model in which demand is not known with certainty and must therefore be described using a probability distribution.

(See also the Glossary for Chapter 15.)

Selected References

Buffa, E. S., and W. H. Taubert. 1972. *Production—Inventory Systems: Planning and Control.* Homewood, Ill.: Irwin.

Dilworth, J. B. 1983. *Production and Operations Management.* New York: Random House.

Greene, J. H. 1974. *Production and Inventory Control.* Homewood, Ill.: Irwin.

Hadley, G., and T. M. Whitin. 1963. *Analysis of Inventory Systems.* Englewood Cliffs, N.J.: Prentice-Hall.

Hillier, F., and G. J. Lieberman. 1980. *Introduction to Operations Research,* 3rd ed. San Francisco: Holden-Day.

Holt, C. C., I. Modigliani, J. F. Muth, and H. A. Simon. 1960. *Production Planning, Inventories, and Work Force.* Englewood Cliffs, N.J.: Prentice-Hall.

Johnson, L. A., and D. C. Montgomery. 1974. *Operations Research in Production Planning, Scheduling, and Inventory Control.* New York: Wiley.

Orlicky, J. A. 1975. *Material Requirements Planning.* New York: McGraw-Hill.

Starr, M. K. and D. W. Miller. 1962. *Inventory Control: Theory and Practice.* Englewood Cliffs, N.J.: Prentice-Hall.

Trueman, R. E. 1974. *An Introduction to Quantitative Methods for Decision Making.* Chicago, Ill.: Holt, Rinehart & Winston.

Wagner, H. M. 1962. *Statistical Management of Inventory Systems.* New York: Wiley.

Whitin, T. M. 1957. *The Theory of Inventory Management.* Princeton, N.J.: Princeton Univ. Press.

Discussion Questions

1. Compare and contrast the procedures for determining the safety stock for the problems addressed in Sections 16.2 and 16.3. Distinguish the objectives of the analysis in these two sections.

2. When are single-period inventory models appropriate?

3. Are there modifications necessary if a continuous distribution other than the normal distribution is used to determine the necessary safety stock for a prescribed service level?

4. Describe a situation in which payoff analysis is appropriate.

5. Discuss the logic used in developing the marginal analysis for single-period inventory models.

PROBLEMS

1. An inventory system has an average yearly demand of 10,000 units. The ordering cost is $100 per order, and the annual holding cost is $5 per unit. The shortage cost per unit is $2. The demand during lead time is described with the following probability distribution.

DEMAND DURING LEAD TIME	PROBABILITY
200	.20
500	.30
800	.30
900	.20

Determine the safety stock and reorder point that minimize total inventory cost.

2. An inventory system has an average yearly demand of 20,000 units. The ordering cost is $150 per order, and the annual per-unit holding cost is $8. The shortage cost is also $8 per unit. The demand during lead time is described using the following probability distribution.

DEMAND DURING LEAD TIME	PROBABILITY
1000	.10
1200	.10
1400	.10
1400	.30
1800	.30
2000	.10

Determine the safety stock and reorder point that minimize total inventory cost.

3. A truck dealer sells custom-built trucks and orders the cab and chassis from the manufacturer. It costs the dealer $2500 to place an order and $500 to carry the truck in inventory for 6 months. The shortage cost per truck is $2500 and the average annual demand for these custom-built trucks is 1500. The demand distribution during lead time is as follows.

DEMAND DURING LEAD TIME	PROBABILITY
25	.05
30	.10
35	.40
40	.30
45	.10
50	.05

Determine the safety stock and reorder point that minimizes total inventory cost. What is the total minimum inventory cost?

4. The average annual demand for a department store brand sleeper sofa is 2000 units. Each time an order is placed it costs the store $2000. The holding cost per sofa per year is $140, while the shortage cost per unit is $100. The demand during lead time for these sofas is as follows.

DEMAND DURING LEAD TIME	PROBABILITY
40	.20
50	.20
60	.20
75	.30
90	.10

Determine the safety stock and reorder point that minimize total inventory cost.

5. Graphically illustrate the order size, safety stock, and reorder point for the inventory system in Problem 4.

6. Give specific demands during lead time for the inventory cycles that span one year, and discuss the behavior of the safety stock for the inventory system in Problem 4.

7. Graphically illustrate the order size, safety stock, and reorder point for the inventory system described in Problem 3.

8. Give specific demands during lead time for the inventory cycles that span one year, and discuss the behavior of the safety stock for the inventory system in Problem 3.

9. The demand for automobile stereos during lead time is normally distributed with a mean of 700 and a standard deviation of 70. Determine the safety stock level and reorder point if our goal is a 75 percent service level during lead time.

10. Determine the safety stock level and reorder point in Problem 9 if no more than one out of twenty orders should result in a stockout.

11. The Wet Elbow Paint Shop sells an average of 400 gallons of paint during lead time. The standard deviation of demand during lead time is 50 gallons. The paint market is very competitive, so the store requires a 90 percent service level. What reorder point should be used to maintain this service level?

12. Determine the safety stock level and reorder point in Problem 11 if no more than one out of five orders should result in a stockout.

13. True Fresh Farm Market sells fresh fruit and orders this fruit weekly. True Fresh pays $20 a case for apples and sells them for $45 a case. Apples not sold during the week are sold to local food wholesalers for $10 a case. The historical demand for apples is given in the following table.

DEMAND (CASES)	PROBABILITY
10	.20
15	.30
20	.30
25	.20

How many cases of apples should be ordered each week?

14. If the local wholesaler will no longer buy the apples, and True Fresh decides to give the apples to a local charitable organization, should the order quantity be modified?

15. A Butcher Shop purchases fresh beef daily to be cut and sold as steaks and roasts. The beef costs $1.85 a pound, and the average selling price of the cut beef is $3.45 a pound. If the beef is not sold by the end of the day, it is ground into hamburger and sold for $1.69 a pound. The historical demand for beef is given in the following table.

DEMAND (LB)	PROBABILITY
50	.10
80	.40
110	.20
140	.20
160	.10

How many pounds of beef should be ordered daily?

16. If in Problem 15 only one-half of the hamburger can be sold for $1.69 a pound, and the remaining must be used as landfill, should the order quantity be modified?

17. Suppose that the distribution for demand of apples in Problem 13 is normally distributed with a mean of 20 cases and a standard deviation of 2 cases. How many cases of apples should be ordered each week?

18. Suppose that the distribution for demand of beef in Problem 15 is normally distributed with a mean of 100 pounds and a standard deviation of 10 pounds. How many pounds of beef should be ordered daily?

19. Slo Joe's Pizza mixes enough pizza sauce in the morning for the day. The cost to make this sauce is $5.00 a gallon, and one gallon of sauce makes 20 pizzas. The profit on a pizza is $1.50. Either Slo Joe makes the correct amount of pizza sauce, he throws some pizza sauce away, or he closes early because he ran out of pizza sauce. If the demand for pizza is normally distributed with a mean of 80 and a standard deviation of 25, how many gallons of pizza sauce should be mixed each morning?

20. How should Slo Joe's decision be modified if the distribution for demand was uniform on the interval from 60 to 100, instead of normally distributed?

Application Review

Determining Target Inventories of Woodchips: An Application to Weyerhaeuser Pulp Mills

Storage of large quantities of wood in chip form has become an integral part of the pulp and paper industry. Maintaining large chip inventories is motivated by several factors, two of which are listed here.

1. The inventory serves as a buffer against differences between mill supply and demand. The reserves reduce the risk of a stockout.

Source: Gary F. Finke, "Determining target inventories of woodchips using risk analysis," *Interfaces* (September 1984), Vol. 14, No. 5, pp. 53–58.

2. Inventories act as a hedge against changes in wood prices and allow timely procurement strategies.

On the other hand, there are some serious problems associated with large quantities of the woodchips. The aging of wood during storage can clearly change its value. Additionally, large inventories tie up dollars that could be employed elsewhere. The inventory carrying cost and inventory loss due to deterioration for a modern pulp mill can be in excess of $1 million annually. These costs can be accurately estimated. Unfortunately, risk is a very real part of the inventory process. Chip supply is influenced by a variety of factors, such as competitor actions, railcar availability, weather, and market conditions. Demand is also plagued with uncertainty. Maintaining an inventory level that will avoid the shutdown of a mill is a problem common to most mills. Shutdown and restart are very expensive, and often the mill never recovers from such an episode.

Historically, the solution to this problem was to carry an excessively large inventory to avoid catastrophic loss. Specific sources of risk were not directly incorporated into the inventory decision. The Springfield Inventory Target Model (SPRINT) is a computer model developed primarily to assist the procurement manager to deal with risk. SPRINT projects chip inflows, outflows, and resulting inventory level by a user-selected time increment for any length of time into the future. The user can select any number of woodchip sources and uses. SPRINT is able to represent each source or use with a probability distribution where the user inputs upper and lower volume estimates and a most likely estimate for each source and each demand in each time period. SPRINT automatically fits the data points to a beta distribution, and Monte Carlo simulation is used to develop probability distributions for expected chip deliveries, usages, and ending inventories at the end of each time period. Thus the probability of a stockout can be calculated for each period. This computer model does more than access risk. It calculates by-product losses, wood substance losses, pulping value losses, and the opportunity cost of capital.

SPRINT helps the wood procurement manager to answer the questions

1. How reliable are inventory projections?
2. What is the stockout risk in each period?
3. What are the total inventory costs in each period?
4. Given the future projections, what is the optimal inventory level?

Determining an optimal target inventory model is the bottom-line problem that must be solved. SPRINT does this using an iterative approach, which is actually a simulation. The output of SPRINT includes many graphical aids to assist the manager unfamiliar or uncomfortable with statistics. For example, Figure 16.6

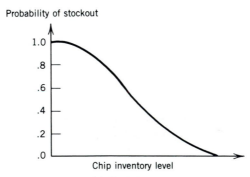

FIGURE 16.6 RISK ANALYSIS.

provides a risk profile. Such data provide the user with an understanding of the tradeoff between inventory level and stockout risk.

The use of SPRINT to aid decision making and inventory management at Weyerhaeuser has had a number of benefits.

1. The model provides a standard, accepted, analytical framework for determining target inventories.
2. The model has quantified risk and has encouraged the sharing of risk between mill management and wood procurement managers.
3. The model points to and illustrates the degree of variability inherent in long-term inventory projections.
4. The model generally demonstrates that inventories can be reduced and still stay within an acceptable risk level.

SPRINT is used at a half dozen Weyerhaeuser pulp mills to help manage chip inventories of close to 200,000 dry tons. At these six mills, the use of SPRINT thus contributed to inventory reductions of 190,000 dry tons over a three-year period. The corresponding reduction in annual inventory cost was over $2 million.

CHAPTER 17

WAITING LINE MODELS

17.1 INTRODUCTION

Waiting lines, or *queues,* are a very common occurrence in our everyday lives. All of us have experienced waiting in line to purchase a ticket at a theater or waiting to pay for groceries at a supermarket. Waiting lines are also a common occurrence in a variety of business and industrial situations. Essentially, waiting lines form whenever the arrivals, or demand, for service from a facility exceeds the capacity of that facility. Waiting lines can consist of people, machines, customer orders, computer jobs to be processed, or other objects awaiting service. Examples of common waiting line situations are presented in Table 17.1.

In this chapter we consider how to analyze waiting lines and how to evaluate the cost and effectiveness of service systems. If the demands to be placed on a service facility were known in advance and could be accurately predicted, it would be a relatively simple chore to schedule the service facility in an efficient manner. It is often very difficult to predict accurately, however, when units will arrive for service and/or how much time will be required to provide the needed service. Consequently, waiting line analysis is characterized by the following.

1. Customers, or arrivals, that require service.
2. Uncertainty concerning the demand for service, and the timing of the demand for service of the customers.
3. Service facilities, or servers, that perform the service operation.
4. Uncertainty concerning the time duration of the service operation.
5. Uncertainty concerning the behavior of the customers as they arrive for service and/or wait in the queue.

Based on these five characteristics the objective of queuing theory becomes the provision of adequate but not excessive service. Providing too much service to the extent that the service facility is often idle or empty represents an incurrence of unnecessary costs, namely the direct cost of the idle employees, or the loss associated with poor employee morale resulting from being idle. Conversely, excessive waiting has a cost in terms of customer frustration and loss of goodwill. Thus, the goal of waiting line modeling is the achievement of an economic balance between the cost of the service and the cost associated with the wait required for that service. The relationship between the level of serv-

TABLE 17.1 EXAMPLES OF COMMON WAITING LINE SITUATIONS

SITUATION	ARRIVALS (DEMAND)	SERVERS	SERVICE MECHANISM
Doctor's office	Patients	Doctors and nurses	Medical care
Movie theater box office	Movie patrons	Ticket seller	Ticket selling
Traffic intersection	Automobiles	Traffic signal	Movement through intersection
Port	Ships	Dock workers	Unloading and loading ships
Garage	Automobiles	Mechanics	Repair automobiles
Registrar's office	Prospective students	Registration clerks	Registration of students
Pizza restaurant	Hungry people	Pizza makers	Make and serve pizzas
Airport	Airplanes	Runways, gates, and terminals	Airplane movement
Mail-order store	Mail orders	Clerks	Filling orders
Telephone exchange	Calls	Switching equipment	Completed call connection

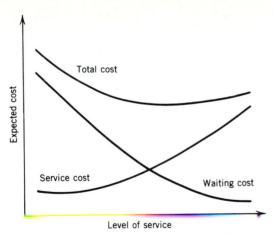

FIGURE 17.1 SERVICE LEVEL: COST RELATION-SHIPS—WAITING LINE MODELS.

ice provided, the cost of the service, the cost associated with the wait required for that service, and the total expected cost (i.e., the sum of the service cost and the waiting cost) is shown graphically in Figure 17.1.

Queuing theory originated in the research of a Danish engineer, A. K. Erlang, who studied the fluctuating demands on telephone service. In 1913 he published some of his findings in a report entitled: *Solution of Some Problems in the Theory of Probabilities of Significance in Automatic Telephone Exchanges.* After World War I, Erlang's work was greatly expanded to encompass numerous applications of waiting lines to business situations.

17.2 THE BASIC STRUCTURE OF WAITING LINE MODELS

In order to analyze waiting lines we must be familiar with the three major components of a waiting line system. The components are

1. the arrivals or inputs to the system;
2. the waiting line, or queue, itself;
3. the service facility.

These components are illustrated in Figure 17.2. These three components have properties and characteristics that must be examined before mathematical models can be developed for waiting line systems.

17.2.1 ARRIVALS OR INPUT PROCESS

The input process for a queuing model is concerned with the manner in which items or customers enter into or arrive at the queuing system. This input process is usually described in terms of three characteristics.

Size of the Calling Population. The source of arrivals is referred to as the *calling population.* The size of the input source is either infinite or finite, and represents the total number of potential customers who will require service for a given period of time. Generally, the size of the calling population is assumed to be infinite because the calculations involving an infinite-size input source are much easier than those involving a finite-size input source. The assumption of an infinite-size input source is applicable to situations in which the number of arrivals at any particular moment is just a small portion of the potential arrivals. Examples of unlimited calling populations include cars arriving at a stoplight, customers arriving at a convenience store, or voters arriving at a poll to vote. A finite-size calling population assumption should be employed if the rate at which the input source generates new customers is significantly affected by the number of customers in the queuing system. For this case, the number of customers within the queuing system affects the number of potential customers outside the queuing system.

Arrival Pattern For the System. Customers, or objects, can arrive at a service facility according to some known, or deterministic, pattern. For example, arrivals at a particular theater might follow a known pattern corresponding to the times at which the movie was being shown.

It is very common, however, for arrivals to occur in a random pattern in everyday situations. For example, calls coming to an 800 telephone number typically arrive randomly, as do the arrivals at fast-food restaurants. A random arrival pattern has two important characteristics. First, a random arrival pattern is one in which each arrival is independent of all other arrivals, or the state of the system. Second, the probability of a particular arrival happening during a specific time period does not depend on when that time period occurs but rather only on its length. Such a random arrival

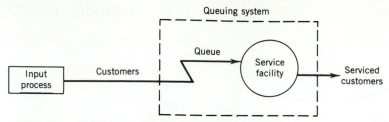

FIGURE 17.2 MAJOR COMPONENTS OF A WAITING LINE SYSTEM.

pattern is said to be "memoryless" (i.e., it has no memory of past events).

The well-known discrete probability distribution, the *Poisson distribution,* is commonly used to describe the random pattern of customer arrivals to a waiting line system. (Refer back to Section 3.5 for a complete discussion of the Poisson distribution.) Using the Poisson distribution, if there is an average of λ arrivals in a time period T, the probability of x arrivals in the same time period is given by

$$P[x \text{ arrivals during time period } T] = \frac{e^{-\lambda T}(\lambda T)^x}{x!} \quad (17.1)$$

WHERE

$e \doteq 2.71828$ (the base of natural logarithms);

$x! = (x) \ (x - 1) \ (x - 2) \cdots (3)(2)(1)$

    (x factorial).

The Poisson distribution is a discrete probability distribution, since it describes the number of customer arrivals for a specific time period. In Figure 17.3 the Poisson distribution is presented for several different values of the mean, λ. As seen in the figure, as the mean becomes larger, the Poisson distribution becomes flatter and more symmetrical. Referring to Figure 17.3b, if the mean arrival rate at a theater ticket window is three customers per time period, the probabilities associated with the different number of arrivals are as shown in Table 17.2.[1]

---

[1]A table of Poisson probability values for various values of x and λ is presented in Appendix C.

With respect to the calling population, if the number of arrivals per time period is Poisson distributed with a mean arrival rate of λ, then the time

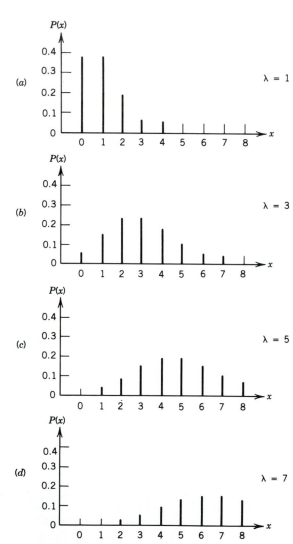

FIGURE 17.3 POISSON DISTRIBUTIONS—VARYING VALUES OF MEAN λ.

TABLE 17.2 PROBABILITIES OF x ARRIVALS AT A THEATER TICKET WINDOW

NUMBER OF ARRIVALS x	PROBABILITY OF x NUMBER OF ARRIVALS $= [e^{-3}(3)^x]/x!$
0	.0498
1	.1494
2	.2240
3	.2240
4	.1680
5	.1008
6	.0504
7	.0216
8	.0027

Note: Poisson arrivals, $\lambda = 3$ customers/time period.

between arrivals (interarrival time) is distributed as the negative exponential probability distribution with mean of $1/\lambda$. For example, if the mean arrival rate per 10-minute time period is 5 customers, then the mean time between arrivals is 2 minutes (10 minutes/5 arrivals = 2 minutes/arrival). The relationship between the arrival rate and the interarrival time can be summarized as follows.

ARRIVAL RATE	INTERARRIVAL TIME
Poisson distributed	Negative exponentially distributed
Mean $= \lambda$	Mean $= 1/\lambda$
$\lambda = 5$ customers per 10-minute time period	$1/\lambda = 1/\left(\dfrac{5 \text{ customers}}{10\text{-minute time period}}\right)$
	$= 2$ minutes/arrival

Behavior of Arrivals. The behavior of arrivals to the waiting line is also taken into consideration as part of the analysis. Waiting line analysis generally proceeds on the basis that the arrivals are patient and form into queues awaiting service. Some waiting line models, however, allow for arrivals to *balk* or *renege*. Balking refers to the phenomena in which arrivals refuse to join the waiting line because it is simply too long. Reneging refers to the situation in which the arrivals initially join the queue, but then leave without completing the service. Virtually all of us have practiced balking or reneging with respect to some type of waiting line. When this happens, the service facility loses a customer and a source of revenue.

17.2.2 THE WAITING LINE (QUEUE)

The focal point of waiting line analysis and the second major component of a waiting line system is the waiting line itself. A waiting line is usually described by two characteristics.

Length of the Waiting Line. The length of a waiting line can be either limited or unlimited. An example of a limited queue situation would be a small theater that can seat a limited number of people for any performance. In general, waiting line models are treated in this chapter under the assumption of unlimited queue length. An example of an unlimited queue situation would be the service facility of a fast-food restaurant.

Queue Discipline. A second characteristic of waiting lines is the queue discipline. The queue discipline specifies the order in which customers entering the queuing system are served. Common types of queue disciplines are as follows.

1. FIRST-COME, FIRST-SERVED Customers are serviced in the order in which they enter the queue. Standing in line to purchase tickets at

a movie theater is an example of a first-come, first-served queue discipline.

2. LAST-COME, FIRST-SERVED   Customers are serviced in the reverse order in which they enter the queue. An elevator in which people move to the rear as they enter is an example of a last-come, first-served queue discipline.

3. RANDOM   In this queue discipline there is no order of service. Question and answer sessions in televised news conferences often appear to be a random queue discipline.

4. PRIORITY   In this queue discipline there is a predefined rule that determines the order of service. For example, people with chronic respiratory problems may be selected first in the general population of a city for a flu inoculation.

17.2.3 THE SERVICE FACILITY

The service facility for the queuing system is concerned with the manner in which items or customers are serviced and leave the queuing system. The service facility is usually described in terms of two characteristics.

Number and Configurations of Service Facilities. The service mechanism may consist of a single-service facility, or multiple-service facilities. A queuing system with multiple-service facilities arranged in parallel is called a multiple-channel queuing system. A queuing system with multiple-service facilities arranged in series is called multiple-stage queuing system. Thus, the number of channels in a queuing system refers to the number of parallel service facilities available for servicing arrivals. The number of stages in a queuing system refers to the number of sequential service steps each individual arrival must pass through. Queuing systems can be categorized into four basic structures, according to the type of service facility present. Each of these four categories is shown graphically in Figure 17.4.

An example of a single-channel, single-stage queuing system would be a small grocery store with only one checkout station. An example of a multiple-channel, single-stage queuing system would be a large grocery store with several checkout stations. An example of a single-channel, multiple-stage queuing system would be a dentist's office in which a patient was first treated by a dental hygienist and then treated by the dentist. If there were several dentists in the office, this would be an example of a multiple-channel, multiple-stage queuing system.

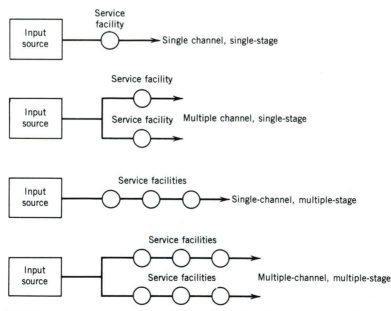

FIGURE 17.4   BASIC CONFIGURATIONS OF QUEUEING SYSTEMS.

Variations of these basic queuing systems do exist, but will not be considered in this book because of their complexity. Indeed, we restrict our queuing analysis in this chapter to single-channel and multiple-channel, single-stage queuing systems.

Service Pattern for the System. The time needed for completing the service is referred to as the *service time* or *holding time*. This service time is generally dependent upon the customer's service requirement, but it may also be partially dependent on the state of the service mechanism. For example, the servers may tend to speed up their service if they perceive that many customers are waiting.

In typical waiting line situations the times required for servicing customers also follow a random pattern. As was the case for the random arrival pattern for customers to a waiting line system, the random service time pattern can be described by a probability distribution. In the case of random arrivals, we were interested in the number of arrivals during a time period. Consequently, we used the discrete Poisson distribution. Service times are continuous, and the well-known continuous probability distribution, the negative exponential distribution (or, as it is often called, simply the *exponential distribution*), is used to describe the random pattern of customer service times in a waiting line system. (Refer back to Section 3.8 for a complete discussion of the exponential distribution.) Using the negative exponential distribution, if μ is the average service rate (i.e., μ is the inverse of the average service time), then the (exponential) probability density function for the service time, t, is given by

$$f(t) = \mu e^{-\mu t} \quad \text{for } t \geq 0 \quad (17.2)$$

WHERE

$e = 2.71828$ (base of natural logarithms)

As noted previously, the negative exponential distribution is a continuous probability distribution, which is used to describe the time required to perform a service. In Figure 17.5, the negative exponential probability distribution is presented for the service time, t. From this figure it can be seen that

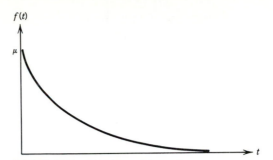

FIGURE 17.5 NEGATIVE EXPONENTIAL PROBABILITY DISTRIBUTION FOR SERVICE TIME, t.

short service times have the highest probability of occurrence. As the service time increases, the probability distribution decreases exponentially toward zero probability.

Using this (exponential) probability density function, we can determine the probability that the service time, t, will exceed some specified length of time, T. This probability is given by

$$P(\text{service time, } t, \text{ exceeds } T)$$
$$= P(t > T) = e^{-\mu T}. \quad (17.3)$$

Conversely, the probability that the service time, t, will be less than or equal to some specified length of time, T, is given by

$$P(\text{service time, } t, \text{ is less than or equal to } T)$$
$$= P(t \leq T) = 1 - e^{-\mu T} \quad (17.4)$$

To illustrate the use of these formulas let us assume that we operate an automobile muffler replacement shop that can service an average of three automobiles per hour. Using Eq. 17.4, we can compute the probability that an automobile has a new muffler installed within a specified time T. For example

$$P[\text{service time} \leq 0.1 \text{ hours}] = 1 - e^{-3(0.1)} = 0.2592$$
$$P[\text{service time} \leq 0.2 \text{ hours}] = 1 - e^{-3(0.2)} = 0.4512$$
$$P[\text{service time} \leq 0.4 \text{ hours}] = 1 - e^{-3(0.4)} = 0.6988$$
$$P[\text{service time} \leq 0.6 \text{ hours}] = 1 - e^{-3(0.6)} = 0.8347$$
$$(17.5)$$

Consequently, using the exponential distribution with $\mu = 3$, we would expect 25.92 percent of the

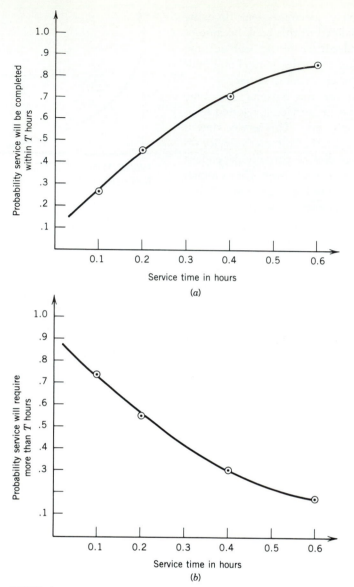

FIGURE 17.6 SERVICE TIME—EXPONENTIAL DISTRIBUTION.

automobiles to have a new muffler installed within 6 minutes or less ($T = 0.1$ hours), 45.12 percent in 12 minutes or less, 69.88 percent in 24 minutes or less, and 83.47 percent in 36 minutes or less. Figure 17.6a shows graphically the probability that an automobile has a new muffler installed within a specified time T, given $\mu = 3$.

Using Eq. 17.3, we can compute the probability that an automobile takes more than a specified

time T to have a muffler installed. For example

$$P[\text{service time} > 0.1 \text{ hours}] = e^{-3(0.1)} = 0.7408$$
$$P[\text{service time} > 0.2 \text{ hours}] = e^{-3(0.2)} = 0.5488$$
$$P[\text{service time} > 0.4 \text{ hours}] = e^{-3(0.4)} = 0.3012$$
$$P[\text{service time} > 0.6 \text{ hours}] = e^{-3(0.6)} = 0.1653$$

$$(17.6)$$

Consequently, using the exponential distribution with $\mu = 3$, we would expect 74.08 percent of the automobiles to require more than 6 minutes ($T > 0.1$ hours) to have a muffler installed, 54.88 percent to require more than 12 minutes, 30.12 percent to require more than 24 minutes, and 16.53 percent to require more than 36 minutes. Figure 17.6b shows graphically the probability that an automobile requires more than a specified time T to have a muffler installed, given $\mu = 3$.

With respect to the service facility, when the expected service completion time, $1/\mu$, follows the negative exponential distribution, then the mean service rate, μ, follows a Poisson distribution. For example, if the mean service completion time is 12 minutes/customer, then the mean service rate is 5 customers/hour. The relationship between the service time and the service rate can be summarized in the following table.

SERVICE TIME	SERVICE RATE
Negative exponentially distributed	Poisson distributed
Mean $= 1/\mu$	Mean $= \mu$
$1/\mu = 1/\dfrac{5 \text{ customers}}{1\text{-hour time periods}}$ $ = 12$ minutes/customer	$\mu = 5$ customers/hours

17.3 DATA COLLECTION AND MODEL VALIDATION

In order to use a particular queuing model we first must collect data on the average arrival rate, λ, and the average service time, $1/\mu$. To determine the average arrival rate we simply keep a tally of the number of arrivals per unit of time, minute, hour, day, week, and so forth. Then, we compute an average arrival rate over all time periods for which we collected data. To determine the average service rate we must tally the times required to perform several individual services. Then these individual service times can be used to compute an average service time, $1/\mu$, and then the average service rate, μ.

After collecting data, and determining the average arrival rate, λ, and the average service time, $1/\mu$, we must next try to validate the queuing model we are attempting to apply to the problem situation. For example, if we propose to use a single-channel waiting line model with a Poisson arrival rate and an exponential service time, we need to try to show that our actual queuing problem "fits" that particular queuing model. To accomplish this we need to show that the system has only one service facility, the (actual) average arrival rate data fit the Poisson distribution, and the (actual) average service time data fit the negative exponential distribution. Given that the data have been collected, the well-known sta-

tistical technique called the chi-square (χ^2) goodness of fit test is typically used to determine if the actual arrival rate data fit the Poisson distribution and the actual service time data fit the negative exponential distribution.

17.4 WAITING LINE MODELS

As we identify and discuss some of the more common types of waiting line models, we should point out that a large number of such models can be derived. This is true because of the uncertainty that exists both for the input process and for the operation of the service facility. Since these two components of queuing models can be described by a myriad of probability distributions, an extremely large number of queuing models potentially exists. Indeed, new types of waiting line models that describe particular situations are being derived constantly. We concentrate on some of the more important and useful results that have been obtained, and focus on the applicability of the results of queuing theory.

As noted previously, the basic objective of waiting line analysis is to balance the level of service provided with the cost associated with providing that level of service. Unlike linear programming or network modeling, however, there is no procedure for the optimization of waiting line problems. For a given waiting line problem, a queuing model may be used to identify the system's *operating characteristics*. Typical operating characteristics include

1. the probability of a specific number of units (customers) in the waiting line;
2. the probability of a specific number of units (customers) in the system (i.e., in the waiting line or being serviced);
3. the average number of units in the waiting line;
4. the average number of units in the system;
5. the average time each unit spends in the waiting line;
6. the average time each unit spends in the system;
7. the percentage of time or probability that an arriving unit will have to wait;
8. the percentage of time or probability that the service facilities are idle.

Given this operating characteristic information together with estimates of service cost and customer waiting time costs, the manager seeks to make decisions that will balance service levels and service costs.

17.4.1 A SINGLE-CHANNEL WAITING LINE MODEL WITH POISSON ARRIVALS AND EXPONENTIAL SERVICE TIMES

The single-channel, single-stage waiting line model is one of the simplest, yet most widely applicable queuing models. Its derivation and use is predicated on the following assumptions.

1. arrivals are described by the Poisson distribution;
2. arrivals come from an infinite population;
3. arrivals are served on a first-come, first-served basis;
4. there is no balking or reneging in the service line (i.e., every arrival waits to be served regardless of the length of the queue that is formed);
5. the average arrival rate is constant over time;
6. service times are described by the negative exponential distribution;
7. the average service time is constant over time;
8. the average service rate is greater than the average arrival rate.

Based on these eight assumptions a set of equations that describe the steady-state operating characteristics of a single-channel waiting line can be developed. The mathematics used to derive these equations is complicated and beyond the scope of this text. Consequently, we simply present these equations and then show how they can be used.

Throughout the material that follows, we will be using the following notation, which was defined earlier.

λ = expected number of arrivals per time period, or mean arrival rate

μ = expected number of customers serviced per time period, or mean service rate

Using this notation the operating characteristics of the single-channel waiting line are as follows.

The probability that the queuing system is idle
= probability that there are 0 units in the queuing system = $P_0 = (1 - \lambda/\mu)$ (17.7)

The probability that there are n units in the queuing system = $P_n = (\lambda/\mu)^n P_0$ (17.8)

The expected number of units in the queuing system
= $L = \lambda/(\mu - \lambda)$ (17.9)

The expected number of units in the queue = L_q
= $\lambda^2/\mu(\mu - \lambda) = L - \lambda/\mu$ (17.10)

The expected waiting time in the queuing system = W
= $1/(\mu - \lambda) = L/\lambda$ (17.11)

The expected waiting time in the queue = W_q
= $\lambda/\mu(\mu - \lambda) = L_q/\lambda = W - 1/\mu$ (17.12)

The probability that an arriving unit has to wait for service = utilization factor for the queuing system
= $P_w = \lambda/\mu$ (17.13)

In Eq. 17.13, we know that the probability that an arriving unit has to wait for service cannot be greater than 1. This means that the utilization factor, λ/μ, cannot exceed one. Moreover, if we attempt to apply a utilization factor of $\lambda/\mu = 1$ or $\lambda = \mu$, we see from Eqs. 17.9 and 17.11 that the average number of units in the queuing system, L, and the expected waiting time in the queuing system, W, both become infinitely large. This means that if we encounter a single-channel waiting line system with Poisson arrivals and exponential service times, with a utilization factor of $\lambda/\mu = 1$, both the waiting line and waiting time will grow infinitely large.

It is also of interest to indicate that the following relationships among the operating characteristics exist, and can be used as alternatives to the equations previously indicated.

$$L_q = L - \lambda/\mu = \lambda W_q \qquad (17.14)$$

$$L = L_q + \lambda/\mu = \lambda W \qquad (17.15)$$

$$W_q = W - 1/\mu = L_q/\lambda \qquad (17.16)$$

$$W = W_q + 1/\mu = L/\lambda \qquad (17.17)$$

Consequently, once we have determined the value of any one of the operating characteristics L_q, L, W_q, or W, the other three operating characteristics can be determined directly by use of Eqs. 17.14 to 17.17.

17.4.2 APPLICATION OF THE SINGLE-CHANNEL WAITING LINE MODEL

Let us now apply the formulas that were presented in the previous section to an actual problem situation. The Like New Auto Cleaning Company operates a facility that cleans and refurbishes used cars for used car dealers. Its current facility can service an average of 12 cars per day (i.e., 8-hour day), and it typically has an average of 10 cars per day (i.e., 8-hour day) needing service. The owner of the Like New Auto Cleaning Company, Hal Timmons, has studied queuing models as a part of an MBA program that he has attended at a local university. He feels that his service facility satisfies all of the assumptions necessary for analysis as a single-channel, single-stage waiting line.

Using the operating characteristic equations given in the proceding section, Hal calculates the values of the operating characteristics of his single-channel service facility. This is done as follows.

$$\lambda = 10 \text{ cars/day arriving}$$

$$\mu = 12 \text{ cars/day being serviced}$$

The expected number of cars in the queuing system

$$= L = \frac{\lambda}{\mu - \lambda} = \frac{10}{12 - 10} = \frac{10}{2} = 5 \text{ cars}$$

$$(17.18)$$

The expected number of cars in the queue $= L_q$

$$= \frac{\lambda^2}{\mu(\mu - \lambda)} = \frac{10^2}{12(12 - 10)} = \frac{100}{24} = 4.17 \text{ cars}$$

$$(17.19)$$

The expected waiting time in the queuing system

$$= W = \frac{1}{\mu - \lambda} = \frac{1}{12 - 10}$$

$$= \frac{1}{2} \text{ day} \quad \left(\text{i.e., } \frac{1}{2} \text{ day} \times 8 \frac{\text{hours}}{\text{day}} = 4 \text{ hours} \right)$$

$$(17.20)$$

The expected waiting time in the queue

$$= W_q = \frac{\lambda}{\mu(\mu - \lambda)} = \frac{10}{12(12 - 10)}$$

$$= \frac{5}{12} \text{ day} \left(\text{i.e., } \frac{5}{12} \text{ day} \times 8 \frac{\text{hours}}{\text{day}} = 3.333 \text{ hours} \right)$$

$$(17.21)$$

The probability that an arriving unit has to wait for service = utilization factor for the queuing system

$$= P_w = \frac{\lambda}{\mu} = \frac{10}{12} = 0.833 \qquad (17.22)$$

The probability that the queuing system is empty
  = probability that there are 0 units in the queuing system $= P_0 = (1 - \lambda/\mu) = (1 - 10/12)$
  $= 0.167$ (17.23)

The probability that there are n units in the queuing system $= P_n = (\lambda/\mu)^n P_0$ (17.24)

Computational results for $n = 1, 2, \ldots, 5$ are presented below in Table 17.3. By looking at the operating characteristics for this waiting line we can determine several important facts about the efficiency of the Like New Auto Cleaning Company. First, it is observed that a typical car has an expected waiting time in the queuing system of 4 hours, and an expected waiting time in the queue of 3.333

TABLE 17.3 PROBABILITY OF n CUSTOMERS IN A SINGLE-CHANNEL QUEUING SYSTEM

n	$P_n = (\lambda/\mu)^n P_0 = (10/12)^n (.166)$
1	.139
2	.116
3	.096
4	.080
5	.067

Note: $\lambda = 10$; $\mu = 12$.

TABLE 17.4 OPERATING CHARACTERISTICS OF SINGLE-CHANNEL QUEUING SYSTEM FOR VARIOUS CUSTOMER ARRIVAL RATES

CUSTOMER ARRIVAL RATE, λ	PROBABILITY OF IDLE SYSTEM, P_0	EXPECTED NUMBER OF CARS IN QUEUING SYSTEM, L	EXPECTED NUMBER OF CARS IN QUEUE, L_q	EXPECTED WAITING TIME IN THE QUEUING SYSTEM, W (HR)	EXPECTED WAITING TIME IN THE QUEUE, W_q (HR)
5 cars/day	.583	0.71	0.30	1.143	0.476
7 cars/day	.417	1.4	0.82	1.6	0.933
9 cars/day	.250	3	2.25	2.667	2
10 cars/day	.166	5	4.17	4	3.333
11 cars/day	.083	11	10.08	8	7.333

Note: Service Rate, μ = 12 cars/day.

hours. This appears to be excessive and inefficient. In addition, the average number of cars in the queue is 4.17, and 83.3 percent of the arriving cars have to wait for service.

Hal Timmons is a little uncertain as to the average customer arrival rate. Consequently, he decides to recompute the operating characteristics for his current service facility configuration, for customer arrival rates of $\lambda = 5, 7, 9$, and 11 cars/day, with the mean service rate for the facility being held constant at $\mu = 12$ cars/day. Using the relationships previously discussed for the single-channel queuing system, Hal computes the operating characteristic information shown in Table 17.4.

From the information shown in the table, Hal can assess the sensitivity of the single-channel queuing system to possible changes in the customer arrival rate. For example, observe what happens if the customer arrival rate is 5 cars/day, or 50 percent of that originally predicted (i.e., 10 cars/day). In this instance, the probability of the system being idle increases from $P_0 = .166$ (for $\lambda = 10$ cars/day) to $P_0 = .583$ (for $\lambda = 5$ cars/day), or more than triples. The expected number of cars in the queuing system decreases from $L = 5$ to $L = 0.71$, or is reduced to less than one-seventh of its original level. The expected number of cars in the queue drops from 4.17 to 0.30, or is reduced to less than one-thirteenth of its original level. The expected waiting time in the queuing system decreases from 4 hours to 1.143 hours, or is reduced to almost a quarter of its original level. Finally, the expected waiting time in the queue drops from 3.333 hours to 0.476 hour, or is reduced to less than one-sixth of its original level. From these comparisons it is evident that the single-channel waiting line system is very sensitive to the customer arrival rate. These results also indicate the importance of trying to measure accurately the queuing model parameters, such as the customer arrival rate, λ, prior to making operating characteristic computations for this waiting line situation. In surveying various used car dealers who provide him with cars for servicing, he arrives at an estimate of $10/hour for customer dissatisfaction and loss of goodwill. He also determines that this figure applies to the time spent in the waiting line (i.e., the car dealers don't really care about the time the car actually requires to be cleaned). Since an average of 10 cars arrive daily, with a car waiting in the queue an average of 3.333 hours, the total

number of hours that cars spend waiting in the queue each day is 10 cars $\times$ 3.333 hours/car = 33.333 hours. Consequently, Hal figures that his daily customer waiting cost for his present service configuration is

$$\begin{aligned} &\text{Daily customer waiting cost} \\ &= (\$10/\text{hour})\,(33.333\ \text{hours/day}) \\ &= \$333.33 \end{aligned} \qquad (17.25)$$

The other major cost for the present service configuration is labor, which is paid at the rate of $10/hour or $80/day. The total anticipated daily cost for the present service configuration is

$$\begin{aligned} &\text{Total daily service facility cost} \\ &= \text{daily customer waiting cost} + \text{daily labor cost} \\ &= \$333.33 + \$80.00 \\ &= \$413.33 \end{aligned} \qquad (17.26)$$

Hal has investigated installing larger and more modern cleaning equipment as well as a conveyor system for the auto cleaning facility. He feels that this can be done at an additional cost of $100/day, based on the discounted anticipated capital expenditure required. With a remodeled facility he estimates that he will be able to service 15 cars/day, instead of the present 12 cars/day. Based on the improved service facility, Hal computes the values of the operating characteristics of his service facility. This is done as follows.

$$\lambda = 10 \text{ cars/day arriving}$$
$$\mu = 15 \text{ cars/day being serviced}$$

The expected number of cars in the queuing system

$$= L = \frac{\lambda}{\mu - \lambda} = \frac{10}{15 - 10} = \frac{10}{5} = 2 \text{ cars} \qquad (17.27)$$

The expected number of cars in the queue $= L_q$

$$= \frac{\lambda^2}{\mu(\mu - \lambda)} = \frac{10^2}{15(15 - 10)} = \frac{100}{75} = 1.333 \text{ cars} \qquad (17.28)$$

The expected waiting time in the queuing system

$$= W = \frac{1}{\mu - \lambda} = \frac{1}{15 - 10}$$
$$= \frac{1}{5} \text{ day} \quad \left(\text{i.e., } \frac{1}{5} \text{ day} \times 8 \frac{\text{hours}}{\text{day}} = 1.6 \text{ hours}\right) \qquad (17.29)$$

The expected waiting time in the queue

$$= W_q = \frac{\lambda}{\mu(\mu - \lambda)}$$

$$= \frac{10}{15(15 - 10)} = \frac{2}{15} \text{ day}$$

$$\left(\text{i.e., } \frac{2}{15} \text{ day} \times 8 \frac{\text{hours}}{\text{day}} = 1.067 \text{ hours} \right)$$

$$(17.30)$$

The probability that an arriving unit has to wait for service = utilization factor for the queuing system

$$= P_w = \frac{\lambda}{\mu} = \frac{10}{15} = .667 \qquad (17.31)$$

The probability that the queuing system is empty = probability that there are 0 units in the queuing system $= P_0 = (1 - \lambda/\mu) = (1 - 10/15)$
$$= .333 \qquad (17.32)$$

The probability that there are n units in the queuing

$$\text{system} = P_n = \left(\frac{\lambda}{\mu} \right)^n P_0 \qquad (17.33)$$

Computational results for $n = 1, 2, \dots, 5$, are presented in Table 17.5. Looking at these new operating characteristics, we see that a typical car now has an expected waiting time in the queuing system of 1.6 hours, and an expected waiting time in the queue of 1.067 hours. Additionally, we see that the average number of cars in the queue is 2, and 66.7 percent of the arriving cars have to wait for service. Therefore, by installing larger and more modern cleaning equipment, as well as a conveyor system, the efficiency of the automobile cleaning facility has been improved significantly. But what about the costs associated with the more efficient facility? Now, an average of 10 cars arrive daily, with each car waiting in the queue 1.067 hours. Therefore, the total number of hours that cars spend waiting is 10 cars × 1.067 hours/car = 10.67 hours. The

TABLE 17.5 PROBABILITY OF n CUSTOMERS IN A SINGLE-CHANNEL QUEUING SYSTEM

n	$P_n = (\lambda/\mu)^n P_0 = (10/15)^n (.333)$
1	.222
2	.148
3	.099
4	.066
5	.044

Note: $\lambda = 10$; $\mu = 15$.

daily customer waiting cost for the improved configuration is

Daily customer waiting cost = $10/hour × 10.67 hours (improved configuration)

$$= \$106.70 \qquad (17.34)$$

The improved configuration will have no effect on labor costs, since the workers will continue to work the same hours and be paid the same labor rate (i.e., $10/hour × 8 hours/day = $80). Hal estimates, however, that the total cost must now include $100/day, which is the daily discounted capital expenditure cost. Consequently, the total anticipated daily cost for the improved facility is

Total daily service facility cost
(improved configuration)
    = daily customer waiting cost
      + daily labor cost
      + daily discounted capital expenditure cost
    = $106.70 + $80.00 + $100.00
    = $286.70 \qquad (17.35)

Since the existing facility has a total daily cost of $413.33, it is clearly preferable to make the improvements that will improve the service rate. The cost savings from the improved service rate more than offset the increased daily cost associated with the capital expenditure.

17.4.3 A MULTIPLE-CHANNEL WAITING LINE MODEL WITH POISSON ARRIVALS AND EXPONENTIAL SERVICE TIMES

The logical extension of the single-channel waiting line is the *multiple-channel waiting line*, with Poisson arrivals and exponential service times. Many queuing systems, such as the teller windows at banks or airline ticket counters, have more than one server and are examples of multiple-channel waiting lines. A typical airline ticket counter with four ticket sellers is shown in Figure 17.7.

In analyzing the multiple-channel waiting line model, we again assume that arrivals are Poisson distributed. These arrivals wait in a single waiting line, and then are serviced on a "first-in, first-out" basis at any of the s service facilities that are avail-

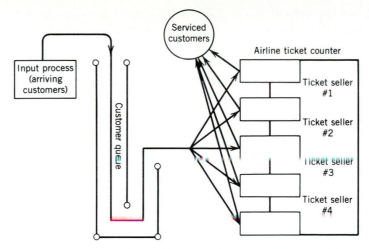

FIGURE 17.7 MULTIPLE-CHANNEL WAITING LINE EXAMPLE—AIRLINE TICKET COUNTER WITH FOUR TICKET SELLERS.

able. Each of the s service facilities has the same mean service rate, μ, which is assumed to be exponentially distributed. The mean service rate for the overall system, $s \cdot \mu$, exceeds the customer arrival rate, λ. The other assumptions listed earlier for the single-channel model still apply.

Initially, let us define the following notation

λ = expected number of arrivals per time period, or mean arrival rate

μ = expected number of customers serviced each time period for each service channel, or mean service rate per channel

s = number of service channels

Using this notation the operating characteristics of the multiple-channel waiting line are as follows

The probability that the queuing system is empty
  = probability that there are 0 units in the
    queuing system

$$= P_0 = \cfrac{1}{\left[\displaystyle\sum_{n=0}^{n=s-1} \frac{(\lambda/\mu)^n}{n!} + \frac{(\lambda/\mu)^s}{s!} \cfrac{1}{1 - (\lambda/s\mu)} \right]}$$

for $s\mu > 2$ (17.36)

The probability that there are n units in the queuing system

$$= P_n = \begin{cases} \cfrac{(\lambda/\mu)^n}{n!} P_0 & \text{for } n \le s \\[3mm] \cfrac{(\lambda/\mu)^n}{s! s^{n-s}} P_0 & \text{for } n > s \end{cases}$$ (17.37)

The expected number of units in the queue

$$= L_q = \frac{(\lambda/\mu)^s (\lambda/\mu s) P_0}{s! \, [1 - \lambda/(\mu s)]^2}$$ (17.38)

The expected number of units in the queuing system

$$= L = L_q + \frac{\lambda}{\mu}$$ (17.39)

The expected waiting time in the queue

$$= W_q = \frac{L_q}{\lambda}$$ (17.40)

The expected waiting time in the queuing system

$$= W = W_q + \frac{1}{\mu} = \frac{L}{\lambda}$$ (17.41)

The utilization factor for the queuing system

$$= \rho = \frac{\lambda}{\mu s}$$ (17.42)

The probability that an arriving unit has to wait for service

$$P_w = \frac{1}{s!} \left(\frac{\lambda}{\mu} \right)^s \frac{s\mu}{s\mu - \lambda} P_0$$ (17.43)

17.4.4 APPLICATION OF THE MULTIPLE-CHANNEL WAITING LINE MODEL

For an application of the multiple-channel waiting line model let us return to the Like New Auto Cleaning Company. Suppose that Hal Timmons, the company's owner, now wishes to consider the desirability of expanding his facility to provide space to clean two cars simultaneously. If this is done, Hal would assign a cleaning crew to each of the two service bays and operate a two-channel waiting line system. Let us compare this alternative with the original single-channel waiting line system presented in Section 17.3.2. Recall that for the original single-channel waiting line system, $\lambda = 10$ cars/day and $\mu = 12$ cars/day.

Using the operating characteristic equations given in the preceding section, Hal calculates the values of the operating characteristics of his two-channel service facility. This is done as follows

$$\lambda = 10 \text{ cars/day arriving}$$

$$\mu = 12 \text{ cars/day being serviced}$$

$$s = \text{two service channels}$$

The probability that the queuing system is empty[2]
$= P_0$

$$= \frac{1}{\left[\displaystyle\sum_{n=0}^{n=s-1} \frac{(\lambda/\mu)^n}{s!} + \frac{(\lambda/\mu)^s}{s!} \frac{1}{1-(\lambda/s\mu)}\right]}$$

$$= \frac{1}{\left[\displaystyle\sum_{n=0}^{n=1} \frac{(10/12)^n}{n!} + \frac{(10/12)^2}{2!} \frac{1}{1-[10/(2\cdot12)]}\right]}$$

$$= \frac{1}{\left[\frac{(10/12)^0}{0!} + \frac{(10/12)^1}{1!} + \frac{(10/12)^2}{2!} \frac{1}{1-(10/24)}\right]}$$

$$= \frac{1}{[1 + .833 + (.347)(1.714)]}$$

$$= \frac{1}{[1 + .833 + .595]}$$

$$= \frac{1}{2.428}$$

$$= .412 \tag{17.44}$$

The probability that there are $n(n \geq 1)$ units in the queuing system (i.e., the queuing system is busy)

$$= P_n = \frac{(\lambda/\mu)^n}{n!} P_0 \qquad \text{for } n \leq 2$$

$$= \frac{(\lambda/\mu)^n}{s!s^{n-s}} P_0 \qquad \text{for } n > 2 \tag{17.45}$$

---

[2]Observe that considerable computational effort is required for computing the value of P_0. To assist you a table of values of P_0, for various combinations of $\lambda/\mu s$ (utilization factor) and s (number of channels) has been provided in Appendix C.

Computational results for $n = 1, 2, \ldots, 5$ are presented below in Table 17.6.

The expected number of units in the queue

$$= L_q = \frac{(\lambda/\mu)^s (\lambda/\mu s) P_0}{s! (1-\lambda/\mu s)^2}$$

$$= \frac{(10/12)^2 (10/12 \cdot 2) (0.412)}{(2 \cdot 1)(1-10/24)^2}$$

$$= \frac{(25/36)(5/12)(0.412)}{(2)(49/144)}$$

$$= \frac{(125/432)(0.412)}{(98/144)}$$

$$= (125/98)(0.412/3) = 0.175 \text{ car} \tag{17.46}$$

The expected number of units in the queuing system

$$= L = L_q + \frac{\lambda}{\mu} = 0.175 + \frac{10}{12} = 1.01 \text{ cars}$$

$$\tag{17.47}$$

The expected waiting time in the queue

$$= W_q$$

$$= \frac{L_q}{\lambda}$$

$$= \frac{0.175}{10}$$

$$= 0.018 \text{ days}$$

$$\left(\text{i.e., } 0.018 \text{ days} \times \frac{8 \text{ hours}}{\text{day}} = 0.144 \text{ hour}\right) \tag{17.48}$$

The expected waiting time in the queuing system

$$= W$$

$$= W_q + \frac{1}{\mu}$$

$$= 0.018 + \frac{1}{12}$$

$$= 0.101 \text{ day}$$

$$\left(\text{i.e., } 0.101 \text{ day} \times \frac{8 \text{ hours}}{\text{day}} = 0.808 \text{ hour}\right) \tag{17.49}$$

TABLE 17.6 PROBABILITY OF n CUSTOMERS IN A MULTIPLE-CHANNEL QUEUING SYSTEM

n	P_n
1	.343
2	.143
3	.060
4	.025
5	.010

Note: $\mu = 10$; $\lambda = 12$; $s = 2$.

The utilization factor for the queuing system ρ

$$= \frac{\lambda}{\mu s} = \frac{10}{12 \cdot 2} = \frac{10}{24} = 0.417 \qquad (17.50)$$

The probability that an arriving unit has to wait for service

$$P_W = \frac{1}{s!} \left(\frac{\lambda}{\mu} \right)^s \frac{s\mu}{s\mu - \lambda} P_0$$

$$= \frac{1}{2!} \left(\frac{10}{12} \right)^2 \frac{2 \cdot 12}{2 \cdot 12 - 10} (.412)$$

$$= (.5)(.694)(1.714)(.412) = 0.245 \qquad (17.51)$$

In keeping with his previous analyses, Hal now proceeds to investigate the economics associated with this multiple-channel ($s = 2$) waiting line situation. With this two-channel configuration an average of 10 cars arrive daily, with a car waiting in the queue an average of 0.144 hour, and the total number of hours that cars spend waiting in the queue each day is 10 cars × 0.144 hour/car = 1.440 hours. Consequently, Hal figures that his daily customer waiting cost for the two-channel service configuration is

Daily customer waiting cost

$$= (\$10/\text{hour})(1.44 \text{ hours/day})$$

$$= \$14.40 \qquad (17.52)$$

The second major cost for the proposed two-channel service configuration is labor. For the two-channel service facility Hal would have to employ two cleaning crews, both of which would be paid at the rate of \$10/hour or \$80/day, or a total daily labor cost of 2 × \$80/day = \$160/day.

In order to have a two-channel service facility, Hal must essentially double the amount of cleaning equipment he currently has. This will require an additional capital expenditure for the additional cleaning equipment. Hal estimates that this additional cost will be \$150/day, on a discounted cost-of-capital basis. Consequently, the total anticipated daily cost for the two-channel service facility is

Total daily service facility cost
(two-channel service facility)

$$= \text{daily customer waiting cost}$$
$$+ \text{daily labor cost}$$
$$+ \text{daily discounted}$$
$$\text{capital expenditure cost}$$
$$= \$14.40 + \$160.00 + \$150.00$$
$$= \$324.40 \qquad (17.53)$$

17.4.5 SUMMARY AND COMPARISON OF SERVICE FACILITY CONFIGURATIONS

Hal can now prepare a summary of the operating characteristics for the three service facility alternatives. This summary of operating characteristics is shown in Table 17.7. In this table the improvement in service comparing the current configuration to the proposed configuration is evident.

Likewise, Hal can prepare a summary of the economic analyses for the three service facility alternatives. The summary of these economic analyses is shown in Table 17.8.

The total daily service facility cost for the two-channel service facility is \$324.40, whereas the total daily service cost for the current one-channel service facility is \$413.33. By upgrading the current one-channel service facility, however, the total daily service cost can be reduced to \$286.70. Although

TABLE 17.7 SUMMARY OF SERVICE FACILITY OPERATING CHARACTERISTICS: LIKE NEW AUTO CLEANING COMPANY

	TYPE OF SERVICE FACILITY		
OPERATING CHARACTERISTIC	SINGLE CHANNEL $\mu = 12$	SINGLE CHANNEL $\mu = 15$	MULTIPLE CHANNEL $s = 2$, $\mu = 12$
Probability that the system is empty, P_0	.166	.333	.412
Average number of cars in the queue, L_q	4.17 cars	1.333 cars	101 cars
Average number of cars in the queuing system, L	5 cars	2 cars	.175 cars
Average time spent in the queue, W_q	3.333 hours	1.067 cars	.808 hours
Average time spent in the queuing system, W	8 hours	1.4 hours	.144 hours

TABLE 17.8 SUMMARY OF SERVICE FACILITY ECONOMIC ANALYSES: LIKE NEW AUTO CLEANING COMPANY

	TYPE OF SERVICE FACILITY		
TYPE OF COST	SINGLE CHANNEL $\mu = 12$	SINGLE CHANNEL $\mu = 15$	MULTIPLE CHANNEL $s = 2, \mu = 12$
Daily customer waiting cost ($)	333.33	106.70	14.40
Daily labor cost ($)	80	80	160
Daily discounted capital expenditure cost ($)	—	100	150
Total daily service facility cost ($)	413.33	286.70	324.40

opening a second service channel would probably improve customer relations and does lower the daily customer waiting cost, it also causes an increase in the overall cost of providing service. Referring back to Figure 17.1, you will observe that this type of tradeoff is the essence of queuing theory. Hal's decision should thus be that of improving his existing one-channel facility rather than creating a two-channel facility.

17.5 MORE COMPLEX WAITING LINE MODELS

We have studied the single-channel and multiple-channel queuing models developed using some eight basic assumptions (refer to Section 17.4.1). Applications of the models have also been discussed. We do not want to leave the impression, however, that these are the only queuing models that you may encounter. For example, both of these models were developed under the assumption that arrivals come from an infinite population. There are queuing models in existence that are based on the assumption that arrivals come from a finite population. There are also queuing models based on limited, or finite, queues. In general, operating characteristics have been derived for more complex waiting line models describing the following situations.

1. Arrivals that follow various probability distributions other than the Poisson.
2. Service times that follow various probability distributions other than the exponential.
3. Arrivals that occur in groups, rather than one at a time.
4. Mean arrival rates that vary depending upon the number of units waiting for service.

5. Queue disciplines that are not first-come first-served.
6. Mean service rates that vary depending upon the number of units waiting for service.
7. Limited, or finite, queues.

The operating characteristics for these waiting line models are generally more complex than those presented in this chapter, which is meant to be an introduction to the basic ideas and applications of queuing theory. A list of references is included at the end of this chapter, and can be consulted if you want to consider more complex queuing models.

Traditionally, in queuing theory a particular model is described by its arrival process, its service process, and by the number of servers utilized. A shorthand notation, developed by a British mathematician D. G. Kendall, is used. This three-symbol *Kendall notation* is as follows.

/	/	/
Code indicating arrival process	Code indicating service process	Code indicating number of parallel servers

The code letter M is used to signify both Poisson arrivals and exponential service times. Consequently, the single-channel waiting line discussed in Sections 17.4.1 and 17.4.2 is the M/M/1 waiting line model, and the multiple-channel waiting line discussed in Sections 17.4.3 and 17.4.4 is the M/M/2 model. Numerous other models can be denoted using this Kendall notation.

17.6 SOLVING WAITING LINE MODELS USING A COMPUTER

Software packages for solving waiting line problems are very common, and can be found in both mainframe and microcomputer versions. They afford the

TABLE 17.9 MICROCOMPUTER PROGRAM OUTPUT: *M/M/*1 WAITING LINE MODEL

INPUT DATA DESCRIBING YOUR PROBLEM Q1 *M/M/*1	
Customer arrival rate (lambda)	= 10.000
Distribution	: Poisson
Number of servers	= 1
Service rate per server	= 12.000
Distribution	: Poisson
Mean service time	= 0.083 DAY
Standard deviation	= 0.083 DAY
Queue limit	= Infinity
Customer population	= Infinity

SOLVING THE MODEL FOR Q1 *M/M/*1

With lambda = 10 customers per DAY and f = 12 customers per DAY

Utilization factor (P) = .8333333

Average number of customers in the system (L) = 5

Average number of customers in the queue (Lq) = 4.166667

Average time a customer in the system (W) = .5

Average time a customer in the queue (Wq) = .4166667

The probability that all servers are idle (P0) = .1666667

The probability an arriving customer waits (Pw) = .8333333

P(1) = 0.13889 P(2) = 0.11574 P(3) = 0.09645 P(4) = 0.08038
P(5) = 0.06698 P(6) = 0.05582 P(7) = 0.04651 P(8) = 0.03876
P(9) = 0.03230 P(10) = 0.02692 P(11) = 0.02243 P(12) = 0.01869
P(13) = 0.01558 P(14) = 0.01298 P(15) = 0.01082 P(16) = 0.00901
P(17) = 0.00751 P(18) = 0.00626 P(19) = 0.00522 P(20) = 0.00435
P(21) = 0.00362 P(22) = 0.00302 P(23) = 0.00252 P(24) = 0.00210
P(25) = 0.00175 P(26) = 0.00146 P(27) = 0.00121 P(28) = 0.00101
P(29) = 0.00084 P(30) = 0.00070

$$\sum_{i=1}^{30} P(i) = 0.829823$$

TABLE 17.10   MICROCOMPUTER PROGRAM OUTPUT: *M/M/2* WAITING LINE MODEL

INPUT DATA DESCRIBING YOUR PROBLEM Q2 *M/M/2*	
Customer arrival rate (lambda)	= 10.000
Distribution	: Poisson
Number of servers	= 2
Service rate per server	= 12.000
Distribution	: Poisson
Mean service time	= 0.083 DAY
Standard deviation	= 0.083 DAY
Queue limit	= Infinity
Customer population	= Infinity

SOLVING THE MODEL FOR Q2 *M/M/2*

With lambda = 10 customers per DAY and f = 12 customers per DAY

Utilization factor (P) = .4166667

Average number of customers in the system (L) = 1.008403

Average number of customers in the queue (Lq) = .17507

Average time a customer in the system (W) = .1008403

Average time a customer in the queue (Wq) = .017507

The probability that all servers are idle (P0) = .4117647

The probability an arriving customer waits (Pw) = .245098

P(1) = 0.34314 P(2) = 0.14297 P(3) = 0.05957 P(4) = 0.02482
P(5) = 0.01034 P(6) = 0.00431 P(7) = 0.00180 P(8) = 0.00075
P(9) = 0.00031 P(10) = 0.00013 P(11) = 0.00005 P(12) = 0.00002
P(13) = 0.00001 P(14) = 0.00000 P(15) = 0.00000 P(16) = 0.00000
P(17) = 0.00000 P(18) = 0.00000 P(19) = 0.00000 P(20) = 0.00000
P(21) = 0.00000 P(22) = 0.00000 P(23) = 0.00000 P(24) = 0.00000
P(25) = 0.00000 P(26) = 0.00000 P(27) = 0.00000 P(28) = 0.00000
P(29) = 0.00000 P(30) = 0.00000

$$\sum_{i=1}^{30} P(i) = 0.588235$$

manager or analyst a great deal of assistance in performing the tedious, and often complex, mathematical computations that are necessary for the solution of waiting line models.

One typical microcomputer software program that can be used for solving waiting line models is that developed by Chang and Sullivan.[3] To illustrate this software program we used it to solve for the operating characteristics of the M/M/1 waiting line model discussed in Section 17.4.2. Output from the microcomputer program applied to this model is presented in Table 17.9. In the bottom part of the table note that we have used the microcomputer program to compute the probability of n customers in the single-channel waiting line system with $\mu = 10$ customers (cars)/day arriving, $\lambda = 12$ customers (cars)/day being serviced, and $n = 1, 2, \ldots, 20$. The microcomputer program performed all of these computations quickly and accurately.

To further illustrate this software we used it to solve for the operating characteristics of the M/M/2 waiting line model in Section 17.4.4. Output for the microcomputer program applied to this model is presented in Table 17.10. In the bottom part of this table note that we have again used the microcomputer program to compute the probability of n customers in the multiple ($s = 2$) -channel waiting line system with $\mu = 10$ customers (cars)/day arriving, $\lambda = 12$ customers (cars)/day being serviced, and $n = 1, 2, \ldots, 20$. The microcomputer program again performed all of these computations quickly and accurately.

17.7   SUMMARY

Waiting line problems occur in many everyday situations, as well as in many business and economic situations. In this chapter we have discussed the general structure of queuing models. We have also presented the operating characteristics for two of the more common queuing models in existence. Applications of these models were also presented, with an emphasis placed on the economic analysis that should accompany the use of a particular queuing model in a decision-making framework. In the following chapter we illustrate how simulation can also be employed to solve waiting line problems.

GLOSSARY

Arrival Rate (λ)   The average number of customers arriving in the queuing system per unit of time.

Balking   The situation in which arriving customers refuse to join the waiting line because they find too many customers ahead of them in the system, and they are not willing to endure a long wait.

Calling Population   The input source for the queuing system.

Channel   A single-service facility or a series of service facilities.

Exponential Distribution   A probability distribution that is often used to describe the random service times in a waiting line system.

Idle   Term that characterizes a queuing system when there are no items to be serviced or customers to be served.

Input Process   The manner in which items or customers enter into or arrive at the queuing system.

Interarrival Time   The time between two arrivals.

---

[3]Yih-Long Chang and Robert S. Sullivan, *Quantitative Systems for Business.* Englewood Cliff, N.J.: Prentice–Hall, 1985.

M/M/1   A queuing system in which the number of arrivals is described by a Poisson probability distribution, the service time is described by an exponential distribution, and there is a single server.

M/M/s   A queuing system in which the number of arrivals is described by a Poisson probability distribution, the service time is described by an exponential distribution, and there are multiple servers.

Multiple-Channel, Multiple-Stage Queuing System   A queuing system characterized by several parallel series of service facilities, each of which provides an identical sequence of servicing operations.

Multiple-Channel Queuing System   A queuing system with multiple-service facilities arranged in parallel.

Multiple-Channel, Single-Stage Queuing System   A queuing system in which service facilities providing one identical service are arranged in parallel.

Multiple-Stage Queuing System   A queuing system with multiple-service facilities arranged in series.

Operating Characteristics   Descriptive characteristics of a queuing system that describes how the queuing system performs.

Poisson Distribution   A probability distribution that is often used to describe the random arrival pattern for a waiting line.

Queue or Waiting Line   One or more units (people, machines, computer programs) waiting for service.

Queue Discipline   A rule specifying the order in which customers entering the queuing system are served.

Queuing or Waiting Line Theory   A body of knowledge concerned with the arrival of customers at one or more service facilities where the demand and timing of the demand of the customers, the time duration of the servicing operations, and the behavior of the customers as they arrive for service and/or wait in the queue are characterized by uncertainty. The objective of queuing theory is the provision of an adequate but not excessive service facility.

Reneging   A situation in which a customer in the queue becomes impatient and leaves the queue before being selected for service.

Service Mechanism   The manner in which items or customers are serviced and leave the queuing system.

Service Rate (μ)   The average number of customers served in the queuing system per unit of time.

Service Time or Holding Time   The time required for completion of a service.

Single-Channel, Multiple-Stage Queuing System   A queuing system in which several service facilities, each providing a different service, are arranged in a single series.

Single-Channel, Single-Stage Queuing System   A queuing system containing a single-service facility.

Stages   The number of sequential service steps that each individual arrival must pass through in a queuing system.

Steady-State Condition   The condition of a queuing system when the startup conditions no longer affect the operating characteristics of the system.

Utilization Factor   The fraction of time the queuing system is busy, computed as the ratio of the arrival rate to the service rate.

Selected References

Beckman, P. 1968. *Introduction to Elementary Queuing Theory and Telephone Traffic.* Boulder, Colo.: Golem Press.

Benes, V.E. 1963. *General Stochastic Processes in the Theory of Queues.* Reading, Mass.: Addison-Wesley.

Cohen, J.W. 1969. *The Single-Server Queue.* Amsterdam: Elsevier-North Holland.

Cooper, R.B. 1972. *Introduction to Queuing Theory.* New York: Macmillan Co.

Cox, D.R., and W.L. Smith. 1961. *Queues.* New York: Wiley.

Gross, D., and C.M. Harris. 1971. *Fundamentals of Queuing Theory.* New York: Wiley-Interscience.

Jaiswal, N.K. 1968. *Priority Queues.* New York: Academic Press.

Lee, A.M. 1966. *Applied Queuing Theory.* New York: St. Martin's Press.

Morse, P.M. 1958. *Queues, Inventories and Maintenance.* New York: Wiley.

Panico, J.A. 1969. *Queuing Theory: A Study of Waiting Lines for Business, Economics and Sciences.* Englewood Cliffs, N.J.: Prentice-Hall.

Discussion Questions

1. Describe the waiting line problem in everyday terms and give examples of typical waiting line situations.

2. What are the basic components in a waiting line model?

3. What will happen if the mean service rate is less than the mean arrival rate in a single-channel queuing system?

4. State an example of an infinite queue.

5. State an example of a finite queue.

6. What are the major assumptions underlying $M/M/1$ and $M/M/s$ queuing models?

7. What is the manager's basic goal in utilizing queuing theory?

8. Explain how you go about making an economic analysis using queuing theory.

9. What do we mean by "steady-state" results in queuing theory?

10. Why would you expect the $M/M/s$ queuing model generally not to be as sensitive to changes in the customer arrival rate as is the $M/M/1$ queuing model?

11. Give examples of waiting line models in which balking could occur.

12. Give examples of queuing models in which reneging could occur.

13. Describe what is meant by the "utilization factor" for the queuing system.

14. Explain how you would obtain data for use in making a waiting line analysis.

PROBLEMS

1. The Burger Doodle fast-food restaurant has a single drive-through order window. Its owner has surveyed activities at the restaurant and has observed that customers arrive according to a Poisson input process at a mean arrival rate of 60 per hour. Customer orders follow an exponential distribution and can be prepared at an average rate of 80 orders per hour. Compute the operating characteristics for this queuing system.

2. An automatic bank teller machine at the C&S National Bank will provide service to customers at the rate of 20 customers per hour. Customers typically arrive at a rate of 15 customers per hour. Compute the operating characteristics for this queuing system. What assumptions did you use in computing these operating characteristics?

3. Police Car 89 is assigned to an area of the Valley Street Precinct. The precinct lieutenant, Mayatano, complains that the car has been arriving late to the scene of its calls, and suggests that the car's officers, Hanko and Rill, are spending too much time at a local restaurant. The officers, however, defend their position by arguing that they are overworked and they suggest that an additional car be assigned to their patrol area. Using your knowledge of queuing theory, develop a quantitative appraisal of this situation. A six-month record of police calls indicates that the rate of police calls has been 4 per hour, and follows a Poisson distribution. The mean service rate for Hanko and Rill is 6 calls per hour, with the service time following the exponential distribution. Compute the operating characteristics for this queuing system. As a part of your analysis determine the probabilities associated with n units in the queuing system for $n = 1, 2, 3, 4,$ and 5.

4. On the Mississippi River at Alton, Illinois, barges arrive according to a Poisson distribution at the rate of 3 barges per hour. On the average it takes 15 minutes to move a barge through the lock. Determine

   a. the probability that the lock is empty;
   b. the expected number in the queue;
   c. the expected number in the queuing system;
   d. the expected waiting time in the queue;
   e. the expected waiting time in the queuing system.

5. Consider a single-channel queuing model. Assume that we want to estimate the mean arrival rate, λ. To estimate λ we do the following.

a. Tally the number of arrivals for the 8-hour time period, 9:00 A.M. to 5:00 P.M..

b. Set λ = arrival rate/hour = 8 hours/number of arrivals during 8-hour period.

Comment on this procedure for estimating λ.

6. Consider a single channel queuing model. Assume that we want to estimate the mean service rate, μ. To estimate μ we do the following.

a. Tally the number of units serviced for the 10-hour time period, 8:00 A.M. to 6:00 P.M..

b. Set μ = service rate/hour = 10 hours/number of arrivals during 10-hour period.

Comment on this procedure for estimating μ.

7. Assume that we are given a single-channel waiting line situation in which arrivals occur at an average rate of 6 per hour (λ = 6) and the mean service rate is 8 per hour (μ = 8). Construct a probability distribution for the probability that there are n units in the queuing system, for values of n = 0, 1, 2, 3, 4, 5, and 6. Suppose that we want to avoid having a waiting line of three or more customers. What is the probability of this happening?

8. Consider a single-channel queuing model, with a mean service rate of μ = 8. Plot the probability that the system is empty for λ = 0, 1, . . . , 8.

9. Assume that we have a single-channel waiting line facility in which arrivals occur at an average rate of 5 per hour (λ = 5). By altering the assignment of personnel within our service facility we can alter the service rate. An increase in the service rate, however, will be accompanied by an increase in the service cost per hour. The service rate and the service cost per hour vary as follows.

SERVICE RATE (μ) CUSTOMERS/HR	SERVICE COST/HOUR ($)
6	4.00
6.5	6.00
7	8.00
7.5	10.00
8	12.00

The cost associated with customers having to wait is $15 per hour. For this situation, perform an economic analysis for an 8-hour time period.

a. Illustrate the economic analysis graphically, showing service cost, customer waiting cost, and total cost for the various possible service rates.

b. What is the optimal service level (service rate) and what is the expected total cost?

10. The jobs to be processed on a particular computer arrive according to a Poisson input process at a mean arrival rate of 10 jobs per hour. Suppose that the computer loses its core storage and that 30 minutes is required to restore the core storage. What is the probability that the number of new jobs that arrive during this time period is

   a. Zero?
   b. One?
   c. Three?
   d. Five?
   e. Six or more?

11. A large southeastern railroad finds that it must steam clean its cars once a year. It is considering two alternatives for its steam-cleaning operation. Under alternative 1, the railroad would operate two steam-cleaning booths, operating in parallel, at a total annual cost of $50,000. The service time distribution under this alternative is exponential with a mean of 6 hours. Under alternative 2, the railroad would operate one large steam-cleaning booth at a total annual cost of $100,000. The service time distribution under this alternative, however, would be exponential with a mean of 7 hours. Under both alternatives, the railroad cars arrive according to a Poisson input process with an arrival rate of one car every 8 hours. The cost of an idle hour is thought to be $10 per hour. Assume that steam-cleaning booths operate (8 hours per day) × (250 days per year) = 2000 hours per year. Which alternative should the railroad choose?

12. During the period of 8:00 P.M. to 9:00 P.M. the arrival of cars at a single toll booth at the Saluda River bridge average 50 cars per hour, according to a Poisson input process. The toll booth has an exponential service time rate of 60 cars per hour. What is the probability of having five or fewer cars in the queue at the toll booth?

13. The number of customers arriving at the single checkout counter in a Kwik Shopper convenience store follows a Poisson input process. The checkout stand receives the customers according to an exponential distribution.

   a. For this M/M/1 queuing system, assume that the expected service rate is 45 customers per hour. Compare L, L_q, W, and W_q for cases where the mean arrival rate is 30 customers per hour, 35 customers per hour, and 40 customers per hour.
   b. Now assume that there are two checkout counters and the expected service rate is the same 45 customers per hour. Make the same comparisons as you did for part (a).

14. Trucks arrive at the Piggly Wiggly supermarket according to a Poisson distribution, at a rate of 4 trucks per hour. A worker unloads them at a rate of 6 trucks per hour, following approximately the exponential distribution of service times. Management of the Piggly Wiggly supermarket is considering the hiring of a second worker to unload trucks, believing that to do so will result in a total of 12

trucks per hour being unloaded. The hourly labor cost associated with each worker unloading trucks is $10. The hourly cost associated with having a truck waiting to be unloaded is $20 per hour spent waiting to be unloaded (i.e., once the truck is actually being unloaded, the waiting cost is not incurred). Perform a queuing analysis and economic analysis for this situation.

15. The manager of the Apple Records store is trying to decide how many cash registers to have open each Saturday (i.e., the busiest day for Apple Records). The decision criteria include the customer waiting time (and the associated waiting cost) and the service costs associated with employing additional checkout clerks. Jane Mahaffey, the manager of Apple Records has conducted a survey of customers and has concluded that the store suffers about $7 in lost sales and goodwill for every hour of customer time spent waiting in the checkout line. Checkout clerks are paid an average of $5 per hour. The customers typically arrive at the checkout stand at a rate of 60 customers per hour. A single clerk can service 70 customers per hour. If two clerks are used, each of the two clerks can service 50 customers per hour. What service configuration should be employed, and why?

16. At Shem Creek in Mt. Pleasant, South Carolina, shrimp boats arrive to be unloaded. The manager of the Low Country Seafood Company estimates that during the shrimping season, shrimp boats arrive at an average rate of two boats per hour, following the Poisson distribution, and each worker can unload $\frac{1}{2}$ boat per hour. He also knows that the workers who unload the shrimp boats earn $10 per hour in wages and benefits regardless of whether they are busy or idle. He estimates that the cost of a shrimp boat being idle (i.e., having to wait to be unloaded) is $100 per hour. How many workers should be employed to unload the shrimp boats?

17. The Discount Shopper Store offers catalogue shopping by telephone. Its current operation has one clerk to answer telephone inquiries. If this clerk is busy, the caller is put on hold and asked to wait. Calls currently are arriving at an average rate of 20 calls per hour, and the clerk can answer calls at an average rate of 25 calls per hour. The calls follow the Poisson distribution, while the service times follow the exponential distribution. The clerk servicing the telephone calls is paid $8 per hour, but the management of the Discount Shopper Store estimates that there is a loss of about $25 per hour of customers time spent waiting for the clerk to take an order.

   a. What is the average time that customers must wait before their order is taken?
   b. What is the average number of customers waiting to place an order?
   c. The management of the Discount Shopper Store is considering the addition of a second clerk to take calls. If this second clerk has the same service rate and receives the same $8 per hour, should he be hired? Explain.

18. Trucks using a single-channel loading dock have a mean arrival rate of 12 trucks per day. The loading/unloading rate is 18 trucks/day.

    a. What is the probability that the loading dock will be idle?

    b. What is the probability that there will be at least one truck waiting to be unloaded?

    c. What is the average number of trucks in the system?

19. Consider the following two waiting line scenarios where λ and μ are expressed in units/hour.

System 1: $s = 1$	$\lambda = 3$	$\mu = 4$	$P_0 = .25$	$L = 3$	$W = 1$	$L_q = 2.25$	$W_q = 0.75$
System 2: $s = 2$	$\lambda = 3$	$\mu = 3$	$P_0 = .45$	$L = 0.873$	$W = 0.291$	$L_q = 0.123$	$W_q = 0.041$

Suppose that the cost per server is $30 per hour and the cost of waiting in the queue is $25 per unit per hour. Which of the two systems is preferred? Explain why.

Application Review

Wyle Data Services: Queuing Theory In Data Processing Networks

Wyle Data Services is a data processing services corporation, headquartered in Huntington Beach, California. Its computer network structure consists of an IBM System 370/3033 central processing unit (CPU) and 3705 controller with 29 available ports. In 1982, its network structure was basically designed as a star configuration, with 21 nodes (i.e., customer terminals) connected to the source node (i.e., the central processing unit in Huntington Beach) by lines of communication, or links. The links, depending on their capacity, could accommodate variable message sizes and speeds. Message speeds, which were controlled by a variable switch modem, varied from 1200 to 9600 bits/second, depending upon traffic volumes. The communication links were either dedicated lines (which allowed messages to be sent directly from one node to another) or multidrop lines (which relayed messages to an ultimate destination node via a number of nodes). The network structure for Wyle Data Services is shown in Figure 17.8.

This company was very interested in analyzing its computer network, and in investigating the cost-effectiveness of alternative network architectures and capabilities. It decided to use a queuing theory approach in its analysis.

The methodology used in the analysis began with a specification of the existing computer network. Initially, the network structure was examined, and a detailed configuration (Figure 17.8) was specified. Next, an average monthly transaction volume was determined for each terminal location. This transaction volume was then translated into the number of messages per month, bits per second, and bits per message for each location in the network structure. Then, the proportion of traffic between, and retained at, the nodes was assigned. Node traffic was then determined at each node, and was converted to link traffic. Finally, message delay

Source: Bruce E. Krell and Maria Arminio, "Queuing theory applied to data processing networks," *Interfaces* (August 1982), Vol. 12, No. 4, pp. 21–33.

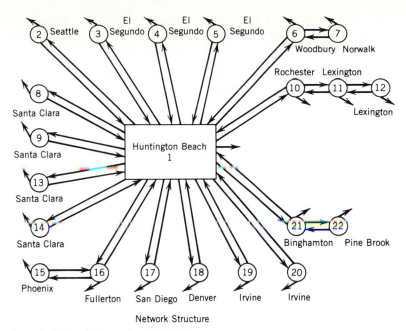

FIGURE 17.8 NETWORK STRUCTURE AND TRAFFIC PROPORTIONS—WYLE DATA SERVICES.

computations were made, with these message delay computations reflecting

1. QUEUING DELAYS: Calculated by standard, single-server queuing theory formulas.
2. TRANSFER DELAYS: Derived as a function of the number of transfers.

After the basic analysis (baseline case) was completed, two alternative network configurations were examined, using the same methodology. Alternative 1 had the same network as the baseline case, but the link capacity was limited to 4800 bits/second. Alternative 2 had a network configuration with dedicated lines only, with a link capacity for all communications of 9600 bits/second.

The results of comparing the baseline case with the two alternatives, in terms of average message delay time were as shown in the following table. These results suggested that the shortest message delay time occurred for Alternative 2, which utilized all dedicated lines with a link capacity of 9600 bits/second.

NETWORK STRUCTURE	TRANSFER + QUEUING DELAY/ TOTAL NUMBER OF LINKS	=	AVERAGE MESSAGE DELAY TIME
Baseline case	162.816 seconds/64 links	=	2.544 seconds/link
Alternative 1	178.688 seconds/64 links	=	2.792 seconds/link
Alternative 2	151.360 seconds/64 links	=	2.365 seconds/link

A cost-efficiency analysis was then performed by Wyle Data Services. Results from this analysis were as shown in the following table. This cost-efficiency analysis indicated that Alternative 2 was the most costly on a per-month basis. Also, it was seen that dropping to 4800 bits/second lines, as reflected in Alternative 1, reduced monthly costs by $1300. This was accomplished with a (minor) impact on average message delay (i.e., an increase of 0.248 second).

NETWORK STRUCTURE	AVERAGE MESSAGE DELAY TIME	TOTAL COSTS PER MONTH
Baseline case	2.544 seconds/link	$14,051.47
Alternative 1	2.792 seconds/link	$12,751.47
Alternative 2	2.365 seconds/link	$18,277.51

The use of queuing theory in the analyses made by Wyle Data Services greatly facilitated the overall appraisal, as well as the consideration of alternatives. Very simple queuing formulas proved to be very valuable in terms of providing information concerning the tradeoffs associated with various network structures.

18

SIMULATION

18.1 INTRODUCTION

If you talk to individuals who are actually applying quantitative methods to managerial decision problems you will quickly learn that *simulation* is one of the most widely used tools in the field. Simulation can be defined as the process of developing a model that represents a particular problem, and then performing experiments using the model to determine performance measures that facilitate making a decision concerning the original problem.

Simulation represents somewhat of a divergence from the topics we have studied in previous chapters. In these previous chapters we have generally been concerned with the formulation of models that could be solved analytically. For example, we formulated linear programming problems and solved them by means of the simplex algorithm. Similarly, we formulated transportation problems and solved them with the modified distribution algorithm. Usually, our goal was to obtain an optimal solution to these problems. Not all real-world problems, however, can be solved using an analytical approach that leads to an optimal solution. For such problems, simulation affords a way of developing a descriptive model rather than an optimization model. Thus, a simulation model provides the decision maker with descriptive information about the problem. The decision maker then makes a decision using this descriptive information, realizing that the choice made is the "best" for the given information, but may not necessarily be optimal. In some instances, we may be able to embed a "search routine" in the simulation model, which will enable us to systematically search for an optimal solution.

Simulation has been extensively applied to decision making. It has been a particularly important tool for physical scientists. For example, chemical engineers routinely simulate new or modified chemical processes by analyzing the operations of a pilot plant. Similarly, airplane flight and the aerodynamic properties of automobiles have been simulated using wind tunnels. Civil engineers have simulated the behavior of entire rivers using physical models. Perhaps the most dramatic use of simulation in recent times was that performed by the National Aeronautics and Space Administration scientists and engineers with respect to the problems and hazards of space flight to the moon prior to actually undertaking it in the manned spacecraft. In the management area, simulation has been applied to inventory control, plant location, transportation systems, queuing problems, and numerous other areas.

18.2 THE SIMULATION PROCESS

The simulation process can be visualized as shown in Figure 18.1.

As an initial step, the problem is defined as a result of analyzing some "real-world" situation. First, we must identify the problem situation that makes the development of the simulation model necessary. Typically, the problem definition step involves the collection of data concerning the input variables and parameters of the model. Also, we need to define how the performance of the model can be evaluated. Finally, we need to specify just how much the model considers (i.e., the model's boundary conditions) and at what level it is constructed (i.e., the model's level of detail).

Second, the simulation model is designed and constructed. This usually entails the development of the overall structure of the model and the writing of a computer program of the model for conducting the actual simulation experiments. Developing the overall structure of the model is often facilitated by a flowchart of the logic to be used, and this flowchart can then be employed in the computer programming of the model. Programming of the model can be done in one of the standard programming languages, such as BASIC, FORTRAN, or PL/1, or it can be written in one of the specialized simulation languages, such as GPSS or DYNAMO. (These special-purpose simulation languages are discussed in more detail in Section 18.8)

Third, the model is tested and validated. This is a critical step in the simulation process, and is usually a difficult task. What we are seeking to do in the testing and validation step is to make sure that the model that has been developed realistically represents the problem being studied, and that it produces results that are reliable and accurate. (Simulation model validation is considered in more detail in Section 18.9.3.)

Fourth, the simulation experiments that are to be performed with the model are designed. In this step we try to devise ways to vary the controllable variables of the model and evaluate the effect of these changes on the performance of the model. The

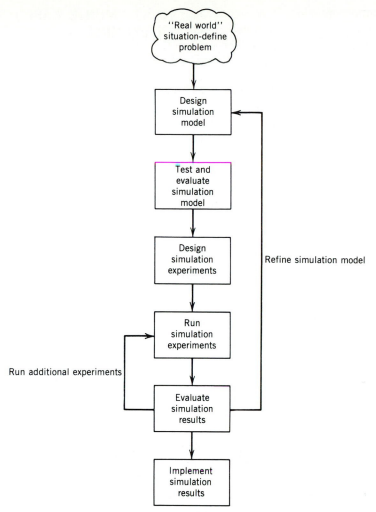

FIGURE 18.1 THE SIMULATION PROCESS.

design of the simulation experiments utilizes statistical concepts and is oriented toward making an intelligent and cost-effective search among the large amount of output data that can be produced by a simulation model. (Design of simulation experiments is considered in more detail in a later section of this chapter.)

Fifth, the simulation model is run on the computer and simulation output results are obtained. Once the initial results are obtained, we must decide whether or not additional experiments are needed. Also, the results may suggest that the original simulation model requires restructuring or "fine-tuning." Thus, it is very important to analyze the sim-

ulation results not only in terms of the solution to the problem but also in terms of its overall accuracy.

The final step in the simulation process involves the implementation of its results. In this step the analyst must make decisions based on the simulation data, and must develop strategies for the implementation of these decisions. (The implementation of modeling efforts is discussed in further detail in Chapter 23.)

18.3 MONTE CARLO SAMPLING

When we perform simulation experiments we often need to take a random sample or samples from some probability distribution describing a population in order to make inferences or generalizations about the population. These sample values are then used as external input or operational values for the simulation model. *Monte Carlo sampling* refers to the process of random sampling that is used in conjunction with probabilistic simulation models.

The use of Monte Carlo sampling originated with Von Neumann and Ulan, who applied it in their research concerning the development of the atomic bomb during World War II. They used the technique in the solution of nuclear shielding problems, and since their work was of a top secret nature, it was given the code name "Monte Carlo." The Monte Carlo method was very successful and quickly spread to various other fields. Indeed, it has become almost synonymous with the term simulation for many people.

The Monte Carlo method involves the generation of artificial experience or data by using a *random number generator* and the cumulative probability distribution being considered. The random number generator may be a mechanical device, such as numbered slips of paper in a hat or a pair of dice, a table of random digits, or a computer subroutine. The cumulative probability distribution being sampled may have been derived from past empirical data, or it may have been obtained from recent statistical experiments. Alternatively, it can be a known theoretical statistical distribution.

The *random numbers* that are produced by the random number generator are then used to reproduce the expected experience corresponding to the probability distribution being examined. The following example explains what we mean by generating a sequence of random numbers. Suppose you take 10 equal-sized squares of paper, number them 0, 1, 2, 3, 4, 5, 6, 7, 8, 9, and place them in a baseball hat. Then, you shake the hat and thoroughly mix the slips of paper. You then select a slip of paper from the hat, without peeking, and record the number. The square of paper is then replaced in the hat, and you repeat the procedure, over and over. The resultant record of numbers (i.e., single digits from 0 to 9) that you would obtain is a sequence of uniform random numbers. By this we mean that any number in this sequence has an equal, or uniform, chance (i.e., 1/10) of being one of the ten digits, 0, 1, 2, . . . , 9.

18.3.1 MONTE CARLO SAMPLING: AN EXAMPLE

To illustrate the Monte Carlo sampling process let us consider an example in which observations are generated from a discrete probability distribution. The data shown in Table 18.1 represent the daily rental demand for video cassette recorders at Al's Video Rental City, as it has been observed for the last 100 business days. Note that daily rentals are in whole numbers of units, from zero to six. Given these observed frequencies we first must establish a probability distribution for the daily rental demand. The probability, or relative frequency, for the daily rental demand is found by dividing the observed frequency by the total number of observations (i.e., 100 days). This demand probability is shown in Table 18.2. We should reiterate that probability distributions are not always based on historical observations as we are doing in this example. Sometimes, the probability distributions will simply be based on managerial experience or judgment. In other cases, we actually collect sample data or perform statistical experiments to determine the probability distribution. In still other cases, known statistical distributions such as the normal, Poisson, binomial, or exponential will be utilized.

Once the probability distribution for the variable of interest has been determined, we convert the probability distribution to a cumulative probability distribution. The cumulative probability distribution for the daily rental demand for videocassette recorders is shown in Table 18.3. In this table

TABLE 18.1 DAILY RENTAL DEMAND FOR VIDEOCASSETTE RECORDERS

NUMBER OF UNITS RENTED DAILY	OBSERVED FREQUENCY (NUMBER OF DAYS)
0	10
1	10
2	15
3	20
4	20
5	15
6	10
	100

TABLE 18.2 PROBABILITY OF DAILY RENTAL DEMAND FOR VIDEOCASSETTE RECORDERS

DAILY RENTAL DEMAND	DEMAND PROBABILITY
0	10/100 = .10
1	10/100 = .10
2	15/100 = .15
3	20/100 = .20
4	20/100 = .20
5	15/100 = .15
6	10/100 = .10
	100/100 = 1.00

corresponds to the probability associated with each daily rental demand probability. For example, the vertical line corresponding to the daily rental demand value of four extends from .55 to .75. This range corresponds to the probability of a daily rental demand for four videocassette recorders, $p(x = 4) = .20$. Similarly, the probability, $p(x)$, for $x = 6$ videocassette recorders, is given by the vertical line from .90 to 1.00, or $p(x = 6) = .10$.

Next, in order to generate a random variable, we now select, or generate, a random number. In simulation studies, this random number is usually defined as a random variable that is uniformly distributed over the interval 0 to 1. This means that each number between 0 and 1 has an equal and independent chance of occurring. In practice, decimal random numbers between 0.0 and 0.9 (i.e., 0.0, 0.1, 0.2, . . . , 0.9). Each of these one-decimal random numbers would have a 1/10 probability of occurring. Or, we could use the 100 two-decimal random numbers between 0.0 and 0.99 (i.e., 0.00, 0.01, 0.02, . . . , 0.99). Each of these two-decimal random numbers would have a 1/100 probability of occurring.

Then, by determining the range in which the random number falls along the vertical axis, an associated value for the daily rental demand can be read from the horizontal axis. For example, assume that we generate the random number 0.25; the associated daily rental demand would be two videocassette recorders. If we generate the random number 0.70, the associated daily rental demand would be four. For the random number 0.98, the associated daily rental would be six. A summary of the random

we see that the cumulative probability for each possible level of demand is the sum of its demand probability added to the previous cumulative probability.

For any cumulative probability distribution a specific probability falls in the interval from 0 to 1. Consequently, a random occurrence (or a random variable) corresponding to a given probability distribution can be generated by selecting a number at random between 0 to 1, finding the interval in the cumulative probability distribution in which the number falls, and identifying the associated outcome of the random variable. To show how this is done let us first plot the cumulative probabilities shown in Table 18.3. The cumulative probability distribution for the daily demand for videocassette recorders is shown in Figure 18.2. In this figure observe that the length of the vertical line at each step

TABLE 18.3 CUMULATIVE PROBABILITY OF DAILY RENTAL DEMAND FOR VIDEOCASSETTE RECORDERS

DAILY RENTAL DEMAND	DEMAND PROBABILITY	CUMULATIVE DEMAND PROBABILITY
0	.10	.10
1	.10	.20
2	.15	.35
3	.20	.55
4	.20	.75
5	.15	.90
6	.10	1.00

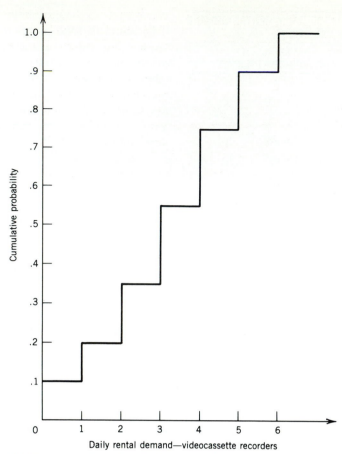

FIGURE 18.2 CUMULATIVE PROBABILITY DISTRIBUTION—DAILY DEMAND FOR VIDEOCASSETTE RECORDERS.

TABLE 18.4 RANDOM NUMBER INTERVALS CORRESPONDING TO DAILY RENTAL DEMAND FOR VIDEOCASSETTE RECORDERS

DAILY RENTAL DEMAND x	DEMAND PROBABILITY $p(x)$	CUMULATIVE DEMAND PROBABILITY $F(x)$	RANGE OF RANDOM NUMBERS, r[a]
0	.10	.10	$0.00 \rightarrow 0.09$
1	.10	.20	$0.10 \rightarrow 0.19$
2	.15	.35	$0.20 \rightarrow 0.34$
3	.20	.55	$0.35 \rightarrow 0.54$
4	.20	.75	$0.55 \rightarrow 0.74$
5	.15	.90	$0.75 \rightarrow 0.89$
6	.10	1.00	$0.90 \rightarrow 0.99$

[a]Note: We have chosen to use the 100 two-digit random numbers in the interval 0.00 to 0.99. Alternatively, we could have chosen to use the 100 two-digit numbers in the interval 0.01 to 1.00

number ranges for the various levels of daily rental demand is presented in Table 18.4.

We now proceed to generate a set of 20 random numbers and obtain the corresponding random variables (i.e., daily rental demands) using either Figure 18.2 or Table 18.4. In this manual random number generation process we use random numbers obtained from the table of random numbers appearing in Appendix C. It should be noted that for large-scale simulation studies, this random number generation process is generally computerized (more will be said later about computer generation of random numbers). In Table 18.5 a summary of the random sampling results from the generation of 20 random numbers is presented.

TABLE 18.5 RANDOM SAMPLING OF DAILY RENTAL DEMAND FOR VIDEOCASSETTE RECORDERS

TRIAL	RANDOM NUMBER r	DAILY RENTAL DEMAND x
1	0.98	6
2	0.09	0
3	0.45	3
4	0.30	2
5	0.50	3
6	0.76	5
7	0.72	4
8	0.66	4
9	0.83	5
10	0.17	1
11	0.28	2
12	0.56	4
13	0.11	1
14	0.22	2
15	0.00	0
16	0.95	6
17	0.86	5
18	0.22	2
19	0.16	1
20	0.76	5

$$\sum_{i=1}^{20} x_i = 61$$

The random sample shown in Table 18.5 simulates the daily rental demand for videocassette recorders for 20 days. The average demand for this 20-day period is 3.05 units (61/20 = 3.05). This simulated average demand can be compared to the expected value of demand computed analytically from this probability distribution using the expected value probability formula for a discrete distribution. Using this formula, we obtain the following results

$$E(x) = \sum_{i=1}^{n} x_i \cdot p(x_i) = \text{expected value of demand}$$

$$(18.1)$$

WHERE

x_i = the demand;

$p(x_i)$ = the probability of demand x_i.

Then

$$
\begin{aligned}
E(x) &= (0)(0.10) + (1)(0.10) \\
&\quad + (2)(0.15) + (3)(0.20) + (4)(0.20) \\
&\quad + (5)(0.15) + (6)(0.10) \\
&= 0 + 0.10 + 0.30 + 0.60 \\
&\quad + 0.80 + 0.75 + 0.60 \\
&= 3.15 \text{ units} \qquad (18.2)
\end{aligned}
$$

The difference between the simulated expected value (3.05 units) and the analytically derived expected value (3.15 units) is a result of the relatively small size of the sample ($n = 20$) that was taken. The results of the Monte Carlo sampling method are a function of the sample size taken, since it is actually a probabilistic sampling procedure. Therefore, the larger the sample size, the more accurate the simulated results should be. As the sample size grows larger we say that the simulated results approach steady-state conditions or equilibrium.

The Monte Carlo method that we have just illustrated can be summarized as five major steps.

1. Establish a probability distribution for the variable of interest.

2. Determine a cumulative probability distribution for the variable of interest.

3. Specify an interval of random numbers for the variable of interest that corresponds to the cumulative probability distribution.

4. Generate a set of random numbers.

5. Use the random numbers to generate a random sample for the variable of interest.

18.4 GENERATING RANDOM NUMBERS

In our previous example we obtained random numbers from a random number table. Throughout our work in simulation we utilize random numbers. In general, we would like the random numbers that we use to have four properties.

1. They must be able to be generated efficiently. That is, the process that we use to generate the random numbers must be one that is rapid and inexpensive.

2. They should have a uniform distribution. Therefore, each random number in the interval (0, 1) should have an equal chance of being selected.

3. They should not repeat until a great many random numbers have been generated. That is, the random numbers should recycle only after long periods.

4. They should not have any pattern.

Four alternative methods can be used to generate random numbers. These methods are

1. manual methods;
2. library tables;
3. analog computer methods;
4. digital computer methods.

Manual methods are extremely simple to employ, but are of little practical value when anything other than a very short sequence of random numbers is needed. Such manual methods include coin flipping, dice rolling, drawing cards, roulette wheel spinning, and the drawing of prenumbered slips of paper or balls out of a container. These methods may be useful for short demonstrations of how to obtain random numbers, but are of little value oth-

erwise. They also have the disadvantage that it is impossible to reproduce a sequence of numbers generated by such devices, and such reproduction may be necessary for the experimental phase of the simulation process.

Several library tables of random numbers are in existence. The earliest was prepared by Tippett[1] in 1927, and many others have appeared since that time. The RAND Corporation library table is probably the table most frequently employed today.[2] *Library tables* offer the advantage that the random numbers they produce can be readily reproduced. Their use is awkward and slow, however, and when they are used in conjunction with a digital computer they must be either stored internally in memory or externally on tape, disk, or cards, and read when random numbers are required.

Analog computers have also been used to generate random numbers, and indeed the RAND Corporation's library table was originally generated by an analog computer. *Analog generation methods* are much faster than either manual methods or library tables, but they again have the handicap of not being reproducible. Also, analog computers are not very common.

When *digital computers* are used to generate random numbers, several alternative procedures are possible. Tocher[3] suggested three: external provision, internal generation by a random physical process, and internal generation of sequences of digits by a recurrence relation. External provison involves the recording of the random number tables on magnetic tape and subsequently using them as direct input to the digital computer. Internal generation by a random physical process usually requires a special adjunct to the digital computer, such as an electronic valve circuit that produces "thermal noise" that can be tracked. The major shortcoming of this method is that its results are not reproducible and thus cannot be checked. The third alternative involves generation of *pseudorandom numbers* by repeatedly transforming an arbitrary set of numbers. At the present time, most computer codes for gen-

---

[1] L. H. C. Tippett, "Random sampling numbers," in *Tracts for Computers,* No. 15. Cambridge Univ. Press, 1927.

[2] RAND Corporation, *A Million Random Digits with 100,000 Normal Deviates.* Glencoe, Ill.: Free Press, 1955.

[3] K. D. Tocher, *The Art of Simulation.* Princeton, N.J.: Van Nostrand 1963, p. 165.

erating random numbers do so by means of this third alternative. Thus the sequence of numbers that is produced is reproducible in a manner such that a "reasonable" statistical test will show no significant departure from randomness. Typical ways of generating pseudorandom numbers include the *midsquare method* and the *multiplicative congruential method*.

18.4.1 THE MIDSQUARE METHOD

The midsquare method is initiated by the selection of a number referred to as a *seed value*. The seed value is then squared, and selected middle digits are used as the random number. The random number just generated is then used as the seed value and is squared. Again, selected middle digits are used as the second random number. For example, assume that we choose the number 1983 as the seed value. Random numbers would be generated as follows.

$$
\begin{array}{llll}
(1983)^2 = & 3 \; \boxed{9322} \; 89 & r = 9322 & \\
(9322)^2 = & 86 \; \boxed{8996} \; 84 & r = 8996 & (18.3) \\
(8996)^2 = & 80 \; \boxed{9280} \; 16 & r = 9280 & \\
(9280)^2 = & 86 \; \boxed{1184} \; 00 & r = 1184 & \\
(1184)^2 = & 1 \; \boxed{4018} \; 56 & r = 4018 &
\end{array}
$$

These four-digit random numbers could then be converted to random numbers in the interval (0, 1) by dividing them by 10,000. For example, the random number 9322 would become the random number 0.9322.

The midsquare method is not a very efficient method for generating random numbers because of the computer time required for squaring numbers and selecting the middle digits as random numbers and new seed values. It has been found that the random numbers generated by the midsquare method tend to have a very short period before repeating, and do not pass the statistical test for randomness. Also, the technique will collapse if a random number composed of all zeros is generated (i.e., using this number as the new seed will result in a series of zeros). Consequently, the midsquare method is not often used in practice.

18.4.2 THE MULTIPLICATIVE CONGRUENTIAL METHOD

The most commonly used methods for generating random numbers utilize congruential relationships.

Congruential methods are very efficient in terms of computer time and cost, and generate long sequences of random numbers before repetition occurs.

The *multiplicative congruential method* is one of several congruential techniques that can be used, and has the following form

$$r_{n+1} \equiv K \, r_n (\text{modulo } m) \qquad (18.4)$$

WHERE

r_{n+1} = the $n + 1$th random number generated;

K = a constant;

r_n = the nth random number generated;

m = positive integer.

The recurrence relationship given by (18.4) indicates that to obtain the random number r_{n+1}, we take the last random number r_n, multiply it by the constant K, and treat the result by modulo m. This means that the product of K times r_n is divided by m and the remainder is the random number r_{n+1}.

To apply the multiplicative congruential method an integer value is selected for r_0 (i.e., the seed value) and the recurrence relationship given by (18.4) is applied. To illustrate, suppose we select $r_0 = 9$, $K = 5$, and $m = 7$ (modulo 7). We can now generate a set of random numbers as follows

$$r_0 \equiv 9 \; (\text{specified as seed value})$$

$$r_1 \equiv (5)(9) \; (\text{modulo } 7) \equiv \frac{45}{7} \equiv 3$$

$$r_2 \equiv (5)(3) \; (\text{modulo } 7) \equiv \frac{15}{7} \equiv 1$$

$$r_3 \equiv (5)(1) \; (\text{modulo } 7) \equiv \frac{5}{7} \equiv 5$$

$$r_4 \equiv (5)(5) \; (\text{modulo } 7) \equiv \frac{25}{7} \equiv 4$$

$$r_5 \equiv (5)(4) \; (\text{modulo } 7) \equiv \frac{20}{7} \equiv 6$$

$$r_6 \equiv (5)(6) \; (\text{modulo } 7) \equiv \frac{30}{7} \equiv 2$$

$$r_7 \equiv (5)(2) \; (\text{modulo } 7) \equiv \frac{10}{7} \equiv 3$$

As we see, the random number sequence 3, 1, 5, 4, 6, 2, 3, . . . is obtained. This is not a valid (i.e., truly random) sequence of random numbers because only 6 of the 10 random digits (0, 1, . . . , 9) are generated, and the sequence of random numbers cycles with a period length of 6. By proper choice of r_0, K, and m, however, we can produce a set of pseudorandom numbers with an acceptably long period, or length of sequence.

In practice the multiplicative congruential method is usually executed on a digital computer. Most computer manufacturers provide random number subprograms that generate uniform random values, given a starting number (seed). For example, IBM furnishes the following subroutine, written in FORTRAN, for use on many of its mainframe computers.

```
SUBROUTINE RANDU(IX,IY,YFL)
  IX = IX*65539
  IF(IY)5,6,6
5 IY = IY + 2147483647 + 1
6 YFL = IY
  YFL = YFL * .4656613 E-9
  RETURN
  END
```

To use this program, the seed value, which must be an odd integer with nine or fewer digits, is specified by the user. The subroutine program then continues to generate random values automatically. The subroutine is a congruential method, based on the internal arithmetic of IBM computers. It will produce a sequence of random values that will not repeat for 2,147,483,647 observations.[4]

18.5 SIMULATION OF A GAME OF CHANCE

As an initial simulation example let us consider a game of chance problem that concerns throwing a

pair of six-sided dice. Each of the two dice is assumed to be "fair," that is, the probability of each of the six sides of the dice appearing is 1/6.

The game that we attempt to simulate is the game of craps, and the following set of rules apply.

1. The player throws the two dice one or more times until an event occurs that determines a win or a loss for the game.

2. The player *wins* if the first throw of the two dice results in a sum of 7 or 11, or, alternatively, if the first sum is 4, 5, 6, 8, 9, or 10, and the same sum reappears *before* a sum of 7 appears.

3. The player *loses* if the first throw of the two dice results in a sum of 2, 3, or 12, or, alternatively, if the first sum is 4, 5, 6, 8, 9, or 10, and a sum of 7 appears *before* the original sum reappears.

In this problem situation, we do not need to gather any data to be able to simulate this game of chance. In fact, the possible combinations that can result from throwing two dice can be illustrated as shown in Figure 18.3. Consequently, the probabilities associated with the possible results of throwing two fair dice are known and follow the multinomial probability distribution. These probabilities are shown in Table 18.6.

From these known probabilities we can then construct the associated random number intervals. This process is summarized in Table 18.7.

Let us now assume that we would like to simulate playing the game of craps 25 times. We define a "play" of the game to involve the (simulated) rolling of the dice until we either win or lose the game. Observe that the rules of the game make it possible, and indeed likely, that several rolls of the dice will be necessary in order for the player to either "win" or "lose."

The logic for this particular simulation can be summarized in the form of a flowchart. (This is often a very useful and informative preliminary step in the simulation process, as it requires you to state clearly just how the simulation process will operate.) This flowchart can then be used to manually perform the simulation experiments, or it can become the basis for writing a computer program for performing the

---

[4]However, depending on the choice of the seed value, it has been shown that only one-fourth of the 2,147,483,647 observations will be obtained. See: Averill M. Law and W. David Kelton, *Simulation Modeling and Analysis.* New York: McGraw–Hill, 1982, pp. 225–228.

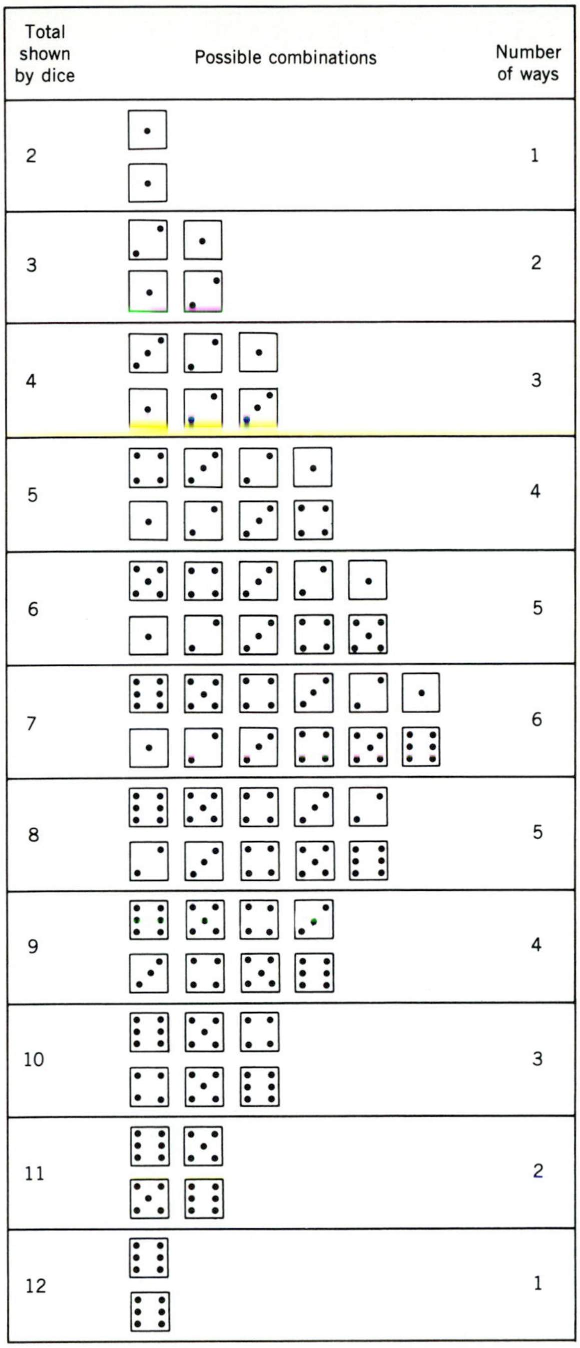

FIGURE 18.3 POSSIBLE COMBINATIONS FROM A ROLL OF TWO FAIR DICE.

TABLE 18.6 PROBABILITIES FOR SUM APPEARING FOR A ROLL OF TWO FAIR DICE

SUM APPEARING FOR A ROLL OF TWO FAIR DICE	POSSIBLE ROLLS TO ACHIEVE SUM (FIRST DIE) AND (SECOND DIE)	P(SUM APPEARING FOR A ROLL OF TWO FAIR DICE)	
2	1 and 1	$(1/6)(1/6)$	$= 1/36$
3	1 and 2 or 2 and 1	$(1/6)(1/6) + (1/6)(1/6)$	$= 2/36$
4	1 and 3 or 3 and 1 or 2 and 2	$(1/6)(1/6) + (1/6)(1/6) + (1/6)(1/6)$	$= 3/36$
5	1 and 4 or 4 and 1 or 2 and 3 or 3 and 2	$(1/6)(1/6) + (1/6)(1/6) + (1/6)(1/6) + (1/6)(1/6)$	$= 4/36$
6	1 and 5 or 5 and 1 or 2 and 4 or 4 and 2 or 3 and 3	$(1/6)(1/6) + (1/6)(1/6) + (1/6)(1/6) + (1/6)(1/6) + (1/6)(1/6)$	$= 5/36$
7	1 and 6 or 6 and 1 or 2 and 5 or 5 and 2 or 3 and 4 or 4 and 3	$(1/6)(1/6) + (1/6)(1/6) + (1/6)(1/6) + (1/6)(1/6) + (1/6)(1/6) + (1/6)(1/6)$	$= 6/36$
8	2 and 6 or 6 and 2 or 3 and 5 or 5 and 3 or 4 and 4	$(1/6)(1/6) + (1/6)(1/6) + (1/6)(1/6) + (1/6)(1/6) + (1/6)(1/6)$	$= 5/36$
9	3 and 6 or 6 and 3 or 4 and 5 or 5 and 4	$(1/6)(1/6) + (1/6)(1/6) + (1/6)(1/6) + (1/6)(1/6)$	$= 4/36$
10	4 and 6 or 6 and 4 or 5 and 5	$(1/6)(1/6) + (1/6)(1/6) + (1/6)(1/6)$	$= 3/36$
11	5 and 6 or 6 and 5	$(1/6)(1/6) + (1/6)(1/6)$	$= 2/36$
12	6 and 6	$(1/6)(1/6)$	$= 1/36$

TABLE 18.7 PROBABILITIES AND RANDOM NUMBER INTERVAL: SUM OF TWO DICE

SUM OF TWO DICE	P(SUM OF TWO DICE)[a]	CUMULATIVE PROBABILITY[a]	INTERVAL OF RANDOM NUMBERS
2	$1/36 = .028$	.028	0–27
3	$2/36 = .056$	.084	28–83
4	$3/36 = .083$	.167	84–166
5	$4/36 = .111$	.278	167–277
6	$5/36 = .139$	.417	278–416
7	$6/36 = .166$	.583	417–582
8	$5/36 = .139$	.772	583–721
9	$4/36 = .111$	.833	722–832
10	$3/36 = .083$	.916	833–915
11	$2/36 = .056$	.972	916–971
12	$1/36 = .028$	1.000	972–999

[a]Slight rounding necessary in order for probabilities to sum to 1.00.

simulation experiments. The flowchart for this game of chance is shown in Figure 18.4.

Table 18.8 presents the simulation of 25 plays of the game of craps. Each play of the game involves the generation of one or more random numbers, in order to simulate one or more rolls of the dice. Each roll of the dice is then evaluated using the set of rules delineated earlier. Consecutive rolls are often necessary in order for a "win" or a "lose" to occur.

Table 18.7 was constructed using the logic summarized in the flowchart presented in Figure 18.4.

As seen in Table 18.8, this simulation of 25 plays of the game of craps resulted in 12 "wins" and 13 "losses," or a probability of winning = .48. Again, a much larger sample size would be required before we could use the results of the simulation to accurately specify the probability of winning the game of craps.

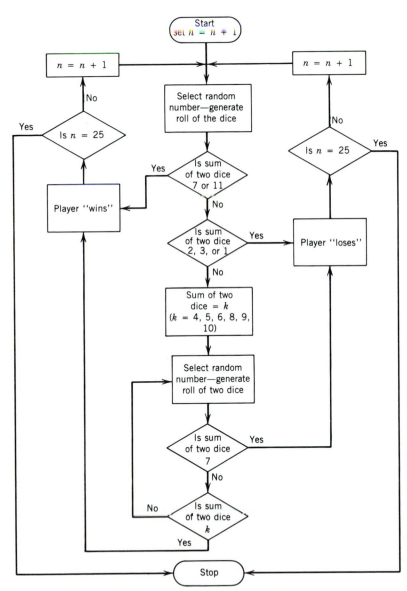

FIGURE 18.4 FLOWCHART FOR SIMULATING A GAME OF CHANCE (n = 25 PLAYS).

TABLE 18.8 SIMULATION OF A GAME OF CHANCE (CRAPS)

PLAY	RN	ROLL OF DICE	PLAY	RANDOM NUMBER	ROLL OF DICE	PLAY	RANDOM NUMBER	ROLL OF DICE
1	455	7 (W)	14	034	3 (L)		006	3 (L)
2	378	6		682	8	24	653	8
	146	4		317	6		593	8 (W)
	798	9		876	10	25	168	5
	185	5		333	6		890	10
	971	11		850	10		243	5 (W)
	754	9		963	11			
	180	5		428	7 (L)		Number of Wins = 12	
	924	11	15	366	6		Number of Losses = 13	
	406	6 (W)		310	6 (W)			
3	140	4	16	804	9		Probability (Winning) =	
	556	7 (L)		153	4		12/25 = .48	
4	207	5		972	12 (L)		Probability (Losing) =	
	203	5 (W)	17	146	4		13/25 = .52	
5	773	9		825	9			
	816	9 (W)		091	4 (W)			
6	315	6	18	906	10			
	498	7 (L)		980	12 (L)			
7	618	8	19	175	5			
	218	5		074	3 (L)			
	768	9	20	337	6			
	545	7 (L)		411	6 (W)			
8	628	8	21	668	8			
	886	10		221	5			
	842	10		347	6			
	575	7 (L)		838	10			
9	493	7 (W)		280	6			
10	067	3 (L)		441	7 (L)			
11	041	3 (L)	22	433	7 (W)			
12	759	9	23	303	6			
	829	9 (W)		654	8			
13	744	9		932	11			

It should again be emphasized that this simulation experiment involved the use of known probabilities, which followed the multinomial distribution. Our next two simulations will involve empirical probability distributions that will be derived from information that has been collected.

18.6 SIMULATION OF A WAITING LINE SYSTEM

In Chapter 17, on waiting line systems, we observed that a variety of such systems can arise in response to a number of business or economic problems. The simple queuing models that we developed and applied in Chapter 17 were based on assumptions that are somewhat restrictive. Unfortunately, more realistic waiting line models often involve very difficult and tedious mathematical computations. For this reason, simulation often affords an excellent means of analyzing waiting line systems.

In this section we simulate a waiting line system involving Ms. Jane Scofield who is about to open a retail photo-finishing store in a suburban shopping center. The store named "Jane's Quik Photo," will be a drive-through operation run by her, but she is contemplating hiring another person to handle anticipated business. Jane would like to use simulation to conduct a series of experiments concerning the operations of her photo-finishing store. She is primarily concerned with the question of operating efficiency, as it relates to the hiring of an additional person for the store.

Jane has observed the operation of a similar retail photo-finishing store in another shopping center and has determined the following set of data.

First, she has observed the pattern of customer arrivals, and has compiled the set of probabilities and associated random number intervals shown in Table 18.9. Second, she has observed the pattern of customer services, and has compiled the set of probabilities and associated random number intervals shown in Table 18.10.

Jane would like to analyze the effect of hiring another person to handle anticipated business. Specifically, she first wants to measure how long a typical customer spends waiting in line and being serviced. This is equivalent to measuring W, the expected waiting time in the queuing system. Second, she wants to measure the average time the current (one worker) is idle. This variable is not one of the standard operating characteristics of a queuing system, but Jane feels that by comparing the average time the one worker is idle to the average time a typical customer is in the queuing system, she will be able to make a decision concerning the desirability of hiring an additional worker. If both measurements are low, Jane will be able to conclude that her business is operating efficiently. If, however, she finds that the average time a typical customer is in the queuing system is high and much greater than the average time the (one) attendant is idle, she would be inclined to hire an additional worker. Alternatively, if she finds that the attendant's average idle time is high and much greater than the customer's average waiting time in the queuing system, then she would be inclined not to hire an additional worker. Jane has also decided she will use a "first-come, first-served" type of queue discipline and that she will initially simulate this queuing system for 30 customers. Her store opens at 8:00 A.M., and she

TABLE 18.9 PROBABILITIES AND RANDOM NUMBER INTERVALS: INTERARRIVAL TIMES AT RETAIL PHOTO-FINISHING STORE

ARRIVAL INTERVAL (MIN)	OBSERVED FREQUENCY	PROBABILITY OF ARRIVAL INTERVAL	CUMULATIVE ARRIVAL INTERVAL PROBABILITY	INTERVAL OF RANDOM NUMBERS
3	14	.07	.07	00 to 06
4	30	.15	.22	07 to 21
5	80	.40	.62	22 to 61
6	40	.20	.82	62 to 81
7	20	.10	.92	82 to 91
8	16	.08	1.00	92 to 99

TABLE 18.10 PROBABILITIES AND RANDOM NUMBER INTERVALS: SERVICE TIMES AT RETAIL PHOTO-FINISHING STORE

SERVICE TIME (MIN)	OBSERVED FREQUENCY	PROBABILITY OF SERVICE TIME	CUMULATIVE SERVICE TIME PROBABILITY	INTERVAL OF RANDOM NUMBERS
3	20	.10	.10	00 to 09
4	40	.20	.30	10 to 29
5	60	.30	.60	30 to 59
6	40	.20	.80	60 to 79
7	40	.20	1.00	80 to 99

assumes that no customer is waiting for service at that time.

The logic for this particular simulation can again be summarized in the form of a flowchart. The flowchart for simulating Jane's Quik Photo queuing problem is shown in Figure 18.5.

Table 18.11 shows the customer-by-customer simulation for "Jane's Quik Photo" queuing problem. The table is constructed according to the flowchart presented in Figure 18.5.

1. For each simulated customer, $n = 1, 2, \ldots,$ 30, generate the interarrival time from the cumulative arrival interval probability distribution in Table 18.9, using a random number. The random number used is recorded in column 2, and the corresponding (simulated) interarrival time is recorded in column 3.

2. For each simulated customer, $n = 1, 2, \ldots,$ 30, generate the service time from the cumulative service time probability distribution in Table 18.10, using a random number. The random number used is recorded in column 4 and the corresponding (simulated) service time is recorded in column 5.

3. In column 6 of Table 18.11, a "running" clock is used to keep track of the arrival times of the 30 simulated customers. To illustrate, the store opens at 8:00 A.M. and the first interarrival time is 6 minutes. Therefore, the first customer arrives at 8:00 A.M. plus 6 minutes, or 8:06 A.M. The second interarrival time is 5 minutes, so the second customer arrives at 8:06 A.M. plus 5 minutes or 8:11 A.M. This same process for arrival times continues throughout the simulation process.

4. In column 7, a "running" clock is used to keep track of when service begins for the 30 simulated customers. Service for a particular customer begins at the time that a customer arrives, if the store's attendant is available (i.e., if the store's attendant is not still busy servicing the previous customer). If the store's attendant is busy, the customer must wait until the store's attendant completes the service for the previous customer. To illustrate, the first customer arrives at 8:06 A.M. and the store's attendant is idle. Therefore, service for the first customer begins at 8:06 A.M., and the first customer does not have to wait at all for service. The second customer, however, arrives at 8:11 A.M. and the attendant does not finish serving the first customer until 8:12 A.M. Consequently, the second customer has to wait one minute for service to begin.

5. In column 8 a "running" clock is used to keep track of when service ends for the 30 simulated customers. The service ending time for a particular customer is simply the sum of the service beginning time plus the (simulated) service time. To illustrate, the service beginning time for the first customer is 8:06 A.M. and the first customer requires 6 minutes for service. Therefore, the service ending time is 8:06 A.M. plus 6 minutes, or 8:12 A.M.

6. The time each customer has to wait is tracked in column 9. The customer waiting time is computed by subtracting the customer arrival time from the time when customer service actually begins. For the first customer, the arrival time is 8:06 A.M. and the customer service

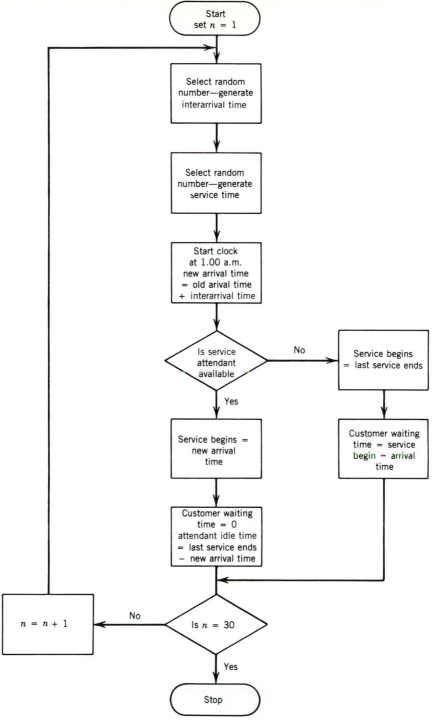

FIGURE 18.5 FLOWCHART FOR SIMULATING JANE'S QUIK PHOTO QUEUING PROBLEM (n = 30 CUSTOMERS).

TABLE 18.11   SIMULATION OF JANE'S QUIK PHOTO QUEUING PROBLEM

(1) CUSTOMER	(2) RANDOM NUMBER (INTERARRIVAL TIME)	(3) INTERARRIVAL TIME (MIN)	(4) RANDOM NUMBER (SERVICE TIME)	(5) SERVICE TIME (MIN)	(6) ARRIVAL TIME	(7) CLOCK SERVICE BEGINS	(8) SERVICE ENDS	(9) CUSTOMER WAITING TIME (MIN)	(10) ATTENDANT IDLE (MIN) (STORE OPEN AT 8:00 A.M.)
1	77	6	62	6	8:06	8:06	8:12		6
2	22	5	78	6	8:11	8:12	8:18	1	
3	72	6	20	4	8:17	8:18	8:22	1	
4	08	4	86	7	8:21	8:22	8:29	1	
5	86	7	67	6	8:28	8:29	8:35	1	
6	63	6	84	7	8:34	8:35	8:42	1	
7	02	3	05	3	8:37	8:42	8:45	5	
8	92	8	14	4	8:45	8:45	8:49		1
9	26	5	36	5	8:50	8:50	8:55		
10	34	5	85	7	8:55	8:55	9:02		
11	77	6	19	4	9:01	9:02	9:06	1	
12	22	5	07	3	9:06	9:06	9:09		
13	66	6	86	7	9:12	9:12	9:19		3
14	96	8	98	7	9:20	9:20	9:27		1

15	88	7	00	3	9:27	9:27	9:30		
16	60	5	19	4	9:32	9:32	9:36		2
17	05	3	65	6	9:35	9:36	9:44	1	
18	95	8	59	5	9:43	9:44	9:49	1	
19	33	5	25	4	9:48	9:49	9:53	1	
20	20	4	74	6	9:52	9:53	9:59	1	
21	77	6	03	3	9:58	9:59	10:02	1	
22	03	3	70	6	10:01	10:02	10:08	1	
23	58	5	92	7	10:06	10:08	10:15	2	
24	22	5	40	5	10:11	10:15	10:20	4	
25	09	4	51	5	10:15	10:20	10:25	5	
26	76	6	61	6	10:21	10:25	10:31	4	
27	59	5	08	3	10:26	10:31	10:34	5	
28	44	5	79	7	10:31	10:34	10:40	3	
29	52	5	81	7	10:36	10:40	10:47	4	
30	88	7	18	4	10:43	10:47	10:51	4	
Totals								48 min	13 min
Average								48/30 = 1.60 min	0.43 min

SIMULATION OF A WAITING LINE SYSTEM

begins at 8:06 A.M. Therefore, customer waiting time is zero minutes. For the second customer, the arrival time is 8:11 A.M. and the customer service begins at 8:12 A.M. Therefore, customer waiting time is one minute.

7. The time the attendant is idle is tracked in column 10. The attendant idle time for a particular customer is the difference between when the service for the current customer begins and the service for the last customer ends. For the first customer, the store opens at 8:00 A.M. and the first customer does not actually arrive until 8:06 A.M. Therefore, the attendant is idle 6 minutes. For the second customer, service begins at 8:12 A.M., which is the same time at which service ended for the previous customer. Consequently the attendant is idle zero minutes.

For the 30 customer simulation shown in Table 18.11 the average time a customer has to wait is 48 minutes/30 customers = 1.60 minutes. Additionally, the attendant is idle an average of 13 minutes/30 customers = 0.43 minute.

It should again be emphasized that this simulation has been done for a relatively small sample size (i.e., 30 customers). In fact, we can observe that the simulation has run only to 10:51 A.M., or for about 3 hours. Therefore, Jane would probably want to at least extend the simulation to about 80 customers in order to obtain results for an entire day. If a computer were available, she might want to run the simulation for an extended period of perhaps a week (i.e., about 400 customers). The results obtained thus far indicate that average customer waiting time and average attendant idle time are both rather small. Therefore, it appears likely that Jane will be able to run her photo shop in an efficient manner using a single attendant.

18.7 SIMULATION OF AN INVENTORY SYSTEM

In the two chapters concerning inventory control we considered both deterministic models (Chapter 15) and probabilistic models (Chapter 16). We observed that the analysis required for probabilistic models was generally a great deal more difficult than that required for deterministic models. Consequently, it is often very useful to analyze probabilistic inventory situations by means of simulation.

In this section we simulate an inventory problem involving a women's shoes retailer. Mrs. Pat Smithfield, owner and manager of Pat's Fashion Shoes, would like to be able to establish both the reorder point and the order quantity for a particular type of women's shoes that has a probabilistic weekly demand and a probabilistic reorder lead time. Pat would like to use simulation to conduct a series of experiments involving various order quantities and reorder points. In each experiment her objective will be that of minimizing the total weekly inventory policy cost for the run, which will be composed of the ordering, holding, and shortage costs.

Pat has collected weekly demand (sales) data for the particular type of women's shoes and has compiled, in Table 18.12, the following set of probabilities and associated random number intervals.

TABLE 18.12 PROBABILITIES AND RANDOM NUMBER INTERVALS: WEEKLY DEMAND FOR A TYPE OF WOMEN'S SHOE

WEEKLY DEMAND FOR PAIRS OF WOMEN'S SHOES	FREQUENCY OF DEMAND	PROBABILITY OF DEMAND	CUMULATIVE DEMAND PROBABILITY	INTERVAL OF RANDOM NUMBERS
25	5	.05	.05	00 to 04
30	10	.10	.15	05 to 14
40	20	.20	.35	15 to 34
50	25	.25	.60	35 to 59
60	25	.25	.85	60 to 84
70	10	.10	.95	85 to 94
80	5	.05	1.00	95 to 99

TABLE 18.13   PROBABILITIES AND REORDER LEAD TIMES FOR A TYPE OF WOMEN'S SHOE

REORDER LEAD TIME (WEEKS)	FREQUENCY OF OCCURRENCE	PROBABILITY OF OCCURRENCE	CUMULATIVE PROBABILITY OF OCCURRENCE	INTERVAL OF RANDOM NUMBERS
1	10	.10	.10	00 to 09
2	30	.30	.40	10 to 39
3	20	.20	.60	40 to 59
4	30	.30	.90	60 to 89
5	10	.10	1.00	90 to 99

Similarly, she has collected reorder lead time data for the particular type of women's shoes and has compiled the following set of probabilities and associated random number intervals. She has determined that the reorder lead time data shown in Table 18.13 apply to both orders that are made as a result of lost sales and orders that occur as a result of the inventory level reaching the reorder point.

Pat has also made an estimate of the various costs associated with her inventory system. She estimates that her inventory holding costs are $0.25 for each pair of shoes held in inventory at the end of a week. A lost sales cost of $2.00 is incurred for each pair of shoes that is not available when demanded by a customer. The cost of placing an order for shoes is $5.00, regardless of the number of pairs of shoes ordered.

Initially, Pat would like to simulate 26 weeks (i.e., one-half year) of retailing operations with a predetermined reorder point of 40 pairs of shoes and a predetermined reorder quantity of 60 pairs of shoes. To begin this simulation experiment she assumes that the beginning inventory is 100 pairs of shoes, and no replenishment or lost sales orders are due in week $n = 1$.

Prior to actually conducting the simulation experiments Pat decides that she will prepare a flowchart of the logic of the simulation process she will utilize. The flowchart for this inventory example is shown in Figure 18.6. Observe that the logic of this simulation problem is more detailed and complex than that of the two previous problems.

The first simulation experiment is summarized for a 26-week period (i.e., $n = 26$) in Table 18.14. This table is constructed in a week-by-week manner, according to the steps shown in the preceding flowchart.

1. Begin each simulated week, $n = 1, 2, \ldots,$ 26, by checking to see whether a previous order has arrived (column 2). If it has, increase the weekly beginning inventory (column 3) by the amount received.

2. Generate the weekly demand from the cumulative demand probability distribution in Table 18.12 by using a random number. The random number used is recorded in column 4 and the corresponding (simulated) weekly demand is recorded in column 5.

3. Compute the weekly ending inventory as weekly beginning inventory minus simulated weekly demand. The weekly ending inventory is recorded in column 6, with a negative weekly ending inventory being recorded as zero. A negative weekly ending inventory means that lost sales of this same amount have occurred. Lost sales in any week are denoted by a "Yes" in column 7, with the amount of lost sales being shown in column 8.

4. When lost sales *do occur* in any week we automatically place a lost sales order equal to the amount of the lost sales. In this manner, if we continue to experience lost sales over several weeks we continue to increase the aggregate amount ordered by the amount of the cumulative lost sales. The lost sales order lead time is generated from the cumulative probability of occurrence in Table 18.13 by using a random number. The random number used to generate the lost sales order lead time is shown in column 9, and the corresponding (simulated) reorder lead time is shown in column 10.

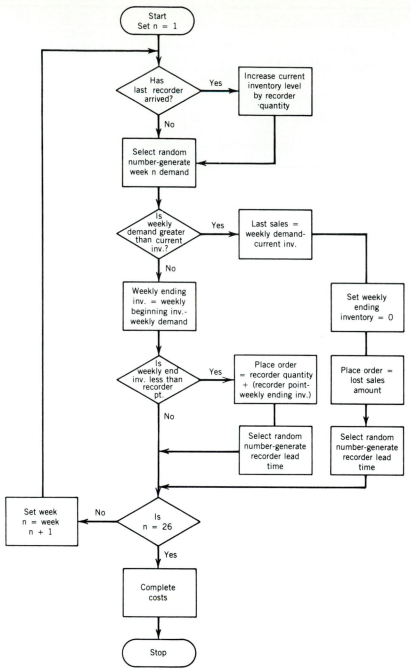

FIGURE 18.6 FLOWCHART FOR SIMULATING PAT'S FASHION SHOES INVENTORY PROBLEM ($n = 26$ WEEKS).

5. When lost sales *do not occur* in any week we compare the weekly ending inventory to the predetermined reorder point. If the weekly ending inventory is above the reorder point, we take no action, and the weekly ending inventory for the current week becomes the weekly beginning inventory for the next week. If the weekly ending inventory is at or below the reorder point, we place a replenishment order equal to the predetermined reorder

TABLE 18.14 INITIAL SIMULATION: PAT'S FASHION SHOES INVENTORY PROBLEM

(1) WEEK	(2) SIZE OF ORDER(S) RECEIVED	(3) WEEKLY BEGINNING INVENTORY	(4) WEEKLY DEMAND (RN)	(5) WEEKLY DEMAND (PAIRS OF SHOES)	(6) WEEKLY ENDING INVENTORY	(7) LOST SALES ?	(8) LOST SALES AMOUNT	(9) REORDER LEAD TIME (RN)	(10) REORDER LEAD TIME (WEEKS)	(11) REORDER POINT ?	(12) ORDER SIZE	(13) REORDER LEAD TIME (RN)	(14) REORDER LEAD TIME (WEEKS)
1	—	100	69	60	40	No		09	1	Yes	60	14	2
2	—	40	99	80	0	Yes	40	43	3				
3	—	0	13	30	0	Yes	30						
4	60+40	100	96	80	20	No		18	2	Yes	80	82	4
5	—	20	93	70	0	Yes	50	74	4				
6	—	0	57	50	0	Yes	50	99	5				
7	30	30	23	40	0	Yes	10	46	3				
8	50	50	81	60	0	Yes	10						
9	80	80	92	70	10	No		23	2	Yes	90	38	2
10	—	10	28	40	0	Yes	30	93	5				
11	50	50	91	70	0	Yes	20						
12	10+90	100	70	60	40	No				Yes	60	60	4
13	10+30	80	03	25	55	No				No			
14	—	55	11	30	25	No		09	1	Yes	75	14	2
15	—	25	31	40	0	Yes	15	23	2				
16	—	0	15	40	0	Yes	40						
17	60+15+75+20	170	83	60	110	No				No			
18	—	110	66	60	50	No				No			
19	40	90	03	25	65	No				No			
20	—	65	75	60	5	No		74	4	Yes	95	13	2
21	—	5	04	25	0	Yes	20	23	2				
22	—	0	11	30	0	Yes	30						
23	95	95	44	50	45	No				No			
24	—	45	68	60	0	Yes	15	99	5				
25	30	30	34	40	0	Yes	10	59	3				
26	20	20	11	30	0	Yes	10	55	3				
Totals		1370			465		380				460		
Weekly averages		52.7			17.9		14.6				17.7		

Note: Reorder point = 40 pairs of shoes; reorder quantity = 60 pairs of shoes.

quantity (i.e., 60 pairs of shoes) plus the difference between the predetermined reorder point (i.e., 40 pairs of shoes) and the weekly ending inventory. In this manner we seek to replenish back to the reorder point (40 pairs of shoes) or to a total inventory of 100 pairs of shoes. The fact that the reorder point has been reached is shown by a "Yes" in column 11. The order size of the replenishment order is shown in column 12. The replenishment order lead time is generated from the cumulative probability of occurrence distribution in Table 18.13 using a random number. The random number for the replenishment order lead time is shown in column 13, and the corresponding replenishment order lead time is shown in column 14.

It should be emphasized that these steps follow the logic specified for this particular simulation model. In another approach to this problem the logic of the simulation model could be different. For example, one could have used logic that specified that when weekly ending inventory was at or below the reorder point, we would always order exactly the reorder quantity (i.e., always order exactly 60 pairs of shoes, regardless of the level to which ending weekly inventory has fallen). Thus, determination of the logic used in a particular simulation model is left to the discretion of the quantitative modeler and/or the manager.

The initial simulation for Pat's Fashion Shoes inventory problem indicates the following summary results:

$$\text{Total weekly ending inventory} = 1370 \text{ pairs of shoes} \quad (18.5)$$

$$\text{Average weekly ending inventory} = \frac{1370 \text{ pairs}}{26 \text{ weeks}} = 52.7 \text{ pairs/week} \quad (18.6)$$

$$\text{Total lost sales} = 380 \text{ pairs of shoes} \quad (18.7)$$

$$\text{Average weekly lost sales} = \frac{380 \text{ pairs}}{26 \text{ weeks}}$$
$$= 14.6 \text{ pairs/week} \quad (18.8)$$

In total 15 orders were placed as a result of lost sales and 6 orders were placed as a result of weekly ending inventory reaching or falling below the reorder point.

$$\text{Total weekly lost sales orders} = 15 \quad (18.19)$$

$$\text{Average weekly number of lost sales orders}$$
$$= \frac{15 \text{ orders}}{26 \text{ weeks}} = 0.58 \text{ order/week} \quad (18.10)$$

$$\text{Total weekly replenishment orders} = 6 \quad (18.11)$$

$$\text{Average weekly number of replenishment orders}$$
$$= \frac{6 \text{ orders}}{26 \text{ weeks}} = 0.23 \text{ order/week} \quad (18.12)$$

$$\text{Total average weekly number of orders}$$
$$= (\text{average of lost sales orders})$$
$$\quad + (\text{average number of replenishment orders})$$
$$= (0.58 \text{ order/week}) + (0.23 \text{ order/week})$$
$$= (0.81 \text{ order/week}) \quad (18.13)$$

Pat would now like to determine the total weekly cost associated with her initial inventory policy. The total weekly inventory policy cost is composed of three parts.

$$\text{Weekly inventory holding cost}$$
$$= (\text{average weekly ending inventory})$$
$$\quad \times (\text{cost of holding a pair of shoes in inventory for one week})$$
$$= (52.7 \text{ pairs/week}) \times (\$0.25 \text{ pair/week})$$
$$= \$13.18 \quad (18.14)$$

$$\text{Weekly lost sales cost}$$
$$= (\text{average weekly lost sales})$$
$$\quad \times (\text{lost sales cost for a pair of shoes})$$
$$= (14.6 \text{ pairs/week}) \times (\$2/\text{pair})$$
$$= \$29.20 \quad (18.15)$$

$$\text{Weekly ordering cost}$$
$$= (\text{total average weekly orders})$$
$$\quad \times (\text{cost of placing an order})$$
$$= (0.81 \text{ order/week}) \times (\$5/\text{order})$$
$$= \$4.05 \quad (18.16)$$

$$\text{Total weekly inventory cost}$$
$$= \text{weekly inventory holding cost}$$
$$\quad + \text{weekly lost sales cost}$$
$$\quad + \text{weekly ordering cost}$$
$$= \$13.18 + \$29.20 + \$4.05$$
$$= \$46.43 \quad (18.17)$$

It should be emphasized that this initial simulation experiment has been tested for only 26 weeks (i.e., one-half year). Before Pat would feel comfortable making an inventory policy decision, she would need to take two additional actions. First, she would need to extend the initial simulation experiment to a much longer time period, say 104 weeks (i.e., 2 years) if she continued to simulate by hand, or to 520 weeks (i.e., 10 years) or 1040 weeks (i.e., 20 years) if she was able to use a computer to make the calculations. Second, Pat would need to test several additional inventory policies to see what policy produced the lowest total weekly inventory cost. Problems 4 and 5 at the end of this chapter ask you to perform simulation experiments, using the same set of data, for different inventory policies, while Problem 6 asks you to compare the economic consequences of these different inventory policies.

18.8 COMPUTERIZING SIMULATION MODELS

The simulation examples we have presented so far in this chapter have been solved manually. In practice, most simulation models are computerized, and then the computerized model is used to make extensive test runs. The computer programming aspects of simulation can be quite complex, and entail the following general activities.

1. Flowcharting of the logic of the simulation model.
2. Computer coding of the logic of the simulation model
   a. General-purpose languages;
   b. Special-purpose languages.
3. Error checking.
4. Data input and starting conditions.
5. Generating test results and output.

The need for flowcharting the basic logic of the simulation model cannot be overemphasized, as it is not uncommon for simulation models to become extremely large and complex. A good flowchart serves to outline the logical sequence of events to be carried out by the computer within a sequential time frame. Note that flowcharts were done for each of the three previous examples.

Once the programming logic for the simulation model has been outlined, the computer code for making simulation runs or tests on the computer can be written. Two types of computer programming languages are available.

First, a general-purpose programming language such as FORTRAN, PL/1, PASCAL, or BASIC can be used. These programming languages afford a great deal of flexibility, are available at most computer installations, and are provided as part of the purchase of the computer itself. They are widely known and understood, and most programmers will have a good working knowledge of one or more of them.

Second, a special-purpose programming language can be used. Because of the widespread application of simulation modeling, a number of special-purpose programming languages designed specifically for simulation work have been developed. These languages typically have several desirable features, such as

1. Random number generators;
2. Clock routines that track events over the simulated time horizon;
3. Process generators that allow the generation of random variates for several probability distributions (e.g., normal, Poisson, exponential);
4. Data plotting routines;
5. Statistical data gathering routines (e.g., means, variances, standard deviations);
6. Output report generating routines that produce a series of fixed-format reports;
7. Diagnostic checking capabilities for the language that automatically check for both syntax and logical errors.

Use of special-purpose simulation languages may reduce the programming flexibility of the modeler. Also, many of these languages are proprietary, so there is a cost associated with their acquisition and use. Finally, one must learn how to program and apply them. Because of the widespread utilization of special purpose simulation languages, a few of the more prominent ones are now briefly described.

18.8.1 SPECIAL-PURPOSE SIMULATION LANGUAGES

A large number of special-purpose simulation languages are in existence. We will not attempt to review a large number of these; rather, we focus on providing a brief review of a few of the more frequently used ones. More extensive details concerning them can be found in the Selected References at the end of the chapter.

DYNAMO. This language was developed at MIT by Fox and Pugh, and was an outgrowth of the modeling approach advocated by Jay Forrester for analyzing industrial systems. DYNAMO utilizes first-order difference equations to model continuous functional relationships. State variables, rate variables, and auxiliary equations are used. The state variables (called level equations in DYNAMO) are used to describe the state of the system at a given point in time. The rate variables are used to describe how the states change with time. The auxiliary equations describe the function of the rate equations, and provide feedback control of the rates. DYNAMO emphasizes information feedback and delays.

DYNAMO has been employed in simulating industrial problems, urban problems, social problems, and even world systems planning. It is fairly easy to use, and does not require prior programming knowledge. The problem to be analyzed must be continuous in structure in order to be modeled using DYNAMO. It does require a language compiler, and thus it is not available on all computers. It is a proprietary product.

GASP IV. This language was developed by Pritsker and Hurst in 1974, as a successor to the GASP II language that was introduced in 1963. GASP IV has the capability of performing both discrete and continuous changes within the same simulation. It utilizes a series of verb-type statements to control the simulation run and produce output reports. It is written entirely in FORTRAN IV, and thus can be used on any computer that has a FORTRAN IV compiler. This is an excellent feature, and allows the programmer to modify the program, using FORTRAN IV, if desired. The programmer must also have a good working knowledge of FORTRAN IV in order to model using GASP IV. It is also a proprietary product.

GPSS. The General Purpose Simulation System, or GPSS, was originally developed in the early 1960s by Geoffrey Gordon of IBM. GPSS is a problem-oriented programming language that is designed primarily for analyzing queuing systems. A GPSS model is constructed by means of block diagrams using GPSS block commands that represent operational functions of the system being analyzed. About 40 different types of blocks are available in GPSS and are used for transactions involving facilities, queues, and storages, over time.

GPSS is fairly easy to use and does not require prior programming knowledge. Although it was developed at IBM and is a proprietary product, it is available on a wide range of computer systems. One problem with its use is that many GPSS programs require lengthy computer run times.

SIMSCRIPT. This language was developed at the RAND Corporation in the early 1960s. It is FORTRAN-based, and is designed for the simulation of discrete systems. It utilizes a series of verb-type statements to control the simulation run and produce output reports. SIMSCRIPT defines the system to be simulated in terms of (1) the *entities*, or components that make up the system; (2) the properties associated with the entities, or the *attributes* of the system; and (3) *sets*, or groups of entities.

SIMSCRIPT requires its own special compiler and is available only on certain computer systems. It is a proprietary product that requires a good knowledge of FORTRAN in order to be used effectively, and most versions require a large amount of computer storage.

18.9 OTHER CONSIDERATIONS IN USING SIMULATION

In the previous section of this chapter we addressed one of the major considerations in using simulation, namely how to go about computerizing simulation models. In this section we briefly discuss some other considerations in using simulation that are important and are likely to be encountered in making a simulation study.

18.9.1 STARTUP CONDITIONS AND EQUILIBRIUM

In most simulation studies we are concerned with the operation of the system under *steady-state*, or equilibrium, operating conditions. When we first begin the simulation process a *transient*, or startup effect can occur. In our example involving the inventory problem (i.e., Pat's Fashion Shoes, Section 18.7), recall that we did not begin the simulation with a zero inventory because this would have been a very atypical condition. Rather we started the simulation with a beginning inventory of 100 pairs of shoes, and assumed that no replenishment orders were due. Even though our assumed starting conditions may be realistic, however, the data collected during the first part of the simulation can be expected to differ from the data collected during later time periods.

Now, there are several ways in which we can reduce the biasing effect of the initial startup period, including

1. exclude a part of the early results produced during the simulation run;

2. use a long time period for the simulation run, so that the results obtained for the transient period at the beginning of the run are not a significant part of the total simulation results;

3. select the initial starting conditions so that they accurately represent the actual steady-state conditions.

Each of these procedures has advantages and disadvantages in terms of cost and accuracy.

Testing of the simulation model should be done under equilibrium conditions. Unfortunately, there are no hard and fast rules that indicate when equilibrium has been achieved. Some general guidelines for obtaining equilibrium conditions, however, have been suggested. Among them are the following.

1. Examine the sequence of results from the simulation run, and compute an average value for some output variable. If the number of observations in which the output value is greater than the average value is about the same as the number of observations in which the output value is less than the average value, then steady-state conditions may have been achieved.

2. Compute a moving average for some output variable. When this moving average no longer changes over time, then equilibrium may have been accomplished.

3. Run the simulation using different seed values and examine the sequence of results. If the results are consistent, then equilibrium may have been accomplished.

18.9.2 SAMPLE SIZE (NUMBER OF ITERATIONS)

A second important consideration is that of sample size, or the number of iterations for the simulation. Herein, the analyst must decide on the sample size required to achieve statistical significance for a given expenditure. Again, it is very difficult to consider all the approaches to sample size determination in this chapter. In general two approaches are used.

1. The sample size is determined prior to, and independently of, the operation of the model.

2. The sample size is determined during the operation of the model as a function of the results generated from the operation of the model.

Using the first approach, the assumption is often made that the responses of the model are independent and normally distributed. Then, a confidence limit approach to determining the required sample size is used. For example, suppose that we are interested in determining the sample size based on a confidence interval for the mean. Suppose that we seek to determine an estimate $\bar{x}$ of the true population mean μ, such that

$$P\{\mu - \epsilon \le \bar{x} \le \mu + \epsilon\} = 1 - \alpha \quad (18.18)$$

WHERE

$\bar{x}$ = sample mean;

μ = population mean;

ϵ = tolerable error of the estimate;

$1 - \alpha$ = probability that the interval $\mu \pm \epsilon$ contains $\bar{x}$.

Under the assumption of normality of the sampling distribution of $\bar{x}$, the required sample size can be shown to be

$$n = \frac{Z_{\alpha/2}^2 \sigma^2}{\epsilon^2} = \text{required sample size} \quad (18.19)$$

WHERE

$Z^2_{\alpha/2}$ = standard normal deviate for $\alpha/2$;

σ = population standard deviation;

ϵ = tolerable error of the mean.

To use this formula we must know σ, $Z_{\alpha/2}$, and ϵ. These values are estimated or determined as a result of a short pilot experiment.

Using the second approach to sample size determination, we compute the confidence intervals for the output values as they are generated during a simulation run and then terminate the run when a predefined confidence interval objective has been met. This approach involves setting automatic stopping rules for the simulation. Two basic approaches can be used.[5]

1. Run the simulation in two stages. First, run a sample of size n and collect the resulting statistical information. Use these results to estimate n^*, using a statistical procedure such as that previously described. If $n^* < n$, the run has been completed. If $n^* > n$, extend the run by $n^* - n$.

2. Specify a minimum n and take a sample. Calculate the sample standard deviation s for this sample. Then compute the quantity

$$d = \frac{(s)t_{1-\alpha, n-1}}{\sqrt{n}} \qquad (18.20)$$

WHERE

s = sample standard deviation;

$t_{1-\alpha, n-1}$ = t statistic for $1 - \alpha$, $n - 1$ degrees of freedom;

n = sample size.

---

[5]For further details, see Robert E. Shannon, *Systems Simulation.* Englewood Cliffs, N.J.: Prentice–Hall, 1975, pp. 197–203.

The quantity d is then compared to ϵ, and the simulation is terminated when $d \leq \epsilon$ for the first time.

18.9.3 SIMULATION MODEL VALIDATION

A very important and necessary step in any simulation study is the validation of the simulation model. Validation basically involves trying to measure how well the simulation model represents the real-world problem or system it is trying to simulate. Before the manager can place confidence in the results obtained from a simulation model, he or she has to be confident that the simulation model accurately reflects the behavior of the real-world system.

In far too many simulation studies very little attention is given to model validation. Often, the primary emphasis is on model design and computerization. As a result, the modeler may spend so much time and effort on model design and computerization that little time is left for analysis and validation of the simulation results.

There are several ways in which a simulation model can be validated. First, the simulation results can be compared to past historical data for the system, assuming such data are in existence. If such data are available, the simulation model is run using these data, and the simulated output data are compared to the actual output data. If major discrepancies exist, flaws in model design or development are indicated.

A second approach to simulation model validation is to have the model, and the results from the model, reviewed by knowledgable persons who are familiar with the operation of the real system. This process is sometimes referred to as "face validity." This approach to validation stresses the reasonableness and completeness of the results. It affords an excellent opportunity to involve knowledgeable managers in the simulation process by making them responsible for validation.

A third approach to validation involves the comparison of the simulated probability distributions to the corresponding probability distributions for the real system. For example, in the Jane's Quik Photo queuing problem the customer interarrival time probability was a key input variable, and we assumed it to be known. In Table 18.15 a comparison of the simulated relative frequencies of interarrival times and the actual probabilities of inter-

TABLE 18.15 COMPARISON OF SIMULATED RELATIVE FREQUENCIES OF INTERARRIVAL TIMES AND ACTUAL PROBABILITIES OF INTERARRIVAL TIMES: JANE'S QUIK PHOTO QUEUING PROBLEM

INTERARRIVAL TIME	ACTUAL PROBABILITY OF INTERARRIVAL TIME	NUMBER OF SIMULATED CUSTOMERS HAVING INTERARRIVAL TIME	SIMULATED RELATIVE FREQUENCIES
3	.07	3	3/30 = 0.10
4	.15	3	3/30 = 0.10
5	.40	11	11/30 = 0.37
6	.20	7	7/30 = 0.23
7	.10	3	3/30 = 0.10
8	.08	3	3/30 = 0.10
	1.00	30	1.00

arrival times for the Jane's Quik Photo queuing problem is presented.

A comparison of the simulated distribution and the actual probability distribution, as seen in Table 18.15, shows general management. Consequently, we could probably conclude that the interarrival time probabilities for this problem are being simulated correctly. This type of analysis can, and should, be done routinely as a part of simulation model validation.

18.10 ADVANTAGES AND DISADVANTAGES OF SIMULATION

There have been numerous applications of simulation modeling in a wide variety of business and managerial situations. Simulation is considered to be a valuable approach to solving a wide range of problems. Among its many advantages are the following.

1. It can be used to analyze and solve large, complex real-world problems that cannot be solved by using other quantitative methods. For example, simulation can be employed in situations where the relationships do not follow the restrictions of linearity.

2. It can be used to study a system without actually disrupting that system. For example, one of the authors has simulated a large distribution network, and has measured the effect of alternative plant and warehouse configurations, without physically disrupting the distribution network.

3. Simulation typically involves the manager in the problem definition, model construction, and results validation phase. Consequently, it greatly facilitates user involvement.

4. The results of simulation studies are often easier to understand than the results from other quantitative models. This is particularly true for the "what-if" types of questions that simulation models allow to be asked.

5. Simulation facilitates the compression of long periods of time. For example, an inventory policy can be tested for several months, or even several years, very quickly by means of a computerized simulation model.

6. Simulation often highlights the importance of specific variables or specific relationships in a particular system.

Although simulation modeling is a very useful and important quantitative method, it should not be regarded as a panacea and used indiscriminately. Simulation also has a number of disadvantages.

1. Simulation models are inherently time-consuming and costly to construct and run on computers.

2. Simulation does not generate optimal solutions, such as those obtained by the use of linear programming, or other quantitative methods.

3. Simulation provides only statistical estimates, not exact results. Thus, the judgments of the analyst and manager are required to compare alternatives and select a course of action.

4. Each simulation model is applicable to a particular problem situation. Transference of results to other problems is generally not possible.

5. Simulation model results may be very difficult to validate.

In summary, simulation modeling is more of an art than a science. Nevertheless, it is a very flexible and useful tool for management decision making.

18.11   SUMMARY

In this chapter we have observed how various problems can be solved using computer simulation. While computer simulation does not always produce the optimal solution, as was the case for linear programming or the transportation method, it is a very important and useful method.

Simulation modeling is particularly useful for problems involving total systems. As such, it is very useful in managerial decision-making situations involving complex systems composed of large numbers of variables, each interacting with the other according to complicated performance rules. Managerial decision making has thus evolved from purely analytical methods to the experimental methods of simulation.

We also noted that there are both pluses and minuses with respect to the use of simulation. Although it is a very useful tool, it should not be used in a haphazard manner. It produces results that are statistical estimates and that may be hard to validate. Therefore, in the final analysis simulation is more of an art than a science, and its effective use requires considerable judgment by both the modeler and the manager.

GLOSSARY

Analytical Techniques   Quantitative techniques that result in the determination of a single "best" answer (e.g., linear programming).

DYNAMO   A special-purpose simulation language that uses first-order difference equations to model continuous relationships.

Experimental Techniques   Quantitative techniques, such as simulation, that usually result in a series of answers, any one of which may be acceptable to the decision maker.

GASP IV   A FORTRAN-based special-purpose simulation language that can be used to model discrete or continuous problems.

GPSS   A special-purpose simulation language used for discrete event problems, particularly those encountered in queuing theory.

Iterations   The run size or number of samples drawn in a simulation study.

Midsquare Method   A mathematical procedure for generating pseudorandom numbers.

Monte Carlo Sampling   A sampling process used to randomly select sample values from a probability distribution.

Multiplicative Congruential Method   A mathematical procedure for generating pseudorandom numbers.

Pseudorandom Numbers   A sequence of numbers that is reproducible, predictable, and that occurs randomly, which is generated by some mathematical process.

Random Number   A random variable uniformly distributed over the unit interval 0 to 1.

Random Number Generator   A mechanical device or computer subroutine that generates the random numbers used in the Monte Carlo method.

Seed   A starting number used to generate a sequence of pseudorandom numbers.

SIMSCRIPT   A FORTRAN-based special-purpose simulation language that can be used to model discrete event problems.

Simulation Modeling   A numerical technique for conducting experiments on a digital computer, which involves certain types of mathematical and logical models that describe the behavior of a business or economic system over extended periods of real time.

Steady-State Conditions   Conditions that specify the operation of a system at equilibrium or at normal conditions.

Transient Conditions   The variability in the output of a simulation experiment that results from the initial starting conditions.

Validation of the Simulation Model   The determination of how closely the simulation model predicts the behavior of the physical system or managerial process being examined.

Selected References

Bonini, Charles P. 1963. *Simulation of Information and Decision Systems in the Firm.* Englewood Cliffs, N.J.: Prentice–Hall.

Chorafas, D.N. 1965. *Systems and Simulation.* New York, Academic Press.

Emshoff, James R., and Roger L. Sisson. 1970. *Design and Use of Computer Simulation Models.* New York: Macmillan Co.

Forrester, J. 1961. *Industrial Dynamics.* Cambridge, Mass.: MIT Press.

Gordon, Geoffrey. 1978. *System Simulation.* Englewood Cliffs, N.J.: Prentice–Hall.

Hammersley, J.M., and D.C. Handscomb. 1964. *Monte Carlo Methods.* London: Methuen.

Hoggatt, Austin C., and Frederick E. Balderstron, Eds. 1963. *Symposium on Simulation Models: Methodology and Applications to the Behavioral Sciences.* Cincinnati, Ohio: Southwestern.

Law, Averill, and W. David Kelton. 1982. *Simulation Modeling and Analysis.* New York: McGraw–Hill.

Markowitz, H.M., B. Hausner, and H.W. Karr. 1963. *SIMSCRIPT: A Simulation Programming Language.* Englewood Cliffs, N.J.: Prentice–Hall.

Meier, Robert C., William T. Newell, and Harold L. Pazer. 1969. *Simulation in Business and Economics.* Englewood Cliffs, N.J.: Prentice–Hall.

Mihram, G. Arthur. 1972. *Simulation: Statistical Foundations and Methodology.* New York: Academic Press.

Mize, Joe H., and J. Grady Cox. 1968. *Essentials of Simulation.* Englewood Cliffs, N.J.: Prentice–Hall.

Naylor, Thomas H. 1971. *Computer Simulation Experiments with Models of Economic Systems.* New York: Wiley.

Naylor, Thomas H., Joseph L. Balintfy, Donald S. Burdick, and Kong Chu. 1966. *Computer Simulation Techniques.* New York: Wiley.

Pritsker, Alan B. 1974. *The GASP IV Simulation Language.* New York: Wiley.

Pugh, Alexander L., III. 1963. *DYNAMO User's Manual.* Cambridge, Mass.: MIT Press.

Schmidt, J.W., and R.E. Taylor. 1970. *Simulation and Analysis of Industrial Systems.* Homewood, Ill.: Irwin.

Shannon, Robert E. 1975. *Systems Simulation.* Englewood Cliffs, N.J.: Prentice–Hall.

Smith, Wilfred Nye, Elmer E. Estey, and Ellsworth F. Vines. 1968. *Integrated Simulation.* Cincinnati, Ohio: Southwestern.

Tocher, K.D. 1963. *The Art of Simulation.* Princeton, N.J.: Van Nostrand.

RAND Corporation. 1955. *A Million Random Digits with 100,000 Normal Deviates.* Santa Monica, Calif.: Free Press.

Watson, Hugh J. 1981. *Computer Simulation in Business.* New York: Wiley.

Discussion Questions

1. What is the main difference between experimental methods (such as simulation) and analytical methods (such as linear programming)?

2. Describe the circumstances for which it may be appropriate to use simulation.

3. Define what we mean by simulation.

4. Describe the steps involved in the simulation modeling process.

5. Why is flowcharting so important in computerizing the simulation model?

6. Compare the advantages and disadvantages of a special-purpose simulation language and a general-purpose programming language.

7. Identify some of the more common special-purpose simulation languages.

8. Describe how random number generators are used in simulation studies.

9. What is the difference between a set of random numbers and a set of pseudorandom numbers?

10. What is meant by the "transient effect" in a simulation study?

11. What are some of the ways to reduce the biasing effect of the initial startup period in a simulation study?

12. What are some of the ways in which we may be able to measure when equilibrium conditions have been reached in a simulation study?

13. Describe approaches that can be used for sample size determination in a simulation study.

14. Why is validation so important in simulation modeling?

15. Describe some approaches to validation that are used in simulation modeling.

PROBLEMS

1. The time between arrivals at a drive-in bank teller's window is defined by the following probability distribution.

INTERARRIVAL TIME (MIN)	PROBABILITY
1	.10
2	.20
3	.30
4	.25
5	.15

Simulate the arrivals of 25 cars at the teller's window. Compute the simulated mean time between arrivals and compare it to the expected value of the time between arrivals.

2. The number of tune-ups done daily at the local Exquisite Tune-Up shop during the last 50 weeks is shown in the following table.

NUMBER OF TUNEUP JOBS	NUMBER OF WEEKS
5	8
6	12
7	16
8	8
9	6

a. Assign random numbers to the number of tune-ups performed corresponding to their relative frequency over the last 50 weeks.
b. Simulate 25 weeks of activity and compute the average number of tuneup jobs done weekly. Compare this number to the expected value of the number of tune-ups.

3. The Great Midwestern Barge Company operates a barge terminal at Cape Girardeau on the Mississippi River. The company's barge facility has a simple dock that is used to load and unload grains from barges. The following set of data has been gathered with respect to barge arrivals and unloadings.

TIME BETWEEN ARRIVALS OF SUCCESSIVE BARGES (HR)	FREQUENCY	TIME REQUIRED TO UNLOAD BARGES (HR)	FREQUENCY
0 to 2.99	15	0 to 4.99	10
3.00 to 6.99	25	5.00 to 8.99	20
7.00 to 10.99	25	9.00 to 13.99	40
11.00 to 14.99	10	14.00 to 23.99	20
15.00 to 18.99	10	24.00 to 30.00	10
19.00 to 24.00	15		

The barges are unloaded on a first-come, first-served basis and the facility operates on a 24-hour basis, 7 days a week. Simulate the arrival and unloading of 30 barges. Compute the average waiting time for unloading a barge, and the percentage of time the terminal facility is idle.

4. For the inventory system described in Section 18.7 rerun the simulation experiment for a reorder point of 20 pairs of shoes and a reorder quantity of 40 pairs of shoes, using a beginning inventory of 100 pairs of shoes, and assuming that no replenishment orders are due.

5. For the inventory system described in Section 18.7 rerun the simulation experiment for a reorder point of 50 pairs of shoes, and a reorder quantity of 50 pairs of shoes, using a beginning inventory of 100 pairs of shoes, and assuming that no replenishment orders are due.

6. Using the information given in Section 18.7, compute the economic characteristics for Problems 4 and 5. How do they compare to those computed in Section 18.7? What inventory system should be used in this situation? Why?

7. Rent-A-Junker rents late model used cars and is interested in determining how many cars to have in its rental fleet. Based on rental records of the last two years, the management of Rent-A-Junker has structured the following probability distributions. Rent-A-Junker makes a $20 net profit per day for each car rented. If a customer wants to rent a junker (oops—a car!) and none is available, the goodwill loss is $25. If a car is in inventory but rented, the daily storage cost is $3. Simulate 20 days of operation, starting with an initial inventory

NUMBER OF CARS RENTED DAILY	PROBABILITY OF RENTAL
0	.20
1	.20
2	.30
3	.15
4	.15

LENGTH OF RENTAL (DAYS)	PROBABILITY
1	.35
2	.30
3	.20
4	.15

of 12 cars on board, and none due to be returned. Assume that cars are immediately available for rental the day after they are returned. Determine the net profit after 20 days of operation.

8. Bob's Quick and Dirty Job Shop does customized machinery of metal parts. It receives a varying number of orders each day, with each order having a variation in the time required to process it. Bob has collected the following data concerning the daily order pattern. Bob estimates that it costs him $15/day for a backordered job resulting from a machine not being available, and $10/day for a machine being idle. Bob would like to have enough machines in his shop to balance the cost of being idle against the backorder cost. Perform a two-part simulation for this problem.

   a. Simulate 15 days of operation to find the proper number of machines to have in the shop.
   b. With this number of machines, rerun the simulation to measure the balance between idle cost and backorder cost.

NUMBER OF ORDERS RECEIVED DAILY	PROBABILITY
1	.05
2	.15
3	.25
4	.40
5	.15

DAYS REQUIRED PER ORDER	PROBABILITY
1	.05
2	.25
3	.30
4	.25
5	.15

9. You are self-employed as a microcomputer consultant. Assume that you have decided that it is time to do some personal budgeting. Over the past two years you have studied your monthly income and expenditure patterns and have developed the following set of information.

MONTHLY INCOME	P(MONTHLY INCOME)	MONTHLY EXPENDITURES	P(MONTHLY EXPENDITURES)
1000	.20	800	.20
1500	.30	1000	.40
2000	.40	1400	.30
2500	.10	1900	.10

a. Simulate your monthly pattern of income and expenditures for the forthcoming 12 months. Assume that you begin with a balance of $500 in the bank. What is your balance at the end of the 12-month period?

b. What is your highest monthly balance during the year? What is your lowest monthly balance during the year? What is your average monthly balance for the year?

10. Bob Blair is a corn farmer in Armstrong, Missouri. Based on last year's experience he has made the following assessment of corn prices, crop yields in bushels per acre, and farming costs in dollars per acre. Assuming that corn prices, crop yields, and farming costs per acre are independent, simulate 20 computations of the profit per acre. What is the average or expected profit per acre?

CORN PRICES ($/BUSHEL)	PROBABILITY
3.00	.05
3.10	.20
3.25	.25
3.40	.30
3.50	.15
3.60	.05

CROP YIELDS (BUSHELS/ACRE)	PROBABILITY
40	.10
60	.20
80	.40
100	.20
120	.10

FARMING COSTS ($/ACRE)	PROBABILITY
40	.05
50	.20
60	.40
80	.30
100	.05

11. Visi-Tech, Inc., is trying to invent and manufacture a new type of self-developing film. It currently has two groups of scientists and engineers working on this project, and has made the following probability estimates of the times required to complete the project. The expected sales from the self-developing film are directly dependent on the time required by the project teams, since a number of other

TIME REQUIRED TO COMPLETE PROJECT	PROJECT TEAM NO. 1	NO. 2
6 months	.25	.30
12 months	.35	.40
18 months	.25	.20
24 months	.15	.10

TIME REQUIRED TO COMPLETE PROJECT	EXPECTED SALES VOLUME (ROLLS OF FILM)
6 months	15,000,000
12 months	13,000,000
18 months	8,000,000
24 months	5,000,000

companies are working on similar films. Visi-Tech, Inc., has made the following estimates of the expected sales volumes, as a function of the time required to complete the project. If Visi-Tech utilizes project team 1, it will need a $1 million capital investment. If Visi-Tech utilizes project team 2, it will need a $2 million capital investment. Simulate 15 trials for each of the two project teams. Which project team should be utilized by Visi-Tech?

12. Consider the following simple game of chance. You can repeatedly flip an unbiased coin until the difference between the number of heads tossed and the number of tails tossed is three. You will be required to pay $1 for each flip of the coin, but you will receive $10 at the end of the game. Simulate ten plays of this game and show whether or not you should play this game.

13. Rusty Parker is the maintenance foreman at a company that produces various machine parts (bolts, nuts, fasteners, screws). He is interested in developing a preventive maintenance plan for the machines in the plant. From past experience, he knows that there is a .15 probability that a machine will suffer a breakdown in any day. If a breakdown does occur, the repair times required for fixing the breakdown are distributed as follows. Perform a simulation experiment for a typical machine for 20 days. What is the average repair time for the simulation, and how does it compare to the expected value of the repair time?

REPAIR TIME (DAYS)	PROBABILITY
1	.30
2	.40
3	.30

14. The football coach at Powerhouse Tech plans to have eight halfbacks on his team for the upcoming season. He wants to evaluate how injuries might affect the availability of halfbacks for any particular game. He has studied injury patterns for the last five years and has made the following observations. Overall, there is a .20 probability of having a major injury (or injuries) in any game, a .60 probability of having a minor injury (or injuries), and a .20 probability of having no injuries. A minor injury puts the player out of the game in which it occurs, and the succeeding game. A major injury puts the player out for the remainder of the season. Draw a flowchart for this problem and simulate the injury pattern for a 13-game season. (Powerhouse Tech always plays in a bowl game.) Determine the availability of halfbacks on a game-by-game basis, and the low, high, and average number of halfbacks available over the season.

MAJOR INJURIES PER GAME	PROBABILITY
1	.80
2	.20

MINOR INJURIES PER GAME	PROBABILITY
1	.55
2	.20
3	.15
4	.10

15. Synergistic Systems, Inc., has been experiencing difficulty with its microcomputer disk drives, which have been experiencing a high

OPERATING HOURS BETWEEN DISK DRIVE PARTS FAILURE (ONE PART/REPAIR)	PROBABILITY
50	.05
60	.20
70	.40
80	.30
90	.05

OPERATING HOURS BETWEEN DISK DRIVE PARTS FAILURE (THREE PARTS/REPAIR)	PROBABILITY
100	.10
120	.15
140	.40
180	.25
200	.10

failure rate. The disk drives have three identical parts that are subject to failure. The disk drives will continue to operate as long as one of the parts has not failed. The company has been replacing these parts, one at a time, as failure occurs. One of the company's engineers feels, however, that it would be better to wait until all three parts fail and replace them all at one time. If only one part is replaced each time a breakdown occurs, the following data are appropriate. It takes about one hour to replace a single part, and each part costs $25. The hourly cost of a disk drive being unusable is $100. If all three parts are replaced only after they all fail, the following data are appropriate. It takes about three hours to replace all three parts at once. Simulate this situation for a total of at least 1000 operating hours for each policy. Which policy should the company follow, and why?

Application Review

Operations Planning in the Bell System Using Simulation

One of the major problems facing operational planners in the telephone utility industry is that of servicing customer complaints. Telephone repair operations are perceived by the telephone using public as being the key indicator of overall telephone service quality. In the early 1980s, the introduction of sophisticated automatic call-delivery systems and information tracking had given operational planners in the Bell System the opportunity to consolidate and centralize its repair service operations, using interactive, computer-controlled video-display terminals.

Operational planners in the Bell System were interested in designing a specific customer complaint configuration that met its operational needs, at a reasonable cost, while achieving a high degree of customer acceptance. For a typical proposed configuration, the planners were interested in answering the following questions.

1. Is the proposed configuration capable of handling the given call-answering load that will be imposed upon it?
2. For a given call-answering load, are sufficient operator positions occupied so that the customer does not experience an unreasonable delay in having his or her call answered?
3. Is the utilization of operator personnel efficient or do they experience excessive idle time?
4. How well does the proposed configuration handle extreme operational conditions such as those occurring at night (i.e., low volume) or during natural disasters (i.e., high volume).
5. How flexible is the proposed configuration in terms of accommodating future growth?

The operational planners had decided that simulation was the appropriate method for trying to answer the preceding questions.

The simulation model that was developed was structured around the the customer maintenance contact center (CMCC). The CMCC was intended to allow customers to report problems and to provide sufficient information about the problems to permit a technician to analyze the problem and make a judgment

Source: James L. Filmer and Joseph M. Mellichamp, "Simulation: An operational planning device for the Bell System," *Interfaces* (June 1982), Vol. 12, No. 3, pp. 54–59.

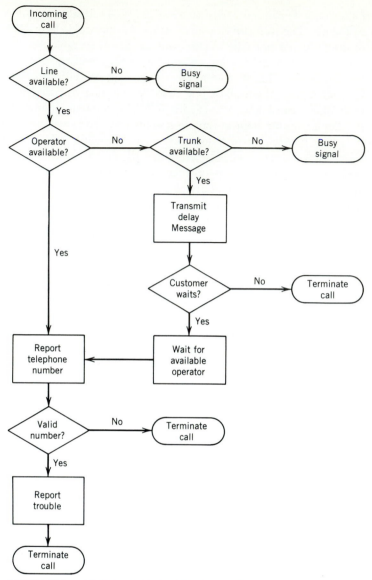

FIGURE 18.7 SCHEMATIC OF CUSTOMER MAINTENANCE CONTACT CENTER (CMCC).

about the probable cause of the problem and its solution. Figure 18.7 presents a simplified schematic of the trouble-call processing system used at the CMCC.

The trouble-call reporting system shown in Figure 18.7 contained the system elements and activities that had to be represented in the simulation model. A simplified diagram of the customer maintenance contact center simulation model is shown in Figure 18.8. The simulation model was composed of two functionally distinct components.

1. A "user-friendly" input/output subroutine.
2. The simulation model, which was written in the General Purpose Simulation Systems (GPSS) language.

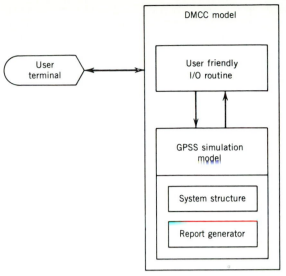

FIGURE 18.8 DIAGRAM OF THE CUSTOMER MAINTE-
NANCE CONTACT CENTER SIMULATION MODEL.

The input/output segment of the model allowed the user to specify the data inputs necessary for describing the CMCC configuration to be simulated. The GPSS simulation model performed the simulation and reported selected system statistics back to the user, using the input/output subroutine. A sample output report is shown in Table 18.16.

TABLE 18.16 SAMPLE OUTPUT REPORT: CMCC SIMULATION MODEL

System Configuration

Number of repair service calls
per 30-minute interval 487

Number of repair service operators available. 35

System Performance

Average number of calls answered
per 30-minute interval 465

Average number of calls delayed
per 30-minute interval 175

Average number of calls transferred
per 30-minute interval 15

Average number of calls overflowed
per 30-minute interval 13

Average number of calls abandoned
per 30-minute interval 1

Average speed of answer (sec) 3.9

Average operator utilization. 86%

Maximum number of lines used 8

Maximum number of delay message trunks used 9

The major application of the CMCC simulation model was in formulating operational plans associated with the Bell System forming a fully separate subsidiary to deal with phone service problems. This was necessitated by legislative and judicial actions. Specifically, the CMCC simulation model was used to configure regional CMCC locations based upon anticipated trouble report volumes. The simulation approach was very valuable in that it facilitated the rapid testing of numerous possible configurations without having to establish "live" operational environments.

19

DYNAMIC PROGRAMMING

19.1 INTRODUCTION

Dynamic programming is a quantitative analysis approach that is applicable to decision-making situations in which a series of interrelated decisions have to be made. Dynamic programming is based on the idea of dividing the problem into stages. The outcome of the decision at one stage affects the decision and outcome at the next stage of the problem. In many ways dynamic programming is similar to decision tree analysis, which we studied in Chapter 4 (refer back to Section 4.6). Its use typically requires that a problem be broken down into a series of smaller subproblems that are solved sequentially.

Dynamic programming is somewhat different than the other techniques that we have presented in this textbook. As mentioned above, it is an approach to decision making rather than a specific solution technique (such as the simplex algorithm or the modified distribution algorithm). This means that there is no standard solution procedure for dynamic programming problems, and it may even utilize other techniques within its overall solution strategy. Since it is a decision-making approach, it is applicable to a wide range of decision-making situations.

Dynamic programming developed initially as a result of studying the sequential decision problems that arose in inventory control theory. The name "dynamic programming" became associated with the computational technique that referred to the types of problems to which it was applied originally. The basic ideas of dynamic programming were developed by Richard Bellman in the 1950s.[1]

Numerous examples of practical applications of dynamic programming to business and managerial problems are in existence. For example, dynamic programming has been used in a variety of production scheduling and inventory control decision-making situations. Similarly, it has been used to solve problems involving spare parts level determination, given space and weight constraints. Capital budgeting, allocation of research and development funds, and long-run corporate planning are other areas that have been analyzed by means of dynamic programming.

In this chapter we present the basic ideas of

---

[1] See Richard E. Bellman, *Dynamic Programming.* Princeton, N.J.: Princeton Univ. Press, 1957.

dynamic programming by illustrating its use in several decision-making situations. In our initial example, we also provide an overview of the dynamic programming solution approach. As we begin our study of dynamic programming, you should be aware that its notation can be confusing and difficult at first. Be prepared to carefully review this notation as it is used throughout the chapter.

19.2 AN ILLUSTRATION OF THE DYNAMIC PROGRAMMING APPROACH: THE SHORTEST ROUTE PROBLEM

The dynamic programming solution approach involves four major steps, which in turn involve a number of important concepts.

1. The overall problem is decomposed into subproblems called *stages.*

2. The final stage of the problem is analyzed and solved for all of the possible conditions or *states.*

3. Each preceding stage is solved, working backward from the final stage of the problem. This involves making an optimal *policy decision* for the intermediate stages of the problem, with each intermediate stage being linked to its preceding stage by a *recursion relationship.* The recursion relationship that is employed involves a *return* at each stage of the problem. The return at a particular stage is the net benefit that accrues at that stage due to the policy decision selected and its interaction with the state of the system. The return can be thought of as the objective function of the dynamic programming problem.

4. The initial stage of the problem is solved, and when this has been accomplished the optimal solution has been obtained.

These four major steps, which comprise dynamic programming, are discussed further in the illustrations in the following sections of this chapter. The various concepts introduced in these four steps are discussed further in the following example.

We now illustrate the methodology of dynamic programming by applying it to the shortest route problem we previously considered in Section 12.3.1. The network for this problem is reproduced below

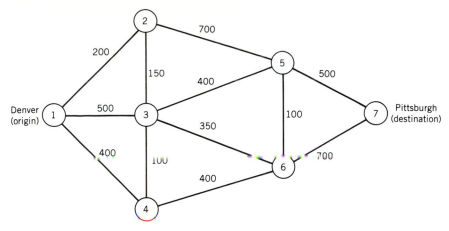

FIGURE 19.1 SHORTEST ROUTE NETWORK.

in Figure 19.1. Recall that the numbers along each branch represent the distances (in hundreds of miles) between the respective nodes. This shortest route problem requires the determination of the minimum distance route from Node 1, Denver, to Node 7, Pittsburgh.

The fundamental relationships between the components of a dynamic programming model are shown pictorially in Figure 19.2. From this figure observe that there are five major components in a dynamic programming model.

First, the problem is subdivided and analyzed by stages. In this problem there are three stages, with each stage involving the choice of a city to which we will next proceed. The three stages of this particular problem can be described by the following subproblems.

1. STAGE 1 SUBPROBLEM. Where should we go from Nodes 5 and 6 in order to reach Node 7 along the shortest route?
2. STAGE 2 SUBPROBLEM. Using the results of stage 1, where should we go from Nodes 2, 3, and 4 in order to reach Node 7 along the shortest route?
3. STAGE 3 SUBPROBLEM. Using the results of stage 2, where should we go from Node 1 in order to reach Node 7 along the shortest route?

It should be mentioned that other dynamic programming problems have stages that represent different time periods, or available resources, associated with the planning horizon of the problem.

Second, at each stage there are a number of *input states* possible. Generally, the input states are the various possible entering conditions for that stage of the problem. The input states provide the information required for making the best decision at the current stage of the problem. In this problem the input states are the individual cities from which we can proceed at any stage of the problem. For example, for the stage 2 subproblem, the input states are Nodes 2, 3, and 4.

Third, at each stage of the problem a policy decision must be made. These policy decisions have a standardized format. In this problem the policy decisions involve the choice of branch on which to proceed from the input nodes. For example, for the stage 2 subproblem we can proceed from the input states (i.e., Nodes 2, 3, and 4) by selecting connecting branches for Nodes 5 and 6.

Fourth, as a policy decision is made at each stage in the solution process, the current state is

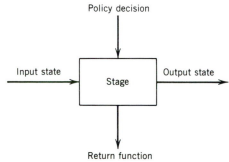

FIGURE 19.2 DYNAMIC PROGRAMMING MODEL COMPONENTS.

transformed into a state that is interrelated to the previous stage of the problem. The *transformation function* specifies the *output state* for the current stage of the problem. It interconnects the various stages of the problem. For example, for the stage 2 subproblem the output states are Nodes 5 and 6. These output states, in turn, become the input states for the stage 1 subproblem.

Fifth, as the result of the policy decision selected as a function of the entering state a *return function* is defined for each stage of the problem. This *return function* measures the increase (or decrease) in some overall measure of system efficiency (i.e., such a profit or cost) that occurs at a particular stage as a function of the entering state and the policy decision. In this problem the return function is defined in terms of the shortest route (distance) for the network.

The symbolic representation of the relationships of the components of a dynamic programming problem for a particular stage, n, is presented in Figure 19.3.

Now, in order to further link the various stages together we need to define a return function that represents not only the return from stage n but also the total return from stage $n - 1$, given the input state for stage $n - 1$ (i.e., s_{n-1}) and the decision for stage $n - 1$ (i.e., x_{n-1}). The total return function for stage n, $f_n(s_n, x_n)$, is defined in terms of the total return function for stage $n - 1$, $f_{n-1}(s_{n-1}, x_{n-1})$. This relationship is the recursion relationship we discussed earlier.

Using this type of recursion relationship, the current value of the total return function is defined

as a function of its value in the previous stage. Therefore $f_2(s_2, x_2)$ is defined as a function of $f_1(s_1, x_1)$, and so forth. Figure 19.4 presents the relationships among the stages, policy decisions, states, and return functions of the dynamic programming problem. The solution of a dynamic programming problem having these structural characteristics is based upon Bellman's *principle of optimality*.

PRINCIPLE OF OPTIMALITY

An optimal policy must have the property that, regardless of the decision made to enter a particular state, the remaining decisions must constitute an optimal policy for leaving that state.[2]

The principle of optimality suggests that given the current system state we are in, an optimal policy for the remaining stages of the problem is independent of the policy adopted in the previous stages of the problem.

In our present problem this means that if we are at a particular state (city) in a particular stage of our travel, then our choice of the next state (city) to be chosen in the next stage of our trip is not dependent upon how we arrived at the current city in the present stage of our trip. Thus, a major characteristic of the dynamic programming solution procedure is

> At each stage in the decision process, given the current state, an optimal policy for the remaining stages of the process is independent of the policy adopted in previous stages of the decision process.

To actually solve a dynamic programming problem, we begin by first solving a one-stage problem, and then we sequentially add a series of one-stage problems that are solved until the overall optimum is found. Usually, this solution procedure is based on a *backward induction process*, where the first stage analyzed is the final stage of the problem and the solution of the problem proceeds by moving back one stage at a time until all stages in the problem

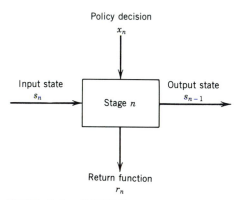

Policy decision
x_n

Input state
s_n

Stage n

Output state
s_{n-1}

Return function
r_n

FIGURE 19.3 SYMBOLIC REPRESENTATION OF DYNAMIC PROGRAMMING MODEL COMPONENTS.

[2]*Ibid.*

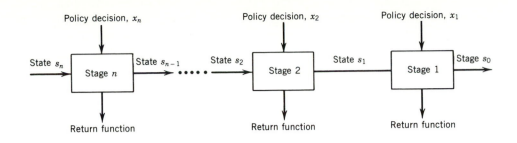

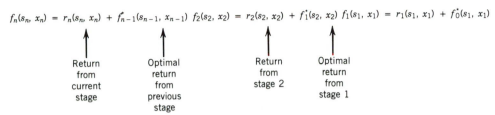

FIGURE 19.4   RELATIONSHIP AMONG THE STAGES, POLICY DECISIONS, STATES, AND RETURN FUNCTIONS OF THE DYNAMIC PROGRAMMING PROBLEM.

are included. It should be mentioned, however, that certain problems alternatively allow the use of a *forward induction process,* where the first stage analyzed is the initial stage of the problem and the solution of the problem proceeds by moving forward one stage at a time until all stages in the problem are included. In general, backward induction is probably more prevalent, and in dynamic programming problems involving uncertainty, backward induction will be required. Thus, another characteristic of the dynamic programming solution procedure is

> The solution procedure for dynamic programming problems generally begins by finding the optimal policy for each state of the last stage of the process.

A final characteristic of the dynamic programming solution procedure is

> The solution procedure proceeds in a fashion that identifies the optimal policy for each state with n stages remaining, given the optimal policy for each state with $n - 1$ stages remaining, using a recursion relationship.

It should be stressed that the exact form of the recursion relationship will vary according to the dy-

namic programming problem being analyzed. The recursion relationship, however, will always be of the general form

$$f_n^*(s_n) = \max/\min \{f_n(s_n, x_n)\} \qquad (19.1)$$

The function $f_n(s_n, x_n)$ is the value associated with the best overall policy for the remaining stages of the problem, given that the system is in state s_n with n stages to go and the decision variable x_n is selected. The function $f_n(s_n, x_n)$ is written in terms of s_n, x_n, and $f_{n-1}^*(\cdot)$.

For our present problem the recursion relationship can be written as follows

$$f_n^*(s_n) = \min_{x_n} \{f_n(s_n, x_n)\}$$
$$= \min_{x_n} \{d_{s_n, x_n} + f_{n-1}^*(x_n)\} \qquad (19.2)$$

In this recursion relationship the first term, d_{s_n, x_n}, is the distance associated with the state variable, s_n, and the decision variable, x_n, for the current stage of the problem. The second term, $f_{n-1}^*(x_n)$, is the minimum distance for the previous stage of the problem, expressed as a function of the decision variable, x_n.

In summarizing the computations associated with dynamic programming problems, it is useful to construct a table such as the following for each stage in the decision process.

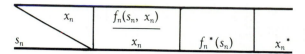

Within this table s_n represents the states for the current stage of the decision process, and the x_n are the decision variables for the current stage (stage = n) of the decision process. The function $f_n(s_n, x_n)$ is the value associated with the best overall policy for the remaining stages of the problem, given that the system is in state s_n with n stages to go and the decision variable x_n is selected. The value $f_n^*(s_n)$ is the maximum (minimum) value of $f_n(s_n, x_n)$ over all possible values of x_n for a particular s_n. The value x_n^* is the value of x_n producing the optimal value, $f_n^*(s_n)$.

The dynamic programming approach to the shortest route problem involves working backward, in stages, from the destination (Pittsburgh) to the origin (Denver). We begin this computational process by determining the shortest route to the destination node (Node 7, Pittsburgh), from state $s_1 = 5$ (Node 5) and state $s_1 = 6$ (Node 6). At this point in our trip there is $n = 1$ more stage to go. We can enter this stage from states $s_1 = 5$ (Node 5) and $s_1 = 6$ (Node 6), and can make a decision only to go to Node 7 (i.e., we can select the decision variable $x_1 = 7$). This computational process results in the following one-stage ($n = 1$) table. Within this one-stage table, $x_1 = 7$ (Node 7) is the immediate

s_1 \ x_1	$f_1(s_1, x_1) = d_{s_1,x_1}$ 7	$f_1^*(s_1)$	x_1^*
5 $\begin{cases} 5 \to 7 \text{ or} \\ 5 \to 6 \to 7 \end{cases}$	500 or 800	500	7(5 → 7)
6 $\begin{cases} 6 \to 7 \text{ or} \\ 6 \to 5 \to 7 \end{cases}$	700 or 600	600	7(6 → 5 → 7)

destination for stage $n = 1$. We can travel to this destination from either state $s_1 = 5$ or state $s_1 = 6$. Each value of $f_1(s_1, x_1)$ in this table is simply the distance, d_{s_1,x_1}, associated with entering this stage of the decision process from state s_1 (i.e., either Node 5 or 6) and moving to the final destination, $x_1 = 7$. The value of $f_1^*(s_1)$ is the minimum value of $f_1(s_1, x_1)$ over all possible values of x_1 for a particular s_1. The value x_1^* is the value of x_1 that produces the optimal (minimum) value, $f_1^*(s_1)$.

The next step in the solution of this shortest route problem by means of dynamic programming involves moving backward one more stage, that is, considering the decision that must be made when there are $n = 2$ more stages to go. The computational process for the two-stage problem becomes slightly more complicated. To illustrate, assume for the moment that we are at state $s_2 = 3$ (Node 3). We can next go to either Node 5 (i.e., choose $x_2 = 5$) or Node 6 (i.e., choose $x_2 = 6$). If we choose to go to Node 5, we can either go directly from Node 3 to Node 5 ($d_{35} = 400$), or we can go from Node 3 to Node 2 to Node 5 ($d_{325} = 150 + 700 = 850$). If we choose to go to Node 6, we can either

go directly from Node 3 to Node 6 ($d_{36} = 350$), or we can go from Node 3 to Node 4 to Node 6 ($d_{346} = 100 + 400 = 500$). If we choose to go from state $s_2 = 3$ (Node 3) to $x_2 = 5$ (Node 5), the minimum additional distance after reaching $x_2 = 5$ will be given in the table for the one-stage problem as $f_1^*(5) = 500$. Thus, the total distances for this decision are

$$d_{35} + f_1^*(5) = 400 + 500 = 900$$
$$d_{325} + f_1^*(5) = 850 + 500 = 1350 \quad (19.3)$$

Similarly, if we choose to go from state $s_2 = 3$ (Node 3) to $x_2 = 6$ (Node 6), the minimum additional distance after reaching $x_2 = 6$ will be given in the table for the one-stage problem as $f_1^*(6) = 600$. Thus, the total distances for this decision are

$$d_{36} + f_1^*(6) = 350 + 600 = 950$$
$$d_{346} + f_1^*(6) = 500 + 600 = 1100 \quad (19.4)$$

Therefore, given that we are at Node 3, we would choose to move from state $s_2 = 3$ to $x_2 = 5$, since this decision results in the minimum total distance of 900 miles. Observe that we have specified a recursion relationship for the two-stage problem, and that this recursion relationship utilizes the optimal solution that we previously determined for the one-stage problem. This recursion relationship is of the form

$$f_2(s_2, x_2) = d_{s_2,x_2} + f_1^*(x_2) \qquad (19.5)$$

The two-stage ($n = 2$) table can now be constructed as follows.

s_2 \ x_2	$f_2(s_2, x_2) = d_{s_2,x_2} + f_1^*(x_2)$ 5	6	$f_2^*(s_2)$	x_2^*
2: $2 \to 5$ or $2 \to 3 \to 5$	1200 or 1050		1050	5 ($2 \to 3 \to 5$)
$2 \to 3 \to 6$ or $2 \to 3 \to 4 \to 6$		1100 or 1250		
3: $3 \to 5$ or $3 \to 2 \to 5$	900 or 1350		900	5 ($3 \to 5$)
$3 \to 6$ or $3 \to 4 \to 6$		950 or 1100		
4: $4 \to 3 \to 5$ or $4 \to 3 \to 2 \to 5$	1000 or 1450		1000	5 ($4 \to 3 \to 5$)
$4 \to 6$ or $4 \to 3 \to 6$		1000 or 1050		6 ($4 \to 6$)

Within this two-stage table, the entries for the values of $f_2(s_2, x_2)$ are obtained using the recursion relationship, as follows.

$$f_2(2, 5) = \begin{cases} d_{25} + f_1^*(5) = 700 + 500 = 1200 \\ d_{235} + f_1^*(5) = 550 + 500 = 1050 \end{cases}$$

$$f_2(2, 6) = \begin{cases} d_{236} + f_1^*(6) = 500 + 600 = 1100 \\ d_{2346} + f_1^*(6) = 650 + 600 = 1250 \end{cases}$$

$$f_2(3, 5) = \begin{cases} d_{35} + f_1^*(5) = 400 + 500 = 900 \\ d_{325} + f_1^*(5) = 850 + 500 = 1350 \end{cases}$$

$$f_2(3, 6) = \begin{cases} d_{36} + f_1^*(6) = 350 + 600 = 950 \\ d_{346} + f_1^*(6) = 500 + 600 = 1100 \end{cases}$$

$$f_2(4, 5) = \begin{cases} d_{435} + f_1^*(5) = 500 + 500 = 1000 \\ d_{4325} + f_1^*(5) = 950 + 500 = 1450 \end{cases}$$

$$f_2(4, 6) = \begin{cases} d_{46} + f_1^*(6) = 400 + 600 = 1000 \\ d_{436} + f_1^*(6) = 450 + 600 = 1050 \end{cases}$$

(19.6)

The entries for the respective values of $f_2^*(s_2)$ are then obtained as the minimum values of the $f_2(s_2, x_2)$ for the respective states. The entries for the respective values of x_2^* are obtained by observing which destinations, and routes, produce the values of $f_2^*(s_2)$.

Continuing this solution process we move backward one more stage, to the situation in which there are $n = 3$ more stages to go. The solution to the three-stage problem is obtained in a similar fashion to the previous stages, except that we now employ a recursion relationship of the form

$$f_3(s_3, x_3) = d_{s_3,x_3} + f_2^*(x_3) \qquad (19.7)$$

In the three-stage problem we have moved backward to the origin (Node 1). Therefore, in the three-stage problem we need to consider moving only from state $s_3 = 1$ to states $x_3 = 2, 3, 4$. These decisions result in the following three-stage table ($n = 3$).

s_3 \ x_3	$f_3(s_3, x_3) = d_{s_3,x_3} + f_2^*(x_3)$ 2	3	4	$f_3^*(s_3)$	x_3^*
1	1250	1400	1400	1250	2

We have now proceeded backward from the one-step problem to the three-stage problem, or from state $s_1 = 7$ (Node 7, Pittsburgh) to state $s_3 = 1$ (Node 1, Denver). The dynamic programming solution to this shortest route problem is now complete. The three-stage table indicates that the minimum-distance route will have a length of 1250 miles.

In terms of the solution to the problem the three-stage table indicates that when we start at Node 1 (Denver), we then go to Node 2 (i.e., we choose $x_3^* = 2$). Setting $x_3^* = 2$, in turn means that $s_2 = 2$ for the two-stage table. Entering the two-stage table with $s_2 = 2$, we see that we should choose $x_2^* = 5$, and that the route is ($2 \rightarrow 3 \rightarrow$

5). Setting $x_2^* = 5$, in turn means that $s_1 = 5$ for the one-stage table. Entering the one-stage table with $s_1 = 5$, we see that we should choose $x_1^* = 7$. We have now determined the optimal solution to this problem. The optimal sequence of nodes, and its associated distances are

	NODES
Sequence:	$1 \rightarrow 2 \rightarrow 3 \rightarrow 5 \rightarrow 7$
Distances:	$200 + 150 + 400 + 500 = 1250$

This is, of course, exactly the same answer that we obtained for this problem when it was solved by

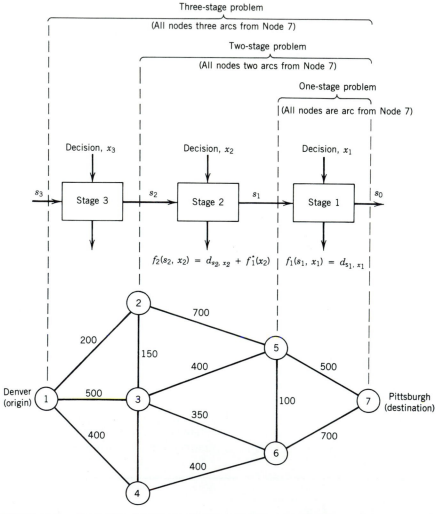

FIGURE 19.5 GRAPHICAL SUMMARY OF THE DYNAMIC PROGRAMMING SOLUTION TO THE SHORTEST ROUTE PROBLEM.

Dijkstra's algorithm in Section 12.3.1. The solution obtained by means of dynamic programming illustrates the fundamentals of this approach and also shows its versatility. A graphical summary of the dynamic programming solution to this shortest route problem is presented in Figure 19.5.

19.3 SOLVING AN ALLOCATION PROBLEM USING DYNAMIC PROGRAMMING

Dynamic programming affords a very effective way of solving problems involving the allocation of scarce resources. In such problems we typically have several competing activities, such as investment projects, which are competing for scarce resources such as investment capital. The general formulation of such a resource allocation problem is

$$\text{Maximize } Z = R_1(A_1) + R_2(A_2)$$
$$+ \cdots + R_n(A_n) \quad (19.8)$$

subject to:

$$A_1 + A_2 + \cdots + A_N \leq T \quad (19.9)$$

with

$$A_1, A_2, \ldots, A_N \geq 0 \quad (19.10)$$

WHERE

$R_1, R_2, \ldots, R_N$ = the returns from the various projects;

$A_1, A_2, \ldots, A_N$ = the resources allocated to the various projects;

T = the total amount of resources available.

Note also that we could replace maximize by minimize, if the objective function involved costs, and the inequality could be replaced by an equality in the constraint.

As an illustration of dynamic programming applied to an allocation problem we will consider a situation that is faced by students everywhere: How do I allocate my available study time? Jane Simpson, an undergraduate business major at Southeastern State University, is in the last semester (she hopes) of her senior year. She still must take final exams in four business courses, and she estimates that she has 50 hours of time available for studying. She has also estimated her grade prospects for these four courses as a function of the amount of study time devoted to the course. The study time estimates are made in 5-hour blocks of time, up to a maximum of 20 hours, which is the most that Jane feels she can study any one subject without becoming unproductive. The possibility of her not studying at all for an exam will not be considered, since this could result in her failing the course and failing to graduate. These study time estimates and associated grade points are as follows. Since Jane is a top ranking student, she wishes to maximize the total grade points she receives for the four courses (A = 5 grade points, B = 4 grade points, C = 3 grade points, D = 1 grade point). You can see that she has many ways in which to allocate her study time. If she allocates large blocks of study time to certain courses, say 15 hours each to Accounting and Finance, however, then she would only be able to allocate 20 hours between Management Science and Business Policy. Since she has recently studied dynamic programming in her Management Science course, she feels that she might be able to make her decision as to the allocation of her study time using dynamic programming.

In solving this problem the various stages of the problem are the four individual courses for which

COURSE	GRADE (GRADE POINTS) EXPECTED AS A FUNCTION OF HOURS STUDIED			
	5 HOURS	10 HOURS	15 HOURS	20 HOURS
Accounting	D(1)	C(3)	B(4)	A(5)
Finance	C(3)	B(4)	A(5)	A(5)
Management Science	D(1)	C(3)	B(4)	A(5)
Business Policy	B(4)	B(4)	A(5)	A(5)

study time allocations must be made. In this case, it does not make any difference which course is considered first, since all four courses must be considered in determining the overall allocation of the 50 hours of study time available.

The states for this particular problem are the number of hours available to allocate to the four courses. The states will be 5-hour increments of time ranging from 5 hours to 50 hours. The decision variables for this particular problem will be the actual number of hours Jane decides to allocate to studying for a particular course. Thus, the decision variables will be one of four values (i.e., 5 hours,

10 hours, 15 hours, or 20 hours). The returns for this problem will be the number of grade points achieved as a function of the number of study hours allocated.

Let us assume that Jane arbitrarily decides to start with the allocation of study time to her Accounting final. Initially, she has all 50 hours of study time available, and she can devote 5 hours, 10 hours, 15 hours, or 20 hours of study time to Accounting. Remember that she cannot allocate more than 20 hours to any course, and that all study time allocations are made in 5-hour time blocks. She can now construct the following one-stage table.

s_1 \ x_1	$f_1(s_1, x_1) = GP_{x_1}$				$f_1^*(s_1)$	x_1^*
	5	10	15	20		
5	1				1	5
10	1	3			3	10
15	1	3	4		4	15
20	1	3	4	5	5	20

Note: $n = 1$, Accounting.

Observe what this table indicates. If Jane has 5 hours of study time available (i.e., $s_1 = 5$), then she can only devote five hours to Accounting (i.e., $x_1 = 5$). This will result in her receiving a D in the course, and she will receive 1 grade point for this D. If Jane has 10 hours of study time available (i.e., $s_1 = 10$), she can devote either 5 or 10 hours to Accounting (i.e., $x_1 = 5$ or $x_1 = 10$). If she chooses $x_1 = 5$, she will get a D and receive 1 grade point. If she chooses $x_1 = 10$, she will get a C and receive 3 grade points. The rest of this table is constructed similarly. It should be apparent to you that the optimal allocation of study hours for this one-stage problem will always be the maximum number of study hours that are available. For example, if 15 hours of study time are available, Jane will want to allocate all 15 hours to studying for her Accounting final. Observe also that there are blank entries in this one-stage table, which occur when a particular assignment is impossible. For example, if she has $s_1 = 10$ hours of study time available, she cannot choose $x_1 = 15$ hours or $x_1 = 20$ hours.

The next step in the solution of this resource allocation problem by means of dynamic programming involves moving backward one more stage,

that is, considering the decision that must be made when there are $n = 2$ more stages to go. In this two-stage problem we make decisions with respect to the allocation of study hours to Finance, and link these decisions to the optimal decisions we previously obtained for the one-stage problem. This is equivalent to considering the allocation of study hours to both Finance and Accounting. The recursion relationship that is employed is of the form

$$f_2(s_2, x_2) = GP_{x_2} + f_1^*(s_2 - x_2) \qquad (19.11)$$

For the two-stage problem, the following table can be constructed. Let us consider how this table was constructed. We are now saying that a maximum of 50 hours of study time is available for both Accounting and Finance. The maximum amount of time that can be devoted to either subject is 20 hours, however, so in total Jane could not study for these two finals more than 40 hours (i.e., the maximum value for s_2 is 40 hours). Given that $s_2 = 40$, Jane could allocate the maximum possible time to studying Finance (i.e., $x_2 = 20$) and still have $s_2 = x_2 = 40 - 20 = 20$ hours available for studying Accounting. If she does this, her return (i.e., grade

s_2 \ x_2	$f_2(s_2, x_2) = GP_{x_2} + f_1^*(s_2 - x_2)$				$f_2^*(s_2)$	x_2^*
	5	10	15	20		
10	4				4	5
15	6	5			6	5
20	7	7	6		7	5 or 10
25	8	8	8	6	8	5, 10, or 15
30		9	9	8	9	10 or 15
35			10	9	10	15
40				10	10	20

Note: $n = 2$, Accounting and Finance.

point expectation) will be given as

$$f_2(s_2, x_2) = GP_{x_2} + f_1^*(s_2 - x_2)$$
$$= GP_{x_2 = 20} + f_1^*(40 - 20)$$
$$= 5 + 5$$
$$= 10 \qquad (19.12)$$

As a further illustration of the construction of this two-stage table, let us see what happens, for example, if $s_2 = 25$, and Jane chooses to study Finance for 15 hours (i.e., $x_2 = 15$). If she does this, her return (i.e., grade point expectation) will be given as

$$f_2(s_2, x_2) = GP_{x_2} + f_1^*(s_2 - x_2)$$
$$= GP_{x_2 = 15} + f_1^*(25 - 15)$$
$$= 5 + 3$$
$$= 8 \qquad (19.13)$$

The remainder of the entries in this table are determined in a similar manner.

Observe that there are places in this table in which there are no entries. For example, if $s_2 = 40$, there is no entry for $x_2 = 15$. This entry essentially has no meaning because $[(s_2 = 40) - (x_2 = 15)] = 25$, and there is no corresponding value for $f_1^*(25)$, since the maximum allowable value for s_1 in the one-stage table is 20 (i.e., she cannot study more than 20 hours in any one course). Also, observe that there is no row corresponding to $s_2 = 5$. This is not allowed, since if $s_2 = 5$ the only possible allocation would be $x_2 = 5$, corresponding to allocating the entire *available* 5 hours to studying Finance. This would leave nothing available for studying Accounting and Jane would fail the course!

Similarly, when $s_2 = 10$, $s_2 = 15$, and $s_2 = 20$, we cannot allocate all of the available hours to studying Finance, or there will be nothing available for studying Accounting. Accordingly, the entries for $s_2 = 10$ and $x_2 = 10$, $s_2 = 15$ and $x_2 = 15$, and $s_2 = 20$ and $x_2 = 20$ are blank.

Continuing this solution process we move backward one more stage, to the situation in which there are $n = 3$ more stages to go. In this three-stage problem we make decisions with respect to the allocation of study hours to Management Science, and link these decisions to the optimal decisions we previously obtained for the two-stage problem. This is equivalent to considering the allocation of study hours to Management Science, Finance, and Accounting.

The solution to the three-stage problem is obtained in a similar fashion to the two-stage problem, except that we now employ a recursion relationship of the form

$$f_3(s_3, x_3) = GP_{x_3} + f_2^*(s_3 - x_3) \qquad (19.14)$$

For this three-stage problem the following table can be constructed. As an illustration of the construction of this table, let us see what happens, for example, if $s_2 = 30$, and Jane chooses to study Management Science for 15 hours. If she does this, her return (i.e., grade point expectation) will be given as

$$f_3(s_3, x_3) = GP_{x_3} + f_2^*(s_3 - x_3)$$
$$= GP_{x_3 = 15} + f_2^*(30 - 15)$$
$$= 4 + 6$$
$$= 10 \qquad (19.15)$$

s_3 \ x_3	$f_3(s_3, x_3) = GP_{x_3} + f_2^*(s_3 - x_3)$				$f_3^*(s_3)$	x_3^*
	5	10	15	20		
15	5				6	5
20	7	7			7	5 or 10
25	8	9	8		9	10
30	9	10	10	9	10	10 or 15
35	10	11	11	11	11	10, 15, or 20
40	11	12	12	12	12	10, 15, or 20
45	11	13	13	13	13	10, 15, or 20
50		13	14	14	14	15 or 20

Note: $n = 3$, Accounting, Finance and Management Science.

Continuing this process we move backward one more stage, to the situation in which there are $n = 4$ more stages to go. In this four-stage problem we make decisions with respect to the allocation of study hours to Business Policy, and link these decisions to the optimal decisions we previously obtained for the three-stage problem. This is equivalent to considering the allocation of study hours to Business Policy, Management Science, Finance, and Accounting. The solution to the four-stage problem is obtained in a similar fashion to the three-stage and two-stage problems, except that we now employ a recursion relationship of the form

$$f_4(s_4, x_4) = GP_{x_4} + f_3^*(s_4 - x_4) \qquad (19.16)$$

In the four-stage problem we have moved backward to the equivalent of studying all four courses, Accounting, Finance, Management Science, and Business Policy, together. For the four-stage problem we need only to consider state $s_4 = 50$ hours, with our choices being $x_4 = 5$ hours, 10 hours, 15 hours, or 20 hours. These decisions result in the following four-stage table.

s_4 \ x_4	$f(s_4, x_4) = GP_{x_4} + f_3^*(s_4 - x_4)$				$f_4^*(s_4)$	x_4^*
	5	10	15	20		
50	17	16	16	15	17	5

Note: $n = 4$, Accounting, Finance, Management Science, and Business Policy.

In terms of the solution to this problem the four-stage table indicates that Jane initially should allocate 5 hours to studying for her Business Policy final (i.e., she chooses $x_4^* = 5$ hours). Setting $x_4^* = 5$ in turn means that $s_3 = s_4 - x_4^* = 50 - 5 = 45$ hours for the three-stage table. Entering the three-stage table with $s_3 = 45$, we see that Jane could choose $x_3 = 10$ hours, 15 hours, or 20 hours (i.e., alternative optimal solutions are possible). Assume that Jane chooses $x_3^* = 10$. Setting $x_3 = 10^*$ in turn means that $s_2 = s_3 - x_3^* = 45 - 10 = 35$ hours for the two-stage table. Entering the two-stage table with $s_2 = 35$, we see that Jane would choose $x_2^* = 15$ hours. Setting $x_2^* = 15$ in turn means that $s_1 = 35 - 15 = 20$ hours for the one-stage table. Entering the one-stage table with $s_1 = 20$ hours, we see that Jane would choose $x_1^* = 20$ hours. We have now obtained one of the optimal solutions to this problem. This optimal solution and its associated grades and grade points are as in the following table.

Another (alternative) optimal solution is given in the following table. Other alternative optimal solutions exist for this problem and you can easily determine them in the same manner as we did above.

A graphical summary of the dynamic programming solution to the resource allocation problem is shown in Figure 19.6.

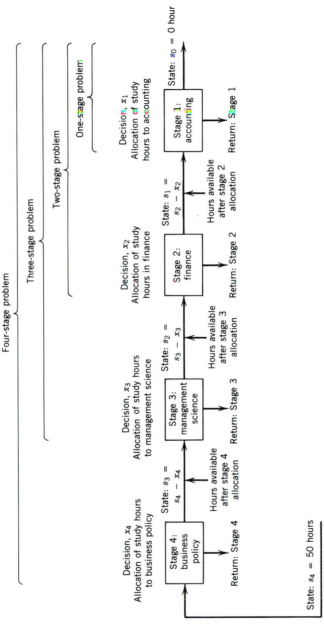

FIGURE 19.6 GRAPHICAL SUMMARY OF THE DYNAMIC PROGRAMMING SOLUTION THE RESOURCE ALLOCATION PROBLEM.

COURSE	STUDY HOURS	GRADE	GRADE POINTS
Business Policy	$x_4 = 5$	B	4
Management Science	$x_3 = 10$	C	3
Finance	$x_2 = 15$	A	5
Accounting	$x_1 = 20$	A	5
		Total	17

COURSE	STUDY HOURS	GRADE	GRADE POINTS
Business Policy	$x_4 = 5$	B	4
Management Science	$x_3 = 15$	B	4
Finance	$x_2 = 10$	B	4
Accounting	$x_1 = 20$	A	5
		Total	17

19.4 DYNAMIC PROGRAMMING APPLIED TO A RELIABILITY PROBLEM

Another area of decision making in which dynamic programming has been applied is that of equipment reliability. In reliability problems the decision maker is typically interested in improving the reliability of a system, where the reliability of the system is a function of the number of a specific type of part installed in a system. For example, commercial airlines typically install two or three of each part in airplanes in order to maintain high reliability.

The typical reliability problem is quite similar to the allocation problem that we presented in the previous section. The reliability problem, however, usually involves the multiplication of the returns (i.e., the reliabilities) from the various stages, rather than adding the returns as we did previously. The general formulation of such a reliability problem is

Maximize $Z = R_1 (A_1) \times R_2(A_2)$
$$\times \cdots \times R_N(A_n) \quad (19.17)$$

subject to

$$A_1 + A_2 + \cdots + A_N \leq T \quad (19.18)$$

with

$$A_1, A_2, \ldots, A_n \geq 0 \quad (19.19)$$

WHERE

$R_1, R_2, \ldots, R_N$ = the reliabilities associated with particular components of the system;

$A_1, A_2, \ldots, A_N$ = the resources associated with particular components of the system;

T = the total amount of resources available.

As an illustration of the use of dynamic programming in solving a reliability problem, let us consider the following problem situation. The Earthworm Tractor Company has been having a problem with the overall reliability of a hydraulic system in one of the tractors it manufactures. The hydraulic system in this tractor has three critical subassemblies, whose individual probabilities of functioning properly (i.e., not failing over a 5-year time period) are as follows.

SUBASSEMBLY	PROBABILITY OF SUBASSEMBLY FUNCTIONING PROPERLY (5-YEAR TIME PERIOD)
A	.80
B	.90
C	.85

Given these individual probabilities, the overall probability of the hydraulic system functioning properly is the product of these individual probabilities, or

P(hydraulic system functioning properly
  — system reliability)
  = P(subassembly A functioning properly)
    × P(subassembly B functioning properly)
    × P(subassembly C functioning properly)
  = (.80) × (.90) × (.85) = .612   (19.20)

The manager of quality control at the Earthworm Tractor Company, Tim Fry, has decided that the hydraulic system reliability is too low. An investigation has indicated that a special type of valve is the critical part in each of the three subassemblies. He has concluded that he may have to install up to three additional valves in the three subassemblies in the hydraulic system in order to improve its overall reliability. He has made the following estimates of the probabilities of the subassemblies working properly, as a function of the number of valves installed.

NUMBER OF VALVES INSTALLED	PROBABILITY OF SUBASSEMBLY FUNCTIONING PROPERLY		
	SUBASSEMBLY A	SUBASSEMBLY B	SUBASSEMBLY C
0	.80	.90	.85
1	.86	.92	.87
2	.92	.94	.90
3	.94	.95	.92

The problem faced by Tim Fry is that of deciding how to allocate the additional valves among the three subassemblies. He could install all three additional valves in subassembly A, thereby improving its reliability to .94. If this were done, the probability of the hydraulic system functioning properly would be

P(hydraulic system functioning properly
  — system reliability)
  = P(subassembly A functioning properly with 3 additional valves)
    × P(subassembly B functioning properly)
    × P(subassembly C functioning properly)
  = (.94) × (.90) × (.85) = .719   (19.21)

Alternatively, he could install one additional valve in all three subassemblies. If this were done, the probability of the hydraulic system functioning properly would be

P(hydraulic system functioning properly
  — system reliability)
  = P(subassembly A functioning properly with 1 additional valve)
    × P(subassembly B functioning properly with 1 additional valve)
    × P(subassembly C functioning properly with 1 additional valve)
  = (.86) × (.92) × (.87) = 0.688   (19.22)

You can see that there are many combinations that he could choose as he attempted to maximize the reliability of the hydraulic system. We now show how dynamic programming can be used to make this choice in the best manner.

Analyzing this problem by dynamic programming, the problem is decomposed into stages, one stage for each of the three subassemblies. For each subproblem we try to determine how many additional valves to allocate. The return for each stage of the problem is the overall probability of the system performing properly. A total of three additional valves can be used, and our overall objective is to maximize the probability of the system performing properly.

Attacking this problem in the typical backward manner initially involves the consideration of subassembly C. Considering only subassembly C, it is obvious that we would allocate any remaining valves that we had to improve the reliability associated with subassembly C. Consequently, the one-stage table can be specified as follows.

In constructing this one-stage table, the following points should be noted. The decision to allocate a certain number of valves to subassembly C can never result in more valves being allocated than there are valves available. This means that the x_1 values can be equal to but cannot exceed the s_1 values. This accounts for the blank entries in this table. We now move backward one more stage. The

s_1 \ x_1	$f_1(s_1, x_1) = R_{x_1}$				$f_1^*(s_1)$	x_1^*
	0	1	2	3		
0	.85				.85	0
1	.85	.87			.87	1
2	.85	.87	.90		.90	2
3	.85	.87	.90	92	.92	3

Note: $n = 1$, subassembly C.

states, the s_2 values, for entering this two-stage problem are the possible remaining number of valves we can allocate. The decision variables, the x_2 values, are the actual number of valves we choose to allocate. The return function values are the overall probabilities of the system performing properly associated with the different allocation decisions. The recursion relationship used in the two-stage table is of the form

$$f_2(s_2, x_2) = R_{x_2} \cdot f_1^*(s_2 - x_2) \qquad (19.23)$$

Notice that this recursion relationship is multiplicative in form. In the two-stage table we are considering subassemblies C and B, together. The two-stage table can now be specified as follows. As an illustration

s_2 \ x_2	$f_2(s_2, x_2) = R_{x_2} \cdot f_1^*(s_2 - x_2)$				$f_2^*(s_2)$	x_2^*
	0	1	2	3		
0	.765				.765	0
1	.783	.782			.783	0
2	.810	.800	.799		.810	0
3	.828	.828	.818	.646	.828	0 or 1

Note: $n = 2$, subassemblies C and B.

of the construction of this table, let us see what happens, for example, if we have two valves available (i.e., $s_2 = 2$), and we decide to put one of them in subassembly B (i.e., $x_2 = 1$). If we do this, the return (i.e., overall reliabiliity of the system) will be given as

$$f_2(s_2, x_2) = R_{x_2} \cdot f_1^*(s_2 - x_2)$$
$$= R_{x_2-1} \cdot f_1^*(2 - 1)$$
$$= .92 \cdot .87$$
$$= .800 \qquad (19.24)$$

Proceeding in this manner we move backward

one more stage, to the three-stage problem. The solution to the three-stage problem is obtained in a similar manner to the two-stage problem, except that we now employ a recursion relationship of the form

$$f_3(s_3, x_3) = R_{x_3} \cdot f_2^*(s_3 - x_3) \qquad (19.25)$$

In the three-stage table, we have moved backward to the consideration of subassemblies C, B, and A, concurrently. For the three-stage problem, we need only to consider the state $s_3 = 3$ parts, since we would want to allocate all three parts that we have. The three-stage table can now be specified as follows.

s_3 \ x_3	$f_3(s_3, x_3) = R_{x_3} \cdot f_2^*(s_3 - x_3)$				$f_3^*(s_3)$	x_3^*
	0	1	2	3		
3	.662	.697	.720	.719	.720	2

Note: $n = 3$, subassemblies C, B, and A.

In determining the solution to this problem the three-stage table indicates that Tim should initially allocate two valves to subassembly A. Setting $x_3^* = 2$, in turn means that $s_2 = s_3 - x_3^* = 3 - 2 = 1$ valve for the two-stage table. Entering the two-stage table with $s_2 = 1$, we see that Tim should allocate zero valves to subassembly B (i.e., $x_2^* = 0$). Setting $x_2^* = 0$, in turn means that $s_1 = s_2 - x_2^* = 1 - 0 = 1$ valve for the one-stage table. Entering the one-stage table with $s_1 = 1$, we see that Tim should allocate one valve to subassembly C (i.e., $x_1^* = 1$). We have now obtained the optimal solution to this problem. This optimal solution can be summarized as follows. For this optimal solution,

SUBASSEMBLY	NUMBER OF ADDITIONAL VALVES ALLOCATED	RELIABILITY OF SUBASSESMBLY
A	2	.92
B	0	.90
C	1	.87

the probability of the hydraulic system functioning properly would be

P(hydraulic system functioning properly
— system reliability)
= P(subassembly A functioning properly with 2 additional valves)
× P(subassembly B functioning properly with 0 additional valves)
× P(subassembly C functioning properly with 1 additional valve)
= $(.92) \times (.90) \times (.87) = .720$ (19.26)

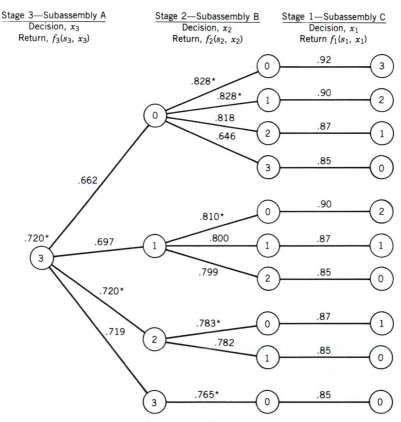

FIGURE 19.7 GRAPHICAL SUMMARY OF THE DYNAMIC PROGRAMMING SOLUTION TO THE RELIABILITY PROBLEM.

A graphical summary of the dynamic programming solution to this reliability problem is presented in Figure 19.7. The nodes in this figure correspond to the decisions concerning the number of parts that can be allocated to the subassembly at that stage. Observe that in stage 1 (subassembly C) we have 10 possible decisions and their associated returns. These decisions and their associated returns are the same as those presented in the one-stage table. You should compare the results of Figure 19.7. with the tables computed earlier for the three stages of this dynamic programming problem.

19.5 PROBLEMS IN USING DYNAMIC PROGRAMMING

Dynamic programming is an extremely useful quantitative decision-making technique that has a very important role in sequential decision making. It affords a great deal of flexibility with respect to the variety of problems and cost functions that it allows to be modeled. Unfortunately, building the model is only part of the task in this instance, and solving the model using dynamic programming may present formidable problems.

Some dynamic programming problems suffer from what is known as the *curse of dimensionality*. This refers to the situation in which the dynamic programming formulation requires several states, which means that there are several state variables rather than the single state variable that we used in solving the previous dynamic programming problems. Recall that in the shortest route problem the single state variable was distance, in the allocation problem the single state variable was study hours, and in the reliability problem the single state variable was parts. In the latter problem, we easily could have had two state variables, for example, parts and the associated cost of the parts.

Although the inclusion of multiple states in a dynamic programming problem does not present a theoretical problem, it does cause significant computational difficulties. For dynamic programming problems in which the single state variable has multiple dimensions, or for which multiple state variables exist, the computational and data storage requirements increase dramatically. For example, assume that we had a single state variable problem in which the state variable could take on any of 25 integer values. For each stage in this problem we would have to make $25^1 = 25$ computations. Then, for two state variables we would have to make $25^2 = 625$ computations; for three state variables, $25^3 = 15,625$ computations; for four state variables, $25^4 = 390,625$; and so forth. This illustrates the so-called "curse of dimensionality," and accounts for the fact that most practical applications of dynamic programming have been limited to one or two states.

A second problem in using dynamic programming is the lack of computer software for solution of dynamic programming problems. Since each dynamic programming problem tends to be unique, there are no standard dynamic programming software packages available as there are for linear programming. Therefore, the quantitative analyst may have to write a computer program in order to be able to solve the dynamic programming problem formulation.

19.6 SUMMARY

In this chapter we have attempted to present the basic concepts of dynamic programming. We would like to emphasize that dynamic programming is an extensive and complex topic, and we have only considered it in a very elementary manner. It has proved to be of considerable value in decision-making situations involving a sequence of interrelated decisions. Hopefully, the examples presented in this chapter are indicative of its usefulness. We would also like to reiterate that dynamic programming is an approach to decision making rather than a decision-making technique or algorithm. This means that you should try to grasp the concepts involved in dynamic programming rather than attempt to focus on specific applications. Finally, it should be mentioned that your possible use of dynamic programming will probably occur after you have developed some modeling expertise using the other techniques discussed in this book. In short, it is somewhat the domain of the advanced analyst or practitioner.

GLOSSARY

Backward Induction   A process in which the first stage analyzed is the final stage of the problem, and solution of the problem proceeds by moving back one stage at a time until all stages in the problem are considered.

Curse of Dimensionality   Reference to the fact that many dynamic programming problems become too large to solve because there are too many states.

Deterministic Dynamic Programming   Or dynamic programming under certainty, involves problem situations in which the state in the next stage of the decision process is completely determined by the interaction of the state and the policy decision, with respect to the decision variable that occurs at the current stage. In deterministic dynamic programming there is no uncertainty nor probability distribution associated with what the next state in the decision process will be.

Dynamic Programming   A quantitative technique applicable to certain types of problems involving a sequence of decisions that are interrelated. It is a general type of problem-solving procedure that can be applied to sequential decision-making situations.

Forward Induction   A process where the first state analyzed is the initial stage of the problem and the solution proceeds by moving forward one stage at a time until all stages in the problem are considered.

"N-Stage" Problem   In dynamic programming, the problem of finding the optimal decision that must be made when there are no more stages to go.

Principle of Optimality   An optimal policy must have the property that, regardless of the decision made to enter a particular state, the remaining decisions must constitute an optimal policy for leaving that state.

Recursion Relationship   A relationship for the N-stage problem that links the optimal decision for the last stage considered ($m = N$) to the optimal decisions made for stages $m = N - 1, \ldots, m = 1$.

Return Function   The value associated with making decision d_n at stage n, for a specific value for the input variable x_n.

Stage   One of the smaller optimization subproblems into which a dynamic programming problem is divided, which requires a standardized policy decision.

State   The various possible conditions in which the system may be at a point in time. The number of states may be finite or infinite for any stage of the decision process.

Transformation Function   Defines, as a functional relationship, the value of the state variable at each stage and serves to interconnect the stages of the dynamic programming problem.

Selected References

Beckman, Martin J. 1968. *Dynamic Programming of Economic Decisions.* Berlin/New York: Springer-Verlag.

Bellman, Richard E., and Stuart E. Dreyfus. 1962. *Applied Dynamic Programming.* Princeton, N.J.: Princeton Univ. Press.

Bellman, Richard E. 1957. *Dynamic Programming.* Princeton, N.J.: Princeton Univ. Press.

Dernardo, E.V. 1975. *Dynamic Programming: Theory and Practice.* Englewood Cliffs, N.J.: Prentice–Hall.

Dreyfus, Stuart E. 1965. *Dynamic Programming and the Calculus of Variations.* New York: Academic Press.

Dreyfus, S., and A.M. Law. 1977. *The Art and Theory of Dynamic Programming.* New York: Academic Press.

Gluss, Brian. 1972. *An Elementary Introduction to Dynamic Programming.* Boston: Allyn & Bacon.

Hadley, G. 1964. *Nonlinear and Dynamic Programming.* Reading, Mass.: Addison–Wesley.

Howard, Ronald A. 1960. *Dynamic Programming and Markov Processes.* Cambridge, Mass.: Mass. Inst. Technol. Press.

Jacobson, H. Davitt, and D. Q. Mayn. 1970. *Differential Dynamic Programming,* Vol. 24. New York: Elsevier–North Holland Publishing.

Kaufmann, A. 1967. *Graphs, Dynamic Programming, and Finite Games.* New York: Academic Press.

Kaufmann, A., and R. Cruon. 1967. *Dynamic Programming: Sequential Scientific Management.* New York: Academic Press.

Nemhauser, G. L. 1966. *Introduction to Dynamic Programming.* New York: Wiley.

White, D. J. 1969. *Dynamic Programming.* San Francisco: Holden–Day.

Discussion Questions

1. What types of problems are suitable for solution by dynamic programming?

2. Why is dynamic programming a method of partial enumeration?

3. What do we mean by a stage in dynamic programming?

4. What does the recursion function involve in dynamic programming?

5. What does the principle of optimality mean in dynamic programming?

6. What is the curse of dimensionality in dynamic programming?

PROBLEMS

1. Find the shortest route for the following network using dynamic programming.

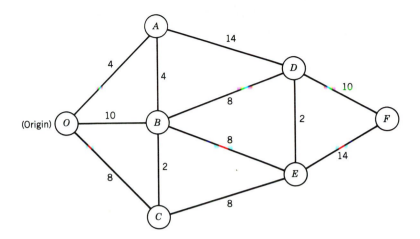

2. Mr. Cleaver has been family vacationing in Washington, D.C., and now is faced with a decision concerning travel back to his home in Los Angeles. Because he has small children, he must make his trip in stages. Because he has spent most of his vacation money in Washington, he must make the trip home using the shortest possible route. His potential travel network is shown in the following insert. The distances associated with the branches of this network are as follows.

$d_{12} = 400$	$d_{25} = 450$	$d_{59} = 400$	$d_{912} = 550$
$d_{13} = 350$	$d_{26} = 460$	$d_{510} = 425$	$d_{1012} = 575$
$d_{14} = 330$	$d_{27} = 440$	$d_{511} = 410$	$d_{1112} = 565$
	$d_{28} = 430$	$d_{69} = 450$	
	$d_{35} = 400$	$d_{610} = 440$	
	$d_{36} = 425$	$d_{611} = 420$	
	$d_{37} = 410$	$d_{79} = 415$	
	$d_{38} = 430$	$d_{710} = 425$	
	$d_{45} = 450$	$d_{711} = 450$	
	$d_{46} = 475$	$d_{89} = 460$	
	$d_{47} = 440$	$d_{810} = 450$	
	$d_{48} = 420$	$d_{811} = 440$	

Determine Mr. Cleaver's shortest route home, using dynamic programming.

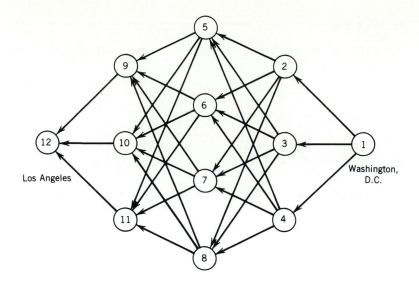

3. Tim Jones ships shrimp from Charleston, South Carolina, to Spartanburg, South Carolina. The possible routes his truck can take and the mileage of each route are shown in the following network. Determine the shortest route from Charleston to Spartanburg using dynamic programming.

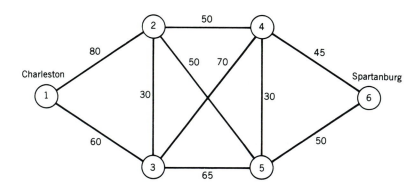

4. Illustrate the optimal solution to problem 3 using the approach shown in Figure 19.5.

5. An aspiring politician, Mr. I. M. Able, is running for county supervisor of garbage dumps. He has six volunteer campaign workers that have agreed to help him in his campaign. He would like to assign these six volunteers to the four major precincts in the county in a way that maximizes their effectiveness. The following table indicates the estimated effectiveness of the assignment of the various number of workers to the four precincts (using a scale of 1–100). Use dynamic programming to determine how many of the six workers should be assigned to each of the four precincts to maximize the total effectiveness of the campaign.

NUMBER OF WORKERS	PRECINCT			
	1	2	3	4
0	0	0	0	0
1	8	15	20	5
2	10	20	25	20
3	20	30	30	35
4	30	35	40	40
5	40	40	50	45
6	50	50	60	50

6. Collegiate Subscriptions, Inc., has divided the state of South Carolina into three sales areas: Piedmont, Midlands, and Low County. It has four sales representatives that it wishes to allocate to these three regions in a manner that will maximize its sales of magazine subscriptions to college students. The company can allocate any number of sales representatives to any one region. The dollar returns expected from the allocations of various numbers of sales representatives to the three sales areas are shown in the following table. Using dynamic programming to determine the optimal number of sales representatives to assign to each sales area in order to maximize the total sales dollars for the company.

NUMBER OF SALES REPRESENTATIVES PER SALES AREA	SALES DOLLARS PER SALES AREA ($000)		
	PIEDMONT	MIDLANDS	LOW COUNTRY
0	0	0	0
1	20	18	24
2	30	36	44
3	45	60	60
4	60	85	75

7. Barnes-Fox Company sells office supplies to businesses throughout Lexington County. It has divided Lexington County into two sales regions: North and South. It currently has three salespeople that it wishes to allocate to these two sales regions as it attempts to maximize its dollar sales of office supplies. The company can allocate any number of salespeople to the two sales regions. The dollar returns expected from the allocation of various number of salespeople to the two sales regions are shown in the following table.

NUMBER OF SALES PEOPLE PER SALES REGION	SALES DOLLARS PER SALES REGION ($000)	
	NORTH	SOUTH
0	0	0
1	12	8
2	20	24
3	30	35

a. Develop a mathematical model for this problem.

b. Use dynamic programming to determine the optimal number of sales-people to assign to each region.

8. A real estate investment firm has $10 million that it can invest, in $2 million increments, during the next calendar year. It is considering investment projects in three midwestern cities: St. Louis, Chicago, and Kansas City. The expected annual returns from the investment projects, for each level of investment are shown in the following table. Use dynamic programming to determine the optimal allocation of the $10 million of available capital among the three investment projects.

CAPITAL INVESTMENT ($ MILLIONS)	EXPECTED ANNUAL RETURN ($ MILLIONS)		
	ST. LOUIS	CHICAGO	KANSAS CITY
0	0	0	0
2	3	4	2
4	6	9	10
6	9	14	11
8	12	18	15
10	15	20	18

9. Rework Problem 8 with the stipulation that a maximum of $4 million can be invested in any one investment project. Compare your answer to that obtained for Problem 8 and explain why it is different.

10. Kathy Woodward has spent the weekend at Murrell's Inlet, South Carolina. While there she has collected 6 gallons of oysters. She is contemplating selling 5 gallons (keeping 1 gallon for herself) to one or more of three friends. The following table presents the expected profits associated with selling various numbers of gallons of oysters to the three friends. Use dynamic programming to determine the optimal allocation of the 5 gallons of oysters among Kathy's three friends.

NUMBER OF GALLONS	TOTAL EXPECTED PROFITS		
	BILL	SUE	TOM
0	0	0	0
1	5	6	4
2	8	10	9
3	11	11	10
4	13	12	14
5	15	14	16

11. Rework Problem 10 assuming that Kathy has decided to sell only 4 gallons of oysters. Compare your answer to that obtained for Problem 10 and explain why it is different.

12. The Education Improvement Act for the State of South Carolina has made $4 million available to the three school districts in Lexington County. This $4 million can be spent in increments of $1 million, and is to be used for improving the mathematical abilities of high school students. In general, the more money allocated to a school district, the greater will be the improvement in mathematical ability of its students, as measured by a standardized test. Past surveys from other states have indicated the following test score measurements for various allocations of funds.

ALLOCATION OF FUNDS ($ MILLION)	EXPECTED TEST SCORES		
	SCHOOL DISTRICT 1	SCHOOL DISTRICT 2	SCHOOL DISTRICT 3
0	30	40	45
1	50	60	55
2	60	80	70
3	70	85	87
4	95	90	92

a. Develop a mathematical model for this problem.
b. Use dynamic programming to determine the optimal allocation of funds for the three school districts.

13. The city of Sumter, South Carolina, is trying to allocate its four new fire trucks to its three fire districts. It has developed the following set of data relating fire losses to the number of fire trucks assigned. Use dynamic programming to determine the optimum allocation of fire trucks to fire districts in order to minimize the total fire losses per month.

NUMBER OF FIRE TRUCKS ALLOCATED	FIRE LOSSES PER MONTH ($000)		
	DISTRICT A	DISTRICT B	DISTRICT C
0	30	40	35
1	20	30	28
2	10	15	14
3	5	7	6
4	3	5	2

14. Pam Thompson, the owner of the Delightful Lily Cosmetics Company is trying to make a decision concerning the allocation of her $5 million advertising budget. She must spend this advertising budget in whole million-dollar increments on some or all of three advertising media. The following table indicates the expected market penetration for various expenditures.

MILLIONS OF DOLLARS SPENT	EXPECTED MARKET PENETRATION		
	MEDIA 1	MEDIA 2	MEDIA 3
0	.00	.00	.00
1	.10	.15	.13
2	.20	.30	.25
3	.30	.45	.40
4	.40	.50	.45
5	.50	.60	.55

a.   Develop a mathematical model for this problem, given that Pam Thompson wishes to maximize the overall market penetration for the entire advertising campaign.

b.   Use dynamic programming to determine the optimal advertising budget allocation.

15. The Jameson Corporation has recently completed the design of a new device that can be used in rescuing people in burning buildings. This device has three major subassemblies, each of which is driven by one or more power cells. The probability that any one component will not fail depends on the number of power cells assigned to that component. Because of cost and weight limitations, a maximum of four power cells can be installed in any component. The following table summarizes these probabilities. Use dynamic programming to determine the optimal allocation of power cells to the three subassemblies.

NUMBER OF POWER CELLS INSTALLED	RELIABILITY OF SUBASSEMBLY		
	SUBASSEMBLY 1	SUBASSEMBLY 2	SUBASSEMBLY 3
0	.76	.90	.80
1	.80	.93	.84
2	.86	.95	.88
3	.92	.97	.92
4	.97	.99	.96

16. The Catch-A-Crook Company manufactures a home burglary detection device, which is composed of three major electronic components. The reliability of each of these three electronic components can be enhanced by installing up to three parallel units of a certain critical switch. The company has made the following estimates of the components working properly, as a function of the number of switches installed.

NUMBER OF SWITCHES INSTALLED	PROBABILITY OF COMPONENT WORKING PROPERLY		
	COMPONENT A	COMPONENT B	COMPONENT C
0	.82	.88	.86
1	.84	.90	.88
2	.90	.92	.90
3	.92	.94	.93

a. Develop a mathematical model for this problem, given that the Catch-A-Crook Company wishes to maximize the overall probability of its burglary detection device working properly.

b. Use dynamic programming to determine the optimal allocation of switches to components.

17. Illustrate the optimal solution to problem 16 using the approach shown in Figure 19.7.

Application Review

Equipment Replacement Using Dynamic Programming

Managers of the transportation fleet at Phillips Petroleum Company were responsible for a fleet of about 1500 passenger cars and 3800 trucks. This fleet included a wide variety of vehicles used directly in petroleum production, transportation, or refining. Specifically, it included a large number of passenger cars and light trucks used for oil-well maintenance and service and for pipeline maintenance, and large highway tractors used to transport petroleum and petrochemical products.

Phillips had historically been very concerned with the equipment replacement problem related to its transportation fleet. It had developed its replacement policies using a dynamic programming model described in the classic book by Churchman et al.[3] The policies were generally stated in the form of: Replace the vehicle after n months of service or after m miles of use, whichever comes first. The company was particularly interested in replacement decisions concerning highway tractors, because of their high unit costs. Because of these high costs the company felt that it needed to make more careful decisions for individual vehicles, rather than use a blanket replacement policy.

Phillips again employed dynamic programming for the new equipment replacement model. The model was based on the assumption that replacement of equipment could occur at a finite set of times. A network was then constructed to represent all of the retain-replace decisions that could occur over the duration

[3]C. West Churchman, Russell L. Ackoff, and E. Leonard Arnoff, *Introduction to Operations Research*. New York: Wiley, 1957.
Source: Richard Waddell, "A model for equipment replacement decisions and policies," *Interfaces* (August 1983), Vol. 13, No. 4, pp. 1–7.

of the activity. An equipment age (state) and time into the activity were associated with each node of the network. Movement through the network was defined in terms of the discounted outgoing cash flow, and the model determined the path from start to termination that minimized the sum of these flows.

The fleet managers at Phillips indicated that this dynamic programming modeling approach to equipment replacement had been heavily utilized. It was very valuable in helping them make some very difficult, highly complex, and costly equipment replacement decisions.

20

MARKOV ANALYSIS

20.1 INTRODUCTION

The term *Markov analysis* refers to a quantitative technique that involves the analysis of the current behavior of some variable in order to predict the future behavior of that same variable. Markov analysis is applicable to systems in which we can determine the probability of movement from one state to another over time. An example of the use of Markov analysis is the determination of the probability that a customer will change brands of toothpaste from one month to the next month. Markov analysis has also been used to describe the probability that a machine that is functioning in one period will continue to function in the next period.

The Markov analysis procedure is named after the Russian mathematician, Andrei A. Markov, who used this technique early in the century to describe and predict the behavior of particles of gas in a closed container. Since that time it has been widely applied to problems in physics, biology, and economics as well as to managerial decision-making problems. Some business and industrial problems to which Markov analysis has been applied include consumer brand switching, equipment maintenance and failure problems, accounts receivable analysis, and stock-market price movements. Markov analysis is similar to dynamic programming in that both involve sequential events. Markov analysis involves the development of a descriptive model, however, while dynamic programming is oriented toward optimization.

A Markov process is a special type of *stochastic process* in which the current state of a system depends only upon the immediately preceding state of the system. For example, assume that you regularly play tennis with three people, and that you played a match with one of the three people last night. Assuming that you do not prefer to play the same person again the next time you play, you could randomly select from among the remaining two players as you schedule your next match. In this case, your decision is dependent only on your immediately preceding opponent, and is probabilistic since there is a one-half probability of selecting any one of the remaining two opponents.

20.2 AN ILLUSTRATION OF MARKOV ANALYSIS: THE ACCOUNTS RECEIVABLE CONTROL PROBLEM

One area in which Markov analysis models have proved to be useful is that of credit or accounts receivable control. To illustrate, let us consider a decision-making situation in which a wholesale distributor is attempting to determine a more effective set of credit-control policies. This wholesale distributor has historically classified all of its accounts receivable into one of the categories above.

In using this set of categories the wholesale distributor uses the following procedure. First, at any point in time in which an accounts receivable balance is paid in full it is immediately placed in the paid in full category. Second, if any portion of an accounts receivable balance exceeds 90 days, that portion is placed in the defaulted category. Third, the wholesaler "ages" the total accounts receivable balance for each customer's account according to the oldest unpaid bill. For example, suppose that a customer's accounts receivable balance on November 30 is as follows. The aging process would assign the total accounts receivable balance of $6000 to the delinquent (31–90 days) category on November 30, since the oldest unpaid bill of October 10 is some 41 days old. Now, let us further assume that on December 5 the customer pays the October 10 bill of $1000. The remaining total balance of $5000 would now be placed in the delinquent (0–30 days) category, since the oldest unpaid amount ($5000), corresponding to the November 20 purchase, is less than 31 days old. Use of this method of accounts

ACCOUNTS RECEIVABLE CATEGORY	STATUS OF ACCOUNTS RECEIVABLE
1	S_1: Paid in full
2	S_2: Defaulted (bad debt)
3	S_3: Delinquent (0–30 days)
4	S_4: Delinquent (31–90 days)

DATE OF PURCHASE	AMOUNT PURCHASED
October 10	$1000
November 20	5000
Total	$6000

receivable aging means that an accounts receivable classified in the delinquent (31–90 days) category at one point in time may appear in the delinquent (0–30 days) category at a later point.

The various accounts receivable categories are the *states* of the system and describe the status of the system at a point in time. They identify all of the possible conditions for this accounts receivable system. In Markov analysis we assume that these states are both *collectively exhaustive* and *mutually exclusive*. By collectively exhaustive we mean that we can list all of the possible states of the system. In our discussion of Markov analysis we assume that there is a finite number of states for the system being analyzed (e.g., four states in the account receivable system). By mutually exclusive we refer to the property that the system can only be in one state at any point in time. As seen earlier, a particular accounts receivable can have only one status at any point in time.

Once the states have been identified, the next step in the Markov analysis process is to determine the probabilities associated with the system being in a particular state. This means that we must initially define the vector of state probabilities for the four states for the current period (i.e., for period i = 1). Assume that we have just analyzed our $100,000 accounts receivable position and have determined that it is distributed as follows.

State 1—Paid in full	$45,000/$100,000	= .45
State 2—Defaulted	$15,000/$100,000	= .15
State 3—Delinquent (0–30 days)	$25,000/$100,000	= .25
State 4—Delinquent (31–90 days)	$15,000/$100,000	= .15

These probabilities can be placed in the vector of state probabilities for the current period as shown

$$V(1) = (.45 \quad .15 \quad .25 \quad .15) \qquad (20.1)$$

WHERE

$V(1)$ = vector of state probabilities for the four account receivable categories;

v_1 = the probability that the accounts receivable is paid in full

= .45;

v_2 = the probability that the accounts receivable is defaulted

= .15;

v_3 = the probability that the accounts receivable is delinquent 0–30 days

= .25;

v_4 = the probability that the accounts receivable is delinquent 31–90 days

= .15.

In general, the vector of state probabilities for period i, $V(i)$, will be given by

$$V(i) = (v_1, v_2, v_3, \ldots, v_n) \qquad (20.2)$$

WHERE

n = the number of states;

$v_1, v_2, \ldots, v_n$ = the probability of being in state 1, state 2, ..., state n in period i.

Once the initial states and the vector of state probabilities have been determined, the next step is to specify the matrix of transition probabilities. This matrix is used in conjunction with the vector of state probabilities in making predictions about the future.

In this particular accounts receivable system it is possible to move between states over time. The probabilities of moving between states are called *transition probabilities*, and are dependent only upon the current state of the system. A transition probability is defined as follows.

p_{ij} = conditional probability of the system being in state j one period, or step, in the future, given that the system is in state i currently

For example, p_{12} is the probability of the system being in state 2 one period (e.g., one month) in the future given that the system is in state 1 currently. These transition probabilities are usually determined empirically. For the problem being considered, let us assume that historical data have been collected and the following *matrix of transition probabilities* has been specified.

$$P = \begin{array}{c} \\ S_1 \\ S_2 \\ S_3 \\ S_4 \end{array} \begin{array}{cccc} S_1 & S_2 & S_3 & S_4 \\ \begin{bmatrix} 1 & 0 & 0 & 0 \\ 0 & 1 & 0 & 0 \\ .5 & .2 & .1 & .2 \\ .4 & .4 & .1 & .1 \end{bmatrix} \end{array}$$

$$= \begin{bmatrix} p_{11} & p_{12} & p_{13} & p_{14} \\ p_{21} & p_{22} & p_{23} & p_{24} \\ p_{31} & p_{32} & p_{33} & p_{34} \\ p_{41} & p_{42} & p_{43} & p_{44} \end{bmatrix}$$

(20.3)

This matrix of transition probabilities summarizes the transition probabilities associated with moving from any one state to any of the other states. To illustrate, consider the meaning of these probabilities for state 3 (row S_3):

Row 3 (state 3) p_{31} = probability of being in state 1 after being in state 3 previous period = .5

p_{32} = probability of being in state 2 after being in state 3 the previous period = .2

p_{33} = probability of being in state 3 after being in state 3 the previous period = .1

p_{34} = probability of being in state 4 after being in state 3 the previous period = .2

Note that this matrix of transition probabilities allows for the probability of being in state 3 (0–30 days delinquent) after being in state 4 (31–90 days delinquent), that is $p_{43} = .1$. Remember, this can occur when a partial payment is received on an accounts receivable that is 31–90 days delinquent. In this case the 31–90 days delinquent accounts receivable is "reclassified" as a 0–30 days delinquent accounts receivable.

Note also that this matrix of transition probabilities has two *absorbing states*. Once an accounts receivable makes a transition to state 1 (paid in full), the probability of making a transition to any other state is zero. Similarly, once an accounts receivable makes a transition to state 2 (defaulted), the probability of making a transition to any other state is zero. Therefore, once an accounts receivable reaches either state 1 or state 2, it will remain in that state forever. This means that all accounts receivable will

eventually be absorbed into either the paid in full or defaulted state. This provides the meaning for the term-absorbing state. We discuss absorbing states more fully later in this chapter.

In general, there are four properties that must be satisfied by the matrix of transition probabilities.

Property 1.
The transition probabilities for a given beginning state of the system sum to 1.0.

Property 2.
The transition probabilities encompass all possibilities for the system.

Property 3.
The transition probabilities are constant over time.

Property 4.
The states of the transition probability matrix are independent over time.

Given the vector of state probabilities and the matrix of transition probabilities we can compute the probabilities associated with the various states n time periods in the future. If we are in any period n, the state probabilities for period $n + 1$ can be computed as follows

$$V(n + 1) = V(n) \cdot P \qquad (20.4)$$

Equation 20.4 can now be used to determine the probabilities associated with the various states in the next period (i.e., in period $n + 1 = 2$). The computations are

$V(2) = V(1) \cdot P$

$$V(2) = (.45\ .15\ .25\ .15) \begin{bmatrix} 1 & 0 & 0 & 0 \\ 0 & 1 & 0 & 0 \\ .5 & .2 & .1 & .2 \\ .4 & .4 & .1 & .1 \end{bmatrix}$$

$= [(.45)(1) + (.15)(0) + (.25)(.5) + (.15)(.4)$

$(.45)(0) + (.15)(1) + (.25)(.2) + (.15)(.4)$

$(.45)(0) + (.15)(0) + (.25)(.1) + (.15)(.1)$

$(.45)(0) + (.15)(0) + (.25)(.2) + (.15)(.1)]$

$= [.635 \qquad .26 \qquad .04 \qquad .065]$

$\qquad \underline{S_1} \qquad\quad \underline{S_2} \qquad\quad \underline{S_3} \qquad\quad \underline{S_4}$

| Paid in full | Defaulted | Delinquent (0–30 days) | Delinquent (31–90 days) |

(20.5)

As you can see the probability of the accounts receivable being paid in full or becoming a bad debt increases, while the probabilities associated with the two various delinquency categories decrease.

20.3 COMPUTING STEADY-STATE PROBABILITIES

In our previous example we noted that the state probabilities for period $n + 1$ can be computed using the state probabilities for period n and the matrix of transition probabilities, P. This means that the following relationships hold

$$
\begin{aligned}
\text{Period 1:} &\quad V(1) = V(0) \cdot P \\
\text{Period 2:} &\quad V(2) = V(1) \cdot P \\
\text{Period 3:} &\quad V(3) = V(2) \cdot P \quad (20.6) \\
\text{Period 4:} &\quad V(4) = V(3) \cdot P \\
\text{Period 5:} &\quad V(5) = V(4) \cdot P \\
&\quad \vdots
\end{aligned}
$$

Previously, we determined [see (20.5)] the state probabilities for period 2 as

$$V(2) = [.635 \quad .26 \quad .04 \quad .065] \quad (20.7)$$

Continuing this computational process

Period 3: $V(3) = V(2) \cdot P$

$V(3) =$

$$[.635 \quad .26 \quad .04 \quad .065]
\begin{bmatrix}
1 & 0 & 0 & 0 \\
0 & 1 & 0 & 0 \\
.5 & .2 & .1 & .2 \\
.4 & .4 & .1 & .1
\end{bmatrix}$$

$$= [.681 \quad .294 \quad .0105 \quad .0145] \quad (20.8)$$

Period 4: $V(4) = V(3) \cdot P$

$V(4) =$

$$[.681 \quad .294 \quad .0105 \quad .0145]
\begin{bmatrix}
1 & 0 & 0 & 0 \\
0 & 1 & 0 & 0 \\
.5 & .2 & .1 & .2 \\
.4 & .4 & .1 & .1
\end{bmatrix}$$

$$= [.6921 \quad .3019 \quad .0025 \quad .0036] \quad (20.9)$$

Period 5: $V(5) = V(4) \cdot P$

$V(5) =$

$$[.6921 \quad .3019 \quad .0025 \quad .0036]
\begin{bmatrix}
1 & 0 & 0 & 0 \\
0 & 1 & 0 & 0 \\
.5 & .2 & .1 & .2 \\
.4 & .4 & .1 & .1
\end{bmatrix}$$

$$= [.6947 \quad .3038 \quad .0006 \quad .0009] \quad (20.10)$$

Period 6: $V(6) = V(5) \cdot P$

$V(6) =$

$$[.6947 \quad .3038 \quad .0006 \quad .0009]
\begin{bmatrix}
1 & 0 & 0 & 0 \\
0 & 1 & 0 & 0 \\
.5 & .2 & .1 & .2 \\
.4 & .4 & .1 & .1
\end{bmatrix}$$

$$= [.6954 \quad .3043 \quad .0001 \quad .0002] \quad (20.11)$$

Period 7: $V(7) = V(6) \cdot P$

$V(7) =$

$$[.6954 \quad .3043 \quad .0001 \quad .0002]
\begin{bmatrix}
1 & 0 & 0 & 0 \\
0 & 1 & 0 & 0 \\
.5 & .2 & .1 & .2 \\
.4 & .4 & .1 & .1
\end{bmatrix}$$

$$= [.69552 \quad .30439 \quad .00004 \quad .00005] \quad (20.12)$$

Period 8: $V(8) = V(7) \cdot P$

$V(8) =$

$$[.69552 \quad .30439 \quad .00004 \quad .00005]
\begin{bmatrix}
1 & 0 & 0 & 0 \\
0 & 1 & 0 & 0 \\
.5 & .2 & .1 & .2 \\
.4 & .4 & .1 & .1
\end{bmatrix}$$

$$= [.6956 \quad .3044 \quad .0000 \quad .0000] \quad (20.13)$$

Note that as we have proceeded from period 2 to period 8, the changes in the state probabilities become smaller and smaller. For periods 7 and 8 the state probabilities are nearly the same.[1] The changes in the state probabilities over time for the various classifications of accounts receivable are shown graphically in Figure 20.1

The virtually constant state probabilities that occur after a certain number of periods are referred to as *steady-state probabilities*. They are the average probabilities that the system will be in certain states

---

[1] It should be noted, however, that they are not exactly the same. Indeed, if we carry out our computations to many decimal places, they will not be exactly the same for future time periods.

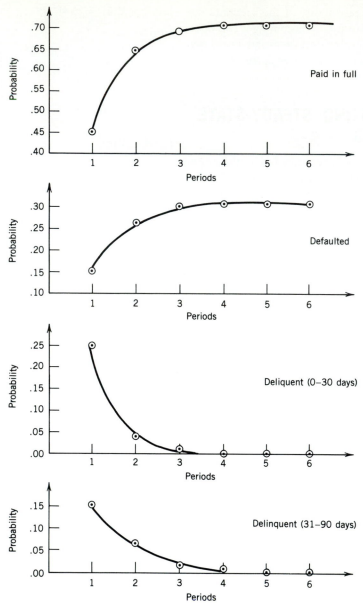

FIGURE 20.1 STEADY-STATE PROBABILITIES OVER TIME.

after a certain number of transition periods. While the system itself can continue to move from state to state over future time periods, after a certain number of time periods the average probabilities associated with the various states will become virtually constant. Therefore, for our accounts receivable problem, the steady-state probabilities are

.6956 = probability of an accounts receivable being paid in full after a number of periods in the future, regardless of its disposition in period 1

.3044 = probability of an accounts receivable being defaulted after a number of periods in the future, regardless of its disposition in period 1

.0000 = probability of an accounts receivable being delinquent 0–30 days after a number of periods in the future, regardless of its disposition in period 1

.0000 = probability of an accounts receivable being delinquent 31–90 days after a number of periods in the future, regardless of its disposition in period 1

The steady-state probabilities that we have just computed for our accounts receivable example indicate the probability of a particular accounts receivable being in a particular category in the long-term future. The steady-state probabilities also indicate the percentage of accounts receivable that will be in each category in the long run. For example, if we currently have 1000 accounts receiv- able worth $1 million outstanding, and the vector of state probabilities for the current period is $V(1) =$ (.45 .15 .25 .15), then in the long run we can expect the following to occur with respect to the number of accounts receivable and dollar amount of accounts receivable in each accounts receivable category:

CATEGORY OF ACCOUNTS RECEIVABLE	STEADY-STATE PROBABILITY	NUMBER OF ACCOUNTS RECEIVABLE	DOLLAR AMOUNT OF ACCOUNTS RECEIVABLE
Paid in full	.6956	1000 × .6956 = 695.6	$1,000,000 × .6956 = $6,956,000
Defaulted	.3044	1000 × .3044 = 304.4	$1,000,000 × .3044 = $3,044,000
Delinquent, 0–30 days	.0000	1000 × .000 = 0	$1,000,000 × .0000 = $0
Delinquent, 31–90 days	.0000	1000 × .000 = 0	$1,000,000 × .0000 = $0

It should also be noted that the steady-state probabilities do not change for different beginning conditions, as long as the matrix of transition prob- abilities is constant and does not contain absorbing states. To illustrate what we mean, refer to Table 20.1 in which we have summarized the behavior of the state probabilities over time, for three sets of beginning conditions, with a constant matrix of transition probabilities which does not contain ab- sorbing states. (This matrix of transition probabil-

TABLE 20.1 SUMMARY OF STATE PROBABILITIES OVER TIME FOR VARYING BEGINNING CONDITIONS

$$P = \begin{matrix} & \begin{matrix} S_1 & S_2 & S_3 \end{matrix} \\ \begin{matrix} S_1 \\ S_2 \\ S_3 \end{matrix} & \begin{bmatrix} .5 & .3 & .2 \\ .4 & .3 & .3 \\ .3 & .3 & .4 \end{bmatrix} \end{matrix} = \text{matrix of transition probabilities}$$

a) Beginning Condition $V(1) = $ (.05 .05 .90)

STATE	PERIOD 1	PERIOD 2	PERIOD 3	PERIOD 4	PERIOD 5	PERIOD 6	
S_1	.3150	.3930	.4086	.4117	.4123	.4125	
S_2	.3000	.3000	.3000	.3000	.3000	.3000	(STEADY-STATE
S_3	.3850	.3070	.2914	.2883	.2877	.2875	PROBABILITIES)

b) Beginning Condition: $V(1) = $ (.50 .40 .10)

STATE	PERIOD 1	PERIOD 2	PERIOD 3	PERIOD 4	PERIOD 5	PERIOD 6	
S_1	.4400	.4180	.4136	.4127	.4125	.4125	
S_2	.3000	.3000	.3000	.3000	.3000	.3000	(STEADY-STATE
S_3	.2600	.2820	.2864	.2873	.2875	.2875	PROBABILITIES)

c) Beginning Condition: $V(1) = $ (.90 .05 .05)

STATE	PERIOD 1	PERIOD 2	PERIOD 3	PERIOD 4	PERIOD 5	PERIOD 6	
S_1	.4850	.4270	.4154	.4131	.4126	.4125	
S_2	.3000	.3000	.3000	.3000	.3000	.3000	(STEADY-STATE
S_3	.2150	.2730	.2846	.2869	.2874	.2875	PROBABILITIES)

ities is shown at the top of Table 20.1). Observe that after six periods the steady-state probabilities are identical for the three beginning conditions.

20.3.1 AN ALGEBRAIC APPROACH TO COMPUTING STEADY-STATE PROBABILITIES

In our previous example we had to compute the state probabilities for six periods before these probabilities became virtually constant. This determi-

nation of the steady-state probabilities required a fair amount of matrix computations, with these computations becoming increasing tedious. For Markov processes involving absorbing states, this procedure must be used to determine the steady-state probabilities. For Markov processes that do not have absorbing states, however, a simpler approach is available.

Referring to our previous example, observe that after period 5 the state probabilities virtually did not change.

Beginning Condition:	a) $V(1) = (.05 \quad .05 \quad .90)$	b) $V(1) = (.50 \quad .40 \quad .10)$	c) $V(1) = (.90 \quad .05 \quad .05)$
	$\vdots \qquad \vdots$	$\vdots \qquad \vdots$	$\vdots \qquad \vdots$
	$V(5) = (.4123 \; .3000 \; .2877)$	$V(5) = (.4125 \; .3000 \; .2875)$	$V(5) = (.4126 \; .3000 \; .2874)$
	$V(6) = (.4125 \; .3000 \; .2875)$	$V(6) = (.4125 \; .3000 \; .2875)$	$V(6) = (.4125 \; .3000 \; .2875)$

$$(20.14)$$

Therefore, we can state in general that after a number of periods in the future the state probabilities in period n equal the state probabilities in period $n + 1$. In our example, we saw that

$$V(7) = V(8) \qquad (20.15)$$

and, in general, we can state that

$$V(n) = V(n + 1) \qquad (20.16)$$

Let us now illustrate how this property can be employed to determine the steady-state probabilities. For this illustration we utilize the matrix of transition probabilities from our previous example

$$P = \begin{array}{c} \\ S_1 \\ S_2 \\ S_3 \end{array} \begin{array}{ccc} S_1 & S_2 & S_3 \\ \begin{bmatrix} .5 & .3 & .2 \\ .4 & .3 & .3 \\ .3 & .3 & .4 \end{bmatrix} \end{array} \qquad (20.17)$$

Recall that this matrix of transition probabilities does not have absorbing states.

Now, to determine the steady-state probabilities for period $n + 1$ according to the procedure of the previous section, we would compute the following

$$V(n + 1) = V(n) \begin{bmatrix} .5 & .3 & .2 \\ .4 & .3 & .3 \\ .3 & .3 & .4 \end{bmatrix} \qquad (20.18)$$

If we now designate the steady-state probabilities as π_1, π_2, and π_3, for both period n and period $n + 1$, we have

$$V(n) = V(n + 1) = [\pi_1 \quad \pi_2 \quad \pi_3] \qquad (20.19)$$

Consequently, the computation given by (20.18) can be rewritten as

$$[\pi_1 \quad \pi_2 \quad \pi_3] = [\pi_1 \quad \pi_2 \quad \pi_3] \begin{bmatrix} .5 & .3 & .2 \\ .4 & .3 & .3 \\ .3 & .3 & .4 \end{bmatrix} \qquad (20.20)$$

Performing matrix operations on (20.20) results in the following set of three simultaneous equations

$$\pi_1 = .5\pi_1 + .4\pi_2 + .3\pi_3 \qquad (20.21)$$

$$\pi_2 = .3\pi_1 + .3\pi_2 + .3\pi_3 \qquad (20.22)$$

$$\pi_3 = .2\pi_1 + .3\pi_2 + .4\pi_3 \qquad (20.23)$$

Furthermore, we know that the steady-state probabilities must sum to 1.0. Thus,

$$1 = \pi_1 + \pi_2 + \pi_3 \qquad (20.24)$$

In Eqs. 20.21 to 20.23 we have similar terms on both sides of the equality sign, so we can rewrite the set of four equations as

$$0 = -.5\pi_1 + .4\pi_2 + .3\pi_3 \quad (20.25)$$

$$0 = .3\pi_1 - .7\pi_2 + .3\pi_3 \quad (20.26)$$

$$0 = .2\pi_1 + .3\pi_2 - .6\pi_3 \quad (20.27)$$

$$1 = \pi_1 + \pi_2 + \pi_3 \quad (20.28)$$

As you can see, we have four simultaneous equations and only three unknowns. So, we can eliminate any one of the first three equations (e.g., we arbitrarily drop Eq. (20.27) and solve the remaining three equations simultaneously for the steady-state probabilities. We now have

$$0 = -.5\pi_1 + .4\pi_2 + .3\pi_3 \quad (20.29)$$

$$0 = .3\pi_1 - .7\pi_2 + .3\pi_3 \quad (20.30)$$

$$1 = \pi_1 + \pi_2 + \pi_3 \quad (20.31)$$

Step 1. Equate Eq. 20.29 to Eq. 20.30

$$-.5\pi_1 + .4\pi_2 + .3\pi_3 = .3\pi_1 - .7\pi_2 + .3\pi_3$$
$$-.5\pi_1 + .4\pi_2 = .3\pi_1 - .7\pi_2$$
$$-.8\pi_1 = -1.1\,\pi_2$$
$$\pi_1 = \frac{1.1}{.8}\,\pi_2$$
$$(20.32)$$

Step 2. Add 3 times Eq. 20.29 to 5 times Eq. 20.30

$$0 = -1.5\pi_1 + 1.2\pi_2 + .9\pi_3$$
$$\underline{0 = 1.5\pi_1 - 3.5\pi_2 + 1.5\pi_3}$$
$$0 = -2.3\pi_2 + 2.4\pi_3$$
$$2.4\pi_3 = 2.3\pi_2$$
$$\pi_3 = \frac{2.3}{2.4}\,\pi_2 \quad (20.33)$$

Step 3. Solve for π_1, π_2, π_3 by substitution

$$1 = \pi_1 + \pi_2 + \pi_3$$
$$1 = \frac{1.1}{.8}\,\pi_2 + \pi_2 + \frac{2.3}{2.4}\,\pi_2$$
$$1 = 3.333\,\pi_2$$
$$\pi_2 = \frac{1.000}{3.333} = .3000 \quad (20.34)$$

$$\pi_1 = \frac{1.1}{.8}\,\pi_2$$
$$= \frac{1.1}{.8}\,(0.300)$$
$$= .4125 \quad (20.35)$$
$$\pi_3 = \frac{2.3}{2.4}\,\pi_2 \quad (20.36)$$
$$= .2875$$

Check:

$$1 = \pi_1 + \pi_2 + \pi_3 \quad (20.37)$$
$$1 = .4125 + .3000 + .2875$$

We need to emphasize that this method for solving for the steady-state probabilities will work only for nonabsorbing Markov processes. If we have an absorbing Markov process, we cannot compute steady-state probabilities for all of the states, because the process must eventually end up in one of the absorbing states. As in the case of our accounts receivable example, however, we may be interested in determining the probability associated with dollars in a particular nonabsorbing state ending up in a particular absorbing state. We now explain how to determine this type of probability in the following section.

20.4 ANALYSIS OF ABSORBING MARKOV PROCESSES

A special case of a Markov process involves an *absorbing* or *trapping state*. An absorbing state is a state that has a zero probability of being left once it is entered. Once the absorbing state is entered, the process either stops completely or stops and then is reinitiated from some other state. A Markov process can be shown to be an *absorbing Markov process* if

1. it has at least one absorbing state;
2. it is possible to move from every nonabsorbing state to at least one absorbing state in a finite number of steps.

Our previous accounts receivable application

exhibits the properties of an absorbing Markov process. It has two absorbing states

1. S_1: paid in full;
2. S_2: default (bad debt).

The probability of being in the paid in full category for an accounts receivable in a future time period, given that the customer in the paid in full category for an accounts receivable for the current time period, is 1.0, or 100 percent. Similarly, if an accounts receivable is in the default category for the current time period, it will be in the default category in a future time period. Observe also that both of the other states, S_3 and S_4, are nonabsorbing but that it is possible to move from any of these nonabsorbing states to the absorbing states, S_1 and S_2. As we observed when we computed the steady-state probabilities for this situation, after period 6 the steady-state probabilities for the two nonabsorbing states, S_3 and S_4, had been reduced to zero. Thus, after period 6 we had moved from the two nonabsorbing states, S_3 and S_4, to the two absorbing states, S_1 and S_2.

A great deal of useful information can be obtained from the matrix of transition probabilities [see (20.3)] for this accounts receivable problem by means of several relatively simple matrix algebra manipulations. In particular, we can determine

1. the probability of absorption by any absorbing state;
2. the expected number of steps before the process is absorbed.

For those unfamiliar with matrix algebra, a review is presented in Appendix A.

To begin the computation process for an absorbing Markov process we initially change the matrix of transition probabilities into the following general form.

$$P = \left[\begin{array}{c|c} I & O \\ \hline A & N \end{array} \right] \qquad (20.38)$$

WHERE

$I =$ an r-by-r identity matrix defining the probabilities of staying within an absorbing state once it is reached;

$O =$ an r-by-s null matrix indicating the probabilities of going from an absorbing state to a nonabsorbing state.

$A =$ an s-by-r matrix containing the probabilities of going from a nonabsorbing state to an absorbing state

$N =$ an s-by-s matrix showing the probabilities of going from one nonabsorbing state to another nonabsorbing state.

For our accounts receivable problem, the matrix of transition probabilities can be structured into the four submatrices just defined, as follows.

$$P = \left[\begin{array}{c|c} I & O \\ \hline A & N \end{array} \right] = \left[\begin{array}{cc|cc} 1 & 0 & 0 & 0 \\ 0 & 1 & 0 & 0 \\ \hline .5 & .2 & .1 & .2 \\ .4 & .4 & .1 & .1 \end{array} \right]$$

$$(20.39)$$

Using the submatrix N from the subdivided transition probability matrix, the *fundamental matrix, F,* can be calculated using the following formula:[2]

$$F = (I - N)^{-1} \qquad (20.40)$$

For a given starting state, the fundamental matrix, F, indicates the expected number of times a process is in each nonabsorbing state before it is absorbed. Using the data from our accounts receivable example, the computation of the fundamental matrix proceeds as follows. First, we determine

$$(I - N) = \begin{bmatrix} 1 & 0 \\ 0 & 1 \end{bmatrix} - \begin{bmatrix} .1 & .2 \\ .1 & .1 \end{bmatrix}$$

$$= \begin{bmatrix} .9 & -.2 \\ -.1 & .9 \end{bmatrix} = \begin{bmatrix} 9/10 & -2/10 \\ -1/10 & 9/10 \end{bmatrix}$$

$$(20.41)$$

---

[2]For computational purposes the identity matrix, *I*, must be of the same magnitude (i.e., *s*-by-*s*) as the matrix, *N*, which shows the probabilities of going from one nonabsorbing state to another nonabsorbing state.

Next, this matrix is inverted to obtain:

$$F = (I - N)^{-1}$$
$$= \begin{bmatrix} 90/79 & 20/79 \\ 10/79 & 90/79 \end{bmatrix} = \begin{bmatrix} 1.14 & .25 \\ .13 & 1.14 \end{bmatrix} \quad (20.42)$$

To interpret the results given by the fundamental matrix, recall that the nonabsorbing states are 3 and 4. The expected number of steps before absorption is the sum of the times the process is in each absorbing state. These summations are as follows.

Beginning State	Expected Steps before Absorption
S_3	90/79 + 20/79 = 110/79 = 1.39
S_4	10/79 + 90/79 = 100/79 = 1.27

To compute the *probability of absorption* of the nonabsorbing states by any of the absorbing states, we employ the following relationship

Probability of absorption
$$= FA = (I - N)^{-1} \cdot A \quad (20.43)$$

Returning to our accounts receivable example

Probability of absorption $= FA = (I - N)^{-1} \cdot A$
$$= \begin{bmatrix} 1.14 & .25 \\ .13 & 1.14 \end{bmatrix} \begin{bmatrix} .5 & .2 \\ .4 & .4 \end{bmatrix} = \begin{bmatrix} .67 & .33 \\ .52 & .48 \end{bmatrix}$$
$$(20.44)$$

The first row of the absorption probability matrix indicates the probability that a delinquent account in state 3 will end up in each of the absorbing states. We observe that there is a .67 probability that a delinquent account beginning in state 3 will end up in state 1 (paid in full) and a .33 probability that a delinquent account beginning in state 3 will end up in state 2 (bad debt). The second row of the absorption matrix indicates the probabilities that a delinquent account beginning in state 4 will end up in each of the absorbing states. We note that there is a .52 probability that a delinquent account beginning in state 4 will end up in state 1 (paid in full) and a .48 probability that a delinquent account beginning in state 4 will end up in state 2 (bad debt).

Finally, let us assume that this company analyzed its current accounts receivable position and has found that it has $25,000 of accounts receivable in state 3 (delinquent, 0–30 days) and $15,000 of

accounts receivable in state 4 (delinquent, 31–90 days). We can use the absorption probability matrix to determine how many of these dollars will eventually end up in state 1 (paid in full) or state 2 (defaulted). Denoting the present composition of the accounts receivable dollars as the vector T

$$T = \begin{array}{cc} S_3 & S_4 \\ (\$25,000 & \$15,000) \end{array} \quad (20.45)$$

The final composition of the accounts receivable dollars, denoted as T' will be

$$T' = T \cdot \text{probability of absorption}$$

$$= \begin{array}{cc} S_3 & S_4 \\ (\$25,000 & \$15,000) \end{array} \begin{array}{c} S_3 \\ S_4 \end{array} \begin{bmatrix} \overset{S_1}{.67} & \overset{S_2}{.33} \\ .52 & .48 \end{bmatrix}$$

$$= \begin{array}{cc} S_1 & S_2 \\ (\$24,550 & \$15,450) \end{array}$$

$$(20.46)$$

Therefore, if this company currently has $25,000 (state S_3) + $15,000 (state S_4) = $40,000 of delinquent accounts receivable, it can expect that eventually $24,550 will be collected, while $15,450 will become bad debts.

The preceding type of analysis is one of the most common and most useful ways of using the Markov process. It is applicable when a matrix of transition probabilities can be defined, absorbing states are present, and decisions about future occurrences are needed.

20.5 SOLVING MARKOV ANALYSIS PROBLEMS USING A COMPUTER

Software packages for solving Markov analysis problems are not as common as software packages for linear programming or network models. Many of the general-purpose management science software packages, however, do contain programs that can be used for solving Markov analysis problems. One such typical Markov analysis program is that contained in *Microsolve/Operations Research* by Jensen.[3]

---

[3]Jensen, *op. cit.*, pp. 163–181.

TABLE 20.2 MICROCOMPUTER PROGRAM OUTPUT: ACCOUNTS RECEIVABLE MARKOV ANALYSIS PROBLEM

STATE PROBABILITIES: PERIODS 1 TO 20; STATES 1 to 4

	S1	S2	S3	S4
PER 1	.635	.26	.04	.065
PER 2	.681	.294	.0105	.0145
PER 3	.69205	.3019	.0025	.00355
PER 4	.69472	.30382	.000605	8.5E − 04
PER 5	.695364	.304283	.000146	.000206
PER 6	.695520	.304394	3.5E − 05	4.9E − 05
PER 7	.695557	.304421	8.5E − 06	1.2E − 05
PER 8	.695566	.304428	2.0E − 06	2.9E − 06
PER 9	.695569	.304429	4.9E − 07	7.0E − 07
PER 10	.695569	.304430	1.1E − 07	1.6E − 07
PER 11	.695569	.304430	2.8E − 08	4.0E − 08
PER 12	.695569	.304430	6.9E − 09	9.8E − 09
PER 13	.695569	.304430	1.6E − 09	2.3E − 09
PER 14	.695569	.304430	4.0E − 10	5.7E − 10
PER 15	.695569	.304430	9.8E − 11	1.3E − 10
PER 16	.695569	.304430	2.3E − 11	3.3E − 11
PER 17	.695569	.304430	5.7E − 12	8.0E − 12
PER 18	.695569	.304430	1.3E − 12	1.9E − 12
PER 19	.695569	.304430	3.3E − 13	4.7E − 13
PER 20	.695569	.304430	8.0E − 14	1.1E − 13

Note: $V(1) = (.45\ .15\ .25\ .15)$ = initial vector of state probabilities.

To illustrate this software program we have used it to compute the steady-state probabilities for the accounts receivable control problem described in Sections 20.2 and 20.3. Recall that we manually computed steady-state probabilities for eight periods into the future, beginning with an initial vector of state probabilities $V(1) = (.45\quad .15\quad .25\quad .15)$.

The output from the Markov analysis microcomputer program is shown in Table 20.2. From this observe that we utilized the computer program to compute the steady-state probabilities for $n = 20$ periods into the future. Also observe that when the computer is used, and the computations are made to many decimal places, the steady-state probabilities are not *exactly* the same in future time periods, even when $n = 20$.

20.5 SUMMARY

In this chapter we have presented an introduction to Markov analysis. This technique is useful in describing the behavior of systems in which we can determine the probability of movement from one state to another over time. We have demonstrated one of the most useful areas of Markov analysis, namely the analysis of accounts receivable. Other application areas include brand switching, and analysis of machine failure. In all of these applications it should be stressed that Markov analysis provides descriptive information that can be used by the decision maker rather than indicating an optimal course of action. In this respect Markov analysis is similar to queuing theory and simulation, which were studied in earlier chapters.

GLOSSARY

Absorbing Markov Chain A Markov chain that has at least one absorbing state, and in which it is possible to move from every nonabsorbing state to at least one absorbing state in a finite number of steps.

Absorbing State A state having a zero probability of being left once it is entered.

Fundamental Matrix A matrix employed in analyzing absorbing Markov chains to determine the expected number of times a process is in each nonabsorbing state before it is absorbed.

Markov Chain or Markov Process A stochastic process for which the occurrence of a future state depends only on the immediately preceding state. Thus, for a Markov process, given that the present state is known, the conditional probability of the next state is independent of the states prior to the present state.

Matrix of Transition Probabilities A matrix containing all of the transition probabilities for a system.

Nonabsorbing State A state that does not have a zero probability of being left once it is entered.

Probability of Absorption The probability of going from a nonabsorbing state i to an absorbing state j.

State The condition of the system at any point in time.

State Probability The probability of an event occurring at a particular moment of time.

Transition Probability The probability that the system will move from state i to state j in one step.

Steady-State Probability The probability that the system will be in any particular state after a large number of periods. A steady-state probability does not change after steady-state, or equilibrium conditions, have been reached.

Vector of State Probabilities A vector of state probabilities for a given system, at a specific point of time (e.g., the initial state).

Selected References

Bhat, U. N. 1972. *Elements of Applied Stochastic Processes.* New York: Wiley.

Chung, K. L. 1960. *Markov Chains with Stationary Transition Probabilities.* Berlin: Springer-Verlag.

Clark, A. Bruce, and Ralph L. Disney. 1970. *Probability and Random Processes for Engineers and Scientists.* New York: Wiley.

Derman, C. 1970. *Finite State Markov Decision Processes.* San Francisco: Holden-Day.

Howard, Ronald A. 1960. *Dynamic Programming and Markov Processes.* New York: Wiley.

Howard, Ronald A. 1971. *Dynamic Probabilistic Models,* Vol. 1, *Markov Models.* New York: Wiley.

Kemeny, J. G., J. L. Snell, and G. L. Thompson. 1959. *Finite Markov Chains.* New York: Van Nostrand.

Parzen, E. 1960. *Modern Probability Theory and Its Applications.* New York Wiley.

Parzen, E. 1962. *Stochastic Processes.* San Francisco: Holden-Day.

Ross, S. M. 1972. *Introduction to Probability Models.* New York: Academic Press.

Discussion Questions

1. What is the nature of a stochastic process?

2. How can we determine the matrix of transition probabilities?

3. What is an absorbing Markov state? What is an absorbing Markov process?

4. What is the fundamental matrix? How is it used in analyzing an absorbing Markov process?

5. What do we mean by an equilibrium condition in a Markov process?

6. What are the basic assumptions that are made in Markov analysis?

7. Explain how Markov analysis is used in decision making.

8. Explain what is meant by steady-state conditions.

9. Cite some practical applications of Markov analysis.

10. Explain what will happen with respect to the steady-state conditions when you have a transition matrix composed of both absorbing and nonabsorbing states.

PROBLEMS

1. A marketing research firm has just completed a survey of consumer buying habits with respect to three brands of breakfast cereal. It estimates that at the present time, 30 percent of the customers buy brand A, 30 percent buy brand B, and 40 percent buy brand C. Additionally, the marketing research firm has analyzed its survey data and has determined that the following brand-switching matrix is appropriate for the three brands of cereal.

$$
\begin{array}{cc}
 & \begin{array}{c} \text{Brand of Cereal} \\ \text{Next Purchased} \end{array} \\
\begin{array}{c} \text{Brand of Cereal} \\ \text{Just Purchased} \end{array}
\begin{array}{c} A \\ B \\ C \end{array}
& \begin{array}{ccc} A & B & C \\ \left[\begin{array}{ccc} .4 & .4 & .2 \\ .2 & .5 & .3 \\ .3 & .4 & .3 \end{array} \right] \end{array}
\end{array}
$$

What will be the expected distribution of customers one time period in the future?

2. Given the following transition matrix with states 1 and 2 as absorbing states:

$$
P = \begin{array}{c} S_1 \\ S_2 \\ S_3 \\ S_4 \end{array}
\begin{array}{cccc}
S_1 & S_2 & S_3 & S_4 \\
\left[\begin{array}{cccc}
1 & 0 & 0 & 0 \\
0 & 1 & 0 & 0 \\
.3 & .3 & .3 & .1 \\
.2 & .4 & .3 & .1
\end{array} \right]
\end{array}
$$

What is the probability that an item that begins in either state S_3 or S_4 ends up in the absorbing states S_1 or S_2? That is, determine the structure of the absorption matrix. How many steps will be required before the process is absorbed, for beginning states S_3 and S_4?

3. Mr. Slim Picker owns an azalea farm in Batesburg, South Carolina. His farm currently has some 4000 azaleas in various stages of growth. Of these 1000 azaleas, 1000 are still too small to be sold and transplanted, while 3000 are available for sale. The operation of this azalea farm can be viewed as a one-year time-period Markov process, with the following four states.

STATE 1. Sold/successfully transplanted

STATE 2. Lost to disease

STATE 3. Too small to be sold

STATE 4. Satisfactory size—available for sale

Slim, who studied Markov analysis while a student at the University of South Carolina, has determined that the following transition matrix is appropriate for his yearly operations.

$$P = \begin{array}{c} \\ S_1 \\ S_2 \\ S_3 \\ S_4 \end{array} \begin{array}{c} \begin{array}{cccc} S_1 & S_2 & S_3 & S_4 \end{array} \\ \begin{bmatrix} 1 & 0 & 0 & 0 \\ 0 & 1 & 0 & 0 \\ .5 & .1 & .2 & .2 \\ .6 & .1 & .1 & .2 \end{bmatrix} \end{array}$$

How many of Slim's currently available 4000 azaleas will eventually be sold, and how many will be lost to disease? How long will it take for this to happen, for states 3 and 4?

4. Your Friend Finance Company categorizes its loans into four categories, as follows.

CATEGORY 1: Loan paid in full

CATEGORY 2: Loan defaulted (bad debt)

CATEGORY 3: Loan payment late (0–30 days)

CATEGORY 4: Loan payment late (31+ days)

From past historical data, the company has derived the following transition matrix as being descriptive of the behavior of its loan categories on a weekly basis.

$$P = \begin{array}{c} \\ S_1 \\ S_2 \\ S_3 \\ S_4 \end{array} \begin{array}{cccc} S_1 & S_2 & S_3 & S_4 \\ \left[\begin{array}{cccc} 1 & 0 & 0 & 0 \\ 0 & 1 & 0 & 0 \\ .4 & .2 & .3 & .1 \\ .3 & .4 & .2 & .1 \end{array} \right] \end{array}$$

a. Compute the expected number of steps before absorption.
b. Compute the absorption matrix associated with states S_1 and S_2.
c. If your Friend Finance Company currently has $50,000 of outstanding loans in category 4, what is the expected amount to eventually be collected and what is the expected amount to eventually be written off as bad debts?

5. Given two products, A and B, the following table indicates the probabilities of a customer buying the same product or a different product in a future period.

Product Purchased this Period	Product Purchased Next Period	
	A	B
A	.6	.4
B	.3	.7

Use Markov analysis to determine the probabilities that a customer will purchase product A or product B in period 4 in the future, given that she purchased product A this period.

6. Given the following transition matrix

This Period	Next Period	
	1	2
1	.2	.8
2	.6	.4

and assuming that the system is in state 2 this period, determine the probabilities that it will be in states 1 and 2 in period 2, in period 3, in period 4, and in period 5.

7. Sue Adamson reads both Ms. and Cosmopolitan regularly. The following transition matrix indicates the probabilities of the magazine Sue will read in a month given the magazine read last month.

| Magazine Read | Magazine Read Next Month | |
This Month	Ms.	Cosmopolitan
Ms.	.60	.40
Cosmopolitan	.50	.50

If Sue read Ms. this month, determine the probability that she will read Ms. in each of the next three months.

0. Determine the steady-state probabilities for the matrix of transition probabilities in Problem 5 using the algebraic method, and explain their meaning.

9. Determine the steady-state probabilities for the matrix of transition probabilities in Problem 6 using the algebraic method, and explain their meaning.

10. Determine the steady-state probabilities for the matrix of transition probabilities in Problem 7 using the algebraic method, and explain their meaning.

11. In Section 20.2 we studied an accounts receivable control problem. What would be the probabilties of being paid in full or defaulted after several periods, if the matrix of transition probabilities changed as follows?

$$P = \begin{array}{c} \\ S_1 \\ S_2 \\ S_3 \\ S_4 \end{array} \begin{array}{c} \begin{array}{cccc} S_1 & S_2 & S_3 & S_4 \end{array} \\ \begin{bmatrix} 1 & 0 & 0 & 0 \\ 0 & 1 & 0 & 0 \\ .4 & .3 & .2 & .1 \\ .4 & .3 & .2 & .1 \end{bmatrix} \end{array}$$

How many steps will be required before the process is absorbed, for beginning states S_3 and S_4?

12. Professor I. M. Tough teaches a course in quantitative methods and requires that all students must pass the final exam in the course in order to pass the course. A student is given three chances on the final exam. For this course, the following states can occur

STATE 1: Pass the final exam, and pass the course;

STATE 2: Fail the final exam three times, and fail the course;

STATE 3: Fail the final exam the first time;

STATE 4: Fail the final exam the second time;

Professor Tough has kept final exam data on several successive classes and has compiled the following matrix of transition probabilities

$$P = \begin{array}{c} \\ S_1 \\ S_2 \\ S_3 \\ S_4 \end{array} \begin{array}{cccc} S_1 & S_2 & S_3 & S_4 \\ \left[\begin{array}{cccc} 1 & 0 & 0 & 0 \\ 0 & 1 & 0 & 0 \\ .6 & .2 & .1 & .1 \\ .4 & .3 & .2 & .1 \end{array} \right] \end{array}$$

a. In the long run what percentage of students will pass the course, and what percentage fail, given that they have failed the final exam the first time?
b. At the present time Professor Tough has 10 students who did not pass the final exam on the first attempt and 20 students who did not pass the final exam on the second attempt. How many students in these two groups will eventually pass the course, and how many will eventually fail the course?

13. Mike Sanchez owns a Zokidata printer that is part of his personal computer configuration. He has kept data on its operating capability on a monthly basis, and has concluded that the printer will work 80 percent of the time if it worked in the previous month. Conversely, it will not work 70 percent of the time if it did not work in the previous month.

a. Construct the matrix of transition probabilities for this situation.
b. What is the probability that the printer will work two months later if it worked this month?
c. What is the probability that it will not work two months later if it worked this month?

14. Sheldon Farnworth is an eminently successful college professor. A measure of his success is his 1976 Ford Pinto, which currently has accumulated over 80,000 miles. On a given day Sheldon is unsure as to whether or not his car will convey him to his university. Ninety percent of the time he will make it if he made it the previous day, and 50 percent of the time he will not make it if he did not make it the previous day.

a. Construct the matrix of transition probabilities for this situation.
b. What is the probability that Sheldon will make it to work two days from now if he made it to work today?
c. What is the probability that Sheldon will not make it to work two days from now if he did not make it to work today?

15. Given the following matrix of transition probabilities with states 1 and 2 as absorbing states

$$P = \begin{array}{c} \\ S_1 \\ S_2 \\ S_3 \\ S_4 \end{array} \begin{array}{cccc} S_1 & S_2 & S_3 & S_4 \\ \left[\begin{array}{cccc} 1 & 0 & 0 & 0 \\ 0 & 1 & 0 & 0 \\ .5 & .3 & .1 & .1 \\ .3 & .3 & .2 & .2 \end{array} \right] \end{array}$$

what is the probability that units in states 3 and 4 end up in each of the absorbing states? How many steps will be required before the process is absorbed, for beginning states S_3 and S_4?

16. Formulate and solve the steady-state equations for the Markov process with the following matrix of transition probabilities

$$P = \begin{bmatrix} .2 & .5 & .3 \\ .1 & .2 & .7 \\ 4 & 4 & ? \end{bmatrix}$$

17. Formulate and solve the steady-state equations for the Markov process with the following matrix of transition probabilities

$$P = \begin{bmatrix} .0 & .5 & .4 & .1 \\ .2 & .4 & .2 & .2 \\ .8 & .2 & .0 & .0 \\ .0 & .0 & 1.0 & .0 \end{bmatrix}$$

18. Dale Carter, coach of the Southern Thunder soccer team is trying to determine the likelihood of his team winning a particular soccer tournament. From past team performances he has determined that there is a .8 probability of the team winning its next game if it wins its current game. Also, there is a .3 probability of it losing its next game if it loses its current game.

    a. Construct the matrix of transition probabilities for this situation.
    b. What is the probability that Southern Thunder will win a three-game tournament given that it wins the first game in the tournament?
    c. What is the probability that Southern Thunder will win a three-game tournament given that it loses the first game in the tournament?

19. A meteorologist at Hilton Head, South Carolina, has determined that the following matrix of transition probabilities describes the daily weather at Hilton Head.

Today's Weather	Tomorrow's Weather		
	Sunny	Cloudy	Rainy
Sunny	.5	.3	.2
Cloudy	.4	.3	.3
Rainy	.2	.2	.6

    a. If it is sunny today, what is the probability that the first rainy day will occur n days ($n \gg 0$) from now?
    b. If it is rainy today, what is the probability that the first rainy day will occur n days ($n \gg 0$) from now?
    c. What assumption is the meteorologist making in applying Markov analysis to this problem situation?

20. Bill Worthington lives in Dillon, Colorado, and is the owner of a ski school. He has been asked to develop prospects for the U.S.

Olympic Ski Team for the forthcoming Winter Olympics. As he contemplates how to undertake the training and development of prospects, he has determined that a typical student can be categorized into one of four states.

STATE 1. Potential Olympic Ski Team member.

STATE 2. No potential—remove from further training.

STATE 3. Daily instruction and practice necessary.

STATE 4. Daily practice and daily competition necessary.

Worthington has kept accurate records concerning the training results of past students. From this historical information, the following matrix of transition probabilities has been developed

$$
\begin{array}{c}
\\
S_1 \\
S_2 \\
S_3 \\
S_4
\end{array}
\begin{array}{cccc}
S_1 & S_2 & S_3 & S_4 \\
\left[\begin{array}{cccc}
1 & 0 & 0 & 0 \\
0 & 1 & 0 & 0 \\
.5 & .2 & .2 & .1 \\
.4 & .2 & .2 & .2
\end{array}\right]
\end{array}
$$

Worthington currently has 200 students enrolled at his ski school, with 110 students in state S_3 and 90 in state S_4. Determine how many of these students will eventually end up in state S_1 or state S_2. How long will it take before the students are absorbed, for beginning states S_3 and S_4?

Application Review

A Highway Pavement Management System for Arizona

Maintenance of roads in Arizona is an extremely complex problem. The state has a large area and its roads vary from heavily traveled interstate highways to sparsely traveled secondary roads. Its climate also varies widely, from the hot deserts of the south to the snowy mountains of the north.

The Arizona Department of Transportation (ADOT) had the responsibility for a road network consisting of 2200 miles of interstate highways and 5200 miles of noninterstate highways. The department was charged with designing, constructing, preserving, and maintaining this extensive road network. The basic maintenance questions it had to answer were

1. How poor should a road segment be before it is repaired?
2. Which of many possible repair actions should be taken?

The need for a pavement management system in Arizona was a function of several factors that were prevalent in the late 1970s.

1. A shift in emphasis from construction of new highways to preserving existing roads.

Source: Kamal Golabi, Ram B. Kulkarni, and George B. Way, "A statewide pavement management system," *Interfaces* (December 1982) Vol. 12, No. 6, pp. 5–21.

2. Existing highways were aging and required an increasing amount of maintenance to preserve the roads in a satisfactory condition.
3. The Federal Highway Administration, which supplied a major portion of the ADOT's budget, had stringent guidelines that required that a substantial proportion of its subsidies be used on preservation in order to avoid the high costs of totally reconstructing roads that were in bad condition.
4. Maintenance costs were increasing dramatically as a function of the rising cost of petroleum-based road-surfacing materials.

In early 1978, the ADOT contracted with Woodward-Clyde Consultants, an engineering consulting firm based in San Francisco, to develop a decision-making tool, called the Pavement Management System (PMS), for Arizona. A team of management scientists, highway engineers, and computer specialists was formed to study the problem. At the same time, a team was formed at the ADOT to assist in defining the problem and collecting the data. The basic objective of the study was to develop a decision-making tool to help the ADOT maintain its roads in the most desirable condition within its budget.

The study team used a modeling approach based on a Markov decision process, the main components of which were the road conditions and condition states, and maintenance actions that could be taken. A state was defined as a combination of the specific levels of the variables relevant to evaluating pavement performance. In the model, transition probabilities linked current road conditions and maintenance actions to future road conditions. A preservation policy for the entire network was the assignment of an action to each state in each time period. The probability that a pavement segment was in a given state or condition was also interpreted as the expected proportion of all pavements that are in that state or condition. This in turn allowed the calculation of the proportion of the statewide network expected to be in the given condition in any year for a given maintenance policy. The performance of the model was evaluated in terms of these proportions. The overall objective was to find the least-cost policy that would maintain at least a certain proportion of pavements in desirable states, and have not more than a certain proportion in undesirable states. Past historical data were used to test and evaluate this Markov modeling approach.

The system was tested with real and hypothetical data, and implemented in May 1980. During the first year of implementation (fiscal year 1980–81), the Pavement Management System saved $14 million of preservation funds. It therefore changed the pavement management decision process in Arizona from a subjective, nonquantitative method to a modern approach that integrated managerial policy decisions and engineering inputs within an optimization system.

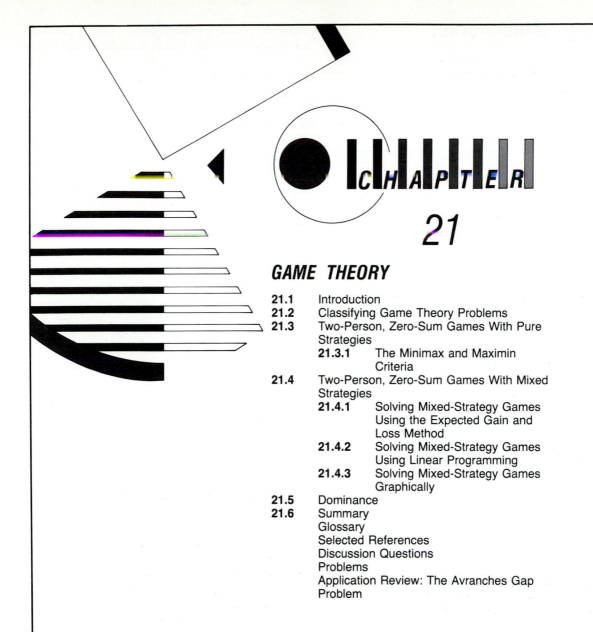

CHAPTER 21

GAME THEORY

21.1 INTRODUCTION

The decision-making techniques that we have studied throughout this book have generally been oriented toward an individual making decisions. Thus, we have focused on a variety of techniques that the individual decision maker can apply to a wide range of problems that might be encountered.

There are, however, certain decision-making situations that basically involve a *game*, which is defined to be a contest involving two or more decision makers, each of whom wants to win the contest. This game situation involves two or more intelligent opponents, each of which tries to optimize his or her decision at the expense of the opponents. The participants in the game employ mathematical procedures and logic in order to develop strategies for winning the game from their competitor(s). The study of how optimal strategies are determined in these competitive decision-making situations is the subject of *game theory*.

Game theory was introduced in 1944 by John von Neumann and Oskar Morgenstern in their classic book, *Theory of Games and Economic Behavior*. Although their book was considered to be a pioneering work in decision making, practical applications of game theory have been somewhat limited. Game theory has been used, however, in military planning, in collective bargaining situations, and in some applications involving life insurance planning. It has also had a major impact on the development of linear programming, and has also been influential in the field of decision theory.

21.2 CLASSIFYING GAME THEORY PROBLEMS

One major way of classifying game theory problems involves the number of competitive decision makers, or *players*, in the game. A game involving two players is referred to as a *two-person game*. A game involving n players ($n > 2$) is called an n-*person game*. Game theory for games involving three or more players is a difficult area, both theoretically and computationally, and has not been used much in practice. Consequently, we limit our discussion in this chapter to two-person games.

Another convenient way of classifying games is according to the total *payoff* from the game that is available to the players. A game in which the sum of the players' gains and losses equals zero is

referred to as a *zero-sum game*. Thus, a game in which the gain of the first player exactly equals the loss of the second player is known as a *two-person, zero-sum game*. This type of game is frequently used to demonstrate the principles of game theory, since it can be easily analyzed mathematically. We utilize it in our subsequent discussion. We should note, however, that there are also games in which the sum of the players' gains and losses do not equal zero. Such games are known as *non-zero-sum games*. Again, we will not consider non-zero-sum games in this chapter because of their theoretical and computational difficulties.

A third way of classifying games is according to the strategies that are employed by the players in the game. In some games the strategies each player follows will always be the same, regardless of the other player's strategy. This type of result is referred to as a *pure strategy*, since each player does not deviate from the strategy that is selected. In game theory pure strategies exist only when the solution has reached an equilibrium state, or *saddle point*. When these is no saddle point, the players will play each strategy for a certain percentage of the time. This type of result is called a *mixed strategy*. We consider both pure strategy and mixed-strategy games in the discussions in this chapter.

21.3 TWO-PERSON, ZERO-SUM GAMES WITH PURE STRATEGIES

To introduce you to the general idea of game theory, let us focus our attention on a simple two-person, zero-sum game. We assume a scenario involving a real estate developer, identified as player A, and the owner of a shopping mall, identified as player B. The real estate investor, player A, has two investment strategies that are a function of trying to secure control of all, or part, of the shopping mall. Strategy A_1 involves the investment of $800,000, while Strategy A_2 involves the investment of $400,000. The owner of the shopping mall, player B, also has two strategies. Under strategy B_1, she can sell all or part of the shopping mall to the real estate developer; under strategy B_2 she can lease him all or part of the shopping mall. The payoffs from the game will be assumed to be the net present values of the incomes that result from the combinations of the strategies selected by the two players.

It is assumed that each player is aware of the exact payoffs that result from every combination of

TABLE 21.1 PLAYER A'S PAYOFF MATRIX

PLAYER A STRATEGIES	PLAYER B STRATEGIES B_1 (SELL)	B_2 (LEASE)
A_1 (Invest $800,000)	$50,000	$100,000
A_2 (Invest $400,000)	$40,000	$-$ 30,000

investment strategies for the two players. Each payoff is a constant dollar amount, and this constant dollar amount is assumed to have exactly the same utility to each player. (You may want to review the concept of utility as it was discussed in Chapter 4.) Furthermore, if player A obtains a payoff, then player B must lose this same payoff, so we have a zero-sum game in which the sum of A's positive payoffs (gains) and B's negative payoffs (losses) is equal to zero.

In Table 21.1, a payoff matrix for player A is presented. By convention, payoffs are shown for only one of the game players (player A in this case). A positive number means that player A gains and player B loses. A negative number means that player B gains and player A loses.

As we now see, the structure of the payoff matrix shown in Table 21.1 makes this situation a pure strategy game. In it, the strategy that each player adopts will always be the same, regardless of the other player's strategy, and the game will have a saddle point.

To illustrate how the game shown in Table 21.1 has a saddle point, let us show how we can determine the strategies for players A and B.

1. Player A will always select strategy A_1, since the worst payoff for selecting strategy A_1 is $50,000, and the best payoff for strategy A_2 is $40,000.
2. Player B knows that player A will always select strategy A_1. Therefore, player B will always

select strategy B_1. Why? Because, by selecting strategy B_1 she will lose $50,000, whereas, if she selects strategy B_2, she will lose $100,000.
3. Both players have a pure strategy to follow, and this game has a saddle point. The numerical value of the saddle point is the payoff, or outcome of the game, in this situation. This numerical value is $50,000, which is the value at the intersection of player's A's pure strategy (i.e., A_1) and Player B's pure strategy (i.e., B_1).

The saddle point solution to this problem can be summarized as shown in Table 21.2. The *value of the game* is the average or expected value of the outcome of the game if the game is played an infinite number of times. In this game, the value of the game for this example is obviously $50,000.

Observe in the table that the numerical value of the saddle point, $50,000, is the largest number in its column and the smallest number in its row. This will be true of all saddle points, and an easy way to determine whether or not a saddle point exists is to see if *both* of the following conditions are met.

1. A numerical value exists that is the largest value in its column, and
2. This same numerical value is the smallest value in its row.

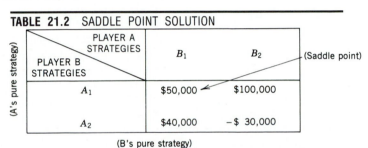

TABLE 21.2 SADDLE POINT SOLUTION

(A's pure strategy) PLAYER B STRATEGIES	PLAYER A STRATEGIES	B_1	B_2	(Saddle point)
	A_1	$50,000	$100,000	
	A_2	$40,000	$-$ 30,000	

(B's pure strategy)

TABLE 21.3 EXAMPLE OF MINIMAX AND MAXIMIN CRITERIA

PLAYER X STRATEGIES \ PLAYER Y STRATEGIES	Y_1	Y_2	MINIMUM OF PLAYER X'S ROW GAINS
X_1	15	7	7
X_2	-8	4	-8
Maximum of player Y's column losses	15	7	

21.3.1 THE MINIMAX AND MAXIMIN CRITERIA

Previously (Chapter 4), we studied the minimax and maximin criteria as they were used in decision theory. The same criteria can be used in game theory. Assuming that we have a two-person game, according to the maximin criterion player A is pessimistic and therefore selects a strategy that maximizes the gains from among the minimum possible payoffs. Concurrently, player B selects a strategy that minimizes the losses from among the maximum possible losses, or uses a minimax criterion. To illustrate the minimax and maximin criteria, consider the game theory example shown in Table 21.3.

The maximin criterion is applied as follows. Player X first identifies the smallest gain for both of the two available strategies (X_1 and X_2). Then, player X selects the maximum gain from among these minimum values. It can be seen in Table 21.3 that 7 is the minimum gain for strategy X_1, and -8 is the minimum gain for strategy X_2. Since the maximum of these two gains is 7, strategy X_1 is selected by player X (i.e., maximin gain criterion). Next, player Y identifies the maximum loss for both of the two available strategies (Y_1 and Y_2). Then, player Y selects the minimum loss from among these maximum losses (minimax loss criterion). It can be seen in Table 21.3 that 15 is the maximum loss for strategy Y_1, and 7 is the maximum loss for strategy Y_2. Since the minimum of these two losses is 7, strategy Y_2 is chosen by player Y (i.e., minimax loss criterion).

Our analysis of the strategies selected by players X and Y indicates that we have obtained a solution that satisfies both players. Each player again has a pure strategy that results in a saddle point solution. It is important to stress that the maximin (minimax)

criterion leads to the optimal solution for each player as long as each of the players adheres to one or the other. If one of the players does not, the solution will not be optimal.

21.4 TWO-PERSON, ZERO-SUM GAMES WITH MIXED STRATEGIES

In many two-person, zero-sum games it will not be possible for the players to employ pure strategies, because the payoff matrix does not have a saddle point. Where there is no saddle point, the players must play each strategy a certain percentage of the time. This situation is referred to as a *mixed-strategy game*.

To illustrate a two-person, zero-sum game with mixed strategies consider the following situation. A professional football player's agent and the management of a professional football team are engaged in contract negotiations. From the football player's agent's point-of-view two strategies are possible. Strategy Q_1 is essentially a "stand pat" strategy based on the performance of the football player during the past season. The football player in question had a great year, but the team did not make the playoffs. Strategy Q_2 is a "go for it" strategy based on the potential of the football player during future seasons. The football player in question is a second-year player and could have the best years of his career ahead of him. From management's point of view, two strategies are also possible. Strategy R_1 is a "free spending" strategy, based on improving the morale of the players on the team. Strategy R_2 is an "arbitration" strategy, in which an outside arbitrator would be used to determine equitable salaries, based on the salaries of other players in the league. The payoff matrix for this situation is shown in Table

TABLE 21.4 PLAYER'S AGENT PAYOFF MATRIX

PLAYER'S AGENT STRATEGIES \ MANAGEMENT STRATEGIES	R_1 ("FREE SPENDING")	R_2 ("ARBITRATION")
Q_1 ("Stand Pat")	−$30,000	$60,000
Q_2 ("Go for It")	$50,000	$20,000

21.4. In this payoff table, the payoffs are in dollars and represent the yearly values of salary and benefits increases. The payoff matrix is structured in terms of gains for the player's agent and losses to management.

In analyzing this payoff matrix we observe that there is no numerical value that fulfills both conditions necessary for a saddle point. Thus, while $50,000 is the largest value in column one, it is not the smallest value in row two. Similarly, while $60,000 is the largest value in column two, it is not the smallest value in row one.

Let us now analyze this situation using the maximin gain criterion for the football player's agent and the minimax loss criterion for management. The payoff table with the two criteria applied is shown in Table 21.5. As can be seen in this table, application of the maximin gain criterion for the player's agent results in the selection of strategy Q_2. Application of the minimax loss criterion for management results in the selection of strategy R_1.

From Table 21.5 we see that the strategies se-lected by the player's agent and management do not result in a saddle point solution, so we do not have a pure strategy game.

There are numerous methods for solving such mixed-strategy games. We now illustrate three such methods: (1) the expected gain and loss method, (2) the linear programming method, and (3) the graphical method.

21.4.1 SOLVING MIXED-STRATEGY GAMES USING THE EXPECTED GAIN AND LOSS METHOD

In solving a two-person, zero-sum game with a mixed strategy the objective is to determine the fraction of time each strategy should be employed in order to maximize gains, or minimize losses. Each player will attempt to formulate a strategy that is indifferent to the opponent's selection of a strategy. This can be accomplished by selecting each strategy a certain percent of time in a manner that the player's expected gains (or expected losses) are equal regardless

TABLE 21.5 PAYOFF TABLE WITH MINIMAX AND MAXIMIN CRITERIA APPLIED TO A MIXED STRATEGY GAME

PLAYER'S AGENT STRATEGIES \ MANAGEMENT STRATEGIES	R_1	R_2	MINIMUM OF PLAYER'S AGENT ROW GAINS
Q_1	−$30,000	$60,000	−$30,000
Q_2	($50,000)	$20,000	$20,000
MAXIMUM OF MANAGEMENT COLUMN LOSSES	$50,000	$60,000	

[minimum of the maximum values (management)]

[maximum of the minimum values (player's agent)]

of the strategy selected by the opponent. This is the same as attaching a certain probability to the selection of a strategy.

In order to determine this probability for the problem at hand we say that the player's agent will select strategies Q_1 or Q_2 such that the expected gains are equal regardless of management's selection of strategies R_1 and R_2. Therefore, if management selects strategy R_1, the possible payoffs for the player's agent are $-\$30,000$ and $\$50,000$. If the player's agent selects strategy Q_1 with a probability of p, and therefore selects strategy Q_2 with a probability of $(1 - p)$, the player's agent's expected gains are

$$(p)(-\$30,000) + (1 - p)(\$50,000)$$
$$= \text{player's agent's gain — strategy } R_1 \quad (21.1)$$

Alternatively, if management selects strategy R_2, the player's agent's expected gains are:

$$(p)(\$60,000) + (1 - p)(\$20,000)$$
$$= \text{player's agent's gain — strategy } R_2 \quad (21.2)$$

If the player's agent is going to be indifferent to the strategy selected by management, then the expected gain of the player's agent for each of the two possible strategy selections for management must be equal. We can thus equate the two gains and solve for p, as follows

$$(p)(-\$30,000) + (1 - p)(\$50,000)$$
$$= (p)(\$60,000) + (1 - p)(\$20,000)$$
$$-\$30,000p + 50,000 - 50,000p$$
$$= 60,000p + 20,000 - 20,000p$$
$$120,000p = 30,000$$
$$p = .25$$
$$1 - p = 1 - .25 = .75 \quad (21.3)$$

Therefore, the player's agent would select strategy Q_1 25 percent of the time and strategy Q_2 75 percent of the time. This will result in the same expected gain, regardless of the strategy selected by management.

Management would determine the probabilities for its strategies, R_1 and R_2, by equating the expected losses for the player's agent selecting strategy Q_1 to the player's agent selecting strategy Q_2. This would

be done as follows

$$(q)(-\$30,000) + (1 - q)(\$60,000)$$
$$= (q)(\$50,000) + (1 - q)(\$20,000)$$
$$-\$30,000q + 60,000 - 60,000q$$
$$= 50,000q + 20,000 - 20,000q$$
$$120,000q = 40,000$$
$$q = .33$$
$$1 - q = .67 \cdot \quad (21.4)$$

Therefore, management would select strategy R_1 33 percent of the time and strategy R_2 67 percent of the time. This would result in the same expected loss, regardless of the strategy selected by the player's agent.

In this game there is a common value for each of the two players that exists in terms of the expected value. These expected values can be computed as follows.

PLAYER'S EXPECTED GAINS:
If management selects strategy R_1:

$$(0.25)(-\$30,000) + (.75)(\$50,000)$$
$$= \$30,000 \quad (21.5)$$

If management selects strategy R_2:

$$(0.25)(\$60,000) + (.75)(\$20,000)$$
$$= \$30,000 \quad (21.6)$$

MANAGEMENT'S EXPECTED LOSSES:
If player's agent selects strategy Q_1:

$$(0.33)(-\$30,000) + (.67)(\$60,000)$$
$$= \$30,000 \quad (21.7)$$

If player's agent selects strategy Q_2:

$$(0.33)(\$50,000) + (.67)(\$20,000)$$
$$= \$30,000 \quad (21.8)$$

Thus, the mixed strategy solution results in an expected game value of $\$30,000$, which is what we would expect to happen if the negotiation process were repeated many times. It should be stressed that

TABLE 21.6 PAYOFF TABLE: MIXED STRATEGY GAME

	R_1	R_2
MANAGEMENT STRATEGIES / PLAYER'S AGENT STRATEGIES		
Q_1	−$30,000	$60,000
Q_2	$50,000	$20,000

in any one negotiation, the actual results would necessitate each player selecting one particular strategy. This means that in any one negotiation the outcome, or payoff, from the game would favor one of the players.

21.4.2 SOLVING MIXED-STRATEGY GAMES USING LINEAR PROGRAMMING

In order to show how linear programming can be used to solve mixed-strategy games, we use the mixed strategy game involving the football player's agent and football team management that was presented in the previous sections. The payoff table for this mixed-strategy game situation, which was originally presented in Table 21.4, is repeated in Table 21.6. We use this in our linear programming formulation of the problem.

The payoff table presented as Table 21.6 can be used to structure two linear programming models. One model can be specified for the player's agent, and a second model can be specified for management. Each model is used for determining the appropriate mixed strategy for that game participant. Recall that the mixed strategy we defined for each of the participants of the game was stated in terms of the percentage of time each strategy was utilized by the participant, or by the probability of occurrence for each strategy utilized by the participant.

Considering first the formulation of the linear programming model for the player's agent, the decision variables can be defined as the probabilities associated with the occurrences of strategies Q_1 and Q_2, namely

p_1 = the probability of occurrence of strategy Q_1

p_2 = the probability of occurrence of strategy Q_2

In terms of our previous solution approach for the mixed strategy for the player's agent, the current decision variable p_1 corresponds to p, and the current decision variable p_2 corresponds to $(1 - p)$. Consequently, we can formulate a set of two constraints, for the two strategies that can be followed by the player's agent, as follows.

PLAYER'S AGENT'S EXPECTED GAINS
Management selects R_1:

$$-30,000p_1 + 50,000p_2 \geq V \qquad (21.9)$$

Management selects R_2:

$$60,000p_1 + 20,000p_2 \geq V \qquad (21.10)$$

where V is the value of the game, which is the expected or average gain for the player's agent, and is identical to the expected or average loss for management. Note that we have used greater-than-or-equal-to inequalities for these two constraints because the player's agent is attempting to maximize gains (i.e., is playing the game using the maximin criterion).

To complete the constraint set for this linear programming model we need a constraint that reflects the fact that the probabilities must sum to 1.0, namely

$$p_1 + p_2 = 1.0 \qquad (21.11)$$

The player's agent will simply want to maximize the value of its gains, V, in this situation. Thus, the objective function for the problem can be written as

Maximize (player's agent's gains) $Z = V$ (21.12)

The complete linear programming formulation can now be written as

Maximize $Z = V$ (21.13)

subject to

$$-30{,}000p_1 + 50{,}000p_2 - V \geq 0$$

$$60{,}000p_1 + 20{,}000p_2 - V \geq 0$$

$$p_1 + p_2 = 1 \qquad (21.14)$$

with

$$p_1, p_2, V \geq 0 \qquad (21.15)$$

Solving this problem using the simplex method produces the following results

$$p_1 = .25$$
$$p_2 = .75$$
$$V = \$30{,}000 \qquad \text{(value of the game)} \quad (21.16)$$

These results are, of course, exactly those obtained using the expected gain and loss method.

A similar model can be derived and solved for the mixed strategy of management. For this model, the decision variables can be defined as the probabilities of the occurrences of strategies R_1 and R_2, namely

q_1 = the probability of occurrence of strategy R_1

q_2 = the probability of occurrence of strategy R_2

In terms of our previous solution approach for the mixed strategy for management, the current decision variable q_1 corresponds to q, and the current decision variable q_2 corresponds to $(1 - q)$. Consequently, we can formulate a set of two constraints that can be followed by management, as follows:

MANAGEMENT'S EXPECTED LOSSES
Player's agent selects Q_1:

$$-30{,}000q_1 + 60{,}000q_2 \leq V \qquad (21.17)$$

Player's agent selects Q_2:

$$50{,}000q_1 + 20{,}000q_2 \leq V \qquad (21.18)$$

where V is the value of the game, which is the expected or average loss for management, and is identical to the expected or average gain for the

player's agent. Note that we have used less-than-or-equal-to inequalities for these two constraints because management is attempting to minimize losses (i.e., is playing the game using a minimax criterion).

To complete the constraint set for this linear programming model we need a constraint that reflects the fact that the probabilities must sum to 1.0, namely

$$q_1 + q_2 = 1.0 \qquad (21.19)$$

Management will simply want to minimize the value of its losses, V, in this situation. Thus, the objective function for this problem can be written as

$$\text{Minimize (management's losses) } Z = V \quad (21.20)$$

The complete linear programming problem can now be written as

$$\text{Minimize } Z = V \qquad (21.21)$$

subject to

$$-30{,}000q_1 + 60{,}000q_2 - V \leq 0$$

$$50{,}000q_1 + 20{,}000q_2 - V \leq 0 \qquad (21.22)$$

$$q_1 + q_2 = 1$$

with

$$q_1, q_2, V \geq 0 \qquad (21.23)$$

Solving this problem, using the simplex method, produces the following results

$$q_1 = .33$$
$$q_2 = .67 \qquad (21.24)$$
$$V = \$30{,}000$$

These results are, of course, the same as those obtained using the expected gain and loss method.

You may have observed that the linear programming formulation describing the player's agent's gain, as given by (21.13), (21.14), and (21.15) is the dual of the linear programming formulation of the management's loss, as given by (21.21), (21.22), and (21.23). Since the two linear programming formulation are duals of each other, they must have the same objective function value, provided, of course, that they do have feasible solutions.

The linear programming method offers a number of advantages in comparison to the expected gain and loss method. First, it can be used for games of any size, (i.e., games larger than 2×2) and this is a major advantage. Second, computer programs for linear programming are readily available so solving for the appropriate mixed strategy can be accomplished without resorting to hand computations.

One note of caution should be made concerning the linear programming approach. It will work *only* if the value of the game, V, is positive. In the linear programming formulation, as given by (21.13)–(21.15) or (21.21)–(22.23), note that V is a decision variable. As such, the nonnegativity restrictions require that $V \geq 0$. One way around this dilemma, if one suspected that the value of the game might indeed be negative, would be to let V be an unrestricted variable, that is, set $V = V' - V''$ where $V' \geq 0$ and $V'' \geq 0$ (refer back to Chapter 8, Section 8.6 for further discussion of this process).

21.4.3 SOLVING MIXED-STRATEGY GAMES GRAPHICALLY

A game with mixed strategies can be solved graphically whenever one of the players has only two possible strategies from which to choose. To illustrate the graphical solution procedure, let us once again consider the mixed-strategy game involving the football player's agent and football team management.

Approaching the problem from the viewpoint of the football player's agent, let his mixed strategies be (x_1, x_2), where $x_2 = 1 - x_1$. We now want to solve for the optimal value of x_1, and this can be done by plotting the expected payoff for each of management's strategies as a function of x_1. This graph can then be used to identify the point that maximizes the minimum expected payoff for the football player's agent. Management's minimax mixed strategy can also be identified from this graph.

Referring back to either Table 21.5 or Table 21.6 for each of the two strategies available for management, the expected payoff for the football player's agent would be

MANAGEMENT STRATEGIES	EXPECTED PAYOFF TO FOOTBALL PLAYER'S AGENT
R_1	$-\$30,000x_1 + \$50,000 (1 - x_1)$
R_2	$60,000x_1 + 20,000 (1 - x_1)$

Next, we plot these expected payoff equations (i.e., straight lines) as shown graphically in Figure 21.1. The expected payoff for management strategy R_1 is plotted as

$$-30,000x_1 + 50,000(1 - x_1)$$
$$= -30,000x_1 + 50,000 - 50,000x_1$$
$$= -80,000x_1 + 50,000 \qquad (21.25)$$

The expected payoff for management strategy R_2 is plotted as

$$-60,000x_1 + 20,000(1 - x_1)$$
$$= 60,000x_1 + 20,000 - 20,000x_1$$
$$= 40,000x_1 + 20,000 \qquad (21.26)$$

As can be seen from Figure 21.1, the optimal value of x_1 is found at the intersection of the two straight lines. This value is $x_1 = .25$, and therefore, $(x_1, x_2) = (.25, .75)$ is the optimal mixed strategy for the football player's agent. The value of the game is

$$V = -80,000(.25) + 50,000$$
$$= \$30,000 \qquad (21.27)$$

This result is, of course, identical to that obtained earlier using the expected gain and loss method or the linear programming method.

To determine the corresponding optimal mixed strategy for management in this situation we make use of the value of the game, \$30,000, which we have just determined. For management, let the mixed strategies be (y_1, y_2), where $y_2 = 1 - y_1$. The expected payoff resulting from the optimal strategy, y_1^*, y_2^*, for management must satisfy the condition

$$y_1^*(-80,000x_1 + 50,000) + y_2^*(40,000x_1 + 20,000) \leq V = 30,000 \qquad (21.28)$$

for all values of x_1 ($0 \leq x_1 \leq 1$). Also, when the football player's agent is playing optimally (i.e.,

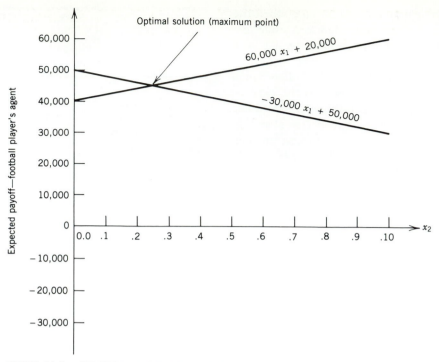

FIGURE 21.1 EXPECTED PAYOFF EQUATIONS.

$x_1 = .25$), this inequality must be an equality, so that

$$y_1^*(-80,000x_1 + 50,000) + y_2^*(40,000x_1 + 20,000) = V = 30,000 \qquad (21.29)$$

for all values of x_1 ($0 \le x_1 \le 1$).

To solve for y_1^* and y_2^*, we can select two values of x_1 (say, 0 and 1), and solve the resulting two simultaneous linear equations. Therefore, we have for $x_1 = 0$

$$50,000y_1^* + 20,000y_2^* = 30,000 \qquad (21.30)$$

For $x_1 = 1$

$$30,000y_1^* + 60,000y_2^* = 30,000 \qquad (21.31)$$

Solving these two simultaneous linear equations, we obtain

$$y_1^* = .33$$
$$y_2^* = .67 \qquad (21.32)$$

These results are, of course, exactly the same as the results obtained previously using either the unexpected gain method, or the linear programming method.

We have illustrated the graphical solution method for a particular problem situation. You should be aware, however, that the graphical approach can only be used to solve any game having mixed strategies in which one player has only two strategies.

21.5 DOMINANCE

Dominance refers to the idea of reducing the size of games by eliminating certain strategies that would never be played. Basically, a strategy for a player can be eliminated if that player has another strategy that will always produce as good, or better, results. After applying the principle of dominance, the resulting game can be solved by using either a mixed or pure strategy.

To illustrate the principle of dominance, let us consider the payoff matrix shown in Table 21.7.

TABLE 21.7 PAYOFF MATRIX: DOMINANCE EXAMPLE

PLAYER A'S STRATEGIES	PLAYER B'S STRATEGIES B_1	B_2	B_3
A_1	-4	2	3
A_2	-2	-5	4
A_3	-7	-1	-8

For player A's strategies we employ the dominance rule for rows, which states that every value in the dominating row(s) must be equal to, or greater than, the corresponding value in the dominated row. Applying the dominance rule for rows to Table 21.7, we see that row three (i.e., strategy A_3) is dominated (by strategy A_1), so it can be eliminated. The reduced payoff matrix with strategy A_3 eliminated is shown in Table 21.8.

For player B's strategies we employ the dominance rule for columns, which states that every value in the dominating column(s) must be equal to, or less than, the corresponding value in the dominated column. Applying the dominance rule for columns to Table 21.8, we see that column three (i.e., strategy B_3) is dominated (by strategy B_1), so it can be eliminated. The reduced payoff matrix with strategy B_3 eliminated is shown in Table 21.9.

We have now reduced the original 3×3 game to a 2×2 game. Observe that the 2×2 game is a mixed-strategy game. We would need to apply either linear programming or the method of expected gains and expected losses to determine the mixed strategies to be employed by each of the two players.

TABLE 21.8 PAYOFF MATRIX: STRATEGY A_3 ELIMINATED

PLAYER A'S STRATEGIES	PLAYER B'S STRATEGIES B_1	B_2	B_3
A_1	-4	2	3
A_2	-2	-5	4

TABLE 21.9 PAYOFF MATRIX: STRATEGIES A_3 AND B_3 ELIMINATED

PLAYER A'S STRATEGIES	PLAYER B'S STRATEGIES B_1	B_2
A_1	-4	2
A_2	-2	-5

Using the method of expected gains and losses, the mixed strategies for the two players and the value of the game can be determined to be

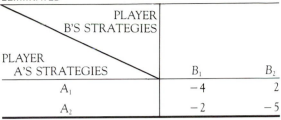

Player A	Player B
$p_1 = 1/3$	$q_1 = 7/9$
$p_2 = 2/3$	$q_2 = 2/9$
$V = -8/3$	$V = -8/3$

21.6 SUMMARY

Game theory affords a convenient way of making decisions involving two or more individuals in a competitive situation. By studying game theory one can gain a better understanding of the logic that is utilized by competing players as they determine either pure or mixed strategies for a particular game.

Game theory has not had a great deal of application in real-world situations. The lack of application is due to several factors. First, it may be difficult, or even impossible, for the players to determine accurate values for the payoff matrix. Second, for games with more than two players, the methods of analysis and solution become very complicated. Third, many games are not zero-sum games, and this complicates the analysis further. Finally, game theory is based on the assumption that the opponents in the game will play the game rationally. All of these factors limit the value of game theory for many managers.

In summary, game theory remains of interest primarily as a means for understanding the thought processes between competing individuals. As such it is most useful for planning efforts and situations in collective bargaining.

GLOSSARY

Game   A competitive decision-making situation involving two or more players, each of whom wants to win the game.

Game Theory   The study of how optimal strategies are formulated in competitive decision-making situations involving two or more players seeking to win the game.

Maximin Criterion   A game theory decision criterion that maximizes a player's minimum gains.

Minimax Criterion   A game theory decision criterion that minimizes a player's maximum losses.

Mixed-Strategy Game   A game in which the overall strategy for a player involves playing each possible strategy a certain percentage of the time.

n-Person Game   A game that has n persons, where $n > 2$.

Payoff   The result of a player selecting a particular strategy in the game.

Pure Strategy Game   A game in which both players will always play just one strategy.

Saddle Point Game   A game that has a pure strategy solution for both players.

Two-Person Game   A game that has only two players.

Value of the Game   The expected results of the game if the game is played a large number of times.

Zero-Sum Game   A game in which the sum of the players' gains and losses equals zero.

Selected References

Davis, M. 1970. *Game Theory: A Nontechnical Introduction.* New York: Basic Books.
Holloway, C. A. 1979. *Decision Making Under Uncertainty.* Englewood Cliffs, N.J.: Prentice–Hall.
Luce, R.D., and H. Raiffa. 1957. *Games and Decisions.* New York: Wiley.
Shubik, M. 1975. *The Uses and Methods of Game Theory.* New York: Amer. Elsevier.
Von Neumann, J., and O. Morgenstern. 1944. *Theory of Games and Economic Behavior.* Princeton, N.J.: Princeton Univ. Press.
Williams, J.D. 1966. *The Compleat Strategist.* New York: McGraw-Hill.

Discussion Questions

1.   What is a game?

2.   What is meant by a zero-sum, two-person game?

3.   What is a pure strategy in game theory?

4.   What is a mixed strategy in game theory?

5. How do we go about solving a mixed-strategy game?

6. What is a saddle point in game theory?

7. Explain how dominance is used in game theory.

8. Why is linear programming useful in solving games that are larger than 2 × 2?

9. What are some of the difficulties associated with using game theory?

10. What are some of the benefits associated with game theory?

PROBLEMS

1. Determine the strategies for players X and Y in the following game. Also indicate the value of the game.

PLAYER X STRATEGIES	PLAYER Y STRATEGIES	
	Y_1	Y_2
X_1	1	-3
X_2	5	7

2. Determine the strategies for players A and B in the following game. Also indicate the value of the game.

PLAYER A STRATEGIES	PLAYER B STRATEGIES	
	B_1	B_2
A_1	25	30
A_2	15	-10

3. Given the following payoff matrix, determine each player's strategy and the value of the game.

PLAYER Q STRATEGIES	PLAYER R STRATEGIES	
	R_1	R_2
Q_1	$-\$15,000$	$\$5000$
Q_2	$\$25,000$	$\$10,000$

4. Given the following payoff matrix, determine each player's strategy and the value of the game.

PLAYER E STRATEGIES	PLAYER F STRATEGIES F_1	F_2
E_1	100	90
E_2	80	85

5. Burger Giant and Taco Grande are competing for a larger share of the fast-food market in Irmo, South Carolina. Both are contemplating the use of promotional coupons. If Burger Giant does not spend any money on promotional coupons, it will not lose any share of the market if Taco Grande also does not spend any money on promotional coupons. Burger Giant will lose 3 percent of the market, however, if Taco Grande spends $2500 on coupons, and it will lose 5 percent of the market if Taco Grande spends $3000 on coupons. If Burger Giant spends $2500 on coupons, it will gain 2 percent of the market if Taco Grande spends $0, it will gain 1 percent of the market if Taco Grande spends $2500 and it will lose 1 percent of the market if Taco Grande spends $3000. If Burger Giant spends $3000, it will gain 4 percent of the market if Taco Grande spends $0, it will gain 2 percent of the market if Taco Grande spends $2500, and it will gain 1 percent of the market if Taco Grande spends $3000.

    a. Develop a payoff table for this game.
    b. Determine the strategies that Burger Giant and Taco Grande should use.
    c. What is the value of the game?

6. Given the payoff matrix as shown in Table 21.9, formulate the linear programming model to determine the mixed strategies to be employed by player A.

    a. Attempt to solve this model using the decision variable V, where $V \geq 0$. Explain why this does not work.
    b. Reformulate and solve this model allowing the decision variable V to be unrestricted in sign (i.e., use $V = V' - V''$, where $V' \geq 0$, $V'' \geq 0$).

7. Determine the saddle point and the value of the game having the following payoff matrix. The payoffs are expressed for Player A.

PLAYER A'S STRATEGIES	PLAYER B'S STRATEGIES B_1	B_2	B_3	B_4
A_1	11	9	5	11
A_2	11	12	7	8
A_3	10	8	6	8

8. Consider the following payoff matrix. The payoffs are expressed for Player A.

PLAYER A'S STRATEGIES	PLAYER B'S STRATEGIES		
	B_1	B_2	B_3
A_1	-2	4	5
A_2	0	-3	6
A_3	-5	1	-6

    a. Apply the principle of dominance to this payoff matrix.
    b. Determine player A's optimal mixed strategy.
    c. Determine player B's optimal mixed strategy.
    d. What is the value of this game?

9. Consider the following payoff matrix. The payoffs are expressed for player Y.

PLAYER Y'S STRATEGIES	PLAYER Z'S STRATEGIES		
	Z_1	Z_2	Z_3
Y_1	7	12	9
Y_2	10	6	10
Y_3	8	9	9

    a. Apply the principle of dominance to this payoff matrix.
    b. Determine player Y's optimal mixed strategy.
    c. Determine player Z's optimal mixed strategy.
    d. What is the value of this game?

10. Management of Pedro's Taco Shell, Inc., is negotiating with its union over the issue of how many taco shells are to be produced during the next contract year. Management wishes to produce as many taco shells as possible, while the union wants to produce as few taco shells as possible. The number of taco shells (in 1,000,000 units) expected to be made yearly for various combinations of management and union actions is shown in the following table.

MANAGEMENT ACTIONS	UNION ACTIONS		
	SLOWDOWN	STRIKE	WORK HARD
LOCK OUT	1.8	1.1	1.3
NEUTRAL	1.3	1.5	1.8
AGGRESSIVE	1.3	1.3	1.8

Determine the strategy to be used by management and the expected value of the game.

11. Downhill Racer Ski Company is currently involved in wage negotiations with its union. Since the management of the company and its union cannot agree, they have called in a mediator. With advice from both parties, the mediator has constructed the following payoff matrix, in which plus figures are hourly wage increases and minus figures are hourly wage reductions. Both sides have agreed that the figures are accurate. You have been called in as a consultant by management to determine its strategy and the expected value of the game.

MANAGEMENT STRATEGIES \ UNION STRATEGIES	U_1	U_2	U_3	U_4
M_1	+ $0.30	+ $0.25	+ $0.12	− $0.08
M_2	+ 0.25	+ 0.22	− 0.05	− 0.09
M_3	+ 0.15	+ 0.06	− 0.07	− 0.11
M_4	+ 0.07	+ 0.08	− 0.10	− 0.15

12. Peach Company and MBI Company are two large microcomputer manufacturers who basically control the personal computer market. As they consider their plans for the forthcoming model year they realize that they both have three major options.

1. Make no changes to microcomputer.
2. Make minor changes to microcomputer.
3. Make major changes to microcomputer.

The resultant market share changes from various combinations of these options for the two competing companies are summarized in the following table. Plus percentages are gains while minus percentages are losses for Peach Company.

PEACH OPTIONS \ MBI OPTIONS	NO CHANGES	MINOR CHANGES	MAJOR CHANGES
NO CHANGES	0	− 5%	− 9%
MINOR CHANGES	+ 4%	0	− 6%
MAJOR CHANGES	+ 7%	− 2%	0

a. Determine the mixed strategy that should be followed by Peach Company.
b. Determine the mixed strategy that should be followed by MBI Company.

c. Determine the value of the game.

13. Sally McWhite and Jim Desmond are playing a board game. In playing this board game, they must choose among three strategies. The payoffs associated with the interactions among these strategies are presented in the following table, and are stated with respect to Sally.

SALLY'S STRATEGIES	JIM'S STRATEGIES		
	WITHDRAWING	NEUTRAL	AGGRESSIVE
WITHDRAWING	20	10	-5
NEUTRAL	40	20	0
AGGRESSIVE	80	60	40

a. Determine the mixed strategy that Sally should use for this game.
b. Determine the mixed strategy that Jim should use for this game.
c. What is the value of this game?

14. South Carolina State is playing Johnson C. Smith in football. South Carolina State utilizes two basic offenses, the veer and the pro-set, while Johnson C. Smith utilizes three defenses, a 5-4-2, 6-3-2, and 8-3. The number of points that South Carolina State expects to score against Johnson C. Smith has been estimated from past games, and is shown in the following table.

S.C. STATE OFFENSES	J.C. SMITH DEFENSES		
	5-4-2	6-3-2	8-3
VEER	28	24	35
PRO-SET	21	31	42

Determine the mixed strategies for each team and the points South Carolina State expects to score.

15. Consider the following game.

PLAYER A'S STRATEGIES	PLAYER B'S STRATEGIES		
	B_1	B_2	B_3
A_1	-3	-1	-1
A_2	0	-4	0
A_3	1	1	-5

a. Verify that the strategies $p_1 = .55$, $p_2 = .27$, $p_3 = .18$ are optimal for player A.

b. Verify that the strategies $p_1 = .23$, $p_2 = .36$, $p_3 = .41$ are optimal for player B.

Application Review

The Avranches Gap Situation: An Application of Game Theory

The Avranches Gap situation provides an example of the application of game theory to a military decision-making problem. It arose in World War II, shortly after the allied invasion at Normandy. In this situation the opposing armies were arrayed according to the drawing presented as Figure 21.2.

General Omar Bradley was in charge of the allied forces in this situation. His basic strategic problem was that of what to do with the reserve of four U.S. divisions just south of the gap in his line, which was at the small French town of Avranches.

Bradley considered three courses of action: one, to order his reserve back to defend the gap; two, to send it eastward to harass or possibly cut off withdrawal of the German Ninth Army; or three, to leave it in position and uncommitted for one day, moving it to the gap if necessary or eastward if the gap was held without reinforcement.

The German commander, General von Kluge, had two logical choices for action: one, to attack toward the west to penetrate to the sea to secure his west flank and cut off U.S. forces south of the gap; or two, to withdraw to the east to take up a more tenable defensive position near the Seine River.

With two courses of action for von Kluge and three for Bradley, six different battles could result, as shown below. Bradley could select the row, von Kluge the column. The two independent choices would determine how the forces met on the battlefield.

Bradley and von Kluge now had to visualize the probable outcome of each

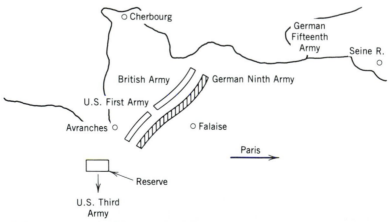

FIGURE 21.2 THE AVRANCHES GAP SITUATION.

Source: O. G. Haywood, "Military decisions and game theory," *Operations Research* (1954), Vol. 2, No. 3, pp. 39–48.

TABLE 21.10 PAYOFFS: AVRANCHES GAP PROBLEM

ALLIED STRATEGIES \ GERMAN STRATEGIES	STRATEGY 1: ATTACK GAP	STRATEGY 2: WITHDRAW
STRATEGY 1: RESERVE TO REINFORCE GAP	Gap holds	Weak pressure on German withdrawal
STRATEGY 2: ORDER RESERVE EASTWARD	Gap cut	Strong pressure on German withdrawal
STRATEGY 3: HOLD RESERVE IN PLACE ONE DAY, TO REINFORCE GAP IF NECESSARY OR STRIKE EASTWARD	Gap hold, possible German enrichment	Moderate pressure on German withdrawal

of these six battles. The outcomes resulting from the interactions among the strategies of the two opponents are presented in Table 21.10.

The next question is: How does Bradley compare these possible outcomes? Before he could judge which was better and which was worse, he had to establish his order of preference for these outcomes. Such an order of preference, from best to worst from the Allied point of view, was: (1) Gap holds, possible German encirclement; (2) strong pressure on German withdrawal; (3) moderate pressure on German withdrawal; (4) weak pressure on German withdrawal; (5) gap holds; and (6) gap cut. In Table 21.11, the original payoff matrix is reconstructed using cardinal numbers.

Having established an order of preference, Bradley could proceed to compare his alternative courses of action. Under the U.S. doctrine of decision making, he desired to select the one that offered the greatest promise of success in view of the enemies opposing capabilities. This was equivalent to using a maximin strategy.

Holding his reserve in position for one day to defend the gap if needed or to strike eastward, Bradley assured an outcome at least as favorable as moderate pressure on German withdrawal. With his other strategies, Bradley recognized

TABLE 21.11 PAYOFFS—CARDINAL NUMBERS ASSIGNED TO ALLIED ORDER OF PREFERENCE

ALLIED STRATEGIES \ GERMAN STRATEGIES	STRATEGY 1: ATTACK GAP	STRATEGY 2: WITHDRAW GERMAN PURE STRATEGY	MINIMUM OF ALLIED GAINS
STRATEGY 1: RESERVE TO REINFORCE GAP	5	4	5
STRATEGY 2: ORDER RESERVE EASTWARD	6	2	6
STRATEGY 3: HOLD RESERVE IN PLACE ONE DAY, TO REINFORCE GAP IF NECESSARY OR STRIKE EASTWARD (ALLIED PURE STRATEGY)	1	3 (saddle point)	3
MAXIMUM OF GERMAN LOSSES	1	3	

that he had to accept the possibility of a less favorable outcome. Bradley adopted the third strategy, as shown in Table 21.11.

The German general, von Kluge, on the other hand, assured a more preferable outcome by deciding to withdraw, which was his minimax decision. This is also shown in Table 21.11.

As we observe in Table 21.11, both sides should have employed a pure strategy, resulting in a saddle point solution. Hitler, however, ordered von Kluge to attack and close the Avranches gap. The U.S. Third Army under General George Patton quickly encircled the German Ninth Army. After most of his forces were destroyed, von Kluge committed suicide.

22

NONLINEAR PROGRAMMING: CALCULUS-BASED SOLUTION PROCEDURES

22.1 INTRODUCTION

Throughout this book we have studied quantitative techniques that have involved linear models and linear optimization. In particular, linear programming (Chapters 6, 7, 8, and 9), goal programming (Chapter 10), the transportation, transshipment, and assignment problems (Chapter 11), network models (Chapter 12), and integer programming (Chapter 14), all utilized various types of linear models. These linear models had linear objective functions and linear constraints. We noted that each of these linear modeling techniques had accompanying solution procedures that were very efficient and powerful. Also, computer programs for these solution procedures have been developed, and the computer programs facilitate the solution of many large-scale, real-world problems.

Unfortunately, there are many practical managerial decision-making problems for which the functions or mathematical relationships involved are not all linear. For example, the objective function in a marketing-type problem may need to be constructed in a manner that describes the nonlinear increase in sales quantities as a function of the reduction in sales price. Similarly, in a production scheduling problem the constraint relationships may need to be stated in a manner that represents nonlinear returns to scale as production volumes are increased. Recall that in our analysis of inventory models in Chapter 15 (Section 15.3), we developed a nonlinear function that expressed the total inventory cost in terms of the order quantity Q, namely:

Total inventory cost (per unit of time)
= Total order cost (per unit of time)
  + total holding cost (per unit of time)
= $K(D/Q) + h(Q/2)$.

Finally, nonlinearities could arise if the coefficients of some mathematical model were themselves random variables subject to uncertainty (i.e., were defined in probabilistic terms).

Although nonlinear models are frequently encountered in practice, they are considerably more difficult to solve than linear models. In general, the solution approaches for nonlinear programming problems involve the use of calculus. We, therefore, employ some rudimentary calculus procedures in several places in this chapter. A brief review of calculus is provided in Appendix B. Nonlinear methods are often quite complex and are not very efficient (i.e., unlike linear programming for which the simplex algorithm is very efficient). Consequently, the topic of *nonlinear programming* is broad and complex, and we only attempt to introduce the subject in this chapter. Our main objective is to show how nonlinear models arise in practice and to indicate some calculus-based solution approaches to their solution.

Most of the methods for solving nonlinear programming problems are of recent origin, and the development of new algorithms for solving various types of nonlinear programming problems is an important area of research. The algorithms that have been developed generally utilize iterative search procedures that are implemented using the computer. Again, we only provide an introduction to some of these solution approaches in this chapter.

This chapter is organized as follows. We begin by presenting some examples of nonlinear programming problems. We then discuss nonlinear programming problems involving a single variable for both the unconstrained and constrained cases. This is followed by a description of nonlinear programming problems involving multiple variables, again for both the unconstrained and constrained cases. We then illustrate how the Lagrange multiplier method can be used in solving nonlinear programming problems composed of a nonlinear objective function and equality constraints.

22.2 EXAMPLES OF NONLINEAR PROGRAMMING

The following two examples illustrate how nonlinear programming problems can arise in managerial decision-making situations.

EXAMPLE 1 NONLINEAR OBJECTIVE FUNCTION.

As a wealthy investor you recently conferred with your investment broker. She has investigated two high-technology stocks, and has indicated that she forecasts a 22 percent return from the first stock and a 19 percent return from the second. Furthermore, since both stocks are somewhat risky, she has also indicated that the variance in the total return resulting from investing in the two projects can be specified by the nonlinear function $4x_1 + 2x_2 + (x_1 + x_2)^2$, where x_1 and x_2 are the amounts allocated to the two investments (in thousands of dollars). This variance measure can be thought of as expressing the risk associated with a portfolio composed of these two investments. Observe that this variance measure is nonlinear and indicates that the risk increases as a nonlinear function of both the total investment and the individual amount of each investment. Furthermore, she has advised you that it would be unwise to invest more than $60,000 in either of the two stocks. You currently have a total of $100,000 that you can invest.

Given these conditions, this investment selection problem can be formulated as follows

Maximize $Z = [.22x_1 + .19x_2]$
$$- K[4x_1 + 2x_2 + (x_1 + x_2)^2] \quad (22.1)$$

subject to:

$$x_1 + x_2 \leq \$100{,}000 \quad \text{(total investment)}$$

$$x_1 \qquad \leq \$60{,}000$$

$$x_2 \leq \$60{,}000 \quad (22.2)$$

with

$$x_1 \geq 0, \qquad x_2 \geq 0 \quad (22.3)$$

Observe that the objective function for this model is nonlinear and is composed of two parts. The first part is the return expected from the two investments (i.e., 22 percent for x_1 and 19 percent for x_2). The second part is the (nonlinear) risk associated with the two investments that is weighted by the dimensionless risk coefficient, K. The risk coefficient, specified at the discretion of the modeler, is used to weight the tradeoff between risk and expected return. If $K = 0$, risk is ignored and the model would revert to a simple linear programming problem. As K increases from 0, the objective function contribution due to expected return becomes less important, and the investor would then be concentrating on minimizing the nonlinear risk term. This problem thus has a nonlinear objective function and three linear constraints.

EXAMPLE 2 NONLINEAR OBJECTIVE FUNCTION AND NONLINEAR CONSTRAINTS.

The Green Gunk Removal Company sells two grades of its famous industrial strength cleaning solvent, "Green Gunk". "Green Gunk-Regular" sells for $5/gallon, but there is also a $0.15 reduction in the selling price that increases with the square of the number of gallons sold. This occurs because of increased costs of distribution. Its second cleaning solvent, "Green Gunk-Super" sells for $8/gallon, and there is a $0.25 reduction in the selling price that increases with the square of the number of gallons sold. The sales revenue function for this firm can thus be written as

Sales revenue
$$= \$5x_1 - \$0.15x_1^2 + \$8x_2 - \$0.25x_2^2 \quad (22.4)$$

WHERE

x_1 = number of gallons of "Green Gunk-Regular" sold;
x_2 = number of gallons of "Green Gunk-Super" sold.

The Green Gunk Removal Company has two restrictions on its sales effort. First, it has a total of 3000 gallons of "Green Gunk-Regular" available, and a total of 5000 gallons of "Green Gunk-Super" available. Second, it has a limited sales force that has a total of 2500 sales force hours available at present. Its sales force productivity function, however, is nonlinear, since there is an increasing return on sales effort as more sales occur. The sales force productivity function can be approximated as

Sales force productivity
$$= 2x_1 - .2x_1^2 + 3x_2 - .4x_2^2 \quad (22.5)$$

Given these conditions this, sales effort determination problem can be written as follows.

Maximize $Z = \$5x_1 - \$0.15x_1^2$
$$+ \$8x_2 - \$0.25x_2^2 \quad (22.6)$$

subject to:

$$x_1 \qquad\qquad \leq 3000$$

$$x_2 \qquad \leq 5000$$

$$2x_1 - .2x_1^2 + 3x_2 - .4x_2^2 = 2500 \quad (22.7)$$

with

$$x_1 \geq 0, \qquad x_2 \geq 0 \quad (22.8)$$

The objective function for this problem is nonlinear, while the constraint set has one nonlinear and two linear constraints.

22.3 NONLINEAR PROGRAMMING: SINGLE VARIABLE MODEL

The simplest type of nonlinear programming problem is that in which we have a nonlinear objective function involving a single variable. The inventory control models that we studied in Chapters 15 and 16 provide examples of situations in which we attempted to determine the optimal value of a single variable that minimizes a total cost function.

Many of the solution procedures used to solve complex, multivariate nonlinear programming problems are based upon, and are extensions of, methods used to optimize objective functions composed of a single variable. Such problems can be graphically presented, and we begin our discussion with such univariate problems. We first consider the unconstrained case in which no constraints are present. Then, we analyze the constrained case in which a set of constraints are present.

22.3.1 UNCONSTRAINED OPTIMIZATION: SINGLE VARIABLE

The *unconstrained univariate optimization problem* is the simplest type of nonlinear programming problem. It involves only an objective function; there are no constraints on the problem. This objective function is expressed in terms of a single decision variable.

To illustrate a typical unconstrained univariate optimization problem, let us consider the following situation. The Zapper Bug Spray Company has maintained historical data that indicate that its yearly revenue (dollars) can be expressed in terms of its production output (gallons of bug spray) by the following equation

$$\text{Yearly revenue (\$)} = \frac{-1}{1000} x^2 + 10x \quad (22.9)$$

where x is gallons of bug spray produced.

The marginal cost of producing a gallon of bug spray is estimated to be \$1, and the yearly fixed cost for the bug spray production operation is \$1000. The yearly total production cost function for the company can be expressed by the following equation

Yearly total production cost (\$)

$$= 1x + 1000 \quad (22.10)$$

The Zapper Bug Spray Company would now like to determine the level at which it should produce in order to maximize yearly profit. Given the yearly revenue function (Eq. 22.9) and the yearly total cost function (Eq. 22.10), the yearly profit function can be expressed by the following equation

$$
\begin{aligned}
\text{Yearly profit} &= \text{yearly revenue} \\
&\quad - \text{yearly total production cost} \\
&= \frac{-1}{1000} x^2 + 10x \\
&\quad - (1x + 1000) \\
&= \frac{-1}{1000} x^2 + 9x - 1000 \quad (22.11)
\end{aligned}
$$

Since the yearly revenue, yearly total cost, and yearly profit can all be expressed as a function of a single variable, they can be plotted as shown in Figure 22.1. From the figure, we can see that profit is maximized to a value of \$19,250 for a production level of approximately 4500 gallons. We now show how differential calculus can be used to obtain the exact answer to this problem.

As we employ differential calculus to solve this problem, we assume that the variable in this problem (i.e., the production quantity, x) is continuous. Also, we assume that the yearly profit function is capable of being continuously differentiated as many times as necessary.

Before we proceed with the actual process of using differential calculus to solve this problem, let us illustrate the properties of a function of a single variable. In Figure 22.2 we have plotted a hypothetical function, $y = f(x)$. In this figure, points x'', x^{**}, x', and x^* are called *inflection points*, *stationary points*, or *critical points*. In differential calculus terms, these points are points at which the first derivative of the function vanishes (i.e., the first derivative has a value of zero). Point x'' is referred to as a *relative* or *local maximum*, and has the property that at point $x = x''$, $f(x'')$ is greater than the value of $f(x)$ for any adjacent value of x. Point x^{**} is referred to as a *relative* or *local minimum*, and has the property that at point $x = x^{**}$, $f(x^{**})$ is smaller

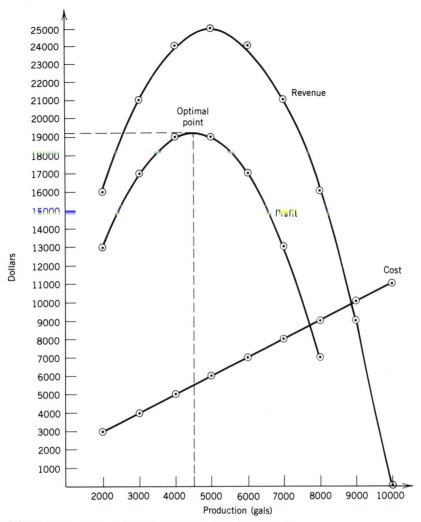

FIGURE 22.1   YEARLY PROFIT, REVENUE, AND COST AS A
FUNCTION OF PRODUCTION LEVELS.

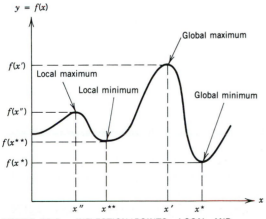

FIGURE 22.2   INFLECTION POINTS—LOCAL AND
GLOBAL OPTIMA.

than the value of $f(x)$ for any adjacent value of x.
Point x' is referred to as an *absolute* or *global maximum*, and has the property that at $x = x'$, $f(x')$ is
greater than $f(x)$ for any allowable value of x. Point
x^* is referred to as an *absolute* or *global minimum*,
and has the property that at $x = x^*$, $f(x^*)$ is smaller
than $f(x)$ for any allowable value of x. From the
definitions presented above and illustrated in Figure
22.2, it should be apparent that a local maximum
or minimum of a function can also be a global maximum or minimum of that function.

Now, the basic concept of differential calculus
is that the slope of a function at any point equals
the derivative of that function. Furthermore, the
slope of any function is equal to zero at a relative

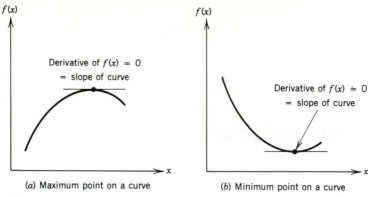

(a) Maximum point on a curve   (b) Minimum point on a curve

FIGURE 22.3   MAXIMUM AND MINIMUM OF A FUNCTION.

maximum or minimum point. Consequently, at the relative maximum and minimum points of a function, the derivative of that function equals zero. These concepts are illustrated graphically in Figure 22.3.

These properties lead to the following definition of the first derivative test for the presence of a local maximum or a local minimum.

First Derivative Test: If a function $f(x)$ has a local maximum or a local minimum at a point x^*, then $df(x^*)/dx = 0$ (i.e., the first derivative vanishes at x^*).

The first derivative test is a *necessary condition* for optimality that means that it must occur at the optimal point. It is important to emphasize that the necessary condition, which requires the first derivative to be equal to zero, must be satisfied at an optimal solution. The necessary condition does not guarantee, however, that the point at which the first derivative is equal to zero is in fact optimal. Assuming that the function being examined is twice differentiable, we can then state a *sufficient condition* for a local optimum (i.e., a condition that guarantees its presence). The sufficient condition, which involves the sign of the second derivative, determines whether a solution meeting the necessary condition is a maximum solution, minimum solution, or indeterminate solution.

Second Derivative Test: If a point x^* is identified such that $df(x^*)/dx = 0$ and $d^2f(x^*)/dx^2 < 0$, then x is a local maximum of $f(x)$. If a point is identified such that $df(x^*)/dx = 0$ and $d^2f(x^*)/dx^2 > 0$, then

x is a local minimum of $f(x)$. If a point x is identified such that $df(x^*)/dx = 0$ and $d^2f(x^*)/dx^2 = 0$, then the test is indeterminate.

To complete our discussion we must consider the importance of functions that are defined as being either concave or convex. Examples of concavity and convexity are shown in Figure 22.4.

From this figure, it can be seen that $f(x)$ is concave if, for each pair of points on the graph of $f(x)$, the line segment joining these two points lies entirely below the graph of the function. A concave function is like an umbrella and will shed water. Conversely, $f(x)$ is convex if, for each pair of points on the graph of $f(x)$, the line segment joining these two points lies entirely above the graph of the function. A convex function is thus like a bathtub and will hold water. A straight line, which we have for the objective function and constraints in a two-variable linear programming problem is both concave and convex, according to the above definition. In Figure 22.4d, we have a nonlinear function that is both nonconvex and nonconcave.

For a single variable function, if $f(x)$ is continuous and possesses a second derivative over the region of interest, then

$f(x)$ is concave if, and only if, $d^2f(x)/dx^2 \leq 0$

$f(x)$ is strictly concave if, and only if, $d^2f(x)/dx^2 < 0$

$f(x)$ is convex if, and only if, $d^2f(x)/dx^2 \geq 0$

$f(x)$ is strictly convex if, and only if, $d^2f(x)/dx^2 > 0$

To illustrate strict convexity consider the function $f(x) = 2x^2$, which is plotted in Figure 22.5.

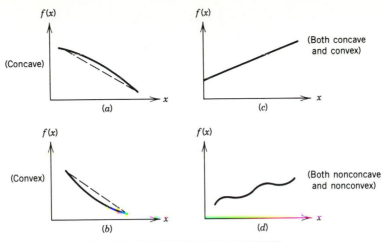

FIGURE 22.4   EXAMPLES OF CONCAVITY AND CONVEXITY.

Taking the first and second derivatives of this function, we obtain

$$\frac{df(x)}{dx} = 4x \qquad (22.12)$$

$$\frac{d^2f(x)}{dx^2} = 4(>0) \qquad (22.13)$$

Therefore, $f(x) = 2x^2$ is strictly convex.

To illustrate strict concavity consider the function $f(x) = -2x^2$, which is plotted in Figure 22.6.

Taking the first and second derivatives of this function, we obtain

$$\frac{df(x)}{dx} = -4x \qquad (22.14)$$

$$\frac{d^2f(x)}{dx^2} = -4(<0) \qquad (22.15)$$

Therefore, $f(x) = -2x^2$ is strictly concave.

In attempting to solve nonlinear programming models, local rather than global optima may be ob-

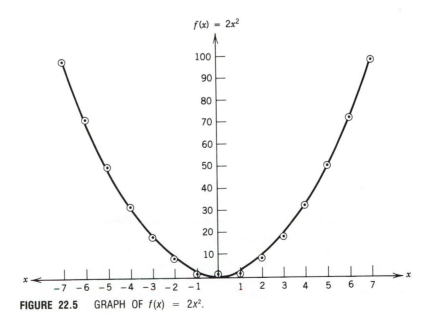

FIGURE 22.5   GRAPH OF $f(x) = 2x^2$.

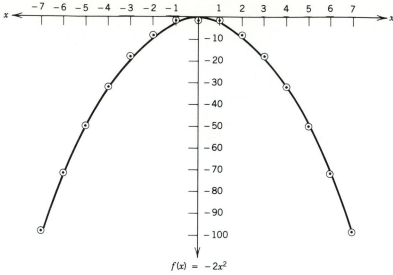

$$f(x) = -2x^2$$

FIGURE 22.6   GRAPH OF $f(x) = -2x^2$.

tained unless certain convexity-concavity conditions are met. In summary, it can be shown that the following relationships for local and global maxima will hold.

1. A local maximum of a concave function is also a global maximum of that function;
2. A local minimum of a convex function is also a global minimum of that function;
3. A local maximum of a strictly concave function is the unique global maximum of that function;
4. A local minimum of a strictly convex function is the unique global minimum of that function.

We now use the concepts that have been discussed earlier to solve our unconstrained univariate optimization problem.

Our objective in this problem is to maximize the yearly profit, which is given by

$$\text{Yearly profit} = \frac{-1}{1000} x^2 + 9x - 1000 \quad (22.16)$$

Taking the first derivative of the yearly profit function, with respect to x, we obtain

$$\frac{df(x)}{dx} = \frac{-2x}{1000} + 9 \quad (22.17)$$

Setting $[df(x)]/dx = 0$, and solving, yields the optimal value, x^*

$$0 = (-1/500)x^* + 9$$
$$x^* = 4500 \quad (22.18)$$

Taking the second derivative of the yearly profit function, with respect to x, we obtain

$$\frac{d^2f(x)}{dx^2} = \frac{-1}{500} \quad (22.19)$$

Since $d^2f(x)/dx^2$ is negative for all values of x, we know that $x^* = 4500$ produces the maximum value of the yearly profit function. By the second derivative test we know that this value produces the global maximum for this yearly profit function. The total (maximum) yearly profit associated with this production quantity is obtained by substituting $x^* = 4500$ into the yearly total profit function, yielding

$$\text{Yearly profit} = \frac{-1}{1000} x^{*2} + 9x^* - 1000$$
$$= \frac{-1}{1000} (4500)^2$$
$$\quad + 9(4500) - 1000$$
$$= -20{,}250 + 40{,}500 - 1000$$
$$= \$19{,}250 \quad (22.20)$$

Observe that this optimal value of the yearly profit function is exactly what was obtained using the graph presented as Figure 22.1.

22.3.2 CONSTRAINED OPTIMIZATION: SINGLE VARIABLE

The *constrained univariate optimization problem* involves a single objective function and one or more constraints. The constraints are often expressed in terms of nonnegativity restrictions on a single decision variable.

To illustrate a typical constrained univariate optimization problem, let us consider the following situation. The Atwater Corporation has determined that the yearly total production cost function for its production of molded plastic cases for computer disk drives can be expressed by the following equation

Yearly total production cost ($)

$$= \frac{1}{2}x^2 - 1000x + 1,000,000 \quad (22.21)$$

where x is the number of molded plastic cases produced. A plot of the yearly total production cost as a function of the number of molded plastic cases that are produced is presented in Figure 22.7. From this figure, we can see graphically that the yearly total production cost is minimized to a value of

$500,000 at a yearly level of production of 1000 molded plastic cases.

Using differential calculus to analytically find the value of x^* that minimizes this function, we take the first derivative of the yearly total production cost with respect to x, set this derivative equal to zero, and then solve for x^*. Taking the first derivative of the yearly total production cost function, with respect to x, we obtain

$$\frac{df(x)}{dx} = 1x - 1000 \quad (22.22)$$

Setting $df(x)/dx = 0$, and solving, yields the optimal value, x^*.

$$0 = 1x^* - 1000$$
$$x^* = 1000 \quad (22.23)$$

Taking the second derivative of the yearly total production cost function with respect to x, we obtain

$$\frac{d^2f(x)}{dx^2} = 1 \quad (22.24)$$

Since $d^2f(x)/dx^2$ is positive for all values of x we know that $x^* = 1000$ produces the minimum value of the yearly total production cost function. The yearly total (minimum) production cost associated

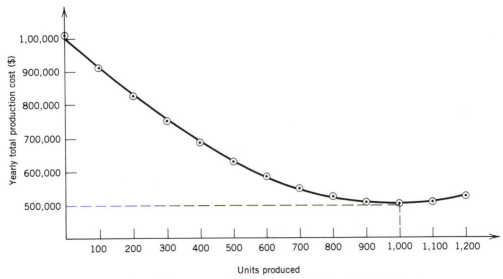

FIGURE 22.7   YEARLY TOTAL PRODUCTION COST AS A FUNCTION OF UNITS PRODUCED.

with this production quantity is obtained by substituting $x^* = 1000$ into the yearly total production cost function yielding

Yearly production cost

$$= \frac{1}{2} x^{*2} - 1000 x^* + 1{,}000{,}000$$

$$= \frac{1}{2} (1000)^2 - 1000(1000) + 1{,}000{,}000$$

$$= 500{,}000 - 1{,}000{,}000 + 1{,}000{,}000$$

$$= \$500{,}000 \qquad (22.25)$$

Note that up to this point all we have done is solve another unconstrained univariate optimization problem. Now, let us transform this situation into a constrained univariate optimization problem. In order to do so we add the constraint

$$x \leq 800 \qquad (22.26)$$

In other words, we are now restricting the number of molded plastic cases that we can produce to be less than, or equal to, 800. The constrained univariate optimization model for this situation is shown in Figure 22.8. In this figure the feasible solution space is shaded. The optimal value, given the feasible solution space, is of course, $x^* = 800$. Note that this point is on the boundary of the feasible

solution space that is formed by the constraint. Substituting $x^* = 800$ into the yearly total production cost function yields

Yearly production cost

$$= \frac{1}{2} x^{*2} - 1000 x^* + 1{,}000{,}000$$

$$= \frac{1}{2} (800)^2 - 1000(800) + 1{,}000{,}000$$

$$= \$520{,}000 \qquad (22.27)$$

Now, let us consider a slightly different situation in which we add the constraint

$$x \leq 1200 \qquad (22.28)$$

In other words, we are now restricting the number of molded plastic cases that we can produce to be less than, or equal to, 1200. The constrained univariate optimization model for this situation is shown in Figure 22.9. In this figure the feasible solution space is again shaded. Note, however, that the optimal value in this case is no longer on the boundary of the feasible solution space. Point C represents a smaller total yearly production cost than point B. Observe that it is inside of the feasible solution space. This means that we must consider not only points on the boundary of the feasible solution space,

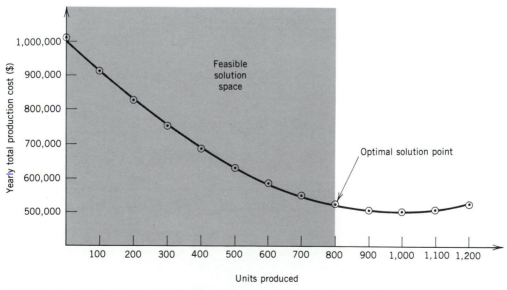

FIGURE 22.8 YEARLY TOTAL PRODUCTION COST AS A FUNCTION OF UNITS PRODUCED, WITH UNITS PRODUCED ≤800.

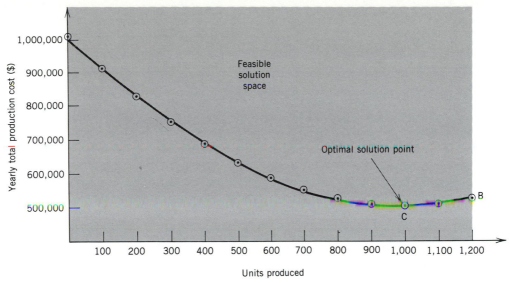

FIGURE 22.9 YEARLY TOTAL PRODUCTION COST AS A FUNCTION OF UNITS PRODUCED, WITH UNITS PRODUCED ≤1200.

but also other points that lie on the objective function. This greatly complicates the process of finding a solution to a nonlinear programming problem such as this.

In summary, in a constrained univariate optimization problem, a global optimum (if one exists) will always occur either at one of the stationary points or at one of the boundary points determined by the constraints. Differential calculus is again employed to determine the stationary points.

22.4 NONLINEAR PROGRAMMING: MULTIPLE VARIABLES MODEL

In general, a nonlinear programming problem that involves a nonlinear objective function having n variables ($n \geq 2$) is harder to solve than a single variable model. This multivariate optimization problem again requires the identification of the stationary points of the nonlinear objective function and then the identification of which of these points represent local or global optima. Unfortunately, the identification of local or global optima is not necessarily easily accomplished for some multivariate functions. Because of these difficulties we only attempt to sketch out the solution methods that can be employed, and indicate some of the difficulties associated with their application.

22.4.1 UNCONSTRAINED OPTIMIZATION: MULTIPLE VARIABLES

The *unconstrained multivariate optimization problem* involves a nonlinear programming problem composed of a single objective function that is represented by multiple variables. Just as we did for the unconstrained univariate optimization problem, we determine the stationary points by setting the first derivatives equal to zero, and solving the resulting equations. For the unconstrained multivariate optimization problem having n variables there will be n first derivatives. Each of these n first derivatives will be a partial derivative with respect to that variable. As was the case for the unconstrained univariate optimization problem, any point at which all of the first partial derivatives are equal to zero is a stationary point, and provides a necessary condition for optimality. The sufficient conditions for optimality for the unconstrained multivariate optimization problem are based on the use of a matrix of all possible second partial derivatives.

The determination of the necessary and sufficient conditions for optimality for the unconstrained multivariate optimization problem poses difficulties in many practical situations. First, setting the first partial derivatives to zero will result in a set of m equations in m unknowns. Unless the original objective function was of simple form, its partial derivatives (i.e., the resulting equations) may be very difficult to solve. Second, the sufficient conditions are quite complex, and require the evaluation of the determinants of the matrix of the second partial derivatives. In some cases it is virtually impossible to solve for the necessary and sufficient conditions. For that reason, various computer codes have been developed to solve for the local optima of nonlinear functions involving several variables. Such codes are based on *steepest ascent* or "hill climbing" methods. This means that, for a maximization problem, the steepest ascent method attempts to move uphill from an initial point along the function, until a point is reached at which the first partial derivatives of the function are sufficiently close to zero. This rather general description of the solution process is meant only to provide the reader with a general understanding of what it involves. A more detailed explanation of the process is beyond the introductory nature of this chapter.

22.4.2 CONSTRAINED OPTIMIZATION: MULTIPLE VARIABLES

The *constrained multivariate optimization problem* is the most difficult type of nonlinear programming problem. It can be stated in mathematical terms, as follows.

Maximize (or minimize) Z
$$= f(x_1, x_2, \ldots, x_n) \quad (22.29)$$

subject to:

$$
\begin{aligned}
g_1(x_1, x_2, \ldots, x_n)\{\leq, =, \geq\}b_1 \\
g_2(x_1, x_2, \ldots, x_n)\{\leq, =, \geq\}b_2 \\
\vdots \qquad\qquad \vdots \quad \vdots \\
g_m(x_1, x_2, \ldots, x_n)\{\leq, =, \geq\}b_m
\end{aligned}
\quad (22.30)
$$

with

$$x_1, x_2, \ldots, x_n \geq 0 \quad (22.31)$$

and with at least one of the functions $f(x_1, x_2, \ldots, x_n)$ or $g_i(x_1, x_2, \ldots, x_n)$ being nonlinear. The constrained multivariate optimization problem may have a number of possible forms, including

1. A linear objective function with some or all of the constraints nonlinear;
2. A nonlinear objective function with a linear constraint set;

3. A nonlinear objective function with some or all of the constraints nonlinear.

Depending on the nature and number of nonlinear functions, and the number of decision variables in the problem, it may become very difficult if not impossible to solve.

In general, we can employ the solution procedures discussed earlier for unconstrained multivariate optimization. For many constrained optimization problems it may be difficult to solve for the stationary points, however, and the constraints of the problem may preclude the use of steepest ascent type methods. Again, the introductory nature of this chapter precludes our attempting to consider this subject in any further detail.

22.4.3 THE LAGRANGE MULTIPLIER METHOD

The *Lagrange multiplier method* is a general mathematical procedure that can be used to solve constrained optimization problems that consist of a nonlinear objective function and a constraint set composed entirely of linear or nonlinear equalities. The Lagrange multiplier method addresses the following type of constrained multivariate optimization problem.

Maximize (or minimize) Z
$$= f(x_1, x_2, \ldots, x_n) \quad (22.32)$$

subject to:

$$
\begin{array}{lll}
g_1(x_1, x_2, \ldots, x_n) = b_1 & g_1(x_1, x_2, \ldots, x_n) - b_1 = 0 \\
g_2(x_1, x_2, \ldots, x_n) = b_2 & g_2(x_1, x_2, \ldots, x_n) - b_2 = 0 \\
\vdots \qquad\qquad = \vdots \text{ or } \vdots & \qquad\qquad\qquad \vdots = \vdots \\
g_m(x_1, x_2, \ldots, x_n) = b_m & g_m(x_1, x_2, \ldots, x_n) - b_m = 0
\end{array}
$$
$$(22.33)$$

with

$$x_1, x_2, \ldots, x_n \geq 0 \quad (22.34)$$

To apply the Lagrange multiplier method we must first state two assumptions.

1. The number of constraints, m, must be less than the number of unknowns, n.

2. The objective function, $f(x_1, x_2, \ldots, x_n)$ and the constraint equations $g_i(x_1, x_2, \ldots, x_n)$, $i = 1, 2, \ldots, m$, must be continuously differentiable functions.

Note also that we can equate each of the constraints to zero. We now write a new function that combines the original objective function and the original constraints into a single function, called the *Lagrangian function*, $L(\mathbf{x}, \boldsymbol{\lambda})$, defined as

$$L(\mathbf{x}, \boldsymbol{\lambda}) = f(\mathbf{x}) - \sum_{i=1}^{m} \lambda_i [g_i(\mathbf{x}) - b_i] \quad (22.35)$$

In this Lagrangian function the sign in front of Σ is arbitrary; it can be either positive or negative. The λ_i used in the function are known as *Lagrange multipliers*. Their interpretation is explained later.

The original constrained problem that had one objective function and m equality constraints has now been transformed into an equivalent unconstrained problem having exactly m Lagrange multipliers. The unconstrained Lagrangian function consists of n original variables, the x_j, and m added Lagrange multipliers, the λ_i. If we take n first partial derivatives with respect to the x_j and m first partial derivatives with respect to λ_i, and equate them to zero, we then obtain a system of $m + n$ equations in $m + n$ unknowns. This system is used to find the stationary points on the Lagrangian function.

To illustrate the Lagrange multiplier method let us consider the following problem situation. Jim Hanifan, the owner of Jim's Boat Shop, has added a new line of bassboats in his boat shop. He now wants to make a decision concerning his monthly advertisement and promotional efforts with respect to this new line of bassboats. He feels that he can either advertise using radio commercials, or use a special advertisement in the Sunday edition of the local newspaper. He currently has $1000 to spend on advertising, and radio commercials cost $300 (i.e., this includes the radio commercial being presented 10 times each month), while the newspaper advertisement costs $200 (i.e., this includes the newspaper advertisement being in 4 consecutive Sunday newspapers). He estimates that his monthly bassboat sales (in thousands of dollars) is approximated by the following function

Bassboat sales: S
$$= 4300x_1 - 300x_1^2 + 2500x_2 - 100x_2^2 \quad (22.36)$$

WHERE

x_1 = number of radio commercials;

x_2 = number of newspaper advertisements.

The complete nonlinear programming problem that describes this situation can now be written as follows

Maximize $Z = f(x_1, x_2)$
$$= 4300x_1 - 300x_1^2 + 2500x_2 - 100x_2^2 \quad (22.37)$$

subject to

$$300x_1 + 200x_2 = 1000 \quad (22.38)$$

with

$$x_1, x_2 \geq 0 \quad (22.39)$$

This nonlinear programming problem has a single Lagrange multiplier. The Lagrangian function for this problem can be written as

$$L(x_1, x_2, \lambda_1) = 4300x_1 - 300x_1^2 + 2500x_2 - 100x_2^2 - \lambda_1(300x_1 + 200x_2 - 1000). \quad (22.40)$$

To minimize this Lagrangian function we must take its first partial derivatives with respect to x_1, x_2, and λ_1; set each of these partial derivatives to zero; and then solve the resulting three equations simultaneously. This is done as follows.

$$\frac{\partial L}{\partial x_1} = 4300 - 600x_1 - 300\lambda_1 = 0 \quad (22.41)$$

$$\frac{\partial L}{\partial x_2} = 2500 - 200x_2 - 200\lambda_1 = 0 \quad (22.42)$$

$$\frac{\partial L}{\partial \lambda_1} = -300x_1 - 200x_2 + 1000 = 0 \quad (22.43)$$

The solution to these three simultaneous linear equations is obtained in the following manner.

1. Using Eq 22.43, define x_1 in terms of x_2.

$$300x_1 = -200x_2 + 1000$$

$$x_1 = -\frac{2}{3}x_2 + \frac{10}{3} \quad (22.44)$$

2. Substitute this expression for x_1 into Eq. 22.41.

$4300 - 600x_1 - 300\lambda_1 = 0$

$4300 - 600(-0.667x_2 + 3.333) - 300\lambda_1 = 0$

$4300 + 400x_2 - 2000 - 300\lambda_1 = 0$

$2300 + 400x_2 - 300\lambda_1 = 0$

$$\lambda_1 = \frac{23 + 4x_2}{3} \qquad (22.45)$$

3. Express Eq. 22.42 in terms of λ_1.

$2500 - 200x_2 - 200\lambda_1 = 0$

$$\lambda_1 = \frac{25 - 2x_2}{2} \qquad (22.46)$$

4. Equate the two expressions for λ_1.

$$\frac{23 + 4x_2}{3} = \frac{25 - 2x_2}{2}$$

$$46 + 8x_2 = 75 - 6x_2$$

$$14x_2 = 29$$

$$x_2^* = \frac{29}{14} = 2.071 \qquad (22.47)$$

5. Substitute this value of x_2 into the expression for x_1 (22.44).

$$x_1^* = -\frac{2}{3}x_2 + \frac{10}{3}$$

$$= \frac{-2}{3(2.071)} + 3.333$$

$$= -1.381 + 3.333$$

$$= 1.952 \qquad (22.48)$$

6. Substitute this value of x_2 into the expression for λ_1 (22.46).

$$\lambda_1^* = \frac{25 - 2x_2}{2}$$

$$= \frac{25 - 2(2.071)}{2}$$

$$= 12.5 - 1(2.071)$$

$$= 12.5 - 2.071$$

$$= 10.43 \qquad (22.49)$$

The optimal value of the objective function can now be computed as

Maximum Z (monthly bassboat sales)

$= 4300x_1 - 300x_1^2$
$\quad + 2500x_2 - 100x_2^2$
$= 4300(1.952) - 300(1.952)^2$
$\quad + 2500(2.071) - 100(2.071)^2$
$= 8394 - 1143 + 5178 - 429$
$= \$12,000 \qquad (22.50)$

In summary, the optimal solution is

$x_1^* = 1.952$ radio commercials;

$x_2^* = 2.071$ newspaper advertisements;

Maximum Z = $12,000 (monthly bassboat sales).

It should be noted that the "optimal" solution we have obtained is really a necessary condition for optimality. As was the case with unconstrained optimization, certain convexity and concavity conditions must be satisfied to guarantee that a local constrained optimal point is also a global optimal point. These conditions also require the use of second partial derivatives and can become complicated. They are beyond the introductory nature of this discussion.

Finally, it should be mentioned that the Lagrange multipliers method can be used for constrained optimization problems in which there are inequality constraints. Necessary optimality conditions for this type of problem involve the *Kuhn-Tucker conditions*, of which the Lagrange multiplier conditions are a special case. Again, because of the introductory level of this chapter, we will not attempt to consider the constrained optimization problem with inequality constraints.

22.4.4 INTERPRETING THE LAGRANGE MULTIPLIERS

The Lagrange multipliers, which are used in the solution of certain types of nonlinear programming problems, have an interesting and important economic meaning. The Lagrange multipliers in nonlinear programming have the same interpretation as the dual variables in linear programming. Therefore, the optimal value of the ith Lagrange multiplier, λ_i^*, reflects the approximate rate of change in the optimal value of the objective function, as the ith right-hand-side value, b_i, is changed, with all other data of the problem remaining constant.

In formal terms the Lagrange multiplier is the partial derivative of $L(\mathbf{x}, \lambda)$ with respect to b, namely

$$\lambda = \frac{\partial f(L)}{\partial b} \qquad (22.51)$$

Therefore, if b increases, the value of λ indicates approximately how much the value of the objective function increases. Alternatively, if b decreases, the value of λ indicates approximately how much the value of the objective function decreases.

The reason that the Lagrange multiplier provides only an approximate estimate of the change in the value of the objective function as a result of the change in b is that it is a partial derivative of the objective function with respect to b. This means that as b changes, we obtain different value of the Lagrange multiplier. The approximation provided by the Lagrange multiplier is a good approximation as long as the change in b is relatively small.

Let us now return to our previous example and show how the Lagrange multiplier is interpreted in that situation. The optimal solution to the problem involving Jim's Boat Shop had the following values for the variables

$$x_1^* = 2.071 \qquad x_2^* = 1.953 \qquad \lambda_1^* = 10.43 \qquad (22.52)$$

Since $\lambda_1^* = 10.43$, the interpretation of the Lagrange multiplier in this case would be that the objective function should increase by approximately $10.43 if b is increased $1. Thus, if the advertising budget was increased from $1000 to $1100, then the objective function should increase approximately by $100 \times \$10.43 = \$1043$.

After increasing the advertising budget to $1100, the revised version of Jim's Boat Shop problem can be written as follows

Maximize $Z = f(x_1, x_2)$
$$= 4300x_1 - 300x_1^2 + 2500x_2 - 100x_2^2 \qquad (22.53)$$

subject to:

$$300x_1 + 200x_2 = 1100 \qquad (22.54)$$

with

$$x_1, x_2 \geq 0 \qquad (22.55)$$

Formulating the Lagrangian for the revised problem, we obtain

$$L(x_1, x_2, \lambda_1) = 4300x_1 - 300x_1^2 + 2500x_2$$
$$- 100x_2^2 - \lambda_1(300x_1 + 200x_2 - 1100) \qquad (22.56)$$

Setting the partial derivatives to zero, we obtain

$$\frac{\partial L}{\partial x_1} = 4300 - 600x_1 - 300\lambda_1 = 0 \qquad (22.57)$$

$$\frac{\partial L}{\partial x_2} = 2500 - 200x_2 - 200\lambda_1 = 0 \qquad (22.58)$$

$$\frac{\partial L}{\partial \lambda_1} = -300x_1 - 200x_2 + 1100 = 0 \qquad (22.59)$$

Solving these three simultaneous linear equations, we obtain

$$x_1^* = 2.095$$
$$x_2^* = 2.357$$
$$\lambda_1^* = 10.14 \qquad (22.60)$$

The optimal value of the objective function can now be computed as:

Maximum Z (monthly bassboat sales)
$$= 4300x_1 - 300x_1^2 + 2500x_2 - 100x_2^2$$
$$= 4300(2.095) - 300(2.095)^2$$
$$+ 2500(2.357) - 100(2.357)^2$$
$$= 9009 - 317 + 5893 - 555$$
$$= \$13,030 \qquad (22.61)$$

This value is $1030 larger than the previous objective function value of $12,000. Thus, a $100 increase in the right-hand-side value of the constraint equation has resulted in an increase of approximately 100 times λ_1 (i.e., $1030 \approx \$1043$) in the objective function. Thus, if Jim Hanifan is able to increase his advertising expenditures from $1000 to $1100, he can expect his monthly boat sales to increase by approximately $1040.

22.5 SUMMARY

In this chapter we have attempted to present an introduction to the topic of nonlinear programming and calculus-based solution procedures. Our presentation has necessarily been brief because many nonlinear programming problems are very difficult to solve, and the mathematical level of this book is not sufficient for an in-depth treatment of this area.

Unlike linear programming, there is no single efficient way to solve nonlinear programming problems. Certain types of nonlinear programming problems can be solved, as long as they do not contain too many variables. Other types can only be considered by using computer search techniques. The field of nonlinear programming is one in which new approaches and procedures are constantly being developed.

GLOSSARY

Absolute or Global Maximum (Minimum) A function $y = f(x)$ is said to have an absolute or global maximum (minimum) at a point $x = x'$ if $f(x')$ is greater (less) than $f(x)$ for any other allowable value of x.

Concave Function A function for which, for each pair of points on the graph of that function, the line segment joining those two points lies entirely below the graph of that function.

Constrained Multivariate Optimization Problem A nonlinear programming problem in several variables that may have a nonlinear objective function and/or nonlinear constraints, plus some type of nonnegativity restrictions.

Constrained Univariate Optimization Problem Involves a nonlinear objective function in one variable that has to be optimized, where there are one or more constraints on the problem.

Convex Function A function for which, for each pair of points on the graph of that function, the line segment joining those two points lies entirely above the graph of that function.

Kuhn-Tucker Conditions The necessary conditions under which a given point, x^*, is a local optimum for the general nonlinear programming problem.

Lagrangian Function A function combining the objective function and the constraints into a single function.

Lagrange Multiplier Method A method that can be used to solve unconstrained nonlinear problems involving the optimization of a function subject to a constraint set composed entirely of equalities.

Lagrange Multipliers Variables utilized in solving certain types of nonlinear programming problems that are analogous to the values associated with the dual variables in a linear programming problem.

Necessary Conditions The conditions that must be satisfied for an optimal solution, but that do not guarantee that a particular solution is optimal.

Nonlinear Programming Problem A mathematical programming problem in which the objective function and/or one or more constraints are not linear.

Relative or Local Maximum (Minimum)   A function $y = f(x)$ is said to have a relative or local maximum (minimum) at $x = x''$ if $f(x'')$ is greater (less) than $f(x)$ for any adjacent value of x.

Stationary Point x^* of a Function $f(x)$ The point x^* that we find by setting the first derivative of $f(x)$ with respect to x equal to zero and solving for x.

Steepest Ascent   A method for solving nonlinear programming problems involving several variables.

Sufficient Conditions   The additional conditions that must be satisfied by a particular solution (i.e., in addition to satisfying the necessary conditions) to guarantee that the particular solution is also an optimal solution.

Unconstrained Multivariate Optimization Problem   A nonlinear programming problem composed of only an objective function, with this objective function having multiple variables.

Unconstrained Univariate Optimization Problem   The most elementary form of a nonlinear programming problem involving an objective function in a single variable.

Selected References

Aoki, Masanao. 1971. *Introduction to Optimization Techniques: Fundamentals and Applications of Nonlinear Programming*. New York: Macmillan Co.

Bracken, J., and G.P. McCormick. 1968. *Selected Applications of Nonlinear Programming*. New York: Wiley.

Bradley, Stephen P., Arnoldo C. Hax, and Thomas L. Magnanti. 1977. *Applied Mathematical Programming*. Reading, Mass.: Addison–Wesley.

Hadley, G. 1964. *Nonlinear and Dynamic Programming*. Reading, Mass.: Addison–Wesley.

Luenberger, David G. 1973. *Introduction to Linear and Nonlinear Programming*. Reading, Mass.: Addison–Wesley.

Mangasarian, Olvi L. 1969. *Nonlinear Programming*. New York: McGraw–Hill.

Zangwill, Willard I. 1969. *Nonlinear Progamming: A Unified Approach*. Englewood Cliffs, N.J.: Prentice–Hall.

Discussion Questions

1.   What characteristics do nonlinear programming problems have?

2.   Why are nonlinear programming problems more difficult to solve than linear programming problems?

3.   What are some of the methods used for solving nonlinear programming problems?

4.   Do you always have a "global" optimum in a constrained univariate optimization problem? Why or why not?

5.   What is the difference between a necessary and a sufficient condition?

6.   Explain the link between the Lagrange multipliers and the dual variables of linear programming.

7. How are the Kuhn-Tucker conditions used?

8. Describe the situation in which the use of the Lagrange multiplier method is appropriate.

PROBLEMS

1. Is the following problem a nonlinear programming problem? If it is, explain why.

$$\text{Maximize } Z = 2x_1 + 5x_2$$

subject to

$$x_1^2 - 5\sqrt{x_2} \geq 8$$
$$3x_1 - 4x_2 \geq 12$$

with

$$x_1 \geq 0, \qquad x_2 \geq 0$$

2. Is the following problem a nonlinear programming problem? If it is, explain why.

$$\text{Minimize } Z = 10x_1 + 3x_2 + 2x_2^2$$

subject to:

$$4x_1 - 2x_2 \leq 10$$
$$11x_1 + 6x_2 \geq 12$$

with

$$x_1 \geq 0, \qquad x_2 \geq 0$$

3. The Bug Doom Chemical Company produces two types of bug spray. The total profit function applicable to these two bug sprays is given by the following function.

$$\text{Profit} = 11x_1 + 7x_2 - 1/100x_1^2 - 1/50x_2^2$$

WHERE
x_1 = gallons of "Bug Doom Regular" produced;

x_2 = gallons of "Bug Doom Super" produced.

The constraints on the resources used in the production process are as follows

RESOURCE	PER-GALLON REQUIREMENT "BUG DOOM REGULAR"	"BUG DOOM SUPER"		RESOURCE AVAILABILITY FOR REQUIREMENT
Chemical 1	2 units	1 unit	≤	40 units
Chemical 2	3 units	3 units	≥	80 units
Mixing hours	4 units	7 units	≤	100 units

Using this information, formulate the appropriate nonlinear programming problem.

4. a. Minimize the function $f(x) = 5x^2 - 7x + 4$.
   b. Determine the sign of the second derivative of this function at the maximizing value of x.
   c. Determine the minimum of this function over the interval $2 \le x \le 12$.
   d. Determine whether this function is concave or convex.
   e. Plot this function and show its minimum.

5. a. Maximize the function $f(x) = -8x^2 - 10x + 20$.
   b. Determine the sign of the second derivative of this function at the maximizing value of x.
   c. Determine the maximim of this function over the interval $2 \le x \le 12$.
   d. Determine whether this function is concave or convex.
   e. Plot this function and show its maximum.

6. Doug Henderson is trying to determine the size of sales territories for his sales force. He has determined that sales in a particular area are related to the population in that area, according to the following function.

$$\text{Sales} = 10,000x - 0.1x^2 + 500,000$$

where x = population. What is the population required in a particular area to maximize sales? What is the maximum sales value?

7. Bubba Goodboy owns Ace Used Cars. He has determined that his yearly sales revenue is a function of the number of cars that he sells, and is given by the following function.

$$\text{Yearly sales revenue} = 5000x - 3x^2 + 100,000$$

where x = number of cars. How many cars should he sell in a year in order to maximize his yearly revenue? What is his maximum yearly sales revenue?

8. The following function indicates the total cost of producting x pounds of cat food.

$$\text{Total production cost} = \frac{1}{4} x^2 - 700x + 500,000$$

where x = pounds of cat food. How many pounds of cat food should be produced to minimize the total cost of production? What is the minimum total production cost?

9. The following function indicates the total cost of inventorying automobile parts at Hank's Parts & Service.

$$\text{Total inventory cost} = -90x + \frac{1}{3} x^2 + 8000$$

where x = number of parts. How many parts should be placed in inventory at Hank's Parts & Service? What is the minimum total inventory cost?

10. Solve the following problem using the Lagrange multiplier method.

$$\text{Maximize } Z = x_1^2 + 3x_2^2 - 7x_1 - 10x_2 + 25$$

subject to

$$x_1 + 3x_2 = 9$$

11. Solve the following problem using the Lagrange multiplier method.

$$\text{Maximize } Z = 3x_1^2 - 10x_1 + 4x_1x_2 + 2x_2^2 - 12x_2 + 60$$

subject to:

$$x_1 + 2x_2 = 6$$

12. a. Solve the following problem using the Lagrange multiplier method.

$$\text{Maximize } Z = 3x_1^2 - 9x_1 + 2x_2^2 - 6x_2 + 50$$

subject to

$$2x_1 + 4x_2 = 20$$

b. Estimate the change in the value of the objective function if the right-hand-side value of the constraint changes to 21.

13. a. Solve the following problem using the Lagrange multiplier method.

$$\text{Minimize } Z = x_1^2 + x_2^2 - 15x_1 - 10x_2 - 45$$

subject to:

$$20x_1 + 40x_2 = 80$$

b. Estimate the change in the value of the objective function if the right-hand-side value changes to 79.

14. The Sweet Passion Perfume Company produces two types of blended perfumes: "Youthful Passion" and "Lust". The total profit function for sales of these two types of blended perfumes is given by the following function.

$$\text{Total profit } f(x_1, x_2) = 8x_1 + 5x_2 - 0.01x_1^2 - 0.02x_2^2$$

WHERE
x_1 = gallons of "Youthful Passion" produced;

x_2 = gallons of "Lust" produced.

At present, the company has a major resource constraint with respect to the distillation hours available for these two perfumes. The distillation hours constraint can be written as

$$2x_1 + 1x_2 = 150 \text{ hours}$$

a. Use the Lagrange multiplier method to determine how many gallons of each of the two perfumes to produce.
b. What is the value of an additional distillation hour?

15. The Billiken Company is a textile manufacturer that produces denim cloth. From historical data it has determined that its yearly revenue (in dollars) can be expressed in terms of its production output (square yards of denim cloth) by the following function.

$$\text{Yearly revenue } (\$) = 10,000x - 1/100x^2$$

where x is the square yards of denim cloth produced. The yearly total production cost function for the Billiken Company can be expressed by the following function.

$$\text{Yearly total production cost} = 2x + 10,000$$

Determine how much cloth should be produced in order to maximize the yearly profit for the Billiken Company. Solve using differential calculus. Also, plot the function and show its maximum.

Application Review

Vehicle Routing at E. I. DuPont, Inc.

The Clinical Systems Division of E. I. DuPont, Inc., manufactures and markets an automatic clinical analyzer. This machine, which automates many of the routine tests made for patients in medical laboratories, is sold to hospitals and other medical institutions as a laboratory labor-saving device. In order to operate the automatic clinical analyzer, consumable products of a chemical nature are required. The consumable chemicals have to be refrigerated, and can be obtained only from DuPont, which ships consumable orders directly to customers.

At the beginning of this study, consumables were being shipped to over 1500 customers located in about 1000 cities throughout the continental United States and Canada. New customers were being added at a rate of about +40 percent per year. Consequently, logistics management at DuPont had become increasingly concerned with the delivery costs associated with consumables, as they were in excess of $1 million annually and were growing rapidly. This lead to the study reported in this case.

DuPont's distribution system for the consumable items was three-tiered in nature. The three tiers, in descending order of product flow, were as follows.

1. *Plants.* Two plants, located in Wilmington, Delaware, and Jonesboro, Arkansas.
2. *Regional Distribution Centers.* Four regional distribution centers, located in Atlanta, Chicago, Los Angeles, and Wilmington.
3. *Truck Terminals.* Five truck terminals, located at each of the four regional distribution centers, and at a satellite terminal in Houston.

Within this distribution system a customer order could be delivered by one of thee alternative modes. The most common delivery mode, called *direct refrigerated delivery* (DRD), involved delivery by one of the DRD trucks that drove weekly loops involving several dozen customers. The second alternative was to use an outside carrier such as air freight or motor freight. The final alternative involved a transshipment from a DRD truck to an outside carrier at a point in the truck's loop that was closer to the customer than the truck's original loading sites. The principal cost items associated with the delivery loops were fuel, truck depreciation, and driver wages.

In the design of delivery loops several constraints were imposed. First, the volume of products to be delivered on a loop could not exceed truck capacity. Second, there was a delivery service policy that permitted only daytime delivery five days per week. Finally, due to driver safety considerations, some constraints on the amount of time a driver could work consecutively were necessary.

The tactical issues considered concerned recurring decisions on the assignment of customers to delivery mode, truck terminal, and specific loops. The goal of redesigning the distribution system was to create loops that minimized the cost of

Source: L. Marshall Fisher, Arnold J. Greenfield, R. Jaikumar, and Joseph T. Lester, "A computerized vehicle routing application," *Interfaces* (August 1982), Vol. 12 No. 4, pp. 42–52.

fuel, driver time, and vehicle depreciation subject to the constraints discussed earlier. Prior to this study, the redesign process was done semiannually in a manual fashion.

The study was also concerned with one major strategic issue, namely the appropriate future role for satellite terminals. While the Houston satellite was very successful, management felt that further analysis was required before the expansion of satellites could be justified. Also, the number, location, and size of satellites were important questions.

To answer the various tactical and strategic questions a project team from the University of Pennsylvania developed and implemented a flexible, computerized vehicle routing program called ROVER (real time optimizer for vehicle routing). This computer package was used to determine which customers should be assigned to each vehicle and specified the order in which customers were assigned to each vehicle in order to minimize total travel cost. The assignment of customers to vehicles was obtained by solving a linear generalized assignment problem whose objective function approximated delivery cost. The optimization method used for this assignment problem was based on the Lagrange multiplier method discussed in this chapter. The algorithm using Lagrange multipliers was about ten times faster than existing generalized assignment problem optimization methods.

Implementation of the ROVER model by E. I. DuPont, Inc., resulted in a greatly improved delivery system. The company reported that its overall delivery costs for consumable products for its automatic clinical analyzer were reduced by approximately 15 percent in the continental United States and Canada. Recent use of the ROVER model has reduced delivery costs in Europe by about 10 percent.

CHAPTER

23

INTEGRATION AND IMPLEMENTATION OF MANAGEMENT SCIENCE TECHNIQUES IN THE DECISION FRAMEWORK

23.1 INTRODUCTION

The previous chapters in this textbook have dealt with the major topical areas of management science, and the focus has been on the quantitative methods most often used by decision makers in complex situations in business. The importance of problem formulation and the interpretation of model solution has been stressed throughout the book. In many cases, the structure of the underlying algorithms needed to solve the formulated mathematical models was emphasized, since a firm grasp of the solution methodology is necessary to intelligently interpret the results of the model solution.

What needs to be emphasized at this point is the fact that these techniques, the quantitative techniques of management science, do not make the decisions—managers make decisions. These techniques do, however, provide important information to the decision maker in the decision-making process. Thus, management science needs to be viewed as more than a collection of models and appropriate algorithms. Certainly, a competent user must be able to formulate the problem, select the appropriate solution technique, generate the solution, and interpret the results of the solution process. These activities alone generally will not assure positive benefit from the modeling process. The results must be *implemented* or the results of the modeling process must be used to delineate the policy or solution that is ultimately implemented. A model is an abstraction of a real-world situation. Simplifying assumptions are necessary in most cases when dealing in complex decision environments and these simplifications are very much a part of the model. They must be considered when the model results are used in formulating policy.

A major role of the management science specialist is to understand how the model results (which requires a complete understanding of the entire modeling process from formulation to solution) relate to the complex environment being modeled. Thus, the model results as well as the model assumptions must be considered when developing a solution to the problem being studied. Many model assumptions are simply omissions of facets of the environment that cannot be adequately modeled. These omissions may be political factors or processes that we do not completely understand or over which

we have no control. Nonetheless, they are a part of the complex decision environment and must be dealt with by the management scientist.

Formulating a model and generating a model solution is often a necessary but not sufficient condition for successful problem solving. The *implementation* of a solution based on a modeling effort requires the interface of the model and its simplifying assumptions with the real world. This is also a function of the management scientist. The successful completion of this function requires: first, a thorough understanding of the models selected and used; second, accurate input into the model; third, a thorough understanding of the situation being modeled; and fourth, a great deal of creativity and imagination.

The first requirement relates directly to the objective of this textbook. The second requirement relates to the maintenance and management of an information system. The third often relates to the organizational support and the position of the management science specialist. The fourth requirement must be developed from a wide variety of life experiences. In this chapter we discuss some implementation issues, a vehicle for accumulating, organizing, and distributing information (the management information system), and the role of management science in the organizational structure.

23.2 IMPLEMENTATION OF THE MANAGEMENT SCIENCE STUDY

The meaning or definition of implementation often varies significantly across the spectrum of individuals involved in a management science study. To the manager, implementation usually means the actual use of the output of the management science project to improve the performance of the operation being modeled. The management scientist, on the other hand, often has a much broader view of implementation. From his or her point of view, implementation also includes new insight into the problem and new information, and does not necessarily require that the results recommended from the management science project be utilized explicitly.

Both of these points of view have a common property: implementation is an objective and an end result that justifies the existence and maintenance

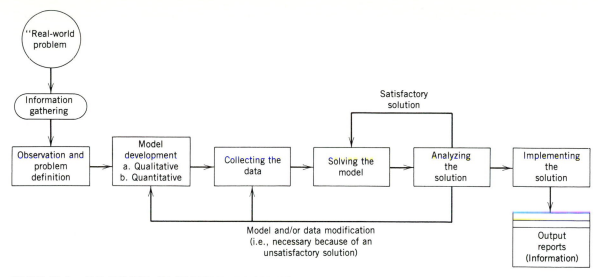

FIGURE 23.1   THE PROCESS OF QUANTITATIVE MODELING.

of a management science project. If implementation is critical, then it is important that implementation, the ultimate goal of the project, be considered in the entire process of quantitative modeling. From this perspective, implementation is not only the end result but is an integral part of the modeling process that begins with the problem definition.

Gupta (1977) supports this position and in summary his article suggests the following strategy for OR/MS studies and implementation.

1. Analyze decision situation and construct its descriptive model.
2. Establish the cause and effect relationship of decision factors influencing the manager's thinking.
3. Explore or develop appropriate information systems to secure the needed data.
4. Construct the mathematical model with explicit recognition of data requirements and availability.
5. Identify the managerial and organizational changes required by the model.
6. Obtain multiple and competitive solutions to the model.
7. Analyze each solution in terms of the consequences on decision factors.
8. Prepare a realistic cost/benefit analysis of each competitive solution.
9. Provide the manager with multiple solutions with consequences and cost/benefit analyses.
10. Aid the manager and his staff in implementing the manager's decision, *if he requests it.*[1]

If we compare these points to the process of quantitative modeling depicted in Figure 23.1 (also Figure 1.1), we see that the quantitative modeling process is not structurally modified but is rather enhanced by these points. Point 1 refers to the problem definition. Point 2 is part of the model development. Point 3 relates to the development of a decision support system that provides a mechanism for collecting the necessary and appropriate data. Points 4 and 5 are again aspects of model development. Points 6, 7, 8, 9 are aspects of solution analysis, while point 10 relates to the "physical" implementation of the solution.

The point of this discussion is that implementation is both an end result and a process. To ensure an appropriate end result, whether it be the "physical" implementation of model results or the indirect impact from the modeling effort itself, implementation must be a conscious objective in each step of the process of quantitative modeling.

---

[1]Jatinder N.D. Gupta, "Management science implementation: Experiences of a practicing O.R. manager," *Interfaces,* **7**(3) (May 1977), 84–90.

Unfortunately, noting and dealing with the fact that implementation is a process is not enough to ensure utilization of results. Grayson, in a 1972 article, indicates the following reasons for the failure to utilize results of a management science project.

1. Shortage of time required to make the management science study.
2. Inaccessibility of the data required for the management science study.
3. Resistance to change by the organization and its managers.
4. Long response time required for the management science study.
5. Invalidating simplifications that are often present in the management science study.[2]

Problems involving data availability, resistance to change, and invalidating assumptions can be addressed in the design of the management science project. The issue of time, indicated in problem areas 1 and 5, cannot be dealt with in the context of the design of the project. The scientific approach to problem solving, which involves many people within the organization, is often tedious and time-consuming. Implementation requires the "sale" of the process to people involved in the problem at various levels in the organization, and this acceptance generally takes time. Instead of focusing directly on the time frame for a management science study, it may be more productive to rely on an educated management's ability to anticipate problems and determine whether a management science project should be undertaken to develop a course of action.

Other studies conducted at Northwestern University under the leadership of Professor Albert H. Rubenstein[3] have identified 10 factors that appear to determine the success of management science groups in industry. These factors are as follows.

1. The level of managerial support including the extent of managerial understanding and ac-

ceptance of the need for management science activities.
2. The organizational location of the management science activity.
3. The adequacy of the resources allocated to the activity.
4. The receptivity of the client as manifested in the charter granted to the management science group to select projects, gather data, and implement results.
5. The strength of the opposition to the management science activity within the organization.
6. The reputation of the management science activity within the organization.
7. The general perception of the level of success of the management science activity within the organization.
8. The organization and technical capability of the management science group.
9. The relevance and practicability of the projects undertaken by the management science group.
10. The influence that the management science group and its leadership could exert within the organization.

These 10 factors indicate the importance of the working relationships among the management science group, operating management, and top management. The worth of the management science activities is also solidly based on the perceived success of the results produced by the management science group.

Even though there are many very good management science models and techniques available, implementation remains an unresolved issue. Successful implementation can become a reality with improved communication, careful planning, and a dynamic control and review process. The bottom line to success, however, rests with the manner in which the management science group presents itself within the organization. The alternatives and preferred decisions presented by the management science group have little chance of being implemented if they are not understood. A necessary condition for implementation is the education of all the individuals in the organization involved in the decision-making process, and this education is probably best provided by making sure that management is

---

[2]C. Jackson Grayson, Jr., "Management science and business practice," *Harvard Business Review,* **51**(4) (July/August 1973), 41–8.

[3]Albert H. Rubenstein *et al.,* "Some organization factors related to the effectiveness of management science groups in industry," *Management Science,* **13**(8) (April 1967), B508–B518.

an active participant in the development and use of the management science model. In the next section we discuss one increasingly important aspect of implementation, the management information system.

23.3 MANAGEMENT SCIENCE, MANAGEMENT INFORMATION SYSTEMS, AND DECISION SUPPORT SYSTEMS

Timely information that can be used as input to the decision-making framework is critical in most organizations that benefit from planning. A production manager needs an accurate demand forecast and information on general market trends in order to develop a reasonable production schedule. A loan officer needs credit information, information that will allow the timely evaluation of assets, as well as up-to-date information on existing loans for the lending institution(s) involved. A system designed to collect, organize, and filter (process) large quantities of information for an organization is known as a *management information system* (MIS). It has become common to refer to management information systems that contain management science models and other decision making tools as *decision support systems* (DSS). The general structure of a management information system is shown in Figure 23.2. An information system contains information that is relevant to a particular decision-making problem, and generally has its own data base, information retrieval capabilities, and report generating software. The

primary purpose of an information system is to support the management and decision-making functions of the organization. To be successful it must produce needed information, in a usable format, when needed.

Any management information system involves the collection of data, and most systems incorporate large volumes of data. This is often one of the most expensive aspects of the information system, since it is very labor intensive. Fortunately, recent technological changes have led to the practice of entering the data into the system at the point of transaction. Recording the transaction at the time it occurs in a form that can be read directly by the computer has lowered the cost of data collection to a point where relevant data, too expensive to record in the past, can now be economically recorded.

The large masses of data that are collected by many organizations must be systematically organized in such a way that the needs of the organization are met. The *data base* is the collection of such data. The actual data in the data base are generally structured so that they can be used for more than one application. Data are stored so that redundancy in information is minimized and so that the data are independent of the computer programs that use them. Access on demand is a vital characteristic of the data base.

The data base is created, accessed, and updated using a *data base management system* (DBMS). The data base management system is actually a collection of software that can quickly retrieve and update data. It has the ability to respond to queries on the

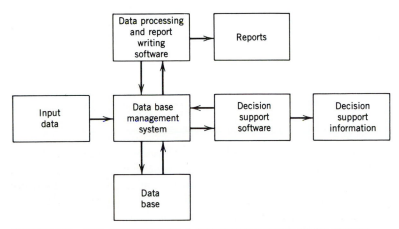

FIGURE 23.2 THE STRUCTURE OF A MANAGEMENT INFORMATION SYSTEM.

data in the data base. The data base management system is also the vehicle used to ensure data security. The development, maintenance, and control of the data base is extremely complex, and the data base management system is the computer software responsible for these tasks.

The information in the data base, managed by the data base management system, is used as input to the general data processing and report generation and the decision support software utilized by the organization. The information processing that takes place in a management information system may be as diverse as the organizations for which the information system is built. The system may simply transform the data base into summary reports that are used for control or reporting purposes. In this case, there is no real analysis of the data except for that implied by its organizational presentation. Examples of these summary reports are profit and loss statements, inventory-level reports, and departmental production reports. This type of information processing allows for timely and accurate reporting of information that describes the status of the organization's activities. Thus, a primary function of an information system is to make reporting routine.

As mentioned earlier, information processing often involves management science models. Although these models generally are not generated by the management information system itself, they can be built into the information system. Any of the management science models presented in this text can be integrated into an information system. When management science models are part of the information system, the relevant information from the data base is processed via the data base management system into a form consistent with the model input requirements. The model results are then transformed into an information format that is most beneficial to the decision maker. These reports often suggest a general course of action to the manager and/or compare alternative courses of action. Providing relevant decision support information to the decision maker is another primary function of a management information system.

As information systems become more sophisticated, they will be used more heavily to provide decision support information, and information processing will no longer be the single primary function of the system. The information system that emphasizes decision models to support the decision process

in the organization has been labeled as a decision support system. Although this term has existed for over 10 years, the implementation of this concept varies widely from one organization to another. Implementation may be slow, but the concept does provide a viable and valuable interface between operations research/management science and management information systems. A true decision support system does more than provide the decision maker with current and useful information. It provides additional information through the use of operations research models, statistical models, or other analytical models.

It is hoped that by using decision support systems we can broaden the range of decision problems that the disjoint areas of operations research and management information systems can support individually. The effective data structuring capabilities of modern information systems may indeed help us deal with many problems that are currently too large or do not fit into the structure of one of the traditional operations research/management science models.

With the development of sophisticated high-speed digital computers has come the study and design of management information systems. We have not attempted in any way to characterize this growing field. The purpose here was simply to indicate that management science models are often an important part of a management information system. The areas of MS/OR and MIS are not in any way disjoint areas that can be developed independently. Management science models and techniques are an important part of a management information system and the integration into a management information system is essential if a management science study (or management science analysis) is to achieve its maximum impact.

23.4 MANAGEMENT SCIENCE IN THE ORGANIZATION

The management science staff in businesses and in governmental, military, and industrial organizations are generally composed of people with training in mathematics, statistics, engineering (principally industrial, mechanical, or electrical), business administration, and economics. Generally, the management science staff brings together many different points of view to the problem-solving process. Often the management science staff is small and works closely with top management on a variety of planning and operational problems. Many of the larger business organizations, however, have management science departments that are quite large, involving 20 or more people.

The actual location of the management staff within the organizational structure depends on the problems addressed by this staff as well as its past success or track record within the organization. If the staff reports directly to top management, it is often involved directly in long-range planning issues and the effective utilization of all the organization's resources. On the other hand, if the management science staff reports to an officer in middle management, it is more likely that the management science staff will be involved in operational issues. The management science staff can be located just about anywhere within the organization, and there does not appear to be one location that is more typical than another.

Probably more important than the actual location of the management science staff within the organization is the integration of the management science approach to decision making within the organization. This integration is often accomplished via what is referred to as the team approach to management science, which involves individuals throughout the organization, including operating personnel. Key leadership roles in the management science staff are typically assumed by the management scientist(s). The diverse backgrounds and different levels of involvement of the individuals in the problem being studied, however, provide valuable insight into the utility and the applicability of the efforts.

The team approach to management science does not necessarily involve a large management science staff within the organization. One or several management scientists with supporting staff can successfully complete a fairly complex study with the appropriate involvement of key personnel within the organization. This is one of the major assets of the team approach to management science. Management science can exist within the organization not only if the management science staff consists of one or two people, but also if there is no management science staff or department. In many cases, members of the management team will be well versed in man-

agement science, and with the help of existing staff will be able to apply management science techniques to their individual problems. As more and more undergraduate and master's students receive thorough training in management science, the frequency of this "in-house" approach to management science will increase.

Even if there are not enough time or resources for management to carry out a management science study, the ability to identify a situation where management science techniques are applicable and potentially useful, is extremely valuable. There are many firms that specialize solely in management consulting, so that the management science staff can also be external to the business organization itself. The management science staff can be located almost anywhere within the organization. It may not formally exist, or it can be external to the organization. In any case, the successful involvement of management science in decision making is facilitated by personnel at all levels of the organizational structure that understand management science models.

23.5 SUMMARY

Management science has been integrated into many aspects of the decision-making process for a wide variety of organizations since its beginnings. More recently, with the development of the high-speed computer has come the development of a support area known as management information systems. Few will argue that the successful implementation is not enhanced by direct involvement of representative (at all levels of the organization) personnel, who will be impacted by the potential change. In order for a management science study to be implemented, it must be accepted and acceptance is usually predicated upon understanding. The necessary understanding not only involves the models and techniques but also the limits of these models and techniques imposed by the necessary simplifying assumptions. The understanding of management science helps emphasize the fact that management science does not replace the decision maker and is not a decision maker. It is simply a tool of the decision maker. Thus, the purpose of this text has been to provide a forum for the development of such understanding.

GLOSSARY

Data Base   A computerized set of raw data.

Data Base Management Systems   A software package that provides for the effective storage, access, and update capability for a data base.

Implementation   Organizational utilization of the results or benefits from a management science study.

Management Information System   A computerized system for collecting and analyzing data and generating reports.

Team Approach to Management Science   The involvement of management scientists, management, and operating personnel in the management science study.

Selected References

Ackoff, Russell, and Patrick Rivett. 1963. *A Manager's Guide to Operations Research.* New York: Wiley.

Churchman, C.N., and A.H. Schainblatt, "The researcher and the manager: A dialectic of implementation," *Management Science,* **2**(4) (February 1965), B69–B87.

Davis, Gordon B. 1974. *Management Information Systems: Conceptual Foundations, Structure and Development.* New York: McGraw–Hill.

Grayson, C. Jackson, Jr., "Management science and business practice," *Harvard Business Review,* **51**(4) (July/August 1973), 41–48.

Gupta, Jatinder N.D., "Management science implementation: Experiences of a practicing O.R. manager," *Interfaces,* **7**(3) (May 1977), 84–90.

Huysmans, Jan H.B.M. 1970. *The Implementation of Management Science.* New York: Wiley.

Markland, Robert E., and Robert J. Newett, "A subjective taxonomy for evaluating the stages of management science research," *Interfaces,* **2**(2) (January 1972), 31–39.

Miller, David W., and Martin K. Starr. 1969. *Executive Decisions and Operations Research.* Englewood Cliffs, N.J.: Prentice–Hall.

Discussion Questions

1. Discuss the inclusion of the implementation objective in each step of the process of quantitative modeling.

2. Why is the involvement of personnel at various levels in the organization important in a management science project?

3. What do you envision as the major problems in achieving the successful implementation of a management science project?

4. What should be the role of MIS within the organizational structure?

5. Why are advances in computer technology so important to the management scientist and the organization?

6. Suppose that an auto manufacturer is considering the production of a new model sports car at a plant that is currently manufacturing a sedan with a stable demand. A management science team needs to be found to study this possibility. What types of people should be included in this project?

Application Review

North American Van Lines, Inc.: A Decision Support System for Fleet Management

North American Van Lines, Inc., is a trucking transportation company with over 3300 vehicles in its independent owner-operator fleet. A Fleet Administration Division assumes the responsibility for managing the company's fleet of tractors. The Fleet Administration Division recruits and trains the contract truckers, procures new tractors, trades used tractors, purchases used tractors as well as sells new tractors to the contract truckers, and provides warranty, insurance, and financing arrangements to the contract truckers. The Fleet Administration Division's charge is to minimize the company's cost of maintaining and carrying equipment. Providing the services mentioned involves a process that is quite complex and incorporates hundreds of variables and constraints. Some of the major components that must be considered are listed here.

1. The net contribution from the sale of tractors of different model years, makes, and axle types to contract truckers and manufacturers during the year.
2. Physical training capacity.
3. Expected demand and preferred number of shipments per contract trucker.
4. Availability of tractor inventory by model year, make, and axle type.
5. Agreement with tractor manufacturers.
6. Complex external financing agreements.

The manual financial planning model used by Fleet Administration generated financial plans through an iterative monthly process. The manual system was excessively costly and time-consuming to generate. The process required one to two weeks to generate a plan so that only a few scenarios could be examined. It is also important to note that the manual system was a descriptive model and thus had little design-aiding capability.

The decision support system developed a minimum expense mix of tractors to sell contract truckers and to trade to manufacturers using a large-scale linear programming model. The system generates a number of descriptive reports that illustrate the financial impact of adopting the suggested sales mix. These reports also provide an operational plan for implementation. An overview flow chart description of the decision support system is given in Figure 23.3.

The project was divided into four phases: the documentation of the existing system, the conceptual design, detail design, and implementation. The project was completed within one fiscal year with a team consisting of seven people. The success of the project was attributed to the following factors.

1. The project enjoyed the enthusiastic support of top management, which provided the necessary resources.
2. The end user of the system had a graduate degree in operations research and understood the conceptual design of the system. He sold the linear programming approach to management.
3. The test time for the system was readily available on the company's computer.
4. The project enjoyed the commitment of individual team members.

Source: Dan Avramovich, Thomas M. Cook, Gary D. Langston, and Frank Sutherland, "A decision support system for fleet management: A linear programming approach," *Interfaces* (June 1982), Vol. 12, No. 3, pp. 1–9.

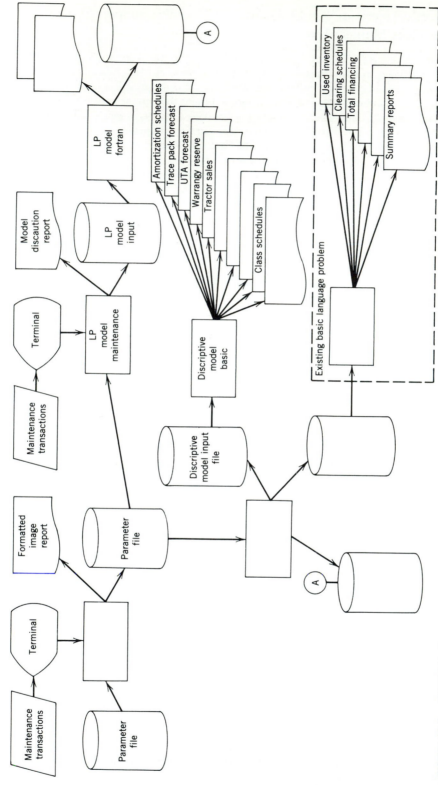

FIGURE 23.3 FINANCIAL PLANNING AND FORECASTING SYSTEM.

The decision support system developed helped fleet management make operating decisions crucial to the profitability of the company. The nonrecurring development cost was approximately $100,000, and implementation resulted in a reduction in average inventory by $3 million and an approximate savings of $600,000 a year in tractor inventory cost. The timeliness of the planning process was also enhanced. Instead of one iteration of the planning process requiring one or two weeks, three iterations could be accomplished in a single day. Probably the most important benefit of the decision support system was the elimination of three man-weeks of labor. Now management can spend its time interpreting the model results rather than supervising the manual effort.

APPENDIX

A

MATRIX NOTATION AND MATRIX ALGEBRA

A *matrix* is a rectangular array of numbers where position in that array is significant. Consider the array of numbers that defines matrix A.

$$A = \begin{bmatrix} 4 & 5 & 6 \\ 2 & 3 & 4 \\ 1 & 0 & 2 \end{bmatrix}$$

Matrix A consists of three rows and three columns. Position is defined in terms of these rows and columns. The numbers 2, 3 and 4 are in the second row and the numbers 5, 3 and 0 are in the second column. The position of the element or number 3 is then said to be in the second row and second column. In general, elements in the matrix are written as a_{ij}, where i designates the row number and j designates the column number. Thus

$$a_{11} = 4$$

$$a_{13} = 6$$

$$a_{31} = 1$$

$$\vdots$$

The dimension of a matrix is "the number of rows by the number of columns." Matrix A, is a three-by-three (3×3) matrix and is also said to be a *square matrix*. The diagonal of a square matrix is the set of all elements a_{ij}, where $i = j$. A square matrix, with $a_{ij} = 1$ if $i = j$, and $a_{ij} = 0$ if $i \neq j$, is called the identity matrix. The three-by-three identity matrix, I_3 is written

$$I_3 = \begin{bmatrix} 1 & 0 & 0 \\ 0 & 1 & 0 \\ 0 & 0 & 1 \end{bmatrix}$$

Some of the standard matrix operations are now reviewed. Matrices can be added or subtracted if they have the same dimension. The addition or subtraction is performed by adding or subtracting the corresponding elements from the original matrices. The result is a new matrix with exactly the same dimension. The following example illustrates these two operations.

$$\underset{(3\times2)}{A} = \begin{bmatrix} 4 & 2 \\ 5 & 6 \\ 0 & -1 \end{bmatrix} \qquad \underset{(3\times2)}{B} = \begin{bmatrix} 1 & -2 \\ 3 & 2 \\ 4 & 5 \end{bmatrix}$$

$$\underset{(3\times2)}{A+B} = \begin{bmatrix} 4+1 & 2-2 \\ 5+3 & 6+2 \\ 0+4 & -1+5 \end{bmatrix} = \begin{bmatrix} 5 & 0 \\ 8 & 8 \\ 4 & 4 \end{bmatrix}$$

$$\underset{(3\times2)}{A-B} = \begin{bmatrix} 4-1 & 2-(-2) \\ 5-3 & 6-2 \\ 0-4 & -1-5 \end{bmatrix} = \begin{bmatrix} 3 & 4 \\ 2 & 4 \\ -4 & -6 \end{bmatrix}$$

Matrix multiplication is slightly more complex. Two matrices may be multiplied only if the number of columns in the first matrix is equal to the number of rows in the second matrix. Thus it should be noted that if the matrix multiplication $A \cdot B$ is defined, the matrix product $B \cdot A$ may not be defined. Also, in general, we cannot say that $A \cdot B = B \cdot A$, even if the products are both defined. The matrix product is determined by the sum of the "products" of the rows in the first matrix and the columns in the second matrix. For example, suppose that A is a 2×2 matrix and B is a 2×3 matrix. We first observe that $A \cdot B$ is defined, while $B \cdot A$ is not defined. We write both A and B in general form to illustrate the concept of matrix multiplication.

$$\underset{(2\times2)}{A} = \begin{bmatrix} a_{11} & a_{12} \\ a_{21} & a_{22} \end{bmatrix} \quad \underset{(2\times3)}{B} = \begin{bmatrix} b_{11} & b_{12} & b_{13} \\ b_{21} & b_{22} & b_{23} \end{bmatrix}$$

$$A \cdot B = \begin{bmatrix} a_{11}b_{11} + a_{12}b_{21} & a_{11}b_{12} + a_{12}b_{22} & a_{11}b_{13} + a_{12}b_{23} \\ a_{21}b_{11} + a_{22}b_{21} & a_{21}b_{12} + a_{22}b_{22} & a_{21}b_{13} + a_{22}b_{23} \end{bmatrix}$$

The dimension of the product matrix is the number of rows in the first matrix by the number of columns in the second matrix. We now illustrate this process for two particular matrices.

$$\underset{(3\times2)}{A} = \begin{bmatrix} 4 & 2 \\ 2 & -1 \\ 2 & 3 \end{bmatrix} \quad \underset{(2\times3)}{B} = \begin{bmatrix} 1 & 0 & 6 \\ 2 & 3 & 5 \end{bmatrix}$$

$$\underset{(3\times3)}{A \cdot B} = \begin{bmatrix} (4)(1)+(2)(2) & (4)(0)+(2)(3) & (4)(6)+(2)(5) \\ (2)(1)+(-1)(2) & (2)(0)+(-1)(3) & (2)(6)+(-1)(5) \\ (2)(1)+(3)(2) & (2)(0)+(3)(3) & (2)(6)+(3)(5) \end{bmatrix}$$

$$= \begin{bmatrix} 9 & 6 & 34 \\ 0 & -3 & 7 \\ 7 & 9 & 27 \end{bmatrix}$$

In matrix algebra, the inverse of a matrix bears the same relationship to that matrix that the reciprocal of a number bears to that number in ordinary arithmetic. In matrix algebra the inverse of a matrix A, A^{-1}, has the property that when it is multiplied with A, the result is an identity matrix of appropriate dimension. That is, A^{-1} is the inverse of A only if

$$A^{-1}A = AA^{-1} = I$$

This definition indicates that the order of multiplication involving a matrix and its inverse does not matter. Therefore, only square matrices can have inverses, although not all do. The definition of the inverse is illustrated with the following example.

$$A = \begin{bmatrix} 3 & -1 & 2 \\ 2 & 1 & 1 \\ 1 & -3 & 0 \end{bmatrix} \quad A^{-1} = \begin{bmatrix} -1/2 & 1 & 1/2 \\ -1/6 & 2/6 & -1/6 \\ 7/6 & -8/6 & -5/6 \end{bmatrix}$$

$$AA^{-1} = \begin{bmatrix} 3 & -1 & 2 \\ 2 & 1 & 1 \\ 1 & -3 & 0 \end{bmatrix}\begin{bmatrix} -1/2 & 1 & 1/2 \\ -1/6 & 2/6 & -1/6 \\ 7/6 & -8/6 & -5/6 \end{bmatrix} = \begin{bmatrix} 1 & 0 & 0 \\ 0 & 1 & 0 \\ 0 & 0 & 1 \end{bmatrix}$$

$$A^{-1}A = \begin{bmatrix} -1/2 & 1 & 1/2 \\ -1/6 & 2/6 & -1/6 \\ 7/6 & -8/6 & -5/6 \end{bmatrix}\begin{bmatrix} 3 & -1 & 2 \\ 2 & 1 & 1 \\ 1 & -3 & 0 \end{bmatrix} = \begin{bmatrix} 1 & 0 & 0 \\ 0 & 1 & 0 \\ 0 & 0 & 1 \end{bmatrix}$$

This example verifies that the matrix labeled as A^{-1} is indeed the inverse of the matrix labeled A. We still need to be able to construct the inverse matrix, however. One convenient way for computing the inverse matrix is known as the Gauss-Jordan elimination procedure. This procedure begins with a matrix called an augmented matrix. That is, we combine matrix A and the identity matrix into a single partitioned matrix

$$[A|I]$$

If matrix A is defined as above, the resulting augmented matrix is as follows

$$\begin{bmatrix} 3 & -1 & 2 & 1 & 0 & 0 \\ 2 & 1 & 1 & 0 & 1 & 0 \\ 1 & -3 & 1 & 0 & 0 & 1 \end{bmatrix}$$

The Gauss-Jordan elimination method involves a sequence of "row operations" that transforms the A matrix to the identity matrix. These row operations when applied to the augmented matrix will also transform the identity matrix to the matrix A^{-1}. In other words, the Gauss-Jordan method transforms $[A|I]$ to $[I|A^{-1}]$.

The term *row operation* refers to the application of simple algebraic operations to the rows of the augmented matrix. The three basic row operations are as follows.

1. Any two rows of a matrix may be interchanged.

2. Any row of a matrix may be multiplied by a nonzero constant.

3. Any multiple of one row may be added to another row of that matrix, element by element.

To illustrate the Gauss-Jordan elimination procedure, we construct the inverse of matrix A. The Gauss-Jordan method systematically transforms columns of the A matrix to columns of an identity matrix. In other words, if

$$A = \begin{bmatrix} 3 & -1 & 2 \\ 2 & 1 & 1 \\ 1 & -3 & 0 \end{bmatrix}$$

the first sequence of row operations transforms the column

$$\begin{bmatrix} 3 \\ 2 \\ 1 \end{bmatrix} \quad \text{to} \quad \begin{bmatrix} 1 \\ 0 \\ 0 \end{bmatrix}$$

To compute the inverse matrix, we augment matrix A with I.

$$\begin{bmatrix} 3 & -1 & 2 & 1 & 0 & 0 \\ 2 & 1 & 1 & 0 & 1 & 0 \\ 1 & -3 & 0 & 0 & 0 & 1 \end{bmatrix}$$

Since our first goal is to perform a row operation that will result in a transformed augmented matrix with a "1" in the first row and first column, a simple exchange of rows 1 and 3 is performed. (It should be noted that the same result could be achieved by multiplying the first row by 1/3.)

$$\begin{bmatrix} 1 & -3 & 0 & | & 0 & 0 & 1 \\ 2 & 1 & 1 & | & 0 & 1 & 0 \\ 3 & -1 & 1 & | & 1 & 0 & 0 \end{bmatrix}$$

Needed next is a row operation that results in an element of zero in the second row and first column. The particular row operation needed is: row 1 is multiplied by -2 and the result is added to row 2.

$$\begin{bmatrix} 1 & -3 & 0 & | & 0 & 0 & 1 \\ 0 & 7 & 1 & | & 0 & 1 & -2 \\ 3 & -1 & 1 & | & 1 & 0 & 0 \end{bmatrix}$$

Next row 1 is multiplied by -3 and the result is added to row 3.

$$\begin{bmatrix} 1 & -3 & 0 & | & 0 & 0 & 1 \\ 0 & 7 & 1 & | & 0 & 1 & -2 \\ 0 & 8 & 2 & | & 1 & 0 & -3 \end{bmatrix}$$

The second sequence of row operations transforms the column

$$\begin{bmatrix} -3 \\ 7 \\ 8 \end{bmatrix} \text{ to } \begin{bmatrix} 0 \\ 1 \\ 0 \end{bmatrix}$$

The first row operation multiplies the second row by 1/7.

$$\begin{bmatrix} 1 & -3 & 0 & | & 0 & 0 & 1 \\ 0 & 1 & 1/7 & | & 0 & 1/7 & -2/7 \\ 0 & 8 & 2 & | & 1 & 0 & -3 \end{bmatrix}$$

The next two row operations are as follows: multiply the second row by 3 and add it to the first row, and multiply the second row by -8 and add it to row 3.

$$\begin{bmatrix} 1 & 0 & 3/7 & | & 0 & 3/7 & 1/7 \\ 0 & 1 & 1/7 & | & 0 & 1/7 & -2/7 \\ 0 & 0 & 6/7 & | & 1 & -8/7 & -5/7 \end{bmatrix}$$

The final set of elementary row operations transforms the column

$$\begin{bmatrix} 3/7 \\ 1/7 \\ 6/7 \end{bmatrix} \text{ to } \begin{bmatrix} 0 \\ 0 \\ 1 \end{bmatrix}$$

The first row operation in this set multiplies the third row by 7/6.

$$\begin{bmatrix} 1 & 0 & 3/7 & | & 0 & 3/7 & 1/7 \\ 0 & 1 & 1/7 & | & 0 & 1/7 & -2/7 \\ 0 & 0 & 1 & | & 7/6 & -8/6 & -5/6 \end{bmatrix}$$

Finally, the third row is multiplied by $-1/7$ and added to the second row, while the third row is multiplied by $-3/7$ and added to the first row.

$$\begin{bmatrix} 1 & 0 & 0 & | & -1/2 & 1 & 1/2 \\ 0 & 1 & 0 & | & -1/6 & 2/6 & -1/6 \\ 0 & 0 & 1 & | & 7/6 & -8/6 & -5/6 \end{bmatrix}$$

Recall that the sequence of nine row operations lead from $[A|I]$ to $[I|A^{-1}]$, and thus A^{-1} can be read from the augmented matrix above.

One of the most important applications of matrix algebra and row operations is in the representation and solution of systems of linear equations. Consider a set of three linear equations in three variables.

$$a_{11}x_1 + a_{12}x_2 + a_{13}x_3 = b_1$$

$$a_{21}x_1 + a_{22}x_2 + a_{23}x_3 = b_2$$

$$a_{31}x_1 + a_{32}x_2 + a_{33}x_3 = b_3$$

Matrix notation can be used to write these three equations as

$$A \cdot x = b$$

where A is the coefficient matrix

$$A = \begin{bmatrix} a_{11} & a_{12} & a_{13} \\ a_{21} & a_{22} & a_{23} \\ a_{31} & a_{32} & a_{33} \end{bmatrix}$$

x is the solution vector

$$x = \begin{bmatrix} x_1 \\ x_2 \\ x_3 \end{bmatrix}$$

and b is the right-hand-side vector

$$b = \begin{bmatrix} b_1 \\ b_2 \\ b_3 \end{bmatrix}$$

Verify this representation by performing the indicated matrix multiplication. That is,

$$\begin{bmatrix} a_{11}x_1 + a_{12}x_2 + a_{13}x_3 \\ a_{21}x_1 + a_{22}x_2 + a_{23}x_3 \\ a_{31}x_1 + a_{32}x_2 + a_{33}x_3 \end{bmatrix} = \begin{bmatrix} b_1 \\ b_2 \\ b_3 \end{bmatrix}$$

and we note that two matrices are equal only if their corresponding elements are identical. Thus the matrix representation is valid.

Given the matrix representation of a linear system

$$A \cdot x = b$$

it is not difficult to see how the matrix inverse can be used to solve the linear system if the coefficient matrix has an inverse. Each side of the matrix equation $A \cdot x = b$ is multiplied by A^{-1}.

$$[A^{-1} \cdot A]x = A^{-1}b$$

Since $A^{-1}A = I$, the equation reduces to

$$Ix = A^{-1}b$$

and since $Ix = x$

$$x = A^{-1}b$$

For example, consider the linear system

$$3x_1 - x_2 + 2x_3 = 18$$

$$2x_1 + x_2 + x_3 = 6$$

$$x_1 - 3x_2 \qquad = 12$$

The coefficient matrix A is

$$A = \begin{bmatrix} 3 & -1 & 2 \\ 2 & 1 & 1 \\ 1 & -3 & 0 \end{bmatrix}$$

and the inverse was calculated to be

$$A^{-1} = \begin{bmatrix} -1/2 & 1 & 1/2 \\ -1/6 & 2/6 & -1/6 \\ 7/6 & -8/6 & -5/6 \end{bmatrix}$$

By the method described we compute x as follows

$$x = A^{-1}b$$

or

$$x = \begin{bmatrix} -1/2 & 1 & 1/2 \\ -1/6 & 2/6 & -1/6 \\ 7/6 & -8/6 & -5/6 \end{bmatrix} \begin{bmatrix} 18 \\ 6 \\ 12 \end{bmatrix} = \begin{bmatrix} 3 \\ -3 \\ 3 \end{bmatrix}$$

Since

$$x = \begin{bmatrix} x_1 \\ x_2 \\ x_3 \end{bmatrix} = \begin{bmatrix} 3 \\ -3 \\ 3 \end{bmatrix}$$

the solution to the linear system is $x_1 = 3$, $x_2 = -3$, and $x_3 = 3$.

If we are solving a linear system of equations, generally we do not compute A^{-1} directly. Instead, we use the following augmented matrix.

$$[A|b] = \begin{bmatrix} 3 & -1 & 2 & 18 \\ 2 & 1 & 1 & 6 \\ 1 & -3 & 0 & 12 \end{bmatrix}$$

The same sequence of row operations used to compute A^{-1} transforms this augmented matrix to

$$[I|A^{-1}b] = \begin{bmatrix} 1 & 0 & 0 & 3 \\ 0 & 1 & 0 & -3 \\ 0 & 0 & 1 & 3 \end{bmatrix}$$

Given the three sequences of row operations directed at each respective column of the coefficient matrix, the first sequence transforms

$$\begin{bmatrix} 3 & -1 & 2 & 18 \\ 2 & 1 & 1 & 6 \\ 1 & -3 & 0 & 12 \end{bmatrix}$$

to

$$\begin{bmatrix} 1 & -3 & 0 & 12 \\ 0 & 7 & 1 & -18 \\ 0 & 8 & 2 & -18 \end{bmatrix}$$

The result of the second sequence is

$$\begin{bmatrix} 1 & 0 & 3/7 & 30/7 \\ 0 & 1 & 1/7 & -18/7 \\ 0 & 0 & 6/7 & 18/7 \end{bmatrix}$$

The result of the third sequence is

$$\begin{bmatrix} 1 & 0 & 0 & 3 \\ 0 & 1 & 0 & -3 \\ 0 & 0 & 1 & 3 \end{bmatrix}$$

Here we have described the use of row operations to solve a linear system of equations when there are the same number of variables as equations and when the inverse of the matrix can be computed.

Typically, in linear programming we must solve linear systems of equations where there are more variables than equations. Certainly, we are not able to find the inverse of the coefficient matrix, since generally it is not square. Elementary row operations, however, are still utilized to identify special solutions to these systems, called basic solutions. The concept of generating basic solutions by the use of row operations to solve linear systems with more variables than equations is discussed in Chapter 8.

APPENDIX

B

DIFFERENTIAL CALCULUS REVIEW

In this textbook we have avoided the use of differential calculus in our presentation, when feasible. Chapter 22 on Nonlinear Programming, however, is an application of differential calculus to some nonlinear optimization models. In this appendix we review the concept of a derivative and a partial derivative and list some of the more important differentiation formulas.

Differential calculus is concerned with the slope, or the rate of change of a function at any given point on the function. To illustrate the basic concept of a derivative, consider the function in Figure B.1. The derivative of a function evaluated at a point a or $(x_0, f(x_0))$ is defined to be the slope of the line tangent to the graph of the function at a. The derivative measures the instantaneous rate of change of a function, $f(x)$, with respect to x. To actually determine this instantaneous rate of change or slope, differential calculus determines a series of successively better approximations to the slope of the tangent line. To illustrate the basic calculation in differential calculus and the interpretation of the derivative as an instantaneous rate of change, consider Figure B.1. Assuming that we move a small distance along the curve to point b or $(x_0 + \Delta x, f(x_0 + \Delta x))$, the slope of the line connecting a and b is given by

$$\frac{\Delta y}{\Delta x} = \frac{f(x_0 + \Delta x) - f(x_0)}{(x_0 + \Delta x) - x_0}$$

As Δx approaches zero, the slope of the line from a to b can be seen to approach the slope of the tangent to the curve at point a. We say that the limit as Δx approaches zero is the slope of the tangent to the curve at point a, and we write

$$\lim_{\Delta x \to 0} \frac{\Delta y}{\Delta x} = \lim_{\Delta x \to 0} \frac{f(x_0 + \Delta x) - f(x_0)}{\Delta x} = f'(x_0)$$
$$= \text{slope of the tangent to the curve}$$
$$\text{at point } a \text{ or } (x_0, f(x_0)).$$

The notation used, $f'(x_0)$, denotes the first derivative of the function f for a particular value of the independent variable x. In general, the common notation for the derivative (first derivative) of a function follows

$$\frac{df(x)}{dx} \quad \text{or} \quad \frac{dy}{dx} \quad \text{or} \quad f'(x)$$

In many cases, we want to compute derivatives of derivatives, higher order derivatives. For example, the second derivative of a function is denoted as

$$\frac{d^2 f(x)}{dx^2} \quad \text{or} \quad \frac{d^2 y}{dx^2} \quad \text{or} \quad f''(x)$$

Geometrically, it represents the rate of change of the slope of the function f. Thus the second derivative is simply the derivative of the function that represents the instantaneous rate of change for the function f. The first and second derivatives are used in Chapter 22 to find points where a nonlinear function assumes a maximum or minimum value.

A number of differentiation formulas have been established and the more common ones are listed here.

$$y = a; \frac{dy}{dx} = 0$$

$$y = x; \frac{dy}{dx} = 1$$

$$y = ax + b; \frac{dy}{dx} = a$$

$$y = x^n; \frac{dy}{dx} = nx^{n-1}$$

$$y = e^x; \frac{dy}{dx} = e^x$$

$$y = [f(x) \pm g(x) \pm \cdots];$$
$$\frac{dy}{dx} = \frac{df(x)}{dx} \pm \frac{dg(x)}{dx} \pm \cdots$$

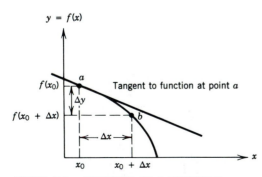

FIGURE B.1 DEFINITION OF A DERIVATIVE.

$$y = f(x) \cdot g(x);$$

$$\frac{dy}{dx} = f(x)\frac{dg(x)}{dx} + g(x)\frac{df(x)}{dx}$$

$$y = \frac{f(x)}{g(x)};$$

$$\frac{dy}{dx} = \frac{g(x)[df(x)/dx] - f(x)[dg(x)/dx]}{[g(x)]^2}$$

$$y = \log_e x; \quad \frac{dy}{dx} = \frac{1}{x}$$

$$y = \log_a u; \quad \frac{dy}{dx} = \frac{1}{u \log_e a}\frac{du}{dx}$$

(where u is a function of x)

$$y = a^x; \quad \frac{dy}{dx} = a^x \log_e a$$

$$y = au; \quad \frac{dy}{dx} = a\frac{du}{dx}$$

(where u is a function of x)

$$y = [f(x)]^n;$$

$$\frac{dy}{dx} = n[f(x)]^{n-1}\frac{df(x)}{dx}$$

$$y = e^{f(x)};$$

$$\frac{dy}{dx} = [e^{f(x)}]\frac{df(x)}{dx}$$

In Chapter 22 the concept of a partial derivative is also employed. This concept is required when a function has more than one independent variable. If y is a dependent variable and x_1 and x_2 are independent variables, the function is written as $y = f(x_1, x_2)$. Partial differentiation treats all but one of the independent variables as a constant and then proceeds as in ordinary differentiation. Partial derivatives characterize the slope of the function relative to one independent variable at a time and thus from a geometric point of view, provide the rate of change of the function in a particular direction.

In this process the partial derivative of the function y with respect to an independent variable x_1 is denoted as

$$\frac{\partial y}{\partial x_1} \quad \text{or} \quad \frac{\partial f(x_1, x_2)}{\partial x_2}$$

A function having n independent variables will have n partial derivatives. Figure B.2 illustrates the two partial derivatives of $y = f(x_1, x_2)$ as rates of change in a particular direction. In the figure the partial derivative of y with respect to x_1, $\partial y/\partial x_1$, can be seen to be the rate of change of the function $y =$

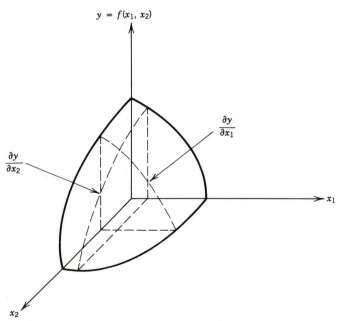

FIGURE B.2 GEOMETRIC INTERPRETATION OF THE PARTIAL DERIVATIVE.

$f(x_1, x_2)$ in the direction that is parallel to the plane defined by the coordinate axes, x_1 and y. It is the slope of the tangent to the curve of intersection of the surface $y = f(x_1, x_2)$ and the plane $x_2 = k$, where k is some specified constant. Similarly $\partial y / \partial x_2$ is the rate of change of the function in the direction that is parallel to the plane defined by the coordinate axes x_2 and y.

A P P E N D I X
C

TABLES

T A B L E

C.1

BINOMIAL PROBABILITY

Reported values are $p(y \le a) = \sum_{y=0}^{a} p(y)$. For example, if $n = 5$ and $p = .40$

$$p(y \le 3) = .913$$
$$p(y = 3) = p(y \le 3) - p(y \le 2)$$
$$= .913 - .683 = .230$$

TABLE C.1 BINOMIAL PROBABILITY

(a) n = 5

a	.01	.05	.10	.20	.30	.40	.50	.60	.70	.80	.90	.95	.99
0	.951	.774	.590	.328	.168	.078	.031	.010	.002	.000	.000	.000	.000
1	.999	.977	.919	.737	.528	.337	.188	.087	.031	.007	.000	.000	.000
2	1.000	.999	.991	.942	.837	.683	.500	.317	.163	.058	.009	.001	.000
3	1.000	1.000	1.000	.993	.969	.913	.812	.663	.472	.263	.081	.023	.001
4	1.000	1.000	1.000	1.000	.998	.990	.969	.922	.832	.672	.410	.226	.049

(b) n = 10

a	.01	.05	.10	.20	.30	.40	.50	.60	.70	.80	.90	.95	.99
0	.904	.599	.349	.107	.028	.006	.001	.000	.000	.000	.000	.000	.000
1	.996	.914	.736	.376	.149	.046	.011	.002	.000	.000	.000	.000	.000
2	1.000	.988	.930	.678	.383	.167	.055	.012	.002	.000	.000	.000	.000
3	1.000	.999	.987	.879	.650	.382	.172	.055	.011	.001	.000	.000	.000
4	1.000	1.000	.998	.967	.850	.633	.377	.166	.047	.006	.000	.000	.000
5	1.000	1.000	1.000	.994	.953	.834	.623	.367	.150	.033	.002	.000	.000
6	1.000	1.000	1.000	.999	.989	.945	.828	.618	.350	.121	.013	.001	.000
7	1.000	1.000	1.000	1.000	.998	.988	.945	.833	.617	.322	.070	.012	.000
8	1.000	1.000	1.000	1.000	1.000	.998	.989	.954	.851	.624	.264	.086	.004
9	1.000	1.000	1.000	1.000	1.000	1.000	.999	.994	.972	.893	.651	.401	.096

(c) n = 15

a	.01	.05	.10	.20	.30	.40	.50	.60	.70	.80	.90	.95	.99
0	.860	.463	.206	.035	.005	.000	.000	.000	.000	.000	.000	.000	.000
1	.990	.829	.549	.167	.035	.005	.000	.000	.000	.000	.000	.000	.000
2	1.000	.964	.816	.398	.127	.027	.004	.000	.000	.000	.000	.000	.000
3	1.000	.995	.944	.648	.297	.091	.018	.002	.000	.000	.000	.000	.000
4	1.000	.999	.987	.836	.515	.217	.059	.009	.001	.000	.000	.000	.000
5	1.000	1.000	.998	.939	.722	.403	.151	.034	.004	.000	.000	.000	.000
6	1.000	1.000	1.000	.982	.869	.610	.304	.095	.015	.001	.000	.000	.000
7	1.000	1.000	1.000	.996	.950	.787	.500	.213	.050	.004	.000	.000	.000
8	1.000	1.000	1.000	.999	.985	.905	.696	.390	.131	.018	.000	.000	.000
9	1.000	1.000	1.000	1.000	.996	.966	.849	.597	.278	.061	.002	.000	.000
10	1.000	1.000	1.000	1.000	.999	.991	.941	.783	.485	.164	.013	.001	.000
11	1.000	1.000	1.000	1.000	1.000	.998	.982	.909	.703	.352	.056	.005	.000
12	1.000	1.000	1.000	1.000	1.000	1.000	.996	.973	.873	.602	.184	.036	.000
13	1.000	1.000	1.000	1.000	1.000	1.000	1.000	.995	.965	.833	.451	.171	.010
14	1.000	1.000	1.000	1.000	1.000	1.000	1.000	1.000	.995	.965	.794	.537	.140

TABLE C.1   755

TABLE C.1 (CONTINUED)

(d) $n = 20$

a	.01	.05	.10	.20	.30	.40	.50	.60	.70	.80	.90	.95	.99	a
0	.818	.358	.122	.002	.001	.000	.000	.000	.000	.000	.000	.000	.000	0
1	.983	.736	.392	.069	.008	.001	.000	.000	.000	.000	.000	.000	.000	1
2	.999	.925	.677	.206	.035	.004	.000	.000	.000	.000	.000	.000	.000	2
3	1.000	.984	.867	.411	.107	.016	.001	.000	.000	.000	.000	.000	.000	3
4	1.000	.997	.957	.630	.238	.051	.006	.000	.000	.000	.000	.000	.000	4
5	1.000	1.000	.989	.804	.416	.126	.021	.002	.000	.000	.000	.000	.000	5
6	1.000	1.000	.998	.913	.608	.250	.058	.006	.000	.000	.000	.000	.000	6
7	1.000	1.000	1.000	.968	.772	.416	.132	.021	.001	.000	.000	.000	.000	7
8	1.000	1.000	1.000	.990	.887	.596	.252	.057	.005	.000	.000	.000	.000	8
9	1.000	1.000	1.000	.997	.952	.755	.412	.128	.017	.001	.000	.000	.000	9
10	1.000	1.000	1.000	.999	.983	.872	.588	.245	.048	.003	.000	.000	.000	10
11	1.000	1.000	1.000	1.000	.995	.943	.748	.404	.113	.010	.000	.000	.000	11
12	1.000	1.000	1.000	1.000	.999	.979	.868	.584	.228	.032	.000	.000	.000	12
13	1.000	1.000	1.000	1.000	1.000	.994	.942	.750	.392	.087	.002	.000	.000	13
14	1.000	1.000	1.000	1.000	1.000	.998	.979	.874	.584	.196	.011	.000	.000	14
15	1.000	1.000	1.000	1.000	1.000	1.000	.994	.949	.762	.370	.043	.003	.000	15
16	1.000	1.000	1.000	1.000	1.000	1.000	.999	.984	.893	.589	.133	.016	.000	16
17	1.000	1.000	1.000	1.000	1.000	1.000	1.000	.996	.965	.794	.323	.075	.000	17
18	1.000	1.000	1.000	1.000	1.000	1.000	1.000	.999	.992	.931	.608	.264	.001	18
19	1.000	1.000	1.000	1.000	1.000	1.000	1.000	1.000	.999	.988	.878	.642	.017	19
													.182	

(e) n = 25

p

a	.01	.05	.10	.20	.30	.40	.50	.60	.70	.80	.90	.95	.99	a
0	.778	.277	.072	.004	.000	.000	.000	.000	.000	.000	.000	.000	.000	0
1	.974	.642	.271	.027	.002	.000	.000	.000	.000	.000	.000	.000	.000	1
2	.998	.873	.537	.098	.009	.000	.000	.000	.000	.000	.000	.000	.000	2
3	1.000	.966	.764	.234	.033	.002	.000	.000	.000	.000	.000	.000	.000	3
4	1.000	.993	.902	.421	.090	.009	.000	.000	.000	.000	.000	.000	.000	4
5	1.000	.999	.967	.617	.193	.029	.002	.000	.000	.000	.000	.000	.000	5
6	1.000	1.000	.991	.780	.341	.074	.007	.000	.000	.000	.000	.000	.000	6
7	1.000	1.000	.998	.891	.512	.154	.022	.001	.000	.000	.000	.000	.000	7
8	1.000	1.000	1.000	.953	.677	.274	.054	.004	.000	.000	.000	.000	.000	8
9	1.000	1.000	1.000	.983	.811	.425	.115	.013	.000	.000	.000	.000	.000	9
10	1.000	1.000	1.000	.994	.902	.586	.212	.034	.002	.000	.000	.000	.000	10
11	1.000	1.000	1.000	.998	.956	.732	.345	.078	.006	.000	.000	.000	.000	11
12	1.000	1.000	1.000	1.000	.983	.846	.500	.154	.017	.000	.000	.000	.000	12
13	1.000	1.000	1.000	1.000	.994	.922	.655	.268	.044	.002	.000	.000	.000	13
14	1.000	1.000	1.000	1.000	.998	.966	.788	.414	.098	.006	.000	.000	.000	14
15	1.000	1.000	1.000	1.000	1.000	.987	.885	.575	.189	.017	.000	.000	.000	15
16	1.000	1.000	1.000	1.000	1.000	.996	.946	.726	.323	.047	.000	.000	.000	16
17	1.000	1.000	1.000	1.000	1.000	.999	.978	.846	.488	.109	.002	.000	.000	17
18	1.000	1.000	1.000	1.000	1.000	1.000	.993	.926	.659	.220	.009	.000	.000	18
19	1.000	1.000	1.000	1.000	1.000	1.000	.998	.971	.807	.383	.033	.001	.000	19
20	1.000	1.000	1.000	1.000	1.000	1.000	1.000	.991	.910	.579	.098	.007	.000	20
21	1.000	1.000	1.000	1.000	1.000	1.000	1.000	.998	.967	.766	.236	.034	.000	21
22	1.000	1.000	1.000	1.000	1.000	1.000	1.000	1.000	.991	.902	.463	.127	.002	22
23	1.000	1.000	1.000	1.000	1.000	1.000	1.000	1.000	.998	.973	.729	.358	.026	23
24	1.000	1.000	1.000	1.000	1.000	1.000	1.000	1.000	1.000	.996	.928	.723	.222	24

TABLE C.1   757

T A B L E
C.2

POISSON PROBABILITY

The Poisson probability function is given by

$$f(x, \lambda) = \frac{\lambda^x e^{-\lambda}}{x!} \quad \text{for } \lambda > 0,\ x = 0, 1, 2, \ldots$$

The following table contains the individual terms of $f(x, \lambda)$ for specified values of x and λ.

TABLE C.2 POISSON PROBABILITY

x	.01	.02	.03	.04	.05	.06	.07	.08	.09	.10	.15
0	.990	.980	.970	.961	.951	.942	.932	.923	.914	.905	.861
1	.010	.020	.030	.038	.048	.057	.065	.074	.082	.090	.129
2				.001	.001	.002	.002	.003	.004	.005	.010

λ

x	.20	.25	.30	.40	.50	.60	.70	.80	.90	1.0	1.1	1.2	1.3	1.4	1.5	1.6	1.7	1.8	1.9	2.0
0	.819	.779	.741	.670	.607	.549	.497	.449	.407	.368	.333	.301	.273	.247	.223	.202	.183	.165	.150	.135
1	.164	.195	.222	.268	.303	.329	.348	.359	.366	.368	.366	.361	.354	.345	.335	.323	.311	.298	.284	.271
2	.016	.024	.033	.054	.076	.099	.122	.144	.165	.184	.201	.217	.230	.242	.251	.258	.264	.268	.270	.271
3	.001	.002	.003	.007	.013	.020	.028	.038	.049	.061	.074	.087	.100	.113	.126	.138	.150	.161	.171	.180
4				.001	.002	.003	.005	.008	.011	.015	.020	.026	.032	.039	.047	.055	.064	.072	.081	.090
5							.001	.001	.002	.003	.004	.006	.008	.011	.014	.018	.022	.026	.031	.036

λ

x	2.1	2.2	2.3	2.4	2.5	2.6	2.7	2.8	2.9	3.0	3.1	3.2	3.3	3.4	3.5	3.6	3.7	3.8	3.9	4.0
0	.122	.111	.100	.091	.082	.074	.067	.061	.055	.050	.045	.041	.037	.033	.030	.027	.025	.022	.020	.018
1	.257	.244	.231	.218	.205	.193	.181	.170	.160	.149	.140	.130	.122	.113	.106	.098	.091	.085	.079	.073
2	.270	.268	.265	.261	.257	.251	.245	.238	.231	.224	.216	.209	.201	.193	.185	.177	.169	.162	.154	.147
3	.189	.197	.203	.209	.214	.218	.220	.222	.224	.224	.224	.223	.221	.219	.216	.212	.209	.205	.200	.195
4	.099	.108	.117	.125	.134	.141	.149	.156	.162	.168	.173	.178	.182	.186	.189	.191	.193	.194	.195	.195
5	.042	.048	.054	.060	.067	.074	.080	.087	.094	.101	.107	.114	.120	.126	.132	.138	.143	.148	.152	.156
6	.015	.017	.021	.024	.028	.032	.036	.041	.045	.050	.056	.061	.066	.072	.077	.083	.088	.094	.099	.104
7	.004	.005	.007	.008	.010	.012	.014	.016	.019	.022	.025	.028	.031	.035	.039	.042	.047	.051	.055	.060
8	.001	.002	.002	.002	.003	.004	.005	.006	.007	.008	.010	.011	.013	.015	.017	.019	.022	.024	.027	.030
9					.001	.001	.001	.002	.002	.003	.003	.004	.005	.006	.007	.008	.009	.010	.012	.013
10									.001	.001	.001	.001	.002	.002	.002	.003	.003	.004	.005	.005

TABLE C.2   759

TABLE C.2 (CONTINUED)

λ

x	4.1	4.2	4.3	4.4	4.5	4.6	4.7	4.8	4.9	5.0	5.1	5.2	5.3	5.4	5.5	5.6	5.7	5.8	5.9	6.0	x
0	.017	.015	.014	.012	.011	.010	.009	.008	.007	.007	.006	.006	.005	.005	.004	.004	.003	.003	.003	.002	0
1	.068	.063	.058	.054	.050	.046	.043	.040	.036	.034	.031	.029	.026	.024	.022	.021	.019	.018	.016	.015	1
2	.139	.132	.125	.119	.112	.106	.100	.095	.089	.084	.079	.075	.070	.066	.062	.058	.054	.051	.048	.045	2
3	.190	.185	.180	.174	.169	.163	.157	.152	.146	.140	.135	.129	.124	.119	.113	.108	.103	.098	.094	.089	3
4	.195	.194	.193	.192	.190	.188	.185	.182	.179	.175	.172	.168	.164	.160	.156	.152	.147	.143	.138	.134	4
5	.160	.163	.166	.169	.171	.173	.174	.175	.175	.175	.175	.175	.174	.173	.171	.170	.168	.166	.163	.161	5
6	.109	.114	.119	.124	.128	.132	.136	.140	.143	.146	.149	.151	.154	.156	.157	.158	.159	.160	.160	.161	6
7	.064	.069	.073	.078	.082	.087	.091	.096	.100	.104	.109	.113	.116	.120	.123	.127	.130	.133	.135	.138	7
8	.033	.036	.039	.043	.046	.050	.054	.058	.061	.065	.069	.073	.077	.081	.085	.089	.092	.096	.100	.103	9
9	.015	.017	.019	.021	.023	.026	.028	.031	.033	.036	.039	.042	.045	.049	.052	.055	.059	.062	.065	.069	9
10	.006	.007	.008	.009	.010	.012	.013	.015	.016	.018	.020	.022	.024	.026	.029	.031	.033	.036	.039	.041	10
11	.002	.003	.003	.004	.004	.005	.006	.006	.007	.008	.009	.010	.012	.013	.014	.016	.017	.019	.021	.023	11
12	.001	.001	.001	.001	.002	.002	.002	.003	.003	.003	.005	.005	.005	.006	.007	.007	.008	.009	.010	.011	12
13					.001	.001	.001	.001	.001	.001	.002	.002	.002	.002	.003	.003	.004	.004	.005	.005	13
14											.001	.001	.001	.001	.001	.001	.001	.002	.002	.002	14
15																	.001	.001	.001	.001	15

x	6.1	6.2	6.3	6.4	6.5	6.6	6.7	6.8	6.9	7.0	7.1	7.2	7.3	7.4	7.5	8.0	8.5	9.0	9.5	10.0
0	.002	.002	.002	.002	.002	.001	.001	.001	.001	.001	.001	.001	.001	.001	.001					
1	.014	.013	.012	.011	.010	.009	.008	.008	.007	.006	.006	.005	.005	.005	.004	.003	.002	.001	.001	
2	.042	.039	.036	.034	.032	.030	.028	.026	.024	.022	.021	.019	.018	.017	.016	.011	.007	.005	.003	.002
3	.085	.081	.077	.073	.069	.065	.062	.058	.055	.052	.049	.046	.044	.041	.039	.029	.021	.015	.011	.008
4	.129	.125	.121	.116	.112	.108	.103	.099	.095	.091	.087	.084	.080	.076	.073	.057	.044	.034	.025	.019
5	.158	.155	.152	.149	.145	.142	.138	.135	.131	.128	.124	.120	.117	.113	.109	.092	.075	.061	.048	.038
6	.160	.160	.159	.159	.157	.156	.155	.153	.151	.149	.147	.144	.142	.139	.137	.122	.107	.091	.076	.063
7	.140	.142	.144	.145	.146	.147	.148	.149	.149	.149	.149	.149	.148	.147	.146	.140	.129	.117	.104	.090
8	.107	.110	.113	.116	.119	.121	.124	.126	.128	.130	.132	.134	.135	.136	.137	.140	.138	.132	.123	.113
9	.072	.076	.079	.082	.086	.089	.092	.095	.098	.101	.104	.107	.110	.112	.114	.124	.130	.132	.130	.125
10	.044	.047	.050	.053	.056	.059	.062	.065	.068	.071	.074	.077	.080	.083	.086	.099	.110	.119	.124	.125
11	.024	.026	.029	.031	.033	.035	.038	.040	.043	.045	.048	.050	.053	.056	.059	.072	.085	.097	.107	.114
12	.012	.014	.015	.016	.018	.019	.021	.023	.025	.026	.028	.030	.032	.034	.037	.048	.060	.073	.084	.095
13	.006	.007	.007	.008	.009	.010	.011	.012	.013	.014	.015	.017	.018	.020	.021	.030	.040	.050	.062	.073
14	.003	.003	.003	.004	.004	.005	.005	.006	.006	.007	.008	.009	.009	.010	.011	.017	.024	.032	.042	.052
15	.001	.001	.001	.002	.002	.002	.002	.003	.003	.003	.004	.004	.005	.005	.006	.009	.014	.019	.027	.035
16			.001	.001	.001	.001	.001	.001	.001	.001	.002	.002	.002	.002	.003	.005	.007	.011	.016	.022
17									.001	.001	.001	.001	.001	.001	.001	.002	.004	.006	.009	.013
18																.001	.002	.003	.005	.007
19																	.001	.001	.002	.004
20																		.001	.001	.002

TABLE C.2   761

T A B L E

C.3

NORMAL PROBABILITY

The following table gives cumulative standard normal probabilities. If z is a standard normal random variable, then

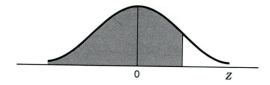

$$P(z \leq 1.33) = .90824$$

$$P(z \geq 1.33) = 1 - .90824 = .09176$$

$$P(0 \leq z \leq 1.33) = P(z \leq 1.33) - P(z \leq 0)$$

$$= .90824 - .50000$$

$$= .40824$$

TABLE C.3 NORMAL PROBABILITY

z	$F(z)$	z	$F(z)$	z	$F(z)$
−4.00	.00003	−3.60	.00016	−3.20	.00069
−3.99	.00003	−3.59	.00017	−3.19	.00071
−3.98	.00003	−3.58	.00017	−3.18	.00074
−3.97	.00004	−3.57	.00018	−3.17	.00076
−3.96	.00004	−3.56	.00019	−3.16	.00079
−3.95	.00004	−3.55	.00019	−3.15	.00082
−3.94	.00004	−3.54	.00020	−3.14	.00084
−3.93	.00004	−3.53	.00021	−3.13	.00087
−3.92	.00004	−3.52	.00022	−3.12	.00090
−3.91	.00005	−3.51	.00022	−3.11	.00094
−3.90	.00005	−3.50	.00023	−3.10	.00097
−3.89	.00005	−3.49	.00024	−3.09	.00100
−3.88	.00005	−3.48	.00025	−3.08	.00104
−3.87	.00005	−3.47	.00026	−3.07	.00107
−3.86	.00006	−3.46	.00027	−3.06	.00111
−3.85	.00006	−3.45	.00028	−3.05	.00114
−3.84	.00006	−3.44	.00029	−3.04	.00118
−3.83	.00006	−3.43	.00030	−3.03	.00122
−3.82	.00007	−3.42	.00031	−3.02	.00126
−3.81	.00007	−3.41	.00032	−3.01	.00131
−3.80	.00007	−3.40	.00034	−3.00	.00135
−3.79	.00008	−3.39	.00035	−2.99	.00139
−3.78	.00008	−3.38	.00036	−2.98	.00144
−3.77	.00008	−3.37	.00038	−2.97	.00149
−3.76	.00008	−3.36	.00039	−2.96	.00154
−3.75	.00009	−3.35	.00040	−2.95	.00159
−3.74	.00009	−3.34	.00042	−2.94	.00164
−3.73	.00010	−3.33	.00043	−2.93	.00169
−3.72	.00010	−3.32	.00045	−2.92	.00175
−3.71	.00010	−3.31	.00047	−2.91	.00181
−3.70	.00011	−3.30	.00048	−2.90	.00187
−3.69	.00011	−3.29	.00050	−2.89	.00193
−3.68	.00012	−3.28	.00052	−2.88	.00199
−3.67	.00012	−3.27	.00054	−2.87	.00205
−3.66	.00013	−3.26	.00056	−2.86	.00212
−3.65	.00013	−3.25	.00058	−2.85	.00219
−3.64	.00014	−3.24	.00060	−2.84	.00226
−3.63	.00014	−3.23	.00062	−2.83	.00233
−3.62	.00015	−3.22	.00064	−2.82	.00240
−3.61	.00015	−3.21	.00066	−2.81	.00248

TABLE C.3 *763*

TABLE C.3 (CONTINUED)

z	$F(z)$	z	$F(z)$	z	$F(z)$
−2.80	.00256	−2.30	.01072	−1.80	.03593
−2.79	.00264	−2.29	.01101	−1.79	.03673
−2.78	.00272	−2.28	.01130	−1.78	.03754
−2.77	.00280	−2.27	.01160	−1.77	.03836
−2.76	.00289	−2.26	.01191	−1.76	.03920
−2.75	.00298	−2.25	.01222	−1.75	.04006
−2.74	.00307	−2.24	.01255	−1.74	.04093
−2.73	.00317	−2.23	.01287	−1.73	.04182
−2.72	.00326	−2.22	.01321	−1.72	.04272
−2.71	.00336	−2.21	.01355	−1.71	.04363
−2.70	.00347	−2.20	.01390	−1.70	.04457
−2.69	.00357	−2.19	.01426	−1.69	.04551
−2.68	.00368	−2.18	.01463	−1.68	.04648
−2.67	.00379	−2.17	.01500	−1.67	.04746
−2.66	.00391	−2.16	.01539	−1.66	.04846
−2.65	.00402	−2.15	.01578	−1.65	.04947
−2.64	.00415	−2.14	.01618	−1.64	.05050
−2.63	.00427	−2.13	.01659	−1.63	.05155
−2.62	.00440	−2.12	.01700	−1.62	.05262
−2.61	.00453	−2.11	.01743	−1.61	.05370
−2.60	.00466	−2.10	.01786	−1.60	.05480
−2.59	.00480	−2.09	.01831	−1.59	.05592
−2.58	.00494	−2.08	.01876	−1.58	.05705
−2.57	.00508	−2.07	.01923	−1.57	.05821
−2.56	.00523	−2.06	.01970	−1.56	.05938
−2.55	.00539	−2.05	.02018	−1.55	.06057
−2.54	.00554	−2.04	.02068	−1.54	.06178
−2.53	.00570	−2.03	.02118	−1.53	.06301
−2.52	.00587	−2.02	.02169	−1.52	.06426
−2.51	.00604	−2.01	.02222	−1.51	.06552
−2.50	.00621	−2.00	.02275	−1.50	.06681
−2.49	.00639	−1.99	.02330	−1.49	.06811
−2.48	.00657	−1.98	.02385	−1.48	.06944
−2.47	.00676	−1.97	.02442	−1.47	.07078
−2.46	.00695	−1.96	.02500	−1.46	.07215
−2.45	.00714	−1.95	.02559	−1.45	.07353
−2.44	.00734	−1.94	.02619	−1.44	.07493
−2.43	.00755	−1.93	.02680	−1.43	.07636
−2.42	.00776	−1.92	.02743	−1.42	.07780
−2.41	.00798	−1.91	.02807	−1.41	.07927
−2.40	.00820	−1.90	.02872	−1.40	.08076
−2.39	.00842	−1.89	.02938	−1.39	.08226
−2.38	.00866	−1.88	.03005	−1.38	.08379
−2.37	.00889	−1.87	.03074	−1.37	.08534
−2.36	.00914	−1.86	.03144	−1.36	.08691
−2.35	.00939	−1.85	.03216	−1.35	.08851
−2.34	.00964	−1.84	.03288	−1.34	.09012
−2.33	.00990	−1.83	.03362	−1.33	.09176
−2.32	.01017	−1.82	.03438	−1.32	.09342
−2.31	.01044	−1.81	.03515	−1.31	.09510

TABLE C.3 (CONTINUED)

z	$F(z)$	z	$F(z)$	z	$F(z)$
−1.30	.09680	−.85	.19766	−.40	.34458
−1.29	.09853	−.84	.20045	−.39	.34827
−1.28	.10027	−.83	.20327	−.38	.35197
−1.27	.10204	−.82	.20611	−.37	.35569
−1.26	.10383	−.81	.20897	−.36	.35942
−1.25	.10565	−.80	.21186	−.35	.36317
−1.24	.10749	−.79	.21476	−.34	.36693
−1.23	.10935	−.78	.21770	−.33	.37070
−1.22	.11123	−.77	.22065	−.32	.37448
−1.21	.11314	−.76	.22363	−.31	.37828
−1.20	.11507	−.75	.22663	−.30	.38209
−1.19	.11702	−.74	.22965	−.29	.38591
−1.18	.11900	−.73	.23270	−.28	.38974
−1.17	.12100	−.72	.23576	−.27	.39358
−1.16	.12302	−.71	.23885	−.26	.39743
−1.15	.12507	−.70	.24196	−.25	.40129
−1.14	.12714	−.69	.24510	−.24	.40517
−1.13	.12924	−.68	.24825	−.23	.40905
−1.12	.13136	−.67	.25143	−.22	.41294
−1.11	.13350	−.66	.25463	−.21	.41683
−1.10	.13567	−.65	.25785	−.20	.42074
−1.09	.13786	−.64	.26109	−.19	.42465
−1.08	.14007	−.63	.26435	−.18	.42858
−1.07	.14231	−.62	.26763	−.17	.43251
−1.06	.14457	−.61	.27093	−.16	.43644
−1.05	.14686	−.60	.27425	−.15	.44038
−1.04	.14917	−.59	.27760	−.14	.44433
−1.03	.15150	−.58	.28096	−.13	.44828
−1.02	.15386	−.57	.24834	−.12	.45224
−1.01	.15625	−.56	.28774	−.11	.45620
−1.00	.15866	−.55	.29116	−.10	.46017
−.99	.16109	−.54	.29460	−.09	.46414
−.98	.16354	−.53	.29806	−.08	.46812
−.97	.16602	−.52	.30153	−.07	.47210
−.96	.16853	−.51	.30503	−.06	.47608
−.95	.17106	−.50	.30854	−.05	.48006
−.94	.17361	−.49	.31207	−.04	.48405
−.93	.17619	−.48	.31561	−.03	.48803
−.92	.17879	−.47	.31918	−.02	.49202
−.91	.18141	−.46	.32276	−.01	.49601
−.90	.18406	−.45	.32636	.00	.50000
−.89	.18673	−.44	.32997	.01	.50399
−.88	.18943	−.43	.33360	.02	.50798
−.87	.19215	−.42	.33724	.03	.51197
−.86	.19489	−.41	.34090	.04	.51595

TABLE C.3 765

TABLE C.3 (CONTINUED)

z	$F(z)$	z	$F(z)$	z	$F(z)$
.05	.51994	.50	.69146	.95	.82894
.06	.52392	.51	.69497	.96	.83147
.07	.52790	.52	.69847	.97	.83398
.08	.53188	.53	.70194	.98	.83646
.09	.53586	.54	.70540	.99	.83891
.10	.53983	.55	.70884	1.00	.84134
.11	.54380	.56	.71226	1.01	.84375
.12	.54776	.57	.71566	1.02	.84614
.13	.55172	.58	.71904	1.03	.84850
.14	.55567	.59	.72240	1.04	.85083
.15	.55962	.60	.72575	1.05	.85314
.16	.56356	.61	.72907	1.06	.85543
.17	.56749	.62	.73237	1.07	.85769
.18	.57142	.63	.73565	1.08	.85993
.19	.57535	.64	.73891	1.09	.86214
.20	.57926	.65	.74215	1.10	.86433
.21	.58317	.66	.74537	1.11	.86650
.22	.58706	.67	.74857	1.12	.86864
.23	.59095	.68	.75175	1.13	.87076
.24	.59483	.69	.75490	1.14	.87286
.25	.59871	.70	.75804	1.15	.87493
.26	.60257	.71	.76115	1.16	.87698
.27	.60642	.72	.76424	1.17	.87900
.28	.61206	.73	.76730	1.18	.88100
.29	.61409	.74	.77035	1.19	.88298
.30	.61791	.75	.77337	1.20	.88493
.31	.62172	.76	.77637	1.21	.88686
.32	.62552	.77	.77935	1.22	.88877
.33	.62930	.78	.78230	1.23	.89065
.34	.63307	.79	.78524	1.24	.89251
.35	.63683	.80	.78814	1.25	.89435
.36	.64058	.81	.79103	1.26	.89617
.37	.64431	.82	.79389	1.27	.89796
.38	.64803	.83	.79673	1.28	.89973
.39	.65173	.84	.79955	1.29	.90147
.40	.65542	.85	.80234	1.30	.90320
.41	.65910	.86	.80511	1.31	.90490
.42	.66276	.87	.80785	1.32	.90658
.43	.66640	.88	.81057	1.33	.90824
.44	.67003	.89	.81327	1.34	.90988
.45	.67364	.90	.81594	1.35	.91149
.46	.67724	.91	.81859	1.36	.91309
.47	.68082	.92	.82121	1.37	.91466
.48	.68439	.93	.82381	1.38	.91621
.49	.68793	.94	.82639	1.39	.91774

TABLE C.3 (CONTINUED)

z	$F(z)$	z	$F(z)$	z	$F(z)$
1.40	.91924	1.85	.96784	2.30	.98928
1.41	.92073	1.86	.96856	2.31	.98956
1.42	.92220	1.87	.96926	2.32	.98983
1.43	.92364	1.88	.96995	2.33	.99010
1.44	.92507	1.89	.97062	2.34	.99036
1.45	.92647	1.90	.97128	2.35	.99061
1.46	.92785	1.91	.97193	2.36	.99086
1.47	.92922	1.92	.97257	2.37	.99111
1.48	.93056	1.93	.97320	2.38	.99134
1.49	.93189	1.94	.97381	2.39	.99158
1.50	.93319	1.95	.97441	2.40	.99180
1.51	.93448	1.96	.97500	2.41	.99202
1.52	.93574	1.97	.97550	2.42	.99224
1.53	.93699	1.98	.97615	2.43	.99245
1.54	.93822	1.99	.97670	2.44	.99266
1.55	.93943	2.00	.97725	2.45	.99286
1.56	.94062	2.01	.97778	2.46	.99305
1.57	.94179	2.02	.97831	2.47	.99324
1.58	.94295	2.03	.97882	2.48	.99343
1.59	.94408	2.04	.97932	2.49	.99361
1.60	.94520	2.05	.97982	2.50	.99379
1.61	.94630	2.06	.98030	2.51	.99396
1.62	.94738	2.07	.98077	2.52	.99413
1.63	.94845	2.08	.98124	2.53	.99430
1.64	.94950	2.09	.98169	2.54	.99446
1.65	.95053	2.10	.98214	2.55	.99461
1.66	.95154	2.11	.98257	2.56	.99477
1.67	.95254	2.12	.98300	2.57	.99492
1.68	.95352	2.13	.98341	2.58	.99506
1.69	.95449	2.14	.98382	2.59	.99520
1.70	.95543	2.15	.98422	2.60	.99534
1.71	.95637	2.16	.98461	2.61	.99547
1.72	.95728	2.17	.98500	2.62	.99560
1.73	.95818	2.18	.98537	2.63	.99573
1.74	.95907	2.19	.98574	2.64	.99585
1.75	.95994	2.20	.98610	2.65	.99598
1.76	.96080	2.21	.98645	2.66	.99609
1.77	.96164	2.22	.98679	2.67	.99621
1.78	.96246	2.23	.98713	2.68	.99632
1.79	.96327	2.24	.98745	2.69	.99643
1.80	.96407	2.25	.98778	2.70	.99653
1.81	.96485	2.26	.98809	2.71	.99664
1.82	.96562	2.27	.98840	2.72	.99674
1.83	.96638	2.28	.98870	2.73	.99683
1.84	.96712	2.29	.98899	2.74	.99693

TABLE C.3   767

TABLE C.3 (CONTINUED)

z	$F(z)$	z	$F(z)$	z	$F(z)$
2.75	.99702	3.20	.99931	3.65	.99987
2.76	.99711	3.21	.99934	3.66	.99987
2.77	.99720	3.22	.99936	3.67	.99988
2.78	.99728	3.23	.99938	3.68	.99988
2.79	.99736	3.24	.99940	3.69	.99989
2.80	.99744	3.25	.99942	3.70	.99989
2.81	.99752	3.26	.99944	3.71	.99990
2.82	.99760	3.27	.99946	3.72	.99990
2.83	.99767	3.28	.99948	3.73	.99990
2.84	.99774	3.29	.99950	3.74	.99991
2.85	.99781	3.30	.99952	3.75	.99991
2.86	.99788	3.31	.99953	3.76	.99992
2.87	.99795	3.32	.99955	3.77	.99992
2.88	.99801	3.33	.99957	3.78	.99992
2.89	.99807	3.34	.99958	3.79	.99992
2.90	.99813	3.35	.99960	3.80	.99993
2.91	.99819	3.36	.99961	3.81	.99993
2.92	.99825	3.37	.99962	3.82	.99993
2.93	.99831	3.38	.99964	3.83	.99994
2.94	.99836	3.39	.99965	3.84	.99994
2.95	.99841	3.40	.99966	3.85	.99994
2.96	.99846	3.41	.99968	3.86	.99994
2.97	.99851	3.42	.99969	3.87	.99995
2.98	.99856	3.43	.99970	3.88	.99995
2.99	.99861	3.44	.99971	3.89	.99995
3.00	.99865	3.45	.99972	3.90	.99995
3.01	.99869	3.46	.99973	3.91	.99995
3.02	.99874	3.47	.99974	3.92	.99996
3.03	.99878	3.48	.99975	3.93	.99996
3.04	.99882	3.49	.99976	3.94	.99996
3.05	.99886	3.50	.99977	3.95	.99996
3.06	.99889	3.51	.99978	3.96	.99996
3.07	.99893	3.52	.99978	3.97	.99996
3.08	.99897	3.53	.99979	3.98	.99997
3.09	.99900	3.54	.99980	3.99	.99997
3.10	.99903	3.55	.99981	4.00	.99997
3.11	.99906	3.56	.99981		
3.12	.99910	3.57	.99982		
3.13	.99913	3.58	.99983		
3.14	.99916	3.59	.99983		
3.15	.99918	3.60	.99984		
3.16	.99921	3.61	.99985		
3.17	.99924	3.62	.99985		
3.18	.99926	3.63	.99986		
3.19	.99929	3.64	.99986		

TABLE C.4 RANDOM NUMBERS

71120	76688	20048	30087	00092	29765	77762	98690	92278	62229	65456	84269	45548	14865	79258	41743	37160	47268	49170	69602
75082	24072	68691	95501	54780	69172	22011	09512	58973	78595	68226	57535	37856	09319	15203	07359	07297	77553	99644	99882
02494	16026	73705	97993	24612	65728	72859	45602	17876	20146	96838	49326	14645	43933	31793	95343	85946	57592	72036	13885
34981	84923	94702	03904	71102	91478	08947	30380	01752	06767	37089	06797	79879	18102	89674	75265	44318	88518	32246	96809
90638	72547	19538	64302	09963	81058	96682	50565	33255	67349	44441	04119	18576	74378	79085	05091	18806	67012	32815	93780
67342	60032	54111	84376	19256	56155	63622	76339	85428	84271	25521	75931	97146	99493	22644	40408	38672	68358	62098	57361
85281	95442	05117	71720	84268	60126	02341	72915	16418	05852	42269	54687	75455	60542	84155	60060	02950	77159	36400	23967
16205	81523	43290	26035	66599	65273	92248	66024	65910	14268	01243	74420	18099	38817	70003	70690	94069	28201	22534	81691
86886	86097	34601	32731	84977	15279	26885	23791	00785	36447	90586	03405	92409	23807	11159	52687	15696	19986	78650	92028
44313	37623	26924	22934	95283	65289	34190	17534	97491	85417	27140	68236	40661	29843	13155	10040	42294	63404	99776	28011
70086	68409	79681	62406	57303	82159	77232	23954	48636	19642	76228	31799	14017	97909	61259	86595	67906	28081	57332	91256
31547	67978	23944	31866	75691	67355	22907	31243	81295	07810	06577	87661	55675	45100	69522	11224	41647	48865	18365	70401
57118	09097	40515	61217	02660	65009	66113	11594	74544	86600	42916	33359	20746	24249	58773	34397	77426	54981	33050	03470
23364	08958	43468	80182	89879	17633	96886	22613	63705	98914	78710	85096	20342	56191	54064	18659	25378	84335	77607	06622
41269	88015	56664	47847	77102	31988	98007	00146	18814	00077	11568	96348	77390	97207	86739	45516	92521	45480	40191	31827
29237	88978	70735	23604	05007	17608	60580	05005	84808	19508	63797	42871	81658	04102	89651	01225	00126	89731	37252	15930
60306	18464	68031	42007	39758	60484	05077	86104	70924	65357	50613	36619	31505	59455	73182	03992	65313	55946	47858	83635
71087	73804	03046	54033	96783	94400	95349	22496	76829	59615	58514	31064	49849	19517	68455	35076	94356	50450	53489	66887
19915	17505	25799	97245	51272	32426	33111	06827	42957	91189	96301	80426	61850	47268	26914	36298	75219	24630	70806	03164
81724	61870	35700	57366	22895	21074	20392	32684	12570	74447	81264	15307	21815	93130	62435	36457	56798	12677	64878	75174
67140	26272	53367	83758	22236	79598	77456	48358	93041	00730	23016	97233	76822	85836	23622	69151	02390	91983	30385	54459
52387	29586	97931	21305	46451	86958	03690	39509	03846	70338	67492	14601	54561	95956	84655	44509	04881	28703	28290	11405
13821	80281	57289	21207	11635	78946	68958	03236	98786	92477	63592	82531	62894	34578	41474	37323	51146	70964	65473	54156
35676	26656	38846	93173	09419	17951	22937	76059	49921	40682	14996	09130	88636	49646	00159	54090	23174	52236	04843	58937
10031	29748	88211	61529	75277	97899	09899	78302	80724	51206	79620	90651	83052	82455	47259	41458	23413	67355	93413	54286
84993	21385	63365	87724	56058	46835	76484	37385	35952	51872	79240	98071	21574	46799	86602	98581	11823	83708	95844	21684
67509	09898	51806	21748	64234	89674	59931	52521	75742	08909	81765	17570	25235	93280	32567	55878	42163	50071	20956	75098
61979	95995	18151	44955	06364	33592	44275	63316	81418	79236	18667	07409	31326	21271	45611	82701	84985	65598	28718	81928
33106	61279	69716	66788	73282	38593	72020	84785	60524	55735	00075	33731	00769	01034	99258	86403	24851	71476	05192	87863
80451	91936	27558	37920	79499	35713	98780	71265	38566	92975	90011	47747	49704	68494	63628	65321	19271	27732	92955	08135
12215	00071	90488	42288	39331	55394	78380	71734	24985	00922	04298	66851	92806	55174	95728	78158	06852	37694	64490	47692
05738	05201	79559	30544	67235	28509	65938	39047	40839	94101	93609	22120	85811	15781	22345	92274	52179	82609	26041	12764
42213	38405	50509	57409	89872	22542	26408	55563	95710	83739	74189	34737	54764	15950	02833	73385	14898	28920	39438	76345
03123	31634	61689	85432	57386	75428	36092	37692	01323	00373	67814	83808	99486	42645	60446	79167	30534	70700	49397	60078
15896	54669	84946	17654	41405	89546	64625	81836	09393	34422	19826	28094	58760	99715	69440	19261	90515	69735	03777	95046

TABLE C.4   769

TABLE C.4 (CONTINUED)

36277	62246	46983	21683	07252	48366	24925	14251	61179	38808	82237	44145	24735	51108	84028	44196	08923	55772	54319	23965
54918	13825	88683	07672	47886	18265	78614	07300	36270	51924	85110	43340	94050	74238	98975	25706	63462	49416	25340	07293
15694	28526	29907	22703	67051	97978	84403	24618	88080	06914	48760	30336	43174	86013	27513	90959	98138	70192	37911	95738
33228	37718	27257	24078	99155	78226	76955	57693	53563	02142	30784	65420	15467	04015	84889	73195	75168	92251	76989	31674
97137	97757	12305	94018	53358	73988	63705	16334	24652	00907	83573	93269	07461	05339	64887	41264	63605	10245	89028	41690
50506	25392	97799	58262	69382	91934	27162	35563	68911	93401	40205	00617	41856	45586	96809	70575	52171	77849	97553	84675
30066	18320	39328	71083	72544	95511	20167	61402	86909	68831	30800	65324	14739	00513	70428	17947	73829	81445	24208	12246
55603	23400	39967	29201	15499	30187	41626	78075	93812	60193	16850	59361	04516	92842	16409	62872	29552	11455	02766	13496
56081	15018	85377	77102	94212	71354	80215	39105	12692	24205	31007	68188	30070	66721	29694	77680	98828	93844	73614	97084
19979	46117	96888	66272	25639	57382	13545	64828	67058	18895	09851	89049	45631	72342	23364	89109	24373	44261	46202	78863
57358	34377	90038	30830	74634	70335	50305	68808	60103	41343	07126	70668	59873	23219	00460	93786	58571	07351	16967	35640
61136	46053	26091	42066	17573	26837	02866	75662	28173	88083	74933	56852	66715	88620	31283	90112	59121	43717	30216	87840
55088	39969	44019	04394	30191	41597	77860	92782	55949	00659	00405	96502	75362	83652	23654	89051	21416	27039	69489	73577
16061	34166	60450	55200	87150	26095	72222	98476	40854	58839	85347	82528	27043	19507	73648	66328	35135	13849	66880	76639
57911	57715	25090	31104	60809	84915	62207	09006	94174	83984	56338	82172	85985	76360	84296	18536	52548	48461	17836	70864

TABLE C.5 EXPONENTIAL FUNCTIONS

x	e^x	e^{-x}	x	e^x	e^{-x}
0.00	1.0000	1.0000	0.45	1.5683	0.6376
0.01	1.0101	0.9900	0.46	1.5841	0.6313
0.02	1.0202	0.9802	0.47	1.6000	0.6250
0.03	1.0305	0.9704	0.48	1.6161	0.6188
0.04	1.0408	0.9608	0.49	1.6323	0.6126
0.05	1.0513	0.9512	0.50	1.6487	0.6065
0.06	1.0618	0.9418	0.51	1.6653	0.6005
0.07	1.0725	0.9329	0.52	1.6820	0.5945
0.08	1.0833	0.9231	0.53	1.6989	0.5886
0.09	1.0942	0.9139	0.54	1.7160	0.5827
0.10	1.1052	0.9048	0.55	1.7333	0.5769
0.11	1.1163	0.8958	0.56	1.7507	0.5712
0.12	1.1275	0.8869	0.57	1.7683	0.5655
0.13	1.1388	0.8780	0.58	1.7860	0.5599
0.14	1.1503	0.8693	0.59	1.8040	0.5543
0.15	1.1618	0.8607	0.60	1.8221	0.5488
0.16	1.1735	0.8521	0.61	1.8404	0.5433
0.17	1.1853	0.8436	0.62	1.8589	0.5379
0.18	1.1972	0.8353	0.63	1.8776	0.5326
0.19	1.2092	0.8269	0.64	1.8965	0.5273
0.20	1.2214	0.8187	0.65	1.9155	0.5220
0.21	1.2337	0.8106	0.66	1.9348	0.5168
0.22	1.2461	0.8025	0.67	1.9542	0.5117
0.23	1.2586	0.7945	0.68	1.9739	0.5066
0.24	1.2712	0.7866	0.69	1.9937	0.5016
0.25	1.2840	0.7788	0.70	2.0138	0.4965
0.26	1.2969	0.7710	0.71	2.0340	0.4916
0.27	1.3100	0.7633	0.72	2.0544	0.4867
0.28	1.3231	0.7558	0.73	2.0751	0.4819
0.29	1.3364	0.7482	0.74	2.0959	0.4771
0.30	1.3499	0.7408	0.75	2.1170	0.4723
0.31	1.3634	0.7334	0.76	2.1383	0.4677
0.32	1.3771	0.7261	0.77	2.1598	0.4630
0.33	1.3910	0.7189	0.78	2.1815	0.4584
0.34	1.4049	0.7118	0.79	2.2034	0.4538
0.35	1.4191	0.7046	0.80	2.2255	0.4493
0.36	1.4333	0.6977	0.81	2.2479	0.4448
0.37	1.4477	0.6907	0.82	2.2705	0.4404
0.38	1.4623	0.6839	0.83	2.2933	0.4360
0.39	1.4770	0.6770	0.84	2.3164	0.4317
0.40	1.4918	0.6703	0.85	2.3396	0.4274
0.41	1.5068	0.6636	0.86	2.3632	0.4231
0.42	1.5220	0.6570	0.87	2.3869	0.4189
0.43	1.5373	0.6505	0.88	2.4109	0.4148
0.44	1.5527	0.6440	0.89	2.4351	0.4106

TABLE C.5   *771*

TABLE C.5 (CONTINUED)

x	e^x	e^{-x}	x	e^x	e^{-x}
0.90	2.4596	0.4066	2.80	16.445	0.0608
0.91	2.4843	0.4025	2.85	16.288	0.0578
0.92	2.5093	0.3985	2.90	18.174	0.0550
0.93	2.5345	0.3945	2.95	19.106	0.0523
0.94	2.5600	0.3906	3.00	20.086	0.0498
0.95	2.5857	0.3867	3.05	21.115	0.0474
0.96	2.6117	0.3829	3.10	22.198	0.0450
0.97	2.6379	0.3790	3.15	23.336	0.0429
0.98	2.6645	0.3753	3.20	24.533	0.0408
0.99	2.6912	0.3716	3.25	25.790	0.0389
1.00	2.7183	0.3678			
1.05	2.8577	0.3499	3.30	27.113	0.0369
1.10	3.0042	0.3329	3.35	28.503	0.0351
1.15	3.1582	0.3166	3.40	29.964	0.0333
1.20	3.3201	0.3012	3.45	31.500	0.0317
1.25	3.4903	0.2865	3.50	33.115	0.0302
1.30	3.6693	0.2625	3.55	34.813	0.0287
1.35	3.8574	0.2592	3.60	36.598	0.0273
1.40	4.0552	0.2466	3.65	38.475	0.0260
1.45	4.2631	0.2346	3.70	40.447	0.0247
1.50	4.4817	0.2231	3.75	42.521	0.0235
1.55	4.7115	0.2122	3.80	44.701	0.0224
1.60	4.9530	0.2019	3.85	46.993	0.0213
1.65	5.2070	0.1921	3.90	49.402	0.0202
1.70	5.4739	0.1821	3.95	51.935	0.0193
1.75	5.7546	0.1738	4.00	54.598	0.0183
1.80	6.0496	0.6153	4.05	57.397	0.0174
1.85	6.3593	0.1572	4.10	60.340	0.0166
1.90	6.6850	0.1496	4.15	63.434	0.0158
1.95	7.0287	0.1423	4.20	66.686	0.0150
2.00	7.3891	0.1353	4.25	70.105	0.0143
2.05	7.7679	0.1287	4.30	73.700	0.0136
2.10	8.1662	0.1224	4.35	77.478	0.0129
2.15	8.5849	0.1165	4.40	81.451	0.0123
2.20	9.0250	0.1108	4.45	85.627	0.0117
2.25	9.4877	0.1054	4.50	90.017	0.0111
2.30	9.9742	0.1003	4.55	94.632	0.0107
2.35	10.486	0.0954	4.60	99.844	0.0101
2.40	11.023	0.0907	4.65	104.58	0.0096
2.45	11.588	0.0863	4.70	109.95	0.0091
2.50	12.182	0.0821	4.75	115.58	0.0087
2.55	12.807	0.0781	4.80	121.51	0.0082
2.60	13.464	0.0743	4.85	127.74	0.0078
2.65	14.154	0.0707	4.90	134.29	0.0074
2.70	14.880	0.0672	4.95	141.17	0.0070
2.75	15.643	0.0639	5.00	148.41	0.0067

TABLE C.5 (CONTINUED)

x	e^x	e^{-x}	x	e^x	e^{-x}
5.10	164.02	0.0061	7.60	1998.2	0.0005
5.20	181.27	0.0055	7.70	2208.3	0.0005
5.30	200.34	0.0050	7.80	2440.6	0.0004
5.40	221.41	0.0045	7.90	2697.3	0.0004
5.50	244.69	0.0041	8.00	2981.0	0.0003
5.60	270.43	0.0037	8.10	3294.5	0.0003
5.70	298.87	0.0033	8.20	3641.0	0.0003
5.80	330.30	0.0030	8.30	4023.9	0.0002
5.90	365.04	0.0027	8.40	4447.1	0.0002
6.00	403.43	0.0025	8.50	4914.8	0.0002
6.10	445.86	0.0022	8.60	5431.7	0.0002
6.20	492.75	0.0020	8.70	6002.9	0.0002
6.30	544.57	0.0018	8.80	6634.2	0.0002
6.40	601.85	0.0017	8.90	7332.0	0.0001
6.50	665.14	0.0015	9.00	8103.1	0.0001
6.60	735.10	0.0014	9.10	8955.3	0.0001
6.70	812.41	0.0012	9.20	9897.1	0.0001
6.80	897.85	0.0011	9.30	10938	0.0001
6.90	992.27	0.0010	9.40	12088	0.0001
7.00	1096.6	0.0009	9.50	13360	0.0001
7.10	1212.0	0.0008	9.60	14765	0.0001
7.20	1339.4	0.0007	9.70	16318	0.0001
7.30	1480.3	0.0007	9.80	18034	0.0001
7.40	1636.0	0.0006	9.90	19930	0.0001
7.50	1808.0	0.0006	10.00	22026	0.0000

TABLE C.5 *773*

TABLE C.6 PROBABILITY OF ZERO UNITS IN THE QUEUING SYSTEM (P_0) FOR MULTIPLE SERVER MODELS

SYSTEM UTILIZATION RATIO $\rho = \lambda/s\mu$	NUMBER OF SERVERS (s)								
	2	3	4	5	6	7	8	9	10
.05	.9048	.8607	.8187	.7788	.7408	.7047	.6703	.6376	.6065
.10	.8182	.7407	.6703	.6065	.5488	.4966	.4493	.4066	.3679
.15	.7391	.6373	.5487	.4724	.4066	.3499	.3012	.2592	.2231
.20	.6667	.5479	.4491	.3678	.3012	.2466	.2019	.1653	.1353
.25	.6000	.4706	.3673	.2863	.2231	.1738	.1353	.1054	.0821
.30	.5385	.4035	.3002	.2228	.1652	.1224	.0907	.0672	.0498
.35	.4815	.3451	.2449	.1731	.1222	.0862	.0608	.0428	.0302
.40	.4286	.2941	.1993	.1343	.0903	.0606	.0407	.0273	.0183
.45	.3793	.2496	.1616	.1039	.0666	.0426	.0272	.0174	.0111
.50	.3333	.2105	.1304	.0801	.0490	.0298	.0182	.0110	.0067
.55	.2903	.1762	.1046	.0614	.0358	.0208	.0121	.0070	.0040
.60	.2500	.1460	.0831	.0466	.0260	.0144	.0080	.0044	.0024
.65	.2121	.1193	.0651	.0350	.0187	.0099	.0052	.0028	.0015
.70	.1765	.0957	.0502	.0259	.0132	.0067	.0034	.0017	.0009
.75	.1429	.0748	.0377	.0187	.0091	.0044	.0021	.0010	.0005
.80	.1111	.0562	.0273	.0130	.0061	.0028	.0013	.0006	.0003
.85	.0811	.0396	.0186	.0085	.0038	.0017	.0008	.0003	.0001
.90	.0526	.0249	.0113	.0050	.0021	.0009	.0004	.0002	.0001
.95	.0256	.0118	.0051	.0022	.0009	.0004	.0002	.0001	.0000

Note: λ = arrival rate (Poisson); s = number of servers; μ = service rate (per individual server and exponential service time).

ANSWERS
TO
EVEN-NUMBERED
PROBLEMS

CHAPTER 2.
PROBABILITY
CONCEPTS

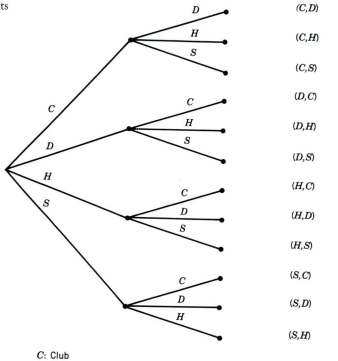

2. a. 12 sample points
   b.

C: Club
D: Diamond
H: Heart
S: Spade

4. Probability of a sample point = 1/24
   $P(A) = 1/6$

6. a. $P(A) = .65$
      $P(B) = .50$
      $P(C) = .33$
   b. .20
   c. No, $A \cap B \neq 0$.

   d. .95
   e. No, $A \cup B \neq S$
   f. 0
   g. .35
   h. .22

8. .51
10. a.

DAYS FROM ORDER TO RECEIPT				
AMOUNT OF ORDER	UNDER 10	11–14	OVER 14	TOTAL
Under $1000	.04	.06	.24	.34
1000 to 5000	.08	.15	.12	.35
Over 5000	.20	.05	.06	.32
	.32	.26	.42	1.00

b. e.g., .32 is the probability that the order is received in under 10 days.
c. .58
d. .69
e. .33
f. .478
g. No

12. a. .50
   b. .571
   c. .04

14. a. .30
   b. .75
   c. .60

CHAPTER 3. PROBABILITY DISTRIBUTIONS

2.
Total Winnings (x)	Probability ($f(x)$)
300	1/6
500	1/6
600	1/6
1100	1/6
1200	1/6
1400	1/6

4. Expected cost of service agreement is $14.75, selling price is $25. The selling price appears to be reasonable.

6.
a. .276
b. .276
c. .047
d. .544
e. .456

8.
a. .500
b. .155
c. .500
d. .998
e. .000

10.
y	$P(y); p = .6$	$P(y); p = .4$
0	.010	.078
1	.077	.259
2	.230	.346
3	.346	.230
4	.259	.077
5	.078	.010

12.
x	$P(x)$	
0	.328	$\mu = 1.0$
1	.409	$\sigma^2 = .8$
2	.205	
3	.051	
4	.007	
5	.000	

14.
a. $e^{-7.5} = 0.000531$
b. $e^{-7.5} + 7.5e^{-7.5} = 0.004679$
c. 0.9409

16.
a. .40
b. .80
c. .60

18. $1 - P(x \leq 5) = .216$

20.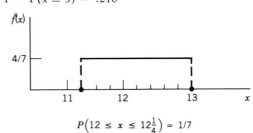

$P\left(12 \leq x \leq 12\frac{1}{4}\right) = 1/7$

22.
a. .494
b. .988
c. .994
d. .894
e. .023
f. .067
g. .017

24. 4.82 years

26.
a. .3679
b. .2231
c. .6065

28. Expected time between arrivals is one minute. $P[t = 1] = 0$.

30. Approximate normal with mean of 45 minutes and standard deviation of 4.74 minutes.

2. a. $EMV(a_1) = 2100$ Choose a_1.
   $EMV(a_2) = 980$
   $EMV(a_3) = 630$

   b. Opportunity Loss Table

	θ_1	θ_2	θ_3
a_1	0	0	0
a_2	100	1900	700
a_3	300	2400	900
	0.3	0.5	0.2

   $EOL(a_1) = 0$ Choose a_1.
   $EOL(a_2) = 1120$
   $EOL(a_3) = 1470$

   c. $EVPI = 0$

4. EMV (season return) = $57,500.
   Since the expected monetary value from the season return is $7500 greater than the $50,000 lease she has been offered, she should operate the resort.

6. a. Payoff Table

		θ_1 (5)	θ_2 (6)	θ_3 (7)	θ_4 (8)	θ_5 (9)	θ_6 (10)
a_1	(5)	25	20	15	10	5	0
a_2	(6)	20	30	25	20	15	10
a_3	(7)	15	25	35	30	25	20
a_4	(8)	10	20	30	40	35	30
a_5	(9)	5	15	25	35	45	40
a_6	(10)	0	10	20	30	40	50
		0.10	0.20	0.15	0.15	0.30	0.10

   $EMV(a_1) = 11.75$
   $EMV(a_2) = 20.25$
   $EMV(a_3) = 25.75$
   $EMV(a_4) = 29.00$
   $EMV(a_5) = 30.00$ Buy 9 cases.
   $EMV(a_6) = 26.50$

   b. Opportunity Loss Table

		θ_1 (5)	θ_2 (6)	θ_3 (7)	θ_4 (8)	θ_5 (9)	θ_6 (10)
a_1	(5)	0	10	20	30	40	50
a_2	(6)	5	0	10	20	30	40
a_3	(7)	10	5	0	10	20	30
a_4	(8)	15	10	5	0	10	20
a_5	(9)	20	15	10	5	0	10
a_6	(10)	25	20	15	10	5	0
		0.10	0.20	0.15	0.15	0.30	0.10

   $EOL(a_1) = 26.5$
   $EOL(a_2) = 18.0$
   $EOL(a_3) = 12.5$
   $EOL(a_4) = 9.25$
   $EOL(a_5) = 8.25$ Buy 9 cases.
   $EOL(a_6) = 11.75$

   c. $EVPI = 8.25$

8. a. Maximax criterion; choose a_1 (10,000,000)
   b. Maximin criterion; choose a_3 (1,000,000)
   c. Criterion of realism; choose a_1 (5,800,000), $\alpha = 0.6$
   d. Equally likely criterion, choose a_1 (4,500,000)
   e. Minimax criterion; choose a_1 (1,500,000)

10. a. Expected value decision criterion
    $EMV(a_1) = 3880$ Choose a_1 (large order).
    $EMV(a_2) = 2350$
    $EMV(a_3) = 900$

    b. Decision tree (see below)

    c. $EVSI = \$3883.48 - \$3880.00 = \$3.48$ (negligible)

    d. $EVPI = \$70$

    e. $E_I = \dfrac{EVSI}{EVPI} = \dfrac{3.48}{70.0} = 0.0497$

12. a. Decision tree – Monetary values (see below)
    $EMV(a_1) = 9.7$ Choose a_1.
    $EMV(a_2) = 9.5$
    $EMV(a_3) = 9.2$
    $EMV(a_4) = 9.6$

    b. Decision tree – Opportunity losses (see below)
    $EOL(a_1) = 3.1$ Choose a_1.
    $EOL(a_2) = 3.3$
    $EOL(a_3) = 3.6$
    $EOL(a_4) = 3.2$

    c. $EVPI = 3.1$

    d. $EOL(a_1) = 8.3$
    $EOL(a_2) = 9.5$
    $EOL(a_3) = 10.8$
    $EOL(a_4) = 11.4$ Choose a_4.

10. b.

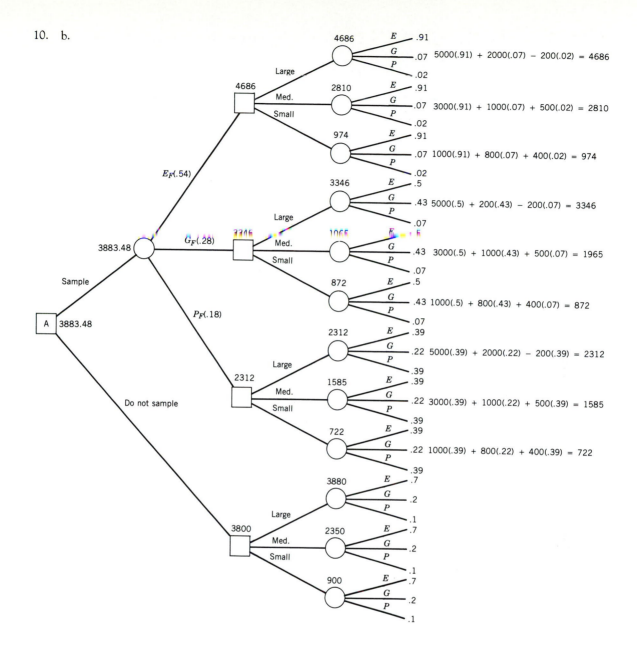

14. a. Payoff matrix

	θ_1 Ship is found	θ_2 Ship is not found	($000)
a_1 Continue search	10,000	−1,000	
a_2 Discontinue search	−5,000	750	
	0.1	0.9	

b. EMV(a_1) = 100
EMV(a_2) = 175   Choose a_2.

c. Decision tree (see below)

d. Yes, should be willing to pay up to $1165 − 175 = $990(000)

16. Certainty Equivalences
(700, 0.5, 100) ~ 500}   given
(100, 0.5, 500) ~ 300 }
(500, 0.5, 700) ~ 600 }   assumed

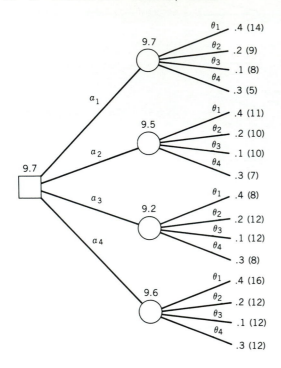

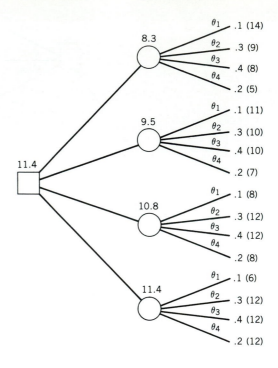

14. c. Decision Tree

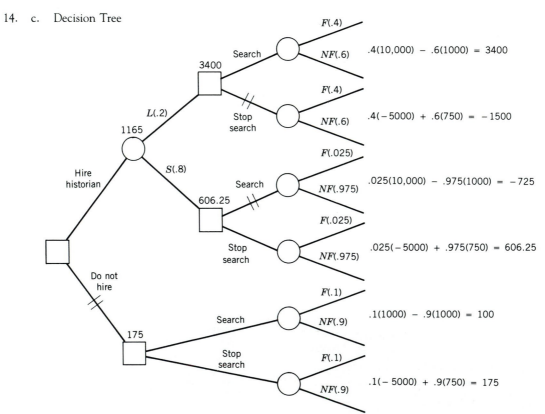

.4(10,000) − .6(1000) = 3400

.4(−5000) + .6(750) = −1500

.025(10,000) − .975(1000) = −725

.025(−5000) + .975(750) = 606.25

.1(1000) − .9(1000) = 100

.1(−5000) + .9(750) = 175

Point	P_i	$U(P_i)$
1	100	0
2	700	1
3	500	

$U(500) = 0.5$
$U(300) = 0.25$ (computed)
$U(600) = 0.75$

Points in order of increasing utility:

Point	Payoff	Utility Index
1	100	0
2	300	0.25
3	500	0.50
4	600	0.75
5	700	1.00

18.

Point	Monetary Payoff (\$K)	Utility Index
1	−1000	0
2	900	1.0
3	500	.75
4	250	.5
5	150	.25

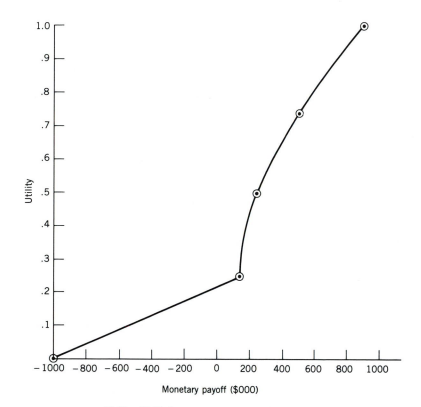

Monetary payoff (\$000)

Utility Table*

	θ_1	θ_2	θ_3
a_1	.1957	.25	.5
a_2	.1087	.5	.75
a_3	0.0	.65	1.0

*Assume linear sections between each set of adjacent points and interpolate for the payoff utilities not given in the problem.

CHAPTER 5.
FORECASTING

2.	MA/3	MA/5	$\alpha = .1$	$\alpha = .5$	$\alpha = .9$
SD	104.47	118.55	134.73	85.50	78.07
MAD	76.67	96.0	113.52	65.56	62.50
Bias	-73.81	-91.43	-94.67	-47.02	-26.18
COV	.0833	.3074	.1096	.0696	.0635
RFE	$-.0588$	$-.0729$	$-.0771$	$-.0383$	$-.0213$

The smallest values of all measures of forecast error occur when the exponential smoothing method is used with $\alpha = .9$. While $\alpha = .9$ gives very little smoothing, this model does react quickly to changes in demand. Given the gradual upward trend in the data, this value of α follows the trend better than the smaller values.

4.	MA/7	$\alpha = .2$	$\alpha = .5$	$\alpha = .9$
SD	748.26	786.61	416.5	284.5
MAD	650.34	656.66	343.44	237.24
Bias	-650.34	-656.66	-343.44	-211.35
COV	.3757	.4109	.2176	.1486
RFE	$-.3265$	$-.343$	$-.1794$	$-.1104$

The exponential smoothing method with $\alpha = .9$ gives the minimum value for all measures of forecast error.

6.

Quarter Number	Diesel Engine Demand	Weighted MA/A
1	50	
2	52	
3	48	
4	50	
5	49	
6	46	
7	48	
8	44	
9	—	45.2

b. There appears to be no trend in the data, and thus, no good reason for weighting the most recent data more highly than previous data. A simple 3-period moving average might be more appropriate, or exponential smoothing with a low α value.

8.

Year	Sales	$\alpha = .3$
1975	545,000	500,000
1976	540,000	513,500
1977	550,000	521,450
1978	575,000	530,015
1979	600,000	543,510
1980	590,000	560,457
1981	620,000	569,320
1982	660,000	584,524
1983	710,000	607,167

1984	725,000	638,017
1985	_____	664,112

10.

Year	Sales	$\alpha = .6$
1975	545,000	500,000
1976	540,000	527,000
1977	550,000	534,800
1978	575,000	543,920
1979	600,000	562,568
1980	590,000	585,027

1981	620,000	588,011
1982	660,000	607,204
1983	710,000	638,882
1984	725,000	681,553
1985	_____	707,621

SD = 41597.3, MAD = 34603.5. The smoothing constant $\alpha = 0.6$ produces the most accurate forecast.

12.   a.   COV = .1466
     b.   RFE = $-.1254$

14.   a.

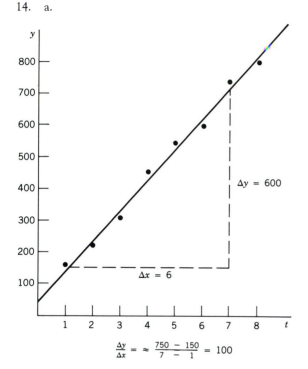

$$\frac{\Delta y}{\Delta x} = \approx \frac{750 - 150}{7 - 1} = 100$$

An increasing linear trend is indicated by the plot.

b.   From the plot the estimated equation is: $y = 45 + 100\,t$.

c. $T_t = 41.43 + 96.91t$

16.   a.

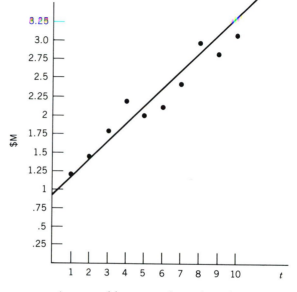

An upward linear trend is indicated

b. $\dfrac{\Delta y}{\Delta x} = \dfrac{3.25 - 1}{10} = \dfrac{3.25}{10} = .325M$

The estimate of the trend equation from the plot is:

$T_t = 1,000,000 + 325,000t$

c. $T_t = 1,080,000 + 203,636t$

18.

Year	Quarter	Sales	MA/4	MA Centered	Seasonal Random Component	Seasonal Factor	Deseasonalized Sales
				a		c	d
1981	1	470				.9708	484.12
	2	400	527.5			.8669	461.39
	3	600	552.5	540.0	1.1111	1.0332	580.73
	4	640	580.0	566.25	1.1302	1.1354	563.71
1982	1	570	572.5	576.25	.9892	.9708	587.13
	2	510	595.0	583.75	.8737	.8669	588.27
	3	570	602.5	598.75	.9520	1.0332	551.70
	4	730	612.5	607.5	1.2017	1.1354	642.98

18.

Year	Quarter	Sales	MA/4	a MA Centered	Seasonal Random Component	c Seasonal Factor	d Deseasonalized Sales
1983	1	600	630.0	621.25	.9658	.9708	618.03
	2	550	615.0	622.5	.8835	.8669	634.41
	3	640	620.0	617.5	1.0364	1.0332	619.45
	4	670	627.5	623.75	1.0742	1.1354	590.13
1984	1	620	667.5	647.5	.9576	.9708	638.63
	2	580	707.5	687.5	.8436	.8669	669.02
	3	800				1.0332	774.31
	4	830				1.1354	731.06

f. $T_t = 485.72 + 14.44t$

18. b.

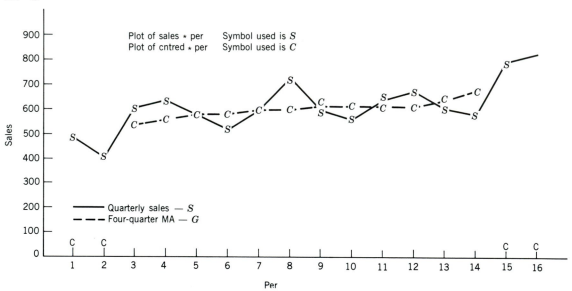

18. e.

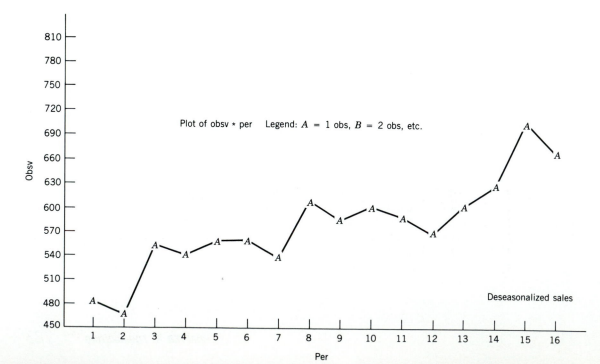

20.

				a		c	d
Year	Quarter	Sales	MA/4	MA Centered	Seasonal Random Component	Seasonal Factor	Deseasonalized Sales
1980	1	60				.9718	61.74
	2	68	70.0			.9884	68.8
	3	72	74.0	72	1.0	1.0020	71.85
	4	80	76.5	75.25	1.0631	1.0388	77.02
1981	1	76	79.0	77.75	.9775	.9718	78.21
	2	78	81.5	80.25	.9720	.9884	78.92
	3	82	84.5	83.0	.9880	1.0020	81.83
	4	90	88.5	86.5	1.0405	1.0388	86.64
1982	1	88	92.5	90.5	.9724	.9718	90.55
	2	94	95.0	93.75	1.0027	.9884	95.12
	3	98	97.5	96.25	1.0182	1.0020	97.4
	4	100	100.0	98.75	1.0127	1.0388	96.27
1983	1	98	103.0	101.5	.9655	.9718	100.84
	2	104	107.0	105.0	.9905	.9884	105.22
	3	110				1.0020	109.78
	4	116				1.0388	111.67

e. $T_t = 61.67 + 3.13t$

20. b.

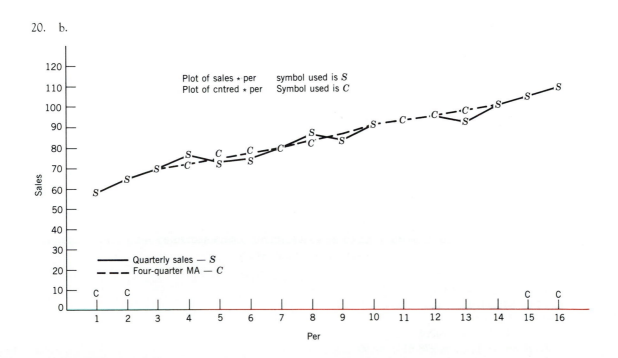

20. e.

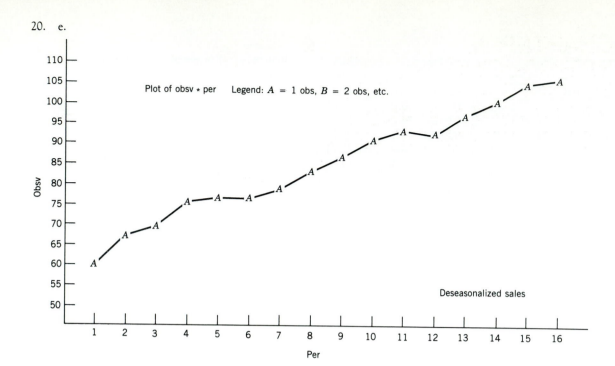

Plot of obsv * per   Legend: A = 1 obs, B = 2 obs, etc.

Deseasonalized sales

22. a. $\hat{Y} = 1.4859 + 6.5663x$
    b. SEE = 2.7169
    c. $r = .99185$
    d. $r^2 = .98377$

24. a.

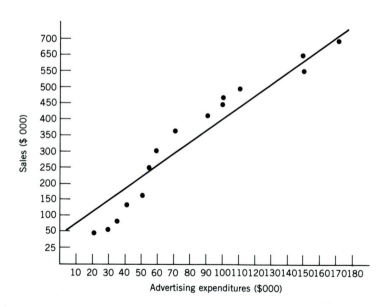

    b. $\hat{Y} = 42.625 + 4.16311x$
    c. $\hat{Y}_{200} = 875.247$
    d. SEE = 51.6831
    e,f. $r = .969537$, $r^2 = .94001$
    g. $P(771.881 \leq Yi_{\text{TRUE}} \leq 978.613) = .95$

CHAPTER 6.
INTRODUCTION
TO LINEAR
PROGRAMMING AND
MODEL FORMULATION

2. Let x_1 = number of pounds of chicken in a batch
   x_2 = number of pounds of turkey in a batch
   x_3 = number of pounds of cereal in a batch
   Minimize $Z = 3x_1 + 4x_2 + 2x_3$
   subject to
   $$x_1 \geq 100$$
   $$2x_1 - x_2 \leq 0$$
   $$x_3 \leq 150$$
   $$x_1 + x_2 + x_3 = 500$$
   with $x_1, x_2, x_3 \geq 0$

4. Let x_1 = number of desk chairs produced
   x_2 = number of desks produced
   x_3 = number of rocking chairs produced
   Maximize $Z = 10x_1 + 50x_2 + 20x_3$
   subject to
   $$2x_1 - x_2 \leq 0$$
   $$x_3 \leq 20$$
   $$10x_1 + 60x_2 + 15x_3 \leq 10{,}000$$
   $$2x_1 + 10x_2 + 3x_3 \leq 1000$$
   with $x_1, x_2, x_3 \geq 0$

6. Let x_1 = number of television advertisements
   x_2 = number of radio advertisements
   x_3 = number of newspaper advertisements
   Maximize $Z = 100{,}000x_1 + 25{,}000x_2 + 50{,}000x_3$
   subject to
   $$500x_1 + 75x_2 + 150x_3 \leq 5000$$
   $$x_1 + x_2 \leq 15$$
   $$x_1 \leq 10$$
   $$x_2 \leq 20$$
   $$x_3 \leq 10$$
   with $x_1, x_2, x_3 \geq 0$

8. Let x_{ij} = number of TV sets produced in quarter i
   by method j
   $i = 1$, first quarter
   $i = 2$, second quarter
   $j = 1$, in-house
   $j = 2$, subcontracted
   I = number of modules in inventory at the end
   of quarter 1.
   Minimize $Z = 5.00x_{11} + 5.00x_{21} + 5.50x_{12} +$
   $6.50x_{22} + 2.00I$

   subject to
   $$x_{11} \leq 1800$$
   $$x_{21} \leq 1800$$
   $$x_{12} \leq 250$$
   $$x_{22} \leq 325$$
   $$x_{11} + x_{12} - I = 1600$$
   $$I + x_{21} + x_{22} = 2200$$
   with $x_{ij} \geq 0, \quad I \geq 0$.

10. Let x_1 = number of type 1 chairs finished
    x_2 = number of type 2 chairs finished
    x_3 = number of type 3 chairs finished
    Maximize $Z = 15.50x_1 + 22.50x_2 + 27.50x_3$
    subject to
    $$.20x_1 + .10x_2 + .08x_3 \leq 80$$
    $$.04x_1 + .20x_2 + .267x_3 \leq 80$$
    $$.10x_1 + .08x_2 + .100x_3 \leq 80$$
    $$.133x_1 + .16x_2 + .133x_3 \leq 80$$
    with $x_1, x_2, x_3 \geq 0$

12. Let x_i = number of service persons hired in month
    i ($i = 1, 2, 3$)
    y_i = number of experienced service persons
    available in month i ($i = 1, \ldots , 4$).
    Minimize $Z = 2000 (y_1 + y_2 + y_3 + y_4) +$
    $1000 (x_1 + x_2 x_3)$
    subject to
    $$y_1 = 40$$
    $$150y_1 - 40x_1 \geq 4000$$
    $$-.90y_1 - x_1 + y_2 = 0$$
    $$150y_2 - 40x_2 \geq 6000$$
    $$-.90y_2 - x_2 + y_3 = 0$$
    $$150y_3 - 40x_3 \geq 5500$$
    $$-.90y_3 + y_4 - x_3 = 0$$
    $$150y_4 \geq 3000$$
    with $x_i, y_i \geq 0$.

14. Let x_1 = number of pounds of corn in a batch
    x_2 = number of pounds of sorghum in a batch
    x_3 = number of pounds of wheat in a batch
    x_4 = number of pounds of vitamins in a batch
    Minimize $Z = .10x_1 + .15x_2 + .15x_3 + .25x_4$
    subject to
    $$x_1 + x_2 + x_3 + x_4 = 1000$$
    $$x_4 \geq 100$$
    $$x_1 \leq 400$$
    $$x_1 + x_3 \geq 500$$

$$3x_1 - 2x_2 - 2x_3 \geq 0$$
with $x_1, x_2, x_3, x_4 \geq 0$

16. x_i = number of square feet allocated to department i $(i = 1, 2, 3, 4)$
    $i = 1$, Men's Clothing
    $i = 2$, Women's Clothing
    $i = 3$, Housewares
    $i = 4$, Auto Supplies
    a. Maximize $Z = 3x_1 + 5x_2 + 2.5x_3 + 2.75x_4$
       subject to
$$x_1 + x_2 + x_3 + x_4 = 75,000$$
$$12x_1 + 15x_2 + 10x_3 + 20x_4 \leq 1,500,000$$
$$1.15x_1 - x_2 \geq 0$$
$$.25x_1 + .25x_2 + .25x_3 - x_4 \geq 0$$
$$x_1 \geq 10,000$$
$$x_2 \geq 15,000$$
$$x_3 \geq 8,000$$
$$x_4 \geq 5,000$$
    with $x_i \geq 0$

    b. Drop the constraint $x_1 + x_2 + x_3 + x_4 = 75,000$.

18. Let x_1 = amount invested in one-year deposit at the beginning of year 1
    x_2 = amount invested in one-year deposit at the beginning of year 2
    x_3 = amount invested in one-year deposit at the beginning of year 3
    x_4 = amount invested in one-year deposit at the beginning of year 4
    x_5 = amount invested in two-year deposit at the beginning of year 1
    x_6 = amount invested in two-year deposit at the beginning of year 2
    x_7 = amount invested in two-year deposit at the beginning of year 3
    x_8 = amount invested in three-year deposit at the beginning of year 1
    x_9 = amount invested in three-year deposit at the beginning of year 2

y_1 = amount not invested at the beginning of year 1
y_2 = amount not invested at the beginning of year 2
y_3 = amount not invested at the beginning of year 3
y_4 = amount not invested at the beginning of year 4

Maximize $Z = 1.10x_4 + 1.22x_7 + 1.35x_9 + y_4$
    subject to
$$x_1 + x_5 + x_8 + y_1 = 5000$$
$$x_2 + x_6 + x_9 + y_2 = y_1 + 1.10x_1$$
$$x_3 + x_7 + y_3 = y_2 + 1.10x_2 + 1.22x_5$$
$$x_4 + y_4 = y_3 + 1.10x_3 + 1.22x_6 + 1.35x_8$$
with $x_i, y_i \geq 0$

20. $x_{ij} = \begin{cases} 1 & \text{if team } i \text{ is assigned to assembly point } j \\ 0 & \text{otherwise} \end{cases}$

Minimize $Z = 20x_{11} + 26x_{12} + 40x_{13} + 30x_{14} + 26x_{15}$
$$+ 22x_{21} + 24x_{22} + 30x_{23} + 32x_{24} + 18x_{25}$$
$$+ 24x_{31} + 26x_{32} + 28x_{33} + 36x_{34} + 18x_{35}$$
$$+ 20x_{41} + 24x_{42} + 36x_{43} + 30x_{44} + 20x_{45}$$
$$+ 20x_{51} + 26x_{52} + 30x_{53} + 40x_{54} + 24x_{55}$$

subject to
$$x_{11} + x_{12} + x_{13} + x_{14} + x_{15} = 1$$
$$x_{21} + x_{22} + x_{23} + x_{24} + x_{25} = 1$$
$$x_{31} + x_{32} + x_{33} + x_{34} + x_{35} = 1$$
$$x_{41} + x_{42} + x_{43} + x_{44} + x_{45} = 1$$
$$x_{51} + x_{52} + x_{53} + x_{54} + x_{55} = 1$$
$$x_{11} + x_{21} + x_{31} + x_{41} + x_{51} = 1$$
$$x_{12} + x_{22} + x_{32} + x_{42} + x_{52} = 1$$
$$x_{13} + x_{23} + x_{33} + x_{43} + x_{53} = 1$$
$$x_{14} + x_{24} + x_{34} + x_{44} + x_{54} = 1$$
$$x_{15} + x_{25} + x_{35} + x_{45} + x_{55} = 1$$
with $x_{ij} \geq 0$

CHAPTER 7.
GRAPHICAL SOLUTION
OF LINEAR
PROGRAMMING
PROBLEMS

2.

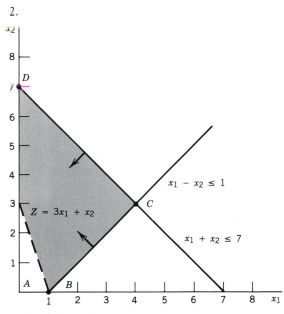

a. (0,0), (1,0), (4,3), (0,7)

b. (4,3)

c. (0,0)

6.

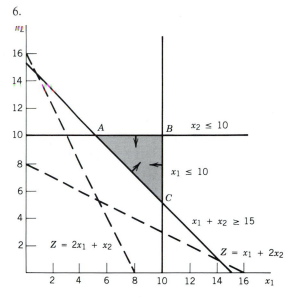

a. (5,10), (10,10), (10,5)

b. $x_1 = 10$, $x_2 = 5$, $Z = 20$

c. $x_1 = 5$, $x_2 = 10$, $Z = 20$

4.

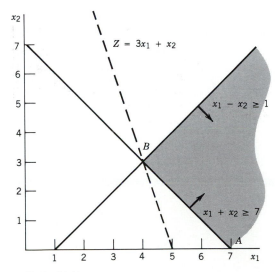

a. (7,0), (4,3)

b. The problem is unbounded

c. (4,3)

8.

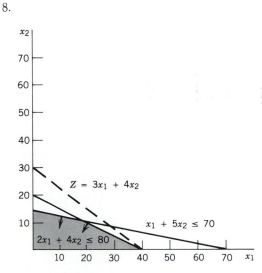

Optimal solution: $x_1 = 40$, $x_2 = 0$

10.

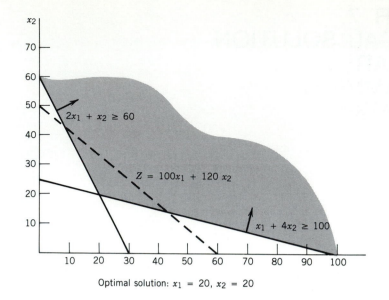

$2x_1 + x_2 \geq 60$

$Z = 100x_1 + 120 x_2$

$x_1 + 4x_2 \geq 100$

Optimal solution: $x_1 = 20$, $x_2 = 20$

12.

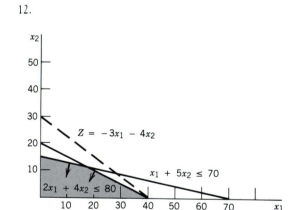

$Z = -3x_1 - 4x_2$

$x_1 + 5x_2 \leq 70$

$2x_1 + 4x_2 \leq 80$

Optimal solution: $x_1 = 40$, $x_2 = 0$

14.

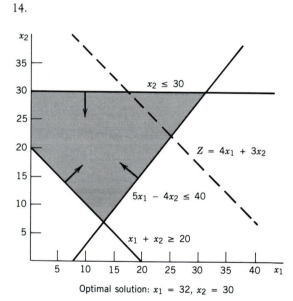

$x_2 \leq 30$

$Z = 4x_1 + 3x_2$

$5x_1 - 4x_2 \leq 40$

$x_1 + x_2 \geq 20$

Optimal solution: $x_1 = 32$, $x_2 = 30$

16.

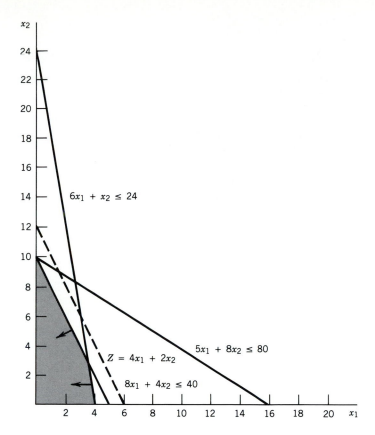

$6x_1 + x_2 \leq 24$

$5x_1 + 8x_2 \leq 80$

$Z = 4x_1 + 2x_2$

$8x_1 + 4x_2 \leq 40$

a. (0,10), (13/4, 7/2), (2,6)

b. $5x_1 + 8x_2 \leq 80$ is redundant.

18. $3x_1 + 2x_2 - S_1 \qquad\qquad = 12$
$\quad -x_1 + 2x_2 \qquad + S_2 \qquad = 12$
$\quad\;\; x_1 - 2x_2 \qquad\quad - S_3 \qquad = 4$
$\quad\;\; x_1 + \;\; x_2 \qquad\qquad + S_4 = 12$

Extreme points   (4, 0, 0, 16, 0, 8)
$\qquad\qquad\qquad$ (12, 0, 24, 24, 8, 0)
$\qquad\qquad\qquad$ (9 1/3, 2 2/3, 21 1/3, 16, 0,
$\qquad\qquad\qquad$ 0)

20. Let x_1 = number of conventional models produced
$\qquad\;\; x_2$ = number of micro-support models produced

Maximize $Z = 75x_1 + 100x_2$

subject to
$$120x_1 + 80x_2 \leq 160,000$$
$$40x_1 + 40x_2 \leq 60,000$$

with $\qquad\qquad x_1, x_2 \geq 0$

with

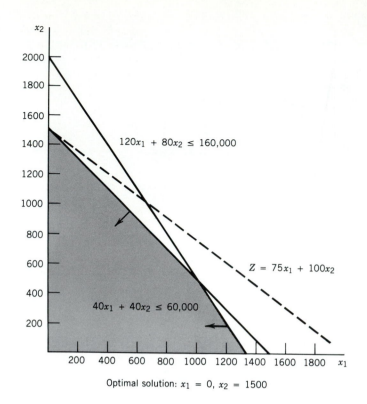

Optimal solution: $x_1 = 0$, $x_2 = 1500$

22. $x_1 = 6\ 2/7$, $x_2 = 1\ 6/7$

24. Note that the slope of equation $2.5x_1 + 3x_2 = 300$ is $-10/3$

26. If the coefficient of x_2 changes to a value greater than 6, the optimal solution changes.

28. An increase of more than 280 will change the optimal solution.

30. Let x_1 = number of sweep-easy brooms produced
    x_2 = number of light-sweep brooms produced

Maximize $Z = 2x_1 + 3.5x_2$

subject to
$$20x_1 + 10x_2 \leq 1440$$
$$12x_1 + 12x_2 \leq 1440$$
$$24x_1 + 4x_2 \leq 1440$$
$$x_1 - 2x_2 \leq 0$$

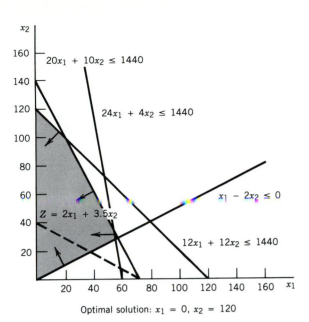

$20x_1 + 10x_2 \le 1440$

$24x_1 + 4x_2 \le 1440$

$x_1 - 2x_2 \le 0$

$Z = 2x_1 + 3.5x_2$

$12x_1 + 12x_2 \le 1440$

Optimal solution: $x_1 = 0$, $x_2 = 120$

32. The only point in the feasible region that represents full utilization of available machine time is (4,2). Therefore, the optimal solution occurs at this point with an objective value of zero.

CHAPTER 8. THE SIMPLEX METHOD

2. Initial simplex tableau

	c_j	3	2	0	0	0		
c_b	BASIS	x_1	x_2	S_1	S_2	S_3	SOLUTION	b_i/a_{ij}
0	S_1	④	1	1	0	0	200	200/4
0	S_2	1	1	0	1	0	80	80/1
0	S_3	1	3	0	0	1	180	180/1
	Z_j	0	0	0	0	0	0	
	$c_j - Z_j$	3	2	0	0	0		

Optimal simplex tableau

	c_j	3	2	0	0	0	
c_b	BASIS	x_1	x_2	S_1	S_2	S_3	SOLUTION
3	x_1	1	0	1/3	−1/3	0	40
2	x_2	0	1	−1/3	1 1/3	0	40
0	S_3	0	0	2/3	−3 2/3	1	20
	Z_j	3	2	1/3	1 2/3	0	200
	$c_j - Z_j$	0	0	−1/3	−1 2/3	0	

4. Initial simplex tableau

	c_j	5	7	0	−M	0	−M	
c_b	BASIS	x_1	x_2	S_1	A_1	S_2	A_2	SOLUTION
0	S_1	1	0	1	0	0	0	10
−M	A_1	1	1	0	1	0	0	12
−M	A_2	①	−2	0	0	−1	1	3
	Z_j	−2M	M	0	−M	M	−M	−15M
	$c_j - Z_j$	5 + 2M	7 − M	0	0	−M	0	

Optimal simplex tableau

	c_j	5	7	0	−M	0	−M	
c_b	BASIS	x_1	x_2	S_1	A_1	S_2	A_2	SOLUTION
0	S_1	0	0	1	−2/3	1/3	−1/3	1
7	x_2	0	1	0	1/3	1/3	−1/3	3
5	x_1	1	0	0	2/3	−1/3	1/3	9
	Z_j	5	7	0	17/3	2/3	−2/3	66
	$c_j - Z_j$	0	0	0	(−17/3 − M)	−2/3	(2/3 − M)	

6. Optimal simplex tableau

c_b	BASIS	c_j x_1 5	x_2 1	S_1 0	S_2 0	S_3 0	SOLUTION
0	S_1	0	2/3	1	0	$-1/3$	200
0	S_2	0	1 2/3	0	1	$-1/3$	800
5	x_1	1	1/3	0	0	1/3	800
	Z_j	5	5/3	0	0	5/3	40,000
	$c_j - Z_j$	0	$-2/3$	0	0	$-5/3$	

8. Initial simplex tableau

c_b	BASIS	c_j x_1 100	x_2 60	x_3 80	S_1 0	S_2 0	S_3 0	SOLUTION	b_i/a_{ij}
0	S_1	8	4	6	1	0	0	1200	1200/8
0	S_2	5	4	5	0	1	0	700	700/5
0	S_3	⑧	3	6	0	0	1	1000	1000/8
	Z_j	0	0	0	0	0	0	0	
	$c_j - Z_j$	100	60	80	0	0	0		

Optimal simplex tableau

c_b	BASIS	c_j x_1 100	x_2 60	x_3 80	S_1 0	S_2 0	S_3 0	SOLUTION
0	S_1	0	0	$-10/17$	1	$-8/17$	$-12/17$	2800/17
60	x_2	0	1	10/17	0	8/17	$-5/17$	600/17
100	x_1	1	0	9/17	0	$-3/17$	4/17	1900/17
	Z_j	100	60	1500/17	0	18/17	10/17	226000/17
	$c_j - Z_j$	0	0	$-140/17$	0	$-18/17$	$-10/17$	

10. Optimal simplex tableau

c_b	BASIS	c_j x_1 20	x_2 40	S_1 0	S_2 0	SOLUTION
0	S_1	3/2	0	1	$-1/4$	4000
40	x_2	1/2	1	0	1/4	4000
	Z_j	20	40	0	10	160,000
	$c_j - Z_j$	0	0	0	-10	

12. Optimal simplex tableau

c_b	BASIS	c_j x_1 3	x_2 6	x_3 2	S_1 0	S_2 0	SOLUTION
0	S_1	1	0	-3	1	-2	0
6	x_2	1/2	1	1	0	1/2	1/2
	Z_j	3	6	6	0	3	3
	$c_j - Z_j$	0	0	-4	0	-3	

14. Optimal simplex tableau

c_b	BASIS	c_j $\to$ 4 x_1	0 x_2	3 x_3	0 S_1	0 S_2	0 S_3	SOLUTION
0	S_1	0	0	0	1	-1	1	1
4	x_1	1	-1	0	0	1	-1	1
3	x_3	0	2	1	0	-1	2	2
	Z_j	4	2	3	0	1	2	10
	$c_j - Z_j$	0	-2	0	0	-1	-2	

16. Initial simplex tableau

c_b	BASIS	c_j $\to$ 1 x_1	1 x_2	-2 x_3	0 S_1	M A_1	0 S_2	M A_2	SOLUTION	b_i/a_{ij}
0	S_1	1	-1	1	1	0	0	0	8	8/1
M	A_1	1	-1	-2	0	1	0	0	4	4/1
M	A_2	2	1	-3	0	0	-1	1	12	12/2
	Z_j	$3M$	0	$-5M$	0	M	$-M$	M	$16M$	
	$c_j - Z_j$	$(1-3M)$	1	$(-2+5M)$	0	0	M	0		

Optimal simplex tableau

c_b	BASIS	c_j $\to$ 1 x_1	1 x_2	-2 x_3	0 S_1	M A_1	0 S_2	M A_2	SOLUTION
-2	x_3	0	0	1	1/3	$-1/3$	0	0	4/3
1	x_1	1	0	0	5/9	$-2/9$	$-1/3$	1/3	68/9
1	x_2	0	1	0	$-1/9$	$-5/9$	$-1/3$	1/3	8/9
	Z_j	1	1	-2	$-2/9$	$-13/9$	$-2/3$	2/3	52/9
	$c_j - Z_j$	0	0	0	2/9	$(13/9+M)$	2/3	$(-2/3+M)$	

18. Optimal simplex tableau

c_b	BASIS	c_j $\to$ 4 x_1	2 x_2	0 S_1	0 S_2	0 S_3	SOLUTION
2	x_2	0	1	3/8	0	$-1/2$	3
0	S_2	0	0	$-43/16$	1	33/12	77/2
4	x_1	1	0	$-1/6$	0	1/4	7/2
	Z_j	4	2	1/2	0	0	20
	$c_j - Z_j$	0	0	$-1/2$	0	0	

20. Let $x_1 = x_1' - x_3$
Initial simplex tableau

c_b	BASIS	c_j $\to$ 1 x_1'	1 x_2	-1 x_3	0 S_1	0 S_2	0 S_3	$-M$ A_1	SOLUTION	b_i/a_{ij}
0	S_1	3	5	-3	1	0	0	0	200	—
0	S_2	2	3	-2	0	1	0	0	1200	—
$-M$	A_1	-3	2	③	0	0	-1	1	400	400/3
	Z_j	$3M$	$-2M$	$-3M$	0	0	M	$-M$	$-400M$	
	$c_j - Z_j$	$(1-3M)$	$(1+2M)$	$(-1+3M)$	0	0	$-M$	0		

Optimal simplex tableau

c_b	BASIS	c_j	1	1	-1	0	0	0	$-M$	
			x_1'	x_2	x_3	S_1	S_2	S_3	A_1	SOLUTION
1	x_2		0	1	0	1/7	0	$-1/7$	1/7	600/7
0	S_2		0	0	0	$-13/21$	1	$-1/21$	1/21	23,000/21
-1	x_3		-1	0	1	$-2/21$	0	$-5/21$	5/21	1600/21
	Z_j		1	1	-1	5/21	0	2/21	$-2/21$	200/21
	$c_j - Z_j$		0	0	0	$-5/21$	0	$-2/21$	$(2/21 - M)$	

Optimal solution

$$x_1 = -1600/21$$
$$x_2 = 600/7$$
$$Z = 200/21$$

Note: Problems 22–40 were solved using a microcomputer. For these problems the solution values of the basic decision variables are provided along with the optimal value of the objective function.

22. $x_1 = 116.7$, $x_2 = 233.3$, $x_3 = 150$, $Z = 1583.33$

24. $x_2 = 94$, $x_3 = 20$, $Z = 5100$

26. $x_1 = 5.59$, $x_2 = 9.41$, $x_3 = 10$, $Z = 1,294,118$

28. $x_{11} = 1675$, $x_{21} = 1800$, $x_{22} = 325$, $I = 75$, $Z = 19,637.5$

30. $x_1 = 298.01$, $x_3 = 254.98$, $Z = 11,631.08$

32. $y_1 = 40$, $y_2 = 40.1434$, $y_3 = 36.6667$, $y_4 = 33$
$x_1 = 4.1434$, $x_2 = .5376$, $Z = 304,301.1$

34. $x_1 = 400$, $x_2 = 400$, $x_3 = 100$, $x_4 = 100$, $Z = 140$

36. a. $x_1 = 28,837.21$, $x_2 = 33,162.79$, $x_3 = 8000$
$x_4 = 5000$, $Z = 286,075.6$
b. $x_1 = 45,128.21$, $x_2 = 51,897.44$,
$x_3 = 8000$, $x_4 = 5000$, $Z = 428,621.8$

38. $x_5 = 5000$, $x_7 = 6100$, $Z = 7442$

40. $x_{14} = 1$, $x_{25} = 1$, $x_{33} = 1$, $x_{42} = 1$, $x_{51} = 1$, $Z = 120$

CHAPTER 9.
POSTOPTIMALITY
ANALYSIS

2. Minimize $Z = 40y + 80y_2$
subject to

$$y_1 + 2y_2 \geq 1$$
$$1/2y_1 + y_2 \geq 2$$
$$1/3y_1 + y_2 \geq 3$$
$$1/4y_1 \geq 4$$

with $y_1, y_2 \geq 0$

4. Minimize $Z = 8y_1 + 5y_2$
subject to

$$4y_1 + y_2 \geq 4$$
$$5y_1 + 3y_2 \geq 1$$

with $y_1 \geq 0$

y_2 unrestricted in sign

6. Minimize $Z = -50y_1 + 10y_2 + 75y_3$
subject to

$$-y_1 + 2y_3 \geq 1/2$$
$$-y_1 + y_2 + 3y_3 \geq 10$$
$$-y_1 + y_2 + y_3 \geq 75$$

with $y_1, y_3 \geq 0$

y_2 unrestricted in sign

8. Minimize $Z = 10y_1 + 4y_2 + 35y_3$
subject to

$$3y_1 - y_2 + 3y_3 = 1$$
$$-8y_1 - y_2 + 7y_3 = 8$$

with $y_1, y_3 \geq 0$

y_2 unrestricted in sign

10. Minimize $Z = 300y_1 + 400y_2 + 150y_3 - 60y_4 - 60y_5$
subject to

$$2.5y_1 + 5y_2 - y_4 \geq 2$$
$$3y_1 + 2y_2 + 2y_3 - y_5 \geq 4$$

with $y_1, y_2, y_3, y_4, y_5 \geq 0$

Note: The dual problem is unbounded.

12. Initial simplex tableau

	c_j	1000	1600	2400	0	0	
c_b	BASIS	x_1	x_2	x_3	S_1	S_2	SOLUTION
0	S_1	-1	-1	-3	1	0	-3
0	S_2	-1	-2	-1	0	1	-4
	Z_j	0	0	0	0	0	0
	$c_j - Z_j$	1000	1600	2400	0	0	

Optimal simplex tableau

	c_j	1000	1600	2400	0	0	
c_b	BASIS	x_1	x_2	x_3	S_1	S_2	SOLUTION
1000	x_1	1	0	5	-2	1	2
1600	x_2	0	1	-2	1	-1	1
	Z_j	1000	1600	1800	-400	-600	3600
	$c_j - Z_j$	0	0	600	400	600	

14. Initial simplex tableau

	c_j	1	2	0	0	0	
c_b	BASIS	x_1	x_2	S_1	S_2	S_3	SOLUTION
0	S_1	1	0	1	0	0	10
0	S_2	0	1	0	1	0	10
0	S_3	-1	-1	0	0	1	-15
	Z_j	0	0	0	0	0	0
	$c_j - Z_j$	1	2	0	0	0	

Optimal simplex tableau

c_b	c_j BASIS	1 x_1	2 x_2	0 S_1	0 S_2	0 S_3	SOLUTION
2	x_2	0	1	-1	0	-1	5
0	S_2	0	0	1	1	1	5
1	x_1	1	0	1	0	0	10
	Z_j	1	2	-1	0	-2	20
	$c_j - Z_j$	0	0	1	0	2	

16. a. $c_1 \geq 0$
$c_2 \geq 0$
$c_3 \geq -16.7$
$-16.7 \leq \text{Coef}(S_1) \leq 7$
$\text{Coef}(S_2) \geq -1.4$
$\text{Coef}(S_3) \geq -2.5$
b. $b_1 \geq -4.6$
$0 \leq b_2 \leq 45$
$b_3 \geq 0$

18. a. 105 units of lamp 2
230 units of lamp 3
b. $y_1 = 0$
$y_2 = 4$
$y_3 = .25$
c. $S_1 = 6.5$
$S_2 = 0$
$S_3 = 0$
d. Resource 1: 0
Resource 2: 4
Resource 3: .25
For an additional unit of resource, the objective function will increase by the amount of the shadow price.
e. For every unit of x_1 produced the objective function will decrease by 6.5.
f.
$$B^{-1} = \begin{bmatrix} 1 & -.5 & -2.5 \\ 0 & .5 & 0 \\ 0 & 0 & .125 \end{bmatrix}$$
$$B = \begin{bmatrix} 1 & 0 & 0 \\ 0 & 1 & 0 \\ 0 & 0 & 1 \end{bmatrix}$$

20. a. 0, an additional ounce of ham will not contribute to the objective function. This marginal change is valid when $b_1 \geq 64$.
b. .125, an additional ounce of turkey will contribute .125 to the objective function value.

This marginal change is valid when $48 \leq b_2 \leq 64$.
c. .25, an additional ounce of cheese will contribute .25 to the objective function value. This marginal change is valid when $64 \leq b_3 \leq 72$.
d. $x_1 = 14$
$x_2 = 5.5$
$S_1 = 2$
$Z = 22.25$
e. $x_1 = 8$
$x_2 = 12$
$S_3 = 4$
$Z = 26$
f. $.75 \leq c_1 \leq 1.125$
$1.33 \leq c_2 \leq 2.00$
g. $x_1 = 0$
$x_2 = 16$
$Z = 33.6$

22. a. Minimize $Z = 19y_1 + 14y_2 + 20y_3$
subject to
$2y_1 + y_2 + y_3 \geq 70$
$y_1 + y_2 + 2y_3 \geq 80$
with $y_1, y_2, y_3 \geq 0$
$y_1 = 20$
$y_2 = 0$
$y_3 = 30$
$S_1 = 0$
$S_2 = 0$
b. 19 hours of production
13 square yards of leather
20 cubic feet of fiber
c. 20, if an additional hour of production time is made available, the objective function value will increase by 20, valid if $10 \leq b_1 \leq 22$
d. 1 square yard
e. $40 \leq c_1 \leq 160$
f. No, the problem is no longer linear!

CHAPTER 10. GOAL PROGRAMMING

2. Let: x_1 = number of hours allocated to production team A

x_2 = number of hours allocated to production team B

The relative productivity between teams A and B is 6 units per hour/4 units per hour = 1.5

Minimize $Z = P_1 d_1^- + P_2 d_2^- + 1.5 P_3 d_3^+ + P_3 d_4^+ + 1.5 P_4 d_3^- + P_4 d_4^-$

subject to

$6x_1 + 4x_2 + d_1^- - d_1^+ = 600$
(production level constraint)

$x_1 \quad + d_2^- - d_2^+ = 45$
(overtime goal constraint—team A)

$x_1 \quad + d_3^- - d_3^+ = 40$
(operation time goal constraint—team A)

$x_2 + d_4^- - d_4^+ = 40$
(operation time goal constraint—team B)

with $x_j \geq 0$, $j = 1, 2$; $d_1^-, d_1^+, d_2^-, d_2^+, d_3^-, d_3^+, d_4^-, d_4^+, \geq 0$

where d_1^- = underachievement of production goal

d_1^+ = overachievement of production goal

d_2^- = deviation below maximum desired overtime for team A

d_2^+ = deviation above maximum desired overtime for team A

d_3^- = underutilization of regular working hours—team A

d_3^+ = overtime operation for team A

d_4^- = underutilization of regular working hours—team B

d_4^+ = overtime operation for team B

Computer solution:

$x_1 = 45.0 \quad d_1^- = 0 \quad d_2^- = 0 \quad d_3^- = 0$
$d_4^- = 0$
$x_2 = 85.5 \quad d_1^+ = 0 \quad d_2^+ = 0 \quad d_3^+ = 5.0$
$d_4^+ = 42.5$

Summary of goal achievement:

PRIORITY	OVER/UNDERACHIEVEMENT
4	0
3	50.0
2	0
1	0

The results of this problem provide an example of how priorities are considered. The primary goal (production level) and the secondary goal (avoiding team overtime in excess of 5 hours) are exactly satisfied. The fourth priority is also satisfied exactly, even though the third priority is not. Given the hours required to meet the first goal, overtime must be incurred by team B since the second priority limits team A overtime. The fourth goal is satisfied since there is no underutilization in either line.

4. Let x_j = number of units of food type j that are included in the diet menu.

$j = 1$—cottage cheese
$j = 2$—fruit
$j = 3$—yogurt
$j = 4$—whole wheat bread
$j = 5$—granola bars

Minimize
$Z = P_1 d_5^- + P_2 d_3^- + P_3 d_2^- + P_4 d_1^- + P_5 d_4^-$

subject to

$1.2x_1 + .7x_2 + 1.3x_3 + .9x_4 + 1.5x_5 \leq 35$
(budget constraint)

$200x_1 + 225x_2 + 175x_3 + 250x_4 + 300x_5$
≤ 15000 (calorie intake constraint)

$1.2x_1 + 2.5x_2 + 1.0x_3 + 1.2x_4 + 1.8x_5 \leq 50$
(protein consumption constraint)

$x_1 + d_1^- = 10$ (cottage cheese goal constraint)
$x_2 + d_2^- = 10$ (fruit constraint)
$x_3 + d_3^- = 10$ (yogurt constraint)
$x_4 + d_4^- = 10$ (whole wheat bread constraint)
$x_5 + d_5^- = 10$ (granola bars constraint)

$x_j \geq 0$, $j = 1, 2, \ldots, 5$; $d_j^- \geq 0$, $j = 1, 2, \ldots, 5$

where d_j^- = underachievement of the aspiration level for food type j.

Computer solution:

$x_1 = 0 \quad d_1^- = 10$
$x_2 = 10 \quad d_2^- = 0$
$x_3 = 10 \quad d_3^- = 0$
$x_4 = 0 \quad d_4^- = 10$
$x_5 = 10 \quad d_5^- = 0$

Summary of goal achievement:

PRIORITY	OVER/UNDERACHIEVEMENT
5	10
4	10
3	0
2	0
1	0

By assigning a relatively low aspiration level to each food type, Joe was able to satisfy his first three priority goals for 10 units each of granola bars, yogurt, and fruit. The solution keeps Joe within his calorie intake constraint (7000 calories are consumed) and satisfies his need for protein (53 units are consumed). The program exactly meets his budget of $35.00.

6. Let x_j = hours allocated to production of casting type to class of customer.

$j = 1$—casting A for old customers
$j = 2$—casting A for new customers
$j = 3$—casting B for old customers
$j = 4$—casting B for new customers
$j = 5$—casting C for old customers
$j = 6$—casting C for new customers

Minimize $Z = P_1 d_1^- + P_1 d_2^- + P_1 d_3^- + P_2 d_4^+ + P_3 d_5^- + P_3 d_6^- + P_4 d_7^-$

subject to

$x_1 + d_1^- - d_1^+ = 80$ hours
(weekly demand for casting type A)

$x_3 + d_2^- - d_2^+ = 40$ hours
(weekly demand for casting type B)

$x_5 + d_3^- - d_3^+ = 25$ hours
(weekly demand for casting type C)

$x_1 + x_2 + x_3 + x_4 + x_5 + x_6 + d_4^- - d_4^+ = 50$
hours   (overtime operation goal constraint)

$\left. \begin{array}{l} x_2 + d_5^- - d_5^+ = 60 \text{ hours} \\ x_6 + d_6^- - d_6^+ = 20 \text{ hours} \end{array} \right\}$
(goal constraints —meet new customer demand for 15 A castings and 20 C castings, respectively)

$x_1 + x_2 + x_3 + x_4 + x_5 + x_6 + d_7^- - d_7^+ = 40$
hours   (operation time goal constraint)

where: d_1^- = underachievement of weekly production goal for type A
d_1^+ = excess production of type A for weekly demand
d_2^- = underachievement of weekly production goal for type B
d_2^+ = excess production of type B for weekly demand
d_3^- = underachievement of weekly production goal for type C
d_3^+ = excess production of type C for weekly demand
d_4^- = deviation below maximum desired overtime level
d_4^+ = operation time above maximum desired overtime level
d_5^- = underachievement of new customer demand, type A
d_5^+ = excess production of type A for new customers

d_6^- = underachievement of new customer demand, type C
d_6^+ = excess production of type C for new customers
d_7^- = underutilization of regular working hours
d_7^+ = overutilization of regular working hours

Computer solution:
$x_1 = 80 \quad x_3 = 40 \quad x_5 = 25 \quad d_1^- = 0$
$d_2^- = 0$
$x_2 = 0 \quad x_4 = 0 \quad x_6 = 0 \quad d_1^+ = 0$
$d_2^+ = 0$
$d_3^- = 0 \quad d_4^- = 0 \quad d_5^- = 60 \quad d_6^- = 20$
$d_7^- = 0$
$d_3^+ = 0 \quad d_4^+ = 95 \quad d_5^+ = 0 \quad d_6^+ = 0$
$d_7^+ = 105$

Summary of goal achievement:

PRIORITY	OVER/UNDERACHIEVEMENT
4	0
3	80
2	95
1	0

The goals assigned priorities 1 and 4 were achieved exactly, the weekly demand for all types of castings, and the underutilization of production capacity, respectively. The goal associated with priority 2 cannot be satisfied since $80 + 40 + 25 = 145$ hours of capacity are required to meet regular weekly demand alone, which is 95 hours more than the plants' weekly regular time capacity. The third priority, production for new customers, is missed entirely $(60 + 20 = 80)$.

8. Computer solution:
$x_1 = 40 \quad d_1^- = 0 \quad d_2^- = 0 \quad d_3^- = 0$
$x_2 = 70 \quad d_1^+ = 80 \quad d_2^+ = 0 \quad d_3^+ = 0$
All priorities are achieved exactly.

10. Computer solution:
$x_1 = 8 \quad d_1^- = 0 \quad d_2^- = 7.0 \quad d_3^- = 0$
$d_4^- = 0$
$x_2 = 15.2 \quad d_1^+ = 0 \quad d_2^+ = 0 \quad d_3^+ = 5.2$
$d_4^+ = 0$

Summary of goal achievement:

PRIORITY	OVER/UNDERACHIEVEMENT
4	0
3	$4 \times 5.2 = 20.8$
2	0
1	0

12. a. Let $x_i = \begin{cases} 1 \text{ if marketing program } i \text{ is chosen} \\ 0 \text{ otherwise} \end{cases}$

$i = 1$—marketing program 1
$i = 2$—marketing program 2
$i = 3$—marketing program 3

Minimize $Z = d_1^- + d_2^-$

subject to

$500{,}000x_1 + 400{,}000x_2 + 500{,}000x_3 + d_1^- = 1{,}400{,}000$ (total profit goal constraint)

$30x_1 + 30x_2 + 20x_3 + d_2^- = 80$ (units sold goal constraint)

$70{,}000x_1 + 10{,}000x_2 + 40{,}000x_3 \le 80{,}000$ (year 1 budget constraint)

$50{,}000x_1 + 30{,}000x_2 + 20{,}000x_3 \le 70{,}000$ (year 2 budget constraint)

with $x_i = 0, 1; d_i \ge 0, i = 1, 2$

where d_1^- = underachievement of total possible unconstrained profit

d_2^- = underachievement of total possible unconstrained number of units sold.

14. Let x_{ijk} = number of students of race i bused from district j to school k

$i = 1, 2$ (black is coded "1")
$j = 1, 2, 3, 4$
$k = 1, 2, 3$

Percent minority:

Black	White
460	30
260	110
30	520
50	390
800	1050

$800/(800 + 1050) = .4324$ = desired proportion of black students

Minimize $Z = P_1 \sum_{i=1}^{3} (d_i^+ + d_i^-) + P_2 d_4^+ +$

$P_3(6d_5^+ + 6d_6^+ + 7d_7^+ + 7d_8^+ + 5d_9^+ + 5d_{10}^+) +$

$P_4 \sum_{i=11}^{13} (d_i^+ + d_i^-)$

subject to

The first racial balance goal constraint is of the form:

$\sum_{j=1}^{4} x_{1j1} + d_1^- - d_1^+ = .4324 \sum_{i=1}^{2}\sum_{j=1}^{4} x_{ij1}$

This and the two remaining racial balance goal constraints may be written as:

1. $.5676 \sum_{j=1}^{4} x_{1j1} - .4324 \sum_{j=1}^{4} x_{2j1} + d_1^- - d_1^+ = 0$

2. $.5676 \sum_{j=1}^{4} x_{1j2} - .4324 \sum_{j=2}^{4} x_{2j2} + d_2^- - d_2^+ = 0$

3. $.5676 \sum_{j=1}^{4} x_{1j3} - .4324 \sum_{j=1}^{4} x_{2j3} + d_2^- - d_3^+ = 0$

4. $\sum_{i=1}^{2}\sum_{j=1}^{4}\sum_{k=1}^{3} c_{jk} x_{ijk} - d_4^+ = 0$

(minimize total transportation cost goal)

To limit the average distance traveled by any student to 8 miles, identify all decision variables that represent district-to-school combinations of greater than 8 miles, then minimize the values of these decision variables in the final solution. This results in the following set of constraints, (5) through (10).

5. $x_{113} - d_5^+ = 0$
6. $x_{213} - d_6^+ = 0$
7. $x_{123} - d_7^+ = 0$
8. $x_{223} - d_8^+ = 0$
9. $x_{131} - d_9^+ = 0$
10. $x_{231} - d_{10}^+ = 0$

11. $\sum_{i=1}^{2}\sum_{j=1}^{4} x_{ij1} + d_{11}^- - d_{11}^+ = 700$

12. $\sum_{i=1}^{2}\sum_{j=1}^{4} x_{ij2} + d_{12}^- - d_{12}^+ = 550$ underutilization/overcrowding goal constraints

13. $\sum_{i=1}^{2}\sum_{j=1}^{4} x_{ij3} + d_{13}^- - d_{13}^+ = 550$

Structural constraints (14) through (21) are included to ensure that every child is assigned to a school:

14. $\sum_{k=1}^{3} x_{11k} = 460$

15. $\sum_{k=1}^{3} x_{21k} = 30$

16. $\sum_{k=1}^{3} x_{12k} = 260$

17. $\sum_{k=1}^{3} x_{22k} = 110$

18. $\sum_{k=1}^{3} x_{13k} = 30$

19. $\sum_{k=1}^{3} x_{23k} = 520$

20. $\sum_{k=1}^{3} x_{14k} = 50$

21. $\sum_{k=1}^{3} x_{24k} = 390$

Note that constraints (14) through (21) could also have been written as:

$\sum_{k=1}^{3} x_{ijk} = \#\ i = 1, 2;\quad j = 1, 2, 3, 4$

with $x_{ijk} \geq 0;$ $i = 1, 2;$ $j = 1, 2, 3, 3\ 4;$
$k = 1, 2, 3$

$d_j^- \geq 0$ $j = 1, 2, 3; 11, 12, 13$

$d_j^+ \geq 0$ $j = 1, 2, \ldots, 13$

where d_k^- = underachievement of racial balance goal in school k; $k = 1, 2, 3$.

d_k^+ = proportion of minorities in excess of racial balance goal in school k; $k = 1, 2, 3$.

d_j^+ = number of students traveling in excess of 8 miles; $j = 5, 6, \ldots, 10$.

d_k^- = underutilization of capacity of school k; $k = 11, 12, 13$.

d_k^+ = number of students assigned in excess of capacity of school k; $k = 11, 12, 13$.

Computer solution: (All decision variables and deviation variables not listed have solution values of zero.)

$x_{111} = 357.72 \simeq 358$ $x_{241} = 323.72 \simeq 324$
$x_{112} = 102.28 \simeq 102$ $x_{243} = 66.28 \simeq 66$
$x_{122} = 260.00$ $d_1^+ = 5$
$x_{132} = 30.00$ $d_4^+ = 83{,}609.69$
$x_{143} = 50.00$ $d_{11}^- = 121.44$
$x_{212} = 30.00$ $d_{12}^+ = 362.28$
$x_{221} = 110.00$ $d_{13}^- = 433.72$
$x_{232} = 520.00$

The following table summarizes the assignments.

Summary of goal achievement:

PRIORITY	OVER/UNDERACHIEVEMENT	
4	917.45	
3	0.0009	(virtually zero)
2	83609.69	
1	5	

The highest priority goal, racial balance in each school, is achieved exactly in schools 2 and 3, and exceeded by 5 students in school 1. Underachievement of the second priority represents the total cost of the program, $83,609.69. No students are bused in excess of 8 miles; however, there is considerable crowding in schools 1 and 2, whereas school 3 is highly underutilized:

SCHOOL	CAPACITY	ASSIGNED
1	700	792
2	550	942
3	550	116

DISTRICT	RACE	SCHOOL 1	SCHOOL 2	SCHOOL 3	TOTAL NUMBER OF PUPILS
1	Black	358	102		460
	White		30		30
2	Black		260		260
	White	110			110
3	Black		30		30
	White		520		520
4	Black			50	50
	White	324		66	390
Total Assigned		792	942	116	1850
Capacity		700	550	550	

16. x_1 = hours spent sunbathing
x_2 = hours spent at the gym
x_3 = hours spent fishing
Minimize $Z = P_1 d_1^- + P_2 d_2^- + P_3 d_3^+ + P_4 d_4^-$
subject to:

$x_1 + d_1^- - d_1^+ = 6$ (sunbathing goal constraint)

$x_2 + d_2^- - d_2^+ = 3$ (time at gym goal constraint)

$x_3 - x_1 - x_2 + d_3^- - d_3^+ = 0$ (total sunbathing and time at the gym goal constraint)

$12.5x_3 - 10x_2 + d_4^- - d_4^+ = 30$ (earnings goal constraint)

$x_1 + x_2 + x_3 = 12$ (12 hours/day)

Since Laura earns $12.50/hr fishing and time at the

gym costs $10.00/hr, she must work 10/12.5 or .8 hours for every hour she spends at the gym.

$x_3 - .8x_2 \geq 0$

with $x_j \geq 0$, $\quad j = 1, 2, 3$; $\quad d_j^-, d_j^+ \geq 0$, $j = 1, 2, 3, 4$.

where: d_1^- = underachievement of sunbathing goal

d_1^+ = hours spent sunbathing in excess of 6 hours

d_2^- = underachievement of time at gym goal

d_2^+ = hours spent at gym in excess of 3 hours

d_3^- = excess of hours spent sunbathing and at gym, relative to hours fishing

d_3^+ = excess of hours spent fishing, relative to sunbathing and time at the gym

d_4^- = excess spent, relative to money earned

d_4^+ = excess earned, relative to money spent

Computer solution:

$x_1 = 6$ $x_3 = 3$ $d_1^+ = 0$ $d_2^+ = 0$
$d_3^+ = 0$ $d_4^+ = 0$
$x_2 = 3$ $d_1^- = 0$ $d_2^- = 0$ $d_3^- = 6$
$d_4^- = 22.5$

Summary of goal achievement:

PRIORITY	OVER/UNDERACHIEVEMENT
4	22.5
3	0
2	0
1	0

The first three goals are satisfied exactly. However, she earns only $30 - 22.5 = \$7.50$ more in a day than she spends at the gym.

18. Let x_j = gallons purchased from source j
$\quad j = 1 -$ Source A
$\quad j = 2 -$ Source B
$\quad j = 3 -$ Source C
Minimize $Z = P_1 d_1^- + P_2 d_2^+ + P_3 d_3^- + P_4 d_4^+$

subject to

$x_1 + d_1^- - d_1^+ = 6000$ (contract purchase goal constraint)

$.10x_1 + .08x_2 + .05x_3 + d_2^- - d_2^+ = 1000$ (shipping cost goal constraint)

$.7x_1 + .9x_2 + .6x_3 + d_3^- - d_3^- = 8000$ (minimum percent ethyl goal constraint)

$.60x_1 + .83x_2 + .30x_3 - d_4^+ = 0$ (total cost minimization constraint)

$x_1 + x_2 + x_3 = 10,000$ (total demand constraint)

with $x_j \geq 0$, $j = 1, 2, 3$; $\quad d_j^-, d_j^+ \geq 0$
$\quad j = 1, 2, 3$;
$\quad j = 1, 2, 3, 4$

where d_1^- = underachievement of contract purchase

d_1^+ = purchase in excess of contract (6000 gallons)

d_2^- = underachievement of shipping cost goal

d_2^+ = shipping cost in excess of $1000

d_3^- = underachievement of percent ethyl goal

d_3^+ = overachievement of percent ethyl goal

d_4^+ = total purchase cost (including shipping)

Computer solution:

$x_1 = 6000$ $x_3 = 0$ $d_1^+ = 0$ $d_2^+ = 0$
$d_3^+ = 0$
$x_2 = 4000$ $d_1^- = 0$ $d_2^- = 80$
$d_3^- = 200$ $d_4^+ = 6920$

Summary of goal achievement:

PRIORITY	OVER/UNDERACHIEVEMENT	
4	6920	(6919.9922)
3	200	
2	0	
1	0	

The first two priorities are satisfied exactly; however, the third priority cannot possibly be satisfied given the large percentage of fuel that must be purchased from source A, which has a relatively low ethyl content.

CHAPTER 11. TRANSPORTATION, TRANSSHIPMENT, AND ASSIGNMENT PROBLEMS

2.

Allocation	Route	Cost
20 units	$O_1 \rightarrow B$	$120
40 units	$O_1 \rightarrow C$	80
30 units	$O_2 \rightarrow A$	120
30 units	$O_3 \rightarrow B$	120
70 units	$O_3 \rightarrow D$	420
Totals 190 units		$860

4.

Allocation	Route	Cost
10 units	$O_1 \rightarrow D_1$	$ 30
40 units	$O_1 \rightarrow D_3$	120
25 units	$O_2 \rightarrow D_4$	25
45 units	$O_2 \rightarrow D_5$	180
15 units	$O_3 \rightarrow D_1$	90
25 units	$O_3 \rightarrow D_2$	125
15 units	$O_3 \rightarrow D_5$	120
40 units	$O_3 \rightarrow D_6$	160
25 units	$O_4 \rightarrow D_2$	100
Totals 240 units		$950

6. a., b.

Allocation	Route	Cost
30 units	$O_1 \rightarrow D_3$	$210
20 units	$O_1 \rightarrow D_5$	0
40 units	$O_2 \rightarrow D_1$	120
40 units	$O_2 \rightarrow D_2$	200
40 units	$O_3 \rightarrow D_3$	160
10 units	$O_4 \rightarrow D_1$	30
80 units	$O_4 \rightarrow D_4$	320
Totals 260 units		$1040

c. Minimize $Z = 6x_{11} + 9x_{12} + 7x_{13} + Mx_{14}$
$+ 3x_{21} + 5x_{22} + 8x_{23} + 10x_{24}$
$+ Mx_{31} + 6x_{32} + 4x_{33} + 7x_{34}$
$+ 3x_{41} + 9x_{42} + 6x_{43} + 4x_{44}$

subject to: $x_{11} + x_{12} + x_{13} + x_{14} = 50$
$x_{21} + x_{22} + x_{23} + x_{24} = 80$
$x_{31} + x_{32} + x_{33} + x_{34} = 40$
$x_{41} + x_{42} + x_{43} + x_{44} = 90$
$x_{11} + x_{21} + x_{31} + x_{41} = 50$
$x_{12} + x_{22} + x_{32} + x_{42} = 40$
$x_{13} + x_{23} + x_{33} + x_{43} = 70$
$x_{14} + x_{24} + x_{34} + x_{44} = 80$

all $x_{ij} \geq 0$

8.

Allocation	Route	Cost
40 canteloupes	Walterboro → Spartanburg	$2400
10 canteloupes	Kingstree → Charleston	350
50 canteloupes	Kingstree → Spartanburg	1500
50 canteloupes	Edgefield → Columbia	2000
20 canteloupes	Dummy → Charleston	0
Totals 170 canteloupes		$6250

10.

Allocation	Route	Cost
50 units	$P_1 \rightarrow W_2$	$200
30 units	$P_1 \rightarrow W_3$	90
40 units	$P_2 \rightarrow W_1$	240
10 units	$P_2 \rightarrow W_4$	50
30 units	$P_3 \rightarrow W_2$	120
10 units	$P_4 \rightarrow W_1$	0
Totals 170 units		$700

12.

Allocation	Route	Cost
30 units	$DC_1 \rightarrow W_1$	$120
10 units	$DC_2 \rightarrow W_1$	50
20 units	$DC_2 \rightarrow W_2$	60
30 units	$DC_2 \rightarrow W_3$	180
40 units	$DC_3 \rightarrow W_4$	160
Totals 130 units		$570

14.

Allocation	Route	Cost
150,000 bushels	Corn → Storage Depot 1	$ 4,500,000
750,000 bushels	Wheat → Storage Depot 2	18,750,000
100,000 bushels	Oats → Storage Depot 2	2,000,000
200,000 bushels	Oats → Storage Depot 3	6,000,000
1,200,000 bushels	Oats → Storage Depot 4	24,000,000
200,000 bushels	Soybeans → Storage Depot 1	10,000,000
200,000 bushels	Soybeans → Storage Depot 3	10,000,000
50,000 bushels	Dummy → Storage Depot 1	0
Totals 2,850,000 bushels		$75,250,000

16.

Allocation	Route	Cost
500 men's suits	Phoenix → Chicago	$13,500
500 men's suits	Dallas → Chicago	13,000
1800 men's suits	Atlanta → St. Louis	46,800
1700 men's suits	Atlanta → New York	40,800
(Transshipment) 200 men's suits	New York → Chicago	1,200
		$115,300

18.

Assignment	Time
Jan → Job 2	4
Bill → Job 1	2
Sue → Job 5	4
Tom → Job 6	4
Mary → Job 4	5
Joe → Job 3	3
Total	22

20.

Assignment	Profit
Customer 1 → Product B	7
Customer 2 → Product E	7
Customer 3 → Product C	9
Customer 4 → Product A	11
Customer 5 → Product D	9
Total	43

CHAPTER 12.
NETWORK MODELS

2. Shortest route: $0 \to D \to T$
   Length: 14 days

8. Minimum spanning tree = 26 days.

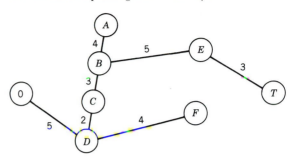

10. Minimum spanning tree = 54 (hundred miles)

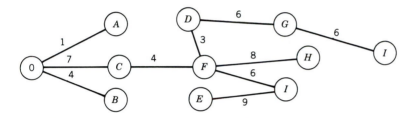

12. Minimum spanning tree = 41.1 miles

Center 1 to Center 2	4 miles
Center 2 to Center 4	4.2 miles
Center 2 to Center 3	4.5 miles
Center 3 to Center 6	5.2 miles
Center 6 to Center 5	5 miles
Center 5 to Center 7	4.2 miles
Center 7 to Center 8	4.5 miles
Center 7 to Center 9	5 miles
Center 9 to Center 10	4.5 miles

14. Flow assignments
   7 to $1 \to 2 \to 4 \to 7$
   6 to $1 \to 3 \to 6 \to 7$
   4 to $1 \to 3 \to 5 \to 7$
   1 to $1 \to 3 \to 4 \to 5 \to 7$
   $\overline{18}$ = Maximum flow

16. Flow assignments
   2 to $1 \to 5 \to 9$
   2 to $1 \to 2 \to 5 \to 9$
   3 to $1 \to 3 \to 5 \to 9$
   1 to $1 \to 2 \to 4 \to 7 \to 5 \to 8 \to 9$
   1 to $1 \to 2 \to 4 \to 7 \to 5 \to 9$
   3 to $1 \to 2 \to 4 \to 7 \to 9$
   2 to $1 \to 3 \to 8 \to 9$
   1 to $1 \to 3 \to 6 \to 8 \to 9$
   $\overline{15}$ = Maximum flow

18. Flow assignments
   7 to $1 \to 5 \to 8 \to 10$
   5 to $1 \to 2 \to 3 \to 6 \to 8 \to 10$
   6 to $1 \to 5 \to 7 \to 9 \to 10$
   4 to $1 \to 4 \to 5 \to 7 \to 9 \to 10$
   4 to $1 \to 2 \to 3 \to 6 \to 8 \to 9 \to 10$
   $\overline{26}$ = Maximum flow

CHAPTER 13.
PERT/CPM

2.

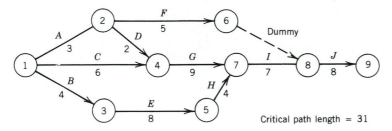

Critical path length = 31

or

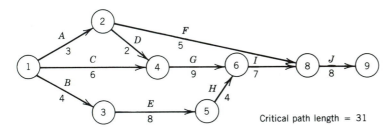

Critical path length = 31

4.   a.–c.

PERT ANALYSIS FOR 13-4						
ACTIVITY NO.	NAME	ACTIVITY EXP. TM.	EARLIEST START	LATEST START	EARLIEST FINISH	LATEST FINISH	SLACK LS-ES
1	a	3.0000	0	2.0000	3.0000	5.0000	2.0000
2	b	4.0000	0	0	4.0000	4.0000	Critical
3	c	6.0000	0	1.0000	6.0000	7.0000	1.0000
4	d	2.0000	3.0000	5.0000	5.0000	7.0000	2.0000
5	e	8.0000	4.0000	4.0000	12.000	12.000	Critical
6	f	5.0000	3.0000	18.000	8.0000	23.000	15.000
7	g	9.0000	6.0000	7.0000	15.000	16.000	1.0000
8	h	4.0000	12.000	12.000	16.000	16.000	Critical
9	i	7.0000	16.000	16.000	23.000	23.000	Critical
10	j	8.0000	23.000	23.000	31.000	31.000	Critical
Expected completion time = 31							

d.   Critical path: $1 \rightarrow 3 \rightarrow 5 \rightarrow 6 \rightarrow 8 \rightarrow 9$;
completion time = 31 days

6. a.–d.

PERT ANALYSIS FOR 13-6							
ACTIVITY NO.	NAME	ACTIVITY EXP. TM.	VAR.	EARLIEST START	LATEST START	EARLIEST FINISH	LATEST FINISH	SLACK LS-ES
1	a	5.8333	0.6944	0	4.5000	5.8333	10.333	4.5000
2	b	6.0000	0.4444	0	5.6667	6.0000	11.667	5.6667
3	c	9.1667	0.6944	0	0	9.1667	9.1667	Critical
4	d	8.8333	0.6944	5.8333	10.333	14.667	19.167	4.5000
5	e	8.0000	1.0000	5.8333	11.000	13.833	19.000	5.1667
6	f	5.8333	0.6944	6.0000	13.333	11.833	19.167	7.3333
7	g	7.3333	1.7778	6.0000	11.667	13.333	19.000	5.6667
8	h	8.0000	0.4444	9.1667	11.167	17.167	19.167	2.0000
9	i	9.8333	0.6944	9.1667	9.1667	19.000	19.000	Critical
10	j	7.0000	0.4444	17.167	19.167	24.167	26.167	2.0000
11	k	7.1667	1.3611	19.000	19.000	26.167	26.167	Critical
Expected completion time = 26.16667							

e. Critical path: 1 → 4 → 6 → 7; completion time = 26.1667 days

f. Probability (meeting schedule completion time of 25 days) = 0.241

8. a.–d.

PERT ANALYSIS FOR 13-8							
ACTIVITY NO.	NAME	ACTIVITY EXP. TM.	VAR.	EARLIEST START	LATEST START	EARLIEST FINISH	LATEST FINISH	SLACK LS-ES
1	a	6.3333	1.0000	0	2.6667	6.3333	9.0000	2.6667
2	b	6.3333	0.4444	0	0	6.3333	6.3333	Critical
3	c	9.0000	1.0000	6.3333	14.333	15.333	23.333	8.0000
4	d	8.3333	0.4444	6.3333	11.500	14.667	19.833	5.1667
5	e	10.667	0.4444	6.3333	9.0000	17.000	19.667	2.6667
6	f	11.333	1.0000	6.3333	9.8333	17.667	21.167	3.5000
7	g	10.333	1.0000	6.3333	13.000	16.667	23.333	6.6667
8	h	13.500	0.6944	6.3333	6.3333	19.833	19.833	Critical
9	i	10.500	0.6944	6.3333	9.1667	16.833	19.667	2.8333
10	j	12.167	0.6944	6.3333	9.0000	18.500	21.167	2.6667
11	k	7.5000	0.6944	16.667	23.333	24.167	30.833	6.6667
12	l	5.3333	0.4444	16.667	23.833	22.000	29.167	7.1667
13	m	4.3333	0.4444	19.833	26.500	24.167	30.833	6.6667
14	n	9.3333	0.4444	19.833	19.833	29.167	29.167	Critical
15	o	9.5000	0.2500	17.000	19.667	26.500	29.167	2.6667

PERT ANALYSIS FOR 13-8							
ACTIVITY NO.	NAME	ACTIVITY EXP. TM.	VAR.	EARLIEST START	LATEST START	EARLIEST FINISH	LATEST FINISH	SLACK LS-ES
16	p	12.667	1.0000	17.000	21.500	29.667	34.167	4.5000
17	q	8.0000	1.0000	18.500	21.167	26.500	29.167	2.6667
18	r	9.1667	1.3611	18.500	25.000	27.677	34.167	6.5000
19	s	9.0000	1.0000	24.167	30.833	33.167	39.833	6.6667
20	t	10.667	1.0000	29.167	29.167	39.833	39.833	Critical
21	u	5.6667	1.0000	29.667	34.167	35.333	39.833	4.5000
Expected completion time = 39.83334							

e. Critical path: $1 \to 3 \to 5 \to 9 \to 11$; completion time = 39.833

f. Probability (meeting schedule time of 40 weeks) = 0.541.

10. a.–d.

PERT ANALYSIS FOR 13-10							
ACTIVITY NO.	NAME	ACTIVITY EXP. TM.	VAR.	EARLIEST START	LATEST START	EARLIEST FINISH	LATEST FINISH	SLACK LS-ES
1	a	6.0000	0.4444	0	0	6.0000	6.0000	Critical
2	b	8.6667	1.0000	0	6.5000	8.6667	15.167	6.5000
3	c	9.0000	1.0000	6.0000	6.0000	15.000	15.000	Critical
4	d	8.1667	0.6944	6.0000	7.0000	14.167	15.167	1.0000
5	e	7.5000	1.3611	15.000	15.000	22.500	22.500	Critical
6	f	7.3333	0.1111	14.167	15.167	21.500	22.500	1.0000
7	g	7.0000	1.0000	22.500	22.500	29.500	29.500	Critical
Expected completion time = 29.5							

e. Critical path: $1 \to 2 \to 3 \to 5 \to 6$; completion time = 29.5 days.

f. Probability (meeting schedule time of 35 days or less) = 0.997.

g. Probability (meeting schedule time of 30 days or less) = 0.40.

12. a.

CPM ANALYSIS FOR 13-12						
ACTIVITY NUMBER	ACTIVITY NAME	EARLIEST START	LATEST START	EARLIEST FINISH	LATEST FINISH	SLACK LS-ES
1	b	0	0	6.0000	6.0000	Critical
2	a	0	1.0000	5.0000	6.0000	1.0000
3	c	6.0000	10.000	11.000	15.000	4.0000
4	d	6.0000	6.0000	14.000	14.000	Critical

CPM ANALYSIS FOR 13-12						
ACTIVITY NUMBER	ACTIVITY NAME	EARLIEST START	LATEST START	EARLIEST FINISH	LATEST FINISH	SLACK LS-ES
5	e	5.0000	6.0000	14.000	15.000	1.0000
6	f	5.0000	7.0000	12.000	14.000	2.0000
7	g	5.0000	19.000	15.000	29.000	14.000
8	h	14.000	17.000	25.000	28.000	3.0000
9	i	14.000	15.000	26.000	27.000	1.0000
10	j	14.000	18.000	25.000	29.000	4.0000
11	k	14.000	18.000	24.000	28.000	4.0000
12	l	14.000	14.000	27.000	27.000	Critical
13	m	25.000	29.000	34.000	38.000	4.0000
14	n	25.000	28.000	35.000	38.000	3.0000
15	o	27.000	27.000	38.000	38.000	Critical
Completion time = 38 Total cost = 0						

Critical Path: 1 → 2 → 3 → 4 → 8 → 9; completion time = 38 days
1 → 2 → 5 → 8 → 9; completion time = 38 days

12. b.

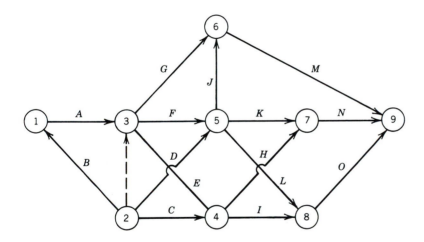

12. c. Time–cost trade-off curve

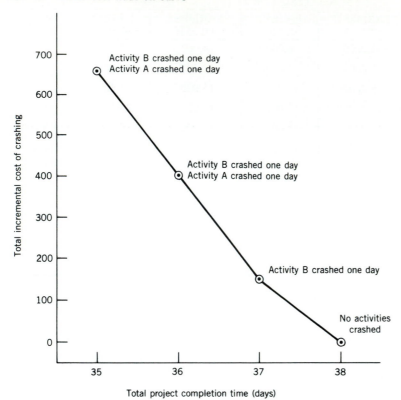

14. a. Budget using earliest start times

Activity	1	2	3	4	5	6	7	8	9	10	11	12
A	4	4	4	4	4							
B			13 1/3	13 1/3	13 1/3							
C					2	2	2	2	2			
D						15	15	15	15			
E						16 2/3	16 2/3	16 2/3				
Cost/ Month	4	4	17 1/3	17 1/3	19 1/3	33 2/3	33 2/3	33 2/3	17			
Total cost	4	8	25 1/3	42 2/3	62	95 2/3	129 1/3	163	180	180	180	180

b. Budget using latest start times

Activity	1	2	3	4	5	6	7	8	9	10	11	12
A	4	4	4	4	4							
B						13 1/3	13 1/3	13 1/3				
C						2	2	2	2	2		
D								15	15	15	15	
E										16 2/3	16 2/3	16 2/3
Cost/ Month	4	4	4	4	4	15 1/3	15 1/3	30 1/3	17	33 2/3	31 2/3	16 2/3
Total cost	4	8	12	16	20	35 1/3	50 2/3	81	98	131 2/3	163 1/3	180

c. Budgeted cost ranges

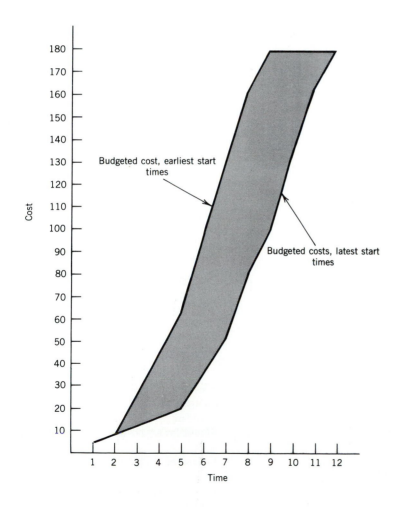

CHAPTER 14. INTEGER PROGRAMMING MODELS

2. Optimal solution: $x_1 = 2$, $x_2 = 3$, $Z = 7$

4. Optimal solution: $x_1 = 2$, $x_2 = 2$, $Z = 12$

6. Optimal solution: $x_1 = 52$, $x_3 = 23$, $Z = 75$

8. a.

$$\text{Minimize } Z = 2x_{11} + 4x_{12} + 3x_{13} + 1x_{14} + 5x_{15}$$
$$+ 1x_{21} + 2x_{22} + 3x_{23} + 4x_{24} + 5x_{25}$$
$$+ 5x_{31} + 4x_{32} + 3x_{33} + 2x_{34} + 1x_{35}$$
$$+ 3x_{41} + 2x_{42} + 4x_{43} + 5x_{44} + 1x_{45}$$
$$+ 3x_{51} + 4x_{52} + 5x_{53} + 1x_{54} + 2x_{55}$$

subject to

$$x_{11} + x_{12} + x_{13} + x_{14} + x_{15} = 1$$
$$x_{21} + x_{22} + x_{23} + x_{24} + x_{25} = 1$$
$$x_{31} + x_{32} + x_{33} + x_{34} + x_{35} = 1$$
$$x_{41} + x_{42} + x_{43} + x_{44} + x_{45} = 1$$
$$x_{51} + x_{52} + x_{53} + x_{54} + x_{55} = 1$$
$$x_{11} + x_{21} + x_{31} + x_{41} + x_{51} = 1$$
$$x_{12} + x_{22} + x_{32} + x_{42} + x_{52} = 1$$
$$x_{13} + x_{23} + x_{33} + x_{43} + x_{53} = 1$$
$$x_{14} + x_{24} + x_{34} + x_{44} + x_{54} = 1$$
$$x_{15} + x_{25} + x_{35} + x_{45} + x_{55} = 1$$

with $x_{ij} \geq 0$ ($i = 1, 2, \ldots, 5$; $j = 1, 2, \ldots, 5$)

$$x_{ij} = \begin{cases} 1 & \text{if carrier } i \text{ is assigned to route } j \\ 0 & \text{otherwise} \end{cases}$$

8. b.   Optimal solution: $x_{13} = 1$, $x_{21} = 1$, $x_{35} = 1$, $x_{42} = 1$, $x_{54} = 1$, $Z = 8$

10. a. $x_1 + x_2 + x_3 + x_5 \geq 2$
    b. $x_3 - x_5 = 0$
    c. $x_1 + x_2 = 1$
    d. $x_3 + x_4 - 2x_5 \geq 0$

12. Let x_i = the amount invested in stock i ($i = 1, 2, \ldots, 25$)

$$\text{Maximize } Z = \sum_{i=1}^{25} (0.10 r_i x_i)$$

subject to

$$\sum_{i=1}^{25} x_i \leq 1,000,000$$
$$x_i - 125,000 y_i \leq 0 \quad (i = 1, 2, \ldots 25)$$
$$x_i - 25,000 y_i \geq 0 \quad (i = 1, 3, \ldots 25)$$

with $x_i \geq 0$ ($i = 1, 2, \ldots 25$)

$$y_i = \begin{cases} 1 & \text{if stock } i \text{ is chosen for investment} \\ 0 & \text{otherwise} \end{cases}$$

14. Let x_{ij} = the number of flatbed cars produced at plant i for distribution center j ($i = 1, 2, 3$; $j = 1, 2, 3, 4$)

$$\text{Minimize } Z = 750x_{11} + 1000x_{12} + 800x_{13}$$
$$+ 900x_{14} + 650x_{21} + 900x_{22}$$
$$+ 1250x_{23} + 500x_{24} + 800x_{31}$$
$$+ 525x_{32} + 675x_{33} + 775x_{34}$$
$$+ 20,000y_1 + 15,500y_2 + 12,000y_3$$

subject to

$$x_{11} + x_{12} + x_{13} + x_{14} - 55y_1 \leq 0$$
$$x_{21} + x_{22} + x_{23} + x_{24} - 50y_2 \leq 0$$
$$x_{31} + x_{32} + x_{33} + x_{34} - 30y_3 \leq 0$$
$$x_{11} + x_{12} + x_{13} + x_{14} - 15y_1 \geq 0$$
$$x_{21} + x_{22} + x_{23} + x_{24} - 15y_2 \geq 0$$
$$x_{31} + x_{32} + x_{33} + x_{34} - 15y_3 \geq 0$$
$$x_{11} + x_{21} + x_{31} = 20$$
$$x_{12} + x_{22} + x_{32} = 15$$
$$x_{13} + x_{23} + x_{33} = 30$$
$$x_{14} + x_{24} + x_{34} = 35$$

with $x_{ij} \geq 0$ ($i = 1, 2, 3$; $j = 1, 2, 3, 4$)

$$y_i = \begin{cases} 1 & \text{if plant } i \text{ is utilized} \\ 0 & \text{otherwise.} \end{cases}$$

16. Let x_i = the number of ounces of food source i ordered

$$y_i = \begin{cases} 1 & \text{if food source } i \text{ is ordered} \\ 0 & \text{otherwise} \end{cases}$$

$$\text{Minimize } Z = .45x_1 + .35x_2 + .38x_3 + .42x_4 +$$
$$5y_1 + 6.5y_2 + 7.5y_3 + 4y_4$$

subject to

$$200x_1 + 50x_2 + 100x_3 + 50x_4 \geq 2000$$
$$100x_1 + 100x_2 + 80x_3 + 100x_4 \geq 1500$$
$$130x_1 + 80x_2 + 90x_3 + 150x_4 \geq 1200$$
$$x_i - M y_i \leq 0 \quad i = 1, \ldots, 4$$

with $x_i \geq 0$

$y_i = 0$ or 1

M = a large positive number

18. Let x_{ij} = number of desks transported from factory i to warehouse j.

$i = 1$: Denmark
    2: Mount Joy
$j = 1$: York
    2: Westhouse
    3: Troy

$$y_{ij} = \begin{cases} 1 & \text{if alternative } i, j \text{ is used} \\ 0 & \text{otherwise} \end{cases}$$

$$\text{Minimize } Z = 100y_{11} + 200y_{12} + 300y_{13}$$
$$+ 350y_{21} + 60y_{22} + 100y_{23}$$

subject to

$$x_{11} + x_{12} + x_{13} = 35$$
$$x_{21} + x_{22} + x_{23} = 30$$
$$x_{11} + x_{21} \qquad = 20$$
$$x_{12} + x_{22} \qquad = 15$$
$$x_{13} + x_{23} \qquad = 30$$
$$x_{ij} - M\,y_{ij} \leq 0 \qquad i = 1, 2$$
$$j = 1, 2, 3$$

with $x_{ij} \geq 0$, integer

$y_{ij} = 0$ or 1

M = a large positive number

CHAPTER 15.
INVENTORY ANALYSIS:
DETERMINISTIC
MODELS

2. EOQ = 12689

6. R = 1643.84

4.

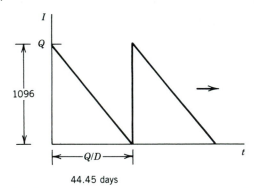

44.45 days

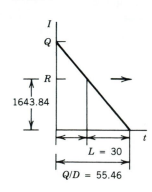

---

8. EOQ $\doteq$ 17889
   Total cost $\doteq$ 5031

10. a. EOQ $\doteq$ 3873
    b. 11.62 days
    c. 1936.5 cases

12. EOQ = 2793
    Total cost = 8593.38.

14. Shortage $\doteq$ 17
    Maximum waiting time $\doteq$ 2.5 days.

16. Optimal order size = 1000, with a total cost of 56,325.

18. The economic order quantity is underestimated by 4.37%.

20. The total cost is underestimated by .14%.

22.

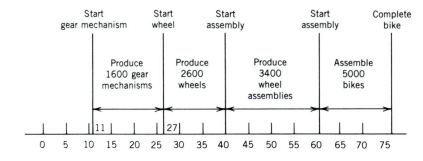

CHAPTER 16.
INVENTORY ANALYSIS:
PROBABILISTIC
MODELS

2. Reorder point = 2000
   Safety stock = 420

4. Reorder point = 75
   Safety stock = 13.5

---

6. Number of cycles = D/Q = 2000/239 = 8
   let d = demand for a cycle
   let I = minimum inventory for a cycle
   let SS = safety stock = 13.5; R = reorder point
   = 75

Cycle	d	I	$I - SS$
1	90	−15	−28.5
2	75	0	−13.5
3	61.5	13.5	0
4	60	15	1.5
5	50	25	11.5
6	40	35	21.5
7	90	−15	−28.5
8	61.5	13.5	0

8. Number of cycles D/Q = 1500/87 = 17
   d = demand for a cycle
   I = minimum inventory for a cycle
   SS = safety stock = 12.75; reorder point = R =
   50

Cycle	d	I	$I - SS$
1	50	0	−12.75
2	45	5	−7.75
3	40	10	−2.75
4	37.5	12.5	0
5	35	15	2.25
6	30	20	7.25
7	25	25	12.75

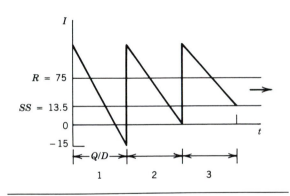

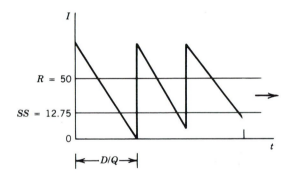

---

10. For a 95% service level the reorder point is 815.15 and the safety stock is 115.15.

12. For a 80% service level the reorder point is 442 and the safety stock is 42.

14. Yes, 15 cases should be ordered.

16. Yes, 140 pounds should be ordered.

18. 113.35 pounds.

20. Enough sauce for 94.29 pizzas should be mixed or 4.71 gallons.

CHAPTER 17. WAITING LINE MODELS

2. L = 3 customers
L_q = 2.25 customers
W = 0.2 hours
W_q = 0.15 hours
Assumptions: 1. Poisson arrivals
2. Exponential service times

4. a. P_0 = 0.25
b. L = 1 customer
c. L_q = 2.25 customers

8.

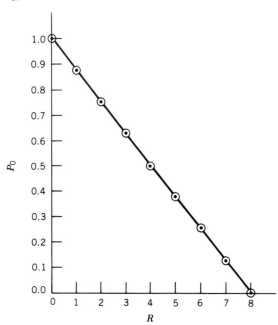

10. a. P(zero arrivals) = 0.0067
b. P(one arrival) = 0.0335
c. P(three arrivals) = 0.1396
d. P(five arrivals) = 0.1745
e. P(six or more arrivals) = 0.3876

12. P(five or fewer cars in the queue) = 0.6652

14. Single channel system: λ = 4 trucks/hour
μ = 6 trucks/hour
W_q = 0.333 hours
Labor cost = $10/hour
Waiting cost = ($20/hour) (0.333 hour)
(4 trucks/hour) = $36.67
Total cost = $10.00 + $36.67
= $46.67/hour

d. W = 1 hour
e. W_q = 0.75 hour

6. Comments: You would need to tally the actual times required to do the individual services rather than just the number of services per time period. Again, you would want to make sure that there were no "wild" fluctuations during any particular time of the day. You might also want to fit the exponential distribution to the data, using the chi-square test.

Multiple channel system: s = 2
λ = 4 trucks/hour
μ = 6 trucks/hour

W_q = 0.021 hours
Labor cost = $20/hour
Waiting cost = ($20/hour) (0.021) (4 trucks/hour)
= $1.68
Total cost = $20.00 + $1.68 = $21.68/hour

16. λ = 2 boats/hour
μ = 1/2(s), where s = number of workers
Therefore at least 5 workers are needed.
For s = 5 workers, W_q = 1.108 hours
Labor cost = $50/hour
Waiting cost = ($100/hour) (1.108 hours) (2 boats/hour) = $221.60
Total cost = $50.00 + $221.60 = $271.60/hour
For s = 6 workers, W_q = 0.285 hours
Labor cost = $60/hour
Waiting cost = ($100/hour) (0.285 hours) (2 boats/hour) = $57.00
Total cost = $60.00 + $57.00 = $117.00/hour
For s = 7 workers, W_q = 0.009 hours
Labor cost = $70/hour
Waiting cost = ($100/hour) (0.009 hours) (2 boats/hour) = $1.80
Total cost = $70.00 + $1.80 = $71.80/hour
For s = 8 workers, W_q = 0.003 hours
Labor cost = $80/hour
Waiting cost = ($100/hour) (0.003) (2 boats/hour)
= $0.60
Total cost = $80.00 + 0.60 = $80.60/hour
Therefore 7 workers should be used.

18. a. P_0 = 1/3
b. P(at least one truck waiting to be unloaded) = P(two or more trucks in the system) = 4/9.
c. L = 2

CHAPTER 18.
SIMULATION

Note: Answers to problems in this chapter will vary as a result of the random numbers selected.

2. a.

NUMBER OF TUNE-UP JOBS	NUMBER OF WEEKS	RELATIVE FREQUENCY (PROB)	CUMULATIVE PROBABILITY	RANDOM NUMBERS
5	8	8/50 = 0.16	0.16	01–16
6	12	12/50 = 0.24	0.40	17–40
7	16	16/50 = 0.32	0.72	41–72
8	8	8/50 = 0.16	0.88	73–88
9	6	6/50 = 0.12	1.00	89–100
Totals	50		1.00	

b. Simulated average number of tune-up jobs per week = 7.08
Expected value − Number of tune-up jobs per week = 6.84

4. See table on following page.

6. a. Reorder point = 20 pairs of shoes; reorder quantity = 40 pairs of shoes.
Total lost sales orders   = 17
Average weekly lost sales orders = 0.65 orders/week
Total replenishment orders   = 3
Average weekly replenishment orders = 0.12 orders/week
Total average weekly orders = 0.65 + 0.12 = 0.77 orders/week

Weekly Costs
Weekly inventory holding cost
= (13.46 pairs/week)($0.25/pair)   = $ 3.37
Weekly lost sales cost = (20.77 pairs/week)
($2.00/pair)   = 41.54
Weekly order cost = (0.77 orders/week)
($5.00/order)   = 3.85
Total = $48.76

b. Reorder point = 50 pairs of shoes; reorder quantity = 50 pairs of shoes.
Total lost sales orders = 6
Average weekly lost sales orders = 0.23 orders/week
Total replenishment orders = 12
Average weekly replenishment orders = 0.46 orders/week
Total average weekly orders = 0.23 + 0.46 = 0.69 orders/week

Weekly Costs
Weekly inventory holding cost
= (39.2 pairs/week)($0.25 pair)   = $ 9.80
Weekly lost sales cost = (8.9 pairs/week)
($2.00/pair)   = 17.80
Weekly ordering cost = (10.69 orders/week)
($5.00/order)   = 3.45
Total = $31.05

8. a. Average number of orders received daily = 44 orders/15 days = 2.9
Average machine days required = 140 machine days/15 days = 9.3
∴ Start with 9 machines in operation, based on average machine day requirement.

b. Number of days idle = 15
Cost = 15 days × $10/day = $150
Number of days backordered = 6
Cost 6 days × $15/day = $90
Might want to redo simulation using 8 machines to try to obtain a better balance between cost of being idle and backordering cost.

10. (Simulated) Profit/Acre = Yield (Bushels/Acre) × Corn Price ($/Bushel) − Farming Cost ($/Acre)
≅ $211.00

12. Win $27   Average gain = $13/10 games =
    Lose   14 $1.30/game
    Net Gain $13

Reorder point = 20
Reorder quantity = 40

Week	Orders Received (# Pairs)	Weekly Beg. Inv.	Random Number (Weekly Demand)	Weekly Demand	Weekly End Inv.	Lost Sales ?	Lost Sales Amt.	Order Size (# Pairs)	Random Number (Reorder Lead Time)	Reorder Lead Time (Weeks)	Reorder Point ?	Order Size (# Pairs)	Random Number (Reorder Lead Time)	Reorder Lead Time (Weeks)
1	—	100	71	60	40	No	—	—	—	—	No	—	—	—
2	—	40	75	60	0	Yes	20	20	02	1	No	—	—	—
3	—	0	34	40	0	Yes	40	40	90	5	No			
4	20	20	67	60	0	Yes	40	40	85	4	No			
5	—	0	16	40	0	Yes	40	40	86	4	No			
6	—	0	44	50	0	Yes	50	50	70	4	No			
7	—	0	31	40	0	Yes	40	40	57	3	No			
8	—	0	23	40	0	Yes	40	40	41	3	No			
9	40 + 40	80	29	40	40	No					No			
10	40	80	60	60	20	No					Yes	80	71	4
11	50 + 40	110	19	40	70	No					No			
12	40	110	81	60	50	No					No			
13	—	50	67	60	0	Yes	10	10	52	3	No			
14	—	0	13	30	0	Yes	30	30	35	2	No			
15	80	80	10	30	50	No					No			
16	—	50	84	60	0	Yes	10	10	67	4	No			
17	10 + 30	40	61	60	0	Yes	20	20	33	2	No			
18	—	0	80	60	0	Yes	60	60	12	2	No			
19	—	0	05	30	0	Yes	30	30	42	3	No			
20	20	20	03	25	0	Yes	5	5	15	2	No			
21	10 + 60	70	36	50	20	No					Yes	80	54	3
22	—	20	15	40	0	Yes	20	20	33	2	No			
23	30 + 45	35	97	80	0	Yes	45	45	50	3	No			
24	—	0	30	40	0	Yes	40	40	55	3	No			
25	80 + 20	100	56	50	50	No					No			
26	—	50	19	40	10	No					Yes	90	57	3
Totals		1055			350	17	540				3			
Weekly average		40.58			13.46	0.65	20.77				0.12			

14. Flow Chart for Powerhouse Tech Halfback Injury
    Simulation

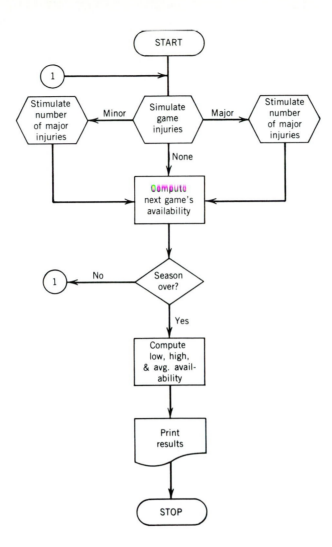

14.

SIMULATION OF POWERHOUSE TECH HALFBACK INJURIES

WEEK	HALFBACKS OUT	HALFBACKS AVAILABLE	RANDOM NUMBER (GAME INJURIES)	INJURIES? TYPE	RANDOM NUMBER (MINOR INJURIES)	NO. MINOR INJURIES	RANDOM NUMBER (MAJOR INJURIES)	NO. MAJOR INJURIES	NO. HALFBACKS NEXT GAME ONLY	NO. HALFBACKS OUT FOR SEASON
1	—	8	71	Minor	75	3			3	
2	3	5	02	None						
3	—	8	34	Minor	90	4			4	
4	4	4	67	Minor	85	3			3	
5	3	5	16	None						
6	—	8	86	Major			44	1		1
7	1	7	70	Minor	31	1			1	
8	1 + 1	6	57	Minor	23	1			1	
9	1 + 1	6	41	Minor	29	1			1	
10	1 + 1	6	60	Minor	71	2			1	
11	2 + 1	5	19	None					2	
12	1	7	81	Major			67	1		1
13	1 + 1	6	52	Minor	13	1			1	

Total halfbacks available 81
Average available/Game 6.2
Low 4
High 8

CHAPTER 19.
DYNAMIC
PROGRAMMING

2. Shortest route: $1 \rightarrow 3 \rightarrow 5 \rightarrow 9 \rightarrow 12$
   Distances: $350 + 400 + 400 + 550 = 1700$

4.

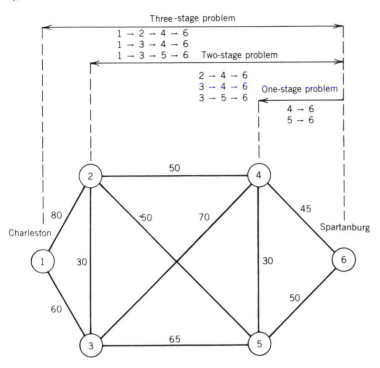

6. Allocate all four sales representatives to the Midlands area; sales will be maximized at $85,000.

8.

Investment Allocation	Expected Annual Return
$0 million → St. Louis	$ 0 million
$6 million → Chicago	$14 million
$4 million → Kansas City	$10 million
	$24 million

10.

Oyster Allocation	Expected Profit
1 gallon → Bill	$ 5
2 gallons → Sue	10
2 gallons → Tom	9
	$24

12. a. Maximize Z = Test scores District 1 + Test scores District 2 + Test scores District 3
    subject to
    Allocation of funds to School District 1 + allocation of funds to School District 2 + allocation of funds to School District 3 ≤ $4 million
    With each allocation ≥ 0

b.

Allocation of Funds	Expected Test Scores
$1 million → School District 1	50
2 million → School District 2	80
1 million → School District 3	55
Total	185

or

Allocation of Funds	Expected Test Scores
$2 million → School District 1	60
2 million → School District 2	80
0 million → School District 3	45
Total	185

14. a. Maximize Z = Market penetration Media 1 + Market penetration Media 2 + Market penetration Media 3

subject to
Dollars spent Media 1 + Dollars spent Media 2 +
Dollars spent Media 3 ≤ $5 million
Dollars spent on each media ≥ 0

b.

Allocation of Advertising Budget	Market Penetration
$0 million → Media 1	0.00
2 million → Media 2	0.30
3 million → Media 3	0.40
Total	0.70

or

Allocation of Advertising Budget	Market Penetration
$0 million → Media 1	0.00
3 million → Media 2	0.45
2 million → Media 3	0.25
	0.70

16. a. Maximize Z = Reliability Comp A · Reliability
Comp B · Reliability Comp C
Subject to: # of switches Comp A + # of switches
Comp B + # of switches Comp C ≤ 3
with # of switches for each Component ≥ 0

b.

Component	Number of Switches Installed	Probability of Component Working Properly
A	2	0.90
B	0	0.88
C	1	0.88

Overall reliability = 0.90 × 0.88 × 0.88 = 0.697

or

Component	Number of Switches Installed	Probability of Component Working Properly
A	2	0.90
B	1	0.90
C	0	0.86

Overall reliability = 0.90 × 0.90 × 0.86 = 0.697

CHAPTER 20. MARKOV ANALYSIS

2.
$$\begin{array}{cc} & S_1 \quad\quad S_2 \\ S_3 \\ S_4 \end{array} \begin{bmatrix} 0.483 & 0.517 \\ 0.383 & 0.617 \end{bmatrix} = \text{Absorption matrix}$$

Beginning State	Expected Steps Before Absorption
S_3	$1.5 + 0.17 = 1.67$
S_4	$0.5 + 1.17 = 1.67$

4. a.

Beginning State	Expected Steps Before Absorption
S_3	$1.48 + 0.16 = 1.64$
S_4	$0.33 + 1.15 = 1.48$

   b.
$$\begin{array}{cc} & S_1 \quad\quad S_2 \\ S_3 \\ S_4 \end{array} \begin{bmatrix} 0.639 & 0.361 \\ 0.475 & 0.525 \end{bmatrix} = \text{Absorption matrix}$$

   c. $23,750—Loan paid in full
      $26,250—Loan defaulted

6. $V(1) = (0 \quad\quad 0)$
   $V(2) = (0.6 \quad\quad 0.4)$
   $V(3) = (0.36 \quad\quad 0.64)$
   $V(4) = (0.456 \quad 0.544)$
   $V(5) = (0.42 \quad 0.58)$

8. Steady-state probabilities

A	B
0.43	0.57

   These are the long-run probabilities associated with a customer buying product A or product B.

10. Steady-state Probabilities

Ms.	Cosmopolitan
0.56	0.44

   These are the long-run probabilities associated with Sue reading Ms. or Cosmopolitan.

12. a.
$$\begin{array}{cc} & S_1 \quad\quad S_2 \\ S_3 \\ S_4 \end{array} \begin{bmatrix} 0.734 & 0.266 \\ 0.607 & 0.393 \end{bmatrix} = \text{Absorption matrix}$$

   b. $19.48\ (\sim19)$ — Pass course
      $10.52\ (\sim11)$ — Fail course

14. a. Matrix of Transition Probabilities

Today		Run	Not run
	Run	0.90	0.10
	Not run	0.50	0.50

(Next Day)

   b. $V(1) = (1 \quad\quad 0)$
      $V(2) = (0.90 \quad 0.10)$
      $V(3) = (0.86 \quad 0.14)$
   c. $V(1) = (0 \quad\quad 1)$
      $V(2) = (0.50 \quad 0.50)$
      $V(3) = (0.70 \quad 0.30)$

16.
$$\pi_1 = 0.2\pi_1 + 0.1\pi_2 + 0.4\pi_3$$
$$\pi_2 = 0.5\pi_1 + 0.2\pi_2 + 0.4\pi_3$$
$$\pi_3 = 0.3\pi_1 + 0.7\pi_2 + 0.2\pi_3$$
$$1 = \pi_1 + \pi_2 + \pi_3$$

Steady-state equations

Steady-state Probabilities: $\pi_1 = 0.2449$
$\pi_2 = 0.3537 \quad\quad \pi_3 = 0.4014$

18. a. Matrix of Transition Probabilities

This game		Win	Lose
	Win	0.8	0.2
	Lose	0.7	0.3

(Next Game)

   b. $V(1) = (1 \quad\quad 0)$
      $V(2) = (0.8 \quad 0.2)$
      $V(3) = (0.78 \quad 0.22)$
   c. $V(1) = (0 \quad\quad 0)$
      $V(2) = (0.7 \quad 0.3)$
      $V(3) = (0.77 \quad 0.23)$

20. $138.92\ (\sim139)$ — Potential Olympic ski team member
    $61.08\ (\sim61)$ — No potential—remove from team

Beginning State	Number of Steps Before Absorption
S_3	1.45
S_4	1.61

CHAPTER 21. GAME THEORY

2. Player A: Strategy A_1 (maximin gain criterion)
   Player B: Strategy B_1 (minimax loss criterion)
   Value of game = 25 (saddle point)

4. Player E: Strategy E_1 (maximin gain criterion)
   Player F: Strategy F_2 (minimax loss criterion)
   Value of game = 90 (saddle point)

6. a. Will not work because $V = -8/3$, and it is impossible to obtain a feasible solution.
   b. $p_1 = 1/2$ (strategy A_1)
      $p_2 = 1/2$ (strategy A_2)
      $V = -8/3$ (i.e., $V' = 0$, $V'' = 8/3$)

8. a. Player A: Row A_3 is dominated (eliminated)
      Player B: Column B_3 is dominated (eliminated)
   b. $p_1 = 1/3$ (strategy A_1)
      $p_2 = 2/3$ (strategy A_2)
      $V = -2/3$
   c. $p_1 = 7/9$ (strategy B_1)
      $p_2 = 2/9$ (strategy B_2)
      $V = -2/3$
   d. $V = -2/3$

10. $p_1 = 0.22$ (lock out) $V = 1.41$ (millions of taco
    $p_2 = 0.78$ (neutral)   shells)
    $p_3 = 0.00$ (aggressive)

12. a. $p_1 = 0.00$ (no changes)
       $p_2 = 0.25$ (minor changes) $V = -1.50\%$
       $p_3 = 0.75$ (major changes)
    b. $p_1 = 0.00$ (no changes)
       $p_2 = 0.75$ (minor changes) $V = -1.50\%$
       $p_3 = 0.25$ (major changes)
    c. $V = -1.50\%$

14. South Carolina State's Optimal Mixed Strategy
    $p_1 = 0.714$ (Veer) $V = 26$ points
    $p_2 = 0.286$ (Pro-set)
    J. C. Smith's Optimal Mixed Strategy
    $p_1 = 0.50$ (5 − 4 − 2)
    $p_2 = 0.50$ (6 − 3 − 2) $V = 26$ points
    $p_3 = 0.00$ (8 − 3)

CHAPTER 22.
NONLINEAR
PROGRAMMING

2. Yes, since the objective function is nonlinear with respect to the variable x_2.

4. a. $x = 7/10$
    b. Positive (>0 for all values of x)
    c. Minimum $= 1.55$ at $x = 7/10$
    d. Strictly convex
    e.

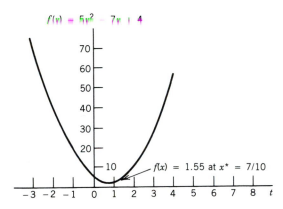

$f(x) = 5x^2 - 7x + 4$

$f(x) = 1.55$ at $x^* = 7/10$

6. Maximum sales $= \$250,500,000$ at a population $= 50,000$

8. Minimum total cost $= \$10,000$ at a production level $= 1400$ pounds

10. $x_1 = 6.25$ Maximum $Z = 13.65$
    $x_2 = 0.92$

12. a. $x_1 = 2.286$ Maximum $Z = 51.714$
        $x_2 = 3.857$
    b. Increases by approximately 2.358

14. a. $x_1 = 11.11$ Maximum total profit $= \$211.12$
        $x_2 = 27.78$
    b. $\$3.89$

CHAPTER 22
NONLINEAR
PROGRAMMING

INDEX